Good
GARDENS
Guide 1995

*Over 1,000 of the best gardens
in the British Isles and Europe*

EDITED BY GRAHAM ROSE AND PETER KING

VERMILION
LONDON

1 3 5 7 9 10 8 6 4 2

Text copyright © Graham Rose and Peter King 1994
Maps © David Perrott 1994
County maps by Clive Dorman & Co.

Project Co-ordinators: Clive Dorman & Co
Copy Editor: Jane Struthers
Botanical Editor: Lizzie Boyd
Disk Editor: Angie Hipkin
Design: Clive Dorman
Photography: Hugh Palmer
Cover design: Jerry Goldie
Cover photograph of The Walled Garden, Biggar Park, by Hugh
Palmer

First published in the United Kingdom in 1994 by Vermilion,
an imprint of Ebury Press Limited
Random House, 20 Vauxhall Bridge Road, London SWIV 2SA

Random House Australia (Pty) Limited
20 Alfred Street, Milsons Point, Sydney,
New South Wales 2061, Australia

Random House New Zealand Limited
18 Poland Road, Glenfield,
Auckland 10, New Zealand

Random House South Africa (Pty) Limited
PO Box 337, Bergvlei, South Africa

Random House UK Limited Reg. No 954009

A CIP catalogue record for this book is available
from the British Library.

ISBN 0 09 178365 8

Typeset from authors' disks by Clive Dorman & Co.

Printed in England by Clays Ltd, St Ives plc

Contents

THE GARDENS

Introduction and Acknowledgements

This is the sixth annual edition of the *Guide*, containing a considerable number of gardens which were not in the 1994 book, as well as deleting those that, for one reason or another, it was not appropriate to repeat. In all nearly 100 'new' gardens are listed this year. All the gardens described are open to the public and there is an emphasis on those which are open frequently or 'by appointment' over several months of the year. Some owners are only able or willing to open once or twice and certain gardens of this kind are included on merit; we hope that such owners may be encouraged to open more frequently if they can. The award of star rating to those gardens which our inspectors believe to be of particular interest continues this year, though there have been some changes from previous editions of the *Guide*, with a few gardens up-rated and others the reverse.

The *Guide* we know is subjective. It is a compilation of the work of a large number of inspectors, each with different gardening interests, each with his or her favourites in the areas on which they have concentrated.

Our thanks to everyone who has helped with the preparation of the *Guide* – to owners, custodians, professional gardening staff, and many others. In particular, we thank our inspectors and those who advised them. Some of those who have given advice do not wish to be listed and, although anonymous they have been every bit as valuable. We are also obliged to staff of The National Trust and The National Trust for Scotland for their co-operation. The names which follow include inspectors (but not all of them) and advisors: Barbara Abbs, Rosie Atkins, David Baldwin, Mrs David Barnes, Kerry Bate, Kenneth and Gillian Beckett, Kathryn Bradley-Hole, Hilary Bristow, Cecil Brown, Adam Caplin, Dr Joan Carmichael, Brian and Gillian Cassidy, Lady Cave, Anne Chamberlain, Sir Jeremy and Lady Chance, Sarah Coles, Anne Collins, E. Anne Colville, Beatrice Cowan, Simon Cramp, Jo, Penelope and Rosie Currie, Wendy Dare, the late Michael Davis, Marilyn Dodd, Rosemary Dodgson, Daphne Dormer, Lady Edmonstone, Matthew Fattorini, Daphne Fisher, Michael and Freda Fisher, Adrian and Audrey Gale, Lucy Gent, Alison Gregory, Elizabeth Hamilton, Camilla Harford, Anne Harrison, Lance Hattatt, Jane Henson, Ronald Higgins, Steve Hipkin, Judith Hitchings, Hilary Hodgson, Mariana Hollis, Caroline Holmes, Jackie Hone, Sophie Hughes, Pam Hummer, Jill Husselby, Judith Jenkins, Valerie Jinks, Vanessa Johnston, Rosemarie Johnstone, Mary Keen, Jo Kenaghan, the late John Last, Jean Laughton, Virginia Lawlor, Anne E. Liverman, Malcolm Lyell, Charles Lyte, Janet Macnutt, Michael Mallett, Rhian de Mattos, Pat McCrostie, Anna McKane, Deirdre McSharry, Hugh Palmer, Lucinda Parry, John and Carol Pease, Victoria Petrie-Hay, Lady Pigot, Stephen Player, Jocelyn Poole, Heather Prescott, Lorna Ramsay, Anne Richards, Christopher Rogers, Alison Rutherford, Sarah Rutherford, Peter de Sausmarez, George and Jane Scott, Gillian Sladen, Dr Gordon Smith, Lady Smith-Ryland, Elaine Snazell, Margaret Soole, Vera Taggart, Sally Tamplin, Bill Tobias, Caroline Todhunter, Michael Tooley, Annetta Troth, Marie-Françoise Valery, Mrs R.E. Vestey, Jackie Ward, Jennifer Wates, Sue Watts, Myra Wheeldon, Susan Whittington, Cynthia Wickham, John Wilks. The editors also express their appreciation of the dedicated assistance of Lizzie Boyd, Angie Hipkin and Wendy Turner.

The Garden Scene

Notable among this year's losses to visitors is the remarkable starred garden at York Gate, Adel. Its owner, Sybil Spencer, one of Northern England's outstanding gardeners, feels that she can no longer maintain it in a fit state for opening. Her decision is doubly sad because she was midwife to the garden when she and her husband bought the bleak farmhouse and its surrounding acre in 1951. They gave it some of its initial form and made the earliest plantings but it was the extraordinary talents of their son who was both a gifted amateur mason and a designer which gave York Gate its special distinction. After his father died, he joined his mother in carrying responsibility for its development until his own tragically-early death. Noting that the garden tour here enabled visitors to experience a series of exciting and unexpected vistas similar to those at Hidcote, which embraces a mixture of fine planting and noble artefacts, the late Arthur Hellyer commented that many of the ideas used at Hidcote on 10 acres could be enjoyed here on one. Alas, no more.

This *Guide* contains over 100 'new' gardens but it is sad to have lost so many others, some of them gardens of considerable distinction which may well not be kept up to standard in the future. The reasons why such gardens become neglected, or at any rate closed to the public, are manifold. Probably the most common is the lack of resources to keep them going, usually a result of the recession, and the difficulty of being able to finance professional help.

Many owners pass on the charge paid by visitors to charities but others quite understandably use income in whole or part to defray the costs of maintenance. This year it has been quite common for an adult entrance charge of £1.50 to be raised to £2. If prices were to continue to rise at this rate, there could well be a resultant decline in the number of visitors, slowing down the extraordinary growth-rate in the public's interest in gardens. This is not to say that garden visiting is necessarily an expensive pursuit – there are parts of Wales where the charge is 75p only and owners believe this is the realistic maximum.

Where gardens and parks are in public ownership and therefore 'free', the harsh economic realities continue to show themselves in occasional deterioration in both content and style. Two societies (The Garden History Society and The Victorian Society) criticise many municipal parks in cities like Manchester which suffer from official neglect. It is not only neglect from which they suffer. Manchester City authorities have embarked on a 'bizarre policy' of removing all shrubs from council-managed land and replacing them with trees, grass and bulbs which are not so likely to catch litter as shrubs. Vandals have a lot to answer for in Britain's public places.

It would be wrong in 1995 to end on this sour note. This is, after all, the year in which two famous gardens are open to the public again after lapses of many years. They come from opposite ends of the historical spectrum. One is Prior Park in Bath, a fine landscape from the city's earliest days. The other is Sutton Place, a fine memorial to the genius of our most famous living landscape gardener, Sir Geoffrey Jellicoe, whose gardens are, alas, in short supply as far as the garden-visiting public is concerned. Perhaps the most notable 'new' event of 1995 will be the opening, after restoration, of a large section of William III's privy garden at Hampton Court. Sir Roy Strong calls this 'undoubtedly the boldest' restoration undertaken since 1939 and 'the single most important site in English garden history'.

Graham Rose and *Peter King*, London 1994

5

How to Use the Guide

The *Guide* is arranged by counties. Within each county the gardens are listed alphabetically by the normal name of the garden/house. The index at the end of the book can also be used to find a garden whose name only is known to the reader.

The maps at the beginning of each county section show numbers which refer to those given against each garden entry. For detailed information about how to reach gardens use the data given in the garden entry itself. The maps at the end of the *Guide* can be used to locate gardens in neighbouring counties which may be close enough to the named county to be visited at the same time.

The information given is believed to be correct at the time of going to press but changes do occur - properties sold or ownership varied and routes improved by motorway extensions etc. There may also be closures of over-visited properties, or limitations imposed on opening times. Prices of entry may be varied without notice.

Gardens in Great Britain which are open by courtesy of the owners for one of the many interested charities are included here where the gardens are of special interest even if, as on some occasions, they are open in this way on only one day in the year. However, many such gardens are also open at other specific times, such as for local charities or church restoration funds, and it is not generally possible to give dates for these locally-publicised openings. Readers should note that other nearby gardens, not listed in this guide for one reason or another, may well be open at similar times to those of listed gardens.

Readers are invited to advise the *Guide* of any gardens which in their opinion should be listed in future editions, and where possible arrangements will be made to review such suggestions.

It has not been possible for *Guide* inspectors to visit every garden which was open to the public at some time in the year, and certain gardens in the *Guide* may not have been visited for over twelve months. In general, inspections have been made on an anonymous basis to ensure objectivity. Readers who would like to add information about gardens listed are warmly invited to write to the *Guide* with their comments, all of which will be acknowledged, and may be used in future editions without attribution.

Detailed use of the *Guide*

Address This is the address given by the owner or some other reputable source.

Telephone Except where owners have specifically requested them to be excluded, telephone numbers to which enquiries may be directed are given for each property. To maintain the support and co-operation of private owners it is suggested that the telephone be used with discretion. Where visits are by appointment, the telephone can of course be used except where written application is specifically requested. Code numbers are given in brackets. In all cases where visits by parties are proposed, owners should be advised in advance and arrangements preferably confirmed in writing. British visitors calling the Republic of Ireland should phone 010353 followed by the code (Dublin is 1) followed by the subscriber's number. WARNING Many

UK codes and numbers are being changed and while those given should be up to date, there may be some which are not.

Owners Names given are those available at the time of going to press. In the case of The National Trust, some properties may be the homes of tenants of the Trust. Some other gardens are owned or managed by other trusts.

Location This information has been supplied by inspectors and is aimed to be the best available to those travelling by car. The unreliability of train and bus services makes it unrewarding to include details, particularly as many garden visits are made on Sundays. However, a number of properties can be reached by public transport.

Access Times of access given are the best available at the moment of going to press, but some may have been changed subsequently. In the entries, the times given are inclusive - that is, an entry such as May to Sept means that the garden is open from 1st May to 30th Sept inclusive and 2 - 5pm also means that visits will be effective during that period, although some gardens may close to visitors beforehand and it is wise to arrive half an hour before closing time. Please note that many owners will open their gardens to visitors by appointment. They will often arrange to give a personally-conducted tour on these occasions.

Best season These are inspectors' suggestions, though the garden concerned may well be highly attractive at other times and usually no garden will be open at a time when it does not merit a visit. The vagaries of climate prevent this information from being anything but a rough guide.

Entrance fees As far as is known, these are correct at time of going to press, but changes may be made without notice. Where there are variations, these will be upwards, but the amount of increase is usually small. Children are often charged at a lower rate, but are expected to be accompanied by an adult. Charges for parties are often at special rates. National Trust charges are explained in their literature with special concessions for members. Accompanied children are normally admitted by The Trust at half-price and this is why no specific charge for children is usually listed for Trust properties. Figures for the Republic of Ireland are given in punts (IR£).

Parking If there is no entry for parking this means no close convenient area available and visitors should allow time to find somewhere suitable.

Refreshments A guide only. Where TEAS is marked, this normally implies that the owners have arranged to serve a simple tea on the property, or near at hand, at reasonable prices during opening hours. An ☆ indicates that the inspector enjoyed a tea of particularly high quality. No entry means that no specific refreshment arrangements were known to the inspector.

Toilet facilities Specific facilities are marked. Where there is no entry there appear to be no specific toilets for visitors and enquiries will have to be directed to staff or owners. Where there are facilities for disabled this is usually indicated.

Wheelchairs Inspectors have indicated where they believe a garden can reasonably be negotiated by someone in a wheelchair. No such entry means that the garden is probably unsuitable.

HOW TO USE THE GUIDE

Dogs If dogs are allowed in a car park, or in the property on a lead, this is indicated. No entry means dogs not allowed. Sometimes Guide Dogs only are permitted.

Plants for sale This often means that the plants are grown on the property but this is not always the case as some owners now buy-in plants from a commercial source for re-sale. No entry means plants not normally for sale.

Shop This entry refers to special shops on the premises, such as National Trust shops, selling souvenirs etc. No entry means no shop.

House open No entry means that the house is not normally open to the visiting public. Where houses are open, there is often an extra charge, usually indicated here, but again subject to change without notice.

Gardens of special distinction To help give the reader the opinion which inspectors and editors have formed about the status of certain gardens, some 80 properties have been marked with ★★ to indicate that in our opinion these are amongst the finest gardens in the world in terms of design and content. Many are of historic importance but some are of recent origin. Readers will appreciate that direct comparisons cannot be made between a vast estate like Chatsworth with its staff of professional gardeners and a tiny plantsman's garden at a terraced house, although that having been said both may be excellent of their kind. Those gardens which are of very high quality, though not perhaps as unique as the ★★ ones, are given a single ★. The latter gardens will be worth travelling a considerable distance to see, and sometimes the general ambience of the property as a whole will make the visit especially rewarding. The bulk of the gardens in the *Guide* which are not given a mark of distinction have considerable merit and will be well worth visiting when in the region. Some of them will have distinctive features of design or plant content, noted in the description, which will justify making a special journey.

Northern Ireland and Republic of Ireland At the end of the section listing these gardens is some general information about these areas.

Two-starred Gardens ★★

BERKSHIRE
Folly Farm
The Old Rectory

BUCKINGHAMSHIRE
Ascott
Cliveden
The Manor House, Bledlow
Stowe Landscape Garden
Waddesdon Manor
West Wycombe Park

CAMBRIDGESHIRE
Peckover House
University Botanic Garden

CHESHIRE
Tatton Park

CORNWALL
Caerhays Castle Garden
Heligan
Trebah
Tresco Abbey
Trewithen

CUMBRIA
Holehird
Holker Hall
Levens Hall

DERBYSHIRE
Chatsworth

DEVON
Castle Drogo
Coleton Fishacre
The Garden House
Knightshayes
Marwood Hill
Rosemoor Garden

DORSET
Cranborne Manor Gardens
Forde Abbey
Shute House

ESSEX
The Beth Chatto Gardens

GLOUCESTERSHIRE
Barnsley House
Hidcote Manor Garden
Kiftsgate Court
Westbury Court Garden
Westonbirt Arboretum

HAMPSHIRE
Exbury Gardens
Jenkyn Place
Mottisfont Abbey Garden
Sir Harold Hillier Gardens

and Arboretum
Ventnor Botanic Garden

HERTFORDSHIRE
Benington Lordship
Gardens of the Rose
Hatfield House
St Paul's Walden Bury

KENT
Hever Castle
Sissinghurst Garden

LEICESTERSHIRE
Wartnaby Gardens

LONDON (Greater)
Chiswick House
Hampton Court Palace
Royal Botanic Gardens,
Kew
Syon Park

MANCHESTER (Greater)
Durham Massey

MERSEYSIDE
Ness Gardens

NORTHAMPTONSHIRE
Cottesbrooke Hall

OXFORDSHIRE
23 Beech Croft Road
Blenheim Palace
Greys Court
Oxford Botanic Garden
Rousham House
Westwell Manor

SHROPSHIRE
Hodnet Hall

SOMERSET
Greencombe
Hadspen Garden and
Nursery

STAFFORDSHIRE
Biddulph Grange Garden

SUFFOLK
Helmingham Hall
Shrubland Hall
Somerleyton Hall

SURREY
Painshill Park
Royal Horticultural
Society's Garden
The Savill Garden
Sutton Place

The Valley Gardens

SUSSEX (East)
Great Dixter
Sheffield Park Garden

SUSSEX (West)
Leonardslee Gardens
Nymans
Standen
Wakehurst Place Garden

WILTSHIRE
Iford Manor
Stourhead

YORKSHIRE (North)
Castle Howard
Studley Royal and
Fountains Abbey

IRELAND
Ard na Mona
Birr Castle Desmesne
Butterstream
Castlewellan National
Arboretum
Glenveagh Castle
Ilnacullin
Mount Congreve
Mount Stewart House
Mount Usher
Rowallane
45 Sandford Road
The Shackleton Garden

SCOTLAND
Arduaine Garden
Brodick Castle
Castle Kennedy and
Lochinch Gardens
Castle of Mey
Crarae Garden
Crathes Castle Garden
Culzean Castle and Country
Park
Drummond Castle
House of Pitmuies
Inverewe Garden
Little Sparta
Logan Botanic Garden
Mellerstain
Royal Botanic Garden
Younger Botanic Garden

WALES
Bodnant Garden
Clyne Gardens
Dyffryn Botanic Garden
Newcastle House
Powis Castle

9

Biographies of the Great Gardeners

SIR CHARLES BARRY (1795 - 1860) A highly successful architect (Houses of Parliament etc), he popularised the formal Italian style of gardening in the mid-nineteenth century, creating impressive designs incorporating terraces, flights of steps, balustrading, urns, fountains and loggias. His most notable gardens were at Trentham Park (Staffordshire), Dunrobin Castle (Highlands), Cliveden (Buckinghamshire) and Shrubland Hall (Suffolk).

CHARLES BRIDGEMAN (- 1738) Famous for the way in which he exploited the outstanding features of the sites for which he designed gardens, Bridgeman provides the link between the rigid formality of much of seventeenth-century garden design and the apparent freedom of the landscape movement pioneered by William Kent and 'Capability' Brown. While retaining features such as geometric parterres close to the house and straight alleys, he also incorporated wilderness and meadow areas linked by meandering paths. By introducing the ha-ha wall he made vistas of the surrounding landscape part of his designs. Apart from work for Royal patrons such as Kensington Gardens (where he was responsible for the Round Pond and the Serpentine), Bridgeman carried out important works at Blenheim (Oxfordshire), Claremont (Surrey), Rousham (Oxfordshire) and Stowe (Buckinghamshire).

LANCELOT 'CAPABILITY' BROWN (1716 - 83) Having worked as head gardener and clerk of works at Stowe early in his career, Brown became familiar with the work of Bridgeman and Vanbrugh and helped to execute the designs of William Kent and James Gibbs. Their influence was particularly noticeable in the buildings he designed for his later schemes. However, he was much more radical than any of them, discarding formality when creating very natural-looking landscapes for his clients. Banishing all flowering plants and vegetables he confined them in walled gardens well away from the house and by using ha-ha walls to prevent the ingress of cattle he made the surrounding meadow land appear to run right up to the house walls. Making lakes by excavation and damming streams, he used the excavated soil to create slopes elsewhere which he clad with distinctive clumps of often quite large specimens of native trees to provide the type of park which seemed to flow naturally into the countryside and suited the hunting requirements of the sporting eighteenth-century squirearchy. To many people it seems that Brown strove to bring the rolling landscapes of his native North Northumberland to his client's parks in the flatter Midlands and South.

PERCY CANE (1881 - 1976) A great admirer of Harold Peto, he was editor and owner of *My Garden Illustrated* and *Garden Design* before World War II. He designed many large gardens in Britain and overseas, in which he resolved the conflict between the formal and naturalistic approach to design by arranging formal features such as terraces close to the house and allowing the treatment to become more and more relaxed as the boundaries of the garden were approached. Some of his best work in England was done at Dartington Hall in Devon.

BRENDA COLVIN (1897 - 1981) Highly-influential landscape architect who worked on large-scale projects such as land reclamation schemes and urban design. A founder member of the Landscape Institute, she became its President from 1951 to 1953 and her 1947 book *Land and Landscape* became a standard work for the professionals.

DAME SYLVIA CROWE (1901 -   ) Responsible for many large-scale projects such as the master planning for new towns like Warrington and Washington as well as being consultant on landscaping for the new towns of Harlow and Basildon. She became an acknowledged expert on the sympathetic integration of development schemes such as the construction of large buildings like power stations with the surrounding landscape. She designed the roof garden for the Scottish Widows Fund in Edinburgh and a park in Canberra, Australia. She was President of the Landscape Institute 1957-59.

MARGERY FISH (1888 - 1969) An informed plantswoman and influential lecturer and author who was a great partisan of the nineteenth-century designer William Robinson's naturalistic approach to gardening. This she developed in her own garden at East Lambrook Manor in Somerset which became a haven for endangered garden plants. Her style for the garden which mixed semi-formal features with traditional planting has been influential.

CHARLES HAMILTON (1704 - 86) Under the influence of William Kent between 1738 and 1773, when he was obliged to sell the estate at Painshill Park in Surrey to pay his debts, Hamilton created one of Britain's most picturesque landscape gardens which is now in process of being restored. As well as being a talented designer, he was an exemplary plantsman incorporating many exotics in his schemes, particularly those from North America. He also designed a cascade and grotto at Bowood in Wiltshire and advised on work at Holland Park in London and Stourhead in Wiltshire.

HENRY HOARE II (1705 - 85) He was the scholarly member of the banking family and greatly influenced the design of the great landscape garden at Stourhead in Wiltshire. A friend of Charles Hamilton, Lord Burlington and William Kent, he shared their naturalistic approach towards landscaping.

GERTRUDE JEKYLL (1843 - 1932) By both her writings and the example of her work (much of it accomplished in partnership with the architect Sir Edwin Lutyens) during the last years of the last century and the first quarter of this, she has probably had as much influence on the appearance of British gardens as any other designer. As someone trained initially as a painter and an embroiderer, her great strength was in carefully considered and subtle use of plant colour. Finding inspiration in the happy informality of cottage gardens, she created large interwoven swathes of plants rather than confining them to precise, 'spotty' patterns and in so doing she changed our attitude towards the way in which borders should be planted. One of the best examples of Gertrude Jekyll's work in partnership with Edwin Lutyens has recently been restored at Hestercombe Court (Somerset).

BIOGRAPHIES OF THE GREAT GARDENERS

SIR GEOFFREY JELLICOE (1900 -   ) Shortly after becoming an architect, Jellicoe made an extensive study of Italian gardens with J.C. Shepheard, which led to their producing in 1925 what has become a classic book, *Italian Gardens of the Renaissance*. The publication of *Gardens and Design* in 1927 confirmed his understanding of basic principles and helped to bring him interesting commissions such as the design of a very large formal garden at Ditchley Park in Oxfordshire. After World War II he was given much public work, including the large water garden in Hemel Hempstead town centre, the Cathedral Close in Exeter, the Kennedy memorial at Runnymede and a large theme park at Galveston in Texas. Among his work for private clients, the gardens at Sutton Place in Surrey and at Shute House in Dorset are notable. His witty designs have a strong architectural quality. In the past his late wife Susan suggested the planting for many of his schemes and she shared the authorship of the very authoritative *The Landscape of Man*, published in 1975, which discusses in great and informative detail the history and art of landscape design.

LAWRENCE JOHNSTON (1871 - 1948) One of the most outstandingly stylish twentieth-century gardeners, Johnston was an American who spent much of his youth in Paris and built two great gardens in Europe and influenced the design of a great many others, such as that of Harold Nicolson and Vita Sackville-West at Sissinghurst in Kent. He began to make the garden at Hidcote Manor in Gloucestershire in 1905 and in Britain pioneered the idea of creating a series of sheltered and interconnected garden 'rooms', each of which surprised by its different content and treatment.   Close to Menton in Southern France, at a property called La Serre de la Madone, Johnston could include in his planting schemes many southern hemisphere plants which were not hardy enough to survive at Hidcote and allow his formal schemes to be softened by the terracotta, orange trees and bougainvilleas of the Mediterranean.

INIGO JONES (1573 - 1652) Best known as a prolific architect, Jones brought formal Palladian ideas acquired on two visits to Italy to garden design at Arundel House in Sussex, Wilton House in Wiltshire and Lincoln's Inn in London. Apart from his own work, he strongly influenced William Kent (see below), who edited a book of his designs.

WILLIAM KENT (1685 - 1748) This former apprentice coach painter from Hull twice made the Grand Tour of Italy with his most influential patron, Lord Burlington. Heavily influenced by the paintings of Claude and Salvator Rosa, he later tried to introduce the type of romantic landscape encountered in their canvases into his gardens, freeing them from much of the formality which had dominated previous British gardening. His work at Rousham (Oxfordshire), Holkham Hall (Norfolk), Chiswick House (London), Claremont (Surrey) and Stowe (Buckinghamshire) had a great influence on Lancelot Brown, Charles Hamilton of Painshill Park and Henry Hoare of Stourhead.

BATTY LANGLEY (1696 - 1751) A landscaper and architect who was an early partisan of the transitional garden in which a formal layout was allied to a slightly freer and more natural planting. While by no means advocating the totally natural approach to landscaping adopted by 'Capability' Brown later in the century, his book *New Principles of Gardening*, which was published in 1728 was probably responsible for changing attitudes. As an architect he remained attached to the idea that landscaped parks should contain temples, pavilions and folly ruins.

NORAH LINDSAY (1866 -1948) A disciple of Gertrude Jekyll and a friend of Lawrence Johnston, she made the famous garden at the Manor House at Sutton Courtenay. Her style tended towards the theatrical and romantic, and gained favour with the Prince of Wales (for whom she worked at Fort Belvedere) and Lord Lothian of Blickling Hall.

JOHN CLAUDIUS LOUDON (1783 - 1843) A prolific author who founded the very successful *Gardener's Magazine* and published a popular and comprehensive *Encyclopedia of Gardening* (first published in 1822 and regularly updated), he had a considerable influence on the design of the middle- and small-sized villa gardens being made in their thousands by the burgeoning middle class. Initially a partisan of picturesque designs, he later favoured more formal arrangements and latterly advocated the adoption of the so-called gardenesque style in which each plant was isolated and displayed to its best advantage - an approach still favoured in the beds of many of our parks. Much of his design work has been lost, but there is a good surviving example in Derby Arboretum.

SIR EDWIN LUTYENS (1869 - 1944) A fine architect who between 1893 and 1912 created approximately 70 gardens in partnership with Gertrude Jekyll. Her subtle planting always softened and complemented the strong architectural nature of his garden designs. And they in their turn splendidly integrated the house in the garden and its site. A fine example of the work of the partnership at Hestercombe in Somerset is in process of being restored. There Lutyens' genius for using classical masonry forms in a highly imaginative and individual way is wonderfully displayed.

WILLIAM A. NESFIELD (1793 - 1881) In a long and adventurous life he was a soldier and talented watercolour painter specialising in the depiction of cascades in Europe and America before becoming a landscaper when he was over 40. He was persuaded by his brother-in-law, the famous architect Anthony Salvin, to use his talent for making pictures to help him design gardens. While his work was eclectic and the style he chose for his gardens usually reflected that of the houses which they surrounded, he was responsible for a reintroduction of the parterre as a garden feature in the nineteenth century. One of the best can still be seen at Holkam Hall in Norfolk. At the Royal Botanic Gardens at Kew, as well as a parterre, he made a pond and created the vistas from the Palm House. In total he is believed to have worked at 260 estates during his career.

SIR HAROLD NICOLSON (1886 - 1968) see Vita Sackville-West

RUSSELL PAGE (1906 - 85) Trained as a painter, he quickly became absorbed by garden design and between 1935 and 1939 worked in association with Sir Geoffrey Jellicoe. After the war he gained an international reputation and worked on many projects in Europe and

BIOGRAPHIES OF THE GREAT GARDENERS

America, including the garden at the Frick Gallery in New York and the Battersea Festival Gardens in London. He encapsulated many of his ideas about garden design in *The Education of a Gardener*, first published in 1962.

JAMES PAINE (1716 - 89) Distinguished designer of garden buildings including the bridge at Chatsworth in Derbyshire, Gibside Chapel in Tyne and Wear and the Temple of Diana at Weston Park in Shropshire.

SIR JOSEPH PAXTON (1803 - 65) Gardened at Chatsworth in Derbyshire for 32 years from 1826, where he made the great fountain and the great conservatory in which he pioneered ideas later used in the design of the Crystal Palace. One of the early designers of public parks including those at Birkenhead and Halifax, he was also influential as a writer and was one of the founders of *The Gardener's Chronicle*.

HAROLD PETO (1854 - 1933) A talented architect who worked for the partnership which later employed the young Edwin Lutyens and who undoubtedly influenced his style. A lover of Italianate formal gardens, one of Peto's best works was his own garden at Iford Manor in Wiltshire, but his canal garden at Buscot Park in Oxfordshire and the garden on Garinish Island, County Cork, are other notable achievements.

HUMPHRY REPTON (1752 - 1818) The most influential eighteenth-century landscaper after the death of Lancelot Brown, he was a great protagonist of Brown's ideas but he did tend to favour thicker planting than Brown, and the buildings he used to draw the eye into the landscape were rustic rather than classical. However, he restored formality to gardens in the form of terracing with flights of steps and balustrading near the house. His success in selling his ideas to clients was due to the production of excellent 'before and after' pictures of their parks, demonstrating the effects to be obtained if his schemes were adopted. These pictures with an explanatory text were bound into books which later became known as Repton's 'Red Books' because red was the colour of their binding. Repton was notable for his energy, producing over 400 Red Books and working on such fine estates as Holkham Hall in Norfolk, Sheffield Park in Sussex, Cobham Hall in Surrey, Woburn Abbey in Bedfordshire and Sheringham Park in Norfolk, which is his best-preserved work.

WILLIAM ROBINSON (1838 - 1935) An Irishman who settled in England and became one of the most prolific writers and influential designers of his epoch. By his teaching and his example he liberated gardeners from the prim rigidity which had begun to dominate garden design in the mid-nineteenth century. Instead of the tightly-patterned bedding displays which the Victorians had adopted in order to show off the host of annual bedding plants which the explorers were sending home, he advocated a very free and natural attitude towards the creation of herbaceous and mixed beds. It was Robinson's attitudes towards planting which early inspired Gertrude Jekyll. He founded a weekly journal, the *Garden* (later absorbed into *Homes and Gardens*), and wrote *The English Flower Garden* which ran to 15 editions during his life and more later.

BIOGRAPHIES OF THE GREAT GARDENERS

LANNING ROPER (1912 - 83) A Harvard graduate from leafy South Orange, New Jersey, who adopted Britain as his home and became one of the most popular landscapers in the 30 years after World War II. His best schemes, such as that at Glenveagh in Ireland, involved a very subtle handling of plants combined with interesting formal features. One of his most controversial designs is the ornamental canal in the R.H.S. garden at Wisley.

VITA SACKVILLE-WEST (1892 - 1962) With her husband, Harold Nicolson, she made two notable gardens. The first at Long Barn, Sevenoaks Weald, Kent was based on a Nicolson design which she planted during and after World War I. The second and most famous, at Sissinghurst Castle, was begun in 1932 and developed during the rest of her life. The Nicolsons were friendly with Laurence Johnston, and their attitude to gardening was certainly influenced by the ideas which he exploited at Hidcote.

WILLIAM SHENSTONE (1714 - 63) An early partisan of picturesque gardening who bankrupted himself making a fine landscape garden of his own, Shenstone wrote an essay entitled 'Unconnected thoughts on gardening' which analysed picturesque gardening and contained advice from which hundreds of landscapers have subsequently benefitted.

SIR JOHN VANBRUGH (1644 - 1726) A considerable dramatist and spectacular architect of palaces like Blenheim in Oxfordshire and Castle Howard in Yorkshire. Although he did not design landscapes himself, he ensured that his houses were magnificently sited and often created buildings for their gardens, such as the bridge at Blenheim. He also adorned landscapes made by other designers of great gardens such as Stowe in Buckinghamshire, and Claremont in Surrey.

ELLEN WILLMOTT (1858 - 1934) She made a famous garden at Warley Place in Essex, part of which became a reserve for the Essex Naturalists' Trust in 1978, though little of her garden remains She became renowned for her knowledge of plants, her patronage of plant hunters (notably Ernest Wilson), the book she published on roses, and her prickly temperament. One of her influential achievements was the development of the garden at Boccanegra on the Italian Riviera.

HENRY WISE (1653 - 1738) Gardener to Queen Anne and taken into partnership by George London who ran the large Brompton Park nurseries in Kensington. The partners planted many of the last of the great formal gardens in the late-seventeenth century tradition at Chelsea Hospital, Longleat House in Wiltshire, Hampton Court, Bushey Park and Kensington Palace.

THOMAS WRIGHT (1711 - 1786) Astronomer and adviser on about 30 gardens owned by great men of the time - including Badminton, Shugborough and Stoke Gifford. His variety of styles included primitive, Chinese, Gothic and classical, and he designed elaborate flower gardens when flower beds (other than parterres) were not common.

Hotels with Fine Gardens

Many garden visitors like to combine their touring with an overnight stay at a hotel or a meal in a hotel restaurant. The *Guide* already lists a number of hotels with fine gardens, but these entries in the main text are limited to those where the owners will welcome visitors to the garden whether they are guests of the hotel or not. It has been decided to extend this by adding a new list to include hotels where the garden is open only to guests or diners. Some of these gardens have not been inspected.

Avon

Thornbury Castle, Thornbury, Nr Bristol BS12 1HH. Tel: (01454) 281182. Claims to have England's oldest Tudor garden.

Buckinghamshire

Cliveden (*see entry*)

Five Arrows, High Street, Waddesdon HP18 0JE. Tel: (01296) 651727. The Five Arrows Hotel was built as part of the Waddesdon Estate by Baron Ferdinand de Rothschild in the 1880s to house those working on the construction of the Manor. The Hotel is still owned by the Rothschild family and stands in the village of Waddesdon. It reopened in March 1993 after being entirely refurbished and the terrace and garden have also been remodelled in the original style with topiary, box hedging and old roses (see Waddesdon entry).

Cornwall

Carwinion (*see entry*)

Long Cross (*see entry*)

Meudon, Mawnan Smith, Nr Falmouth TR11 5HT. Tel: (01326) 250541. *Open for charity three times a year. Visitors calling at reception are welcome to wander especially if they have tea or coffee.* Terraced gardens landscaped by 'Capability' Brown. A steep-sided sheltered ravine running down from the hotel to the sea with paths winding through glades of giant Australian tree ferns, magnolias, embothriums, drimys, cordylines, hoberias, and clumps of the huge *Gunnera manicata* and many other rare and exotic species. The climate here permits groups of graceful banana trees. There are extensive plans for development of the garden.

Cumbria

Leeming House Hotel, Watermillock, Ullswater, Penrith CA11 0JJ. Tel: (017684) 86622. The *Michelin* describes this as 'an elegant installation' whatever that may mean. The gardens, originally conceived in 1869 as a series of grand terraces in the Italian style with a central staircase with views over the lake, still retain much of their nineteenth-century glory. A central feature on the middle terrace has been converted into a pool with fountain. Clipped yew and hedges of variegated yew and laurel link the various areas of garden and woodland with the lakeside setting and the backdrop of fells, dredged with naturalised daffodils, bluebells and primroses in Wordsworthian proportions. Azaleas and rhododendrons (350 varieties) in profusion. Most splendid of all are the trees from many parts of the world, glorious in their autumn colours.

Sharrow Bay Country House, Pooley Bridge, Ullswater. Tel: (018536) 301. According to the *Good Food Guide* 'The charm of this lakeside villa is best appreciated by lying in bed listening to torrents streaming down the hillside, and the susurration of waterfowl'. Shorter-term visitors are however welcome to view the gardens with a lakeside setting.

Derbyshire
Riber Hall, Matlock. Tel: (01629) 582795. Elizabethan manor house which stands in its own grounds with old English walled garden and orchard, with many rare plants, plus a conservatory.

Devon
Buckland-Tout-Saints Hotel, Kingsbridge TQ7 2DS. Tel: (01548) 853055. Queen Anne house and park.
Endsleigh House (*see entry*)
Gidleigh Park (*see entry*)

Dorset
Summer Lodge, Evershot DT2 0JR. Tel: (01935) 83424. Described as a peaceful Georgian home (formerly dower house) with sheltered walled garden. Stunning views from every hill on which wild flowers abound. Afternoon cream teas for non-residents.

Gloucestershire
The Lygon Arms, Broadway. Tel: (01386) 852255. A fine Tudor building much modernised in the heart of the Cotswolds. Guests will enjoy a walk in the typically English gardens of lawns, borders and clipped hedges.
Upper Court, Kemerton, Tewkesbury. Tel: (01386) 725351. Described in the *Yellow Book* as 15 acres of garden and grounds mostly landscaped in the 1930s. Grounds include a two-acre lake where visitors are welcome to bring picnics. Doomsday watermill, thirteenth-century dovecot and two acres of wilderness. The hotel will show the garden to non-guests provided they telephone first to make an appointment.

Hampshire
Lainston House Hotel, Sparsholt, Winchester. Tel: (01962) 863588. Approached through parkland, this handsome William and Mary house has a large circular bed in quadrants filled with perennials, herbs and annuals, a shaggy topiary garden with a ruined chapel, good shrub borders, a courtyard with a pergola planted with roses and clematis and flower borders with day lilies, Japanese anemones, hostas, etc. Most spectacular is the vista down a magnificent lime avenue. For an elegant tea, or quiet weekend with the ping of tennis balls in the background.
Rhinefield House Hotel, Rhinefield Road, Brockenhurst. Tel: (019590) 22922. A Victorobethan mansion built by Romaine-Walker for the coal heiress Mars Walker-Monroe. Have lunch or tea – or neither, the hotel is welcoming – beside the broad spaces of the newly-restored Italian gardens, with canals, fountains, wrought iron gates, redwoods, topiary yew and three stunningly contrived views over the New Forest. A Hampshire Gardens Trust protegé.
Tylney Hall Hotel (see entry)

Hereford & Worcester
Grafton Manor, Grafton Lane, Bromsgrove. Tel: (01527) 579007 Formal herb garden in 26 acres of grounds, a two-acre lake and a sixteenth-century stewpond.
Hope End Hotel, Ledbury. HR8 1JQ. Tel: (01531) 633613. *Open first weekend in Feb to mid-Dec.* The house was commissioned from the architect Loudon by Elizabeth Barrett Browning's father (not Charles Laughton) and the grounds were laid out by him in the Picturesque manner, recently restored and forming part of a larger listed park. The present owners, the Hegartys, grow food organically here in the splendid eighteenth-century walled garden in the 40-acre estate.
Upper Court (*see* Gloucestershire above)

HOTELS WITH FINE GARDENS

Hertfordshire

Hanbury Manor (see entry)
West Lodge Park Hotel (see entry for The Beale Arboretum)

Norfolk

Congham Hall (see entry)
The Plantation Garden (see entry)

Oxfordshire

Le Manoir aux Quat' Saisons, Church Road, Great Milton, Oxford OX44 7PD. Tel: (01844) 278881. Completely re-modelled gardens, including a vegetable garden and herb garden which supplies the kitchen. There is also an orchard and formal flower gardens, the swimming pool garden (reserved for resident guests) and cut flower garden. The water gardens are currently being refurbished, culminating in the opening of a new Japanese garden.

Shropshire

Hawkstone Park Hotel (see entry)

Somerset

Ston Easton (see entry)

Suffolk

Hintlesham Hall, Hintlesham, Ipswich IP8 3NS. Tel (01473) 652334. The Tudor and Georgian hall sits elegantly in its gardens which have been greatly improved in the last five years. The herb garden is of special interest – designed by Beth Chatto for Robert Carrier (a previous owner) to supply the kitchens. Hedged by beech and espaliered apple trees it is divided into a series of mirrored geometric patterns. The patterns are edged in santolinas, rosemarys, lavenders and thymes, infilled with cooking and salading herbs leading to rectangular *potager* beds. There is a wild garden, rose bank, water gardens, mixed borders, croquet lawn and tender plants in the orangery. Golf course. Pleasant for both the plantsman or stroller.

Sussex, West

Gravetye Manor, Vowels Lane, Nr East Grinstead. Tel: (01342) 810567. This historically important garden has been carefully restored in the style set out by William Robinson. It has a wild meadow leading down to trout lakes from terraced formal gardens. The elliptical kitchen garden enclosed by Sussex sandstone walls is unique and is cultivated to produce fresh vegetables for the hotel kitchen. It is worth giving yourself a treat, either spending a weekend at Gravetye, or going for lunch, but enquire about prices and availability before making plans. Either way guests will be able to appreciate the garden, lakes and woods.

Little Thakeham (see entry)

South Lodge Hotel, Lower Beeding, Nr Horsham. Tel: (01403) 891711. Splendid Victorian baronial mansion built by Ducane Godman, a noted explorer and botanist. Ducane Godman competed with Sir Edmund Loder in the planting of hybrid rhododendrons, and the last member of his family, Miss Edith Godman, died aged 85 in 1982, while waiting for a taxi to take her to the Chelsea Flower Show. The south face of the house looking towards the Downs is hung, in May, with yellow Banksian roses, amongst other beauties, including clematis and the most magnificent *Wisteria macrobotrys* with racemes over two feet long. Earlier there are huge camellias, one of which is reputedly 200 years old and grows up a section of wall from the original Tudor house. Terrace with herbaceous border. Extensive grounds with walks to lake. Rock garden. Walled garden, incorporating a brick from the Great Wall of China, is being restored and has a fine *Actinidia kolomikta*. Leonardslee, Nymans and Wakehurst (see entries) are all 20 minutes drive from South Lodge.

Warwickshire

Welcombe Hall, Nr Stratford-upon-Avon. Tel: (01892) 295252 W.S. Nesfield was called in here by the owner and builder of the Jacobean-style mansion (1869). He developed elaborate parterres now restored for Orient Express Hotels to his designs, which had stone instead of box edging. His terracing, statuary, etc. to the rear of the property have survived, and a cascade has been added at the point furthest from the hotel. An extraordinary sight.

Wiltshire

Woolley Grange, Woolley Green, Bradford-on-Avon BA15 1TX. Tel: (01225) 864705. Jacobean stone manor house standing in open countryside. Victorian walled vegetable garden. Pool.

Yorkshire

Middlethorpe Hall, Bishopthorpe Road, York YO2 1QB. Tel: (01904) 641241. William and Mary house, gardens and park, given by Michelin its top 'pleasant' rating with the gardens and park a 'particularly attractive feature'.

Ireland

Dunloe Castle (*see entry*)

Scotland

Ardanaiseig Hotel and Garden (*see entry*)

Crinan Hotel, Argyll, Strathclyde PA31 8SR Tel: (0154683) 235/245. Visitors can view the beauty of Crinan Loch and canal. Situated on a very steep hillside, much of the garden was hewn out of the rockface over 100 years ago and, because of this, the spectacular herbaceous beds are slightly unexpected.

Greywalls, Muirfield, Gullane, East Lothian EH31 2EG. Tel: (01620) 842144. Designed in 1901 by Sir Edwin Lutyens with the gardens attributed to Gertrude Jekyll. Open to non-residents, many of whom visit the garden to view progress which includes the development of a rose garden, yellow and white border, a herbaceous border and a shade border. Also herbs for the hotel kitchen and cut flowers for the house.

Glenborrowdale Castle, Ardnamurchan Peninsula, Argyll. Tel: (019724) 266. Michelin says this is a Victorian castle in extensive gardens to which it gives an accolade.

Kildrummy (*see entry*)

Wales

Bodysgalen Hall (*see entry*)
Portmeirion (*see entry*)
Ynyshir Hall (*see entry*)

HOTELS

Please note the introduction to this section which explains that the gardens of hotels in the main section of the *Guide* are open to the public on the terms explained in their entry. Those described in this section are not usually open unless the visitor is a guest of the hotel, although there are exceptions.

AVON

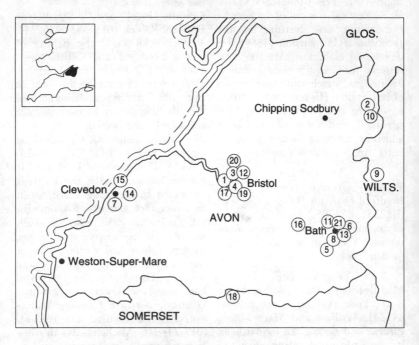

ASHTON COURT ESTATE 1
Long Ashton, Bristol, Avon. Tel: (0117) 963 9174

Bristol City Council ★ SW of Bristol off A370 ★ Parking ★ Toilet facilities ★
Open daily until dusk ★ Entrance: free

Ashton Court Mansion dates from the early sixteenth century with the addition of a remarkable seventeenth–century wing and some features of this period are incorporated in the predominantly Victorian gardens. The terraced lawn is bounded by an early eighteenth–century wall with steps down to the sunken garden with redwood trees and a pond. The pets' graves of the Smyth family overlook the ha-ha. A rose garden now graces an area that used to be greenhouses. The picturesque landscape park with its curving drive, tree belt and clumps has a rare survival (one indebted to Bristol City Council for its maintenance) in the form of a deer park. The nearby Clarkencombe wood has a large collection of ancient dramatic oaks.

BADMINTON ★ 2
Badminton, Avon.

The Duke and Duchess of Beaufort ★ 5m E of Chipping Sodbury, B4040, N of M4 junction 18 ★ Parking ★ Teas on open day ★ Toilet facilities ★ Suitable for wheelchairs ★ Open 25th June for charity, 2 – 6pm. Park open all year round but no cars ★ Entrance on charity day: £1.50, OAP £1, children under 10 free

This private garden has been designed over the last decade to the south and east sides of the house. Very cleverly planted, they manage to answer both the grandeur and the muddle of the house. Two orangeries on the east side are exuberant with the best conservatory plants – large myrtle bushes in tubs and clambering cobaea, with the new formal garden on this side designed by Russell Page shortly before his death. The orangeries lead to immaculate matching box parterres in front of Kent's pavilions with clipped yews beyond framing the vista to the park (fittingly Page is buried in the nearby church-yard). On the south side is the most extensive of the recent modern work – a series of enclosures or rooms, most walled by hornbeam hedges, containing very successful mixed planting. Vistas erected, and paths and borders divide neat plots of fruit and vegetables.

BLAISE HAMLET ★   3
Blaise Castle House, Henbury, Bristol, Avon.

The National Trust ★ 4m N of Bristol, W of Henbury village, N of B4057 ★ Parking ★ Suitable for wheelchairs ★ Dogs on lead ★ House and museum open Tues – Sun and Bank Holiday Mon, 10am – 1pm, 2 – 5pm ★ Entrance: free

A picturesque village with a green surrounded by nine cottages with private gardens, a hamlet designed by John Nash with George and John Repton in 1809 for the pensioners of John Harford's estate. The village pump and sundial of 1812 remain. Jasmines, ivies and honeysuckles were planted around the cottages and ornamental shrubs to add to the woodland setting. A spec-tacular drive can be made from Henbury Hill to the entrance lodge of Blaise Castle House (owned by Bristol City Museum) – a charming 'cottage *orné*' is half-way. The driveway into the gorge and up to the house passes a 'Robber's Cave' and the 'Lovers Leap'. The view is exceptional. Near the house is the delightful ornamental dairy and elegant orangery also by John Nash.

BRISTOL ZOO   4
Clifton, Bristol, Avon.

Bristol Zoo Gardens ★ Signposted from M5 junctions 17 and 18 and from Bristol city centre ★ Parking ★ Refreshments: in restaurant ★ Toilet facilities ★ Suitable for wheelchairs ★ Shop ★ Open daily except 25th Dec, 9am – 6pm (5pm in winter) ★ Entrance: £5.50, concessions £4, children (3-13) £2.50. Special rates for parties of 20 or more (1994 prices)

Fashions in gardening are whimsical, and everyone has different likes and dislikes. In Bristol Zoo, a gorgeous tapestry of colour, including fuchsias, pelargoniums, begonias, marigolds, busy Lizzies and innumerable other bedding plants in island beds and herbaceous borders will greatly impress those whose tastes run to great splashes of colour. It is very well contrived, with evident love and care and the trees are labelled. The zoo is definitely worth a visit!

CITY OF BATH BOTANICAL GARDENS   5
Royal Victoria Park, Bath, Avon.

City of Bath ★ In Royal Victoria Park ★ Best season: spring ★ Parking ★ Toilet facilities in Royal Victoria Park ★ Suitable for wheelchairs ★ Dogs on lead ★ Open daily, 9am – dusk ★ Entrance: free

Located in the city's Royal Victoria Park the botanical gardens were formed in 1887 to house a life-long collection of plants belonging to Mr C.E. Broome of Batheaston, who had been an enthusiastic amateur botanist and plant collector. It has become one of the finest collections of plants on limestone, certainly in the West Country. To mark the centenary in 1987, the Gardens were extended to take in the adjacent Great Dell in the Park itself. The herbaceous border was replanted in 1990. A ten-year improvement scheme was begun in 1992 to develop and create new collections and improve labelling. Entered through a wrought iron gate the Botanical Gardens are a nine and a half-acre green refuge from busy city life.

CLAVERTON MANOR   6
Claverton, Bath, Avon. Tel: (01225) 460503

The American Museum ★ 2m SE of Bath off A36, signposted American Museum ★ Parking ★ Refreshments ★ Toilet facilities ★ Partly suitable for wheelchairs ★ Herbs for sale ★ Shop ★ Museum and New Gallery ★ Garden open 25th March to 5th Nov, daily except Mon, 2 – 5pm; Bank Holiday Sun and Mon, 11am – 5pm ★ Entrance: Grounds and galleries: £2, children £1. House, grounds and galleries: £5, OAP £4.50, children £2.50 (1994 prices)

The house, designed by Jeffry Wyatville, and garden are set on the side of the valley of the Avon in a stunning position with splendid views from the terrace. Despite the storms of 1989 which brought down the cedar of Lebanon on the main lawn, and many trees in the park, the grounds display good beech, ilex and cedars and have been replanted. The rather stark high walls of the house and the terrace support honeysuckle, clematis and old rose climbers, and fastigiate yews make strong buttress shapes up the south-facing wall. The Colonial Herb Garden is modest in size but the little herbarium is popular for seeds, herbs, tussie-mussies and so on. The Mount Vernon garden, a re-creation of George Washington's famous garden, with rampant old-fashioned roses, trained pear trees and box and beech hedges, is surrounded by white palings. There is a replica of the octagonal garden house used as a school room for Washington's step-grandchildren. The seven-acre arboretum containing a very fine collection of exclusively native American trees and shrubs is believed to be the only one of its kind outside the US. There is extensive labelling and a map listing trees and shrubs is available. An orchard contains American apple varieties.

CLEVEDON COURT   7
Tickenham Road, Clevedon, Bristol, Avon. Tel: (01275) 872257

The National Trust ★ 1½m E of Clevedon on B3130. M5 junction 20 ★ Best season: summer ★ Parking ★ Refreshments in tea room ★ House open ★ Garden open April to Sept, Wed, Thurs, Sun and Bank Holiday Mon, 2 – 5pm. Closed 14th April ★ Entrance: £3.40, children £1.60 (house and garden)

The fourteenth-century house is magnificently sited with steeply terraced gardens. The upper terrace is backed by ornamental woodland of ilex and holm oaks, London planes and a mulberry tree which was said to be 'ancient' in 1822. The bowling green on one of the terraces is flanked by a Gothic gazebo which counterbalances an eighteenth-century octagonal summerhouse on the other. The Trust suggests these south-facing terraces may have housed apricots and figs but they have been replanted with species such as the strawberry tree, *Canna iridiflora*, palms, myrtles, fuchsias, a Judas tree and fine magnolias (best in spring) which flourish in the sheltered microclimate.

CROWE HALL ★ 8
Widcombe Hill, Bath, Avon. Tel: (01225) 310322

Mr John Barratt ★ Behind Bath Spa station off the A36 within walking distance of station ★ Best season: late March to mid-July ★ Parking on Widcombe Hill ★ Teas ★ Partly suitable for wheelchairs ★ Dogs ★ Plants sometimes for sale ★ Open 26th March, 23rd April, 14th, 28th May, 18th June, 16th July, 2 – 6pm and for groups by appointment ★ Entrance: £1.50, children 30p

These gardens, which extend to 11 acres on the hillside above Widcombe, are some of the most mysterious and beautiful in Bath. Through the gates there is an intriguing view of a drive, portico and terrace, and once inside the grounds few gardens in the area offer so many surprises and delights. As the owner says 'The garden is an island of classical simplicity surrounded by romantic wilderness'. Around the Regency-style house are Italianate terraces, a pond, grottos, tunnels, woods, glades, kitchen gardens and a long walk with a stone statue facing a stunning view of Prior Park, a Palladian mansion (see entry). Vistas and views are a feature of this steeply-banked garden where down one walk you suddenly come on the roof of the fifteenth-century church of St Thomas à Becket. The loss of 20 trees in recent storms is regarded as an improvement by the owner because new vistas have opened up. Beyond the recently restored grotto is a new meadow garden and an amusing garden dedicated to Hercules, with a theatrically ferocious hero. Magnificent trees include mulberries and nut. For its stunning setting in the meadows above and facing away from Bath and for the romantic ambience, Crowe Hall is an experience not to be missed.

DYRHAM PARK 9
Nr Chippenham, Avon. Tel: (0117) 937 2501

The National Trust ★ 8m N of Bath, 12m E of Bristol on A46. Take M4 junction 18 in direction of Bath ★ Parking on grass ★ Refreshments in Orangery and picnics in park ★ Toilet facilities ★ Suitable for wheelchairs on ground floor of house and terrace only. Park suitable but many inclines ★ Dogs in dog walking area on lead only ★ House, garden and park: April to 29th Oct, daily except Thurs and Fri, 12 noon – 5.30pm (last admission 5pm or dusk if earlier) ★ Entrance: Park only £1.60, children 80p (house, garden and park £5, children £2.50)

Only a tiny fragment of the London and Wise extensive 'Dutch' Garden shown in the view by Kip in 1712 survives. The terraces were all smoothed out in the late eighteenth century to form an 'English' landscape with fine mature beech, Spanish chestnut, Lucombe oak, red oak and black walnut. Avenues of elms survived until the mid-1970s when they were wiped out by Dutch elm disease. They have since been replanted with limes. The cascade in the garden on the west side is still working and one can make out the form of the original garden and enjoy the terrace and the orangery which is by Talman. It is the views towards Bristol and the elegance of the 'natural' landscape with the house tucked into the hillside that still make this an outstanding example of English landscape gardening. In all, 263 acres of ancient parkland.

ESSEX HOUSE   10
Badminton, Chipping Sodbury, Avon. Tel: (01454) 218288

Mr James Lees-Milne ★ 1m N of Acton Turville on B4040. M4 junction 18 ★ Toilet facilities nearby ★ Partly suitable for wheelchairs ★ Open by appointment only to the seriously-interested, May to Aug ★ Entrance: £2

The late Mrs Lees-Milne held Open Days for over 25 years but said what she really enjoyed was showing people around herself. Her widower says he will do his best to keep this impressive garden open. Although not large, until 1990 it was dominated by two very large and very old cedars of Lebanon. These both crashed in the great gale of that year and now the upper part of the garden has been replanned and planted. One could spend longer and learn more than in any number of more showy plots. It demonstrates what intelligence in dealing with site, sureness of hand in planting, lightness of touch in design can achieve. This garden is broken up by surprises but always maintains a consistency of thought behind it. Many old roses and some topiary. Climbers, bulbs, alliums and annuals are woven throughout to reinforce the bones of the planting as the season progresses. The beds are full enough and the plants vigorous, everything is just in check but never too clipped or too manicured.

THE GEORGIAN GARDEN   11
Gravel Walk, Bath, Avon.

Bath Museums Service ★ Enter garden by the Gravel Walk ★ Parking in Charlotte Street, 5 minutes walk across Victoria Park ★ Toilet facilities in Park ★ Open May to Oct, Mon – Fri, 9am – 4.30pm ★ Entrance: free

Anyone interested in seeing how a Georgian town garden looked should not miss the newly restored garden behind The Circus (entry via Gravel Walk). Designed to be seen from the house, the garden plan is based on excavations conducted by the Bath Archaeological Trust of the original garden, laid out in the 1760s. Surprisingly simple, there is no grass but a bed of yellow gravel edged with stone paving. Three flower beds are on a central axis. Box-rimmed borders planted starkly with scented varieties of phlox, stocks, asters and a good deal of love-lies-bleeding. Honeysuckle clings to a central white pole. An eye-catcher is a curious bench copied from an eighteenth-century original. The planting sets out to show how a Georgian garden might have evolved between 1760 and 1836.

GOLDNEY HALL   12
Lower Clifton Hill, Clifton, Bristol, Avon. Tel: (0117) 926 5698

University of Bristol ★ In centre of Bristol at top of Constitution Hill, Clifton ★ Teas on open days ★ Garden open 30th April, 14th May, 2 – 6pm. Grotto open by special appointment for those with a serious interest ★ Entrance: £1.50, OAP and children 75p

Although not large or notably planted this is historically an important garden with much packed into it and a rare survival of a medium-sized garden covering nine acres. The grotto is astonishingly elaborate, water really gushes through it and its walls are literally encrusted with shells and minerals. Its facade is a very striking example of early but sophisticated Gothic. The grotto is now justly famous but the entire garden (or what remains) is a thrilling discovery in the middle of this busy, once bombed, city. It is full of surprises not least of which is the small formal canal with orangery at its head. From the house one is led through the shadows of an *allée* of yews to the dank grotto entrance. Passing through the grotto and out by narrow labyrinthine passages, suddenly there is a terrace, a broad airy walk with magnificent views over the old dock. At the far end of this terrace is the Gothic gazebo and towering above the other end is the castellated tower. Garden follies, parterre and herb garden.

HOLBURNE MUSEUM AND CRAFTS STUDY CENTRE 13
Bath, Avon. Tel: (01225) 466669

Trustees of the Museum ★ On A36 south junction of Great Pulteney Street ★ Best season: summer ★ Parking ★ Refreshments: licensed teahouse in grounds ★ Toilet facilities in museum ★ Suitable for wheelchairs ★ Dogs on lead ★ Shop ★ Museum open Mon – Sat, 11am – 5pm, Sun, 2.30 – 6pm. Closed Mons from Nov to Easter ★ Garden open all year ★ Entrance: free

The gardens provide a delightful complement to the Holburne Museum which houses an exceptional collection of decorative and fine art. Originally part of Sydney Gardens, little remains of the early fashionable eighteenth-century pleasure gardens modelled on Vauxhall Gardens.

JASMINE COTTAGE 14
26 Channel Road, Clevedon, Nr Bristol, Avon. Tel: (01275) 871850

Mr and Mrs M. Redgrave ★ 12m W of Bristol. From M5 use junction 20. Take the road to the seafront continuing N on B3124 and turn right at St Mary's church ★ Parking on road ★ Teas ★ Toilet facilities ★ Plants for sale ★ Open 13th April to Aug, Thurs, 2.30 – 5.30pm and 26th March, 23rd April, 21st May, 25th June, 23rd July, 27th Aug, 2 – 6pm and by appointment ★ Entrance: £1, children free

There is something for everyone here: old-fashioned roses, mixed shrubs, herbaceous borders, island beds, pergola walk, and a vegetable garden all crammed into one-third of an acre. Inspiration for suburban enthusiasts.

THE MANOR HOUSE 15
Walton-in-Gordano, Clevedon, Bristol, Avon. Tel: (01275) 872067

Mr and Mrs S. Wills ★ 2m NE of Clevedon on B3124. Entrance on N side of entry to village nearest Clevedon ★ Parking. Coaches by appointment only ★ Suitable for wheelchairs ★ Plants for sale ★ Open all year by appointment. Also mid-April to mid-Sept, Wed and Thurs, 10am – 4pm; mid-Oct to mid-Nov, and some weekends for charity (telephone for details) ★ Entrance: £1.50, children under 14 free

A most unusual plantsman's garden of about four acres which is basically

AVON

only 18 years old although the owners have taken advantage of some plantings, mostly trees, which remain from the mid-eighteenth century onwards.
The Wills have aimed mainly at an informal effect and they have planted
ornamental trees, shrubs, herbaceous plants and bulbs to give colour and
structure throughout the year. The colour in autumn is particularly remarkable. The new plantings to the south of the house, which include the
White and Silver beds, retain something of the original layout but on the
other side the owners have transformed the conventional sloping lawn and
rose beds by including a sensitive mixture of plants, many of which are
unusual. There is one formal area, hedged with yew, called the Pool
Garden. It contains rectangular pools and fountains, and at one end, the
raised Asian bank is planted to reflect the pink, blue, white and silver
colours of the plantings around the pools. Overall the Wills have achieved a
remarkably attractive garden, the very opposite of what is usually meant by
the description 'plantsman's'. Note, too, their emphasis on labour-saving
such as gravel mulch in the white bed.

PRIOR PARK ★ 16
Bath, Avon.

*The National Trust ★ From Bath take A36 left at the White Hart pub to Prior
Park Road ★ Parking ★ Opening Sept 1995*

There can be few more dramatic settings than the Prior Park landscape
park which has recently been acquired and is undergoing extensive restoration by the National Trust. The Palladian mansion by the architect John
Wood from 1734, designed for Bath's leading entrepreneur and philan-
thropist Ralph Allen, dominates the steeply sloping landscape and provides
stunning views of the city. Landscaped and planted continuously over a
period of twenty years from 1734 to 1764 the park is approached on a
circular walk from the lower gate off Prior Park Road which leads directly
into the Wilderness. This area includes a rococo sham bridge and the ruins
of Mrs Allen's grotto. The walk continues from the mansion viewpoint
down the east side of the valley to the lakes and to the Palladian bridge of
1755 returning by the west side of the valley via the Chinese gate.

THE RED LODGE 17
Park Row, Bristol, Avon. Tel: (0117) 921 1360

*Bristol Corporation ★ Located in city centre ★ House open. Extra charge ★
Garden open June and July, Sat only. Opening hours are 'constrained by staffing
levels' (telephone before travelling any distance) ★ Entrance: free*

Good reconstruction of the early seventeenth-century town garden of a
merchant's house. Trellis work re-created from a seventeenth-century
design and knot garden based on the plasterwork pattern in the house. Old
varieties of roses, shrubs and other plants. A list of plant names is available
for a small charge.

SHERBORNE GARDEN 18
Pear Tree House, Litton, Avon. Tel: (01761) 241220

Mr and Mrs J. Southwell ★ 15m S of Bristol, 7m N of Wells on B3114 ¼m beyond Litton and Ye Olde Kings Arms ★ Best season: June/July ★ Field car park and picnic area ★ Refreshments: tea and coffee ★ Suitable for wheelchairs ★ Dogs on lead ★ Open 4th June to 25th Sept, Sun and Mon, also 2nd April, 7th May and 1st Oct, 11am – 6pm. Other days by appointment ★ Entrance: £1.50, children free

A rather surreal garden that displays a very personal choice of species trees, grasses and water garden features in a three and a half-acre site reclaimed from farmland. The owner gardeners are compulsive tree people who since 1963 have planted hundreds of species and exotic trees, expanding the original cottage garden and paddock into a mini-arboretum. The garden now boasts a pinetum, nut hedges, collection of species roses and the latest manifestation, a prickly wood that offers 180 varieties of holly (a list is provided for real holly lovers), and a collection of over 100 ferns. Most trees and plants are clearly labelled. This garden is an interesting example of how natural pasture land may be tamed and surface water channelled into ponds.

UNIVERSITY OF BRISTOL BOTANIC GARDEN 19
Bracken Hill, North Road, Leigh Woods, Bristol, Avon.
Tel: (0117) 973 3682

University of Bristol ★ Cross the Suspension Bridge from Clifton, turn first right (North Road) and go ¼m up on the left ★ Parking ★ Partly suitable for wheelchairs ★ Open Mon – Fri except Bank Holidays, 9am – 5pm; weekends, Friends of the Botanic Garden only ★ Entrance: free

The Botanic Garden relocated to this site in 1959 and is a very interesting garden for the keen plantsman. Large collections of both New Zealand and South African floras as well as comprehensive collections of aeonium, cistus, hebe, paeonia, pelargonium, salvia and sempervivum are all cultivated in this attractive five-acre garden. Collections of native trees and shrubs, and plants peculiar to the Avon Gorge, plus conservation collections of rare native south west species are also grown. Glasshouses contain ferns, orchids, bromeliads, cacti and succulents, insectivorous plants and tender bulbs. The garden aims to be educational and illustrate the diversity of the plant kingdom. Plants and borders are well-labelled and arranged with various themes: poisonous, dye, economic, medicinal, sand dune and woodland are just some of the groupings in this fascinating garden. Access at the weekend is only to Friends of the garden; details of becoming a Friend and partaking of the annual seed list and plant sales can be obtained from the Superintendent.

VINE HOUSE ★ 20
Henbury, Bristol, Avon. Tel: (0117) 950 3573

Mrs T.F. Hewer ★ 4m N of Bristol centre, in Henbury, next to 'Salutation' ★ Suitable for wheelchairs ★ Dogs on lead ★ By appointment all year for NGS. Please ring in advance ★ Entrance: £1, OAP and children 50p

Two acres of garden developed by the present owner and her late husband since 1946 which although within the city boundary has the good fortune to back on to the woodland of the large Blaise estate landscaped by Repton.

AVON

This is a particularly interesting garden because its owners started by reducing it to 'brown earth' and planned the planting positions by using canes, checking them from the house. The result is 'in part a wild garden' with glades with bulbs, cyclamen and other carpeting plants and ponds, a bog and 'cliff' garden. There are surprises round every corner. The specimen trees are labelled.

WILLIAM HERSCHEL MUSEUM   21
19 New King Street, Bath, Avon. Tel: (01225) 311342

Trustees of the Museum ★ On New King Street close to Queen's Square and Green Park Station ★ Best season: summer ★ Toilet facilities ★ Shop ★ Museum open ★ Garden open March to 1st Nov, daily, 2 – 5pm, Nov to Feb, Sat and Sun, 2 – 5pm ★ Entrance: £2.50, children under 18 £1, family ticket (2 adults and up to 4 children) £5

This museum is one of the smaller and more fascinating museums, from whose garden William Herschel discovered the planet Uranus in 1781. Over the years the garden has suffered from neglect, but recent replanting has now re-created a charming small town garden such as might well have existed in William Herschel's time.

OPENING DATES AND TIMES

Times of access given are the best available at the moment of going to press, but some may have been changed subsequently. In the entries, the times given are inclusive – that is, an entry such as May to Sept means that the garden is open from 1st May to 30th Sept inclusive and 2 - 5pm also means that entry will be effective during that period. Please note that many owners will open their gardens to visitors by appointment. They will often arrange to give a personally-conducted tour on these occasions.

TELEPHONE NUMBERS

Except where owners have specifically requested that they be excluded, telephone numbers to which enquiries may be directed are given for each property. To maintain the support and co-operation of private owners, it is suggested that the telephone be used with discretion. Where visits are by appointment, the telephone can of course be used except where written application, particularly for parties, is specifically requested. Code numbers are given in brackets. For the Republic of Ireland phone 010353 followed by the code (Dublin is 1) followed by the subscriber's number. In all cases where visits by parties are proposed, owners should be advised in advance and arrangements preferably confirmed in writing.

BEDFORDSHIRE

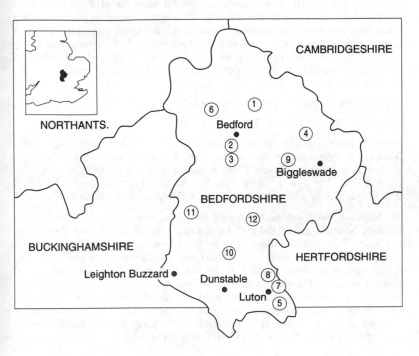

BROADFIELDS   1
Keysoe Row East, Keysoe, Bedford, Bedfordshire.
Tel: (01234) 376326

*Mr and Mrs Chris Izzard ★ Leave Bedford on B660 Kimbolton road. After
10m, turn right at Keysoe crossroads by White Horse public house, then ½ m on
right ★ Parking ★ Cream teas available mid-June to mid-Sept (pergola cover if
wet), daily, 2 – 5pm (Sat, 10am – 2pm) (telephone for details) ★ Toilet facilities ★ Suitable for wheelchairs ★ Dogs on lead ★ Open for charity (telephone for
details) and by appointment*

An immaculate, two-acre weed-free garden. Mr Izzard has a full-time job
and this is a hobby. Formal planting-out with wonderful standard fuchsias
and clipped box trees. Vistas with heather, mature trees, shrubs, conifers
for winter interest and beautifully-grown begonias and bedding plants. A
model kitchen garden and lots of spring bulbs.

EMBANKMENT GARDENS   2
The Embankment, Bedford, Bedfordshire. Tel: (01234) 267422

*North Bedfordshire Borough Council ★ Russell Park, near the town centre ★
Parking ★ Suitable for wheelchairs ★ Dogs ★ Open all year ★ Entrance: free*

A charming Victorian set piece, begun in 1890 by the Corporation and later incorporated with Russell Park, started in 1894. It runs along the banks of the River Ouse with swans and a wonderful vista to Mill Meadow with John J. Webster's delightful iron bridge. A mature avenue of plane and lime trees lines the river embankment. John Lund designed the layout which is formal with a statue and urns, and symmetrical beds of seasonal bedding. Balanced by miniature pampas grasses and yuccas. A tranquil and delightful spot. The 'Riverside Walks' leaflet includes Embankment Gardens and the Russell Park area.

KINGS ARMS PATH GARDENS 3
Ampthill, Bedfordshire. Tel: (01525) 402030

Ampthill Town Council ★ Opposite Market Square, Ampthill, down Kings Arms Yard via public footpath ★ Best season: spring ★ Parking in town centre car parks ★ Teas at adjacent Bowls Club on some open days ★ Suitable for wheelchairs ★ Open 12th Feb, 2 – 4pm; 16th April, 28th May, 18th June, 15th Oct, 2.30 – 5pm and for groups by appointment ★ Entrance: 50p, children 25p

An unusual woodland walk created between 1968 and 1986 by the late William Nourish, full of delightful surprises, planted for interest throughout the year. Very skilful foliage contrasts – *Cornus controversa* 'Variegata', a lovely *Liriodendron tulipifera*, rodgersias and *Lysichiton americanus*. A peaceful garden, maintained since 1987 by the 'Friends of the Garden'. Good ground cover and underplanting including many varieties of snowdrops, narcissi, hellebores, primulas and epimediums. Collections of geraniums, haemerocallis, ilex, magnolias and many others. The *Acer tetramerum* is thought to be the finest of the species in the country. On some opening days there is music by the Ampthill Town Band.

THE LODGE 4
Sandy, Bedfordshire. Tel: (01767) 680551

Royal Society for the Protection of Birds ★ 1m E of A1 off B1042 Sandy – Potton road ★ Best season: spring ★ Parking ★ Toilet facilities ★ Suitable for wheelchairs ★ Shop ★ Open daily, dawn to dusk ★ Entrance: £2, OAP £1, children 50p (1994 prices). RSPB members free

One of over 100 reserves established by the RSPB throughout the country. The garden has many woodland walks and nature trails with extensive bird life and the rare Natterjack toad reintroduced and breeding happily. The Lodge was bought in 1934 by Sir Malcolm Stewart, who improved the garden and made a terraced fish pond on the south side. There is a Victorian terrace and fine trees in good lawns. Of particular interest is the 'RSPB Memorial Garden', a tranquil garden where the names of those who have left bequests to the RSPB are honoured. Other features include a large weeping birch, Wellingtonias, azalea walks to a woodland heath, colchicums, acers, sweet chestnuts. A large bignonia on the house. A huge wisteria, camellias and many big mature conifers. Two small walled gardens with *Garrya elliptica*, old wisterias and many *Clematis tangutica*. A very well planted vista of old cedar trees. No peat is used and organic principles reign supreme.

LUTON HOO 5
Luton, Bedfordshire. Tel: (01582) 30909

The Wernher family ★ 2m SE of Luton, entrance W off A6129. Enter by Park Street gates ★ Best season: summer ★ Parking ★ Restaurant ★ Toilet facilities ★ Suitable for wheelchairs ★ Plants for sale most spring and summer weekends ★ House open ★ Garden open 14th April to mid-Oct, Fri – Sun, 12 noon – 6pm and Bank Holiday Mons, 10.30am – 6pm (last admission 5pm) ★ Entrance: £2.50, OAP and students £2.25, children £1 (house and garden £5, OAP and students £4.50, children £2) (1994 prices)

The house stands magnificently in a landscape by 'Capability' Brown with an abundance of large cedars, oaks, ashes and other mature trees. On the south side of the house is the formal garden with a large herbacous border, recently replanted, and two vast *Magnolia* x *soulangiana*. The lower terrace forms the rose garden in eight large beds edged with box and with a sheltering yew hedge. The walls of the terrace are covered in musk roses, *Garrya elliptica* and *Wisteria sinensis*. The rock garden has small pools and waterfalls running through the centre with many water lilies. There has been much new work with scree beds of *Iris reticulata*, sedum, lewisia, thymus etc. and peat walls with erica, abies, picea and pinus. But recently much of the older masonry has begun to tumble into disrepair.

ODELL CASTLE 6
Odell, Bedfordshire. Tel: (01234) 720240

The Rt. Hon. Lord Luke ★ From A6 turn W through Sharnbrook to Odell ★ Best seasons: spring and early summer ★ Parking ★ Refreshments ★ Open 14th May, 16th July, 2 – 6pm ★ Entrance: £1, children free

A wonderful site on the side of a valley sweeping down to the River Ouse with lawns and lovely trees. Wellingtonias, ilex, mulberries and willows. Shrub roses. Secret paths wind down the hillside. Magnificent borders against old balustraded walls. Banks of daffodils.

SEAL POINT ★ 7
7 Wendover Way, Luton, Bedfordshire. Tel: (01582) 26841

Mrs Danae Johnston ★ In NE Luton. Turn N off Stockingstone Road into Felstead Way ★ Parking in road ★ Refreshments ★ Plants for sale ★ Open 9th July, 2 – 6pm and at other times by appointment. Coaches and small groups welcome ★ Entrance: £2

A most exciting small sloping town garden with many interesting plants and features. A sheltered paved patio with *Jasminum mesnyi* and *Euphorbia rigida* (syn. *E. biglandulosa*). Home-made ornaments with a Japanese theme. A pool with a waterfall, and very well-grouped contrasting foliage. Giant rhubarb, cut-leaved elder, grasses, etc. A fern area and two beds, yin and yang: yin being blues and pale colours and yang berberis and brown sorrel – an exciting and original idea. Trees include *Cercis canadensis* and a fine specimen, *Sophora japonica*, 20 years old and beginning to flower. *Clematis texensis* and a charming clipped box cat with tail, and much more.

STOCKWOOD PARK 8
Stockwood Craft Museum, Farley Hill, Luton, Bedfordshire.
Tel: (01582) 38714

Borough of Luton ★ From M1 take junction 10 to Luton. Take Farley Hill (Chapel Street) turn off the A505 Dunstable road out of Luton. Signposted from A1081 old London road ★ Parking ★ Refreshments: in Conservatory tea room ★ Toilet facilities ★ Suitable for wheelchairs ★ Shop ★ Stockwood Craft Museum in stable block ★ Open April to Oct, Tues – Sat, 10am – 5pm, Sun and Bank Holidays, 10am – 6pm; Nov to March, Sat and Sun, 10am – 4pm. Guided tours available all year by appointment ★ Entrance: free

A series of period gardens have been laid out within the walled gardens of the old house – a Victorian garden, a cottage garden, a seventeenth-century knot garden – designed by Robert Burgoyne, Luton's gifted master gardener, ably assisted by Peter Ansell, the head gardener at Stockwood Park. In the park is a landscape garden with sculpture by Ian Hamilton Finlay – the one artist to have given a convincing continuity to the landscape gardening tradition. His modern fragments of 'antique' buildings, partly buried, suggest the eighteenth-century ideal of a harmonious blend of planting, architecture and sculpture – arguably the greatest art form to have originated in Britain.

THE SWISS GARDEN 9
Old Warden, Biggleswade, Bedfordshire. Tel: (01234) 228330

Bedfordshire County Council ★ Take A1 to Biggleswade and follow signposts from A1 Biggleswade roundabout. Signposted on A600, Shefford – Bedford road ★ Best season: end May/June ★ Parking opposite Shuttleworth Collection ★ Refreshments at Aerodrome. Lakeside picnic area ★ Toilet facilities inc. disabled ★ Suitable for wheelchairs (wheelchairs for loan) ★ Dogs in woodland and picnic area only ★ Shop ★ Open Jan to Oct: Jan to Feb, Suns only, 11am – 4pm; March to Sept, daily except Tues: weekends, Bank Holiday Mons and whole of Aug, 10am – 6pm, weekdays 1.30 – 6pm (last admission 5.15pm); Oct, Suns only, 11am – 4pm. Guided tours available ★ Entrance: £2, concessions £1, children 75p, family ticket £4, season ticket £8. Discount of 25% in Jan and Feb. Special rates for parties

This fascinating romantic landscaped garden is said to have been created in 1830 by Lord Ongley of the East India Company for his Swiss mistress. It was closed for 40 years from 1939, then leased by Bedfordshire County Council and restored. It has wonderful trees; cedar of Lebanon, the largest Arolla pines in England, vast pieris 300 years old underplanted with *Helleborus orientalis* and a most unusual variegated sweet chestnut. Innumerable curly iron bridges cross over miniature canals. Little Swiss period summerhouses with sheets of bulbs in the spring underplanting azaleas, rhododendrons and spring-flowering shrubs. The gloom of the grotto and the dazzling light of the fernery provide a dramatic contrast.

TODDINGTON MANOR ★ 10
Toddington, Bedfordshire. Tel: (01525) 873924 (11am – 5pm) and (01525) 872576 (evenings)

Sir Neville and Lady Bowman-Shaw ★ 1m NW of Toddington, 1m from M1 junction 12. Signposted ★ Best seasons: June and July ★ Parking ★ Refreshments ★ Dogs on lead ★ Plants for sale ★ Shop ★ Rare Breeds Centre and vintage tractor collection ★ Garden open 15th April to Sept, daily, 11am – 6pm, and possibly some open days in Oct ★ Entrance: £2.50, children £1 (1994 prices). Special rates for parties

The Bowman-Shaws moved here in 1979 to find a wilderness, since reclaimed and planted with spring bulbs, flowering trees and other plants which lend colour on into the summer. They also inherited some wonderful old trees: beeches, ashes, yews and Wellingtonias set in extensive lawns. The pleached lime walk, set along a lovely old paved path, has a hosta/fern border on one side and large herbaceous borders on the other. A large walled garden is filled with interesting and complementary plants (most recently three delphinium beds) undergoing constant improvement. Particularly beautiful are the many shrub and climbing roses. There is a large and comprehensive herb garden alongside restored timber greenhouses which contain vines, peaches and many exotic pot plants. Water plays an important role. A stream and several ponds add interest to the garden. In the woods the walks go past two lakes and include plenty of wildlife for plant and animal lovers.

WOBURN ABBEY 11
Woburn, Bedfordshire. Tel: (01525) 290666

The Marquess of Tavistock and the Trustees of the Bedford Estates ★ From M1 junction 13 follow signs ★ Parking ★ Restaurant ★ Toilet facilities ★ Shop ★ Pottery and Antiques Centre ★ Open weekends only from Jan to 27th March and then daily to Oct, 10am – 4.45pm ★ Entrance: £5 per car inc. one passenger's entry to house. Pedestrians 50p (1994 prices)

Humphry Repton, who designed the park and garden, considered Woburn to be one of his finest achievements. Today, huge magnificent sweeping lawns are meticulously mown in diamonds and stripes lining up with the house. The private gardens, which are open to the public at stated times, contain a large hornbeam maze. They have good herbaceous borders, massed beds of 'Iceberg' roses edged with lavender, and a most successful new rose garden. Lovely ponds with rare water lilies. In the spring there are 122 varieties of daffodils and narcissi. Also fritillaries and orchids naturalised in the grass. There are many fine trees, including tulip trees. The owners are concentrating on viburnums and hope to hold a National viburnum collection. An old camellia house (frost-free) contains large camellias, still with the odd flower in June. The deer park is landscaped down to the Shoulder-of-Mutton pond, with lovely groups of trees, and with many species of deer. A really historic wonderful site.

WREST PARK 12
Silsoe, Bedfordshire. Tel: (01525) 860152

English Heritage ★ ½m E of Silsoe village off A6 ★ Parking ★ Refreshments ★ Toilet facilities ★ Dogs on lead ★ Shop ★ House open ★ Garden open April to Sept, Sat, Sun and Bank Holidays only, 10am – 6pm ★ Entrance: £1.85, OAP £1.35, children (5-15) 90p (1994 prices)

BEDFORDSHIRE

Wrest Park is one of the few places in England where it is possible to see an early eighteenth-century garden in the manner of Bridgeman. A very rigid and formal layout dominates the main axis of the grounds which feature an impressive canal; many subsidiary and frequently meandering cross-axes cut through thick blocks of natural and unrestrained woodland leading to statues and giant vases set in grassy glades. Later in the eighteenth century 'Capability' Brown worked at Wrest Park and made several alterations without destroying much of its earlier plan. He made a highly naturalistic artificial river to surround the grounds and loosened the planting at their perimeter. In the nineteenth century, when the house was rebuilt in the French style, it was fronted by Italianate terraces with parterres. There are several fine buildings. Two deep mixed borders separated by a wide turf alley have recently been refurbished and should look well for much of the summer if the rabbits can be kept at bay.

BERKSHIRE

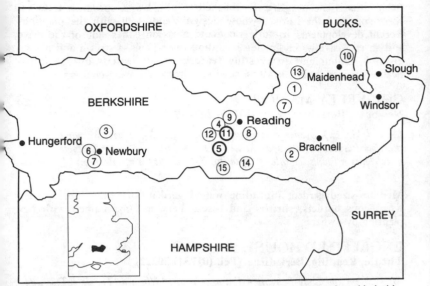

Two-starred gardens are ringed in bold.

ASHDOWN HOUSE
(see Oxfordshire)

BEAR ASH
Hare Hatch, Nr Reading, Berkshire. Tel: (01734) 402639

Lord and Lady Remnant ★ 2m E of Wargrave, ½m N of A4 at Hare Hatch ★ Teas ★ Toilet facilities ★ Plants for sale ★ Open 4th June for charity, 2 – 6pm ★ Entrance: £2, children free

A delightful and immaculately-kept two–acre garden with a pleasant view over parkland. Gold border and silver sundial garden. Shrubs, old-fashioned roses, swimming pool garden, Pandora's secret garden and a small vineyard. Small herb garden in kitchen garden. The new lake in the park can be viewed from the garden.

BLENCATHRA
Finchampstead, Berkshire. Tel: (01734) 734563

Dr and Mrs F.W. Gifford ★ At NW end of Finchampstead Ridges on B3348 between Crowthorne Station and Finchampstead War Memorial. Entrance off joint private drive ★ Teas on open days ★ Toilet facilities ★ Partly suitable for wheelchairs ★ Dogs on lead ★ Plants for sale on open days ★ Open 9th April, 21st May, 2 – 6pm and by appointment ★ Entrance: £1.80, accompanied children free. Parties welcome

The owners started this 11-acre garden in 1964, when they purchased an unmanaged woodland site and built their house. With minimal budget and help – none professional – the garden has evolved. Their enthusiasm for fresh ideas is encouraging. Established shrubs, lawns, specimen trees and roses surround the house, whose design blends well with the plantings. Recent developments include woodland areas on either side of the drive, and an extensive water garden including three pools, a stream and marshy ground. Colour and interesting features in all seasons due to use of heathers, spring bulbs, azaleas, rhododendrons and many conifers.

CHIEVELEY MANOR 3
Newbury, Berkshire. Tel: (01635) 248208

Mr and Mrs C.J. Spence ★ ½m from M4 in Chieveley village, Manor Lane by church ★ Parking in field near house ★ Teas ★ Toilet facilities ★ Suitable for wheelchairs ★ Plants for sale ★ Open 9th July, 2 – 6pm ★ Entrance: £1, children free

Medium-sized garden, including walled garden, swimming pool garden, herbaceous borders, shrubs and roses. Very well-maintained with new planting by owners.

ENGLEFIELD HOUSE ★ 4
Theale, Reading, Berkshire. Tel: (01734) 302221

Sir William and Lady Benyon ★ Entrance is on A340, near Theale ★ Teas and toilet facilities on Sun openings only ★ Suitable for wheelchairs ★ Plants for sale ★ Open all year, Mons; also April to June, Tues – Thurs, all 10am – dusk and 14th May, 2 – 6pm ★ Entrance: £1.50, children free

A beautiful garden with a spectacular view. Deer park. Seven acres of woodland with interesting trees and shrubs. Stream and water garden. Terrace with borders, all excellently maintained.

FOLLY FARM ★★ 5
Sulhamstead, Nr Reading, Berkshire.

The Hon. Hugh and Mrs Astor ★ 7m SW of Reading. 2m W of junction 12 on M4. Onto A4 and turn left at road marked Sulhamstead at Mulligan's Fish Restaurant 1m after Theale roundabout; entrance ¾m on right through a brown gate marked 'Folly Farm Gardens' ★ Parking ★ Teas on charity open days only ★ Toilet facilities ★ Partly suitable for wheelchairs ★ Open probably 23rd April, 29th May, 25th June, 2 – 6pm. Individual or group applications in writing ★ Entrance: £1.50, children free on open days. Groups or individuals at other times £2.50 per person (applications in writing) (1994 prices)

A sublime example of the Lutyens and Jekyll partnership in its vintage years before World War I. The intimate relationship of house and garden personifies Lutyens' genius for design and craftsmanship. A complex arrangement of spaces and courts is linked by herringbone-patterned brick paths, enhancing the vernacular origins of an attractive Edwardian country house. The gardens retain much of their original character, although some planting has been chosen to suit the taste of the present owners. The herbaceous borders are mainly shrub roses, which look wonderful in the second half of June, with old-fashioned herbaceous plants in between giving colour as late as August. The formal sunken rose garden surrounded by a high yew hedge is particularly notable for its masterful design on several levels and this has been substantially replanted in more subtle colours. Other features include formal entrance court, barn court, Dutch-inspired canal garden, flower parterre and tank cloister. This is one of the country's most important twentieth-century gardens.

FOXGROVE FARM 6
Enborne, Newbury, Berkshire. Tel: (01635) 40554

Miss Audrey Vockins ★ Enborne is 2½m SW of Newbury. From A343 turn right at The Gun Inn for 1½m, then right down Wheatlands Lane and right at T-junction ★ Teas on open days ★ Suitable for wheelchairs ★ Nursery open daily except Mon, Tues and whole of Aug (but open all Bank Holidays) ★ Garden open for snowdrops, crocuses and cyclamen during Feb and March by telephone appointment only and 26th March, 29th April, 11th June, 2 – 6pm ★ Entrance: £1, children free

This small garden adjoins a nursery run by the Vockins family. They specialise in bulbs especially species snowdrops, also primroses, auriculas, alpines and small herbaceous plants. The apple tree which fell to the gales has made way for an enlarged peat bed.

HAZELBY HOUSE ★ 7
North End, Nr Newbury, Berkshire. Tel: (01635) 253544

Mr and Mrs M.J. Lane Fox ★ 5m SW of Newbury. Turn right off A343 to Ball Hill. The garden is about ¼m beyond Ball Hill on Kintbury road. Turn left just before Hazelwood Stud ★ Parking ★ Suitable for wheelchairs ★ Plants sometimes for sale ★ Open by written appointment only ★ Entrance: £3

An outstanding garden marrying rich and thoughtful planting with many interesting design features, especially the pergola. Extending to more than five acres, there is a rose garden with heavily-trained old-fashioned roses like 'Ispahan' underplanted with hardy and tender herbaceous perennials, a long shrub walk, herbaceous borders between beech hedges, two lily ponds, an extensive terrace with conservatory, bold shrub borders, a lake with a temple on an island and a newly-planted stream and woodland garden.

HURST LODGE 8
Broadcommon Road, Hurst, Berkshire.

Mr and Mrs A. Peck ★ On A321 Twyford – Wokingham road ★ Parking ★ Teas ★ Suitable for wheelchairs ★ Dogs on lead ★ Plants for sale ★ Open 14th, 20th Aug, 2 – 5.30pm ★ Entrance: £2, children free (joint entrance with Reynolds Farm, Hurst)

This old five-acre garden was developed by Lady Ingram who died in 1989. Her placing of trees and shrubs to give sensitive colour combinations makes for attractive views. The displays of flowers, bulbs, magnolias, hydrangeas, camellias and rhododendrons give a pleasing year-round effect. The most notable features of the garden are the fine trees, old yews, copper beeches and scarlet oaks, a huge old oak and a Scots pine, plus a new rockery beside the enlarged pond. New walks have been opened up and borders developed and extended during the year. Large kitchen garden.

LITTLE BOWDEN 9
Pangbourne, Berkshire. Tel: (01734) 842210

Mr and Mrs Geoffrey Verey ★ 1½m W of Pangbourne on the Pangbourne – Yattendon road ★ Best seasons: mid–May, late June/early July ★ Parking: small groups in front of house. Open days parking in field ★ Teas on open days ★ Toilet facilities ★ Suitable for wheelchairs ★ Dogs on lead ★ Plants for sale ★ Open for charity 28th May, 9th July, 2.30 – 6pm and by appointment ★ Entrance: £2, children free. Swimming 50p

Much of this three-acre semi-formal garden and three acres of woodland garden has been developed by the Vereys since 1950. But a glade with specimen trees and borders was developed by Percy Cane early this century. In May the canopy of the cherry wood is so thick with blossom, from far off it looks like snow; underfoot there is a carpet of bluebells below flowering shrubs, especially magnolias, azaleas, camellias. In July the herbaceous border along the whole length of the house is at its best, as are two other mixed borders of roses, shrubs and herbaceous plants. In October the visitor should look out for the weeping lime. The terrace garden with original 1920s Italian olive jars and paved sunken garden with white flowers adjoins the house; also in the paved area is a pond with water lilies, surrounded with plantings of roses and lilies. A silver plant border leads to a swimming pool area which is landscaped and sheltered by yew hedges and walls bearing roses and clematis.

ODNEY CLUB 10
Cookham, Berkshire.

John Lewis Partnership ★ Off A4094 near Cookham Bridge ★ Parking in grounds ★ Teas ★ Toilet facilities ★ Suitable for wheelchairs ★ Dogs on lead ★ Plants for sale as available ★ Open 23rd April, 2 – 6pm ★ Entrance: £1.50, children 25p

Although only open one day this is a huge 120-acre site along the Thames and makes a long afternoon visit. Well-cared for and continuously developing. A favourite with Stanley Spencer who visited often to paint the magnolia which featured in his work. There is a magnificent wisteria walk, and also specimen trees, herbaceous borders, small side gardens, and terraces with spring bedding plants.

THE OLD RECTORY ★★ 11
Burghfield, Reading, Berkshire.

Mr and Mrs R.R. Merton ★ 5m SW of Reading. Turn S off A4 to Burghfield village and right after Hatch Gate Inn ★ Parking only June to Oct (after hay is cut), otherwise on road ★ Suitable for wheelchairs ★ Plants for sale inc. unusual plants ★ Open last Wed in each month Feb to Oct, 11am – 4pm and for parties by appointment in writing ★ Entrance: £1, private parties £2.50

This garden has achieved wide renown and its maturity and the amazing generosity of plants skilfully planted are remarkable in a site started from scratch in 1950. Mrs Merton, described by herself as 'a green-fingered lunatic', has collected plants from all over the world, notably some rare items from Japan and China. The terrace has a fine display most of the year, the herbaceous border and beds are impressive with collections of hellebores, pinks, violas, peonies, snowdrops, old roses and many others. In the spring there are drifts of daffodils and rather rare cowslips and so many other plants to see that it is well worth making a visit month by month if you live within reasonable range. There is something here for every type of gardener most of the year. The Mertons propagate everything so sales on open days are fascinating, and there is a 'mini-market' of stalls by other plantsmen.

OLD RECTORY COTTAGE ★   12
Tidmarsh, Pangbourne, Berkshire. Tel: (01734) 843241

Mr and Mrs A.W.A. Baker ★ ½m S of Pangbourne towards Tidmarsh. Turn E down narrow lane ★ Parking ★ Plants for sale ★ Open by appointment for individual members of the RHS Lily Group, Alpine Garden Society and Hardy Plant Society and garden societies and 23rd April, 21st May, 18th June, 9th July, 2 – 6pm ★ Entrance: £1, children free

This two-acre garden is full of rare and exciting plants, many of them collected by the owner. It has an area with early spring bulbs and a wild garden round a small lake. Lilies, roses, unusual shrubs and climbers. It is worth visiting on each of the open days as there is always something new to stimulate the interest of a keen gardener. In addition there are ornamental pheasants, white doves and Arab horses. Quite rightly this garden has had much media coverage.

THE SAVILL GARDEN
(see Surrey)

SCOTLANDS   13
Cockpole Green, Berkshire. Tel: (01628) 822648

*Mr M. and the Hon. Mrs Payne ★ Halfway between Wargrave and Henley. At top of Remenham Hill on A423 take turning to Cockpole Green ★ * Teas ★ Suitable for wheelchairs ★ Dogs on lead ★ Plants for sale ★ Open 23rd April, 2 – 6pm and small parties by appointment at other times ★ Entrance: £2, children free*

Happily located in a small clay valley, the present owners have created an extensive water garden from a mere trickle, the edges of which are lush with moisture-loving plants complemented with shrub, fuchsia and ground cover borders. On the high ground to the west side of the house (attractive chalk and flint, formerly a barn), fine specimen trees, catalpas, cedars, Spanish chestnuts mark the boundary of this four-acre site; the trees make way for the formal gardens; a terrace awash with crevice plants; a lead statue of a drummer boy standing guard over the paved pool garden, decorated with planted stone tubs; herbaceous borders and, closest to the corner of which stands a brick and flint gazebo designed to give pleasing views from ground floor windows. On the east side of the drive, lawns sweep down to the large pond which has a new shallow flight of steps and retaining wall at the southern end to facilitate additional planting. At the north end of the pond a Repton-style summerhouse marks the merging of the landscaped water garden with natural woodland. Mown grass paths invite the visitor to the waterfall pool and a small rectangular gazebo, and up a gentle slope to the eastern boundary of the garden. Here a long, shallow flight of steps has been added leading from the trees, through the plants and shrubs to the water's edge, and affording a tranquil and secluded view back across the garden.

STRATFIELD SAYE HOUSE
(See Hampshire)

SWALLOWFIELD PARK   14
Swallowfield, Reading, Berkshire. Tel: (01734) 883815

Country Houses Association Ltd ★ 5m S of Reading in Swallowfield village. Entrance by the village hall ★ Parking in front of house ★ Toilet facilities ★ Suitable for wheelchairs ★ Dogs on lead ★ Open May to Sept, Wed and Thurs, 2 – 5pm ★ Entrance: house and gardens £2.50, children £1

Swallowfield Park has 25 acres of garden, all maintained to the highest standard. There is a six and a half-acre walled garden, much of it built by Thomas Pitt, grandfather of the Prime Minister, in which there are colourful herbaceous borders, scented roses, an orchard, a laburnum and wisteria-covered pergola and a large and productive vegetable garden. In other parts of the grounds are fine lawns and specimen trees, many of them brought to the park in the nineteenth century. There is a dogs' cemetery in which one of Charles Dickens' dogs is buried. Visitors are encouraged to walk past the active croquet lawn, past a large decoy pond to the banks of the River Loddon, which forms the northern boundary of the park.

VIRGINIA WATER
(see VALLEY GARDENS, Surrey)

WYLD COURT RAINFOREST   15
**Streatley Road, Hampstead Norris, Nr Newbury, Berkshire.
Tel: (01635) 200221**

Wyld Court Rainforest Ltd ★ M4 junction 13 then travel N to B4009 ★ Parking ★ Light refreshments ★ Plants for sale ★ Open daily except 25th Dec: April to Oct, 10am – 5.30pm, Nov to March, 10am – 4.30pm ★ Entrance:£3.50, Children £3, under14 £2

A remarkable 25,000 sq ft of glasshouse with a fine collection of exotic plants, splendidly grown, which educates visitors in the beauty and diversity of the jungle. A feature is the tasteful and imaginative way in which the plants are displayed in a carefully-studied interior landscape with paths at various levels which allow them to be enjoyed from above. There are three distinct environments – a cloud forest area; an area known as the Orinoco House which mimics conditions in a mangrove area; the third area has the visually high-light intensity of the lowland tropics. In each of the separate environments is a representative collection of the animals found here, chosen to illustrate the symbiotic relationship between animals and plants in the natural environment.

BUCKINGHAMSHIRE

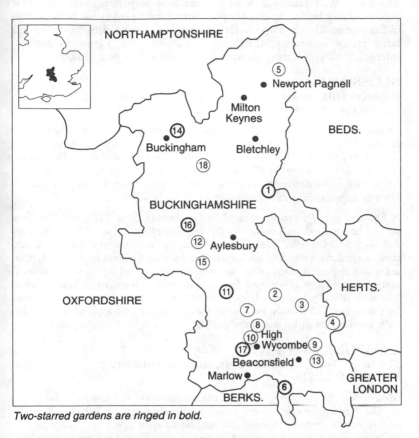

NORTHAMPTONSHIRE

⑤
● Newport Pagnell

Milton
Keynes

BEDS.

⑭
Buckingham

● Bletchley

⑱

①

BUCKINGHAMSHIRE

⑯

⑫ ● Aylesbury

⑮

HERTS.

⑪ ② ③

OXFORDSHIRE

⑦

⑧ High
⑩ ● Wycombe ⑨
⑰ ●
⑬
Beaconsfield ●

④

Marlow ●

⑥

BERKS.

GREATER
LONDON

Two-starred gardens are ringed in bold.

ASCOTT ★★ 1
Wing, Buckinghamshire. Tel: (01296) 688242

The National Trust ★ ½m E of Wing, 2m SW of Leighton Buzzard on S of A418
★ Best season: spring/summer ★ Parking 220 yards from house ★ Toilet facilities ★
Partly suitable for wheelchairs ★ Dogs in car park only ★ House and garden open
5th April to 7th May, and in Sept, Tues – Sun, 2 – 6pm (last admission 5pm) ★
Garden only open 10th May to 30th Aug: every Wed and last Sun in month, 2 –
6pm (last admission 5pm) ★ Entrance: £3 (house and garden £5)

Thirty acres of Victorian gardening at its very best, laid out with the aid of
James Veitch and Sons of Chelsea. Formidable collection of mature trees of
all shapes and colours set in rolling lawns. Fascinating topiary includes
evergreen sundial with yew gnomon and inscription: 'Light and shade by
turn but love always' in golden yew. Wide lawns slope away to magnificent
views across the Vale of Aylesbury glimpsed between towering cedars.
Formal gardens include the Madeira Walk with sheltered flower borders

and the bedded-out Dutch garden. More topiary has been added to the garden, as shown in old prints, and there are new plantings of magnolias. The Long Walk has been reconstructed as a serpentine walk with new beech hedging leading to the lily pond and a wild garden has been planted in Coronation Grove. Two stately fountains were created by Story – one a large group in bronze, the other a slender composition in marble. Interesting all year, spring gardens feature massed carpets of bulbs.

BLOSSOMS 2
Cobblers Hill, Nr Great Missenden, Buckinghamshire.
Tel: (01494) 863140

Dr and Mrs Frank Hytten ★ From Great Missenden follow Rignall Road towards Butlers Cross. After about 1m turn right into Kings Lane and up to top of Cobblers Hill. At T-junction see yellow stone marker in hedgerow. Turn right. After 50 yards turn right at Blossoms sign ★ Best seasons: spring and early summer ★ Limited parking ★ Teas ★ Suitable for wheelchairs ★ Plants for sale ★ Open by appointment only ★ Entrance: £1.50 for NGS

A five-acre garden, mainly created by the owners since 1975, including one acre of beechwood with bluebells. Spring-flowering bulbs, shrubs and trees followed by bluebells. There is an old apple orchard and new rock and cutting gardens, including an herbaceous border. Collections of eucalyptus, acers and salix and many other specimen trees, including *Euodia hupehensis* and a magnificent ivy-leaved beech. Interesting features include a small lake with island where it is hoped mallard will make a home, and sculpture by the owner and friends; two other water gardens and a paved well garden with sundial linked by woodland paths.

CAMPDEN COTTAGE 3
51 Clifton Road, Chesham Bois, Buckinghamshire.
Tel: (01494) 726818

Mr and Mrs P. Liechti ★ On A416 between Amersham and Chesham. Turn into Clifton Road by Catholic Church (opposite primary school). Close to traffic lights at a pedestrian crossing ★ Parking in road, but on open days in school car park by arrangement ★ Refreshments in Old Amersham ★ Toilet facilities in Amersham on the Hill and Old Amersham ★ Unusual plants for sale ★ Open by appointment for parties (but no coaches) and 12th March, 9th April, 14th May, 11th June, 16th July, 6th Aug, 3rd Sept, 1st Oct, 2 – 6pm ★ Entrance: £1, accompanied children free

A generation ago the owner described herself as 'never having given gardening a thought', and started to 'tidy' the neglected garden while builders took over the house. Straight lines have given way to a design adapted to take advantage of a magnificent weeping ash and the original network of stone paths has become a sunny York stone terrace which has a large and ever-increasing collection of terracotta pots, planted for seasonal colour. The owner's speciality is rare and unusual plants – when asked to point out those of interest in early September for a TV programme Mrs Liechti counted more than 400. She is also skilled in finding interesting associations of colour, shape and foliage. Mrs Liechti has created a new formal area with yew hedge, walled border and extended lawns. The busiest open day is in March for the well-known collection of hellebore species and hybrids but worth visiting month by month to keep in touch with all developments.

CHENIES MANOR HOUSE ★ 4
Chenies, Rickmansworth, Hertfordshire. Tel: (01494) 762888

Lt Col. and Mrs MacLeod Matthews ★ Off A404 between Amersham and Rickmansworth. If approaching via M25, take junction 18 ★ Best season: late April to Sept ★ Parking ★ Teas ★ Toilet facilities ★ Suitable for wheelchairs ★ Herbs for sale ★ Shop ★ House open. £1.95 extra ★ Garden open April to Sept, Wed, Thurs and Bank Holidays, 2 – 5pm ★ Entrance: £1.80, children 90p

The owners have created several extremely fine linked gardens in keeping with their fifteenth/sixteenth–century brick manor house. The gardens are highly decorative and maintained to the highest standards. Planted for a long season of colour and using many old-fashioned roses and cottage plants, there is always something to enjoy here. Formal topiary in the 'white' garden, collections of medicinal and poisonous plants in a 'physic' garden, an historic turf maze and a highly productive kitchen garden. On her visits here, Queen Elizabeth I had a favourite tree and the Royal Oak survives. In 1991 'The Sunday Times Maze' was planted in yew hedging with a layout based on the geometric figure of the icosahedron.

CHICHELEY HALL 5
Chicheley, Newport Pagnell, Buckinghamshire. Tel: (01234) 391252

Trustees of the Hon. Nicholas Beatty and Mrs John Nutting ★ On A422 between Bedford and Newport Pagnell, 3m from M1 junction 14 ★ Parking ★ Teas ★ Toilet facilities ★ Suitable for wheelchairs ★ Shop ★ House open ★ Garden open 2nd April to 28th May, and Suns in Aug, 2.30 – 5pm. Parties at any time by appointment ★ Entrance: £1.50 (house and garden £3, children £1.50, parties of 20 or more £2.40 per person)

One of the best and least altered Georgian houses in the country is surrounded by an elegant park with fine avenues and views. Mature trees include oaks, cedars and limes. C-shaped canal lake attributed to London and Wise in 1709. Formal avenues (lime and laburnum) recently planted near the house.

CLIVEDEN ★★ 6
Taplow, Maidenhead, Berkshire. Tel: (01628) 605069

The National Trust ★ 2m N of Taplow ★ Parking ★ Refreshments: light lunches, coffee, teas, in Conservatory Restaurant ★ Toilet facilities ★ Partly suitable for wheelchairs ★ Dogs in specified woodlands only, not in gardens ★ Shop ★ House open April to Oct, Thurs and Sun, 3 – 6pm (last admission 5.30pm) ★ Gardens open March to Oct, daily, 11am – 6pm and Nov to Dec, 11am – 4pm. Closed Jan and Feb ★ Entrance: £4 (house £1 extra. Timed ticket)

A famous house built in 1666 by the Duke of Buckingham in the grand manner overlooking the Thames which flows at the foot of a steep slope below. The present house and terrace designed by Sir Charles Barry incorporates a famous balustrade brought by the 1st Viscount Astor from the Villa Borghese in Rome in the 1890s. The water garden, rose garden and herbaceous borders are attractive in spring, summer and autumn respectively. The formal gardens below the house and the Long Garden, fountains, temples and statuary are pleasing throughout the year. Amongst famous designers who have worked on the grounds are John Fleming (the parterre), Leoni (The Octagon Temple), Bridgeman (walks and the amphitheatre), Nesfield (contribution uncertain) and Jellicoe (rose garden). The Trust is restoring Jellicoe's rose garden of 1959, re-laying paths to the abstract design and incorporating the designer's secret garden in the shape of a cabbage rose. The house is now a luxury hotel, and there is an Open Air Theatre Festival in the summer.

GRACEFIELD 7
Lacey Green, Nr Bradenham, Buckinghamshire.

Mr and Mrs B. Wicks ★ Take A4010 High Wycombe – Aylesbury road. In Bradenham turn right by Red Lion inn towards Walters Ash. Turn left at T-junction to Lacey Green. Brick and flint house is beyond the church facing Kiln Lane ★ Best season: May to Sept ★ Parking at village hall , Lunches and teas on open day ★ Suitable for wheelchairs ★ Dogs on lead ★ Plants for sale if available ★ Open 25th June, 11.30am – 5pm. Parties by written arrangement ★ Entrance: £1.50, children free

A steeply-terraced water garden is a fine feature in this one and a half-acre garden. Plants for the flower arranger; new designs for paved terraces, statuary and trough gardens; collections of clematis and shrub roses; specimen trees include a special malus 'Marshal Oyama' giving fantastic jelly. The owner is a self-confessed plantaholic and has thoughtfully named many specimens in her unusual collection.

GREAT BARFIELD 8
Bradenham, High Wycombe, Buckinghamshire. Tel (01494) 563741

Mr Richard Nutt ★ 4m NW of High Wycombe. From A4010 at the Red Lion turn into village. At bottom of village green turn right ★ Teas ★ Suitable for wheelchairs ★ Plants for sale ★ Open 19th Feb, 2 – 5pm, 23rd April, 2 – 5.30pm, 2nd July, 2 – 6pm, 17th Sept, 2 – 5pm and by appointment. Groups and coaches welcome but please check first ★ Entrance: £1, children under 16 free (conducted tours £2 per person)

A plant connoisseur's garden of one and a half acres designed by the owner for interest over a long season, which starts in February with snowdrops, hellebores and spring bulbs. The position and choice of plants and unusual trees in the island beds combine with the axis of the garden in relation to the house to show to great advantage the many varieties of trees, shrubs and climbing plants. There are generous plantings of roses, lilies, bulbs and herbaceous plants.

HAREWOOD 9
**Harewood Road, Chalfont St Giles, Buckinghamshire.
Tel: (01494) 763553**

Mr and Mrs J. Heywood ★ From A404 Amersham – Rickmansworth road, at mini-roundabout in Little Chalfont turn S down Cokes Lane. Harewood Road is

200 yards on left ★ Best season: spring to autumn ★ Parking on street ★ Teas ★ Toilet facilities for disabled ¼m away ★ Suitable for wheelchairs once beyond gravel driveway ★ Plants for sale ★ Open by appointment only ★ Entrance: £1.50, children free

This one-acre garden has been developed over the last decade but specimen trees planted a century ago and mature yew and box hedges give it a sense of privacy and enclosure. Many unusual roses and clematis. Interesting hardy plants have been chosen for foliage effect and climbers trained into neighbouring shrubs and trees. Other features include a pool garden with statuary and a superb trellis-supported white wisteria. The condition throughout is very good all year round. Extensive plant list available.

HUGHENDEN MANOR   10
High Wycombe, Buckinghamshire. Tel: (01494) 532580

The National Trust ★ 1½m N of High Wycombe on A4128 ★ Parking ★ Toilet facilities inc. disabled ★ Suitable for wheelchairs ★ National Trust shop ★ House open ★ Garden open 4th to 26th March, Sat and Sun only, 2 – 6pm, April to Oct, Wed – Sat, 2 – 6pm, Sun and Bank Holiday Mon, 12 noon – 6pm (Oct 5pm) (last admission ½ hour before closing) ★ Entrance: £3.60, family ticket £9. Party rates on application

High-Victorian garden created by Mrs Disraeli in 1860s and recently restored. Particularly pleasing is the human scale of house and gardens. Five acres with lawns, terraced garden with herbaceous border, formal annual bedding and woodland walks. Orchard with old varieties of apples and pears. Unusual chimaera shrub *Laburnocytisus adamii* produces yellow and mauve laburnum flowers and mauve sprays of *Cytisus purpureus* in late spring/early summer. The additional Victorian flowerbeds, usually at their best in July, have recently been restored.

THE MANOR HOUSE ★★   11
Bledlow, Buckinghamshire.

The Lord and Lady Carrington ★ ½m from B4009 in middle of Bledlow village ★ Parking at farm next door ★ Teas served at the church on 7th May and in the garden 18th June ★ Partly suitable for wheelchairs ★ Open by written appointment, May to Sept and for charity 7th May, 18th June, 2 – 6pm ★ Entrance: £2, children free. Lyde Garden open free every day

With the help of landscape architect Robert Adams, Lord and Lady Carrington have created an elegant English garden of exceptionally high standard. Visit the highly productive and colourful walled vegetable garden, with York stone paths and central gazebo. Formal gardens are enclosed by tall yew and beech hedges. Mixed flower and shrub borders feature many roses and herbaceous plants around immaculately manicured lawns. A garden approached through a yew and brick parterre, incorporating several modern sculptures (displayed with a wit typical of their owners), planned around existing mature trees on a contoured and upward sloping site with open views, is now thoroughly established, with its trees and lawns fulfilling the original landscaping designs. The Lyde Garden (always open) is a water garden of great beauty and tranquillity supporting a variety of species plants.

BUCKINGHAMSHIRE

NETHER WINCHENDON HOUSE 12
Nether Winchendon, Nr Aylesbury, Buckinghamshire.
Tel: (01844) 290101

Mr and Mrs R. Spencer Bernard ★ 7m SW of Aylesbury, 5m from Thame. Near the church in Nether Winchendon village ★ Parking on road nearby ★ Suitable for wheelchairs ★ Open 30th April, 23rd July, 2.30 – 6pm for charity and at other times by appointment ★ Entrance: £1.30, children free (1994 prices)

These gardens surround a romantic brick and stone Tudor manor which is approached by an unusual line of dawn redwoods planted in 1973 continuing a centuries-old tree planting tradition by the Spencer Bernard family. Small orchards on either side of the house combine with fine specimen trees, including mature acers, catalpas, cedars, paulownias, liquidambars and, dominating the lawns at the back of the house, an eighteenth-century variegated sycamore and a late-1950s oriental plane of almost equal height. Well-kept lawns, shrub and flower borders, walled gardens including a productive kitchen garden.

SPINDRIFT 13
Jordans Village, Nr Beaconsfield, Buckinghamshire.
Tel: (01494) 873172

Mr and Mrs E. Desmond ★ N of A40 in Jordans village, at far side of green turn right into cul de sac near school ★ Best seasons: spring and summer ★ Parking in school playground on open days ★ Refreshments: coffee and tea ★ Partly suitable for wheelchairs ★ Dogs ★ Plants for sale ★ Open 1st May, 28th Aug and by appointment ★ Entrance: £1.50, children under 12, 20p

A series of linked 'secret gardens' on different levels are to be found on this sloping site. Fine trees and hedges set off a wide range of unusual plants and shrubs. A miniature version of Monet's flower garden has been created recently and features iris, poppies, peonies and arches with climbing nasturtiums. A model fruit and vegetable garden is terraced on a hillside. Large collection of hostas and hardy geraniums. Three greenhouses with vines.

STOWE LANDSCAPE GARDEN ★★ 14
Buckingham, Buckinghamshire. Tel: (01280) 822850

The National Trust ★ 3m NW of Buckingham via Stowe Avenue off A422 Buckingham – Brackley road ★ Parking ★ Light refreshments in temporary tearoom. Contact Administrator for party bookings. Picnic area in car park and Grecian Valley ★ Toilet facilities inc. disabled ★ Batricars, inc. two two-seaters, may be pre-booked, free of charge ★ Dogs on lead ★ Shop ★ House (Stowe School) may be open in holidays ★ Garden open 26th March to 16th April, daily; 17th April to 21st July, Mon, Wed, Fri and Sun; 3rd July to 3rd Sept, daily; 4th Sept to 29th Oct, Mon, Wed, Fri and Sun; 27th Dec to 7th Jan 1996, daily. All 10am – 5pm or dusk if earlier (last admission 1 hour before closing) ★ Entrance: £3.80. All parties must book in advance

Hurry to visit Stowe as The National Trust scheme here gathers momentum, an undertaking of garden restoration on a scale unlikely to have been previously matched in this country. The plan is to bring Stowe back to its condition in mid-nineteenth century, using the immense mass of documentation available in the United States and elsewhere as source material. The garden was diversified in the nineteenth century with a number of distinct 'scenes' each having a complete character of its own, and the aim now is to reinstate these 'character' areas. The Trust has some £12 million at its disposal to complete the project, including £2m from a mystery donor. The concept is brilliantly planned using the Trust's considerable management and computer resources to resite lost plantings or remove recent redundant additions. The work on the buildings alone deserves whatever medal the country gives to citizens who do fine work for posterity. Stowe has had enormous influence on garden design – starting from the mid-seventeenth century under a succession of distinguished designers including the owner, Viscount Cobham, Bridgeman, Vanbrugh, Kent, 'Capability' Brown and then the new owner Lord Temple who thinned out Brown's plantings after 1750. There are two ways of visiting Stowe – one just to enjoy the wonderful views, the water, the trees and the buildings and sculpture. The other is to try to step back in time and understand what was meant by political/philosophical design which led to the landscape movement which was exemplified at its finest by Stowe, so influencing not only Britain but the gardening world at large. Whichever approach is adopted, the views are breathtaking and it is wise to allow a minimum of two hours to walk round, preferably with a map. Visitors must understand that the site has been a school since 1923, and that while the staff did their best to keep things going, what is now happening is a wondrous change of quite a different order. Amazingly, the practical work is in the hands of an imaginative manager plus only five permanent gardeners, though supported by many volunteers and a Community Action team. Part of the school's contribution is to be some flower gardens, four in all.

TURN END ★   15
Townside, Haddenham, Buckinghamshire.
Tel: (01844) 291383/291817

Mr and Mrs P. Aldington ★ From A418 turn to Haddenham. From Thame Road turn at the Rising Sun into Townside. Turn End is 250 yards on left ★ Best season: spring/early summer ★ Restricted parking ★ Teas on charity open days ★ Plants for sale ★ Open April to June, Wed, 2 – 5pm; also for NGS 11th, 18th June, 17th Sept, 2 – 6pm. Parties by appointment at other times ★ Entrance: £1.50, children 50p. Party rates on application

Peter Aldington's RIBA award-winning development of three linked houses is surrounded by a series of garden rooms evolved over the last 25 years. A sequence of spaces, each of individual character, provides focal points at every turn. There is a fishpond courtyard, a shady court, a formal box court, an alpine garden, hot and dry raised beds and climbing roses. A wide range of plants is displayed to good effect against a framework of mature trees. This plantsman's garden is created within a one-acre village centre site.

WADDESDON MANOR ★★   16
Waddesdon, Nr Aylesbury, Buckinghamshire. Tel: (01296) 651282

The National Trust ★ 6m NW of Aylesbury on A41, 11m SE of Bicester. Entrance in Waddesdon village ★ Best season: spring – autumn ★ Parking, inc.

disabled car park ★ Refreshments: light lunches and teas. Picnics except on lawns at house ★ Toilet facilities inc. disabled ★ Partly suitable for wheelchairs ★ Guide dogs only ★ Plants for sale ★ National Trust shop ★ House open 6th April to 15th Oct, Thurs – Sat, 1 – 5pm, Sun and Bank Holidays, 11am – 5pm; also July and Aug, Wed, 1 – 5pm ★ Gardens open March to 22nd Dec, Wed – Sun, 11am – 5pm; also 6th April to 15th Oct, Sun and Bank Holidays, 10.30am – 5pm. Lord Rothschild's Water Garden only open to groups by prior arrangement. Nursery and Plant Centre open daily ★ Entrance: £3, children (5–17) £1.50 (house and grounds £5.95 – £8.95). Family tickets and grounds season tickets available

Baron Ferdinand de Rothschild's remarkable chateau (built 1874 to 1889), which houses a formidable art collection, is set in an appropriately grand park with fountains, vistas, terraces and walks. The gardens contain an extensive collection of Italian, French and Dutch statuary. An ornate, semi–circular aviary of sixteenth–century French style, built 1889, provides a distinguished home to many exotic birds. The park today benefits from its 100-year old plantings of native yews, limes and hornbeams with a liberal sprinkling of exotic pines, cedars, Wellingtonias and cypresses. Ironically, the fact that all the planting was completed within a period of 10 to 15 years means that a massive programme of replanting is now required, not only of large trees such as oaks, but also of overgrown shrubberies. This horticultural renewal is now reaching completion and at the time of writing the grounds should be back in order by spring 1995. The extensive parterre and fountains, intended to be viewed from the south side of the house, have undergone the most extensive restoration of all, requiring 40,000 plants to provide the 'former glory' here. Daffodil Valley is another spring attraction with thousands of snakeshead fritillaries and wild flowers encouraged to seed. Well away from the house Lord Rothschild has redeveloped the famous Dairy, with its adjacent Water Garden (a nineteenth–century extravaganza in artificial stone) excavated and restored by the Bannermans with all their usual creative skills. This is well worth a visit but is only open by prior arrangement with the Marketing Office at Waddesdon (Tel (01296) 651 282).

WEST WYCOMBE PARK ★★   17
West Wycombe, Buckinghamshire. Tel: (01494) 24411

The National Trust ★ At W end of West Wycombe, S of A40 Oxford road ★ Parking ★ Suitable for wheelchairs ★ Dogs in car park only ★ House open June to Aug, Sun – Thurs, 2 – 6pm (last admission 5.15pm) ★ Grounds open April to May, Sun and Wed, 2 – 6pm; June to Aug, Sun – Thurs, 2 – 6pm; Bank Holiday Suns and Mons, 2 – 6pm (last admission 5.15pm) ★ Entrance: £2.50 (grounds), £4 (house and grounds), family ticket £9.50 (1994 prices)

The park was largely created by the second Sir Francis Dashwood and was influenced by his experiences on the Grand Tour which included visits to Asia Minor and Russia. The first phase involved the creation of the lake with meandering walks completed by 1739. Subsequently numerous classical temples and statues were added as well as delightful little flint and wooden bridges which span the streams. Later still in the 1770s the park was enlarged; Nicholas Revett was employed to design even more temples and follies including the Music Temple on an island which is particularly fine.

Thomas Cook, a pupil of 'Capability' Brown, was entrusted with the planting of trees and alterations to the landscape. There are splendid vistas especially towards the lake which is in the shape of a swan. This is not the place to visit if you seek flower gardens and rose beds. Those who know a little about Dashwood's Hell Fire Club will enjoy seeing the other side of his nature.

WINSLOW HALL 18
Winslow, Buckinghamshire. Tel: (01296) 712323

Sir Edward and Lady Tomkins ★ 10m N of Aylesbury, 6m S of Buckingham on A413 ★ Parking ★ Refreshments: by arrangement. Teas served in village ★ Suitable for wheelchairs ★ House open ★ Garden open throughout the year by appointment; also July and Aug, Wed and Thurs, 2.30 – 5.30pm. Also Bank Holidays ★ Entrance: £2 (house and garden £4)

The original gardens were created around the house completed in 1702 by Sir Christopher Wren. Apart from an English oak older than the house itself, the early London and Wise design has disappeared. Although set on a very busy main road the garden is exceptionally tranquil with a formal and high-walled terrace garden in front. Behind the house a sweep of lawn is bordered by shrubs and specimen trees mainly planted over the last 30 years by the owners and providing an unusual example of dedicated and consistent pruning to show the trees to their best advantage; among them American scarlet oak, willow oak, a fascinating weeping 'creeping' cedar resembling a prehistoric animal, and an 'immature' sequoia of only 100 years old. Where the 300-year-old oaks and elms have died, low stumps remain and provide a base for honeysuckle, roses, clematis, berberis and other climbers which are regularly clipped to make unusual flowering domes. Planted chiefly for foliage effect and autumn colour, mixed shrub and flower borders and rose beds add summer interest.

1996 GUIDE

The 1996 *Guide* will be published before Christmas 1995. Reports on gardens for consideration are welcome at all times of the year but particularly by early summer (June) 1995 so that they can be inspected that year.

Please address letters reporting on gardens to the publishers, Vermilion, 20 Vauxhall Bridge Road, London SW1V 2SA. All letters are acknowledged by the editors.

All descriptions and other information are as accurate as possible at the time of going to press, but circumstances change and it is wise to telephone before making a long journey.

The *Guide* makes no charge for entries which are written by our own inspectors. The factual details are supplied by owners. It is totally independent and its only revenue is from sales of copies in bookshops.

CAMBRIDGESHIRE

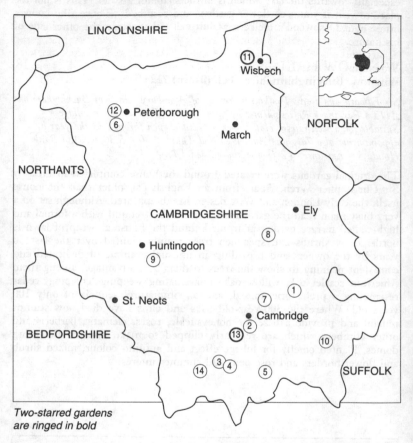

LINCOLNSHIRE

NORFOLK

NORTHANTS

CAMBRIDGESHIRE

BEDFORDSHIRE

SUFFOLK

⑪ Wisbech

⑫ ⑥ Peterborough

March

Ely

⑧

Huntingdon
⑨

St. Neots

⑦ ①

② Cambridge
⑬

③ ④

⑭

⑤

⑩

*Two-starred gardens
are ringed in bold*

ANGLESEY ABBEY ★   1
Lode, Cambridgeshire. Tel: (01223) 811200

*The National Trust ★ In village of Lode, 6m NE of Cambridge, on B1102 ★
Parking ★ Refreshments: restaurant ★ Toilet facilities ★ Suitable for wheelchairs.
Powered scooter (golf cart), Batricars and two–seater vehicle available ★ Plants
for sale ★ National Trust shop ★ House open ★ Garden open 29th March to 9th
July, Wed – Sun and Bank Holiday Mon (but closed 14th April), 11am –
5.30pm; 10th July to 5th Sept, daily, 11am – 5.30pm; 6th Sept to 29th Oct,
Wed – Sun, 11am – 5.30pm (last admission 4.30pm) ★ Entrance: weekdays £3,
Sun and Bank Holiday Mons £3.50 (house and garden: weekdays and Sat
£4.80, Sun and Bank Holiday Mons £5.80. Pre–booked parties £3.80 per
person). NT members charged for Snowdrop weekends in February. Lode Mill
free (demonstrations on first Sun of each month)*

The grounds cover 100 acres and were created in the last 50 years in the park of an abbey which was later converted to an Elizabethan manor. The garden was 'improbably created from naked fenland' in the 1930s with advice from Lanning Roper. A very visual garden with magnificent vistas down avenues of mature trees and statuary and hedges enclosing small intimate gardens. 4500 hyacinths, spring bulbs and superb mature herbaceous borders. Silver pheasants. A new riverside walk beside the River Lode links the dahlia garden (best in summer) with the hedged herbaceous area and opens up splendid views down the river to the working mill.

CAMBRIDGE COLLEGE GARDENS 2

Most colleges are helpful about free access to their gardens although the Masters' or Fellows' gardens are often strictly private or rarely open. Specific viewing times are difficult to rely on because some colleges prefer not to have visitors in term time or on days when a function is taking place. The best course is to ask at the Porter's Lodge or to telephone ahead of visit. However, some college gardens will always be open to the visitor, by arrangement with porters, even if others are closed on that particular day.

Amongst the College gardens of particular interest are the following: *Christ's*; note particularly Milton's mulberry; the cypress grown from seed from the tree on Shelley's grave in Rome; Charles Darwin's garden with canal with false perspective; roof garden on the new building [Open weekdays, 10am – 12 noon. Closed Bank Holidays, Easter Week and May to mid-June and 23rd Dec to 2nd Jan]. *Clare Fellows' Garden*; two-acre garden beside the River Cam impressively redesigned in 1946 [Normally open July to Sept, daily inc. Bank Holidays, 10.30am – 4pm. £1.50 for College and gardens]. *Emmanuel Gardens*; large gardens with herb garden designed by John Codrington [Open daily, 9am – 5pm; College Gardens and Fellows' Garden open 8th July for charity]. *Jesus College*; a must for those interested in sculpture to see the Flanagan Venetian horse. Sensitive planting elsewhere and do not miss the head in the cloisters [Open daily, 9am – 5.30pm, but closed May to mid-June to parties of four or more]. *King's College*; one of the greatest British architectural experiences set off by fine lawns. Spring bulbs [College open daily until 6.30pm but access limited mid-April to mid-June and closed 14th, 15th Aug and 23rd Dec to 3rd Jan. £2]. King's Fellows' Garden with magnificent old specimen trees [Open only 16th April, 23rd July, 2 – 6pm. £1. Teas]. *Leckhampton* (part of Corpus Christi) at 37 Grange Road. Laid out by William Robinson, originally seven acres with two acres added [Open 5th June for charity]. *Magdalene Fellows' Garden* [Open daily 1 – 6pm. Closed May and June]. *Pembroke*; courtyard gardens with modern plantings [Daily during daylight hours. Closed May and June]. *Peterhouse*; varied, smallish gardens and interesting octagonal court with hot and cool sides [Open Mon – Fri, 1 – 5pm. Limited access mid-April to mid-June]. *Robinson College Warden and Fellows' Garden*, Grange Road; although one of the newest institutions, many believe the garden is one of the finest in the city. The eight-acre site has been extensively landscaped incorporating a number of established Edwardian gardens into the grounds. Bin Brook bisects the garden, with a pond at its centre. Notable for its trees, shrub collection and shade-tolerant species. The wild garden provides a good display of bulbs [Open daily, 10am – 6pm, except 14th to 17th April and some periods during May and June for examinations]. *St John's*; huge park-like garden with eight acres of grass, fine trees and good display of bulbs in spring. Wilderness (two and three quarter acres) introduced by 'Capability' Brown, has spring bulbs including from June to July the spectacular Turk's cap lily (martagon lily). In the Master's Lodge are quantities of *Arabus turnata*, probably the only specimens in the country. Rose garden [Open daily 10.30am to 5.30pm but College closed to visitors May and June]. *Trinity*; a garden and grounds of 45 acres with good trees. [Grounds open daily although restricted access, with charge for entry, March to Sept; opening times from Porter's Lodge. Fellows' Garden open 9th April, 2 – 6pm]. *Little St Mary's Church*; wild and natural garden which has been developed since 1925 [Open all year round].

CROSSING HOUSE GARDEN ★   3
Meldreth Road, Shepreth, Cambridgeshire. Tel: (01763) 261071

Mr and Mrs Douglas Fuller ★ 8m SW of Cambridge, ½m W of A10 ★ Some parking ★ Suitable for wheelchairs ★ Open all year, daily ★ Entrance by collecting box

This is a tiny garden, started by the present owners over 30 years ago. No matter what time of the year you visit it there is always something fascinating growing. In all there are 5000 species to see. It is also an eye-opener as to what can be achieved in such a small space – from the use of diminutive box edges, to the yew arches that are beginning to grow, to the three tiny greenhouses packed with unusual plants. Highly recommended, a delightful garden. Docwra's Manor (see entry) is within easy walking distance.

DOCWRA'S MANOR   4
Shepreth, Royston, Hertfordshire. Tel: (01763) 261473/261557/260235

Mrs John Raven ★ 8m SW of Cambridge, ½m W of A10. Opposite war memorial ★ Best seasons: May to July and Sept ★ Parking in village hall car park ★ Toilet facilities ★ Suitable for wheelchairs ★ Small nursery with hardy plants for sale ★ Open all year, Mon, Wed, Fri, 10am – 4pm and 2nd April, 7th May, 4th June, 2nd July, 6th Aug, 3rd Sept, 1st Oct, 2 – 6pm. Also by appointment. Parties welcome ★ Entrance: £1.50, accompanied children under 16 free. Extra charge for guided parties and for parties out of opening hours

This two and a half-acre garden round a Queen Anne house has been created by the owner since 1954. It is divided into different areas by using buildings, hedges and walls, thus enabling choice and tender plants to be protected from winds. Collections of euphorbias and clematis species. The garden has been encouraged to grow jungle-like and seedlings are left to develop where they will. Many bulbs and unusual plants. The Docwra's garden was described by the late John Raven in his book, *The Botanist's Garden*, recently republished (see also entry for Ardtornish, Scotland). The Crossing House (see previous entry) is within easy walking distance.

DUXFORD MILL   5
Mill Lane, Duxford, Cambridgeshire. Tel: (01223) 832325

Mr Rupert and Hon. Mrs Lea. Contact: Mr Terry Bailey ★ From M11 junction 10 take A505 towards Newmarket, taking the second turn to Duxford village ★

Best season: early July ★ Parking ★ Refreshments by arrangement ★ Toilet facilities ★ Suitable for wheelchairs ★ Plants for sale occasionally ★ Open by appointment ★ Entrance: £1, children 50p

This nine-acre garden, started in 1948, took 20 years to complete and was planned to save upkeep with lawns which flow into each other for easy mowing and rose borders in long curves with access at front and back. Roses were bred at Duxford (there are over 2000) to give as constant a display as possible and to produce cut blooms. Vistas were planned to take advantage of the river and mill pools with statues and a Regency temple as focal points. Five hundred trees provide windbreaks, interest and winter colour, notably silver birch and other betula species, such as *B. costata*, *B. jacquemontii* and *B. papyrifera*, the paper birch. Also a maple collection and specimens of the fossil tree, better known as dawn redwood (*Metasequoia glyptostroboides*), raised from cuttings from the first specimen sent to the UK in 1948. The gardens attract a variety of wildfowl.

ELTON HALL ★ 6
Peterborough, Cambridgeshire. Tel: (01832) 280454

Mr and Mrs William Proby ★ 8m W of Peterborough in the village of Elton, just off the A605 ★ Best season: July ★ Parking ★ Refreshments ★ Toilet facilities ★ Hall open ★ Open 16th April to Aug, Bank Holiday Suns and Mons; also July, Wed and Sun; Aug, Wed, Thurs and Sun, 2 – 5pm ★ Entrance: £1.65, children 70p (hall and garden £3.90, children £1.90) (1994 prices)

Elton Hall and gardens have many regular visitors enjoying the Proby family's progress in restoring the seventeenth-century hall which has been in their family ever since. The magnificent rose garden has been replanted with old roses under the guidance of Peter Beales. There is a new herbaceous garden round the lily pond planted with an unusual selection of foliage and blue and white flowering plants, including *Crambe cordifolia* and *Romneya coulteri*. The hornbeam and yew hedging planted in the early 1980s is now well advanced and provides marvellous shelter for the shrub garden. A Gothic orangery and new garden are planned for 1995. A 'must' for rose lovers. Arboretum, knot garden, box walk and eight acres of grounds in total.

HARDWICKE HOUSE ★ 7
High Ditch Road, Fen Ditton, Nr Cambridge, Cambridgeshire. Tel: (01223) 292246

Mr J. Drake ★ 3½m NE of Cambridge. From A45 Newmarket Road turn N by the borough cemetery ★ Best season: spring/summer ★ Parking in road opposite ★ Teas in Cambridge ★ Partly suitable for wheelchairs ★ Plants for sale ★ Open two or three times for charity and by appointment (if you are unable to keep the appointment please let the owner know) ★ Entrance: £1.50, children 50p

This medium-sized garden can be visited at any season; the spring gives a stunning display of bulbs and the colchicums give September interest. Mr Drake holds the National collection of aquilegias – 120 different varieties. There are hedges everywhere to protect the garden from its very exposed position. These have been carefully planned to create varying environments.

Within the hedged enclosures there are collections of plants available in this country prior to 1660, Turkish borders and tight plantings of ground cover interspersed with plants of great rarity.

THE HERB GARDEN 8
**Nigel House, High Street, Wilburton, Ely, Cambridgeshire.
Tel: (01353) 740824**

Mrs Yate ★ 5m SW of Ely on A1123 in the centre of Wilburton near the church ★ Best season: May to July ★ Parking in drive and by church ★ Toilet facilities ★ Suitable for wheelchairs ★ Dogs on lead ★ Plants for sale ★ Open May to Sept, most days, 10am – 6pm. Telephone to check ★ Entrance: free (collection box for charity)

For the enthusiast with a keen interest in herbs, Mrs Yate has created a very special garden. The narrow plot has been divided in such a way that a surprise is just around each partition. The herbs are well displayed in named collections covering the aromatics, culinary, astrological, medicinal, biblical, dyers, Roman and Shakespearian herbs.

THE MANOR 9
**Hemingford Grey, Nr Huntingdon, Cambridgeshire.
Tel: (01480) 463134**

Diana and Peter Boston ★ 4m from Huntingdon, in Hemingford Grey ★ Plants for sale ★ Open by appointment all year round ★ Entrance: £1.50

This moated Norman manor house was the setting for Lucy Boston's *Green Knowe* books for children. A small garden (four acres) but very private, divided into different areas planted with old roses. Walk around the back of the moat to the wild garden. There is an inner garden with herbaceous border and small circular beds in grass with a dominant shrub in each. Topiary crowns avenue and chessmen. The weeds do sometimes become noticeable, but Lucy Boston (died 1990) didn't mind a few here and there anyway. The charm of the garden overpowers any weeds present.

ODSEY PARK
(See Hertfordshire)

PADLOCK CROFT ★ 10
West Wratting, Cambridgeshire. Tel: (01223) 290383

Mr and Mrs P.E. Lewis ★ On the outskirts of the village by West Wratting Park. With the Chestnut Tree public house on your right take the first right and first right again. Signed on the left ★ Best season: May to July ★ Limited parking ★ Toilet facilities ★ Suitable for wheelchairs ★ Plants for sale ★ Open April to 15th Oct, Wed – Sat and Bank Holiday Mon, 10am – 6pm. At other times by appointment ★ Entrance: £1.50, children 50p combined with other local gardens on charity open days. Charity box at other times

A two-thirds of an acre garden created during the last 12 years solely by the owners. Mr and Mrs Lewis hold the National collections of campanula and *Campanulaceae* and are great plant enthusiasts, growing plants from all over the world including the St Helena ebony (once thought to be extinct).

The garden offers a number of imaginative plantings for dry, damp and alpine collections and has extensive rockeries and a *potager*. Nearby properties Scarlett's Farm (01223) 290812 and Weaver's Cottage (01223) 892399 open with Padlock Croft on charity open days.

PECKOVER HOUSE ★★   11
North Brink, Wisbech, Cambridgeshire. Tel: (01945) 583463

The National Trust ★ In centre of Wisbech on N bank of the River Nene ★ House open April to Oct, Sun, Wed and Bank Holiday Mons, 2 – 5.30pm ★ Garden open April to Oct, Sat – Wed and Bank Holiday Mons, 2 – 5.30pm ★ Entrance: £1 (house and garden £2.40)

For a hundred years or so this Victorian garden has been 'the product of prudent tidiness, a period piece'. Given in 1943 to The National Trust by Alexandrina Peckover, it had been in the same family since the second half of the eighteenth century. A town house, with two and a quarter acres of garden, it contains some very interesting trees. A maidenhair tree, one of the largest in England, was planted two centuries ago by the donor's Peckover grandfather. Hardy palms withstand the English winter, and in the Orange House are three orange trees bearing fruit which was bought at the Hagbeach Hall sale and is at least 200 years old. In the conservatory are billbergias, daturas and monsteras. Another small house contains tender ferns. Trees and plants are rather in the Victorian taste, such as Wellingtonias and Lawson cypresses, yuccas and spotted-leaved aucubas. The garden is divided by walls; imaginative planting of bulbs, climbers and herbaceous plants make for continuous interest throughout the year. An elegant summerhouse is joined to the conservatory by matching borders edged with pinks.

THORPE HALL   12
Longthorpe, Peterborough, Cambridgeshire. Tel: (01733) 330060

The Sue Ryder Foundation ★ On W edge of Peterborough between A47 and A605 ★ Parking ★ Refreshments. coffee shop ★ Toilet facilities ★ Suitable for wheelchairs ★ Shop ★ Ground floor of house open as garden ★ Garden open daily except 25th, 26th Dec and 1st Jan, 10am – 5pm (for charity 4th June, 2 – 5.30pm) ★ Entrance: £1 for charity

The Sue Ryder Foundation Home at Thorpe Hall opened in spring 1991 and with it the Victorian gardens largely neglected since c. 1920 but now benefiting from a restoration programme started in 1989. The garden's architecture, proportions and vistas are elegant, and the restoration thus far promising, although hampered by drought in 1990. Visits to see progress would be most rewarding for Victorian garden enthusiasts. The adjacent garden centre is separately managed with a good selection of well-labelled shrubs. One section of the main garden is being restored to Cromwellian style. Grade II listed.

UNIVERSITY BOTANIC GARDEN ★★   13
Cambridge. Tel: (01223) 336265

University of Cambridge ★ In S Cambridge, on E side of A1309 (Trumpington Road). There are two entrances: one in Bateman Street and one in Hills Road ★ Pay and display parking in road ★ Refreshments ★ Toilet facilities ★ Suitable for

*wheelchairs ★ Open all year except 25th, 26th Dec: summer 10am – 6pm, winter
10am – 4pm ★ Entrance: a charge is made March to Oct, Mon – Fri and
weekends and Bank Holidays throughout the year; Nov to Feb, Mon – Fri, free*

This garden covers a huge area (40 acres) and is so diverse that a brief
description will not do it justice. It admirably fulfils its three purposes –
research, education and amenity. A visit at any time is worthwhile – even in
winter when the stem garden, especially on a sunny day, is dramatic. The
various dogwoods with red, black, green and yellow-ochre stems contrast
with *Rubus biflorus*, while the pale pink trunk of the birch *Betula albo-sinen-
sis* var. *septentrionalis* is stunning. There is a splendid collection of native
trees as well as exotic ones, including *Asimina triloba* and a good specimen
of *Tetracentron sinense*. Among the collections is a fine one of willows and
poplars. *Populus nigra* is now rare in England. A central area is reserved for
research. There are also rockeries (both sandstone and limestone), a collection of species tulips, a scented garden, a fine range of glasshouses (hot and
cool), a library and a herbarium of cultivated plants. Every specimen is
clearly labelled. The Gilmour building, named after a director who greatly
expanded the garden in the 1950s and 1960s, offers gifts and refreshments.
A major benefactor was Reginald Cory (d. 1934) who was also responsible
for Dyffryn (see entry).

WIMPOLE HALL 14
Arrington, Nr Royston, Cambridgeshire. Tel: (01223) 207257

*The National Trust ★ 7m SW of Cambridge signposted off A603 at New
Wimpole ★ Best season: spring ★ Parking ★ Refreshments: teas and lunches ★
Toilet facilities ★ Suitable for wheelchairs. 'Self-drive vehicle' available ★
Minimal number of plants for sale ★ National Trust shop ★ House open ★ Garden
open 25th March to 5th Nov, daily except Mon and Fri, 1 – 5pm (Bank
Holiday Sun and Mon, 11am – 5pm); also 4th to 25th Aug, Fri, 1 – 5pm. Pre-
booked guided tours for parties with head gardener ★ Entrance: £4.50, children
£2 (hall and garden) (1994 prices)*

The gardens of this eighteenth-century house followed almost every fashion
in landscaping from 1690 to 1810. Today it is much changed due to Dutch
elm disease. However, parterres, simplified by The National Trust, have
been recently reinstated to the north of the house and there has been major
restoration of the lower lake in the north park. Extensive and beautifully
kept lawns but little else for the discerning plantsman, although the gardens
are undergoing continuous restoration. The surrounding landscape is of
great historic and aesthetic interest and includes a two and a quarter-mile
avenue, originally planted in elm in 1720, recently replanted with limes by
The National Trust. Grand folly and Chinese bridge. The Hall is notable
for the library of 1720 and the later drawing room by Soane. This architect
also designed the Model Home Farm which now contains rare breeds and
has a museum of agricultural equipment in the Great Barn. There is also
an adventure playground and film loft.

CHESHIRE

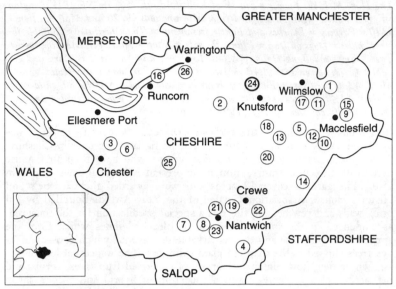

Two-starred gardens are ringed in bold

ADLINGTON HALL 1
Macclesfield, Cheshire. Tel: (01625) 829206

Mrs A.S. Barnett Legh ★ 5m N of Macclesfield off the A523. Signposted in the village of Adlington ★ Best season: May/early June ★ Parking ★ Refreshments in tea rooms ★ Toilet facilities ★ Partly suitable for wheelchairs ★ Dogs on lead ★ Small shop ★ House open ★ Garden open April to 2nd Oct, Sun and Bank Holidays, 2 – 5.30pm ★ Entrance: £4, children £1.50, parties of 25 or more £3.50 per person, children £1 (hall and gardens)

To the front of the house (fifteenth and sixteenth-century with Georgian additions) a gravel drive encircles an oval of lawn with a sundial at its centre. Beyond there is more grass, then through a pair of iron gates is a short avenue of limes dating from 1688. After these a path leads eastwards to the Shell House, a small brick building dating from 1794, in which shells were stuck around the walls in the mid-nineteenth century. To the west is a wood through which there are walks open to the visitor. The walk along the small river bank is particularly pleasant. In the centre, close to a bridge, is the Temple to Diana. Various follies in the wilderness have been restored including the Chinese bridge, black and white Tig house, and the old Hermitage. On the north front of the house more formal gardens have been created. East from the house across a cobbled area is a formal pool. A large statue of Father Tiber lies at the back with water pouring into the pool from a pitcher on which he leans. Not much interest, then, for the plantsperson but an attractive woodland park, mostly landscaped in the eighteenth century in the style of 'Capability' Brown.

ARLEY HALL AND GARDENS ★ 2
Nr Great Budworth, Northwich, Cheshire. Tel: (01565) 777353

The Hon. M.L.W. Flower ★ 5m W of Knutsford off A50, 7m SE of Warrington off A49. Follow signs. Also signed from M6 junctions 19/20 and M56 junctions 9/10 ★ Parking ★ Lunches and light refreshments ★ Toilet facilities ★ Suitable for wheelchairs ★ Dogs on lead ★ Plants for sale ★ Shop ★ Hall open May to August, Tues – Sun, and Bank Holiday Mons, 1 – 5pm; also Suns in late April and Sept ★ Garden open 14th April to 1st Oct, Tues – Sun, and Bank Holiday Mons, 12 noon – 5pm ★ Entrance: grounds, garden and chapel £2.80, children (5–16), £1.40, reduced rates for organised groups (hall, grounds, garden and chapel £4.20, children £2.10) (1994 prices)

It is thought that one of the earliest herbaceous borders in England was planted at Arley Hall. One of the few remaining landed estates in Cheshire, this is the ancestral house of the Warburtons who built their first house here in the fifteenth century, though the present Arley Hall dates only from 1840. The gardens cover 12 acres and were awarded the Christie's and Historic Houses Association Garden of the Year Award. Bounded by old brick walls and yew hedges, there is a special predilection for the tonsured, as evidenced in the splendid avenue of pleached limes which form the approach to the house and the remarkable ilex avenue which consists of 14 ilex trees clipped to the shape of giant cylinders. The walled garden, once a kitchen garden, now contains a variety of cordoned fruit trees, shrubs and herbaceous plants. There is also a collection of hybrid and species shrub roses, a rock garden planted with azaleas and rhododendrons, and a contemporary addition of a woodland garden.

ASHTON HAYES 3
Ashton, Chester, Cheshire.

Michael Grime ★ On the B5393 between Ashton and Mouldsworth ★ Parking ★ Refreshments ★ Toilet facilities ★ Dogs on lead ★ Open 29th May, 2 – 6pm ★ Entrance: £1.50, OAP £1, children 50p

A gravel drive leads the visitor under a huge cut-leaved beech to a recently-built house set in a lawned area with small beds of mixed shrubs. The house overlooks a valley that has been dammed to create a pool at its base surrounded by rhododendrons, azaleas, large pines and other fine trees. Back up the bank towards the house is a group of more exotic shrubs that include camellias and a Chilean fire bush. The south garden, a large lawned dell, has a good collection of mature conifers and more rhododendrons; note the circular gate set in the wall. These gardens are extensive, covering 12 acres altogether.

BRIDGEMERE GARDEN WORLD 4
Bridgemere, Nr Nantwich, Cheshire. Tel: (019365) 239/381/382

Mr J. Ravenscroft ★ On A51 S of Nantwich. From M6 take junction 15 or 16 and follow signs ★ Parking ★ Refreshments: coffee shop ★ Toilet facilities, inc. disabled ★ Suitable for wheelchairs ★ Plants for sale ★ Shop ★ Open daily, 10am – dusk (summer 8pm, winter 5pm) ★ Entrance: nominal admission fee

Begun in 1961 with one field of roses, this 25-acre garden centre now claims to be Europe's largest. There are areas with all types of plants for sale including garden ornaments and conservatories. Although some of these areas are attractively laid out, the main area of interest as a garden to view is the Garden Kingdom with over 20 different gardens including three Chelsea Flower Show Gold Medal winners. This has been made mainly to show what the plants offered for sale will come to look like, and most plants are labelled. There is a cottage garden, the Hill containing dwarf or slow-growing plants, the rhododendron and azalea garden, the Winter garden, the rock and water garden, the silver grey border, French rose garden, Folly garden, white garden, Mediterranean garden, Victorian garden, the autumn border plus herbaceous borders and annual borders. Fruit and vegetable garden and the Old Bridgemere – a re-construction of the very early nursery. All this plus woodlands and lawns.

CAPESTHORNE HALL AND GARDENS ★ 5
Macclesfield, Cheshire. Tel: (01625) 861221; Fax: (01625) 861619

Mr W.A. Bromley Davenport ★ 7m S of Wilmslow, 1m from Monks Heath on A34 ★ Parking ★ Refreshments: lunch, afternoon teas, supper by arrangement ★ Toilet facilities ★ Suitable for wheelchairs ★ Dogs in park only ★ Shop ★ House open as gardens but 1.30 – 3pm only ★ Garden open April, Sun; May, Aug and Sept, Wed and Sun; June and July, Tues – Thurs and Sun, 12 noon – 6pm. Also open all Bank Holidays during the summer months ★ Entrance: gardens and chapel £2.25, OAP £2, children (5-16) £1 (hall, gardens and chapel £4, OAP £3.50, children £1.50)

Capesthorne is one of East Cheshire's fine historic parks showing the English style of eighteenth- and nineteenth-century landscape design with belts of trees enclosing a broad sweep of park and with the house as the focal element. The gardens are best enjoyed by following the suggested woodland walks, because the outstanding features are the range of mature trees, and the views and plant-life associated with the series of man-made lakes. There is much, too, to interest those with a taste for the history of gardens – for example the site of a conservatory built by Sir Joseph Paxton. There is a pair of outstanding rococo Milanese gates, and more convention-ally a formal lakeside garden planned in the 1960s by garden designer Vernon Russell-Smith.

CHESHIRE HERBS 6
Fourfields, Forest Road, Nr Tarporley, Cheshire. Tel: (01829) 760578

Libby and Ted Riddell ★ On the A49 close to the crossroads with the A54 ★ Best season: mid- to late-summer ★ Parking ★ Plants for sale ★ Shop ★ Open daily except 24th Dec to 2nd Jan, 10am – 5pm ★ Entrance: free

This is principally a nursery which stocks over 200 varieties of herbs but there is also a small garden in a lawned area enclosed by a yew hedge. It is a circular knot garden small enough to be emulated by most gardeners; the raised bank around it reminds us that such gardens are best when seen from a higher level. Beyond is a larger area of beds again circular in pattern containing many herbs and planted in an informal manner. A plan in the nursery's Herbal Guide names them. There is also a polytunnel full of large tubs of plants. The aroma here and in other parts of the nursery more than makes a visit worthwhile.

CHOLMONDELEY CASTLE GARDENS ★   7
Cholmondeley Castle, Malpas, Cheshire. Tel: (01829) 720383/203

The Marchioness of Cholmondeley ★ On A49 between Tarporley and Whitchurch ★ Parking ★ Refreshments. Lakeside picnic area ★ Toilet facilities ★ Plants for sale ★ Shop ★ Open 2nd April to 1st Oct; April: Sun and Bank Holiday Mon; May to Oct: Wed, Thurs, Sun and Bank Holiday Mon, all 12 noon – 5.30pm ★ Entrance: £2.60, OAP £1.80, children 75p

Although the Cholmondeley family have lived at Cholmondeley since the twelfth century, the present castle was commenced only in 1801 and completed some 20 years later. It is not open to the public but visitors may enjoy the park and gardens which were laid out in the nineteenth century and have been extensively replanted since the 1960s. As a site it is magnificent, with the castle straddling a hill-top and a view across parkland to a distant mere, and the classic ground in between. There are mature trees, interesting (and acid-loving) plants in an attractive setting. In particular the Temple Garden – bordered walkways around a water garden – is most satisfying with its rock garden and a fine view of the lake that leads to a stream garden planted with moisture-lovers. The grass round the tea-room is filled with wild orchids and backing away from this is a good planting of rhododendrons – indeed throughout the garden are many varieties of rhododendrons and azaleas. The rose garden contains an interesting mixture of old and new.

DORFOLD HALL   8
Nantwich, Cheshire. Tel: (01270) 625245

Mr R. Roundell ★ 1m W of Nantwich, S of A534 ★ Best seasons: spring and early summer ★ Parking ★ Toilet facilities ★ Partly suitable for wheelchairs (garden only) ★ Hall open ★ Garden open April to Oct, Tues and Bank Holiday Mons, 2 – 5pm ★ Entrance: £3, children £2

Dorfold Hall, impressive from the front, is approached through an avenue of limes with open parkland to each side and a large pool just to the west. The approach to the house is thought to have been laid out by William Nesfield who was chosen to design various parts of Kew. To the rear or south of the house is a large lawn at the east side of which is a statue of Shakespeare standing between two modern shrub borders, all the borders to the south having been replanted. Beyond a low wall is another large lawn from where there are views across a ha-ha to the flat countryside in the south. A broad grass walk leads eastwards to a dell. Here rhododendrons and other acid-loving shrubs have been planted amongst mature trees around a small stream, an area developed by the present owner. To the west is another grassed area with specimen trees and two fine gates.

DUNGE FARM GARDENS   9
Kettleshulme, Stockport, Cheshire. Tel: (01663) 733787

David and Elizabeth Ketley ★ In the village of Kettleshulme. Signposted from

*B5470 Macclesfield – Whaley Bridge road ★ Best season: May to Aug ★ Parking
★ Teas ★ Toilet facilities ★ Plants for sale ★ Open April to Aug, daily, 10.30am
– 6pm, evening groups by appointment (only mini buses and 35-seater coaches
acceptable) ★ Entrance: £2 (weekdays), £2.50 (weekends and Bank Holidays),
children 50p*

Many gardens in Cheshire are magnificently situated but Dunge Farm
perhaps comes out best of all. Nestling in a small valley high up in the
Peak District, every view is provided with a marvellous backdrop by the
surrounding hills. There is much of horticultural interest as well, beds of
diverse herbaceous plants and shrubs surround the old stone farmhouse and
many alpines grow around the terrace. A small trout pool to the south of
the house is the starting point for a number of walks. One leads into the
rhododendron dell, where amongst a great variety of rhododendrons and
azaleas there are also acers, magnolias and other shrubs. There are perennials, too, rodgersias, euphorbias, meconopsis, corydalis and others, mainly
moisture-lovers as a small stream keeps this area damp. Another walk goes
around the side of the valley and joins the stream further up. As well as
more rhododendrons there are a number of seats positioned carefully at the
best viewpoints back down the valley. Planting only began here in 1982 but
the garden is already well worth a visit; shrub and species roses are plentiful, giving further interest after the rhododendrons have finished.

DUNHAM MASSEY
(see Manchester (Greater))

GAWSWORTH HALL 10
Macclesfield, Cheshire. Tel: (01260) 223456

*Mr and Mrs T. Richards ★ 3m S of Macclesfield off A536. Signposted ★ Best
season: midsummer ★ Parking ★ Refreshments: tearooms at pavilion in car park ★
Toilet facilities ★ Suitable for wheelchairs ★ Small shop ★ Hall open ★ Garden
open Easter to 4th Oct, daily, 2 – 5.30pm ★ Entrance: £1.50 (house and garden
£3.40, children £1.70, parties of 20 or more £2.90) (1994 prices)*

Gawsworth Hall is approached by a drive leading between two lakes which
arrives at the north end of the hall where there is a large yew tree and
lawns sloping down to one of the lakes. A formal garden on the west side
of the house has beds of modern roses edged by bright annuals and many
stone ornaments including a sundial and circular pool with a fountain.
Stone steps lead to a sunken lawn area with borders of shrubs and perennials. To the south is another lawned garden surrounded by a high yew
hedge and herbaceous borders. A grassed area containing mature trees lies
to the west of these formal areas, from where there is a view of the
medieval tilting ground and site of the Elizabethan pleasure gardens. A path
back to the house passes a small conservatory containing classical statues.
Open-air theatre in garden mid-June to mid-August.

HARE HILL GARDENS 11
**Hare Hill, Over Alderley, Nr Macclesfield, Cheshire.
Tel: (01625) 828981**

*The National Trust ★ N of B5087 between Alderley Edge and Prestbury at
Greyhound Road ★ Best season: spring/ early June ★ Parking ★ Toilet facilities ★
Partly suitable for wheelchairs ★ Open April to Oct, Wed, Thurs, Sat, Sun and
Bank Holiday Mons, 10am – 5.30pm. Special for rhododendrons and azaleas,
probably 12th May to 2nd June, daily, 10am – 5.30pm. Parties by appointment
★ Entrance: £2.50, children £1.25. £1.50 per car refundable on entry to garden*

This garden consists of two distinct areas, a walled garden, once used for
growing vegetables, and surrounding it a large woodland garden. The
walled garden is rather sparsely planted. Climbing plants around the walls
include vines, roses, ceanothus and wisteria, and in the centre are a few
small rosebeds. A seat set into the north wall is surrounded by a white
trellis pergola and nearby are two wire statues. The woodland garden is
perhaps of greater interest. It contains over 50 varieties of holly, many
fine rhododendrons and magnolias and there are spring-flowering bulbs
and some climbing roses growing high into their host trees. In the centre is
a pond spanned by two wooden bridges. Dredging work has been carried
out to clear the woodland pools, and a new bridge has been built linking
one of the garden paths to the island.

HENBURY HALL 12
Nr Macclesfield, Cheshire.

*Mr S.Z. de Ferranti ★ Parking in field ★ Teas ★ Toilet facilities ★ Partly suit-
able for wheelchairs ★ Open twice a year for charity ★ Entrance: £2, children
50p (1994 prices)*

Henbury Hall was built in 1986 based on Palladio's Villa Rotunda and its
light creamy stone goes well with its parkland setting. To the north of the
hall the land slopes down to a lake. The 12 acres around are well-landscaped and planted with many mature trees, azaleas and rhododendrons,
etc. There is a fountain in the centre of the lower lake and ornamental
bridges at each end. The land to the north rises again, and beyond more
banks of trees and shrubs there is a walled kitchen garden. Close by is a
unique design of tennis court and a large modern conservatory housing a
swimming pool, a fernery and a grotto. At the other side of the kitchen
garden is a cottage recently renovated in the gothic style.

JODRELL BANK ARBORETUM 13
Jodrell Bank Science Centre and Arboretum, Macclesfield,
Cheshire. Tel: (01477) 571339

*Manchester University ★ On the A535 between Holmes Chapel and Chelford, 5m
from M6 junction 18. Signposted ★ Parking ★ Refreshments: self-service cafeteria
★ Toilet facilities ★ Partly suitable for wheelchairs ★ Shop ★ Open 18th March to
29th Oct, daily, 10.30am – 5.30pm. Otherwise Sat and Sun, 11am – 4.30pm ★
Entrance: £3.50, OAP £2.50, children £1.90 (arboretum, science centre and
planetarium), children under 5 free but not admitted to planetarium. Family
ticket £10.50*

The arboretum was begun in 1972 largely at the instigation of Professor Sir
Bernard Lovell and with financial support from the Granada Foundation. It
is set in a flat landscape with all views to the south dominated by the

massive radio telescope. Large collections of trees, heathers and old-fashioned roses are its main attractions. There are broad grass walkways and many small natural ponds in this 40-acre garden. The National collections of malus and sorbus are here, together with the Heather Society's calluna collection. An Environmental Discovery Centre with 'The Tree Planet' exhibition stands at the Arboretum entrance. A visit to Jodrell Bank represents good value when all its attractions are considered and is a day out for a family.

LITTLE MORETON HALL   14
Congleton, Cheshire. Tel: (01260) 272018

The National Trust ★ 4m SW of Congleton on the E side of the A34 between Congleton and Newcastle-under-Lyme ★ Parking ★ Refreshments: drinks and light meals ★ Toilet facilities, inc. disabled ★ Suitable for wheelchairs. Wheelchair and scooter available on loan ★ Dogs in car park and areas outside moat only ★ Shop ★ Herbs usually for sale ★ Open April to Sept, Wed – Sun, 12 noon – 5.30pm. Closed 14th April but open Bank Holiday Mons, 11am – 5.30pm. Oct, Sat and Sun, 12 noon – 5.30pm (last admission 5pm) ★ Entrance: £3.50, children £1.80, family £8.80; joint ticket with Biddulph Grange Gardens £6, children £3, family £15

Little Moreton Hall is one of the best-known timber-framed buildings in the country, and its gardens too are very pleasant in their own quiet way. They cover about an acre and are set within a moat. There is a cobbled courtyard in the centre of the hall and to the west a large lawn with fruit trees and an old grassed mound. To the north of the hall is a yew tunnel and the best feature of all, a knot garden, laid out under the guidance of Graham Stuart Thomas following a seventeenth-century model. It is a simple design of gravel and lawn separated by a low box hedge. Behind the knot garden, four new beds have been planted with medieval and culinary herbs and a selection of seventeenth-century vegetables. There are herbaceous borders around the hall and a gravel walk that follows the inside perimeter of the moat. The garden is largely the creation of the Trust and is a fitting complement to the house.

MELLORS GARDENS   15
Hough Hole House, Sugar Lane, Rainow, Nr Macclesfield, Cheshire. Tel: (01625) 572286

Mr and Mrs G. Humphreys ★ Ten minutes from the centre of Macclesfield. Take the Whaley Bridge road. In the village of Rainow turn off to the north, opposite the church into Round Meadow. Then turn at the first left into Sugar Lane and follow this down to the garden ★ Parking ★ Refreshments ★ Toilet facilities ★ Partly suitable for wheelchairs ★ Dogs on lead ★ Open 28th, 29th May, 27th, 28th Aug, 2 – 5pm (but please telephone first as possible new owner) or by appointment for parties of more than 10 ★ Entrance: £1.50, children free

Where can you pass through the valley of the shadow of death, climb Jacob's ladder, see the mouth of hell and visit the Celestial City all within 10 minutes of Macclesfield? Here in the second half of the nineteenth century, James Mellor, much influenced by Swedenborg, designed this allegorical garden which attempts to re-create the journey of Christian in

CHESHIRE

Bunyan's *Pilgrim's Progress*. Most areas are grassed with stone paths running throughout. There are many small stone houses and other ornaments to represent features of the journey. At one end a large pond is overlooked by a small octagonal summerhouse. The garden stands in a small valley in a rugged but attractive part of the Peak District. Be sure to be shown round by the owner or buy one of the excellent guide books in order to get the best from this small garden.

NORTON PRIORY MUSEUM AND GARDENS 16
Tudor Road, Manor Park, Runcorn, Cheshire. Tel: (01928) 569895

Norton Priory Museum Trust ★ From M56 at junction 11 turn for Warrington and follow Norton Priory signs. From all other directions follow Runcorn then Norton Priory signs ★ Parking ★ Refreshments: teas and snacks in Museum ★ Toilet facilities, inc. disabled ★ Suitable for wheelchairs ★ Dogs permitted but not in walled garden ★ Plants for sale ★ Shop ★ Museum open ★ Gardens open March, daily, 12 noon – 4pm; April to Oct, weekdays, 12 noon – 5pm, Sat, Sun and Bank Holidays, 12 noon – 6pm. Walled garden closed Nov to Feb ★ Entrance: £2.50, OAP and children £1.30. Museum and grounds £1.90, OAP, children and students £1. Walled garden £1.20, OAP, children and students 80p

Norton Priory was built as an Augustinian foundation in the twelfth century and transformed into a Tudor then Georgian mansion before being abandoned in 1921. The 30 acres of woodland gardens contain the ruins of the Priory, and also an authentic eighteenth-century walled garden. Originally built by Sir Richard Brooke in 1770 this eventually fell into disrepair, but since 1980 it has been restored to reflect both the Georgian and modern designs and tastes. Its range of specialities include a culinary and medicinal herb garden, plants for household uses, a fruit arch and cordon fruit, traditional vegetables, a new orchard and a number of herbaceous borders.

PENN 17
Macclesfield Road, Alderley Edge, Cheshire.

Mr R.W. Baldwin ★ ¾m E of Alderley Edge village, N of B5087 ★ Parking on Woodbrook Road ★ Refreshments ★ Plants for sale ★ Open 14th, 16th, 17th, 30th April, 1st, 28th, 29th May, 2 – 5pm ★ Entrance: £2, OAP £1.25, children 50p

This garden is most noted for its fine collection of rhododendrons and azaleas and there are over 500 varieties here. But the situation high on Alderley Edge and its layout contribute much to the garden's charm. An Edwardian house stands at the centre facing south and overlooks a large lawn, surrounded by banks of trees and shrubs including camellias and magnolias as well as rhododendrons. Behind the house is a steeply rising woodland garden with narrow paths running among the trees and shrubs, and it is here that the best views are obtained, both back across the Cheshire plain and over the Edge towards Manchester. A fruit and vegetable garden and some small herbaceous beds lie to the west of the house.

PEOVER HALL 18
Peover Hall, Over Peover, Nr Knutsford, Cheshire.

Mr R. Brooks ★ 3m S of Knutsford on A50 ★ Teas on Mons ★ Toilet facilities ★

*Partly suitable for wheelchairs (many grass paths) ★ Dogs in park only ★ Plants
for sale on special occasions ★ Hall open, Mon only, 2.30 – 4.30pm ★ Gardens
open May to Sept, Mon and Thurs, 2.30 – 4.30pm ★ Entrance: £1.50, children
50p (hall and garden £2.50, children £1.50) (1994 prices)*

Peover Hall (pronounced Peever) and its gardens are surrounded by a large
expanse of flat parkland laid out in the early eighteenth century, but the
gardens are mainly Edwardian. On the northern side of the hall is a forecourt, from where a broad grass walk leads through an avenue of pleached
limes to a summerhouse. This overlooks a small circular lawn and both are
enclosed by a high yew hedge. On the west side of the gardens is a wooded
area containing many rhododendrons and a grassed dell that is particularly
attractive. Clustered around the south and west of the hall are several small
formal gardens, separated by brick walls and yew hedges. Some contain yew
topiary. There is a rose garden, a herb garden, a white garden and a pink
garden. The lily pool garden has a summerhouse with a tiled roof
supported by Doric columns. Fine Georgian stables and a church to visit.

QUEEN'S PARK, CREWE ★   19
**Victoria Avenue, Wistaston Road, Crewe, Cheshire.
Tel: (01270) 69176**

*Crewe and Nantwich Borough Council ★ 2m W of Crewe town centre, S of the
A532 ★ Parking off Queen's Park Drive ★ Refreshments: cafeteria in park ★
Toilet facilities, inc. disabled ★ Partly suitable for wheelchairs ★ Dogs on lead ★
Open all year, 9am – sunset ★ Entrance: free*

Queen's Park is a very well landscaped Victorian park created in 1887-8 by
the London & North Western Railway as a gift to the people of Crewe. It
is oval in shape and covers 48 acres, with large grassed areas and a wide
variety of mature trees. From an ornate entrance with two 'gothic' lodges
and a clock tower, a drive leads through an avenue of birches to the centre
of the park. Here a modern café with a terrace looks down upon the large
boating lake that is surrounded by banks of trees and shrubs. From the
west of the park a stream runs through a lightly wooded valley to join the
lake. A path linking the entrance to this valley passes some raised beds of
heathers and goes through a tunnel of laburnum. It merits a high grade for
the quality of landscaping, the trees and the Victorian buildings, but in
essence it is a large municipal park where a fight against vandalism and
litter is fought hard.

THE QUINTA ★   20
Swettenham, Cheshire.

*Sir Bernard Lovell ★ E off the A535 Holmes Chapel – Alderley Edge road near
Tremlow Green in the village of Swettenham, next to the church ★ Parking ★
Teas on Bank Holidays ★ Open daily, 2pm to sunset. Parties by arrangement ★
Entrance: £2*

Sir Bernard Lovell began planting this garden in 1948 to satisfy his love of
trees. It has steadily expanded and now contains a large variety of trees and
shrubs. There are good collections of pines and birches, five of the six varieties of wingnut and an oriental plane directly descended from the

Hippocratic tree on the island of Cos. Most areas are informally planted and interspersed with grassed glades; a number of avenues pass up and down the garden including one of limes planted in 1958 to celebrate Sir Bernard's Reith lectures. Across the more recently planted areas to the west of the garden a walk (one mile from the car park and back) passes some marvellous views across the Dane Valley. It leads to the 39 steps that descend into the wooded valley of a small brook. Take good walking shoes and a tree guide as some specimens have lost their labels and can be quite a challenge to identify.

REASEHEATH 21
Reaseheath College, Nr Nantwich, Cheshire. Tel: (01270) 625131

Reaseheath College ★ 1½m N of Nantwich on A51 ★ Parking ★ Toilet facilities ★ Partly suitable for wheelchairs ★ Plants for sale ★ Open for College Open Days 20th, 21st May, and 25th May to 27th July, Wed only, 1 – 5pm ★ Entrance: Donations to the Gardens Scheme. Guided tours will also be conducted for a small fee. Prices on application

The College is fortunate in being housed in the grounds of Rease Heath for its attractive gardens must constantly provide the students with inspiration. From the old brick hall a large lawn sweeps southwards to a lake, flanked on one side by a heather garden and by a rockery on the other. The lake is spanned by a wooden bridge and stocked with a good variety of water lilies and marginals. On the south side is a woodland garden, with many fine trees including a large cut-leaved beech. Underplanting is of primulas, hostas, azaleas and other shade-loving plants. To the west of the lake is another lawned area; this has island beds with a variety of small trees, shrubs and perennials. There is also a formal rose garden enclosed by a berberis hedge. Other small gardens are scattered around the campus.

RODE HALL 22
Church Lane, Scholar Green, Cheshire. Tel: (01270) 882961

Sir Richard and Lady Baker Wilbraham ★ 5m SW of Congleton between A34 and A50 ★ Best seasons: spring and early summer ★ Parking ★ Toilet facilities ★ House open as garden ★ Garden open 5th April to 27th Sept, Weds and Bank Holidays, 2 – 5pm ★ Entrance: £2 (house and garden £3.50. Special groups at other times £4)

A long drive leads through parkland to an attractive red brick house with fine stable buildings and a gravel forecourt. The gardens lie to the north and east of the house, with many areas remaining as planned by Repton in 1779. The rose garden and formal areas close to the house however were planned by Nesfield in 1860; these are mainly lawn, with gravel paths and clipped yews, with good views from here of the surrounding countryside and Repton's lake. In a dell to the west is a woodland garden with flowering shrubs including many rhododendrons, azaleas and some fine climbing roses. Old stone steps lead up the opposite side of the dell to a grotto and early nineteenth-century terraced rock garden. A small stream is dammed at the open end of the dell with the resulting pond surrounded by marginals. A path leads from here to the lake. The ice-house in the park is worth a visit and the two-acre Victorian walled kitchen garden in working order is now open to the public.

STAPELEY WATER GARDENS 23
**London Road, Stapeley, Nantwich, Cheshire. Tel: (01270) 623868 or
The Palms (01270) 628628**

*Mr R.G.A. Davies ★ 1m SE of Nantwich on A51 ★ Parking ★ Refreshments:
restaurant and café ★ Toilet facilities ★ Suitable for wheelchairs and some wheelchairs available ★ Open all year, daily except 25th Dec: summer, Mon – Fri,
9am – 6pm, Sat, Sun and Bank Holidays, 10am – 6pm; winter, Mon – Fri,
9am – 5pm, Sat, Sun, 10am – 5pm. The Palms open from 10am ★ Entrance:
The Palms £2.90, OAP £1.95, children £1.45, parties of 20 or more £2.50 per
person, OAP £1.75, children £1.35 (1994 prices)*

This is an area with two acres under cover claimed by the owners to be the
world's largest water garden centre. Within it a few areas are attractive
gardens in their own right. At the back are many pools containing a good
variety of aquatic plants and the land around is landscaped with lawns and
shrub borders. Another area has small demonstration gardens. Across the
car park is The Palms Tropical Oasis. This huge greenhouse has none of
the architectural merit of a Victorian Palm House, but the main hall is
impressive. It has a long rectangular pool stocked with Koi and is flanked
by huge palm trees; on the right is a rockery with streams and pools, on the
left a tropical house with a giant Amazonian water lily.

TATTON PARK ★★ 24
Knutsford, Cheshire. Tel: (01565) 654822

*Cheshire County Council ★ Signposted from M6 and M56 ★ Parking £2 per car
★ Refreshments: hot and cold lunches and snacks but from Oct to March, Suns
only, 11.30am – 4.30pm ★ Toilet facilities ★ Partly suitable for wheelchairs ★
Plants for sale ★ Shop ★ House open April to Sept, 12 noon – 4pm ★ Gardens
open April to Sept, daily except Mons (but open Bank Holiday Mons), 10.30am
– 6pm. Oct to March 1996, daily except Mons and 25th Dec, 11am – 4pm ★
Entrance: gardens £2.50, park £2 per car, Tatton Explorer (to house, old hall
and farm, park and gardens) £6 (1994 prices)*

The gardens here cover 50 acres and warrant an extensive exploration. On
passing through the entrance visitors see to their left the Orangery. Built in
1820 by Lewis Wyatt, and recently restored to his original 1818 plan, it
contains orange trees, lemon trees and plants appropriate to 1818. Next
door is Paxton's fernery of 1850, again recently restored. This has large
New Zealand tree ferns in its distinctively Victorian interior. To the east
passing a large L-shaped herbaceous and shrub border, the Edwardian rose
garden is reached. This is formal in design with a pool at its centre and
fine stone paths and ornaments around. To the south lie large informally
planted areas, an arboretum containing many conifers and rhododendrons
and a lake containing water lilies which has a good variety of marginal
plants growing around its banks. On the west side of the lake is a unique
Japanese garden built in 1910 by workers brought especially from Japan. To
the south of the house is the Italian garden, possibly designed by Paxton
and best viewed from the top floor of the house. The garden also contains a
maze and is surrounded by very attractive parkland.

TIRLEY GARTH ★ 25
Utkinton, Nr Tarporley, Cheshire. Tel: (01829) 732301

Tirley Garth Trust ★ 2¹/₂m N of Tarporley, just N of village of Utkinton on the road to Kelsall. Signposted ★ Parking ★ Teas ★ Toilet facilities ★ Partly suitable for wheelchairs ★ Dogs on lead ★ Open 21st, 28th, 29th May and 4th June, 2 – 6pm ★ Entrance: £2.50, children 50p

Tirley Garth is a magnificent Edwardian house with gardens that complement it perfectly. They are still in much the same layout as originally designed by T.H. Mawson and C.E. Mallows and some of the stonework in the paths, ornaments and buildings is particularly notable. There is a circular courtyard at the western entrance and a small sunken garden to one side which leads to the large terrace on the south front which has lawns and rose beds. To the east is a lawned terrace with a view across the large semicircular rose garden that spreads below it. In the centre of the house is a courtyard with a circular pool and fountain. Outside these formal gardens are areas of parkland and woodland; to the east is a stream running through a small valley planted with fine azaleas, rhododendrons and other shrubs.

WALTON HALL GARDENS 26
Walton Lea Road, off Chester Road, Walton, Warrington, Cheshire. Tel: (01925) 601617

Warrington Borough Council ★ 2m SW of Warrington on S side of A56 in the village of Walton ★ Best seasons: spring and autumn ★ Parking, for which a charge is made ★ Refreshments ★ Partly suitable for wheelchairs ★ Toilet facilities ★ Dogs on lead, some restricted areas ★ Children's zoo and play area ★ Gardens open daily, 8am – dusk ★ Entrance: free

Walton Hall, the former home of the Greenall family, is a dark brick house with a distinctive clock tower. In front is a large lawn and to one side a modern pool and rockery, with a variety of shrubs, alpines and aquatic plants. Behind the Hall is a series of formal gardens separated by yew hedges and planted with bright annuals. Further south is a lawned area with herbaceous borders, with a path leading under some large beech trees to a rose garden. This has beds of modern roses set in an area of grass enclosed by a high conifer hedge. A walk back around the west side of the garden passes through an attractive area of shrubs and trees amongst which are many acers. Banks of mature woodland and large parkland surround the garden. The Council keeps the whole area in good condition, and there are games for children and others. A Ranger Service operates within the park, providing information and organising public events.

HISTORIC GARDENS

The Garden History Society founded in 1965 has published a journal *Garden History* since 1972. Membership is open to those interested. Details from the Secretary, Roger White, 76 Clapham Common North Side, London SW4 9SD Tel: (0171) 350 0085.

CORNWALL

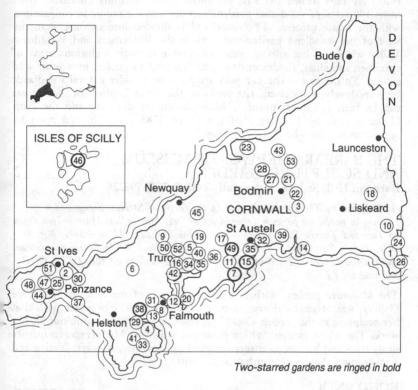

Two-starred gardens are ringed in bold

ANTONY 1
**Torpoint, Cornwall. Tel: NT office (01752) 812191;
woodland garden office (01752) 812364**

*The National Trust and the Trustees of the Carew Pole Garden Trust ★ From
Plymouth use Torpoint car ferry. Antony is 2m W of Torpoint on A374, 16m SE
of Liskeard ★ Parking ★ Refreshments: in tea room ★ Toilet facilities ★ Partly
suitable for wheelchairs ★ Shop ★ House open as Formal Garden ★ Formal
Garden open April to Oct, Tues, Wed, Thurs and Bank Holiday Mons; also
June to Aug, Suns, all 1.30 – 5.30pm (last admission 4.45pm). Woodland
Garden open 31st March to Oct, Mon – Sat, 11am – 5.30pm, Sun, 2 – 5.30pm
★ Entrance: £1 (woodland garden (not NT)); combined gardens only £2.50
(house and formal garden £3.60, pre-booked parties £2.80 per person)*

Antony House is a little off the beaten track but it is well worth the effort
to visit one of the country's finest eighteenth–century houses, in a truly
magnificent natural setting. The great garden designer, Humphry Repton,
was consulted by Reginald Pole Carew but they disagreed over the initial
plans, and it has been successive generations of the Carew Pole family who
have presided over the evolution of the formal garden, parkland and natural

69

woodland. The house and formal garden with its terrace overlooking park-land which sweeps down to the River Lynher (glimpsed through a series of rides) are now owned by The National Trust. A family charitable trust owns 100 acres of woodland garden, also open to the public in conjunction with the house gardens. The woodland is divided into two areas: to the west of the woodland garden car park is the Wilderness and Westdown Valley where, in late spring, one can ramble through a glorious array of specimen camellias, rhododendrons, azaleas and magnolias in a semi-wild setting. To the east of the car park are 50 acres of older natural woodland; here are lovely walks along the banks of the River Lynher. In these areas can be seen a 'fishful' pond, a fifteenth-century dovecote and the Bath House – built by Thomas Parlby between 1788 and 1790 and open by appointment with The National Trust.

THE BARBARA HEPWORTH MUSEUM AND SCULPTURE GARDEN 2
Barnoon Hill, St Ives, Cornwall. Tel: (01736) 796226

Administered by The Tate Gallery ★ In the centre of St Ives. Signposted ★ Parking in public car parks ★ Open April to Oct, Mon – Sat, 11am – 7pm (9pm on Tues and Thurs), Sun, 11am – 5pm, Bank Holidays, 11am – 5pm; Nov to Mar, Tues – Sat, 11am – 5pm, Sun, 1 – 5pm. Closed Mon ★ Entrance: museum and sculpture garden £1 (combined ticket to Tate Gallery St Ives £2.50, OAP and students £1.50)

The sculpture garden, within walking distance of the new St Ives Tate Gallery, was originally designed by the artist herself. It was her wish that her sculpture in the garden should represent a permanent exhibition of her work. The whole garden, which possesses a distinct Mediterranean quality in its trees and bushes, is interconnected by intricate pathways. Native and semi-tropical flowers also enhance the setting.

BOCONNOC 3
The Stewardry, Boconnoc, Lostwithiel, Cornwall.
Tel: (01208) 872546

Mr and Mrs J.D.G. Fortescue ★ South of A390. Well-signed on open days between Lostwithiel and Middle Taphouse ★ Best season: spring ★ Parking in field ★ ☆Teas ★ Toilet facilities ★ Special route for wheelchairs ★ Dogs on lead ★ Plants for sale ★ Shop selling charity goods ★ Open for various charities 30th April, 7th, 14th, 21st May, 2 – 6pm ★ Entrance: £1.50, children free

The extensive grounds were first laid out by Thomas Pitt, Lord Camelford, in the eighteenth century. Great landscape effects. The magnificent woodland garden covers some 20 acres. It contains fine flowering shrubs and many very large and unusual trees (including a Japanese umbrella tree). This magnificent garden is best seen by taking a walk along the well-kept paths.

BOSAHAN ★ 4
Manaccan, Helston, Cornwall. Tel: (01326) 231330

Mrs Vivian ★ 10m SE of Helston, 1m NE of Manaccan village ★ Parking in field if dry. If wet, firm area near farm ★ Cream teas ★ Toilet facilities ★ Partly suitable for wheelchairs ★ Dogs on lead ★ Plants for sale ★ Open 9th, 23rd April, 14th May, 2 – 5.30pm ★ Entrance: £1.50, children free

This valley garden of five acres started 100 years ago leads down to the Helford river and will give pleasure to the keen plantsman as it has both mature and newer planted trees and shrubs, including some New Zealand varieties. In spring colour is provided by masses of camellias, rhododendrons, azaleas and magnolias along with bog plants in the water garden. There are formal beds with herbaceous plants at the top of the garden and one walks down through the valley to find the more mature specimens including pittosporums and dicksonias. There is some additional colour from ornamental pheasants. Fine views from the top of the valley.

BOSVIGO HOUSE 5
Bosvigo Lane, Truro, Cornwall. Tel: (01872) 75774

Mr Michael and Mrs Wendy Perry ★ From the A390, just before reaching Highertown, take turning into Dobbs Lane adjacent to Shell garage. Entrance to Bosvigo House is 500 yards down Dobbs Lane and is clearly marked on the left ★ Some parking in carriage drive, otherwise in lane ★ Refreshments on charity Suns only ★ Toilet facilities ★ Partly suitable for wheelchairs ★ Rare and unusual plants for sale at nursery ★ Open March to Sept, Wed – Sat, 11am – 6pm and some Suns for charity ★ Entrance: £1.50, children 50p

The three-acre garden surrounding a Georgian house consists of many delightful enclosed and walled areas. The 'hot garden' displays red, yellow and orange plants. The 'Vean Garden' has white and yellow flowers, and the walled garden many rare plants. Within this last section stands a Victorian conservatory where the owners have placed comfortable chairs for visitors. The woodland garden is resplendent with many plants, some rare. A garden with subtle mixtures of colour and foliage where the plantsman will find many unusual and rare specimens.

BURNCOOSE NURSERIES AND GARDEN 6
Gwenap, Redruth, Cornwall. Tel: (01209) 861112

C.H. Williams ★ On the A393 Redruth – Falmouth road between the villages of Lanner and Ponsanooth. Signposted ★ Parking ★ Refreshments ★ Toilet facilities ★ Suitable for wheelchairs ★ Dogs on lead ★ Very large nursery ★ Garden open daily 9am – 5pm (Sun 11am – 5pm) ★ Entrance: £1, children free

A sister garden to Caerhays Castle Garden (see entry), Burncoose covers 30 acres in a woodland setting, originally laid out by the Williams family at the turn of the century. It is now a commercial nursery whose garden contains 25 species of bamboo and a fine collection of camellias, azaleas, magnolias and rhododendrons. Each section of the woodland is easily accessible by well-kept paths.

CAERHAYS CASTLE GARDEN ★★ 7
Caerhays, Gorran, St Austell, Cornwall. Tel: (01872) 501310

Mr F.J. Williams ★ 10m S of St Austell. On the coast by Porthluney Cove between Dodman Point and Nare Head ★ Parking at beach car park ★ Teas ★ Toilet facilities ★ Dogs on lead ★ Plants for sale ★ Castle open for conducted tours

CORNWALL

*27th March to 5th May (excluding Bank Holidays), Mon – Fri, 2 – 4pm ★
Garden open 20th March to 5th May, Mon – Fri, 11am – 4pm; also 26th
March, 16th April, 8th May for charity, 11am – 4pm ★ Entrance: £2.50,
children under 16 £1.50, for charity days £1.50, children under 14 free (castle
only £3, castle and garden £5)*

An internationally noted garden with unrivalled collections of magnolias and
shrubs raised from seed and material brought back by such plant hunters as
George Forrest and E.H. Wilson, who were assisted financially in their
expeditions by the Williams. The house, a vast romantic castle in the
'Gothick' style, was built by John Nash between 1805 and 1807. The garden
began to take on its present form from 1896. The woodland stretches down
to the sea and there are many rare specimens to be seen including tree ferns,
acers, oaks, azaleas and nothofagus. J.C. Williams originally specialised in the
cultivation and hybridising of daffodils, but turned his sheltered clearings
over to a refuge for the nineteenth-century influx of new plants, and many
in British gardens today, including camellias which he bred, originated at
Caerhays. A place to be visited by the family as well as the plantsman.

CARWINION 8
Mawnan Smith, Nr Falmouth, Cornwall. Tel: (01326) 250258

*Mr H.A.E. Rogers ★ From Mawnan Smith, take the road by the Red Lion pub.
500 yards up the hill on the right is a white gate marked Carwinion ★ Parking in
drive and field opposite ★ ☆Teas ★ Toilet facilities ★ Partly suitable for wheelchairs ★ Dogs on lead ★ Plants for sale ★ Open all year, daily, 10am – 5.30pm ★
Entrance: £2, children free*

The Rogers family has been living at Carwinion since the eighteenth
century. The garden, a conservation area, is some 10 acres with a wild
subtropical woodland area leading to the River Helford. Here is the most
comprehensive collection of bamboos in Europe (over 100 specimens), all
labelled. Also a *Gunnera manicata* said to be the largest in Europe, with a
crown as large as a man's body, plus an 18-foot *Dicksonia antarctica*. A
natural un-manicured garden.

CHYVERTON ★ 9
Zelah, Truro, Cornwall. Tel: (01872) 540324

*Mr and Mrs N. Holman ★ 1m W of Zelah on A30. Turn off N at Marazanvose
(end of new bypass), the entrance is ¹/₂m on right ★ Parking ★ Dogs on lead ★
Open by appointment only March to June. Parties of 20 or more by arrangement
★ Entrance: £3, bona fide horticultural students and children under 16 free.
Visitors personally conducted around by owners*

The outstanding feature of this garden originally landscaped in the eighteenth
century is its collection of magnolias, including some bearing the name of the
property and also the owner's father 'Treve' Holman. Superb trees of copper
beech, cedars of Lebanon, eucryphia and a collection of nothofagus make a
beautiful backcloth to a vast collection of camellias and rhododendrons. The
garden is planted to give vistas and is always being further developed. A
collection of acers is being planted and there are good colour combinations
with azaleas and photinias. There is an unusual hedge of *Myrtus luma* and by

the stream are vast gunneras and lysichitums. Note the new water garden and primulas. Trees and shrubs have room to develop freely here but it is hard to realise that this beautiful and vast garden is maintained solely by the owners. Visitors have also rated this one of the most beautiful of Cornish gardens because of its naturalness – no spraying, hence a profusion of wild flowers.

COTEHELE ★ 10
St Dominick, Nr Saltash, Cornwall. Tel: (01579) 50434

The National Trust ★ 1m W of Calstock, 8m SW of Tavistock, 4m from Gunnislake. Turn at St Anne's Chapel ★ Best season: May/June ★ Parking ★ ✩Refreshments in the Barn Restaurant ★ Toilet facilities (and mother and baby room) ★ Partly suitable for wheelchairs ★ Plants for sale ★ Shop ★ House open April to Oct, daily except Fri, 12 noon – 5.30pm ★ Film Room: an eight-minute slide presentation of the history of the estate ★ Garden open daily, 11am – 5.30pm (or dusk if earlier) (last admission ½ hour before closing) ★ Mill open daily except Fri (but open 14th April), 12 noon – 5.30pm (5pm during Oct) ★ Entrance: garden and mill £2.50 (house, garden and mill £5, pre-booked parties £4 per person). Garden by donation in honesty box Nov to March

This ten-acre garden with terraces falling to a sheltered valley has developed gradually from Victorian times. It should give pleasure to most visitors with its combination of formal courtyards, fine terraces, walled garden, pools, herbaceous borders and valley garden. The grey granite walls of the house are a background to many climbers and from the rose terrace one walks down to the pool and dovecote. In the valley are giant conifers, hydrangeas, palms, acers and betulas. There is a small acer plantation and yew hedges along with herbaceous borders.

COUNTY DEMONSTRATION GARDEN
(see **PROBUS GARDENS**)

CREED HOUSE 11
Creed, Grampound, Cornwall. Tel: (01872) 530372

Mr and Mrs W.R. Croggon ★ Take A390 to Grampound, then take road signposted 'To Creed' in the main street. After 1m turn left opposite Creed church. Entry to house and garden on left ★ Parking in lane ★ Teas ★ Toilet facilities ★ Partly suitable for wheelchairs ★ Dogs on lead ★ Open by appointment and 14th May, 4th, 11th June for charity, 2 – 5.30pm ★ Entrance: £1.50, children free

A Georgian rectory garden of seven acres successfully restored over the past 20 years. The very large lawn, originally the site of a bowling green and a tennis court, looks across to a magnificent view of the surrounding countryside. At the far end of the lawn is a delightful well-stocked fish pond. A good collection of trees and rhododendrons. Walled herbaceous gardens. Many new plantings. A woodland walk.

FALMOUTH GARDENS 12
Carrick District Council ★ From A39 follow signs to beaches and hotels ★ Best seasons: spring and summer ★ Parking in roads nearby ★ Suitable for wheelchairs ★ Dogs on lead ★ Open all year, 8am – dusk ★ Entrance: free

CORNWALL

Fox Rosehill Gardens, Melvill Road. A truly remarkable long-established small park of two acres. Famous for its many exotic trees and shrubs, including an *Embothrium coccineum* (Chilean firebush) and an *Arecastrum romazoffianum* (palm). All shrubs and trees are labelled and are set against paths and two lawns. A delight for the ordinary visitor and of great interest to the plantsman.

Gyllngdune Gardens, Princes Pavilion, Melvill Road. A garden with a very attractive lawn, a long Victorian veranda with hanging baskets, and a newly-renovated bandstand. A place for a peaceful rest during holiday exertions.

Queen Mary Gardens, Cliff Road. A seaside park retaining a typical early twentieth-century atmosphere, with formal bedding, subtropical plants and two recently re-designed 100-metre long herbaceous borders.

GLENDURGAN GARDEN 13
Helford River, Mawnan Smith, Nr Falmouth, Cornwall.
Tel: (01326) 250906

The National Trust ★ 4m SW of Falmouth, ½m SW of Mawnan Smith on the road to Helford Passage ★ Parking ★ Refreshments: in tea-room ★ Toilet facilities ★ Plants for sale ★ Shop ★ Open March to Oct, Tues – Sat and Bank Holiday Mons, 10.30am – 5.30pm (last admission 4.30pm). Closed 14th April ★ Entrance: £2.80

This 40-acre valley garden was originally planted by Alfred Fox in the 1820s with the village of Durgan at its foot alongside the Helford river. The woodland valley contains many specimen trees and conifers including two tulip trees and a swamp cypress. There are also many sub-tropical plants especially tree ferns. In spring camellias, rhododendrons and magnolias, including a fine *Magnolia campbellii* 'Alba', flower as do many wild flowers, including primroses, bluebells and wild daffodils. In summer there are drimys, eucryphias, embothriums and many hydrangeas, wild pink campions, aquilegias and foxgloves. There is also the fastest growing tree recorded in National Trust gardens, a *Populus* 'Androscolggin' which has reached 79 feet in 14 years. There is an 1833 laurel maze, a giant stride and many fine views of the Helford river.

HEADLAND 14
3 Battery Lane, Polruan-by-Fowey, Cornwall. Tel: (01726) 870243

Mr and Mrs J. Hill ★ Use public car park. Turn left (on foot) down St Saviour's Hill, left again at intersection near Coastguard Office. Gate on right ★ Best season: June/July ★ Cream teas ★ Beach for swimming ★ Open 18th, 25th May, and June to Sept, Thurs, 2 – 8pm ★ Entrance: £1, children 50p for charity

This cliff garden 100 feet above sea level, created from an old quarry on the headland, has been developed by the present owners since 1974. It is a great credit to the owners for the excellent range of plants they grow with sea on three sides of the garden where plants must withstand spray and gales. It is designed with narrow paths and archways leading round corners to discover secret areas with Australian and New Zealand plants – cordylines and olearias; sub-tropical succulents – agaves, echeverias, crassulas and lampranthus. There is a path with various eucalyptus trees. In crevices one sees sempervivum, sedum and erigeron. Monterey pines, tamarisk, Torquay palms, yuccas and a fatsia all thrive and there are good plant combinations. It is surprising to find vegetables and fruit trees and bushes doing well on such a windswept slope. With the vast range of plants and clever design it is hard to believe the garden is only one and a quarter acres.

HELIGAN ★★ 15
Pentewan, St Austell, Cornwall. Tel (01726) 844157/843566

The Heligan Manor Gardens Project ★ From St Austell take the B3273 sign-posted Mevagissey. Pass by the village of Pentewan. Signposted ★ Parking in grounds ★ Light refreshments ★ Toilet facilities ★ Partly suitable for wheelchairs ★ Dogs on lead ★ Plants for sale ★ Open all year, daily, 10am – 4.30pm. Gates close at 6pm. Guided tours by arrangement ★ Entrance: £2.80, OAP £2.40, children £1.60, family ticket (2 adults, 2 children) £7.80

The gardens cover 57 acres including 27 acres known as 'The Jungle'. A garden existed on the site in 1603. The area increased in the early eighteenth century and later in 1780 expanded to its present size. The entire area had been virtually untended since 1914 when in 1991 reclamation began. The ground was covered with fallen trees and brambles 10 feet high. Now the omnipresent bramble undergrowth has been cleared and 1500 tons of timber removed. Plants have now been reinstated and 5000 trees have been placed in shelter belts. The work is done by a team of contractors and constant supply of volunteers. Heligan is one of the largest on-going restorations in Europe. Paths have been restored in their original locations and metal detectors have been used to find lead labels denoting the original position of plants. The entire area is being reclaimed to become one of the most important gardens in the country. In the various sections of the terrain are found a man-made rockery some 150 yards long, an avenue of palms, a grotto, summerhouses, a wishing well, bee boles (vaulted cells for keeping bees), the melon garden with its pineapple pit, a vinery, the remains of a 300-foot-long herbaceous border (now being reclaimed), a large vegetable garden and an Italian garden fully restored with its pool and summerhouse. Among many outstanding specimens are a *Pinus thunbergii* (Japanese black pine), a *Cedrela sinensis*, a *Podocarpus totara* (Chilean yew) and a 'Cornish Red' rhododendron, all reputed to be the largest in the world.

HIGH NOON 16
Nansawen, Ladock, Nr Truro, Cornwall. Tel: (01726) 883030

Mr R.E. Sturdy ★ 7m E of Truro on the A39. Parking in Ladock village and at Ladock House (see entry) ★ Dogs on lead ★ Toilet facilities ★ Open 30th April and by appointment ★ Entrance: £2 (combined with Ladock House), children free

A three and a half-acre garden with a woodland walk and, in contrast, formal lawns with south-facing views of the neighbouring hillside. The garden is well-stocked with rhododendrons, magnolias and camellias. There is a rose garden. In spring the entire area is covered with a mass of daffodils. Formal pool.

THE HOLLIES 17
Grampound, Truro, Cornwall. Tel: (01726) 882474

Mr J.R. and Mrs N.B. Croggon ★ 6m from St Austell on A390 Truro road in the village of Grampound next to post office ★ Parking in side lanes – Creed Lane, Bosillian Lane, Pepo Lane ★ Teas ★ Toilet facilities ★ Suitable for wheelchairs ★ Plants for sale ★ Open for charity 9th April, 14th May, 11th, 18th June, 9th July, 2 – 5.30pm and by appointment. Private visits welcomed ★ Entrance: £1, children 50p

This two-acre garden has a charming 'cottage' garden effect created by the unusual design. It consists of a number of sections, each different in character. Island beds contain a wide range of trees and shrubs with underplanting to provide interest throughout the year, although spring is the peak time. Many rare plants, including alpines.

KEN CARO   18
Bicton, Nr Liskeard, Cornwall. Tel: (01579) 62446

Mr and Mrs K.R. Willcock ★ 5m NE of Liskeard. Take A390 to Callington, turn off at Butcher's Arms, St Ive, take the Pensilva Road to next crossroads and take the road signposted Bicton ★ Parking ★ Toilet facilities ★ Plants for sale ★ Open 15th April to 28th June, Sun – Wed; July and Aug, Tues and Wed, 2 – 6pm ★ Entrance: £2, children 50p

A formal series of well-designed small gardens (including one Chinese) begun by the owners 20 years ago. Very well-labelled shrubs, conifers and rhododendrons. Aviary with birds and a collection of water fowl. Total area four acres – a new area taken in for 1994. Some very rare specimens including a *Eucryphia* x *nymansensis*. A good visit for the plantsman and the gardener alike.

LADOCK HOUSE   19
Ladock, Nr Truro, Cornwall. Tel: (01726) 882274

Mr G.J. and Lady Mary Holborow ★ 7m E of Truro on the A39. Entrance by the church ★ Parking ★ Teas ★ Toilet facilities ★ Suitable for wheelchairs ★ Open 30th April, 2 – 5.30pm ★ Entrance: £2 (combined with High Noon (see entry)), children free

An old Georgian rectory set in six and a half acres of garden and woodland. The whole area has been reclaimed and planted during the past 16 years. Large expanse of lawns with shrubs and flowerbeds. A spring garden with clearings in wooded areas with rhododendrons, azaleas and camellias. The garden continues on the other side of a park-like field with bluebells, primroses and a further shrub area.

LAMORRAN HOUSE ★   20
Upper Castle Road, St Mawes, Cornwall. Tel: (01326) 270800; Fax (01326) 270801

Mr and Mrs R. Dudley-Cooke ★ At garage above village of St Mawes turn right – signposted at Castle. In about ½m Lamorran is on left of road set behind a line of pine trees ★ Parking for cars in road. Coaches by prior appointment ★ Toilet facilities ★ Partly suitable for wheelchairs ★ Plants for sale ★ Open for various charities 16th, 30th April, 14th, 28th May, 4th, 11th June. Also April to Oct, Wed and Fri, 10am – 5pm and by appointment ★ Entrance: £2, children free

This four-acre garden developed since 1980 contains a large and excellent collection of sub-tropical and warm temperate species which one would not expect to find on a hillside adjacent to the sea. In the main it has been designed in the Italian style with columns and other artefacts. There are over 500 azaleas, many different palms and eucalyptus, yuccas, 250 rhododendrons, a wide range of conifers, a range of Australian and New Zealand plants and a large collection of tree ferns. There are little gardens and round every corner more unusual plants. A Japanese garden and many water features. The plantsman will enjoy this and so will other visitors as the owner has incorporated good design features and interesting colour and foliage combinations.

LANCARFFE ★ 21
Nr Bodmin, Cornwall. Tel: (01208) 72756

Mr and Mrs R. Gilbert ★ 2m NE of Bodmin. Turning off old A30 which is parallel to Bodmin bypass ★ Parking. No coaches ★ Refreshments ★ Toilet facilities ★ Dogs on lead ★ Open for charity 2nd, 9th, 16th and 23rd May, 2 – 5pm ★ Entrance: £1.50, children free

Walking through this four and a half-acre garden one can enjoy one of the best collections of plants in the west of England which includes *Davidia involucrata* (pocket-handkerchief tree) and beds of roses. Some beautiful trees form a backcloth to a fine collection of azaleas, camellias and rhododendrons. There is a delightful walled water garden with shrubs and climbers on the walls. Hydrangeas, eucryphias, acers, *Desfontainea spinosa*, *Campsis radicans* and *Edgworthia papyrifera*, one of the largest *Paulownia fargesii* (foxglove tree) in Britain, various cornus and embothriums are some of the specimens to be enjoyed. The owners are continuing to develop this very pleasant garden.

LANHYDROCK ★ 22
Bodmin, Cornwall. Tel: (01208) 73320

The National Trust ★ 2½m SE of Bodmin off A38, or off B3268 ★ Best season: spring ★ Parking 600 yards but inc. disabled adjacent to garden ★ Refreshments ★ Toilet facilities inc. disabled and mothers' and childrens' room ★ Partly suitable for wheelchairs ★ Dogs on lead in park ★ Plants for sale ★ Shop in house ★ House open (closed Mon except Bank Holiday Mons and closed Nov to March 1996) ★ Garden open April to Oct, daily, 11am – 5.30pm (5pm in Oct); Nov to March 1996 daily during daylight hours ★ Entrance: garden and grounds £2.50, (house, garden and grounds £5.40, family ticket (2 adults and 2 children) £14.50, pre-booked parties £5 per person). Garden free Nov to March

This superb 30-acre garden started in 1857 contains gardens within a garden and has some exceptional trees and shrubs both in the park, woodland and the more formal areas. The collection of trees started before 1634. Banks of colour are provided by magnolias, camellias and rhododendrons, and followed by roses which are in beds in the lawn adjacent to the house interspersed with cone-shaped Irish yews. In the terraces beds of annuals are edged with box. A circular yew hedge surrounds the herbaceous borders which contain a wide range of choice plants and provide summer colour. The woodland has walks amongst rare trees and hydrangeas and other flowering shrubs. There is a stream with moisture-loving plants. A

Victorian cob and thatched summerhouse has recently been rebuilt.

LONG CROSS VICTORIAN GARDENS 23
Trelights, Nr Port Isaac, Cornwall. Tel: (01208) 880243

Mr and Mrs D.J. Crawford ★ 7m N of Wadebridge on B3314 near St Endellion church and Trelights village. Signposted ★ Parking ★ ☆Refreshments ★ Toilet facilities ★ Suitable for wheelchairs ★ Dogs on lead ★ Plants for sale ★ Open all year, daily ★ Entrance: £1 and accompanied children under 14 free, season ticket £1.75

In reconstructing this late-Victorian garden the former owners discovered paths which were not known to exist, also rockeries, steps, shrubs and plants. Hedges act as effective windbreaks against the strong west winds in this salt-laden coastal region. The layout produces a maze-like effect. Among the many sections are a central area with an ornamental pond, a pets corner and a children's playground – in all, three acres. There is a good supply of attractive seats. Fine views of Port Quin to the west and Tintagel Head to the north. Long Cross is a hotel, open at all times.

MARY NEWMAN'S COTTAGE 24
Culver Road, Saltash, Cornwall.

Tamar Protection Society on lease from Caradon District Council ★ ¼m from Saltash town centre ★ Parking on waterside nearby ★ Open 14th to 17th April, 8th, 29th May, 28th Aug, 11am – 4pm ★ Entrance: £1, children 50p

The cottage was built in the fifteenth century. Mary Newman, first wife of Sir Francis Drake and Mayoress of Plymouth, lived here. The garden overlooks the River Tamar and Brunel's famous Royal Albert Bridge. The small cottage garden is in a peaceful, riverside setting. Herbs are a speciality. Within a small area are herbaceous plants, shrubs, such old-fashioned roses as 'Sir Walter Raleigh' and 'Fisherman's Friend', and a sundial.

MORAB SUBTROPICAL GARDEN 25
Penzance, Cornwall. Tel: (01736) 62341 ext. 3322 (Garden Manager)

Penwith District Council ★ In the centre of Penzance. Entrances in St Mary's Terrace, Morab Road and Coulson's Place ★ Best season: spring, but exceptional climate allows camellias to bloom as early as mid-Nov ★ Parking in public car parks ★ Toilet facilities ★ Suitable for wheelchairs ★ Dogs on lead ★ Open all year, dawn – dusk ★ Entrance: free

The three-acre garden designed by Reginald Upcher, a well-known garden architect in his day, remains exactly in accordance with his plan. The land was bought by Penzance Corporation in 1888 and opened in 1889. The garden contains two ponds, a large highly ornamental fountain and a magnificent bandstand. Many rare trees and plants including a *Cordyline australis* (New Zealand cabbage palm), a *Dicksonia antarctica* (a tree fern) and a *Clethra arborea* (a lily-of-the-valley tree). The garden is in two sections, the main one joined to a smaller area beside the Morab Library.

MOUNT EDGCUMBE HOUSE AND PARK ★   26
Cremyll, Torpoint, Cornwall. Tel: (01752) 822236

Plymouth City Council and Cornwall County Council ★ Access from Plymouth by Cremyll ferry (pedestrian) to Park entrance or Torpoint ferry (vehicle) A374 and B3247. Access from Cornwall A38 to Trerulefoot roundabout then A374 and B3247 ★ Parking for cars and coaches, but advance booking for coaches helpful ★ Refreshments: lunches, teas and light refreshments April to Oct daily in Orangery (01752) 822586. Picnics ★ Toilet facilities ★ Suitable for wheelchairs ★ Dogs on lead in Park and formal gardens only ★ Shop ★ House open as Earl's Garden ★ Park and formal gardens open daily, 8am – dusk. Earl's Garden open April to Oct, Wed – Sun and Bank Holiday Mons, 11am – 5.30pm ★ Entrance: Park and formal gardens free. Earl's Garden and house £3, concessions £2.20, children under 17 £1.50

The gardens and landscaped park were created by the Mount Edgcumbe family in the eighteenth century. They have been praised by Pepys, William Kent and Humphry Repton. The site covers 865 acres, and stretches from Plymouth Sound to Rame Head. Surrounding the house the Earl's Garden is an informal terrace and shrub garden which contains a rare shell grotto and on the east front re-established late Victorian flowerbeds. The formal gardens at the lower end of the old tree-lined avenue encompass English, French and Italian Gardens (complete with ornamental orange trees) and two new gardens to commemorate the family's historical connection with America and New Zealand. Planted in the Amphitheatre is the National collection of camellias. There are fine sea views to Drake's Island from the Park, where fallow deer may sometimes be seen.

THE OLD MILL HERBARY   27
Helland Bridge, Bodmin, Cornwall. Tel: (01208) 841206

Mr and Mrs Whurr ★ Take the A30 1m N of Bodmin and follow signs to Helland and then Helland Bridge. The Herbary is adjacent to the bridge ★ Parking. Coaches by appointment only ★ Toilet facility ★ Plants for sale ★ Open April to October, 10am – 5pm ★ Entrance: £2, children 75p

Five acres of semi-wild terraced gardens with woodland area, adjacent to the River Camel. Active leat, bog/water garden, fishpond, statuary and camomile lawn. Labelled displays of unusual culinary, medicinal and aromatic herbs and also shrubs, climbers and a mini-arboretum.

PENCARROW ★   28
Washaway, Bodmin, Cornwall. Tel: (01208) 841369

The Molesworth-St Aubyn family ★ 4m NW of Bodmin. Signposted from the A389 Bodmin – Wadebridge road and B3266 at Washaway ★ Best season: spring ★ Parking ★ Refreshments in tearoom. Picnics ★ Toilet facilities ★ Partly suitable for wheelchairs ★ Dogs on lead near house ★ Plants for sale ★ Shop ★ House and Craft Centre open 3rd April to mid-Oct, daily except Fri and Sat, 1.30 – 5pm (June to 10th Sept and Bank Holiday Mon open 11am) ★ Garden open daily, dawn – dusk ★ Entrance: £1.50, children free (house and gardens £3.50, children £1.50) (1994 prices)

The drive, one mile long, leads to the imposing Palladian mansion built in

CORNWALL

1760. A formal garden with a circular lawn is laid out on two sides of the house. Nearby on a higher level, shrubs are placed in a rock garden made with boulders transported from Bodmin Moor when the gardens were designed by Sir William Molesworth from 1831 onwards. There are 50 acres of woodland and parkland where over 600 different varieties of rhododendrons and a large collection of camellias grow. Among the many trees stands a *Picea orientalis* (Caucasian spruce), the second earliest known to have been planted in Britain. There are a large number of Monkey Puzzle trees (*Araucaria araucana*). The English name is said to have originated at Pencarrow when, in 1834, the parliamentary barrister Charles Austin who was staying at Pencarrow rashly touched the prickly leaves and quickly withdrew his hand, saying: 'It would puzzle a monkey'.

PENJERRICK   29
Budock, Nr Falmouth, Cornwall. Tel: (01872) 870105

Mrs R. Morin ★ 3m SW of Falmouth between Budock and Mawnan Smith. Entrance opposite the Penmorvah Hotel ★ Best season: spring ★ Parking on grass verge along drive. Parking for one coach only at gate ★ Dogs on lead ★ Plants for sale ★ Open March to Sept, Wed, Fri and Sun, 1.30 – 4.30pm and by appointment ★ Entrance: £1, children 50p

A 15-acre garden set in parkland created by the Fox family in the late eighteenth century. The home of the 'Barclayi' and 'Penjerrick' rhododendron hybrids. The upper garden is planted with rhododendrons, camellias, tree ferns and bamboos and many rare trees (it also contains the second largest beech in Britain). The wilder lower garden has ponds enhanced by tree ferns, first planted *c.* 1824.

PENPOL HOUSE   30
Penpol Avenue, Hayle, Cornwall. Tel: (01736) 753146

Major and Mrs T.F. Ellis ★ 4m SE of St Ives. Turn left at White Hart Hotel, Penpol Road, then second left into Penpol Avenue. ★ Parking in adjacent field ★ Teas ★ Suitable for wheelchairs ★ Plants for sale on open days ★ Open by appointment May to July and 25th June, 2nd July, 2 – 6pm ★ Entrance: £2 (£1.50, children 50p on open days)

Situated in the extreme south-west overlooking the Hayle estuary and surrounding the sixteenth-century house, the three and a half-acre garden was formerly sheltered by a belt of elms which succumbed to Dutch elm disease. Old yew and fuchsia hedges and more recently trees and shrubs have reshaped a garden over a hundred years old. The garden leads from one colourful pocket to another with old walls and low-growing box, fuchsia and yew dividing the various areas. The walled garden with espaliered apple and pear trees surrounded by amaryllis lilies, contains a water garden, bordered by shrub and patio roses. Along one wall a large bed of delphiniums grown from seed. The little 'Grey Garden' planned years ago for quiet colours is now bright with shrubs and plants. An old lemon verbena fills one wall, japonica climbs another and beneath are crinum lilies. The main garden has roses everywhere, over trellises, a garden of nineteenth-century roses and a formal rose garden. There are beds of flag iris, borders of herbaceous plants and peonies and more delphiniums, all set off by sweeping lawns and terraces. Plenty of ideas here for what can be done in alkaline soil.

PENWARNE 31
Mawnan Smith, Nr Falmouth, Cornwall. Tel: (01326) 250585/250325

Mr and Mrs H. Beister ★ 3¹/₄m SW of Falmouth and 1¹/₄m N of Mawnan Smith off the Falmouth to Mawnan Smith road ★ Parking. Coaches by prior arrangement ★ Toilet facilities ★ Partly suitable for wheelchairs ★ Dogs on lead ★ Open 12th March, 2 – 5pm ★ Entrance: £1, children 50p

There are many large trees including *Cryptomeria japonica*, beeches and oaks which form a backcloth to this woodland garden planted about 1900 in which is set a fine Georgian house. The old walled garden has roses, clematis and lilies and there are banks of azaleas, rhododendrons, camellias and magnolias, together with shrubs from New Zealand. The pool with ornamental ducks and the stream running through the garden provide areas for primulas and tree ferns. There are fruit trees and bushes along with bamboos. Many new plantings.

PINE LODGE ★ 32
Cuddra, St Austell, Cornwall. Tel: (01726) 73500

Mr and Mrs R. Clemo ★ Just E of St Austell off A390 between Holmbush and the turning to Tregrehan. Signs on open days ★ Parking ★ Teas ★ Toilet facilities ★ Suitable for wheelchairs ★ Plants for sale ★ Open 28th May, 25th June, 1 – 5pm or parties of 20 or more by appointment all year ★ Entrance: £3 (£2 on open days), children free

This five-acre garden, started in the 1950s, has been extended and now includes parkland. The property amounts to some 30 acres. It contains a wide range of plants, original colour combinations and good design features. The whole area contains some 5500 different plants, all of which are labelled. Besides the usual rhododendrons and camellias so familiar in Cornish gardens there are herbaceous borders with rare plants, a pinetum, a pergola with clematis and ivies and other climbers. A large wildlife pond, a lake with an island, a marsh garden and an arboretum with a large variety of trees.

POLDOWRIAN 33
Coverack, Helston, Cornwall. Tel: (01326) 280468

Mr and Mrs P. Hadley ★ Take B3293 Helston to St Kereme road. 2m after Goonhilly Earth Station, turn right at BP garage at Zoar. Take second right signposted 'Gwenter', then second left at Poldowrian sign ★ Plants for sale ★ Open April to June by appointment only ★ Entrance: by donation to charity

Four-acre woodland garden, well-pathed, leading to unspoilt coast. Bronze Age wells, museum. Two Japanese umbrella pines, Norway maples, many camellias, hydrangeas, rhododendrons and other shrubs. Woodland flowers. Pond with an island in the middle. Water garden.

POLGWYNNE 34
Feock, Nr Truro, Cornwall. Tel: (01872) 862612

Mrs P. Davey ★ 5m S of Truro. Take A39, then B3289 to first crossroads. Carry straight on past garage on right following signposts to Feock. At T-junction turn left down steep hill and the house is situated on the right at the bottom ★ Best seasons: spring and summer ★ Parking ★ Refreshments on open days ★ Toilet facilities ★ Partly suitable for wheelchairs ★ Plants for sale on open days only ★ Open 30th April, 21st May, 4th June, 2 – 5.30pm and by appointment all year round ★ Entrance: £1.50 for charity, children free

A three and a half-acre garden with woodlands extending to the shore of Carrick Roads. Many unusual shrubs and fine trees including what is reputed to be the largest female *Gingko biloba* in Britain. Fine early-Victorian greenhouses stand in the large vegetable garden. Beautiful setting with fine views.

PORTHPEAN 35
Porthpean House, St Austell, Cornwall. Tel: (01726) 72888

Mr and Mrs C. Petherick ★ Take A390 and then the road signposted Porthpean, past Mount Edgcumbe Hospice, turn left down Porthpean Beach Road. Porthpean House is the white building at the bottom of the hill just before the car park ★ Best season: spring ★ Parking in car park nearby ★ Refreshments: teas for parties ★ Toilet facilities ★ Suitable for wheelchairs ★ Dogs on lead ★ Plants for sale ★ Open 19th, 26th March, 2nd, 9th and 23rd April for charity, 2 – 5pm. Also by appointment ★ Entrance: £1.50, children free

This three-acre garden was first developed by Maurice Petherick some 40 years ago. It contains a special collection of camellias, also many azaleas and rhododendrons. The grounds have access to the beach and from the main lawn one has a magnificent view of St Austell Bay. On spring days cherry blossoms stand out sharply against the blue of the sea. There is also a nursery garden with Victorian greenhouses.

PROBUS GARDENS
(formerly County Demonstration Garden) 36
Probus, Nr Truro, Cornwall. Tel: (01726) 882597; Fax: (01726) 883868

Cornwall County Council Education Committee ★ Just E of Probus village on A390 ★ Best season: June to Sept ★ Parking, inc. coaches ★ Refreshments: café ★ Toilet facilities ★ Suitable for wheelchairs ★ Plants for sale ★ Shop ★ Gardens open Jan to 13th April, Mon – Fri, 10am – 4pm; 15th April to 6th Oct, daily, 10am – 5pm; 9th Oct to 22nd Dec, Mon – Fri, 10am – 4pm ★ Entrance: £2.35, children free. Parties of 20 or more £1.90 per person. Pre-booked guided tours of 15 or more £3 per person

This seven and a half-acre demonstration garden was started from a green field site in 1969 to serve the needs of the local community as a centre for horticulture. Many aspects of gardening are explained with displays of annuals, herbaceous perennials, shrubs, trees, conifers and hedges. Also layouts for fruit, vegetables and general garden designs. Annually, trials are grown and these add to the interest of this diverse garden. Here the visitor can receive expert advice and information.

ST MICHAEL'S MOUNT 37
Marazion, Nr Penzance, Cornwall. Tel: (01736) 710507

The National Trust ★ ½m from the shore at Marazion, ½m S of A394. Access by ferry or across causeway ★ Best season: spring/early summer ★ Parking in Marazion ★ Refreshments: restaurant/café ★ Toilet facilities ★ Plants for sale ★ Shop, April to Oct ★ Castle and Abbey open ★ Gardens open April to Oct, Mon – Fri, 10.30am – 5.30pm (last admission 4.45pm), for Cornwall Gardens Festival and most weekends from June to Sept for charity when NT members are asked to pay for admission, Nov to March guided tours can be arranged if tide, weather and circumstances permit. Check by telephone ★ Entrance: £3.50, children £1.75, family ticket £9, pre-booked parties £3

A unique and extraordinary 20-acre maritime garden which has been created in terraces just above the sea at the foot of a 300-foot perpendicular cliff. Here, in spite of apparent total exposure to gales and salt spray, sub-tropical species abound. The walled garden was planted in the eighteenth century by two young ladies, ancestors of the St Aubyn family who still live in the Castle. A remarkable example of micro-climate effect is in itself a fascinating study for the keen gardener. Planting has been done amongst granite boulders, some weighing hundreds of tons. There are yuccas, geraniums, euryops, hebes, phormiums, fuchsias and in spring sheets of wild narcissus. Kniphofias grow wild in bracken – great splashes of colour.

TREBAH ★★ 38
Mawnan Smith, Nr Falmouth, Cornwall. Tel: (01326) 250448

Major and Mrs J.A. Hibbert (The Trebah Garden Trust) ★ 1m W of Falmouth. Signposted from A39 Hillhead roundabout, 500 yards W of Glendurgan Garden ★ Best season: March to Oct ★ Parking ★ Refreshments ★ Toilet facilities ★ Partly suitable for wheelchairs ★ Dogs on lead ★ Plants for sale ★ Open all year, daily, 10.30am – 5pm ★ Entrance: £2.80, disabled and children £1, children under 5 free (Nov to Feb, £1, disabled and children 50p)

A 25-acre ravine garden started by Charles Fox in the 1840s which contains many beautiful and mature trees and shrubs that provide an undulating carpet of colour. The deep ravine leads to a private beach on the Helford River. A stream runs through a water garden and a series of ponds with mature Koi carp. Extensive plantings of sub-tropical Mediterranean plants at the top of the garden blend into the rain forest of the lower reaches with glades of giant tree ferns, bananas and bamboos. Three acres of blue and white hydrangeas carry the colour through to Christmas. A paradise for the artist, the plantsman and the family.

TREGREHAN 39
Par, Cornwall. Tel: (0172681) 4389

The Carlyon Estate. Mr T. Hudson ★ On A390 Lostwithiel to St Austell road. The entrance is opposite the Britannia Inn ★ Best season: spring ★ Parking ★ Refreshments ★ Toilet facilities ★ Partly suitable for wheelchairs ★ Plants for sale, esp. camellias ★ Open mid-March to June, daily except 16th April, 10.30am – 5pm ★ Entrance: £2, children 50p. Guided tours by prior arrangement

CORNWALL

The 20-acre garden contains many large and interesting trees and rhododendrons in addition to the large collection of camellias raised by the late owner. There are woodland walks carpeted with bluebells in spring and a walled garden. Other plants include clivias and nerines, but the camellias, rare trees and vast rhododendrons are of particular interest to the keen plantsman. Much planting of material grown from seed, and plants of known provenance. Magnificent Victorian greenhouses.

TREHANE 40
Nr Probus, Cornwall. Tel: (0187252) 0270

David and Simon Trehane ★ Turn N off A39 between the Wheel Inn and Tresillian Bridge. Follow the road for 1½m to Trehane. Signposted ★ Best season: spring/summer ★ Parking off the drive. Coaches by special arrangement for a different route ★ Teas ★ Toilet facilities ★ Partly suitable for wheelchairs ★ Dogs on lead ★ Plants for sale ★ Open by appointment and 19th March, 2nd, 16th, 30th April, 7th, 21st May, 4th, 18th June, 2nd, 16th July, 20th Aug, 2 – 5pm ★ Entrance: £1.50, children free

This is a plantsman's garden containing a wonderful variety and many good collections – geraniums, hemerocallis, romneyas and trilliums. There are lovely camellias. Interesting climbers cover the old walls and in spring the woodland area is carpeted with bluebells, claytonias and campions. In the central courtyard of the ruined mansion you find a great Holboellia. A very old *Pieris japonica* and a davidia and vast rhododendrons, azaleas and magnolias provide a background to a large collection of herbaceous plants. This garden will also be enjoyed by the general visitor as it has a great sense of peace and half of its 10 acres is woodland.

TRELEAN 41
St Martin-in-Meneage, Nr Helston, Cornwall. Tel: (01326) 231255

Squadron Leader Witherwick ★ 7m SE of Helston on B3293. After 4m turn left for Mawgan. 1m from the village of St Martin-in-Meneage ★ Parking in field ★ Teas ★ Toilet facilities ★ Dogs on lead ★ Plants for sale ★ Open May to Oct for individuals or parties by appointment. Tours by the owner if convenient ★ Entrance: £1.50, children free

This three-acre garden set in a wooded estate with superb views of the River Helford is for the keen plantsman as it contains a superb collection of beautiful and rare trees and shrubs including 14 different nothofagus, 50 different acers, various eucalyptus, cistus, enkianthus, olearias and robinias. The winding steep paths are bordered on either side by holly, hazel, Scots pine and many varieties of rhododendrons and 70 different conifers. The owners, who started this garden from an area of woodland and bracken in 1980, are certainly creating a paradise for the botanist.

TRELISSICK ★ 42
Feock, Nr Truro, Cornwall. Tel: (01872) 865808

The National Trust ★ 4m S of Truro on B3289 above King Harry Ferry ★ Best season: April/May ★ Parking £1 (refundable) ★ Refreshments: restaurant open 11am – 5.30pm; Suns, 12 noon – 5.30pm (5pm in March and Oct) ★ Toilet facilities ★ Partly suitable for wheelchairs ★ Dogs on lead on woodland walk and park only ★ Plants for sale ★ Shop ★ Art and Craft Gallery in grounds open ★ Garden open March to Oct, Mon – Sat, 10.30am – 5.30pm, Sun, 1 – 5.30pm (5pm in March and Oct) ★ Entrance: £3.40, family ticket £8.50, pre-booked parties £3 per person

This 25-acre garden with woodland was originally planted with exotic things and became known as the fruit garden of Cornwall. Now it contains a wide variety of interest with its collection of hydrangeas, a dell, aromatic, fern and fig gardens along with some very large trees including *Quercus ilex*, *Fagus sylvatica* and a beautiful Japanese cedar *Cryptomeria japonica* in a lawn backed by herbaceous borders containing a range of perennials. Near the entrance is a lovely border of heliotrope – a tradition of Trelissick. The dell has tree ferns, hostas and hellebores and there are many beautiful shrubs. Small walled garden with aromatic plants.

TREMEER 43
St Tudy, Nr Bodmin, Cornwall. Tel: (01208) 850313

The Haslam-Hopwood family ★ NW of St Tudy between A39 and B3266. Take Wadebridge road from the centre of St Tudy ★ Best season: April to June ★ Parking in garden. Coaches at village hall by arrangement ★ Toilet facilities ★ Dogs on lead ★ Open April to Sept, daily, 9 – 6pm ★ Entrance: free. Donations to charity at the entrance

By Cornish standards this seven-acre garden is exposed and cold and has a high rainfall, but manages to produce vivid colour and pervading scent. A large bank of heathers is backed by dwarf rhododendrons and camellias. The terrace beneath the house looks out to a backcloth of fine mature trees. After crossing the lawn, walks meander through beautiful shrubs – rhododendrons, azaleas, camellias – and at the bottom of the garden are two small lakes with primulas, hostas and other water plants. Herbaceous borders provide summer colour and the walls have good climbers and perennials beneath.

TRENGWAINTON GARDEN ★ 44
Nr Penzance, Cornwall. Tel. (01736) 63021

The National Trust ★ 2m NW of Penzance on B3312, or ½m off A3071 ★ Best season: spring ★ Parking ★ Teas usually at Trengwainton Farm ★ Toilet facilities ★ Suitable for wheelchairs ★ Dogs on lead ★ Open March to Oct, Wed – Sat and Bank Holiday Mons, 10.30am – 5.30pm (5pm in March and Oct) (last admission ½ hour before closing). Closed 14th April ★ Entrance: £2.80, children £1.40

Trengwainton means 'House of the Spring' and was acquired by the Bolitho family in 1867. It will appeal to both the plantsman and the ordinary gardener because it contains a magnificent collection of magnolias, rhododendrons and camellias and a series of walled gardens with many tender and exotic shrubs and plants that would not survive in less mild areas of England. The stream garden alongside the drive backed by a beech wood provides masses of colour from candelabra primulas, lilies, lysichitums and other bog plants. Many of the rhododendrons were raised from seed collected by Kingdon Ward's expedition to NE Assam and the Mishmi

Hills of Burma. New Zealand tree ferns, pittosporums from China, Japanese maples, embothriums, olearias, acacias, eucryphias, and Chatham Island forget-me-nots are just a few of the beautiful plants to be seen during the spring and summer. There are magnificent views of the hills leading down to the sea and a space has been cut in the woodland to reveal St Michael's Mount.

TRERICE   45
Kestle Mill, Newquay, Cornwall. Tel: (01637) 875404

The National Trust ★ 3m SE of Newquay via A392 and A3058. Turn right at Kestle Mill ★ Best season: summer ★ Parking ★ Refreshments ★ Toilet facilities ★ Partly suitable for wheelchairs ★ Plants for sale ★ Shop in house ★ House open ★ Garden open April to Oct, daily except Tues, 11am – 5.30pm (5pm in Oct) (last admission ½ hour before closing) ★ Entrance: £3.60, pre-booked parties £3 per person (house and garden)

A small garden by Cornish standards developed around an Elizabethan manor house where one can enjoy many unusual and lovely rare plants. It has been planted with shrubs, climbers and perennials to provide very good foliage and colour combinations. In the front walled courtyard are herbaceous borders. The back court has a range of cottage garden plants – fuchsias, honeysuckles, roses and climbers on the house. An orchard has been planted with apples, pears, quinces, plums in the quincunx pattern used in the seventeenth century, and there are figs elsewhere in the garden. The design features of the garden are of particular interest. Lawn mowers of different sizes and from different periods are displayed in the former stable hay loft.

TRESCO ABBEY ★★   46
Tresco, Isles of Scilly. Tel: (01720) 22849
Mike Nelhams (Head Gardener)

Mr R.A. Dorrien-Smith ★ On the Island of Tresco. Travel: by helicopter from Penzance Heliport to Tresco Heliport – 12 months (reservations (01736) 63871 and (01720) 22646) or from St Mary's by launch ★ Refreshments ★ Toilet facilities ★ Suitable for wheelchairs (available at garden gate) but paths steep in places ★ Dogs on lead ★ Plants for sale ★ Shop ★ Open daily, 10am – 4pm ★ Entrance: £3.50, children £1.50 (1994 prices)

One of the most spectacular of all Britain's 'sub-tropical' gardens on an island which lies in the warming Gulf Stream. Usually protected from Atlantic gales, this was not the case in 1990 and as a result of the devastation several thousand trees are being replanted and massive clearance work done with financial assistance from English Heritage. Robin Lane Fox calls this 'a paradise...one of the most important recoveries in British garden history' and the amazing fact is that it is tended by a mere four full-timers. The garden is arranged on several terraces mounting a hillside which are linked by flights of steps. They serve as a home for myriad exotic plants like proteas from South Africa, the tender geranium *G. maderense* from Madeira and trees and shrubs from the North Island of New Zealand and Australia which could not thrive out-of-doors in many places on the British mainland. This 17-acre garden is both formal and nformal. Many of the plants are self-seeded. The grounds also house the Valhalla collection of ship figureheads from the National Maritime Museum.

TREVEGEAN 47
9 Manor Way, Heamoor, Penzance, Cornwall. Tel: (01736) 67407

Mr and Mrs P.G. Cousins ★ Take Penzance bypass, turn left at first roundabout towards Treneere, turn sharp right, straight up hill to Manor Way. Concealed entrance to garden marked 7 and 9 ★ Parking on road ★ Cream teas ★ Toilet facilities ★ Plants for sale ★ Open by appointment from April to June ★ Entrance: £1

Third-of-an-acre garden a delight for the plantsman and general gardener. The different concealed sections are edged with box hedging and they intercommunicate by brick paths. This remarkable garden, placed at the rear of a housing estate, is completely concealed from the outside by trees and hedges. There are many interesting shrubs: *Viburnum odoratissimum*, *Muehlenbeckia*, and among the flowers you find *Rosa chinensis* 'Mutabilis', *Geranium palmatum* and *Lobelia tupa* and old-fashioned roses. This garden has won various prizes.

TREWIDDEN 48
Penzance, Cornwall. Tel: (01736) 62087 (Head Gardener)

Captain A.R. Bolitho ★ Follow the Penzance distributor road as for Land's End. Entrance is on the right beyond crossroad to Newlyn. Signed 'Trewidden Nursery' ★ Parking. Coaches by appointment ★ Toilet facilities ★ Dogs on leads ★ Woodland garden open all year except Bank Holidays, Mon – Sat, and for charity 19th March, 16th, 30th April, 14th May, 8am – 1pm, 2 – 5pm ★ Entrance: £1.50, children 50p

This woodland garden contains a large number of fine specimens of the best kinds of flowering shrubs. A *Magnolia* x *veitchii*, possibly the largest in Britain, overshadows a large pond. In this section, too, one finds other fine magnolias. In the Fern Pit, once an open tin mine, stands a magnificent group of *Dicksonia antarctica* (tree ferns) which are 100 years old. The nurseries, originally a kitchen garden, are now used to produce a wide range of trees and shrubs for sale. The private garden of the house is also open for four afternoons during the year.

TREWITHEN ★★ 49
Grampound Road, Nr Truro, Cornwall. Tel: (01726) 883647

Mr and Mrs A.M.J. Galsworthy ★ On A390 between Truro and St Austell, adjacent to the County Demonstration Garden ★ Parking ★ Tea shop ★ Toilet facilities ★ Suitable for wheelchairs ★ Dogs on lead ★ Plants for sale ★ Garden shop ★ House open April to July, Mon, Tues, 2 – 4pm. ★ Gardens open March to Sept, Mon – Sat, 10am – 4.30pm (also Sun in April and May) ★ Entrance: Gardens £2.80, children £1.50, group rate (12 plus) £2.20. House £3, children £1.50

This is an internationally famous garden, known for its great collection of magnolias, rhododendrons and camellias along with many other beautiful and rare trees and shrubs. It is fitting that its founder George Johnstone named a camellia after his daughter 'Elizabeth Johnstone', and there are rhododendrons 'Alison Johnstone' after his wife, 'Trewithen Orange' and 'Jack Skelton' after his head gardener. The lawn in front of the house is edged with banks of a wide range of shrubs including viburnums, azaleas, potentillas, euonymus, berberis. There is a sunken garden with tree ferns, azaleas and acers. There are many nothofagus, embothriums, pieris, enkianthus, eucryphias, griselinias. The walled garden has a pool and some choice climbers including *Clianthus puniceus* and *Mutisia decurrens*, and there is a pergola with wisteria. Newly planted beds of young trees of sorbus and birch, mahonia, cornus, phygelius and roses and island beds with heathers and dwarf conifers. The beech trees that provide shelter for the garden are magnificent. A half-hour video describes the creation of the garden over the years.

TREWORDER MILL 50
Kenwyn, Nr Truro, Cornwall. Tel: (01872) 73314

Mr and Mrs D. Rutter ★ 2¹/₂m W of Truro. Take A390 Redruth road. Turn at Treliske hospital roundabout, past Duchy hospital. Turn left at T-junction ★ Parking at bottom of the hill in lane ★ Toilet facilities ★ Open 17th May to 28th June, Wed, 10am – 12 noon, 2 – 5pm ★ Entrance: £1.50, children free

The two and three-quarter-acre garden has been formed within the surrounding woodland. An escarpment, covered with tall trees and bushes, borders one side of the area and other trees and bushes margin the section along the road. The sophisticated arrangement of the garden itself contrasts successfully with the natural beauty of the surroundings. There is a natural pond and a trout stream running through its length. The wide range of moisture-loving plants includes particularly impressive primulas and hostas.

TREWYN GARDEN 51
St Ives, Cornwall. Tel: (01736) 62341 ext. 3322 (Garden Manager)

Penwith District Council ★ In St Ives, near the Barbara Hepworth Museum (see entry) ★ Parking in public car parks ★ Toilet facilities in town ★ Special wheelchair slope in main section ★ Dogs on lead ★ Open all year ★ Entrance: free

The garden is divided into three sections: a main garden with a superbly-kept lawn, bright flowers and well-matured deciduous trees as well as numerous palms; a shrubbery section and a third section, a series of flowerbeds and a lawn leading to pensioners' flats – in all about one acre. About 150 yards away from Trewyn Garden is the Memorial Garden under the same management (though not suitable for wheelchairs and locked at night). A small lawn represents Flanders fields and red roses the Flanders poppies. A rest haven, well-furnished with benches, and with very attractive flowerbeds.

VICTORIA GARDENS 52
Truro, Cornwall. Tel: (01872) 74555

Carrick District Council leased to Truro City Council ★ In Truro city centre, next to Crown Court ★ Car park next to Crown Court ★ Toilet facilities ★ Partly suitable for wheelchairs, but a few steps. Enter by SW or N gate ★ Dogs on lead ★ Open daily except 25th, 26th Dec, 8am – dusk ★ Entrance: free

A delightful Victorian public park of seven acres complete with a contemporary fountain in a circular pond adjacent to a fine bandstand still very much in use during summer. The park rises steeply from a brook at the bottom to a large fishpond at the top. At the lower level beneath the brook there is a small additional section of grass and flowerbeds. Apart from the numerous flowerbeds throughout the park there are some fine mature trees including copper beeches and a weeping beech.

WATERGATE   53
Trelill, Bodmin, Cornwall. Tel (01208) 850712

Lieutenant Colonel and Mrs G.B. Browne ★ 5m SW of Camelford, N of St Kew Highway, NE of Trelill. Turn right at Methodist Chapel in the village ★ Parking in road ★ Teas ★ Toilet facilities ★ Dogs on lead ★ Plants for sale ★ Open 16th April, 21st May, 2 – 5.30pm and by appointment ★ Entrance: £1.50, children under 16 free

This pleasing three-acre garden with a stream running through it contains a comprehensive display of narcissus, camellias, magnolias and primulas. Also a water garden, and herbaceous borders and rare roses. All are set against dramatic scenery of wooded hills.

HOW TO FIND THE GARDENS

Directions to each garden are included in the entry. This information has been supplied by the owners and garden inspectors and is aimed to be the best available to those travelling by car. However, it has been compiled to be used in conjunction with a road atlas.

The unreliability of train and bus services makes it unrewarding to include details, particularly as many garden visits are made on Sundays. However, many properties can be reached by public transport, and National Trust guides and the NGS Yellow Book sometimes give details.

The numbers on the maps correspond to the numbers of the gardens in each county. The maps show the proximity of one garden to another so that visits to several gardens can be planned for the same day. It is worthwhile referring to the maps of bordering counties to see if another garden visit can be included in the itinerary, and to look at the maps at the end of the *Guide*.

CUMBRIA
& THE ISLE OF MAN

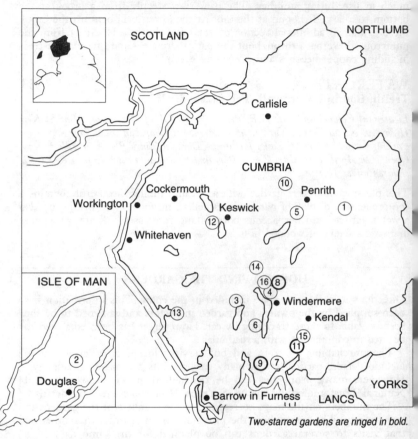

Two-starred gardens are ringed in bold.

ACORN BANK GARDEN
Temple Sowerby, Penrith, Cumbria. Tel: (017683) 61893

1

The National Trust ★ 6m E of Penrith off A66 N of Temple Sowerby ★ Best seasons: spring and early summer ★ Parking ★ Picnic area only ★ Toilet facilities, inc. disabled ★ Mostly suitable for wheelchairs ★ Guide dogs only in gardens, on lead in picnic area and woodland walk ★ Plants for sale ★ Shop ★ Admission to house by prior written permission Sue Ryder Foundation ★ Garden open April to Oct, 10am – 5.30pm (last admission 5pm) ★ Entrance: £1.60, children 80p (special rates for pre-booked parties)

The 'acorn bank' is the ancient oakwood sloping down to the Crowdundle Beck behind the house. In spring it is a mass of daffodils and narcissi in many varieties planted profusely in the 1930s (e.g. some 60,000 Lenten lilies). The walled gardens are then also a mass of blossom from the old varieties of apple, medlar, pear and quince in the sheltered orchards, with their carpet of wild tulips, anemones and narcissi. The orchard's trees include apple varieties which blossom late and are therefore suitable for cooler northern areas. Along the three sheltering walls are carefully modulated herbaceous and shrub borders, with good clematis and climbers. A bed of species roses (rugosa and others) flanks the steps to a picturesque sunken garden (a pond and alpine terraces). Through a gateway lies a splendid herb garden – a well tended collection of some 250 medicinal and culinary herbs, all comprehensively labelled and documented.

BALLALHEANNAGH ★ 2
Glen Roy, Lonan, Isle of Man. Tel: (01624) 861875

Clif and Maureen Dadd ★ In Glen Roy on E side of island, 2m inland from Laxey ★ Parking ★ Plants for sale at nursery ★ Open daily, 10am – 5pm ★ Entrance: £2, children 50p

Take a steep-sided valley, a ladder, some seedlings of exotic rhododendrons and forget all about digging pits to accommodate the roots. Just stick them into crevices among the mosses and ferns. Wait a few years, never giving up. Outcome – paradise for plant-lovers. You expect to find a garden like Ballalheannagh in Cornwall or Kerry but this is the middle of the Isle of Man. Every visitor with an interest in gardening who is marooned on that island need not fear boredom. This is a botanical garden, not in name, but surely in content. Steep winding paths cling to the valley sides. Crystal water cascades below carry the bells of pieris to the Irish Sea. The lower portion is well-stocked with lofty rhododendrons while the upper parts of the valley contain newer plantings that will certainly delight in years to come. Here are pieris, eucalyptus, drimys, epacris, epigaeas, megacarpeas and betula (species with wonderful names like *Betula tatewakiana*), and a host of others too, and the native mosses and ferns are a wonderful sight. The garden has been extended to more than 20 acres with gravel walks exceeding four miles and has new oriental features.

BRANTWOOD 3
Coniston, Cumbria. Tel: (015394) 41396

Brantwood Trust ★ E side of Coniston Water off B5285, signposted. Steam yacht 'Gondola' sails regularly from Coniston Pier ★ Best seasons: spring, autumn ★ Parking ★ Tea room and restaurant ★ Toilet facilities, inc. disabled ★ Plants for sale ★ Shop ★ House open, £3, children under 18 free ★ Garden open mid-March to mid-Nov, daily, 11am – 5.30pm, winter, Wed – Sun, 11am – 4pm ★ Entrance: £1.50p, children free (nature trail) (1994 prices)

This is a superb site with wonderful views, atmosphere and potential. The rocky hillside behind the house is threaded with a wandering network of paths created by Ruskin (who lived here 1872-1900) to delight the eye and please the mind. Rhododendrons and azaleas flourish in the acid soil to make a lovely woodland garden. Now in the capable hands of Sally Beamish, it is being restored to its former glory after long neglect and enhanced by imaginative planting. The Zig-Zaggy garden has been cleared of its rhododendrons, etc., the cottage garden restored and new areas made, such as a fernery and, down to the lake, a trellis walk bordered by 200 varieties of plants. The water features will also be revived.

BROCKHOLE ★   4
Lake District National Park Centre, Windermere, Cumbria.
Tel: (015394) 46601

Lake District National Park Authority ★ 1½m N of Windermere on A591 ★ Parking ★ Refreshments: restaurant and tearoom ★ Toilet facilities inc. disabled ★ Partly suitable for wheelchairs ★ Dogs on lead ★ Shop ★ Exhibition, slide theatres and lake cruises from the jetty ★ Centre open 6th April to 5th Nov, 10am – 5pm ★ Grounds open all year, daily, 10am – dusk ★ Entrance: parking fee only: cars £2.20, minibuses and coaches free if pre-booked otherwise £7

A garden blessed with the Lakeland combination of western aspect and water to the hills beyond, in this case notably the Langdale Pikes. To frame this view Mawson worked closely (c.1900) with his architect colleague, Gibson. The ornamental terraces drop through rose beds, herbaceous borders and shrubbery to a wild flower meadow flanked by mature woodland. The original kitchen and herb garden has been restored; other special features are herbaceous plants, Chilean and other half-hardy shrubs and rarities and the constantly changing colour from spring rhododendrons and azaleas through to the late Chilean hollies.

DALEMAIN   5
Dalemain Estate, Dacre, Penrith, Cumbria. Tel: (017684) 86450

R.B. Hasell-McCosh ★ On A592 2m N of Pooley Bridge on Penrith road ★ Best season: early summer ★ Parking ★ Licensed restaurant and tea room ★ Toilet facilities ★ Suitable for wheelchairs ★ Plants for sale ★ Shop ★ House open ★ Garden open 8th April to 8th Oct, Sun – Thurs, 11.15am – 5pm ★ Entrance: £3, children free (house and garden £4, children £3, family £11 (2 adults plus own children)). Special prices for pre-booked parties. Guided tours of gardens £3.80 per person

Dalemain has evolved in the most natural way from a twelfth-century pele tower with its kitchen garden and herbs. The Tudor-walled knot garden is there, as is the Stuart terrace (1680s) and the walled orchard where apple trees like 'Nonsuch' and 'Keswick Codling', planted in 1728, still bear fruit. The gardens have been finely re-established by Mrs Sylvia McCosh during the last twenty years with shrubs, species roses and other rarities, together with herbaceous replanting along the terraces and around the orchard. There is a wild garden on the lower ground featuring the Himalayan blue poppy in early summer and a walk past the Tudor gazebo into woods overlooking the Dacre Beck. Some thoughtful planting for future shapes and form in woodland.

GRAYTHWAITE HALL ★   6
Ulverston, Hawkshead, Cumbria. Tel: (015395) 31248

Graythwaite Estate ★ 4m up W side of Windermere from Newby Bridge, A590 ★ Best season: spring ★ Parking ★ Toilet facilities ★ Dogs on lead ★ Open April to mid- or late July, daily, 10am – 6pm ★ Entrance: £2, children free

Essentially a spring garden landscaped by the late Victorian Thomas Mawson in partnership with Dan Gibson in a beautiful parkland and woodland setting. Azaleas and rhododendrons lead to late cultivars of spring-flowering shrubs. Formal terraced rose garden. The finely wrought sundials and gate by Gibson, the Dutch garden and the stream and pond all add charm to this serene garden. For topiary admirers, Mawson employed interesting effects to contrast with his more billowy plantings. Notable are the battlemented yew hedge and some globe yews with golden yews in the top half and green in the bottom.

HALECAT   7
Witherslack, Grange-over-Sands, Cumbria. Tel: (015395) 52229

Mrs M. Stanley ★ Off A590. Signposted ★ Parking ★ Plants for sale in adjoining nursery ★ Garden open April to Oct, Mon – Fri, 9am – 4.30pm, Sun, 2 – 4pm ★ Entrance: free

This two acres is the front garden of the mid-nineteenth-century house which stands at the head of a small valley with distant views of Arnside Knott and the Forest of Bowland. Mrs Stanley has created the garden over the past 45 years. It is a series of terraces and squares and the limestone quarried from the borders has been used to build the retaining walls and the perimeter wall separating the garden from the surrounding woodland. An azalea bed has been made on the bottom terrace by the removal of rock and filling the beds with peat from a nearby moss. The herbaceous borders are very well-maintained and filled with many shrubs, clematis, herbaceous plants, and shrub and climbing roses. A pleasing, personal garden. The adjoining nursery has many interesting plants including a collection of over hydrangea and hybrids. There is a beautiful gazebo with stained glass quarries designed by Francis Johnson.

HOLEHIRD ★★   8
Troutbeck, Windermere, Cumbria. Tel: (015394) 46008

Lakeland Horticultural Society ★ 1m N of Windermere on A592 Troutbeck road ★ Parking ★ Toilet facilities ★ Partly suitable for wheelchairs ★ Annual plant sale first Sat in May in local school ★ Open all year, daily, sunrise – sunset. Garden guides available April to Oct, 11am – 5pm ★ Entrance: by donation

This is a garden run by members of a Society dedicated to promoting 'knowledge on the cultivation of plants, shrubs and trees, especially those suited to Lakeland conditions'. It lies on a splendid site with a natural water course and rock banks looking over Windermere to Scafell Pike. The Society has part of the former orchard, the rock garden and now the walled kitchen garden. Much earlier planting has been preserved, including survivors from plant-hunting expeditions to China and many fine specimen trees (e.g. 60-foot handkerchief tree). Highlights are the summer-autumn heathers, winter-flowering shrubs, alpines and the National astilbe, hydrangea and polysticum fern collections. The walled garden now has herbaceous specimens, herbs and climbers.

HOLKER HALL ★★ 9
Cark-in-Cartmel, Grange-over-Sands, Cumbria. Tel: (015395) 58328

Lord and Lady Cavendish ★ 4½m W of Grange-over-Sands on B5278 between Haverthwaite (A590) and Grange-over-Sands ★ Best seasons: spring and summer ★ Parking ★ Refreshments: cafeteria lunches, snacks and teas ★ Toilet facilities inc. disabled ★ Mostly suitable for wheelchairs ★ Plants for sale ★ Shop ★ Hall and Motor Museum open. Extra charge ★ Open April to Oct, daily except Sat, 10.30am – 6pm (last admission 4.30pm) ★ Entrance: £3, children over 6 £1.70, family ticket (2 adults and up to 4 children) £8.90. Parties £2.25 per person, OAP £2, children over 6 £1.55 (gardens, grounds and exhibitions) (1994 prices)

Set in acres of parkland, the woodland walks and formal gardens have been constantly developed by the family ever since Lord George Cavendish established his 'contrived natural landscape' over 200 years ago. The woods now contain many rare and beautiful specimens, all tagged and chronicled in the excellent guide to the walks. Other features are the cascade, evocative of the Villa d'Este, and a beautifully contrived transformation of the croquet lawn into summer gardens. This combination of formal beds and inventive planting (e.g. spire lilies rising out of massed rue) makes a wonderful Italianate-cum-English garden that typifies the spirit of Holker. There is also Mawson's rose garden, which has been sensitively renewed (his pergola and balustrade still survive). New additions include an elliptical formal garden, a rhododendron and azalea walk and a wild flower meadow. The early blaze of rare rhododendrons and azaleas, carpets of spring bulbs and the colour and scent of summer and autumn displays provide year-round interest and pleasure. Venue for The Great Garden and Countryside Festival 2nd to 4th June 1995.

HUTTON-IN-THE-FOREST ★ 10
Skelton, Penrith, Cumbria. Tel: (017684) 84449

Lord and Lady Inglewood ★ 3m from M6 junction 41, along B5305 to Wigton ★ Best season: early summer ★ Parking ★ Teas when house open. Other meals on request ★ Toilet facilities ★ Possible for wheelchairs – gravel paths ★ Dogs on lead ★ House open: 16th, 17th April, then 30th April to 24th Sept, Thurs, Fri, Sun and Bank Holiday Mons; also Weds in Aug, all 1 – 4pm. Private parties by arrangement from April ★ Garden and grounds open daily, except Sat and 25th Dec, 11am – 5pm ★ Entrance: £1.50, children free (house and grounds £3, children (7-16) £1)

This garden is a mixture of seventeenth-, eighteenth-, nineteenth- and twentieth-century features. It has great visual appeal, with a magnificent view from the seventeenth-century terraces now embellished with Victorian topiary. There are good herbs and fruit trees and excellent beds and borders in the walled garden. Some of the mature woodland trees were planted by Henry Fletcher, an ancestor of the owners, in the early eighteenth century. Recent planting includes rhododendrons and other spring displays in the woodland low garden and there is an extensive woodland walk. Other features include a seventeenth-century dovecote and eighteenth-century lake.

LEVENS HALL ★★ 11
Levens Hall, Kendal, Cumbria. Tel: (015395) 60321

Mr C.H. Bagot ★ 5m S of Kendal on A6 (M6 junction 36) ★ Best season: summer ★ Parking ★ Teas ★ Toilet facilities inc. disabled ★ Suitable for wheelchairs ★ Plant centre ★ Shop ★ House open ★ Garden open 2nd April to 28th Sept, Sun – Thurs, 11am – 5pm. Closed 14th April ★ Entrance: £2.60, children £1.60, parties of 20 or more and others £2.20 per person (house and garden £3.90, children and students £2.30, parties of 20 or more and others £3.20 per person) (1994 prices)

James II's gardener, Guillaume Beaumont, designed this famous topiary garden in 1694. It is one of very few to retain its original trees and design. To mark the 300th anniversary a new garden feature has been especially created. The impeccably clipped yews and box hedges are set off by colourful spring and summer bedding and borders. The primroses in the seventeenth-century garden may be the start of a permanent collection, and a new area, the Fountain Garden, has been created with lime avenues meeting at the pool. Indeed there is much to see in addition to the topiary. Massive walls of beech hedge open to vistas over parkland. One avenue leads to the earliest designed ha-ha. There is a picturesque herb garden behind the house, and another now planted up to match the recently discovered seventeenth-century plan. The record of only 10 gardeners in 300 years, and the affectionate care by the Bagot family, account for the rare harmony of this exceptional garden.

LINGHOLM GARDENS ★ 12
Lingholm, Keswick, Cumbria. Tel: (017687) 72003

The Viscount Rochdale ★ W side of Derwentwater, 3m from Keswick off A66 ★ Best seasons: spring, early summer and autumn ★ Parking ★ Teas ★ Toilet facilities ★ Suitable for wheelchairs ★ Plants for sale ★ Open April to Oct, daily, 10am – 5pm ★ Entrance: £2.60, accompanied children free, groups £2.10 per person (1994 prices)

A most pleasing lakeland garden with a long view south to Borrowdale. Colour from early spring with daffodils and a long-lasting display of rhododendrons and azaleas (*Rhododendron auriculatum* flowers in July/August) in native woodland with silver firs, maples and cedars. Long herbaceous border, sunken garden with pool, and a delightful woodland walk; careful labelling throughout. Beatrix Potter stayed and whilst here wrote *Squirrel Nutkin* (see also Beatrix Potter Garden, Birnam, Scotland).

MUNCASTER CASTLE ★ 13
Ravenglass, Cumbria. Tel: (01229) 717614/717203

Mr and Mrs Gordon-Duff-Pennington ★ 15m S of Whitehaven on A595 ★ Best season: April to June ★ Parking ★ Teas ★ Toilet facilities ★ Suitable for wheelchairs ★ Dogs on lead ★ Plant Centre ★ Shops ★ Owl Centre ★ Castle open 26th March to 29th Oct, Tues – Sun and Bank Holiday Mons, 1 – 4pm ★ Gardens and owl centre open all year, daily, 11am – 5pm ★ Entrance: £3, children £1.60, family (2 adults and 2 children) £8 (gardens and owl centre); £4.90, children £2.50, family £12.50 (castle, gardens and owl centre) (1994 prices)

The splendid backdrop of Scafell and the hills, the acid soil and the Gulf Stream warmth provide ideal conditions. One of the finest collections of species rhododendron in Europe has been built up, many from plant-hunting expeditions to Nepal in the 1920s (Kingdon Ward, Ludlow and Sheriff). There are excellent azaleas, camellias, magnolias, hydrangeas and maples, plus many unusual trees (e.g. nothofagus species). The garden is at its best in May and June but intensive new planting is ensuring constant pleasure for visitors in all seasons. Due to a shortage of labour to maintain the 77 acres of gardens, some areas are rather wild (and overgrown) in appearance.

RYDAL MOUNT 14
Ambleside, Cumbria. Tel: (015394) 33002

Rydal Mount Trust ★ 1m N of Ambleside on A591 ★ Best season: spring ★ Parking ★ Toilet facilities ★ Dogs on lead ★ Shop ★ House open ★ Gardens open Mar to Oct, daily, 9.30am – 5pm, Nov to Feb, daily except Tues, 10am – 4pm ★ Entrance: £2.50, children £1, groups £2 per person

The carefully maintained grounds of Wordsworth's house still follow the lines of his own plan and it is easy to imagine the poet wandering along the upper terrace walk ('the sloping terrace') and down through winding, shaded paths to the lawns, or across a terrace to the ancient mound with its distant glimpse of Windermere. Apart from its poetic association the garden is also a visual delight with good herbaceous borders, shrubs and unusual trees (e.g. the fern-leaved beech). An addition to the spring display is the bank of dancing daffodils in nearby Dora's field. Wordsworth's other house at Cockermouth has a pleasant town garden, now restored, but it is only worth a visit if the house, too, is to be inspected.

SIZERGH CASTLE ★ 15
Kendal, Cumbria. Tel: (015395) 60070

The National Trust ★ 3½m S of Kendal on A591 (M6 junction 36) ★ Best season: spring to autumn ★ Parking ★ Teas: 1.30 – 5.30pm ★ Toilet facilities ★ Partly suitable for wheelchairs ★ Shop ★ Castle open same days, 1.30 – 5.30pm ★ Open April to Oct, Sun to Thurs, 12.30 – 5.30pm (last admission 5pm) ★ Entrance: £1.70 (castle and garden £3.30). Parties of 15 or more reduced rate by arrangement

An exceptionally varied garden with colour from early spring daffodils to summer borders and climbers culminating in glorious autumn tints (the vine-clad tower all fiery red is a memorable spectacle). Other features encountered along shady paths are the Rock Garden (in the midst of a 10-year replan), the Herbaceous Border, the Terrace Wall (with half-hardy shrubs and climbers not expected this far north), the Rose Garden (with many species roses, including Musk and Moss Roses). There are also wild flower banks with native limestone flora including six species of orchids, a water garden and lake.

STAGSHAW   16
Ambleside, Cumbria. Tel: (015394) 35599

The National Trust ★ ½m S of Ambleside on A591 ★ Best seasons: spring, early summer ★ Limited parking, access dangerous ★ Open April to June, daily, 10am – 6.30pm, July to Oct, by appointment (please send SAE to The National Trust North West Regional Office, The Hollens, Grasmere, Cumbria) ★ Entrance: £1

Created by the Trust's former Regional Agent, Cubby Acland, this is a carefully blended area of azaleas and rhododendrons among camellias, magnolias and other fine shrubs on a west–facing hillside of oaks looking over the head of Lake Windermere. Rather difficult of access but worth the effort.

NATIONAL COUNCIL FOR THE CONSERVATION OF PLANTS AND GARDENS

The NCCPG has just published the latest version of its *National Plant Collections Directory*. Anyone interested in particular families of plants who wants to see some of the rarer species and garden varieties will find this is an invaluable publication indicating where and when they can be seen. This edition, which offers information on about 550 collections comprising more than 50,000 plants, also contains articles by holders of the collections.

NATIONAL TRUST EVENTS

For a list of Summer events at National Trust properties members of the public should write with a large SAE (28p stamp) to: The National Trust, 'Summer Events', 36 Queen Anne's Gate, London SW1H 9AS.

OPENING DATES AND TIMES

Times of access given are the best available at the moment of going to press, but some may have been changed subsequently. In the entries, the times given are inclusive – that is, an entry such as May to Sept means that the garden is open from 1st May to 30th Sept inclusive and 2 – 5pm also means that entry will be effective during that period. Please note that many owners will open their gardens to visitors by appointment. They will often arrange to give a personally-conducted tour on these occasions.

DERBYSHIRE

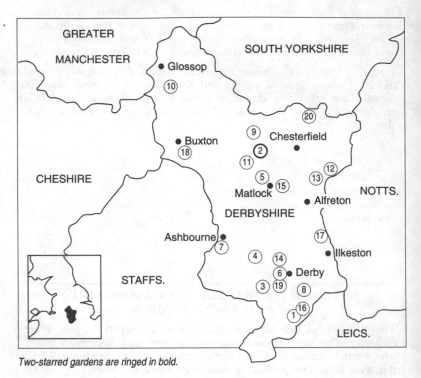

Two-starred gardens are ringed in bold.

CALKE ABBEY
1

Ticknall, Derbyshire. Tel: (01332) 863822 (office)

The National Trust ★ 10m S of Derby, off A514 at Ticknall ★ Parking ★ Refreshments: restaurant ★ Toilet facilities ★ Partly suitable for wheelchairs ★ National Trust shop ★ House open as garden but 1 – 5pm (tickets are timed and there may be some waiting) ★ Garden open April to Oct (closed 14th April), Sat – Wed and Bank Holiday Mons, 11am – 5pm ★ Entrance: £2, children £1 (house and garden £4.50, children £2.20). £2 vehicle charge entry to park, which is open during daylight hours all year, refundable on entry to house

Previously owned by the Harpur Crewe family and taken on by the Trust in 1985, Calke Abbey gardens have a long history and with a sympathetic approach could be another Trust jewel. Frames, pits, an orangery and grotto, and an auricula theatre have been restored. The gardeners are growing fruit, vegetables and flowers in the two walled compartments formerly kept for flowers and physic herbs. The third and biggest compartment is the old kitchen garden, now disused, overlooked by a derelict orangery plus a head gardener's office of 1777 and the Trust is appealing for funds to restore this to its former beauty. The staff's aim is to grow old varieties, including an apple and plum orchard, wherever possible, and the renewal of this garden will interest all those who yearn for traditional fruit and vegetables grown in the old manner, labour-intensive, but providing weekly fare for the luncheon menu in the restaurant.

CHATSWORTH ★★ 2
Bakewell, Derbyshire. Tel: (01246) 582204

The Duke and Duchess of Devonshire ★ 4m E of Bakewell, 10m W of Chesterfield on B6012, off A619 and A6 ★ Parking: cars £1, coaches free ★ Refreshments: home-made food in the Carriage House restaurant, snacks near Orangery Shop ★ Toilet facilities ★ Suitable for wheelchairs (but not house) ★ Dogs on lead ★ Plants for sale ★ Shop ★ House open ★ Garden open 22nd March to 29th Oct, daily, 11am – 5pm ★ Entrance: £3, OAP and students £2.50, children £1.50, family £8 (house and garden £5, OAP and students £4.25, children £2.50, family £13) (1994 prices)

The 100 acres of garden at Chatsworth have developed over 300 years and many areas still reflect the garden fashions of each century. The seventeenth-century gardens of London and Wise remain only as the cascade and canal pond to the south and the copper 'willow tree' with water pouring from its branches. During the eighteenth century 'Capability' Brown destroyed much of the formal gardens to create a landscaped woodland park. Notable is the vista created by Brown from the Salisbury Lawn to the horizon, which remains unchanged as does the lawn itself since no liming or fertiliser has been used, allowing many varieties of wild flowers, grasses, moss and sedges to thrive. The orange borders and blue and white borders are twentieth-century additions as are the terrace, display greenhouse, rose garden and old conservatory garden which has lupin, dahlia and Michaelmas daisy beds and a yew maze planted in 1963. The Duke and Duchess continue to work on the garden improving the arboretum and pinetum by removing the suffocating rhododendrons, laurels and sycamores and planting many new trees – labelling of these different trees is excellent. The serpentine hedge of beech was planted in 1953 and the double rows of pleached red-twigged limes were planted in 1952, both now rewarding features. Paxton's work still gives pleasure: there is the large rockery, some rare conifers, the magnificent 276-ft water jet from the Emperor fountain. Alas, the Great Conservatory was a casualty of the 1914–18 war and three and a half foot stone walls in the old conservatory garden are all that remain to give an idea of its size. The epitome of a cottage garden has been created near the 'Plant Sales' area. The kitchen garden has been resited and redesigned – it has been called 'indelibly British'. The first major piece of garden statuary to be placed in the garden for 150 years, *War Horse* by Dame Elisabeth Frink, was purchased in 1992 and placed at the south end of the canal. Another recent addition is up the yew stairs to a 'bedroom' where the four poster is ivy and the dressing table privet, which future generations may regard as a folly. A more conventional introduction by the present owners is the plan of Chiswick House laid out in yellow box with a pool for the dome. Make sure to see the Display Greenhouse (1970) with its bananas introduced by Paxton. Indeed to ensure missing nothing, obtain a guide. A useful booklet 'The Garden at Chatsworth' and two children's booklets 'Water Trail' and 'History Trail' can be bought in the shop.

CHERRY TREE COTTAGE 3
18 Sutton Lane, Hilton, Derbyshire. Tel: (01283) 733778

Mr and Mrs R. Hamblin ★ 8m SW of Derby. Take A516 from Derby. Sutton Lane is on the right in Hilton, opposite The Old Talbot pub. Cherry Tree Cottage is a few yards down on the right ★ Parking in Hilton car park ★ Plants for sale ★ Open by appointment May to July, Mon – Fri. Parties welcome ★ Entrance: £1, children free

Despite being a small area, there are many unusual plants, including snow-drops, hellebores, specie aquilegias, dianthus and variegated plants, as well as a scree garden, pool and herb garden. The garden achieves so much yet remains neat and charming.

DAM FARM HOUSE 4
Yeldersley Lane, Brailsford, Derbyshire. Tel: (01335) 360291

Mrs S.D. Player ★ 5m SE of Ashbourne on A52. Opposite the Ednaston village turn, the gate is 500 yards on right ★ Parking in field next to garden ★ Suitable for wheelchairs ★ Plants for sale ★ Open April to Oct by appointment only (also open some Sundays with teas) ★ Entrance: £2, children free, parties £2 per person

The scree garden has a large number of choice alpines. Climbers are used abundantly for clothing walls, trees, pergolas – even spilling down over high retaining walls and all achieved since 1980. Collections of plants, shrubs and roses. Plenty of informative labelling. This garden promises to be a most important one as it continues to develop under the expertise of Mrs Player.

DARLEY HOUSE ★ 5
Darley Dale, Matlock, Derbyshire. Tel: (01629) 733341

Mr and Mrs G.H. Briscoe ★ 2m N of Matlock on A6 to Bakewell, on right just past Whitworth Hospital ★ Best season: spring/summer ★ Limited parking beside entrance ★ Refreshments: tea and biscuits ★ Partly suitable for wheelchairs ★ Plants for sale. Extensive seed list ★ Open 15th May to 16th Sept by appointment ★ Entrance: £1, children free. Special arrangements for private parties

This serene garden was originally set out by Paxton in 1845. Plantsman's gardens can be bogged down by the sheer number of different plants but here, although there is a wealth of beautiful and unusual plants, all harmonise. There are a number of mature tender shrubs and plants which surprisingly survive the Derbyshire weather – thoughtful planting obviously paying dividends. Extensive seed list. Additional areas of the garden have recently been restored.

DERBY ARBORETUM 6
Arboretum Square, Derby, Derbyshire. Tel: (01332) 255802

Derby City Council ★ Situated between Reginald Street and Arboretum Square with entrances on either side of the Royal Crown Derby Factory ★ Parking in car parks nearby or on streets ★ Toilet facilities ★ Suitable for wheelchairs ★ Dogs on lead ★ Open all year ★ Entrance: free

The first specifically designed urban park in Britain, this was designed to a commission by John Claudius Loudon whose original plans involved the planting of 1000 trees. A useful (and free) leaflet now lists 40 varieties, many from around the world, all individually numbered.

DOVE COTTAGE GARDENS 7
Clifton, Ashbourne, Derbyshire. Tel: (01335) 43545

Mr and Mrs S.G. Liverman ★ 1½m SW of Ashbourne off A515. In Clifton turn right at crossroads then first left (signposted Mayfield Yarns). The house is 200 yards down lane on the left by the River Dove ★ Parking ★ Teas ★ Toilet facilities ★ Plants for sale ★ Open by appointment for party bookings of 10 or more and on certain days for charity, 1.30 – 5pm ★ Entrance: Parties £1.50 per person for guided tour and for charity £1, children free (1994 prices)

It is only to be expected that this richly-stocked cottage garden is above the average for it has had the benefit of being developed and nurtured by an owner who is a qualified horticulturalist. She began replanting it in 1979. There are several hardy plant collections including alliums, campanulas, euphorbias, geraniums and variegated plants.

ELVASTON CASTLE COUNTRY PARK ★ 8
Nr Derby, Derbyshire. Tel: (01332) 571342

Derbyshire County Council ★ 6m SE of Derby on B5010 between Borrowash A6005 and Thulston A6. Signposted from A6 and A52 ★ Parking: mid-week 60p, weekends and Bank Holidays £1.20 (1993 prices) ★ Refreshments: in Parlour tearoom, Easter to Oct ★ Toilet facilities ★ Suitable for wheelchairs ★ Dogs on lead in Old English Garden ★ Shop ★ Estate Museum open April to 30th Oct, daily except Mon and Tues (but open Bank Holiday Mons). £1.20, children 60p (1994 prices) ★ Garden open all year, daily, 9am – dusk ★ Entrance: free

A fine Grade II historic garden worthy of a visit at any time of the year. Within the 200 acres there is a large variety of mature trees, many of them evergreen. A tree trail is planned. The Italian garden with its clipped yews has limited appeal visually. The original walled kitchen garden is now the Old English Garden containing herbaceous borders, rose garden and herb garden. The history of the garden is displayed in the Information Centre; of particular interest is that in 1851 there were 90 gardening staff. William Barron, the professional gardener who developed the garden at that time, was an expert on transplanting mature trees.

FIR CROFT 9
Froggatt Road, Calver, Derbyshire.

Dr and Mrs S.B. Furness ★ 4m N of Bakewell. Between the Q8 filling station and the junction of B6001 and B6054 ★ Best season: spring/early summer ★ Limited parking ★ Partly suitable for wheelchairs ★ Plants for sale at adjoining nursery ★ Open 23rd April, 14th May, 4th, 18th June, 2 – 6pm ★ Entrance: by collection box for charity

The owner is a botanist and botanical photographer who has put his expertise into an extensive alpine garden – a 'must' to visit if interested in alpine and scree gardens, particularly as the garden was started from scratch in 1985.

GAMESLEY FOLD COTTAGE 10
Glossop, Derbyshire. Tel: (014578) 67856

Mr and Mrs G. Carr ★ Off A626 Glossop – Marple road near Charlesworth.
Turn down the lane opposite St Margaret's School. Signposted on open days ★
Parking ★ Teas ★ Plants for sale ★ Open 21st May, 25th June, 1 – 4pm and
private parties by appointment only ★ Entrance: £1, children free (1994 price)

Although all gardeners will find much of interest here, those who like
native or 'wild' flowers will be particularly impressed. The many loosely-
planted beds are crammed with primulas, violets, campions and poppies, a
lot of which are self-seeded. Mixed in is a good variety of perennials,
notably campanulas, euphorbias, geraniums, verbascums and others that go
well with their wild neighbours. Much wildlife is to be found and particularly butterflies are lured here by the flowers. The lovely views of the
surrounding countryside and hills are another bonus. Many other gardens
in this area tend to be dominated by rhododendrons, so Mrs Carr's very
different approach on her less acid soil presents a refreshing change.

HADDON HALL 11
Bakewell, Derbyshire. Tel: (01629) 812855

The Duke of Rutland ★ 2m SE of Bakewell, 6½m N of Matlock on A6 ★
Parking: cars 50p, coaches free ★ Refreshments: lunches and teas in Stables
tearoom ★ Toilet facilities ★ House open ★ Garden open April to Sept, daily
except Sun in July and Aug, but open Bank Holiday Sun, 11am – 5.45pm ★
Entrance: hall and gardens £4.50, OAP £3.50, children £2.80, family (2 adults
and 2 children) £12.50, parties £3.50 per person, school parties £2.40 per child
(no garden–only ticket)

The medieval castle and gardens of seventeenth-century origin – reconstructed this century – stand on a limestone bluff. The gardens are mainly
on the south side and are laid out in a series of stone-walled terraces with
the River Wye at their feet. The thick stone walls of the castle and terrace
walls face south and west and look well as a background for the extensive
collection of climbing and rambling roses. The plants, shrubs and roses all
have legible labels. Winner of Christie's/Historic Houses Association
Garden of the Year award in 1994.

HARDWICK HALL ★ 12
Doe Lea, Chesterfield, Derbyshire. Tel: (01246) 850430

The National Trust ★ 9½m NW of Mansfield, 9½m SE of Chesterfield.
Approach from M1 junction 29 then A6175 ★ Best season: summer ★ Parking.
Gates close at 6pm ★ Refreshments in Great Kitchen of Hall on days Hall is
open 12 noon – 4.45pm ★ Toilet facilities ★ Suitable for wheelchairs ★ Dogs in
park only, on lead ★ National Trust shop ★ House open April to Oct on Wed,
Thurs, Sat, Sun and Bank Holiday Mon (closed 14th April), 12.30 – 5pm or
sunset if earlier (last admission 4.30pm) ★ Garden open April to Oct, daily, 12
noon – 5.30pm. Country park open, daily, dawn – dusk ★ Entrance: £2 (house
and garden £5.50, children £2.70). No reduction for parties

This famous Elizabethan mansion house was built for Bess of Hardwick by
Robert Smythson in the late sixteenth century. Mature yew hedges and

stone walls provide necessary shelter to an otherwise exposed escarpment site. The borders of the South Court have spring-flowering shrubs to give colour for a longer period than herbaceous plants can provide. Some herbaceous borders have strong, hot colours as an overall grouping, others have soft hues. In order to rest the soil to rid it of a build-up of pests and diseases the borders were replanted in October 1989. The herb garden is outstanding in variety of plants and display.

THE HERB GARDEN 13
Hall View Cottage, Hardstoft, Pilsley, Nr Chesterfield, Derbyshire.
Tel: (01246) 854268

Mrs Raynor ★ 5m SE of Chesterfield on B6039 Holmewood − Tibshelf road. 3m from M1 junction 29 ★ Parking ★ Refreshments: in tea room with herb recipes ★ Suitable for wheelchairs ★ Plants for sale ★ Shop ★ Garden open March to Sept, daily, 10am − 6pm ★ Entrance: free

A rich herb garden in a rural setting with a now established parterre. Three speciality gardens have been added: a physic garden, a scented pot pourri garden and a lavender garden. A very large range of herbs for sale including rare and unusual species. This garden is only a short distance from the other excellent herb garden in Hardwick Hall (see entry).

KEDLESTON HALL ★ 14
Kedleston, Derbyshire. Tel: (01332) 842191

The National Trust ★ 4½m NW of Derby on the Derby − Hulland road between A6 and A52. Well signposted ★ Best season: summer/autumn ★ Parking ★ Refreshments: tearoom, 12 noon − 5pm ★ Toilet facilities ★ Suitable for wheelchairs by prior arrangement ★ Shop ★ Hall open, April to Oct (closed 14th April), Sat − Wed, 1 − 5.30pm (last admission 5pm). Contains Lord Curzon's Indian Museum ★ Park open April to Oct, daily, 11am − 6pm and Nov to 17th Dec, Sat and Sun only, 12 noon − 4pm. Garden open April to Oct, Sat − Wed, 11am − 6pm ★ Entrance: park, £2 vehicle entry charge; hall and garden £4.20, children £2.10. Coach parties must pre-book by writing to the Administrator

The ancient home of the Curzon family, their most famous member being George Nathaniel, Viceroy of India 1899−1905. The extensive gardens do not compete with this classical Robert Adam palace, but are of mature parkland where the eye is always drawn to the house. The rhododendrons when in flower are worth visiting in their own right, otherwise visit the gardens as a pleasurable way not only to view Adam's magnificent south front but his hexagonal-domed summerhouse, his orangery, a Venetian-windowed fishing house, the bridge across the lake, the aviary and slaughterhouse − now a loggia − and the main gateway. The formal gardens have a sunken rose garden. The Sulphur Bath House, one of the earliest eighteenth-century landscape garden features, where a small spa used to operate, has been restored but is not accessible to the public.

LEA GARDENS 15
Lea, Nr Matlock, Derbyshire. Tel: (01629) 534380/534260

Mr and Mrs Tye ★ 5m SE of Matlock E off A6 ★ Parking. Coaches by appoint-

ment ★ Refreshments: light lunches, teas ★ Suitable for wheelchairs ★ Plants for sale ★ Open 20th March to 16th July, daily, 10am – 7pm, and rest of year by appointment ★ Entrance: £2.50, children 50p (season ticket £3.50)

This garden has a comprehensive collection of rhododendrons, azaleas, alpines and conifers all brought together here in a beautiful woodland setting. An excellent booklet describes the contents of the garden with a suggested route. John Marsden Smedley started his rhododendron garden in 1935, inspired by his visits to Bodnant and Exbury. Under the Tye family the collection now comprises some 550 varieties of rhododendrons and azaleas in a much increased area.

MELBOURNE HALL GARDENS ★ 16
Melbourne, Derbyshire. Tel: (01332) 862502

Lord Ralph Kerr ★ 8m S of Derby off B587 in village of Melbourne (between A514 and A453) ★ Best season: spring/summer ★ Limited parking ★ Refreshments: hot and cold meals in tea room ★ Toilet facilities ★ Suitable for wheelchairs ★ Shop ★ House open, Aug, daily except 7th, 14th, 21st, 2 – 5pm. £2.50, OAP £2, children 75p ★ Garden open April to Sept, Wed, Sat, Sun and Bank Holiday Mon, 2 – 6pm ★ Entrance: £2, OAP £1 (1994 prices)

There has been very little alteration to the Rt Hon. Thomas Coke's formal garden so this is a visual record of a complete late seventeenth/early eighteenth-century garden in the style of Le Nôtre laid out by London and Wise. It is in immaculate condition with avenues culminating in exquisite statuary and fountains, including the lead urn *The Four Seasons* by van Nost, whose other lead statuary stands in niches of yew. A series of terraces run down to a lake, the Great Basin. A grotto has an inscription thought to be that of Byron's troublesome mistress Caroline Lamb. Unique in English gardens is the Birdcage iron arbour of 1706 which can be seen from the house along a long walk hedged with yews. It is well worth buying the booklet 'Melbourne Hall Gardens' at the entrance, giving the history and a suggested guided tour.

210 NOTTINGHAM ROAD 17
Woodlinkin, Nr Codnor, Derbyshire. Tel: (01773) 714903

Mr and Mrs R. Brown ★ 12m NW of Nottingham on A610 1m from Codnor. It is the first house past a garage on the left ★ Best season: late spring/early summer ★ Limited parking ★ Suitable for wheelchairs ★ Dogs on lead ★ Open 25th June, 2 – 5pm ★ Entrance: £1

A plantsman's garden of half an acre with an emphasis on shrub roses – the garden is packed with many good examples. There are also some rarer shrubs and trees. Geraniums, hellebores, symphytums and similar plants provide all-year interest in the herbaceous section.

PAVILION GARDENS 18
St Johns Road, Buxton, Derbyshire. Tel: (01298) 23114/23910

High Peak Borough Council ★ Near the centre of Buxton. Enter from Burlington Road ★ Parking ★ Refreshments in complex ★ Toilet facilities ★ Dogs on lead ★ Open all year ★ Entrance: free

Twenty-three acres of landscaped municipal park, woodland and two ornamental lakes, this updated pleasure garden of 1871 has the distinction of having been laid out by Edward Milner of Sydenham (site of the Crystal Palace to whose designer, Paxton, Milner was chief assistant). The gardens are well-maintained and the pleasing 1875 Octagon (now a conference centre) is a graceful backdrop. The conservatory is well-stocked.

57 PORTLAND CLOSE   19
Mickleover, Derbyshire. Tel: (01332) 515450

Mr and Mrs A.L. Ritchie ★ From A111 (Derby ring road) take A516. At first roundabout take B5020 (signposted Mickleover). In Mickleover take right turn into Cavendish Way, then second left into Portland Close ★ Best season: spring/summer ★ Limited parking ★ Plants for sale ★ Open by appointment ★ Entrance: 75p, children free

A plantsman's small garden with something unusual planted in almost every inch of it. The knowledgeable owner propagates most of the huge variety of hostas, primulas, auriculas, violas and cyclamen, with many of the plants for sale. Alpines, sink gardens.

RENISHAW HALL   20
Eckington, Derbyshire. Tel: (01246) 432042

Sir Reresby and Lady Sitwell ★ 6m from Sheffield and Chesterfield on A616. From M1 at junction 30, take A616 towards Sheffield for 3m through Renishaw village ★ Parking ★ Teas ★ Toilet facilities ★ Partly suitable for wheelchairs ★ Dogs on lead ★ Plants for sale ★ Antique, gift and wine shops ★ Museum and Arts Centre in Georgian stables ★ Open 17th April, 1st, 29th May, 28th Aug; also June to Aug, Fri – Sun, all 10.30am – 4.30pm ★ Entrance: £3, OAP £2, children £1

For nearly 20 years Renishaw had 'the most northerly vineyard in western Europe'. Also astonishing to see at this northerly latitude and on top of a hill (albeit on a south facing wall) are enormous specimens of *Acacia dealbata*, *Cytisus battandieri* and *Fremontodendron californicum*. There are other rare, slightly tender specimen shrubs within the garden. Presumably the fact that the soil is light, the aspect southerly and shelter provided by yew hedges and parkland trees overcome the disadvantages of latitude and height. Sir George Sitwell spent much of his life in Italy and hence this is the style he re-created at Renishaw nearly 100 years ago, all vividly described in Osbert Sitwell's memoirs. The sound of splashing water, always in the background, adds to the Italianate atmosphere, and the present owner has added a stupendous water jet to increase the effect. Good guide by Sir Reresby Sitwell who has enlarged the borders, introduced innovative planting (Sir George had rejected Miss Jekyll's designs for being too colourful) and linked the garden to the wood by new planting and paths. The Sitwell Museum is another new feature. George Plumptre says this is a garden 'of rare, all-round quality, a joy to garden design enthusiasts and plantsmen'.

DEVON

Two-starred gardens are ringed in bold.

ANDREW'S CORNER   1
Belstone, Nr Okehampton, Devon. Tel: (01837) 840332

*H.J. and Mr and Mrs R.J. Hill ★ 3m E of Okehampton, signposted to Belstone
★ Parking ★ Teas on open days ★ Suitable for wheelchairs ★ Plants for sale ★
Open by appointment and 23rd April, 7th, 28th May, 4th, 18th June, 16th July,
2.30 – 6pm ★ Entrance: £1, children free*

Nine hundred feet above sea level, on north Dartmoor, facing the Taw valley
and across to the high moor. In only two thirds of an acre (amazing that it is
not larger) grow a wide variety of plants of all sorts not normally seen at such
an altitude. The sense of space is achieved by the division of the garden into
different levels by rhododendrons and trees, each area being a small region with
its own micro–climate, and all with glimpses through to other areas and to the
wide landscape. There are herbaceous plants and lilies, conifers and heathers in

island beds; in spring flowering bulbs and meconopsis; in autumn colour from maples (many grown from seed) and gentians. There are dry stone walls (a speciality of the area), a paved area and a pond with water plants; among the stone and paving are lewisias and other alpines. The owner does not like the description 'plantsman'; he says it is a hobby he loves.

ARLINGTON COURT 2
Arlington, Nr Barnstaple, Devon. Tel: (01271) 850296

The National Trust ★ 7m N of Barnstaple on A39, turn E ★ Parking 300 yards away ★ Refreshments: in tearoom and restaurant when house open ★ Toilet facilities near house ★ Dogs in grounds only on leads ★ Shop open during open hours, and weekends before Christmas ★ House open ★ Garden open April to 1st Nov, daily except Sat (but open Sat of Bank Holiday weekends), 11am – 5.30pm (last admission ½ hour before closing). Footpaths through woods and park open Nov to April during daylight hours ★ Entrance: garden and carriage museum £2.40, children £1.20 (house, museum and garden £4.60, children £2.30, family ticket £11 (2 adults and 2 children), parties of 15 or more £3.50 per person, children £1.75)

The Georgian house is set in a magnificent park where Shetland ponies and Jacob sheep graze. There are a number of woodland walks with remains of the old stone-built water courses or leats that were used to irrigate the park in times of drought two centuries ago. The planned 'wilderness' was a popular eighteenth-century feature, a semi-wild area between the garden and the parkland. The woodland is managed to protect wildlife including red deer. The lake is approached by an avenue of monkey puzzle trees.

AVENUE COTTAGE GARDENS 3
Ashprington, Totnes, Devon. Tel: (01803) 732769

Mr R.C.H. Soans and Mr R.J. Pitts ★ Take the A381 from Totnes towards Kingsbridge. Turn left to Ashprington. Facing the Durant Arms in Ashprington turn left uphill past the church (no through road). The gardens are 300 yards on the right ★ No coaches ★ Open April to Sept, Tues – Sat, 11am – 5pm. Also by appointment ★ Entrance: £1, children 25p by collecting box

These were originally part of the eighteenth-century landscape gardens of Sharpham House, separated 50 years ago. They are approached along a splendid avenue of Turkey oaks planted in 1844. Many of the rhododendrons and azaleas planted in the last century are enormous and magnificent. Over the years parts of the garden had become very overgrown so a clearing programme was started. The new plantings are now developing and the garden is worth visiting at any time although probably best in spring. The owner/gardeners are always delighted to point out some of their more unusual treasures.

BICKHAM BARTON 4
Bickham, Roborough, Plymouth, Devon. Tel: (01822) 852478

Helen, Lady Roborough ★ 8m N of Plymouth on A386. Take Maristow road turn left on Roborough Down and follow poster directions ★ Parking ★ Plants for sale ★ Open 2nd April to 4th June, Suns only, 2 – 5.30pm, 17th April, 8th, 29th May, 18th June, and by appointment at other times ★ Entrance: £2

This is a spring garden in a valley with magnificent views. There is a mass of bulbs and many camellias as well as magnolias and rhododendrons. A walled garden with old roses.

BICKHAM HOUSE   5
Kenn, Exeter, Devon. Tel: (01392) 832671

Mr and Mrs John Tremlett ★ 6m W of Exeter on A38 Plymouth – Torquay road. Leave the dual carriageway at Kennford Services and follow signs to Kenn. Take first right in the village and follow lane for ¾m to end of no-through road ★ Parking ★ ☆Teas ★ Toilet facilities ★ Suitable for wheelchairs ★ No shade for dogs ★ Plants for sale ★ Open 19th, 22nd March, 16th, 19th April, 21st, 24th May, 18th, 21st June, 16th, 19th July, 20th, 23rd August, 17th, 20th September, 2 – 5pm and at other times by appointment ★ Entrance: £1.50, children 50p

A five-acre garden gazing upon characteristically rolling Devon parkland. The immediate foreground is dominated by a deceptively venerable lake – in fact construction work began in 1990. Much of the planting is also of comparatively recent vintage, for the Tremletts started redeveloping the garden only six years ago – testimony to the fertile soil of the region. Bickham, however has been in the family since 1682 and there remains an overwhelming sense of homogeneity. Its many fine individual features include an enormous *Liriodendron tulipifera* (tulip tree) and a delightful *Davidia involucrata* (pocket-handkerchief tree), a passion flower that dominates the conservatory and a rampaging wisteria. The parterre at the back of the house is seasonally planted out and the small water garden is another feature luxuriant beyond its years. Summer colour is predominant in the walled garden which also has a positively pristine vegetable area. All-year interest in the shape of a host of naturalised bulbs, azaleas and rhododendrons for the early season, colour-coordinated mixed herbaceous beds for a little later and lovely autumn colour from the acers.

BICKLEIGH CASTLE   6
Nr Tiverton, Devon. Tel: (01884) 855363

Mr O.N. Boxall ★ 4m S of Tiverton off A396. At Bickleigh Bridge take A3072 and follow signs ★ Best season: spring/early summer ★ Parking ★ Teas ★ Suitable for wheelchairs (ground floor of house only) ★ Castle open. Private tours for groups by appointment ★ Garden open 14th to 21st April, daily; 23rd April to 29th May, Sun, Wed and Bank Holiday Mons; June to early Oct, daily except Sat, all 2 – 5.30pm ★ Entrance: £3.20, children (5-15) £1.60 (castle, garden and exhibitions) (1994 prices). Family tickets available

These gardens are situated in the valley of the Exe around the ancient buildings which are historically fascinating with much to see. The Castle became the home of the Carew family, Sir George Carew being the Vice Admiral of the *Mary Rose*. Beyond the eighteenth-century Italian wrought iron gates is a large mound planted in the 1930s with every known variety of rhododendron. There is a 300-year-old wisteria and many more mature trees including *Gingko biloba*, magnolias, a Judas tree and a tulip tree. The moat is planted with iris and water lilies.

BICTON COLLEGE OF AGRICULTURE 7
East Budleigh, Devon. Tel: (01395) 68353

By Sidmouth Lodge, halfway between Budleigh Salterton and Newton Poppleford on A376 ★ Parking in garden car park beyond student car park, short walk to garden ★ Refreshments ★ Toilet facilities ★ Suitable for wheelchairs ★ Dogs on lead ★ Wide range of unusual plants for sale ★ Open all year, daily except 25th, 26th Dec ★ Entrance: £2, children free. Membership of Friends of the College gives unlimited access and free gardening advice on Fri afternoons

The gardens of this Georgian house form the horticultural department of Bicton College, and as such contain a large number of plants laid out for both study and general interest – truly a plantsman's paradise. As well as the fascinating herbaceous beds there is an arboretum with spring-flowering trees and an old walled garden with glasshouses, all approached by an avenue of araucarias (monkey puzzle trees). Amongst the plants which provide both information and effect are the NCCPG collections of agapanthus and pittosporums. There is a large area of parkland and a lake. Garden and arboretum guides are available.

BICTON PARK ★ 8
East Budleigh, Budleigh Salterton, Devon.
Tel: (01395) 568465; Fax: (01395) 568889

Bicton Park Trust Company ★ 2m N of Budleigh Salterton on A376 ★ Parking ★ Refreshments: self-service restaurant and licensed bar, picnic areas ★ Toilet facilities ★ Suitable for wheelchairs (wheelchair loan available) ★ Dogs on lead ★ Shop ★ Museum, woodland railway ride and children's play areas ★ Park open April to Oct, daily, 10am – 6pm ★ Entrance: all inclusive prices £3.75, OAP £2.75, children (3–15) £2.75, family ticket £12 (2 adults and 4 children) (1994 prices). Special rates for parties of 20 or more

There is much to see here in the 50 acres – don't be put off by the 'fun and family entertainment'. The formal and informal gardens date from 1734 and the Italian garden is attributed to Le Nôtre; there is an Oriental garden with a 150-year-old mulberry, azaleas, camellias, flowering cherries and a peony border (bush and tree); an American Garden established in the 1830s with a snowdrop tree (*Halesia carolina*), calico bushes and a pocket-handker-chief tree (*Davidia involucrata*); a Hermitage Garden with lake and water garden and a pinetum with some rare conifers including a Mexican juniper, yuccas, Korean thuya and Tasmanian cedar. The pinetum was established in 1838 and extended in 1910 to take the collection of the famous botanist and explorer 'Chinese' Wilson. Perhaps Bicton's greatest glory is the Palm House built between 1815 and 1820, one of the oldest in the country and recently refurbished; in it, Kentia palms up to 20 feet, tree ferns and bromeliads, and outside an Assam tea plant. There are also geranium and fuchsia houses and a tropical and a temperate house for bananas, coffee trees and bougainvilleas. Bicton College of Agriculture is also open (see entry).

BUCKLAND ABBEY 9
Nr Yelverton, Devon. Tel: (01822) 853607

The National Trust and Plymouth City Council ★ 6m S of Tavistock, 11m N of

DEVON

Plymouth. Turn off A386 ¼m S of Yelverton ★ Parking ★ Licensed restaurant and tea-room ★ Toilet facilities ★ Partly suitable for wheelchairs (steep site). Motorised buggy may be available ★ Dogs on lead ★ Shop ★ Open April to Oct, 10.30am – 5.30pm, also Nov to March, Sat and Sun, 2 – 5pm ★ Entrance: £2 (house and gardens £4). Increased charges (which also apply to NT members) when special events are in progress

Buckland Abbey garden is largely a twentieth-century creation. There is a box hedge parterre between the 100-foot-long medieval Dutch barn and the abbey, its pockets filled with over 50 different herbs, reputedly inspired by Vita Sackville-West. *Magnolia delavayi* and *M. grandiflora* grow against the abbey tower and a line of surprisingly tall yews on the north border of the lawn surround the abbey. From the lawn, close and distant views of Devon and Cornwall loom beyond the boundary.

BURROW FARM GARDENS ★   10
Dalwood, Axminster, Devon. Tel: (0140483) 1285

Mr and Mrs John Benger ★ 4m W of Axminster. Take A35 Honiton road from Axminster. After 3½m turn north near Shute garage on to the Stockland road. Garden is ½m on right ★ Parking ★ Cream teas on Weds and Suns ★ Toilet facilities ★ Suitable for wheelchairs (not woodland garden) ★ Dogs on leads ★ Plants for sale in nursery ★ Open April to Sept, daily, 2 – 7pm and mornings by appointment ★ Entrance: £2, children 50p, parties (discount rate) by appointment

These lovely gardens, created from pasture land, are the inspiration of Mary Benger and her family. The five-acre site is still being developed. Foliage effect was the prime consideration during the planning stages and this has been admirably achieved with a lovely array of azaleas and rhodo-dendrons. A former Roman clay pit is graded from top to bottom through mature trees and shrubs to an extensive bog garden with a marvellous show of candelabra primulas and native wild flowers during the early part of the season. In summer the pergola walk, with its old-fashioned roses and herbaceous borders, is a picture. The setting and sense of grandeur are more typical of gardens of greater repute. Magnificent views.

CASTLE DROGO ★★   11
Drewsteignton, Devon. Tel: (016473) 3306

The National Trust ★ 4m S of A30 or 4m N of Moretonhampstead on A382, follow signs from Sandy Park ★ Parking. Coaches by appointment only ★ Refreshments: coffee and light lunches (licensed) and teas, 10.30am – 5pm ★ Toilet facilities inc. disabled ★ Suitable for wheelchairs. Special parking and access by arrangement at reception. Scented plants for visually handicapped ★ Shop ★ Castle open at extra charge (but closed Fri). Croquet can be played with hired equipment ★ Garden open April to Oct, daily, 10.30am – 5.30pm (last admission ½ hour before closing) ★ Entrance: £2 (garden and grounds only). Reduced rates for parties by appointment

The last castle to be built in England (begun 1910) was designed by Sir Edwin Lutyens. Gertrude Jekyll had some involvement with the planting of trees around the drive, but the plans for the planting of the garden were by George Dillistone of Tunbridge Wells. Apart from the evergreen oaks above the magnificent views over the Teign Gorge, and a valley planted with rhododendrons, magnolias, camellias, cherries and maples, there is a series of formal terraces and borders with walls of granite, sharp-edged yew hedges with rose beds and arbours of yew and *Parrotia persica*, 'the iron tree'. In the main formal gardens, with galleries round a sunken centre, paths are serpentine (an Indian touch typical of Lutyens who built New Delhi in the 1920s when he was supervising here), and herbaceous borders are full of old varieties of lupins, lychnis, campanulas, hollyhocks and red hot pokers. Under the granite walls are perennials like euphorbias, hellebores, alchemillas and veronicas, with spring bulbs. Steps lead to a second terrace with yuccas and wisterias and herb borders; more steps to shrub borders of lilacs, azaleas, magnolias and lilies, and finally a splendid circular lawn surrounded by a tall yew hedge at the top, a huge green circle and a perfect stage set for croquet.

CASTLE TOR 12
Wellswood, Torquay, Devon. Tel: (01803) 214858

Mr L. Stocks ★ In Torquay. From Higher Lincombe Road, turn E into Oxlea Road. Entrance is 200 yards on right with eagle-topped pillars ★ Parking ★ Open by appointment ★ Entrance: £1, children 25p

Half a century ago the then owner of Castle Tor approached Sir Edwin Lutyens and asked him to design a smaller version of Castle Drogo; being too busy Sir Edwin nominated a pupil of his, Frederick Harrild, and the result is this fascinating architectural garden with magnificent views over Lyme Bay and Tor Bay. Gertrude Jekyll's ideas about garden colour – no violent juxtapositions or circular beds full of salvias – were incorporated, and the whole is framed in terraces of Somerset limestone (a pleasant change from granite) and cubic green walls of yew hedges; there is topiary in both green and golden (Irish) yew. There are architectural-type follies like a pillared orangery with a domed roof and a tower with portcullis and gatehouse; best of all a long ornamental water course or small canal. Over the years the owner has collected suitable statuary and bright annual flowers are seen as accents in urns and tubs against the stone background. About five years ago, Reg and Carole Burnside acquired the three lower terraces, flanking Lincombe Drive, and part of the round garden on the fourth terrace. They have constructed a magnificent residence in matching Somerset stone, called Lincombe Keep. It has received acclamation all round and has won an architectural award. Visitors to Castle Tor are permitted to enter their part of the garden which is maintained as a harmonious whole.

CLEAVE HOUSE 13
Sticklepath, Okehampton, Devon. Tel: (01837) 840481

Ann and Roger Bowden ★ 3¹/₂m E of Okehampton on the old A30 towards Exeter. Cleave House is on the left, in the village, just past small right turn for Skaigh ★ Parking ★ Toilet facilities ★ Partly suitable for wheelchairs ★ Dogs on lead ★ Plants for sale ★ Open by appointment and for charity 10th, 14th May, 25th June, 10.30am – 5.30pm ★ Entrance: 50p

For the Bowdens hostas are not just a business, they are an abiding passion.

Their one-acre garden, tucked away at the heart of a small Devon village, does boast some delightful mixed planting – both trees and shrubs – but hostas are the dominant feature. Hostas are propagated by division from existing stock, while some are micropropagated and grown on for two years. A few varieties, notably the brightly coloured, have been imported from the United States. This Mecca for the hosta enthusiast includes demonstration beds resplendent with over three hundred and fifty different varieties, displaying fascinating variation of both colour and size. People from all over the world have made the pilgrimage to view the extensive range of plants on show and for sale, and to take advantage of the Bowdens' specialist knowledge. The collection has been designated an NCCPG reference (of modern hybrids).

COLETON FISHACRE GARDEN ★★   14
Coleton, Kingswear, Dartmouth, Devon. Tel: (01803) 752466

The National Trust ★ 2m from Kingswear, take Lower Ferry Road and turn off at toll house ★ Parking ★ Very limited for wheelchairs ★ Open March, Suns, 2 – 5pm, and April to Oct, Wed – Fri, Sun and Bank Holiday Mons, 10.30am – 5.30pm ★ Entrance: £2.80, children £1.40, pre-booked parties of 15 or more £2 per person

Oswald Milne, who was a pupil of Edwin Lutyens, designed the house and the architectural features of this garden for Sir Rupert and Lady D'Oyly Carte; the house was completed and the garden begun in 1926. Exceptionally mild and sheltered, it is in a Devon combe, sloping steeply to the cliff tops and the sea, and sheltered by belts of Monterey pines and holm oaks planted in 1923. The streams and ponds make a humid atmosphere for the moisture-loving plants like the magnificent bamboos (inch-thick canes) and mimosas, and many other sub-tropical plants, rarely growing outside in this country. There is a collection of unusual trees like dawn redwood, swamp cypress and Chilean myrtle, and dominating all a tall tulip tree and 'Tree of Heaven' the same age as the house. Formal walls and terraces make a framework round the house for a large number of sun-loving tender plants. There are various water features, notably a stone-edged rill and a circular pool in the herbaceous-bordered walled garden. Scented herbs and plants. A brilliant garden.

CROFTDENE   15
Ham, Nr Dalwood, Axminster, Devon.

Mr and Mrs P. Knox ★ From A35 3¹/₂m W of Axminster turn N near Shute garage signed Dalwood and Stockland. Keep left up Stockland Hill until just past television mast. Turn right signed Ham. Continue 1¹/₂m to Ham Cross. From A30 5m E of Honiton turn right signed Axminster and Stockland. Continue 3m to television mast and turn left to Ham. Garden is near telephone box ★ Parking on road ★ Cream teas at Burrow Farm Gardens (see entry) ★ Toilet facilities ★ Open 28th May, 25th June, 2 – 6pm and by appointment ★ Entrance: £1, children free

It is hard to believe that this garden is only a few years down the road to maturity. Near-fanatical devotion on the part of the owners has resulted in the creation of a plantsman's paradise. The one and a half-acre garden supports a huge range of shrubs, herbaceous and ericaceous plants, a marvellous rock garden with a fine collection of alpines, island beds and pond with waterside plants. A delightful acre of natural woodland provides the perfect contrast to the more formal setting.

CROSSPARK 16
Northlew, Nr Okehampton, Devon. Tel: (01409221) 518

Mrs G. West ★ 8m NW of Okehampton. From Okehampton take old A30 Launceston road for 1m, turn right onto Holsworthy road for 6m and right to Northlew by telephone mast, go over bridge and left to Kimber, then follow road for 2½m ★ Parking ★ Toilet facilities ★ Only a small area suitable for wheelchairs ★ Plants for sale ★ Open 30th April to 26th June, Suns and Mons, 2 – 6pm, and all year by appointment ★ Entrance: 75p

This one-acre plantswoman's garden, created from a field by the owner, would provide interest for a visit at most times of the year. A heather bed and pleasant separate colour beds and also an attractive white garden. The pool and waterfall are surrounded by a range of bog plants and there is a good selection of climbers on the house. Also dwarf conifers and a rockery.

DARTINGTON HALL ★ 17
Dartington, Nr Totnes, Devon. Tel: (01803) 862271

Dartington Hall Trust ★ 2m NW of Totnes, E of A384 ★ Parking. Coaches by appointment (01803) 863614 ★ Toilet facilities ★ Plants for sale ★ Open daily, dawn – dusk ★ Entrance: by donation

The gardens were begun by Dorothy and Leonard Elmhirst in 1925 when the Hall was derelict and the estate and parkland overgrown. Several garden designers have been advisers – Beatrix Farrand designed the courtyard and opened up the woodland walkways. There are three woodland walks using bay, yew and holly as a background for a collection of camellias, magnolias and rhododendrons. Landscape designer Percy Cane made the glade and the azalea dell. The overall design is strongly architectural with sunken lawns and terraces and formal clipped yews contrasting with the mature woodland. Fine sculpture by Henry Moore and others.

DOCTYN MILL ★ 18
Spekes Valley, Nr Hartland, Devon. Tel: (01237) 441369

Mr M.G. and Mrs E.G.N. Bourcier ★ Off A39 from north Devon via Hartland to Stoke or from north Cornwall to West Country Inn, turn left and follow Elmscott signs towards Lymebridge in Spekes Valley ★ Parking ★ Cream teas ★ Toilet facilities ★ Open March to Oct, daily, 10am – 5pm ★ Entrance: £2, OAP £1.50, children 50p

Created by Mr and Mrs Pugh, the previous owners, from a derelict water mill about 1980. They embarked upon a large-scale clearance of the waterways; there are ponds, leats, footbridges over the river and many smaller streams as it is only 1500 yards from Speke's Mill Mouth coastal waterfall and the beach. A boggy area was drained to make a stream and a bog garden with ligularias, primulas and ferns; the whole purpose has been to make everything as natural as possible, integrating the garden into the wild. In spring there are displays of narcissi, camellias, primulas, azaleas and magnolias with bluebells; in summer the garden abounds in roses, mostly old shrub roses, there is a hedge of 'Felicia' and 'Pax' hybrid musk roses and a climbing 'Felicia' – a rarity. Roses are underplanted with many varieties of perennial geraniums, another favourite plant, and these are also used on the rockery (which is wet clay and north-facing and not suitable for alpines) together with hebes and small conifers. New ownership since December 1993.

ENDSLEIGH HOUSE AND GARDENS 19
Milton Abbot, Nr Tavistock, Devon. Tel: (0182287) 248

Endsleigh Charitable Trust ★ 4m W of Tavistock on the B3362 ★ Parking ★ Refreshments: hotel open by appointment for lunch and tea ★ Gardens open April to Sept, Sat, Sun and Bank Holidays, 12 noon – 4pm, and by appointment, Tues and Fri, 12 noon – 4pm ★ Entrance: by donation (suggested minimum £1)

Endsleigh was built, starting in 1811, for the 6th Duke of Bedford from designs by architect Jeffry Wyatville and landscape gardener Humphry Repton. The house is a good example of the 'Cottage *orné*' and was used as a fishing and hunting lodge by the Duke. It is now a quiet country house hotel popular with salmon fishermen. The house and the immediate garden have tight views overlooking the almost stream-like character of the upper Tamar, wooded on either bank. The garden is undergoing gradual restoration in an endeavour to establish the nineteenth-century vision. There is an uneasy truce between the rich wilderness that has invaded Repton's landscape and the slow process of ongoing authentication. Rare tree species in the arboretum have largely survived the storms of the late 1980s. Buzzards and cormorants command the sky.

FARDEL MANOR 20
Ivybridge, Devon.

Dr A.G. Stevens ★ 1¼ m NW of Ivybridge, 2m SE of Cornwood, 200 yards off railway bridge ★ Parking ★ Teas ★ Plants for sale ★ Open 24th July, 11am – 4.30pm ★ Entrance: £1.50, children 50p

Five acres, about half of it recently planted, with secluded areas or 'rooms', including a herb garden, a formal pond garden, herbaceous borders and shrubberies surrounding the fourteenth-century manor house. Climbing roses cover the garden walls together with Canary creeper and clematis. There is an orangery with pond and fountain and many established tender plants. Vegetable and fruit gardens and an orchard, a bog area with parsley, thistles, day lilies and wild iris and the giant *Gunnera manicata*. A stream leads to a lake with iris and native plantings – a habitat for waterfowl of all kinds. The cultivation is totally organic.

THE GARDEN HOUSE ★★ 21
Buckland Monachorum, Yelverton, Devon. Tel: (01822) 854769

The Fortescue Garden Trust ★ 10m N of Plymouth, W of Yelverton off A386 ★ Parking ★ Refreshments: coffee, light lunches and cream teas ★ Plants for sale ★ Open March to Oct, daily, 10.30am – 5pm ★ Entrance: £2.75, OAP £2.25, children 50p

A 10-acre garden created after 1945 by Lionel Fortescue, a great plant collector and a perfectionist. The walls, thatched barn and tower date from the sixteenth century, and the tower was once part of a vicarage. The delightful two–acre walled garden has been described as one of the most beautiful in the country. It contains a fine collection of herbaceous plants, and hedges planted for shelter on different levels have enhanced the 'secret' ambience of this very special garden. There are some lovely old specimen trees and shrubs, herbaceous plants and alpines. A further 10 trees have been planted in a six-acre development (limes) and there are plans for a stream and bog garden, a small lake, a peat garden, a wisteria wood and a water garden.

GIDLEIGH PARK ★ 22
Chagford, Devon. Tel: (01647) 432367

Kay and Paul Henderson ★ In Chagford Square turn right into Mill Street by Lloyd's Bank. In 150 yards fork right (virtually straight across junction). Go to end of the road – about 2m ★ Parking ★ ☆ Lunches and teas served in hotel ★ Toilet facilities ★ Dogs on lead ★ Open all year except Bank Holidays, Mon – Fri ★ Entrance: £5 (inc. coffee or tea with biscuits)

Gidleigh Park, the acclaimed hotel and restaurant, is set in 45 acres of magnificent and secluded grounds on the North River Teign, within the Dartmoor National Park. The woodland garden and parkland were created between 1850 and 1930, but then fell into decay for the next 50 years. Since 1980, under the direction of head gardener Keith Mansfield, the owners have undertaken an extensive programme of restoration. Among the many interesting features is a delightful water garden rebuilt and planted in 1986. Visitors can take this in on their way round the 'Boundary Walk' – a 45-minute stroll through natural mixed woodland, underplanted with azaleas and rhododendrons. The River Teign is never far away, tumbling over granite boulders, past spring displays of rhododendrons. The mock-Tudor house gives way to a terrace resplendent in summer colour; while a parterre and herb garden add a touch of formality. There is an interesting avenue of young pleached limes (*Tilia platyphyllos*) adjacent to the front lawn and one must mention the croquet lawns and the pavilion – the final decadent flourishes.

THE GLEBE HOUSE 23
Whitestone, Nr Exeter, Devon. Tel: (01392811) 200

Mr and Mrs John West ★ 4m W of Exeter, adjoining Whitestone church ★ Parking but narrow lanes unsuitable for coaches ★ Open 4th June to 23rd July, Suns only, 2 – 5pm and by appointment ★ Entrance: £1, children free

A two and a half-acre garden round a former rectory, fifteenth-century with a Georgian facade, and a fourteenth-century tithe barn (Ancient Monument), with magnificent views to the south over the estuary of the Exe, and towards Dartmoor. On the lower level are lawns, trees and a heather garden; above, divided by coniferous hedges and windbreaks, are walks among clematis, honeysuckle and a collection of over 300 varieties of shrub roses – species, old-fashioned, climbing and modern. The middle level of the garden, with the house and tithe barn, features many varieties of climbing roses, clematis, jasmine and honeysuckle. The most impressive and memorable plant is an enormously vigorous *Rosa filipes* 'Kiftsgate' which is trained along the tithe barn, and extends over 130 feet – flooding the courtyard with scent when in flower in early July. This must be one of the largest climbing roses in the country, as the original at Kiftsgate Court (see entry) is said to be 100 feet in length. From this remarkable plant an equally vigorous 'sport' has emerged (double flowerets budding pink and opening white). This is called 'St Catherine' after the adjoining church, and a cutting of this new plant is thriving at the R.H.S. Garden at Rosemoor (see entry).

GREENWAY HOUSE 24
Nr Greenway Ferry, Churston Ferrers, Brixham, Devon.
Tel: (01803) 842382 (Greenway Gardens)

Mr and Mrs A.A. Hicks ★ 4m W of Brixham. From B3203 Paignton – Brixham road, take road to Galmpton, then towards Greenway Ferry ★ Parking ★ Tea and biscuits ★ Suitable for wheelchairs ★ Plants for sale in nursery open Mon – Fri except Bank Holidays, 2 – 5pm, Sat, 10am – 12 noon and by appointment ★ Garden open 27th April, 4th May, 2 – 6pm ★ Entrance: £1, children 50p

Another large (30-acre) and ancient Devon garden on a steep slope, here on the bank of the tree-lined Dart river which has woodland walks. There is a large number of indigenous trees over 150 years old and a giant tulip tree. In the walled garden are many camellias, 30 varieties of magnolias, many ceanothus, wisterias and abutilons. The banks of primroses and bluebells make it magical in spring. On the Georgian facade are *Magnolia grandiflora*, *Akebia quinata* and *Mutisia oligodon*; in the natural glades are foxgloves, white iris, herb Roberts, pennyworts, ivies and hart's tongue and male ferns.

HIGHER KNOWLE 25
Lustleigh, Devon. Tel: (016477) 275

Mr and Mrs D.R.A. Quicke ★ 8m NW of Newton Abbot, 3m NW of Bovey Tracey on A382 towards Moretonhampstead. In 2½m, turn left at Kelly Cross for Lustleigh; after ¼m left then right at Brookfield along Knowle Road; after ¼m steep drive on left ★ Teas in village ★ Open mid-March to mid-May, Sun and Bank Holiday Mons, 2 – 6pm ★ Entrance: £2, children free

A woodland garden some 40 years old situated on a steep hillside with Dartmoor views. The old oak wood is carpeted with primroses and blue-bells in spring, and magnolias, camellias and rhododendrons, ornamental cherries and heather banks; there are also tall embothriums (*Embothrium coccineum*) flowering in early summer. A beech hedge encloses a lawn, with the main display of deciduous and evergreen azaleas. Giant Dartmoor granite boulders add much natural sculpture to the woodland walks. There is also a water garden.

HILL HOUSE NURSERY AND GARDEN ★ 26
Landscove, Nr Ashburton, Devon. Tel: (01803) 762273

Mr and Mrs Raymond Hubbard ★ From Plymouth-bound A38, take second exit signed Ashburton, then left signed Landscove 2½m. Hill House on right a few hundred yards after a group of dwellings on left. Travelling via the A384 Totnes

– Buckfastleigh road follow signs to Landscove ★ Parking ★ Teas ★ Toilet facilities ★ Suitable for wheelchairs ★ Dogs on lead ★ Open all year, daily, 11am – 5pm. Booking required for parties ★ Entrance: free

Hill House and the adjoining church are Gothic-style buildings designed by the architect of Truro cathedral, John Loughborough Pearson. The garden is largely the brainchild of the late-lamented Edward Hyams, who featured Hill House in his book *An Englishman's Garden*. For the past eleven years the present owners have been restoring Hyams's garden, endeavouring to continue his emphasis on the exotic and the unusual. In spring a giant cedar protects a mass of snowdrops and cyclamen, while daffodils stand like sentinels along peripheral woodland walks. Colour abounds right up to Christmas and it is quite amazing that so many tender varieties – salvias, unusual magnolias and vulnerable roses to name but a few – appear to flourish within sight of Dartmoor. The conservatory bordering the pond has been rebuilt to Hyams's original design and contains a grape vine, passion flowers and a lemon tree. The garden temple (thought to date from the eighteenth century) is soon to be restored. An integral feature of the Hill House Garden is the commercial nursery. There are over 18,000 square feet of glasshouses providing the ideal microclimate for a colourful profusion of exotic plants. The display beds of fuchsias, rare passion flowers, salvias and many more are a joy to behold.

KILLERTON ★   27
Broadclyst, Nr Exeter, Devon. Tel: (01392) 881345

The National Trust ★ 7m NE of Exeter, on W side of B3181 ★ Parking ★ Licensed refreshments same time as house. Tearoom limited opening in winter ★ Toilet facilities ★ Partly suitable for wheelchairs but motorised buggies with drivers available ★ Plants for sale ★ Shop and produce shop ★ House and costume museum open 18th March to Oct, daily except Tues, 11am – 5.30pm (last admission 1/2 hour before closing) ★ Park and garden open all year, 10.30am – dusk ★ Entrance: £2.80 (Nov to Feb 1996 £1) (house, park and garden £4.60)

This large hillside garden surrounded by woods and parkland extends to over 4000 acres. It was created by John Veitch in the 1770s and later involved the famous Victorian William Robinson. The actual garden area of 18 acres will provide pleasure and interest to all but particularly to the tree and shrub enthusiast; it is a haven of delight. Beside the avenue of beeches, there are Wellingtonias (the first plantings in England), Lawson cypresses, oaks, maples and many fine broadleaved trees. Trees and shrubs introduced by Veitch are now reaching an imposing size. Terraced beds provide summer colour, as well as extensive herbaceous borders. Killerton has a rare rhododendron collection with 95 different species, many brought back from China and Japan. The collection is currently undergoing restoration; propagating and renewing those that are under threat or already lost. The storms of recent years have had a dramatic effect on the garden, in some cases opening up new vistas; 20 per cent has been lost over the past 15 years. There is also an early nineteenth-century summerhouse, the Bear's Hut, ice-house and rock garden.

KNIGHTSHAYES ★★ 28
Bolham, Tiverton, Devon.
Tel: (01884) 254665 (Administrator) (01884) 253264 (Garden Office)

*The National Trust ★ 2m N of Tiverton, turn right off A396 at Bolham ★
Parking inc. disabled ★ Refreshments: restaurant for coffee, lunches and teas.
Licensed ★ Toilet facilities ★ Suitable for wheelchairs ★ Dogs on lead in park and
Impey Walk only ★ Plants for sale ★ Shop ★ House open, daily except Fri (but
open 14th April), 1.30 – 5.30pm (last admission 5pm) ★ Garden open April to
Oct, daily, 11am – 5.30pm ★ Entrance: £2.80 (house, garden and grounds
£4.80. Parties of 15 or more £3.80 per person)*

This 50-acre garden is the setting for a most extraordinary late-Victorian
Gothic-style house in warm red Devon sandstone. On the terrace nearest to
the house subtly-coloured borders reflect the sensitivity and skill of Lady
Heathcoat Amory's original plantings since 1946. In bold contrast, the
famous pool garden is enclosed by tall, dark battlemented hedges while on a
lower terrace hedge, topiary hounds are in full cry. Extensive woodland
which forms 'The Garden within the Wood' shelters magnolias and rhododendrons; acers and tree peonies flourish, together with many tender and
unusual plants, some in raised peat block beds, and in surrounding parkland
magnificent trees frame views across the Exe valley farmland.

LEE FORD 29
Budleigh Salterton, Devon. Tel: (01395) 445894

*Mr and Mrs N. Lindsay-Fynn ★ 3½m from Exmouth ★ Parking ★ Teas on
charity open day, 3 – 5.30pm ★ Partly suitable for wheelchairs ★ Plants for sale
★ Open 28th May for charity, 1.30 – 5.30pm, also by appointment for parties
only ★ Entrance: £1.20, OAP £1, children 60p. Parties of 20 or more £1 per
person*

Inspired by the Savill Gardens at Windsor, the present owner's father
developed this woodland garden in the 1950s and 1960s and it is one of the
longest established open-to-the-public gardens in Devon, best seen perhaps
in early summer when the rhododendrons, azaleas and magnolias are in
flower. The mown glades are surrounded with masses of species and
ponticum rhododendrons, and there is a large collection of camellias, some
from the Channel Islands, including white camellias which are often in
flower on Christmas Day. There is also a treat of an old-fashioned walled
vegetable garden with an Adam pavilion in the formal garden.

MARWOOD HILL ★★ 30
Marwood, Nr Barnstaple, Devon. Tel: (01271) 42528

*Dr J.A. Smart ★ 4m NW of Barnstaple. Turn off A361 signed Marwood Hill
Gardens ★ Best season: April to Aug ★ Parking in roadway ★ Teas on Sun and
Bank Holidays or for parties by prior arrangement ★ Partly suitable for wheelchairs ★ Dogs on lead ★ Plants for sale ★ Open daily except 25th Dec, dawn –
dusk ★ Entrance: £2, OAP £1.50, accompanied children under 12 free*

With the wonderful collection of plants this 20-acre garden is of special
interest to the connoisseur but could not fail to give pleasure to any visitor.
Over 3000 different varieties of plants covering collections of willows, ferns,

magnolias, eucryphias, rhododendrons and hebes, and a fine collection of camellias in a glasshouse. Large planting of eucalyptus and betulas. Recently-built pergola with 12 varieties of wisteria. Raised alpine scree beds. Three small lakes with extensive bog garden and National collections of astilbe, *Iris ensata*, and tulbaghia.

THE MOORINGS 31
Rocombe, Uplyme, Lyme Regis, Dorset. Tel: (01297) 443295

Mr and Mrs A. Marriage ★ 2m NW of Lyme Regis. Take A3070 out of Lyme Regis, turn right to Rocombe and Rhode Hill. After ½m fork left (unsuitable for Heavy Goods Vehicles). Fourth house on right, drive is beyond house. ★ Parking ★ Plants for sale ★ Visitors welcome any time, but please telephone in advance ★ Entrance: 75p, accompanied children free

Especially rewarding to visit in spring and autumn, this garden has been made by Mr Marriage since 1961 out of three small fields on a sheltered, steep, west-facing slope. Impressively, most of the newly-planted arboretum trees have been grown from seed; there is a collection of eucalyptus, many unusual pines including umbrella and maritime pines (grown from seed gathered in the south of France) and nothofagus, including *N. obliqua* and *N. procera*, and the woodland is underplanted with snowdrops, daffodils and bluebells. *Hibiscus paramutabilis*, a hardy shrub with very large flowers in August, is very rare in this country; there are camellias and a 35-foot high magnolia, and a buddleia flowering rose-red in June. A great point of interest is the collection of over 50 different species of fern, nearly all grown from spores.

THE OLD RECTORY 32
Woodleigh, Nr Loddiswell, Devon. Tel: (01548) 550387

Mr and Mrs H.E. Morton ★ 3½m N of Kingsbridge, E off Kingsbridge – Wrangaton road at Rake Cross (1m S of Loddiswell), 1½m to Woodleigh itself ★ Parking ★ Suitable for wheelchairs ★ Open by appointment only ★ Entrance: £1, children 20p

A three-acre woodland garden, and walled garden, rescued from neglect 34 years ago. In the woodland are several individual glades of mature trees, underplanted with magnolias, azaleas, camellias and rhododendrons. There is great attention to form in the planting; evergreens and shrubs are planted for scent and winter effect, and the wild garden is most colourful in spring with crocus and daffodils, while the walled garden is designed with summer in mind. The garden is a haven for wildlife, no chemicals are used and it is managed without outside help.

OVERBECKS MUSEUM AND GARDEN ★ 33
**Sharpitor, Salcombe, Devon.
Tel: (0154884) 2893 or Gardener-in-Charge (0154884) 3238**

The National Trust ★ 1½m S of Salcombe, SW to South Sands ★ Best season: spring – early summer ★ Parking. No coaches ★ Refreshments: in tea room. Picnic area ★ Toilet facilities ★ Shop ★ Museum open April to Oct, daily except Sat, 11am – 5.30pm ★ Garden open all year, daily, 10am – 8pm or sunset if earlier ★ Entrance: £2 (museum and garden £3.40)

Palms stand in this exotic garden high above the Salcombe estuary, giving a strongly Mediterranean atmosphere. The mild, maritime climate enables it to be filled with exotics such as myrtles, daturas, agaves and an example of the large camphor tree, *Cinnamomum camphora*, a great rarity. The Himalayan *Magnolia campbellii* is over 90 years old and 40 feet high and wide and a sight to see in March. The steep terraces were built in 1901 and lead down through fuchsia trees, fruiting banana palms and myrtle trees to a wonderful *Cornus kousa*. In formal beds near the house is the Chatham Island forget-me-not – *Myosotidium hortensia* (hydrangea-like) with flowers as clear as blue china – phormiums, and tender roses among the rocks. There is a new parterre of classical design, using the traditional coloured gravels surrounded by box, and enlivened with orange and lemon trees in season.

PAIGNTON ZOO AND BOTANICAL GARDEN 34
Totnes Road, Paignton, Devon. Tel: (01803) 527936

The Whitley Wildlife Trust ★ 1m from centre of Paignton on Totnes Road ★ Parking ★ Refreshments: restaurants ★ Toilet facilities ★ Suitable for wheelchairs ★ Shops ★ Open daily except 25th Dec from 10am (closing times vary according to season) ★ Entrance: £5.75, OAP £4.60, children £3.50 (1994 prices). Rates for parties available

Those with mixed views on zoos may be won over by Paignton; it is in the forefront of animal and plant conservation and one of the zoos worldwide involved in the breeding of endangered species. As well as the very healthy and happy animals there are the plants. Paignton (over 100 acres in size) was the first zoo in the country to combine animals and a botanic garden, laid out 60 years ago and added to over the years. Choice of plants has been dictated by their harmlessness to teeth and beaks and their ability to provide shade, perches and swinging and basking places; there are geographical collections of plants in the paddocks, and plants also make the fences safer. Hardy Chinese plants surround the baboon rocks. Paignton has the R.H.S. National collection of sorbaria and buddleia. There are two large plant houses, one sub-tropical with tender plants and trees and magical birds flying, and a tropical house with a jungle pool and areas of tropical plants (indoor plants par excellence) and small areas of different plant families – orchids, African violets and lilies; everything well-labelled.

ROSEMOOR GARDEN ★★ 35
Great Torrington, Devon. Tel: (01805) 624067

The Royal Horticultural Society ★ 1m SE of Great Torrington on B3220 ★ Best season: May to Sept ★ Parking ★ Refreshments: in restaurant (licensed) ★ Toilet facilities ★ Suitable for wheelchairs ★ Plants for sale in plant centre ★ Shop in Visitors' Centre open March to Dec, 10am – 6pm (summer) ★ Garden open all year ★ Entrance: £3, children £1

First opened to the public 35 years ago, the original eight-acre garden was made by Lady Anne Berry; it contains a collection of 3500 plants from all over Europe, North and South America, New Zealand and Japan. There is a large collection of rhododendrons and old roses; it is also the home of specialist collections of ilex (hollies) and cornus (dogwoods) – over 100 varieties. There are scree gardens, an arboretum, alpines and bulbs.

Recently Rosemoor was given to the Royal Horticultural Society as its first regional centre, second only to Wisley. An extra 32 acres have been given, and the new garden already includes 2000 roses in 200 varieties, colour theme gardens, a herb garden, ornamental vegetable garden, stream and bog gardens and herbaceous borders. A cottage garden and foliage and plantsman's garden now open. A fruit and vegetable garden opened in 1994. The *Rosemoor Explorer*, a children's guide to the garden, is free for children aged six to sixteen. A great National Garden in the making.

SALTRAM HOUSE 36
Plympton, Plymouth, Devon. Tel: (01752) 336546

The National Trust ★ 3m E of Plymouth. On A379 turn N to Billacombe. After 1m turn left to Saltram ★ Best season: April to June ★ Parking ★ Licensed refreshments ★ Toilet facilities ★ Suitable for wheelchairs ★ Shop ★ House open as garden but open 12.30pm ★ Garden open April to Oct, daily except Fri and Sat (but open 14th April), 10.30am – 5.30pm (last admission 5pm) ★ Entrance: £2.20 (house and garden £5)

The original garden dates from 1770, slightly altered in the last century; there are three eighteenth-century buildings – a castle or belvedere, an orangery (due to the mild climate the orange and lemon trees are moved outside in the summer) and a classical garden house named Fanny's Bower after Fanny Burney who came here in 1789 in the entourage of George III. There is a long lime avenue underplanted with narcissi in spring, *Cyclamen linearifolium* in autumn and a central glade with specimen trees like the stone pine and Himalayan spruce. There is a beech grove, a Melancholy Walk, and walks with magnolias, camellias, rhododendrons and Japanese maples which, with other trees, make for dramatic autumn colour.

TAPELEY PARK ★ 37
Instow, Devon. Tel: (01271) 860528

Mr H.T.C. Christie ★ 2m N of Bideford S off A39 Barnstaple – Bideford road ★ Parking ★ Teas in Queen Anne dairy. Picnic places ★ Toilet facilities ★ Suitable for wheelchairs ★ Dogs ★ Plants for sale ★ House open. £1.50, children £1. Tours for parties of 6 or more ★ Medieval jousting displays ★ Open April to Oct, daily except Sat, 10am – 6pm ★ Entrance: £1.90 (non-jousting days) to £4.50 (Bank Holiday Sun and Mon competitive jousting days), OAP £1.50 to £3.50, children £1 to £2 (1994 prices)

The house is basically William and Mary, set on a splendid site above the River Torridge and Bideford, with much to see and a family with a fascinating history – the Christies of Glyndebourne. There are three formal terraces, an Italian garden with ornamental water, yew hedges, an ilex tunnel, a shell house, ice-house, and a variety of roses, fuchsias, lavenders, dahlias as well as more exotic plants like *Abelia floribunda*, sophora and feijoa from Brazil. On the south of the house are yuccas, *Magnolia grandiflora*, agapanthus and mimosas; on the east, wisteria and *Drimys winteri*, a rare honeysuckle. A woodland walk is lined with camellias, hydrangeas and rhododendrons with primroses and primulas in spring under the giant beeches and oaks; this leads to a water lily-covered pond in late summer, in the background tall firs and *Thuya plicata*. Walled kitchen garden.

TUDOR ROSE TEA ROOMS AND GARDEN 38
36 New Street, The Barbican, Plymouth, Devon.

Plymouth Corporation ★ In the centre of the old town ★ Parking difficult ★ Dogs ★ Open daily, 10am – 6pm ★ Entrance: free

An integral part of an area of Plymouth that is being refurbished, this is an interesting reconstruction of the type of Tudor garden that would have existed behind the house in this ancient street. As far as possible only plants which grew in Elizabethan England have been established. Elsewhere in Plymouth the Corporation commemorates great Victorian seaside gardening with colourful carpet bedding by traditional methods.

UNIVERSITY OF EXETER ★ 39
Northcote House, The Queen's Drive, Exeter, Devon.
Tel: (01392) 263263

University of Exeter ★ On N outskirts of Exeter on A396, turn E on to B3183 ★ Best season: April to June ★ Parking ★ Dogs on lead ★ Shop open weekdays sells guide book ★ Open daily ★ Entrance: free. Coaches by appointment only

There is much to see on a one-mile tour of these extensive gardens based on those made in the 1860s by an East India Merchant millionaire who inherited a fortune made by blockade-running in the Napoleonic Wars. The landscaping and tree planting was carried out by Veitch whose plant collectors went all over the world (among them E.H. 'Chinese' Wilson) and at that time many of the trees were unique in Europe. There is a series of lakes with wildfowl, dogwoods, birches, hazels and alders, callistemon shrubs (bottle brushes), wingnut trees (*Pterocarya stenoptera*) brought from China in 1860 and a maidenhair tree (*Gingko*) sacred in Buddhist China. Rockeries have collections of alpines; there is a banana tree (*Musa basjoo*), a large *Gunnera chilensis* and palm trees introduced by Robert Fortune in 1849. Formal gardens and bedding plants lead to a sunken, scented garden. Exeter will house the National collection of azara, evergreens from Chile, with scented yellow flowers. There are, of course, rhododendrons, magnolias, camellias in a woodland walk; roses, eucalyptus and *Opuntia humifusa*, the prickly pear cactus flowering in summer.

VICAR'S MEAD 40
Hayes Lane, East Budleigh, Devon. Tel: (013954) 42641

Mr and Mrs H.F.J. Read ★ From A376 Newton Poppleford – Budleigh Salterton road, turn off left for East Budleigh ★ Car park 50 yards from entrance ★ Teas in village ★ Toilet facilities ★ Partly suitable for wheelchairs ★ Plants for sale ★ Open on certain NGS days and by appointment ★ Entrance: £1, children free

On and around a red sandstone escarpment this five-acre garden has been created since 1977. It is most interesting to keen plantsmen in that it contains many rare and unusual plants and houses four National collections – dianellas, libertias, liriopes and ophiopogons.

WOODSIDE 41
Higher Raleigh Road, Barnstaple, Devon. Tel: (01271) 43095

Mr and Mrs M. Feesey ★ Off A39 Barnstaple – Lynton road, turn right 300 yards above fire station ★ Parking in quiet road outside ★ Open 7th May, 18th June, 2 – 5.30pm ★ Entrance: £1, children 50p (1994 prices)

A sloping two-acre garden in semi-woodland suburban area with unusual collection of plants including ornamental grasses, bamboos and sedges. Many parts of the garden are shaded but rare dwarf shrubs, trees and conifers survive. There are raised beds and troughs with alpines and dwarfs. A collection of New Zealand plants along with peat-loving shrubs make this a garden with a difference.

WYLMINGTON HAYES GARDENS AND WATERFOWL COLLECTION ★ 42
Wilmington, Honiton, Devon. Tel: (01404) 831751

Mr and Mrs P. Saunders ★ 5½m N of Honiton, on A30, turn right, signposted Stockland 3 and Axminster 10. After 3½m entrance is on right, before Stockland TV mast ★ Best seasons: April to June and autumn ★ Parking ★ Cream teas and light refreshments ★ Toilet facilities ★ Plants for sale ★ Open 14th to 19th April then Suns and Bank Holiday Mons only until end of June, 2 – 5pm ★ Entrance: £2.50, wheelchair visitors and children £1

Wylmington Hayes is 83 acres of reclaimed gardens and woodland originally created in 1911. There is much to interest both the dedicated gardener and those who merely seek a quiet stroll amid lovely surroundings. For the gardener there are spectacular hybrid rhododendrons, azaleas, magnolias, camellias and acers; there are also some majestic trees, including numerous oaks, a handkerchief tree, tree peonies, tulip trees and several sequoias. Two woodland walks – one short, one longer – extend to the extremities of the garden. Of particular interest is the newly-completed Italian garden. The influence of water is apparent for all to see. There are several small ponds (some containing koi carp) and a fine lake which is home to an interesting collection of ornamental and domestic waterfowl, including black swans. Wylmington Hayes is lovely throughout the year but April, when the lawns and hollows are a carpet of bulbs, and May through to June when the rhododendrons and azaleas are a blaze of colour, are perhaps the optimum months for a special visit.

CUTTINGS

Readers may wish to be reminded that the taking of cuttings without the owners' permission can lead to embarrassment and, if it continues on a large scale, may cause owners to close their gardens to the public. This has to be seen in the context of an increasing number of thefts from gardens. At Nymans, the famous Sussex garden, thefts have reached such a level that the gardener will not now plant out any shrub until it is semi-mature and of such a size that its theft would be very difficult. Other owners have reported the theft of artefacts as well as plants.

DORSET

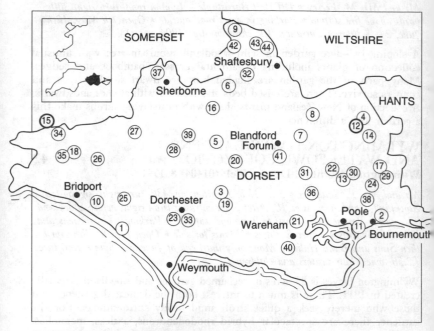

SOMERSET WILTSHIRE

⑨
㊷ ㊸㊹
Shaftesbury
㊲ ⑥ ㉜
Sherborne
HANTS
⑯ ⑧
⑮ ④
㉞ ㉗ ㊴ ⑫ ⑭
⑤ Blandford
  Forum ⑦
㉟⑱ ㉖ ㉘ ㊵ ⑰
  ⑳ ㉒ ㉚ ㉙
  DORSET ⑬ ㉔
Bridport ㉛ ㊱ ㊳
⑩ ㉕ ③ ②
  Dorchester ⑲ Poole
  Wareham ㉑ ⑪ Bournemouth
① ㉓㉝ ④
  ㊵
  Weymouth

Two-starred gardens are ringed in bold.

ABBOTSBURY GARDENS ★ 1
Abbotsbury, Dorset. Tel: (01305) 871387

*Ilchester Estates ★ 9m NW of Weymouth, 9m SW of Dorchester off B3157 ★
Parking ★ Refreshments ★ Toilet facilities ★ Partly suitable for wheelchairs ★ Dogs
on lead ★ Plants for sale ★ Shop ★ Open March to Oct, daily, 10am – 5pm, Nov
to Feb, daily except 25th, 26th Dec and 1st Jan, 10am – 3pm ★ Entrance:
£3.50, OAP £3, children free (1994 prices). Group booking discounts available*

Proximity to the sea helps to provide the microclimate which makes
Abbotsbury so special. Within its 20 acres there is much of great interest to
the plantsperson in the many rare species on display, while amateur gardeners can get pleasure from the banks of colour and the shaded walks –
particularly in the spring, but also at other seasons. People travel a long
way to visit these gardens – often called 'sub-tropical', but probably techni-
cally better described as 'wet Mediterranean'. The new visitor centre, shop
and refreshment area are an excellent additional bonus for the many coach
parties who come for both gardens and nearby Swannery (not to be missed
when open!) There is also a woodland trail and a children's play area. Pure
garden enthusiasts will be more interested in the redesigned plant sales area
which, while not extensive, has a good range of healthy stock on display.

ARNMORE HOUSE 2
57 Landsdowne Road, Bournemouth, Dorset. Tel: (01202) 551440

Mr and Mrs David Hellewell ★ On B3064 just S of the hospital ★ Parking in road ★ Toilet facilities ★ Suitable for wheelchairs ★ Open all year by appointment only ★ Entrance: £1, children free

The special features of this garden have developed through a mixture of the owner's interest in Chinese gardening and a pragmatic approach to ease of management. Trees and shrubs have been chosen for their shape and foliage, and, where desired, have been trained or pruned to fit the overall picture. Flower borders are eschewed in favour of grey slab paths alongside raised beds containing rows of shaped yew and privet, box and bay. Wherever possible these small to medium-sized trees are grown in pots so that trimming can take place over a suitable receptacle for the clippings. The formal parterre consists of neat diagonals of *Buxus sempervirens* complemented with clipped balls of *B.* 'Aureovariegata' and features grey concrete slabs to minimise maintenance. All this may sound rather austere, but it nevertheless suits the composer/owner who has created it and published a booklet about its development. It is worth a visit for its originality.

ATHELHAMPTON HOUSE ★ 3
Puddletown, Dorchester, Dorset. Tel: (01305) 848363

Patrick Cooke ★ On A35 1m E of Puddletown, near Dorchester ★ Best season: May/June ★ Parking ★ Refreshments ★ Toilet facilities ★ Partly suitable for wheelchairs ★ Shop ★ House open ★ Garden open Easter to Oct, Tues, Wed, Thurs, Sun and Bank Holidays (also Mon and Fri in July and Aug), 12 noon – 5pm ★ Entrance: £2.50, children free (house and garden £4.20, parties of 20 or more £3.50 per person)

Athelhampton garden was rescued and re-designed by Alfred Cart de La Fontaine in 1891, a process continued by subsequent owners, latterly the late Robert Cooke. Courts and walls follow the original plan with beautiful stonework in walls and arches. Apart from some of the most impressive topiary in England there are also pools, fountains, a rectangular canal with water lilies and a pleached lime walk. Tulips, rambling roses, clematis and jasmine (in their seasons) make it memorable. The gardens are encircled by the River Piddle and on the west lawn stands a sixteenth-century dovecote.

BOVERIDGE FARM 4
Cranborne, Dorset. Tel: (01725) 517241

Mr and Mrs Michael Yarrow ★ Nr Cranborne on Martin Road (unclassified). Take 2nd turn on right ★ Parking ★ Teas at Ashley Park in next village of Damerham ★ Toilet facilities ★ Plants for sale at Ashley Park ★ Open 16th April, 14th May, 11th June, 2 – 5pm ★ Entrance: £1, children free

The house lies on a steep north-facing slope, and the garden has been laid out below it, to the west of it and above. The plants and shrubs on the lower side are on chalk, whilst the fern bank and shrubbery above are on neutral clay. There is a fine view across the rooftops and along the valley, which is largely arable with wooded hilltops. It has taken over 35 years to create the garden as it is today, a colourful and interesting collection much of which the previous owner, a farmer called Mr Dampney, grew from seed or cuttings.

BROADLANDS ★ 5
Hazelbury Bryan, Nr Sturminster Newton, Dorset.
Tel: (01258) 817374

Mr and Mrs M.J. Smith ★ 4m S of Sturminster Newton off A357 Blandford – Sherborne road at signpost. ½m beyond Antelope pub ★ Parking ★ Toilet facilities ★ Suitable for wheelchairs ★ Plants for sale ★ Open by appointment and 2nd, 17th April, 7th May, and May to Aug, Weds, 2 – 5.30pm ★ Entrance: £1.70, accompanied children free

This is a two-acre garden in which the design and planting have the intriguing effect of obscuring the full size of the area while at the same time extending the apparent distance the visitor covers in walking round it. This is achieved by the clever siting of island beds, with grass walkways leading to features such as ponds, rockeries and paved seating areas. There are screening hedges to enhance the surprise of discovering the cottage garden, the vegetables, the ornamental woodland. Round every corner the visitor comes upon some new feature of interest and delight, and everywhere there are uncommon plants to give pleasure in all seasons. Begun in 1975, this is a most successful layout, excellently labelled and refreshingly imaginative, which should inspire gardeners of all levels of competence. New features include an area devoted to shrub and climbing roses with an attractive but simply-constructed pergola, and further development and underplanting in the woodland area.

CARTREF 6
Station Road, Stalbridge, Dorset. Tel: (01963) 363705

Mrs Nesta Ann Smith ★ From A30 at Henstridge traffic lights turn S for 1m into Stalbridge village. Turn left opposite PO, house is 80 yards on right ★ Parking nearby ★ Open April to Sept (but please telephone before arriving in June), Tues and Fri only: Tues, 2 – 6pm, Fri, 10am – 6pm and by appointment ★ Entrance: £1.50, children free

If one is to question what makes a good garden, a visit to this quarter-acre behind an unassuming semi-detached village house has the answer for inveterate collectors. In this comparatively small area, winding paths, lawn and small woodland are crammed with clearly-labelled rarities, each tree is a framework for interesting climbers, and the microclimate encourages plants such as *Cytisus battandieri*, *Pittosporum tobira* and terrestrial orchids. Mrs Smith is happy to talk about plants from their provenance to maintenance; her vast knowledge is gleaned from experience gained by working in well-known nurseries under such masters as Jim Archibald and the hosta expert, Eric Smith. Many of the varieties are for sale.

CHARLTON COTTAGE 7
Tarrant Rushton, Blandford Forum, Dorset. Tel: (01258) 452072.

The Hon. Penelope Piercy ★ 3m SE of Blandford on B3082. Fork left at top of hill, right at T-junction, first left to village ★ Parking in adjacent field ★ Suitable for wheelchairs ★ Open 7th May, 2 – 6pm and possibly again later in the year ★ Entrance: £1.50, children free

Charlton Cottage is at the south end of the village and the garden is on both sides of the street which continues as a farm track to a ford. The back garden has two lawn areas separated by flower borders and shrubs, and slopes up to a soft fruit garden and a view over the valley. At the other side of the street are two herbaceous borders sloping down to a withy bed, where the owner has made a small water garden, and which continues to the River Tarrant and provides a pleasant shady walk.

CHETTLE HOUSE   8
Blandford Forum, Dorset. Tel: (01258) 830209

Mr and Mrs P. Bourke ★ 6m NE of Blandford on A354, turn left to Chettle ★ Parking ★ Refreshments usually available ★ Toilet facilities ★ Suitable for wheelchairs ★ Plants for sale ★ House open ★ Garden open 14th April to 8th Oct, daily except Tues and Sat, 11am – 5pm ★ Entrance: £2, children free

Beyond the wide lawns framing this impressive Queen Anne house (designed by Thomas Archer of rounded style and reversed capitals fame), vistas appropriate to that period are preserved with a vineyard on the south slope. Lavish herbaceous borders contain many (some rare) chalk-loving plants, including no fewer than 20 varieties of honeysuckle, a buddleia collection, and some fine clematis. The owners are always on the lookout for the unusual, and plants seen in the garden are sometimes available for sale in the plant centre. The tranquil site is approached through mature trees where a number of different horse chestnut species may be seen. There is an art gallery, a tea room, and a pretty church in the grounds.

CHIFFCHAFFS   9
Chaffeymoor, Bourton, Gillingham, Dorset. Tel: (01747) 840841

Mr and Mrs K.R. Potts ★ 3m E of Wincanton. Leave A303 (Bourton bypass) at sign marked 'Bourton' and continue to end of village ★ Best season: spring ★ Parking in road ★ Teas on last Sun in the month and Bank Holiday weekends ★ Toilet facilities ▲ Plants for sale ★ Open 26th March to 24th Sept, Sun, Wed and Thurs (but closed the second Sunday of each month), 2 – 5.30pm. Also open by appointment ★ Entrance: £1.50, children 50p

An impressive avenue of flowering cherries leads to the house and garden, the nursery and the woodland walk through the surrounding fields, which extend to a total of 12 acres. The terraces and viewpoints afford fascinating glimpses of open country around and the varied and colourful beds and borders are delightful. Special interest is provided by the new underplanting in the woodland area and by the collection of dwarf rhododendrons and old-fashioned roses. The nursery is well-stocked with a wide variety of healthy-looking plants.

CHILCOMBE HOUSE ★   10
Chilcombe, Nr Bridport, Dorset. Tel: (01308) 482234

Mr and Mrs J. Hubbard ★ 5m E of Bridport off A35 ★ Open June, Weds only: 28th June, 2 – 6pm but other Weds by appointment ★ Entrance: £2, children free

To visit Chilcombe is something of a pilgrimage for it isn't easy to find and the long single-track road can cause problems for vehicles. The very rare opening days at this outstanding garden ensure that enthusiasts and devotees throng to it even in the most uncertain summer weather. Their determination is rewarded by a delightful display of skilled and knowledgeable plantsmanship within a number of very small areas. There are lawns, courtyards, an orchard and a walled garden divided by hedges and sub-divided by box and other borders. Multi-patterned paths between massed plantings of shrubs, flowers and herbs, reflecting the owners' artistic eye for colour and form; charming details include the mixed thyme bank and the small conservatory packed with colour and rare specimens. Set beside the tiny church, backed by tall trees over grassy banks, and with views to the distant coastal hills, this garden is a marvellous creation in a beautiful setting.

COMPTON ACRES ★   11
Canford Cliffs, Poole, Dorset. Tel: (01202) 700778

Mr and Mrs L. Green ★ From Poole/Bournemouth Road onto Canford Cliffs road (near Sandbanks) ★ Parking ★ Refreshments ★ Toilet facilities ★ Suitable for wheelchairs (can be supplied) ★ Guide dogs only ★ Plants for sale ★ Shop ★ Open March to Oct, daily, 10.30am – 6.30pm ★ Entrance: £3.70, OAP and students £2.70, children £1, family ticket (2 adults and 2 children) £8. Parties of 20 or more £3 per person, OAP and students £2.30, children 90p (1994 prices)

Keen gardeners might be put off by the huge coach park and frankly commercial approach. They should persevere, because the gardens themselves are well-designed, immaculately kept and stocked with many interesting and well-labelled plants, trees and shrubs. There is also a Japanese garden. Water abounds in streams, waterfalls, ponds and formal lakes, the home of fat, multi-coloured carp. An enterprise aimed obviously (and very accurately) at the tourist, Compton Acres has the feel of a very opulent public park, a sort of pop-concert of the gardening world – but none the worse for that.

CRANBORNE MANOR GARDENS ★★   12
Cranborne, Dorset. Tel: (01725) 517248

The Viscount and Viscountess Cranborne ★ 10m N of Wimborne on B3078 ★ Parking ★ Toilet facilities ★ Partly suitable for wheelchairs ★ Garden centre open all year, but closed Mons ★ Shop ★ Gardens open March to Sept, Weds, 9am – 5pm and 10th June for charity ★ Entrance: £2.50, OAP £2

Tradescant established the basic framework in the early seventeenth century, but little is left of the original plan. Neglected for a long period, the garden has been revived in the last three generations and now includes several smaller areas surrounded by tall clipped yew hedges, a walled white garden at its best in midsummer, wide lawns (again yew-lined) and extensive woodland and wild areas. Best of all is the high-walled entrance courtyard to the south which is approached through an arch between the two Jacobean gatehouses. Here the plant selection along the lengthy borders is delightfully imaginative, providing the perfect introduction to what has been called 'the most magical house in Dorset' (not least for the garden which surrounds it). The excellent nursery garden specialises in traditional rose varieties, but also carries a wide selection of other plants, particularly clematis and herbaceous.

DEAN'S COURT   13
Wimborne Minster, Dorset.

Sir Michael and Lady Hanham ★ In the centre of Wimborne off B3073 ★ Parking nearby ★ Wholefood teas ★ Toilet facilities ★ Suitable for wheelchairs ★ Organically-grown herb plants for sale ★ Open April to Sept, Bank Holidays, 10am – 6pm; Suns preceeding Bank Holidays and every Thurs, 2 – 6pm. Contact Wimborne Tourist Information Office for details. Tel: (01202) 886116 ★ Entrance: £1.50, children 70p

A mellow brick house set in 13 acres of parkland containing a number of interesting and very large trees. A swamp cypress towers near the house, also a 92-foot tulip tree. The many fine specimens include Wellingtonias, Caucasian wing nut, Chilean fire bush, Japanese pagoda tree, blue cedars and horse chestnuts. There are few formal beds, but a courtyard contains an unusually comprehensive herb garden with over 170 different plants. The walled kitchen garden, in which many of the old varieties of vegetable are grown by chemical-free production methods, is extensive and obviously successful. Monastic stewpond where the medieval monks bred their carp can still be seen in this peaceful haven just a few yards from a busy town.

EDMONDSHAM HOUSE   14
Edmondsham, Nr Cranborne, Wimborne, Dorset.
Tel: (01725) 517207

Mrs J. Smith ★ 1m S of Cranborne. From the A354 turn at Sixpenny Handley crossroads to Ringwood and Cranborne ★ Best season: spring ★ Parking ★ Refreshments on open days ★ Toilet facilities ★ Suitable for wheelchairs ★ Plants for sale ★ House open 17th April, 8th, 29th May, 28th Aug, and Weds in April and Oct, 2 5pm ★ Garden open when house is open and May to Sept, Weds and Suns, 2 – 5pm. Also by appointment ★ Entrance: £1, children 50p (house and garden £2, children £1, under 5 free)

A vast, walled kitchen garden in which only organic methods are used provides the major interest here. This is very much a Victorian kitchen garden in origin, having been intensively cultivated since the mid-nine-teenth century, but several modern and interesting vegetable variants are grown. Herbaceous borders line the walls. Wide lawns surround the house, bordered by many fine and rare trees growing to a good height. An unusual circular grass hollow is said to be a cockpit, one of only a very few 'natu-ralised' areas of the sort in the country. The massed spring bulbs together with the many spring-flowering shrubs make this the best season to visit, but the peaceful, mellow atmosphere pervades the garden at all seasons.

FORDE ABBEY ★★   15
Chard, Somerset. Tel: (01460) 21366

Mr M. Roper ★ 7m W of Crewkerne, 4m SE of Chard off A30 ★ Parking ★ Refreshments ★ Toilet facilities ★ Suitable for wheelchairs ★ Dogs ★ Plants for sale

★ House open April to Oct, Sun, Wed, and Bank Holidays ★ Garden open all year, daily, 10am – 4.30pm ★ Entrance: £3.25, OAP £2.75, children free. Parties £2.75 per person (house and garden £4.50, OAP £4, children free. Parties of 20 or more £3.50 per person), children free (1994 prices)

This unique and fascinating former Cistercian abbey, inhabited as a private house since 1649, is set in a varied and pleasing garden. Old walls and colourful borders, wide sloping lawns, lush ponds and cascades, graceful statuary and huge mature trees combine to create an atmosphere of timeless elegance. There is something here for every gardener to appreciate; the bog garden displays a large collection of primulas and other Asiatic plants; the shrubbery contains a variety of magnolias, rhododendrons and other delightful specimens. The rock garden has been revolutionised by Mr Jack Drake, now retired from Aviemore, and a very fine arboretum has been built up since 1947; at the back of the abbey is an extensive kitchen garden and a nursery selling rare and unusual plants which look in fine health. Allow plenty of time as the grounds extend to 30 acres in all. Winner of the Christie's Garden of the Year award.

FRITH HOUSE 16
Stalbridge, Nr Sturminster Newton, Dorset. Tel: (01963) 250232

Urban Stephenson ★ Between Milborne Port and Stalbridge, 1m S of A30 or turn west by Stalbridge PO, 2m along narrow lane, lodge on left ★ Parking near farm entrance ★ Toilet facilities ★ Suitable for wheelchairs ★ Plants occasionally for sale ★ Open 2nd April, 4th June, 6th Aug, 2 – 6pm ★ Entrance: £1.50 children free

In an open valley surrounded by unspoilt pastoral views, this friendly Edwardian house lies beneath a shelter-belt of woodland and looks south across sweeping lawns studded with orchard and fine old cedars. The four-acre grounds are very well-maintained, in particular the immaculately-trimmed yew hedges and the shrub borders within sunny walled areas. Below the terrace is a bed filled with a striking array of 20-year-old scarlet 'Frensham' roses: there is also an excellent kitchen garden, and shady avenues through the Woodland Walk. Further down are two lakes, fed by a stone conduit which has been developed as an ornamental area of shrubs and water plants. Pleasant grassy walks surround the lakes, where crayfish are bred.

HIGHBURY 17
West Moors, Dorset. Tel: (01202) 874372

Mr Stanley Cherry ★ 8m N of Bournemouth off B3072. In Woodside Road, the last road at the N end of West Moors village ★ Parking in road ★ Refreshments ★ Toilet facilities ★ Suitable for wheelchairs ★ Plants for sale ★ Open by appointment, April to Sept ★ Entrance: 75p (pre-booked parties for house and garden £1 per person inc. teas)

Mr Cherry has amassed in his small botanical garden a fascinating collection of unusual specimens which will interest plantsmen and botanists rather than amateurs. With excellent labelling and much other general information available, this is a garden which delivers more to the enthusiast than is conveyed by the initial impression. It must be admitted that the average gardener might find the closely surrounding trees and the emphasis on rarity as against form and colour rather less than exciting.

HORN PARK   18
Beaminster, Dorset. Tel: (01308) 862212

Mr and Mrs John Kirkpatrick ★ On A3066 1¹/₂m N of Beaminster on left before tunnel ★ Parking ★ Lunches and teas in Beaminster and in Craft Centre, Broadwindsor ★ Toilet facilities ★ Plants for sale ★ Open April to 1st Oct, Tues, Wed and Sun, also Bank Holiday Mons, 2 – 6pm ★ Entrance: £2.50

Although the impressive house by a pupil of Lutyens dates from 1910, the garden is a developing re-creation based partly on features discovered as the work progresses. A drive through parkland leads to the wide gravel sweep before the entrance porch, with terraced lawns to the front of the house and a panoramic view east and south towards Beaminster and the distant coast. Other features include rock areas, herbaceous and rose borders, a water garden beneath a steep azalea bank, ponds, a woodland garden and walks with wild flowers, including orchids and bluebells in spring. The natural wild flower meadow is listed as a Site of Nature Conservation Interest, with over 100 wild flowers and grasses, including wild orchids.

ILSINGTON HOUSE   19
Puddletown, Dorset. Tel: (01305) 848454

Mr and Mrs Peter Duff ★ Off A35 in centre of Puddletown ★ Best season: May to July ★ Parking ★ Refreshments and home-made lunches by arrangement ★ Toilet facilities ★ Suitable for wheelchairs ★ Plants sometimes for sale ★ House open ★ Garden open May to Sept, Wed and Thurs only, 2 – 6pm (last admission 5pm) ★ Entrance: £2 (house and garden £3)

An oasis of tranquillity in the middle of the village, these formal gardens in William and Mary style echo the age of the house. There are secrets and surprises; behind the ancient yew hedge the visitor will find a continuous bed of bearded iris, the colours chosen with an artist's eye for subtlety and impact. Part of the ha-ha (which is the longest in Dorset) is being developed into a canal and wildlife pond for rare and endangered species, and much emphasis is given overall to natural habitats and wild flower meadows. This contrasts with the formality of the peony bed, containing rare Victorian varieties, the Compass garden for quiet reflection and magnificent beds of iris and catmint which draw the eye to the tree-lined boundary. Unusual statues and sculptures.

IVY COTTAGE ★   20
Aller Lane, Ansty, Dorchester, Dorset. Tel: (01258) 880053

Anne and Alan Stevens ★ 8m W of Blandford, 12m N of Dorchester. Take A354 Puddletown/ Blandford road, turn first left after Blue Vinney, through Cheselbourne ★ Parking in road ★ Teas on Suns only ★ Partly suitable for wheelchairs ★ Plants for sale ★ Open April to Oct, Thurs, 10am – 5pm and on 9th April, 21st May, 27th Aug, 24th Sept, 2 – 5.30pm. Parties by appointment only ★ Entrance on Thurs, April to Oct, £1.50, on Suns, £2.50 (combined with Aller Green – see below)

Mrs Stevens trained and worked as a professional gardener before coming to her cottage 30 years ago. Although chalk underlies the surrounding land, this garden is actually on greensand; it has springs and a stream that keep it well watered and is therefore an ideal home for plants such as primulas, irises, gunneras, and in particular trollius and moisture-loving lobelias, for both of which this is the NCCPG National collection. A thriving and ordered vegetable garden (which hardly ever needs a hose), large herbaceous borders giving colour all year round, drifts of bulbs and other spring plants surrounding specimen trees and shrubs and three most interesting raised beds for alpines. This garden has been justifiably featured in print and on television, and merits a wide detour. Just up the road is Aller Green, a typical peaceful Dorset cottage garden of approximately one acre in an old orchard setting. The two share some charity opening days with a combined admission charge, and the cottage is particularly worth seeing in its autumn colours.

KESWORTH   21
Kesworth Farm House, Sandford, Wareham, Dorset.
Tel: (01929) 551577

Mr H.J.S. Clark ★ 1¹/₂m N of Wareham off A351 opposite Sandford School (Keysworth Drive) ★ Parking ★ Toilet facilities ★ Dogs ★ Open 14th, 21st May, 12.30 – 7pm (last admission 5.30pm) ★ Entrance: £1, children free

Kesworth is a twentieth-century park and garden scheme conceived on the scale of 'Capability' Brown, but carried out under unfavourable conditions. Bordered on the south side by the marshy edge of Poole Harbour, to the north by a railway line, and with industrial estates, both active and derelict, formerly in full view. Mr Clark's intention of revitalising the farmland and building his own residence there was to prove even more difficult than he imagined. Poor soil, voracious wildlife, wind and fire took constant toll of his plantings. Twenty-five years of effort and 27,000 trees have gone into the project, with the result that Kesworth farm house (a modern evocation of the mid-eighteenth century) now stands fronted by a wide yew-lined lawn, with flagged courts and borders to the rear linking it with the original farm outbuildings. On all sides are graduated screens of trees set in broad grassland. The eyesores have been successfully obliterated, the land revived. Kesworth may not stand among the foremost as a gardener's treasure trove, but with its avenue, groves and marshland scenery and wildlife it illustrates conservation started long before the concept became fashionable.

KINGSTON LACY ★   22
Wimborne, Dorset. Tel: (01202) 883402

The National Trust ★ 1¹/₂m W of Wimborne on B3082 ★ Best season: spring ★ Parking 100 yards ★ Licensed refreshments and teas, 11.30am – 5.30pm. Picnics in north park only ★ Toilet facilities ★ Suitable for wheelchairs. Self-drive vehicle available ★ Dogs on lead in car park and north park only ★ Shop ★ House open as garden, 12 noon – 5.30pm (last admission 5pm) ★ Garden open April to Oct, daily except Thurs and Fri, 11.30am – 6pm ★ Entrance: park and garden: £2.20, children £1.10 (house, garden and park: £5.50, children £2.70, parties £4.80 per person, children £2.50)

The terrace displays urns, vases and lions in bronze and marble. There are six interesting marble wellheads or tubs for bay trees, also an Egyptian obelisk and a sarcophagus. The small informal 'Dutch Garden' was laid out in 1899 for Mrs Bankes in memory of her husband and is still planted in the seasonal schemes designed for her. The restored Victorian fernery leads to the once fine Cedar Walk where one of the trees was planted by the Duke of Wellington in 1827, others by visiting royalty and family members. The garden has recovered well from tree loss in the 1990 storms and there is a laurel walk and an ancient lime avenue. Spectacular roses near the restaurant. The Trust has planted extensive Victorian ground-cover and overall their maintenance is to a high standard. In spring, there are many areas of spring bulbs in the 250-acre park to enjoy. The sunken garden has been restored to the 1906 plan.

KINGSTON MAURWARD ★   23
Dorset College of Agriculture, Dorchester, Dorset.
Tel: (01305) 264738

Kingston Maurward Gardens ★ E of Dorchester off A35. Turn off at roundabout at end of bypass ★ Best season: spring/summer ★ Parking ★ Toilet facilities ★ Partly suitable for wheelchairs ★ Open daily 14th April to 15th Oct, 1 – 5pm. Guided tours by appointment ★ Entrance: £2.50, children £1.50, under 3 free. Family season tickets available (gardens and Farm Animal Park)

The original parkland around Kingston Maurward encompasses 32 acres of specimen trees, water features and woodland, which overlooks the water-meadows of the Frome Valley. The formal gardens to the west of the house were laid out between 1910 and 1915 by the Hanbury family, who also owned La Mortola in Italy. The splendid stone terraces, balustrading, steps and yew hedges have been used to create many intimate gardens and carefully-planned vistas. The refurbishment of the stone features is nearly complete, with the statuary on long loan from the Palace of Westminster and the Grecian temple being recarved from the original design. The gardens contain a large collection of roses, herbaceous perennials and half hardy plants, including the National collections of penstemons and salvias. Large drifts of spring bulbs, cyclamens and autumn crocus surround fine specimen trees. The original large lake has a nature trail around its margin, is full of wildlife and gives superb views of the gardens and watermeadows. The garden is entered through the Farm Animal Park, which has an interesting collection of unusual breeds, set in a beautiful wooded paddock overlooking Stinsford Church of Hardy fame.

KNOLL GARDENS ★   24
Hampreston, Nr Wimborne, Dorset. Tel: (01202) 873931

Mr K. Martin ★ Between Wimborne and Ferndown, off Ham Lane. Leave A31 at Canford Bottom roundabout and forward 1½m. Signposted ★ Parking ★ Refreshments ★ Toilet facilities ★ Suitable for wheelchairs ★ Plants for sale ★ Shops ★ Gardens open March to Oct, daily, 10am – 5.30pm ★ Entrance: £3.45, OAP £2.90, students £2.40, children £1.70. Reductions for parties of 20 or more

Alterations and new developments continue to provide added interest to what has already become a magnet for garden-loving tourists. The waterfall and ponds have been redesigned and extended to feature a striking dragon sculpture, beneath whose arched body thin streams of water form the strings of a harp. A brick 'ruin' provides a backcloth to yet another pond below, and all around are borders and shrubberies, island beds and rockeries, interesting trees (particularly in the Australian section) and pleasant lawns. Holds the NCCPG collection of mahonias. Everywhere the condition is immaculate, the labelling informative – a thoroughly professional production backed by a well-stocked nursery, restaurant and shop.

LANGEBRIDE HOUSE   25
Long Bredy, Nr Bridport, Dorset. Tel: (01308) 482257

Mrs Greener ★ Off A35 Dorchester – Bridport road, turn S to Long Bredy ★ Best season: early spring ★ Parking ★ Toilet facilities ★ Partly suitable for wheelchairs ★ Open March to July by appointment ★ Entrance: £1

This garden has so many desirable features it is difficult to avoid making a list: 200-year-old copper beeches rising from wide, lush lawns, underplanted with carpets of spring bulbs; a thriving enclosed vegetable garden of manageable size, backing onto a sloping grass area with colourful mixed borders along the old tile-topped walls; a rising slope to the mixed wild woodland behind, where favourite trees have been planted in groups to allow for culling as they enlarge; a formal yew-lined lawn with pond, fountain and old stone features, from which steps descend through sloping shrubberies towards the front of the house; a miniature area of greensand allows a patch of acid-loving plants to provide contrast; a long line of pleached limes runs parallel with the bi-colour beech hedge along the road; there is a sloping orchard, a tennis court with a tall rockery behind as a viewing point and sun-trap, there are beds and borders, trellises for climbing plants and low stone walls for those that prefer to hang; and all around thousands of bulbs hide in waiting for the spring explosion which, in the owners' opinion, is the best season to visit.

MAPPERTON ★   26
Beaminster, Dorset. Tel: (01308) 862645

The Montagu family ★ 5m NE of Bridport, 2m SE of Beaminster ★ Parking ★ Toilet facilities ★ House open to parties of 15 or more by appointment ★ Garden open March to Oct, daily, 2 – 6pm ★ Entrance: £2.50, children (5-18) £1.50, under 5 free

A garden with a difference, Mapperton runs down a gradually steepening valley dominated by the delightful sixteenth/seventeenth-century manor house. Terraces in brick and stone descend through formal Italian-style borders towards a summerhouse, which itself stands high above two huge fish tanks (how have they resisted turning them into an Olympic-length swimming pool?) On all sides there is topiary in yew and box. Beyond the tanks, the valley becomes a shrubbery and arboretum, much of it planted since the 1950s by the present owners. Some statuary depicting animals and birds, both natural and stylistic. Numerous ornaments (many supplied by a local firm founded in 1885 and still going strong) provide interest and surprise. Tour with gardener can be arranged in advance.

MELBURY HOUSE 27
Evershot, Dorset. Tel: (01935) 83699 (Garden Office)

The Hon. Mrs Morrison ★ 13m N of Dorchester on A37 Yeovil – Dorchester road. Signposted ★ Best season: spring/summer ★ Parking ★ Toilet facilities ★ Suitable for wheelchairs ★ Plants for sale ★ Open for a few days in the summer (telephone for information) ★ Entrance: £2, OAP and children £1 (1994 prices)

This historic house (not open to the public) is approached by a long drive through open parkland. Visitors are directed round the east side, passing the ancient family church (open) set above a wooded valley. Lawns sweep down to a small lake beyond which rise more wooded hills. A shrub-enclosed lawn leads to a flower garden on the west side, with colourful herbaceous borders beneath mellow brick walls. Beyond this are two other vast walled areas largely used as open lawn, but with a good part still maintained as a productive kitchen garden. To the south-west of the house lies an interesting arboretum with shrubs and massed spring bulbs. Last season saw much alteration and replanting, so this garden will be a source of continuous interest and in time it will be one of the best in Dorset.

MINTERNE 28
Minterne Magna, Dorchester, Dorset. Tel: (01300) 341370

Lord and Lady Digby ★ 9m N of Dorchester on A352 ★ Parking ★ Toilet facilities ★ Dogs on lead ★ Open April to Oct, daily, 10am – 7pm ★ Entrance: £2, children (accompanied only) free

An interesting collection of Himalayan rhododendrons and azaleas, spring bulbs, cherries and maples. Many rare trees. One and a half miles of walks with palm trees, cedars, beeches, etc. Alas no labelling to help the amateur. The first half of the walk is disappointing in midsummer although evidence remains of some spectacular spring colour. At the lower end of the valley the stream with its lakes and waterfalls is surrounded by splendid tall trees, among which the paths wind back towards the house. A very restful and attractive atmosphere, but both lakes and undergrowth could do with attention. Tree colour in autumn should be special.

THE MOORINGS
(see Devon)

MOULIN HUET 29
15 Heatherdown Road, West Moors, Dorset. Tel: (01202) 875760

Mr H. Judd ★ 8m N of Bournemouth. Look for cul-de-sac off the road ★ Parking in road ★ Open May to Sept by appointment only ★ Entrance: 70p, children free

Mr Judd (90 years old) and his late wife built their garden from open heath over 20 years. Although only a third of an acre and triangular in shape, it seems to stretch and enlarge as the visitor is conducted from area to area through archways and along winding paths. All the plants, some of them quite rare, have been grown from seed or cuttings. There is also a fine collection of bonsai, grown by Mr Judd's own unique method which apparently defies all the rules.

NORTH LEIGH HOUSE 30
Colehill, Wimborne, Dorset. Tel: (01202) 882592

Mr and Mrs S. Walker ★ 1m NE of Wimborne. Turn off B3073 by Sir Winston Churchill pub into North Leigh Lane (¾m) ★ Parking ★ Refreshments ★ Toilet facilities ★ Partly suitable for wheelchairs ★ Dogs on lead ★ House open by appointment ★ Open 7th May, 30th July, 2 – 6pm ★ Entrance: £1, children 20p

The restoration of this delightful house and its once impenetrable grounds has taken over 22 years to achieve, and the work continues. There are five acres of informal parkland, with mature trees, a small lake and grassy banks covered in drifts of wild orchids and naturalised spring bulbs. The Victorian features include a balustraded terrace, a fountain, a walled garden and a magnificent conservatory in which a heavily-fruiting vine flourishes alongside other interesting specimens. There is a strong sense of the past being recaptured here; it is not difficult to imagine in such surroundings the tennis or croquet parties of 100 years ago, with the urbane butler bringing forth cooling drinks on a long-distant summer afternoon. Today, figs from the tree may be taken with afternoon tea.

THE OLD MILL 31
Spetisbury, Blandford, Dorset. Tel: (01258) 453939

The Rev. and Mrs J. Hamilton-Brown ★ Take A350 Blandford – Poole road. Opposite school at entrance to the village, sign marked Footpath ★ Best season: summer ★ Parking ★ Teas on charity days ★ Toilet facilities ★ Partly suitable for wheelchairs ★ Dogs on leads ★ Plants for sale ★ Open 7th June to 30th Aug, Weds, 2 – 5pm and for charity 11th June, 16th July. Other days by appointment ★ Entrance: £2, children free

For best effect approach along the public footpath, a narrow concrete bridge four feet above the undulating grass. From this vantage point the visitor can immediately appreciate the quiet mill stream glowing with well-chosen, water-loving plants along its banks, the ponds and dips sheltering lushly-planted boggy areas, the graceful willows rising and weeping above banks of balsam, rushes and tall grasses, the River Stour flowing clear and full inches below the mown lawns. Water naturally predominates (and sometimes overwhelms!) in this fascinating garden, developed over 18 years.

THE OLD RECTORY 32
Fifehead Magdalen, Gillingham, Dorset. Tel: (01258) 820293

Mrs P. Lidsey ★ S of Gillingham, and ½m S of A30, just W of East Stour crossroads ★ Parking in road ★ Toilet facilities ★ Plants for sale ★ Open spring and summer by appointment and 11th June, 2 – 6pm ★ Entrance: £1, children free

This charismatic garden of one and a half acres encircles an attractive early eighteenth-century thatched rectory that has unusual stone facings (house not open). It has been carefully cultivated by the owner who enjoys colour by mixing shrubs, herbaceous plants and annuals; there are collections of violas, and hardy geraniums and hebes, as well as five varieties of elder. There is a natural carp pond; also a small rose arbour. Many pots and tubs at the front of the house. The tiny ancient church is at the other end of this picturesque hamlet.

THE OLD RECTORY   33
Litton Cheney, Nr Dorchester, Dorset. Tel: (01308) 482383

Mr and Mrs Hugh Lindsay ★ 1m S of A35, beside the village church ★ Limited parking in centre of village ★ Teas ★ Plants for sale ★ Open two days, probably late April and May, for charity, 2 – 6pm or by appointment ★ Entrance: £1, children 20p

The Rectory rests comfortably below the church and is approached by a gravel drive which circles a small lawn. A thatched summerhouse stands to one side, like a massive beehive. A small walled garden has outhouses and a large barn on two sides and borders around three, prolifically stocked with well-chosen and favourite plants in specific colour bands. A steep path leads in to the four acres of natural woodland, a surprisingly extensive area of mature trees with many springs, streams and ponds – never a water shortage here, even in the driest of summers. This area was reclaimed by the current owners, who are adding new young trees and shrubs as well as successfully encouraging many spring-flowering plant colonies, mostly native. Climbing back up to the house, the visitor arrives at the terrace – a belvedere giving views over the trees to open farmland on the other side of the valley. Spring and autumn are the best times to see this garden, from which Reynolds Stone, the wood-engraver, drew inspiration.

THE OLD RECTORY   34
Seaborough, Nr Beaminster, Dorset. Tel: (01308) 868426

Mr and Mrs C.W. Wright ★ 3m S of Crewkerne. Take B3165, turn second left after de-restriction sign, first right after ½m, second left in Seaborough village (house near corner). Signposted on open day ★ Best season: April to July ★ Parking but no coaches ★ Teas on open day ★ Toilet facilities ★ Dogs on lead ★ Open once a year in spring or early summer and by appointment all year ★ Entrance: £1, children 20p

Pleasant views from the terraces, with stone steps down to the lower garden. Magnolias, rhododendrons and camellias give colour in their season; the Himalayan and other trees, shrubs and herbaceous plants, the ferns and bulbs, over 1000 species and cultivars in all, provide a wealth of interest throughout the year. This garden specialises in providing suitable conditions for interesting plants rather than their arrangement in colour schemes.

PARNHAM HOUSE ★   35
Beaminster, Dorset. Tel: (01308) 862204

Mr and Mrs J. Makepeace ★ ½m S of Beaminster on A3066 ★ Parking ★ Refreshments: licensed buttery. Picnicing allowed on grass areas adjoining the car park and overlooking the river ★ Toilet facilities ★ Partly suitable for wheelchairs ★ Dogs on lead ★ Shop ★ House and workshop open ★ Open April to Oct, Wed, Sun and Bank Holidays, 10am – 5pm. Group visits by appointment only ★ Entrance: £4.20, children (10-15) £2, under 10 free (house, workshop and garden)

The imposing stone terracing to the west of the house frames the many large clipped yews through which descend spring-fed water channels. A wide lawn leads to a balustrade and a small lake. There are large woodland

and wild areas to the north and east, and sheltered borders along the brick wall of the old kitchen garden – the earliest part. Here Mrs Makepeace has used her gift for colour and form to create some splendid displays, notable as much for their shape and texture as for the well-chosen colour schemes. There are also delightful small and large courtyards to the south of the house with interesting plantings.

THE PRIEST'S HOUSE MUSEUM AND GARDEN   36
23-27 High Street, Wimborne Minster, Dorset. Tel: (01202) 882533

The Priest's House Museum ★ In the centre of Wimborne ★ Parking in town car parks ★ Refreshments in summer ★ Toilet facilities ★ Suitable for wheelchairs ★ Museum shop on Sat only ★ Museum open (Special Christmas exhibition, 27th Dec – 12th Jan) ★ Garden open April to 29th Oct, Mon – Sat, 10.30am – 5pm and 27th, 28th Aug, 2 – 5pm ★ Entrance: £1.50, OAP £1, children 50p (museum and garden)

In the heart of this small town lies a 300ft long walled garden, hidden from the busy shopping thoroughfare by the frontage of the Museum. Both are well worth a visit. A long narrow level garden laid out with some formal beds but mostly lawn, herbaceous and herb borders. A few unusual plants but further labelling is required. In late spring the wisteria on the back of the house is particularly appealing. Sit on one of the seats dotted around and enjoy the peaceful atmosphere in this well-cared for garden staffed by volunteers who are only too pleased to answer questions about the plants.

SANDFORD ORCAS MANOR   37
Nr Sherborne, Dorset. Tel: (01963) 220206

Sir Mervyn Medlycott, Bart ★ 2½m N of Sherborne, turning off B3148, next to village church ★ Parking ★ Toilet facilities ★ Dogs on lead ★ House open ★ Garden open 17th April, 10am – 6pm, then May to Sept, Sun, 2 – 6pm and Mon, 10am – 6pm ★ Entrance: £2, children £1 (house and garden). Pre-booked parties of 10 or more at reduced rates on other days if preferred

Looked at purely as a garden, Sandford Orcas is not exceptional. An old, flagged path slopes up between bordered lawns towards an open field. The stone walls at either side are attractive enough, but they stop suddenly at the wire fence and the view lacks a frame and a focal point. There is a herb garden with small box-bordered beds and a pleasant view across a lower lawn along the south side of the house. At the end of this lawn another viewpoint back towards the south front allows the attractive planting below the herb garden to show at its best. Roses and other climbing plants clinging to the honey-grey walls harmonise well with this gracious setting. It is the house, ancient and redolent of its long history, which permeates the scene and transforms the garden.

STAPEHILL ABBEY GARDENS   38
Ferndown, Wimborne, Dorset. Tel: (01202) 861686

Mr and Mrs J. Pickard (Managers) ★ On the old A31 Wimborne – Ferndown road, ½m E of Canford Bottom roundabout ★ Best season: early summer ★ Parking ★ Lunches and teas ★ Toilet facilities ★ Partly suitable for wheelchairs ★

Guide dogs only ★ Craft workshops ★ House open ★ Garden open April to Oct, daily, 10am – 5pm; Nov to March, daily except Mon and Tues (but closed 24th Dec to 1st Feb) 10am – 4pm ★ Entrance: £4.50, OAP and students £4, children (4–16) £3

Formerly home for 200 years to Cistercian nuns, this lovely old abbey has now been restored and the grounds transformed into gardens. There is a Victorian cottage garden, wisteria walk, orchid house, lake and picnic area, also a large rock garden with waterfall and pools which will be a fine feature when more mature. There are a number of craft shops in the old Abbey with demonstrations of traditional crafts on most days. The restaurant is in the former rectory, off a lovely walled terrace so one can eat out of doors in summer. The Country World museum features tractors etc.

STICKY WICKET 39
Buckland Newton, Dorset. Tel: (01300) 345476

Peter and Pam Lewis ★ 11m from Dorchester and Sherborne, 2m E of A352 or take B3143 from Sturminster Newton. At T-junction midway between church and school ★ Parking in meadow ★ Refreshments ★ Toilet facilities ★ Partly suitable for wheelchairs ★ Plants for sale ★ Open 18th June to 14th Sept, Thurs, 10.30am – 8pm and some Suns for charity, 2 – 6pm. Parties welcome by appointment ★ Entrance: £1.50, children 75p

A design of concentric circles and radiating paths has enabled the creation of many separate beds showing different planting styles. A very fragrant and colourful display is enhanced by many unusual and/or variegated plants and bordered by species roses. The garden is designed to attract birds, butterflies and bees and to provide spectacular flowerheads for drying. There is a small pond and a wet area which is also attractive to wildlife. This is very much the garden of conservationist-minded plant-lovers; an informal white garden is being developed. If the progress of recent years is maintained this garden is destined to become outstanding.

STOCKFORD 40
East Stoke, Wareham, Dorset. Tel: (01929) 462230

Mrs A.M. Radclyffe ★ 3½m W of Wareham on A352 opposite Stokeford Inn ★ Parking ★ Toilet facilities ★ Partly suitable for wheelchairs ★ Dogs on lead ★ Open 16th April, 7th, 28th May, 2 – 6pm ★ Entrance: £1, children 25p

A longish drive through woodland leads to this quaint, thatched house closely surrounded by mature trees. Underplanting of camellias, rhododendrons and azaleas among the lush grass gives evidence of attractive spring colour, while in the part-walled garden well-established shrubs and border plants nestle in the dappled shade. Three acres of woodland.

STOUR HOUSE 41
41 East Street, Blandford, Dorset. Tel: (01258) 452914

Mr T.S.B. Card ★ In Blandford, 100 yards from Market Place on the one-way system ★ Parking in town ★ Toilet facilities ★ Suitable for wheelchairs ★ Open 2nd April, 2 – 5pm; 9th July, 13th Aug, 2 – 6pm ★ Entrance: 80p, children 20p

A garden that appeals to both formal and informal tastes. The formal part is walled with long wide-bordered lawns, a small pond, many unusual and some tender shrubs and long vistas towards a modern sculpture and a wooden bridge of unusual design which leads to a delightful and romantic island in the River Stour. The island has many beautiful mature trees, both native and non-native species. The owner has planted many varieties of younger trees himself. There are over 60 roses, and a rose hedge. After disruption by the Blandford Flood Relief Scheme, vistas have been opened up and new beds planted. A beautiful town garden, well worth a visit.

WESTON HOUSE   42
Buckhorn Weston, Gillingham, Dorset. Tel: (01963) 371005

Mr and Mrs E.A.W. Bullock ★ 4m W of Gillingham, 4m SE of Wincanton. From A30 turn N to Kington Magna, continue towards Buckhorn Weston and after railway bridge take left turn towards Wincanton. House is second on left ★ Parking ★ Open by appointment May to July. Telephone (01963) 371005 ★ Entrance: £1, children free

When the Bullocks moved into their Georgian farmhouse eight years ago, the large garden to the rear was mostly rough grass. Now, thanks to their hard work and imaginative flair, design and colour are highlighted by the beautiful array of old-fashioned and English roses. This harmonious collection is particularly comprehensive and can be explored via stepping stones thoughtfully arranged behind the borderlines and around the boundary walls. York paving was introduced to create roundels and pathways bordered by carefully-toned blues with white. A mixed border, yellow, white and blue, is backed by an old wall supporting interesting climbers. 'Hot' colours are staged in herbaceous borders later in the season and a woodland area is now being developed. Although main flowerbeds are near the house, general design is enhanced by a well-kept lawn and areas of meadow and rough-cut grass, interspersed with some unusual trees and shrubs, leading the eye to rougher areas, thence to fields. The effect is both restful and original. Mrs Bullock is a knowledgeable plantswoman.

WINCOMBE PARK   43
Shaftesbury, Dorset. Tel: (01747) 852161

The Hon. Martin Fortescue ★ 2m from Shaftesbury signed to Wincombe off A350 to Warminster ★ Parking ★ Teas ★ Toilet facilities ★ Dogs on lead ★ Unusual plants occasionally for sale ★ Open 19th May, 18th Oct, 2 – 5.30pm, also to groups by appointment ★ Entrance: £1.50, children free (1994 prices)

This is essentially a beautifully landscaped park. The house is set upon the side of a valley, screened behind tall trees and approached by a winding drive. There is a high bank beside the drive containing an interesting and well-judged selection of shrubs and small trees. Below and to the side of the house are small lawns and a walled kitchen-garden, itself worth a look. The borders are full of specimens to interest the plantsperson. But the real pleasure for the visitor lies in the wide, sloping lawn, below it the lake, and then up the steep wooded valley side beyond.

DURHAM

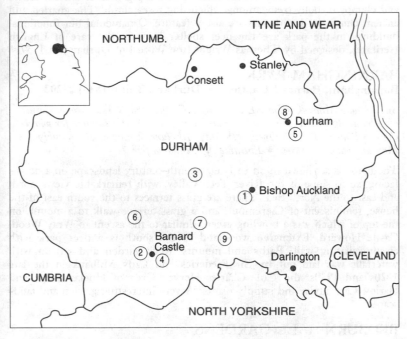

AUCKLAND PARK
Auckland Castle, Bishop Auckland, Co. Durham.

Bishop of Durham; Managed by Wear Valley District Council ★ Leave A1(M) at Bishop Auckland sign and follow A689 west, through Rushyford, past Windlestone Hall and Coundon into Bishop Auckland ★ Best season: early summer ★ Parking in Market Square, W of Castle ★ Refreshments: cafés in Market Square ★ Toilet facilities in bus station ★ Partly suitable for wheelchairs ★ Dogs on lead ★ Auckland Castle State Rooms and Chapel open during summer, Suns pm, Tues am, Weds pm and Thurs pm and also Sat pm in Aug ★ Gardens open daily throughout year: summer, 7.30am – 9pm; winter, 7.30am – dusk ★ Entrance: free (castle £1.50 (1994 price))

A remarkable survival, poorly maintained, of an eighteenth-century and earlier deer park in the well-wooded valleys of the Coundon Burn and Gaunless River, tributary to the River Wear. Enter the park via a gatehouse designed by Sir Thomas Robinson with touches of Thomas Wright, and walk past Auckland Castle, glimpsed through a *clairvoyée*. Suddenly, through the gateway in James Wyatt's screen of 1796 for Bishop Barrington there is a glimpse of the twelfth-century banqueting hall converted to a chapel by Bishop Cosin in the late seventeenth century. There is an inner and an outer park covering 80 acres, all that remains of a deer park that once extended to 500 acres. Within them the River Gaunless traces a meandering course with precipitate bluffs such as Kitty Heugh and craggy outcrops. The river has been canalised in places with a weir, dating from the eighteenth century. There are avenues of Austrian pine and sweet chestnut and circular platoons of trees. There are groves of ancient alders and clumps of holly trees among which dog roses climb. The gnarled and ancient clumps of hawthorns are also a feature. Ornamental but functional buildings in the park are the deer shelter (now in the care of English Heritage), designed by Thomas Wright (the Wizard of Durham) in 1757.

BARNINGHAM PARK 2
Barningham, Barnard Castle, Co. Durham. Tel: (01833) 21202

Sir Anthony Milbank ★ 5m SE of Barnard Castle, 10m NW of Scotch Corner off A66 at A66 Motel crossroads ★ Parking ★ Teas ★ Partly suitable for wheelchairs ★ Plants for sale ★ Open 28th May, 4th June, 2 – 6pm, also possibly 21st May and one day in Sept ★ Entrance: £2, children free

The house is set down in an early eighteenth-century landscape on a north-facing, steep slope of the River Tees Valley, with remarkable views north and east to the North Sea. There are grass terraces to the south east of the house, reminiscent of Claremont, and a grass terrace walk to a mount, on the top of which was a bowling green, similar to the ascent to Wray Wood, Castle Howard. Extensive woodland to the south is a deer park with circumvallating wall. Paths and mounts. Rock garden and stream with waterfalls was laid out by Sir Frederick and Lady Milbank in the late 1920s and 1930s: did Col. Charles Hervey Grey of Hocker Edge and Harlow Carr advise and supply plants? A very interesting garden and landscape.

BEDBURN HALL GARDENS 3
Hamsterley, Bishop Auckland, Co. Durham. Tel: (0138888) 231

Mr I. Bonas ★ 9m NW of Bishop Auckland. W off A68 at Witton-le-Wear. 3m SE of Wolsingham off B6293 ★ Parking ★ Teas ★ Partly suitable for wheelchairs ★ Open by appointment and as advertised on certain days in summer, 2 – 6pm ★ Entrance: £1.50, children 50p

A medium-sized terraced garden, largely developed by the present owner, it is beautifully situated by Hamsterley Forest. The garden is dominated by a lake with associated rhododendrons and bamboos. A new conservatory contains figs, bougainvilleas, passion flowers and other exotics. Woodland.

THE BOWES MUSEUM GARDEN 4
Barnard Castle, Co. Durham. Tel: (01833) 690606

Durham County Council ★ From Barnard Castle E on the road towards Westwick ★ Best season: spring/summer ★ Parking ★ Refreshments: coffee, lunch, teas in museum restaurant and picnic areas all during summer ★ Toilet facilities ★ Suitable for wheelchairs ★ Museum closed for rewiring to 1st April. Phone for details of opening ★ Shop in museum ★ Garden open daily, dawn – dusk ★ Entrance: free

The garden and grounds are dominated by the museum buildings and only the terrace, parterre and drives constitute an integrated whole. Pevsner describes it as 'a sudden apparition at the end of Newgate, big, bold and incongruous, looking exactly like the town hall of a major provincial town in France. In scale it is just as gloriously inappropriate to the town to which it belongs (and to which it gives some international fame) as in style'. The formal garden complements the building. The rest of the grounds contain 100 different species of trees, some of considerable anti-quity and predating the opening of the museum in 1892 (it was designed in 1869 by the French architect Jules Pellechet for John Bowes, son of the tenth Earl of Strathmore and kinsman of the Queen). Specimen trees are dotted about – an araucaria, a *Robinia pseudoacacia*, a *Juglans regia*. To the north-east, there is a delightful small bowling green pavilion, and to the south a shrub and rose garden. The standard of maintenance is not high as only one full-time gardener is employed. Opposite the museum is Spring Lodge, now a hotel, with a collection of trees and shrubs assembled by the late Col. Watson.

DURHAM COLLEGE OF AGRICULTURE AND HORTICULTURE   5
Houghall, Durham, Co. Durham. Tel: (0191) 386 1351

Durham County Council ★ 1m SE of Durham city on the south side of the A177 from Durham to Stockton-on-Tees. Leave A1(M) at A177 signposted Peterlee and follow A177 towards Durham ★ Parking ★ Toilet facilities ★ Suitable for wheelchairs ★ Plants for sale ★ Open all year, 1 – 4.30pm ★ Entrance: free

Houghall College campus grounds have been developed over the last 35 years as the county's main horticultural educational and training facility for both amateur and professional gardeners. The campus grounds comprise some 24 acres of sportsfields and ornamental features and within them contain one of the largest collections of hardy plants in north east England. The gardens are situated in a frost pocket, where some of the lowest temperatures in the country are recorded annually. Ornamental features include: water garden, woodland garden, alpine house, display greenhouses, rock garden, raised beds, troughs, narcissi naturalised under trees, heather garden and arboretum. The College is holder of the National collections of sorbus and meconopsis.

EGGLESTON HALL GARDENS   6
Eggleston, Barnard Castle, Co. Durham. Tel: (01833) 650378

Mrs W.T. Gray ★ 5m NW of Barnard Castle on B6278 ★ Parking ★ Catering for parties can be arranged ★ Partly suitable for wheelchairs ★ Plants for sale ★ Gardens open daily, 10am – 5pm ★ Entrance: £1 for the season or 50p for a single visit

The house (not open but glimpsed) was designed by Ignatius Bonomi for the antiquarian William Hutchinson. The Lodge at the entrance, also by Bonomi, gives access to the gardens – Doric gate piers, wrought iron gate bought from The Great Exhibition by William Gray, and lodge with pedimented, columned porch in warm stone greet the visitor. What is attractive about these gardens are the shrub and herbaceous plantings between the drive and the walled garden. The conservatory is well-stocked and the noisette rose 'Alister Stella Gray' is a delight. The walled garden has great potential, with its cobble-lined rill and high stone walls on the north and east sides. Open the gate in the wall to find the plant sale area – fine glasshouses full of rare and interesting species. The reserve garden north of the rill is well-maintained as is the soft fruit and vegetable garden; but it is interesting to contemplate how it would look if the shrub and herbaceous plantings were integrated with the walled garden.

RABY CASTLE GARDENS 7
Staindrop, Co. Durham. Tel: (01833) 660202

The Rt Hon. The Lord Barnard ★ 1m N of Staindrop on A688 Barnard Castle – Bishop Auckland road ★ Parking ★ Teas ★ Toilet facilities ★ Partly suitable for wheelchairs ★ House open from 1pm (extra charge). Buildings by Paine and Garrett by appointment only ★ Garden open 14th to 19th April; May and June, Weds and Suns only; July to Sept, daily except Sat, 11am – 5.30pm. Bank Holiday openings Sat until following Wed ★ Entrance: £1, OAP and children 75p

This formal garden dating from the mid-eighteenth century was designed by Thomas Wright (the Wizard of Durham) for the 2nd Earl of Darlington, and has a wide array of trees, shrubs and herbaceous plants. Thomas White advised on the landscaping along with Joseph Spence. The garden walls from locally hand-made bricks have flues which used to enable sub-tropical fruits to be grown on the south terrace. The famous white Ischia fig tree brought to Raby in 1786 still survives. Rose garden, shrub borders, original yew hedges, lakes and ornamental pond, though the best bits (*ferme ornée*, Gothic cottage and Roman baths) are alas not open to the public except by appointment.

UNIVERSITY OF DURHAM BOTANIC GARDEN ★ 8
Hollingside Lane, Durham, Co. Durham. Tel: (0191) 3742670

Durham University ★ 1m from centre of Durham City, E of A1050. Accessible from the A1(M). From S leave A177 and drive NW through Bowburn and Shincliffe to Durham. From N leave at A690 and drive SW to Durham. Garden off Hollingside Lane ★ Parking ★ Refreshments ★ Toilet facilities ★ Partly suitable for wheelchairs ★ Plants for sale ★ Shop in Visitor Centre ★ Garden open all year. Glasshouses open daily, 9am – 4pm. Visitor Centre open April to Oct, daily, 10am – 5pm; Nov to March, daily except Christmas week and bad weather, 2 – 4pm ★ Entrance: suggested 50p donation

Established in 1970 as a centre for botanical study, this is now one of the few botanical gardens in the north of England. Special features include a water and bog garden (the gazebo garden), a new rose pergola garden, a heather garden, in addition to the collections of Himalayan, South American, East and West North American tree and shrub species, many from seeds collected on plant expeditions in these areas. The Prince Bishop's Garden is new, comprising six figures, carved in elm by Colin Wilbourn, which have been transferred from the Gateshead Garden Festival. The arboretum has grass walks and is cut once a year. The grasses and ox-eye daisies are a delight – unplanned and unexpected.

WESTHOLME HALL 9
Winston, Darlington, Co. Durham. Tel: (01325) 730442

Mr and Mrs J.H. McBain ★ On B6274 between Staindrop and Winston ★

Parking in field ★ Home-made teas ★ Toilet facilities ★ Dogs on lead ★ Plants for sale ★ Open 28th May, 2nd, 23rd July, 27th Aug, 2 – 6pm. Parties welcome by arrangement ★ Entrance: £1.50, children 50p

The Jacobean house and the garden (which was laid out in 1890) are reached by a short drive of limes with mature hollies on the north side. To the south is parkland. Immediately inside the garden enclosure (about five acres), there are lawns: on the right an old tree supports 'Felicité et Perpetue' rose and clematis 'Comtesse de Bouchaud'. From the front door in the south elevation, an axial line to a stone–flagged bridge over a stream, the Westholme Beck – a tributary of the Alwent Beck – and thence to the River Tees. A stone retaining wall parallel and south of the house forms the backing for a long shrub and herbaceous border with long grass walk running east-west: then a grass slope to a wide croquet lawn with bold plantings of rhododendrons. Beyond are grass walks with cherries and specimen trees. Cross the stream that bisects the garden and there is a paddock, and more walks through maturing woodland: one vista through what will one day become an avenue of beeches is closed by a massive stone plinth. Elsewhere in the garden, the long grass terrace walk is terminated by a wall and an urn. Stone parapets were salvaged from the Streatlam Park demolition sale of the 1930s, and now adorn this garden. There is a delightful shrub rose garden to the west of the house, partly sunk and overlooked by a summerhouse, with a good collection of albas, bourbons, etc. At Headlam Hall about five miles east, excellent lunches and dinners are available.

TELEPHONE NUMBERS

Except where owners have specifically requested that they be excluded, telephone numbers to which enquiries may be directed are given for each property. To maintain the support and co-operation of private owners, it is suggested that the telephone be used with discretion. Where visits are by appointment, the telephone can of course be used except where written application, particularly for parties, is specifically requested. Code numbers are given in brackets. For the Republic of Ireland phone 010353 followed by the code (Dublin is 1) followed by the subscriber's number. In all cases where visits by parties are proposed, owners should be advised in advance and arrangements preferably confirmed in writing.

BEWARE CHANGED PHONE NUMBERS

While every attempt has been made to include correct telephone numbers for 1995, there have been changes as we went to press and some owners have not amended their numbers so it may be necessary to check with 192 Directory Enquiries. Apologies.

ESSEX

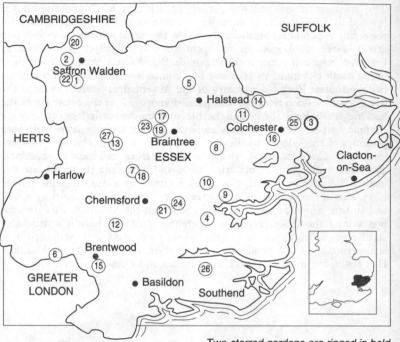

CAMBRIDGESHIRE

SUFFOLK

⑳

② Saffron Walden
㉒①

⑤

● Halstead ⑭

HERTS

⑰
㉓⑲
Braintree
ESSEX

⑪
Colchester ㉕ ③
⑯

㉗⑬

⑧

Clacton-on-Sea

● Harlow

⑦
⑱

⑩

⑨

Chelmsford ●

㉑ ㉔

④

⑫

Brentwood

⑥
⑮

⑳⑥

GREATER
LONDON

● Basildon

Southend

Two-starred gardens are ringed in bold

AMBERDEN HALL   1
Widdington, Nr Saffron Walden, Essex. Tel: (01799) 40402

*Mr and Mrs D. Lloyd ★ 6m from Saffron Walden. E off B1383 near Newport,
follow signs to Mole Hall Wildlife Park ¹/₂m past park on right ★ Parking ★
Cream teas on 11th June ★ Toilet facilities ★ Suitable for wheelchairs ★ Open
10th, 11th, 14th June, 2 – 6pm ★ Entrance: £2*

Some lovely old walls enclose this medium–sized garden set at one side of a
fine house. The borders are well designed, so that not all of the garden is
visible at once. All are planted in specific colours – the red border being the
newest with roses, dahlias, hemerocallis, etc. The walls are covered in a variety
of climbers, many rare, like *Trachelospermum jasminoides*. To hide a barn roof,
a Leylandii hedge has been clipped at 15 feet and the sides corrugated. Good
vegetable garden with raised beds to make it easier to cope with heavy clay
soil. Garden extended beyond the walls with ivy *allée*. This has two viburnum
hedges with poles rising out of them each carrying different ivies.

AUDLEY END   2
Saffron Walden, Essex. Tel: (01799) 522399/522842

English Heritage ★ 1m W of Saffron Walden on the B1383 ★ Parking ★

Refreshments: in restaurant. Picnics in park ★ Toilet facilities ★ Dogs on lead ★ Shop ★ House open 1 – 5pm ★ Garden open April to Sept, daily except Mon and Tues (but open Bank Holiday Mons), 12 noon – 6pm ★ Entrance: £2.70, OAP £2, children £1.30 (house and grounds £4.90, OAP £3.70, children £2.40) (1994 prices)

The Jacobean house has always been a gem but now visitors can enjoy an early version of the parterre garden restored to the plans developed by Lord Braybrooke and his wife *c.* 1830, advised by William Sawrey Gilpin. The design was inspired by the classic seventeenth-century French parterres, with sheltering shrubberies which relate to contemporary (ie. 1830) interiors. English Heritage have introduced the whole repertory of the flower garden of the period – irises, gladioli, martagon lilies, bergamots, peonies and astrantias, *Viola cornuta*, hypericums – all planted in some 170 beds. Restoration has taken 10 years and has been completed without interfering with the surrounding 'Capability' Brown landscape park, which features a circular temple, bridge and Lady Portsmouth's column by Adam, with fine plane, oak and beech trees. The whole is immaculately maintained.

THE BETH CHATTO GARDENS ★★ 3
Elmstead Market, Colchester, Essex. Tel: (01206) 822007

Mrs Beth Chatto ★ ½m E of Elmstead Market on A133 ★ Parking ★ Toilet facilities ★ Plants for sale in nursery adjoining gardens ★ Open March to Oct, Mon – Sat, 9am – 5pm, Nov to Feb, Mon – Fri, 9am – 4pm. Closed Suns and Bank Holidays. Groups by arrangement ★ Entrance: £2, children free

Beth Chatto designed this garden in the 1960s from a neglected hollow which was either boggy and soggy or exceedingly dry. She, more than anyone else, has influenced gardeners by her choice of plants for any situation – dry, wet or shady – and her ability to show them off to perfection. The planting of her garden is a lesson to every gardener on how to use both leaf and flower to best advantage. The large new gravel garden which she planted recently to replace the old car park is maturing well as a home for beautiful plants which can thrive in very dry conditions. Adjoining the garden is the excellent Unusual Plants nursery – many plants are available in too small a quantity to appear in the catalogue.

CAMEO COTTAGE 4
Chapel Lane, Purleigh, Nr Maldon, Essex. Tel: (01621) 828334

Mrs Joan Cook ★ S of Maldon between the B1010 and 1012. Locate the hill that leads to the church. Facing the hill, turn right, take first left (Howe Green Road), take first right by a black house (Chapel Lane). Cameo Cottage is first house on the right ★ Parking ★ Open by appointment ★ Entrance: donation for charity

Set around a cottage, the early part of which dates back to the seventeenth century, this three-quarter-acre cottage garden is immediately captivating. It is entirely filled with plants that tumble and spill gloriously around a maze of narrow paths and small courtyards, yet the apparent informality is restrained within particular colour schemes, forming the cameos that give the cottage its name. Additional depth and texture are provided by a variation in levels, statuary and numerous raised troughs made by the owner's late husband. A diverted field ditch has allowed the creation of a bog garden. This is an enthralling place for the plantsman as it contains many rare treasures among more familiar herbaceous varieties. It is also known as a garden for all seasons, as it provides interest from February onwards. RHS Garden Hyde Hall (see entry) is nearby.

CRACKNELLS ★   5
Great Yeldham, Essex. Tel: (01787) 237370

Mr and Mrs T. Chamberlain ★ Off A604 between Halstead and Haverhill ★ Parking ★ Suitable for wheelchairs ★ Open by appointment ★ Entrance: by charity box donation

Mr Chamberlain started contouring this large garden even before he started building his house. The garden rolls away from the house down to the lake, also excavated at the start. This is not a garden in the accepted sense but 'a garden picture painted with trees', to use Mr Chamberlain's own words. He has collected trees from all over the country and has an impressive collection. Here is the rare cut-leaved beech, *Fagus sylvatica* var. *heterophylla* and its purple and pink-leaved forms, 'Rohanii' and 'Roseomarginata', as well as the variegated tulip tree *Liriodendron tulipifera* 'Aureomarginatum'. There are also collections of birches, acers, sorbus and oaks. If you are a lover of trees, make your pilgrimage.

7A ELLESMERE GARDENS   6
Redbridge, Ilford, Essex. Tel: (0181) 550 5464

Cecilia Gonzalez ★ Travelling E, off A12 Eastern Avenue between Redbridge roundabout (M11 interchange) and Gants Hill roundabout ★ Parking in street ★ Open by appointment only (garden only takes two at a time) ★ Entrance: £1

A charming split-level courtyard garden, only 20 feet square, and a treasure trove of unusual plants. The number of species here is remarkable, given the garden's size, but all growth is restricted and imaginative use is made of container planting. As a result, a real plant-lover can spend as much time here as in a far larger garden. The upper level is filled with containers, while dense planting in the lower level creates a microclimate that allows some unusual tropical plants to flourish. The owner knew little about gardening when she moved here at the beginning of the 1980s and the site was covered with paving stones, most now removed.

FANNERS GREEN   7
Great Waltham, Nr Chelmsford, Essex. Tel: (01245) 360035

Dr and Mrs T.M. Pickard ★ 4m N of Chelmsford. Take the B1008 from Chelmsford to Great Waltham, turn left into South Street, opposite the church. Drive 1¼m ★ Limited parking ★ Plants for sale ★ Open 7th, 8th May, 11th, 12th June, 17th July, 2 – 6pm and parties by appointment ★ Entrance: £1, children free

Mrs Pickard is a garden designer and it certainly shows in this small country garden. Here are compartments in miniature with hedges of thuya and beech, each compartment having a different theme. The vegetable garden is divided by paths into tiny squares with vegetables grown for their decorative qualities as well as their culinary uses. There is a large range of plants and shrubs, including a half-standard purple-leaved sambu-cus, a herb garden and a well-kept conservatory.

FEERINGBURY MANOR   8
Coggeshall Road, Feering, Essex. Tel: (01376) 561946

Mr and Mrs Giles Coode-Adams ★ On B1024 between Coggeshall and Feering ★ Parking ★ Toilet facilities ★ Suitable for wheelchairs ★ Open 2nd May to 28th July, weekdays, 9am – 1pm and by appointment. Closed Bank Holidays ★ Entrance: £1.50

With all its size (seven acres) and variety this is also a very peaceful garden. The large natural ponds are well planted with rare and unusual bog plants – gunneras and primulas, iris, astilbes and kirengeshomas. There are fine trees, shrub borders and a long 'old rose' border backed up by a trellis with clematis growing up it. Clematis are Mr Coode-Adams' speciality. Many exciting plants tucked into unexpected corners.

FOLLY FAUNTS HOUSE   9
Goldhanger, Maldon, Essex. Tel: (01621) 788213 or 788611 (office)

Mr and Mrs J.C. Jenkinson ★ On B1026 between Maldon and Colchester ★ Parking ★ Teas ★ Toilet facilities ★ Suitable for wheelchairs ★ Dogs on lead ★ Plants for sale ★ Open by appointment and 28th May, 11th, 25th June, 2 – 5pm. Groups welcome. Telephone for appointment ★ Entrance: £1.50, children 75p

A large five-acre garden around an eighteenth-century manor house has been created by the owners since 1963. The garden is divided into 'compartments' each with a different theme and has a wide variety of unusual trees and shrubs. The plantings around the informal and formal ponds are a special feature. In recent years a further 20 acres of park and woodland divided by five double avenues has been planted to make attrac-tive walks.

GLEN CHANTRY   10
Wickham Bishops, Nr Witham, Essex. Tel: (01621) 891342

Mr and Mrs W.G. Staines ★ SE of Witham. Turn left off B1018 towards Wickham Bishops. Pass the golf course, cross River Blackwater bridge and turn left up track by Blue Mills ★ Parking ★ Teas on Suns and Mons only ★ Toilet facilities ★ Partly suitable for wheelchairs ★ Large range of unusual plants for sale ★ Open 16th, 17th April, 7th, 8th, 28th, 29th May, 11th June, 2nd July, 3rd, 17th Sept, 2 – 5pm; also June and July, Fri and Sat, 10am – 4pm ★ Entrance: £1, children 50p

This large undulating garden has been created by the owners since 1977. The huge informally-shaped borders are filled with a variety of herbaceous plants, bulbs, shrubs and shrub roses. Large rock gardens and a stream with waterfalls running through them to a pond make a dominant feature. Colour-theme beds, foliage areas featuring grasses and hostas and a more formal white garden are recent additions. However it is always the plants themselves that take centre stage.

HILL HOUSE 11
Chappel, Nr Colchester, Essex. Tel: (01787) 222428

Mr and Mrs R. Mason ★ On A604 between Colchester and Earls Colne ★ Limited parking ★ Plants for sale ★ Open by appointment ★ Entrance: donation to charity

This is a large garden at the beginning of its life. It has been designed by the owners on formal lines using yew hedging and walls to create vistas. A mixed planting of tough native trees, sorbus and hawthorn, etc. has been established as a windbreak. A new lime avenue is the latest addition – sited to lead the eye out into the country. The bones of the garden are now in place including urns, statues and seats. All the colour and secondary planting is being introduced gradually. In a small courtyard, reminiscent of a London garden, is a raised pool planted only with green-leaved plants and white flowers. Another feature is a pond with two black swans and other ornamental ducks.

HYDE HALL GARDEN
(see RHS GARDEN HYDE HALL)

INGATESTONE HALL 12
Ingatestone, Essex. Tel: (01277) 353010

Lord Petre ★ From Ingatestone main street, take turning opposite the fire station. Signposted ★ Parking ★ Refreshments: tea-room ★ Toilet facilities ★ Suitable for wheelchairs ★ Shop ★ House open ★ Garden open 15th April to Sept, Fri – Sun and Bank Holiday Mon; also 12th July to Aug, Wed, Thurs, all 1 – 6pm ★ Entrance: £3.50, OAP and students £3, children £2

There have been buildings here since 950AD and the present house was built in the 1540s. There are gardens and immaculate lawns. A large stew-pond contemporary with the house provided fish and fresh-water mussels; it is now bordered by huge gunnera and shady walks. The walled garden has magnificent standard roses and a lily pond. There are various walks: a nut walk and a grass walk, but the lime walk is haunted by Bishop Benjamin Petre's dog which saved his life when he was set upon in 1740, and which still patrols. The extensive lawns have specimen trees: mulberries, *Magnolia grandiflora* and weeping beeches. The house, which is in a remarkable state of preservation, is well worth a visit.

LANGTHORN'S PLANTERY 13
Little Canfield, Dunmow, Essex. Tel: (01371) 876731

Mr and Mrs David Cannon ★ 5m E of M11 junction 8, on A120 ★ Parking ★ Toilet facilities (not disabled) ★ Suitable for wheelchairs ★ Plants for sale ★ Plantery open daily, 10am – 5pm ★ Garden open March to Oct, last week of every month ★ Entrance: free

The Cannons are avid collectors of unusual plants. They propagate in the nursery and Langthorn's stocks one of the widest ranges of plants in the country, over 1200 varieties of herbaceous perennials, many unusual forms of diascias, geraniums and salvias; 1300 varieties of shrubs and conservatory plants. Alpines, clematis and honeysuckles. The garden has now been re-vamped and will be open to the public on a limited basis.

LOWER DAIRY HOUSE   14
Little Horkesley, Colchester, Essex. Tel: (01206) 262220

Mr and Mrs D.J. Burnett ★ 7m N of Colchester off A134. Left at bottom of hill before Nayland Village, into Water Lane. Garden ½m on left after farm buildings ★ Parking ★ Teas ★ Toilet facilities ★ Plants for sale ★ Open April to 9th July, Sat, Sun and Bank Holiday Mons (but closed 22nd, 23rd April, 13th, 14th May), 2 – 6pm and by appointment ★ Entrance: £1, children 50p (1994 prices)

This plantsman's garden of one and a half acres is a riot of colour. Mrs Burnett fills any spaces in between the perennials with annuals – marigolds and larkspur and geraniums – all old-fashioned plants. Many unusual plants intermix with cottage garden varieties, including a good selection of cistus, diascias and other sun lovers. There is a pond where the thick planting consists of primulas, hostas and mimulus. A natural stream runs along one side providing bog gardens, a woodland dell, and bank of shrubs, roses and a variety of foliage trees. Spring bulbs are also a feature of the garden.

THE MAGNOLIAS   15
18 St Johns Avenue, Brentwood, Essex. Tel: (01277) 220019

Mr and Mrs R.A. Hammond ★ From A1023 turn S to A128. After 300 yards turn right at traffic lights, over railway bridge. St Johns Avenue is third on right ★ Restricted parking ★ Teas ★ Plants for sale ★ Open 26th March, 2nd, 16th, 23rd April, 7th, 14th, 28th May, 18th June, 23rd July, 20th Aug, 24th Sept, 22nd Oct, 10am – 5pm. Parties by appointment ★ Entrance: £1, children 50p

This fascinating half-acre plantsman's garden illustrates what can be achieved in a small space. Lawns are minimal. Paths wind through jungle-like borders filled with acers, camellias and magnolias underplanted with smaller shrubs and ground-cover plants. There is a large collection of hostas and unusual and rare bamboos. Some huge koi live in raised pools. Something of interest here at any time of the year.

OLIVERS   16
Olivers Lane, Colchester, Essex. Tel: (01206) 330575

Mr and Mrs David Edwards ★ 3m SW of Colchester between B1022 and B1026 (signposted 'Roman River Centre'). From Colchester via B1022 Maldon Road turn left at Leather Bottle pub mini-roundabout into Gosbeck's Road, right into Olivers Lane ★ Parking ★ Toilet facilities ★ Suitable for wheelchairs ★ Open 1st, 2nd, 29th, 30th April, 1st May, 1st, 2nd July, 2 – 6pm; also April to June, Wed, 2 – 5pm, and by appointment ★ Entrance: £1.50, children free

The moment you drive down to the attractive Georgian-fronted house and step on to the large York paved terrace, beautifully planted in soft sympathetic colours, you are entranced. Around you are 20 acres of garden and woodland in fine condition. From the terrace you look down over lawn, pools and woods to a natural meadow (cut only to encourage wild flowers and grasses) and to trees bordering the river. A 'willow pattern' bridge crosses the first of a succession of pools which drop down to an ancient fish pond. *Taxodium distichum*, metasequoia and gingko flourish by the pools. There are yew hedges and the delightful woodland walk. Here mature native trees shelter rhododendrons, azaleas and shrub roses in the rides.

PANFIELD HALL   17
Nr Braintree, Essex. Tel: (01376) 324512

Mr and Mrs R. Newman ★ 2m from Braintree. N off A120 through Great Saling, right to Panfield, through village and right into Hall Road ★ Parking ★ Cream teas ★ Toilet facilities ★ Suitable for wheelchairs ★ Dogs on lead ★ Plants for sale ★ Open by appointment and one day for charity, 2 – 6pm ★ Entrance: £1.50, OAP £1, children 50p

This four-acre garden surrounding an old house (1520) has been restored in the last few years and the herbaceous and shrub borders have been replanted. The rose garden is completed. Leading from there is a pergola with laburnum, wisterias and clematis already looking established. Crossing the bridge over the ponds is a box maze with roses in the triangular corner beds. There is a box and topiary maze here too. The long formal canal-like pool and statue are in memory of Mr Newman's parents. The clipped box crowns add to the feeling of formality which admirably offsets the house.

PARK FARM   18
**Chatham Hall Lane, Great Waltham, Chelmsford, Essex.
Tel: (01245) 360871**

Mr D. Bracey and Mrs J.E.M. Cowley ★ 5m N of Chelmsford. Take B1008 N through Broomfield. On Little Waltham bypass turn left into Chatham Hall Lane signposted to Howe Street; Park Farm is ½m on left ★ Parking ★ Teas ★ Toilet facilities ★ Plants for sale ★ Open 16th, 17th, 30th April, 1st, 7th, 8th, 28th, 29th May, 4th, 5th, 11th, 12th, 25th, 26th June, 9th, 10th July, 2 – 6pm. Parties by appointment ★ Entrance: £1, children 50p

Two acres of garden in separate 'rooms' formed by yew hedges with climbers obscuring the old farmhouse and dairy in the centre. Many different species of bulbs, shrubs, roses and herbaceous perennials. Design is still proceeding with new projects underway. The drought-affected pond is a current problem which will no doubt be solved by the enthusiastic Mrs Cowley.

POUND FARMHOUSE   19
Rayne, Nr Braintree, Essex. Tel: (01376) 326738

Mr and Mrs J.F. Swetenham ★ Off A120, 2m W of Braintree on the Shalford road from Rayne ★ Parking ★ Suitable for wheelchairs ★ Open by appointment and for charities 18th June, 2 – 6pm ★ Entrance: £1.50

This medium-sized garden with its imaginatively-planted and well-kept borders has been created over the last twenty years. The densely-planted wind-break trees, producing shade and dry conditions, block a view of the countryside from the house and consequently dictate the designs and choice of plants. It is a garden which can be seen all year, either for the blossom and bulbs in the spring, the roses and pond a little later, the flame border in July or the late-summer border in September.

REED HOUSE 20
Manor Lane, Great Chesterford, Saffron Walden, Essex.
Tel: (01799) 30312

Mrs Felicity Mason ★ 11m S of Cambridge, 4m N of Saffron Walden, 1m S of Stump Cross M11 junction. On B184 turn into Chesterford High Street. Turn left at Crown and Thistle public house into Manor Lane ★ Open by appointment to gardening groups of up to 30 and others ★ Entrance: £1.50 per person

Mrs Mason moved to her present house a few years ago, leaving a large garden (crammed with treasures) that used to be open to the public four times a year. Her new garden is a revelation as to what can be achieved in a short time. She designed the garden and planted everything herself. Features include sink gardens, koi carp in the pool, bulbs everywhere, clematis, a greenhouse bursting at its panes, and a new conservatory rapidly filling up with rare plants.

RHS GARDEN HYDE HALL ★ 21
Rettendon, Nr Chelmsford, Essex. Tel: (01245) 400256

The Royal Horticultural Society ★ 7m SE of Chelmsford, signposted from A130 ★ Parking ★ Light refreshments, hot and cold lunches ★ Toilet facilities ★ Suitable for wheelchairs ★ Plants for sale ★ Open 26th March to 29th Oct, Wed, Thurs, Sat, Sun and Bank Holidays, 11am – 6pm ★ Entrance: £2.50, children (6-16) 50p. Groups of 20 or more £2 per person

This attractively landscaped hill-top garden has a lily pond with beautifully-planted raised beds surrounding it. A dell with huge arum lilies, smilacinas, *Hydrangea villosa*, hellebores and autumn cyclamen. The National viburnum collection is here including *Viburnum cylindricum* with shiny leaves and large rather loose flowers, flowering in August. Also the prunus collection. Bupleurum with drifts of dark blue agapanthus and thorn apples. A rose walk with posts and ropes and climbers with clematis growing through them. A marvellous border with mixed shrubs and herbaceous plants – a rather startling but most successful mixture. Finally masses of crinums, pink and white. Everything beautifully grown and flourishing. And a greenhouse with datura 'Grand Marnier' covered in flowers even escaping from the open windows.

R. AND R. SAGGERS 22
Waterloo House, High Street, Newport, Saffron Walden, Essex.
Tel: (01799) 540858

R. and R. Saggers ★ On B1383 through Newport ★ Parking ★ Refreshments in adjoining café ★ Toilet facilities ★ Suitable for wheelchairs, but gravel paths ★ Plants for sale ★ Shop ★ Open Tues – Sun and Bank Holiday Mons, 10am – 5pm ★ Entrance: free

This small, immaculately-kept nursery has a charming town garden running down to a stream between flint walls. The nursery stocks old-fashioned roses, rare and unusual plants, grown and propagated by Mr R. Saggers who is a keen plantsman. Almost everything on sale is grown in the wide borders in front of the flint walls. Many exciting shrubs and herbaceous plants. A good range of statuary, lead urns, delightful stone pigs and square white wooden planters, Whichford pots, etc. On a small scale but excellent quality.

SALING HALL ★ 23
Great Saling, Nr Braintree, Essex.

Mr and Mrs Hugh Johnson ★ 6m NW of Braintree, halfway between Braintree and Dunmow on A120 turn N at the Saling Oak ★ Parking ★ Suitable for wheelchairs ★ Open for NGS May to July, Wed, 2 – 5pm and 25th June, 2 – 6pm. Parties by written appointment ★ Entrance: £2, children free

Hugh Johnson's wonderful garden is essentially for tree lovers. The huge elms died, and he turned the 12 acres of chalky boulder clay into an arboretum of genera that thrive on alkaline clay or gravel. A marvellous collection of pines, quercus, sorbus, aesculus, robinias, prunus, salix and betulas. Many rarities like *Cercis canadensis* 'Forest Pansy', *Eriobotrya japonica*, *Staphylea pinnata*, an unknown weeping juniper, incense cedars from Oregon seed and unusual pines on the east slope. The walled garden faces south west. Fruit trees are trimmed into mushroom shapes to contrast with a file of clipped cypress and a matching file of Irish junipers and pyramid box bushes. The borders are informal with grey and blue plants of rather typical Mediterranean associations – agapanthus, euphorbias, etc. The disciplined planting in the various sections creates a distinct atmosphere in each. There is a vegetable garden, a Japanese garden, a water garden (planted with gunneras, primulas, iris, etc.), a valley garden and a rose glade. The old moat with its cascade boasts some substantial carp.

STONE PINE ★ 24
Hyde Lane, Danbury, Chelmsford, Essex. Tel: (01245) 223232

Mr and Mrs David Barker ★ E of Chelmsford 1m S off A414 ★ Limited parking ★ Plants for sale occasionally ★ Open by appointment ★ Entrance: by charity box

This small plantsman's garden is owned by the former Chairman of the Hardy Plant Society. Mr Barker has filled it with choice and unusual plants. The area of grass is minimal and paths wind around borders crammed with trees, acers being particularly popular, and shrubs. Surprising plants appear around each corner like the rarely-seen *Paris quadrifolia*. Mr Barker is also knowledgeable on lilies, hemerocallis, hostas and grasses. National reference collections of epimedium and Japanese anemones.

TYE FARM 25
Elmstead Market, Colchester, Essex. Tel: (01206) 822400

Mr and Mrs C. Gooch ★ 2m from Colchester on A133, ½m before Elmstead Market ★ Parking ★ Suitable for wheelchairs ★ Open by appointment ★ Entrance: £2

This one-acre garden is cleverly planted with hedges to make compartments to break the prevailing wind. There is a neat vegetable garden with espaliered peach trees, a white garden and over 60 varieties of old roses planted with spring-flowering or autumn-colouring shrubs. Outside the conservatory is a formally-planted area for herbs, box-edged. The conservatory has many unusual plants in it, including a lemon tree and a mature *Rhododendron fragrantissima*.

VOLPAIA 26
54 Woodlands Road, Hockley, Essex. Tel: (01702) 203761

Mr and Mrs D. Fox ★ 2¼m NE of Rayleigh. On B1013 Rayleigh – Rochford road, turn S from Spa Hotel into Woodlands Road ★ Limited parking ★ Refreshments: tea ★ Open 16th April to 25th June, Thurs and Sun, 2.30 – 5.30pm and by appointment ★ Entrance: £1, children 30p

Here is a garden for plant lovers – not a garden for lovers of massed colour. From the lawn at the rear of the house, paths lead into natural woodland of mature oak, hornbeam and birch where all kinds of rhododendron, camellia and magnolia have been planted and now flourish. *Davidia involucrata*, cornus and eucryphia flower in turn. Woodland plants seldom seen elsewhere are at home here: trilliums, uvularias, disporums, erythroniums and Solomon's seal. Corners have been cut back to allow lilies to flower in summer and the willow gentian in autumn. There is a bog garden where primulas, gunneras, ferns, and hostas and the skunk cabbage find the moisture they love.

WARWICK HOUSE 27
Easton Lodge, Little Easton, Great Dunmow, Essex.
Tel: (01371) 873305

Mr and Mrs B. Creasey ★ 1m N of Great Dunmow on B184 then left to Little Easton. In ½m turn left to Easton Lodge and on 1¼m to white gates. House is ½m on right ★ Best season: May/June ★ Parking ★ Refreshments ★ Toilet facilities ★ Suitable for wheelchairs ★ Plants for sale ★ Open Feb, Sat and Sun, 12 noon – 4pm (subject to weather); 16th, 30th April, 6th May to 2nd July, Sat and Sun, 2 – 6pm and at other times by appointment. Parties welcome ★ Entrance: £1.50, children under 12 free

This wing of the former home of the Countess of Warwick (house now demolished) has a charming garden divided into a cobbled herringbone courtyard with a fountain and raised brick beds with massed agapanthus, clematis, and good colour contrast. Pots of orange and lemon trees, large azaleas and brugmansias. A good fernery. Heavy pergolas with wisteria and clematis, and a well-stocked conservatory. Lovely dovecot. A barbeque area and swimming pool, both well planted up. The garden is surrounded by woodland with mature birch trees. Part of the abandoned gardens, designed by Harold Peto at the turn of the century, has now been acquired.

WHEELCHAIR USERS

Please note that entries which describe a garden as 'suitable for wheelchairs' refer to the garden only. If there is a house open, it may or may not be suitable for wheelchairs.

GLOUCESTERSHIRE

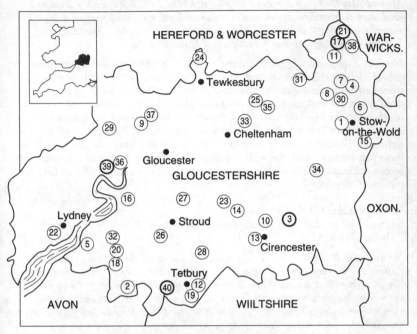

Two-starred gardens are ringed in bold

ABBOTSWOOD ★

1

Stow-on-the-Wold, Gloucestershire. Tel: (01451) 830173

Dikler Farming Co ★ 1m W of Stow-on-the-Wold on B4077 ★ Best season: spring ★ Parking free in grounds but no coaches. Coaches can drop passengers at the top gate and park in Stow ★ Teas ★ Toilet facilities ★ Partly suitable for wheelchairs ★ Open 16th April, 7th, 21st May, 4th, 18th June, 1.30 – 6pm ★ Entrance: £2, children free

The house is in one of the most beautiful of Cotswold settings. From the car park it is approached up a descending stream and pools towards the woodland carpeted with spring flowers and bulbs, including one of the largest displays of fritillaries. The woods continue above and beyond the house and have been planted with rhododendrons, flowering shrubs and specimen trees. Near the house are formal gardens and terraces including a box-edged rose garden and a water garden. Extensive heather plantings. The gardens round the house (once owned by Harry Ferguson, the tractor man) are by Lutyens. Note especially his lily pool running up to the house; there is a jet of water there which, if the angle of the sun is right, shimmers spectacularly. Alas other vertical features by Lutyens were removed by an earlier owner, though the planting remains faithful to his design.

ALDERLEY GRANGE ★ 2
Alderley, Gloucestershire. Tel: (01453) 842161

Mr Guy and the Hon. Mrs Acloque ★ 2m S of Wotton-under-Edge. Turn NW off A46 Bath – Stroud road at Dunkirk ★ Best season: April to July ★ Parking ★ Suitable for wheelchairs ★ Open by appointment during June ★ Entrance: £1.50, children free

A garden of exceptional beauty and character in tranquil walled setting, renowned for its collection of aromatic plants and scented flowers. Designed by the late Alvilde Lees-Milne and believed to be the last garden in which Vita Sackville-West had a hand, Alderley Grange was acquired by the present owners in 1974 and has been immaculately maintained and developed with discretion and style. The fine house and a mulberry tree date from the seventeenth century; a pleached and arched lime walk leads to a series of enclosed gardens. There is a notable hexagonal herb garden with many delightful perspectives of clipped, trained or potted shrubs and trees. There are abundant plantings of old roses. Many tender and unusual subjects flourish in this cherished and exquisite space, which has been much photographed and drawn.

BARNSLEY HOUSE ★★ 3
Barnsley, Cirencester, Gloucestershire. Tel: (01285) 740281

Mrs Rosemary Verey ★ 4m NE of Cirencester on A433/B4425 in village of Barnsley ★ Parking, inc. coaches ★ Toilet facilities ★ Partly suitable for wheelchairs ★ Plants for sale ★ Open all year, Mon, Wed, Thurs and Sat, 10am – 6pm ★ Entrance: £2, OAP £1, children free. Season ticket £4. Dec to Feb no charge. Parties by appointment

A splendid small garden of four acres, but comprising many garden styles from the past, carefully blended by the Vereys since they acquired the house in 1951. The William and Mary stone house is set in the middle of the garden, surrounded on two sides by a stone wall built in 1770. Borders create vistas and divide the garden into different areas with their own interesting features. The standard of horticulture and maintenance is very high. Great attention has been given to colour and texture. The kitchen garden is a particular delight with numerous small beds, ornate paths, box hedges, trained fruit trees, etc. A very popular garden with visitors so if you require solitude try to avoid peak-hour travel.

BATSFORD ARBORETUM ★ 4
Moreton-in-Marsh, Gloucestershire.
Tel: (01608) 650722 (weekdays), (01386) 700409 (weekends)

The Batsford Foundation ★ 1½m NW of Moreton-in-Marsh on A44 to Evesham. Opposite the entrance to Sezincote (see entry) ★ Best season: spring and autumn ★ Parking ★ ✩Refreshments: coffees, light lunches and teas. Picnic area ★ Toilet facilities ★ Dogs on lead in arboretum ★ Plants for sale at garden centre open all year 10am – 5pm ★ Falconry Centre open ★ Arboretum open March to mid-Nov, daily, 10am – 5pm ★ Entrance: £2, OAP and children £1.50, under 14 free, pre-booked groups of 12 or more £1.50 per person (1994 prices)

Over 1500 species of different trees in 50 acres of typical Cotswold countryside plus an unusual collection of exotic shrubs and bronze statues from the Far East, originally collected for the garden by Lord Redesdale. It was expanded by the first Lord Dulverton in the 1960s. For students, a guide-book gives the details, but everyone will enjoy the effects, particularly the autumn colours. The late Arthur Hellyer used to enjoy the Japanese rest house and the bronzes Redesdale brought back from Japan. Fine views of the house (not open). There is also a water garden and, nearby, a falconry centre. Sezincote (see entry) is opposite, and up the hill is the new garden at Bourton House (see entry).

BERKELEY CASTLE 5
Berkeley, Gloucestershire. Tel: (01453) 810332

Mr R.J.G. Berkeley ★ W of M5 between junctions 13 and 14 just off A38 ★ Parking ★ Tea rooms and picnic lawn ★ Toilet facilities ★ Shop ★ House open ★ Butterfly farm ★ Garden open April, daily except Mon, 2 – 5pm, May to Sept, Tues – Sat, 11am – 5pm, Sun, 2 – 5pm, Oct, Sun, 2 – 4.30pm, Bank Holiday Mon, 11am – 5pm ★ Entrance: £1, children 50p (castle and gardens £3.90, OAP £3, children £1.90) (1994 prices). Special prices for parties

Apart from Windsor, Berkeley is the oldest inhabited castle in Britain. Its history, full of incident, includes the brutal murder of Edward II after his failure to succumb to the stench of putrefying carcasses in the dungeon below his prison room. An entertaining guided tour of the immaculately-maintained castle may be followed by a walk in the extensive parkland, with lovely views over gentle, unspoilt Gloucestershire landscape. There is an Elizabethan bowling lawn, a lily pond and terraced beds simply planted with many unusual shrubs and ramblers which tumble and climb against the imposing castle walls, their colours in the sun reminiscent of rose and lavender pot pourri.

BLOCKLEY VILLAGE GARDENS 6
Nr Moreton-in-Marsh, Gloucestershire.

There are nine gardens open for charity during the summer in this picturesque hilly Cotswold village. Most of them are on steep hillsides, and often tricky for visitors with creaking knees, and impossible for wheelchairs ★ Parking difficult ★ Teas available ★ Entrance: £2 for nine gardens (1994 price)

Three of the gardens are also open by appointment. *Old Mill Dene.* Mr and Mrs B.S. Dare, (01386) 700457 [Open by appointment and 22nd, 29th June, 6th, 13th July]. A charming garden nestling at the bottom of the valley, and built around the mill pond and stream, and climbing in terraces up the steep hillside. Each terrace has a different character and planting scheme, and the top garden is Mrs Dare's *potager* – productive and beauti-ful, with a gardener's seat in an arbour enjoying lovely views. *Peartrees.* Mrs J. Beckwith, (01386) 700464 [Open by appointment]. A walled cottage garden, crammed with treasures, and with happy planting associations. The front garden is planted in gravel, and is south-facing, for dry-heat-loving plants. *Paxton House.* Mr and Mrs P. Cator, (01386) 700213 [Open by appointment and 1st May, 25th July]. A garden sheltered by magnificent walls, clothed with roses and clematis – again on different levels, and with many mature interesting shrubs and ornamental trees.

BOURTON HOUSE 7
Bourton-on-the-Hill, Nr Moreton-in-Marsh, Gloucestershire.

Mr and Mrs R. Paice ★ 2m W of Moreton-in-Marsh on A44 ★ Parking across road ★ Refreshments: DIY tea and coffee in historic barn ★ Toilet facilities ★ Unusual plants for sale ★ Open 25th May to 29th Sept, Thurs and Fri and 29th May, 28th Aug, 12 noon – 5pm ★ Entrance: £2.50, children free

This exceptionally handsome eighteenth-century Cotswold village house with fine views is enhanced by a medium-sized garden largely created under the present ownership. The diminutive geometrical *potager* is a particular delight. Well-kept lawns, quiet fountains, a knot garden and Cotswold stone walls set off a number of herbaceous borders in which the choice and arrangement of plants and shrubs skilfully use current fashions in garden design. Each year there are new delights – the raised pond in the top garden, a topiary walk, and long terraces on the main lawn now planted with low-growing shrubs, perennials and alpines. Nearby Sezincote and Batsford, and Hidcote as well as Kiftsgate (see entries) are less than half an hour away and make Bourton House a sensible location to include in garden touring in this part of Gloucestershire.

BURNT NORTON 8
Near Chipping Campden, Gloucestershire. Tel: (01386) 840162

The Earl of Harrowby ★ 1½m N of Chipping Campden on road to Mickleton, left into farm lane as road goes downhill, then through wood for ½m ★ Parking ★ Teas ★ Suitable for wheelchairs ★ Plants for sale ★ Open by appointment (phone caretaker) ★ Entrance: £2, children free

Burnt Norton is famous because T.S. Eliot, staying in 1934 at a nearby house (now a grand hotel), went over to see the estate in the belief that it belonged to a Birmingham businessman. In fact it was one of several residences of the Harrowby family whose ancestor had purchased it in the mid-eighteenth century, and its extensive terraces, rose gardens, etc., appealed to the poet whose mind at the time was concentrating on the thought that 'Time present and time past/Are both perhaps present in time future/And time future contained in time past.' The result was the most famous poem in the *Four Quartets* series. Visitors with literary interests will find it useful to have a copy to hand. Others will enjoy the bluebell walk, the classical pavilion, the deserted pools and the brick terraces. Good views. Reminiscent of Hidcote.

CAMP COTTAGE 9
Highleadon, Gloucestershire. Tel: (01452) 790352

Mr L.R. Holmes and Mr S. O'Neill ★ 6m W of Gloucester. From Gloucester take A40 Ross road, turn right onto B4215 Newent road. 2½m along, turn right at sign for Upleadon (Highleadon garage on left side at turn). Cottage is 100 yards up lane on left hand side ★ Best season: May to July ★ Parking on main road outside ★ Refreshments: tea and soft drinks ★ Plants for sale ★ Open 26th Feb, 5th, 12th, 19th, 26th March, 11am – 3pm; 16th April to 29th Aug, every Sun, Tues and Bank Holiday Mon; also 22nd May to 10th July, Mon, 2 – 6pm and by appointment ★ Entrance: £1, children 50p

Picturesque seventeenth-century timbered cottage in a sheltered setting surrounded by richly-planted cottage garden. An extensive network of pergolas and arches bears a splendid collection of old roses, honeysuckles, unusual climbers and ramblers. Old-fashioned herbaceous plants and self-sown annuals pack every niche in the garden, whose rich river silt base supports prodigious colonies of opium and Welsh poppies. It is hard to believe that the present owners have built up this lavish, multi-tiered display only since 1988. Newly-created bog garden.

CERNEY HOUSE   10
North Cerney, Nr Cirencester, Gloucestershire.
Tel: (01285) 831300/831205

Sir Michael and Lady Angus ★ 4m N of Cirencester on A435 Cheltenham road, behind famous thirteenth-century church ★ Best season: May/June ★ Parking ★ ☆Teas. Lunches and high teas by prior arrangement ★ Toilet facilities ★ Suitable for wheelchairs ★ Plants for sale ★ Shop ★ Open Feb to Oct, Tues, Wed and Fri, 2 – 6pm and one Sun in May for charity (when adjacent Scrubditch Farm is also open). Open at other times and for parties by appointment ★ Entrance: £1.50, children free

Around the house, remodelled by Decimus Burton in 1791, goats and sheep graze and wild flowers flourish in their meadow. The pleasantly unmanicured three and a half-acre garden is not for those who like everything tickety-boo – the plants are happy and unrestrained. There are lawns, shrubs and trees around the house, and behind it a large walled garden restored since the mid-1980s with riotous herbaceous borders, vegetables, many old roses, clematis and a delightful children's story-book pig (a Gloucester Old Spot, of course) beneath the apple trees nearby. A woodland walk is carpeted with snowdrops in February and bluebells in May. There is a colourful rockery behind the house, with a waterfall. The herb garden and pink border beside the swimming pool are now well established. The area is rich in Roman history, with Chedworth Roman Villa a few miles away.

CHIPPING CAMPDEN GARDENS   11
Chipping Campden, Gloucestershire.

N of A44 between Evesham and Stow-on-the-Wold and S of Stratford-upon-Avon off A46 E of Broadway ★ Parking ★ Refreshments: ample facilities in town for all needs ★ Public toilets in town

Because of its position near Hidcote, Kiftsgate and Stratford the town is a popular holiday stopping-off point for garden visitors, so it is fortuitous that it has two small gardens frequently open.

Mr and Mrs Lusty's is entered through their house *The Martins* in the main street, which is itself next door to Mrs Lusty's interior decorating shop The Green Dragon and behind the butter market. It is a long, narrow town garden, with houses and a drive on one side, which has triumphed over its location by being cleverly designed to give surprises, informality, shelter and a wide variety of plants. Two levels are used, forming divisions with grass paths around small borders and beds. There is a spendid mulberry tree. Visitors are invited to contribute to charity, and the garden is open from April to Oct, although it is occasionally closed on Sun or when it rains hard so check with the shop (01386) 840379 in case.

Another town garden normally open all the year is the *Ernest Wilson Memorial Garden*, also in the High Street. It was opened in 1984 in memory of 'Chinese' Wilson, who was born in Chipping Campden in 1876. The famous collector is estimated to have introduced 1200 species of trees and shrubs during his career and the garden includes several of his finds including *Acer griseum*, the paperbark maple, *Davidia involucrata*, the pocket-handkerchief tree, and the plant for which he wished to be remembered, the *Lilium regale*. It is a peaceful oasis, with seats and shade, backed by the beautiful church tower. Admission is free with a box for contributions to its upkeep set in the stone wall beside the entrance arch.

Other gardens in Campden and neighbouring Broad Campden are open for charity and for the past three years a charity has arranged for 30 gardens to open over a June weekend. This will probably become an annual event. The choice of gardens appears to have been dictated by a desire for quantity rather than quality, and in general their appeal will be to those who like what is now called the traditional Cotswold style.

THE CHIPPING CROFT   12
The Chipping, Tetbury, Gloucestershire. Tel: (01666) 503570

Dr and Mrs P. Taylor ★ In the centre of the town proceed between The Snooty Fox and Barclays – past parking in Chipping Square – garden is on left at bottom behind stone wall with tall trees, entrance in driveway to courtyard ★ Teas on 23rd April and 11th June ★ Dogs ★ Open by appointment and 23rd April, 11th, 18th June for charity, 2 – 6pm ★ Entrance: £2

This is a most unusual town garden because of its size and character. Entering through a courtyard leading to a large and immaculately-maintained lawn bordered by mature trees and a wooded walk, it extends to about two acres and is on three levels. At one time, the eighteenth-century house was used as a school, and since 1985 Dr Taylor has transformed a hard-surfaced playground area into a courtyard with a small rectangular raised pool, replanted extensively, constructed a summerhouse/potting shed and new steps connecting the various levels. Three formal terrace-gardens contain a variety of cottage garden flowers as well as unusual plants, vegetables and herbs with the kitchen garden proper laid out as a *potager* on a higher level. Beneath the terraces is a wide walk with borders either side and arches covered with roses, honeysuckle and clematis leading back to the house.

CIRENCESTER GARDENS   13
Cirencester, Gloucestershire.

On W side of Cirencester, leading up to entrance to Cirencester Park ★ Parking ★ Toilet facilities ★ Plants for sale

The grandest garden in the town, *Cirencester Park*, is sometimes only open once a year in aid of charity but the park is open all the year round, courtesy of Lord Apsley. Note the perimeter hedge, claimed to be the largest in the world, planted in 1720 by the first Earl Bathurst. It is 40ft high. Some gardens in Cecily Hill, near the park gates, are open occasionally for charity but alas the gardens at *Little Tulsa* which were of such grandeur under the Becks have gone to seed while the house was being sold. Perhaps the new owners will be able to work a miracle. *Cecily Hill House*, owned by Mr and

Mrs Rupert de Zoete, has a small ornamental kitchen garden of original design and unusual vegetables. It is open once a year in July but can be visited by appointment, (01285) 653766. Five to ten minutes walk from Cecily Hill at *20 St Peter's Road* is a 70 foot garden entirely without grass, with a small rockery, cascade and pond and 18 varieties of clematis which would be of considerable interest to anyone having to design for such a small space. Meg and Jeff Blumson open by appointment as well as their charity Sun openings twice in the summer, (01285) 657696. The Becks have moved to *25 Bowling Green Road* and their new garden will be open some Sunday afternoons in June, July and August, so ring (01285) 653778 for details.

CONDERTON MANOR
(see Hereford and Worcester)

COTSWOLD FARM   14
Duntisbourne Abbots, Gloucestershire. Tel: (01285) 653856

Major and Mrs P.D. Birchall ★ 5m N of Cirencester on A417; signed immediately W of Five Mile House Inn ★ Best season: May to July ★ Parking at house ★ Toilet facility ★ Open by appointment (adequate notice appreciated) ★ Entrance: £2

Mature garden planted in grand style and sustained with sensitive artistry surrounding fine old house in superb Cotswold setting. Terrace designed by Norman Jewson in 1938. Formal walled gardens with pools and planted with shrub roses, lavender and a collection of scented flowers. Established plantings of shrubs, herbaceous plants and many small treasures overlooking an unspoilt wooded valley. A charmed garden redolent of another age in a remote and lovely situation.

DAYLESFORD HOUSE ★   15
Daylesford, Stow-on-the-Wold, Gloucestershire. Tel: (01608) 659777

Sir Anthony and Lady Bamford ★ Off A436 between Stow-on-the-Wold and Chipping Norton ★ Parking ★ ☆Teas ★ Toilet facilities ★ Suitable for wheelchairs ★ Plants for sale ★ Open one Wed in mid-April and one late June, 2 – 6pm ★ £1.50

Like nearby Sezincote, Daylesford House was designed by Samuel Pepys Cockerell. Warren Hastings, the first Governor General of India, bought the Daylesford Estate in 1785; he was very interested in gardening and built the large walled garden before the house was complete. This was stocked with exotic plants and fruits, and a yak which he brought back from India roamed around the grounds which were extensive. John Davenport was employed to design the layout of the garden, the lakes and the Gothic orangery. The garden is a delight, with its magnificent lawns and lakes complete with swans and Canada geese, woodland walks (carpeted with primroses in April, bluebells in May), orangery full of unusual shrubs, trellised rose garden and the decorative formal fruit and vegetable walled garden with orchid house, peach house and working glasshouses. A great deal for the plantsman and others to see, even though Lady Bamford says 'the garden is still being developed and not yet in anything like finalised state'.

FRAMPTON COURT 16
Frampton-on-Severn, Gloucestershire.
Tel: (01452) 740267 (home); (01452) 740698 (office)

Mrs Peter Clifford ★ SW of Gloucester near Stonehouse, 2m from M5 junction 13. Signposted. Left hand side of village green, entrance through imposing gates in long wall between two large chestnut trees ★ Best season: May to Sept ★ Parking ★ Refreshments in village hall on selected days ★ Suitable for wheelchairs ★ House open by appointment with guided tours by owner. £3.50 per person; £4 per person for parties of four or fewer ★ Garden open all year by appointment ★ Entrance: £1

Home of their lady ancestors, the botanic artists who painted *The Frampton Flora* 1830-1860, Frampton Court remains an elegant family establishment on land owned by the Clifford family since the twelfth century. The house, dating from the 1730s, is of the Vanbrugh school, with exquisite interior woodwork and furnishings which may be shown by appointment to visitors, preferably in parties, by the present owner Mrs Peter Clifford. The five-acre grounds are maintained with a minimum of labour and contain a lake, fine trees and a formal water garden of Dutch design, believed to have been built by the architects of the larger Westbury Court Garden on the other side of the Severn. A Strawberry Hill Gothic Orangery 1750 (not always open but available for holiday letting), where the ladies are believed to have executed their work, stands reflected in the still water, planted with lilies and flanked by a mixed border. This garden is open in association with that of Frampton Manor, also occupied by Cliffords, where a strongly-planted walled garden with many old roses is splendidly set off by a fine fifteenth-century timbered house.

HIDCOTE MANOR GARDEN ★★ 17
Hidcote Bartrim, Chipping Campden, Gloucestershire.
Tel: (01386) 438333

The National Trust ★ Follow signposts from Chipping Campden or Mickleton near Stratford-on-Avon ★ Parking but coaches by prior arrangement ★ Refreshments: in licensed restaurant or in Plant Centre light refreshment area. No picnics ★ Toilet facilities ★ Partly suitable for wheelchairs ★ Plants for sale ★ Shop ★ Garden open April to Oct, daily except Tues and Fri, 11am – 7pm (last admission 6pm or 1 hour before sunset if earlier). Parties by written appointment only. Liable to overcrowding on Bank Holiday Mons and fine Suns ★ Entrance: £5, children £2.50, family (2 adults and up to 4 children) £13.75. No party concessions

It is unnecessary to describe this garden in detail, as it is one of the most famous in Britain and an essential visit for garden lovers of every persuasion. Created by Lawrence Johnston in the early years of the twentieth century. Johnston had a strong sense of design and great skill in planting, using mainly nineteenth-century specimens. Many varieties now bear the name Hidcote. Given to The National Trust in 1948, its splendid architectural effects and bold plantings have been retained, and those visitors who query the use of annuals may like to know that Johnston also used several half-hardy varieties, even more of which are used today to prolong the flowering season in the Old Garden, Red Borders, etc. Johnston's achievement is all the more remarkable because of the isolation of the hill-top site whose scale can be appreciated by the view from the entrance to Kiftsgate garden which is within walking distance (see entry). See also Vale House, Chipping Camden and Sezincote.

HILL HOUSE ★   18
Wickwar, Nr Wotton-under-Edge, Gloucestershire.
Tel: (01454) 294304

Dr and Mrs Richard Adlam ★ Take A46 then A432 to Chipping Sodbury, A4060 to Wickwar and B4509 down the hill. Hill House is on the left ★ Parking in lane and paddock beyond house ★ ☆Teas ★ Toilet facilities ★ Suitable for wheelchairs ★ Plants for sale ★ Open 14th May, 11th June and at other times for parties by arrangement ★ Entrance: £1.50, children 50p

To enter this garden is to be enticed into a magical world of grass walks, leafy arbours, pools and woodland, the whole exuding an atmosphere of mystery and romance. For this is a very romantic garden, the creation of the late Duchess of Westminster whose overriding philosophy of rare trees and shrubs planted in exuberance is very much in evidence today. But the present owners, drawing on the firm foundation and experience of their predecessor, are imposing their own personalities, and their enthusiasm and commitment continue to carry the garden forward. In an area of some four acres, mainly walled, roses tumble from trees, the June ox-eye daisy, informally planted throughout, carries the eye along sweeping borders into enclosures where wild flowers mingle with drifts of spring bulbs. A pair of herbaceous borders, framed by pleached limes, are a particular delight. So, too, is a handsome specimen of the rarely-seen *Berberis temolaica* whose purplish shoots become glaucous with age. Vegetables, neatly planted on a sloping site, provide additional interest as do the aviaries of exotic birds.

HODGES BARN ★   19
Shipton Moyne, Tetbury, Gloucestershire. Tel: (01666) 880202

Mr and Mrs Charles Hornby ★ 3m S of Tetbury on the Malmesbury side of Shipton Moyne. From the A433 Tetbury – Bath road, Shipton Moyne is sign-posted. Drive through the village, past the Cat and Custard Pot pub, bear left and a few hundred yards after leaving the village, the towers of Hodges Barn will be visible on the left ★ Parking ★ Teas by arrangement for parties ★ Suitable for wheelchairs ★ Unusual lime-tolerant plants for sale ★ Open April to 15th Aug, Mon, Tues, Fri, 2 – 5pm and 16th April, 28th May, 2nd July, 2 – 6pm. Also by appointment. Parties welcome ★ Entrance: £2.50, groups of 25 or more £2 per person, children free

In 1499 this was built as a dovecot or columbarium to a large house nearby, the latter burnt down in 1556. It was converted to a home in 1938 and bought by the Hon. Mrs Arthur Strutt, the present owner's grandmother, in 1946, and she set about creating the basic structure of the garden with good stone walls and topiary. She also planted most of the trees before her death in 1973. Another influence on the present garden was the once-famous Pusey House, near Faringdon, owned by Mr Hornby's parents, who supplied some of the fine plants at Hodges Barn. It is an extensive eight-acre garden, with plenty of interest for everyone – above all those who like roses (there are well over 100 different varieties). The spring garden, water garden, little wild woodland, the large cleared wood, the topiary and the splendid lawns are all enjoyable. The plantings reflect the owners' interest in colour, scent and variety, and they have not been inhibited by a desire to prevent one flower or shrub from growing into another. Note the planting in gravel along some of the many beds, and the tapestry hedges. This is a garden which reeks of enthusiasm and long may it continue.

HUNTS COURT   20
North Nibley, Dursley, Gloucestershire. Tel: (01453) 547440

Mr and Mrs T.K. Marshall ★ 2m NW of Wotton–under–Edge near North Nibley. Turn E off B4060 in Nibley at the Black Horse Inn and fork left after ¼m ★ Best season: June ★ Parking ★ ☆Teas on Suns only ★ Toilet facilities ★ Suitable for wheelchairs ★ Nursery open 9am – 5.30pm ★ Garden open all year except Aug, Tues – Sat, 2 – 6pm. Also 11th June to 9th July, Suns and by appointment ★ Entrance: £1

A must for those with a love of old roses. June sees in excess of 400 varieties – species, climbing and shrub – filling the borders, cascading the rails, pergolas and trees and spilling out over the informal grass paths which weave a passage through rare shrubs and herbaceous perennials. A more formal sundial garden, recently developed, the beds intersected with gravel paths, is colour co–ordinated and provides a home for hardy geraniums, penstemons and diascias. In another area mown paths draw the eye towards the Cotswold escarpment which commands the eastern landscape. Summer is inevitably dominated by roses but this is not to deny interest in other seasons for this is a garden to provide something of note for the greater part of the year. In the adjoining nursery many of the plants growing in the garden are on sale and the owner is on hand with helpful advice. A useful leaflet is available.

KIFTSGATE COURT ★★   21
Chipping Campden, Gloucestershire. Tel: (01386) 438777

Mr and Mrs J.G. Chambers ★ 3m NE of Chipping Campden and near Mickleton. Kiftsgate is next to Hidcote Manor which is signposted ★ Parking ★ Plants for sale ★ Open April to Sept, Wed, Thurs, Suns, 2 – 6pm. Also Sats in June and July, and Bank Holiday Mons, 2 – 6pm (NB not identical opening times with Hidcote). Coach parties by appointment only ★ Entrance: £3, children £1

The house was built in the mid–nineteenth century on this magnificent site surrounded by three steep banks. The garden was largely created by the present owner's grandmother, who with her husband moved there after World War I. Her work was continued by her daughter, Diana Binny, who made a few alterations but continued the colour schemes of the borders. In spring, the white sunken garden is covered with bulbs and there is a fine show of daffodils along the drive. June and July are the peak months for colour and scent but the magnificent old and species roses are the glory of this garden, home of *Rosa* 'Kiftsgate'. Other features are perennial geraniums, a large wisteria and many species of hydrangea, some very large. In autumn, Japanese maples glow in the bluebell wood. This garden should not be missed, not only because of its proximity to Hidcote, but because of its profusion of colour and apparent informality. Unusual plants are sometimes amongst those available for sale. Vale House (see entry) is nearby.

LYDNEY PARK GARDENS 22
Lydney, Gloucestershire. Tel: (01594) 842844

Lord Bledisloe ★ 20m SW of Gloucester. N of A48 between Lydney and Aylburton ★ Parking ★ Refreshments: teas. Picnics in deer park ★ Toilet facilities ★ Dogs on lead ★ Shrubs for sale ★ Roman site and museum open ★ Gardens open 16th April to 28th May, Suns, Weds and Bank Holiday Mons; 29th May to 4th June, daily, 11am – 6pm. Parties by appointment in season ★ Entrance: £2 except Wed when £1. Car and accompanied children free

The park dates back to the seventeenth century and although it has been in the hands of one family since 1723, a new house was built in 1875 and the old one demolished. A new start was made on the garden in 1950 when the terrace was paved and a line of cypresses 'Kilmacurragh' planted to frame the view. An area near the house has an interesting collection of magnolias but the most picturesque sight is the bank of daffodils and cherries, splendid in season. From 1957, a determined attempt has been made to plant rhododendrons and azaleas in the wooded valley, behind and below the house, with the aim of achieving bold colour at different times between March and June. Near the entrance to the main part of the gardens there is a small pool surrounded by azaleas and a collection of acers. From here the route passes through carefully-planted groups of rhododendrons and by a folly, brought from Venice as recently as 1961. This overlooks a valley and bog garden. Criss-crossing the hillside, there are rare and fine rhododendrons and azaleas, including an area planted with un-named seedlings. Enormous effort has gone into the plant design, colour combination and general landscaping, and those who are enthusiastic about rhododendrons, azaleas and camellias will find enough to enjoy for a whole day. Nearby is the Roman camp and museum containing the famous bronze Lydney dog. Guide book with map available.

MISARDEN PARK GARDENS ★ 23
Miserden, Stroud, Gloucestershire. Tel: (01285) 821303

Major M.T.N.H. Wills ★ 7m SW from Gloucester, 3m from A417. Signposted ★ Parking ★ Toilet facilities ★ Suitable for wheelchairs ★ Nursery adjacent to garden ★ Garden open 4th April to 28th Sept, Tues, Wed and Thurs, 9.30am – 4.30pm and probably 9th April, 2nd July, 2 – 6pm. Pre-booked parties by appointment ★ Entrance: £2 (inc. printed guide), children free. Reduction for parties of 20 or more

This lovely, timeless English garden has most of the features that one expects from a garden of the early twentieth century. There are extensive yew hedges (some topiary by Lutyens), a York stone terrace, a loggia overhung with wisteria, a good specimen of *Magnolia* x *soulangiana*. The south lawn sports very splendid grass steps. West of the house the ground ascends to the nursery in a series of grassed terraces. There are two very good herbaceous borders leading to a traditional rose garden beyond. Many fine specimen trees. The spring show of blossom and bulbs is particularly good. The gardens command excellent views over the famous Golden Valley. The Manor House (seventeenth–century) is not open.

THE OLD MANOR 24
Twyning, Nr Tewkesbury, Gloucestershire. Tel: (01684) 293516

Mrs Joan Wilder ★ 3m N of Tewkesbury via A38; follow signs to Twyning. The garden is at the T-junction at west end of the village ★ Best season: April to June ★ Parking ★ Tea and biscuits on Bank Holiday Mons only ★ Toilet facilities ★ Suitable for wheelchairs ★ Small specialist nursery ★ Garden open March to Oct, Mons, 2 – 5pm (or dusk if earlier) ★ Entrance: £1.50, children 50p

Plantswoman's garden packed with treasures developed over 35 years partly on the site of a Queen Anne manor. Ancient abbey masonry, churchyard headstones and old brick walls with pineapples give atmosphere to a series of separated contained spaces featuring a pool garden, fern, peat and scree beds, troughs and a renowned 'snake bed'. A connoisseur's collection of plants including many species; unusual plants available from nursery.

ORCHARD COTTAGE 25
Duglinch Lane, Gretton, Nr Winchcombe, Gloucestershire. Tel: (01242) 602491

Mr Rory Stuart ★ In Gretton (off B4078) up Duglinch Lane to the left of the Bugatti Inn. Approximately 300 yards up lane on right opposite black railings ★ Limited parking in driveway ★ Plants for sale ★ Open all year by appointment only ★ Entrance: £1 for charity

Well past the somewhat unpromising suburban beginnings of Duglinch Lane and tucked into the hillside near the famous Bugatti Club's Prescott Hill Climb is this romantic cottage garden created largely by the present owner's aunt, the late Mrs Nancy Saunders, in the 1950s, and featured in *The Englishwoman's Garden*. She was helped by the late John Codrington, whom she met on a botanical expedition. Its approximately one and a half acres consist of an old orchard with a variety of unusual shrubs and trees, from which there is a splendid view towards Bredon Hill, and the garden around the cottage. Mrs Saunders derived great pleasure from collecting plants during her travels abroad, bringing them home in her sponge-bag. The wide range of planting is for all-year interest but if hellebores are your particular passion February to March would be the best time to see the extensive collection. Sudeley Castle (see entry) is nearby.

OWLPEN MANOR ★ 26
Uley, Nr Dursley, Gloucestershire. Tel: (01453) 860261

Mr and Mrs N. Manders ★ 3m E of Dursley on B4066. 1m E of Uley ★ Parking ★ Refreshments ★ Toilet facilities ★ House open ★ Garden open April to Sept, Tues, Thurs, Sun and Bank Holiday Mons, 2 – 5pm ★ Entrance: £3.20, children £1.50

Situated in a remote Cotswold valley surrounded by hills is this half-acre 'little hillside garden' as Gertrude Jekyll described it. The formal garden, laid out on five terraces and partially hidden by a regiment of yews, dates from the 1720s. A bowling green remains from an earlier period, as well as a yew room and a small typical manor house garden, still in process of restoration.

PAINSWICK ROCOCO GARDEN ★ 27
The Stables, Painswick House, Painswick, Gloucestershire.
Tel: (01452) 813204

Lord and Lady Dickinson ★ ½m from Painswick on B4073. Signposted ★ Best season: spring ★ Parking ★ Refreshments: teas and lunches ★ Toilet facilities ★ Plants for sale ★ Shop ★ Garden open 11th Jan to Nov, Wed – Sun and on Bank Holiday Mons, 11am – 5pm ★ Entrance: £2.60, OAP £2.20, children £1.30. Coaches by appointment

A great deal of time, money and effort is going into the restoration (almost complete redevelopment) of this rare rococo survival. Much of the work is now completed with new plantings becoming established. At present, the best features are the eighteenth-century garden buildings, the views into especially beautiful surrounding countryside, and the marvellous snowdrop wood spanning a stream that flows from a pond at the lower end. This must be one of the best displays of naturalised snowdrops in England. There are some splendid beech woods and older specimen trees. Wildflowers are allowed complete freedom. Rococo gardening was an eighteenth-century combination of formal geometric features with winding woodland paths, revealing sudden incidents and vistas – in essence, a softening of the formal French style, apparent from about 1715 onwards in all forms of art. A painting by Thomas Robins (1716-1778) is the basis for Painswick's restoration, done in 1748 for Benjamin Hyett who created the garden in the grounds of the house built by his father in 1735. It is a large estate and visitors (who should be fit for some steep inclines) must allow three-quarters of an hour or more even for a brisk walk round its many beauties. Alas no picnicing, but pleasant tearooms near the house for refreshment after a worthwhile effort.

THE PRIORY
(see Hereford and Worcester)

RODMARTON MANOR ★ 28
Rodmarton, Gloucestershire. Tel: (01285) 841253

Mr and Mrs Simon Biddulph ★ 6m SW of Cirencester, 4m NE of Tetbury off A433 ★ Teas by prior arrangement ★ Suitable for wheelchairs ★ A few plants for sale ★ Open 13th May to 26th Aug, Sats only, 2 – 5pm and at other times by appointment ★ Entrance: £1.50 on Sats and £2 at other times

This much praised garden has been featured in numerous books and magazines over the years. It is a good example of an 'English' garden in the classical sense, but firmly of this century. The garden is famous for its fine hedges of yew, beech and holly. The drive to the manor house, designed by Ernest Barnsley, lies between two immaculately clipped tall beech hedges. There is much good topiary, a lovely hornbeam avenue and many fine vistas. The herbaceous borders, terrace and leisure gardens are of particular interest. Great emphasis has had to be placed on labour-saving schemes. This garden will appeal to those who like their design strong and undiluted, and there is a very useful leaflet.

RYELANDS HOUSE   29
Taynton, Gloucestershire. Tel: (01452) 790251

*Captain and Mrs E. Wilson ★ 8m W of Gloucester, midway betwen Huntley (A40)
and Newent (B4215) ★ Best season: spring ★ Parking ★ Refreshments ★ Toilet
facilities ★ Suitable for wheelchairs in dry weather ★ Dogs welcome on country and
woodland walk ★ Plants for sale ★ Open by appointment for parties and on 2nd, 9th,
16th, 17th, 23rd, 30th April, 2 – 6pm ★ Entrance: £2, children free*

Carefully cultivated garden designed, developed and maintained by owners
since 1964 surrounding a fine creeper-clad early-nineteenth-century Grade
II Listed house in a peaceful country setting. Yew and box hedges subdi-
vide a sunken garden, pergolas and arches frame well-placed statuary and
lead the eye to inviting seats, a water garden and specimen shrubs. Mature
trees shade immaculately-maintained beds planted with an experienced eye,
in sophisticated tonal harmonies. A half-mile walk with outstanding views
across the owners' land to a tranquil two-acre secluded lake, rich with
wildlife, should not be missed especially in spring when wild daffodils
carpet the woodland.

SEZINCOTE ★   30
Bourton-on-the-Hill, Nr Moreton-in-Marsh, Gloucestershire.

*Mr and Mrs D. Peake ★ 1½m from Moreton-in-Marsh on A44 just before
reaching Bourton-on-the-Hill ★ Parking ★ Teas on charity open day ★ Toilet
facilities ★ House open May to July and Sept, Thurs, Fri, 2.30 – 6pm (no
children in house) ★ Garden open Jan to Nov, Thurs, Fri and Bank Holiday
Mons, 2 – 6pm (or dusk if earlier). Also 9th July for charity. Closed Dec ★
Entrance: £2.50, children £1, children under 5 free (house and garden £4)*

The entrance to Sezincote is up a long dark avenue of holm oaks that open
into the most English of parks, with a distinct feel of Repton influence – fine
trees and distant views of Cotswold hills. Turning the last corner is the
surprise, for there is Sezincote, that fascinating rarity, an English country
house built in the Moghul architectural style. The form of the garden has not
changed since Repton's time but the more recent planting was carried out by
Lady Kleinwort, with help from Graham Thomas, and on her return from
India in 1968 she laid out the 'Paradise Garden' with canals and Irish yews in
the south garden. Behind this is the curved orangery, home to many tender
climbing plants. The house is sheltered by fine copper beeches, cedars, yews
and limes, which provide a fine backdrop for the exotic shrubs. Streams and
pools are lined with great clumps of bog-loving plants and the stream is crossed
by an Indian bridge, adorned with Brahmin bulls. The garden is planted for
interest all year round. It is particularly strong on autumn colours, and the
instructive guide to the garden, by Graham Thomas, is highly recommended.

SNOWSHILL MANOR ★   31
Nr Broadway, Gloucestershire. Tel: (01386) 852410

*The National Trust ★ 3m S of Broadway off A44 ★ Parking. Coaches by
appointment. New car park with entry via new footpath (no entry from
Snowshill village) ★ Refreshments in restaurant near new shop and ticket office,
all open from 12 noon ★ Braille guide available, but otherwise unsuitable for*

disabled ★ Shop ★ Manor open 1pm ★ Grounds open April to Oct, daily except Tues and 14th April, 12 noon – 6pm (5pm in April and Oct) (last admission ½ hour before closing). Timed ticket system as liable to overcrowding particularly on Suns and Bank Holiday Mons ★ Entrance: grounds £2 (manor and grounds £5, family ticket £13.75). Parties by written appointment only

From a design by M.H. Baillie-Scott, the owner Charles Wade transformed a 'wilderness of chaos' on a Cotswold hillside into an interconnecting series of outdoor 'rooms' in Hidcote style from the 1920s onwards. Wade was, according to the *Oxford Companion*, a believer in the Arts and Crafts rustic ideal and the garden, like the house, expresses his eccentricities. Seats and woodwork are painted 'Wade' blue, a powdery dark blue with touches of turquoise which goes well with the Cotswold stone walls. The simple cottage style conceals careful planting with blue, mauve and purple as the motif. Organic gardening is employed here.

STANCOMBE PARK ★ 32
Dursley, Gloucestershire. Tel: (01453) 542815

Mrs Barlow ★ Between Wotton-under-Edge and Dursley on B4060 ★ Best season: June ★ Parking in field by park ★ Teas and home-made cakes ★ Toilet facilities ★ Partly suitable for wheelchairs ★ Plants for sale ★ Open by appointment for parties and 4th June, 2 – 6pm ★ Entrance: £2, children 50p for both gardens

When Stancombe Park – built in the 1840s – is open for charity people rush to view the most curious park and garden south of Biddulph Grange. Set on the Cotswold escarpment, it boasts the ingredients of a Gothic best-seller. A narrow path drops into a dark glen, roots from enormous oaks, copper beeches and chestnuts trip your feet, ferns brush your face, walls drip water, and amonites and fossils loom in the gloom. A dark lake reflects an eerie Doric temple. Rocks erupt with moss. Egyptian tombs trap the unwary. Tunnels turn into gloomy grottos. Even plants live in wire cages. Metal arches flake with rust. Family parties become confused, divided and lost. Folly freaks are in their element, though it has to be admitted that some people do not find it gloomy since the droughts have stopped the springs. Indeed the secret garden can be light and friendly when it is not raining. Everyone has a good time in this Victorian theme park turned horror movie. Escape can be found in the pretty rose garden, tea and further twentieth-century follies around the charming house. Also interesting tree and shrub planting and a fine double border.

STANWAY HOUSE 33
Cheltenham, Gloucestershire. Tel: (01386) 584469

Lord Neidpath ★ 1m E of B4632 Cheltenham – Broadway road, 4m from Winchcombe ★ Parking ★ Refreshments: coffee and tea, Bakehouse tea rooms in village. Picnics permitted in park ★ Toilet facilities ★ Partly suitable for wheelchairs ★ Dogs ★ House open ★ Garden open June to Sept, Tues and Thurs, 2 – 5pm and for afternoon shows. Other times by appointment ★ Entrance: £1.50 (house and garden £3, OAP £2.50, children £1) (1994 prices)

Stanway is a honey-coloured Cotswold village with its Jacobean 'great house' which has been in the hands of only two families. It was much frequented by Arthur Balfour and 'The Souls' in the latter years of the last century. Behind the house, the garden rises in a series of dramatic lawns and a (rare) formal terraced mound to the pyramid folly which, in the eighteenth century was the pivot of the vast cascade descending to a lake or canal by the house. This was reputedly designed by Stephen Switzer and exceeded in length its famous rival at Chatsworth. The present owner plans to restore this with its 185-yard-long waterfall, its canal 38 yards wide, and to extend the lime avenue and vista. Alas the estimated cost is £¼ million. However a good start has been made on the canal excavations and it is hoped to restore the pyramid which was a banqueting hall from which guests, on a summer evening, would watch the cascade gates being opened and the water falling down towards the house. Other features include the fourteenth-century tithe barn, church and a dog cemetery whose inmates go back to 1700. Little for the plantsperson to study, but if you are suffering from a surfeit of National Trust manicuring, try this for sheer style.

STOWELL PARK   34
Northleach, Gloucestershire. Tel: (01285) 720308

Lord and Lady Vestey ★ 2m SW of Northleach on A429. The drive entrance is on right after a long stone wall ★ Parking to the right of drive ★ Teas ★ Toilet facilities ★ Open 14th May, 25th June, 2 – 5pm ★ Entrance: £1.50, children free

The original house dates from around 1600 but it was enlarged for the Earl of Eldon in the 1880s and 90s by Sir John Belcher, the architect of the Mappin & Webb building in the City of London. Stowell Park was used as a shooting lodge. This is a large garden in a magnificent setting: the terrace on the south side of the house overlooks the River Coln, with Chedworth Woods across the valley. The original garden is thought to have been laid out in the 1870s, but since 1981 Lady Vestey has introduced new ideas and new plantings. The approach to the house is along an avenue of pleached limes planted in 1983, and there are fine walled kitchen gardens containing vegetables, fruit, flowers for cutting and a range of glasshouses. A good collection of old-fashioned and climbing roses. Twelfth-century church.

SUDELEY CASTLE ★   35
Winchcombe, Gloucestershire. Tel: (01242) 602308

Lord and Lady Ashcombe ★ 8m N of Cheltenham Spa on B4632. Entry through the town of Winchcombe ★ Parking ★ Refreshments: in restaurant April to Oct. Picnic facilities in play area and park only ★ Toilet facilities ★ A good selection of plants for sale. Plant centre open March to Oct ★ Shop ★ Castle open as gardens, 11am – 5pm ★ Gardens open March, daily, 11am – 4pm; April to Oct, daily, 10.30am – 5.30pm (March 11am – 4pm) ★ Entrance: £3.35, OAP £2.95, children £1.60 (castle and grounds £4.95, OAP £4.55, children £2.75). Party rates available for parties of 20 or more

There has been a house on this magnificent site for over 1000 years and today the emphasis is on tourism with pleasant facilities, craft and other exhibitions. The main attraction of the extensive grounds is the Queen's Garden, an outstanding collection of old-fashioned roses, surrounded by the sculptural yew hedges with openings and tunnel walks and clipped yews by the park balustrade. These were laid out in the nineteenth century by an

GLOUCESTERSHIRE

ancestor of the present owners on the site of the original Tudor parterre and have been renovated in recent years. Among the Castle's eight gardens are the Chapel Garden and the Tithe Barn Garden which have been introduced under the guidance of Rosemary Verey and Jane Fearnley Whittingstall. Sudeley aims to become one of the major rose gardens of England.

SUNNINGDALE   36
Grange Court, Westbury-on-Severn, Gloucestershire.
Tel: (01452) 760268

Mr J. Mann Taylor ★ From Huntley take the A40 to Westbury-on-Severn. Continue for 2m (signposted Grange Court). Sunningdale is just before Northwood Green ★ Parking on roadside ★ Plants for sale ★ Open 11th, 22nd, 25th June, 9th July, 6th, 10th, 13th, 17th Aug, 2 − 5pm and by appointment June to mid-Aug ★ Entrance: £1.50

This south-facing, three-quarter-acre garden abounds in choice plants from around the world. Notwithstanding the inhospitable clay, informal borders and island beds are literally crammed with unusual, often rare, trees, shrubs and herbaceous perennials. Amongst a wide range of grasses *Oryzopsis miliacea* is particularly striking, whilst on the terrace the shrub *Grevillea* 'Canberra Gem' displays cerise flowers for most of the year. Of special interest is the National collection of phlomis housed in the garden. Clearly labelled and well-documented, this is best seen during June and July. Elsewhere, greenhouses contain rarities too tender to be exposed outside even in this favoured spot.

TREVI GARDEN   37
Hartpury, Gloucestershire. Tel: (01452) 700370

Gilbert and Sally Gough ★ 5m NW of Gloucester via A417. In village turn sharp back right Over Old Road before war memorial ★ Parking in road outside ★ ☆Teas, except on 3rd April ★ Suitable for wheelchairs ★ Plants for sale ★ Open 16th March to 21st Sept, Thurs, 2 − 6pm. Also 2nd, 16th, 17th, 30th April, 1st, 7th, 28th, 29th May, 6th, 27th, 28th Aug, 2 − 6pm. Coaches and groups at other times by appointment ★ Entrance: £1.50, accompanied children free

This carefully-planned and maintained garden gives the impression of more space than its one acre and aims to be full of interest and variety at all times of the year. Meandering paths lead through arches, around well-planted beds, under a laburnum and clematis walk, through a stream garden and alongside a decorative vegetable garden flanked with espaliered fruit trees. The owners have invested much hard work in achieving a garden displaying colour and good-looking plants at every season and have created a sense of an enclosed and charmed oasis. There are unusual species and cultivars to catch the plantsman's eye as well as old favourites.

VALE HOUSE   38
Hidcote Boyce, Chipping Campden, Gloucestershire.
Tel: (01386) 438228

Miss Bettine Muir ★ On the road from Chipping Campden to Hidcote Manor and Kiftsgate Gardens (see entries). On the edge of Hidcote Boyce ★ Parking in

*mown paddock ★ Partly suitable for wheelchairs ★ Plants for sale ★ Open May to
July, Weds, 2 – 5pm ★ Entrance: £1.50, children 50p*

Miss Bettine Muir is the second daughter of Heather Muir, the creator of
Kiftsgate, and remembers the planting of the famous rose. She is a born
gardener and her skill is reflected in the most unusual and exciting planting
in her own garden. She moved to Vale House in the early 1970s, beginning
work on the 'flat field' which surrounded it in 1972. Within dense windbreaks which do not impede the lovely view west across the Cotswolds to
Bredon is a series of small gardens linked by paved paths. Around the
house are climbers and borders of unusual plants, to the east a small
enclosed garden with many interesting plants, shrubs and roses, edged with
a border of nerines and new shrub plantings.

WESTBURY COURT GARDEN ★★ 39
Westbury-on-Severn, Gloucestershire. Tel: (01452) 760461

*The National Trust ★ 9m SW of Gloucester on A48, close to the church ★
Parking ★ Picnic area ★ Toilet facilities, inc. disabled ★ Suitable for wheelchairs.
Braille plan of garden available ★ Open April to Oct, Wed – Sun and Bank
Holiday Mon (but closed 14th April), 11am – 6pm. Other months by appoint-
ment only ★ Entrance: £2.30, children £1.15. Parties of 15 or more by written
arrangement*

A remarkable seventeenth-century Dutch water garden and, as such, one of
the rarest types of garden to have survived more or less intact in this
country. A contemporary Tall Pavilion dominates a Long Canal which is
flanked by clipped yew hedges regularly spaced with pyramids and holly
balls. Parallel to this is a T–Canal where, in the centre of the arm, Neptune
bestrides a dolphin. To the north-east is a charming gazebo, one side of
which overlooks a small, walled garden where in box-edged beds are species
of plants to be found growing in England prior to 1700. Beyond is the
parterre: beds of simple shape containing topiary, this time in box. This in
turn is surrounded by the Quincunx, a formal arrangement of small trees
and clipped evergreens. A specimen of *Quercus ilex* is thought to be one of
the oldest in the country, with a girth of 26 feet at a point of five feet
above ground. Westbury Court is a garden of *allée*, canal, *claivoyée*, and
vista, all carefully restored and maintained to a high standard by the Trust.
The historic houses on this site were destroyed, one as late as the 1950s,
and there is now a home for elderly people here.

WESTONBIRT ARBORETUM ★★ 40
Westonbirt, Gloucestershire. Tel: (01666) 880220

*The Forestry Commission ★ 3m SW of Tetbury on A433, 5m NE of junction
with A46 ★ Best seasons: spring and autumn ★ Parking ★ Light refreshments at
café (closed Jan). Picnic areas ★ Toilet facilities, inc. disabled ★ Suitable for
wheelchairs ★ Dogs allowed in most areas ★ Rare trees and shrubs for sale in plant
centre ★ Visitor Centre with exhibition and shop (closed Jan) ★ Grounds open all
year, 10am – 8pm or dusk ★ Entrance: £2.60, OAP £1.70, children £1*

This is perhaps the finest arboretum in Britain. Started in 1829 by R.
Staynor-Holford, Westonbirt was expanded and improved by successive

generations of the same family until it was taken over by the Forestry Commission in 1956. Numerous grass rides divide the trees into roughly rectangular blocks, within which are various open spaces and glades used for special plantings such as the famous Japanese maple collection. Westonbirt is noted for its vast range of notable mature specimen trees. Colour is best in spring (rhododendrons, magnolias, etc.) and autumn (Japanese maples, fothergilla). The Forestry Commission is continuing with new planting, for example the Hillier Glade with ornamental cherries. Across the valley from the original arboretum is Silkwood with collections of native and American species that in spring are carpeted with primroses, wood anemones and bluebells. There are 18,000 numbered trees and 17 miles of paths.

GARDENING FOR THE DISABLED

Demonstration gardens to assist the disabled are available at a number of properties open to the public. These include the following:

Battersea Park, London. Horticultural Therapy Unit (Wandsworth Borough Council). Telephone for appointment (0171) 720 3419

Disabled and Older Gardeners' Association, Herefordshire Growing Point, Herefordshire College of Agriculture, Holme Lacy, Hereford.
Tel: (01432) 870316

Hadlow College, Tonbridge, Kent. Telephone for appointment
(01732) 850551

Park House Garden, Horsham, West Sussex

Royal Horticultural Society's Garden, Wisley (see *Guide* under Surrey)

Ryton Organic Gardens, Ryton-on-Dunsmore (see *Guide* under Warwickshire)

Syon Park, Middlesex (see *Guide* under London)

Open days for the disabled are also held from time to time at the following gardens:

Dolly's Garden (see *Guide* under London)

Hillsborough Community Development Trust (see *Guide* under South & West Yorkshire)

Iden Croft Herbs (see *Guide* under Kent)

The Gardening for Disabled Trust is a registered charity which collects donations from the public and uses them to assist disabled people with improvements to their gardens, or to supply equipment which will enable them to continue to garden. Donations should be sent to Mrs Felicity Seton, Hayes Farmhouse, Hayes Lane, Peasmarsh, Rye, East Sussex.

HAMPSHIRE &
THE ISLE OF WIGHT

Gardens on the Isle of Wight will be found at the end of the Hampshire section.

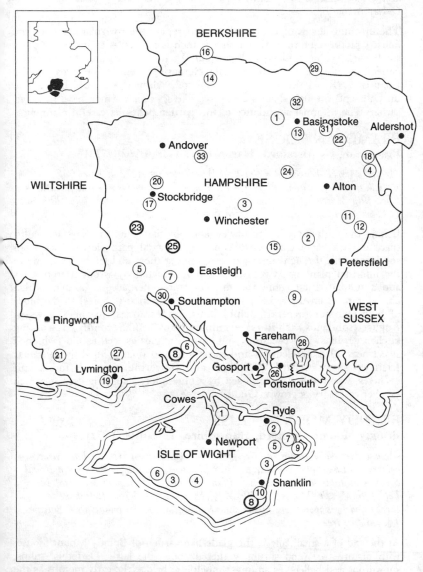

Two-starred gardens are ringed in bold

THE BARN HOUSE 1
Rectory Road, Oakley, Nr Basingstoke, Hampshire.
Tel: (01256) 780271

Brigadier and Mrs H.R.W. Vernon ★ 5m W of Basingstoke. From Basingstoke take B3400 Whitchurch road. ½m W of Newfound turn left at Station Road ★ Parking in road or at Oakley Manor ★ Tea and toilet facilities at Oakley Manor next door ★ Open for NGS 6th Aug, 2 – 5.30pm ★ Entrance: (combined with Oakley Manor) £2

The ups and downs of this small garden repeat the irregular levels of the house's picturesque roof. Every square inch is packed with interest, with a small rockery, perennials and particularly in late summer the splendid collection of texensis and viticella clematis ('Venosa Violacea', 'Alba Luxurians', 'Royal Velours', 'Etoile Violette', 'Minuet', etc.) which scramble up walls and through shrubs and roses like *R. glauca* which have flowered earlier. The informal abundance of this garden belies its careful planning.

BRAMDEAN HOUSE ★ 2
Bramdean, Nr Alresford, Hampshire. Tel: (01962) 771214

Mr and Mrs H. Wakefield ★ 9m E of Winchester on A272 at W end of Bramdean ★ Best season: summer ★ Parking ★ Refreshments ★ Toilet facilities ★ Open 19th March, 16th, 17th April, 21st May, 18th June, 16th July, 20th Aug, 2 – 5pm ★ Entrance: £1.50, children free (1994 prices)

Behind the undulating hedge of yew and box like some vast abstract sculpture, and the eighteenth-century house, an axial path slowly rises from south to north through these gardens, linking them and lending a frame to the informal plantings. Cross axes are punctuated by wrought iron gates and a sundial. First come the mirror-planted herbaceous borders which change tone from the reds of May (peonies, oriental poppies) to the blues of high summer (nepetas, delphiniums, tradescantias) to the yellows of August (solidagos, achilleas, evening primroses). Secondly, a working kitchen garden with vegetables and cordon apples as well as old-fashioned sweet peas, gladioli, clematis and carnations and finally, lined by columnar Irish yews, an orchard with fruit and flowering trees, daffodils and beehives, where the vista is closed by a blue-doored apple house, up which espalier rosemary is grown. Good hop tree.

BRANDY MOUNT HOUSE 3
Brandy Mount, Alresford, Hampshire. Tel: (01962) 732189

Mr and Mrs M. Baron ★ In Alresford town centre. First right in East Street before Sun Lane. No vehicular access ★ Best season: spring ★ Parking in Broad Street ★ Suitable for wheelchairs ★ Plants for sale ★ Open probably 11th, 12th Feb, 19th March, 23rd April, 7th May, 18th June, 2 – 5pm (telephone to check) and by appointment in the snowdrop season and on most Sats ★ Entrance: £1, children free

At the end of a small lane is the glade-like garden of Brandy Mount House, with mature trees and shrubs gathered about the lawn. Daffodils, tulips, snowdrops and hellebores amongst much else bridge the early months as the many and varied herbaceous borders first swell then burst with a true plantsman's collection. The National collections of galanthus and daphne are here.

BROADHATCH HOUSE 4
Bentley, Nr Alton, Hampshire. Tel: (01420) 23185

Bruce and Elizabeth Powell ★ 4m NE of Alton. In Bentley turn N from A31 up School Lane, by pond. After 300 yards bear right, and proceed another 300 yards to garden up drive on right ★ Parking ★ Suitable for wheelchairs ★ Dogs on lead ★ Plants for sale ★ Open by appointment from 10th June to 10th July ★ Entrance: £1.50, children free

These three and a half acres are well laid out. Best here are the herbaceous borders, their height maintained by wires carrying ramblers, clematis and perennial sweet peas, which lead to a circular sunken garden recently replanted in hot and cold shades like a colour wheel. Pleasant rose garden with many old roses and grey foliage plants. Pink, purple and grey borders with cotton lavender, purple berberis, etc. Kitchen garden.

BROADLANDS 5
Romsey, Hampshire. Tel: (01794) 516878

Lord Romsey ★ S of Romsey on A31. Signposted ★ Parking ★ Refreshments and picnic site ★ Toilet facilities ★ Suitable for wheelchairs ★ Shop ★ Open July and Aug, daily, 12 – 5.30pm (last admission 4pm) ★ Entrance: £5, OAP £4, children (12-16) £3.40 (1994 prices)

This former home of Lord Louis Mountbatten has a smooth lawn running from the steps of the porticoed west front to the River Test. Spreading parkland trees of beech and cedar come together in a composition that epitomises the eighteenth-century English Landscape School. The elegant Palladianism of Broadlands could only be the work of 'Capability' Brown.

CADLAND HOUSE ★ 6
Fawley, Hampshire.

Mr and Mrs Maldwin Drummond ★ 16m SE of Southampton off A326 ★ Parking ★ Tea by arrangement ★ Partly suitable for wheelchairs ★ Plants for sale ★ Open May and June by written appointment to parties only (minimum 20) ★ Entrance £2

Unique landscape garden of eight acres overlooking the Solent designed by 'Capability' Brown in 1776 for the banker Robert Drummond and his wife Winifred, restored since recent hurricanes to the original plan using period plants. A path with tiered shrubs (roses, brooms, philadelphus, *Lavandula stoechas*, laurels, *Ptelea trifoliata*) winds from the modern house (replacing the original three-roomed cottage *orné*), along the shore and back through a lime walk and Georgian flower border. Broad vistas alternate with carefully orchestrated glimpses of the sea. Also, kitchen garden with well-maintained traditional fruit houses. Walled garden with red border, cool border and rare plants (*Astelia chathamica*, *Pileostegia viburnoides*, tender acacias) as well as the National collection of leptospermum.

CROYLANDS 7
Old Salisbury Lane, Nr Romsey, Hampshire. Tel: (01794) 513056

The Hon. Mrs Charles Kitchener ★ From Romsey take A3057 Stockbridge road, after 1m turn left at the Duke's Head, fork left after the bridge and the garden is 1m further on the right ★ ☆Teas on NGS days ★ Suitable for wheelchairs ★ Plants for sale ★ Open mid–May to June, daily (inc. NGS open days) ★ Entrance: £1.50, children free

The curving lines of this informal plantsman's garden echo the lines of the wheelwright's cottage roof. The vistas appear to be the result of happy chance but have been skilfully prepared. From the cottage there is a view across the lawn between shrubs to a stand of gold-leaved plants, and paths (brick from the local Michelmarsh brickworks) wind through trees like *Arbutus unedo* and *Populus candicans* to reach glades furnished with arbours, pots of New Zealand cabbage or phormiums, shrubs wreathed in clematis, a large Australian mint bush, a white abutilon, and *Elaeagnus angustifolia*. Shade border and a white border with ornamental grasses, cerastium, etc. In June the former vegetable plot has 200 peonies in flower.

EXBURY GARDENS ★★ 8
Exbury, Nr Southampton, Hampshire. Tel: (01703) 891203

Mr E.L. de Rothschild ★ 2½m SE of Beaulieu, 15m SW of Southampton, via B3054 SE of Beaulieu after 1m turn right for Exbury ★ Best season: spring/autumn ★ Parking ★ Refreshments ★ Toilet facilities ★ Suitable for wheelchairs ★ Dogs on short lead ★ Plants for sale ★ Shop ★ Open mid-Feb to Oct, 10am – 5.30pm (or dusk if earlier) ★ Entrance: £4, OAP £3.50 (£4.50 at mid-season weekends and Bank Holiday Mons), children (10-16) £3, parties of 15 or more £3.50 per person (seasonal discounts)

Established between the wars by Lionel de Rothschild, these outstanding gardens are synonymous with rhododendrons and azaleas. The 200 acres of winding paths, with a canopy of oaks, pines, cedars, Japanese maples and rare trees like *Emmenopterys henryi*, are planted with rhododendrons, many such as *R. yakushimanum* and Hawk 'Crest' introduced here. In March early rhododendrons, camellias and the daffodil meadow flower. In April the rock garden, miniature mountain scenery with screes and valleys, is at its peak with dwarf alpine rhododendrons galore, azaleas reflected in the ponds, candalabra primulas by the cascades, and bluebells. In June/early July the rose garden, mostly standard miniatures and HTs, has a small but similar mix of the Exbury fruit gum colours. May is the busy month for visitors but there is much to see all year round. Good autumn spectacle.

FAIRFIELD HOUSE ★ 9
Hambledon, Portsmouth, Hampshire. Tel: (01705) 632431

Mrs Wake ★ 10m SW of Petersfield in Hambledon ★ Best season: June to July ★ Parking ★ Refreshments ★ Toilet facilities ★ Suitable for wheelchairs ★ Dogs on lead ★ Plants for sale ★ Open by appointment ★ Entrance: £1.50, children free (suitable for groups)

There can be little doubt that Lanning Roper, who assisted 20 years ago in the establishment of this excellent garden, would approve of the continuing development of the planting at Fairfield, particularly the climbing, shrub and bush roses around and on the elegant white Regency 'colonial' house. This largely informal, skilfully shaped garden is set on a south-facing slope beneath chalk down and sheltered by yew hedges, walls and a legacy of fine trees, cedars of Lebanon and a stooled lime and spreading copper beech (span of some 120 feet). The five and a half acres not only host an impressive range of shrub and climbing roses, of which there are over 160 in number, but mixed borders of choice specimens, and in spring drifts of bulbs. The owner's own tree planting includes a tulip tree, fern-leaved beech, various malus, sorbus, prunus, betulas and robinias. Roses are the speciality. An excellent list is supplied, and an interesting method of supporting large shrub roses has been developed which is worth examining. The latest venture is a meadow garden in an adjacent field recently acquired where over 2000 wild flowers have been planted.

FURZEY GARDENS ★   10
Minstead, Nr Lyndhurst, Hampshire. Tel: (01703) 812464

Mrs M.A. Selwood (Manager) ★ 8m SW of Southampton, 1m S of A31, 2m W of Cadnam and the end of M27, 3¹/₂m NW of Lyndhurst ★ Best season: spring ★ Parking ★ Refreshments at Honey Pot café ¹/₂m away ★ Toilet facilities ★ Plants for sale ★ Gallery of crafts ★ Sixteenth-century cottage open daily in summer, weekends in winter ★ Gardens open daily except 25th and 26th Dec, 10am – 5pm (earlier in winter) ★ Entrance: summer: £3, OAP £2.50, children £1.50; winter: £1.50, children 75p. Reductions for parties by arrangement

This eight-acre garden was laid out by Hew Dalrymple in the early 1920s using plants from the nursery at nearby Bartley. The range of plants, particularly those of Australasian descent, make this garden a must for horticulturalists and plant historians. Situated on a south-facing slope, winding paths lead to many noteworthy and surprisingly large specimens. There is relatively little herbaceous planting but this is more than compensated for by the boldness and density of some of the most colourful planting schemes, with the vermilion of Chilean Fire trees in May/June outstanding. Recent replanting has left some gaps in the borders but there docs not sccm to be anything, from lawns to the shaded plants of the water garden, that will not flourish here.

GILBERT WHITE'S HOUSE AND GARDEN   11
The Wakes, Selborne, Alton, Hampshire. Tel: (01420) 511275

Oates Memorial Trust ★ 4¹/₂m S of Alton, 8m N of Petersfield. On B3006 ★ Parking in public car park behind Selborne Arms ★ Picnic area ★ Toilet facilities ★ Suitable for wheelchairs ★ Unusual plant fair 24th, 25th June ★ Shop ★ House open ★ Garden open late March to Oct, daily; Nov to March, weekends, 11am – 5pm ★ Entrance: £2.50, OAP and students £2, children £1 (first child free)

Gilbert White, the great naturalist, has left us with a well-documented eighteenth-century garden, through his writings in the *Garden Kalendar*. Gradually being extended and restored to period form, the garden contains many fascinating and unusual plants grown by White, such as species foxgloves, hollyhocks, Painted Lady sweet peas and Venus-looking-glass, *Legousia speculum-veneris*, as well as part of his original fruit wall and the

179

brick path leading to a ha-ha and sundial. There are splendid vistas towards the beech-clad hanger which forms a magnificent backdrop to this secluded garden. Additions since Gilbert White's time include a laburnum arch, 'old rose' garden, herb garden, wild garden, fine tulip tree and yew topiary. Visitors may ponder on the fact that it was at The Wakes that White made the first observations of the value of the earthworm to gardens and farms.

GREATHAM MILL 12
Greatham, Nr Liss, Hampshire. Tel: (01420) 538425

Ed and Cindy Grove ★ 7m SE of Alton. From Alton take B3006 signposted Liss. Through Selbourne and Empshot to bottom of hill. Then ¹/₂m to point where two lanes join road from right. Take first lane (no through road) to garden. From the south take A3 to roundabout near Greatham, follow A325 (marked Farnham), turn left onto B3006 for ¹/₄m and into lane marked No Through Road to garden ★ Parking ★ Refreshments: tea-room ★ Toilet facilities ★ Plants for sale ★ Open 14th April to 15th Oct, Sat, Sun and Bank Holiday Mons, 2 – 6pm. Also by appointment ★ Entrance: £1, children free at weekends. Other days by appointment £2, children free

This cottage-style garden beside the seventeenth-century millhouse on a bend of the River Rother is now run by the late Mrs Pumphrey's granddaughter with her husband. Water garden with ferns, hostas, rodgersias and gunneras. Clematis, wisteria and the fuchsia gooseberry *Ribes speciosum* ramble up the house, and a riotous mass of old-fashioned perennials, campanulas, gypsophilas, inulas, etc. grow nearby. A winding path leads past alpines and over bridges to a dell with foliage shrubs and trees, such as *Acer pseudoplatanus* 'Brilliantissimum', *Acer griseum* and *Prunus serrula*.

HACKWOOD PARK (The 'Spring Wood') 13
Basingstoke, Hampshire. Tel: (01256 23107)

The Viscount and Viscountess Camrose ★ 1m S of Basingstoke. The entrance is off Tunworth Road. Signposted ★ Parking ★ Refreshments ★ Toilet facilities ★ Open 2nd April, 14th May, 8th Oct, 2 – 5.30pm ★ Entrance £2, OAP £1, children free

Furnished with follies to the design of James Gibbs, architect of St Martin-in-the-Fields, and almost certainly laid out under the direction of the same hand, 'Spring Wood' is the only complete example in England of a garden wood in the French manner. Eight Le Nôtre-styled avenues radiate from a central round point leading the visitor beneath an impressive canopy of specimen and forest trees and revealing in turn the surprisingly subdued follies by Gibbs and others, the impressive earthworks of the woodland boundary and ampitheatre and distant prospects of the south and east fronts of Hackwood House. Reinstated in the *Guide* following restoration after the depredations of the gales.

HIGHCLERE CASTLE 14
Highclere, Nr Newbury, Hampshire. Tel: (01635) 253210

Lord and Lady Carnarvon ★ 4¹/₂m S of Newbury on W side of A34 ★ Parking ★ Refreshments and picnic area ★ Toilet facilities ★ Suitable for wheelchairs ★ Shop

★ House open ★ Garden open July to Sept, Wed, Thurs, Sat, Sun and Bank Holidays (Easter, May and Spring: Sun and Mon; August: Mon), 11am – 6pm (last admission 5pm) ★ Entrance: £5, OAP £4, disabled and children under 16, £3 (1994 prices). Garden-only tickets available and special group rates

Though much altered by 'Capability' Brown in the 1770s, Highclere Park will still reward students of the earlier rococo style with a rare and fine collection of early eighteenth-century follies. Around Charles Barry's huge battlemented house an equally fine collection of cedars – North Indian Deodar, Mount Atlas and Lebanon – may be identified, the near horizontal branches of the latter framing views first to the house and then seemingly all the district. Relegated to the slopes away from the house, the walled and secret garden is planted in an uncharacteristically cautious manner for Highclere and saved only by James Russell's eye for good spring and summer colour. It was on Lord Carnarvon's estate here that in 1909 the young Geoffrey de Havilland made some of the early powered tests in his wood and fabric flying machine. See also entry for Hollington Herb Garden.

HINTON AMPNER ★   15
Hinton Ampner, Bramdean, Nr Alresford, Hampshire.
Tel: (01962) 771305

The National Trust ★ 1m W of Bramdean village, 8m E of Winchester on A272 ★ Parking. Special entrance for coaches through village ★ Homemade teas in tearoom 2 – 5pm ★ Toilet facilities ★ Suitable for wheelchairs ★ House open Tues and Wed only and Sat and Sun in Aug, 1.30 – 5.30pm (last admission 5pm) ★ Garden open April to Sept, Sat, Sun, Tues, Wed and Bank Holiday Mons (but closed 14th, 17th April), 1.30 – 5.30pm (last admission 5pm) ★ Entrance: £2.40 (house and garden £3.70). Pre-booked parties to house and garden £3.20 per person. Bookings to the Administrator

Located on the shoulder of a ridge, the ascent to the house through parkland in no way prepares the visitor for the view to the south of classic English downland scenery over a series of descending terraces. From his inheritance of the estate in 1935 onwards Ralph Dutton, later Lord Sherborne, set about transforming the remnants of a Victorian/Edwardian park into a series of gardens on different levels linked by the 'Long Walk' and the 'main terrace'. The skill with which features such as the temple, obelisk and statue of Diana are sited and with which many surprise vistas were created is testimony to Lord Sherborne's knowledge of garden history. While areas of the garden are in the process of restoration which will be complete in 1996, the masterly design and the elegance of its topiary, yew and box hedges deserve wide recognition. The lily pond has been drained and cleared and a chalk pit dug out and replanted as a Dell Garden.

HOLLINGTON HERB GARDEN   16
Woolton Hill, Nr Newbury, Berkshire. Tel: (01635) 253908

Mr and Mrs S.G. Hopkinson ★ 4m S of Newbury off A343. Follow signs to Herb Garden ★ Best season: summer ★ Parking ★ Refreshments ★ Toilet facilities ★ Suitable for wheelchairs ★ Plants for sale ★ Shop ★ Open March to Sept, daily, 10am – 5.30pm, Sun and Bank Holiday Mons, 11am – 5pm; Oct to Mar, Mon – Fri, 10am – 5pm ★ Entrance: free. Collecting box for charity

Interestingly laid out, this small garden modestly but successfully combines the function of a sales pitch for its specimen plants with the art of garden design. Set within an old walled garden, a small fountain, knot garden and rampant hop climbing over gnarled espalier provide the visual treats, but it is the pot-pourri of aromas that distinguishes this garden and nursery. It could be combined with a visit to Highclere Castle nearby (see entry).

HOUGHTON LODGE   17
Stockbridge, Hampshire. Tel: (01264) 810177/810502

Captain and Mrs M. Busk ★ 6m S of Andover, 1½m S of Stockbridge on minor road signposted Houghton ★ Best season: spring ★ Parking ★ Suitable for wheelchairs ★ Plants sometimes for sale ★ House open by appointment only ★ Gardens, greenhouse and hydroponicum open March to Sept, Sat and Sun, 10am – 5pm, Mon, Tues and Fri, 2 – 5pm. Other times by appointment. Coach parties welcome by prior appointment ★ Entrance: £2.50

Built towards the end of the eighteenth century, Houghton Lodge is probably among the most 'picturesque' of Gothic cottage *ornés*, both in its architectural fantasy and its perfect garden setting alongside the River Test. Marie Antoinette would certainly have approved of this idyll. A succession of snowdrops and massed daffodils beneath fine parkland specimens of plane, oaks and horse chestnuts clothe the ridge beyond the lawns from where a unique rustic flint grotto can be reached; in autumn the colours of Indian gums and maples can be observed reflected in the river. The Hampshire Hydroponicum, believed to be the first in England set up for public display of plant culture without soil, occupies a large greenhouse within the chalk cob walls of the kitchen garden. Replanting of the gardens has been undertaken with the advice of the landscape historian David Jacques.

JENKYN PLACE ★★   18
Bentley, Nr Alton, Hampshire. Tel: (01420) 23118

Mrs Patricia Coke ★ 4m SW of Farnham on A31, signposted 400 yards N of Bentley crossroads ★ Parking ★ Toilet facilities ★ Suitable for wheelchairs ★ Unusual plants for sale from Green Farm Nursery ★ Open 6th April to 10th Sept, Thurs – Sun and Bank Holiday Mons, 2 – 6pm ★ Entrance: £2, children 75p (1993 prices)

This remarkable garden is reminiscent of Hidcote, both in spirit and structure. The high ground is occupied by a series of formal rooms arranged on terraces. These include the Sundial Garden with pots of tender plants such as daturas, acidantheras and scented pelargoniums, the former Rose Garden now a medley of greys, pinks and purples, and the classically-perfect double herbaceous border at its peak from late May to July. Leaf Garden with plants of foliage interest, Herb Garden surrounded by a circular fence of espalier apples. The succession of flowering trees includes magnolias and the pocket handkerchief tree *Davidia involucrata* in May and the rare *Cladrastis sinensis* in late July, a sight for sore eyes.

THE LITTLE COTTAGE   19
Lymington, Hampshire. Tel: (01590) 679395

Wing Commander and Mrs Peter Prior ★ On the outskirts of Lymington on A337 opposite the Tollhouse Inn ★ Parking in layby opposite or down side lane ★ Plants for sale ★ Open by appointment June to Sept, Tues only, 10am – 6pm ★ Entrance: £1

Amazingly, within this quarter-acre garden off the busy A337, are the six variously-coloured formal rooms of Hidcote or Sissinghurst. The miniature set-up works because of Mrs Prior's attention to colour, tone, scale and detail. Furnished with box hedging, rows of standard box, holly and variegated euonymous, there is the blue and pale yellow garden, the white garden with lime, the mauve and silver garden, the pink and light green, blue and white and the apricot and copper gardens. Red will be the 1995 project. Pots, varied paving, focal garden buildings and furniture are carefully sited among the soft planting. Rhinefield House Hotel is not far off (see entry in hotels section).

LONGSTOCK PARK GARDENS ★ 20
Longstock, Nr Stockbridge, Hampshire. Tel: (01264) 810894

John Lewis Partnership (Leckford Estates Ltd) ★ 2m N of Stockbridge. From A30 turn N on A3057. Signposted ★ Parking ★ Refreshments in tea room at nursery ★ Toilet facilities ★ Suitable for wheelchairs ★ Plants for sale at nursery ★ Open April to Sept, first and third Sun of each month, 2 – 5pm ★ Entrance: £2, children 50p

The huge leaves of gunnera, the stilts (pneumatophores) of *Taxodium distichum*, varied nymphaeas and a giant white lily, *Cardiocrinum giganteum*, are just a few of the many interesting features and unusual plants to be found in this most immaculate and loveliest of water gardens. Developed between 1946 and 1953 the garden is fed by the River Test and is located some way from the house. Approached with an air of increasing expectation between a high hedge and old oak trees the garden reveals itself all at once as a veritable archipelago connected by narrow bridges and causeways beneath which clear waters and golden carp slowly move. The background is formed by woodland trees into which a variety of acid-loving trees and shrubs and wild flowers have been introduced as a contrast to the sometimes over-disciplined planting of this successful garden. The surrounding 45 acres of parkland feature an arboretum, nursery and walled garden. The National collection of *Clematis viticella* can be found adjacent to the walled garden where there is also a splendid herbaceous border and old roses.

MACPENNYS NURSERIES AND WOODLAND GARDENS 21
Burley Road, Bransgore, Nr Christchurch, Hampshire. Tel: (01425) 672348

Mr and Mrs T.M. Lowndes ★ Midway between Christchurch and Burley. Turn N off A35 Lyndhurst – Bournemouth road at Hinton Admiral (Cat and Fiddle), right at Bransgore crossroads (Crown) on ¼m on right ★ Best season: spring ★ Parking ★ Teas at Holmsley Old Station Tearooms or Burley Forest Tearooms ★ Suitable for wheelchairs ★ Dogs on lead ★ Plants for sale ★ Open daily inc. Bank Holidays except 25th, 26th Dec and 1st Jan, Mon – Sat, 9am – 5pm, Sun, 2 – 5pm ★ Entrance: collecting box for donations to charity which are not required for customers visiting nursery

There is something about the very name Macpennys that promises the well-stocked nursery that one finds at Bransgore. The gravel pit alongside provides a highly successful way of extending the plant collection into a most unusual woodland garden. Magnolias, camellias, pieris and rhodo-dendrons all flourish beneath a canopy of mixed trees somewhat savaged by the recent severe winter storms. A labyrinthine series of paths (from which one is invited to scramble to reach labels) eventually return to the nursery.

THE MANOR HOUSE   22
Upton Grey, Nr Basingstoke, Hampshire. Tel: (01256) 862827

Mr and Mrs J. Wallinger ★ 6m SE of Basingstoke in Upton Grey village on hill immediately above church ★ Parking. Coaches by appointment only ★ Teas available if notice given ★ A few plants for sale ★ Open May to July for groups by appointment ★ Entrance: £2

Here are formal gardens and terraces with excellent herbaceous borders and dry-stone walling, as well as Jekyll's only surviving restored wild garden. Over the past 10 years they have been meticulously restored by the present owners to the original 1908 Gertrude Jekyll plans. Copies of those plans, a short history of the garden, and photographs covering the deterioration and restoration of the garden are on display. The garden illustrates many of the designer's techniques; her use of plants in flowing drifts of colour and her good eye for proportion and structure. The house was designed by Ernest Newton for Charles Holme, editor of *The Studio* magazine.

MOTTISFONT ABBEY GARDEN ★★   23
Mottisfont, Nr Romsey, Hampshire. Tel: (01794) 341220/340757

The National Trust ★ 4¼m NW of Romsey, ½m W of A3057 ★ Best season: midsummer ★ Parking ★ Refreshments at local post office ★ Toilet facilities ★ Suitable for wheelchairs. Four-seater golf buggy available ★ Dogs in car park only (no shade) ★ Shop ★ The Abbey is closed for restoration in 1995, but re-opens with tea room facilities in 1996 ★ Garden open 19th, 26th March; April to Oct, Sat – Wed, 12 noon – 6pm or dusk if earlier (last admission 5pm) (open in June, Sat – Thurs, 12 noon – 8.30pm for rose season) ★ Entrance: £2.50 (£3.50 in rose season)

Established in only 1972, the walled rose garden designed by Graham Stuart Thomas is already famous and deservedly so. Between the gravel paths, meeting at a small pool and fountain, are assembled one of the most comprehensive collections of old French roses of the nineteenth century, seen and smelt at its best in midsummer. Broad herbaceous borders containing pinks, aubretias, saponarias and much else ensure that from very early in the season there is always something to enjoy. It is to be hoped that the visitor will not miss, if it is possible to miss, the enormous London plane trees, *Platanus* x *hybrida (acerfolia)* (the largest in the country) that occupy parkland sweeping down to the River Test. Pockets of formal gardens can be found around the house created by such accomplished designers as Geoffrey Jellicoe (the pleached lime walk underplanted with *Chionodoxa luciliae*) and Norah Lindsay.

MOUNDSMERE MANOR 24
Preston Candover, Nr Basingstoke, Hampshire. Tel: (0125687) 207

*Mr and Mrs Andreae ★ 6m S of Basingstoke on B3046. Drive gates on left just
after Preston Candover sign ★ Parking. Coaches by appointment ★ Dogs on lead ★
Open 2nd July, 2 – 6pm ★ Entrance: £2, children 50p*

Inspired by Hampton Court and designed in 1908, the pleasing relationship
of house to garden to landscape marks Moundsmere Manor as one of Sir
Reginald Blomfield's (1856–1942) best surviving gardens. To the south of the
'Wrenaissance' house the principal formal garden descends in terraces framed
by clipped yews with deep herbaceous borders. This is Edwardian gardening
on a grand scale, characteristically architectural, and will not disappoint
students of Blomfield's *The Formal Garden in England* in which he attacked
the informal style of gardening supported by William Robinson. Other examples of his work are found at Godinton Park (Kent) and Athelhampton
House (Dorset) (see entries). There is a pinetum to the north.

THE SIR HAROLD HILLIER GARDENS AND
ARBORETUM ★★ 25
Jermyns Lane, Ampfield, Nr Romsey, Hampshire.
Tel: (01794) 68787

*Hampshire County Council ★ 3m NE of Romsey, 9m SW of Winchester, ¾m W
of A31 along Jermyns Lane. Signposted from A31 and A3057 ★ Parking ★ Light
refreshments at weekends and Bank Holidays April to Oct, 12 noon – 5pm ★
Toilet facilities ★ Suitable for wheelchairs ★ Plants for sale at Hilliers
Nursery/Garden Centre ★ Open all year except 25th, 26th Dec and 1st Jan,
10.30am – 6pm (Nov to March 5pm or dusk) ★ Entrance: £3, OAP £2.50,
children under 15 £1, Friends' season ticket £15. Parties of 30 or more £2.50
per person (1994 prices)*

Administered by Hampshire County Council since 1977, this enormous
collection of trees and shrubs was begun in 1953 by the late Sir Harold
Hillier using his house and garden as a starting point. Extends to 160 acres
and includes approximately 14,000 different species and cultivars, with
many rarities. With a total of 40,000 plants it is impossible not to be
impressed or to learn something about how, what and where to plant.
Seasonal interest maps and labelling will lead the visitor to herbaceous,
scree, heather and bog gardens. Amongst the trees and shrubs *Eucalyptus
nitens* and *niphophila*, *Magnolia cylindrica* and the acers are worthy of note.
Much more than an arboretum this attractively laid-out garden can be
enjoyed at many levels and can only increase in interest as the immense
collection of young trees gains in maturity. Nearby at Broadlands (see
entry) there is a 'Capability' Brown landscape.

SOUTHSEA COMMON AND ESPLANADE
SEAFRONT GARDENS 26
Clarence and Southsea Esplanade, Portsmouth, Hampshire.
Tel: (01705) 834148

*Follow directions for Old Portsmouth but from Anglesey Road one-way system
turn left into Hampshire Terrace, continue to Pier Road and turn left down*

Clarence Esplanade ★ Best season: June to Sept ★ Southsea Castle car park and public parking nearby ★ Toilet facilities ★ Suitable for wheelchairs ★ Dogs ★ Open all year ★ Entrance: free

The heathland origins of Southsea Common and Esplanade could not be further from the minds of the many thousands of tourists as they admire year after year the extensive bedding out and manicured gardens. Quintessentially English, a tour of approximately four and a half miles will brazenly confirm the highest, or worst, expectations of what the pleasure grounds of a seaside resort should be. Telephone for free colour gardens tour leaflet.

SPINNERS ★ 27
School Lane, Boldre, Nr Lymington, Hampshire.
Tel: (01590) 673347

Mr and Mrs P.G.G. Chappell ★ 1½m N of Lymington. From A337 Brockenhurst – Lymington road, turn E for Boldre. Signposted ★ Parking ★ Wide selection of plants for sale in nursery ★ Open 14th April to 14th Sept, Wed – Sat, 10am – 5pm; also Suns in May. At other times nursery and part of the garden open. Telephone for details ★ Entrance: £1.50

This informal woodland garden on the acid soil of the New Forest, created by the Chappells, and praised by Roy Lancaster and other plantsmen, is remarkable for its plant association, and the owners' careful choice of scale. Nothing is over large, or dwarfs the smaller pleasures. In spring the sun shines through the canopy of trees, lighting camellias and dwarf rhododendrons, exochordas, magnolias, *Cornus kousa* and the brilliant coral leaves of *Acer palmatum* 'Shishio Improved'. At ground level, carpets of cyclamen, and *Erythronium revolutum* like pale pink stars, as well as white and strange maroon trilliums. Beside the spring near the house the yellow greens of ferns and variegated iris synchronise with white and yellow skunk cabbage. Ferns, primulas, hostas in the small bog garden. Good autumn colouring with *Nyssa sinensis* and other trees.

STANSTED PARK
(see Sussex (West))

STAUNTON COUNTRY PARK 28
Havant, Hampshire. Tel: (01705) 453405

Hampshire County Council and eight other public bodies ★ NW of Havant. Signposted ★ Light refreshments ★ Toilet facilities ★ Shop and Visitors' Centre ★ Ornamental farm ★ Park open daily, summer 10am – 5pm, winter 10am – 4pm ★ Entrance: £2.70, OAP £2.30, children £2 (1994 prices)

Formerly the Leigh estate, belonging to the nineteenth-century horticulturalist and orientalist Sir George Staunton. The largest restoration of Victorian greenhouses in the country has been completed (costing over £1 million) within the walled garden. Inside the crinkle crankle wall are passion flowers, pepper vines and exotics grown by Staunton including the giant *Victoria amazonica* lily in its original circular pool. The great house has gone and much work has been done and fine specimen trees remain, as well as the Gothic library, the shell house and the beacon, the terrace and lakes, the Chinese bridge, and the remains of the lake fort where Staunton used to fire guns and fly the imperial yellow flag of China.

STRATFIELD SAYE HOUSE 29
Reading, Berkshire. Tel: (01256) 882882

The Duke of Wellington ★ 1m W of A33, halfway between Reading and Basingstoke. Turn off at Wellington Arms Hotel ★ Parking ★ Refreshments ★ Toilet facilities ★ Suitable for wheelchairs ★ Shop ★ House open. Wellington Country Park, 3m from house caters for many tastes, and can be visited on combined entry ticket with house and gardens ★ Gardens open May to last Sun in Sept, daily except Fri, 11.30am – 4pm ★ Entrance: £4.50, children £2.25. Special rates for parties of 20 or more

Horticulture and history are inextricably linked, from Pleasure Gardens laid out in the seventeenth century for the first owners with thousands of fine trees including many varieties of oaks, maples and walnuts to the 155-year-old *Quercus cerris* or Turkey oak under which the first duke's horse Copenhagen is buried; from *Sequoiadendron giganteum*, also known as Wellingtonia after the first duke, to the avenue of plane trees planted in 1972. In the pleasure gardens around 300 trees were victims of the gales and storms, among them the famous liquidambar and *Nyssa sylvatica*, but the damage has been cleared and new plantings are in hand. The walled gardens and American garden were designed for the first duke who also placed the traditional Victorian summerhouse in the Pleasure Gardens. A large walled garden for vegetables and fruit is laid out in the Victorian manner, and contains a camellia house (possibly built by Paxton whose boss, the Duke of Devonshire, was a chum of the Iron Duke) from where a substantial herbaceous border leads down the centre to the Rose Garden which was replanted in 1972. Here all the roses have been chosen for their scent and new varieties are added every year. Additions also in the American garden designed for the first duke by his head gardener. This still retains many of the original plants introduced from North America with the emphasis on azaleas, rhododendrons and kalmias but now contains plants from all over the world selected to give year-round interest.

THE TUDOR HOUSE MUSEUM 30
**Tudor House, Bugle Street, Southampton, Hampshire.
Tel: (01703) 332513**

Southampton City Council ★ A36 to West Quay Road or Western Esplanade or A33, follow signs to Docks and Town Quay ★ Public car parks nearby ★ Toilet facilities ★ Suitable for wheelchairs ★ Shop ★ Museum open ★ Open Tues – Fri, 10am – 12 noon, 1 – 5pm, Sat, 10am – 12 noon, 1 – 4pm, Sun, 2 – 5pm ★ Entrance: £1.50 (concessions available)

This delightful museum with its dark polished floors and gallery includes a garden designed by Dr Sylvia Landsberg. It incorporates many features from Tudor gardens, such as heraldic beasts on poles, a camomile seat, a knot garden with twisting lines of santolina, germander and box, a skep for bees, a fountain surrounded by flowering camomile and hyssop, an arbour hung with vines, and many herbs, labelled with details of their associations and use. Surrounded by old walls and buildings, this is a peaceful and romantic corner in the heart of Southampton.

TYLNEY HALL HOTEL
Rotherwick, Nr Hook, Hampshire. Tel: (01256) 764881

31

Access from M3 junction 5, take A287 via Newnham or from M4 junction 11, take B3349 via Rotherwick ★ Parking ★ Teas ★ Partly suitable for wheelchairs ★ Open for meals to non-residents and also open to the public for NGS ★ Entrance: £1.50, children free (1994 prices)

An Edwardian period piece. This house with gardens stretching to 67 acres was built by Seldon Wornum for Sir Lionel Phillips in 1900. In 1906 Wornum asked Gertrude Jekyll for designs and planting plans for the water garden. After the last war Tylney Hall became a Brent Council school. In 1984 the property was acquired by a hotel consortium and since then the gardens have been restored, although not entirely. The original gates to the Dutch garden (which now has a modern swimming pool) have been recovered, the iris border has been replanted and the rose pergola in the kitchen garden rebuilt. Wornum's splendid Italian garden with terrace, herbaceous border and fountain overlooking parkland and lake have been restored in place of the school's tarmac tennis courts. Jekyll's water garden to the south, with kiosk, two lakes, streams, stepping stones and bogside plants, has great charm. Avenue of Wellingtonias, specimen trees and fine vistas.

THE VYNE
Sherborne St John, Nr Basingstoke, Hampshire. Tel: (01256) 881337

32

The National Trust ★ 4m N of Basingstoke between Sherborne St John and Bramley on A340, turn E at NT signs ★ Parking ★ Refreshments: light lunches, homemade teas, 12.30 – 2pm, 2.30 – 5.30pm. Picnics in car park only ★ Toilet facilities ★ Suitable for wheelchairs ★ Dogs in car park only ★ Shop ★ House open 1.30 – 5.30pm (last admission 5pm) ★ Garden open 25th March to Sept, daily except Mon and Fri (but open 14th April), 12.30 – 5.30pm. Open Bank Holiday Mons (but closed Tues following), 11am – 5.30pm. Please telephone for opening details after Sept ★ Entrance: £2 (house and garden £4, family ticket £10). Parties of 15 or more for house and garden £3 per person Tues – Thurs only

This example of the English School was landscaped by John Chute between 1755 and 1776 to complement the early classical portico and garden houses designed by John Webb, disciple of Inigo Jones. Though not as grand or extensive as many country houses in the ownership of The National Trust this early sixteenth-century house provides to the west of its modest entrance one of the best, though small, herbaceous borders of such properties and to the north broad lawns and fine trees that perfectly match the famous Corinthian portico. The framed views to the house from across the lake will amply reward those who venture on the woodland walk. Other features include stone seats in architectural yews, great oaks, the Garden House lake and *Phillyrea latifolia* specimens.

WHITE WINDOWS ★ 33
Longparish, Nr Andover, Hampshire. Tel: (01264) 720222

Mrs J. Sterndale-Bennett ★ 5m E of Andover. Off A303 to Longparish village on B3048 ★ Parking ★ Suitable for wheelchairs ★ Plants for sale ★ Open two days for charity, 2 – 6pm and by appointment April to Sept, Weds, 2 – 6pm ★ Entrance: £1

There is a curiously theatrical air to the garden at White Windows. So carefully staged is the layout and the planting combinations that the whole display is like a series of windows swung open to public view. Begun in 1980, Jane Sterndale-Bennett has already assembled an impressive collection of plants. Specimen plants playfully sited within an imaginatively choreographed 'chorus line' delight with the unusual and the clever use of foliage.

ISLE OF WIGHT

BARTON MANOR 1
Whippingham, East Cowes, Isle of Wight. Tel: (01983) 292835

Robert Stigwood ★ From East Cowes A3021, 500 yards beyond Osborne House on left ★ Parking ★ Refreshments: Cafeteria and wine bar – all day licence ★ Toilet facilities ★ Suitable for wheelchairs ★ Plants for sale ★ Shop ★ Garden open April to 8th Oct, daily, 10.30am – 5.30pm ★ Entrance: £3.50, OAP £3 (inc. souvenir tasting glass, wine tasting and guide leaflet), children (one per adult) free, parties £3 per person

Prince Albert's original design included fine trees and the cork grove. The grand terraces were added by Edward VII, and slope down towards Osborne Bay. In 1924 no less than 225,000 daffodils were planted around the lake, which give a fine display in spring. There is also a secret garden planted with azaleas and roses, impressive herbaceous borders and a productive vineyard, wine from which is on sale. In 1968 Hilliers laid out an intriguing water garden on the far side of the lake, on what was originally Queen Victoria's skating rink. The present owner (a keen conservationist) running the garden and vineyard as a commercial operation has spared no effort in restoring and maintaining the estate. The NCCPG's National collection of red hot pokers (kniphofia) and watsonia is here. The most recent addition to the estate is an original hedge maze which is the largest such attraction on the island – it is now large enough to get lost in.

MORTON MANOR 2
Brading, Sandown, Isle of Wight. Tel: (01983) 406168

J.B., J. and J.A. Trzebski ★ 3m from Ryde on A3055, turn right at Brading traffic lights, signposted 100 yards up hill ★ Parking ★ Refreshments: morning coffee, lunch, cream teas. Fully licensed ★ Toilet facilities ★ Suitable for wheelchairs ★ Dogs on lead ★ Home-grown plants and vines for sale ★ Shop ★ Manor open. Guided tours ★ Vineyard and winery ★ Garden open 2nd April to Oct, daily except Sat, 10am – 5.30pm ★ Entrance: £3, OAP £2.50, children £1, parties of 15 or more £2 per person (house and garden)

The history of Morton dates back to the thirteenth century. The Elizabethan sunken garden is surrounded by a 400-year-old box hedge and old-fashioned roses and shaded by a magnificent *Magnolia grandiflora*. The terraces are nineteenth-century with extensive herbaceous borders and a huge London plane. Masses of spring bulbs are followed by rhododendrons and traditional herbaceous displays. Among the wide range of fine trees is an Indian Bean (*Catalpa bignonioides*) and a *Cornus kousa*. Another feature is a pagoda covered with the wine variety 'Baco'. There are also 50 different varieties of Japanese maple. Little remains of the old walled garden but in the corner behind the herbs are the restored bee boles; also a turf maze has been made for children, and there is a vineyard growing seven varieties of grape.

MOTTISTONE MANOR 3
Mottistone, Isle of Wight. Tel: (01983) 740552

The National Trust ★ SW of Newport on B3399 between Brighstone and Brook ★ Best season: May/June ★ Parking ★ Dogs on lead ★ Manor open 28th Aug only ★ Garden open 5th April to 27th Sept, Weds and Bank Holiday Mons, 2 – 5.30pm (last admission 5pm) ★ Entrance: £1.80 (manor and gardens £3.60). Bookings and enquiries to: Moreys Lodge, Brook, Isle of Wight PO30 4EJ

A terraced garden, best seen in late spring for a glorious display of irises and in August for its colourful herbaceous borders, laid out to gain maximum effect from the views over the Channel and south-west coast of the island. Not so much a plantsman's garden as an impressive frame for the Manor.

NORTHCOURT ★ 4
Shorwell, Newport, Isle of Wight. Tel: (01983) 740415

Mr and Mrs J. Harrison ★ 4m S of Newport on B3323. Entrance on right after rustic bridge, opposite thatched cottage ★ Parking ★ Refreshments ★ Partly suitable for wheelchairs ★ Dogs on lead (under sufferance) ★ Plants sometimes for sale ★ Open one day in May and June for charity, 2 – 5pm. Groups of 10 or more can book for special opening ★ Entrance: approx. £1.50 (varies according to charity)

Twelve acres of wooded grounds surround a Jacobean manor house. There are three varied gardens (divided between members of the Harrison family) consisting of landscaped terraces leading down to the stream and water gardens; herbaceous borders, woodland walks, walled rose garden and walled kitchen garden. The garden specialises in more tender plants. Abutilons, salvias, diascias and argyranthemums thrive especially in the new Mediterranean garden. Shrub roses and later hydrangeas are a particular feature and there are over 50 varieties of hardy geraniums spread around the gardens.

NUNWELL HOUSE 5
Coach Lane, Brading, Ryde, Isle of Wight. Tel: (01983) 407240

Col. and Mrs J.A. Aylmer ★ 3m S of Ryde, signed off the A3055 in Brading into Coach Lane ★ Best seasons: July and September ★ Parking ★ Toilet facilities ★ Shop ★ House open ★ Garden open 2nd July to 28th Sept, Sun, 1 – 5pm, Mon, Wed, 10am – 5pm ★ Entrance: £3, OAP £2, accompanied children £1 (house and garden)

Nunwell House stands in six acres of gardens with wonderful views across the park to Spithead. The rose garden (originally a bowling green in the seventeenth century) is set at the top of a slope, in front of the walled garden (not open), which leads down the Long Walk past the side of the house, where stand two very handsome paulownias, to the front. The fountain came from the Crystal Palace and below the balustrade is a lily pond, formerly a swimming pool. Among the varied shrubs and plants in the borders there are several pretty mallows 'Barnsley', a notable acanthus, an enormous *Elaeagnus* x *ebbingei* and a *Cotoneaster* x *watereri* 'Cornubia'. There is also a 50 yard run of Frensham and a *Cornus kousa* and on the front of the house are two large myrtles. A steep flight of steps bordered by lavender leads up to the woods. To the rear of the house is an arboretum laid out by Vernon Russell-Smith in 1963. The Aylmers are gradually restoring the gardens to their former glory.

OWL COTTAGE ★ 6
Hoxall Lane, Mottistone, Newport, Isle of Wight. Tel: (01983) 740433

Mrs A.L. Hutchinson ★ From B3399 turn down Hoxall Lane by Mottistone Green. Owl Cottage is 200 yards on right ★ Best season: late June/early July ★ Refreshments: home-made teas by appointment ★ Toilet facilities ★ Suitable for wheelchairs ★ Dogs ★ Open May to Aug, 2 – 5pm, by appointment for parties of 10 or more persons ★ Entrance: £1.50

A brilliant cottage garden with sea views (the thatched cottage is sixteenth century), planted to give year-round colour. There are 23 flowering cherries and over 50 varieties of clematis, including the *balearica* flowering in sequence from January to October and the *armandii*. In addition to a large herbaceous section there are colourful bulbs and flowering shrubs, euphorbias, amaryllis lilies, agapanthus, delphiniums, penstemons, alstroemerias (including a new species called Princess lilies) and the green arum lily. The garden is the creation of the present owners, whose knowledge and enthusiasm enhance one's visit.

PITT HOUSE 7
Love Lane, Bembridge, Isle of Wight.

J.L. Martin ★ Nr the centre of the village; drivers can enter Ducie Avenue before the museum ★ Suitable for wheelchairs ★ Open 28th May, 10.30am – 5pm ★ Entrance: £1, children 20p

Four acres with lovely views of the Solent through the trees. On a lower level from the house is a delightfully shady dell with ponds and water plants. In the main part of the garden are pergolas hung with roses and honeysuckle, and a Victorian greenhouse with two magnificent yellow daturas. A variety of interesting trees including a crinodendron. Full of unexpected pleasures.

VENTNOR BOTANIC GARDEN ★★ 8
The Undercliffe Drive, Ventnor, Isle of Wight. Tel: (01983) 855397

South Wight Borough Council ★ Follow signs from A3055 ★ Paying car park ★ Refreshments: restaurant/café, licensed bar ★ Toilet facilities ★ Suitable for wheelchairs ★ Dogs on lead ★ Limited plants for sale ★ Shop ★ Garden open all

*year. Temperate House, 7th to 30th March, Tues and Thurs only, 10am – 5pm;
2nd April to Oct, daily, 10am – 5pm; Nov to Feb, Sun only, 11am – 5pm; 1st
to 19th March, Tues – Thurs, 11am – 3pm and Sun, 1 – 4pm ★ Entrance: free
(Temperate House 50p, children 20p, parties of 15 or more 45p per person, school
parties 15p per child subject to variation)*

Twenty-two acres, moderately sheltered from the south and north by
Quercus ilex and escallonia. The shelter belt which was decimated in the
1987 and 1990 gales is being replanted. Many tender plants (including
olives; *Berberis asiatica* and *Acer sikkimensis* from the Himalayas; *Cestrum
elegans* from Mexico; *Pittosporum daphniphylloides* from China) all flourish in
the mild climate. Banana plants from Japan and *Cistrus ichangensis* are but a
few of the rare plants displayed to maximum effect in surroundings which
are now designed as a Victorian sub-tropical garden. There is also a magnificent temperate house with a worldwide collection of plants from the warm
temperate zones, together with written and pictorial displays. There is an
Australian section, a central bed of flowers from southern Africa, an island
section with palms from Crete and a collection of plants from St Helena.
New planting includes an extensive New Zealand garden and a
Mediterranean terrace. A Japanese terrace is in the making and will be
planted up in October. The medicinal garden which contains plants used in
folk medicine around the world is outstanding. *Teucrium chamaedrys*
(germander) makes a very effective low hedge in the small formal area. The
garden is particularly well supplied with seats throughout.

THE WATCH HOUSE 9
Bembridge, Isle of Wight. Tel: (01983) 872019

*Sir William Mallinson, Bart ★ Travel round Bembridge harbour from St Helens
on the B3395. The house is down an unmade road to the left about 100 yards
from the Bembridge Sailing Club ★ Best season: May/June ★ Plants for sale ★
Open by appointment ★ Entrance: £1, children 50p*

A delightful sheltered garden, originally laid out as a *potager* by Vernon
Russell Smith in the grounds of a house built for the Admiralty. Now
updated by Stanley Peters as a charming re-creation of a seventeenth-century
idea. There are plenty of old roses such as 'Blairii Number 2', 'Souvenir du
Docteur Jamain', 'Variegata di Bologna' and various mosses. A pleached
apple walk adds interest and all is interspersed with herbaceous plants and
bulbs. The sea on the other side of the house forms a dramatic backdrop.

Illustrations – The Best of Their Kind

If it is difficult to describe a garden in words, it is doubly difficult to give
the essence of a garden in one single photograph. We have therefore
chosen one outstanding garden to illustrate each of the main categories
which appear in the *Guide* – from the stately landscape at one end of the
scale to the pocket-handkerchief at the other. Each edition of the *Guide*
will illustrate a new garden from each of the ten categories, the chosen
gardens being, in the opinion of the editors, amongst the best in the land.

ARBORETUM *It is a little over 50 years since the late Sir Harold Hillier used his garden as a starting point for this now world-renowned collection of trees and shrubs in Hampshire. Open all year except at Christmas and New Year, the garden extends to 160 acres and includes a total of 14,000 plants. More young trees are coming to maturity every day.*

JAPANESE *This garden of solitude and contemplation is hidden in one of the busiest commercial gardens in the country, Compton Acres in Dorset. Japanese gardens did not become fashionable in the West until after 1868 when the country was first opened to the outside world, and they reached the height of their popularity here in the early years of the twentieth century.*

WATER LILIES

Aquatic gardens are currently very popular, and at Burnby Hall in Humberside there is one of the most comprehensive as well as beautiful collections, established 60 years ago in the former trout ponds. June to September are the optimum months for seeing the lilies at their best.

BOTANIC Oxford has the oldest botanic garden in the country, founded in 1621. The heart of the garden is still surrounded by the original high stone walls and the splendid gateway seen here. The collection is supplemented by the University Arboretum a short drive away.

MODERN British gardeners are often criticised for their passion for the past, their nostalgia and their reluctance to develop a new style which can be recognised as typical of our times. Here at **Turn End**, Buckinghamshire, an award-winning housing project is surrounded by a series of garden rooms developed over the past 25 years. This attempt at a modern style is rightly much admired.

LARGE COUNTRY The grounds of this eighteenth–century house contain walled gardens, rhododendron glades with other unusual trees and shrubs, and spectacular semi-formal gardens. There are notable herbaceous borders. Here is an example of a garden which has developed into the present century rather than remaining a 'museum' based on its design from 200 years ago. It is the House of Pitmuies in Tayside, Scotland.

YAFFLES 10
Bonchurch, Ventnor, Isle of Wight. Tel: (01983) 852193

Mrs Wolfenden ★ Immediately above St Boniface Church in Bonchurch ★ Best season: April/May ★ Parking in road ★ Refreshments: tea or coffee ★ Dogs on lead ★ Plants for sale ★ Open by appointment. Parties of 10 or more preferred ★ Entrance: £1, children free

A quarter of an acre of sheltered cliff garden with spectacular sea views, sculpted by Mrs Wolfenden from a precipice overgrown with weeds and scrub. Years of very hard work have made this garden of ledges and glades, with a variety of flowering shrubs, spring bulbs and plants of botanical interest. Taking advantage of the mild climate of the island's undercliff the owner has succeeded in creating a sheet of colour all the year round, and has turned the lower wilderness into a productive vegetable garden. Although it is not a garden, the grassy setting of nearby ruined Appuldurcombe House, near Wroxall, is also well worth a visit (open to Sept, daily, 10am – 6pm and, in winter, 10am – 4pm).

1996 GUIDE

The 1996 *Guide* will be published before Christmas 1995. Reports on gardens for consideration are welcome at all times of the year but particularly by early summer (June) 1995 so that they can be inspected that year.

A report form is included in the *Guide* although experience shows that most people prefer to write a letter. Please address letters to the publishers, Vermilion, 20 Vauxhall Bridge Road, London SW1V 2SA. All letters are acknowledged by the editors.

All descriptions and other information are as accurate as possible at the time of going to press, but circumstances change and it is wise to telephone before making a long journey.

The *Guide* makes no charge for entries which are written by our own inspectors. The factual details are supplied by owners. It is totally independent and its only revenue is from sales of copies in bookshops.

HEREFORD
& WORCESTER

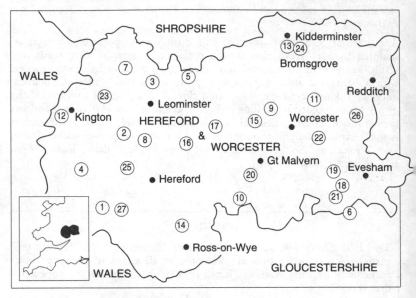

ABBEY DORE COURT ★   1
Abbey Dore, Hereford, Hereford and Worcester. Tel: (01981) 240419

Mrs C.L. Ward ★ 11m SW of Hereford ★ Parking ★ Refreshments: from 11am ★ Toilet facilities ★ Partly suitable for wheelchairs ★ Plants for sale ★ Gift gallery ★ Garden open 4th March to 22nd Oct, daily except Wed, 11am – 6pm and by appointment before 4th March to see hellebores ★ Entrance: £1.75, children 50p

Mrs Ward is a noted plantswoman (although she disclaims the soubriquet) and the large garden has much of interest. Through the garden wall entrance an herbaceous area beckons with flowers, both unusual and better-known, tumbling over the paths. Beyond is an orchard. To the south of the house is the upper lawn, with two big, old *Sequoiadendron giganteum* leading towards the lower lawn with the main herbaceous borders, a small herb garden, and, beyond, the formal garden which is rapidly becoming less formal. Then along to the river walk by the Dore and borders which are full of ferns. Across the river to the west is the pond with its rock garden and the Salix Bed and there have been further developments here. There is an excellent plan by John Meehan, with all the major plants and areas carefully named. Notes accompanying a smaller version of the map explain how Mrs Ward has developed the garden over the past 20 years.

ARROW COTTAGE GARDEN ★   2
Ledgemoor, Weobley, Hereford and Worcester. Tel: (01544) 318468

*Mr and Mrs L. Hattatt ★ 10m NW of Hereford ★ Best season: May/June ★
Parking on roadside ★ Open April to July, Sept, Wed – Fri and Sun, 2 – 5pm.
Closed Aug. At other times by appointment ★ Entrance: £1.50, children free*

Designed as a series of small gardens by the present owner and his family
since 1972. The older part of the garden, planted long ago, is reached by a
painted arched wooden bridge. The transformation from what was an old
apple orchard is very well-planned. A fact sheet is provided to help identify
plants. Meander through the white garden, red border, rock garden, old
rose garden and kitchen garden. Extending over two acres and maintained
to a high standard this garden is a delight.

BERRINGTON HALL   3
Leominster, Hereford and Worcester. Tel: (01568) 615721

*The National Trust ★ 4m N of Leominster on W side of A49 ★ Parking ★
Refreshments: lunches and teas in restaurant (opening 12.30pm) (telephone for
wheelchair access). Picnic tables in car park ★ Toilet facilities, inc. disabled ★
Suitable for wheelchairs ★ Shop ★ Hall open from 1.30pm ★ Grounds open April
to Sept, daily except Mon, Tues and 14th April (but open Bank Holiday Mons),
12.30 – 6.30pm; Oct, Wed –Sun, 12.30 – 5.30pm (last admission ½ hour before
closing). Park walk open July to Oct same days as garden, closes 5.30pm. Parties
of 15 or more by written arrangement ★ Entrance: £1.65 (hall and grounds
£3.60, family ticket £9.90)*

This late eighteenth-century house designed by Henry Holland is set in
mature grounds landscaped by 'Capability' Brown. The gardens are well-
maintained, formally-organised with many shrubs plus a woodland walk
with unusual trees, some recently planted. The walled garden is a young
orchard of 50 varieties of pre-1900 apples. Park walk down to 'Capability'
Brown's pool. Croft Castle (see entry) is nearby.

BROBURY GARDENS AND GALLERY   4
Brobury, Hereford and Worcester. Tel: (01981) 550229

*Mr E. Okarma ★ 11m W of Hereford ★ Parking ★ Toilet facilities ★ Art Gallery
open ★ Garden open all year except 25th Dec and 1st Jan, Mon – Sat, 9am –
4.30pm (4pm in winter) ★ Entrance: £2, OAP £1.50, children 50p*

The garden is what might be expected to be enjoyed by a well-to-do
Victorian gentleman. Conifers, some formal terracing, good trees, herbaceous borders as well as modern planting including a nice young stand of
Betula jacquemontii and clever use of conifers to conceal electricity poles.
More interesting plants can be found in antique prints in the Gallery which
has a very wide selection, both horticultural and general. Brobury, facing, as
it does, both Moccas and Bredwardine where the diarist Kilvert was vicar
for the last few months of his life and where he is buried, is a convenient
stop on the Kilvert Trail and Brobury House offers bed and breakfast.

BURFORD HOUSE GARDENS ★ 5
Tenbury Wells, Hereford and Worcester. Tel: (01584) 810777

Mr M. Chesshire ★ 1m W of Tenbury Wells on A456 ★ Best season: summer ★ Parking close to garden ★ Refreshments: Burford Buttery ★ Toilet facilities ★ Suitable for wheelchairs ★ Plants for sale in the Plant Centre open daily, 10am – 6pm ★ Gardens open daily, 10am – 5pm ★ Entrance: £1.95, children 80p. Parties of 25 or more by prior arrangement £1.60 per person

The Georgian house dates from 1728 but the present gardens from only 1954 when Mr J. Treasure took over. The garden and adjoining plant centre is best known for its collection of clematis. However, it is very diverse in its plants and plantings. Formal water gardens at the rear of the house give way to a variety of informal shrub and herbaceous borders. Good autumn colour is provided by the woodland planting.

CONDERTON MANOR 6
Conderton, Tewkesbury, Gloucestershire.

Mr and Mrs William Carr ★ 5½m NE of Tewkesbury between the A435 and the B4079 ★ Parking ★ Refreshments at Yew Tree Inn ★ Toilet facilities ★ Suitable for wheelchairs ★ Open 13th April, 18th May, 22nd June and by appointment for groups ★ Entrance: £2, children 25p (1994 prices)

A very fine example of what most people think of as the traditional Cotswold Manor House. The seven-acre garden has interesting plantings of trees, mixed beds and a long border with some unusual plants. There is a newly-built formal terrace, a stream garden and, above all, a position commanding a panorama of the countryside.

CROFT CASTLE 7
Leominster, Hereford and Worcester. Tel: (01568) 780246

The National Trust ★ 5m NW of Leominster off B4362 ★ Parking ★ Refreshments: in restaurant at Berrington Hall (see entry) nearby. Picnics in car park only ★ Toilet facilities ★ Partly suitable for wheelchairs. Two braille guides available ★ Dogs in parkland only on lead ★ Castle open ★ Garden open 15th to 17th April, 2 – 6pm and rest of April and Oct, Sat and Sun, 1.30 – 4.30pm; May to Sept, Wed – Sun and Bank Holiday Mons, 1.30 – 5.30pm (last admission ½ hour before closing). Parties of 15 or more by prior written arrangement. Parkland and Croft Ambrey open all year ★ Entrance: £3.10, children £1.55, family £8.50

This is a traditional estate garden with formal beds around the house which dates from the fourteenth century. It is well-kept and pleasant to walk through but lacks specific interest for the specialist, except for the walled garden which is in good condition. The park is notable for its fine avenue of Spanish chestnuts, possibly 350 years old, and for its venerable pollarded oaks. There are charming walks in the Fishpool valley. Berrington Hall is nearby (see entry).

DINMORE MANOR 8
Dinmore, Leominster, Hereford and Worcester. Tel: (01432) 830322

Mr R.G. Murray ★ 6m N of Hereford on A49. 1m driveway signposted in summer ★ Best season: summer ★ Parking ★ Teas most afternoons ★ Toilet facilities ★ Suitable for wheelchairs ★ Open daily, 9.30am – 5.30pm ★ Entrance: £2.50, accompanied children under 14 free. Party bookings by arrangement

The site includes the twelfth to fourteenth-century church of the Knights Hospitaller. An unusual garden centred around the small church, its outstanding feature is the rock garden with some excellent specimens of *Acer palmatum*. This part of the garden is bordered on two sides by modern cloisters linking the house to a small tower which help to evoke a medieval atmosphere. The house and garden are built on high ground with surrounding stone wall giving way to lower ground and some fine views.

EASTGROVE COTTAGE GARDEN NURSERY ★   9
Sankyns Green, Nr Shrawley, Little Witley, Hereford and Worcester. Tel: (01299) 896389

Mr and Mrs J. Malcolm Skinner ★ 8m NW of Worcester between Shrawley (B4196) and Great Witley (A443) ★ Best seasons: June/July and Sept/Oct ★ Parking ★ Toilet facilities ★ Plants for sale ★ Open April to July, daily except Tues and Wed; Sept to 14th Oct, Thurs – Sat, all 2 – 5pm. Closed Aug ★ Entrance: £1.50, children 20p

This delightful cottage garden, with a profusion of colour has been carefully planted to give each plant maximum impact, the interaction of variegated foliage and strongly-coloured shrubs creating backdrops for a variety of herbaceous plants. A collection of flowers and foliage by the front door, looking stunningly casual, turn out to be all in pots. The brick paths lead through areas of clever colour combinations. A recent addition is the arboretum, again artistically planted to give maximum effect to the various coloured foliage. Most plants are labelled and Mr and Mrs Skinner are always on hand with helpful advice. A wide range of well-grown, less usual plants are for sale, all grown at the nursery.

EASTNOR CASTLE   10
**Eastnor, Ledbury, Hereford and Worcester.
Tel: (01531) 633160/632302**

Eastnor Estates ★ 2m E of Ledbury on A438 ★ Best seasons: spring and early autumn ★ Parking ★ Refreshments on Castle open days ★ Toilet facilities ★ Dogs on lead ★ Shop ★ Castle open selected days for collections of armour, tapestries and fine art. Parties of 20 or more by appointment any day ★ Garden open 6th April to Sept, Sun; also Aug, daily except Sat; open Bank Holiday Mons, all 12 noon – 5pm ★ Entrance: £1.75, children £1 (house and garden £3.50, children £1.75)

Essentially an arboretum, Eastnor has one of the best nineteenth-century plantings in the country with many mature specimens. It is worth visiting early in the year for the display of spring bulbs. The house is an early nineteenth-century castle in medieval style surrounded by grounds now brought under control as an extensive restoration and replanting plan gathers momentum (maintenance until recently was largely confined to the vicinity of the castle). A newly-stoned path around the lake gives striking views of the castle, although an area of the water is covered in summer with 'Pattypans', *Nuphar lutea*, the common yellow water lily, and around the edges are clumps of khaki shelters which, by day, partially conceal the common white fisherman. There is a great variety of both conifers and broad-leaved trees, most with discreet aluminium labels, relating to the tree guide. Paths have been kept clear, and the keen tree enthusiast will enjoy the long walks in the woodland. From time to time the park is the venue for a variety of large events, including pop concerts, so those more interested in the quieter things of life should check before visiting.

HANBURY HALL   11
Droitwich, Hereford and Worcester. Tel: (01527) 821214

The National Trust ★ 4¹/₂m E of Droitwich, 1m N of B4090, 6m S of Bromsgrove, 1¹/₂m W of B4091 ★ Parking ★ Refreshments: in tearoom ★ Toilet facilities, inc. disabled ★ Suitable for wheelchairs. Batricar available ★ Dogs on lead in parkland on footpaths only ★ Shop ★ House open ★ Garden open April to Oct, Sat – Mon, 2 – 6pm; also Aug, Tues and Wed, 2 – 6pm. Closed 14th April ★ Entrance: £3.70, family ticket £10. Parties of 15 or more by written arrangement with Property Manager. Evening guided tours for pre-booked parties from May to Sept on Mons £3.70 per person inc. NT members (minimum charge £74)

The National Trust is in process of restoring this garden, parts of which narrowly escaped destruction 30 years ago. The original was by London, the prolific designer of the William and Mary period, though none of his work survives. However, the Trust believes it has enough information to rebuild a large part thereof. The main features will be (1) a yew alley, (2) a topiary fruit garden, (3) a Wilderness with wide paths converging on (4) the Cedar Walk (the latter has survived from London's time) (5) a sunken parterre described as 'spectacular'. The garden may still be raw and thin in parts in 1995 but will be of interest to those who like to see acorns grow.

HERGEST CROFT GARDEN ★   12
Kington, Hereford and Worcester. Tel: (01544) 230160

W.L. Banks and R.A. Banks ★ ¹/₂m W of Kington off A44 ★ Parking ★ Teas ★ Toilet facilities ★ Partly suitable for wheelchairs ★ Dogs on lead ★ Plants for sale ★ Shop ★ Open 14th April to 29th Oct, daily, 1.30 – 6.30pm ★ Entrance: £2.50, children under 15 free, season ticket £9, parties of 20 or more £2 per person

This has been the family home of the Banks family since 1896, and the garden design was much influenced by the writings of William Robinson and Gertrude Jekyll. There is an interesting collection of plants including huge rhododendrons in delightful woodland setting which extends to 50 acres and has general appeal as well as to the plantsperson. Formal garden. Half a mile through the park is a wood containing vast sheets of rhododendrons quite 30 feet high. By following the path at the top of the dingle you can look down on a scene not far removed from those in their native habitat. In late May, Wellington boots are usually necessary, not least in crossing the park in which many sheep safely graze.

28 HILLGROVE CRESCENT ★ 13
Kidderminster, Hereford and Worcester. Tel: (01562) 751957

Malley and David Terry ★ Hillgrove Crescent is a short semicircle linking A449 and A448 near their junction, the three roads enclosing a school ★ Limited parking in road ★ Plants for sale ★ Open 21st May, 25th June, 6th Aug, 2 – 6pm and by appointment ★ Entrance: £1.50, children free

Malley Terry has transformed the area behind her semi-detached house into a miniature Paradise Garden. An immense variety of material, much of it uncommon, has been expertly grown and cunningly combined to form contrasts of shape, texture and colour which blend into a whole which is much more than the sum of the parts. An object lesson for every gardener with restricted space, it has the appearance of being three times its actual size without the least impression of crowding. A masterpiece.

HOW CAPLE COURT 14
How Caple, Hereford, Hereford and Worcester. Tel: (01989) 86626

Mr and Mrs Peter Lee ★ 10m SE of Hereford on B4224, turn right at How Caple crossroads ★ Best season: summer ★ Parking ★ Refreshments on Sun and Bank Holidays. Parties by appointment ★ Toilet facilities ★ Dogs on leads ★ Plants for sale ★ Shop ★ Open Easter to Oct, Mon – Sat, 9.30am – 5pm, also May to Oct, Sun, 10am – 5pm ★ Entrance: £2.50, children £1.25

A large house and medieval church set in 11 acres of grounds with fine trees lining a valley which flows down to a bend in the River Wye. Much of the Edwardian planting is being re-established, there are good formal terraces, and a big pool surrounded by a curious pergola. The Florentine garden and water supply has now been restored and the owners are working on the water steps below – a spectacular feature. In the stable yard is a small area selling some unusual shrubs and old roses. Recent plantings in the valley are maturing well. Open air concert on 16th June and full dress opera on 17th June 1995.

LAKESIDE 15
Gaines Road, Whitbourne, Nr Worcester, Hereford and Worcester.

Mr D. Gueroult and Mr C. Philip ★ 9m W of Worcester off A44. Turn left at county boundary sign, signposted Linley Green (ignore sign to Whitbourne) ★ Teas ★ Plants for sale ★ Open 23rd April, 14th May, 18th June, 2 – 6pm ★ Entrance: £1.50, children free

The first glimpse of this six-acre garden is a moment of sheer delight: a dramatic vista of the lake at the bottom of a steep grassy slope. The main part of the garden is situated within the walls of what was the fruit garden of Gaines House nearby and consists of mixed beds and borders with many unusual shrubs and plants, bulbs and climbers. It has been created by the present owners since 1984 and is now well–established, with continuing expansion, particularly the newly-planted bog garden. At least one plant of every variety in the garden is labelled. The main lake – complete with fountain – is the largest of three medieval stewponds which are thought to have provided fish for the Bishop of Hereford's palace nearby at Whitbourne Court. There is a short woodland walk bordered with ferns and different varieties of holly, leading to the very attractive lakeside walk, where there are various kinds of daffodil in spring. An exceptionally-situated garden, with great variety and interest. Don't miss the view from the top of the heather garden.

LOWER HOPE 16
Ullingswick, Hereford and Worcester. Tel: (01432) 820557

Mr and Mrs Clive Richards ★ At the roundabout on the A465 near Burley Gate take the A417 towards Leominster. After 2m turn right. Lower Hope is about ½m on left. Signposted ★ Parking ★ Refreshments ★ Toilet facilities ★ Suitable for wheelchairs ★ Guide dogs only ★ Open 9th April, 28th May, 9th July, 2 – 6pm ★ Entrance: £2, children £1

On entering this five-acre garden through a gate in the hedge which largely conceals it from the road, the effect is of finding the south banks of the Chelsea Flower Show transported bodily to Herefordshire. Artfully contrived streams meander, crossed by Japanese-type bridges under which swim Koi carp; beds backed with shrubs and filled with perennials and annuals in profusion; serried masses of roses; herbaceous borders; a laburnum tunnel; fruit and vegetable gardens; two conservatories full of giant begonias, ferns and the grander kind of indoor pot display, a swimming pool surrounded by fashionable garden furniture, a paved yard with a weather-vaned stable block. There are some interesting shrubs and everything is a great tribute to the Richards' gardeners. In addition, the prize-winning herd of pedigree Hereford cattle and flock of pedigree Suffolk sheep graze in adjoining paddocks.

MARLEY BANK 17
**Bottom Lane, Whitbourne, Hereford and Worcester.
Tel: (01886) 821576**

Mr and Mrs R. Norman ★ 10m W of Worcester on A44. Turn right to Whitbourne. At T junction by church after 1m turn left for 600 yards ★ Plants for sale ★ Open by appointment all year and generally first and third Suns in the month from April to Sept ★ Entrance: £1.50

Sue and Roger Norman are experts and the garden not only contains a great variety of plants in terraced beds but has been created with a designer's eye for form and texture. Very few of these plants are at all common, unusual cultivars are the norm, and rare treasures, particularly alpines, abound. The many paths are carefully constructed of different materials to complement the plantings and the whole looks out over a very fine view. All plants for sale are propagated at Marley Bank and purchasers need have no qualms about nomenclature and provenance – factors not always found in sales from private gardens.

OVERBURY COURT ★   18
Overbury, Hereford and Worcester.

Mr and Mrs Bruce Bossom ★ 5m NE of Tewkesbury. 2¹/₂m N of Teddington Hands roundabout (A435 and A438 crossing) ★ Parking in field off lane by church ★ Teas nearby ★ Suitable for wheelchairs ★ Plants usually for sale ★ Open 26th March, 2 – 6pm ★ Entrance: £1.50, children free

The south side of this magnificent Georgian house boasts a fine stone terrace overlooking a great sweep of formal lawned garden with hundreds of yards of clipped hedges, specimen clipped yews and a formal pool. To the east, the lawn is framed by a silver and gold border with a crinkle–crankle edging of golden gravel, leading to a gazebo overlooking the road and the country to the south. On the west the frame is completed by more hedging and a sunken garden of attractively underplanted species roses leading to the west side of the house where, under enormous plane trees, a stream winds its way from a grotto over vast lawns, falling gently into pools before it disappears underground. Elsewhere, shrub and flower borders and aged cherries merge and blend into the adjacent Norman churchyard. Everything, from the family totempole near the grotto to the polished plate on the Estate Office door, speaks of a continuity that is rare today. An exceptionally restful garden. Nevertheless, visitors with children should note that there is an unguarded opening in the south hedge which is immediately above a considerable drop to the road beneath.

PERSHORE COLLEGE OF HORTICULTURE   19
Avonbank, Pershore, Hereford and Worcester. Tel: (01386) 552443

1m S of Pershore on A44. 7m from M5 junction 7 ★ Best season: summer ★ Parking ★ Toilet facilities ★ Suitable for wheelchairs ★ Garden centre open daily except Mon ★ College gardens open 3rd June for College Open Day and 40th Anniversary celebrations, and weekdays by appointment for large parties ★ Entrance: £1 on Open Day

The gardens are designed with an educational bias and so include a wide selection of 'model gardens' created by students as well as the major features in the RHS Regional Centre's grounds. Additionally, the grounds include an arboretum, orchards, automated glasshouses and a hardy plant production nursery. The RHS West Midlands Regional Centre is on the college campus. The Alpine Garden Society has its national HQ here and is developing gardens.

THE PICTON GARDEN   20
Old Court Nurseries, Colwall, Malvern, Hereford and Worcester. Tel: (01684) 40416

Mr and Mrs P. Picton ★ 3m W of Malvern on B4218 ★ Best season: June to Oct ★ Limited parking ★ Suitable for wheelchairs ★ Plants for sale ★ Open April to Oct, daily except Mon and Tues, 10am – 1pm, 2.15 – 5.30pm ★ Entrance: £1.50

A one–and–a–half–acre plantsman's garden on the site of Ernest Ballard's

Old Court Nurseries. Recently-constructed alpine and rose gardens together with the existing large collection of herbaceous perennials ensure plenty of summer interest. Shrubs create year-round diversity. Holds the NCCPG Michaelmas daisy collection, a genus on which the owner, Paul Picton, the son of the late Percy Picton, is an acknowledged expert. At the end of September and in early October it is possible to see a vast array of these useful autumn-flowering plants in every imaginable variety and Mr Picton is always ready with advice.

THE PRIORY ★   21
Kemerton, Tewkesbury, Gloucestershire. Tel: (01386) 725258

The Hon. Mrs Healing ★ 5m NE of Tewkesbury off B4080 ★ Parking ★ Suitable for wheelchairs ★ Dogs on lead ★ Unusual plants for sale at small nursery ★ Open June to 28th Sept, Thurs and 28th May, 18th June, 9th July, 6th, 27th Aug, 10th Sept, 2 – 7pm ★ Entrance: £1.50, children 50p, under 7 free

This mature garden is a splendid example of clever tree planting. A plan of the garden lists 67 varieties. The garden was started in 1938 by the present owner and her husband although they were not able to begin developing and designing the garden until after the war. Well-manicured lawns are backed by colourful herbaceous borders full to overflowing, carefully planted in subtle colour combinations. The red border is particularly striking. The 400-year-old yew is like a huge green dome. Through the pergola with informal flowerbeds and shrubs there is an 'off-centre' turning circle, designed by the late John Codrington, in front of the eighteenth-century house, with clever shrub planting and the formal fountain garden with neat box hedges and tender plants in tubs down steps to the pool where water lilies in various colours echo lilium colours in the adjoining borders. Past the raised alpine bed is an extremely well-stocked vegetable garden bordered with herbs and some fine dahlias.

SPETCHLEY PARK ★   22
Spetchley, Nr Worcester, Hereford and Worcester.
Tel: (0190565) 224/213

Mr R.J. Berkeley ★ 3m E of Worcester on A422 ★ Parking ★ Refreshments ★ Toilet facilities ★ Suitable for wheelchairs ★ Open April to Sept, Tues – Fri, 11am – 5pm, Suns, 2 – 5pm, Bank Holidays, 11am – 5pm. Closed all other Mons and all Sats ★ Entrance: £2.20, children £1.10

Rose Berkeley was sister of the great Ellen Willmott and in her day the garden was one of the wonders of England. Now, this formal garden provides many vistas along borders and walls, through clipped yew hedges and open arches. Combined with the successive planning and planting it has a rich and abundant feel. The old kitchen garden is now surrounded by splendid borders although the beds within the walls would be improved by thinning out. There are large drifts of naturalised Turk's Cap lilies in early July, and the new rock beds near the entrance are maturing well. As one would expect, fine specimen trees abound and the wooden rusticated arbour must be one of the best examples of Victorian taste in garden furniture still standing.

STAUNTON PARK 23
Staunton-on-Arrow, Leominster, Hereford and Worcester.
Tel: (015447) 474

*Mr E.J.L. and Miss A. Savage ★ 3m from Pembridge, 6m from Kington on the
Titley road. Signposted ★ Best season: spring/summer ★ Parking inside garden ★
Teas ★ Toilet facilities ★ Suitable for wheelchairs ★ Dogs on lead ★ Plants for sale
★ Shop ★ Norman church adjoining open ★ Garden open April to Sept, Wed, Sun
and Bank Holiday Mons, 2 – 6pm ★ Entrance: £1.50, children 50p*

52 acres of parkland surround the house (not open), originally a deer park,
and the 14-acre garden, designed and planted between 1842 and 1884. The
part of the garden open to the public appears to have maintenance difficulties, but the woodland walk, the lake and the beautiful setting go some way
towards making up for a few weeds. Set out in the traditional country
house style with ha-ha flanking the park, there are old oak trees, a 100
year-old *Davidia involucrata* and a magnificent *Liriodendron tulipifera* (tulip
tree) which flowers late June/early July. A herb garden near the north
herbaceous border and a new bog garden will interest specialists. The
scented walk for the visually disabled, and a shrubbery of golden foliage are
now completed. Future projects include a butterfly walk.

STONE HOUSE COTTAGE GARDENS ★ 24
Stone, Kidderminster, Hereford and Worcester. Tel: (01562) 69902

*Mr and Mrs James Arbuthnott ★ 2m SE of Kidderminster via A448 ★ Parking ★
Toilet facilities ★ Suitable for wheelchairs ★ Plants for sale ★ Open March to Oct,
Wed – Sat and May and June, Suns, 10am – 6pm ★ Entrance: £1.50, children
free*

This garden has been created since 1974 and looking round it now it is
difficult to believe that the whole area was once flat and bare. The owners
have skilfully built towers and follies to create small intimate areas in the
garden and at the same time provide homes for very many unusual climbers
and shrubs. Yew hedges break up the area to give a vista with a tower at
the end, covered with wisteria, roses and clematis. Hardly anywhere is a
climber growing in isolation – something will be scrambling up it, usually a
small late-flowering clematis. Raised beds are full to overflowing, shrubs
and unusual herbaceous plants mingle happily. In a grassed area shrubs are
making good specimens. All plants are labelled so the visitor knows what to
look for in the adjacent nursery. (But buy with care. Some of the plants are
tender, and this is a very sheltered garden.) In June during two evenings of
music the towers have a secondary purpose as platforms for the wind
ensembles. You are invited to picnic in the garden for a modest fee. The
effect is akin to non-pretentious Glyndebourne transplanted to San
Gimingnano. At other times you may ascend the towers to view the garden
as a whole for the price of a donation to the Mother Theresa charity.

THE WEIR GARDEN 25
Swainshill, Hereford and Worcester.

The National Trust ★ 5m W of Hereford on A438 ★ Best season: spring ★

Parking. No coaches ★ Open 15th Feb to Oct, Wed – Sun and Bank Holiday Mons, 11am – 6pm. Open 14th April ★ Entrance: £1.50

This garden offers a pleasant walk along the banks of the Wye. The main time to visit is in the spring since the chief charm resides in the drifts of bulbs. It is terraced in an informal way on a cliffside and is being improved by extensive replanting. Recent bank protection work has yet to be disguised but a new rustic elevated bridge permits a fine general view. Features include a small rockery and from June to August, wild flowers on the river banks.

WHITE COTTAGE (Cranesbill Nursery) 26
Earls Common Road, Stock Green, Nr Redditch, Hereford and Worcester. Tel: (01386) 792414

Mr and Mrs S.M. Bates ★ 7m E of Worcester off A422 ★ Best season: May/June ★ Limited parking ★ Teas at Coneybury Farm and Plant Centre 1½m away ★ Suitable for wheelchairs ★ Plants for sale ★ Open 14th April to 1st Oct, daily except Wed and Thurs, 10am – 5pm but by appointment only in Aug ★ Entrance: £1, OAP 75p for charity, children free

A two-acre garden with large shrub and herbaceous borders containing many unusual perennials. A small stream bordered by bog beds provides suitable conditions for primulas, hostas, ligularias, etc. The spring wild flower meadow is home to fritillaries, primroses and cowslips. Within an old hornbeam hedge is a more formal area. A large collection of hardy geraniums can be seen around the garden. Part of the garden has been set aside for a small nursery containing many of the plants featured in the garden.

WHITFIELD ★ 27
Wormbridge, Hereford and Worcester.

Mr G.M. Clive ★ 8m SW of Hereford on A465 to Abergavenny ★ Teas. Picnic parties welcome ★ Suitable for wheelchairs ★ Open 4th June, 2 – 6pm and occasionally for local charities (see local press for details) ★ Entrance: £1.50, children 50p

Within this large park, the owner has created one of the largest private gardens made in Britain in the last half-century. The park itself has some fine old trees which may be seen on the one-and-a-half-mile woodland walk, including an 1851 redwood grove. Near the house, a new terrace with fine planting and statuary was the first step towards developing the grand garden which expands across the lawn to the south of the house. To the east a large cedar dominates an area now managed as a wildflower meadow, cut only twice a year. To the north, Mr Clive has created superb water features, including a lake and, rare in this century, a folly ruin.

HERTFORDSHIRE

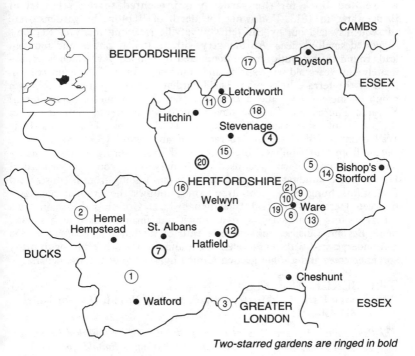

Two-starred gardens are ringed in bold

THE ABBOT'S HOUSE   1
10 High Street, Abbots Langley, Hertfordshire. Tel: (01923) 264946

Dr and Mrs Peter Tomson ★ In Abbots Langley. Approach via M25 junction 19 (from W) and 21a (from E) or M1 junction 6 ★ Parking in village car park ★ Refreshments ★ Toilet facilities ★ Suitable for wheelchairs ★ Plants for sale in nursery ★ Garden open 14th May, 18th, 20th June, 27th Aug, 2 – 5pm ★ Entrance: £1.50

One and three quarter acres of plantsman's garden full of delightfully rare species: *Mahonia gracilipes*, *Dipelta floribunda*, *Itea ilicifolia*, *Leptospermum scoparium* 'Red Damask' and *Magnolia sieboldii*. Many exciting specimens some of which must be doubtfully hardy. The sunken garden has plants thriving between the brickwork. There is flourishing *Myosotidium hortensia* mulched with seaweed, and a shrub border with contrasting foliage.

ASHRIDGE MANAGEMENT COLLEGE   2
Berkhamsted, Hertfordshire. Tel: (01442) 843491

Ashridge (Bonar Law Memorial) Trust ★ 3½m N of Berkhamsted (A41), 1m S of Little Gaddesden ★ Parking ★ Toilet facilities, inc. disabled ★ Suitable for wheelchairs ★ Dogs on lead ★ Open April to Oct, Sat and Sun, 2 – 6pm ★ Entrance: £2, OAP and children £1

HERTFORDSHIRE

A total of 150 acres comprising 90 acres of garden with the rest woodland. The nineteenth-century garden design was influenced by Humphry Repton whose Red Book for the garden was presented to the 7th Earl of Bridgewater in 1813. Following the death of Repton the gardens were subsequently laid out by Sir Jeffry Wyatville retaining many of Repton's suggested small gardens. An orangery with an Italian garden and fountain leads round to the south terrace dominated by clipped yew which is appoximately 160 years old with spring and summer bedding. The main lawn in front of the terrace links many small gardens and has planted within it a group of ancient yews and a large oak planted by Princess (later Queen) Victoria. The circular Rosarie sited virtually where Repton intended is in the process of being restored and replanted. The Monk's Garden and Holy Well comprises box laid out to represent an Armorial Garden depicting shields from four families closely associated with Ashridge. The conservatory dates from 1854 and was used as a fernery. The grotto, constructed of Hertfordshire pudding stone, and the *souterrain* leading from it constructed from flints hung on an iron framework, follows the original boundary between Hertfordshire and Buckinghamshire. Crossing the main lawn brings visitors to a sunken garden which was formerly used as a skating pond. Beyond a disused moat is an avenue of Wellingtonia planted in 1858 and underplanted with rhododendrons, leading to the arboretum with many specimen trees and a Bible garden formed by a circle of incense cedars.

THE BEALE ARBORETUM 3
West Lodge Park, Cockfosters Road, Hadley Wood, Hertfordshire.
Tel: (0181) 440 8311

The Beale family ★ Leave M25 at junction 24 and take road marked Cockfosters (A111). West Lodge Park 1m further on left ★ Parking ★ Suitable for wheel-chairs but gravel paths undulating ★ Dogs on lead ★ Open all year for organised groups of 10 or more by appointment (conducted tours, teas and luncheon by arrangement) and April to Oct, Wed, 2 – 5pm; also for NGS 4th June, 2 – 5.30pm, 22nd Oct, 12 noon – 4pm. Conducted tours available ★ Entrance: £1.50, children 30p

Edward Beale bought the West Lodge Park Hotel in 1945 with the intention of enriching its fine eighteenth-century park with many more trees and creating the important arboretum which it has now become. To help him Mr Beale enlisted the professional advice of Frank Knight, a former director of the Royal Horticultural Society, consultant Derek Honour and Frank Hillier. Today, there are 10 acres of arboretum with some fine rare trees and now Edward Beale plans to add a further 18 acres to the arboretum. The trees at West Lodge Park plus the three acres of more formal garden, many azaleas, rhododendrons and a lake, coupled with the impressive four-star hotel, can make a visit to this little-known gem, only 12 miles from central London, memorable. And certainly if he was to visit the property today, as he did in 1675, the diarist John Evelyn would still be able to say that it was 'a very pretty place – the garden handsome'. He would probably fail to recognise the strawberry tree which was believed to be there at the time of his visit and which has become one of the largest in England.

BENINGTON LORDSHIP ★★ 4
Benington, Nr Stevenage, Hertfordshire. Tel: (01438) 869668

*Mr and Mrs C.H.A. Bott ★ 5m E of Stevenage ★ Parking ★ Refreshments ★
Toilet facilities ★ Plants and pots for sale ★ Open April to Sept, Wed and Bank
Holiday Mons, 12 noon – 5pm, April to Aug, Sun, 2 – 5pm ★ Entrance: £2.50,
children free*

Here is a garden that has almost everything: wonderful views, lakes to
wander round, a Victorian folly and a Norman keep and moat, as well as a
colourful rockery and big double herbaceous borders. Borders in the kitchen
garden, one in shades of gold and silver, another full of penstemons.

BROMLEY HALL 5
Standon, Ware, Hertfordshire. Tel: (0127984) 2422

*Mr and Mrs A.J. Robarts ★ 6m W of Bishop's Stortford near A120 and A10 on
Standon – Much Hadham road ★ Parking ★ Suitable for wheelchairs ★ Open
14th, 28th June, 2.30 – 5.30pm ★ Entrance: £1.50, children 25p (1994 prices)*

Mrs Robarts has created this garden entirely herself over the last 20 years.
Improvements and alterations are going on all the time. It is both an architectural garden making good use of walls and hedges, statuary and seats,
and also a plantsman's garden. Mr Robarts looks after the vegetable garden,
and it is immaculate. The wide border on the edge of the drive is backed
by a tall hedge and is a well–designed mixture of shrub and foliage planting
with unusual and elegant perennials.

CAPEL MANOR Horticultural and Environmental Centre
(see London (Greater))

CHENIES MANOR HOUSE
(see Buckinghamshire)

DOCWRA'S MANOR
(see Cambridgeshire)

FANHAMS HALL 6
Ware, Hertfordshire. Tel: (01920) 460511

*Sainsbury Business Training Centre ★ Leave A10 at Harlow turn (A414). Take
next left for Ware. In town centre, at roundabout, turn right into New Road. At
T-junction turn right again into Fanhams Hall Road. The Hall is ½m further on
left ★ Parking ★ Toilet facilities ★ Suitable for wheelchairs ★ Open April to Oct
except Bank Holidays, Mon – Fri, 10am – 3pm. Parties by appointment only ★
Entrance: £2, OAP £1*

Owned and built by the Page-Croft family. Set in 27 acres of park and
gardens. The rose garden with lily pond is magnificent, as are the shrub
borders with magnolias. Before World War I, gardeners came from Japan
every year to carry out improvements in the Japanese garden. Sweeping
lawns with good trees, including a ginkgo, three large catalpas and a parrotia. There is a wisteria walk with tree peonies. Brilliant autumn colours
with acers of many sorts. The head gardener, Carmel Ovenden, is still

struggling with a lovely garden that got out of hand, and is making excellent headway.

GARDENS OF THE ROSE ★★ 7
Chiswell Green, St Albans, Hertfordshire. Tel: (01727) 850461

Royal National Rose Society ★ 2m S of St Albans on B4630 (signposted) ★ Parking ★ Refreshments: licensed cafeteria ★ Toilet facilities ★ Suitable for wheelchairs with good facilities for disabled ★ Dogs on lead ★ Miniature and patio rose plants for sale, growers' catalogues available ★ Open 10th June to 15th Oct, Mon – Sat, 9am – 5pm, Suns and Bank Holidays, 10am – 6pm ★ Entrance: £4, disabled £3, groups £3.50 per person. Members and children free

The Royal National Rose Gardens provide a wonderful display of one of the best and most important collections of roses in the world. There are some 30,000 rose trees and at least 1700 varieties including hybrid teas, floribundas and climbing roses of every kind, miniature roses and ground-cover roses. Some are thought to differ little from the roses admired by writers in the classical world. Part of the gardens is the trial grounds for roses from all over the world. The Society has introduced other plants which harmonise with roses and enhance the planting schemes to give a more natural effect. There are many such companion plants including clematis and hardy geraniums. H.M. The Queen Mother is particularly fond of old roses and the garden named for her contains a fascinating collection of Gallicas, Albas, Damasks, Centifolias, Portlands and Moss roses. Here can be seen what is thought to be the original red rose of Lancaster and white rose of York. Among the Gallicas is the 'Rosa Mundi' said to have been named for Fair Rosamond, the mistress of Henry II. This is an historic wonderland which could be explored indefinitely by rose lovers and will have interest for all gardeners. (Note: for those who wish to be up-to-date, hybrid teas and floribundas are now known as large-flowered and cluster-flowered roses respectively.) The garden is being enlarged over the next ten years from its current 12 to some 60 acres.

1 GERNON WALK 8
Pixmore Way, Letchworth, Hertfordshire. Tel: (01462) 686399

Mrs R. Crawshay ★ Best season: early June ★ Parking ★ Suitable for wheelchairs ★ Open by appointment ★ Entrance: by collecting box

In this long narrow area, 100 feet by 8 feet at its narrowest point, the owner has over the past decade devised a successful garden out of a quite impossible site. A patio with a tiny pool, a seat and a mirror at an angle to suggest a vista beyond. A winding path with raised beds. *Prunus laurocerasus*, *Deutzia setchuenensis*, *Elaeagnus commutata*. At the end there is a paved space with a seat.

GREAT MUNDEN HOUSE 9
Nr Dane End, Ware, Hertfordshire. Tel: (01920) 438244

Mr and Mrs D. Wentworth-Stanley ★ 7m N of Ware off A10. Turn off W of Puckeridge bypass ★ Parking ★ Teas ★ Partly suitable for wheelchairs ★ Plants for sale ★ Open 23rd April, and one day in June for charity, 2.30 – 5.30pm. Private visits welcome for small parties ★ Entrance: £2, children 50p

A charming small garden, beautifully planned and immaculately kept. It is situated down the side of a valley with a backdrop of wheat fields and trees. Good windbreaks of beech hedges as the wind funnels down the valley. Kitchen garden with vegetables planted in patterns. Good mixed borders imaginatively planted with shrubs, shrub roses and excellent foliage plants. Intimate secret corners and a paved area surrounded by silver plants and a *Juniperus virginiana* 'Skyrocket' in each corner. The redesigned island border is becoming well established with shrub roses and shrubs. Many more climbing roses have been planted to ramble through apple trees.

HANBURY MANOR HOTEL   10
Ware, Hertfordshire. Tel: (01920) 487722

Hanbury Manor Hotel ★ 2m N of Ware on A10 ★ Parking ★ Refreshments: restaurants and public bar in hotel ★ Toilet facilities ★ Suitable for wheelchairs ★ Dogs on lead ★ Shop in hotel ★ Garden open all year ★ Entrance: free (charge on charity days)

Edmond Hanbury inherited the property (known then as Poles) in 1884. He pulled down the old house, replacing it with a Jacobean-style mansion designed by Sir Ernest George. The Hanbury family were gifted horticul-turalists and the original gardens, now part of the hotel complex, were widely acclaimed both for their species trees and orchid houses. Today, a colourful pre-Victorian walled garden with listed Moon Gate shows off extensive herbaceous borders, herb garden and fruit houses. The original pinetum with centuries-old sequoias still stands, and major restoration work has seen the revival of the period rose gardens and bulb-planted orchard. A more recent secret garden in a woodland setting is well worth a visit.

R. HARKNESS & CO. LTD   11
The Rose Gardens, Hitchin, Hertfordshire. Tel: (01462) 420402

R. Harkness & Co. Ltd ★ On A505 Hitchin – Letchworth road ★ Best season: summer ★ Parking ★ Refreshments: in restaurant ★ Toilet facilities, inc. disabled ★ Suitable for wheelchairs ★ Dogs ★ Plants for sale ★ Shop ★ Open all year, daily, 9am – 5.30pm (Bank Holidays 10am – 5.30pm) ★ Entrance: free

This famous rose grower has an extensive nursery and exhibits at Chelsea. Here there are two and a half acres of rose garden and nursery with 25,000 container plants, mostly roses but also some excellent and unusual shrubs. A beautifully-managed garden with all the roses grafted and grown by Harkness themselves. The stock field has 17 acres of roses and a further 17 acres of roses waiting to be grafted. This is at a separate location and can only be visited by appointment.

HATFIELD HOUSE ★★   12
Hatfield, Hertfordshire. Tel: (01707) 262823

The Marquess and Marchioness of Salisbury ★ Opposite Hatfield railway station on A1000, 2m from A1(M) junction 4 ★ Parking ★ Refreshments: light meals and teas, 11am – 5pm ★ Toilet facilities ★ Suitable for wheelchairs ★ Plants for sale ★ Garden and gift shops ★ House open daily except Mon and 14th April ★

Garden open 25th March to 8th Oct. West Gardens, daily except 14th April, 11am – 6pm. East Garden (Lord and Lady Salisbury's private garden) Mon except Bank Holiday Mons, 2 – 5pm ★ Entrance: £2.80, OAP £2.50, children £2 (house supplement £2.20, children £1.10). Enquire for party rates and garden guide

Originally laid out in the early seventeenth century by Robert Cecil and planted by John Tradescant the Elder. Nothing new can be written about this fascinating garden with its presiding genius the Marchioness of Salisbury, except to say do visit it. Try to choose a Monday afternoon in season when the gardens east of the house are open for it is here that some of the most beautiful plants are to be seen. See the mop-headed *Quercus ilex* imported especially for the garden and the wild garden around the New Pond (formed in 1607), newly landscaped and planted since the devastation of two hurricanes. Amongst the many features are the varied knot gardens planted by Lady Salisbury in the early 1980s following her own designs, sited, like those in Tudor times, to be viewed from above, and all filled with plants used from the fifteenth to seventeenth centuries. Make sure to see also the wilderness and the scented gardens. There is an annual midsummer festival at Hatfield, part country fair, part garden party and part flower show, which gives an opportunity to visit the gardens, including the splendid East Garden mentioned above. There is a lovely wild garden bank behind the Old Palace, and a charming herb garden.

HILL HOUSE ★   13
Stanstead Abbotts, Ware, Hertfordshire. Tel: (01920) 870013

Mr and Mrs R. Pilkington ★ Halfway between Hertford and Harlow. From A10 turn E on to A414, and at roundabout take B181 for Stanstead Abbots, left at end of High Street and first right past church ★ Parking ★ Teas ★ Toilet facilities ★ Dogs on lead ★ Unusual plants for sale ★ Picture gallery ★ Open 7th May, 4th, 11th June, 16th July, 2 – 5pm ★ Entrance: £2, OAP £1.50, children 50p

Six acres of very varied garden including woodland, a bog garden, a fine herbaceous border and a highly-recommended Victorian conservatory. Immaculate borders, extensive lawns and walls and a wide variety of plants. The position is an interesting one, on a south-facing slope with a magnificent view overlooking the Lea valley.

HOPLEYS ★   14
Much Hadham, Hertfordshire. Tel: (0127984) 2509

Mr A. Barker ★ 50 yards N of Bull public house in centre of Much Hadham ★ Parking ★ Toilet facilities ★ Suitable for wheelchairs ★ Plants for sale ★ Open all year except Jan; Sun, 2 – 5pm, Mon, Wed – Sat, 9am – 5pm and also on special days for charities ★ Entrance: £1.50, children under 16 free

The owner and his parents have been working on this garden for many years and it has been expanding annually. The relatively new pool and bog area look well established. There are numerous borders filled with shrubs and hardy plants, most of which are for sale in the nursery. The long-established conifer bed illustrates the different sizes and shapes of mature conifers. There is also a border for tender plants which have come through the last few winters well. Not far from Hopleys is the headquarters of Andrew Crace, who designs and sells a wide range of fine garden furniture and bronze and stone ornaments. He is planning to open on a regular basis and visitors to Much Hadham would be well advised to watch the press for details.

KNEBWORTH HOUSE 15
Knebworth, Nr Stevenage, Hertfordshire. Tel: (01438) 812661

The Lord Cobbold ★ 30m N of London, 2m from Stevenage. Direct access from A1(M) junction 7 ★ Parking ★ Refreshments: in sixteenth-century tithe barn ★ Toilet facilities ★ Open 1st, 2nd, 8th to 23rd April, daily except Mons (but open 17th April); 29th April to 21st May, weekends and 8th May; 27th May to 29th June, 4th July to 4th Sept, daily except Mon (but open 29th May, 29th Aug); 9th Sept to 1st Oct, weekends only, all 12 noon – 5pm ★ Entrance: £4.50, OAP and children £4 (house and garden) (1994 prices)

As the historic home of the Lytton family, the garden evolved from a simple Tudor green and orchard to Sir Edward Bulwer Lytton's elaborate design of the mid-1800s. Edwin Lutyens made alterations and simplified the main central area. His twin pollarded lime avenues lead to an upper lawn of rose beds, lily ponds and herbaceous borders, with tall yew hedges behind. Beyond lies the Gold garden, in striking contrast to the mainly blue theme of the adjacent Lutyens brick garden and pergola, featuring herbaceous plants with old-fashioned and shrub roses. There is also a unique quincunx-patterned herb garden designed by Gertrude Jekyll for Knebworth in 1907, but not laid out until 1982. Other features are the Lutyens garden bothy and wall border, many fine trees, the dogs' graveyard, and wildlife pond. The 'Wilderness' area is a carpet of daffodils in spring followed by blue alkanets, foxgloves and other wild flowers.

MACKERYE END HOUSE 16
Harpenden, Hertfordshire.

Mr and Mrs David Laing ★ From Wheathampstead follow signs for Luton. The house is ½m on right ★ Parking ★ Refreshments ★ Toilet facilities ★ Suitable for wheelchirs ★ Plants for sale ★ Open 18th June, 11am – 5pm ★ Entrance: £1.50, children 50p

A Grade I manor house (1550) in 11 acres of park and garden. Its Victorian walled garden is now divided by magnificent yew hedges with wonderful peonies of all shades. There is a path maze, a cutting garden, a new garden enclosed by a pergola walk of old English roses and vines, a paved walk around the house with camellias, magnolias and a patio with a large ginkgo tree. The rough grass in front of the house has a mass of wild daffodils in the spring and a vast tulip tree planted in the seventeenth century.

ODSEY PARK 17
Ashwell, Hertfordshire. Tel: (01462) 742237

Mr and The Hon. Mrs Jeremy Fordham ★ Equidistant between Royston and Baldock (4½m) on N carriageway of A505. Enter by lodge on road ★ Parking ★ Teas ★ Suitable for wheelchairs ★ Open 23rd April, 1 – 5pm, 25th June, 2 –

6pm ★ Entrance: £1.50, children under 12 free

In a fine park setting with mature trees and grazing cattle this immaculate garden was re-made by Mr and Mrs Fordham from an earlier garden of the 1860s. Spring bulbs, especially tulips, a superb herbaceous border against a honey-coloured wall with huge delphiniums and clematis behind and good contrasting planting in front. There are imaginative shrub borders, good specie roses and an unusual standard grey salix walk. An interesting cast-iron conservatory dating from 1870.

PELHAM HOUSE   18
Brent Pelham, Buntingford, Hertfordshire. Tel: (01279) 777473

Mr David Haselgrove and Dr Sylvia Martinelli ★ E of Brent Pelham on B1038 Newport road ★ Parking ★ Suitable for wheelchairs ★ Plants for sale ★ Open 16th April, 14th May, 11 June, 2 – 5pm and by appointment for parties at other times ★ Entrance: £1.50

A most interesting and ambitious garden in a most unprepossessing cold and windy site covering in all three and a half acres. In raised beds there are hardy orchids, erythroniums, corydalis, trilliums, euphorbias and hellebores (a spectacular 'Boughton Beauty'). There are wild bee orchids in profusion. *Daphne cneorum* flourishes in shingle beds and *Cornus kousa* is magnificent in unadulterated clay. Birches and oaks are among the many other trees and shrubs. Bulb frames.

SCOTTS GROTTO   19
Scotts Road, Ware, Hertfordshire. Tel: (01920) 464131

East Hertfordshire District Council ★ In Scotts Road, Ware, off A119 Hertford road ★ Parking in road ★ Open April to Sept, Sat and Bank Holiday Mon only, 2 – 4.30pm. Group visits by prior arrangement ★ Entrance: £1

Recently restored by the Ware Society, this is the largest grotto in the country, decorated with exotic shells and lined with flints. It is truly 'grotto-esque' with a council chamber, committee room, consultation room and several passages. Take a torch!

ST PAUL'S WALDEN BURY ★★   20
Whitwell, Nr Hitchin, Hertfordshire. Tel: (01438) 871218

Mr and Mrs Simon Bowes Lyon ★ 5m S of Hitchin, 1/2m N of Whitwell on B651 ★ Best season: April to July ★ Parking ★ Teas ★ Suitable for wheelchairs ★ Dogs on lead ★ Open 16th April, 21st May, 11th June, 2nd July 2 – 7pm. Also other times by appointment ★ Entrance: £2, children 50p

The formal landscape garden has retained intact its original design of 1730, one of the few to survive the landscape movement. It covers an area of 40 acres though it seems larger. The long rides (or *allées*) lined with beech hedges fan out from the house through woodland as well as open fields to temples, statues, ponds and the medieval church. The eighteenth-century house is the principal ornament in this layout. The Bowes Lyon family who have lived here for over 200 years have created more recent flower gardens with interesting and unusual plants, and woodland shrub gardens with rhododendrons, magnolias and camellias. Daffodils, bluebells and mixed flowers form an important feature. This is a listed Grade I garden. It was the childhood home of HM the Queen Mother.

VAN HAGE'S NURSERY AND GARDEN CENTRE   21
Great Amwell, Nr Ware, Hertfordshire. Tel: (01920) 870811

Van Hage's Nursery ★ On the outskirts of Ware. M25 junction 25, A10 towards Cambridge, A1170 towards Ware ★ Parking ★ Refreshments in coffee shop ★ Toilet facilities ★ Suitable for wheelchairs ★ Plants for sale ★ Shop ★ Open daily, 9am – 6pm (opens 9.30am on Mon) ★ Entrance: free

A superbly-run nursery with an unusually comprehensive selection of plants and shrubs. The stock includes very good Dutch bulbs. There is a range of containers, pots and chimneys, paving and dried flowers, books and garden accessories. Informative staff.

HUMBERSIDE

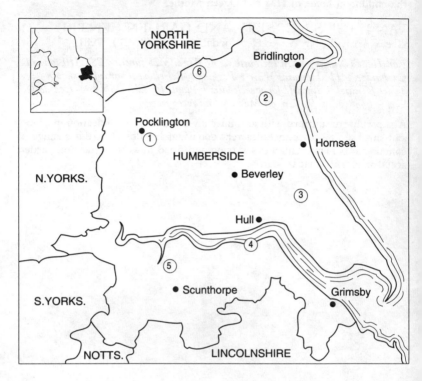

BURNBY HALL GARDENS AND MUSEUM   1
Pocklington, Humberside. Tel: (01759) 302068

Stewart's Burnby Hall Gardens and Museum Trust ★ 13m E of York on B1247 in Pocklington ★ Best season: June to Sept ★ Parking, inc. coaches ★ Refreshments: cafeteria for teas in garden ★ Toilet facilities, inc. disabled ★ Suitable for wheelchairs ★ Shop ★ Open 2nd April to Sept, daily, 10am – 6pm ★ Entrance: £2, OAP £1.50, children (5-16) 50p, under 5 free. Parties of 20 or more £1.30 per person

When the gardens were established on twelve acres of open farmland in 1904 by Major Stewart, the original ponds, which covered two acres, were constructed for fishing, but in 1935 they were converted to water lily cultivation. They are now under the direction of Mt Davies of Stapeley Water Gardens (see entry) who has acquired a substantial water garden in France for *Nymphae* cultivation. This large collection of hardy water lilies forms part of the National collection. Lilies may be seen from June to mid-September in a normal year and in July the two lakes are covered in colourful blooms from 80 different varieties.

BURTON AGNES HALL 2
Burton Agnes, Great Driffield, Humberside. Tel: (01262) 490324

Hon. Nicholas and Mrs Susan Cunliffe-Lister (Preservation Trust Ltd) ★ 5m E of Great Driffield on A166 York – Bridlington road ★ Best season: summer ★ Parking ★ Refreshments: in coffee shop ★ Toilet facilities ★ Plants for sale ★ Shop with extensive selection of dried flowers ★ House open ★ Garden open April to Oct, daily, 11am – 5pm ★ Entrance: £1.80 (hall and garden £3.50, OAP £3)

The beautiful Elizabethan hall – designed by Robert Smithson, master mason to Elizabeth I and builder of Longleat and Hardwick – is approached through the gatehouse archway, up a wide gravel drive flanked by rows of onion-shaped yew hedges, with lawns beyond. Little evidence remains of the garden's history, any former flower planting in sight of the hall having succumbed to lawn on all sides. However the walls of the former enormous kitchen garden conceal a recently-created (1990) riot of colour (including campanulas, thymes, clematis, hardy geraniums and old roses): a *potager* of vegetables and herbs supply the needs of the household, two herbaceous borders, a scented garden, a jungle of bamboos and giant exotic species, and also a newly-planted maze. A series of large-scale games (including chess, draughts and snakes and ladders) are laid out on paving at the far end of the walled garden. Behind the hall is an area of woodland garden, and also a woodland walk of approximately one mile.

BURTON CONSTABLE HALL 3
Nr Hull, Humberside. Tel: (01964) 562400

Burton Constable Foundation ★ 7½ m NE of Hull. Take A165 between Hull and Skirlaugh and follow signs ★ Parking ★ Refreshments: coffee shop ★ Toilet facilities ★ Shop ★ Hall open as garden, 1 – 4.15pm ★ Garden open 16th April to Sept, Sun – Thurs, 12 noon – 5pm. Also Sats in July and Aug. Parties at any time by arrangement ★ Entrance: £3.50 (hall and grounds)

A fine Elizabethan house surrounded by parkland which 'Capability' Brown, whose plans can still be seen, laid out in the 1770s. His 20 acres of lakes are spanned by a good stone bridge, and while his trees have not all survived they are being replaced by new plantings, still in their infancy. Around the house is a four-acre garden with handsome eighteenth-century orangery, statuary and borders. This is one of the grandest establishments in the North East and with the help of a £3.5m endowment from the National Heritage Memorial Fund should soon regain its former glory.

THE COTTAGES 4
Ferry Road, Barrow Haven, Nr Barton-on-Humber, South Humberside. Tel: (01469) 531614

Mr and Mrs E.C. Walsh ★ 4m E of Barton-on-Humber off A1077 adjacent to Barrow-Haven railway station ★ Parking ★ Teas ★ Partly suitable for wheelchairs ★ Plants for sale ★ Open 28th, 29th May, 18th June, 16th July, 27th, 28th Aug, 11am – 5pm and by appointment ★ Entrance: £1, children under 10 free

Situated on a disused tile works near the River Humber this one and a quarter-acre garden is on a direct flight path for many migratory birds. By careful management the owners have maximised the number of food sources, nest sites and habitats for visiting and resident species. There are bird-watching hides for the enthusiast. The result is a pastoral haven of old thorn trees intermingled with more recently-planted trees, shrubs and herbaceous plants. Grassy paths meander to a dyke planted with bog plants, a pond and reed bed and an organic vegetable plot on raised beds. In contrast, the well-manicured area around the house has beds, borders and trellises brimming with plants providing year-round colour.

NORMANBY HALL 5
Normanby Hall Country Park, Nr Scunthorpe, South Humberside. Tel: (01724) 280444

Run by Scunthorpe Borough Council ★ 4m N of Scunthorpe on B1430 ★ Best season: June/July ★ Parking ★ Refreshments ★ Toilet facilities ★ Suitable for wheelchairs ★ Dogs on lead ★ Shop ★ Hall and Farm Museum open April to Oct, daily, 1 - 5pm ★ Park open all year: 9am - 5pm (up to 9pm in summer) ★ Entrance: small admission fee paid in car park

Although the parkland and woodland at Normanby is extensive, with superb nature trails, rhododendron walks, lakes and accessible deer park, the actual pleasure gardens are rather limited. They are, however, well-maintained and as an addition to the many attractions here are worth seeing. Next to the Regency house are formal rose beds and a lavender-edged sunken garden with a fish pond. Further away, and easily missed, is a lovely, walled 'secret garden'. Enclosed by mellow brick walls, holly and conifer hedges are double-sided herbaceous borders, grass paths and good wall shrubs and climbers, a peaceful retreat from the often busy park. Within the grounds is a farm museum which, like the house, has no entry charge and allows all the family to find something of interest at a minimal cost.

SLEDMERE HOUSE 6
Sledmere, Great Driffield, Humberside. Tel: (01377) 236637

Sir Tatton Sykes, Bart ★ 9m NW of Great Driffield, signposted off A166 ★ Parking ★ Teas ★ Toilet facilities ★ Suitable for wheelchairs ★ Shop ★ House open ★ Garden open 14th April to 24th Sept, daily except Fri and Mon (but open 14th April and Bank Holiday Mons), 12 noon - 5pm ★ Entrance: £1.50, children £1 (house, park and garden £3.25, OAP £2.75, children £1.75)

A listed garden, Sledmere is among the most well-preserved of 'Capability' Brown's landscape schemes. Dating from the 1770s it clearly reveals his characteristic belting and clumping of trees and carefully controlled diagonal vistas to distant 'eye-catchers'. His use of a ha-ha allows the park to flow up to the windows of the house (whence it is best seen) across extensive tree-planted lawns. To the rear of the house is a well-stocked herbaceous border, a newly planted knot garden and an interesting Italian paved sculpture court (1911) which is undergoing restoration. The eighteenth-century walled gardens are now grassed over and planted with mainly roses and herbaceous plants and are entered through a small but attractive rose garden set off by garden urns.

KENT

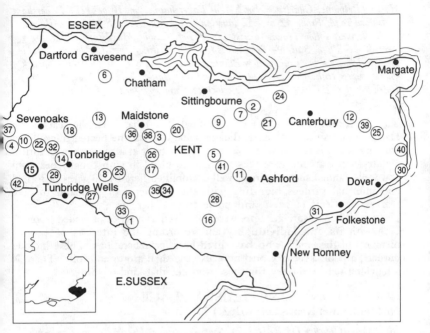

Two-starred gardens are ringed in bold.

BEDGEBURY NATIONAL PINETUM ★   1
Nr Goudhurst, Cranbrook, Kent. Tel: (01580) 211044 (Curator)

*Forestry Commission ★ On B2079 Goudhurst – Flimwell road off the A21 ★
Parking. Disabled persons may be brought to and collected from lake or park in
the office car park nearby ★ Refreshments: ice creams and light refreshments
available in car park ★ Toilet facilities ★ Dogs on lead ★ Shop open 17th April to
Sept, 10am – 5pm ★ Arboretum open daily, 10am – 7pm (4pm in winter) ★
Entrance: £1.50, OAP £1, children 75p. Exact money required at certain times*

The Pinetum lies on Hastings clay over sandstone too infertile for sustained
agriculture, being silty, very acid and deficient in phosphates. Specimen
trees were initially cultivated with the addition of essential nutrients.
However, although the size of some of the conifers is inevitably limited, the
variety of species is not, and the Pinetum offers the most comprehensive
collection of the conifers that can be grown in Britain. It has been planted
so that the form, colour and texture of the mature trees can readily be seen.
As well as being a valuable educational resource for schools and students of
forestry and related subjects, it is also a place for quiet enjoyment.

KENT

BELMONT ★   2
Belmont Park, Throwley, Faversham, Kent. Tel: (01795) 890202

*Harris (Belmont) Charity ★ 4m SW of Faversham, 1½m W of A251 Faversham
– Ashford road. From A2 or M2 junction 6, take the A251 S towards Ashford.
At Badlesmere follow brown tourist signs ★ Best season: May/June ★ Parking ★
Teas, 3 – 5.30pm. Suitable for picnics ★ Toilet facilities, inc. disabled ★ Suitable
for wheelchairs ★ Dogs on lead ★ Plants usually for sale ★ Shop ★ House open ★
Garden open 16th April to Sept, Sat, Sun and Bank Holiday Mons, 2 – 5pm ★
Entrance: £2, children 75p (house, clock museum and gardens £4, children
£2.50)*

The eighteenth-century house by Samual Wyatt has been the seat of the
Harris family since 1801 and, though somewhat off the beaten track down
winding lanes, it is well worth a visit. It was built at a time when beautiful
country house architecture was required to blend in with equally beautiful
and well-planned surroundings; well exemplified here by 40 acres of formal
and informal gardens blending with the 150 acres of parkland to give
marvellous vistas of aged and noble trees. There is a yew walk and a
pinetum. The pleasure gardens were conceived as a series of walled 'rooms',
each with its own individuality and recording the interests of various
members of the family who have lived here for generations. These include
borders, a pool, a rockery and note also the shell grotto and folly. There is
a touching pets' cemetery for those who like that kind of thing.

BOUGHTON MONCHELSEA PLACE   3
Nr Maidstone, Kent. Tel: (01622) 743120

*Mr Charles Gooch ★ On B2163 5m S of Maidstone. Use M20, junction 8 ★
Parking ★ Refreshments: tearoom ★ Toilet facilities ★ Shop ★ Grounds open 14th
April to 15th Oct, Sun and Bank Holiday Mons; also June to Aug, Wed, 2 –
6pm ★ Entrance: £2.75, OAP £2.50, children £1.50 (house and gardens £3.75,
OAP £3, children £2.50). Parties welcome by appointment*

This is an attractive walled garden built and established behind the main
house, full of roses and herbaceous plants in season. It is not a plantsman's
garden but is very peaceful in the wider context of the old ragstone walls
and the rooftops of Boughton Monchelsea Place. This is situated on the
greensand ridge and the lawn in front of the house gives fine views over the
Weald, with a steep drop almost immediately below. It is said that a herd
of deer in the park has been there for at least 300 years. The old church
nearby is also well worth a visit.

CHARTWELL   4
Westerham, Kent. Tel: (01732) 866368

*The National Trust ★ 2m S of Westerham off B2026 ★ Parking ★ Refreshments:
licensed self-service restaurant ★ Toilet facilities ★ Partly suitable for wheelchairs
★ Dogs on lead ★ Shop ★ House open ★ Garden open April to Oct, Tues to
Thurs, Sat, Sun and Bank Holiday Mon, 11am – 5.30pm (last admission
4.30pm). Closed 14th April and Tues following Bank Holiday Mon ★ Entrance:
£2, children £1 (house and garden £4.50, children £2.25)*

The lawns to the front of the house slope down to two large lakes and a swimming pool (constructed by Sir Winston Churchill). A walled rose garden at the side of the house leads to a loggia, with grapevine, adjoining the Marlborough Pavilion which contains bas reliefs of the Battle. Another main feature, adjoining an orchard, is the Golden Rose Garden and Walk – extending to the kitchen garden, where Sir Winston built the summerhouse and the brick wall. Lady Churchill had a good deal to do with the original design of the garden. This is a garden worth exploring and enjoying for the sense of space and history, but it is not of particular interest to the plantsperson.

CHURCH HILL COTTAGE GARDENS 5
Charing Heath, Ashford, Kent.

Mr and Mrs M. Metianu ★ Leave M20 at junction 8 from Maidstone or junction 9 from Folkestone to join A20. Follow sign S from dual-carriageway section of A20, ½m W of Charing, to Charing Heath and Egerton. Fork right at Red Lion pub after 1 mile, take next right and 250 yards on right ★ Best season: May to July ★ Parking ★ Toilet facilities ★ Suitable for wheelchairs ★ Plants for sale in nursery open as garden and Feb, Oct and Nov ★ Garden open March to Sept, daily except Mon (but open Bank Holiday Mons) ★ Entrance: £1.50, children free

Church Hill Cottage Gardens have an air of peace and tranquillity rarely equalled in much larger gardens. There is a strong sense of design in the curves of borders and island beds but these are so well matched by the fine and well-developed planting that the whole seems natural and much more established than one normally expects after only a decade. Established birches form a central point. Beds are varied, some with colour themes, others with shrubs heavily underplanted with a wide range of unusual hardy plants, bulbs in season, foliage plants, etc. One point of plantsman's interest is the large collection of dianthus, which includes between 30 and 40 types of old forms dating from the sixteenth to eighteenth centuries. The woodland area is developing well.

COBHAM HALL 6
Cobham, Kent. Tel: (01474) 824319/823371

The Westwood Educational Trust ★ 3½m W of Rochester, S of the A2 on the B2009 ★ Parking ★ Teas ★ Toilet facilities ★ House open ★ Garden open 29th, 30th March, 2nd, 5th, 6th, 9th, 14th to 17th (Medway Craft Fair), 19th, 20th April, 1st, 2nd June, 5th, 6th, 12th, 13th, 16th (Jaguar Drivers Club Day), 19th, 20th, 23rd, 26th, 27th, 30th July, 2nd, 3rd, 6th, 9th, 10th, 13th, 16th, 17th, 20th, 23rd, 24th, 27th, 28th Aug, 2 – 5pm ★ Entrance: £2.50, OAP and children £2

This, Humphry Repton's first major work, is being returned to something like its original condition of around 1790, including fragments of his 'invisible fence' designed to exclude deer from the pleasure ground he created here. There are a number of delightful buildings; a Gothic dairy by James Wyatt, a grotto, an aviary and a classical temple. On the south lawn is a modern re-creation of a knot garden by Kathleen Faure to a design taken from a plaster ceiling in the house and the west lawn boasts a pair of grand Coadestone vases. Remarkably, a number of trees have survived from early plantings; a row of four limes are all that remain of the five great seventeenth-century lime avenues, an ancient oak said to have been planted about 1550 and a two hundred year old holly. There is a group of mature hornbeams and a fine ginkgo. In the spring the park is filled with drifts of daffodils, narcissi and many rare bulbs. The house has a history too, home to the lady who modelled for Britannia. Restoration continues by the Cobham Hall Heritage Trust, established in 1993, which has completed much survey work and is gradually clearing and planting. Guided tours lasting approximately 1½ hours are provided and because the site is so overgrown these are recommended for a full appreciation of the detail as well as the scale of Repton's scheme. Aside from the Repton interest, this is one of the area's great historic sites, with Celtic and Roman associations.

COPTON ASH GARDENS 7
105 Ashford Road, Faversham, Kent.
Tel: (01795) 535919 (day) and (01227) 751968 (evening)

Mr and Mrs John Ingram and Drs Tim and Gillian Ingram ★ 1m S of Faversham. Leave M2 at junction 6. On A251 Faversham – Ashford road, opposite eastbound junction with M2 ★ Best seasons: spring and autumn ★ Parking in road ★ Suitable for wheelchairs ★ Plants for sale from nursery open March to Oct, Tues – Thurs, Sat and Sun, 2 – 6pm ★ Garden open by appointment and on certain days for charity ★ Entrance: £1, accompanied children free

Despite its position close to the M2 there is a pleasant atmosphere at Copton Ash. This a plantsman's garden created since 1978 on the site of an old cherry orchard. About one and a half acres in extent, it accommodates some 2000 species in herbaceous borders and island beds with specimen plantings. There is a collection of fruit varieties, alpines are grown in raised beds, and experiments are under way to examine the hardiness of species from Australia, New Zealand and South America. Helpfully, many plants and shrubs are labelled. From the garden, Tim Ingram has developed a specialist nursery. Belmont and Longacre (see entries) are nearby.

CRITTENDEN HOUSE ★ 8
Crittenden Road, Matfield, Nr Tonbridge, Kent. Tel: (01892) 832554

Mr B.P. Tompsett ★ 6m SE of Tonbridge on B2160. Turn left in village along Chestnut Lane, house on right after 1m ★ Parking ★ Refreshments: at Cherrytrees on Matfield Green ★ Toilet facilities ★ Partly suitable for wheelchairs ★ Open 2nd, 16th, 17th, 30th April, 14th, 28th May, 2 – 6pm ★ Entrance: £2, children under 12 25p. Parties by appointment

An extraordinary range of soil types has led to a wide variety of species blending within the labour-saving concept of the owner's design; with spring bulbs, rhododendrons, roses, lilies, waterside plantings and autumn colours, this garden teems with interest throughout the year. Curved lawns sweep to island beds and interestingly-planted water fringes within a framework of trees. The local native flora, such as *Primula vulgaris* and *Dactylorhiza fuchsii*, mingle strikingly with more rarified species such as *Paeonia lutea ludlowii* ('Sherriff's Variety'), a gift from George Sherriff, and *Malus* 'Crittenden' (awarded First Class Certificate in 1971). *Crataegus* varieties, such as *monogyna* 'Pink May', x *lavallei* and *laciniata*, contrast with *Davidia involucrata* var. *involucrata* (with its outstanding autumn colours) and *Rhododendron* 'Elizabeth', *R.* 'Unique', *R. yakushimanum* 'Exbury' and *R. auriculatum* 'Lady Chamberlain'. Several trees have been raised from seeds collected by the owner – *Pinus ayacahuite* from Popacatapetl, Mexico, and *Hippophae salicifolia* from Nepal, for example. The local stone used in the garden has many fossil sand-ripples and even a fossil footprint of a dinosaur – possibly Iguanodon.

DODDINGTON PLACE 9
Doddington, Nr Sittingbourne, Kent. Tel: (01795) 886101

Mr R. and the Hon. Mrs Oldfield ★ 6m S of Sittingbourne. From A20 turn N at Lenham. From A2 turn S at Teynham. Signposted ★ Best season: May/June ★ Parking ★ Refreshments: morning coffee, light lunch, afternoon tea ★ Toilet facilities ★ Suitable for wheelchairs ★ Dogs on lead ★ Plants for sale when available ★ Shop ★ Open 17th April to Sept, Weds and Bank Holidays, 11am – 6pm; also Suns in May. Other days for parties by appointment ★ Entrance: £2, children 25p

Ten acres of landscaped grounds created by Nesfield in the nineteenth century and further developed in the 1910s and the 1960s. The main attractions here are the views of open countryside and the spaciousness which offer pleasant walks at any time of year. Other features are a rather fine rock garden, excellent yew hedging (some cut to resemble undulating mountain scenery), a new *allée* and, in season, the woodland garden's collection of rhododendrons.

EMMETTS GARDEN ★ 10
Ide Hill, Sevenoaks, Kent. Tel: (01732) 750429

The National Trust ★ 1½m S of A25 on Sundridge to Ide Hill road. 1½m N of Ide Hill off B2042 ★ Best season: spring to midsummer ★ Parking. Buggy available from car park to entrance ★ Teas 2 – 5pm ★ Partly suitable for wheelchairs ★ Dogs on lead ★ Open March, Sat and Sun; April to Oct, Wed – Sun and Bank Holiday Mons, 1 – 6pm (last admission 5pm) ★ Entrance: £2.50, children £1.30. Pre-booked parties £2, children £1

Set on the top of Ide Hill, Emmetts Garden gives a superb view over the Weald of Kent and provides an impressive setting for this plantsman's collection of trees and shrubs. This is a garden to visit at any time of the year, but is particularly fine in spring, with its bluebell woods and flowering shrubs. First planted by Frederick Lubbock, the owner, from about 1890 until his death in 1926, it is specially noted for its rhododendrons and azaleas. It follows the late-nineteenth-century style of combining exotics with conifers to provide a 'wild' garden, all well listed in the Trust guide. Recent additions to extend the interest throughout the season include a rose garden, a rock garden and extensive planting of acers for autumn colour. The enforced clearance of some trees and shrubs after the gales of 1987 has enabled new planting to keep the traditions of the garden but also to expand it. Recent planting is continuing to develop well. The new rock garden in particular has grown on and is becoming established. It is still a wonderful site and a fascinating garden.

GODINTON PARK ★ 11
Ashford, Kent. Tel: (01233) 620773

*Mr Alan Wyndham Green ★ 1½m W of Ashford on A20 at Potter's Corner ★
Best season: summer ★ Parking ★ Toilet facilities ★ Partly suitable for wheelchairs
★ Dogs on lead ★ Plants for sale sometimes ★ House open ★ Garden open 2nd,
3rd, 4th April, 30th May, 29th Aug and June to Sept, Sun, 2 – 5pm and
parties by appointment ★ Entrance: 70p (house and garden £2, children 70p.
Parties of 20 or more £1.50 per person)*

The key features of the formal areas are the water garden, well stocked with
lilies and surrounded by shrubs and beds, and the small enclosed Italian
garden; four statues, draped in wisteria, guard the entrance to this peaceful
spot with its cruciform pool, statuary, loggia and summerhouse. There are
also several shrubbed areas, a rose garden with triangular beds of annuals,
and much statuary, reflecting the architectural interest of the designer. The
layout was developed by Sir Reginald Blomfield when remodelling the
house between 1902-6, and he used yew hedges to separate the gardens
from the park, marking the different areas with lesser hedges and level
changes, evolving a happy mix of balance and order. Much of the topiary
reflects the outlines of the Jacobean house, although some of the symmetry
has been lost with time. The garden is important evidence of Blomfield's
formal style which was so much at variance with Robinson's. Round the
house and gardens is an ancient park, of some 240 acres, containing some of
the oldest trees in England.

GOODNESTONE PARK ★ 12
Nr Wingham, Canterbury, Kent. Tel: (01304) 840107

*The Lord and Lady FitzWalter ★ 5m E of Canterbury on A257 turn S onto
B2046, after 1m turn E ★ Parking ★ Teas on Suns and Weds from April to Sept
★ Toilet facilities ★ Suitable for wheelchairs ★ Plants for sale ★ Shop ★ House open
by appointment for parties of 20 to 25. £1.50 per person ★ Garden open 28th
March to 27th Oct, Mon, Wed, Thurs, Fri, 11am – 5pm; also 2nd April to 15th
Oct, Sun, 12 noon – 6pm. Closed Tues and Sat, except for pre-booked parties ★
Entrance: £2, OAP £1.80, disabled in wheelchairs £1, children under 12 30p,
parties over 25 or more £1.80 per person (£2.20 per person for guided tour)*

Goodnestone (pronounced Gunston) Park is a 14-acre garden in rural setting
round the eighteenth-century house. First built in 1700, by Brook Bridges,
this Palladian-style house was rebuilt and enlarged by his great-grandson, Sir
Brook Bridges, 3rd Bart whose daughter, Elizabeth, married Jane Austen's
brother, Edward. Jane Austen refers frequently to Goodnestone and her
Bridges cousins in her letters. There are pleasant vistas within the garden
and good views out to open countryside. The garden ranges in planting
from the mid-eighteenth-century parkland with fine trees and cedars to the
walled area behind the house which dates back to the sixteenth and seventeenth centuries. The garden tour leads along a broad terrace in front of the
house, planted with an abundance of roses and mixed shrubs. Behind the
house a small woodland garden, laid out in the 1920s, gives pleasant walks
and welcome shade. Here are rhododendrons, camellias, magnolias and
hydrangeas among many others. A cedar walk leads, between spring borders
on the left and more roses on the right, to a walled garden overlooked by

the church tower. Old roses mingle with mixed underplanting. Walls bear clematis, jasmine, climbing roses. New planting in the woodland area shows continued development of this fine garden.

GREAT COMP ★ 13
Platt, Borough Green, Sevenoaks, Kent. Tel: (01732) 882669/886154

Great Comp Charitable Trust ★ Leave M20 at junction 2, take A20 towards Maidstone and leave it at Wrotham Heath (B2016). Follow brown tourist signs ★ Parking ★ Teas on Suns and Bank Holidays or by arrangement for parties ★ Toilet facilities, inc. disabled ★ Suitable for wheelchairs ★ Plants for sale ★ Open April to Oct, 11am – 6pm ★ Entrance: £2.50, children £1. Annual ticket £7.50 (OAP £5)

A half-day is likely to be required to do justice to this imaginatively-planned, seven-acre garden, which offers all-year interest. Although the setting for an early seventeenth-century house, it has only been created since 1957 by Mr Roderick Cameron and the late Mrs Joyce Cameron out of the neglected earlier garden, rough woodland and paddock. Long grass walks intersect the beds and borders creating ever-changing views to tempt the visitor to stray from their intended route. Some areas are somewhat overgrown, although generally this does not detract from the garden's overall character. Focal points and interest are created by statuary, a temple and ruins built from the tons of ironstone dug up over the years. There are woodland areas, herbaceous borders, a heather garden, rose garden, formal lawns and a new Italianate garden, designed to set off the collection of Mediterranean plants. Specimen trees include a young dawn redwood, *Metasequoia glytostroboides*, and a Californian redwood, *Sequoia sempervirens* 'Cantab'.

115 HADLOW ROAD 14
Tonbridge, Kent. Tel: (01732) 353738

Mr and Mrs Richard Esdale ★ 1m N of Tonbridge. Take A26 from Tonbridge High Street signposted Maidstone. The house is 1m on left in a service road ★ Limited parking ★ Refreshments: tea and biscuits ★ Open by appointment and 16th July, 27th Aug, 2 – 6pm ★ Entrance: £1

A third-of-an-acre terraced suburban garden with many interesting specimen plants such as *Catalpa bignonioides* 'Aurea', *Acer negundo* 'Flamingo', *A. japonicum* 'Aureum', *Picea pungens* 'Koster', golden elm and *Sorbus cashmiriana*. Herbaceous border, clematis, roses and summer bedding provide additional colour and a small pool with fountain contains a range of water-loving plants. There is a small well-stocked fruit and vegetable garden.

HEVER CASTLE ★★ 15
Hever, Edenbridge, Kent. Tel: (01732) 865224

Broadlands Properties Ltd ★ 3m SE of Edenbridge, midway between Sevenoaks and East Grinstead off B2026 ★ Refreshments ★ Toilet facilities ★ Suitable for wheelchairs ★ Plants for sale ★ Shop ★ Castle opens 12 noon ★ Garden open 14th March to 5th Nov, 11am – 6pm (last admission 5pm) ★ Entrance: £3.80, OAP £3.30, children (5-16) £2.20, family ticket (2 adults, 2 children) £9.80. Groups of 15 or more per person: £3.20, students (17-19) £3, children £2 (castle and gardens, £5, OAP £4.50, children £2.50). Pre-booked private guided tours of the gardens by the Head Gardener for parties of 10 or more £6 per person (1994 prices)

The gardens were laid out between 1904–8 to William Waldorf Astor's designs. One thousand men were employed, 800 of whom dug out the 35-acre lake; steam engines moved rock and soil to create apparently natural new features and teams of horses moved mature trees from Ashdown Forest. Today the gardens have reached their maturity and are teeming with colour and interest throughout the year. Amongst the many superb features is an outstanding four-acre Italian garden, the setting for a large collection of classical statuary. Opposite, there is a magnificent pergola, supporting camellias, wisteria, crab apple, Virginia creeper and roses. It fuses into the hillside beyond which has shaded grottos of cool damp-loving species such as hostas, astilbes and polygonums. Less formal areas include the rhododendron walks, Anne Boleyn's orchard and her walk, which extends along the full length of the grounds and is particularly attractive in autumn.

HOLE PARK 16
Rolvenden, Near Cranbrook, Kent. Tel: (01580) 241251

Mr D.G.W. Barham ★ On B2086 between Cranbrook and Rolvenden ★ Parking ★ Teas on 21st May ★ Toilet facilities ★ Suitable for wheelchairs ★ Dogs can be exercised near car park ★ Open 9th, 16th, 26th, 30th April, 7th, 17th, 21st, 28th May, 7th June, 8th, 15th Oct, 2 – 6pm and parties by arrangement ★ Entrance: £2, children under 12 50p

The present owner moved to Hole Park in 1960 and used the framework of the gardens created by his grandfather to develop a garden offering interest throughout the year. The yews planted after World War I are precisely cut and are a special feature here. They enclose fine lawns and trees and extensive borders. There are walled areas, terraces and other distinctly individual parts offering plenty of opportunity for wall and climbing plants and for views over parkland and the Weald of Kent. A period piece is the sunk garden placed centrally between the two long borders whilst the pool forms an integral part of the garden design in providing a foreground to a stunning view of Rolvenden's postmill as seen from the vineyard pavilion. Statuary, fountains and seats provide interest at every turn. The woodland areas contain rhododendrons and azaleas, daffodils and bluebells in profusion and the dell is a cool feature throughout. Autumn colours are a very special attraction to provide continuous colour for all the opening season in this garden which is being constantly improved and planted.

IDEN CROFT HERBS 17
Frittenden Road, Staplehurst, Kent. Tel: (01580) 891432

Rosemary and David Titterington ★ Sign from A229 S of Staplehurst. Turn down Frittenden Road at Elf garage and follow signposts ★ Parking ★ Light refreshments ★ Toilet facilities ★ Suitable for wheelchairs ★ Plants for sale ★ Shop ★ Gardens open all year, Mon – Sat, 9am – 5pm, additional opening from March to Sept, Sun and Bank Holidays, 11am – 5pm ★ Entrance: free but voluntary donation of £1 appreciated

Gardens situated in quiet backwater near Staplehurst. There are acres of herbs bordered by grass paths and a large walled garden. A variety of demonstration gardens help the garden planner and over 1000 varieties of herbs and aromatic plants are available in pots for planting according to seasonal variations. The origanums and mints here were designated as the National collections in 1983 and 1993 respectively. The latest garden is specially designed for the enjoyment of blind and disabled visitors.

IGHTHAM MOTE 18
Ivy Hatch, Nr Borough Green, Kent. Tel: (01732) 810378

The National Trust ★ 6m E of Sevenoaks, off A25 and 2¹/₂m S of Ightham off A227 ★ Parking ★ Refreshments: in tea pavilion ★ Toilet facilities, inc. disabled ★ Suitable for wheelchairs with special parking available ★ Shop ★ House open (can be very busy on Sun pm and Bank Holidays. Timed ticket system may be in operation) ★ Garden open April to Oct, daily except Tues and Sat, 12 noon – 5.30pm (Sun and Bank Holiday Mons, 11am – 5.30pm) (last admission 5pm). Pre-booked guided tours on weekdays 11am – 12 noon ★ Entrance: £4, children £2, pre-booked parties of 20 or more £3 per person, children £1.50 (1994 prices)

Situated in a wooded cleft of the Kentish Weald, this medieval and Tudor manor house lies in the valley of Dinas Dene, where a stream has been dammed to form small lakes and the moat which surrounds the house. The medieval design of the gardens have evolved over several centuries. The present lawn replaces the stew pond, which was used for breeding fish for the table. Further household needs were satisfied with vegetables and herbs for culinary and medicinal purposes, and flowers for decorating and scenting the house were also prevalent. During the nineteenth century the garden emerged as an excellent example of the ideal 'old English' garden and The National Trust is gradually restoring this with extensive replanting. Six acres of woodland walks with fine rhododendrons are re-established and the long border has returned to its former glory.

LADHAM HOUSE ★ 19
Goudhurst, Kent. Tel: (01580) 211203

Betty, Lady Jessel ★ NE of village off A262 ★ Parking ★ Teas ★ Toilet facilities ★ Dogs on lead ★ Open 16th April, 28th May, 9th July, 11am – 6pm. Open at other times by appointment and for coaches ★ Entrance: £2, children 50p. £2.50 for private visits at other times

This Georgian house with additional French features has been in the family for over 100 years and the garden developed over that period. Interesting to see the bog garden, replacing a leaking pond, and the arboretum replacing the old kitchen garden. The mixed shrub borders are attractive; notable are the magnolias – two watsonii over 30ft and a deep-red-flowering 'Betty Jessel', a seedling from Darjeeling. Amongst the other rarer trees and shrubs are *Cornus kousa*, embothriums, American oaks, *Aesculus parviflora*, *Carpenteria californica* and *Azara serrata*. The arboretum is maturing and has some unusual and interesting trees, such as golden oak. The Fountain Garden has been completely reconstructed.

LEEDS CASTLE AND CULPEPER GARDENS   20
Maidstone, Kent. Tel: (01622) 765400

Leeds Castle Foundation ★ On B2163 off junction 8 of M20 ★ Best seasons:
Culpeper Gardens in spring, rose season and high summer, Castle grounds, spring
and autumn ★ Refreshments ★ Toilet facilities ★ Suitable for wheelchairs with
transport from car park to castle ★ Dogs in car park only ★ Shop ★ Castle opens
10.30am ★ Park and gardens open March to Oct, daily, 10am – 5pm; Nov to
Feb, daily, 10am – 3pm. Closed on 25th Dec and prior to ticketed events on 24th
June, 1st July and 4th Nov ★ Entrance: £5.50, OAP and students £4.50,
children (5-15) £3.30, family ticket £15 (castle, park and gardens £7, OAP
and students £6, children (5-15) £4.80, family ticket £19.50) (1994 prices)

Visit Leeds Castle and grounds for its romantic, wooded setting, covering
some 500 acres. The woodland garden with old and new plantings of shrubs
is especially beautiful in daffodil time. The atmosphere is also much
enhanced by wildfowl. The Culpeper Garden, in a secluded area beyond the
Castle, provides the main interest for the keen gardener. This is not a herb
garden as often thought, though a small area does include some herbs, but is
named after a seventeenth-century owner of Leeds Castle, distantly related to
the herbalist. Started in 1980 by Russell Page on a slope overlooking the
River Len, and surrounded by high brick walls of stabling and old cottages,
the garden already gives an established feel of old world charm. A simple
pattern of paths lined with box contains areas full of old roses (40 varieties),
riotously underplanted with herbaceous perennials. The National collection of
nepetas and monardas is situated in one corner. The spectacular grotto built
in 1987 beneath the maze has been much publicised. The garden is complemented by some rare and attractive birds in the duckery and aviary.

LONGACRE   21
Perry Wood, Selling, Nr Faversham, Kent. Tel: (01227) 752254

Dr and Mrs G. Thomas ★ 5m SE of Faversham. From A2 (M2) take A251 S
then follow signs for Selling. Pass White Lion on left, second right, then left,
continue for ¼m. From A252 at Chilham, take road to Selling at Badgers Hill
Fruit Farm, turn left at 2nd crossroads, first right, next left, then right. ★ Best
seasons: spring and summer ★ Parking ★ Teas on NGS open days: 16th, 17th,
30th April, 1st, 14th, 28th, 29th May, 11th, 25th June, 9th, 23rd July, 27th,
28th Aug, 10th Sept ★ Suitable for wheelchairs ★ Plants for sale from own
nursery ★ Garden open April to Oct, daily, 2 – 5pm and by appointment ★
Entrance: £1, children free

This is a jewel of a small garden in a tranquil country setting next to Perry
Woods into which the borders of the garden melt. Created entirely by the
present owners, it presents all-year interest of colour and form, replicating in
miniature woodland, alpine and damp areas. The enthusiast can spend an
absorbing time in the nursery alone, which carries a wealth of unusual herbaceous plants.

LONG BARN ★   22
Long Barn Road, Weald, Nr Sevenoaks, Kent.

Brandon and Sarah Gough ★ 3m S of Sevenoaks. Follow signs to Weald from junc-

tion of A21 and B245. Continue through village ★ Parking ★ Toilet facilities ★ Open probably 18th June, 23rd July, 2 – 5pm ★ Entrance: £2, OAP £1, children 50p

An impressive three-acre garden set on different levels round the fourteenth-century Wealden hall that was the home of Harold Nicolson and Vita Sackville-West before Sissinghurst. Since 1986, keeping to the Nicolsons' basic design, the owners have extensively renovated and replanted it. Although formal areas effortlessly give way to the informal, romantic and classical, each is constrained within the linear control that reached its apogee at Sissinghurst. The garden has many fine features including raised beds that contain (in season) herbaceous plants that explode in vibrant but controlled bursts of colour, a cool and shady classical grove and a secret garden whose understated classical design gives it the air of an aesthete's study. A box parterre, terraces, banks, rose gardens, small courtyards, ponds and pergolas all add variety of this exciting garden, which continues to develop with new plantings of trees and shrubs. A nearby property with Nicolson connections is Knole, much featured in the TV series, where the park is open to the pedestrian and Lord Sackville's garden on the first Wed in each month, May to Sept, only.

MARLE PLACE 23
Brenchley, Nr Tonbridge, Kent. Tel: (0189272) 2304

Mr and Mrs G. Williams ★ 2m S of Brenchley, 1m NW of Horsmonden and 1½m N of Lamberhurst. Signposted ★ Parking ★ Refreshments ★ Toilet facility ★ Suitable for wheelchairs ★ Plants for sale ★ Open April to Oct, 10am – 5.30pm and also by appointment ★ Entrance: £2, OAP and children £1.50 (1994 prices)

The present owners have worked for over 30 years on the soil and with constant digging in of compost, the unyielding clay has become productive. The fact that some of the garden is made on the site of old farm buildings has led to the creation of a series of varied terrace enclosures surrounding the seventeenth-century listed house. The owners particularly favour aromatic, culinary and medicinal herbs and wild flowers. There is a nursery which specialises in these and the National collections of santolina and calamintha are here. Other features include a walled fragrant garden, ornamental ponds and a Victorian gazebo. For the plantsman, there are borders featuring many unusual plants. The herbaceous garden is new, and an adjoining natural wildflower grassland is planned. There is a woodland walk and a variety of bantams which wander through what is described by the owners as a 'family garden'.

MOUNT EPHRAIM 24
Hernhill, Nr Faversham, Kent. Tel: (01227) 751496

Mrs M.N. Dawes and Mr and Mrs E.S. Dawes ★ Take A299 N from A2/ M2, then left to Hernhill at Duke of York pub, signposted through village on left ★ Parking ★ Refreshments. Licensed to sell wine from own vineyard ★ Toilet facilities ★ Partly suitable for wheelchairs ★ Dogs on lead ★ Craft centre shop on Suns only ★ Garden open 16th April to Sept, daily except Tues, 1 – 6pm; Bank Holiday weekends 11am – 6pm ★ Entrance: £2, children 50p, groups £1.50 per person

Mount Ephraim is set on seven sloping acres, surrounded by orchards and a vineyard, and with distant views of the Thames estuary from its highest parts.

It is not a plantsman's garden; its attractions stem largely from its favoured position. However there is something to see throughout the season as there are rose gardens, a lake, a small Japanese garden, a rock garden, water garden and herbaceous borders, as well as some unusual topiary. On Sundays it is possible to take a three-quarter-mile educational tour of one of the orchards and at the end of June there are usually performances of Shakespeare.

NORTHBOURNE COURT 25
Northbourne, Deal, Kent. Tel: (01304) 511281 (office hours)

The Hon. Charles James ★ 1½m W of Deal. From A258 at W of Deal take turning W towards Great Mongeham and Northbourne ★ Best season: June and July ★ Parking ★ Refreshments sometimes ★ Toilet facilities: unisex ★ Partly suitable for wheelchairs ★ Plants for sale ★ Open June to Aug, Suns, 2 – 5pm ★ Entrance: £2.50, OAP and children £1.50. Coach parties by arrangement. Enquiries to Hon. Charles James, Home Farm, Betteshanger, Kent.

Originally created in Tudor times, with Jacobean structure providing the basis, the garden in its present form was the creation of the father of the present Lord Northbourne. The main feature of this delightful garden, set within high walls to protect it from easterly winds, is the series of small and enclosed gardens with profuse and colourful, cottage-style planting. The old tiered terraces give further character and a distinctive setting for chalk-loving plants. Specially noticeable are grey-foliage plants, including lavenders and dianthus. Also distinctive fuchsias and geraniums.

THE OLD PARSONAGE 26
Sutton Valence, Kent. Tel: (01622) 842286

Dr and Mrs Richard Perks ★ From A274 Maidstone – Headcorn road, turn E into Sutton Valence. At King's Head Inn take upper road up hill. House is at the top on right with clearing by tree at gate ★ Best season: late June ★ Parking at entrance ★ Toilet facilities ★ Partly suitable for wheelchairs ★ Plants for sale ★ Open 17th, 20th, 23rd, 25th June, 2 – 6pm and by appointment ★ Entrance: £1.50, children 50p

This is a delightful garden, set on the steep slopes of the greensand ridge with remarkable views southwards over the Weald of Kent. Shrub roses, an exceptional tree peony (*Paeonia delavayi*) and a wide variety of foliage plants feature strongly and provide a profusion of contrast and interest along the well-kept paths that lead along the various levels of the hillside. There is strong emphasis on ground cover, with hostas, geraniums and hellebores a special feature, presumably a gesture towards labour-saving maintenance claimed modestly by Dr Perks.

OWL HOUSE GARDENS 27
Lamberhurst, Kent. Tel: (01892) 890230

Maureen, Marchioness of Dufferin and Ava ★ 6m S of Tunbridge Wells, S of Lamberhurst. Turn right off A21. Signposted ★ Best season: April to June ★ Parking ★ Toilet facilities ★ Suitable for wheelchairs ★ Plants for sale ★ Dogs on lead ★ Open daily, except 25th Dec and 1st Jan, 11am – 6pm. Coach parties by arrangement ★ Entrance: £3, children £1

A large (16½ acre) garden set amongst orchards developed since 1952 around a sixteenth-century cottage which was used by wool smugglers. The cottage was so-called because smugglers warned one another of the approach of police by hooting. Swathes of bluebells and daffodils start the season followed by camellias, azaleas and rhododendrons. The summer interest is maintained by very large numbers of old roses (*Rosa filipes* 'Kiftsgate', *R. longicuspis*, *R.* 'Rambling Rector', etc.) climbing into the many fine trees throughout the garden. Philadelphus and clematis also abound. Statues of owls are dotted around the garden with many seats strategically placed to overlook beautiful viewpoints. There is a wisteria temple, a grove of *Parrotia persica*, an iris walk, an appleblossom walk, laburnum walk and for late summer a blue hydrangea walk. Three small ponds provide a peaceful setting for contemplation.

PEDDAR'S WOOD 28
14 Orchard Road, St Michael's, Tenterden, Kent. Tel: (015806) 3994

Mr and Mrs B.J. Honeysett ★ From A28 1m N of Tenterden turn W to Grange Road at Crown Hotel, second right Orchard Road ★ Refreshments: coffee and cake ★ Open 6th May, 3rd June, 15th July, 5th Aug, 2 – 6pm and by appointment ★ Entrance: £1, children 20p

This plantsman's garden of exceptional opulence and interest is approximately a quarter of an acre behind a typical small semi-detached town house. Great imagination and expertise have been used to develop it over the last 10 years into a garden of many delights. Other than potash only the usual organic composts are used but a two inch mulch of peat has been laid over the loamy soil. Amongst the clematis which trail rampantly are 'Victoria' and 'Margo Kosta'. Pink abutilons, solanums, vines, wisterias and roses vie for space while specimens such as cannas, the unusual red rose 'Baron Giro de l'Aln' and tree ferns are evident. There are in fact over 100 varieties of clematis including some of the owner's own seedlings as well as 40 varieties of lilies, 50 varieties of climbing roses and ferns in abundance. It takes ages to go round this garden as there are layers upon layers of plantings and every square inch is packed with interesting plants. The owner is a mine of information.

PENSHURST PLACE 29
Penshurst, Tonbridge, Kent. Tel: (01892) 870307

Lord De L'Isle ★ S of Tonbridge on B2176, N of Tunbridge Wells on A26 ★ Parking ★ Refreshments: in restaurant, 11am – 5.30pm ★ Toilet facilities ★ Suitable for wheelchairs in grounds ★ Guide dogs only ★ Shop ★ House open, 12 noon – 5.30pm (last admission 5pm) ★ Garden open weekends in March; April to 1st Oct, daily; weekends in Oct, 11am – 6pm. Garden tours available for parties of 20 or more ★ Entrance: £4.95, OAP £4.50, children under 16 £2.75, family ticket £13 (house and garden, toy museum and adventure playground)

The 600-year-old gardens, contemporary with the house, reflect their development under their Tudor owner Sir Henry Sidney and the restoration by the present owner, his father and his grandfather Lord De L'Isle. The many separate enclosures, surrounded by trim tall yew hedges, offer a wide variety of interesting planting, with continuous displays from spring to early autumn. The Italian garden with its oval fountain and century-old gingko dominates the front of the magnificent house. The herbaceous border is teeming with colour from irises, phlox, anemones, anchusas, coreopsis and yuccas amongst others. Contrast is made by the nut trees and over a dozen different crab apples underplanted with daffodils, myosotis, tulips, bluebells, Lenten lilies and a magnificent bed of peonies which borders the orchard. Even in late summer the rose garden is colourful with 'King Arthur' and 'Elizabeth Glamis' and their perfumes mingle with that from mature lavender bushes. A new lake and nature trail have been developed so that the style of design so much enjoyed here by Gertrude Jekyll and Beatrix Farrand is fully recaptured. Numerous seats make it easy to enjoy the garden and the views. Two medieval fish ponds have been reclaimed and stocked with fish.

THE PINES GARDEN 30
Beach Road, St Margaret's Bay, Kent. Tel: (01304) 852764

St Margaret's Bay Trust ★ 3m NE of Dover off B2058, S of the village of St Margaret's at Cliffe ★ Best seasons: spring and summer ★ Parking nearby in road ★ Toilet facilities ★ Suitable for wheelchairs ★ Plants for sale when available ★ Open daily except 25th Dec, from 10am ★ Entrance: small admission charge

It is hard to believe that this well-stocked and perfectly maintained garden was a rubbish dump until 1970. Fred Cleary, founder of St Margaret's Bay Trust, and his wife transformed the original three acres, with a second three-acre site known as the Barrack Field, once home and training ground for soldiers during the Napoleonic Wars. Now the garden is established, with a good variety of trees, including conifers, flowering shrubs, bulbs and bog plants. An avenue of elms is an encouraging sight. A lake, well-stocked with fish, and a rockery provides further interest. A huge bronze statue of Sir Winston Churchill seems intrusive but is understandable in this cliff-top situation near to Dover cliffs.

PORT LYMPNE 31
Lympne, Nr Hythe, Kent. Tel: (01303) 264646/7

Mr J. Aspinall ★ 3m W of Hythe, 18m S of Canterbury ★ Parking ★ Refreshments: restaurant and bar ★ Shop ★ Mansion open: a Lutyens-style house with Rex Whistler and Spencer Roberts murals ★ Garden open daily, 10am – 5pm (summer) and to 1 hour before dusk (winter) ★ Entrance: £6.50, OAP and children £4.50 (house, garden and wild animal park)

This is one of those gardens which some people enjoy very much and leaves others cold. It stands in a 300-acre wild animal park with views across the Channel. Before World War I Sir Philip Sassoon began building a new house and garden with the help of Sir Herbert Baker and Ernest Willmote and, after the war, with much assistance from the architect Philip Tilden. After a period of distinction in the 1920s and 30s it fell into decay until it was rescued in the 1970s by John Aspinall who wanted the surrounding land for his private wild animal park. He has reconstructed the 15-acre garden to something like its original design with advice from experts like the late Russell Page. Visitors enter down a great stone stairway of 125 steps, flanked by clipped Leyland cypress, to the paved West Court with lily pool. Beyond is the Magnolia Walk and a series of terraces planted with standard fig trees and vines. Everywhere there is fine stone paving and walls with appropriately-placed urns, statues from 'Stowe', etc. There is extensive bedding and use of bedding-out. Arthur Hellyer admitted that 'for years it has been fashionable to denigrate Port Lympne' but he admired it. Others, however, feel that it lacks 'soul' - that vital element that every great garden must have, however extensive the resources that have been poured into it. The late Arthur Hellyer waxed lyrical about the beautiful wrought ironwork by Bainbridge Reynolds.

RIVERHILL HOUSE GARDENS   32
Sevenoaks, Kent. Tel: (01732) 458802/452557

Mr John Rogers (correspondence to Mrs John Rogers) ★ On A225 left-hand side of road, 2m S of Sevenoaks ★ Best seasons: spring and early summer ★ Parking. Coaches by appointment ★ Home-made teas ★ Toilet facilities ★ Shop ★ House open only to bona fide booked parties. No children inside house ★ Garden open April to June, Suns and Bank Holiday weekends, 12 noon – 6pm ★ Entrance: £2, children 50p (house and garden £3 per person for coach bookings during the above period for parties of 20 or more)

This was originally one of the great smaller country-house gardens, housing a plantsman's collection of trees and species shrubs as introduced by John Rogers, a keen horticulturist, in the mid-1800s. Massive rhododendrons, many of them species, topped by cedar of Lebanon planted in 1815, also azaleas, and outstanding underplanting of bulbs make Riverhill a fine sight in spring and early summer. Other features include wood garden, rose walk and old orchard with Wellingtonia (planted in 1860), magnolias, etc.

SCOTNEY CASTLE ★   33
Lamberhurst, Tunbridge Wells, Kent. Tel: (01892) 890651

The National Trust ★ 1m S of Lamberhurst on E side of A21, 8m SE of Tunbridge Wells ★ Best seasons: spring and autumn ★ Parking ★ Toilet facilities ★ Partly suitable for wheelchairs but hilly approach ★ Shop ★ Old Castle open May to 17th Sept same times as garden ★ Garden open April to 29th Oct, Wed – Fri, 11am – 6pm, Sat and Sun, 2 – 6pm or sunset if earlier. Bank Holiday Suns and Mons, 12 noon – 6pm (last admission 1 hour before closing) ★ Entrance: £3.20, children £1.60. Pre-booked parties (weekdays only) £2 per person, children £1

This is an unusual garden designed in the romantic manner by the Hussey family following the tradition established by William Kent and using the services of William Gilpin, the artist and landscape gardener who also advised on the site of the new house, completed in 1843. Of the old fourteenth-century castle only one of the four towers remains, plus some seventeenth-century red brick. The landscape garden includes many smaller garden layouts in the overall area. A formal garden overlooks a quarry garden. The grounds of the old castle enclose a rose garden. Herb garden. Lakeside planting adds an air of informality. Evergreens and deciduous trees provide the mature planting. They link shrubs and plants to give something in flower at every season. Daffodils, magnolias, rhododendrons and azaleas are the most spectacular. Also notable are the kalmias and hydrangeas. In a good autumn, the colours are spectacular. In some ways the planting seems occasional and haphazard, but visit this garden for its setting on a slope that gives fine views of open countryside, and for the romantic eighteenth- to nineteenth-century theme uniting it. A great pity there are no refreshments as there is plenty of space.

SISSINGHURST GARDEN ★★   34
Sissinghurst, Nr Cranbrook, Kent. Tel: (01580) 712850

The National Trust ★ 2m NE of Cranbrook, 1m E of Sissinghurst on A262, 13m S of Maidstone ★ Parking. Coaches by appointment only ★ Refreshments: Tues – Fri, 12 noon – 5.30pm, Sat and Sun, 10am – 5.30pm. Picnic area beyond car park and on grass in front of castle only ★ Toilet facilities ★ Wheelchairs restricted to two chairs at one time because of narrow and uneven paths. Pushchairs not admitted ★ Shop ★ Garden open April to 15th Oct, Tues – Fri, 1 – 6.30pm (last admission 6pm), Sat, Sun and 1st April, 10am – 5.30pm (last admission 5pm). Closed Mons, inc. Bank Holidays. Parties by appointment. A timed ticket system is in operation, and at peak times visitors may have a short wait to enter the garden ★ Entrance: £5, children £2.50

'Profusion, even extravagance and exuberance within the confines of the utmost linear severity' is Vita Sackville-West's description of her design when creating Sissinghurst with her husband Harold Nicolson. It is a romantic garden with seasonal features throughout the year. Certain colour schemes have been followed, as in the purple border, the orange and yellow cottage garden, and the white garden, which is probably the most beautiful garden at Sissinghurst, itself one of the outstanding gardens in the world. The Nicolsons added little to, but saved much of the Elizabethan mansion. The site was first occupied in the twelfth century, when a moated manor was built where the orchard now stands. The long library and Elizabethan tower are open and the latter is well worth climbing in order to see the perspective of the whole garden and surrounding area. The garden is in immaculate condition, well-labelled, with changing vistas at every turn of the winding paths or more formal walks. The rose garden contains many old-fashioned roses as well as flowering shrubs such as *Ceanothus impressus*, *Hydrangea villosa* which together with iris, clematis and pansies fill the area. There is a thyme lawn leading to the herb garden filled with fragrance and charm. It is a truly magnificent example of Englishness and has had immense influence on garden design because of its structure of separate 'outdoor rooms' within the garden. See also Long Barn and Knole entries.

SISSINGHURST PLACE GARDENS   35
Sissinghurst Place, Sissinghurst, Kent.

Mr and Mrs Simon macLachlan ★ 2m N of Cranbrook, E of the village of Sissinghurst on the A262 ★ Parking ★ Teas for May openings ★ Toilet facilities ★ Suitable for wheelchairs ★ Open 8th, 9th April, 20th, 21st May, 2 – 6pm ★ Entrance: £1

The original house at Sissinghurst Place was destroyed by fire in 1948, watched by Vita Sackville-West and then described in 'The Easter Party'. The servants' wing is now the house and the ruins are a garden with herbs, climbers, a collection of cistus, a pool and a very large fig tree. The large garden has lawns, fine trees, daffodils, shrubs, rhododendrons, roses and herbaceous plants in a tranquil country setting. A lime avenue leads past a 500–year–old oak to a wild spring garden with pond.

SMITH'S HALL 36
Lower Road, West Farleigh, Maidstone, Kent. Tel: (01622) 814617

Mr and Mrs Stephen Norman ★ 4¹/₂m W of Maidstone, turn S off A26 Maidstone – Tonbridge road at Teston Bridge. Turn right at T- junction. Garden on left, opposite Tickled Trout pub ★ Parking ★ Teas ★ Toilet facilities ★ Partly suitable for wheelchairs ★ Open one Sun in late June/July for NGS ★ Entrance: £1.50, children free

This large walled garden was created by the present owner's grandmother and apart from making the original vegetable garden considerably smaller, the garden layout is unchanged. There are many fine trees, shrubs, lawns, a rose garden, an old rose walk, a wild garden, spring and peony borders, four herbaceous borders each with a different colour scheme and a new avenue of climbing roses.

SQUERRYES COURT 37
Westerham, Kent. Tel: (01959) 562345/563118 Fax: (01959) 565949

Mr and Mrs John Warde ★ ¹/₂m W of Westerham on A25, 10 minutes from M25 junctions 5 or 6 ★ Parking ★ Teas ★ Toilet facilities, inc. disabled ★ Partly suitable for wheelchairs ★ Dogs on lead ★ House open ★ Garden open March, Suns only; April to Sept, Wed, Sat, Sun and Bank Holiday Mons, 2 – 6pm. Parties of 20 or more by appointment ★ Entrance: £2, OAP £1.80, children £1 (house and garden £3.50, OAP £3.20, children £1.60). Reduced rates for parties

The gardens are divided into about 20 acres of formal areas and 200 of park-land. Lime groves, which are the oldest in the country, lead to a gazebo, built around 1740, from where a former member of the family used to watch his racehorses in training; nearby is a fine old dovecot. The main feature is the newly restored formal area to the rear of the house; a 1719 print has been used as an outline on which to base the ongoing develop-ments, which reflect the mellowed brickwork of this handsome house. Beds, edged with box, contain lavender, rue, purple sage and *Nicotiana affinis*, with contrasting magenta and pink of penstemon and verbena; all are framed by well-kept yew hedges. There are several rose gardens, heather beds and azalea and rhododendron shrubberies and fine examples of topiary, which, together with a broad variety of spring bulbs, make this a garden for all seasons. Many fine magnolias around the house, a cenotaph in memory of General Wolfe (a family friend), and a large lake complete this most attrac-tive garden. The house is worth a visit, too, for its collection of paintings. Those with a historical bent will wish to visit nearby Chartwell (see entry), which has a much less interesting garden horticulturally speaking.

STONEACRE 38
Otham, Maidstone, Kent. Tel: (01622) 862871

The National Trust ★ 1m S of A20 from Bearsted, at north end of Otham village ★ Best seasons: spring and summer ★ Parking in field. Limited disabled parking at gate ★ House open ★ Garden open April to 28th Oct, Wed and Sat,

2 – 6pm (last admission 5pm) and parties by appointment ★ Entrance: £2, children £1 (house and garden) (1994 prices)

This is a Kentish hall house restored and embellished from 1920 to 1926 by Aymer Vallance, Oxford aesthete, writer and friend of William Morris. Rosemary Alexander, as tenant of the Trust, is restoring the garden after some years of neglect. The acre of cottage garden contains a gingko, mulberry and *Staphylea colchica*. There is a small herb garden with beds divided by low box hedging. A grass path leads to the summerhouse in the two-acre wild garden which includes apple orchards and two ponds. Mrs Alexander was helped in her work by old reports on the garden by Trust adviser Graham Stuart Thomas which included suggestions that the football posts on the lawn be removed. The result is a charming cottage-type garden within the framework of yew hedges and ragstone walls, plus all the delights of the wild garden, a suitable setting for Mrs Alexander's English Gardening School whose pupils spend some of their time here.

UPDOWN FARM 39
Betteshanger, Deal, Kent. Tel: (01304) 611895

Mr and the Hon. Mrs Willis-Fleming ★ 3m S of Sandwich. From A256 Sandwich – Dover road, turn S off the Eastry bypass signposted Northbourne and Finglesham. Turn first left and into first house on the right ★ Parking ★ Refreshments ★ Toilet facilities ★ Suitable for wheelchairs ★ Open 14th May, 11th June, 10am – 6pm ★ Entrance: £1.50, OAP 80p, children 30p

Standing on chalk downland in open country, this is a delightful garden with many facets. A mixture of formal, enclosed areas lead on to open and informal gardens with a good variety of shrubs and with quiet woodland area. The present owners have created it over the last fifteen years and it is continually developing. Shrub and climber roses are a special feature. Well worth visiting in conjunction with nearby Northbourne Court (see entry).

WALMER CASTLE 40
Kingsdown Road, Deal, Kent. Tel: (01304) 364288

English Heritage ★ On coast, S of Walmer, 2m S of Deal signposted from the A258 Deal – Dover road ★ Parking ★ Toilet facilities ★ Partly suitable for wheelchairs ★ Guide dogs only ★ Castle open ★ Garden open April to Oct daily, 10am – 6pm; Nov to Dec and March, Wed – Sun, 10am – 4pm. Closed 24th to 26th Dec, and Jan and Feb. Also closed when Lord Warden is in residence. Telephone in advance of visit to check if open ★ Entrance: £3, concessions £2.60, children £1.80 (castle and garden £3.50). Discount for parties of 11 or more

English Heritage is restoring the gardens to their former status in the early twentieth century, when the castle was the official residence of the Warden of the Cinque Ports. Opening details are provided but the garden is not yet inspected, as it will be at least two years before completion of the work.

WALNUT TREE FARM GARDENS 41
Swan Lane, Little Chart, Nr Ashford, Kent. Tel: (0123384) 214

Mr and Mrs M. Oldaker ★ 3m NW of Ashford off A20 Ashford – Maidstone road. From Little Chart by The Swan Inn take road towards Pluckley. The gardens are 500 yards on left ★ Parking ★ Teas subject to weather ★ Suitable for wheelchairs ★ Plants for sale in nursery ★ Open 28th, 29th May, 4th, 11th, 18th, 25th June, 2nd, 9th, 16th, 23rd, 30th July, 2 – 5pm. Coaches by appointment ★ Entrance: £1.50

Already well-developed, this four-acre Romantic garden is one to watch over the years as it has promise of more delights to come. Carefully-selected herbaceous plants combine with shrubs in island beds. A walled garden beside the house provides the setting for a wide variety of climbing roses. A bog garden created in the last four years contains a mixture of moisture-loving plants. Views to the North Downs take in shrub roses and also young trees planted with care – native trees on the garden edge and ornamental trees further in. Two new shrub borders have been added and a scented garden is being created. Mrs Oldaker has searched hard for rare plants and has some on sale.

WAYSTRODE MANOR 42
Cowden, Kent. Tel: (01342) 850695

Mr and Mrs Peter Wright ★ 4½m S of Edenbridge, off B2026 Edenbridge – Hartfield road ★ Parking in road ★ Teas ★ Toilet facilities ★ Partly suitable for wheelchairs ★ Plants for sale ★ Shop ★ Garden open by appointment for parties of 20 or more and some Weds and Suns in May and June for NGS ★ Entrance: £2, children 50p. Party prices on application

The half-timbered sixteenth-century house and its surrounding gardens, developed by the present owners over the past 25 years, are set deep in the wooded Kentish countryside on Wealden clay. Plants tumble over the paving stones around the house and borders of shrubs and perennials, the wisteria walk and the laburnum tunnel all make more formal contrasts. Clipped yew hedges. Island beds are arranged in varying colour schemes; for example the oranges and reds of dahlias and roses in one and grey-foliage plants in another. The plants are well-labelled. Water garden and winter garden.

WEST FARLEIGH HALL
(change of name, see SMITH'S HALL)

KENT AND GREATER LONDON

We have included some gardens with Kent postal addresses in the Greater London section for convenience. So before planning a day out in Kent it is worthwhile consulting the Greater London section.

LANCASHIRE

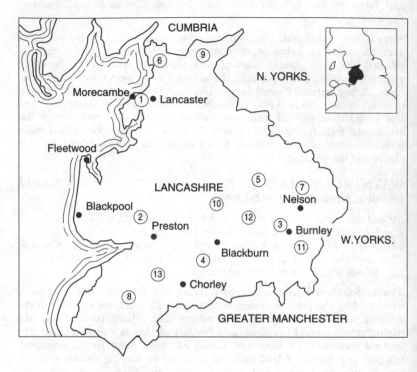

ASHTON MEMORIAL 1
Williamson Park, Lancaster, Lancashire. Tel: (01524) 33318

E of Lancaster town centre. Signposted ★ Best season: spring ★ Parking ★
Refreshments: tea shop ★ Toilet facilities inc. disabled ★ Suitable for wheelchairs
★ Dogs ★ Shop ★ Memorial open. Entrance to viewing gallery 50p, ground floor
with exhibition free ★ Garden open daily except 25th, 26th Dec and 1st Jan,
April to Sept, 10am – 5pm, Oct to March, 11am – 4pm ★ Entrance: free
(butterfly house, mini-beast house, conservation garden and free-flying bird
enclosure £2.50, OAP £2, children £1.50

Ashton Memorial was described by Pevsner as 'the grandest monument in
England'. It stands at the highest point of Williamson Park looking down on
the town of Lancaster. There are many views of the surrounding country
from various points in the superbly landscaped park. Broad paths run
through the grounds much of which is woodland with an underplanting of
rhododendrons and other shrubs. There is a small lake spanned by a stone
bridge, and from near here is a large stairway that leads to the huge domed
monument. Near to the folly is the butterfly house and pavilion. Both monument and the butterfly house were designed in 1906 in the style of the
Baroque revival.

CATFORTH GARDENS ★ 2
Roots Lane, Catforth, Preston, Lancashire. Tel: (01772) 690561/690269

Mr and Mrs T.A. Bradshaw and Mr and Mrs W. Moore ★ 5m NW of Preston. Turn S off the B5269 to the village of Catforth. Roots Lane is at the S end of the village. Signposted ★ Parking ★ Refreshments on charity days ★ Suitable for wheelchairs ★ Plants for sale ★ Nursery and gardens open 18th March to 17th Sept, daily, 10.30am – 5pm ★ Entrance: £1.50 (combined price), accompanied children free

There are three gardens here separated by a nursery which stocks an excellent range of perennials. *The Bungalow Garden* is informally laid out with grass paths running amongst well-planted beds. Some unusual small trees and shrubs provide height and a good selection of ferns and grasses give variety to the foliage, but it is perennials that will most impress. This is the home of the National collection of hardy geraniums, and the charm and usefulness of the genus is well demonstrated as they are grown in many different situations. Most perennials are well represented here, flowering throughout the season. Euphorbias, pulmonarias and dicentras are particularly plentiful. There is also a pond surrounded by banks of alpines, and a small woodland area with hydrangeas and dwarf rhododendrons. *The Farmhouse Garden* was created as a cottage garden. It has a good collection of perennials, sidalceas, phloxes, lythrums and crocosmias, an alpine scree and newly-made ponds. Newly constructed in 1994, and still being developed, the one-acre *Paddock Garden* consists of a series of clay-lined ponds and associated waterside planting; a large raised bank for plants more difficult to grow in the low-lying, wet North West; and long, boldly-planted herbaceous borders in a colour-complementary fashion.

GAWTHORPE HALL 3
Padiham, Nr Burnley, Lancashire. Tel: (01282) 778511

Lancashire County Council (on lease from The National Trust) ★ N of A671 just E of Padiham town centre ★ Best season: spring ★ Parking ★ Refreshments daily except Mon and Fri, 12.30 – 4.15pm ★ Toilet facilities inc. disabled ★ Partly suitable for wheelchairs ★ Dogs on lead ★ Shop ★ House open April to Oct, daily except Mon and Fri but open 14th April and Bank Holiday Mons, 1 – 5pm (last admission 4.15pm) ★ Gardens open all year 10am – 6pm ★ Entrance: free (house £2.30, children £1)

This garden, though not particularly special in botanical terms, does set off the Elizabethan hall. To the front is a formal layout of lawns and gravel paths, to the rear a parterre by Barry in the form of a sunburst overlooks the River Calder. The woodlands that surround the formal garden are planted with rhododendrons and azaleas. Through them are many walks with views back to the house and across the valley.

HOGHTON TOWER 4
Hoghton, Nr Preston, Lancashire. Tel: (01254) 852986

Sir Bernard de Hoghton ★ 5m SE of Preston N of A675 midway between Preston and Blackburn ★ Best season: summer ★ Parking ★ Refreshments: tearoom

★ Toilet facilities ★ Shop ★ House open ★ Garden open Easter to Oct, Suns and Bank Holidays, 1 – 5pm; also July and Aug, Tues – Thurs, 11am – 4pm. Telephone for details of other opening dates ★ Entrance: grounds £1 (house extra £2.50, children £1.25)

Hoghton Tower, a sixteenth-century house built of local stone, occupies a hilltop position with good views to all sides. The house and outbuildings are built around two courtyards which although not qualifying as gardens are fine areas. Surrounding the house are three walled gardens; the first contains a large lawn and herbaceous borders. The second has a rectangular lawn at the centre of which is a raised square pond with an elaborate stone fountain; to one end is a statue and at the other a sundial on a stone pedestal; clipped yews flank two sides of the lawn. The third is mainly lawn with access to the tops of two crenellated towers. Around the walled gardens runs 'the long walk' which passes under some large beech trees and is planted with shrubs, mainly rhododendrons and azaleas. Good views of the surrounding countryside.

HOLDEN CLOUGH NURSERY   5
Holden, Bolton-by-Bowland, Nr Clitheroe, Lancashire.
Tel: (01200) 447615

Peter Foley ★ 7m N of Clitheroe turn N off A59 to Sawley and follow road towards Bolton by Bowland, turn left to Holden before Bolton and fork left in village ★ Parking in road ★ Toilet facilities ★ Plants for sale ★ Open all year except 25th Dec to 1st Jan, Mon – Thurs, 1 – 5pm, Sat, 9am – 5pm, Bank Holidays, 9am – 5pm, and Suns in April and May only, 2 – 5pm ★ Entrance: free

It is refreshing after visiting so many modern garden centres to find a nursery that is dedicated simply to plants. Much of this two-acre site is given to display areas where a large range of perennials, shrubs, heathers, rhododendrons and conifers are grown. Alpines are also prominent with areas of raised beds and sink and trough gardens on show. Astilbes, hostas, primulas and saxifrages are amongst the nursery's specialities, and many other plants are available in great variety, too. The beautiful local countryside is another attraction in visiting this garden.

LEIGHTON HALL   6
Carnforth, Lancashire. Tel: (01524) 734474

Mr R.G. Reynolds ★ 2m W of Yealand Conyers, signposted from M6 junction 35 ★ Parking ★ Teas ★ Toilet facilities ★ Suitable for wheelchairs ★ Dogs on lead in park only ★ Shop ★ Hall open ★ Gardens open May to Sept, daily except Sat and Mon, 2 – 5pm ★ Entrance: £3.20, OAP £2.70, children £2, parties of 25 or more £2.70 per person, schools £1.70 per child (hall and grounds) (1994 prices)

Very striking when first seen from the entrance gates, the white stone façade (c. 1800) shines out in its parkland setting with the hills of the Lake District visible beyond. The most interesting area of the gardens, which lie to the west of the house, is the walled garden with its unusual labyrinth in the form of a gravel path that runs under an old cherry orchard. Opposite is a vegetable garden made in a geometric design with grass paths. There are also herbaceous borders and a very aromatic herb garden containing a wide variety of perennials with climbing roses on the wall behind.

PENDLE HERITAGE CENTRE 7

Park Hill, Barrowford, Nelson, Lancashire.
Tel: (01282) 695366; Fax: (01282) 611718

*The Lancashire Heritage Trust ★ In the centre of Barrowford at the
A682/B6247 junction, N of Nelson and near M65 junction 13 ★ Best season:
June/July ★ Parking ★ Refreshments ★ Toilet facilities ★ Partly suitable for
wheelchairs ★ Plant sale 7th May with NCCPG stand ★ Shop ★ House and
buildings open ★ Garden open all year daily except 25th Dec, 10am – 4.30pm*

In the centre of Barrowford among a group of fine old stone buildings (eight Grade II Listed) is a walled garden dating from the 1780s. This has been restored and replanted under the guidance of the NCCPG using only plants that were available in the eighteenth century. There are culinary and medicinal herbs and plants that were used in the production of dyes, as well as traditional varieties of fruit and vegetables. All plants are organically grown in beds divided by gravel paths and edged in clipped box. A woodland walk takes the visitor up a steep wooded bank planted with native wild flowers to a viewing point that looks back over the garden and surrounding countryside. The Heritage Centre will be organising a garden open day when eight or so private gardens in the area will be open to the public.

RUFFORD OLD HALL 8

Rufford, Nr Ormskirk, Lancashire. Tel: (01704) 821254

*The National Trust ★ 7m N of Ormskirk, N of Rufford village on E of A59 ★
Best season: spring ★ Parking ★ Refreshments: lunches and teas ★ Toilet facilities
★ Suitable for wheelchairs ★ Dogs on lead ★ Shop ★ Hall open as garden (last
admission 4.30pm) ★ Garden open April to Oct, daily except Thurs and Fri, 1 –
5pm ★ Entrance: £1.60 (house and garden £3)*

Rufford Old Hall is an exceptional fifteenth-century timber-framed house whose gardens complement it perfectly, having been laid out by the Trust in the style of the 1820 period. On the south are lawns and gravel paths laid out in a formal manner. The many island beds are formal in layout, too, but the shrubs, small trees and herbaceous plants they contain are planted in a more relaxed way. In the centre a path leads from two large topiary squirrels to a beech avenue that goes beyond the garden towards Rufford. There are many mature trees and rhododendrons in this area. To the east of the house by the stables is an attractive cobbled space with climbing plants on the surrounding walls. When visiting, look for the gardener's own garden to the north side of the house, in which grow many old-fashioned plants enclosed by a rustic wooden fence.

SELLET HALL GARDENS 9

Kirkby Lonsdale, via Carnforth, Lancashire. Tel: (015242) 71865

*Mr and Mrs G.P. Gray ★ 1m SW of Kirkby Lonsdale, signposted from B6254 ★
Best seasons: spring and summer ★ Parking ★ Light refreshments ★ Toilet facilities
★ Partly suitable for wheelchairs ★ Nursery ★ Shop ★ Garden open March to
Oct, 10am – 5pm ★ Entrance: £1, children 50p*

Created over the last 20 years, this garden is set around an old and attractive grey stone house in a beautiful part of North Lancashire. A fairly large herb garden is its best feature, formal in layout and surrounded by a high yew hedge. The symmetrical beds contain a great number of herbs and other perennials; there are good collections of lavenders, thymes and artemisias. Behind the herb garden is a woodland garden and to one side a bee garden. Also a small Japanese garden and other areas of shrubs, perennials, dwarf conifers and heathers. The small courtyard has been attractively planted. Some areas are still being developed, and the results are impressive for this exposed part of the country.

STONYHURST COLLEGE 10
Hurst Green, Lancashire. Tel: (0125) 4826 345

Stonyhurst College ★ 10m E of M6 junction 31, just off B6243 Longridge – Clitheroe road on outskirts of Hurst Green ★ Parking ★ House open 25th July to 28th Aug, Tues – Sun only ★ Garden open 8th July to 28th Aug, Tues to Sun only and 28th Aug ★ Entrance: house and garden £3.50, OAP and children £2.50

The rather severe stone buildings of Stonyhurst College are surrounded by long-established parkland. Two long rectangular pools that flank the drive date from the seventeenth century. An area of formal gardens to the south of the college are of less interest for the plants than for the stonework which, although in a state of poor repair, is still quite magnificent. Steps lead up to a circular pool overlooked by an unusual cross-shaped stone building; more steps beyond lead down to a gravel terrace. This has two gazebos placed symmetrically at each end and a fine view across the low wall that connects them. Photographs in Gertrude Jekyll's book *Garden Ornament* show this garden in its former glory and it is hoped that the restoration will achieve something approximating to its previous bliss.

TOWNELEY PARK 11
Todmorden Road, Burnley, Lancashire. Tel: (0128?) 424213

Burnley Borough Council ★ 1¹/₂m SE of Burnley town centre on A671 ★ Best season: spring ★ Refreshments: cafeteria ★ Toilet facilities ★ Suitable for wheelchairs ★ Dogs on lead ★ Gift shop in Hall ★ Hall open daily except Sat, weekdays, 10am – 5pm, Sun, 12 noon – 5pm. Closed Christmas week ★ Park open all year during daylight hours ★ Entrance: free

The Hall dates from 1500 but its exterior is largely the work of 1816 – 20. The frontage looks out over a pond and beyond a ha-ha to open parkland laid out in the late eighteenth century. There are some formal beds to the east of the house planted with bright arrangements of annuals. Herbaceous plants and shrubs have been chosen for the area around the Hall and the Small Lime Walk opened up by removing old rhododendrons and replacing with a better selection of choice shrubs and ground cover. Further to the east as well as to the south and west are extensive woodlands containing many large rhododendrons and long walks. There is also a museum of local crafts and industries and a nature centre and aquarium.

WHALLEY ABBEY 12
Whalley, Clitheroe, Lancashire. Tel: (0125482) 2268

Diocese of Blackburn ★ 11m from M6 junction 31, Whalley is S of A59 between Clitheroe and Blackburn ★ Best season: summer ★ Refreshments: in coffee shop. Picnic area ★ Toilet facilities ★ Partly suitable for wheelchairs ★ Shop and exhibition area ★ Open all year, dawn – dusk ★ Entrance: £1.50, OAP £1, children 25p

Whalley Abbey is visited mainly by those wishing to see the ruins of the fourteenth-century abbey, and the gardens run round their periphery. These gardens are of recent creation and consist mainly of herbaceous borders and shrubs; in one area there are conifers and heathers. The stone terraces that have been made against the north outer wall of the garden are perhaps its most attractive feature. To the south of the ruins is an avenue of mixed trees flanking the River Calder that runs behind them. Development of the gardens is continuing.

WORDEN PARK 13
Leyland, Lancashire. Tel: (01772) 421109

Borough of South Ribble ★ Take B5248 S from Leyland and at Leyland Cross follow signs to Worden Park ★ Parking ★ Refreshments: coffee shop and snacks at Craft Centre ★ Toilet facilities, inc. one adapted on RADAR key scheme ★ Partly suitable for wheelchairs ★ Dogs ★ Craft centre ★ Open daily, 8am – sunset ★ Entrance: free, except first Sat in June when a charge is made

These gardens are set around part of an old house and a stable block that now contains a craft workshop (the rest of the house was burnt down in the 1950s). There are formal areas with brightly planted beds amongst cobbled paths and a garden for the blind with scented plants grown in raised beds. The maze is quite unusual, being made of hornbeam hedges in a circular pattern. A little distance away is a large conservatory with a rockery to one side and a herbaceous border to the other. They face a formal sunken lawned area that is enclosed by a low balustrade and some fine ironwork gates. Large areas of open parkland surround the gardens, which contain a children's adventure play area, mini golf, a model railway, an ice-house and an arboretum.

THE NATIONAL TRUST

The National Trust celebrates its cetenary in 1995. It has grown to become Britain's largest conservation charity and now permanently protects over half a million acres of countryside, 200 houses and 160 gardens open to the public in England, Wales and Northern Ireland. A host of commemorative events during the year will include concerts, lectures, childrens' activities and outdoor events with fireworks. The Trust will welcome participation. A book on the 'first hundred years' has been published and there will be an accompanying BBC TV programme.

LEICESTERSHIRE

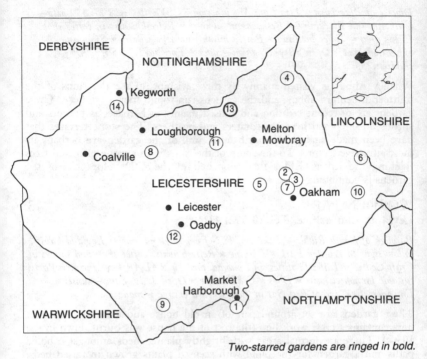

Two-starred gardens are ringed in bold.

ARTHINGWORTH MANOR   1
Arthingworth, Leicestershire. Tel: (0185886) 219

Mr and Mrs W. Guinness ★ 5m S of Market Harborough. Follow A508 and after 4m turn left to village. From Northampton via A508 turn right at bottom of hill at Kelmarsh. In village turn right at church, then first left ★ Parking ★ Dogs on lead ★ Open May to July, Weds and 18th June, 2 – 5pm ★ Entrance: £1.50, children 50p

A compilation of two homes, their seven acres of gardens sympathetically connected in detailed contrasting arrangements. A sunken formal terrace with lily pond leads upwards to a gold border and through into wide herbaceous beds. The garden seems to be on several levels rising to imposing gates into the vegetable and cutting garden. Each house has its own perfect croquet lawns and wide south terraces. A small secret white garden, a hidden corner of old roses, extensive glasshouses and a three-acre arboretum which is beginning to show its future promise. Small secret white garden.

ASHWELL HOUSE   2
Ashwell, Nr Oakham, Leicestershire. Tel: (01572) 722833

Mr and Mrs S.D. Pettifer ★ 3m N of Oakham via B668 towards Cottesmore, turn left to Ashwell ★ Parking ★ Refreshments: Lunches or teas ★ Toilet facilities ★ Suitable for wheelchairs ★ Plants sometimes for sale ★ Open for parties by appointment ★ Entrance: £1 per person

An old walled garden, well-planned with colour combinations to provide all-year colour, and golden plants to light up the various borders. There are peaches, plums, pears and blackberries on the old walls and soft fruits in the garden along with a range of vegetables, and some nut trees. A wide range of shrubs and perennials in the borders, and a large variety of flowers grown for drying. Pleasure garden with summer pavilion in classical style and architectural features by George Carter.

ASHWELL LODGE ★ 3
Ashwell, Nr Oakham, Leicestershire. Tel: (01572) 722825

Mrs B.V. Eve ★ 3m N of Oakham between A606 to Melton Mowbray and B668 Oakham – Cottesmore road ★ Parking in street ★ Teas ★ Toilet facilities ★ Suitable for wheelchairs ★ Plants for sale ★ Open 23rd April, 2.30 – 6pm ★ Entrance: £1, children free (1994 prices)

A one and a half-acre garden redesigned by Percy Cane about 1973 and divided up into little gardens by hedges of beech and yew. A paved rose garden with shrub and pillar roses and a crown-shaped trellis with roses, as well as clematis with roses on arches provide masses of colour. A peony border. A good range of cottage-garden plants in the herbaceous borders and also shrubs and acers. Water and a greenhouse are other features in this very pleasant garden which in spring is colourful with bulbs. There are fruit trees, and smaller plants on the patio.

BELVOIR CASTLE 4
Belvoir, Grantham, Leicestershire. Tel: (01476) 870262

The Duke of Rutland ★ 6m from Grantham, S of A52 Nottingham – Grantham road and N of Melton Mowbray road. By Belvoir village. Signposted ★ Parking ★ Refreshments: lunches and teas. Picnics in car park ★ Toilet facilities ★ Partly suitable for wheelchairs ★ Shop ★ Castle open ★ Garden open April to Sept, Tues, Wed, Thurs, Sat and Sun, Oct, Sun only, 11am – 5pm (last admission to house 4.30pm). Open Bank Holiday Mons. Groups at other times by appointment. Spring garden open all year for pre-booked parties ★ Entrance: castle and garden £4.25, OAP £3 and children £2.65. Spring garden £3.25 per person for pre-booked parties of 10 to 40 persons

From a distance this castle (pronounced Beaver) has all the appearance of a medieval fortress, although on arrival it is clearly a more solid eighteenth-century erection. The house is famous for its rooms by James Wyatt. The mid-nineteenth century garden descends from the castle in a series of terraces and slopes with some small gardens created by hedging. Bulbs, early-flowering shrubs, roses and arbours. Some seating. Good views of Belvoir Vale. Friendly peacocks. Also available for viewing by pre-booked groups is the Duchess of Rutland's private woodland garden, known as the Spring garden, a delightful informal garden situated in a natural ampitheatre in the middle of dense woodland.

BURROUGH HOUSE ★ 5
Burrough on the Hill, Melton Mowbray, Leicestershire.
Tel: (01664) 454226

Mrs Barbara Keene ★ 6m W of Oakham, 5m S of Melton Mowbray. From A606 at Langham take road signposted to Cold Overton and Somerby, continue through Somerby to Burrough on the Hill ★ Parking ★ Home-made refreshments ★ Toilet facilities ★ Suitable for wheelchairs ★ Plants for sale ★ Lecture rooms available ★ Open 16th, 17th April, 7th, 8th, 28th, 29th May, 27th, 28th Aug, 11am – 5pm; also June to Aug, Thurs and Sun, 2 – 5pm. At other times by appointment. Parties by prior arrangement only ★ Entrance: £1.50 (Bank Holidays £2), accompanied children free

Four and a half acres of garden laid out in 1924 by the plant collector Sir Raymond Greene containing many interesting features including a woodland walk through rhododendrons and azaleas. Recently-designed triple cascading ponds and rose and alpine gardens. A new white garden is under construction. The wooden bower house came from the now-destroyed Burrough Court which was the first meeting place of the late Prince of Wales and Wallis Simpson.

CLIPSHAM HOUSE ★ 6
Clipsham, Leicestershire. Tel: (01780) 410238

Mr and Mrs R. Wheatley ★ 10m NE of Oakham, E of A1 on B668 ★ Parking in grounds ★ Toilet facilities ★ Suitable for wheelchairs ★ Dogs on lead ★ Open for groups by appointment in June and for charity on 25th June ★ Entrance: £2, children 25p

This romantic three-acre garden is as one with the pretty Regency rectory (1820) set in parkland with fine trees and rolling pasture. The exceptional walled garden, laid out in 1939 and designed by Dame Brenda Colvin, features old-fashioned roses, shrubs with contrasting foliage and hardy perennials in muted colours. An elevated summerhouse with pool gives added dimension. A pleached hornbeam walk takes the eye to the perfect folly.

LANGHAM LODGE 7
Langham, Nr Oakham, Leicestershire. Tel: (01572) 722912

Mr and Mrs H.N. Hemsley ★ ½m out of Langham on Burley Road. Go up farm drive beside pair of cottages ★ Parking ★ Teas ★ Suitable for wheelchairs ★ Dogs on lead ★ Plants for sale ★ Open 25th June, 11am – 6pm ★ Entrance: £1, children free

This one-acre garden, with rich soil, should be of interest to plantspersons for its imaginative foliage combinations and good sense of shape and colour contrasts. Old-fashioned roses, a peony border, iris, azaleas, hebes, sedums, berberis, dogwoods, eucalyptus, elaeagnus and hostas. There is a hot-coloured bed, an evergreen border, and bulbs in spring. A delightful walled garden with water and a wide range of cottage-garden plants, a greenhouse and a vegetable garden are other features to enjoy.

LONG CLOSE ★ 8
60 Main Street, Woodhouse Eaves, Leicestershire.
Tel: (01509) 890616 (business hours)

Mrs George Johnson ★ S of Loughborough off B591 between A6 and M1 junctions 22 and 23 ★ Parking in village car park ★ Teas (tea and biscuits only on 7th May) ★ Toilet facilities ★ Partly suitable for wheelchairs ★ Dogs on lead ★ Plants for sale ★ Open 2nd April, 2 – 5pm, 7th, 28th May, 2 – 6pm and by appointment March to June ★ Entrance: £1.50, children 20p

When Mrs Johnson and her husband bought Long Close in 1949, they began a project of restoration based on the framework and potential left by their predecessor, Colonel Gerald Heygate. Taking advantage of the lime-free loam they nurtured a collection of rhododendrons, azaleas and magnolias, both rare and complementary. These are now in magnificent maturity. The limitations of a long rectangular shape have been overcome in this five-acre garden by a clever design and increasingly informal terraces. Old rhododendrons stretch in a solid bank in massed irregular shapes to lead the eye along winding paths to fine specimens of trees and finally to an informal dappled pool. Many rare and interesting trees, shrubs and plants. There is also a courtyard which plays its sheltered part with magnificent wall-covering plants, many hardly to be found elsewhere so far north. Truly a plantsman's garden, featured in *Country Life*.

ORCHARDS 9
Hall Lane, Walton, Nr Lutterworth, Leicestershire.
Tel: (01455) 556958

Mr and Mrs G. Cousins ★ 8m S of Leicester. Take A50, turn right for Bruntingthorpe then follow signs for Walton ★ Best season: summer ★ Parking in nearby roads ★ Toilet facilities ★ Suitable for wheelchairs ★ Dogs on lead ★ Plants for sale ★ Open for NGS 18th, 21st June and June to Sept by appointment ★ Entrance: £1.20, children free

A fine example of how to create variety in a small area round a village bungalow. There are raised beds around a pool, old brick paths, troughs with alpines, island beds, a cottage garden with shrub roses, lavenders, verbascums and geraniums. Full of ideas and original plant combinations.

PREBENDAL HOUSE 10
Empingham, Oakham, Leicestershire.

Mr and Mrs J. Partridge ★ 4m from Stamford, just off A606 in Empingham behind the church ★ Parking ★ Teas in Tithe Barn ★ Toilet facilities ★ Suitable for wheelchairs ★ Open 11th June, 2 – 6pm ★ Entrance: £1, children 50p (1994 prices)

The medium-sized garden of the old bishop's palace has yew hedges dividing the garden into smaller areas and forming backing for herbaceous borders. The walled kitchen garden has a wide range of vegetables, fruit trees and bushes as well as herbaceous borders with masses of dahlias and peonies. Also in this area are greenhouses and a fig growing on the wall. The sunken garden contains three pools with fish and water lilies and a beautiful beech tree. There are several large trees in the garden and drive which blend the garden into the adjacent parkland. Many shrub roses along with cottage-garden plants give the garden a great feeling of peace.

ROCKINGHAM CASTLE
(see Northamptonshire)

ROOF TREE COTTAGE   11

Hoby, Nr Melton Mowbray, Leicestershire. Tel: (01664) 434214

D. Headley ★ 8m NE of Leicester, 1m NW of A607 Leicester – Melton road. Turn at Brooksby Agricultural College ★ Open May to June by written appointment and 30th April, 2 – 6pm ★ Entrance: £1, children free

This is a small cottage garden planned and planted with skill to complement the exceptionally fine Constable landscape beyond. The garden slopes gently down from the medieval cottage with paths winding through unusual plantings, many descendants from those popular in the seventeenth century and others related to indigenous species; a few have been included for sentimental reasons. The garden has singular charm, brought about by the informal but thoughtful design which combines the quiet, peaceful beauty of the planting and open spaces with timeless pastoral views, which unfold and change as the onlooker descends.

UNIVERSITY OF LEICESTER BOTANIC GARDEN 12
Stoughton Drive South, Oadby, Leicestershire. Tel: (0116) 271 7725

Leicester University ★ 3m SE of city centre, just off the A6 opposite Oadby race course ★ Parking in nearby roads ★ Toilet facilities ★ Suitable for wheelchairs ★ Plants for sale when available ★ Open all year, Mon – Fri (except Bank Holidays), 10am – 4pm (3.30pm on Fri) or dusk if earlier ★ Entrance: free

A 16-acre garden founded in the early 1900s incorporating the gardens of four large houses with many interesting features ranging from large specimens of *Pinus nigra*, *Sequoiadendron giganteum*, *Fraxinus excelsior* and *Juglans regia* to glasshouses containing collections of alpines, cacti and succulents and plants of economic importance. Shrub borders with a wide range of acers and conifers, herbaceous borders and heather garden. Climbers on walls and on a stone pergola. A formal pool, a parterre garden and a typical Leicestershire meadow have been created. National collections of aubretias, hardy fuchsias and skimmias. Visitors can learn much botanically.

WARTNABY GARDENS ★★   13
Wartnaby, Nr Melton Mowbray, Leicestershire.

Lord and Lady King ★ 4m NW of Melton Mowbray. From A606 turn W in Ab Kettleby for Wartnaby ★ Best season: end May to mid-Aug ★ Parking ★ Refreshments ★ Toilet facilities ★ Partly suitable for wheelchairs ★ Dogs on lead ★ Plants for sale ★ Open 21st May, 25th June, 23rd July, 2 – 6pm, also by appointment at other times ★ Entrance: £1.20, children 30p (1994 prices)

This garden has delightful little gardens within it, including a grey garden, a sunken garden and a purple border of shrubs and roses, and there are good herbaceous borders, climbers and old-fashioned roses. A large pool has an adjacent bog garden with primulas, ferns, astilbes and several varieties of willow. There is an arboretum with a good collection of trees and shrub roses, and alongside the drive is a beech hedge in a Grecian pattern. Greenhouses contain peaches, orchids and a vine and there is a fruit garden with fruit arches and cordon trees. Fine views.

WHATTON HOUSE   14
Nr Kegworth, Leicestershire. Tel: (01509) 842268

Lord Crawshaw ★ 4m NE of Loughborough on A6 between Kegworth and Hathern. 1m from M1 junction 24 ★ Parking in grounds ★ Refreshments in tea room ★ Toilet facilities ★ Partly suitable for wheelchairs ★ Dogs on lead ★ Plants for sale ★ Open 16th April to Aug, Sun, Wed and Bank Holiday Mons, 2 – 6pm. Weekdays by appointment ★ Entrance: £1.50, OAP and children 75p (1994 prices)

This 15-acre garden created by Lord Crawshaw's family and developed over the years contains wide interest with the lovely herbaceous border, large trees, flowering shrubs and more recently-planted arboretum. Note the Art Nouveau gate. There is an ice-house, a dog cemetery, rose garden, woodland garden and the Canyon garden. Water adds to the beauty with pools and there are brick channels that can be filled with water. There is a large walled kitchen garden and in the early part of the year masses of wild flowers. Some areas are somewhat overgrown but an air of peace surrounds the whole.

HOW TO FIND THE GARDENS

Directions to each garden are included in the entry. This information has been supplied by the garden inspectors and is aimed to be the best available to those travelling by car. However, it has been compiled to be used in conjunction with a road atlas.

The unreliability of train and bus services makes it unrewarding to include details, particularly as many garden visits are made on Sundays. However, many properties can be reached by public transport, and National Trust guides and the NGS Yellow Book sometimes give details.

The numbers on the maps correspond to the numbers of the gardens in each county. The maps show the proximity of one garden to another so that visits to several gardens can be planned for the same day. It is worthwhile referring to the maps of bordering counties to see if another garden visit can be included in the itinerary, and to look at the maps at the end of the Guide.

CUTTINGS

Readers may wish to be reminded that the taking of cuttings without the owners' permission can lead to embarrassment and, if it continues on a large scale, may cause owners to close their gardens to the public. This has to be seen in the context of an increasing number of thefts from gardens. At Nymans, the famous Sussex garden, thefts have reached such a level that the gardener will not now plant out any shrub until it is semi-mature and of such a size that its theft would be very difficult. Other owners have reported the theft of artefacts as well as plants.

LINCOLNSHIRE

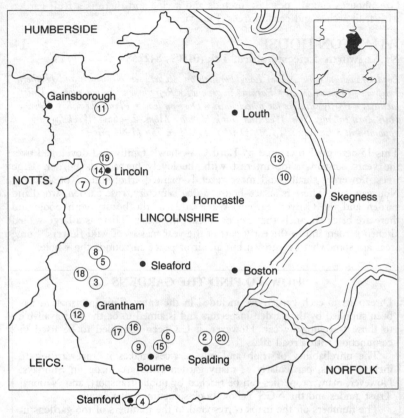

AUBOURN HALL ★

Aubourn, Nr Lincoln, Lincolnshire.

Sir Henry Nevile ★ 7m SW of Lincoln between A46 and A607 ★ Parking ★ Limited toilet facilities ★ Suitable for wheelchairs ★ Plants sometimes for sale ★ Open 21st May, 4th, 18th June, 2nd July; July and Aug, Weds, all 2 – 6pm ★ Entrance: £2.50, OAP £2

First impressions of the gardens at this lovely red-brick hall (*c.* 1600) are of spacious simplicity. Glorious undulating lawns and borders sweep through rose arches or along grassy swathes to more lawns and gardens beyond. The enviably deep and diverse borders are carefully planted to give maximum effects of colour, shape and texture. There are, however, secluded areas in which to linger; the newly-planted rose garden, the old apple orchard thick with spring bulbs and hedge parsley, the ponds and the woodland dell, and a swimming pool surrounded by a late-flowering rose and clematis-covered pergola. The nearby church, one of the smallest in Lincolnshire, is also open to visitors on garden open days.

AYSCOUGHFEE HALL AND GARDENS 2
Churchgate, Spalding, Lincolnshire. Tel: (01775) 725468

South Holland District Council ★ Centre of Spalding ★ Parking on Churchgate ★ Refreshments: café open seasonally ★ Toilet facilities inc. disabled ★ Suitable for wheelchairs ★ Dogs on lead ★ Hall open daily, 9am – 5pm (4.30pm on Fri). Closed weekends Oct to Feb ★ Gardens open weekdays, 8am – dusk, Sun, 10am – dusk. Closed 25th Dec ★ Entrance: free

Next to the River Welland the gardens of this public park are in a beautiful setting. Entirely enclosed by lovely old walls, they are worth visiting for the bizarrely-shaped, clipped yew walks, its old rectangular fish pond with fountains and the fascinating medieval red-brick hall now housing the museum of South Holland. In addition there are good bedding displays, lawns, pergola and wall shrubs including a fruiting vine.

BELTON HOUSE ★ 3
Belton, Nr Grantham, Lincolnshire. Tel: (01476) 66116

The National Trust ★ 3m N of Grantham off A607 ★ Parking ★ Refreshments: light lunches, teas, etc., 12 noon – 5.30pm ★ Toilet facilities inc. disabled ★ Suitable for wheelchairs ★ Dogs on lead ★ Gift shop ★ House open 1 – 5.30pm. ★ Gardens open April to 1st Oct, Wed – Sun and Bank Holiday Mons (but closed 14th April), 11am – 5.30pm (last admission 5pm). Free access to park on foot from Lion Lodge gates all year but this does not give admittance to house, garden or adventure playground ★ Entrance: £4.30, children £2.10 (house and gardens) (1994 prices)

The gardens at Belton are large and impressive. The extensive woodland area has two lakes, a small canal and good cedars; a children's adventure playground makes it ideal for families. However, it is the formal area to the north of the house, completed with the superbly restored and replanted Jeffry Wyatville orangery, that makes the garden memorable. The 'Dutch garden' has clipped yew hedging, formal beds with lavender edging, standard 'Iceberg' roses and well-planted stone urns. The earlier Italian garden has a large central pond with fountain, a lion-headed exedra, lawns and clipped yews.

BURGHLEY HOUSE 4
Stamford, Lincolnshire. Tel: (01780) 52451

Burghley House Preservation Trust. Custodian: Lady Victoria Leatham (née Cecil) ★ ½m E of Stamford on the Barnack road, close to A1. Well signposted ★ Parking ★ Refreshments ★ Toilet facilities ★ Limited access for wheelchairs ★ Dogs on lead in park ★ Shop ★ House and parkland are open April to 8th Oct but to visit the garden itself obtain open dates by telephoning the number above ★ Entrance: £1 (house £5.10, OAP £4.80, children £2.50, accompanied children free) (1994 prices)

The main attraction at Burghley is the magnificent Elizabethan house with its immense collection of art treasures, built by William Cecil, created Lord Burghley by his Queen. Both the house and its present custodian, Lady Victoria Leatham, have appeared on many television antiques programmes. The parkland, landscaped by 'Capability' Brown, is delightful and extensive. There is only a small area of formal rose garden with oval pond, lavender, fountain and urns so Burghley is of limited interest to visitors with more botanical leanings. In addition to creating a large serpentine lake, Brown built a new stable block, an orangery, a gamekeeper's lodge, a dairy and an ice-house. The finest surviving small building is a lakeside summerhouse. The planting, over the last three years, of nearly four acres of spring bulbs means that openings in March/April are quite spectacular.

CAYTHORPE COURT 5
School of Agriculture and Horticulture, Caythorpe, Grantham, Lincolnshire. Tel: (01400) 72521

De Montfort University ★ 10m N of Grantham off A607 ★ Parking ★ Refreshments on open day ★ Toilet facilities ★ Partly suitable for wheelchairs ★ Plants and produce for sale ★ Open 10th June, 1 – 5pm for College Open Day ★ Entrance: £2.50 per car

One of three centres for the School of Agriculture and Horticulture in Lincolnshire, this is reflected in the glasshouses and display beds of roses, shrubs, bedding and herbaceous plants. However, it is the original garden around the 1899 hunting lodge that makes a visit worthwhile. Three large terraces built on a west-facing slope are wonderfully romantic with Ancaster stone walls, balustrades and stairways. For ease of maintenance all are quite simply planted. The upper terrace has a good shrub border and lawn with a specimen monkey-puzzle tree. The middle terrace, a delight in spring, has walls covered in aubretia, and a row of flowering cherries. The third has Virginia creeper and wisteria swathing the balustraded stairs, and a wide rose border underplanted with flag irises and backed by clematis-covered walls. From the upper terrace walks lead to woodland.

21 CHAPEL STREET 6
Hacconby, Nr Bourne, Lincolnshire. Tel: (01778) 570314

Mr and Mrs C. Curtis ★ 3m N of Bourne off A15, turn E at crossroads to village ★ Parking on road ★ Teas on open days ★ Toilet facilities ★ Plants for sale ★ Open 18th, 19th Feb (if weather adverse telephone for alternate dates), 2nd March, 16th April, 4th May, 1st June, 6th July, 3rd Aug, 7th Sept, 5th Oct and by appointment ★ Entrance: £1, children (under 16) free

The gay and cottagey impression of this village garden has been achieved by minimising lawn area and replacing it with planting space. The circuitous path passes rockeries and scree beds, small trees and shrub roses, rustic arches, troughs and a pond. All have been exuberantly planted and under-planted to ensure year round colour and interest. There are hundreds of varieties of bulbs, alpines and herbaceous plants here to satisfy both the casual gardener and the seeker of the rare. The ornamental garden is in the process of being enlarged by the addition of paths, box edging and flowers to the neighbouring vegetable plot.

DODDINGTON HALL 7
Doddington, Lincoln, Lincolnshire. Tel: (01522) 694308

Mr and Mrs A.G. Jarvis ★ 5m W of Lincoln on B1190 ★ Parking ★ Refreshments: restaurant open from 12 noon ★ Toilet facilities inc. disabled ★ Suitable for wheelchairs ★ Dogs on lead ★ Shop ★ House open ★ Garden open

12th March to 27th April, Suns only (but closed 16th April and open 17th April); May to Sept, Wed, Sun and Bank Holiday Mons, 2 – 6pm. Parties at other times by arrangement ★ Entrance: £1.80, children 90p (house and garden £3.60, children £1.80), family tickets available and special rates for disabled in wheelchairs and parties of 20 or more

The romantic gardens of the Elizabethan house successfully combine many different styles and moods. The simplicity of the gravel, box and lawned courtyard, the formal croquet lawn and the gravel walk along the kitchen garden wall contrasts with the walled west garden with its elaborate parterres of roses, iris and clipped box edging with borders of herbaceous plants and old roses. (The parterres were restored in Elizabethan style in 1900.) Fine eighteenth-century Italian gates open from here on to a formal yew alley, more old roses and a good wild garden. Here the meandering walks take in a turf maze, stream, ancient specimens of sweet chestnut, cedar, yew and holly, and the Temple of the Winds built by the present owner. The more recently-planted herb garden, pleached hornbeams and dwarf box-edging continue to harmonise the different areas.

FULBECK HALL   8
Fulbeck, Nr Grantham, Lincolnshire. Tel: (01400) 72205

Mr and Mrs Fry ★ On A607 Lincoln – Grantham road ★ Parking ★ Picnic area ★ Toilet facilities ★ Suitable for wheelchairs ★ Dogs on lead ★ Plants for sale in July ★ Hall open ★ Garden open 17th April, 8th, 29th May, 2nd to 30th July, daily and 28th Aug, 2 – 5pm. Groups by appointment at any time ★ Entrance: £1.50, children 50p (hall and garden £3, OAP £2.50, children £1) (1994 prices)

The 11-acre garden at Fulbeck is varied and interesting with recent planting within the formal Victorian design laid out at the end of the last century. Many of the trees here are as old as the house (1733). The top terrace with a gravel walk is backed by a superbly-shaped clipped yew hedge. The bottom lawn has shrubs, roses, unusual clematis and ramblers climbing into the surrounding trees. Against a limestone wall at the south of the house is a herbaceous border with many choice plants. Beyond the immediate garden is a pleasant wild garden and nature trail. In 1990, 200 native trees and shrubs around the north and western edge of the garden were planted, and a pond was constructed near the northern boundary by the nature trail.

GRIMSTHORPE CASTLE   9
Grimsthorpe, Nr Bourne, Lincolnshire.
Tel: (01778) 32205; Fax: (01778) 32259

Grimsthorpe and Drummond Castle Trust Ltd ★ 4m NW of Bourne on A151 Colsterworth – Bourne road ★ Parking ★ Teas ★ Toilet facilities inc. disabled ★ Suitable for wheelchairs ★ Castle, park and gardens will probably be open as usual during the summer but telephone for details of times and prices

The impressive house, part-medieval, part-Tudor and part-eighteenth-century, of Vanbrugh design, is surrounded on three sides by good pleasure gardens in which 'Capability' Brown had a hand. The Victorian knot garden to the east of the house has beds of lavender, roses and catmint with edges of clipped box. To the south are two yew-hedged rose gardens with topiary, a yew 'broad walk' and a retreat. Leading to the west terrace is a double yew walk with classic herbaceous borders and beyond a shrub rose border and row of 70-year-old cedars. The yew hedging throughout the garden is superbly maintained and differs in design from one area to another. Beyond the pleasure gardens are the arboretum, wild garden, an unusual geometrically-designed kitchen garden with clipped box and bean pergola, and extensive parkland. Views of the old oak and chestnut avenues and the parkland with its lake and Vanbrugh summerhouse are provided by cleverly positioned vistas and terraces.

GUNBY HALL ★   10
Gunby, Nr Spilsby, Lincolnshire.

The National Trust ★ 2½m NW of Burgh-le-Marsh on S of A158 ★ Parking ★ Toilet facilities ★ Suitable for wheelchairs ★ Dogs on lead ★ Plants for sale ★ Hall and garden open April to Sept, Wed only, 2 – 6pm (last admission 5.30pm). Garden also open Thurs, 2 – 6pm. Also Tues, Thurs and Fri by written appointment to Mr and Mrs J.D. Wrisdale. Coaches and parties pre-book in writing ★ Entrance: £1.80, children 90p (house and garden £3, children £1.50)

The early eighteenth-century house, with its walls smothered in fine plants, is set in parkland with avenues of lime and horse chestnut. The shrub borders, wild garden, lawns with old cedars and the restrained formal front garden of catmint and lavender beds backed by clipped yew provide a startling contrast to the main attraction of Gunby – its walled gardens. The dazzling pergola garden with its apple-tree walkway has a maze of paths leading to beds of old roses, herb garden and brimming herbaceous and annual borders. The second walled area houses an impressive kitchen garden reached after passing more borders of perfectly-arranged herbaceous plants and hybrid musk roses. Backing on to its wall is another wonderfully classic herbaceous border and beyond an early nineteenth-century long fish pond and orchard completing an altogether enchanting garden. It is fitting that it was the subject of Tennyson's 'Haunt of Ancient Peace'.

HALL FARM AND NURSERY   11
Harpswell, Gainsborough, Lincolnshire. Tel: (01427) 668412

Mr and Mrs M Tatam ★ 7m E of Gainsborough on A631 ★ Best season: summer ★ Parking ★ Teas on charity day only ★ Toilet facilities ★ Partly suitable for wheelchairs ★ Dogs on lead ★ Plants for sale ★ Open daily, 10am – 6pm, but closed from Nov to Feb at weekends except by appointment ★ Entrance: donation to charity

This garden has been carefully planned and exuberantly planted. The owners' sheer delight in plants, satisfied by their adjoining nursery, is evident everywhere. A santolina-edged rose pergola leads down the side of the farm house to two large terraced lawns and a large informal pond. The wide borders here are of mainly shrub roses (there are 84 rose varieties in the garden) underplanted with herbaceous plants. From the top terrace old stone pillars make an imposing entrance to a round sunken garden with miniature box edging and seasonal bedding. A short walk away is an interesting medieval moat.

HARLAXTON MANOR GARDENS   12
Grantham, Lincolnshire. Tel: (01476) 592101

*University of Evansville, USA ★ 1m from A1 on A607 Melton Mowbray road ★
Parking ★ Toilet facilities ★ Partly suitable for wheelchairs ★ Dogs on lead ★
Plants sometimes for sale ★ House occasionally open ★ Garden open April to Oct,
daily except Mon (but open Bank Holiday Mons), 11am – 5pm ★ Entrance:
£2.50, OAP £2, children under 12 £1.25, parties of 20 or more £2 per person.
Guided tours extra*

This fantastic Victorian mansion and garden was built to delight and impress –
'I have not read of such a place even in a fairy tale,' wrote Disraeli in 1846.
The formal gardens were built on seven terraces and designed as a tour round
Europe. These, and the cottage gardens of the estate, were held up as models
of their time. Many of the original features remain. There are beautiful
Ancaster stone steps, balustrades, colonnades, ponds and even a Tuscan-style
tower. Sadly most of the plantings and paths have been lost or overgrown over
the last 20 years. Recently the landscape designer Alan Mason has begun the
daunting task of renovating the gardens. Shrubberies and yew walks have been
ruthlessly cut back, and the incredibly ornate six and a quarter-acre walled
garden has been replanted. Harlaxton will be of great interest to the garden
historian or to anyone who likes a 'before and after' transformation.

HARRINGTON HALL   13
Harrington, Spilsby, Lincolnshire.

*Mr and Mrs D.W.J. Price ★ 5m E of Horncastle, 2m N of A158 ★ Parking ★
Refreshments ★ Toilet facilities ★ Suitable for wheelchairs ★ Dogs on lead ★ Plants
for sale ★ Open 13th May, 11th June, 9th, 23rd July, 13th Aug, 2 – 6pm ★
Entrance: £1, children free*

Red-brick Tudor and eighteenth-century walls provide the perfect backdrop
for wall shrubs and a variety of borders. Referred to in Tennyson's 'Maud,' it
is hard to imagine that these walled gardens and terrace have changed,
although they were in fact replanted in the 1950s after wartime vegetable
cultivation. The present owner is in the process of remaking the formal one-
acre vegetable garden with gravel paths, miniature box edging and espalier
fruit trees. The tiny church next to the hall is open to those visiting the
garden.

THE LAWN   14
Union Road, Lincoln, Lincolnshire. Tel: (01522) 560306

*Lincoln City Council ★ Off Burton Road beside Lincoln Castle ★ Parking
(charged) ★ Refreshments ★ Toilet facilities ★ Suitable for wheelchairs ★ Shop ★
National Cycle Museum and Lincoln Archaeological Centre open ★ Garden open:
summer weekdays, 9am – 5pm; weekends 10am – 5pm. winter Mon – Thurs,
9am – 5pm; Fri, 9am – 4.30pm; weekends, 10am – 4pm ★ Entrance: free*

When Lincoln City Council bought this disused Georgian mental hospital in
1985 they hoped to establish a botanic collection to represent Lincoln's partnership with cities and countries around the world. Central to this is the Sir
Joseph Banks conservatory. Here excellent use of water, and arrangements of
plants in areas corresponding with parts of the world visited by Banks on his

three-year voyage with Captain Cook, have made this small area both exotic and interesting. The nearby walled John Dawber Garden continues this international theme, with mini gardens representing England, Germany, China and Australia. The gardens are still very new and it will be some years before the natural elements balance the dominating architecture.

32 MAIN STREET   15
Dyke, Nr Bourne, Lincolnshire. Tel: (01778) 422241

Mr and Mrs D. Sellars ★ 1m N of Bourne, off A15 ★ Parking ★ Refreshments at nearby pub ★ Dogs on lead ★ Open by appointment. Groups especially welcomed ★ Entrance: £1, children 25p

This small area of 100 x 50 feet is subdivided into tiny compartments allowing an astonishing number of planting schemes. Every available space is crammed with a choice plant, ornament, trough or architectural feature and careful planning and underplanting ensures continuous colour.

MANOR FARM   16
Keisby, Nr Lenton, Bourne, Lincolnshire. Tel: (01476) 585607

Mr and Mrs C.A. Richardson ★ 9m NW of Bourne, N of A151 ★ Parking ★ Teas ★ Toilet facilities on ground floor ★ Suitable for wheelchairs ★ Dogs on lead ★ Plants for sale ★ Open 18th, 19th Feb, 11am – 4pm, and one Sun in June (telephone for details) ★ Entrance: £1, children free

This pretty, informal garden is a delight with its artistic planning and colour harmonisation. The tiny paths to the herb garden, pergola and stream meander through the beds and so allow close inspection of the many choice plants, including herbaceous shrub roses, ramblers and clematis.

MANOR HOUSE   17
Bitchfield, Grantham, Lincolnshire. Tel: (01476) 585261

Mr John Richardson ★ Centre of Bitchfield village on B1176 SE of Grantham ★ Parking ★ Toilet facilities ★ Open mid-June to mid-July. Parties only by appointment. No children ★ Entrance: donations to charity. £2 per person

The restrained courtyard entrance has walls of soft apricot-pink, perfectly matching the gravel, and is decorated merely with clipped box in French-style planters. Just south of the house is a formal box-edged garden with a central armillary sphere, planted with the grey-foliaged, white-flowering *Cerastium tomentosum* var. *columnae* that gives a welcome winter colour and interest, for this is a summer garden. There are over 100 rose varieties mixed with herbaceous plants in formal and informal borders. Roses also provide colour round the pond and ramble happily through old apple trees in the lawn and over the house walls. By careful design, views over a ha-ha to the paddock are never lost, even with the owner's generous planting schemes. Much recommended for lovers of shrub roses and summer-flowering herbaceous plants. Robin Lane Fox helped with the design.

MARSTON HALL   18
Marston, Nr Grantham, Lincolnshire. Tel: (01400) 50225

Reverend Henry Thorold ★ 6m NW of Grantham, 1½m off A1 ★ Teas ★ Toilet

Facilities ★ Suitable for wheelchairs ★ Dogs on lead ★ Plants for sale when available ★ House open ★ Garden open 18th, 25th June, 30th July, 13th Aug, 2 – 6pm. Other times by appointment ★ Entrance: £2, children £1

The gardens reflect the intimate nature of the beautiful and ancient Ancaster stone house. A series of small, walled and high-hedged gardens, courtyards and walks house formal rose beds, cottage garden, knot garden planted with herbs, and vegetables screened by herbaceous borders and trellising. To the south of the house are lawns, clipped yews and walks through the newly-planted laburnum avenue and ancient trees including an enormous laburnum and a 400-year-old wych elm. The avenue of Lombardy poplars stretches from the orchard to the river perfectly uniting the garden with the parkland beyond.

RISEHOLME HALL 19
Lincolnshire College of Agriculture and Horticulture, Riseholme, Lincoln. Tel: (01522) 522252

Lincolnshire County Council ★ 2m N of Lincoln off A15 or A46 ★ Parking ★ Coffee shop open daily, refreshments on Open Day and in evenings if booked ★ Toilet facilities inc. disabled ★ Suitable for wheelchairs ★ Plants for sale ★ Farm shop ★ Open 14th May, 10.30am – 5pm for College Open Day and some evenings by appointment ★ Entrance: £2.50 per car

Typically eighteenth-century landscaped parkland, with a picturesque lake, surrounds the house and gardens. Reflecting its educational as well as decorative function the garden provides a rare opportunity to view a vast selection of labelled plants. The horticultural department's demonstration plots show rock, water, low maintenance and heather gardens as well as demonstration hedges, genus beds, bedding, vegetables and glasshouses. The long Bishop's Walk has a yew hedge to the north and a warm brick wall to the south allowing the cultivation of many tender wall shrubs and climbers normally only found in more southerly districts. Along the walk is a herbaceous border and island beds of flowering shrubs, plus an arboretum planted in 1971, mixed borders, rose beds and conservation areas.

SPRINGFIELDS SHOW GARDENS 20
Springfields, Spalding, Lincolnshire. Tel: (01775) 724843

Springfields Horticultural Society ★ 1½m from Spalding on A151 ★ Parking ★ Refreshments: café, tea shop and licensed restaurant ★ Toilet facilities ★ Suitable for wheelchairs ★ Plants for sale ★ Shop ★ Open 18th March to 1st Oct, daily, 10am – 5pm (last admission 5pm) ★ Entrance: £2.50, OAP £2.30, accompanied children free (special events £3.50 to £5, OAP £3.50 to £4.50, children (5-16) free)

The 25 acres of gardens have been designed to maximise areas of show bedding – whether of the colourful spring displays of thousands of bulb varieties or of the later roses and annuals. Subdivided into smaller areas by shrub borders and small copses, the garden boasts many different features all easily accessible for wheelchairs. However, with the exception of an excellent herbaceous border, with its bold plantings, the gardens and glasshouse can be monotonous. New features are a drought garden and a refurbished glasshouse with palms and semi-tropical plants. The colour schemes are dazzling but wearing and the gardens themselves – the lake, the pergolas and the architecture – are all somewhat dated.

LONDON (Greater)

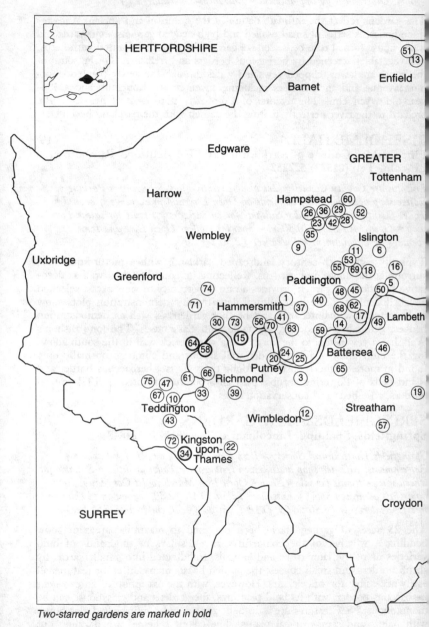

Two-starred gardens are marked in bold

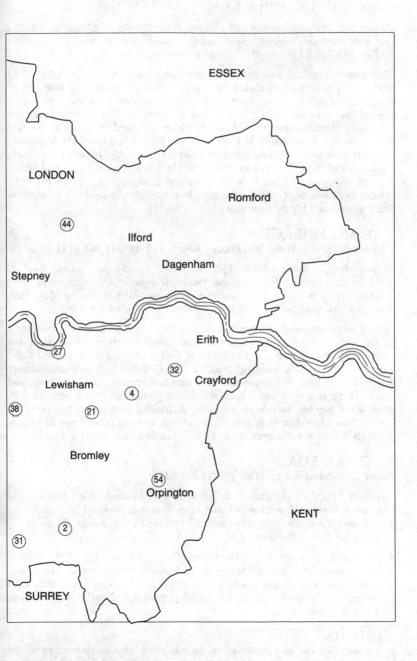

ESSEX

LONDON

Romford

Ilford

Dagenham

Stepney

(44)

Erith

(27)

(32)

Crayford

Lewisham

(4)

(38)

(21)

Bromley

(54)

Orpington

KENT

(2)

(31)

SURREY

29 ADDISON AVENUE 1
London W11. Tel: (0171) 603 2450

Mr and Mrs D.B. Nicholson ★ Off Holland Park Avenue, W of tube station.
Cars must enter via Norland Square and Queensdale Road ★ Parking ★ Open
23rd or 30th July, 2 – 6pm (but telephone to check) ★ Entrance: £1

Meticulously kept and well-designed small town walled garden (about 30 x 40
feet) with a profusion of plants on every surface. It makes the best use of
every inch of space. A tiny lawn is dominated by two venerable pear trees.
Beyond them are perennial borders, slightly raised, and formally laid out but
informally planted with an emphasis on phlox and hardy geraniums. To one
side of the studio workshop at the end of the garden is a small shade garden,
complete with statue. In late summer *Solanum jasminoides* blossoms profusely
on one of the walls. The colour themes of the borders (pink, blue and white)
and the variegated foliage help to unify the garden, which is an excellent
balance between design and planting. Interestingly 'everything is used to
being moved and hardly ever sulks.'

THE ANCHORAGE 2
8 Croydon Road, West Wickham, Kent. Tel: (0181) 462 4141

Mr and Mrs G. Francis ★ From A232 and A2022 roundabout, continue along
A232 for approximately 100 yards and turn right opposite Manor House public
house ★ Parking in road ★ Refreshments ★ Plants for sale ★ Open 21st May, 18th
June, 2nd, 5th, 30th July, 2 – 5.30pm ★ Entrance: £1, children 25p

Behind an unassuming suburban semi lies this third-of-an-acre plantsman's
garden whose owners have given free reign to their admiration for
Sissinghurst by creating a mini version of that celebrated spot. Several beds,
separated by low box hedging, make a series of 'rooms' each individually
designed for colour. These contain some rare herbaceous plants, old roses and
irises. There is a fruit and vegetable plot, a pond and paved herb garden,
while some patches have been left wild. A fruitful hour or so can be spent
here and an added bonus is that the plants on sale are more unusual than is
generally found at such open days. Dolly's Garden (see entry) is nearby.

32 ATNEY ROAD 3
Putney, London SW15. Tel: (0181) 785 9355

Mrs Sally Tamplin ★ Off Putney Bridge Road ★ Best season: May, then mid to
late June ★ Parking in street ★ ☆Teas ★ Open by appointment and for charity
several times during the year, often with 17 Fulham Park Gardens. Please
telephone for dates ★ Entrance: £1

A spacious London garden with attractively planted terrace. Wide borders
along the boundaries are packed with herbaceous plants, roses, hydrangeas
and other shrubs to ensure a long season of interest. A central rose arch leads
to the rear of the garden giving a sense of perspective. Nearby is 17 Fulham
Park Gardens (see entry).

ATRIUMS

It is ironic that the newspaper group which owns what is claimed to be the
biggest atrium in Europe, 115ft high with waterfalls and fully-grown trees,

requests that their London garden should be denied publicity 'for security reasons'. Would they give the same protection to private persons? A similar shyness overcomes other commercial organisations in the South of England despite their investment in a green 'public face' in their office entrances. However, for connoisseurs of the atrium, flamboyant examples can be found at *Triton Court* on Finsbury Square in the City and at the offices of *Robert Fleming Holdings Ltd*, 25 Copthall Avenue, EC2. Another fascinating new office garden in London is that created at the *Cannon Bridge* development. Alas, though it can be enjoyed by resident office workers, the magic created on less than half a yard depth of soil remains closed to the public. Owners please relent.

AVERY HILL PARK 4
Eltham, London SE9. Tel: (0181) 850 3217

London Borough of Greenwich ★ Off Bexley Road and Avery Hill Road ★ Parking ★ Refreshments: small café ★ Toilet facilities ★ Suitable for wheelchairs ★ Some restrictions on dogs ★ Open 7.30am – dusk. The winter garden open Mon – Thurs, 1 – 4pm, Fri, 1 – 3pm, Sat and Sun, 10am – 4pm. Closed 24th, 25th Dec and 1st Jan ★ Entrance: free

More remains of the gardens at Avery Hill than the 50-room mansion, which was badly damaged in the Blitz. The house was built by Colonel John North, known as The Nitrate King because he made a fortune from Chilean nitrates which were much in demand as fertiliser. Since 1906 it has been used as a teachers' training college, while the gardens are enjoyed by the local inhabitants. There are rose gardens and three giant conservatories which look like icebergs which have come to a halt on the southern slope of Shooter's Hill. The domed temperate house is bursting with bougainvillaeas and staghorn ferns. The tropical house attracts school parties to see bananas, coffee and ginger plants while the camellias draw the crowds to the cold house in the spring. There is also an aviary.

BARBICAN CONSERVATORY 5
The Barbican, Silk Street, London EC2. Tel: (0171) 638 4141

City of London ★ In the Barbican Centre, on the 8th floor ★ Parking. Lift and stairs ★ Toilet facilities ★ Partly suitable for wheelchairs ★ Shops on Levels 4 and 7 of Barbican Centre ★ Open weekends and Bank Holidays only, 12 noon – 5.30pm. Telephone to confirm opening times as the conservatory is sometimes used for conferences ★ Entrance: 80p, OAP and children 60p, family ticket (1 or 2 adults and up to 4 children) £2.25. Pre-booked guided tours available – telephone for details

The lift to the eighth floor of the Barbican transports you from the centre of the City to a lush jungle of temperate and semi–tropical plants. Planted in the autumn of 1980-81, using 1600 cubic metres of soil, the conservatory was opened in 1984. Twin *Cupressus cashmeriana* grace the main entrance while a vast banyan tree (*Ficus bengalensis*) in the eastern section threatens to burst through the roof. Many familiar houseplants like *Ficus benjamina* have reached gigantic proportions and a colossal Swiss cheese plant (*Monstera deliciosa*) produces edible fruits after flowering. The Arid House on the second level, added in 1986, contains epiphyllum and cacti, including the largest

Carnegiea gigantea in Europe. Fred, as it is affectionately known, was a gift from the Mayor of Salt Lake City. There are finches in the aviary and the ponds are alive with fish and terrapins. Natural predators and pathogens are used to keep down pests, and the hard Thames water is softened to stop nutrients becoming locked in the soil. On Sundays through the winter at 2pm there is usually a talk on gardening for those who buy £1.50 tickets (0171 382 7021).

28 BARNSBURY SQUARE   6
London N1. Tel: (0171) 607 2001

*Mr F.T. Gardner ★ Off Thornhill Road ★ Parking in road ★ Refreshments ★
Open 11th June, 2 – 6pm, and other times by prior appointment ★ Entrance: £1*

A real period piece! For the most part, an un-reconstructed Victorian garden, cared for by the third and fourth generation of owners. There is a re-discovered grotto dating from the nineteenth century, linked with a pool (exceptionally full of frogs), waterfall and fountain, all previously run with rationed mains water but now pumped in the conventional manner. A Victorian gazebo of real distinction, though slightly askew. Magnificent trees lent by surrounding gardens create the London oasis effect. Interesting planting reflects changing fashions and styles and gives year-round interest.

BATTERSEA PARK   7
Battersea, London SW11. Tel: (0181) 871 7530/1

*Wandsworth Borough Council ★ S side of Thames, from Chelsea Bridge to Albert
Bridge ★ Parking free in car park ★ Refreshments ★ Toilet facilities ★ Suitable for
wheelchairs ★ Dogs ★ Open daily, 7am – dusk ★ Entrance: free*

Laid out 1852–8 on Battersea Fields, an old duelling rendezvous. It was much improved by the late-lamented GLC and contains many interesting features such as the Buddhist temple, zoo, aviary, sculptures, large boating lake and also frequent entertainments in tented accommodation. The plantsperson should make a point of visiting the glasshouses near Albert Bridge. Interesting sub-tropical garden, water garden and modern wooden arbourwork. It is to be hoped that the improvements will continue, though there are disturbing signs: for example, the historic rock garden has been 'restored' by spraying it with gunnite which has changed its colour from white to red and destroyed the sharpness of the forms, turning them to a 'jellymould'. It will be 50 years before the gunnite erodes.

BROCKWELL PARK   8
Tulse Hill, London SE24. Tel: (0171) 926 0105

*London Borough of Lambeth ★ Take A205 then A215, entrances at Herne Hill
Gate, Norwood Road, Brockwell Gardens Road etc. ★ Best season: summer
(July) ★ Parking: Herne Hill Gate, Norwood Road, Brockwell Gardens Road ★
Refreshments ★ Toilet facilities inc. disabled ★ Partly suitable for wheelchairs ★
Dogs, except in walled garden ★ Open daily, 9am – dusk ★ Entrance: free*

A peaceful and attractive refuge from nearby Brixton shopping centre, within a surprisingly large park, Brockwell has both a pretty and secluded old English walled garden, with rose beds, and a delightful mixture of herbaceous bedding, providing almost year-round interest. (Radios, cassettes, and dogs are banned from the walled garden – and children under 14 have to be accompanied by an adult.) On the hilltop surrounding the clock-tower are a variety of shrubs and trees and formal bedding. Both park and gardens are very well-maintained. The parkland is well provided with benches. Ground staff are helpful and informative. There are three ponds. Good views to the north over a London of many towers and a few spires which looks surprisingly attractive and even romantic.

15A BUCKLAND CRESCENT ★   9
London NW3.

Lady Barbirolli ★ Near Fitzjohn's Avenue at Swiss Cottage end. 5 minutes from Swiss Cottage tube station and various buses ★ Parking in neighbouring streets ★ Suitable for wheelchairs ★ Plants for sale ★ Open 18th June, 2.30 – 6.30pm ★ Entrance: £1, children 50p

The strong sense of space and line that musicians often possess is expressed in this dignified third-of-an-acre town garden. The ground plan combines flowing unfussy lines and ingenious geometry. Planting ranges from a functional but decorative vegetable patch to some remarkable mature tree specimens, such as *Cornus alternifolia* 'Variegata' and *Metasequoia glyptostroboides*; it is everywhere discriminating. A generous terrace is enhanced by boldly planted urns.

22 CAMBRIDGE ROAD   10
Teddington, Middlesex. Tel: (0181) 977 5692

Mr and Mrs Roger Storr ★ Turning off Teddington High Street near St Alban's Church ★ Parking ★ Toilet facilities ★ Suitable for wheelchairs ★ Plants sometimes for sale ★ Open 25th June, 2 – 6pm ★ Entrance: 50p, children free

Mr and Mrs Storr are professional gardeners and have created an imaginative garden to incorporate their differing ideas: a His 'n' Hers garden! 'Hers' is immediately beyond the patio which has tender plants and a water feature. It is well-shaped and planted for delectable colour. 'His' is mostly vegetables, both unusual and beautifully arranged. In between, their young children have been accommodated with a tree house in an old pear, connected by a drawbridge to a bridge over the whole garden and down a ladder on the other side, all covered with clematis and honeysuckles. Visitors should not use the tree house! The children also have their own garden for planting at the back. There are unusual plants such as albizia.

CAMLEY STREET NATURAL PARK   11
12 Camley Street, London NW1. Tel: (0171) 833 2311

London Borough of Camden; managed by the London Wildlife Trust ★ Off Goods Way, behind King's Cross railway station ★ Parking in nearby streets ★ Toilet facilities, inc. baby changing and disabled ★ Partly suitable for wheelchairs ★ Open daily, Mon – Thurs, 9am – 5pm, Sat and Sun, 11am – 5pm (both 6pm in summer) ★ Entrance: free. Donations welcome

Now threatened by the King's Cross Channel Tunnel link, this is an example of an extremely successful urban wildlife park and garden created against all the odds. Plants, wildlife and people thrive in it. In two and a fifth acres set between the Regent's Canal, imposing black and red gasometers and a noisy skipyard, it has been landscaped with a large pond and includes a visitors' centre with environmental education classroom. This tranquil space has a fine record of sighted birds and other wildlife. Views of the canal and passing narrow boats are somewhat romantically offset by relics of Victorian industry.

CANNIZARO PARK ★   12
West Side Common, Wimbledon, London SW19.
Tel: (0181) 946 7349

London Borough of Merton ★ West Side Common, Wimbledon ★ Best season: March to early June ★ Parking: West Side Common and surrounding side roads ★ Teas on summer Suns only, 2 – 6pm, provided by Wimbledon Guides and Brownies ★ Toilet facilities ★ Wheelchairs have reasonable access to top garden ★ Dogs on lead ★ Open daily, Mon – Fri, 8am – sunset, Sat, Sun and Bank Holidays, 9am – sunset ★ Entrance: free

Formerly the grounds of Cannizaro House, the approach is through imposing gates and a formal drive, lined with beautifully-kept seasonal bedding. Cannizaro's trees are its principal attraction: cork oaks, mulberry and sassafras (until a few years ago it had the oldest sassafras in England). Some enormous and beautiful beeches, mature red Japanese maples, magnolias and a Chilean flame tree (flowering late May/June) are among the many attractions here. At the southern wooded end of the park, Lady Jane's Wood, the main feature is the magnificent azalea dell. Throughout the long spring flowering season, the whole wood appears to be in flower. There is floral colour even in the coldest moments. In the midst of the trees a secluded picnic area, set with tables, contains – somewhat unexpectedly – a bust of the Emperor Haile Selassie of Ethiopia, who sought refuge in Wimbledon. There is a small aviary, a pretty walled rose garden, an azalea and rhododendron collection and a heather garden. The old garden, a formal garden and the pool are found down a steep slope directly in front of Cannizaro House and a wild garden is being created in the same location. A sculpture exhibition is held in the park in June.

CAPEL MANOR   13
Horticultural and Environmental Centre, Bullsmoor Lane, Enfield, Middlesex. Tel: (01992) 763849

Capel Manor Charitable Corporation ★ From the M25 junction with the A10, it is AA signposted via Turkey Street/Bullsmoor Lane ★ Parking ★ Teas ★ Toilet facilities ★ Suitable for wheelchairs ★ Dogs on lead ★ Plants for sale sometimes at special events and shows ★ Shop ★ Open daily, 10am – 5.30pm (dusk in winter) ★ Entrance: £3, OAP £2, children £1.50. Special prices for Show weekends

These gardens are intended to show the history of gardening from the sixteenth century to the present. They also function as a design centre for the garden industry. The contrast with Myddelton House, nearby (see entry) could not be stronger: at Capel, maintenance is excellent but a unifying sensibility completely lacking. The gardens here are from first to last a curate's egg; good areas, such as the garden for the disabled, jostle with aberrations and queasy inventions, such as 'A Lover's Garden'. Detailing is mixed; jagged rocks are sunk in the middle of smooth, rounded pebbles. But there is much of interest for the family outing, enhanced by a few rare breeds of farm livestock. In 1990 the *Sunday Times* Beginner's Garden, featured at Chelsea, was moved here for display, and funds are being collected for further development. *Gardening from 'Which?'* has established an area of demonstration and theme gardens here, including a 'live' A-Z of shrubs. This is home for the National collection of achilleas and sarcoccas. There is a Japanese garden, a garden for wildlife and another garden from Chelsea.

CHELSEA PHYSIC GARDEN ★ 14
66 Royal Hospital Road, Chelsea, London SW3. Tel: (0171) 352 5646

Trustees of Chelsea Physic Garden ★ One entrance in Swan Walk, off Chelsea Embankment and another in Royal Hospital Road ★ Parking: meters in side street and in Battersea Park on opposite side of river ★ Teas ★ Toilet facilities ★ Partly suitable for wheelchairs ★ Plants for sale ★ Open April to Oct, Wed, 2 – 5pm, Sun, 2 – 6pm; also during Chelsea Flower Show and Chelsea Festival Week, 12 noon – 5pm. There are sometimes Sun openings and sales for all in the winter months (telephone for details) ★ Entrance: £3.50, students, children and unemployed £1.80

Founded to train London's apothecaries in herbal medicine in the seventeenth century, the Chelsea Physic Garden is still actively involved in research into herbal medicine, as well as playing an important botanical role. Its three and a half acres, tucked between Cheyne Walk and Swan Walk, are well worth visiting, not only for the fascinating range of medicinal plants grown there, but also for their rare and interesting ones, including beautiful trees like the magnificent golden rain tree (*Koelreuteria paniculata*). The garden also houses what is believed to be one of the earliest rock gardens in Europe, created with basaltic lava brought back by the botanist Joseph Banks from Iceland in 1772. The main part of the garden is devoted to systematicly ordered beds of plants, but there are also displays associated with the plant hunters and botanists who have played their part in the development of the garden, including Banks, Philip Miller, William Hudson and Robert Fortune, as well as an attractive woodland garden and a new Garden of World Medicine showing the use of medicinal plants by tribal peoples. The National collection of cistus is housed here. You can become a Friend of the Chelsea Physic Garden for £20, entitling you and a guest to free entry on all public open days and to entry at other times in office hours.

CHISWICK HOUSE ★★ 15
Burlington Lane, Chiswick, London W4. Tel: (0181) 742 1225

London Borough of Hounslow ★ 5m W of central London, just off A4 ★ Parking. Entrance on A4 ★ Refreshments ★ Toilet facilities ★ Suitable for wheelchairs ★ Dogs on lead, not admitted in Italian garden ★ House open April to Oct, daily, 10am – 6pm, Nov to March, 10am – 4pm. Closed 24th to 26th Dec ★ Gardens open all year, daily, 10am – dusk ★ Entrance: garden free (house £2.30, concessions £1.70, children £1.15) (1994 prices)

Handsome, semi-classical gardens, stretching over many acres, with lake, statues, monuments and magnificent trees. Created by William Kent to complement the Palladian villa built by Lord Burlington in 1729, the gardens are full of splendid vistas, avenues and changes of contour. There is a formal Italian garden with parterres filled with technicolour bedding plants in front of the handsome conservatory (both introduced after Kent's day) and a large canal-shaped lake, with informal woodland planting around it. The gardens are well worth visiting at any time of the year, but particularly in autumn and winter when many other gardens have lost their charm. Once or twice during the year there are special events here.

CITY OF LONDON PARKS AND GARDENS 16

Although there is inevitably a certain similarity in the design and planning of any group of gardens administered by a public body, those within the City of London (numbering nearly 100), being principally located on bomb sites, churchyards and former churchyards, perhaps have more variety than might be expected. For tourists and workers they provide a welcome respite from the dirt and noise of the City and almost all are provided with lots of benches. They are open 8am – 7pm or dusk, 7 days a week unless otherwise stated.

EC1: *Bunhill Fields Burial Ground.* Between Bunhill Row and City Road. [Open Mon – Fri, 7.30am – 7pm (4pm Oct to March), weekends 9.30am – 4pm] A burial ground, unused since 1853, containing many fine tombs and memorials, including those of William Blake and John Bunyan. Most of the tombs are behind railings, but part of the grounds which were bomb-damaged have been planted with grass, trees and shrubs. Fine planes and a mulberry. *Christchurch – Greyfriars Rose Garden*, Newgate Street. [Open daily] A collection of hybrid teas and climbing roses trained up wooden pillars with rope linking them. *Postman's Park*, St Martins Le Grand. [Open daily, 7am – dusk. Closed weekends and Bank Holidays] Close to St Paul's Cathedral. An area of formal bedding in the centre with mature trees, bushes and shrubs. There is also a small fountain with goldfish, and tombs and headstones from the time when it was a churchyard. An arcade protects a tiled wall commemorating the deeds of those who died in their efforts to save others, called the Watts Memorial.

EC2: *Finsbury Circus.* The largest public open space in the City and London's first public park (1606). Apart from the ubiquitous London plane trees, it also boasts the only bowling green in the City, surrounded by low box hedges, bedding plants, shrubs, a drinking fountain and a small bandstand. *St Anne and St Agnes Churchyard*, Gresham Street. [Permanently open] Here the church still stands, alongside the remains of part of London Wall and those of a Roman fort, surrounded by trees and shrubs. *St Botolph-without-Bishopsgate Churchyard*, Bishopsgate [Permanently open] Apart from the usual planting, there is also a tennis court (summer) and netball courts (winter) and a former school house, restored in 1952 by the Worshipful Company of Fan Makers to serve as a church hall. *St Mary Aldermanbury*, Love Lane. [Permanently open] Made within the low ruined walls of a Wren church destroyed in the Blitz, the stumps of remaining pillars mark different levels of the garden. A shrubbery encloses a monument to Shakespeare's pals, John Heminge and Henry Condell. There is also a small knot garden. *St Mary Staining.* [Permanently open] Another patch of grass surrounded by shrubs, roses and benches.

EC3: *Pepys Garden*, Seething Lane. [Open weekdays only, 9am – 5.30pm] A splinter of garden on the site of the Navy Office, where Samuel Pepys lived and worked. A surprising number of trees in a tiny area. *St Dunstan-in-the-East Church Garden*, St Dunstans Hill. The most romantic garden in the City, it has been created within the walls of a Victorian Gothic church which was bombed during World War II. Only the Wren tower survived and was restored. The remaining walls, containing arched windows and doorways, are covered with creepers and climbing plants and the spaces between planted with small trees and shrubs. There is a small fountain surrounded by benches and large tubs planted with standard fuchsias and bedding plants.

EC4: *St Laurence Pountney*, Laurence Pountney Hill. [Closed weekends] Two pocket-handkerchief patches of greenery with benches on the site of St Laurence Pountney Church and Corpus Christi College, destroyed in the Great Fire, 1666. *St Paul's Churchyard*. [Open 6am – 7.30pm] Winding paths surround the back of the Cathedral with welcome shade and a resting place for the weary tourist. Apart from the usual municipal planting, there is a rose garden in the SE corner with hybrid teas and climbing roses on the fine early wrought-iron railings.

E1: *Portsoken Street Garden*, between Portsoken Street and Goodman's Yard. A tiny oasis with a bubbling fountain, brick walls, small trees and shrubs in raised beds behind low brick walls.

ADJACENT TO CITY OF LONDON

EC1 (London Borough of Islington): *Fortune Street Garden*, NW of the Barbican between Beech Street and Old Street. *Myddleton Square*, St John Street, which houses St Mark's Church.

EC3 (Borough of Tower Hamlets): *Trinity Square*, Tower Hill, home to Wyatt's Trinity House.

N1: *New River*, a narrow man-made stream and park off Canonbury Road. *St Mary Churchyard Gardens*, Upper Street, opposite the King's Head Theatre.

COLLEGE GARDEN AND LITTLE CLOISTER   17
Westminster Abbey, London SW1. Tel: (0171) 222 5152

Dean and Chapter of Westminster ★ Off Dean's Yard (entrance in The Sanctuary, outside west end of the Abbey) and past Great Cloister ★ Best season: spring ★ Suitable for wheelchairs ★ Abbey shop ★ Band concerts July and Aug, Thurs, 12.30 – 2pm ★ Open all year, Tues and Thurs only (but closed 31st March), 10am – 6pm (Oct to March closes 4pm) ★ Entrance: 20p

The eleventh-century College Garden (a little over one acre) has been under cultivation for more than 900 years, making it possibly the oldest garden in England. Originally the source for herbs that were used to prepare simple remedies for the monks of the Benedictine Abbey, it is now a communal garden for the staff of the Abbey and members of Westminster School. As part of a development project, there has been some landscaping, which gives the garden a coherent shape and purpose, encouraging visitors to move towards the southern end of the Abbey, and to the eastern side. In the south-west corner, there is a quiet area, guarded by shrubs. The next phase of the development is to reconstruct a medieval garden. The tiny Little Cloister Garden is a small study in green and white, with a fountain and fish pond in the centre. Fine trees throughout and good labelling.

LONDON (Greater)

COLVILLE PLACE   18
London W1

*London Borough of Camden ★ Between Charlotte Street and Whitfield Street,
near Tottenham Court Road ★ Parking very difficult ★ Suitable for wheelchairs ★
Open 7.30am – dusk ★ Entrance: free*

Fortunate houses in Colville Place look across a paved path on to what is a
cross between a *hortus conclusus* and a small piazza. This imaginative tiny
public garden was created a few years ago on a bomb site. There is a lawn, a
pleasing pergola, fruit trees and, slightly tucked away, a children's play area.
Planting is bold, simple and pleasing, with lots of lavender. This seems to be
London's nearest equivalent to modern garden design in the public arena,
and the result has enormous charm. A haven from Oxford Street.

CRYSTAL PALACE PARK   19
Crystal Palace Road, London SE22.
Tel: (0181) 313 4407 (Bromley Leisure Services)

*London Borough of Bromley ★ Entrance at junction of Thicket Road and Crystal
Palace Road ★ Parking ★ Refreshments ★ Toilet facilities ★ Partly suitable for
wheelchairs ★ Open all year, 7.30am – dusk ★ Entrance: free (£1, children 50p
for farmyard) (1993 prices)*

After the success of his Crystal Palace at the Great Exhibition of 1851 Sir
Joseph Paxton was asked to re-erect it in Sydenham in what has become
known as Crystal Palace Park. He was also responsible for creating the fine
gardens which surrounded his 'glass cathedral'. Sadly the Crystal Palace was
burnt down in 1936 but the terraces remain and give a true impression of the
massive scale of the former building. There are plenty of features from the
200-acre park's glory days remaining, particularly the 29 life-sized statues of
pre-historic monsters, the world's first dinosaur theme park. See also the
large maze, the farmyard with live animals, the symphony concerts and fireworks. A day out for all the family.

29 DEODAR ROAD   20
London SW15. Tel: (0181) 788 7976

*Mr and Mrs P. Assinder ★ Off Putney Bridge Road. On bus routes 14, 22, 37,
74, 80, 85, 93, 220, or nearest Underground stations Putney Bridge or East
Putney ★ Open by appointment and 16th April, 4th June, 16th July, 2 – 5pm ★
Entrance: £1*

A long, thin garden sloping down to the Thames in three sections, the last,
on the riverside, separated from the rest by a screen of clematis and roses on
arches making a secluded sitting area. Many camellias (Mrs Assinder is a
Director of the International Camellia Society), hardy geraniums, unusual and
variegated shrubs, ceanothus, roses, eupatoriums, penstemons and so on – an
idiosyncratic mixture.

DOLLY'S GARDEN   21
43 Layhams Road, West Wickham, Kent. Tel: (0181) 462 4196

Mrs Dolly Robertson ★ Layhams Road is off A232/A2022. No 43 is a semi-

detached house recognisable by a small sunken garden in the front. Opposite Wickham Court Farm ★ Open all year by appointment only ★ Entrance: collecting box for charity

This is a raised vegetable garden purpose-built for the disabled owner with easy access to wide, terraced walkways. The owner, who maintains the entire 24ft by 70ft area herself, is pleased to pass on her experiences as a disabled gardener so that others may share her joy and interest, even if they are wheelchair gardeners.

THE ELMS   22
13 Wolverton Avenue, Kingston upon Thames, Surrey.
Tel: (0181) 546 7624

Professor and Mrs R. Rawlings ★ 1m E of Kingston on A308, 100 yards from Norbiton station. Entry opposite Manorgate flats in Manorgate Road ★ Parking in street ★ Teas by Home Farm Trust/ Princess Alice Hospice ★ Seeds and plants for sale ★ Open 18th, 19th March, 22nd, 23rd April, 13th, 14th May, 2 – 5pm and groups by appointment ★ Entrance: £1

This is a true collector's garden with some rare and unusual plants, featuring rhododendrons, magnolias, camellias, dwarf conifers and a wide range of evergreen and deciduous shrubs. Small trees, ground cover (herbaceous), a two-level pool with geyser and well-planted margins, also interesting alpine trays featured. This very small garden (only 55 x 25 feet) even has plums, pears and soft fruit.

FENTON HOUSE   23
Hampstead Grove, London NW3. Tel: (0171) 435 3471

The National Trust ★ Centre of Hampstead in area known as Holly Hill behind Heath Street ★ Parking difficult ★ Toilet facilities only if house is also visited ★ Partly suitable for wheelchairs ★ House open ★ Garden open March, Sat and Sun, 2 – 5pm; April to Oct, Sat, Sun and Bank Holiday Mons, 11am – 5.30pm and Mon – Wed, 1 – 5.30pm (last admission ½ hour before closing) Parties on weekdays by appointment ★ Entrance: free (house £3.50)

Handsome seventeenth-century house and walled garden (about one acre). The formal south garden is seen through an impressive iron gate (now open). The entrance to the house is via the side door. Directly behind the house the walled garden is formal with standard *Prunus lusitanica* in tubs, gravel walks and herbaceous borders edged with neatly-clipped box. Standard hollies are an unusual feature, and here as in the rest of the garden the walls are particularly well-planted. There is an interesting collection of varieties of *Clematis viticella*. The garden is terraced on several levels with yew hedges (10 years old) dividing the areas, which become less formal further from the house. There is a sunken rose garden with secluded seating, good vistas and many scented plants. The far wall hosts a beautifully-trained *Magnolia grandiflora*. Adjacent to the main garden below another wall is an old orchard, carefully cut at three mower heights, and a small kitchen/cottage garden. The garden is surprisingly peaceful and has the delightful, unhurried atmosphere of the traditional old-world garden. Particularly good views of it are to be had from the attic floor of the house. It is remarkable what the Trustees have achieved in the first decade of Fenton House's development, and their improvements continue.

FULHAM PALACE   24
Bishops Avenue, Off Fulham Palace Road, London SW6.
Tel: (0171) 736 7181 (general enquiries), (0171) 736 3233 (Museum only)

London Borough of Hammersmith and Fulham ★ Fulham Palace Road and
Bishop's Avenue to the North ★ Parking in road ★ Suitable for wheelchairs ★
Plants for sale in nearby nursery ★ Museum open Wed – Sun and Bank Holiday
Mons, 2 – 5pm (Nov to Feb, 1 – 4pm) ★ Garden open daily except 25th Dec,
1st Jan, 8am – dusk ★ Entrance: free (Museum 50p, concessions 25p, children
free. Private tours £3.50 per person) (1994 prices)

The palace, surrounded by a moat in its prime, was the former home of the
Bishops of London where in the sixteenth century Bishop Compton used his
missionaries to help him establish here a collection of shrubs and trees sent
back from America. Today it is rather sad in a faded way, like an overgrown
country house garden, but it is a charming place for a peaceful walk, far
superior to many other open spaces in London. The 15-acre area to wander
round is seldom crowded. The south front of the house looks over lawns
with enormous cedars and other trees, including an ancient evergreen oak.
The remains of the old walled garden contain a very long ruined glasshouse
built along a curved wall, and a box-edged herb garden, enclosed by a
magnificent old wisteria hedge. Another part has order beds as well as an
orchard which has recently been replanted using historic varieties of
apple/pear and other fruit trees. The small courtyard at the front of the
house (part Henry VII, part Victorian) has euphorbias, some climbers and
other plants and a fountain. Do not mistake Fulham Palace for Bishop's Park
which extends to the south as far as the river.

17 FULHAM PARK GARDENS ★   25
London SW6. Tel: (0171) 736 4890

Anthony Noel ★ From Putney Bridge underground station, turn along Kings
Road and left at Threshers off-licence, then right into Fulham Park Gardens ★
Parking ★ Open 9th July, 17th Sept, 2.30 – 6pm ★ Entrance: £2, OAP £1

This tiny garden measuring 40ft by 17ft has the advantage of a paved walk
round its environs so you can stroll for half an hour and really appreciate its
originalities. Each year Anthony Noel, actor turned landscape designer, experiments with new colour schemes in this romantic stage set of a garden. Plants
are usually grown in tiers for maximum decorative effect in a small space.
Great emphasis is placed on foliage and colour combinations with rare clematis, ferns and hostas. An air of pastoral seclusion is created by the fountain,
water falling into a raised pool containing large pebbles and broken terracotta
shards and surrounded by white flowering plants. On open days this garden is
usually open for charity at the same time as 32 Atney Road (see entry), and
queues of visitors have been known to stretch down the street.

GOLDERS HILL PARK   26
North End Way, Hampstead, London NW3. Tel: (0181) 455 5183

Corporation of London ★ From Hampstead, past Jack Straw's Castle on road to
Golders Green, opposite Bull and Bush pub. The flower garden is on right of
park, past café ★ Refreshments: North End Way entrance, March to Oct ★ Toilet

*facilities ★ Partly suitable for wheelchairs ★ Dogs on lead ★ Greenhouse open
weekends, 2 – 4pm ★ Park open daily, 7.30am – dusk ★ Entrance: free*

The manicured 36-acre park was created in 1899 in the grounds of a manor
house (bombed in World War II). The two-acre flower garden on the north
side is claimed to be as good as you will see anywhere in London, with a
mixture of perennial and bedding plants. It has an almost Victorian feel with
its neat, brilliantly coloured displays of flowers. The colour schemes and
designs are different and exciting though some feel they err on the vulgar
side. On a less strident note is the canal feature planted with water-loving
and woodland plants, leading down to the ornamental pool with its ducks and
flamboyant flamingos. Plenty of seats at strategic points ensure that the
garden is much used by elderly local residents. (The park itself has a large
menagerie with deer, goats, wallabies, blackbuck and many birds.)

GREENWICH PARK 27
Greenwich, London SE10. Tel: (0181) 858 2608

*Royal Parks ★ Entrances in Greenwich (Romney Road) and in Blackheath
(Charlton Way). Good service to Greenwich by river, telephone (0171) 376
3676 or (0181) 305 0300 for winter timetables ★ Parking easier at Blackheath
entrance ★ Refreshments ★ Toilet facilities ★ Suitable for wheelchairs but quite
steep in places ★ Dogs ★ Observatory and Maritime Museum, Greenwich Theatre
and Ranger's House. Ships at Greenwich pier. Thames Barrier Visitors' Centre ★
Park open dawn – dusk ★ Entrance: free*

Situated on a hilltop overlooking London, Greenwich is the oldest enclosed
Royal Park. Covering 73 hectares (183 acres), the Park is associated with a
pageant of kings and queens and provides a setting for several historic buildings, including the Old Royal Observatory. The Park was particularly popular
with Henry VIII and his daughter Queen Elizabeth I, who, legend has it, took
refreshment within the hollow oak that bears her name. Probably open to the
public from George IV's reign, it continues to be popular with the local
community and tourists. The Flower Garden, with its brilliant displays of
summer colour, is particularly popular. Sunday afternoon band performances
and entertainments for children. Superb views of the park and the River
Thames from the upper floor of the café which has a pleasant enclosed garden.

4 THE GROVE ★ 28
Highgate, London N6.

*Mr Cob Stenham ★ In Highgate village, off Hampstead Lane ★ Parking in street
★ Open 18th June, 2 – 5pm ★ Entrance: 50p*

The seventeenth-century house sits behind a dignified front courtyard, beautifully paved with brick (as is the rear terrace) with restrained planting of
skimmias and other evergreens. A side passage brings the visitor through to
an outstanding vista; the terrace, with a formal pool surrounded by dramatic
planting, is the foreground to an immaculate lawn with well-planted, mixed
borders. Beyond this is an extensive backdrop to the wooded slopes of
Hampstead Heath. An arbour of silver pears overlooks this stunning view and
a ceanothus arch leads one down, through a tunnel of *Vitis coignetiae*, to the
lower garden. This comprises an orchard with an old mulberry tree and

some good statuary. One yew hedge conceals the well-ordered compost/bonfire area, and another balances this to enclose a tiny secret garden dominated by a *Cladrastis lutea*. *Rosa laevigata* 'Cooperi' flourishes on the south wall of the house, and the whole garden, which is beautifully designed and maintained, has exceptional charm.

7 THE GROVE ★ 29
Highgate, London N6. Tel: (0181) 340 7205

Thomas G. Lyttelton ★ In Highgate village ★ Parking in street ★ Teas on 18th June only ★ Suitable for wheelchairs ★ Open 30th April, 18th June, 2 – 6pm ★ Entrance: £1, OAP and children 50p

A half-acre London walled town garden behind a very handsome Georgian house *c*.1815, splendidly designed by the owner for low-maintenance, but with lots of interest. Tunnels, arbours, screens abound. A series of brick-built arches across the width of the garden separate it into two compartments. The area near the house is formal with a lawn, the area beyond the screen much less so, with many fine compartments and features. Full of secret paths and unexpected views. A magic garden for children. Much use is made of ever-greens and there are some exquisite shrubs, including a row of camellias down one wall and a massive *Hydrangea petiolaris* with a trunk as thick as a boxer's biceps! There are many species and varieties of a particular genus – five varieties of box and even more of ivies, for example. The owner describes it as a gold, green and red garden. The canal feature, planted with yellow irises, and the *allées* and tunnels provide inspiration for busy garden–owners who would still like to have an interesting garden. Several other gardens in The Grove are open on the charity day in June, including No 4 (see entry).

GUNNERSBURY PARK 30
London W3. Tel: (0181) 992 1612

London Borough of Ealing and Hounslow ★ ½m N of Chiswick roundabout turn left off A406 ★ Parking: entrance from Popes Lane, no coaches ★ Refreshments ★ Toilet facilities ★ Suitable for wheelchairs ★ Dogs ★ Museum open Mon – Fri, 1 – 5pm (winter, 1 – 4pm), weekends and Bank Holidays, 1 – 6pm. Closed Christmas ★ Park open daily, 7.30am – dusk ★ Entrance: free

Little remains of the grandiose gardens of the Rothschild days except the rose gardens in the traditional 'Clock' pattern, with a background of parkland. Alas the formal beds have been grassed over and planted with shrubs. Beyond the trees the sports grounds, golf course and tennis courts are hidden from view from the terrace where it is difficult to realise one is only a few miles from Marble Arch. Amongst the gardeners who have toiled here were William Kent and J.C. Loudon. For children, there is a boating pool and two play areas.

HALL GRANGE 31
Shirley Church Road, Croydon, Surrey.

Methodist Homes ★ In Shirley Church Road, near the junction with Upper Shirley Road ★ Parking on road ★ Teas ★ Suitable for wheelchairs ★ Open probably 14th May, 2 – 5.30pm (last admission 5pm) (telephone 0181 777 3389 to check) ★ Entrance: £1, children free

The garden at Hall Grange, originally called the Wilderness, was created by the Reverend William Wilkes, breeder of the Shirley Poppy and secretary of the Royal Horticultural Society from 1888 to 1920. He acquired seven acres of Shirley Common in 1910 to build his retirement home and planted the garden with informal groups of trees, shrubs, rhododendrons and tree heathers in the existing turf. He added any British wild plants which he found interesting. To botanists the most interesting area is the sphagnum bog which the London Ecology Unit has designated a Site of Metropolitan Importance. There are 126 species of wild flowers and native shrubs and trees in the garden and 22 mosses including four types of sphagnum.

HALL PLACE 32
Bexley, London. Tel: (0181) 303 7777

London Borough of Bexley ★ Just N of A2 near junction of A2 and A223 ★ Parking ★ Restaurant and café ★ Toilet facilities ★ Garden open daily, Mon – Fri, 7.30am – dusk, weekends and Bank Holidays, 9am – dusk. Model allotment, parts of nursery and glasshouses open daily except 25th Dec, Mon – Fri, 9am – 6pm (4pm in winter) ★ Entrance: free

Surrounding a splendid Jacobean mansion, this is arguably the most interesting and best-kept public garden in South East London. Although there is a strong emphasis on municipal annual bedding plants, like ageratum, *Senecio* x *hybrida* and African marigolds to provide summer colour, they are used with great restraint and good taste as are the roses in the large classical rose garden. So, too, are the herbaceous plants in two splendid borders separated by a turf *allée* and backed by a characterful old brick wall on one side and a tightly-clipped yew hedge on the other. Features include a raised walk overlooking one of Britain's finest topiary gardens, several rich shrubberies, a large and beautifully designed patterned herb garden, a rock garden, meandering stretches of the River Cray, a heather garden and acres of lawn studded with an interesting mixture of evergreen and deciduous trees to provide vistas.

HAM HOUSE ★ 33
Ham Street, Richmond, Surrey. Tel: (0181) 940 1950

The National Trust ★ On S bank of Thames, W of A307 at Petersham ★ Parking 400 yards by river, disabled on terrace ★ Refreshments: April to Oct, daily except Fri, 11am – 5.30pm ★ Toilet facilities inc. disabled ★ Partly suitable for wheelchairs ★ House open daily except Thurs and Fri, 1 – 5pm (Sun 11.30am – 5pm) ★ Garden open daily except Fri, 10.30am – 6pm (or dusk if earlier) ★ Entrance: free (house £4, children £2)

Currently undergoing restoration by The National Trust, the gardens at Ham House aim to retain their seventeenth-century appearance in which formality predominates. In the south garden, below a wide gravel terrace, are eight square lawns divided by paths. The strong architectural nature of the wilderness, gravel terraces and parterres of box lavender and cotton lavender mean that the restoration, down to replicas of the seventeenth-century garden furniture, adds to its charm. In 1995 a cut-flower border of period plants is being established. The orangery is late seventeenth-century, the earliest surviving example of its type in the country, and in front of it is a wide lawn with rose beds and a peony border. During the summer months, orange trees in period-style boxes will be displayed on the Orangery terrace. The garden is well-maintained. Marble Hill (see entry) is across the river and can be reached by ferry.

HAMPTON COURT PALACE ★★   34
East Molesey, Surrey. Tel: (0181) 977 8441

Historic Royal Palaces Agency ★ On A308 at junction of A309 on N side of Kingston bridge over Thames ★ Limited parking ★ Toilet facilities ★ Mostly suitable for wheelchairs ★ Dogs on lead ★ Shop ★ Palace open (admission charge) ★ Gardens open daily, dawn – dusk ★ Entrance: free (Pre-booked morning tours of garden £2 for garden visitors, but included in Palace admission charge)

Hampton Court Palace is worth a visit to study the activities of British monarchs from Henry VIII onwards, and the gardens, which provide the setting for the palace, are an exciting and eclectic mixture of styles and taste, with many different character areas of interest. Most famous for its Great Vine, planted in 1768 (probably the oldest in the world), which still produces hundreds of 'Black Hamburg' grapes each year (on sale to the public when harvested in September) and its maze, the oldest hedge-planted maze in Britain, planted in 1690. The pond gardens offer a magnificent display of bedding plants, and there is a Tudor knot garden with interlocking bands of dwarf box, thyme, lavender and cotton lavender, infilled with plants of the period. On a truly grand scale, the great fountain garden, an immense semi-circle of grass and flower beds with a central fountain, is probably the most impressive element, but the wilderness garden in spring, with its mass of daffodils and spring-flowering trees – principally cherry and crab – has the most charm. The laburnum walk off the wilderness garden – a tunnel of trained trees with butter-coloured rivulets of flowers in May – is another great attraction. The former kitchen garden now houses a rose garden. The newest garden is a restoration of William III's formal area outside his apartments, completed in 1702 and running south of the palace, designer uncertain but construction by Henry Wise, the partner of London. The original was depleted after the king's death in 1704 and disappeared completely in Victorian times. Guided walks of the Palace gardens take place daily from April to the end of October and special pre-booked morning tours can also be arranged. An area of the gardens sometimes missed by visitors is the secluded twentieth-century garden, an area developed originally for the training of apprentices, but now also open to all. It is located just over the canal in the great fountain garden (signposted) and is open April to Oct, daily, 8am – 6.30pm; Nov to March, Mon – Fri, 8am – 4pm. Too much to see in one day – plan at least two trips; one in spring and one in summer to walk in only part of the 66 acres of gardens and the informal deer park ten times that size. Hampton Court Park is the venue for the annual Hampton Court Palace International Flower Show in July, which is establishing itself alongside Chelsea as a major horticultural event.

37 HEATH DRIVE   35
London NW3. Tel: (0171) 435 2419

Mr and Mrs C. Caplin ★ Off Finchley Road ★ Best seasons: late spring and summer ★ Parking ★ Refreshments ★ Suitable for wheelchairs ★ Unusual plants for sale ★ Open 7th May, 16th July, 2.30 – 6pm ★ Entrance: £1, children 50p

Largish, square garden (about one-fifth of an acre) with a vast number of plants packed into it. There is an attractive pergola walk and unusual and interesting plants. Lots of lavatera, tree peonies, rhododendrons, palms (Trachycarpus), broom trees, large bamboos, a tamarisk tree, a fig and a mulberry tree. Other features of the garden include pools and rockeries, a fruit tree tunnel (apples, pears and plums), raised beds and a greenhouse and conservatory for exotics. The garden has a very effective compost heap hidden behind a hedge of delightful cut-leaved alder. In the front garden there is a particularly good semi-evergreen *Buddleia colvillei* with magenta hanging flowers in June and July, and a very large *Pieris formosa forrestii*. The Caplins have won the Frankland Moore Trophy (for gardens with help) seven times and are well featured in Arabella Lennox-Boyd's book *Private Gardens of London*.

THE HILL GARDEN 36
Inverforth Close, North End Way, London NW3.
Tel: (0181) 455 5183

Corporation of London ★ From Hampstead past Jack Straw's Castle on road to Golders Green, on left hand side. Inverforth Close is off North End Way (A502) ★ Partly suitable for wheelchairs ★ Open daily, 9am – dusk ★ Entrance: free

Overgrown in parts, the chief charm here lies in its secluded setting. A major restoration project is underway at the Pergola, built between 1906 and 1925 to a design by Thomas H. Mawson as a screen between Lord Leverhulme's house, The Hill (now known as Inverforth House), and its kitchen gardens and to shield it from people walking on the Heath. The structure is one of the best examples of a pergola. Wonderful views across the Heath from many points in the garden. There is a large formal lily pond as well as herbaceous borders, undulating lawns, and many shrubs and trees.

HOLLAND PARK 37
Kensington, London W8/W11. Tel: (0171) 602 9483

Royal Borough of Kensington and Chelsea ★ Between Kensington High Street A31 and Holland Park Avenue, with several entrances ★ Parking from Abbotsbury Road entrance ★ Refreshments: light lunches etc, in café and kiosk, or restaurant ★ Toilet facilities, inc. disabled ★ Dogs on lead in some areas ★ Open daily, 7.30am – sunset ★ Entrance: free

Most of the famous Holland House was destroyed by bombs in World War II. The formal gardens, created in 1812 by Lord Holland, have been maintained. The 53-acre park contains some rare trees such as Pyrenean oak, Chinese sweet gum, Himalayan birch, violet willow and the snowdrop tree which flowers in May. The rose walk has now been replanted with a variety of azaleas. There is a small iris garden round a fountain. Peacocks strut the lawns and drape the walls with their tail feathers and in the woodland section birds and squirrels find sanctuary from London's noise and traffic. There are children's play areas. In 1991, a one-acre Kyoto Garden was opened in Holland Park as a permanent souvenir of the Japanese Festival. One of the most pleasant small London parks.

HORNIMAN GARDENS 38
100 London Road, Forest Hill, London SE23. Tel: (0181) 699 8924

Horniman Museum ★ On the South Circular where Lordship Lane joins London Road ★ Refreshments: at café in Museum and available in the gardens in summer. Picnics allowed in gardens ★ Toilet facilities ★ Horticultural demonstrations March to Sept, first Wed in the month at 2.30pm ★ Open all year except 25th Dec, Mon – Sat, 7.15am – dusk, Sun, 8am – dusk ★ Entrance: free

Charming, rather old-fashioned park in fine situation with extensive views over, alas, rather hideous south London, on three sides. Formal bedding, rose pergola, bandstand (with band on summer Sunday afternoons and children's entertainment on Tues (11am) and Thurs (3pm) in August), steep hill garden with rocks, stream, conifers, etc. Large and impressive Victorian conservatory rebuilt recently behind the Horniman Museum which does not contain any plants in winter but is used for functions from time to time and for the concert series held in spring and autumn. There are two nature trails, one in the gardens and one along a stretch of disused railway line with a pond and wild flower meadow. Also an animal enclosure. Not far away is Dulwich Art Gallery (not to be missed).

ISABELLA PLANTATION ★ 39
Richmond Park, Richmond, Surrey. Tel: (0181) 948 3209

Royal Parks ★ Richmond Park, Broomfield Hill ★ Best season: late spring ★ Parking: Broomfield Hill car park, Pembroke Lodge (Roehampton Gate), disabled at north entrance by way of Ham Gate ★ Refreshments (Pembroke Lodge) ★ Toilet facilities (summer only) ★ Suitable with care for wheelchairs ★ Dogs on lead ★ Open daily, dawn – dusk ★ Entrance: free

A wooded enclosure, this features many fine indigenous forest trees – oaks, beeches and birch – as well as more exotic specimens like magnolias, camellias, witch hazels and styrax trees. The principal glory, however, is the collection of rhododendrons and azaleas, the earliest rhododendron 'Christmas Cheer' blossoming in the New Year, but the garden is at its best from April until June, when the dwarf azaleas and the waterside primulas around the pond are also in flower. The garden is a notable bird sanctuary – nuthatches, treecreepers, kingfishers, woodpeckers and owls have all been spotted, and herons fish regularly in the ponds. The Waterhouse Plantation in neighbouring Bushy Park is also very fine (see entry).

KENSINGTON GARDENS 40
London W2. Tel: (0171) 298 2100

Royal Parks ★ Entrances off Bayswater Road, Kensington High Street and West Carriage Drive, Hyde Park ★ Best seasons: spring and summer ★ Refreshments: Orangery Tea Room and Broadwalk Kiosk ★ Toilet facilities, inc. disabled ★ Palace State Apartments open Mon – Sat, 9am – 5pm, Sun, 11 am – 5pm. Outdoor sculpture sometimes on display at Serpentine Art Gallery open weekly, 10am – 6pm (dusk in winter) ★ Gardens open daily, 6am – closing times displayed at gate ★ Entrance: free

These 274 acres of finest park, adjoining Hyde Park, have their own pleasures, including sculpture by Henry Moore and G.F. Watts and, for children and older enthusiasts, the Peter Pan statue. The orangery, probably by Hawksmoor, with decoration by Grinling Gibbons, is well worth a visit. So, too, is the sunken water garden surrounded by beds of bright seasonal flowers which can be viewed from 'windows' in a beech walk. From the Broad Walk south to the Albert Memorial, semi-circular flower beds are kept planted against a background of flowering shrubs. Many different species of nannies and prams are in evidence along the Flower Walk at the south side near the Albert Memorial. English Heritage has been appointed to manage the restoration of the Albert Memorial, which is scheduled to be completed by 1999.

KENSINGTON ROOF GARDEN   41
99 High Street, Kensington, London W8. Tel: (0171) 937 7994

Virgin Group ★ In Derry Street off Kensington High Street by lift ★ Toilet facilities ★ Telephone to check that gardens are open before attempting to visit ★ Entrance: free

Fantasy one and a half-acre garden 100 feet above the ground on the sixth floor of what was Derry and Tom's 1938 department store. A private member's club with restaurant facilities, the gardens which surround the Art Deco bar and dining room are also used for functions and conferences. Ralph Hancock designed them to give three distinct illusions – a formal Spanish garden with canal, an English woodland garden and a Tudor garden. The soil is nowhere thicker than three feet so it is remarkable that more than 500 varieties of trees and shrubs, including palms, figs and vines survive up here. Ducks swim about in their high-rise ponds, watched over by two flamingos, and there is a delightful maze of small paths, bridges and walkways with peepholes in the outer walls giving glimpses across the city skyline. No great horticultural interest but remarkable for its very existence. London's latest roof garden, Cannon Bridge, alas has even more restricted public access.

KENWOOD   42
Hampstead Lane, London NW3. Tel: (0181) 348 1286

English Heritage ★ N side of Hampstead Heath, on Highgate to Hampstead road ★ Parking at West Lodge car park, Hampstead Lane ★ ☆Excellent refreshments: hours as house ★ Toilet facilities ★ Suitable for wheelchairs ★ Dogs on lead ★ House open 14th April to Oct, 10am – 6pm, Nov to 13th April, 10am – 4pm ★ Park open daily, summer: 8am – 8.30pm, winter: 8am – 4.30pm ★ Entrance: free

A picturesque landscape laid out by Humphry Repton at the end of the eighteenth century. Vistas, sweeping lawns from the terrace of Kenwood House and views over Hampstead Heath (and London) predominate. Magnificent mature trees, mainly oak and beech. Large-scale shrubberies, dominated by rhododendrons. There is also some magnificent modern sculpture including a Henry Moore and a 1953 Barbara Hepworth. The garden slopes down towards two large lakes known as the Wood Pond (the largest) and the Thousand Pound Pond (where open air concerts are held in summer). Woods to the south of the lakes fringe the heath side of the gardens, with several gates onto the heath itself. A good place to walk at any season, but particularly when the trees are turning in autumn, to recall that the lime walk was a favourite of that great gardener of the eighteenth century, Alexander Pope. Conservation work is in progress to repair the surviving features of Repton's layout. The sham bridge on the Thousand Pound Pond, site of the concert stage, has been faithfully rebuilt with one upside-down baluster, and natural regeneration of the ancient woodlands is being encouraged, though elsewhere they are being thinned. The felling of trees dear to the hearts of present-day walkers is currently the subject of a public consultation exercise.

227 KINGSTON ROAD   43
Teddington, Middlesex. Tel: (0181) 943 0202

Mr Ben Sunlight ★ On the main Kingston – Twickenham road, almost on the corner of Holmesdale Road and opposite a petrol station ★ Parking in side streets ★ Open by appointment and 11th June, 2.30 – 6pm ★ Entrance: £1

Working in a restricted space (90 x 30 feet) and using a limited palette (mostly white and pink), Mr Sunlight has created an amazingly peaceful English garden redolent of Japan. He held a competition to find the firm that would put his ideas into practice. The result is a tiny gravel path around three interlinked ponds, where normally one would find grass, each tinkling into the next. One can look down into the water from the black zig-zag bridge or sit and take in the vista to the small temple at the end of the garden. Perspective is cheated with a not-quite-life-sized figure standing on an island, contemplating the water. Nearer the house a group of three silver birches have a stag's horn fern suspended invisibly between them. The planting is carefully chosen for colour, form, length of season as dictated by the restrained space.

1 LISTER ROAD ★   44
London E11. Tel: (0181) 556 8962

Mr Myles Challis ★ Off High Road, Leytonstone about 10 minutes walk from the tube station ★ Parking on Lister Road ★ Toilet facilities ★ Plants for sale ★ Open July to Sept by appointment ★ Entrance: £1, children 50p

Here is a garden to stretch the imagination and encourage a daring planting of tender plants. Myles Challis's remarkable creation of sub-tropical and temperate plants is grown with a designer's eye to evoke a mysterious atmosphere – a jewel of a garden. It contains palms, bamboos, daturas, tree ferns, rice-paper plants and bananas including a rare red Abyssinian banana, all allowed to grow to their natural size. Water gurgles from a Challis-designed fountain contributing to this special garden. Book in advance for an appointment. The owner is an excellent educator who will patiently explain the origin of his many exciting plants.

LONDON SQUARES   45

Many other cities have squares but probably none has more than London. They were mostly built in the eighteenth and nineteenth centuries to provide an outlook for the fashionable houses which surrounded them and in not so fashionable areas like Pimlico so that the lesser classes could imitate the behaviour of their betters. A few squares still remain the joint property of the owners of houses (and today, flats) round them, the grandest being Belgrave Square built by Basevi in 1825, Eaton Square and Cadogan Square. Other private squares, hardly less grand, include Montpelier, Brompton, Carlyle, Lowndes, Onslow and others to the west of Hyde Park Corner. One enthusiast,

LONDON (Greater)

Roger Phillips of Eccleston Square, says that in order to keep the squares going for the benefit of the residents and the visual pleasure of others passing by, it is necessary to wage a horrendous battle against potential developers. Some squares (and 'gardens' as other areas are called) have over the years become places where the public may be admitted and these include the following:

Central area: *Berkeley Square*; *Cavendish Square*; *Grosvenor Square*; *Phoenix Gardens* is a community-run site with a 20-year lease which shows what can be done by London residents, and, unlike many others, is open 24 hours a day and *St James's Square* (this is the earliest, begun 1665, and the quietest). Also in this area is *St Pauls Churchyard*, *Covent Garden* and *Soho Square*. Eastern area: *Embankment Gardens*, if rather municipal, are leafy and tranquil; *Gray's Inn* (where Field Court is open to the public during weekday lunchtimes in the summer); *Inner and Middle Temple Gardens*, with entrance in Fleet Street; *Lincoln's Inn*, with one of its 'squares' New Hall open to the public Mon – Fri, 12 noon – 1.30pm only. A journalist recently wrote that he was 'struck dumb ... by the vast encampment of bedraggled humanity that now fills the square, protected from the elements by pitifully inadequate shelters lashed together from old boxes and blankets ... a sight to leave one chastened.' Northern area: Despite its name probably the least romantic is the home of the Bloomsberries *Bloomsbury Square*, now litter-full rather than literary; *Brunswick Square* beyond which is the walled garden, usually a haven of peace – *St George's Gardens*; *Fitzroy Square*, the work of Geoffrey Jellicoe, not open but viewable; *Gordon Square*, closed weekends; *Queen Square* with its statue of Queen Charlotte, after whom it is named; *Russell Square*, once the prettiest but alas no longer, with a café reputed to sell the worst coffee in London and *Tavistock Square* (quietest in the area).

One London square has begun limited opening to the public, *Eccleston Square* in Pimlico [Open for charity 23rd April, 4th June. Telephone (0171) 834 7354 for details]. This three-acre square, run by a committee of residents, and normally reserved for the use of the residents, has something for everyone – a tennis court, areas for children to play in and a paved area. It is also of considerable horticultural interest and contributes to the National collection of ceanothus. Many different roses and 110 different camellias. Another two, *Cadogan Place* (above the car park halfway down Sloane Street to its E) and *Cadogan Square* (to the W) are usually open for two to three days in early June for the Chelsea Festival.

The newest square in London is surrounded by offices, not houses. This is *Arundel Great Court* which may be viewed from The Strand, south of Aldwych and entered from Arundel and Norfolk Streets. To the south is the luxurious courtyard garden of the Norfolk Hotel. Further north still are the City gardens like *Finsbury Circus Gardens*, Moorgate, unusually quiet except on sunny weekday lunchtimes (see also City of London Parks and Gardens).

4 MACAULAY ROAD 46
Clapham, London SW4. Tel: (0171) 627 1137

Mrs Jonathan Ross ★ Off Clapham Common Northside ★ Parking in street ★ Plants for sale ★ Open 18th June, 2 – 6pm ★ Entrance: £1, OAP 50p

A walled garden, 80 feet by 50 feet set out in strong, clear lines with formality heightened by box hedges, topiary and lots of pots. Two circular lawns surrounded by dense, mixed planting, arches and pergola. A grotto with

277

fernery around it and many exotic shrubs and herbaceous plants chosen for their strong foliage. The garden has been designed to look as good in winter as in summer. With a large range of plants, many grey or variegated, the overall effect is of profusion and soft colours.

MARBLE HILL   47
Richmond Road, Twickenham, Middlesex.

English Heritage ★ S of Richmond Bridge off Richmond Road. Additional access by river launch ★ Parking ★ House open daily, 10am – 6pm (Nov to Jan 4pm) ★ Park open daily, 7.30am – dusk

English Heritage is still in the process of reviving these gardens, originally laid out in the 1740s. Alexander Pope, a neighbour of the Countess of Suffolk, took an interest in the layout and recent excavations have revealed one of the two grottoes known to have been constructed. Traces of pebble and flint patterns exist, though hard to see; the main objective of the grotto would have been the view of Richmond Hill, now overgrown. There is an ice-house and a very young 'Sweet Walk'. The gardens (if they can be called that as largely they are sports pitches and a venue for Summer Music concerts) lay claim to the largest and probably the oldest black walnut in the country and also the tallest bay willow and Italian alder trees. Take the ferry to Ham House (see entry) over the river.

MOUNT STREET GARDENS   48
Mount Street, London W1. Tel: (0171) 798 2063/4

Westminster City Council ★ Access from Mount Street, South Audley Street near the Public Library and South Street, Mayfair ★ Dogs on lead ★ Open spring and summer, weekdays, 8am – up to 9.30pm; autumn and winter, 8am – 4.30pm. Suns and Bank Holidays, open from 9am ★ Entrance: free

This well-hidden leafy retreat is much loved by locals while the throng of the city seems to pass it by. Tasteful planting and lofty trees make it the perfect spot to take your ease after shopping. Versailles tubs planted with palms, beds of sugar pink and white geraniums or other interesting and varied schemes can be enjoyed from dozens of wooden benches donated by those who have enjoyed this garden's charm.

MUSEUM OF GARDEN HISTORY   49
Lambeth Palace Road, London SE1. Tel: (0171) 261 1891

The Tradescant Trust ★ Lambeth Palace Road, parallel to River Thames on S bank, hard by Lambeth Bridge ★ Best seasons: spring and summer ★ Refreshments ★ Toilet facilities ★ Suitable for wheelchairs ★ Plants for sale ★ Shop ★ Antique collection of garden tools and artefacts which include Gertrude Jekyll's desk, lectures, exhibitions and concerts ★ Open 5th March to 10th Dec, Mon – Fri, 11am – 3pm, Sun, 10.30am – 5pm. Closed Sat ★ Entrance: free, donations requested

The garden in the churchyard was begun in 1981. It commemorates the two John Tradescants (father and son), gardeners to Charles I and II, who are buried in a fine tomb in the replica seventeenth-century garden. The garden contains examples of plants brought back by the Tradescants from their plant-hunting travels in Europe and America in the seventeenth century. Lady

Salisbury's knot garden design incorporates some of the Tradescants' plants that are now seen as indigenous to this country. Well-labelled herbs abound amongst pretty perennials making a delightful backcloth for the table tombs, whilst the walls are clothed in Virginia creeper, ivy, roses and clematis. Although small the garden has a few well-placed benches. A planting plan of the knot is available in the shop, and some of the plants featured are on sale. See *Yellow Book* for possible opening of nearby Lambeth Palace one or two days in summer.

MUSEUM OF LONDON NURSERY GARDEN 50
The Museum of London, London Wall, London EC2. Tel: (0171) 600 3699

Museum of London ★ Underground: St Paul's, Barbican or Moorgate ★ Best season: summer ★ Refreshments: licensed restaurant ★ Toilet facilities ★ Suitable for wheelchairs but steps make assistance necessary ★ Museum shop ★ Open 16th April to Oct, Tues – Sat, 10am – 5.50pm, Sun, 12 noon – 5.50pm (last admission 5.30pm). Closed Mon ★ Entrance: £3.50, concessions £1.75 (museum)

In 1990 the Museum of London put on a much welcomed exhibition called 'London's Pride' which traced the history of the capital's gardens. The exhibition offered an opportunity to bring in garden designers Colson and Stone and totally revamp the internal courtyard. The team transformed an almost lifeless area into a living history of plantsmanship in the City from medieval times to the present day. Legendary names like Henry Russell, who sold striped roses in Westminster, to James Veitch, who sold exotica like the monkey puzzle tree from his nursery in Chelsea, are represented. This tiny roof garden is flanked on four sides by high buildings yet the designers have still managed to incorporate a tumbling rill and a rock garden. A visit here should be combined with the Barbican Conservatory (see entry).

MYDDELTON HOUSE GARDENS ★ 51
Bulls Cross, Enfield, Middlesex. Tel: (01992) 717711

Lee Valley Regional Park Authority ★ From M25 go S on A10 (junction 25), turn first right on to Bulls Moor Lane, bear left into Bulls Cross and Myddelton House is on the right at the junction with Turkey Street ★ Parking ★ Toilet facilities ★ Suitable for wheelchairs ★ Plants for sale on special open days ★ Open weekdays, 10am – 3.30pm. Closed weekends and Bank Holidays except special open days which are usually last Sun in the months Feb to Oct from 2 – 5pm ★ Entrance: £1.20, concessions 60p

A magnificent diverse plant collection set in four acres was built up by the famous E.A. Bowles and now is restored. Splendid spring bulbs, followed by iris, followed by autumn crocus and impressive varieties of autumn-remontant iris make this garden a joy all year round. Zephyranthus and nerines are but a few of the autumn bulbs and there is a fine *Crinum moorei* near the conservatory. This is by no means a municipal garden and the impressive plant collection is displayed attractively, in a well-designed garden surrounding the impressive Regency house of mellow golden brick. Understaffing has resulted in some untidiness but the garden is still unified by Bowles's plants and vision and it is worth reading details of his plan, which included a Lunatic Asylum planted with botanical misfits.

NOEL-BAKER PEACE GARDEN 52
Elthorne Park, Hazelville Road, London N19.

London Borough of Islington ★ There are several entrances to Elthorne Park, including those in Beaumont Road and Sunnyside Road ★ Best season: summer ★ Parking in adjacent roads ★ Toilet facilities in adjacent playground ★ Suitable fo. wheelchairs ★ Open daily, Mon – Fri, 8am – dusk, Sat, 9am – dusk, Sun, 10am – dusk ★ Entrance: free

This is a small well-designed formal garden within a London park, create in 1984 in memory of Philip Noel-Baker, winner of the Nobel Peace Priz in 1959. It is a lovely example of late twentieth-century garden design an planting, centering on an interesting water feature and a striking bronz figure (with horizontal bronze reflection). Much use is made of brick an York stone paving, and raised beds together with lawns; the overall effect i softened and enlivened by the excellent planting, with many unusual specie (e.g. *Feijoa sellowiana*, *Clerodendrum bungei* and *C. trichotomum*). Th emphasis is on green, grey and white, lifted here and there by splashes o colour and linked by the strong lines of the asymmetric design whic creates several secluded sitting areas. It receives extensive use and suppor from the local community and although the results of limited maintenanc are sometimes apparent, the overall impression is of well-loved amenity There is a good children's playground and a fitness trail in adjacen Elthorne Park.

1F OVAL ROAD 53
Flat 1, 1F Oval Road, London NW1. Tel (0171) 267 0655

Sheila Jackson ★ In Oval Road. Nearest tube Camden Town. Buses to Camden Town or Camden High Street, stops C2 and 274 very near ★ Parking difficult, especially on Suns ★ Open 9th June, 5.30 – 8.30pm, 11th June, 2 – 5pm. Also by appointment ★ Entrance: £1, children 50p

A tiny space squeezed between a tall Victorian house and the Euston railwa line has been transformed into a miniature garden of great charm and horti cultural interest by the owner. Despite its small size one needs to wall through and around the garden to explore all the hidden places and vistas and to appreciate the huge variety of unusual plants. Most of these grow i containers and have thrived this way for years.

PRIORY GARDENS 54
Orpington, Kent Tel: (0181) 313 1113

London Borough of Bromley ★ Behind library, Church Hill off Orpington High Street ★ Toilet facilities ★ Separate area for dogs ★ Open daily, 8am – dusk (9pm in summer) ★ Entrance: free

Skirting the Old Priory which is now the Orpington Public Library, this i one of the most tastefully-gardened public spaces in outer London. It has a excellent example of patterned annual bedding, a recently-replanted herba ceous garden, a rich rose garden, fine mature trees and shrubs and a refur bished lake. Considering the recent cutbacks in public spending, the level o husbandry and maintenance in these gardens is exemplary.

QUEEN MARY'S ROSE GARDEN   55
Inner Circle, Regent's Park, London NW1. Tel: (0171) 486 7905

Department of the Environment ★ Off Marylebone Road. Many other entrances to the park ★ Best season: June to Aug ★ Parking: Inner Circle, weekdays, from 11am, Sat and Sun, all day ★ Refreshments ★ Toilet facilities ★ Suitable for wheelchairs ★ Open daily, dawn − dusk ★ Entrance: free

These sedate, well laid-out and beautifully manicured gardens are justly famous. Playing host to more than 60,000 roses − dominated by hybrid teas and floribundas, although also including old-fashioned, shrub and species roses − the sight and scent of the gardens in high summer is a magnet for thousands of visitors. It must be said, however, that this style of rose garden is not to everyone's taste. The roses are grown with almost military precision and are in perfect condition. Swagged and garlanded climbers surround the circular rose garden, but the herbaceous borders are also worth visiting, particularly in late July and August, as is the large ornamental lake with its central island. It attracts many varieties of waterfowl, including herons which nest on the island. The Broad Walk (five minutes from the Rose Gardens) between the Inner and Outer Circle towards Cambridge Gate is another exquisitely-maintained Victorian-style area of planting. St John's Lodge, on the north side of the Inner Circle and now part of what was Bedford College, has a secluded garden including a rose garden. The Avenue Gardens, south of Chester Road, are being extensively renovated, reviving the original plans of Nesfield (1862–63). There will be gravel paths, turf panels, formal beds and specimen trees. The display beds will carry spring bulbs and summer bedding. There will be 32 ornamental vases and tazzas and eight fountains. The park as a whole is one of the most pleasant in London.

RANELAGH GARDENS
(see ROYAL HOSPITAL, CHELSEA)

RAVENSCOURT PARK   56
King Street, London W6.

Hammersmith and Fulham Borough Council ★ Near junction of King Street and Chiswick High Street ★ Best season: June/July ★ Parking outside ★ Refreshments: summer, 10am − 7pm, winter, 10am − 5pm ★ Toilet facilities ★ Suitable for wheelchairs ★ Dogs in exercise areas ★ Plant shop Under the Arches, Wed − Sat, 10.30am − 4.45pm, Sun, 10.30am − 5.45pm ★ Park open daily, 7.30am − dusk ★ Entrance: free

A delightful park thought to be a Repton landscape, with a variety of trees and shrubs relatively unscathed by recent gale damage. A scented garden, a pond with Canada geese and other waterfowl, a bowling green, an impressive cactus house and extensive playing facilities for children plus frequent events throughout the summer months. One of the best park cafeterias in London in a former coach house.

THE ROOKERY   57
Streatham Common South, London SW16. Tel: (0171) 926 9334

Lambeth Council ★ Streatham High Road, then Streatham Common South ★ Best season: July ★ Parking top of Streatham Common ★ Light refreshments ★

Toilet facilities ★ Partly suitable for wheelchairs ★ Dogs on lead on top terrace only ★ Open daily, 9am – dusk. Closed 25th Dec ★ Entrance: free

A secluded and beautifully-kept mixed garden. Formerly the walled garden of a private house and the surrounding hillside – with sloping lawns and terraces. Views over Croydon. Walled garden, the beautiful white garden best seen in July, extensive rock garden with a small stream and goldfish pond. Delightful old English garden, beautifully scented, with large variety of annual and perennial plants. An orchard picnic area with tables. Abundance of benches donated by grateful Streatham residents for this peaceful and pretty garden a quarter of a mile (uphill) off the busy High Road. Plenty of litter bins. Children enjoy the orchard area (no ball games), the dense shrubbery and hidden, winding paths leading up through the rock garden area and stream.

ROYAL BOTANIC GARDENS ★★ 58
Kew, Richmond, Surrey. Tel: (0181) 940 1171

Trustees ★ Kew Green, S of Kew Bridge ★ Parking Kew Green/Brentford Gate car park in Ferry Lane. Coach parking Kew Road/Old Deer Park, Richmond ★ Refreshments: Orangery Restaurant, Pavilion Restaurant and Bakery ★ Toilet facilities, inc. disabled ★ Suitable for wheelchairs which may be reserved in advance free of charge ★ Shops ★ Kew Palace open summer, Queen Charlotte's Cottage open summer weekends and public holidays (April to Sept) ★ Gardens open daily, except 25th Dec and 1st Jan, 9.30am – 4/6pm (depending on season), glasshouses, 9.30am – 4.30pm. Guided tours daily from the Victoria Gate visitor centre, 11am and 2pm ★ Entrance: £4 (last hour of admission £1.50), OAP and students £2, children (5–16) £1.50, under 5 free, blind, partially-sighted and wheelchair occupants free (attendant at appropriate rate), family day ticket (2 adults and up to 4 children) £10, season ticket (for Kew and Wakehurst Place) £17, family season £33 (1994 prices). Other season tickets and Friends of Kew membership available. Guided tours £1 per person

Internationally renowned, and primarily a botanic institution, collecting, conserving and exchanging plants from all over the world, Kew's delightful and varied gardens and grounds of more than 300 acres have something for everyone. In spring, the flowering cherries, crocuses, daffodils, and tulips and the lovely rock garden, in May and June, the bluebell wood, its lilacs (made famous by the song) and the water-lily house, in summer the herbaceous garden, the rose garden, in the autumn bulbs and trees, and in the winter, the heath garden, the winter flowering cherries and (indoors) the alpine house, as well as the year-round pleasure of Decimus Burton's Palm House, the Temperate House, and the Princess of Wales Conservatory with its computer-controlled microclimates. The recently-opened Sir Joseph Banks building houses an exhibition on the way mankind uses plants.

Kew's grounds also contain four temples, the famous Pagoda, a campanile, the Marianne North Gallery (filled with over 800 oil paintings of plants) and the Kew Gardens Gallery, showing botanical paintings, besides Kew Palace itself, and the charming Queen Charlotte's Cottage. The grass garden has over 500 taxa of grasses – besides those of the bamboo garden. A large percentage of the herbaceous stock is of known wild origin. There is a somewhat formal rose garden, a delightful rock garden – originally of limestone, but completely replaced by sandstone. The Cambridge Cottage Garden and the Queen's Garden (in the style of a seventeenth-century garden) should not be missed.

The huge glasshouses, some of which are kept at tropical temperatures, are well worth visiting in winter, with their unique collections of exotic and unusual plants, ranging from banana trees to giant water lilies. In the Princess of Wales Conservatory are imaginative mangrove swamps and deserts, carnivorous plants and orchids.

The trees range from ash and birch collections, through conifers, eucalyptus and mulberry to walnut. The lake, once a disused gravel pit, has an abundance of wildfowl. The Orangery does not contain oranges – which are to be found in the Citrus Walk in the Temperate House. The Orangery now has a shop and a restaurant.

It is well worth buying the souvenir guide and planning a route for the elderly or unenergetic. The disabled will find all parts of Kew except the Marianne North Gallery easily accessible. Children will particularly enjoy the Princess of Wales Conservatory, with its Mohave desert and carnivorous plants, as well as the Palm House to see 'real' bananas and the Marine Display showing seaweeds and fish from around the world. Tree-climbing, ball-games and other sports are not allowed. Neither are radios, cassettes, etc.

ROYAL HOSPITAL, CHELSEA
RANELAGH GARDENS ★   59
Royal Hospital Road, London SW3. Tel: (0171) 730 0161

Royal Hospital Chelsea ★ Through Chelsea Hospital London Gate in Royal Hospital Road, and through next gate into the South Gardens, then through small gate on left ★ Parking difficult in street ★ Suitable for wheelchairs ★ Open daily (except 25th Dec and May and June due to preparatory work for the Chelsea Flower Show), Mon – Sat, 10am – 1pm, 2pm – sunset, Sun, 2pm – sunset ★ Entrance: free

Elegant and attractive gardens with over a mile of wide walkways through undulating park-like grass and handsome tree and shrub planting, with a few perennial and shrub borders. Formerly the pleasure grounds of Ranelagh, complete with a large rotunda (now demolished) and laid out in formal style, they were redesigned by Gibson in the nineteenth century, but turned into allotments for pensioners between the World Wars. They were later reconstructed according to Gibson's plan. A summerhouse by Sir John Soane, near the entrance to the garden, houses several seats plus glass cases with a history and a map of the gardens with the major trees marked on it. These include many species of poplar, birch, beech, holly, cherry, chestnut, lime, oak and so on, with a couple of more exotic ones – the tree of heaven and the maidenhair tree. The serenity of the gardens is slightly marred by traffic in Chelsea Bridge Road. To one side of the park is the area used to house the Chelsea Flower Show. A long avenue of plane trees marks the western edge of the gardens.

SOUTHWOOD LODGE   60
33 Kingsley Place, Highgate, London N6.

Mr and Mrs Christopher Whittington ★ Off Southwood Lane, Highgate village ★ Parking in street ★ Plants for sale ★ Open 7th May, 11th June, 2 – 6pm and by written appointment ★ Entrance: £1, children 50p

An imaginatively-designed garden created in 1963 from a much larger, older garden, set at the highest part of London with a magnificent view to the east 'as far as the Urals'. In approximately a third of an acre of a fairly steep site, there is much variety of mood and planting. By the house, which is clad in many fine clematis, a densely-planted paved area is enclosed on two sides by a high beech hedge through which steps lead down to a grassy walk planted with bushes, shrubs, more clematis and herbaceous plants. A wooded area in the lowest part of the garden, with many shade-loving plants, leads one up past two pools with the soothing sound of trickling water and suitable bog plants. There are alpines growing in troughs on a low wall.

7 ST GEORGE'S ROAD ★   61
St Margaret's, Twickenham, Middlesex. Tel: (0181) 892 3713

Mr and Mrs R. Raworth ★ Off A316 between Twickenham Bridge and St Margaret's roundabout ★ Best season: May to July ★ Parking in road ★ Teas on open day ★ Unusual plants for sale ★ Open by appointment and 4th, 18th June, 2 – 6pm ★ Entrance: £1, children 50p

A most successful result of garden design inspired by Hidcote and Tintinhull, on a miniature scale, nearly a generation ago. Mature garden of grace and peacefulness, yet not far from one of London's main routes to the west. The various rooms, Italianate patio, herb and knot garden, rose-covered pergola terrace leading onto an emerald carpet of grass and flower borders backing onto old trees in a private park. There are many old roses and rare shrubs, containerised plants to interest the plantsperson and also the contents of a large elegant conservatory on the north-facing wall of the wisteria-covered house. Recent additions are a sunken Mediterranean garden and small gravel garden.

ST JAMES'S PARK ★   62
Horse Guards Parade, London SW1. Tel: (0171) 930 1793

Royal Parks ★ From Buckingham Palace on the W to Horse Guards Parade on the E, the Mall on the N and on the S by Birdcage Walk ★ Refreshments in park ★ Toilet facilities ★ Suitable for wheelchairs ★ Dogs allowed but must be on lead in certain areas ★ Open daily ★ Entrance: free

One of the smaller royal parks but one of the prettiest, though the Garden History Society and the Victorian Society criticise those who have replaced its original path system with 'a crude and quite unplanned overlay' of tarmacked straight lines. It was Henry VIII who turned this swampy field into a pleasure ground and nursery for deer. After the Restoration, in 1660, Charles II employed the French garden designer Le Nôtre, who planned the gardens at Versailles, to refashion the park into a garden. Le Nôtre drew up plans for a formal canal and included a 600-yard pitch for King Charles to play the old French game of Paille Maille (a crude form of croquet). The game gave its name to Pall Mall. Nash remodelled the lake and gardens in 1827-29. The islands are still home to a wide variety of birds from ducks to pelicans. The park is also a sanctuary for politicians and civil servants as well as weary sightseers who can doze on deckchairs. Free band performances on most days during summer.

SUNDAY MARKETS
North Wharf Road, London W2.

Off Bishops Bridge Road and Edgware Road. The Westway (A40) runs parallel with North Wharf Road ★ Parking ★ Suitable for wheelchairs

Small Sunday market with stalls for standard bedding plants, hanging flowers and cut flowers huddle together in this empty lot behind Westway. Aficionados of the Goldhawk Road end of Portobello Road know the first stallholder on the left where wild flowers and unusual plants have been on sale for some years now.

Columbia Road, London E2.
Off Hackney Road or Gosset Street (Shoreditch or Bethnal Green underground) ★ Refreshments: salmon bagels ★ Suitable for wheelchairs ★ Dogs ★ Open all year, Sun only, 7am – 2pm

The other famous market is Columbia Road, recently given a reprieve by the dreaded planners. Stallholders set out their wares of bedding plants, shrubs, small trees and indoor plants while others sell direct from the back of a lorry. Hanging baskets of honeysuckle and roses in flower can all mean your empty garden spots may have a replacement before Sunday lunch. The biggest drawback is parking so get there early and don't even think about remaining on a yellow line as you may be clamped immediately.

SYON PARK ★★
Brentford, Middlesex. Tel: (0181) 560 0881

His Grace the Duke of Northumberland ★ 2m W of Kew Bridge, road marked from A315/310 at Bush Corner ★ Parking ★ Refreshments ★ Toilet facilities ★ Suitable for wheelchairs ★ Plants for sale ★ National Trust Shop ★ House open April to Sept, daily except Mon and Tues; Oct, Suns only, all 11am – 5pm ★ Garden open daily except 25th, 26th Dec, 10am – 6pm or dusk ★ Entrance: £1.75, OAP and children £1.25 (house and gardens £4, OAP and children £3.60) (1994 prices)

The Tudor house with interiors redesigned by Robert Adam *c.*1760 is the London seat of the Percy family which also employed 'Capability' Brown. From woodland garden to Charles Fowler's Great Conservatory (1830), Syon Park shows British gardening on a grand scale and is one of the oldest landscapes in the country. A few statistics: 3200 trees here, 211 different species recorded. One in four of these are over 100 years old and about one in seven over 200 years old. The Great Conservatory was used by Joseph Paxton as the model for his famous greenhouses at Chatsworth. Now open to the public all year, it is gardened organically and planted largely for scent. There are fern and cactus collections. In the formal garden in front is the large basin and fountain surmounted by a copy of the Giovanni da Bologna *Mercury*. On the banks beyond is a fine display of azaleas. Surrounding the Conservatory are gardens and lakes as in Brown's original plan. The lakeside walk is of great interest; specimen trees planted in the eighteenth century by Brown still survive, supplemented by irises, day lilies and clumps of Chilean rhubarb. Syon is now not only a garden-cum-park, but also a garden centre and a kind of entertainment circuit with shops, art centre, butterfly house, motor museum, restaurants and seasonal events such as music concerts and craft shows. Nearby Osterley Park (not at present in the *Guide*) may be worth a visit as The National Trust are attempting to beautify the grounds.

TRINITY HOSPICE ★   65
30 Clapham Common North Side, London SW4.
Tel: (0171) 735 3104

Trustees of the Hospice ★ Off N side of the Common ★ Best seasons: spring, mid-summer ★ Parking on Common ★ Refreshments ★ Toilet facilities ★ Suitable for wheelchairs ★ Plants for sale ★ Open for charity on some weekends in April, June, July and Sept, 2 – 5pm and by appointment at other times ★ Entrance: 50p, children free

The gardens at Trinity Hospice were designed primarily for the benefit of patients, their families and the staff. Stretching over nearly two acres, the gardens are set out on slightly rolling park-like terrain and designed by John Medhurst and David Foreman of London Landscape Consortium on the principles adhered to by Lanning Roper. The latter had originally been asked by the Sainsbury Family Charity Trust to design these gardens on a dilapidated site but his illness caught up with him before he could do much. The gardens were finished because of donations made by his friends and called the Lanning Roper Memorial Garden. Perennials and shrubs predominate but there is also a wild garden at one end and a large pool with a mobile sculpture.

TRUMPETER'S HOUSE AND LODGE GARDEN ★   66
Old Palace Yard, Richmond, Surrey. Tel: (0181) 940 7731

Mrs Pamela and Miss Sarah Franklyn ★ On Richmond Green ★ Best season: May/June ★ Parking ★ Toilet facilities ★ Suitable for wheelchairs ★ Plants for sale inc. old-fashioned pinks ★ Open for groups by appointment ★ Entrance: £3

Three acres of garden stand on the site of the former Richmond Palace. The gardens feature ponds, many varieties of roses, Judas and mulberry trees and extensive lawns. Behind ironwork gates lies a 'secret garden' where Queen Elizabeth I walked and where a raised Georgian gazebo overlooks one of the loveliest stretches of the river. Here the garden has been laid out with plants of the Elizabethan period and the eye is drawn to a fine white aviary housing white doves. Contains National collection of old-fashioned pinks. A knot garden has now been added. Very well maintained, this is one of the most interesting middle-sized gardens in the London region.

15 UPPER GROTTO ROAD   67
Strawberry Hill, Twickenham, Middlesex. Tel: (0181) 891 4454

Mrs Jeane Rankin ★ Nearest stations Strawberry Hill or Twickenham. Buses 68, 33 to Popes Grotto, then Popes Grove, first right into Radnor Road and second right into Upper Grotto Road, or 90B, 267, 281, 290 to Heath Road, into Radnor Road and second left into Upper Grotto Road ★ Best season: late June/early July ★ Refreshments: teas ★ Open 2nd, 9th July and by appointment ★ Entrance: 50p, children 25p

This garden is very small, but it has been laid out by a plantswoman with, as she says, advancing age and arthritis in mind. So it is practical and absolutely delightful: a tiny colourful, sunny courtyard with a cleverly-designed conservatory which makes the house and garden all one. It will take at least an hour to take in the variety of plants, to sniff the scents set to trap you and to listen to the gentle sound of water, all in proportion, on pebbles. Pay a reverential visit to Pope's Grotto after leaving.

VICTORIA AND ALBERT MUSEUM
(The Pirelli Garden) 68
Cromwell Road, London SW7.

Board of Trustees of the Victoria and Albert Museum ★ Cromwell Road, close to South Kensington tube station and in walking distance of Harrods ★ Parking difficult ★ Refreshments: in Garden Café during summer ★ Toilet facilities ★ Suitable for wheelchairs ★ Open daily, Mon, 12 noon – 5.50pm, Tues – Sun, 10am – 5.50pm ★ Entrance: suggested voluntary donation £4.50, OAP, students and children over 12 £1, Friends and Patrons of the V&A and children under 12 free for museum and garden

This large area within the splendid Victorian pile originally had a large number of cherry trees which had reached the end of their natural life and a big ash tree due for demolition. At the time, the early 1980s, the then–director of the museum, Sir Roy Strong, had just staged an epoch-making The Garden exhibition. Thanks to the sponsorship of Pirelli it was possible to employ two architects, Douglas Childs and Maggie Davies, who produced a design of classic geometry sympathetic to the Italianate style of the museum buildings. It is very elegant and maintained to a high standard. The central fountain is floodlit in the evening.

WALLACE COLLECTION 69
Hertford House, Manchester Square, London W1.
Tel: (0171) 935 0687

Trustees of the Wallace Collection ★ N of Wigmore Street, behind Selfridges ★ Parking difficult ★ Toilet facilities (most elegantly tiled in London) ★ Suitable for wheelchairs ★ Shop ★ Gallery open ★ Garden open daily, weekdays, 10am – 5pm, Sun, 2 – 5pm. Closed 14th April, 1st May and 24th to 26th Dec ★ Entrance: free

A secluded paved courtyard in the centre of Hertford House, a mansion built in 1776-88 for the then Duke of Manchester. When this storehouse of paintings, china and other treasures, collected by the Marquess of Hertford, was bequeathed to the nation, the government bought this mansion to display them. This stylish courtyard is like a stage set, dramatised by eight magnificent bronze urns, all of which once stood in the Chateau de Bagatelle, the home of the Marquess. Sponsorship of flowers and plants for the urns would be warmly welcomed, according to the Museum. The centrepiece is an elegant fountain with a golden snake recoiling from the fish in the pool. The planting is kept simple with beds edged with clipped box.

WALPOLE HOUSE ★ 70
Chiswick Mall, London W4.

Mr and Mrs Jeremy Benson ★ S of Great West Road (A4) between Hammersmith flyover and Hogarth roundabout. Approach from Eyot Gardens South or Church Street, off Hogarth roundabout ★ Parking in adjacent roads ★

LONDON (Greater)

Seeds for sale from excellent lists, packed with information and from 10p a packet ★ Open (dependent on tides for easy access and safe parking) one Sun in mid-April, 2 – 6pm, and one Sun in late May, 2 – 7pm ★ Entrance: £1, OAP 40p, children 20p (1994 prices)

This is one of the beautiful old houses on the Mall with two-thirds of an acre of formally-designed and informally-planted garden whose sheer size (for London) takes your breath away as you come out into it from the house. A large paved area leading up steps to wide lawns with mature and handsome trees including two poplars, a tulip tree, several large ornamental cherries, acers and magnolias. Beyond a yew hedge is a woodland area, heavily shaded, and intersected with old brick paths. A formal lily pond (larger than many town gardens) is surrounded by borders and a fence covered with climbers. Many varieties of specie peonies (including the spectacular *P. cambessedesii*), climbing roses, clematis, etc. There is much self-seeding in the borders which accounts for the informality within the mostly formal lay-out. A strawberry grape, from which cuttings are sometimes for sale, grows on the front of the house. Note the 'front' gardens across the road (other owners) which are regularly flooded by the river. The nearby Strawberry House, splendidly developed by the previous owners, has changed hands and it may soon be opened with Walpole House.

WALPOLE PARK 71
Ealing, London W5. Tel: (0181) 579 2424

London Borough of Ealing ★ Centre of Ealing, access from Uxbridge Road and High Street ★ Parking in surrounding residential roads ★ Toilet facilities ★ Suitable for wheelchairs ★ Dogs on lead ★ Open daily, 8am – dusk ★ Entrance: free

The gardens were acquired by the Borough Council and opened to the public in 1901. Large walled rose garden with a pergola. Formal beds set in lawn framed by old cedar trees. Centrepiece of floral sculpture in the shape of a peacock, its tail a bed of suitably-coloured flowering plants. There is also a water garden in Oriental style.

THE WATER GARDENS
(see COOMBE WOOD, Surrey)

WATERHOUSE PLANTATION 72
(also known as Woodland Garden) ★
Bushy Park, Hampton, London. Tel: (0181) 979 1586

Royal Parks ★ On A308 Hampton Court road, ¼m W of Hampton Court roundabout. Short walk from car park, gate on main road alongside ★ Best season: spring ★ Parking ★ Suitable for wheelchairs ★ Open daily, 9am – dusk ★ Entrance: free (park and plantation)

There are two Plantations, both in Bushy Park, adjoining Hampton Court. Planting similar to the Isabella Plantation in Richmond Park (see entry) concentrating on masses of shrubs – rhododendrons, azaleas and camellias. The paths wind round shrubs and open onto small lakes and the canalised Longford River with many small bridges. The Bushy Park Association has recently planted a fritillary meadow and there are many other spring bulbs. The gardens are sensitively well cared for and worth seeing at all times of year. Investment is being made in new seating.

GREATER LONDON AND SURROUNDING COUNTIES

A few gardens with Kent and Surrey addresses are included in the Greater London section for convenience, but check the county section as another beautiful garden may be nearby.

MANCHESTER (Greater)

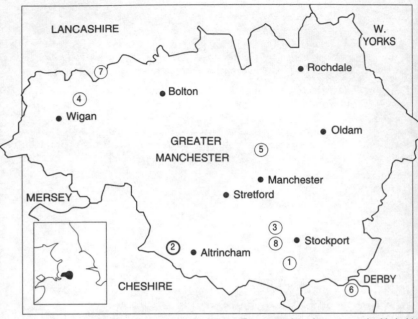

LANCASHIRE

W. YORKS

⑦

④

● Bolton

● Wigan

GREATER MANCHESTER

● Rochdale

● Oldam

⑤

● Manchester

● Stretford

MERSEY

③

⑧

● Stockport

②

● Altrincham

①

CHESHIRE

DERBY

⑥

Two-starred gardens are marked in bold

BRAMALL HALL   1
Bramall Park, Bramhall, Stockport, Greater Manchester.
Tel: (0161) 485 3708

Stockport Metropolitan Borough Council ★ 2m S of Stockport on A5102 between Bramhall and Stockport, follow signposts ★ Best season: late spring/early summer ★ Parking ★ Refreshments in tea shop in converted stables ★ Toilet facilities ★ Partly suitable for wheelchairs ★ Dogs on leads in some areas ★ Shop in Hall ★ Hall open April to Sept, daily, 1 – 5pm; Oct to Dec, daily except Mon and 25th, 26th Dec, 1 – 4pm; Jan to March, weekends only ★ Grounds open daily all day ★ Entrance: free (hall £2.75, OAP and children £2)

The gardens of Bramall Hall are a missed opportunity. At the front of this magnificent black and white timber-framed house is a courtyard covered in tarmac. To the back a slope down from the house has been terraced using brick retaining walls. These are in bad repair and of an unfortunate choice of brick. The best parts of the gardens are a little distance to the front of the house where, in a narrow strip of land, are some formal beds containing bright annuals and a herbaceous border enclosed by a hedge. The parkland is another matter. In the valley of a small river are broad areas of grassland and a number of small lakes. Woods, which contain some very large beech trees, surround the park and hide all sign of the suburbs of Stockport. The riverside walk has banks covered in wild flowers.

DUNHAM MASSEY ★ ★ 2
Nr Altrincham, Cheshire. Tel: (0161) 941 1025

The National Trust ★ 3m SW of Altrincham off A56 ★ Parking ★ Refreshments: licensed self-service restaurant ★ Toilet facilities ★ Suitable for wheelchairs. Manual and electric wheelchairs and Batricar available ★ Dogs on lead in park only ★ Shop ★ House open April to Oct, daily except Thurs and Fri, 12 noon – 5pm (last admission 4.30pm) ★ Garden open April to 29th Oct, daily, 11am – 5.30pm ★ Entrance: £2 (house and garden £4.50)

Dunham Massey has extensive parkland with much of its layout dating from the eighteenth century and earlier. The gardens close to the house have many historic elements, too. The lake that borders the north and west sides of the house was formerly part of a moat and overlooking it is a mount that dates from the Tudor period, now grassed over and planted with false acacias. On the north side of the house, in front of the lake, is an Edwardian parterre planted in purple and gold; to the east is a large lawn bordered by shrubs and trees where there is an eighteenth-century orangery and an old well house. The Trust has carried out much replanting with the aim of restoring it 'in the character of the late-Victorian Pleasure Ground'. The result appears extremely successful. In the centre of the house is an attractive courtyard with four beds of shrubs and herbaceous plants. A new walk, planted with oaks, has been created starting from Langham Grove and curving around Old Man Pool in the Deer Park.

FLETCHER MOSS BOTANICAL GARDENS AND PARSONAGE GARDENS ★ 3
Mill Gate Lane, Didsbury, Greater Manchester. Tel: (0161) 434 1877

Manchester City Council (Recreational Services) ★ 5m S of Manchester city centre on Mill Gate Lane which runs S of the A5145 close to the centre of the village of Didsbury ★ Limited parking ★ Refreshments: in small café (the building where the first meeting of the RSPB took place) but opening times uncertain ★ Toilet facilities inc. disabled ★ Partly suitable for wheelchairs ★ Dogs allowed in certain areas only ★ Open all year, 9am – dusk ★ Entrance: free

Much of this well-maintained garden is set on a steep south-facing bank planted with a variety of shrubs, heathers, bulbs, alpines, azaleas and small trees. Rocky streams run down to a water garden and lawned area where there are moisture-loving plants including gunneras. Across some tennis courts is a large grass area containing specimen trees. Within a short walking distance are the Parsonage Gardens, laid out in Victorian times and more formal, containing lawns, good herbaceous borders, camellias and rhododendrons. There is also an Orchid House and some fine trees, notably a swamp cypress and a mulberry.

HAIGH HALL GARDENS 4
Haigh Country Park, Haigh, Nr Wigan, Greater Manchester. Tel: (01942) 832895

Metropolitan Borough of Wigan (Department of Leisure) ★ 2m NE of Wigan on N side of B5238. Signposted ★ Parking (60p during peak summer season) ★ Refreshments: café ★ Toilet facilities ★ Suitable for wheelchairs which are available from the information centre ★ Dogs on lead ★ Shop ★ Parkland open all year, daily during daylight hours. Zoo open, daily except 25th, 26th Dec and 1st Jan ★ Entrance: mainly free, but some areas are entered through the zoo

Haigh Hall is surrounded by mature parkland, and a short distance to the east are some formal gardens probably of Victorian and Edwardian origin. In an open area of lawn is an oval pool around which are rose beds and specimen shrubs. Close by are three adjoining walled gardens, the middle one containing a good herbaceous border and a well-stocked shrub border. The second, to the south, has shrubs around the walls and young specimen trees planted in a lawn in the centre; the wall to the south is low and gives a view across a wild garden with a pond. The third walled garden at the northern end can only be entered from the zoo, and here against the south-facing wall is a cactus house. On the west side is a landscaped area with heathers and conifers. The rest is a formal layout with roses, yew hedges and lawns and, against the east wall, a border of shrub roses. The arboretum set in woodlands is developing well.

HEATON HALL   5
Heaton Park, Prestwich, Greater Manchester.
Tel: (0161) 236 5244 (Hall enquiries); (0161) 773 1085 (Park enquiries)

Manchester City Council ★ 4m N of the city centre on A576 just S of junction with M66 ★ Best season: spring/early summer ★ Parking. Charge on Suns and Bank Holiday Mons ★ Refreshments: café ★ Toilet facilities ★ Some areas suitable for wheelchairs, but ring for advice before visiting ★ Dogs ★ Shop ★ House open summer months only ★ Garden open all year during daylight hours ★ Entrance: free

Heaton Hall, built in 1772 by James Wyatt, was described by Pevsner as 'the finest house of its period in Lancashire'. Now it is used to display items from the City Art Gallery's collection. The 650-acre park, landscaped between 1770 and 1830, contains a number of other Neo-Classical buildings. To the front of the Hall is an area of formal, brightly planted gardens that would perhaps go better with a Victorian house. To the rear are some stables, with a small heather garden at their front and behind a large formal rose garden. A path leads through a tunnel to an attractive dell of mature trees and many rhododendrons. From here a path follows a stream through a series of pools and waterfalls to a large boating lake. On the Prestwich side of the park is an old walled area of small demonstration gardens.

LYME PARK ★   6
Disley, Stockport, Greater Manchester. Tel: (01663) 762023/766492

The National Trust ★ 6m SE of Stockport just W of Disley on A6 ★ Parking ★ Refreshments: in tearoom or at car park kiosk ★ Toilet facilities ★ Special help is available for wheelchairs (telephone in advance) ★ Shop ★ Garden open April to Oct, daily, 11am – 5pm; Oct to 23rd Dec, weekends, 12 noon – 4pm. Guided tours by arrangement ★ Entrance: £1 for garden (park: pedestrians free, car £3 to include occupants)

Lyme Hall, a Palladian-style mansion, is set in over 1300 acres of spectacular parkland in the foothills of the Pennines with panoramic views of the

Cheshire Plains. The 17-acre gardens are of great historic importance, retaining many original features from Tudor and Jacobean times. Lyme Park is regarded as the foremost National Trust garden for high-Victorian-style bedding in magnificent formal beds using many rare and old-fashioned plants including penstemon 'Rubiconda' (bred at Lyme in 1906). Important features include a well-planted Georgian orangery (Lewis Wyatt 1814) containing two venerable 150-year-old camellias; a seventeenth-century formal ampitheatre; a spectacular Dutch garden with a fine and rare example of a *parterre de broderie* using Irish ivy and golden box hedging; an elegant Edwardian rose garden; a fine Gertrude Jekyll-style herbaceous border designed by Graham Stuart Thomas; a wooded ravine garden with stream and fine collections of rhododendrons, azaleas, ferns and shade-loving plants; a collection of rare trees and plants associated with the eminent plantsman, Hon. Vicary Gibbs; a large reflection lake; a 300-year-old lime avenue, wildflower avenue and extensive lawns.

RIVINGTON TERRACED GARDENS 7
Rivington, Greater Manchester.
Tel: (01204) 691549 (Rivington Information Centre)

North West Water ★ 2m NW of Horwich. Follow the signposts to Rivington from the A673 in Horwich or in Grimeford village. The gardens are reached by a 10-minute walk from Rivington Hall and Hall Barn ★ Best season: June ★ Parking, refreshments, toilet facilities at Hall Barn and refreshments, toilet facilities and information at Great House Barn ★ Dogs ★ Open at all times ★ Entrance: free

These are not gardens as such but the remains of gardens that were built by Lord Leverhulme and designed by T.H. Mawson in the early part of this century. They are set mainly in woodland on a steep west-facing hillside and have fine views across Rivington reservoirs. It is worth buying the guide which leads the visitor round and explains the various features. Particularly impressive is a rocky ravine, the remains of a Japanese garden and the restored pigeon tower. There is a variety of mature trees and many rhododendrons and once this must have been a very grand estate. When visiting be prepared for a stiff walk and beware of the paths which can be slippery.

WYTHENSHAWE HORTICULTURAL CENTRE 8
Wythenshawe Park, Wythenshawe Road, Baguley, Greater Manchester. Tel: (0161) 945 1768

Manchester City Council ★ 7m S of Manchester city centre, ¼m from M63 junction 9, ½m from M56 junction 3, S of B5167 ★ Parking ★ Refreshments: cafeteria at hall, open July to mid-Sept, daily, 10am – 4.30pm (Sun 5.30pm). Rest of year closed on Tues ★ Toilet facilities inc. disabled ★ Partly suitable for wheelchairs ★ Plants for sale Wed, 1 – 4pm, also Sat and Sun, 10am – 4pm ★ Open daily, 10am – 4pm ★ Entrance: free

This centre is the nursery that provides most of the bedding stock for the city's parks. It also houses many surprisingly large collections of plants. Outside are herbaceous beds, vegetable plots and a fruit garden, heather beds and an area of small trees and conifers. Among the many greenhouses is a cactus house, a temperate house, a fern and orchid house and an alpine house.

MERSEYSIDE

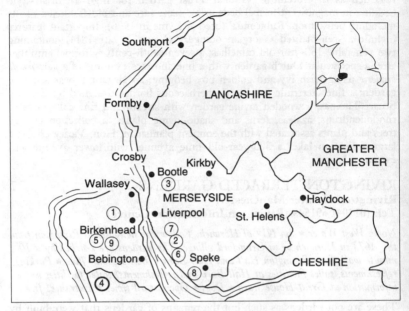

Two-starred gardens are ringed in bold.

BIRKENHEAD PARK ★
Birkenhead, Wirral, Merseyside.
Tel: (0151) 647 2366 or Ranger (0151) 652 5197

1

Metropolitan Borough of Wirral ★ 1m from the centre of Birkenhead on S of A553 ★ Best seasons: spring and summer ★ Parking around park ★ Refreshments: tea kiosk sometimes open ★ Partly suitable for wheelchairs ★ Code of practice for dog owners and poop scoop by-laws introduced ★ Open during daylight hours ★ Entrance: free

Birkenhead Park is rich in history. Opened in 1847, it was the world's first park to be built at public expense. Joseph Paxton produced its design which was highly influential in the creation of New York's Central Park. It is split into two by a road; on the eastern side is a lake with well-landscaped banks planted with trees and shrubs. A Swiss-style bridge links two islands and to one end is a fine stone boathouse that has been recently restored. In the west part is another lake with weeping willows and rhododendrons planted round its edge. There is also an enclosed area of more ornamental plants. This park is so well landscaped and planted that it is possible to overlook the litter and vandalism from which it suffers. Recent restoration works include entrances, railings and adjustments to tree plantings. A ranger is now based in the Grand Entrance, a Grade II listed building on the edge of the park.

CALDERSTONE PARK ★   2
Liverpool, Merseyside. Tel: (0151) 225 4835

Liverpool City Council, Environmental Services ★ 4m SE of Liverpool city centre, S of A562 ★ Parking ★ Refreshments in teashop ★ Toilet facilities ★ Suitable for wheelchairs ★ Dogs in park only ★ Park open at all times. Old English Garden and Japanese Garden open daily except 25th Dec, April to Sept, 8am – 7.30pm, Oct to March, 8am – 4pm ★ Entrance: free

This is a large landscaped park with mature trees, shrubs, a lake and rhododendron walk. In its centre are three gardens set around an old walled garden which are a credit to the city council gardener here. The first is the Flower garden which has semiformal beds of perennials and grasses, formal beds of annuals and a long greenhouse. Next is the Old English garden, where amongst a formal layout of paths are beds containing a huge range of perennials, bulbs and shrubs. There is a circular pond at the centre and pergolas carrying clematis, vines and other climbers cross the paths at various points. Finally the Japanese garden has a chain of rocky streams and pools around which are pines, acers and clumps of bamboo. A greenhouse contains the National collection of the genus *Aechmea*. Altogether this must be one of the best 'free' gardens in the country.

CROXTETH HALL AND COUNTRY PARK   3
Liverpool, Merseyside. Tel: (0151) 228 5311

Liverpool City Council, Leisure Services ★ Turn N off A5058 Liverpool ring road into Muirhead Avenue on NE side of city. Signposted ★ Best season: summer ★ Parking ★ Restaurant ★ Toilet facilities ★ Partly suitable for wheelchairs ★ Dogs in outer park only ★ Shop in house ★ Hall and Victorian Farm also open ★ Garden open April to Sept, daily, 11am – 5pm, winter times on request ★ Entrance: grounds free; walled garden 60p, OAP and children 30p; all facilities £2.50, OAP and children £1.25 (1994 prices)

Croxteth Hall stands in 500 acres of parkland in which there are large areas of woodland and many rhododendrons. The centre of interest to gardeners is the large walled garden to the north of the house. Interpreted as a working Victorian kitchen garden and divided up by gravel paths, this garden contains areas growing a great variety of fruit, vegetables and decorative plants; fruit espaliers are grown against the walls and trained on wire fences and the south-facing wall has a broad herbaceous border containing a good variety of perennials and ornamental grasses. In the north east corner several greenhouses and a mushroom house are all open to the visitor. To the south end is a weather station surrounded by herb beds.

ISLE OF MAN
(see Cumbria)

NESS GARDENS ★★   4
University of Liverpool Botanic Gardens, Ness, South Wirral, Merseyside. Tel: (0151) 336 2135/7769

University of Liverpool ★ 2m off A540 on Neston Road between Ness and Burton ★ Parking ★ Refreshments ★ Toilet facilities ★ Partly suitable for

*wheelchairs ★ Guide dogs only ★ Plants for sale ★ Shop ★ Open daily except 25th
Dec, March to Oct, 9.30am – dusk, Nov to Feb, 9.30am – 4pm ★ Entrance:
£3.50, OAP and children (10–18) £2.50, family ticket £8*

A Mr Bulley began gardening on this site in 1898 using seeds from plants
collected for him by George Forrest, the noted plant hunter. His daughter gave
the gardens to the University in 1948. They extend to over 60 acres. Those who
have experience of the north west winds blowing off the Irish Sea will marvel at
the variety and exotic nature of the plant life. The secret is in the Lombardy
poplars, holm oaks and Scots pines which have been planted as shelter belts
shielding the specialist areas. The aim has been to provide all-year-round interest from the spring, through the herbaceous and rose gardens of the summer to
the heather and sorbus collections of the autumn. There are in addition areas of
specialist interest such as the Native Plant Garden which houses plants raised
from seed or cuttings from wild plants and used for propagation or the re-stock-
ing of natural habitats. With the introduction of an academic chair at the
Gardens in 1991 there has been a positive attempt made to improve labelling
and signposting. Maps, coloured guide and interest trails have been updated and
in the shop there is a computer-based display system for locating plants.
Specialisms include sorbus, betulas, salix, rhododendrons and primulas.

THE OLD HALL ★   5
Hadlow Road, Willaston, South Wirral, Cheshire.
Tel: (0151) 327 4779

*Dr and Mrs M.W.W. Wood ★ 8m NW of Chester, in the centre of Willaston on
Hadlow Road (B5151) ★ Parking in roads nearby and in small car park nearly
opposite ★ Toilet facilities ★ Suitable for wheelchairs ★ Plants for sale ★ Open by
appointment and some Suns for charity ★ Entrance: £1.50*

These are attractive and well–established gardens set around an equally attractive old stone and brick house. Shrubs and perennials are the mainstay of the
garden although some large broadleaved trees and good conifers give form
and structure to the planting. Many shrubs are chosen for their foliage
colour; there are different forms of berberis, salix and some fine purple
smoke bushes. Among the huge range of perennials are poppies, aquilegias,
astrantias, violas, euphorbias and perennial geraniums. The planting in the
shaded areas is particularly good. One area that has been liberally treated with
gravel contains many tender plants and the lawns are full of daffodils. There
is a vegetable garden with fruit cage and greenhouses.

REYNOLDS PARK WALLED GARDEN   6
Church Road, Woolton, Liverpool, Merseyside. Tel: (0151) 724 2371

*Liverpool City Council (controlled by Environmental Services, Calderstone Park)
★ 4½m SE of Liverpool city centre. Turn left off A562 up Beaconsfield Road to
end and right into Church Road. Park is on left ★ Refreshments in nearby
Woolton village ★ Open all year, Mon – Fri, 9am – 4pm ★ Entrance: free*

A walled garden with herbaceous borders, large dahlia beds and excellent wall
climbers. All in very good condition, litter-free and maintained with only two
staff. Large grass area with mature trees. Unusual clipped yew garden. Small
rose garden.

SEFTON PARK 7
Liverpool, Merseyside. Tel: (0151) 724 2371

Liverpool City Council (controlled by Environmental Services, Calderstone Park)
★ 3m SE of Liverpool city centre, N of A561 ★ Best season: spring ★ Parking at
various points around park ★ Refreshments at café in centre of park ★ Suitable for
wheelchairs ★ Dogs ★ Open at all times ★ Entrance: free

Although this large park suffers badly from litter and vandalism it remains an
extremely fine Victorian park, with many of its monuments, gateways and
shelters as well as the large houses surrounding it built in the Gothic style of
the late 1800s. A large serpentine boating lake has two small streams entering
at its northern end. One stream flows from the east through a lightly wooded
valley that has been landscaped with large rocks and planted with rhododendrons. The other flows from the north through a series of small lakes passing
a replica of Piccadilly's Eros, a statue of Peter Pan and an ornate bandstand.
In the centre of the park is a palm house now in bad repair, as are the
statues. The Garden History Society and the Victorian Society, which call
Sefton 'a site of national historic importance', are highly critical of its present
sad state. Paxton's Stanley Park also arouses their ire, as do the other
Liverpool parks Prince's Park and Newsham Park which they say are suffering from 'savage vandalism'. It is hoped that reglazing of the palm house will
be complete by 1996, the centenary of the gift of the Park to Liverpool by
the Victorian millionaire Harry Thompson.

SPEKE HALL 8
The Walk, Liverpool, Merseyside. Tel: (0151) 427 7231

The National Trust ★ 8m SE of Liverpool city centre, S of A561. Signposted ★
Best season: spring ★ Refreshments in teashop from 12 noon. Picnics in orchard ★
Toilet facilities, inc. disabled ★ Partly suitable for wheelchairs ★ Shop ★ Hall
open April to 30th Oct, daily except Mon ★ Garden open daily except Mon, 12
noon – 5.30pm (winter 12 noon – 4pm). Closed 1st Jan, 14th April, 24th to
26th, 31st Dec ★ Entrance: £1 (hall and gardens £3.60)

The gardens at Speke are neither as old nor as impressive as the Elizabethan
Hall. They are remarkable, however, for although they are situated amidst the
industrial areas of south Liverpool they seem to be set in the heart of the countryside, despite their proximity to Liverpool airport. In front of the house is a
large lawn with shrub borders to the sides containing mainly rhododendrons
and hollies. On the side opposite the house is a ha-ha allowing views to the
fields and woodland. A stone bridge leads over a drained moat to the ornate
stone entrance of the hall. The moat continues to the west where there is a
herbaceous border with a variety of perennials; a large holm oak stands opposite. To the south is a formal rose garden containing fragrant varieties of old-
fashioned roses. In the centre of the house is a large cobbled courtyard in
which grow two enormous yews. The Trust is continuing to develop many
areas of the gardens and a mid-Victorian-style stream garden has been planted
with rhododendrons, azaleas, camellias, ferns and other plants.

THORNTON MANOR ★ 9
Thornton Hough, Wirral, Merseyside.
Tel: (0151) 336 4828 (Estate Office)

The Viscount Leverhulme ★ Situated on the minor road that links the A5137 to the B5136 at Thornton Hough village ★ Parking ★ Refreshments ★ Toilet facilities ★ Partly suitable for wheelchairs ★ Dogs on lead ★ Plants for sale ★ Open three Suns in spring, 2 – 7pm and probably 27th Aug (telephone for details) ★ Entrance: £1.50, OAP and children 50p (1994 prices)

Thomas Mawson created two gardens for Lord Leverhulme. One, Rivington (see entry under Greater Manchester) is perched high on a hillside, the other, Thornton Manor, lies in the very different flat, lush countryside of the Wirral. Here, instructed to create 'a garden for promenading and walking' Mawson came up with a wonderfully spacious design. In front of the house is a large lawn with a formal layout of broad stone paths; no planting, just good views of the surrounding countryside. To the east is a loggia and a lime walk. To the west, a long, straight path takes the visitor past some of the garden's main features. First the Forum, a rectangular lawn surrounded by a colonnade covered in climbers, then the teahouse, an impressive stone building that was once the entrance to the walled garden and it, too, is covered in climbers. The path eventually reaches an area that is the most abundantly planted part of the garden. Here gravel paths lead amongst mixed beds of shrubs, perennials and annuals. Starting here, a long walk leads to the lake and then to the east side of the house via a dell, an attractive planting of shrubs and trees surrounding a pool. Like Mawson's other gardens, Thornton Manor retains a leisurely Edwardian atmosphere that makes it a great joy to visit.

TELEPHONE NUMBERS

Except where owners have specifically requested that they be excluded, telephone numbers to which enquiries may be directed are given for each property. To maintain the support and co-operation of private owners, it is suggested that the telephone be used with discretion. Where visits are by appointment, the telephone can of course be used except where written application, particularly for parties, is specifically requested. Code numbers are given in brackets. For the Republic of Ireland phone 010353 followed by the code (Dublin is 1) followed by the subscriber's number. In all cases where visits by parties are proposed, owners should be advised in advance and arrangements preferably confirmed in writing.

WARNING
Many UK codes and numbers are being changed and while those given should be up to date, there may be some which are not.

MIDLANDS (West)

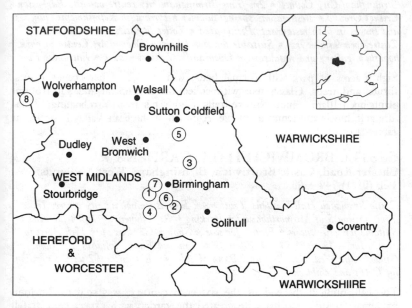

STAFFORDSHIRE

Brownhills

Wolverhampton   Walsall

⑧

Sutton Coldfield

WARWICKSHIRE

Dudley   West
          Bromwich   ⑤

⑦ ●Birmingham
WEST MIDLANDS   ③
① ⑥ ②
Stourbridge   ④

Solihull

● Coventry

HEREFORD
&
WORCESTER

WARWICKSHIIRE

BIRMINGHAM BOTANICAL GARDENS
AND GLASSHOUSES ★   1
Westbourne Road, Edgbaston, Birmingham, West Midlands.
Tel: (0121) 454 1860

*2m from city centre. Approach from Hagley Road or Calthorpe Road following
tourist signs ★ Parking ▲ Refreshments: restaurant. Picnics allowed ★ Toilet
facilities ★ Suitable for wheelchairs. Manual and electric wheelchairs available for
use free of charge ★ Plants for sale ★ Shop and gallery ★ Open daily, 9am (10am
on Suns) – 7.30pm (or dusk if earlier) ★ Entrance: £3 (£3.30 on summer
Suns), OAP, disabled, students and children £1.70. Parties £2.70 per person
(£1.50 for concessions)*

This 15-acre ornamental garden will appeal to the keen plantsperson and also
to the everyday gardener. In addition to the unusual plants in the Tropical
House and the Orangery, there is a Cactus and Succulent House, and cages
with parrots and also guinea fowl, ducks, peacocks, geese and other birds.
Some beautiful old trees, a border for E.H. Wilson plants, a raised alpine bed
and a raised garden area to give ideas and enjoyment to disabled visitors. The
rock garden contains a wide variety of alpine plants, primulas, astilbes and
azaleas and there are also herbaceous borders and a rose garden. There is a
small display of carnivorous plants. The model domestic theme gardens cover
low maintenance, children, colour and a plantsman's garden. An attractive
courtyard now houses the National bonsai collection. A children's playground
and adventure trail makes the garden a pleasant place for a family outing.
Bands play every Sunday in summer.

CANNON HILL PARK 2
Moseley, Birmingham, West Midlands. Tel: (0121) 442 4226

Birmingham City Council ★ 2m from Birmingham city centre opposite Edgbaston Cricket Ground ★ Best season: spring/summer ★ Parking ★ Refreshments: lunches and snacks in park restaurant. Picnic area ★ Toilet facilities in Midlands Art Centre open 9am – 9pm ★ Suitable for wheelchairs ★ Dogs ★ Art Centre in park, bookshop, gallery and restaurant ★ Open daily, 7.30am – dusk ★ Entrance: free

Eighty acres of park with formal beds, wide range of herbaceous plants, shrubs and trees. Glasshouse with collection of tropical and sub-tropical plants open 10am – 4pm. Nature trails. Children's area. Also boating, miniature golf, bowls and tennis available. A model of the Elan Valley is set in the garden area.

CASTLE BROMWICH HALL GARDENS ★ 3
Chester Road, Castle Bromwich, Birmingham, West Midlands. Tel: (0121) 749 4100

Castle Bromwich Hall Gardens Trust ★ 4m E of Birmingham city centre. 1m from junction 5 of M6 northbound ★ Parking ★ Refreshments ★ Toilet facilities ★ Suitable for wheelchairs ★ Plants for sale ★ Shop ★ Gardens open 15th April to Sept, Mon – Thurs, 1.30 – 4.30pm. Sat, Sun and Bank Holidays, 2 – 6pm. Guided tours Wed, Sat, Sun and Bank Holidays ★ Entrance: £2 with concessions for OAPs and children

The hall, built at the end of the sixteenth century, was sold to Sir John Bridgman in 1657 and his wife created the garden with expert help. It fell into decay, and now a series of formal connecting gardens is being restored to give them the appearance and content of a garden of 1680-1740. The perimeter wall and orangery have been rebuilt. There are fan- and espalier-trained fruit trees and orchard, a kitchen garden, ponds, cold bath, archery ground, maze, wilderness and historic borders. New orchards of period varieties were planted winter 1990-91. A wild flower meadow and nut grounds have been established. Visitors have the rare opportunity to see a period garden being restored.

MARTINEAU ENVIRONMENTAL STUDIES CENTRE 4
Priory Road, Edgbaston, Birmingham, West Midlands. Tel: (0121) 440 4883

City of Birmingham Education Department ★ Turn off A38 road into Priory Road and entrance is 100 yards on right opposite Priory Hospital ★ Parking ★ Tea on open days ★ Toilet facilities ★ Suitable for wheelchairs ★ Plants for sale ★ Open three times a year (contact Centre for dates), 10.30am – 6pm ★ Entrance: £1, children 50p

This is a two-acre educational garden designed for teachers and children but the wide range of features makes it interesting for all, and a good place for the family with children interested in gardening. There are annuals, herbaceous and shrub borders, roses, raised beds, herbs, alpines, bulbs, miscanthus and the greenhouse with a collection of cacti, tomatoes and peppers along with tropical things such as a banana, tea and coffee plant. In the woodland area there are native plants and a pool with plenty of wildlife. The vegetable plots contain brassicas, root crops and legumes and the fruit trees and soft fruit include a medlar, fig, greengage, apricot, blueberry and tayberry. Plants are grown for their educational value, which sometimes means that weeds are left, or actively encouraged. There are now some sheep, ducks and hens.

26 SUNNYBANK ROAD 5
Wylde Green, Sutton Coldfield, Birmingham, West Midlands.
Tel: (0121) 384 8474

Chris and Margaret Jones ★ From S take A5127, turn left on to A452 Chester road, right at next traffic lights, B4531. The third right is Sunnybank Road. From N follow signs through Sutton Coldfield for Birmingham, turn right for Wylde Green station into Station Road and left under bridge into Sunnybank Road ★ Parking in road ★ Refreshments ★ Plants for sale ★ Open 28th May, 25th June, 23rd July, 2 – 6pm and by appointment for horticultural groups ★ Entrance: £1, accompanied children free

This garden has been made over the past decade from a sandy lawn filled with builder's rubbish and one silver birch tree. A terrace outside the house is bordered by beds with all-year interest, and tubs of annuals. Winding paths lead down to a pool and a bog garden beyond which is a lawn, surrounded by recently created and planted new beds, also a small herb garden. Beds and borders contain a good variety of shrubs and plants, many raised from seed by the owners, and are full of attractive different shapes and colours. It shows what can be created from an unpromising, rectangular suburban back garden and will be interesting to plantspersons or just to enjoy for its colour and variety.

THE UNIVERSITY OF BIRMINGHAM BOTANIC GARDEN ★ 6
Winterbourne, 58 Edgbaston Park Road, Edgbaston, Birmingham.
Tel: (0121) 414 5590

The University of Birmingham School of Continuing Studies ★ Off A38 Bristol road leading out of the city, adjacent to the University campus ★ Parking ★ Toilet facilities ★ Suitable for wheelchairs ★ Plants sometimes for sale on open days ★ Open by prior arrangement ★ Entrance: £1, children 50p (1994 prices)

About seven acres of garden originally belonging to a large house owing much to the landscape style developed by Edwin Lutyens and Gertrude Jekyll. Because of its wide range of plants and different features it should be of interest to the botanist as well as the ordinary gardener. There are geographical beds showing typical trees and shrubs from Europe, Australasia, the Americas, China and Japan. The pergola is covered with clematis and roses and there are herbaceous borders backed by brick walls covered with climbers. A miniature arboretum contains interesting specimens including giant oaks, acers, conifers and a *Gingko biloba* along with hedges of yew, *Taxus baccata* and copper beech. In a fairly new Commemorative Garden is a black mulberry planted to mark the 100th anniversary of the City of Birmingham. The range of plants continues with the sandstone rock garden, troughs, rhododendrons, heathers and alpines. There is an unusual nut walk containing several varieties of *Corylus avellana* trained over an iron frame-

MIDLANDS (West)

work. A special feature is the walled garden laid out with beds of roses showing the History of the Rose, and elsewhere are more recent plantings of roses. Clearing of old shrubs at one side of the house has opened up the small paved garden attractively.

8 VICARAGE ROAD 7
Edgbaston, Birmingham, West Midlands. Tel: (0121) 455 0902

Charles and Tessa King-Farlow ★ 1½m W of city centre off A456 Hagley road. Going out of the city, turn left into Vicarage Road ★ Best season: May to Sept ★ Parking in local roads ★ Suitable for wheelchairs ★ Plants for sale at certain times ★ Open by appointment only ★ Entrance: £1, OAP and children 50p

A visit to this garden should give pleasure to most gardeners as there is a sense of mystery as one moves from one area to the next. Plenty of good planting ideas can be seen with the clever use of colour and foliage combinations – a range of grey and variegated foliage. Roses and clematis scramble through old fruit trees and other shrubs. There is a bank of shrub roses, and four mixed borders containing a wide range and some rare plants. There is a conservatory, pool and 1920s rock garden providing year-round colour. The walled kitchen garden has fruit and vegetables, and has recently been redesigned and laid out in a geometric pattern.

WIGHTWICK MANOR 8
Wightwick Bank, Wolverhampton, West Midlands.
Tel: (01902) 761108

The National Trust ★ 3m W of Wolverhampton off A454. Turn by the Mermaid Inn up Wightwick Bank ★ Parking ★ Refreshments: tea room ★ Toilet facilities ★ Suitable for wheelchairs, although sloping site. Braille guides ★ Dogs on lead ★ Shop ★ House open same days as garden, 2.30 – 5.30pm. Timed tickets ★ Garden open March to Dec, Thurs and Sat, Bank Holiday Sun and Mon, 2 – 6pm. Also open any weekday by appointment. Pre-booked parties accepted Wed and Thurs ★ Entrance: £2 (house £4.20, students £2)

This 10-acre garden, designed by Alfred Parsons and Thomas Mawson, surrounds an 1887 house strongly influenced in its design by William Morris and his movement; it contains a collection of pre-Raphaelite paintings. Large trees form a delightful framework to the garden with a central octagonal arbour with climbing roses and clematis. Through an old orchard is a less formal area with pools surrounded by shrubs and rhododendrons. There are herbaceous borders, two rows of barrel-shaped yews and beds containing plants from gardens of famous men. As a surprise round a corner one comes across a line of boulders from Scotland and the Lake District which were left when the great glaciers melted in the last Ice Age. The Peach House has been restored and the Mathematical Bridge giving access to the Bridge garden, with spring bulbs, is now reconstructed.

NORFOLK

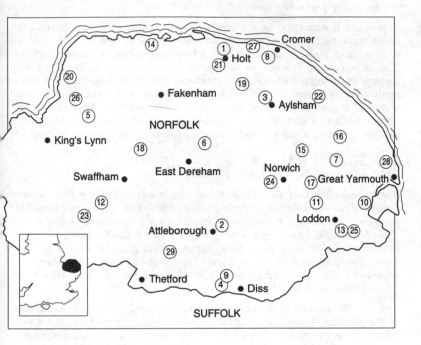

BAYFIELD HALL

1

Nr Holt, Norfolk. Tel: (01263) 712219

Mr and Mrs R. Combe , 1m N of Holt off A148 ★ Parking ★ Teas on open day in Old Servants' Hall overlooking lake ★ Plants for sale at Wildlife Garden next door ★ Open 25th June for charity, 2 – 5pm and by appointment ★ Entrance: £2, children (under 10) free

The house commands one of the most beautiful views in Norfolk. The grounds are thought to have been landscaped by Repton and the wooded valley of the Glaven has been dammed to form a lake. A formal garden designed in the mid-twentieth century with borders containing many rare and semi-hardy shrubs is sited on rising ground at one side, so it does not interfere with the relationship between the house and the landscape. A ruined Saxon church forms part of this arrangement. The gardens immediately around the house are well planned and contain many unusual plants including a mature *Schizophragma hydrangeoides*.

BESTHORPE HALL ★

2

Besthorpe, Attleborough, Norfolk. Tel: (01953) 452138

Mr J.A. Alston ★ 1m E of Attleborough on Bunwell Road. Entrance on right,

*past church ★ Best season: May to Sept ★ Parking ★ Refreshments ★ Toilet
facilities ★ Suitable for wheelchairs ★ Plants for sale ★ Open 11th June, 2 – 5pm
and by appointment ★ Entrance: £2*

A pool and fountain occupy the centre of the entrance forecourt. Beyond the
house, more pools and fountains are set among lawns skirted by high clematis-
hung walls of Tudor brick which form a backdrop to long herbaceous borders.
The largest lawn, believed to have once been a tilt yard, has developing
topiary, while on another is an enormous and shapely Wellingtonia. There are
many other fine trees among which are paulownia, and a variety of birches,
acers and magnolias including the sumptuous *M. delavayi*. There are walled
kitchen gardens, a nuttery, a herb garden, and a small lake with wildfowl. On
another pool lives a pair of black swans. Bearded iris are the June feature.

BLICKLING HALL ★   3
Aylsham, Norfolk. Tel: (01263) 733084

*The National Trust ★ 1½m NW of Aylsham on N side of B1354 ★ Best seasons:
spring and summer ★ Parking ★ Refreshments 11am – 5pm. Picnic area in walled
garden ★ Toilet facilities ★ Suitable for wheelchairs ★ Dogs in park on lead ★
Plant Centre open 10am – 5pm ★ Shop ★ House open ★ Garden open 25th
March to 5th Nov, daily except Mon (but open Bank Holiday Mons) and
Thurs, 1 – 5pm; daily in July and Aug, 11am – 5pm. Closed 14th April ★
Entrance: £2.50 (house and gardens £4.90 (Sun and Bank Holiday Mons
£5.50)). Garden walks £3*

Although the gardens of Blickling Hall seem so suited to the style and beauty
of the Jacobean house, they consist of a blend of features from the seventeenth to the twentieth centuries. From the earliest period come the massive
yew hedges flanking the south approach. To the east is the parterre planned
by Nesfield and Wyatt in 1870 with its topiary pillars and blocks of yew
shaped like grand pianos. Complicated flower beds were replaced in 1938
with Norah Lindsay's four large square beds of herbaceous plants in selected
colours with surrounding borders of roses edged with catmint. The central
pool has a seventeenth-century fountain bought from nearby Oxnead Hall. A
high retaining wall bounds the southern side while in the centre of the
eastern side flights of steps mount up to the highest terrace with a central
vista through blocks of woodland to the Doric temple of 1730 raised above
parkland beyond. The two blocks are intersected by *allées* in seventeenth-
century style although planted in 1861-64. Gales did much damage but
replanting has been completed using Turkey oak, lime and beech. On the
southern side is the Orangery of 1782 by Samuel Wyatt which houses half-
hardy plants and a statue of Hercules by Nicholas Stone made for Oxnead in
the 1640s. In the corner of the northern block is the secret garden, a remnant
of a larger eighteenth-century garden for which Repton made recommenda-
tions. It now consists of a lawn with a central sundial surrounded by high
beech hedges. The shrub border through which it is approached is by Norah
Lindsay who was also responsible for the planting of the dry moat around the
house. North of the parterre is a raised grassy area, possibly a remnant of the
Jacobean mount; here grows an enormous, sprawling Oriental plane. To the
north-west is landscaped parkland where woods descend to the curving lake
formed before 1729 and later extended. West of the house are cedars of

Lebanon and a collection of magnolias around a nineteenth–century fountain. Elsewhere in the park are the Gothic Tower of 1773 and the Mausoleum of 1796, a pyramid 45 ft square by Joseph Bonomi. Recently, the Trust restored the park to its 1840 limits and replanted 12 hectares of the Great Wood.

BRESSINGHAM STEAM MUSEUM AND GARDENS ★   4
Bressingham, Diss, Norfolk. Tel: (0137988) 386/382 (24 hours)

Mr Alan Bloom ★ 3m W of Diss on A1066 ★ Parking ★ Refreshments ★ Toilet facilities ★ Suitable for wheelchairs ★ Plants for sale ★ Shop ★ Open April to Oct, daily, 10am – 5pm ★ Entrance: £3.30 – £3.70 according to season, OAP £2.70 – £3, children (4-16) £2.30 – £2.70 (1994 prices)

Alan Bloom's garden consists of five acres of island beds set in undulating meadow with mature trees. Almost all beds are informal, devoted to mainly hardy perennials and alpine plants, approximately 5000 different kinds. A smaller garden of conifers and shrubs adjoins. Such a variety and setting have been favourably compared to Wisley. Provides interest for most of the year. The nearby steam museum, with narrow gauge rides round the 400–acre estate and a large collection of static exhibits including express locomotives, does not in the opinion of the owners impinge on the garden appeal, but enhances the overall interest. They run to a predetermined programme with the busiest time during school holidays, but still leaving quiet days for those who come solely for the garden. The large Plant Centre offers a very wide range of plants of all kinds including shrubs and trees and has separate refreshment facilities. See also entry for Foggy Bottom.

CONGHAM HALL HOTEL   5
Lynn Road, Grimston, Nr King's Lynn, Norfolk. Tel: (01485) 600250

Mr and Mrs T. Forecast ★ NE of King's Lynn. Go to A149/A148 interchange, then follow A148 signed Sandringham/Fakenham/Cromer for 100 yards. Turn right for Grimston. Hotel is 2½m on left hand side of road ★ Parking ★ Suitable for wheelchairs ★ Open April to Sept, daily except Sat, 2 – 4pm. Small parties by arrangement at other times. No coaches ★ Entrance: free

Herb garden. Over 300 varieties grown in about two acres of hedged *jardinière* set near the Georgian manor house, now a hotel, which is itself surrounded by 40 acres of parkland. Mrs Forecast began the herb garden a few years ago as part of a vegetable and soft fruit supply for the kitchen. Now it has become an obsession, and includes medicinal herbs which, it goes without saying, are rarely if ever required by diners. Anyone interested in herbs should certainly visit. *Bon viveurs* will find the hotel in the *Good Food Guide*.

ELSING HALL ★   6
Elsing, Nr East Dereham, Norfolk. Tel: (01362) 637224

Mr and Mrs D.H. Cargill ★ 5m NE of East Dereham. Signposted off A47 ★ Parking ★ Refreshments ★ Dogs on lead ★ Open June and July, Suns only, 2 – 6pm and by appointment ★ Entrance: £2, children free

The romantic appearance of this garden is in complete harmony with the moated flint and half-timbered house which it surrounds. The garden is rich, lush and unrestrained and in mid-summer is filled with the scent of the old garden roses which cover the walls and fill the borders. The lawn between the house and the moat has been abandoned to wild orchids; wildfowl nest among the reeds. Both the moat and a nearby stewpond are encircled by moist borders supporting luxuriant growth. On the walls of the kitchen garden grow old roses, many of which seem unique to this place. A large variety of trees has been planted, a formal garden has been developed, and an avenue of gingkos established.

FAIRHAVEN GARDEN TRUST ★   7
South Walsham, Norwich, Norfolk. Tel: (01603) 270449

Fairhaven Garden Trust ★ 9m NE of Norwich off B1140 at South Walsham ★ Best season: May/June ★ Parking ★ Refreshments ★ Toilet facilities ★ Partly suitable for wheelchairs ★ Dogs on lead ★ Plants for sale ★ Open 14th April to 1st Oct, daily except Mon (but open Bank Holiday Mons); 22nd to 29th Oct, daily, all 11am – 5.30pm (Sat, 2 – 5.30pm). Walks with the warden (pre-booking required) Suns in July, 2.30pm ★ Entrance: £3, OAP £2, children £1. Season tickets £7, family season ticket £20, bird sanctuary £1. Walks with the warden £4, OAP £3.50

A garden created in natural woods of oak and alder extending to about 230 acres surrounding the unspoiled (private) South Walsham Inner Broad. Paths wind among banks of azaleas and large-leaved rhododendrons and lead to the edge of the broad itself. Much of the area is wet and supports a rich variety of primulas especially candalabras, with lysichitums, hostas, astilbes, ligularias and gunneras of exceptional size, merging into the natural vegetation among which are many royal ferns and some majestic oaks. Although particularly colourful during the flowering of the azaleas in the spring, this garden gives pleasure at all times of the year when natural beauty is preferred to man-made sophistication.

FELBRIGG HALL ★   8
Roughton, Norwich, Norfolk. Tel: (01263) 837444

The National Trust ★ 2m SW of Cromer off A148. Main entrance on B1436 ★ Best season: summer ★ Parking ★ Refreshments: 25th March to 5th Nov, daily except Tues and Fri, 11am – 5pm ★ Toilet facilities ★ Suitable for wheelchairs. Self-drive scooter available ★ Dogs in park only on leads ★ Shop ★ Hall open as garden, 1 – 5pm (Bank Holiday Mons, 11am – 5pm) ★ Garden open 25th March to 5th Nov, daily except Tues and Fri, 11am – 5pm. Estate only 6th Nov to March 1996, dawn – dusk. Woodland walks all year except 25th Dec, daily, dawn – dusk ★ Entrance: £1.80 (house and gardens £4.60. Parties Mon, Wed, Thurs and Sat £3.40 per person)

The house faces south across the park which is notable for its fine woods and lakeside walk. A ha-ha separates the park from the lawns of the house where there is an orangery planted with camellias. To the north the ground rises and there are specimen trees and shrubs. At some distance to the east there is a large walled kitchen garden now richly planted with a combination of fruit, vegetables and flowers in a formal design behind clipped hedges. There is also a vine house and a great brick dovecot. In early autumn there is a display of many varieties of colchicums: the National collection is kept here. The gardens are kept in immaculate order. Sheringham Park is nearby (see entry).

FOGGY BOTTOM 9
Bressingham, Diss, Norfolk.

Mr Adrian Bloom ★ 3m W of Diss on A1066 adjoining Bressingham Gardens ★ Open April to Oct, every Mon and first Sun in each month, 11am – 5pm ★ Entrance: £2, children £1

Adrian Bloom's garden is of six acres, planted over the last 25 years and is a little distance away from Alan Bloom's garden at Bressingham (see entry). It is designed with broad meandering pathways, the main structure provided by a colourful display of conifers, interplanted with a wide range of trees and shrubs, perennials and ornamental grasses. There are over 3000 different species and varieties of plants planned for year-round interest.

FRITTON LAKE 10
Fritton, Great Yarmouth, Norfolk. Tel: (01493) 488208

Lord and Lady Somerleyton ★ 5m SW of Great Yarmouth off the A143 ★ Best season: summer ★ Parking ★ Refreshments ★ Toilet facilities ★ Suitable for wheelchairs ★ Shop ★ Falconry, heavy horses, golf, putting, boat hire and craft workshops ★ Garden open April to 24th Sept, daily, 10am – 5.30pm ★ Entrance: £3.50, OAP and children £2.50, family (2 adults, 2 children) £11, group discounts available

The large lake remains almost unspoilt and separate from the tea rooms and other commercial attractions of this country park. An unusual feature is a Victorian garden of about half an acre in the gardenesque style with irregular beds surrounded by clipped box hedges and filled with shrubs and herbaceous perennials that give a colourful display in the summer.

THE GARDEN IN AN ORCHARD 11
Mill Road, Bergh Apton, Norwich, Norfolk. Tel: (01508) 480322

Mr and Mrs R.W. Boardman ★ 6m SE of Norwich off A146 at Hellington Corner ★ Parking ★ Refreshments on Suns ★ Toilet facilities ★ Suitable for wheelchairs ★ Dogs on lead ★ Plants for sale ★ Open May to Sept, Sat, Sun and Bank Holiday Mons, 11am – 6pm (advisable to check before visiting) ★ Entrance: £1 (1994 price)

The garden started as a three and a half-acre commercial orchard and over the years has been planted up bit by bit with rare and unusual plants and trees. Narrow paths meander through dense plantings of species roses giving eye to eye contact with their flowers and these open up to similar plantings of herbaceous walks giving the garden a sense of mystery. Mr Boardman is a professional plantsman and among his rare trees are *Phellodendron amurense*, *Prunus padus* 'Colorata', *Paulownia tomentosa* and nine species of eucalyptus. *Lonicera ledebourii* catches the eye, along with *Malva sylvestris mauritiana* and many special clematis scrambling through trees.

GOODERSTONE WATER GARDENS 12
Crow Hall, Gooderstone, King's Lynn, Norfolk. Tel: (01366) 21208

Mr and Mrs W.H. Knights ★ 4m SW of Swaffham. E of Gooderstone village. Signposted. Gardens on opposite side of road to car park ★ Best season: summer ★

Parking ★ Tea and biscuits on Suns (tea machine on weekdays) ★ Toilet facilities ★ Suitable for wheelchairs ★ Open early April to early Oct, weekdays, 10.30am – 6pm, Sun for charity, 1.30 – 6pm ★ Entrance: £1, children 30p (1994 prices)

Somewhat difficult to find, the entrance to these gardens is along a concreted path between modern industrial buildings. A series of broad streams with many recently added trees and shrubs has been excavated in open woodland. These are bordered by a variety of aquatic plants and crossed by numerous wooden bridges connecting wide grassy paths. There is no great variety of design and one part of this extensive garden is very much like another but the effect is pleasing.

HALES HALL   13
Hales, Loddon, Norfolk. Tel: (01508) 548395

Mr and Mrs Terence Read ★ 12m SE of Norwich, signposted off A146 ★ Parking ★ Plants for sale in nursery ★ Fifteenth-century Great Barn open ★ Garden open Tues – Sat, 10am – 5pm (closed 1 – 2pm), Sun, 2 – 5pm and some Bank Holidays. Party visits by arrangement ★ Entrance: collection box

A moat surrounds the remaining wing of a vast house of the late fifteenth century and a central lawn with well-planted borders and topiary of box and yew (grown from cuttings) backed by high brick walls. Work is continuing on the restoration of the garden after centuries of neglect. The owners specialise in growing rare and unusual perennial plants, and look after the National collection of citrus, figs and greenhouse grapes. The associated century-old nurseries offer an extensive range of conservatory plants, vines, figs and mulberries.

HOLKHAM HALL ★   14
Holkham, Wells-next-the-Sea, Norfolk.
Tel: (01328) 710374 (garden centre) or (01328) 710227 (estate office)

The Viscount Coke ★ 2m W of Wells on A149 ★ Parking ★ Refreshments in tea room ★ Toilet facilities ★ Suitable for wheelchairs ★ Plants for sale in garden centre ★ Pottery and gift shop ★ House open as terrace gardens ★ Terrace gardens open 16th, 17th, 30th April and 1st, 28th, 29th May, 11.30am – 5pm; 30th May to 28th Sept, daily except Fri and Sat, 1.30 – 5pm. Garden centre gardens open throughout the year Mon – Sat, 10am – 1pm, 2 – 5pm, Sun, 2 – 5pm ★ Entrance: £3, children £1.50 (state rooms and terrace gardens). Discounts for pre-paid parties of 20 or more. Garden centre gardens free

The vast park at Holkham was laid out originally by William Kent and later worked on by both Brown and Repton. The park is famous for its holm oaks. On the west side of the house, lawns sweep down to the great lake. The terrace which fronts the south facade was added in 1854 but the scale of the house and park is so large that, from a distance at least, this does not seriously disrupt the vision of the two. The formal beds designed by W.A.Nesfield flank a great fountain representing Perseus and Andromeda said to be designed by C. Smith. The garden centre in walled gardens in the grounds extend to over six acres, subdivided into six areas with perennial borders and the original greenhouses. Alpines, shrubs, perennials, herbs, roses, bedding and house plants for sale.

HOVETON HALL GARDENS 15
Nr Wroxham, Norfolk. Tel: (01603) 782798

Mr and Mrs Andrew Buxton ★ 1m N of Wroxham Bridge on A1151 ★ Best season: May/June ★ Parking ★ Teas ★ Toilet facilities ★ Suitable for wheelchairs ★ Plants for sale ★ Open 16th April to 17th Sept, Wed, Fri, Sun and Bank Holiday Mons, 2 – 5.30pm. Coach parties and tours by arrangement ★ Entrance: £2, children 50p

Set in the Norfolk Broads area, the gardens are amply supplied with water and streams. For mid-May and early June the rhododendrons and azaleas, many rare varieties, are spectacular, dominating and scenting the woodland walks. The formal walled garden, planted and enclosed in 1936, with herbaceous borders of that period, is now in the process of additional planting. A delightful gardener's cottage is set picturesquely in one corner, covered in roses. The adjoining walled kitchen garden is a good example of traditional vegetable planting, with herbaceous plants from the garden for sale. The entrance to the two walled gardens has an intriguing iron gate in the shape of a spider, hence the formal garden is called 'The Spider Garden'. A water garden, leading to the lake, has good water plants, vast examples of *Gunnera manicata*, peltiphyllums, hostas and good stands of bamboos. The whole area is laced with streams and interesting bridges, adding calm and reflection at every corner. Birds, both migratory and native, abound.

HOW HILL FARM ★ 16
Ludham, Norfolk. Tel: (01692) 678558

Mr P.D.S. Boardman ★ 2m W of Ludham. Follow signs to How Hill, Farm Garden S of How Hill ★ Parking ★ Refreshments ★ Toilet facilities ★ Partly suitable for wheelchairs ★ Open 14th May, 2 – 5pm. Party visits at other times by arrangement ★ Entrance: £1.50, children free

The garden around the farm is comparatively conventional except for a large Chusan palm planted in a dog cage from which it threatens to escape. Here, too, is a collection of over 50 varieties of *Ilex aquifolium* as well as many rare species of the holly genus. Over the road in the river valley is a rich combination of exotics mingled with native vegetation. Around a series of pools, banks of azaleas merge into reed beds, rhododendron species rise over thickets of fern and bramble, wild grasses skirt groves of the giant *Arundo donax*, with birches and conifers against a background of a recently-created three-acre broad, thick with water lilies. The soil in places is exceptionally acid, as low as pH 2.8, other parts vary up to pH 7.5, supporting a wide variety of trees and shrubs.

LAKE HOUSE WATER GARDENS 17
Brundall, Norwich, Norfolk.

Mr and Mrs Garry Muter ★ 5m E of Norwich. From A47 roundabout take Brundall turn and turn right at T-junction into Postwick Lane ★ Best season: May ★ Limited parking ★ Refreshments: tea and biscuits ★ Dogs on lead ★ Unusual plants for sale ★ Open 16th, 17th, 30th April, 1st May, 11am – 5pm. Coach parties by appointment ★ Entrance: £2

An acre of water gardens set in a steep cleft in the river escarpment unsuitable for the infirm and young children. From the top of the hill the gardens fall away to a lily-covered lake at the bottom. They were once part of a 76-acre private estate and arboretum planted about 1880. The fascinating history has been researched and written by the owners and can be purchased by visitors. This is a feature throughout the whole garden, reflecting Mrs Muter's talent as a flower arranger. Surrounding the formal gardens are drifts of primroses, bluebells and daffodils in season; wild flowers abound. The formal planting has many rare and interesting species. *Zantedeschia* 'Green Goddess' and 'Crowborough' in a large clump cool down a flamboyant *Hemerocallis* 'Frans Hals'. A pale blue galega blends with *Hydrangea* 'Quadricolor' – a combination of lettuce-green-edged leaves and pink and blue flowers. A wide variety of hardy geraniums bloom in succession and a good collection of hybrid helianthemums in June.

LEXHAM HALL   18
King's Lynn, Norfolk. Tel: (01328) 701288/701341; Fax (01328) 700053

Mr and Mrs Neil Foster ★ 2m W of Litcham off B1145 ★ Best season: spring/summer ★ Parking ★ Refreshments: teas and lunches ★ Toilet facilities ★ Suitable for wheelchairs ★ Plants for sale ★ Open 28th May and May to July by appointment for parties ★ Entrance: £3

The seventeenth- and eighteenth-century hall sits well amid beautiful parkland with sheep and interesting trees. The ground falls away to the river forming a lake, and canals crossed by elegant bridges, largely the creation of the Wodehouse and Keppel families. The garden was the inspiration of the present owner's mother who, with the help of Dame Sylvia Crowe, laid out the bones of the garden; massive yew hedges reveal intimate views of the park, taking the eye to the distance beyond; wide terracing to the south of the house, well-planted and colourful, and a long grass walk edged with herbaceous plants and shrubs progressing to woodland full of rhododendrons, azaleas and spring bulbs. Colourful rose garden. The kitchen garden, maintained in the old style, has an early eighteenth-century crinkle-crankle wall covered with fruit, a cutting border, greenhouses with plants for the house and tender vegetables, the whole a picture of health. A wood to the south, always known as the American Gardens, is reputedly planted from seeds collected in America.

MANNINGTON HALL ★   19
Nr Saxthorpe, Norfolk. Tel: (01263) 3874175

Lord and Lady Walpole ★ 18m NW of Norwich, signposted at Saxthorpe off B1149 ★ Best season: June/July ★ Parking ★ Refreshments ★ Toilet facilities ★ Suitable for wheelchairs ★ Plants for sale ★ Shop ★ Open April to Oct, Sun, 12 noon – 5pm, also June to Aug, Wed – Fri, 11am – 5pm ★ Entrance: £2.50, OAP and students £2, children free

The romantic appearance of this garden of 20 acres is only matched in Norfolk by Elsing Hall where the house is also of the fifteenth century. Lawns run down to the moat which is crossed by a drawbridge to herbaceous borders backed by high walls of brick and flint. The moat also encloses a secret, scented garden in a design derived from one of the ceilings of the house. Outside the moat are borders of flowering shrubs flanking a Doric temple, and beyond are woodlands containing the ruins of a Saxon church and nineteenth-century follies to deceive the visitor, if only temporarily. Within the walls of the former kitchen garden, a series of rose gardens has been planted following the design of gardens from medieval to modern times and featuring roses popular at each period. A lake, woods and meadowland with extensive walks are other features.

NORFOLK LAVENDER 20
Caley Mill, Heacham, King's Lynn, Norfolk.
Tel: (01485) 570384; Fax: (01485) 571176

Norfolk Lavender Ltd ★ 13m N of King's Lynn on A149 ★ Best season: June to Sept ★ Parking ★ Refreshments ★ Toilet facilities ★ Suitable for wheelchairs ★ Plants for sale ★ Shop ★ Open all year except two-week Christmas holiday ★ Entrance: free

Here is the National collection of lavenders (Norfolk), displaying many of the species and varieties which can be grown in this country, set in two acres around a nineteenth-century watermill on the banks of the Heacham river. The fields of lavender are a fine sight in July and August, and there is also a rose garden and a herb garden.

THE OLD RECTORY 21
Holt, Norfolk. Tel: (01263) 712204

Lady Harrod ★ ½m W of Holt on A148 ★ Parking ★ Refreshments ★ Partly suitable for wheelchairs ★ Plants for sale ★ Open two Tues in late Feb/ early March (please telephone for details) ★ Entrance: £2 inc. coffee

As Lucinda Lambton remarks, 'the countryside has been woven into this garden in the most wild and wonderful way'. A meadow full of wild orchids is by the gate, laurels have grown into shady groves, a fast-flowing stream emerges from a rushy pool to make its way into the heart of the garden and then to disappear into a mysterious long-hidden moat. Banks of cow parsley rise above it. There is a walled garden where old roses and vegetables mingle. But it is in late winter that this garden should be seen, when a carpet of snowdrops spreads over the wooded hillside which rises above the stream.

THE OLD VICARAGE ★ 22
East Ruston, Nr Stalham, Norfolk. Tel: (01603) 632350 (daytime)

Graham Robeson and Alan Gray ★ N of Stalham beside East Ruston church ★ Parking ★ Partly suitable for wheelchairs ★ Plants sometimes for sale ★ Open 7th June to 25th Oct, Wed, 2.30 – 5pm and by appointment for coach parties ★ Entrance: £2.50

The profusion of plants in this garden has to be seen to be believed and because of its coastal setting, many are semi-hardy. Rare plants are everywhere with an artistic slant, and the value of theatre in the garden is not forgotten with tall dark hedges with openings beckoning the visitor on to yet further discoveries from box parterre to sunken garden, superb double herbaceous borders and, one of the most striking elements, the tropical border. How rare to find bananas growing one and a half miles from the North Sea, their leaves intact, surrounded by equally luxurious foliage of cannas and many other exotics. Outside the formal gardens surrounding the house, the Norfolk countryside opens up to several churches and the Happisburgh lighthouse which become focal points, with avenues of trees or simply a vista to stumble upon. Wild flower meadows and borders contain rare and interesting shrubs, many from the southern hemisphere. It is hard to believe that this garden has been created by the owners within the last 11 years.

OXBURGH HALL   23
Oxborough, Nr King's Lynn, Norfolk. Tel: (01366) 328258

The National Trust ★ 7m SW of Swaffham off A134 ★ Parking ★ Refreshments ★ Toilet facilities ★ Suitable for wheelchairs ★ Shop ★ House open as garden, 1 – 5pm (Bank Holiday Mons, 11am – 5pm) ★ Garden open 25th March to 5th Nov, daily except Thurs and Fri, 12 noon – 5.30pm ★ Entrance: £2 (hall and garden £3.80, pre-booked parties £3 per person)

The neat gardens of this fine moated house, carefully tended by The National Trust, lack the romantic appeal of Elsing or Rainthorpe, but there are some good trees, pleasant lawns, and well-stocked herbaceous borders. On the east side of the house is a parterre with bedding plants in colour masses, said to be of French design but somewhat modest by French standards and, while worth inspecting, somehow seeming inappropriate. However, the house has been lived in by the Bedingfeld family since 1482 and it is pleasant to muse on their past while walking through the woods.

THE PLANTATION GARDEN   24
4 Earlham Road, Norwich, Norfolk.
Tel: (01603) 611669 (Mrs E. Bickerton)

Plantation Garden Preservation Trust ★ Entrance off Earlham Road, behind The Beeches Hotel ★ Best season: summer ★ Partly suitable for wheelchairs ★ Open mid–April to Oct, Suns, 2 – 5pm and special openings three times a year. Groups by arrangement ★ Entrance: £1, accompanied children free (£1.50 special openings). Group visits £15 minimum (1994 prices)

An Italianate, high-Victorian garden of the 1850s undergoing restoration. Design influenced by Sir Charles Barry's garden at Shrubland Park (see entry for Shrubland Hall, Suffolk), was created by Henry Trevor in a disused chalk quarry just outside the city's St Giles Gate (now demolished). Framed by mature trees, the garden is a series of terraces linked by architectural features combining classical and Gothic elements. An extraordinary conglomeration of materials is used: industrial waste, brick ornaments, flint and stone, in medieval (randon-rubble) constructional method. A multi-tiered fountain some 30 feet high replaces the lost palm house as a focal feature. Conservation and restoration of this garden is an on-going process. It is also an area of ecological interest with lime-loving wild flowers, birds and is Grade II English Heritage registered.

RAVENINGHAM HALL ★   25
Raveningham, Norwich, Norfolk. Tel: (0150846) 222

Sir Nicholas Bacon ★ 14m SE of Norwich off A146, left at Hales on B1136, then first right ★ Parking ★ Refreshments ★ Toilet facilities ★ Suitable for wheelchairs ★ Plants for sale ★ Open April to Sept, Suns and Bank Holidays, 2 – 5pm, Wed, 1 – 4pm. Nursery open all year, weekdays; also Sats from March to Oct, and Suns and Bank Holidays Easter to mid–Sept ★ Entrance: £2, children free

This garden, in a fine landscaped park, has a rich variety of trees, shrubs and herbaceous plants dating from the eighteenth century to the present day. There is a large collection of galanthus species and varieties. The walled kitchen garden and greenhouses are still in use, and the associated nurseries offer an exceptional range of shrubs, climbers and herbaceous plants, many rarely available elsewhere. An arboretum is being developed, and a herb garden will be completed in 1995.

SANDRINGHAM HOUSE ★ 26
Sandringham, King's Lynn, Norfolk. Tel: (01553) 772675

H.M. The Queen ★ 9m NE of King's Lynn on B1440 near Sandringham Church ★ Best seasons: spring and autumn ★ Parking ★ Refreshments in restaurant and tea room ★ Toilet facilities ★ Suitable for wheelchairs ★ Plants for sale ★ Shop ★ House open as garden but closed 19th July to 4th Aug ★ Ranger's Interpretation Centre and country park ★ Garden open 13th April to 1st Oct (except 23rd July to 3rd Aug), daily, 11am (12 noon on Sun) – 4.45pm ★ Entrance: £2.50, OAP £2.00, children £1.50 (house and grounds £3.50, OAP £2.50, children £2.00) (1994 prices)

The house stands among broad lawns with an outer belt of woodland through which a path runs past plantings of camellias, hydrangeas, cornus, magnolias and rhododendrons with some fine specimen trees including *Davidia involucrata* and *Cercidiphyllum japonicum*. The path passes the magnificent cast and wrought iron 'Norwich Gates' of 1862. In the open lawn are specimen oaks planted by Queen Victoria and other members of the Royal Family. To the south-west of the house is the upper lake whose eastern side is built up into a massive rock garden using blocks of the local carrstone, and now largely planted with dwarf conifers. Below the rock garden, opening onto the lake, is a cavernous grotto, intended as a boathouse, while above is a small summerhouse built for Queen Alexandra. There are thick plantings of hostas, agapanthus and various moisture-loving plants around the margin of the lake. The path passes between the upper and largest lower lake set in wooded surroundings. To the north of the house is a garden designed by Sir Geoffrey Jellicoe for King George VI. A long series of beds is surrounded by box hedges and divided by gravel and grass paths and is flanked by avenues of pleached lime, one of which is centred on a gold-plated statue of a Buddhist divinity.

SHERINGHAM PARK ★ 27
Upper Sheringham, Norfolk. Tel: (01263) 823778

The National Trust ★ 4m NE of Holt off A148 ★ Best season: May/June ★ Parking ★ Refreshments at Felbrigg Hall (also NT) during their opening hours (see entry) ★ Partly suitable for wheelchairs ★ Dogs on lead in park ★ Park open daily, dawn – dusk ★ Entrance: £2.30 per car inc. parking and all occupants. Coaches £6.90 (book in advance with Warden)

Sheringham Park stands in a secluded valley at the edge of the Cromer/Holt ridge, close to the sea but protected from its winds by steep wooded hills. Both house and park are now the property of The National Trust although the house remains in private occupation. The park is remarkable not only for its great beauty and spectacular views but also for an extensive collection of rhododendrons which thrive in the acid soil. Crowning an eminence is a classical temple based on a design by Repton and erected to mark the 70th birthday of Mr Thomas Upcher, the last descendant of the original owner to live at Sheringham. This is the favourite and best-preserved work of Repton.

THRIGBY HALL WILDLIFE GARDENS 28
Filby, Great Yarmouth, Norfolk. Tel: (01493) 369477

Mr K.J. Sims ★ 6m NW of Great Yarmouth, signposted at Filby on A1064 ★ Best season: summer ★ Parking ★ Refreshments ★ Toilet facilities ★ Suitable for wheelchairs ★ Shop ★ Open daily, 10am – 6pm or dusk ★ Entrance: £4.40, OAP £3.90, children £2.60

The chief attraction of these gardens is a collection of Chinese plants arranged to form the landscape of the Willow Pattern plate, complete with pagodas and bridges across a small lake. Complementing the collection of Asiatic animals, the plants are those particularly associated with temple gardens and include *Gingko biloba*, *Pinus parviflora*, *Paeonia suffruticosa*, *Nandina domestica* and *Chimonobambusa quadrangularis*, set against a background of willows of many species. Otherwise Thrigby is a wildlife park with many facilities for children.

WRETHAM LODGE ★ 29
East Wretham, Thetford, Norfolk. Tel: (01953) 498366

Mrs A. Hoellering ★ 6m NE of Thetford off A1075. Left by village sign, right at crossroads then bear left ★ Best season: April to July ★ Parking ★ Home-made teas ★ Toilet facilities ★ Suitable for wheelchairs ★ Plants for sale ★ Open 30th April, 7th May and one Sunday in summer, 2.30 – 5.30pm and by appointment. Parties by appointment ★ Entrance: £1.50, children free (1994 price)

Extensive lawns surround the handsome flint-built former rectory set in its own walled park. There are wide, mixed borders around the house and within the walled kitchen garden; hundreds of old, species and climbing roses are massed in informal beds and cover the high flint walls. There are espalier and fan-trained fruit trees and a large indoor fig. Many unusual vegetables are grown in the well-tended kitchen garden. In the spring there is a display of daffodils (Daffodil walk on 2nd April, 11am – 6pm) and many varieties of specie tulip. A wide grassy walk runs round the park through a range of mature and recently established trees where spring-flowering bulbs are naturalised, with a mass display of bluebells and narcissi in May.

NORTHAMPTONSHIRE

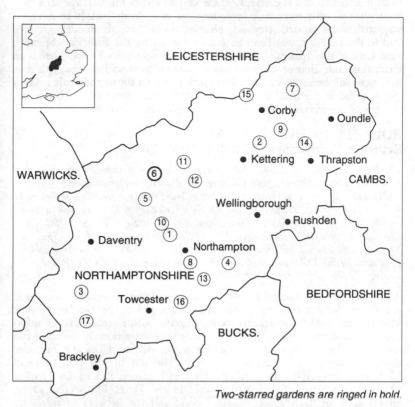

LEICESTERSHIRE

⑮

⑦

● Corby

● Oundle

⑨

② ⑭

WARWICKS.

⑪

⑥

● Kettering ● Thrapston

⑫

CAMBS.

⑤

Wellingborough

⑩

● Rushden

①

● Daventry

⑧ ● Northampton

④

NORTHAMPTONSHIRE ⑬

③

Towcester ⑯

BEDFORDSHIRE

⑰

BUCKS.

Brackley ●

Two-starred gardens are ringed in bold.

ALTHORP HOUSE 1
Althorp, Northampton, Northamptonshire.
Tel: (01604) 770107 (house and park office)

Earl and Countess Spencer ★ W of Northampton on A428 Northampton – Rugby
road ★ Parking ★ Teas ★ Toilet facilities ★ Suitable for wheelchairs ★ Shop ★
House open ★ Gardens open 14th to 17th April and Aug, daily, 1 – 5.30pm.
Please telephone for further opening times and events ★ Entrance: £4.50, OAP
£3.50, disabled persons in wheelchairs free, children under 15 £2.50 (1994 prices)

The main attraction of Althorp, the family home of the Princess of Wales, is
the fine house (largely remodelled after 1786 from the original Elizabethan
building) with its collections of pictures, furniture and china brought together
over the centuries by the Spencer family. Early prints suggest that the original formal gardens were swept away during the fashionable eighteenth-
century improvements by the architect Henry Holland, helped by Samuel
Lapidge, 'Capability' Brown's assistant. The present gardens were laid out in
the 1860s by the architect W.M. Teulon and enclosed by stone walls and

balustrades. Blue-painted Versailles boxes containing clipped bay trees enhance the courtyard. To the side and rear the gardens are also mainly laid to lawn, although this is currently under development. To date five beds have been planted with roses and lavender, and two shrub beds with a raised octagonal shape created. Beyond, pleasant walks through wooded grounds lead to the lake and the Temple, bought for £3 by the fifth Earl Spencer, First Lord of the Admiralty, from the garden of Admiralty House. Here is an interesting collection of conifers and deciduous trees and shrubs with new specimens still being added. The large park in which sheep and cattle graze is still managed in the traditional way. It contains many trees which commemorate family anniversaries. It is the venue for various public events.

BOUGHTON HOUSE GARDEN 2
Kettering, Northamptonshire. Tel: (01536) 515731

The Duke and Duchess of Buccleuch and Queensberry ★ Signposted off A43, N of Kettering, between Weekley and Geddington ★ Parking ★ Refreshments: light snacks and teas during weekends and daily in Aug; at other times by appointment ★ Toilet facilities inc. disabled ★ Suitable for wheelchairs ★ Dogs on lead in park only ★ Plants for sale ★ Shop ★ House open Aug to 1st Sept, 2 – 5pm (last admission 4.30pm) ★ Grounds open May to Sept, daily except Fri, 1 – 5pm. Specialist and educational groups welcome at other times by prior arrangement ★ Entrance: £1.50, OAP and students 75p (house and grounds £4, OAP and students £2.50) (1994 prices)

Although with only limited formal gardens remaining, Boughton House will nonetheless be attractive to garden enthusiasts and the whole family. The large sixteenth- and seventeenth- century house, with a strong French influence and monastic origins, contains an extensive collection of paintings and furniture. The magnificent surrounding park, with its lakes and canalised river, and avenues of trees, was originally laid out by the first Duke of Montagu before 1700 with the help of a Dutch gardener, Van der Meulen, who had experience of reclamation work in the Fens. The second Duke, known as 'John the Planter', added a pond and the network of rides and avenues of elms and limes in the 1720s. These avenues originally extended to 70 miles before Dutch elm disease took its toll. The limited planting close to the house includes herbaceous borders and some fine planted vases. To the south of the house a small circular rose garden leads on to the outstanding rectangular lily pond, beyond which the walled garden houses a long herbaceous border and the well-stocked nursery and plant shop. In the 350–acre park there are walks and trails, including one for the disabled, and a woodland adventure play area for children.

CANONS ASHBY HOUSE ★ 3
Canons Ashby, Nr Daventry, Northamptonshire.
Tel: (01327) 860044

The National Trust ★ 6m S of Daventry. Easy access from either M40/ M1/ A5 (please phone for details) ★ Parking 200 yards from house. Disabled telephone in advance and park near house ★ Refreshments: light lunches and teas ★ Toilet facilities ★ Wheelchairs available. Taped guide for visually handicapped visitors ★ Dogs on lead in home paddock only ★ House open ★ Garden and brewhouse open

*April to Oct, Sat to Wed inc. Bank Holiday Mon (but closed 14th April),
1 – 5.30pm or dusk if earlier (last admission 5pm) ★ Entrance: garden free
(house and garden £3.20, children £1.60, family ticket £8. Reductions for
pre-booked parties)*

This well-maintained garden is being extensively restored by The National
Trust. Formal with axial arrangements of paths and terraces, high stone
walls, lawns and gateways, it dates almost entirely from the beginning of the
eighteenth century. Borders with majestic plants such as acanthus and giant
thistles. Yew court with fine topiary. Old varieties of pear, apple, plum trees
and soft fruit. Cedar planted in 1715. Espaliers grown from original stock
planted by Edward Dryden, whose family owned the house.

CASTLE ASHBY GARDENS ★ 4
Castle Ashby, Northamptonshire. Tel: (01604) 696696

*The Marquess of Northampton ★ 5m E of Northampton, between A45
Northampton – Wellingborough road and A428 Northampton – Bedford road ★
Best seasons: March to May, July to Sept ★ Parking ★ Refreshments at tea
rooms in village, 400 yards ★ Suitable for wheelchairs but paths not very smooth
★ Dogs on lead ★ Plants for sale ★ Farm shop and Rural Craft Centre in village
★ 'Country Fair', first week July ★ Gardens open daily, 10am – dusk, with
occasional closures for events. Tours for parties by appointment ★ Entrance: £2,
OAP and children £1 (tickets from machine when entrance unattended)*

Originally Elizabethan, then a park landscaped by 'Capability' Brown, and
later a Matthew Digby Wyatt Terrace, Italian garden and arboretum, Castle
Ashby is now primarily an 'all function centre' for company and private
events. There is public access to most of the gardens (except East terrace
although good views from near the church) which present a glorious combination of views. A nature walk past mature trees leads over a terracotta
bridge and to the 'knucklebone arbour', a summerhouse with what are probably sheep or deer knuckles set in the floor. Among the wild and naturalised
plants are carpets of aconites and snowdrops, winter heliotropes, butterburs,
daffodils, bluebells, wood anemones, celandines, bush vetches, wood butter-
cups and a wide selection of lake and pondside plants. Features include an
orangery and archway greenhouses, topiary and well-planted large vases.
Restoration of the garden and its architectural features is continuing.

COTON MANOR GARDENS 5
Ravensthorpe, Northamptonshire. Tel: (01604) 740219

*Mr and Mrs Ian Pasley-Tyler ★ 10m N of Northampton, signposted on A428
and A50 ★ Parking ★ Home-made lunches and teas ★ Toilet facilities ★ Partly
suitable for wheelchairs ★ Dogs on lead ★ Unusual plants and shrubs for sale ★
Shop ★ Open 16th April to 9th Oct, Wed – Sun and Bank Holiday Mons, 12
noon – 6pm ★ Entrance: £2.70, OAP £2.20, children £1*

Abundant natural spring water keeps this 10-acre garden looking green and
fresh even during a very dry summer. Separated by hedges, a series of garden
areas and water features occupy the slopes and terraces below the house. The
garden dates from the 1920s and is still being developed by the third generation of the family: new features include an attractive herb garden. The excel-

lent herbaceous borders display interest throughout the summer, while the emphasis on foliage in the woodland and water gardens will inspire visitors with similar conditions in their own gardens. Maintenance standards are high throughout. The waterfowl collection is mainly kept in the Goose Park and the orchards and dells at the bottom of the site.

COTTESBROOKE HALL ★★ 6
Cottesbrooke, Northampton, Northamptonshire. Tel: (01604) 505808

Captain and Mrs J. Macdonald-Buchanan ★ 10m N of Northampton between A50 and A508 (A14 – A1/M1 link road) ★ Parking ★ Teas ★ Toilet facilities ★ Unusual plants for sale ★ House open ★ Gardens open 20th April to Sept, Thurs only. Also Bank Holiday Mons Easter to Aug, 2 – 5.30pm (last admission 5pm). Parties by appointment when possible ★ Entrance: £2.50, children £1.25 (house and gardens £3.50)

An excellently-maintained formal garden surrounding a fine Queen Anne house, set in a large park (also open) with lakes and a stream, vistas and avenues. Design and planting work by Edward Schultz, Geoffrey Jellicoe, Sylvia Crowe and the late Hon. Lady Macdonald-Buchanan is being continued by the present owners and their head gardener, Mrs Daw. The result is a series of delightful enclosed courtyards and gardens around the house with superb borders, urns and statues. Be sure to visit the intriguingly-named Dilemma garden, and to examine the Statue Walk. The spinney garden is at its best in spring with bulbs and azaleas. New trees, borders, yew hedges, walls, gates and vistas have only recently been added. Beyond the thatched Wendy house the wild garden surrounds a series of small lakes and cascades, with azaleas, rhodendrons, acers, cherries, spring bulbs and wild flowers. The magnolia, cherry and acer collections and the ancient cedars are notable. The house contains fine paintings, including distinguished Stubbs, and was possibly the model for Jane Austen's Mansfield Park.

DEENE PARK 7
Corby, Northamptonshire. Tel: (01780) 450278/450223

Mr Edmund Brudenell ★ 6m N of Corby off A43 Kettering to Stamford road ★ Parking ★ Teas ★ Toilet facilities ★ Partly suitable for wheelchairs ★ Dogs in car park only ★ Shop ★ House open ★ Gardens open 16th, 17th April, 7th, 8th, 28th, 29th May; then June to Aug, Suns and 28th Aug, all 2 – 5pm. Groups by appointment ★ Entrance: £2, children £1 (house and gardens £3.50, children £1)

The glory of Deene, which was created by generations of the Brudenell family, is its trees. Fine mature specimens and groups fringe the formal areas and frame tranquil and enchanting views of the parkland and countryside. Main features of its garden are the long borders, old-fashioned roses and the lake. The gardens, parkland, church and house together provide a delightful, interesting and relaxing afternoon for visitors in what was the home of the Earl of Cardigan who led the Charge of the Light Brigade in 1854.

DELAPRE ABBEY 8
London Road, Northampton, Northamptonshire.
Tel: (01604) 761074

Northampton Borough Council Leisure Department ★ 1m S of Northampton on

A508 ★ Best season: summer ★ Parking ★ Toilet facilities ★ Suitable for wheelchairs ★ Dogs on lead ★ Open March to Sept, daily, 10am − sunset. Park open all year ★ Entrance: free

Largely rebuilt in the seventeenth century, the house on the site of the former nunnery of St Mary of the Meadow, together with 500 acres of land, passed into public ownership in 1946. With improving standards of maintenance (although some associated buildings are in need of repair) it is still possible to glimpse the hey-day of a lovely garden. Beyond the walled former kitchen garden well-tended lawns, perennial, annual and rose beds and an eighteenth-century thatched game larder are walks through the wilderness garden with fine trees, shrubberies and lily ponds. There are lakes and a golf course in the park, and at the roadside close to the entrance, one of the Queen Eleanor Crosses commemorates the funeral procession in 1290 of Edward I's queen.

HILL FARM HERBS   9
Park Walk, Brigstock, Northamptonshire. Tel: (01536) 373694

Eileen and Mike Simpson ★ 8m from Kettering via A43. 5m from Corby, 6m from Thrapston. Signposted in Brigstock, just off A6116 ★ Best season: early summer ★ Parking ★ Refreshments: in tearoom 14th April to Sept ★ Toilet facilities ★ Suitable for wheelchairs ★ Plants for sale ★ Shop with wide range of herbs, dried flowers and pots ★ Open daily except 25th, 26th Dec, 10.30am − 5.30pm (Nov to Feb 4.30pm) ★ Entrance: free

Hill Farm Herbs is set at the back of an old stone farmhouse. Many herbs and cottage garden plants are grown in a number of garden areas, some in informal cottage mixtures, others laid out with specific themes. Garden owners planning a new or remodelled cottage or herb garden will find these areas a great inspiration. Many of the plants are available for sale. Two new garden areas are the Cook's garden, a small formal garden full of culinary herbs and the Lavender and Thyme garden, an informal garden, designed to display a wide range of herbs.

HOLDENBY HOUSE GARDENS   10
Holdenby, Northampton, Northamptonshire. Tel: (01604) 770074

Mr and Mrs James Lowther ★ 7m NW of Northampton, signposted A50 and A428 ★ Parking ★ Refreshments: home-made teas. Meals by appointment ★ Toilet facilities ★ Partly suitable for wheelchairs ★ Dogs on lead ★ Shop inc. croquet mallet hire ★ House open 17th April, 29th May, 28th Aug ★ Garden open (through the Falconry Centre) 4th April to Sept, Mon − Fri, 1 − 5pm, Sun, 2 − 6pm and Bank Holiday Mons, 1 − 6pm. Groups by appointment ★ Entrance: £2.75, OAP £2.25, children £1.75

Two grassed terraces, a fish pond and the palace forecourt with its original arches remain of the extensive Elizabethan garden which surrounded the vast mansion built by Elizabeth I's chancellor, Sir Christopher Hatton, in the late sixteenth century. The recent gardens still link the surviving remnant of the house (only one-eighth of its former size) to its past, especially the delightful Elizabethan garden, planted in 1980 by Rosemary Verey as a miniature replica of Hatton's original centrepiece, using only plants available in the 1580s. Other features include the fragrant border, part of the nineteenth-century garden also replanted by Mrs Verey, the Falconry Centre and some rare breeds of farm animals. Occasional events in the gardens on Bank Holiday weekends.

KELMARSH HALL 11
Kelmarsh, Northamptonshire. Tel: (01604) 686276

Miss C.V. Lancaster ★ On A508 5m S of Market Harborough, 11m N of Northampton ★ Best season: spring ★ Parking ★ Refreshments ★ Toilet facilities ★ Dogs on lead ★ Plants and produce for sale occasionally ★ James Gibb's Palladian house open with escorted visits ★ Garden open 16th April to 27th Aug, Sun and Bank Holidays, 2.15 – 5pm and by appointment (minimum 30 persons) ★ Entrance: £1.50, OAP and children over 12 £1, children under 12 free (house and garden) (1994 prices)

The drive is an avenue of lime trees bordering the park of 20 acres where a herd of rare British white cattle graze. Maze-like close-clipped box and yew hedges and colonnades lead to secret and quiet gardens with views of a lake. There are herbaceous borders and a rose garden. Seats are provided at vantage points and spring flowers and rhododendrons are special features. Keen gardeners will probably wish to visit only if they are combining it with a tour of the house. Nearby is the Haddonstone Show Garden, which those contemplating ornamental additions to their gardens may well wish to visit. The firm has been one of the most imaginative in producing replicas which sometimes are difficult to distinguish from the originals.

LAMPORT HALL GARDEN 12
Lamport, Northampton, Northamptonshire.
Tel: (01604) 686272

Lamport Hall Trust ★ 8m N of Northampton on A508 ★ Parking ★ Refreshments ★ Toilet facilities ★ Suitable for wheelchairs ★ Dogs on lead in picnic area only ★ Shop ★ Hall open ★ Garden open April to Sept, Sun and Bank Holiday Mons, 2.15 – 5.15pm. Details of other days available on request. Coach parties/groups at any time by arrangement ★ Entrance: £3, OAP £2.50, children £1.50 (house and gardens) (1994 prices)

The main attraction here is Lamport Hall itself, which organises gift, craft, antique and doll fairs every month except November. It also has a school study centre and agricultural museum. Its principal facade is by John Webb and the Smiths of Warwick. Grounds initially laid out by Gilbert Clarke in 1655 have been the subject of comprehensive restoration. There are now extensive herbaceous and mixed borders and lawns and the lily pond and rose garden are mature. Sir Charles Isham's local ironstone rockery, the home of the first garden gnome, has been painstakingly restored and his box bowers are growing back to their original style. The unusual shell and coral fountain at the centre of the Italian garden is in working order again after many years. There is also public access to the park.

THE MENAGERIE 13
Horton, Northamptonshire. Tel: (01604) 870957

Mr G. Jackson-Stops and Mr I. Kirby ★ 6m S of Northampton, on B526 turn left 1m S of Horton into field ★ Parking in field ★ Partly suitable for wheelchairs ★ Plants for sale ★ House open to parties of 20 or more by appointment ★ Garden and shell grotto open April to Sept, Thurs, 10am – 4pm and for parties of 20 or more by appointment ★ Entrance: £2.50, children £1

The informal approach through a farm gateway and across fields gives no hint of the delights of the fascinating journey beyond. This is a garden in the making with formal water gardens and wetlands surrounding the house, an eighteenth-century folly, where Lord Halifax had his private zoo. One of the most important surviving works of Thomas Wright of Durham, with magnificent rococo plasterwork in the salon, the house is open to parties by appointment. The garden is a recent development, very attractively situated with views across to where Horton Hall once stood. The central lime avenue, planted in the 1980s, leads to a mount with a spiral path up it and an obelisk on top, and the two hornbeam *allées* lead to eighteenth-century ponds with fountains. Two thatched arbours have just been built – one circular and classical, the other triangular and Gothic, with newly-planted shrubberies designed to hide them from the house in due course. The charming rose garden enclosed by yew hedges was designed by Vernon Russell-Smith in 1989. A most unusual garden, it is of great interest to see its 'grand scheme' developing.

THE OLD RECTORY ★   14
Sudborough, Kettering, Northamptonshire. Tel: (01832) 733247

Mr and Mrs Anthony Huntington ★ Off A6116 Corby – Thrapston road ★ Best season: April to July ★ Toilet facilities ★ Suitable for wheelchairs ★ Plants for sale occasionally ★ Open by appointment. Parties welcome ★ Entrance: £2 (£2.50 with tea and biscuits), children under 16 free

Delightful three-acre rectory garden in beautiful stone and thatch village. Much has been accomplished in recent years to develop a garden of interest to all throughout the year, with a fine collection of hellebores and many planted containers. Copious planting in the mixed borders, around the pond and many climbers. The vegetable garden (*potager*) is fascinating with small beds and brick paths leading to a central wrought-iron arbour. Standard roses, gooseberries and tents of runner beans provide vertical features. A small wild garden with interesting trees and a woodland walk along the stream completes the picture, with excellent labelling throughout.

ROCKINGHAM CASTLE GARDENS   15
Corby, Northamptonshire. Tel: (01536) 770240

Commander Michael Saunders Watson and family ★ 2m N of Corby on A6003. Signposted ★ Best seasons: April and June/July ★ Parking. Disabled may park near entrance ★ Teas ★ Toilet facilities ★ Partly suitable for wheelchairs ★ Dogs on lead ★ Shop ★ House open ★ Garden open 16th April to Sept, Sun and Thurs, Bank Holiday Mons and the Tues following, also Tues in Aug, 1.30 – 5.30pm. Groups by appointment at other times ★ Entrance: £2.30 (castle and gardens £3.80, OAP £3.20, children £2.30, family ticket (2 adults and 2 children) £10, parties of 20 or more £3.20 per person)

Rockingham sits on a hilltop fortress site with stunning views of three counties. Features remain from all periods of its 900-year history. The garden's major features range from formal seventeenth-century terraces and yew hedges to the romantic wild garden of the nineteenth century. There is a circular rose garden surrounded by a yew hedge and also good herbaceous borders. The wild garden was replanted with advice from Kew Gardens in the late 1960s and it includes over 200 species of trees and shrubs. The result is a delightful blend of form, colour, light and shade. Recommended for group/family outings and for those who combine interest in horticulture with history.

STOKE PARK   16
Stoke Bruerne, Towcester, Northampton, Northamptonshire.
Tel: (01604) 862172

Mr A.S. Chancellor ★ Clearly signposted from A5, N of Milton Keynes. ¼m W of village, opposite junction to Blisworth ★ Best season: summer ★ Parking ★ Suitable for wheelchairs ★ Dogs on lead ★ Pavilion open ★ Garden open June to Aug, weekends and 28th Aug, 2 – 6pm, rest of year by appointment ★ Entrance: £1

Stoke Park was the first house to display the Palladian plan in Britain but now (due to a fire) only the splendid pavilions with colonnaded walls remain. However, the svelte lawns, herbaceous borders, herb garden and a large fountain basin with water lilies are the features at Stoke Park which will be enjoyed by all who visit.

SULGRAVE MANOR   17
Sulgrave, Northamptonshire. Tel: (01295) 760205

Trustees, endowed by Colonial Dames of America ★ 7m NE of Banbury, 5m from M40 junction 11, 2m off B4525 ★ Parking ★ Refreshments sometimes available, otherwise at Thatched House Hotel opposite ★ Toilet facilities ★ Manor open ★ Garden open April to Oct, daily except Wed: weekends, Bank Holiday Mons and Aug, 10.30am – 1pm, 2 – 5.30pm, otherwise weekdays except Wed, 2 – 5.30pm; Nov, Dec and March, Sat, Sun and 27th to 29th Dec, 10.30am – 1pm, 2 – 4.30pm (last admission 1 hour before closing); also Nov, Dec, Feb and March, weekdays by appointment. Closed 19th June, 25th and 26th Dec and whole of Jan ★ Entrance: £3, children £1.50 (house and garden). Discounts for parties of 12 or more

The house was built in 1539 by a distant ancestor of George Washington, then acquired in 1914 and restored after World War I, with the benefit of U.S. generosity. All visitors are taken round the house in regularly organised conducted tours. The gardens, like the house, bear little relation to their sixteenth-century condition, but the rose garden, herb garden, herbaceous borders and kitchen garden are attractive examples of their kind, designed by Sir Reginald Blomfield (d. 1942), author of *The Formal Garden of England* and an opponent of Robinson (see also Godinton Park, Kent).

NORTHUMBERLAND

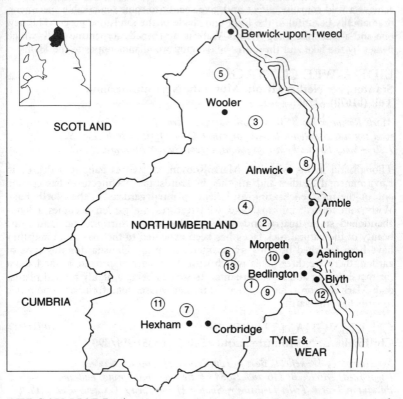

BELSAY HALL ★ 1
Belsay, Nr Newcastle-upon-Tyne, Northumberland.
Tel: (01661) 881636

English Heritage ★ 14m NW of Newcastle on A696 ★ Parking. Coaches please notify in advance ★ Refreshments: tea room, Easter to Sept, 11am – 5pm. Picnic area ★ Toilet facilities inc. disabled ★ Suitable for wheelchairs (available on loan) ★ Dogs on lead ★ Annual regional NCCPG plant sale usually held here in June ★ Shop ★ Hall and Castle open ★ Gardens open April to Oct, daily, 10am – 6pm, Nov to March, daily, 10am – 4pm. Closed 24th to 26th Dec and 1st Jan ★ Entrance: £2.40, OAP £1.80, children £1.20 (1994 prices)

The gardens are the creation of two men who between them owned the Hall in succession from 1795 to 1933. Sir Charles Monck built the severe Neo-Classical mansion with formal terraces leading through woods to a 'garden' inside the quarry from which the house was built. His grandson took over in 1867, adding Victorian features. Both were discerning plantsmen. The result is a well-cared-for collection of rare, mature and exotic specimens in a fascinating sequence. The terrace looks across to massed June rhododendrons.

Other areas (flower garden, magnolia terrace, winter-flowering heathers) lead to woods, a wild meadow and the quarry garden itself. Reminiscent of the ancient Greek quarries in Syracuse, it was carefully contrived and stocked to achieve a wild romantic effect and give shelter to some remarkable specimens, dramatically beautiful in the light and shade of the sandstone gorge. The new one-and-a-half-mile Crag Wood Walk is a stepped, serpentine walk which passes by the lake and through the hanging woodlands opposite the Hall.

BIDE-A-WEE COTTAGE ★ 2
Stanton, Nr Netherwitton, Morpeth, Northumberland.
Tel: (01670) 72262

Mark Robson ★ 3m SSW of Longhorsley. Turn off A697 Morpeth – Coldstream road towards Stanton ★ Plants for sale ★ Open April to 26th Aug, Sats only, 1.30 – 5pm. Parties by arrangement, except Suns ★ Entrance: £1.75

Though still in his twenties, Mark Robson, as well as gaining a degree in Environmental Studies and another in Landscape Architecture, has created one of the most enchanting and richly-planted gardens in the North East. With both formal, informal and wild features the garden occupies a long-abandoned stone quarry and some of the higher surrounding land. The beauty of the natural rock faces has been exploited to the maximum and they have been enriched by truly sympathetic planting. Unusual for this type of garden, there are three pools which with their margins provide a fine habitat for marsh-loving and aquatic plants. As well as being a highly refined plants-man Mark Robson is also a splendid mason whose stonework has done much to embellish the garden.

CHILLINGHAM CASTLE 3
Chillingham, Northumberland. Tel: (016685) 359/390

Sir Humphrey Wakefield, Bart ★ 12m NNW of Alnwick between A1 (signposted), A697, B6346 and B6348 ★ Best seasons: spring, midsummer ★ Parking ★ Teas ★ Toilet facilities ★ Shop ★ House open ★ Gardens open 14th to 17th April and May to Sept, daily except Tues, 1.30 – 5pm and in winter by appointment only ★ Entrance: £3.30, OAP £2.80, children over 5 £2.20, family (2 adults and 2 children) £9, parties of 20 or more £2.80 per person

Not easy to find but well worth an effort, this has been the family home of the Earls Grey and their relations since the 1200s. Sir Humphrey is vigor-ously restoring the castle along with the grounds, landscaped in 1828 by Wyatville (of Hampton Court and Windsor fame). The Elizabethan-style walled garden has been virtually excavated to rediscover its intricate pattern of clipped box and yew (enlivened by scarlet tropaeolum), with rose beds, central avenue and a spectacular herbaceous border the whole length of the garden. Outside are lawns and a rock garden, delightful woodland and lake-side walks through drifts of snowdrops and spring displays of daffodils, blue-bells and, later, rhododendrons.

CRAGSIDE HOUSE, GARDEN AND GROUNDS 4
Rothbury, Morpeth, Northumberland. Tel: (01669) 20333

The National Trust ★ 13m SW of Alnwick off A697 between B6341 and B6344

*★ Parking (select car park nearest to house) with ½m walk to Formal Garden ★
Refreshments: coffee, lunch and teas in Vickers Room Restaurant. Picnics in
grounds ★ Toilet facilities in Visitor Centre (away from garden) ★ Dogs on lead
in grounds only ★ Visitor Centre (inc. shop, Information Centre and Armstrong
Energy Centre) ★ House open as grounds, 1 – 5.30pm (last admission 4.45pm) ★
Grounds open April to Oct, daily except Mon (but open Bank Holiday Mons),
10.30am – 7pm, 4th Nov to 17th Dec, Tues, Sat and Sun, 10.30am – 4pm ★
Entrance: £3.50 (house, garden and grounds £5.50, family (2 adults and 2
children) £14)*

Lord Armstrong, one of the greatest of Victorian engineers, clothed this hillside above the Coquet Valley with millions of trees and shrubs as the setting
for a house designed by R. Norman Shaw (the first ever lit by hydro-elec-
tricity) that was then the wonder of the world. From the car park the path
(signposted 'Garden') affords views of the rock gardens below the house.
These have been cleared after years of neglect and are now planted with an
impressive display of heathers, shrubs and alpines. The path descends sharply
into the Debdon gorge, crosses the river by a rustic bridge (magnificent
views of the elegant iron bridge soaring above) and climbs through majestic
conifers to the Clock Tower (1864) which overlooks the Cragside Formal
Garden. This walled garden, laid out in 'high-Victorian' style, is set in three
terraces and is in the process of extensive restoration. On the upper terrace
are rock ferneries, grottoes and a small canal. The middle terrace contains the
imposing Orchard House (with its rotating fruit pots) to one side of which is
a carpet bed (7 x 59 feet) planted with small foliage plants in a formal star
and diamond pattern typical of the 1870s. The lower terrace is laid out and
planted in Italian style and is presided over by the cast iron rose loggia built
at Lord Armstrong's works and now planted with annuals. The walk back to
the car park impresses on the visitor the contrasting forces of a wild
Romanticism and industrial technology which influenced this estate in equal
measure.

ETAL MANOR 5
Etal, Nr Ford, Wooler, Northumberland. Tel: (0189082) 205

*Elizabeth, Lady Joicey ★ On the B6354 10m N of Wooler ★ Parking ★ Toilet
facilities ★ Partly suitable for wheelchairs ★ Dogs on lead ★ Open April to June,
Suns only, 1 – 6pm; Sept and Oct, Suns only, 11.30am – sunset ★ Entrance:
£1.50, children 25p, under 5 free*

It is delightful to stroll on the grass in this spacious woodland garden (the
house is 1748) under a canopy of fine old trees, discovering colourful vistas at
every turn. The interest in both spring and autumn is provided by many
different trees and shrubs giving great variety of colour in flower, leaf and
bark. In September and October drifts of autumn crocus add to the spectacular colour of the foliage.

HERTERTON HOUSE ★ 6
Hartington, Cambo, Morpeth, Northumberland. Tel: (0167074) 278

*Frank and Marjorie Lawley ★ 2m N of Cambo on B6342 ★ Best season: summer
★ Parking ★ Toilet facilities ★ Plants for sale ★ Open April to Sept, daily except
Tues and Thurs, 1.30 – 5.30pm ★ Entrance: £1.40*

The Lawleys took over this land and near-derelict Elizabethan building, with commanding views over picturesque upland Northumberland, in 1976. With vision and skill they have created three distinct areas. In front, a winter garden with tranquil vistas; alongside, a cloistered 'monastic' knot garden of mainly medicinal, occult and dye-producing herbs; and to the rear, their most impressive achievement, a flower garden with perceptively mingled hardy flowers chosen with an artist's eye. Many are unusual traditional plants (including many species from the wild) that flourish within the newly-built sheltering walls. A gem of a place, of great interest to the plantsperson.

HEXHAM HERBS ★ 7
The Chesters Walled Garden, Humshaugh, Nr Hexham, Northumberland. Tel: (01434) 681483

Kevin and Susie White ★ 5m N of Hexham, ½m W of Chollerford on B6318 ★ Best season: March to Sept ★ Parking ★ Refreshments: planned ★ Suitable for wheelchairs, if accompanied (gravel paths) ★ Plants for sale ★ Shop ★ Open March to Oct, daily, 10am – 5pm, reduced hours in winter. Also by appointment ★ Entrance: £1, children (under 10) free

The tall brick walls of the old kitchen garden slope gently south from the very line of Hadrian's Wall, echoing the Roman forts that lie to east and west. Within these ramparts, still with vestiges of the Victorian glasshouses and heating system, the Whites have fashioned a superb herb collection (over 900 varieties), including most fittingly a unique Roman garden with plants (myrtle, etc.) identified by archaeologists through pollen analysis. A major feature is the national NCCPG thyme and marjoram collections. A rose garden (over 60 species), extensive herbaceous borders (also some 1500 varieties) and terraced lawns against an architectural backdrop (Norman Shaw's Chesters mansion) fill out this splendid intriguing 'fort'. A new feature is a formal round pool with fountain set in a gravelled area with benches. A labelled wildflower meadow and woodland walk with pond are also open.

HOWICK HALL ★ 8
Howick, Northumberland. Tel: (01665) 577285

Lord Howick of Glendale (Howick Trustees Ltd) ★ 6m NE of Alnwick off B1339 ★ Best season: spring/summer ★ Parking ★ Toilet facilities ★ Partly suitable for wheelchairs ★ Open April to Oct, 1 – 6pm ★ Entrance: £1.50, children and concessions 75p (1994 prices)

Acquired by the Grey family in 1319, the accident of woodland which sheltered this site from the blasts of the North Sea enabled Lord and Lady Grey to come here during World War I and start building a fine collection of tender plants which would do credit to a Scottish west coast garden. The lower terrace has a pool and excellent borders and the lawns run down through feature shrubs to a stream. Winding paths lead through shrubbery or parkland to the 'Silverwood', under whose magnificent trees one passes among numerous fine shrubs and woodland flowers planted by Earl and Countess Grey from 1931, the year of their silver wedding. There are good varieties of rhododendron and azalea, and outstanding species hydrangea (*H. villosa*) apart from unusual flower varieties. A large pond-side garden is developing well. A catalogue of plants would be helpful. This is a plantsperson's garden but there are many delights for the aesthete such as the agapanthus of varying blues on the terrace. In early April visitors will be impressed by the spectacular view of drifts of daffodils in the meadow and parkland.

KIRKLEY HALL COLLEGE 9
Ponteland, Northumberland. Tel: (01661) 860808

11m NW of Newcastle off A696, right at Ponteland on C151 for 2½m. RAC signposted ★ Parking ★ Refreshments and picnic spots ★ Toilet facilities ★ Suitable for wheelchairs ★ Plants for sale ★ Open daily, 10am – dusk ★ Entrance: £1.50, OAP and children (8–16) 70p, family ticket £3, parties of 13 or more (no guide) £1.20 per person, guided tours of 13 or more by prior arrangement £2.50 per person (1994 prices)

The 10-acre grounds with their three-acre walled garden form a showcase for all the gardening arts from propagation onwards. Inside the walls are climbers, borders and bedding plants in profusion, all pleasingly grouped and labelled. The grounds contain a succession of beds, skilfully shaped to follow the rolling contours of the land, each carefully composed for variety of profile and continuity of colour. Then to the Hall with its outstanding array of beautifully-planted containers on terraces down to a most attractive sunken garden and a wildlife pond. National collections include beech, ivy and willow. The whole is thoroughly professional: all plants are labelled. Series of evening talks.

MELDON PARK 10
Morpeth, Northumberland. Tel: (01670) 72661

Mr and Mrs M.J.B. Cookson ★ 6m W of Morpeth on B6343 ★ Best season: early June ★ Parking ★ Light refreshments on Suns and Bank Holidays only ★ Toilet facilities, inc. disabled ★ Suitable for wheelchairs ★ House open ★ Garden open 27th May to 25th June, 26th to 28th Aug, 2 – 5pm ★ Entrance: £3, children 50p

When, in 1832, Newcastle glassmaster Isaac Cookson purchased a 700-acre estate enclosing a stretch of the steep Hartburn dene, he simply asked John Dobson to pick his spot and design the house. His trust was rewarded. Dobson built a broad plateau on which he planted a fine Neo-Classical house facing squarely south over terrace and ha-ha to the dene below. This was flanked by shrubberies and mature imported trees of which at least one fine cedar still survives – as does the serene charm of the original vision, a tribute to the continuing care of the Cookson family. Attractions include rose beds, a small orangery, woodland and wild meadow walks, and in particular the walled garden, quartered by pathways in part apple-hedged, where kitchen beds and venerable plums are accompanied by much innovative planting. Rose beds bordered by trim box hedges will give colour later, and there is a well-planted herbaceous border with an attractive variety of plants including notable peonies and iris on the east side of the house.

NUNWICK ★ 11
Simonburn, Nr Hexham, Northumberland.

Mr and Mrs L.G. Allgood ★ On B6320 3m N of Chollerford ★ Parking in field

★ ✩*Teas on open days* ★ *Toilet facilities* ★ *Partly suitable for wheelchairs* ★ *Dogs on lead* ★ *Open 18th June and for parties by appointment* ★ *Entrance: £1.50*

A 'very perfect house for its date' (1760) says Pevsner, though there are early nineteenth-century additions. It looks over lawns, a ha-ha and parkland with many fine trees. A short walk leads to the gardens – on one hand herbaceous borders sheltered by hedges of beech and shrub roses adjoining the orchard, and on the other a large Victorian walled kitchen garden. This is well-planted with many varieties of vegetables, the walls clothed with fruit trees and old roses, and colourful flower borders along the central paths. Rustic bridges cross the burn to a special feature of this garden – the eighteenth-century Gothic Kennels – planted with a spectacular collection of hostas in four 'rooms' open to the sky. Purple erinus, variegated ivy and toadflax cling to old walls. The woodland walk by the stream passes groups of newly-planted shrubs and trees (carefully-labelled) and a recently-created bog garden. Other features include an impressive collection of old stone troughs planted with alpines and a small orangery containing a large camellia over 100 years old.

SEATON DELAVAL HALL   12
Seaton Sluice, Near Whitley Bay, Northumberland.
Tel: (0191) 2373040/2371493

Lord Hastings ★ *10m NE of Newcastle, ¹/₂m inland from Seaton Sluice on A190* ★ *Best season: June to Aug* ★ *Parking* ★ *Refreshments: in tea room* ★ *Toilet facilities* ★ *Partly suitable for wheelchairs* ★ *Souvenir stall* ★ *Parts of house open* ★ *Garden open May to Sept, Wed, Sun and Bank Holiday Mons, 2 – 6pm* ★ *Entrance: £2, children 50p*

The original grounds of this architectural masterpiece by Vanbrugh no doubt matched its magnificence, but little is known save for an early painting showing a swan lake. A notable weeping ash survives from that time, and there is a venerable rose garden. Since 1948 an excellent parterre has been laid out, now embellished by a large Italianate pond and fountain. An attractive shrubbery (rhododendron, azalea, etc.) and herbaceous borders have also been established on the south side towards the fine Norman chapel. Replanting continues and the garden is obviously in good hands.

WALLINGTON ★   13
Cambo, Morpeth, Northumberland. Tel: (0167074) 283

The National Trust ★ *20m NW of Newcastle off A696 (signed on B6342)* ★ *Best season: spring – autumn* ★ *Parking* ★ *Refreshments: coffee, lunch and teas in Clock Tower Restaurant (0167074) 274. Picnics in car park* ★ *Toilet facilities inc. disabled* ★ *Suitable for wheelchairs. Two self-drive scooters available* ★ *Dogs on lead in garden, free in grounds* ★ *Shop* ★ *House and children's museum open April to Oct, daily, except Tues, 1 – 5.30pm (last admission 5pm)* ★ *Walled garden open April to Sept, daily, 10am – 7pm; Oct, daily, 10am to 6pm; Nov to March 1996, daily, 10am – 4pm (or dusk if earlier). Grounds open all year round during daylight hours* ★ *Entrance: £2.30, children £1.15 (house and grounds £4.60 children £2.30)*

The superb house in a 100-acre landscape of lawns, terraces and flowerbeds has an excellent walled garden, with a great variety of climbers. There is a garden house designed in Tuscan style by Daniel Garrett. Lancelot 'Capability' Brown, growing up locally, would have been aware of the first 'landscaping' works at Wallington and he later made partly-extended plans for a separate park on the estate at Rothley. The Victorian Peach House in the walled garden is now restored. Over 400 metres of new hedges have been planted. In the Edwardian conservatory is a great tree fuchsia planted in 1908 plus many other treasures. Outside, the walks step down from a classical fountain past beds re-designed by Lady Trevelyan in the 1930s, including notable heathers and many herbaceous varieties, through to the water meadow planted by the Duke of Atholl in 1738. Trees include a great larch, the survivor of six, by the China Pond. New circular walk. The Hall is steeped in the history of the Trevelyan family and is associated with Ruskin and the Pre-Raphaelite painters who assisted with its floral decorations.

GARDENING FOR THE DISABLED

Demonstration gardens to assist the disabled are available at a number of properties open to the public. These include the following:

Battersea Park, London. Horticultural Therapy Unit (Wandsworth Borough Council). Telephone for appointment (0171) 720 3419

Disabled and Older Gardeners' Association, Herefordshire Growing Point, Herefordshire College of Agriculture, Holme Lacy, Hereford. Tel: (01432) 870316

Hadlow College, Tonbridge, Kent. Telephone for appointment (01732) 850551

Park House Garden, Horsham, West Sussex

Royal Horticultural Society's Garden, Wisley (see *Guide* under Surrey)

Ryton Organic Gardens, Ryton-on-Dunsmore (see *Guide* under Warwickshire)

Syon Park, Middlesex (see *Guide* under London)

Open days for the disabled are also held from time to time at the following gardens:

Dolly's Garden (see *Guide* under London)

Hillsborough Community Development Trust (see *Guide* under South & West Yorkshire)

Iden Croft Herbs (see *Guide* under Kent)

The Gardening for Disabled Trust is a registered charity which collects donations from the public and uses them to assist disabled people with improvements to their gardens, or to supply equipment which will enable them to continue to garden. Donations should be sent to Mrs Felicity Seton, Hayes Farmhouse, Hayes Lane, Peasmarsh, Rye, East Sussex.

NOTTINGHAMSHIRE

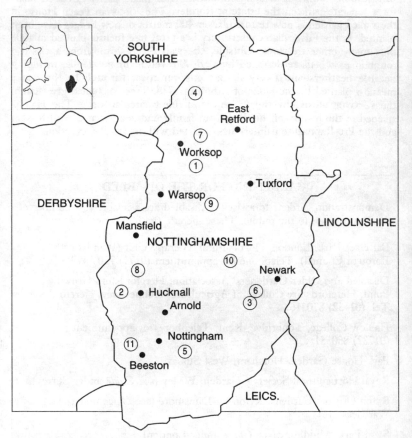

CLUMBER PARK 1
Clumber Estate Office, Clumber Park, Worksop, Nottinghamshire. Tel: (01909) 476592

The National Trust ★ 4¹/₂m SE of Worksop off A1 and A57, 11m from junction 30 off M1 ★ Parking ★ Refreshments: cafeteria and restaurant, daily, 10.30am – 5pm and in summer to 6pm ★ Toilet facilities ★ Partly suitable for wheelchairs (wheelchairs inc. those for children available) ★ Dogs ★ Plant sales centre open 27th March to 22nd Oct, 10.30am – 6pm ★ National Trust shop ★ Chapel open except 25th Dec, 10 – 4pm ★ Park always open during daylight hours. Garden, Vineries and Tools exhibition open April to Sept, Sat, Sun, Bank Holiday Mons, 10am – 5pm (last admission 4.30pm) ★ Entrance: 60p, children 30p. Vehicle charge for park: cars £2.50, coaches £6 (£12 at weekends and Bank Holidays). Bicycle hire

In 1707 the Park was enclosed from Sherwood Forest and the Dukes of

Newcastle had their seat here. Only the stable block, chapel and entrance gates remain as the great house was demolished in 1938. The National Trust purchased the park in 1946. The Lincoln terrace and pleasure gardens were laid out by William Sawrey Gilpin in the early nineteenth century. Twenty-five acres out of the 3800 acres of parkland are managed by just two garden-ers. The vinery and palm house has been restocked and the extensive glasshouses (450 feet) are the best and longest in The National Trust's prop-erties. The kitchen garden exhibition of late nineteenth-century and early twentieth-century tools is fascinating and reminds us that modern powered-garden tools have taken much of the heavy work out of gardening. The walled kitchen garden has a fruit and vegetable border, a herb border and a collection of old varieties of apple trees. The Lincoln terrace reached its height of excellence in the 1920s and after years of neglect has been restored. The cedar avenue has Atlantic cedars and sweet chestnut trees of breath-taking size enhance the pleasure grounds.

FELLEY PRIORY ★   2
Underwood, Jacksdale, Nottinghamshire. Tel: (01773) 810230/812056

The Hon. Mrs Chaworth Musters ★ From M1 junction 27, take A608 for Heanor and Derby and the garden is on the left, 1/2m W of M1 ★ Parking on open days in field adjacent ★ Refreshments on open days ★ Toilet facilities ★ Suitable for wheelchairs ★ Plant sales every Tues, Wed, Fri, 9.30am – 12.30pm and on other open days. Plant Fair 4th June, 12 noon – 4pm ★ Open March to Oct, second and fourth Weds in the month, 9am – 4pm; also 23rd April, 25th June for NGS, 11am – 5pm and by appointment for parties ★ Entrance: £1.50 on NGS days otherwise £1, children free

Despite the M1 being only half a mile away, above the house, but out of sight, the first impression is of a garden with quiet English countryside as a backdrop. The owners have, with the use of hedging, created several gardens within the one, the original ancient walls unifying the separate parts as well as providing shelter and support for many unusual and slightly tender shrubs and climbers. The new rose garden will be glorious when more mature – at present domed pergolas add instant height.

FLINTHAM HALL ★   3
Flintham, Nottinghamshire.

Mr Myles Thoroton Hildyard ★ 6m SW of Newark on A46 ★ Parking in adjacent field ★ Teas ★ Toilet facilities ★ Dogs on lead ★ Open one Sunday in June for charity and at other times by appointment ★ Entrance: £1.50, children 50p (1994 prices)

Do set aside plenty of time to visit this garden; it will not be wasted. The hall and extensive gardens are obviously loved and lavish amounts of time and effort are spent on them. It is therefore remarkable to learn that Michael Blagg is the sole gardener, though Mr Hildyard regularly attends to the gardens. The unique Victorian conservatory is a heady experience; the exotic plants and ornate architecture vying with each other for your attention. In the *Shell Guide to Nottinghamshire* it is described as the most spectacular in the country. It is only one of many surprises; the Regency pheasantry, recently imaginatively restored, has been frescoed by Ricardo Cinalli.

HODSOCK PRIORY ★ 4
Blyth, Worksop, Nottinghamshire. Tel: (01909) 591204

*Sir Andrew and Lady Buchanan ★ 2m from A1 at Blyth off B6045 Blyth –
Worksop road ★ Parking. Coaches must book ★ ☆Teas in the conservatory on
Suns only, unless pre-booked for 20 persons or more ★ Toilet facilities, inc.
disabled ★ Dogs in park only ★ Plants for sale ★ Open Feb to 1st March, daily
(weather permitting): weekends, 10am – 4pm, weekdays, 1 – 4pm; then April to
30th July, Sun, Tues, Wed, Thurs, 2 – 5pm (but closed 28th May) ★ Entrance:
£2, disabled persons in wheelchairs and accompanied children free. Discount for
pre-booked groups of 20 or more*

An historic five-acre private garden with Grade I listed gatehouse *c.* 1500 and
a dry moat. The part-acid, part-neutral soil allows a wide range of plants to
be grown here so that there is an unusual mix of garden styles. There are
fine trees including a huge cornus, a very old catalpa (Indian bean), tulip tree
and swamp cypress, and much replanting is going on so that there is a
profusion of flowers and interest all year round. In late winter, there is the
Snowdrop Spectacular, in the spring there are the bulbs (over a tonne of new
bulbs planted in 1994), and later, mixed borders with perennials and old
roses, the latter much admired. There is a special 'Lily Week' from 19th
July. Interesting holm oak hedge. Good walks, mainly grass, beyond the
small lake and bog garden and into the old moat, which are accessible to the
disabled. Some of the turn-of-the-century gravel paths have been restored,
and three new arbours have been built.

HOLME PIERREPONT HALL 5
Radcliffe-on-Trent, Nottinghamshire. Tel: (0115) 933 2371

*Mr and Mrs R. Brackenbury ★ 5m SE of Nottingham off A52/A6011.
Approach past the National Water Sports Centre and continue for 1½m ★
Parking ★ Teas. Other refreshments by prior arrangement ★ Toilet facilities ★
Suitable for wheelchairs ★ Dogs on lead ★ Shop ★ Hall open ★ Garden open 16th
to 18th April, 28th to 30th May; June, Suns; July, Thurs and Suns; Aug,
Tues, Thurs, Fri and Sun and Bank Holiday Mon, all 2 – 5.30pm. Groups by
appointment all year, inc. evening visits ★ Entrance: house and garden £3,
children £1*

The Hall is a medieval brick manor house but the listed garden and parterre
of 1875 have been restored by the present owners. The box parterre is the
outstanding feature of the gardens and the newly created herbaceous borders
next to the York stone path (replacing old rose beds) enhance the courtyard
garden further. (The Jacob sheep are very friendly lawnmowers.) Mr and
Mrs Brackenbury work hard with improvements to this peaceful house and
garden and willingly provide ample information. Their innovations include a
winter garden, outer east garden, yews, shrubs and roses.

MILL HILL HOUSE 6
**Elston Lane, East Stoke, Newark, Nottinghamshire.
Tel: (01636) 525460**

*Mr and Mrs R.J. Gregory ★ 5m S of Newark. Take A46, turn left into Elston
Lane (signposted to Elston) and the house is the first on the right ★ Parking 100*

yards past the house in nursery ★ Toilet facilities ★ Suitable for wheelchairs ★
Dogs on lead ★ Plants for sale ★ Open April to Oct, Wed – Sun, 10am – 6pm,
some of the Suns being for the NGS. Also by appointment. Groups welcome by
appointment ★ Entrance: £1, accompanied children free

A half-acre cottage garden generously filled with a wide variety of plants
provides year-round interest and tranquillity. The garden demonstrates how
to overcome the problems of an exposed northward-sloping site with an electricity pylon and marl subsoil. If you have similar obstacles, a visit to this
garden will uplift your spirits. The plants provide a wealth of propagating
material for the adjacent nursery.

MORTON HALL 7
Ranby, Retford, Nottinghamshire. Tel: (01777) 702530

Lady Mason ★ 4m W of Retford. Entrance on link road from A620 to
southbound A1 ★ Teas. Picnics permitted ★ Toilet facilities ★ Partly suitable for
wheelchairs ★ Dogs on lead ★ Morton Hall nurseries adjacent to garden ★ Open
9th April, 7th, 14th, 21st June, 15th Oct, 2 – 6pm ★ Entrance: £2 per car or
£1.25 per person whichever is the least

'The gardens are celebrated' wrote Henry Thorold in his *Shell Guide to*
Nottinghamshire. It is not surprising for there is a large number of mature and
rare specimen trees and shrubs in a relatively small park. They were planted
over 100 years ago by the Mason family, all amateur botanists. The well-
stocked nursery next to the gardens was started 30 years ago by Sir Paul and
Lady Mason and is run by Mrs McMaster. The soil is sandy and poor but
obviously suits the slightly more tender shrubs – romneyas thrive next to the
house. Enjoy the rare and unusual and the colours in spring and autumn in
this peaceful garden but do not expect immaculate lawns and flowerbeds.
The forestry walk features modern planting by William Mason, the present
landowner.

NEWSTEAD ABBEY ★ 8
Linby, Nottinghamshire. Tel: (01623) 793557

Nottingham City Council ★ 11m N of Nottingham on A60 ★ Parking ★
Refreshments: tea room in grounds open April to Sept ★ Toilet facilities ★ Partly
suitable for wheelchairs ★ Dogs on lead ★ Shop ★ House open at extra charge,
April to Sept, 12 noon – 6pm (last admission 5pm). Contains Byron memorabilia
and period rooms ★ Gardens open all year, daily, 10am – dusk ★ Entrance:
£1.35, children 65p (1994 prices)

Water predominates in this estate that the poet Byron inherited but could
rarely afford to live in. In most of the extensive and immaculate gardens
there is much of interest. The Japanese gardens are justly famous and the
rock and fern gardens worth visiting. Indeed the waterfalls, wildfowl, passage-
ways, grottos and bridges provide plenty of fun for children, but in addition
there is an excellent, imaginatively-equipped play area with bark mulch for
safety. The tropical garden and the monks' stewpond are visually uninterest-
ing but they are of laudable age. It is a pity that the large walled kitchen
garden is now a rose garden – rose gardens however pretty are commonplace,
but large kitchen gardens to the great houses are rare now and of more

interest. The old rose garden is now the iris garden – an insipid area with gladioli planted in the regular plots in an effort to liven up the place.

RUFFORD COUNTRY PARK 9
Nottinghamshire. Tel: (01623) 824153

Nottinghamshire County Council ★ 2m S of Ollerton on A614 ★ Parking ★ Refreshments: main meals – the Buttery, Mon – Sat, 12 noon – 2.30pm, Sun, 12 noon – 3.30pm, snacks at the Coach House daily, 10am – 5pm ★ Partly suitable for wheelchairs, four available which can be booked in advance ★ Dogs (guide dogs only in shops and restaurants) ★ Shops ★ Rufford Abbey Cistercian area open ★ Park open daily, dawn – dusk ★ Entrance: free. Parking charge from April to Oct at weekends and Bank Holidays

Rufford Country Park contains almost everything that might be expected of an important country park, e.g. lakes, lime avenues, mature cedars, etc. The promise has been fulfilled – a visit to the newly-established eight themed gardens within the Formal Gardens are well worthwhile. Large areas are managed with wildlife in mind hence plenty of birdlife. Ball games are allowed on the lawns beneath cut-leaved beeches and cedars. Ample picnic areas. Conducted walks arranged during the week and weekends. Telephone for dates and times. The Reg Hookway Arboretum, established in 1983, shows promise with a good collection of oaks and birches – all well-labelled. There is a new rose garden in front of the abbey ruins.

ST HELEN'S CROFT 10
Halam, Nr Southwell, Nottinghamshire. Tel: (01636) 813219

Mrs E. Ninnis ★ 3½m W of Southwell, ½m from Halam (pronounced Haylam) towards Edingley on the left, with name on recessed gate ★ Parking in adjacent field ★ Suitable for wheelchairs ★ Plants for sale ★ Garden and conservation meadow open by appointment only ★ Entrance: £1, children 25p (1994 prices)

A charming three-quarter-acre garden which is an inspiration for all elderly gardeners as it is still cared for by its creator. Undaunted by the heavy clay soil she constantly introduces changes and has plans for future plantings. A new rose border has been made using old and new roses. An informative leaflet is provided at the entrance. A seven-acre conservation meadow adjoins the garden with 20,000 fritillaries, other wildlings and trees, wild violets, cowslips, primroses, and honeysuckles – a sight reminiscent of a Monet painting. There is access to the meadow for wheelchairs and cars for severely disabled on mown paths. An additional half acre is being turned into a woodland garden with ferns, hostas and bluebells, with rotting logs for mosses, lichens and insect life. Superb views.

WOLLATON HALL 11
Nottingham. Tel: (0115) 928 1333

Nottingham City Council ★ 2½m from the city centre on A609. From M1 junction 25 take A52, turn left onto A614 and left onto A609 ★ Parking ★ Refreshments: snacks near Wollaton Road car park ★ Toilet facilities ★ Partly suitable for wheelchairs ★ Dogs on lead because of deer ★ Shop ★ Natural history museum in Hall open April to Sept, Mon – Sat, 10am – 7pm, Sun, 2 – 5pm,

*Oct to March, Mon – Sat, 10am – dusk, Sun, 1.30 – 4.30pm. Closed 25th Dec.
Free except small charge on Sun and Bank Holidays ★ Garden open daily all
year ★ Entrance: free*

This large park and garden is surrounded by the city but because of its size
the visitor feels deep in the country – unfortunately near the park periphery
the roar of traffic dispels that illusion. The polyanthus in spring are spectacular as is the summer bedding where castor-oil plants and ornamental
cabbages have their place in the schemes. The formal gardens at the top of
the hill give onto views of huge cedars and holm oaks and thence on to the
lime avenues and the deer in the park.

COUNTY GARDEN TRUSTS

The County Gardens Trust are independent charitable trusts which rely
for their funding upon contributions, grants, sponsorship and
membership income. Trust funds are dedicated to promote their
objectives, which are to work with and alongside Parish, District and
County Councils, The National Trust and garden or conservation
societies to provide education, information, protection and creative
projects for the improvement and conservation of the country's extensive
garden heritage for the benefit of everyone. Examples can be found in
many counties, for example in Hampshire, where the Trust has
supported several new gardens and has been instrumental in reviving two
hotel gardens listed in this year's *Guide*.

CUTTINGS

Readers may wish to be reminded that the taking of cuttings without the
owners' permission can lead to embarrassment and, if it continues on a
large scale, may cause owners to close their gardens to the public. This
has to be seen in the context of an increasing number of thefts from
gardens. At Nymans, the famous Sussex garden, thefts have reached
such a level that the gardener will not now plant out any shrub until it is
semi-mature and of such a size that its theft would be very difficult.
Other owners have reported the theft of artefacts as well as plants.

DOGS, TOILETS & OTHER FACILITIES

If these are not mentioned in the text, then facilities are not available.
For example if dogs are not mentioned, owners will probably not permit
entry, even on a lead.

HISTORIC GARDENS

The Garden History Society founded in 1965 has published a journal
Garden History since 1972. Membership is open to those interested.
Details from the Secretary, Roger White, 76 Clapham Common North
Side, London SW4 9SD Tel: (0171) 350 0085.

OXFORDSHIRE

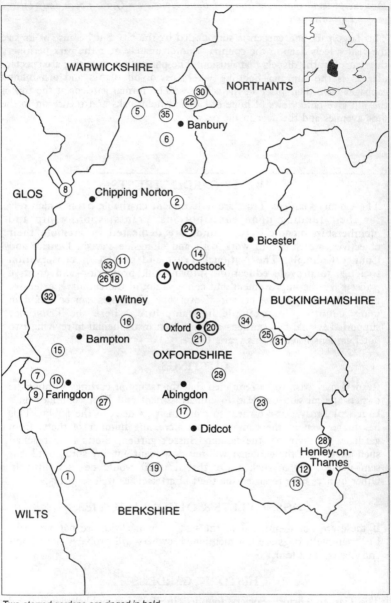

Two-starred gardens are ringed in bold.

ASHDOWN HOUSE 1
Lambourn, Newbury, Berkshire.
Tel: Regional Office (01494) 328051

The National Trust ★ 2½m S of Ashbury, 3½m N of Lambourn on W side of B4000 ★ Parking 250 yards from house ★ Grounds suitable for wheelchairs ★ Dogs on lead ★ House open. £2 ★ Woodlands open all year, Sat – Thurs, dawn – dusk ★ Grounds free

Seen from the main road, Ashdown House appears to have a tall central section replete with cupola flanked by two lower wings. It is only when the visitor approaches the front entrance that it becomes obvious that the wings are quite separate from the central block – one was the kitchen and the other the servants' quarters of this fine hunting lodge built by the first Lord Craven for Elizabeth of Bohemia. The remains of a large formal park are present in a western lime avenue. A complementary lime avenue planted in 1970, to the north of the house, is now maturing well. Also an appropriately intricate parterre, designed by A.H. Brookholding–Jones, was planted by The National Trust in the 1950s. Sadly the avenue west of the parterre was practically destroyed in the 1990 storm and new planting is being put into effect using trees propagated from those which survived. The garden is best enjoyed in spring when thousands of snowdrops, naturalised in the avenue and woodland, are at their showiest.

BARTON ABBEY 2
Middle Barton, Oxfordshire. Tel: (01869) 40227

Mrs R Fleming ★ 10m S of Banbury, turn W off A423 on the B4030 for 1m ★ Parking ★ Teas ★ Toilet facilities ★ Suitable for wheelchairs ★ Dogs on lead ★ Plants for sale ★ Open 23rd April, 2 – 6pm ★ Entrance: £1.50, children free

Gardens which are only open once or twice a year to the public are rarely included in the *Guide* but an exception is made for Barton Abbey (it has appeared before) as it has been open for the NGS for a total of over 60 years. Gilling Castle in North Yorkshire (see entry) also has the distinction of being open to the public for this period.

23 BEECH CROFT ROAD ★★ 3
Summertown, Oxford. Tel: (01865) 56020

Mrs A. Dexter ★ Summertown, 2m from centre of Oxford. Beech Croft Road runs between the Banbury and Woodstock roads which connect Oxford centre to ring road ★ Parking limited in Beech Croft Road. Advisable to use public parking in Summertown ★ Open April to Sept by appointment only ★ Entrance: £2.50 for charity

Clever use of perspective creates the effect of a much larger garden than would seem possible in an area of 23 x 7 yards. Foliage of different colours, textures, sizes and shapes is planted and pruned to form a backdrop to a variety of well-chosen plants. Ramondas and ferns are given room in the lower, damper end of the garden, alpines in stone troughs are placed in a sunnier position near the house. This is a tapestry garden, every inch containing unusual and interesting plants displayed with great skill.

BLENHEIM PALACE ★★ 4
Woodstock, Oxfordshire. Tel: (01993) 811091

The Duke of Marlborough ★ 8m NW of Oxford on A44 at Woodstock. Entrances off A44 and through the town of Woodstock ★ Parking ★ Refreshments: cafeterias, Indian Room Restaurant on Water Terraces ★ Toilet facilities, inc. disabled ★ Partly suitable for wheelchairs ★ Dogs on lead in Park only ★ House open, mid-March to Oct, 10.30am – 5.30pm (last admission 4.45pm) ★ Park open daily except 25th Dec, 9am – 5pm ★ Entrance: park only, pedestrians 90p, children 50p. Cars including occupants £4 (includes admission to park, butterfly house, train, adventure play area, nature trail and car parking. Optional extras: the Marlborough Maze and rowing boat hire); gardens only £3; house and gardens £6.90, OAP £4.90, children £3.30 (1994 prices)

The visitor who walks through Hawksmoor's Triumphal Arch into Blenheim Park sees one of the greatest contrived landscapes in Britain. The architect Vanbrugh employed Bridgeman and Henry Wise, Queen Anne's master gardener and the last of the British formalists. Wise constructed a bastion-walled 'military' garden, kitchen gardens, planted immense elm avenues and linked Vanbrugh's bridge to the sides of the valley. The gardens were ready when the first Duke of Marlborough moved into the palace in 1719. Major alterations were made by the 4th, 5th and 9th Dukes, one of the earliest of which was the grassing over of Wise's formal gardens by 'Capability' Brown after 1764. Brown also landscaped the park, installing the lake and cascade, and removed Wise's military garden. It is possible to spend several hours walking through the grounds. The gardens include formal areas restored by Achille Duchêne early this century from those grassed by Brown in the North forecourt. He made formal gardens to the east and west, the latter two water terraces in the Versailles style. To the east of the Palace is the elaborate Italian garden of patterned box and golden yew, interspersed with various seasonal plantings. To the south west from the terraces are the rose garden and arboretum. From the vast south lawn 'one passes through a magnificent grove of cedars...part shrubberies of laurel and an exedra of box and yew, the whole exemplifying the Victorian pleasure grounds' in the words of the *Oxford Companion*. As a contribution to the celebration of the 300th anniversary of the replanting of the maze at Hampton Court, the Duke of Marlborough planted a maze in 1991 in part of the kitchen garden, which is maturing well. In a few years it should provide visitors with a puzzling and pleasurable experience. The former garden centre has been redeveloped as a herb garden.

BROOK COTTAGE ★ 5
**Well Lane, Alkerton, Nr Banbury, Oxfordshire.
Tel: (01295) 670303/670590**

Mr and Mrs D. Hodges ★ 6m W of Banbury. From A422 Banbury – Stratford road, turn W at sign for Alkerton. Soon after entering village, small war memorial on right. Turn left into Well Lane and right at fork ★ Teas for groups booked in advance and DIY tea or coffee every weekday ★ Partly suitable for wheelchairs ★ Unusual plants for sale ★ Open April to Oct, Mon – Fri, 9am – 6pm. Evenings, weekends and all group visits by appointment only ★ Entrance: £2, OAP £1.50, children free, for NGS

This garden, designed and planted since 1964, is on a steeply-sloping, west-facing site of four acres to create areas totally differing in character. The owners have used the natural features in an interesting way, for example by planting large species, old-fashioned and modern shrub roses in the grass on a steep slope. Good use is made of water and there is a large unusual-shaped pond. Indeed shape is a feature of the overall effect, such as in a sweeping crimson copper beech hedge. Note the interesting grouping of hollies and conifers. There is something here for everyone in all seasons, from the alpine scree to the small 'cottage' and vegetable gardens above the house. Most plants are labelled. Upton House (see Warwickshire entry) nearby shows an earlier and more formal use of slopes.

BROUGHTON CASTLE ★   6
Broughton, Nr Banbury, Oxfordshire. Tel: (01295) 262624

The Lord Saye and Sele ★ 2½m SW of Banbury on B4035 ★ Parking ★ Teas on open days, refreshments for parties by arrangement ★ Toilet facilities ★ Suitable for wheelchairs ★ Castle open ★ Garden open 16th, 17th April, 7th, 8th May; then 17th May to 13th Sept, Wed, Sun and Bank Holiday Mons; also Thurs in July and Aug, all 2 – 5pm. Also by appointment for groups throughout year ★ Entrance: £3.20, OAP and students £2.70, children £1.50 (1994 prices)

More of a house than a castle, the gardens are unexpectedly domestic within the confines of the moat. In 1900 there were 14 gardeners but the present owner and his inspired gardener have reduced the workload somewhat while retaining the overall splendour. The most important changes were made after 1969 following a visit from Lanning Roper who suggested opening up the views across the park. There are now two magnificent borders. The west-facing one, backed by the battlement wall, has a colour scheme of blues and yellows, greys and whites. The other long border is based on reds, mauves and blues. Great planting skill is evident in the serpentine flows of colour. On the south side is the walled 'ladies garden' with box-edged fleur-de-lys shaped beds holding floribunda roses. Another wonderful border rises up to the house wall. Everywhere is a profusion of old-fashioned roses and original planting.

BUSCOT PARK ★   7
Faringdon, Oxfordshire. Tel: (01367) 242094

The National Trust ★ On A417 between Lechlade and Faringdon ★ Parking ★ Teas and light refreshments. Lunches for parties by prior arrangement ★ Toilet facilities ★ Plants for sale ★ House open ★ Garden open April to Sept, Wed – Fri (inc. 14th April) and every 2nd and 4th Sat and Sun immediately following, 2 – 6pm (last admission 5.30pm). Closed Bank Holiday Mon ★ Entrance: £3, (house and garden £4)

Although the house was built in 1780, this garden has been developed during the twentieth century. The water garden was created by Harold Peto in 1912, though the avenues linking lake to house were added later using a goose-foot plan from the house, with fastigiate and weeping varieties of oak, beech and lime. The Egyptian avenue created by Lord Faringdon in 1969 is guarded by sphinxes and embellished with Coade stone statues copied from an original from Hadrian's Villa. The large walled kitchen garden was rearranged in the mid-1980s, and is now intersected by a pleached tunnel of ostrya (hop hornbeam) and a Judas tree tunnel. Deep borders under the outside walls have unusual and skilled planting by Tim Rees, mixing old roses and climbing vegetables (gourds, marrows, beans, cucumbers) which lay themselves out over the rose bushes, after their flowering is over. Walkway outside kitchen garden between two wide borders using exterior wall and trellis as screens. Exceptionally effective planting by the late Peter Coats and, over the years, imaginative development by Lord Faringdon. The planting of the kitchen garden and the double borders is so skilful that even in drought conditions none of the effect is lost.

CHASTLETON GLEBE 8
Chastleton, Oxfordshire.

Mr and Mrs C.R. Kruger ★ 3m SE of Moreton-in-Marsh off A44 ★ Parking in field ★ ☆Teas ★ Toilet facilities ★ Suitable for wheelchairs ★ Dogs on lead ★ Plants and jams for sale ★ Open 16th July, 2 – 6pm ★ Entrance: £2

A Cotswold house surrounded by lawns and fine old trees on three sides, and open on the south side to views across the lake and island with its enchanting Chinese bridge and pagoda. Enjoy this view from the red planted terrace. A wide long border of blue and yellow herbaceous plants shading to hot colours in the middle and cool greys and pinks at the end is backed by a 10-foot stone wall. A newly-erected, 40-foot rose tunnel is sheltered by hedges of beech and yew. Croquet lawn is bordered with old shrub roses, and the kitchen garden is very attractively planted with flowers for picking and drying, vegetables and herbs. Other gardens in the village are normally open on the same days, and are well worth visiting. Chastleton House has been bought by The National Trust and is currently closed for renovation, but look over the churchyard wall at the charming topiary garden, probably a Victorian re-creation of a seventeenth-century design. The property will reopen in the autumn of 1996, with the first full season in 1997. Another fine Chastleton garden which has changed hands is The Old Post Office. This may be opened when others in the village do so for charity. There are many magnificent gardens in the vicinity – Ilmington Manor, Batsford and Sezincote.

CLOCK HOUSE ★ 9
Coleshill, Nr Swindon, Wiltshire. Tel: (01793) 762476

Michael and Denny Wickham ★ 3¹/₂m SW of Faringdon on B4019 ★ Best season: June/July ★ Parking ★ Teas in courtyard in fine weather ★ Toilet facilities ★ Suitable for wheelchairs ★ Plants for sale ★ Open 14th May, 18th June, 2nd July, 10th Sept, 2 – 6pm ★ Entrance: £1.50, children free

Situated on a hillside with inspiring views over the Vale of the White Horse, this exuberant, delightful garden was created by the present owners in the last 30 years in the grounds of Coleshill House, burned then demolished in the 1950s. The groundplan of the original house is being planted out in box, to show layout of walls and windows. Courtyard with collection of plants in pots, and a sunny walled garden in the old laundry-yard with roses and mixed planting and a fine greenhouse. Lime avenue at the front of the house sweeps down to the views, and a pond and terrace are sheltered by tall shrubs. Mixed herbaceous borders with interesting and unusual plants. This is an original garden, designed by an artist, with a large collection of plants in imaginative settings, the atmosphere being prolific rather than tidy.

FARINGDON HOUSE ★   10
Faringdon, Oxfordshire. Tel: (01367) 240240

Dr S. Zinovieff ★ Entered from centre of town which is off the A420 between Oxford and Swindon ★ Parking ★ Teas on charity days ★ Partly suitable for wheelchairs ★ Open by appointment and 16th April, 2 – 5pm ★ Entrance: £1, accompanied children free

Medium-sized apparently conventional park with fine terrace, views and trees. Its charm is renowned, particularly the 'fun' features introduced by Lord Berners and his successor Robert Heber-Percy, grandfather of the present owner, who has introduced some splendid, if more conventional floral innovations, for example, the two new rose borders on the south-east lawn. Visitors at the end of May may also benefit from the profusion of honeysuckle on the front of the house and, with luck, the peony borders. To return to the 'fun' features, there are Berners' coloured fantail doves and in the orangery pool, half-submerged and looking as though he might have lunched rather too well, is a bust of General Havelock, of the Indian Mutiny. The swimming pool has a medieval influence. A rare fruit walk between two high sheltering walls. Good autumn border, lined in box, and massed bulbs down the drive in spring. All sorts of strange and amusing things went on here during the times of Lord Berners and his successor Robert Heber-Percy, chronicled in Nancy Mitford's novel *The Pursuit of Love* whose Merlinford is modelled on Faringdon. On Folly Hill, about ½m away, Lord Berners built a folly for Heber-Percy when he was 21; he wanted it to be classical and though the architect preferred Gothic, Berners made him add a classical top. It has its own dates for opening with separate admission charge.

GOTHIC HOUSE   11
Charlbury, Oxfordshire. Tel: (01608) 810654

Mr and Mrs Andrew Lawson ★ In centre of Charlbury village on B4022 Witney – Enstone road ★ Parking in street ★ Teas ★ Suitable for wheelchairs ★ Plants for sale ★ Open 7th May, 10th Sept, 2 – 6pm ★ Entrance: £1.50

Gothic House, a third of an acre walled town garden, recently designed by one of the country's leading garden photographers and his sculptress wife. Artistic flair is evident everywhere, from the entrance through a fine Gothic glass structure to the tour round the many gems picked out in miniature. The planting is highly imaginative. So is the clever use of green wood structures in treillage style including a romantic seat, and the railway sleepers which define the pond. Note the *trompe l'oeil* painting on wood. Briony Lawson's sculptures are everywhere, numbered and for sale. *Objets trouvées* amid the foliage and the whole effect delightful.

GREYS COURT ★★   12
Rotherfield Greys, Henley-on-Thames, Oxfordshire.
Tel: (01491) 628529

The National Trust ★ 3m W of Henley-on-Thames E of B481 ★ Best season:

April to June ★ Parking ★ Teas April to Sept, Mon, Wed, Fri and Sat ★ Toilet facilities ★ House open April to Oct, Mon, Wed, Fri (but closed 14th April), 2 – 6pm ★ Garden open April to Sept, daily except Thurs and Sun, 2 – 6pm (last admission 5.30pm) ★ Entrance: £3, children £1.50, family ticket £7.50 (house and garden £4, children £2, family ticket £9.50)

The statue of St Fiacre, the protector of gardeners, stands modestly in this beautiful garden, or several gardens, set against the ruins of a fourteenth-century fortified house. The largest area, an orchard, is divided by lines of morello cherries and parallel hedges of 'Rosa Mundi'. An ancient wisteria forms a canopy over a walled area, approached on one side through a tunnel of younger wisterias in pinks and blues. Impeccably kept peony bed and rose garden glow against the ancient walls. Beyond the kitchen garden – now a new ornamental garden of designer vegetables, etc – across the nut avenue, is the maze, designed by Randoll Coate and inspired by one seen in a dream by the then Archbishop of Canterbury. Donkey wheel and restored ice-house open.

GREYSTONE COTTAGE ★   13
Colmore Lane, Kingwood Common, Henley-on-Thames, Oxfordshire. Tel: (01491) 628559

Mr and Mrs W. Roxburgh ★ 5m N of Reading between B481 Nettlebed – Reading road, and Sonning Common – Stoke Row road. 1m down Colmore Lane, next to Unicorn pub ★ Best season: spring/summer ★ Parking in lane (March open day) and field (May open day) ★ Home-made teas on special opening days ★ Suitable for wheelchairs ★ Plants for sale ★ Open 5th March (for hellebores and snowdrops), 7th May, 18th June, all 2 – 6pm and by appointment March to 1st Sept ★ Entrance: £1, children free

The owners have created this garden over the past 20 years. Sunny courtyard in front of house contains beds planted with white-flowered regale lilies, mallows and perennial stock following on from spring bulbs. A large border is partly Mediterranean, with Cistus species, myrtle, yuccas, etc., and blue harebells. Pots of *Lilium longiflorum* and non-hardy plants by the door. Pear-tree *allée* (80 years old) leading away from house, with vegetable garden to right, hedges of beech beyond; lawns and woodland with long border to the west, full of unusual plants, especially a large number of hostas. Woodland with primroses, primulas and fritillaries, hellebores, azaleas, bilberries and blueberries. Golden garden behind house with wildlife pond. Fritillary and wild flower area.

HILL COURT   14
Tackley, Oxfordshire.

Mr and Mrs Andrew C. Peake ★ 9m N of Oxford, just E of A423. Coming from Oxford turn opposite Sturdy's Castle; if driving south turn off at earlier sign marked Tackley ★ Parking ★ Teas ★ Suitable for wheelchairs ★ Plants for sale ★ Open 17th, 18th June, 2 – 6pm ★ Entrance: £1.50, children free

A two-acre, sixteenth-century walled garden, no longer physically attached to the house which was demolished *c.* 1960. Remains of the manor house, also demolished, can be seen across the park which dates from 1787. The garden, the design of which was influenced by Russell Page, is unusual because it is terraced uphill from the entrance. The rose beds had to be removed about seven years ago and the sensitive and original planting which replaced them is the work of Rupert Golby. Designers will find it pleasurable.

KELMSCOTT MANOR 15
Kelmscott, Nr Lechlade, Oxfordshire. Tel (01367) 252486

The Society of Antiquaries ★ 2m SE of Lechlade ★ Parking ★ Toilet facilities ★ House open as garden and with group tour by appointment on Thurs and Fri ★ Garden open April to Sept, Wed, 11am – 1pm, 2 – 5pm ★ Entrance: £5

Described by *Country Life* as a magical house in a remarkably unchanged village, its strange atmosphere will be relished by those who are attracted by William Morris in particular, or the Pre-Raphaelite Brothers in general. The small garden was for years rather a let-down, but the curator and his wife have changed its character so that the formal but pleasing arrangement and the trees are just what would be expected at Morris's romantic summer home for 25 years. He himself described it as 'a heaven on earth...and such a garden! Close down on the river, a boat house and all things handy.'

MANOR HOUSE ★ 16
Stanton Harcourt, Oxfordshire. Tel: (01865) 881930

Mr and The Hon. Mrs Gascoigne ★ 9m W of Oxford, 5m SE of Witney on B4449 ★ Best season: late spring/early summer ★ Parking ★ Teas ★ Toilet facilities ★ Suitable for wheelchairs ★ Dogs on lead ★ Plants for sale ★ House open ★ Garden open 16th, 17th, 27th, 30th April, 1st, 7th, 8th, 11th, 14th, 25th, 28th, 29th May, 8th, 11th, 22nd, 25th June, 6th, 9th, 20th, 23rd July, 10th, 13th, 24th, 27th, 28th Aug, 7th, 10th, 21st, 24th Sept, 2 – 6pm ★ Entrance: £1.50, OAP and children £1 (house and garden £3, OAP and children £2)

Twelve acres of gardens incorporated in and around ruins of a fourteenth- and fifteenth-century manor house. An avenue of clipped yew leads from the house to the chapel, and there are herbaceous and rose borders, with clematis, hydrangeas and roses clambering up the magnificent old walls. The kitchen garden is still in the process of redesign as a formal rose garden using David Austin's new English roses, espaliered apple trees, and a fountain in the middle. The stewponds are sadly low in water, but covered with water lilies in high summer, and fringed with water-loving plants, and are crossed by some enchanting old bridges. It would take an army of gardeners to keep this garden immaculate, so enjoy it for its nostalgic atmosphere and history, magnificent walls and urns, and romantic paths winding through nut-walks which are underplanted with bulbs and primulas in the spring. Don't miss the teas in the medieval kitchens.

THE MILL HOUSE ★ 17
Sutton Courtenay, Abingdon, Oxfordshire. Tel: (01235) 848219

Mrs Jane Stevens ★ The village is 1½m S of Abingdon (leave the town over the river bridge). Entrance gates in main street just opposite the Fish public house ★ Parking ★ Teas ★ Suitable for wheelchairs ★ Open 2nd April, 18th June, 1st Oct, 2 – 6pm and by prior appointment ★ Entrance: £2, children £1, under 4 free (1994 prices)

Although the stone house behind high walls suggest promise, the romantic experience of The Mill cannot be guessed at as the visitor approaches it through the winding main street of the village. Of course few gardeners have the gift of the Thames in their territory, but the use of it which Mrs Stevens has conjured up since she acquired it in 1981 is quite remarkable. She had the benefit of a structure laid out by Colonel Peter Laycock, a colleague of Eric Savill, who planted some splendid trees around the ruined paper mill, and she has added highly imaginative touches of her own. This is a garden to be walked in, sat in and savoured so do not attempt to rush round the eight and a half acres. There are formal areas on either side of the early Georgian house, but once past these, the wanderer amongst the water, trees and groves will be lost in a sylvan idyll. Fine bulbs in spring, old-fashioned roses planted by Mrs Stevens in summer, and charming colours in autumn. Very high standard of maintenance mixed with original touches like the circles of comfrey. For those who like to conjure up dreams of previous owners, Asquith and Margot lived here and entertained all the great figures of the day for Fridays-to-Mondays during his period of office before 1916. The nearby Manor House, with garden by Norah Lindsay, is open once a year for the NGS.

MOUNT SKIPPET ★   18
Ramsden, Oxfordshire. Tel: (01993) 868253

Dr and Mrs M.A.T. Rogers ★ 4m N of Witney off B4022 to Charlbury. At crossroads marked to Finstock turn E and almost immediately turn right. Then after 400 yards turn left up No Through Way lane ★ Parking ★ Refreshments by arrangement. Picnic area available ★ Suitable for wheelchairs ★ Plants usually for sale ★ Open April to Sept by appointment ★ Entrance: £1 for charity

Dr Rogers, now retired after a career as a research chemist, is a dedicated plantsman, preferring to grow everything from seeds or cuttings. He took over this family house of two acres and has developed a very attractive garden in a beautiful Cotswold setting. Plants are his love and there are many rare ones. He has two rock gardens, an alpine house and interesting shrubs and trees. Everywhere there are collections of pots with rare treasures, some of which are sometimes for sale. Almost everything in the garden is labelled, and if you are lucky, Dr Rogers will delight in giving you an enthusiastic and highly informative tour of his garden. Swot up on your Latin names and plant origins before you go!

THE OLD RECTORY ★   19
Farnborough, Wantage, Oxfordshire. Tel: (01488) 638298

Mrs Michael Todhunter ★ 4m SE of Wantage off B4494 ★ Best season: mid-April to mid-July ★ Parking ★ Teas nearby sometimes on charity open days ★ Plants for sale ★ Open 23rd April, 14th May, 25th June and by written appointment ★ Entrance: £1.50, children free on open days, and £3 by appointment

Outstanding four-acre garden created over 30 years on good original structure of large trees and hedges with magnificent views over the Downs. Deep, parallel herbaceous borders, backed by yew hedges. Subtle and effective planting next to front of house; smaller areas laid out for sun or shade-loving plants; woodland and shrubs, lawns; swimming pool surrounded by large

Hydrangea sargentiana, potted lilies, agapanthus, with mixed roses around outside walls. Collection of old roses and small-flowered clematis. Wild flowers at edge of front lawn by ha-ha. Incidentally, those who like John Betjeman's poetry will be interested to know that he lived here 1945-50 and can look for the ghost of Miss Joan Hunter Dunn in the shrubberies. A John Piper window in the church is in his memory. One of Oxfordshire's highest gardens, 800 feet, prey to winds from the Downs.

OXFORD BOTANIC GARDEN ★★ 20
Oxford. Tel: (01865) 276920

University of Oxford ★ In centre of Oxford opposite Magdalen College near bridge ★ Parking difficult ★ Picnics, while not specifically authorised, could be taken overlooking river ★ Suitable for wheelchairs ★ Professional photography and music prohibited ★ Open daily, 9am – 5pm (4.30pm during GMT). Greenhouses 2 – 4pm. Closed 14th April and 25th Dec ★ Entrance: free except during mid-June to Sept £1 (1994 price)

This is the oldest botanic garden in Britain and one of the most attractive to the general visitor. Founded in 1621, it is surrounded by a high wall and entered through a splendid gateway by Nicholas Stone. One yew survives from the early plantings and there is a series of beds containing herbaceous and annual plants in systematic and labelled groups. The old walls back beds with tender plants, including roses and clematis. To the left is the greenhouse area, modern ones replacing those built in 1670. There is also a rock garden. Outside the front entrance is a large rose garden donated by Americans in memory of those university staff who developed penicillin. Several miles away at Nuneham Courtenay (south of the A423) is the University Arboretum opened in 1968 (see entry).

OXFORD COLLEGE GARDENS 21
Most colleges are helpful about free access to their gardens although the more private ones, such as the Master's or Fellows', are rarely open. Specific viewing times are difficult to rely on because some colleges prefer not to have visitors in term time or on days when a function is taking place. The best course is to ask at the Porter's Lodge or to telephone ahead of visit. However, it is fair to say that some Oxford college gardens will always be open to the visitor, by arrangement with porters, even if others are closed on that particular day. Some colleges have a policy of allowing public entrance on official guided tours only.

Amongst the college gardens of particular interest are the following: *Christ Church*; although famous for Lewis Carroll's reference to the Cheshire Cat's chestnut tree in the Deanery garden and the Oriental plane planted 1636. Neither of these horticultural heritages can be visited by the public. However, they can visit the Memorial garden on St Aldates [Memorial garden open winter 8am – 4.30pm, summer 8am – 8pm. Deanery and Masters' garden only open once a year for charity. Meadow open daily]. *Corpus Christi*; the smallest college with an attractive small garden overlooking Christ Church Meadow [Closed over Easter, but otherwise normally open 1.30 – 4pm]. *Green College*; alas this institution with its environmental name is only open to the public once a year. *Holywell Manor*; part of Balliol, a restful, well-maintained garden of one acre [Open 10.30am – 6.30pm]. *Kellogg College*; an unusual and pleasant roof garden [Open all year – ring (01865) 270360]. *Lady Margaret Hall*; eight acres of formal and informal, mainly designed by the Victorian architect Blomfield, also responsible for some of the buildings [Open 2 – 6pm or dusk if earlier. All visitors are requested to call at the Porter's Lodge.] *Magdalen College Meadows* [Normally open 2 – 6pm, but during July to Sept, 11am – 6pm. £1.50 for college and gardens], entered off the north side of the bridge, link the college quads to 5 acres of deer park surrounded by Addison's Walk, named after the eighteenth-century essayist and garden enthusiast, which circuits the River Cherwell. Visitors in May should see the water meadow with its fritillaries. *New College*; admirers of the writings of Robin Lane Fox will be able to see examples of his plantings, outstanding mixed borders against Oxford city wall, rose borders, cloister garden; mound, completed in 1649. [Open term time 2 – 5pm, vacation 11am – 5pm. There is an admission charge of £1 on summer weekends in term and during parts of the Easter and summer vacations, but this includes entry to Chapel, Hall, Quadrangles and Cloisters as well as Gardens]. *Nuffield College*; formal gardens in two quadrangles with water features [Open 9am – 5pm]. *The Queen's College*; a garden with a fourteenth-century history, today pleasantly modernised. Good herbaceous borders in Fellows' garden [Open once a year for charity but not to casual visitors during year except those on guided tours through the Information Centre]. *Rewley House*; Wellington Square, has an interesting roof garden, opened in 1986 [Open by appointment and on one afternoon in July for charity]. *Rhodes House*; not a college and not a pretty building but an unexpectedly pleasant garden behind [9am – 5pm weekdays only]. *St Catherine's College*; in the midst of so much ancient charm in garden design it is pleasing to be able to strongly recommend a modern garden (1960-4) created by the distinguished Danish architect Arne Jacobsen (1902-71). Noted for his concern for integrating building and landscape, this is a remarkable example. Fine water feature. *St Hugh's College*; an interesting 10-acre garden largely created by Annie Rogers, a Fellow. [All visitors are requested to call at the Porter's Lodge]. *St John's College*; landscaped in the eighteenth century and immaculately kept still Striking in spring when bulbs in flower [Open daily, 1 – 5pm or dusk if earlier. Better to go during the week, rather than at weekends, to avoid crowds]. *Templeton College*; 37 acres landscaped by Alan Mitchell and planted with over 20,000 trees [Open 25th Sept, 2 – 5.30pm and other times for groups who apply in writing]. *Wadham College*; herbaceous borders, new 'fragrant' garden and fine old trees [Open 1 – 4.30pm]. *Wolfson College*; nine acres designed around modern college buildings by Powell and Moya [Open daily, 8am – 10pm]. *Worcester College*; the only true landscaped garden in Oxford, including a lake, made from a swampy area in 1817. Brightly-coloured beds in front quad [Open term time 2 – 6pm, vacation 9am – 12 noon and 2 – 6pm]. The Provost's Garden, open on special occasions, has a charming rose garden stretching to wooded lakeside walks and orchards. The *University Parks* laid out in 1864, are the perfect place for walking in all weathers and across the bridges to Mesopotamia or the Spalding nature reserve. The shrub and herbaceous borders near South Lodge Gate are laid out on colour themes. The Parks have a fine collection of mature trees mixed with newer plantings. [Open daily, except St Giles Fair on 4th Sept, 8am – dusk]

PETTIFERS 22
Lower Wardington, Nr Banbury, Oxfordshire. Tel: (01295) 750232

Mr J. and the Hon. Mrs Price ★ 5m NE of Banbury, on the Daventry road, from M40, junction 11. Opposite Lower Wardington church ★ Best seasons: April to June and Sept ★ Plants sometimes for sale ★ Open by appointment and on NGS days with Wardington Manor (see entry) ★ Entrance: £1

This is a 10-year old garden, still evolving, but with an air of maturity and peace which partly stems from the stunning view that dominates the landscape. Interesting foliage plants ensure plenty of colour all year round. Bold planting of some more unusual plants, and attention to detail – for instance in the elegant patterns made in the paths – make this a garden to linger in now, and to watch mature with pleasure. There is a box-edged herb and kitchen garden, herbaceous borders, a foliage border, a green and white shrub border and old rose borders. A very good plan and plant list is supplied.

ROFFORD MANOR 23
Little Milton, Oxfordshire.

Mr and Mrs J.L. Mogford ★ 10m SE of Oxford, 1m from Little Milton on Chalgrove Road, signposted 'Rofford Only' ★ Teas ★ Suitable for wheelchairs ★ Plants for sale ★ Open 10th Sept, 2 – 6pm and by written appointment for parties at any time of year ★ Entrance: £2, children free

From initial planning to planting, and now in early maturity, this has been a fascinating garden. A courtyard lined with juvenile pleached limes leads to a traditional kitchen garden with an apple and pear arbour. Next a box garden, with a raised lily pool, surrounded by box hedges, white flowerbeds, and white garden seats – a cool and tranquil place to sit down. Then stroll down a medlar walk and enter a paved rose garden, with romneyas, shrub roses, white cranesbills and silver thyme at your feet. The expansive lawn is edged with two wide herbaceous borders, and the ha–ha at the end of the lawn allows them to be viewed with pastoral views forming a backdrop. A prolific orchard hides the tennis court, and the swimming pool is exuberantly surrounded with vines, roses, clematis and salvias. Close to the house is a walled herb garden, where roses loll about with the herbs. A new cottage pot garden has been added.

ROUSHAM HOUSE ★★ 24
Steeple Aston, Oxfordshire. Tel: (01869) 347110 or (01860) 360407

Charles Cottrell-Dormer ★ 2m S of Steeple Aston off A4260 Oxford – Banbury road and B4030 ★ Parking ★ Picnics welcome anywhere in garden ★ Toilet facilities ★ House open April to Sept, Wed, Sun and Bank Holidays, 2 – 4.30pm ★ Garden open all year, daily, 10am – 4.30pm ★ Entrance: £2.50, no children under 15

This is much admired because William Kent's design of 1738 is effectively frozen in time. Historical enlightenment can be combined with the enchantment of the setting and the use he made of it. In fact, before Kent it was already a famous garden described by the poet Pope as 'the prettiest place for water-falls, jetts, ponds, inclosed with beautiful scenes of green and hanging wood, that ever I saw.' Kent's design, influenced perhaps by stage scenery, created a series of effects, and the best way to view the garden is to follow these one by one, rather than to attempt to grasp the design as a whole, although it is important to follow the various effects in the order Kent intended, and for this a guidebook is necessary. By taking the effects one-by-one, a feeling for the whole will then gradually emerge. In fact this was one of the first places where the garden took in the whole estate, also 'calling-in' the surrounding country-side, to use Pope's words. There are splendid small buildings and follies, fine sculpture, water and many seats and vantage points. The walled gardens next to the house are earlier than Kent and the owners have made them into a major attraction with herbaceous borders, parterre, rose garden and vegetable garden. Those who are not particularly interested in the historic spendours of Rousham will find this area most rewarding, as will everyone else.

SHOTOVER HOUSE   25
Shotover, Oxfordshire.

Lt Col Sir John Miller ★ 6m E of Oxford on the A40 on S side of dual carriageway ★ Best season: spring ★ Parking ★ Teas (with fine views) ★ Toilet facilities ★ Suitable for wheelchairs if the weather has been dry although some paths surfaced ★ Plants sometimes for sale ★ Open one Sun in April for NGS ★ Entrance: £1, children free

Rare cattle and sheep (including black varieties) greet the visitor as he walks from the car park at the end of the drive round to the colonnaded back of the eighteenth-century house (not open). Pevsner calls the exterior dull but the owner is doing much to enliven the planting in the formal garden surrounding it and to revive the statuary. From the rear arcade the view is of a long canal ending in a Gothic folly, which can be reached by walking via the pet cemetery and interesting decorated wood chalet. This garden was begun *c.* 1718. Round to the west front of the house, visitors will enjoy strolling down the long vistas carved out of what was once part of the royal forest of Wychwood. William Kent was involved in this design in the 1730s, building a domed octagonal temple, now ringed by cherries, and, on another axis, an obelisk (Kent was working at nearby Rousham (see entry) from 1738). Allow an hour to survey this pleasant park.

SHUCKLETS   26
High Street, Ramsden, Oxfordshire. Tel: (01993) 868659

Dr and Mrs G. Garton ★ 3m N of Witney off B4022, near the centre of the village opposite Stag and Hounds pub ★ Best season: May to July ★ Parking in road ★ Partly suitable for wheelchairs (some steep paths) ★ Plants sometimes for sale ★ Open April to Sept by appointment ★ Entrance: £1.50

This cottage swagged with roses, honeysuckle and apricots, has a deceptively large two-acre garden behind it. Close to the house is a hot, dry bed for Mediterranean plants, and a meandering rock garden. Then you reach a blue and pink border, and an apricot and cream border. Further up the hill is a circular garden of shrub roses, which leads into an orchard – trees festooned in more shrub roses and climbers. At the top is an ornamental vegetable garden, and a small, but delightfully productive vineyard. A plantsman's garden, full of interest and surprise.

STANSFIELD ★ 27
49 High Street, Stanford-in-the-Vale, Oxfordshire.
Tel: (01367) 710340

*Mr and Mrs D. Keeble ★ 3½m SE of Faringdon, turn off A417 opposite Vale
Garage ★ Best season: June to Aug ★ Parking in street ★ Suitable for wheelchairs
by consultation with owners ★ Plants for sale ★ Open 4th April to 26th Sept,
Tues, 10am – 4pm. Also by appointment ★ Entrance: £1*

A one-acre-plus plantsman's garden, not yet finished, with many island beds
and borders. Large collection of plants, both for damp and dry conditions.
All-year round interest in wide use of foliage and seasonal flowers, starting
with species spring bulbs. Many shrubs interplanted. A new woodland area
has been underplanted and a new grass border created. Alpines in sinks and
troughs. A new scree garden has been made. Attention is focused on number
and variety of plants rather than layout and design.

STONOR PARK 28
Henley-on-Thames, Oxfordshire. Tel: (01491) 638587

*Lord Camoys ★ 5m N of Henley-on-Thames on B480 ★ Best season: June/July
★ Parking ★ Teas. Party lunches by arrangement ★ Toilet facilities ★ Suitable for
wheelchairs by special arrangement ★ Dogs on lead ★ Shop ★ House open ★
Garden open: April, Sun and Bank Holiday Mon, 2 – 5.30; May, June and
Sept: Wed and Sun, 2 – 5.30pm, Bank Holiday Mons, 12 noon – 5.30pm; July
and Aug: Wed, Thurs, Sat (Aug only), Sun, 2 – 5.30pm, Bank Holiday Mon,
12 noon – 5.30pm. Parties by arrangement, Tues, Wed or Thurs (am and pm)
and Sun pm ★ Entrance: £3.50, children under 14 in family parties free (1994
prices). Party rates on application*

The house, a red-brick Tudor E-shaped building, with twelfth century
origins, is the main attraction at Stonor Park. It is set in a bowl on the side
of a hill with open parkland and large trees in front, and with flower and
vegetable garden behind and to the side sheltered against the hill. Lawns
lead up to a terrace with pools, stone urns and planting along the steps.
Orchard with cypresses and espaliered fruit trees, lavender hedges. Stone
sculpture exhibition.

UNIVERSITY ARBORETUM 29
Nuneham Courtenay, Nr Oxford, Oxfordshire.

*Oxford University ★ S of Oxford on A423 ★ Best seasons: May to June and
Sept to Oct ★ Parking ★ Open all year except 14th to 17th April and 23rd Dec
to 3rd Jan: May to Oct, daily, 10am – 5pm; Nov to April, Mon – Fri, 10am –
4.30pm ★ Entrance: free*

The village and church of Nuneham were demolished in the 1670s in order
to construct a classical landscape to be seen from the house; Oliver
Goldsmith's poem 'The Deserted Village', written in 1770, may be based on
that upheaval. Horace Walpole, in 1780, described the gardens, designed by
'Capability' Brown and William Mason (the poet gardener) as the most beautiful in the world. Most of those gardens, with the house, became part of
Nuneham Park Conference Centre in the 1960s. The remaining 55 acres of
garden, now with the Botanic Garden under the University's care, include

OXFORDSHIRE

rhododendron walks, camellia and bamboo collections under magnificent conifers, a 10-acre bluebell wood and a 12-acre meadow.

UPTON HOUSE
(see Warwickshire)

WARDINGTON MANOR   30
Wardington, Nr Banbury, Oxfordshire. Tel: (01295) 750202/758481

Lord and Lady Wardington ★ 5m NE of Banbury off A361 ★ Parking ★ Teas ★ Toilet facilities ★ Suitable for wheelchairs ★ Plants sometimes for sale ★ Open 21st May, 2 – 5.30pm and by appointment ★ Entrance: £2.50 (with Pettifers, see entry), otherwise £1.50

Great lawns spread themselves in front of the Carolean manor house with its wisteria-covered walls. The topiary is impeccable too, and there are attractive borders. Away from the house, the owners have created a flowering shrub walk with interesting ground cover, which leads to a walled area planted with hostas. To the left is a rockery and large pond with walk around. On the NGS open day Wardington is twinned with Pettifers, an interesting one-acre garden with unusual foliage, which also opens on its own later in the year.

WATERPERRY GARDENS ★   31
Nr Wheatley, Oxfordshire. Tel: (01844) 339226/339254

9m E of Oxford, 2¹/₂m N of Wheatley. Turn off M40 junction 8 and follow signs ★ Parking ★ Refreshments: tea shop open 10am to ¹/₂ hour before closing. Light lunches, wine licence ★ Toilet facilities ★ Suitable for wheelchairs ★ Plants for sale in large nursery ★ Shop ★ Craft Gallery ★ Church open (Saxon origins) all year round ★ Garden open daily, March to Oct, 10am – 5.30pm or 6pm at weekends; Nov to Feb, 10am – 4.30pm. Closed Christmas and New Year holidays. During the three days 20th to 23rd July open only to visitors to Art in Action (enquiries (0171) 381 3192) ★ Entrance: Nov to Feb, 75p; March to Oct, £2.20, OAP £1.70, children £1, coach parties (of 20 or more) by appointment only £1.60 per person (1994 prices)

Waterperry has to be included in this *Guide* although its 20 acres are difficult to categorise. There is a strong institutionalised/education atmosphere going back to the 1930s when a Miss Havergal opened up a small horticultural school. There is also a commercial garden centre which occupies large areas of the so-called garden, with row upon row of flowers and shrubs being grown from seeds or cuttings. Intermixed with all this are major features of the old garden, lawns and a substantial herbaceous border; also new beds containing collections of alpines, dwarf conifers and other shrubs. The South Field is a growing area for soft fruit. The Clay Bank is planted with shade lovers. Almost all the plants are labelled and the owners describe the place as one where 'the ornamental and the utilitarian live side by side'. The greenhouses in the nursery are interesting too: containing a good stock of houseplants for sale, usually including orchids and tall ficus; another, in the old walled garden, has an enormous citrus tree (it's worth the detour just to catch the scent of blossom) and other Mediterranean specimens, which are not for sale. Several hours need to be spent here to do it justice and if the visitor is overpowered by the 'utilitarian' aspect, he or she can stroll down the shady path by the little River Thame. A guide is sold at the shop. Several Wheatley gardens are also open in spring for charity, together with Shotover House (see entry), a rare survival of the early eighteenth-century styles, including Gothic revival, with only minor alterations to the original layout.

WESTWELL MANOR ★★ 32
Nr Burford, Oxfordshire.

Mr and Mrs T.H. Gibson ★ 2m SW of Burford off A40 ★ Parking in village ★ Plants for sale ★ Open 21st May, 2nd July, 2 – 6.30pm ★ Entrance: £2, children 50p

Six acres of garden divided into different 'rooms' by stone walls and topiary in yew and box surround a large house with a sixteenth-century centre, and later additions. Stone terraces with steps to different levels shelter many stone-carpeting plants, and interesting bulbs. Good *potager* with box and lavender hedges, and fruit trees trained over hoops make you feel as if you are standing in a Kate Greenaway painting. Wild garden, herbaceous and rose gardens, and a calm lily pool flanked by peonies, and a wonderful wisteria-clad pergola.

WILCOTE HOUSE ★ 33
Wilcote, Finstock, Oxfordshire. Tel: (01993) 868606

The Hon. Charles Cecil ★ 3m S of Charlbury E off B4022 ★ Best season: May to July ★ Parking ★ Toilet facilities ★ Suitable for wheelchairs ★ Plants for sale ★ Open 30th April, 28th May, 8th Oct, 2 – 5.30pm ★ Entrance: £1.50, children free. Conducted tours by arrangement

It is worth visiting this garden in May/June in order to walk down the laburnum tunnel planted as recently as 1984. The house is a splendid seventeenth/nineteenth-century copy in Cotswold stone of earlier periods and the large garden is also a period piece with extensive beds of old-fashioned roses and mixed borders. An unusual feature is the vast wild garden planted with an interesting selection of trees and intersected by grass paths. Very fine setting in this beautiful part of England. Arrive early for best plant sales. Mount Skippet (see entry) is nearby.

WOODPERRY HOUSE 34
Nr Stanton St John, Oxfordshire.

Mr and Mrs Robert Lush ★ 4m E of Oxford. From Headington roundabout on ring road, take turning to Horton-cum-Studley. After 1½m cross over B4027. Road is signed to Horton-cum-Studley. Woodperry House is ⅓m down this road on right ★ Parking ★ Refreshments in aid of charity ★ Toilet facilities ★ Plants for sale ★ Open 21st May, 2 – 5pm. Also open to special interest groups by prior appointment ★ Entrance: £1.50, children free

There is something here for most visitors, particularly those who want to see a five-acre garden built more or less from scratch (started *c.* 1987) in a style suited to the early eighteenth-century country house (not open), which Pevsner rightly described as 'strikingly beautiful'. A large formal lawned area at the back of the house looks out over Otmoor. Lime tree avenue. Elaborate beds. Stone summerhouses. Beyond is a well-planted herbaceous border on one side, matched by the one opposite. Below is a very large walled vegetable garden. Water gardens and parkland are being planned. Plane and cherry avenues planted.

WROXTON ABBEY   35
Wroxton, Nr Banbury, Oxfordshire. Tel: (01295) 730551

Wroxton College of Fairleigh Dickinson University of New Jersey USA ★ 3m W of Banbury off A422 ★ Parking in village. Vehicles are not permitted into the grounds ★ Suitable for wheelchairs ★ Dogs on lead ★ House (now used for academic purposes) open only by appointment ★ Grounds open all year, dawn – dusk ★ Entrance: free

The historical interest of this garden and park is that in 1727 Tilleman Bobart (a pupil of Wise) was commissioned to construct a Renaissance-style garden with canals by the owner of the large Jacobean manor house, the 2nd Baron Guilford. But by the late 1730s his son had this grassed over to convert it to the then fashionable landscape-style. Sanderson Miller designed some of the garden buildings *c.* 1740. The present American owners have restored much of this early landscape garden since 1978. On entering the long drive up to the house, it appears to be a conventional park, but beyond are interesting features including a serpentine river, lake, cascade which can be seen from a viewing mount, Chinese bridge, Doric temple, Gothic dovecot, obelisk, and ice-house all restored from their derelict state. There is a rose garden and a newly-created knot garden. The steps have all been renovated. In all, the grounds cover 56 acres and offer many hours of pleasant walks. A garden guide is available.

HOW TO FIND THE GARDENS

Directions to each garden are included in the entry. This information has been supplied by the owners and garden inspectors and is aimed to be the best available to those travelling by car. However, it has been compiled to be used in conjunction with a road atlas.

The unreliability of train and bus services makes it unrewarding to include details, particularly as many garden visits are made on Sundays. However, many properties can be reached by public transport, and National Trust guides and the NGS Yellow Book sometimes give details.

The numbers on the maps correspond to the numbers of the gardens in each county. The maps show the proximity of one garden to another so that visits to several gardens can be planned for the same day. It is worthwhile referring to the maps of bordering counties to see if another garden visit can be included in the itinerary, and to look at the maps at the end of the *Guide*.

SHROPSHIRE

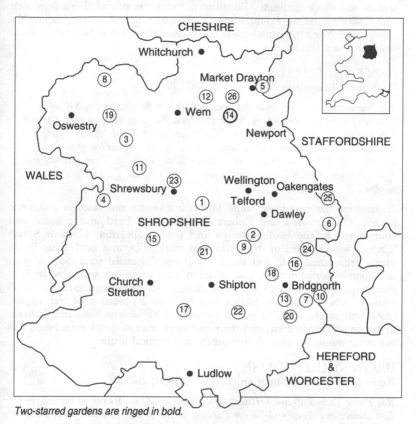

CHESHIRE

Whitchurch ●

⑧

Market Drayton
⑫ ⑳ ⑤
● Wem ⑭
⑲
● Oswestry

Newport ●
⑤
STAFFORDSHIRE

③

⑪
⑳
Shrewsbury Wellington
④ ① Telford Oakengates
SHROPSHIRE ● Dawley ㉕
⑮ ② ⑥
㉑ ⑨
㉔
⑯
⑱
Church ● Shipton Bridgnorth
Stretton ⑬ ⑦ ⑩
⑰ ㉒ ⑳

WALES

HEREFORD
&
● Ludlow WORCESTER

Two-starred gardens are ringed in bold.

ATTINGHAM PARK   1
Attingham, Nr Shrewsbury, Shropshire. Tel: (01743) 709203

*The National Trust ★ 4m SE of Shrewsbury. Turn off B4380 at Atcham ★
Parking ★ Tearoom. Picnics allowed along Mile Walk ★ Toilet facilities ★ Partly
suitable for wheelchairs. Self-drive electric scooter available but prior booking
essential ★ Dogs on lead in grounds (not allowed in deer park) ★ Shop ★ House
open April to 27th Sept, Sat – Wed, 1.30 – 5pm; Bank Holiday Mons, 11am –
5pm; Oct, Sat and Sun, 1.30 – 5pm (last admission for all 4.30pm). Parties by
arrangement ★ Grounds and park open daily except 25th Dec during daylight
hours ★ Entrance: £1.40, children 70p (house and grounds £3.50, children
£1.75, family £8.70). Party and out-of-hours rates available*

The house is really the main attraction, but after a tour of it one can enjoy a half-mile walk by the River Tern with daffodils in the spring followed by azaleas and rhododendrons. In autumn, colour is provided by dogwoods and American thorns. Foundations of the old mill can be seen below the upper weir. A few perennials near the house but this is a garden mainly of large trees and shrubs.

BENTHALL HALL   2
Broseley, Shropshire. Tel: (01952) 882159

The National Trust. Tenants: Mr and Mrs James Benthall ★ 1m SW of Broseley off B4375, 4m NE of Much Wenlock, 8m S of Wellington ★ Parking 150 yards down road ★ No picnics ★ Toilet facilities ★ Partly suitable for wheelchairs ★ Part of house open same times as garden ★ Garden open 2nd April to 27th Sept, Wed, Sun and Bank Holiday Mon, 1.30 – 5.30pm (last admission 5pm). Parties at other times by arrangement ★ Entrance: £2 (£3 house and gardens)

A small garden containing some interesting plants and features and some topiary. George Maw and Robert Bateman both lived in the house and contributed to the garden design and plant collection. Graham Stuart Thomas was involved in the restoration work. The rose garden has lovely plants and a small pool and there is a delightful raised scree bed. A good collection of geraniums and ground-cover plants together with a peony bed, clematis and roses through trees and shrubs create a pleasant garden to stroll through. The old kitchen garden now contains a collection of crab apples, roses, wall plants, etc. The crocus introduced by George Maw and daffodils in spring provide interest, and the many large trees of Scots pine, beech and oak are stunning features. A monument to botanical history.

BROWNHILL HOUSE   3
Ruyton XI Towns, Shropshire. Tel: (01939) 260626

Roger and Yoland Brown ★ 10m NW of Shrewsbury on B4397 in the village ★ Best season: end May/mid-July ★ Parking at the Bridge Inn 100 yards away ★ Teas ★ Toilet facilities ★ Plants for sale ★ Open 14th, 27th, 28th May, 18th June, 15th, 16th July, 10th Sept, 2 – 6pm and by appointment May to Aug ★ Entrance: £1.50, children free

Out of an impossible north-facing cliff a garden of great variety has been created. Since 1972 the slope has been transformed from a scrap-covered wilderness to a series of terraces and small gardens connected by over 450 steps that wander up and down the hill through plantings of trees and shrubs, patches of wild flowers and open flower-filled spaces. At the bottom a riverside garden runs from an open lawn to a bog garden. A series of formal terraces includes a laburnum walk and at the top there are paved areas with a pool, gazebo, parterre, a long walk with herbaceous border, flowerbeds and a large kitchen garden with glasshouses. Also a folly, Thai spirit house, sculptures. A grotto is under development.

BURFORD HOUSE GARDENS
(see Hereford and Worcester)

CHURCH BANK 4
Rowley, Shropshire. Tel: (01743) 891661

Mr and Mrs P.M. Kavanagh ★ 12m SW of Shrewsbury on B4386 Montgomery road, continuing through Westbury. After ⅓m turn right towards Rowley. After 3½m turn left at crossroads for Brockton. Church Bank is 120 yards on left ★ Best season: mid-July ★ Parking ★ Picnics allowed ★ Plants for sale when available ★ Open by appointment from May to Sept and on 23rd July and 20th Aug for NGS ★ Entrance: £1.20, children free (1994 prices)

Two-acre garden on a south-facing hillside created by the owners over the past five years. It contains a considerable range of plants and has some good design features. Standing on the terrace one looks down on a mass of colour and at the bottom is the pool and conservation area which fits well into the surrounding countryside. Either side of the drive are raised beds with heathers and evergreens as well as many perennials. A vegetable garden with soft fruit. Features include a collection with betula and grasses, various containers, a pergola and many shrubs. All-year interest and colour.

THE COVERT 5
Pheasant Walk, Burntwood, Loggerheads, Market Drayton, Shropshire. Tel: (01630) 672677

Mr and Mrs Leslie Standeven ★ Turn off A53 Newcastle – Market Drayton road onto Burntwood, S of Loggerheads crossroads. Follow Burntwood until Pheasant Walk opens off ★ Parking nearby ★ Teas ★ Toilet facilities ★ Partly suitable for wheelchairs ★ Plants for sale ★ Open 9th July, 2 – 6pm and by appointment ★ Entrance: £2, children 50p

Everyone will enjoy the patterns, colours and vistas here, but for the plantaholic, it is a box of delights. The owner is a designer and has brought her training to the display of plants. In three-quarters of an acre there is an extraordinary variety commencing with a scree garden of Mediterranean plants at the front of the house and continuing through a bog garden, a pool garden, alpines in scree and tufa beds, architectural and herbaceous plants (many of uncommon species), shrubs and trees. Labelling is excellent.

DAVID AUSTIN ROSES 6
Bowling Green Lane, Albrighton, Nr Wolverhampton, Shropshire. Tel: (01902) 373931

Mr and Mrs David Austin ★ 8m NW of Wolverhampton, 4m from Shifnal, between the A41 and A464. Take junction 3 off M54 towards Albrighton. Turn right at sign 'Roses and Shrubs' then take the second right (Bowling Green Lane) ★ Best season: late June/July ★ Parking ★ Refreshments: tea, coffee and biscuits ★ Toilet facilities ★ Suitable for wheelchairs ★ Dogs on leads ★ Plant centre ★ Garden open March to Oct, Mon – Fri, 9am – 6pm, Sat, Sun and Bank Holiday Mons, 10am – 6pm. Nov to Feb, Mon – Fri, 9am – 5pm, Sat, 10am – dusk, Sun, 12 noon – dusk. Closed 25th, 26th Dec and 1st Jan ★ Entrance: free

David Austin is one of the country's leading rose breeders so this is an ideal place for inspecting roses. There are about 900 varieties, including shrub, old roses, climbing and species. At flowering time there is a riot of colour. They are well displayed and elsewhere there are iris, a peony garden and hardy plants. The nursery stocks a good range of plants other than roses. David Austin's private garden is occasionally open to the public.

THE DOROTHY CLIVE GARDEN
(see Staffordshire)

DUDMASTON 7
Quatt, Nr Bridgnorth, Shropshire. Tel: (01746) 780866

The National Trust ★ 4m SE of Bridgnorth on A442 ★ Best season: late May but planted for spring, summer and autumn colour ★ Parking ★ Teas ★ Toilet facilities ★ Partly suitable for wheelchairs. Batricar available ★ Dogs on lead in Dingle only ★ Plants for sale ★ Shop ★ House open ★ Garden open 29th March to 1st Oct, Wed and Sun, 2 – 5.30pm (last admission 5pm). Special opening for pre-booked parties only, Thurs, 2 – 5.30pm. Estate open free of charge for pedestrian access throughout the year ★ Entrance: £2.50 (house and garden £3.50 (applies to Thurs special openings), parties £2.90 per person)

An eight-acre garden of appeal and interest with its large pool and bog garden and the associated plants along with island beds with shrubs, azaleas, rhododendrons, viburnums and lovely old roses. Some large specimen trees bring an air of peace to the garden, and there are old fruit trees including mulberry and medlars to add to the interest of old shrubs. Alas, there are no plant labels to help identify the specimens. There are two estate walks of between 4 to 5½ miles starting from Hampton Cope off A442. This is one of half-a-dozen gardens near Bridgnorth, and, if there is time to spare, it is worth going in to town to see the Telford church and the town gardens beside it.

ERWAY FARM HOUSE 8
Nr Ellesmere, Shropshire. Tel: (0169175) 479

Mr and Mrs Alan Palmer ★ 3m N of Ellesmere, 2m S of Overton on Dee. On B5068 Ellesmere – St Martins road after Dudleston Heath, turn right then second left ★ Best season: late May ★ Parking ★ Toilet facilities ★ Rare plants for sale ★ Open 15th to 17th April and last Sun in every month, 2 – 6pm ★ Entrance: £1, children free. Parties by appointment

It is difficult to describe adequately the wonderful range of plants this garden contains. Starting early in the year are masses of galanthus, hellebores, aconites and Sprengeri tulips, followed by hostas, iris, peonies and roses. There are many shrubs and trees, including rare willows, beneath which grow lilies, alliums, hardy cyclamen and fritillarias. Other rare specimens include *Lathraea clandestina* and *Abutilon vitifolium*. A charming cottage garden adds summer interest. There is an interesting collection of contemporary sculpture and a new wildlife area with pond is planned.

FARLEY HOUSE 9
Nr Much Wenlock, Shropshire. Tel: (01952) 727017

Mr and Mrs R.W. Collingwood ★ In Much Wenlock on the A458, turn on to A4169 (formerly B4378) signed Ironbridge, garden is 1m on left ★ Parking very limited on main road ★ Toilet facilities ★ Plants for sale if available ★ Open by arrangement April to Oct. Coach parties welcome ★ Entrance: £1

This one-acre garden has been created on a hillside since 1980 by the present owners, and it is interesting to see how they have gradually cleared land to create island beds containing a wide variety of plants. The garden is not yet finished. It has a cottage-garden feel and this is reflected in the plants. Paved area with alpines and raised beds and a peat bed. Troughs and range of conifers.

GATACRE PARK 10
Six Ashes, Nr Bridgnorth, Shropshire. Tel: (01384221) 211

Lady Thompson ★ 6m SE of Bridgnorth on A58 Stourbridge – Bridgnorth road ★ Parking ★ Refreshments: tea and biscuits ★ Toilet facilities ★ Plants for sale ★ Open 7th, 14th May, 2 – 6pm ★ Entrance: £1.50, children free. Parties by arrangement

This eight-acre garden has a wide range of features and plants. Vast rhododendrons and azaleas in the woodland area contrast with the Italianate sunken garden with a rectangular lily pool, and columnar trees and a yew arch. Island beds of shrubs and herbaceous plants provide good colour and foliage contrasts and include a vast yucca. Nearby on the lawn is a wonderful specimen of *Liriodendron tulipifera* and a large mulberry tree. Elsewhere is fascinating topiary, ranging from teapots, teddy bears and a corkscrew to the Gatacre monster. There are roses, acers, herbaceous borders, an excellent walled garden and good climbers around the house.

HAUGHMOND 11
Felton Butler, Shropshire. Tel: (0174381) 473

Mr and Mrs G.E. Pearce ★ 8m N of Shrewsbury, turn off the A5 to Felton Butler and in 1½m turn left ★ Best season: June ★ Parking in field ★ Teas ★ Toilet facilities ★ Suitable for wheelchairs ★ Plants for sale ★ House is up for sale so may not be open in 1995 but if still in the hands of present owners they will be open by appointment

Beautiful colour and foliage contrasts offer the visitor plenty of ideas. The owner reckons to create a new bed every year and raises many plants from cuttings – there is a hedge of various specimens raised this way. The range of plants is considerable and one has the advantage of being able to purchase many of them from the little nursery. Clematis scramble through and onto the pergola, along with a golden hop and roses. A hedge created from hips makes the boundary. There is a shade border, range of herbs, euphorbias, pool with lilies, astilbes and ligularias. A range of conifers, bottle brush plants, buddleias and a hedge of golden leylandii.

HAWKSTONE 12
**Weston-under-Redcastle, Nr Shrewsbury, Shropshire.
Tel: Hotel: (01939) 200611; Information: (01939) 200300;
Hall: (01630) 685242**

13m NE of Shrewsbury, 6m SW of Market Drayton ★ Park open April to Oct, daily, 10am – 6pm. Hall gardens open 29th May and 5th to 31st Aug (principal rooms of hall also open). ★ Entrance: park £4, OAP £3, children £2, family (2 adults and 3 children) £10; hall and gardens £2, children 75p

SHROPSHIRE

What Marcus Binney describes as 'a heroic new chapter' in the rescue of these historic gardens has just taken place. In their day they were as famous as Stowe and Stourhead and through the generosity of the proprietors of the *Hawkstone Park Hotel*, the grounds have been returned to their eighteenth-century grandeur and sublimity (the latter was supposed to induce awe if not fear). A series of monuments now reconstructed is linked by winding paths and tunnels. Ascending towards the White Tower the visitor passes the thatched buildings in one of which was a mechanical hermit famous for his artificial cough (now replaced by a hologram), then a grotto (used to house Santa at Xmas) and a so-called Swiss bridge, a fallen tree across a gorge. Much remains to be done to the Red Castle, which is genuinely medieval. The whole thing is a triumph for all involved, including English Heritage who rate this Grade I. There are three set walks through the park (3½m, 2½m and 1¾m) but visitors should be warned that all involve climbing and descending many steps, often of uneven height, totally unsuited for those with walking or visual difficulties. About a mile from the car park is *Hawkstone Hall*, owned by the Redemptorists, which has fine formal gardens around it, a colourful indoor winter garden and a courtyard garden. The terraced gardens include a lily pool, rockery and many fine trees including a monkey puzzle. The owners are proud of their own antiquities.

HAYE HOUSE   13
Eardington, Nr. Bridgnorth, Shropshire. Tel: (01746) 764884

Mrs Eileen Paradise ★ 2½m S of Bridgnorth on the B4555 Highley road. Through village of Eardington, then farmhouse 1m on left ★ Parking in courtyard ★ Teas with home-made cakes by prior arrangement ★ Toilet facilities ★ Partly suitable for wheelchairs ★ Plants possibly for sale ★ Open April to Sept by appointment ★ Entrance: £2

The owner is a National Flower Demonstrator and accepts parties for demonstrations. The garden was created to provide appropriate material and specimens. The vegetable garden and old tennis court on the outskirts also contain flower and plant material to be used in flower arranging.

HODNET HALL ★★   14
Hodnet, Shropshire. Tel: (01630) 685202

Mr A.E.H. and The Hon. Mrs Heber-Percy ★ 5½m SW of Market Drayton, 12m NE of Shrewsbury at junction of A53 and A442 ★ Best season: early summer ★ Parking for cars and coaches ★ Refreshments: snacks and teas ★ Toilet facilities ★ Partly suitable for wheelchairs ★ Dogs on lead ★ Plants for sale ★ Shop ★ Open April to Sept, Tues – Sat, 2 – 5 pm, Sun and Bank Holiday Mons, 12 noon – 5.30pm ★ Entrance: £2.60, OAP and parties per person £2.10, children £1 (1994 prices)

This garden has been superbly planted to give interest through the seasons – daffodils and blossom in spring, then primulas, rhododendrons, azaleas, laburnums and lilacs, followed by roses, peonies and astilbes merging in summer with the hydrangeas and shrubs that continue until the autumn foliage and berries round off the year. There are great trees on the estate and a magnolia walk along with many unusual plants. Arranged around a chain of lakes which comprise one of the largest water gardens in England, it is the home of a romantic bevy of black swans. Magnificent at all seasons. The walled kitchen garden is set aside for the sale of shrubs, fruit, flowers, etc.

LONGNOR HALL 15
Nr Dorrington, Shrewsbury, Shropshire. Tel: (01743) 718543

Mr and Mrs A.V. Nicholson ★ Off A49 S of Shrewsbury, turn to Longnor and enter the garden through the grounds of Longnor Church ★ Parking ★ Teas and toilet facilities at village hall ★ Plants for sale ★ Open 28th, 29th May, 2 – 6pm ★ Entrance: £1.50, children 50p

This beautiful garden has the tallest native black poplar in England, and the tallest Scots pine in the county. The arboretum is continually being planted and contains several varieties of oaks and cedars, along with maples, limes and copper beeches. The area around the house is grassed, surrounded by high beech and yew hedges with fine wrought iron gates leading into a deer park. The walled garden has good herbaceous borders, roses and clematis-clad walls. A row of cottages has rose beds alongside them and there is a wall of pear trees. The ornamental garden has a lily pool. The walled kitchen garden contains an extensive range of apples, vegetables, soft fruit and flowers for cutting. In the greenhouses are peaches, apricots and a vine. The owners hope to develop a water garden. Thirteenth-century church. In all, 70 acres, with over 2000 trees planted in the past few years.

LOWER HALL ★ 16
Worfield, Nr Bridgnorth, Shropshire. Tel: (017464) 607

Mr and Mrs C.F. Dumbell ★ A454 Wolverhampton/ Bridgnorth road, turn right to Worfield and after passing village stores and pub turn right ★ Best season: April to July ★ Parking in driveway or nearby roads ★ Garden room available for party catering. Catered events and tea and biscuits can also be arranged ★ Toilet facilities ★ Suitable for wheelchairs ★ Plants for sale ★ Open by appointment and 11th, 18th, 25th, 26th June ★ Entrance: £2, children under 12 free

This modern plantsman's garden has been created by the present owners since 1964, helped originally by the designer Lanning Roper. The walled garden has old brick paths and fruit trees through which climb roses and clematis; over the walls the village cottages and the Tudor house provide a fine backcloth to the garden. Everywhere the use of colour combinations and plant associations is good – a red border, another of white and green, giving a cool effect. The water garden is separated from the woodland garden by the River Worfe with two bridges and two weirs. The woodland garden includes rare magnolias, a collection of birch with bark interest, acers, amelanchiers – all-year variety and colour.

MILLICHOPE PARK 17
Munslow, Craven Arms, Shropshire. Tel: (0158476) 234

Mr and Mrs L. Bury ★ 8m NE of Craven Arms, 11m from Ludlow on B4368 Craven Arms road ★ Parking ★ Teas on open days. Picnics allowed in woodland ★ Toilet facilities ★ Dogs on lead ★ Plants for sale when available ★ Open 24th June, 2 – 6pm and by appointment ★ Entrance: £1.50, children 50p (1994 prices)

SHROPSHIRE

This 13-acre garden stands on the slopes of Wenlock Edge looking across to the Brown Clee Hill, and the view from the house includes a splendid artificial lake and vast trees, including a cedar of Lebanon, Douglas firs, copper beeches, Californian redwoods and an 140-foot *Abies procera*. Wandering through the woodland in spring, visitors enjoy masses of wild flowers – primroses, violets, bluebells and rhododendrons. The herbaceous borders are in the form of several small gardens surrounded by yew hedges. There is a series of small lakes and a pool surrounded by bog plants. Good pieces of sculpture and a fine old temple.

MORVILLE HALL GARDENS   18
Morville, Nr Bridgnorth, Shropshire.

The National Trust ★ 3m NW of Bridgnorth on A458 ★ Best season: summer ★ Parking ★ Teas ★ Toilet facilities ★ Partly suitable for wheelchairs ★ Open by written appointment to Mrs R. Norbury and twice a year for NGS ★ Entrance: £2, children 50p (joint entrance with The Dower House and Gatehouse gardens)

In 1985 reconstruction work on the garden commenced and photographs show the transformation effected by Trust volunteers. Mixed borders contain a wide range of shrubs, fuchsias and roses. Plums and cherries grow on the walls, there is a stewpond, ha-ha, glasshouse with vines and peaches, pool with lilies and irises. A vineyard was planted in 1989 and a box parterre containing 1000 plants is planted in the same pattern as the Tudor plasterwork in the kitchen. A frame is being covered with honeysuckle, roses and clematis and stone sculptures from monastic buildings mingle with old shrub roses. A sense of peace prevails in the garden. *The Dower House* garden started in 1989 features an Elizabethan knot garden, cloister garden, Victorian rose garden and maze. *The Gatehouse* garden includes a wide range of golden plants and a small area planted to give woodland effect, providing a pleasing contrast to the other two gardens.

OTELEY   19
Ellesmere, Shropshire.

Mr and Mrs R.K. Mainwaring ★ From S entrance opposite convent. Near A528/495 junction 1m E of Ellesmere. From N past The Mere turn left opposite convent. Drive through park to house ★ Parking ★ Teas ★ Toilet facilities ★ Suitable for wheelchairs if dry ★ Dogs on leads ★ Plants for sale ★ Open 29th May, 2 – 6pm, possibly one day in Sept, 1 – 5pm and by appointment ★ Entrance: £1.50, children 50p (1994 prices)

A magnificent 10-acre garden set in park and farmland with glimpses of The Mere beyond surrounding trees. Extensive lawns with architectural features, interesting and old handsome trees set about the lawns. Herbaceous borders backed by high walls covered with roses, clematis and other climbing plants. Grey silver border. Walled kitchen garden. Decorative island beds. Rhododendrons, azaleas, roses, shrubs in a gracious setting. Collection of peonies flowering simultaneously. Folly. All this plus what an inspector describes as 'one of the best plant stalls we have come across in 20 years of garden visiting, both for unusual plants and modest prices'.

THE PADDOCKS 20
Chelmarsh Common, Chelmarsh, Nr Bridgnorth, Shropshire. Tel: (01746) 861271

Mr and Mrs P. Hales ★ 3m S of Bridgnorth on Highley Road ★ Best season: late spring/early summer ★ Open by appointment ★ Entrance: £1 (£1.50 with tea and biscuits) for charity, children free

A 'cottage' garden with good use of old materials to make paths, pergolas, pagoda and rockeries. Typical cottage plants have been used and the garden is divided into 'room' areas. There is a stream garden with a bog area with good ideas for the amateur gardener. It contains a good range of plants. A charming small knot garden and a pond has been added with waterfall and fountain. A wild garden is also being created.

PREEN MANOR ★ 21
Church Preen, Nr Church Stretton, Shropshire. Tel: (01694) 771207

Mr and Mrs P. Trevor-Jones ★ 5m SW of Much Wenlock on B4371, 3m turn right for Church Preen and Hughley and after 1½m turn left for Church Preen, over crossroads and drive ½m on right ★ Parking ★ Teas ★ Plants for sale if available ★ Open 1st, 15th, 29th June, 13th, 27th July, 2 – 6pm, 1st Oct, 2 – 5pm and to parties of 15 or more by arrangement in June and July only ★ Entrance: £1.75, children 50p

An exceptional garden with many interesting features. A kitchen garden wall and garden gate remain of the now demolished manor house designed by Norman Shaw and set in a park with fine old trees. The present owners have restored and replanned it and round every corner or through a gateway there is always a surprise. The gravel garden has a yellow and white border and elsewhere is a silver border. The chess garden has replaced the swimming pool and there is a pot garden filling a corner. The vegetable garden has a parterre design and each bed has variety. The bog garden is attractive, and the unusual fernery is sited amongst some ruins. One could spend a day here.

RUTHALL MANOR ★ 22
Ditton Priors, Bridgnorth, Shropshire. Tel: (0174634) 608

Mr and Mrs G.T. Clarke ★ From Morville take B4368 and turn off for Ditton Priors. After entering the village turn right. Ruthall is ¾m ★ Best season: Easter to Oct ★ Parking in adjacent field ★ Tea shop in Ditton Priors open daily except Wed ★ Toilet facilities ★ Partly suitable for wheelchairs ★ Open by appointment and for parties ★ Entrance: £1.50

This one-acre garden has been cleverly designed since 1972 for ease of maintenance and planted to give pleasure to keen plant lovers. There are some unusual specimens and a collection of daphnes and birches and a group of sorbus, ilex, robinias and willows. By the pool is a collection of primulas, astilbes and iris. Good foliage and colour contrasts and something of interest all through the year. Small vegetable garden and fernery.

THE SHREWSBURY QUEST MEDIEVAL GARDEN 23
193 Abbey Foregate, Shrewsbury, Shropshire. Tel: (01743) 366355

Shrewsbury Quest ★ In Abbey Foregate, Shrewsbury ★ Car park next door 50p all day but beware of parking elsewhere ★ Refreshments: lunch and tea rooms ★ Suitable for disabled ★ Open daily except 25th Dec and 1st Jan, 10am – 5pm

Inside this medieval monastery 'experience' is a recently completed reproduction of a Tudor physic and herb garden designed by the well-known expert on medieval gardens, Dr Sylvia Landsberg. The work was completed in six months at a cost of £50,000, but this 'old' garden is so 'new' that it has not been inspected this year.

SWALLOW HAYES ★ 24
**Rectory Road, Albrighton, Nr Wolverhampton, Shropshire.
Tel: (01902) 372624**

Mrs Michael Edwards ★ 7m NW of Wolverhampton. Use M54 junction 3. Turn off A41 into Rectory Road after Garden Centre ★ Best seasons: May/June and autumn ★ Parking in drive and nearby road ★ Teas on open days ★ Toilet facilities ★ Suitable for wheelchairs ★ Dogs on lead ★ Plants for sale when available ★ Open 8th Jan (for National collection of witch hazels), 11am – 4pm and 30th April, 14th, 28th May, 2 – 6pm and for parties by arrangement ★ Entrance: £1.20, children 10p

A delightful two-acre modern garden with many design features and a beautiful display of plants, shrubs and trees. Although planted for easy maintenance, it contains nearly 3000 different types of plants and provides all-year interest. Alpine border divided into various soil conditions, Mediterranean wall with tender plants. Small pools, ferns, a woodland area, colour and foliage contrasts. The National collection of witch hazels and lupins and an interesting area of small gardens to copy at home. Vegetables and fruit trees; nursery stock beds and hardy geranium trial.

WESTON PARK ★ 25
Weston-under-Lizard, Nr Shifnal, Shropshire. Tel: (0195276) 207

Weston Park Foundation ★ On A5 7m W of junction 12 on M6 and 3m N of junction 3 on M54 ★ Best season: May/June ★ Parking ★ Stable Tea Rooms providing home baking and estate produce ★ Toilet facilities ★ Partly suitable for wheelchairs ★ Dogs ★ Shop ★ House open on certain occasions at additional entrance fee ★ Garden open April to 17th Sept (please enquire for dates and times) ★ Entrance: £3, OAP £2.50, children £2 (1994 prices)

A distinctive 'Capability' Brown creation covering almost 1000 acres of delightful woodland planted with rhododendrons and azaleas, together with beautiful pools. Some magnificent trees form a handsome backcloth to many shrubs. A rose walk leads to the deer park. The rose garden by the house and the Italian parterre garden have been restored. There are many architectural features – The Temple of Diana, Roman bridge and the Orangery all designed by James Paine. For those who wish to spend more time at Weston there are gourmet dinners and open-air cultural events in the park and gardens – details from owners. For children there is an adventure playground, the Weston Park Railway and a pets corner.

WOLLERTON OLD HALL ★ 26
Wollerton, Hodnet, Shropshire. Tel: (01630) 685769/685756 (daytime)

Mr and Mrs John Jenkins ★ From Shrewsbury take A53 to Hodnet. Turn right towards Market Drayton for ½m, then right just after Wollerton sign. Keep right at brick animal pound and turn left into drive after 80 yards ★ Parking ★ Refreshments: light lunches and teas ★ Toilet facilities ★ Plants for sale ★ Open 2nd June to 25th Aug, Fri only and 25th June, 6th, 28th Aug, all 1 – 5pm ★ Entrance: £2, children 50p

This two-acre garden is structured around the sixteenth-century house which has demanded formal lines of wall, beech and yew, resulting in at least 10 separate gardens each with its own character and theme. Priority in planting has been given to design, colour and plant association. This has been achieved by the intensive cultivation of perennials. At least 1300 species, some rare and tender. The garden is being carefully extended into shrub and wildflower areas overlooking the Tern valley.

NATIONAL COUNCIL FOR THE CONSERVATION OF PLANTS AND GARDENS

The NCCPG has just published the latest version of its *National Plant Collections Directory*. Anyone interested in particular families of plants who wants to see some of the rarer species and garden varieties will find this is an invaluable publication indicating where and when they can be seen. This edition, which offers information on about 550 collections comprising more than 50,000 plants, also contains articles by holders of the collections.

NATIONAL TRUST EVENTS

For a list of Summer events at National Trust properties members of the public should write with a large SAE (28p stamp) to: The National Trust, 'Summer Events', 36 Queen Anne's Gate, London SW1H 9AS.

WHEELCHAIR USERS

Please note that entries which describe a garden as 'suitable for wheelchairs' refer to the garden only. If there is a house open, it may or may not be suitable for wheelchairs.

SOMERSET

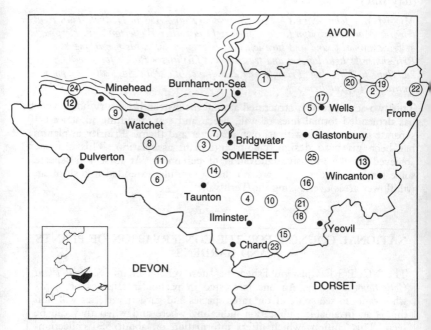

Two-starred gardens are ringed in bold.

AMBLESIDE AVIARIES AND GARDENS   1
Lower Weare, Nr Axbridge, Somerset. Tel: (01934) 732362

*Mrs T.K. Pickford ★ 1¹/₂m SW of Axbridge on A38 ★ Best season: May ★
Parking ★ Coaches by appointment ★ Refreshments: licensed restaurant, cream teas,
ice-creams ★ Toilet facilities ★ Suitable for wheelchairs ★ Souvenir and gift shop ★
Open March to Oct, daily, 10am – 5pm ★ Entrance: £2, OAP and children (over
3) 75p*

The trees around the large pool, which is bisected by a bridge, are really all
that remain of the original plan by the owner of some 40 years ago who
conceived the idea of a water garden as depicted on the 'Willow Pattern'
plate. The cherry blossom reflected in the lily pond, silhouetted by willows of
different varieties, give an oriental effect. The aviaries do not intrude on the
water garden and the variety of ducks adds to the atmosphere of rural peace
in spite of the busy road running alongside a high hedge.

AMMERDOWN HOUSE ★   2
Kilmersdon, Radstock, Somerset.

*Lord Hylton ★ On the B3139, ¹/₂m off A362 Radstock to Frome road ★ Parking
★ Open Bank Holiday Mons only: 17th April, 8th, 29th May, 28th Aug, 11am
– 5pm ★ Entrance: £2.50 for charity, children free*

A Bath-stone house originally designed by James Wyatt, with panoramic views on one side and a Lutyens garden on the other, the garden was a brilliant conception by Lutyens who wanted to link the house with the orangery. When one walks through the Italianate 'rooms' of yew and sculpture and parterre, one is unaware of the tricks of space that are being played. Massive yew planting, now mature and fully 12 foot high, creates enclosed formal areas which lead irresistibly one from another – the spaces between being almost entirely filled with hedging. The originality and grandeur remain as do some particularly clever details such as the clipped Portuguese laurels, honeysuckles trained over wire umbrellas, ancient lemon verbenas in pots in the orangery, and terraces. Daffodils, narcissi and cowslips are spring features, together with fountains and statues at all seasons.

BARFORD PARK ★   3
Spaxton, Nr Bridgwater, Somerset. Tel: (01278) 671269

Mr and Mrs M. Stancomb ★ 5m W of Bridgwater. Turn left to Enmore off the Spaxton road from Bridgwater ★ Best season: May to July ★ Parking ★ Teas for parties by arrangement ★ Toilet facilities ★ Partly suitable for wheelchairs ★ Dogs on lead ★ House open ★ Garden open May to 15th Sept, Wed, Thurs and Bank Holiday weekends, 2 – 5.30pm. Parties by arrangement at any time ★ Entrance: £2.50, children free (house and garden)

This is a garden in the eighteenth–century style developed over the last 32 years. Set in parkland and protected by a ha-ha on three sides, it has many features. After watching the golden orfe darting around the lily pond, stroll down a sweep of lawn to a stand of tall trees. There, in the woodland glade, is a carpet of many shades of primulas. The eighteenth–century walled garden is unusually situated in view of the house – a sweep of lawn with deep herbaceous borders on each side make a colourful vista.

BARRINGTON COURT GARDEN ★   4
Barrington, Somerset.

The National Trust ★ 5m N of Ilminster, in the village of Barrington on B3168 ★ Parking ★ Refreshments ★ Toilet facilities ★ Suitable for wheelchairs. Self-drive buggy available ★ Plants for sale ★ Court House open 5th April to 27th Sept, Wed only, 11am – 5.30pm (last admission 5pm). £1 ★ Garden open April to 1st Oct, daily except Fri, 11am – 5.30pm (last admission 5pm) ★ Entrance: £3.10, children £1.50. Parties (by arrangement with NT Wessex Regional Office) £2.60 per person, children £1.20

In 1917, Gertrude Jekyll planned planting for this derelict property for the Lyle family. Set in a park with avenues of mature chestnut trees, the gardens follow the Hidcote style of separate 'rooms'. The lily pool area has surrounding beds of golden lilies, coppery wallflowers and shades of coral pink azaleas. The white-flowering and silver-leaved plants are seen in the White Garden, though this is a Lyle scheme *à la* Sissinghurst, not Jekyll. It is fascinating that this was part of the farm, before the Lyle lease, and the cattle troughs can still be seen in the beds. Beyond, a pergola, also not Jekyll, supports clematis, wisteria and honeysuckles in profusion. Note the cattle sheds *c.* 1800 of considerable visual appeal. The vast walled kitchen garden produces a wide variety of fruit and vegetables. Further afield a cider orchard provides raw material for the liquid refreshments. The Trust is restoring these gardens to their Jekyll plantings and design but will not decide for 10 years whether to restore the White Garden in similar fashion. In addition to its great charm, Barrington offers visitors an unusual opportunity to see a garden being restored to Jekyll origins. Although Jekyll had other plans for the remains of the garden these were never carried through and the three 'rooms' are the only areas the Trust plans to restore.

THE BISHOPS PALACE 5
Wells, Somerset. Tel: (01749) 678691

The Church Commissioners ★ In centre of Wells, adjacent to Cathedral ★ Public parking in city car parks nearby ★ Refreshments ★ Toilet facilities ★ Bishop's Chapel open ★ Garden open 4th April to Oct, Tues, Thurs and Bank Holiday Mons, 11am – 6pm, Sun 2 – 6pm. Also Aug, daily, 11am – 6pm (last admission 5.30pm) ★ Entrance: £2, UB40 holder £1, accompanied children free. Parties of 10 or more £1.50 per person (1994 prices)

The ruins of the banqueting hall have been 'room scaped' with shrubs and herbaceous plants. A shrub rose garden has been planted near the water (from the wells). An unusual garden ornament has been carved from the root of a very old yew tree, depicting Adam and Eve being expelled from the Garden of Eden by an angel with a flaming sword. There are fine mature trees from plantings in the mid-nineteenth century, e.g. black walnut, gingko; and an acre of the walled garden was laid out as an arboretum to commemorate the Queen's Silver Jubilee in 1977. An interesting collection includes the Chinese foxglove tree and a European hornbeam.

BITTESCOMBE MANOR 6
Upton, Nr Wiveliscombe, Taunton, Somerset. Tel: (0139) 87240

Mr and Mrs D. Wood ★ 6m W of Wiveliscombe. Leave M5 at junction 25. Take B3227 Wiveliscombe road ★ Parking ★ Teas ★ Toilet facilities ★ Partly suitable for wheelchairs ★ Dogs on lead ★ Plants for sale ★ Open 28th, 29th May, 2 – 5.30pm ★ Entrance: £1.50, children free (1994 prices)

A formal walled rose garden surrounded by shrubs – brilliant rhododendrons in tall clumps glow against the foliage of the trees growing up the hillside. The water garden is formed from a series of large pools, with water falling gently down the hillside to a small lake in a grassy setting. Woodland walks.

CANNINGTON COLLEGE GARDENS ★ 7
Cannington, Nr Bridgwater, Somerset. Tel: (01278) 652226

Cannington College ★ 3m NW of Bridgwater on A39 ★ Parking ★ Teas for parties by arrangement ★ Toilet facilities ★ Guide dogs only ★ Plant centre ★ Open 17th April to Oct, daily, 2 – 5pm ★ Entrance: £1.50, OAP and children 75p. Groups contact Mr Rudhall (ext. 234)

The College was founded in 1922 in the grounds of an old Benedictine priory. Plant specialists may find here the National collections of abutilon, argyranthemum, ceanothus, cordyline, osteospermum, phormium, wisteria and yucca. Various glasshouses reproduce the conditions – temperate, subtropical, tropical – for houseplants of a different clime. A plant centre close to the garden sells some of the National collection species and a range of other plants and shrubs. Visitors are also encouraged to view the landscaped gardens across the A39.

COMBE SYDENHAM COUNTRY PARK   8
Monksilver, Taunton, Somerset. Tel: (01984) 56284

Mr and Mrs W. Theed ★ 5m S of Watchet on B3188 between Monksilver and Wiveliscombe ★ Parking inc. coaches ★ Refreshments: home-made lunches, cream teas ★ Toilet facilities ★ Plants for sale ★ Shop (inc. trout from estate) ★ Courtroom (west wing) Mon – Fri, 11am – 4pm ★ Country Park open 27th March to Oct, daily except Sat, 10am – 5pm ★ Entrance: £4, children £1.50 (garden and country park)

Surrounded by a deer park, the small formal Elizabethan parterre-garden is being restored and restocked with old types of roses. The pink lavender is a source of pride to Mrs Theed who also cultivates the old herb garden. Quince trees and a peacock house create the atmosphere of a domestic garden in Tudor times.

DUNSTER CASTLE ★   9
Dunster, Nr Minehead, Somerset. Tel: (01643) 821314

The National Trust ★ 3m SE of Minehead on A39 ★ Best season: May/June ★ Parking ★ Refreshments in Dunster ★ Toilet facilities ★ Electrically-operated self-drive Batricar, and volunteer-driven multi-seater, available for disabled and infirm ★ Dogs in park only ★ Shop ★ Castle open different dates ★ Garden and park open Feb to 10th Dec, daily, 11am – 5pm (closes 4pm Feb and March, and Oct to Dec). Garden and park open 14th April ★ Entrance: £2.70, children under 16 £1.30, family ticket (2 adults and 3 children) £6.50 (castle, garden and park £4.80, children under 16 £2.40, pre-arranged parties £4.30 per person)

The family which had lived here since the fourteenth century gave it to The National Trust in 1976. A very fine herbaceous border backed by rare shrubs surrounds a lawn by the keep and is well worth the steep climb to view. On the formal terraces below thrive a variety of sub-tropical plants, camellias and azaleas. Thousands of bulbs have been planted and after the daffodils and snowdrops come fine displays of forsythias, camellias and early rhododendrons. There is the National collection of arbutus and a huge 60ft *Magnolia campbellii*. There are views across to Exmoor, the Quantocks and the Bristol Channel. The park totals 28 acres in all.

EAST LAMBROOK MANOR ★   10
Nr South Petherton, Somerset. Tel: (01460) 240328

Mr and Mrs A. Norton ★ 2m NE of South Petherton off A303 ★ Parking ★ Coaches by arrangement ★ Refreshments: coffee and biscuits only but parties by arrangement ★ Toilet facility ★ Plants for sale (mailing list) ★ Shop for Margery Fish publications ★ Open March to Oct, Mon – Sat, 10am – 5pm ★ Entrance: £2, OAP £1.90, school age children 50p

Margery Fish established these gardens for endangered species and the present owners have carried on her tradition. The result is an impression of luxuriant growth. The garden's ring paths are half-hidden by the profusion of plants and its controlled wilderness of colour and scent give the discerning a chance to find rare plants and shrubs. National collection of geranium (cranesbill) species and cultivars is here.

FORDE ABBEY
(see Dorset)

GAULDEN MANOR ★   11
Tolland, Lydeard St Lawrence, Nr Taunton, Somerset.
Tel: (019847) 213

Mr J.H.N. Starkie ★ 9m NW of Taunton off A358 ★ Parking ★ Teas (by arrangement for parties) ★ Toilet facilities ★ Shop ★ House open ★ Garden open 16th, 17th April and 30th April to 3rd Sept, Suns, Thurs and Bank Holiday Mons, 2 – 5.30pm. Also parties at other times by prior arrangement ★ Entrance: £1.50 (house and gardens £3)

Garden seats at vantage points give the visitor a chance to appreciate the many different vistas provided in this country garden which includes a bog garden, herb garden, butterfly garden and herbaceous borders of selected colour. A short walk through a woodland glade leads to a secret garden of white flowering plants. Visitors should not miss the small duck garden with carvings on the fence posts near the tea house.

GREENCOMBE ★★   12
Porlock, Somerset. Tel: (01643) 862363

Greencombe Garden Trust (Miss Joan Loraine) ★ ½m W of Porlock off B3225 ★ Parking ★ Coaches by arrangement ★ Toilet facility ★ Partly suitable for wheelchairs ★ Plants for sale ★ Open April to July, Sat – Tues, 2 – 6pm or by appointment ★ Entrance: £2.50, children 50p (1994 prices)

Created in 1946 by Horace Stroud, this garden was extended by the present owner over the last 21 years. Overlooking the Severn, set on a hillside where the sun cannot penetrate for nearly two months in the winter, it glows with colour. The formal lawns and beds round the house are immaculate and by contrast the woodland area, terraced on the hillside, provides a nature walk of great interest. A wide variety of rhododendrons and azaleas flower in the shelter of mature trees, where ferns and woodland plants flourish. No sprays or chemicals are used in the cultivation of this completely 'organic' garden which contains the National collections of erythronium, gaultheria, polystichum and vaccinium.

HADSPEN GARDEN AND NURSERY ★★   13
Castle Cary, Somerset. Tel: (01749) 813707

Mr N.A. Hobhouse and N. and S. Pope ★ 2m SE of Castle Cary on A371 ★ Parking ★ Coaches by arrangement ★ Light refreshments Thurs to Sat and teas on Sun and Bank Holidays ★ Toilet facilities ★ Partly suitable for wheelchairs ★ Plants for sale ★ Open March to 1st Oct, Thurs – Sun but open Bank Holiday Mon, 9am – 6pm ★ Entrance: £2, children 50p

The basic plan in this garden was created by Margaret Hobhouse in the

Victorian gardening 'boom' days to provide a setting for the eighteenth-century hamstone Hobhouse home. Over the years the garden became overgrown and formless with an interval in the 1960s when Penelope Hobhouse endeavoured to restore some order. In the last few years the present owners have reclaimed the garden, retaining the best of the original plan and embellishing it with a variety of planting to provide colour, shape and interest. It is now a classic country house garden, with carefully colour-schemed herbaceous borders, a lily pond in a formal setting, shrub walks, a curved walled garden contrasted by wild flowers in the meadow, all framed in parkland. Recent visitors write that they found this an amazing display of colour and interest in July.

HESTERCOMBE HOUSE GARDENS ★   14
Cheddon Fitzpaine, Taunton, Somerset. Tel: (01823) 337222

Somerset County Council ★ Close to the village of Cheddon Fitzpaine just N of Taunton, follow the 'daisy' sign to the garden ★ Best season: June/July ★ Parking ★ Coaches by arrangement only ★ Picnics on lawn ★ Toilet facilities in house ★ Wheelchairs limited to four main areas ★ Part of the interior of the house open ★ Garden open all year, Mon – Fri, 9am – 5pm, also May to Sept, Sat and Sun, 2 – 5pm ★ Entrance: £2, OAP £1.50, children free. Garden plan and guide available 50p (1994 prices)

This is a superb product of the collaboration between Edwin Lutyens and Gertrude Jekyll, blending the formal art of architecture with the art of plants. On a limited budget the Somerset County Council has endeavoured to maintain the gardens, respecting the colour groupings of the original designs and keeping the water courses flowing as they would have in Edwardian days. The *Oxford Companion* describes this as Lutyens at his best in the detailed design of steps, pools, walls, paving and seating. The canal, pergola and orangery are fine examples of his work. The Council's programme to restore the gardens to Gertrude Jekyll's original plant design is proceeding well, and the leaflet which details this and Lutyen's stonework is most useful.

LOWER SEVERALLS   15
Haselbury Road, Crewkerne, Somerset. Tel: (01460) 73234

Audrey and Mary Pring ★ 1½m NE of Crewkerne off B3165 ★ Parking on road ★ Teas on charity open days ★ Suitable for wheelchairs ★ Plants for sale in nursery ★ Open March to Oct, weekdays except Thurs, 10am – 5pm, Sun, 2 – 5pm ★ Entrance: £1

A typical cottage garden with herbaceous border against stone-walled house. The garden extends through stone pillars which make a frame for the view of the valley over lawn and varied shrubs and a bog garden. Specialists in herbs, geraniums and salvias. A water garden has now been created, fed from a spring in adjacent farmland, together with a 'wadi' or dry garden built up to form a windbreak for a sheltered valley.

LYTES CARY MANOR   16
Nr Somerton, Somerset. Tel: (01458) 223297

The National Trust ★ 2½m NE of Ilchester, signposted from large roundabout on

*A303 ★ Best season: late June/early July ★ Parking ★ Suitable for wheelchairs ★
Plants for sale inc. good selection of perennials ★ Open April to 28th Oct, Mon,
Wed and Sat, 2 – 6pm or dusk if earlier (last admission 5.30pm) ★ Entrance:
£3.70, children £1.90*

This garden was revived by its present tenants with advice from Graham
Stuart Thomas who designed a wide border with a mixture of roses, shrubs
and herbaceous plants. There are also pleasing lawns with hedges in
Elizabethan style and some topiary as well as a large orchard with naturalised
bulbs and mown walks with a central sundial.

MILTON LODGE ★   17
Wells, Somerset. Tel: (01749) 672168

*Mr D.C. Tudway Quilter ★ ½m N of Wells. From A39 to Bristol turn N up Old
Bristol Road ★ Best season: midsummer ★ Car park for cars and minibus only.
First gate on the left ★ Teas on Sun and Bank Holidays ★ Toilet facilities ★
Open 14th April to Oct, daily except Sat, 2 – 6pm ★ Entrance: £2, children
under 14 free. Private parties and coaches by special arrangement*

The garden, replanted by the present owners in the 1960s, is cultivated
down the side of a hill overlooking the Vale of Avalon, affording a magnificent view of Wells Cathedral. A wide variety of plants all suitable for the
alkaline soil provide a succession of colours and interest from March to
October. Many fine trees can be seen in the garden and in the seven-acre
arboretum opposite the entrance to the car park.

MONTACUTE HOUSE ★   18
Montacute, Yeovil, Somerset. Tel: (01935) 823289

*The National Trust ★ 4m W of Yeovil. NT signs off A3088 and A303 near
Ilchester ★ Best season: June to Sept ★ Parking ★ Refreshments: light lunches and
teas ★ Toilet facilities ★ Suitable for wheelchairs ★ Dogs on lead in park only ★
Plants for sale March to mid-Dec ★ Shop ★ House open April to 30th Oct, 12
noon – 5.30pm. Closed 14th April ★ Park and garden open throughout year,
daily except Tues, 11.30pm – 5.30pm. Other times by arrangement with
administrator ★ Entrance: £2.70 (Nov to April £1.30) (house and garden
£4.80)*

This Elizabethan garden of grass lawns surrounded by clipped yews set in
terraces is a triumph of formality. The surrealism of the topiary, which some
claim was inspired by a dramatic snowfall, adds immensely to the effect. A
large water feature has replaced the original Elizabethan high circular mount.
Colours are provided by herbaceous borders from mid-summer. There is a
charming raised walk, two original pavilions, and an arcaded garden house
probably devised by George Curzon during the tenancy when he lived here,
first with Elinor Glyn, then with his second American wife. The gardens are
surrounded by graceful parklands giving vistas and an impression of space. A
new avenue of 72 limes to replace the existing one, which has several trees
either missing or reaching the end of their lives, is underway.

THE OLD RECTORY (Seaborough)
(see Dorset)

R.T. HERBS AND GARDEN 19
Kilmersdon, Radstock, Somerset. Tel: (01761) 35470

*Mr and Mrs R. Taylor ★ 6m NE of Shepton Mallet on B3139 ★ Best season:
spring/summer ★ Public car park adjacent ★ Refreshments in local pub ★ Plants
for sale ★ Open daily, 9am – 6pm or dusk ★ Entrance: donation box for charity*

This is a working garden far removed from the gracious lawns of a stately
home but demonstrating the potential of a narrow plot to become a graceful
and attractive garden. The wide variety of herbs mingled with herbaceous
plants and wild flowers attracts bees, butterflies and insects during the
summer and provides feeding grounds for wildlife during the winter months.

SHERBORNE GARDEN
(See Avon)

STON EASTON PARK ★ 20
Ston Easton, Somerset. Tel: (01761) 241631

*Peter and Christine Smedley ★ 11m from Bath, 6m from Wells on A37 ★
Parking ★ Teas at hotel ★ Toilet facilities in hotel ★ Open by appointment only ★
Entrance: free*

Ston Easton Park is a listed Grade I Palladian house and park. The grounds
were laid out and planned by Humphry Repton in 1792-3. Penelope
Hobhouse is working with the Smedleys on the restoration of the park, now
the grounds of their hotel. For the opportunity to study the restoration of a
great eighteenth-century park in progress it is worth making an appointment
to visit. A suitably impressive drive winds past old stables to the plain
Palladian magnificence of the house. As always Humphry Repton made a Red
Book with his proposals for improvements. There is a terrace, wide lawns,
woods, cedars, beeches, oaks, willows and some new yew hedges. The glory is
the view from the great Saloon – or the terrace – over the River Norr which
has a bridge and cascades for the correct romantic effect. Vast kitchen garden
with glasshouses, a cutting garden and yards of beautifully presented fruit
and vegetables. As an example of the dedication of the restoration it took
seven years to repair the kitchen garden walls, three and a half years for each
side. A rose garden, sited in the kitchen garden, has recently been completed
also with the help of Mrs Hobhouse.

TINTINHULL HOUSE GARDEN ★ 21
Tintinhull, Yeovil, Somerset.

*The National Trust ★ 5m NW of Yeovil, ½m S of A303 ★ Parking ★ Teas in
courtyard ★ Suitable for wheelchairs and special parking by arrangement ★ Open
April to Oct, Wed – Sun and Bank Holiday Mons, 12 noon – 6pm ★ Entrance:
£3.50, children £1.60*

A relatively small modern garden, barely one and a half acres, which achieves
an impression of greater size with a series of vistas created under the influence of Gertrude Jekyll and Hidcote. Developed from the 1930s by Phyllis
Reiss, it was in the tender care of Penelope Hobhouse from 1980 to 1993
when she moved to a house of her own. The wide variety of plants is not

labelled in order to retain the charm of a private garden but an inventory is available for interested visitors.

THE TROPICAL BIRD GARDENS 22
Rode, Nr Bath, Somerset. Tel: (01373) 830326

Mrs E.S. Risdon ★ 5m NE of Frome, signed off A361 ★ Parking ★ Refreshments: licensed cafeteria in summer, light refreshments in winter ★ Toilet facilities ★ Suitable for wheelchairs ★ Clematis for sale in season ★ Shop ★ Gardens open all year except 25th Dec, summer 10am – 6pm, winter 10am – dusk (last admission 1 hour before closing) ★ Entrance: £3.90, OAP £3.40, children (3–16) £2 (1994 prices)

The gardens have been developed to provide the background and natural habitat, as far as possible, for the birds. The clematis collection was started in 1985 and is now established. Mrs Risdon is the membership secretary of the British Clematis Society. Underplanting in the tree trail is going on continuously. Special clematis weekend 8th/9th July 1995.

WAYFORD MANOR ★ 23
Crewkerne, Somerset. Tel: (01460) 73253

Mr and Mrs R.L. Goffe ★ 3m SW of Crewkerne off B3165 at Clapton ★ Parking ★ Teas ★ Dogs on lead ★ Plants for sale ★ Open 9th, 30th April, 14th, 28th May, 2 – 6pm. Parties by appointment ★ Entrance: £1.50, children 50p (1994 prices)

A very well-maintained garden of flowering shrubs and trees, rhododendrons and spring bulbs, against the stonework of an Elizabethan house. This is a fine example of the work of Harold Peto who redesigned the garden in 1902 and whose original plans are being restored by the present owners and their dedicated gardener, Michael. The loss of mature trees and larger shrubs in the 1990 gale opened up an area which led to the discovery of a waterway previously buried. This has been cleared and now runs from the lower of a series of small pools down to a very much larger pool whose original shape had been lost by the force of peltiphyllum rhizomes pushing out the retaining stonework. Order has now been restored. Restoration of the winter garden is one of the new projects, with the introduction of more reliable dwarf trees than were available in Peto's day (such as *Cupressus sempervirens* 'Stricta'). The garden has also some rare and colourful maples.

WOODBOROUGH 24
Porlock Weir, Somerset. Tel: (01643) 862406

Mr and Mrs R.D. Milne ★ From A39 take B3226 towards Porlock Weir. At Porlock Vale House on right, take left tarmac lane uphill. Garden is the first on right ★ Best season: May ★ Limited parking. No coaches ★ Dogs on lead ★ Open 30th April, 7th, 8th, 28th, 29th May for charity, 11am – 5.30pm and at other times by appointment ★ Entrance: £1.50, children under 10 free

Sturdy footwear is recommended when visiting this fascinating garden created on a steep (1 in 4) hillside with magnificent views over Porlock Bay. The wide variety of shrubs includes some of the lesser-known hybrid rhododendrons and a number of Ghent azaleas. A bog garden and two pools add interest over a longer season. Mr and Mrs Milne are hoping to share with visitors their hard-won experience in garden restoration and battle with the dreaded honey fungus.

WOOTTON HOUSE ★ 25
Butleigh Wootton, Nr Glastonbury, Somerset.

The Hon. Mrs J. Acland-Hood ★ 3m S of Glastonbury. Minor road to Butleigh from Glastonbury, turn right to Butleigh Wootton. Continue through the village to house ★ Parking in road ★ Teas on charity day ★ Suitable for wheelchairs ★ Dogs on lead ★ Open for charity and by appointment. Telephone Mrs Ray (0164383) 586 ★ Entrance: £1.50 (1994 price)

The present garden design has been developed since 1900. It is a beautiful example of a private country-house garden. A terrace with a view to the Beacon Hill in the Mendips framed by herbaceous beds set in a sweep of lawn. The old-fashioned rose garden against a stone wall leads to the woodland area where anemones and fritillaries grow as well as cyclamen.

1996 GUIDE

The 1996 *Guide* will be published before Christmas 1995. Reports on gardens for consideration are welcome at all times of the year but particularly by early summer (June) 1995 so that they can be inspected that year.

A report form is included in the *Guide* although experience shows that most people prefer to write a letter. Please address letters to the publishers, Vermilion, 20 Vauxhall Bridge Road, London SW1V 2SA. All letters are acknowledged by the editors.

All descriptions and other information are as accurate as possible at the time of going to press, but circumstances change and it is wise to telephone before making a long journey.

The *Guide* makes no charge for entries which are written by our own inspectors. The factual details are supplied by owners. It is totally independent and its only revenue is from sales of copies in bookshops.

BEWARE CHANGED PHONE NUMBERS

While every attempt has been made to include correct telephone numbers for 1995, there have been changes as we went to press and some owners have not amended their numbers so it may be necessary to check with 192 Directory Enquiries. Apologies.

DOGS, TOILETS & OTHER FACILITIES

If these are not mentioned in the text, then facilities are not available. For example if dogs are not mentioned, owners will probably not permit entry, even on a lead.

STAFFORDSHIRE

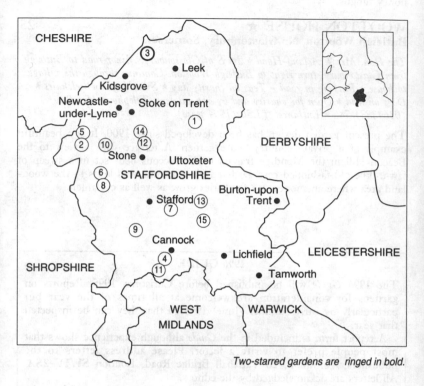

CHESHIRE

Leek

Kidsgrove

Newcastle-under-Lyme

Stoke on Trent

DERBYSHIRE

Stone

Uttoxeter

STAFFORDSHIRE

Burton-upon-Trent

Stafford

LEICESTERSHIRE

Cannock

SHROPSHIRE

Lichfield

Tamworth

WEST MIDLANDS

WARWICK

Two-starred gardens are ringed in bold.

ALTON TOWERS ★   1
Alton, Staffordshire. Tel: (01538) 702200

Alton Towers ★ From N take M6 junction 16 or M1 junction 28, from S take M6 junction 15 or M1 junction 23A. Signposted ★ Best season: spring/summer ★ Parking ★ Refreshments: restaurants, kiosks, picnic areas ★ Toilet facilities ★ Suitable for wheelchairs ★ Shops ★ Ruins open ★ Grounds open all year, 9am – 6pm, 7pm or 8pm according to time of year (one hour before rides open to one hour after they close) ★ Entrance: mid–Nov to mid–March grounds only (theme park closed) for a nominal charge but decision to open in winter in 1994/95 is uncertain at press date so check before travelling; mid–March to mid–Nov (grounds and theme park) £15.50 (full-day), OAP and accompanied wheelchair users £5.50, children £11.50 (full-day), second-day tickets £5 extra per person (1994 prices). Group rates available

This fantastic garden of ornamental architecture was one of the last great follies, created in the early nineteenth century. W.S. Nesfield was active here (one of his parterres is still *in situ* though in need of restoration). It contains many beautiful and unusual features including the Chinese Pagoda fountain, a copy of the To Ho pagoda in Canton. The enormous rock garden is planted with a range of conifers, acers and sedums. The fine conservatory houses geraniums and other colour according to the season, and the terraces have rose and herbaceous borders. There is a Dutch garden, Her Ladyship's Garden featuring yew and rose beds, the Italian garden, a yew arch walkway and woodland walks. There is water to add further beauty and interest. In addition, there are all the attractions of the pleasure park in season, but if intending to visit grounds out of season check by telephone first.

ARBOUR COTTAGE 2
Napley, Nr Market Drayton, Shropshire.

Mr and Mrs D.K. Hewitt ★ 4m N of Market Drayton. From A53 take B5415 signposted Woore. In 1¾m turn left at telephone box ★ Teas ★ Open May and June, Thurs, 2 – 5.30pm; also by appointment. Parties welcome ★ Entrance: £1.50, children 50p

This is the first entry in the *Guide* to be based on a video (it features in the NGS programme No 3). It is two acres of colour all the year round, planted particularly for winter, so there are grasses, bamboos, etc. and many trees and shrubs. The 'mixture' (the owners' words) include alpine and scree beds and there are plans for a rockery. Plenty for the plantsman, especially the daphne collection. It has to be said that it is difficult to experience the atmosphere of any garden from photograph or video so there will be a personal inspection before the next edition of the *Guide*.

BIDDULPH GRANGE GARDEN ★★ 3
Biddulph Grange, Biddulph, Stoke-on-Trent, Staffordshire.
Tel: (01782) 517999 (Garden Office)

The National Trust ★ 3½m SE of Congleton, 7m N of Stoke-on-Trent. Access from A527 Tunstall road ★ Best seasons: May/June and Sept ★ Parking ★ Refreshments ★ Access for disabled difficult ★ Shop ★ Open April to 29th Oct, Wed – Fri (but closed 14th April), 12 noon – 6pm, Sat, Sun and Bank Holiday Mon, 11am – 6pm (last admission 5.30pm or dusk if earlier). 4th Nov to 17th Dec, Sat and Sun, 12 noon – 4pm ★ Entrance: £3.90, children £1.95, family ticket £9.75; Nov and Dec: £2, children £1, family £5

About three-quarters of the restoration of this 15-acre garden is complete with the Dahlia Walk finished, the Shelter House rebuilt and the auraucana, rose and verbena parterres now planted. This is one of the most remarkable and innovative gardens of the nineteenth century. Designed by James Bateman and Edward Cooke, it contains a series of smaller gardens separated by rocky outcrops, tunnels, walls and tree-lined banks. An Egyptian Garden contains a pyramid of clipped yews and stone sphinx and a stone monster. In the Chinese Garden is a pagoda, joss house and water buffalo and a fine pool. Masses of rhododendrons reflect in the waters of a lily pool. A towering pinetum has unusual conifers, such as monkey puzzles, and there is a walk fashioned to resemble an obelisk. Behind the house are terraces falling to a pond and many wonderful discoveries for the explorer. The Stumpery, a Victorian invention, is on view. Even now, this is one of the country's most remarkable gardening discoveries and when fully restored it will be one of its most important period pieces.

12 DARGES LANE 4
Great Wyrley, Nr Cannock, Staffordshire. Tel: (01922) 415 064

Mrs A. Hackett ★ 2m SW of Cannock. From A5 (Churchbridge junction) take A34 towards Walsall. First turning on right over brow of hill. House on right on the corner of Cherrington Drive ★ Parking in road ★ Refreshments ★ Plants for sale ★ Shop selling dried flower arrangements ★ Open 21st May, 30th July, 27th Aug, 2 – 6pm ★ Entrance: £1

Quarter-acre garden on two levels, well-stocked and of great interest to plantsmen. Attractive trees and large variety of shrubs and foliage plants as background to comprehensive collection of flowering plants and small shrubs, some unusual, even rare. Holder of the National collection of lamiums. Borders and island beds. Small water garden. Every inch is used to grow or set off the collection which has year-round appeal to flower-arrangers. The overall effect is attractive as well as enticing to the plant lover. Plants for sale include some more unusual ones.

THE DOROTHY CLIVE GARDEN ★ 5
Willoughbridge, Nr Market Drayton, Shropshire.
Tel: (01630) 647237

Willoughbridge Garden Trust ★ 7m N of Market Drayton, 1m E of Woore on A51 between Nantwich and Stone ★ Parking inc. car park for disabled ★ Refreshments in tea room ★ Toilet facilities ★ Partly suitable for wheelchairs ★ Open April to Oct, daily, 10am – 5.30pm ★ Entrance: £2.60, children £1

Created by the late Colonel Clive in memory of his wife with the help of distinguished gardeners including the late John Codrington, this garden has wide appeal because of both its design and inspired planting. The coloured guide identifies the highlights season by season. These include the rhododendrons and azaleas in the quarry garden and the pool with the scree garden rising on the hillside above it. In spring there are unusual bulbs and primulas, in summer colourful shrubs, unusual perennials and many conifers; other trees provide autumn colour. The scree garden must give gardeners many good ideas. The garden is being extended and new features include a laburnum arch with roses and other climbers and a small pool with bog garden.

ECCLESHALL CASTLE GARDENS 6
Eccleshall, Staffordshire. Tel: (01785) 850151

Mr and Mrs Mark Carter ★ ½m N of Eccleshall on A519. 6m from M6 junction 14 or 10m from M6 junction 15 ★ Best seasons: April/May and July ★ Parking ★ Dogs on lead ★ Open 16th to 23rd April, daily and 28th May to 27th Aug, Wed and Sun, 1 – 5.30pm. Other times by prior arrangement in writing ★ Entrance: by donation

The entrance is along the lime avenue, probably over 200 years old; there are many other old trees in the grounds, and new ones are being planted. The 650-year-old walls of the moat garden and the beautiful arches of the bridge and the renovated fourteenth-century tower are features of this old-world garden. The rose garden, espalier pear trees, rows of indigenous hornbeam, herbaceous borders and masses of rhododendrons create a sense of tranquillity.

THE GARTH 7
2 Broc Hill Way, Milford, Staffordshire. Tel: (01785) 661182

Mr and Mrs David Wright ★ 4½m SE of Stafford. On A513 Stafford – Rugeley road, at the Barley Mow turn right, then left after 1m ★ Parking ★ Teas ★ Toilet facilities ★ Dogs on lead ★ Plants for sale ★ Open 4th, 25th June, 2 – 6pm and by appointment for parties ★ Entrance: £1, children 50p

This half-acre garden surrounded by countryside contains specialist areas which should give inspiration and ideas to any gardener. There is a sense of surprise as one moves through the garden on different levels and at the bottom discovers old caves. The range of plants includes six unusual beeches, 20 different ferns, magnolias, rhododendrons, pulmonarias, hostas, azaleas, penstemons and astilbes. A good range of shrubs include berberis, fothergillas, garryas, amelanchiers and *Holodiscus discolor*, all planted to provide foliage interest and colour combinations. Archways are covered with roses and loniceras and in the herbaceous borders are heathers, campanulas and osteospermums. Climbers, herbaceous borders, a pool and bog garden.

HEATH HOUSE 8
Offley Brook, Nr Eccleshall, Staffordshire. Tel: (01785) 280318

Dr and Mrs D.W. Eyre-Walker ★ 3m W of Eccleshall. Take B5026 towards Woore. At Sugnall turn left and after 1½m turn right immediately by stone garden wall. After 1m straight across crossroads and the garden is on right in few yards ★ Limited parking ★ Teas ★ Toilet facilities ★ Plants for sale when available ★ Open 21st May, 16th July, 2 – 6pm and by appointment ★ Entrance: £1.50, children free

A one and a half-acre garden round a country house with varied features, including a delightful bog garden and wide herbaceous borders with good plantings to provide a succession of colour. A fruit and vegetable garden, raised alpine bed, an old mulberry tree, and rose border. The woodland area with various ground-cover plants make a good contrast to the formal front garden. There are large shrubs and a good selection of unusual plants.

LITTLE ONN HALL 9
Church Eaton, Nr Stafford, Staffordshire. Tel: (01785) 840154

Mr and Mrs I.H. Kidson ★ 6m SW of Stafford, 2m S of Church Eaton, midway between the A5 and A518 ★ Parking ★ Teas ★ Partly suitable for wheelchairs ★ Open 21st May, 11th June, 2 – 6pm ★ Entrance: £1.50, children 50p

Entering this six-acre garden the driveway is flanked with long herbaceous borders backed by yew hedges and elsewhere are more herbaceous borders. The large rose garden has standards, shrub and hybrid teas. An unusual-shaped pool known as the 'Dog Bone' has water lilies and elsewhere in the garden are bog plants. Since 1971 the present owners have been planting new trees and are trying to maintain the original design by Thomas H. Mawson of Windermere. There are many rhododendrons, spring bulbs and large beeches and conifers thus ensuring colour for a long season. The moat garden gives the garden a sense of mystery and charm.

MANOR COTTAGE 10
**Chapel Chorlton, Nr Newcastle-under-Lyme, Staffordshire.
Tel: (01782) 680206**

*Mrs Joyce Heywood ★ From A51 Nantwich – Stone road turn behind Cock Inn
at Stableford. House on village green ★ Parking on road around the village green
★ Toilet facilities ★ Suitable for wheelchairs ★ Plants for sale ★ Open 17th April
to Sept, Mons only, 2 – 5pm and at other times by appointment ★ Entrance:
£1.50, children 50p*

This two-thirds of an acre garden has been created by the present owner over
several years and is beautifully designed with excellent colour combinations
and varieties of foliage, including many variegated forms. It is a flower
arranger's paradise with a wide range including collections of ferns, geraniums, hellebores, grasses and hostas. Small paths lead one to find beauty
round each corner, and there are roses climbing through old fruit trees and a
good range of conifers and a lovely alpine area. All year round colour and
interest.

MOSELEY OLD HALL 11
**Moseley Old Hall Lane, Fordhouses, Wolverhampton,
Staffordshire. Tel: (01902) 782808**

*The National Trust ★ 4m N of Wolverhampton. Traffic from S on M6 and
M54 take junction 1 to Wolverhampton. Traffic from N on M6 leave motorway
at junction 11 then take A460. Coaches must go on A460 ★ Best season:
June/July ★ Refreshments: in tearoom. Light lunches, July and Aug, Suns from
12.30pm ★ Shop ★ House open (Elizabethan house where Charles II hid after the
Battle of Worcester) ★ Garden open April to 29th Oct, Wed, Sat and Sun (and
Tues in July and Aug), 2 – 5.30pm. Also Bank Holiday Mons, 11am – 5pm ★
Entrance: £3.30, children £1.65, family ticket (2 adults and 2 children) £8
(house and garden)*

A garden mainly for the specialist interested in old plants as all specimens are
seventeenth-century except for a few fruit trees. The knot garden is from a
design of 1640 by the Reverend Walter Stonehouse. A wooden arbour is
covered with clematis and *Vitis vinifera* 'Purpurea'. The fruit trees include a
mulberry, medlars and a morello cherry. The walled garden has topiary and
herbaceous borders, and fritillaries grow in the nut walk. There is a small
herb garden and boles for bees. Interesting to see plants grown in former
days to provide dyes and for cleansing and medicinal purposes.

OULTON HOUSE 12
Oulton, Nr Stone, Staffordshire. Tel: (01785) 813556

*Mr and Mrs J.E. Bridger ★ ½m NE of Stone. From Stone take the Oulton road
and after the Oulton village sign turn left. After passing a few houses turn right
up a long drive ★ Parking ★ Teas ★ Toilet facilities ★ Plants for sale ★ Open by
appointment 25th June to 8th July ★ Entrance: £1.50, children 75p*

This three-acre garden with fine views has been developed by the present
owners over 15 years and is surrounded by parkland; a range of large trees
provides shelter for the garden. A conservatory contains vines, camellias and
roses, and large greenhouses have nectarines, figs and peaches. There is a

rhododendron walk, large rockery, herbaceous borders containing interesting colour combinations and a wide range of plants including geraniums, delphiniums, euphorbias and astrantias. There are masses of old shrub roses, a grey and silver border by the house, which has clematis and roses climbing its walls. There is a patio area, a golden corner, white area and a large vegetable and fruit garden. Although not a weed-free garden, there is plenty to delight the eye and it is hoped it may be open more often as the spring bulbs must be a delight to see. Something of interest all summer.

RODE HALL
(see Cheshire)

SHUGBOROUGH ★   13
Great Haywood, Milford, Staffordshire. Tel: (01889) 881388

Staffordshire County Council/ The National Trust ★ 6m E of Stafford on A513 ★ Best season: July ★ Parking ★ Refreshments: lunches and snacks in tea room, also picnic areas ★ Toilet facilities ★ Suitable for wheelchairs. Batricars available ★ Dogs on lead in park only ★ Shop ★ House, museum and adjacent farm open ★ Garden open 25th March to 27th Oct, daily, 11am – 5pm. Open for pre-booked parties all year except 24th Dec to 2nd Jan 1995 from 10.30am. Guided walk of the grounds 7th, 8th Jan 1995, 2 – 3.30pm ★ Entrance: £1.50 per vehicle to parkland. House, servants' quarters and farm £7.50, OAP and children £5, under 5 free, or £3.50, OAP and children £2 for single-site ticket. National Trust members free to house, reduced rate to museum and farm

Of interest to garden historians because Thomas Wright of Durham worked here and because there are many buildings and monuments ascribed to James 'Athenian' Stuart and built for Thomas Anson from the 1740s onwards. These are some of the earliest examples of English Neo-Classicism and there is also an early example of Chinoiserie based on a sketch made by one of the officers on Admiral Anson's voyage round the world. The *Oxford Companion* suggests that the buildings were 'randomly scattered' but another view is that they were put in place as 'hidden architectural treasures' to surprise. As for the garden, the Victorian layout with terraces by Nesfield was revitalised for the Trust in the mid-1960s by Graham Stuart Thomas who also worked on the Edwardian rose garden. The first stage of a major tree planting scheme has begun, with over 1000 young oak trees, the aim being to restore Shugborough to its original eighteenth-century layout with more hedgerows and wooded areas. There is also a woodland walk and guided tours of the garden for those who prefer it. Floral arrangement events in the house.

TRENTHAM GARDENS   14
Trentham, Stoke-on-Trent, Staffordshire. Tel: (01782) 657341

Trentham Leisure Ltd ★ On A34 S of Stoke-on-Trent. 2m from M6 junction 15 ★ Best season: summer ★ Parking ★ Refreshments: in restaurant ★ Toilet facilities ★ Suitable for wheelchairs ★ Dogs on lead ★ Garden centre and conference centre with restaurant facilities adjacent ★ Open early April to early Oct, daily, 10am – 6pm ★ Entrance: £1.50, OAP 75p, children (4–14) 50p, under 4 free

These 1000 acres of parkland were designed by 'Capability' Brown. Nesfield added a large Italian garden and Sir Charles Barry laid out formal gardens for the Duke of Sutherland. The gardens have been greatly simplified but still retain many features such as Brown's large lake on which one can now enjoy water sports (including jetskiing and waterskiing). Rose garden and displays of bedding plants, a good selection of shrubs including hebes, potentillas and buddleias. Magnificent trees both alongside the River Trent, which flows through the gardens, and in the woodland area by the lake. The Italian garden has masses of colour from annuals and also some yew trees. A clematis walk has been replanted. A good place for a family day-out as there are picnic areas, wildfowl centre and hatchery, a children's farm with deer, play area and funfair. There is also a Print Museum and a newly opened Nature Trail and Heritage Trail.

WOLSELEY GARDEN PARK ★   15
Wolseley Bridge, Stafford, Staffordshire. Tel: (01889) 574888

Sir Charles and Lady Wolseley ★ At junction of A51 with A513 between Rugeley and Stafford ★ Parking ★ Refreshments sometimes available ★ Toilet facilities ★ Suitable for wheelchairs ★ Plants for sale at Wyevale garden centre adjacent ★ Open daily. Times vary seasonally but 10am – 6pm in summer ★ Entrance: April to Oct: £2, OAP £1.50, children (5-16) £1; Nov to March: £1.50, OAP £1, children (5-16) 50p. Reduced rates for parties of 20 or more

An interesting new 45-acre garden development as part of the owners' plan to make the site a major leisure and educational centre. Important features include a two-acre walled rose garden, a water bog garden with board walk, rockery, a collection of willows, a large new lake set in a water meadow, a woodland spring garden with flowering shrubs and bulbs. There is a scented garden for the particular enjoyment of the blind and partially sighted and a winter garden aimed at giving colour from November to March. Excavated remains of a twelfth-century castle may also be viewed. Alas on a recent visit there were signs of neglect in some areas due to severe staffing 'cut-backs' in light of the recession.

THE NATIONAL TRUST

The National Trust celebrates its cetenary in 1995. It has grown to become Britain's largest conservation charity and now permanently protects over half a million acres of countryside, 200 houses and 160 gardens open to the public in England, Wales and Northern Ireland. A host of commemorative events during the year will include concerts, lectures, childrens' activities and outdoor events with fireworks. The Trust will welcome participation. A book on the 'first hundred years' has been published and there will be an accompanying BBC TV programme.

SUFFOLK

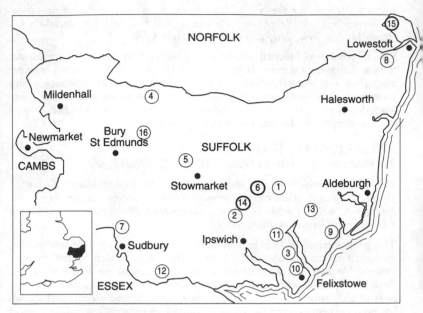

NORFOLK

⑮ Lowestoft
⑧

Mildenhall ● ④

Halesworth ●

Bury ⑯
Newmarket ● St Edmunds

CAMBS

SUFFOLK

⑤

Stowmarket ● ⑥ ① Aldeburgh ●

⑭
②

⑬

⑦ ⑪ ⑨

Sudbury ● Ipswich ● ③

⑫ ⑩

ESSEX Felixstowe

Two-starred gardens are ringed in bold.

AKENFIELD   1
1 Park Lane, Charsfield, Woodbridge, Suffolk. Tel: (0147337) 402

*Mrs Peggy Cole ★ 3m W of Wickham Market on B1078 ★ Plants for sale ★
Open 16th April to Sept, daily, 10.30am – 7pm ★ Entrance: £1, OAP 75p*

Akenfield, formerly a council house, has a half-acre cottage garden full of
charm, overflowing with flowers and vegetables and including a small
orchard. To one side the front garden is planted with roses and bedding
plants, to the other a small honeysuckle arch leads to a patio with containers
of flowers, hanging baskets – and a shed full of home-made wines which is
an irresistible attraction to robins who nest among the bottles. Opposite the
patio is a tiny water garden complete with waterfall and wishing well. The
back garden is divided in two; to one side is a vegetable garden with about 30
different kinds of vegetables and a hen house at the far end. On the other
side there are two large greenhouses, overflowing with pot plants, tomatoes
and cucumbers. Beyond are small gardens connected by archways, apple
trees and a grape vine; hanging baskets and even bottles hold more plants.

BLAKENHAM WOODLAND GARDEN 2
Little Blakenham, Ipswich, Suffolk.

Viscount Blakenham ★ 4m NW of Ipswich, 1m off the B1113. Follow signs from the Beeches in Little Blakenham ★ Parking in field ★ Suitable for wheelchairs ★ Open March to June, daily except Sats, 1 – 5pm ★ Entrance: £1

Set in five acres of bluebell wood, planted with a huge variety of ornamental trees and flowering shrubs. It is at its best in spring, full of cornus, azaleas, magnolias and rhododendrons, later followed by roses, hydrangeas and abutilons. Grass paths wind through and one can sit on one of the many seats, listening to the birds in perfect peace. As summer advances it gets more overgrown, which only adds to its charm.

BUCKLESHAM HALL ★ 3
Bucklesham, Ipswich, Suffolk. Tel: (01473) 659263

Mr D.R. Brightwell ★ 6m E of Ipswich, ½m E of Bucklesham village. Entrance opposite and just N of Bucklesham primary school ★ Parking. Coaches by appointment ★ Refreshments by special arrangement ★ Plants often for sale ★ Shop ★ Open by appointment ★ Entrance: £2

The great interest of Bucklesham is how these seven acres of interlocking gardens, terraces and lakes have been created from scratch by the previous owners, Mr and Mrs Ravenshear, since 1973. Round the house are secret gardens so packed with flowers that no weed could survive; newly planted beds of old-fashioned roses overflow their borders, and a courtyard garden has been created with the use of every kind of container. Descending terraces of lawns, ponds and streams lead to the woodland and beyond; round each corner is a new vista. Skill, wide horticultural knowledge and imagination have enabled the previous owners to achieve their aim of displaying plants, shrubs and trees of interest to the plantsman in tranquil surroundings appealing to the layman, all with minimum maintenance.

EUSTON HALL ★ 4
Euston, Thetford, Suffolk. Tel: (01842) 766366

The Duke and Duchess of Grafton ★ 3m S of Thetford on A1088 ★ Best season: June and July ★ Parking ★ Refreshments ★ Toilet facilities ★ Suitable for wheelchairs (garden, shop and tearoom only) ★ Plants for sale ★ Shop ★ House open ★ Garden open June to 28th Sept, Thurs, 2.30 – 5pm, and 25th June and 3rd Sept, 2.30 – 5pm ★ Entrance: £2.50, OAP £2, children 50p, parties of 12 or more £2 per person

Fronted by terraces, the Hall stands among extensive lawns and parkland along a winding river, the work of William Kent in the 1740s (followed by 'Capability' Brown) as is the splendid domed temple isolated on an eminence to the east, and also the pretty garden house in the formal garden by the house, developed by the present Duke. The pleasure grounds, laid out in the seventeenth century by John Evelyn, have grown into a forest of yew but straight rides trace out the original formal layout. Also from this period are the stone gate piers which, together with the remnants of a great avenue, mark the original approach to the house. A small lake reflects the house across the park, and there are many fine specimen trees and a wealth of shrub roses.

HAUGHLEY PARK ★   5
Nr Stowmarket, Suffolk. Tel: (01359) 40205

The Williams family ★ 4m NW of Stowmarket, signposted Haughley Park (not Haughley) on A45 ★ Parking. Coaches by appointment ★ Picnics in grounds ★ Toilet facilities inc. disabled ★ Suitable for wheelchairs ★ Dogs on lead ★ House open ★ Garden open May to Sept, Tues, 3 – 5.30pm ★ Entrance: £2, children £1

A hundred acres of rolling parkland edged by 100 more acres of woodland surround the seventeenth-century Jacobean mansion. Unexpected secret gardens edged by clipped hedges or flint and brick walls hide their immaculate flowerbeds, climbers and flowering shrubs; each garden has its own character. The main lawn is surrounded by herbaceous borders, with, at the end, a splendid lime avenue drawing the eye across many miles of open countryside. Rhododendrons, azaleas and camellias grow on soil which is, unexpectedly for Suffolk, lime-free. The trees include a splendid *Davidia involucrata*, a 40 foot-wide magnolia and a flourishing oak, over 30 foot in girth, reputed to be 1000 years old. Beyond is the walled kitchen garden, the greenhouses and the shrubbery. In spring the broad rides and walks through the ancient woodland reveal not only the newly planted trees, specimen rhododendrons and other ornamental shrubs but 10 acres of bluebells and, more remarkably, two acres of lilies-of-the-valley, and half a mile of mauve Ponticum rhododendrons.

HELMINGHAM HALL ★★   6
Stowmarket, Suffolk. Tel: (01473) 890363 (Contact Mrs MacGregor)

Lord Tollemache ★ 9m NE of Ipswich on B1077. 6m E of A45 on B1077 then signposted ★ Parking ★ Teas in coach house, picnic facilities ★ Toilet facilities ★ Suitable for wheelchairs ★ Dogs on lead ★ Plants for sale ★ Gift shop. Safari rides to see deer, Highland cattle and Soay sheep ★ Open 30th April to 10th Sept, Sun, 2 – 6pm. Parties of 30 or more on Wed pm by prior appointment ★ Entrance: £2.80, OAP £2.60, children £1.50, parties of 30 or more £2.30 per person

Eighteen generations of Tollemaches have lived here, and though there have been many changes over the past five centuries the property retains a strong Elizabethan atmosphere. The double-moated Tudor mansion house of great splendour and charm, built of warm red brick, stands in a 400-acre deer park. A nineteenth-century parterre, edged with a magnificent spring border, leads to the Elizabethan kitchen garden which is surrounded by the Saxon moat with banks covered in daffodils. Within the walls the kitchen garden has been transformed into an enchanting garden most subtly planted; the meticulously maintained herbaceous borders and old-fashioned roses surround beds of vegetables separated by arched tunnels of sweet peas and runner beans. Beyond is a meadow garden with, leading from it, a yew walk with philadelphus and shade-loving plants. On the other side of the Hall is a newly created garden dating from 1982. It is an historical knot garden and herb garden, with a magnificent collection of shrub roses underplanted with campanulas and geraniums, framed by a yew hedge. All the plants are chosen to be contemporary with the house.

MELFORD HALL ★   7
Long Melford, Sudbury, Suffolk. Tel: (01787) 880286

The National Trust. Sir Richard Hyde Parker, Bart ★ E side of A134, 14m S of Bury St Edmunds, 3m N of Sudbury ★ Parking ★ Refreshments in Long Melford, picnics in car park ★ Toilet facilities by main entrance ★ Mostly suitable for wheelchairs, one wheelchair provided. Disabled driven to Hall ★ House open with special Beatrix Potter exhibition ★ Garden open May to Sept, Wed, Thurs, Sat, Sun and Bank Holidays, 2 – 5.30pm; April and Oct, Sat and Sun only ★ Entrance: £2.70 (principal rooms and garden) (1994 price)

This magnificent sixteenth-century Hall of mellow red brick is set in a park and formal gardens. A plan by Samuel Pierse of 1613 shows that the park was separated from the Hall by a walled enclosure outside which was the moat. Part of this is now the sunken garden. The avenue at the side of the house is currently being replanted with oak grown from acorns taken from the existing trees. The octagonal brick pavilion, a rare and beautiful example of Tudor architecture, on the north side of the path, overlooks the village green and the herbaceous borders inside the garden which are being restored to their original Victorian and Edwardian design and planting. Outside the pavilion are clipped box hedges and a bowling green terrace which lead past dense shrubbery. The garden has many good specimen trees including the rare Oriental tree *Xanthoceras sorbifolium*. Great domes of box punctuate the lawns and an interesting detail is the arrangement of yew hedges and golden yew to the north of the house. Outside the walls are topiary figures. Round the pond and fountain are beds originally planted with herbs in 1937 and now being gradually improved. However it is all a far cry from the 1930s when the head gardener, Mr Pomfret, and his four assistants planted out annuals in the wide border which ran the whole length of the tall brick wall. In the house as well as outside, Pomfret (in his bowler) reigned supreme.

NORTH COVE HALL ★   8
North Cove, Beccles, Suffolk. Tel: (01502) 476631

Mr and Mrs B. Blower ★ 3½m E of Beccles, 50 yards off A146 Lowestoft road ★ Best season: summer ★ Parking ★ Teas ★ Toilet facilities ★ Suitable for wheelchairs ★ Dogs on lead ★ Plants for sale ★ Open probably 25th June, 2.30 – 6pm and by appointment ★ Entrance: £1.50, children free

Climbing roses adorn this sunny Georgian house which is set in lawns surrounded by mature park trees. The walled garden partly encloses the half-acre pond with water lilies and bordered by majestic *Gunnera manicata*, *Taxodium ascendens* 'Nutans', a group of *Betula jacquemontii* and *Alnus glutinosa* 'Imperialis'. Inside the walls are herbaceous, shrub borders, pergolas and the house kitchen garden. Small scree garden. Outside are woodland walks among mature trees and various younger conifers.

THE OLD RECTORY   9
Orford, Woodbridge, Suffolk. Tel: (01394) 450063

Mr and Mrs Tim Fargher ★ Take the B1084 from Woodbridge to Orford. The Old Rectory is on the left behind the church ★ Parking for disabled only ★ Small

*selection of plants for sale ★ Open mid-June to mid-July, Mon to Fri, 10am –
4pm, by appointment only. Visitors are asked to make themselves known to the
gardener, Mr Denny ★ Entrance: £3, OAP and children £1*

This extensive five-acre garden, tucked behind Orford church, is immaculate,
secluded and unexpected. It was designed for the owners' parents by Lanning
Roper, with additions by Mark Rumary and its beautifully-planned borders
and vistas surround the house, which has a large conservatory.

PETER'S GARDEN 10
**The Mill, 194 Kirton Road, Trimley St Martin, Ipswich, Suffolk.
Tel: (013948) 241**

*Diana Hewett ★ From A45 Ipswich – Felixstowe road turn left at roundabout
signed for Kirton. Pass Trimley St Martin school, and Mill is on the right ★
Parking off road ★ Partly suitable for wheelchairs ★ Open by appointment only ★
Entrance: donations towards upkeep appreciated*

The half-acre plantsman's garden was developed over 45 years around a
converted post-mill by literature teacher and poet, Peter Hewett. It is now
funded largely by Trevor Nunn and maintained by local volunteers. It
features an orchard, vegetable plot, pond, bog garden and lavender border.
Dominating the garden are deep beds of shrubs and old roses underplanted
with cottage garden flowers.

PLAYFORD HALL 11
Playford, Nr Ipswich, Suffolk. Tel: (01473) 622509

*Mr and Mrs Richard Innes ★ 1m off old A12 between Ipswich and Woodbridge,
on the edge of Playford ★ Parking ★ Open by appointment only ★ Entrance:
£1.50*

A beautiful moated Elizabethan house set in 10 acres of outstanding gardens.
Trees, lawns and a lake surround the house, with yew hedges dividing herbaceous and shrub borders full of unusual plants. Roses cascade over the house
and moat walls, and there is also a pergola rose garden underplanted with
lavender and other old favourites.

THE PRIORY ★ 12
Stoke by Nayland, Suffolk. Tel: (01206) 262216

*Mr and Mrs Henry Engleheart ★ 8m N of Colchester on B1068 to Sudbury ★
Parking ★ Teas ★ Suitable for wheelchairs ★ Open 28th May, 25th June, 2 –
6pm ★ Entrance: £1.50, children free*

An exceptional nine-acre garden, with fine views over Constable countryside.
Around the house is a splendid selection of plants and roses in terraces and
mixed borders. Lawns slope down to a series of six lakes, thickly planted with
a mass of water plants and lilies. A Chinese bridge links to a tea pavilion by
one of the lakes. In the spring rhododendrons and azaleas ring the lakes
under large trees. A new garden of mixed planting is planned in the walled
garden which will lead into the greenhouse/conservatory, with its colourful
collection of tender plants.

THE ROOKERY ★   13
Eyke, Woodbridge, Suffolk. Tel: (01394) 460226

Captain and Mrs Robin Sheepshanks ★ 5m E of Woodbridge. Turn N off B1084 Woodbridge – Orford road when sign says Rendlesham 2 before double bend sign ★ Parking ★ Refreshments, inc. cream teas ★ Suitable for wheelchairs ★ Vineyard and farm shop selling wine, plants and produce ★ Open 30th April, 14th, 28th May, 18th June, 10th Sept, 2 – 5.30pm ★ Entrance: £1.50, children 50p

The gales which devastated so many fine gardens had occasionally the unexpected benefit of opening up large areas which were subsequently, as at The Rookery, developed in new and interesting ways. The informal garden designed on differing levels has a wide variety of trees and shrubs. The owners are now increasing the already large stock of roses, making new vistas; the visitors' curiosity is constantly aroused as to what is round the next corner. A small pond, a bog garden, shrubbery and evergreen walk, spring bulbs and rhododendrons add to the general interest. The old vegetable garden is now a flourishing vineyard of one acre and wine can be bought.

SHRUBLAND HALL ★★   14
Coddenham, Suffolk. Tel: (01473) 830404

Lord de Saumarez ★ 4m N of Ipswich. Turn off A14 to B1113 at Claydon ★ Parking ★ Refreshments and picnic area in car park ★ Toilet facilities ★ Suitable for wheelchairs ★ Plants for sale ★ Open probably 16th July, 2 – 6pm ★ Entrance: £2, OAP and children £1

The magnificence of Shrubland Hall is reflected in the Victorian gardens, laid out by Sir Charles Barry and later modified by William Robinson. They are amongst the most important of their type remaining in England. From the upper terrace outside the house one descends by a stunning cascade of a hundred steps and descending terraces to a garden of formal beds, fountain and eye-catcher loggia. Beyond is the wild garden which merges into the woods and is bordered by the park with its many fine trees, some reputed to be 800 years old. The gardens are punctuated by a series of enchanting follies ranging from a Swiss chalet to an alpine rockery and magnificent conservatory. Lord and Lady de Saumarez have an extensive programme of restoration which includes the box maze and the old dell garden. Many trees blown down in the gales are being cleared and replaced.

SOMERLEYTON HALL ★★   15
Nr Lowestoft, Suffolk. Tel: (01502) 730224/730308

Lord and Lady Somerleyton ★ 8m from Yarmouth, 6m NW of Lowestoft off B1074 signposted ★ Parking ★ Teas and picnics ★ Toilet facilities inc. disabled ★ Suitable for wheelchairs ★ Gift shop ★ House opens 2pm. On certain days the miniature railway runs ★ Gardens open 16th April to Sept, Thurs, Sun and Bank Holiday Mons; July and Aug, Tues, Wed, Thurs, Sun and Bank Holiday Mon, 12.30 – 5pm ★ Entrance: £3.50, OAP £3, children £1.60, parties of 15 or more £2.70 per person, children £1.40 (1994 prices)

An Elizabethan house extensively rebuilt in the mid-nineteenth century as a grand Italianate palace and the gardens splendidly reflect this magnificence with 12 acres of formal gardens, a beautiful walled garden, an aviary and a loggia surrounding a sunken garden displaying statues from the old, now demolished, winter garden. A major programme of replanting and restoration has included replacing many of the great trees in the park which were lost in the gales and cutting back the overgrown yews of the maze, originally laid out by William Nesfield in 1846. Not to be missed are the extraordinary peach cases and ridge-and-furrow greenhouse designed by Sir Joseph Paxton, and now containing peaches, grapes and a rich variety of tender plants. The Victorian kitchen garden and a museum of gardening are being developed.

WYKEN HALL ★   16
Stanton, Ixworth, Bury St Edmunds, Suffolk.
Tel: (01359) 250287/250240

K.M. Carlisle ★ 9m from Bury St Edmunds on A143. Leave A143 between Ixworth and Stanton. Signposted Wyken Vineyards ★ Parking ★ ☆Refreshments: in The Leaping Hare Café ★ Toilet facilities ★ Suitable for wheelchairs ★ Dogs on lead ★ Plants for sale ★ Shop ★ Hall open ★ Garden open Feb to 24th Dec, Thurs, Fri, Sun and Bank Holiday Mons, 10am – 6pm ★ Entrance: £2, OAP £1.50, children under 12 free

This outstanding garden covers four acres, most of which have been planted in the last twelve years. It is divided into a series of rooms, starting with the wild and winter garden, which leads into the south and woodland garden, and so into the dell. Mown paths meander between shrubs and so into the newly-planted copper beech maze, which is next to the nuttery and gazebo. Then to the rose garden, enclosed on three sides by a hornbeam hedge and on the fourth by a rose-laden pergola. Beyond the wall are the knot and herb gardens, separated by yew hedges, and designed by Arabella Lennox-Boyd. A new 'edible garden' and a kitchen garden have just been planted to the north of the house. Remarkable for its colours and scents, this is a garden not to be missed.

OPENING DATES AND TIMES

Times of access given are the best available at the moment of going to press, but some may have been changed subsequently. In the entries, the times given are inclusive – that is, an entry such as May to Sept means that the garden is open from 1st May to 30th Sept inclusive and 2 – 5pm also means that entry will be effective during that period. Please note that many owners will open their gardens to visitors by appointment. They will often arrange to give a personally-conducted tour on these occasions.

SURREY

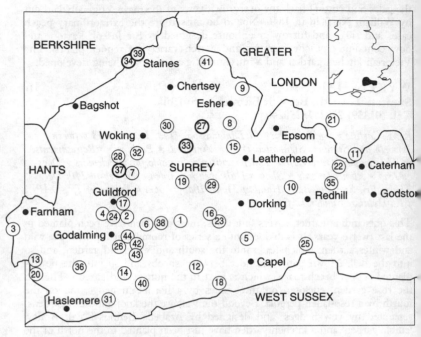

BERKSHIRE

GREATER

LONDON

● Bagshot

39
34
Staines

41

● Chertsey

9

Esher ●

Woking ●

30

27

8

15

Epsom ●

21

HANTS

28
32

37
7

SURREY

33

Leatherhead ●

11

22

Caterham ●

19

29

10

35

Godsto

Guildford

17

Dorking ●

Redhill ●

● Farnham

4
24
2

16
23

3

Godalming ●

6
38

1

44

5

25

26
42

43

13

36

14

12

● Capel

20

40

18

Haslemere
31

WEST SUSSEX

Two-starred gardens are ringed in bold.

ALBURY PARK MANSION   1
Albury, Guildford, Surrey. Tel: (0148641) 2964 (Administrator)

Country Houses Association Ltd ★ Turn off A25 onto A248 (signposted Albury).
Turn left just before village and entrance is immediately left ★ Best seasons:
spring and early summer ★ Parking ★ Toilet facilities ★ House open (Pugin), also
old Saxon church ★ Garden open May to Sept, Wed and Thurs, 2 – 5pm ★
Entrance: £2.50, children under 16 £1, members of C.H.A. free

The gardens remaining around the house are mainly under grass with gravel
walks, a ha-ha and stream providing the boundaries. A small formal rose
garden, azaleas and rhododendrons are to be seen and an herbaceous border.
However it is the trees that are most impressive – several oaks, a tulip tree
and a very old London plane amongst them. There is a tree chart of the
estate in the house. Although not open to visitors, the azaleas and rhododendrons on the estate are visible from the garden in spring and are a beautiful
sight when in bloom. The pleasure grounds which lie north of the
Tillingbourne remain in the ownership of the Trustees of the Albury Estate
and are not open to the public. This is unfortunate as the layout owes much
to the assistance given by John Evelyn to his neighbour, later 6th Duke of
Norfolk, in or before the 1660s. These included the terraces, one in the style
of a Roman bath, a tunnel, now walled in at one end, and a canal. In 1882

William Cobbett on one of his rural rides described them as 'without exception the prettiest in England; that is to say, that I ever saw in England.'

BARNETT HILL 2
Wonersh, Guildford, Surrey. Tel: (01483) 893361

The Red Cross ★ Leave Guildford on A281 towards Horsham. After 1½m cross railway bridge and turn left at Shalford village green for Wonersh. Continue for 1½m and turn first left signposted Conference Centre. Entrance is at the top of the hill on the right ★ Parking ★ Cream teas ★ Toilet facilities ★ Plants for sale ★ Open 21st May, 2 – 5.30pm ★ Entrance: £1.50, children 20p

The attractive house was built in 1906 by the grandson of the great travel agent Thomas Cook, at the cost of £35,000. It was a site of 26 acres in all with 10 acres of formal and planted gardens on which he employed 14 gardeners: now there are three. During the war Mrs Cook gave the property to the Red Cross for eventual use as a training and conference centre. The main lawns are backed by a decorative wall, yew hedge and interesting borders and give an amazing view to the South Downs. There are fine shrubs, rhododendrons, azaleas and a Judas tree, while the woodland walk is bordered with bluebells and foxgloves, and also affords extensive views. An apple store is thatched with heather.

BIRDWORLD 3
Holt Pound, Nr Farnham, Surrey. Tel: (01420) 22140

The Harvey family ★ 3m S of Farnham on A325 ★ Best season: June to Sept ★ Parking ★ Refreshments: café for light lunches, coffee and teas ★ Toilet facilities ★ Suitable for wheelchairs. Wheelchairs available for hire ★ Shop ★ Open daily except 25th Dec, summer 9.30am – 6pm, winter 9.30am – 3.30pm ★ Entrance: £3.65, OAP £2.75, children £2 (1994 prices)

First-time visitors to Birdworld will be surprised by the extensive gardens which provide a backdrop to the bird sanctuary. With its wide flat paths and ample seating there is plenty of space to enjoy the variety of planting on show. Although lacking a unifying theme (and the family disagree over which comes first, the birds or the gardens), the variety ensures that the gardens are attractive and colourful on all of the 364 days a year that they are open. Features include summer bedding, hanging baskets, wall baskets, rose garden, heather bed, ornamental grasses border, pergola and climbing roses, pond and white garden.

BRADSTONE BROOK 4
Shalford, Guildford, Surrey. Tel: (01483) 68686

Scott, Brownrigg & Turner ★ 3m S of Guildford on A281 towards Horsham then A248 to Dorking. Sign on left past the Common ★ Parking ★ Teas ★ Open for charity 16th July, 2 – 6pm ★ Entrance: £1.50, children 50p

The layout for this 20-acre garden was Gertrude Jekyll's, particularly the water garden, but the area was derelict for 25 years until discovered by the present owners 10 years ago. Set against the background of the Surrey hills, the Edwardian house is framed by lawns and an ornamental rose garden with lavender and box hedges. Other features include an alpine garden, a lily tank and several woodland walks to a variegated beech and the snowdrop tree, *Halesia carolina*, that flowers in late spring/early summer, and swamp cypresses. Over 150,000 bulbs and some trees under preservation orders including a *Betula nigra* said to be the largest in the country. A video showing the gardens in all their former glory is available in the tea room.

BROOK LODGE FARM COTTAGE   5
Blackbrook, Dorking, Surrey.

Mrs Basil Kingham ★ 3m S of Dorking off A24 ★ Parking in farm opposite ★ Home-made refreshments ★ Toilet facilities ★ Suitable for wheelchairs ★ Plants for sale May and June ★ Open 28th, 31st May, 18th, 21st June, 23rd, 26th July, 20th Aug (Suns 2 – 6pm, Weds 11am – 3pm) ★ Entrance: £1.50, children free

This plantsman's garden was made from a three and a half-acre field about 45 years ago by the present owner. The entrance provides a vista of spacious lawns with curving borders of shrubs and flowering trees and shrub roses, with hosts of unusual plants framing the main house. A fine collection of conifers cradles a small summerhouse. At the top of the garden a swimming pool, hidden by a Hoathley stone wall, leads to a waterfall and rockery with a woodland garden beyond. Leaving the garden, past herbaceous border and roses, there is a well-kept herb and kitchen garden, and finally two separate cottage gardens, full of interest.

CHILWORTH MANOR   6
Chilworth, Surrey. Tel: (01483) 61414

Lady Heald ★ 3m SE of Guildford on A248. Turn off in village centre up Blacksmiths Lane ★ Best seasons: spring and June ★ Parking ★ Refreshments: teas in house on Sat and Sun. Picnicking from 12.30pm in car park ★ Toilet facilities ★ Partly suitable for wheelchairs ★ Dogs on lead ★ House open Sat and Sun only ★ Garden open 8th to 12th April, 6th to 10th May, 3rd to 7th June, 8th to 12th July, 5th to 9th Aug, 2 – 6pm and by appointment ★ Entrance: £1.50 (house £1), children free

A lovely old garden, particularly in spring and autumn, but something to see all the year round. Laid out in the seventeenth century, a walled garden was carved in three tiers out of the side of the hill early in the following century by Sarah, Duchess of Marlborough before she moved to Blenheim. The high walls, backed by wisteria, shelter many fine plants, a herbaceous border, lavender walk and shrubs. There is also a rock garden and a woodland area with magnolias, rhododendrons, azaleas, an oak tree reputed to be 400 years old and a Judas tree. Our inspector, who visited in spring, was impressed by the candelabra primulas along the stream and golden carp in the monastic stewponds. At weekends, the house is decorated by various Surrey flower clubs in turn. The ideal time to visit is on a day warm enough to sit on one of the strategically placed seats so as to absorb the atmosphere created by time past and time present.

CLANDON PARK   7
West Clandon, Guildford, Surrey. Tel: (01483) 222482

The National Trust ★ 3m E of Guildford. Take A247 or A3 to Ripley and join A247 via B2215 ★ Parking. Disabled drivers only near front of house ★

Refreshments: licensed restaurant when house is open, lunches from 12.30pm, teas 3.15 – 5.30pm. Picnic area ★ Toilet facilities inc. disabled ★ Suitable for wheelchairs ★ Dogs on lead in picnic area and car park only ★ Shop ★ House open ★ Garden open April to 29th Oct, daily except Thurs and Fri (but open 14th April), 1.30 – 5.30pm; Bank Holiday Mons 11am – 5.30pm ★ Entrance: free (house £4, children £2)

Built by a Venetian architect in the early 1730s for the 2nd Lord Onslow, whose family still owns the park, although the house and seven-acre garden are owned by the Trust. An interesting feature is the Maori meeting house, known as Hinemihi, brought from New Zealand over 100 years ago by the then Lord Onslow, and said to be one of the oldest in existence. Also note the grotto and parterre. The garden is on a hillside and gives a fine view of the lake in the park.

CLAREMONT LANDSCAPE GARDEN ★   8
Portsmouth Road, Esher, Surrey Tel: (01372) 469421

The National Trust ★ E of A307, S of Esher just out of the town ★ Parking ★ Refreshments in tea room ★ Toilet facilities ★ Partly suitable for wheelchairs ★ Dogs, Nov to March only, on lead ★ Shop ★ House, not NT, not open ★ Garden open all year: Jan to March, daily except Mon, 10am – 5pm; April to Oct, Mon – Fri, 10am – 6pm, Sat, Sun and Bank Holiday Mon, 10am – 7pm (but 12th to 16th July garden closes 4pm); Nov to March 1996, daily except Mon, 10am – 5pm or sunset if earlier (last admission ½ hour before closing) but closed Mons and 25th Dec, 1st Jan ★ Entrance: Mon – Sat £1.80, Sun and Bank Holiday Mon £2.60. Guided tours for 15 or more £1.40 extra by prior booking. All coaches must book

The *Oxford Companion* describes this as one of the most significant historic landscapes in the country. The 50 acres restored by the Trust are only part of the original estate which was broken up in 1922 and part became a school. The great landscape designers of the eighteenth century each adapted it in turn for the owner, the immensely wealthy man who eventually became Duke of Newcastle. First he retained Vanbrugh, then Bridgeman, then Kent. Later, when Clive of India purchased the estate he brought in 'Capability' Brown who also designed the house, now the school and, in typical form, diverted the London-Portsmouth road to improve the viewpoints, the most striking of which is the grass amphitheatre. In the nineteenth century it was a favourite retreat of Queen Victoria and her younger son. A useful leaflet describes the various contributions to the park, which will appeal to everyone with its sensitive reconstruction of the eighteenth-century English style, even if it has nothing specific to offer the plantsperson, except perhaps the magnolia walk. The garden is a very popular recreation park for local families, sunbathers and picnickers. Special twilight guided walks take place each week from April to October.

COOMBE WOOD ★   9
Warren Road, Kingston Hill, Kingston, Surrey.

The Water Garden's Residents Association ★ From Kingston take the A308 (Kingston Hill) towards London. About 1½m on the right, turn right into Warren Road ★ Parking on street ★ Partly suitable for wheelchairs ★ Open twice for NGS

7th May, 1st Oct, 2 -5pm ★ Entrance: £1, children 50p (1994 prices)

An unusual and historic Japanese water garden. This was the original site of Veitch's famous nursery to which the owner's eldest son, resident in Japan, sent hundreds of plants for commercial development. This was in the 1860s and at the turn of the century more oriental plants arrived from Ernest Wilson's expeditions to China. When the nursery was sold in 1914, General Sir Arthur Paget and his wife, who lived next door, bought the two acres which contained the stream and a pond which they incorporated within their own Japanese-style garden, saving many Veitch plantings. The Paget estate changed hands again and today part is a residential development of 10 acres of which the water gardens form a most beautiful area. The Japanese features have been retained and improved. First-rate and well-restored bridges, tea-house, etc. in the Japanese style induce a sense of excitement for visitors exploring the winding paths, as the maturity of the planting creates a full woodland effect. The upkeep is above average. The rhododendrons are a particular attraction and include many Wilson species. Note also the fine magnolias, camellias and Japanese maples which show to advantage at the spring and autumn openings. The blue hydrangeas are a remarkable sight and there are many unusual trees.

THE COPPICE 10
Coppice Lane, Reigate, Surrey. Tel: (01737) 243158

Mr and Mrs B. Bushby ★ Leave M25 at junction 8 and take A217 for Reigate, down Reigate Hill. Immediately before level crossing turn right into Somers Road which continues as Manor Road. At end turn right into Coppice Lane. The Coppice is the last big house ★ Careful parking in Coppice Lane ★ ☆Teas ★ Toilet facilities ★ Partly suitable for wheelchairs ★ Dogs on leads ★ Open 19th, 26th April, 26th July, 2nd Aug, 2 – 5pm for charity ★ Entrance: £1.50, children 50p (1994 prices)

Mr and Mrs Bushby have redeveloped this six and a half-acre garden on heavy clay over the past five years. Even outside the front hedge, the grass is impeccably kept and there are perfectly clipped boxes of hawthorn at the roadside. The front garden is formal with standard roses and bedding plants. At the back, there is a rose pergola, a decorative yew hedge surrounding a croquet lawn and water garden with two ponds, rocky streams and waterfalls. Good shrubs and herbaceous plants – many unusual species. Conservatory.

2 COURT AVENUE 11
Old Coulsdon, Surrey. Tel: (017375) 54721

Dr K. Heber ★ In Old Coulsdon, opposite the Tudor Rose pub ★ Best season: summer ★ Parking in Court Avenue ★ Teas ★ Suitable for wheelchairs ★ Plants for sale ★ Open by appointment ★ Entrance: £1, children 50p

From the corner of a busy road, visitors step into a colourful oasis. Dr Heber began this garden 25 years ago and now grows around 3000 different plants in a level third of an acre. Against a background of shrubs, roses and clematis are many unusual varieties of herbaceous and foliage plants. The design is open and informal, with every inch of earth covered by plants, leaving no room for weeds. Knightsmead (see entry) is nearby.

COVERWOOD LAKES AND GARDEN 12
Peaslake Road, Ewhurst, Cranleigh, Surrey. Tel: (01306) 731103

Mr and Mrs C.G. Metson ★ 7m SW of Dorking. Off A25 1¹/₂m S of Peaslake ★ Parking ★ Home-made teas, and for 23rd Oct, hot soup and sandwiches ★ Toilet facilities ★ Suitable for wheelchairs ★ Plants for sale ★ Open 23rd, 30th April (gardens only), 7th, 14th, 21st, 24th, 28th May (gardens and farm), 2 – 6pm. Also 22nd Oct (gardens and farm), 11am – 4.30pm ★ Entrance: April: £1.50, children £1; May and Oct: £2, children £1. Large or private parties by prior arrangement

The original gardens were designed in 1910 by a rich Edwardian business-man. Now it is a woodland estate surrounding four lakes, the water for which arises from the natural springs in the bog garden. Each lake has a different character, from the towering rhododendrons reflecting in the calm water of the highest to the largest alongside the arboretum. This was planted early in 1990 and contains 100 different kinds of trees which are prospering in this natural setting. Bordering the paths are a great many varieties of hostas, trilliums and candelabra primulas. Lilies of the valley form a carpet below a dazzling display of rhododendrons and azaleas.

CROSSWATER FARM 13
Millais Nurseries, Crosswater Farm, Churt, Farnham, Surrey. Tel: (01252) 792698

Mr and Mrs E.G. Millais ★ 6m from Farnham and Haslemere. ¹/₂m N of Churt. Follow signs for Millais Nurseries ★ Parking in field beside garden ★ Teas available on charity days 27th to 29th May ★ Toilet facilities ★ Suitable for wheelchairs ★ Plants for sale in specialist rhododendron nursery ★ Open May, daily, 2 – 5pm ★ Entrance: £1.50, children free

These six acres of woodland gardens were begun in 1946 by Mr and Mrs Millais who specialise in rhododendrons and azaleas. Among the mature and some more recent plantings are rare species collected in the Himalayas, and hybrids raised by the owners, including 'High Summer'. The family main-tains the gardens which contain an exceptional range of rhododendrons from all over the world. These are labelled for identification and most are available from the adjoining nursery which grows more than 600 different varieties. The surrounding garden features a stream, ponds and companion plantings including young rare species which the owners have collected as seed from remote corners of the Himalayas, some being the first to be grown outside China and Bhutan.

FEATHERCOMBE GARDENS 14
Feathercombe, Hambledon, Nr Godalming, Surrey. Tel: (01483) 860257

Miss Parker ★ 5m S of Godalming, E of A283 between Hydestile and Hambledon ★ Parking ★ Picnic area available ★ Toilet facilities ★ Partly suitable for wheelchairs ★ Dogs on lead ★ Plants for sale ★ Open 30th April, 1st, 28th, 29th May, 2 – 6pm ★ Entrance: £1.50, children 10p

Although mainly worth visiting for the good display of rhododendrons and azaleas, there are fine views across three counties framed by larches and some tree heaths which are now 20 to 30 feet high. Now that the garden is maintained solely by the family, some of the features in the original design of 1910 by Eric and Ruth Parker have had to be changed through lack of labour. Ruth Parker was one of Ludwig Messel's daughters and there must have been strong connections between her garden at Feathercombe and his at Nymans (see entry) in West Sussex.

90 FOLEY ROAD   15
Claygate, Surrey. Tel: (01372) 462538

Mr and Mrs B. Mathew ★ Claygate is SE of Esher. Signposted ★ Parking in road ★ Refreshments nearby ★ Dogs on lead ★ Open two Suns in March and April, 2 – 5pm ★ Entrance: £1.50, children free

The south-facing front garden is entirely gravelled over and planted with interesting subjects which enjoy hot, dry conditions. At the back, the north slope has been terraced with a rill running through. There are effective design ideas for both sunny and shady areas. The owner, who has written 14 books on plants and bulbs, has gardened here since 1975, and the result is described as 'a treat'. There are collections of bulbs, species iris, hellebores, daphnes and lewisias, and, in the greenhouse, insectivores and tender plants. Although the garden is not large, allow plenty of time to see it, every plant is interesting, and many are rare.

GODDARDS   16
Abinger Common, Nr Dorking, Surrey. Tel: (01306) 730487

The Lutyens Trust ★ From Guildford take the A25 Dorking Road. At Wotton take a right turn for Abinger Common. The house is on the Green opposite a Victorian well ★ Limited parking ★ Teas ★ Suitable for wheelchairs ★ House open ★ Garden open April to Oct, Tues – Sat (telephone the Administrator for details of times) ★ Entrance: house and garden £3.50 (£2 concessions) (1994 prices)

Sir Edwin Lutyens designed the house originally in 1898 as a home of rest for ladies of small means. He planned it around a courtyard garden, facing slightly west of south and overlooked by all the principal rooms – in effect an outdoor room. Gertrude Jekyll collaborated on the structure of the garden which remains intact. The Lutyens Trust will use Gertrude Jekyll's planting plans, discovered in America, to restore the garden to her original design over the next five years. A dipping well in the centre provides water for the plants and around it are paved paths, low walls, curved beds and a raised sundial. There are flower borders under the windows and vines and wisteria grow against the house walls. Architectural yew hedges enclose the formal gardens around the house and yew arches give vistas over lawns, a ha-ha and across a meadow to a curved backdrop of woods. The Administrator Anthony Smith usually conducts personal tours.

GUILDFORD CASTLE GARDENS   17
Castle Street, Guildford, Surrey. Tel: (01483) 505050

Guildford Corporation ★ From the High Street walk through the arches into Tunsgate. The Castle is opposite at the far end ★ Best season: spring and summer ★ Parking in Sydenham Road car park ★ Partly suitable for wheelchairs ★ Dogs

★ *Castle keep open 10am – 5pm. 65p, children 35p (1994 prices)* ★ *Gardens open daily, dawn – dusk* ★ *Entrance: free*

This ruined keep built by William the Conqueror (close to the present city centre) once formed part of the garden of a private house bought by Guildford Corporation in 1885. Clever use has been made of the original moat. A path runs around the bottom, and shaped beds, retaining their interesting Victorian designs, are cut into the sloping, turfed sides. They are bedded out for spectacular spring and summer display with much the same plants as the Victorians would have used. There are plenty of seats here in a wider level area for the weary or contemplative. A tunnel, its damp, shady approach brightly planted, leads up to a bowling green and a bandstand, with attractive borders and clipped hedges, well-maintained like the whole of the garden.

HAMPTON COURT PALACE
(see London)

HANNAH PESCHAR GALLERY
AND SCULPTURE GARDEN   18
Black and White Cottage, Standon Lane, Ockley, Surrey.
Tel: (01306) 627269

Hannah Peschar ★ *1m SW of Ockley. Signposted from Cat Hill Lane onwards with a tourist sign 'Garden'* ★ *Parking* ★ *Refreshments for group visits by arrangement* ★ *Toilet facilities* ★ *Suitable for wheelchairs (but not the indoor gallery)* ★ *Open May to Oct, Fri and Sat, 11am – 6pm, Suns and Bank Holidays, 2 – 5pm. Any other day, except Mons, by appointment only* ★ *Entrance: £4, OAP £3, children £2. Guided tours for parties £6 per person, group picnics £4 per person. Special leaflet on request*

This delightful Surrey woodland garden designed by Anthony Paul is of primary interest to those who enjoy contemporary outdoor sculpture, as Mrs Peschar represents a wide range of artists whose work is displayed in natural settings, featuring architectural plants and water. The exhibits change, of course, as they are sold, and anyone planning to place objects of art outdoors will find a study of the sculptures here a source of inspiration. Note the bridge, too, which demonstrates the way art contributes to function. The garden has expanded in size and retains its native character.

HATCHLANDS   19
East Clandon, Guildford, Surrey. Tel: (01483) 222482

The National Trust ★ *E of East Clandon, N of A246* ★ *Best seasons: spring and summer* ★ *Parking. Batricar for disabled visitors available from car park* ★ *Home-made teas* ★ *Toilet facilities* ★ *Suitable for wheelchairs* ★ *House open* ★ *Garden open April to Oct, Tues, Wed, Thurs, Sun and Bank Holiday Mon, also Fri in Aug, 2 – 5.30pm (last admission 5pm)* ★ *Entrance: park walks and grounds (when open) £1.50 (house and gardens £4)*

The restoration of these gardens has now been successfully completed. The Gertrude Jekyll garden has been returned to its original size and planted to her 1914 plans. Plants were specially propagated, some having come from abroad. The result is very effective. Beside the garden is a magnificent mature London plane. A wild flower meadow is left uncut until July. The garden at the front has been restored from the Italianate to Humphry Repton's original design of lawns and vistas. There are three woodland walks and the park has been restored to Reptonian principles.

HIGH MEADOW 20
Tilford Road, Churt, Surrey. Tel: (01428) 606129

Mr and Mrs John Humphries ★ 3m N of Hindhead. Take A287 from Hindhead then fork right to Tilford. House is nearly 2m on right ★ Parking at Avalon PYO farm on left past turning to house. Disabled may park in drive to house ★ Teas ★ Toilet facilities ★ Plants for sale ★ Open 16th, 17th April, 28th, 29th May, 25th, 26th June, 27th, 28th Aug, 2 – 6pm ★ Entrance: £1.50, children free

As the name suggests this garden is situated high on a meadowside protected by a series of hedges of beech, holly and cupressus. A small terrace is overlooked by a pergola with a variety of climbers. Unusually-shaped beds surround grass of putting-green quality and contain a wealth of colour co-ordinated shrubs, roses and herbaceous plants which are cleverly graded by height. There is a small pool set in a rock garden, a bog plant section, rockery and small peat garden. A plantsman's garden.

HILEY NURSERY 21
25 Little Woodcote Estate, Wallington, Surrey. Tel: (0181) 647 9679

Mr and Mrs Brian Hiley ★ Off Woodmansterne Lane which links B278 and A237. Signposted SCC Smallholding ★ Best season: summer ★ Parking in field beside garden ★ Toilet facilities ★ Suitable for wheelchairs ★ Plants for sale in nursery ★ Open April to Sept, Wed and Sat, 9am – 5pm ★ Entrance: £1.20 for charity (1994 price)

Twenty years ago Brian and Heather Hiley came here to market-garden. Now they specialise in rare and tender perennials and display them in a chalky acre divided into a series of small gardens. There are herbaceous borders, a rockery and an alpine house all packed with rare and unusual plants. There are also hardy perennials, a blaze of annuals and many varieties of penstemons, diascias and osteospermums, as well as some plants which the Hileys have saved from near extinction.

KNIGHTSMEAD 22
Rickman Hill Road, Chipstead, Surrey. Tel: (01737) 551694

Mrs C. Jones and Miss C. Collins ★ 1m SW of Coulsdon, 3m SE of Banstead, off the B2032 ★ Parking in Bouverie Road/Rickman Hill Road ★ Refreshments: soup, tea and coffee (April) and teas (June) ★ Plants for sale ★ Open 19th April, 11am – 4pm, 24th, 25th June, 2 – 5.30pm and by appointment ★ Entrance: £1.30, accompanied children 50p

When the present owners came here 12 years ago, the half-acre garden was overshadowed by vast Lawson's cypresses. Now there are shrub roses and clematis, with arcs of smaller trees underplanted with spring bulbs and woodland plants such as erythroniums, trilliums and pure colour-bred hellebores.

A graceful 60ft Deodar cedar dominates this well–designed plantsman's garden. A lily pond, a rose arch and beds of shrubs and perennials give year-round interest. On heavy clay soil, a bog garden, peat bed and limestone scree provide ideal conditions for choice plants. Walls support climbers and a conservatory extends the range. 2 Court Avenue (see entry) is nearby.

LEITH HILL RHODODENDRON WOOD 23
Tanhurst Lane, Leith Hill, Surrey. Tel: (01306) 712434

The National Trust ★ From Dorking take the Coldharbour Road and continue to Leith Hill. At the next junction keep right, then fork left. The wood is immediately on the left ★ Best season: April/May ★ Parking ★ Light refreshments at tower when open. Picnic area ★ Dogs on lead (not allowed in picnic area) ★ Leith Hill Tower open April to Sept, Wed, 2 – 5pm, Sat, Sun and Bank Holidays, 11am – 5pm (last admission 4.30pm). Also fine weekends Oct to March, 11am – 3.30pm (last admission 3pm) ★ Rhododendron Wood open during daylight hours ★ Entrance: £1 per car for the wood and 50p for the tower

The wood was originally part of the estate of Leith Hill Place, once the home of the composer, Ralph Vaughan Williams. Beside the car park there is a picnic area, thickly carpeted with wild marguerites. Below this the rhododendrons and azaleas have recovered well from damage inflicted by the 1987 storm, which removed most of their canopy of trees. They are a blaze of colour in April and May. An immense tulip tree, *Liriodendron tulipfera*, can be seen in the field beyond and there are spectacular views. Further on, where the storm caused less damage, the mature trees create a contrasting shady area.

LOSELEY PARK 24
Nr Guildford, Surrey. Tel: (01483) 304440

Mr and Mrs J.R. More-Molyneux ★ 3m SE of Guildford off B3000 ★ Parking ★ Refreshments: restaurant offering wholefood lunches, snacks and teas. Open 11am – 5pm in season ★ Toilet facilities ★ House open May to Sept, Wed – Sat, 2 – 5pm ★ Garden open May to Sept, Wed – Sun, 11am – 5pm. Also 29th May and 28th Aug ★ Entrance: £1.50, children 50p (1994 prices)

The house, garden and farm provide interest and entertainment for all the family by offering such attractions as farm tours and trailer rides. The Elizabethan house is set in a sweep of lawn surrounded by parkland. The secluded garden to the side of the house has yew hedges creating 'rooms', an herbaceous bed with familiar plants and a moat walk. A new rose garden was planted in November 1993 and a herb garden in 1994. Future plans include vegetable, white and sunken gardens.

THE MOORINGS 25
14 Russells Crescent, Horley, Surrey.

Dr and Mrs C.J.F.L. Williamson ★ Near town centre, 400 yards from railway station ★ Parking in Russells Crescent ★ Teas ★ Suitable for wheelchairs ★ Dogs on lead ★ Plants for sale ★ Open 24th, 25th, June, 2 – 6pm ★ Entrance: £1.25, children 25p

Here is a retreat, a secret garden, close to the bustle of a town centre, full of rare and interesting plants, with rocks, pools and ornaments hidden amongst them. There are lawns, too, with unusual specimen trees and wide borders of roses. Long paths make the garden seem bigger than its one acre.

MUNSTEAD WOOD ★ 26
Heath Lane, Busbridge, Godalming, Surrey.

Sir Robert and Lady Clark ★ From Godalming take B2130 to Busbridge. Heath Lane is on the left opposite the church ★ Park just before Heath Lane or in Munstead Wood Road (next left) ★ Teas ★ Toilet facilities ★ Suitable for wheelchairs ★ Open 16th April, 28th May,14th Sept, 2 – 6pm ★ Entrance: £2, children 50p

The house was designed by Edwin Lutyens for Gertrude Jekyll in 1896, but she had begun the garden 13 years earlier with no definite plan. She lived here until her death in 1932. Sir Robert and Lady Clark have been here 26 years. *Hydrangea petiolaris* clothes the wall around the unusual entrance. There are narrow borders and wall plants against the house and a cool courtyard at the back with paving and pools. Well-kept lawns lead to a rock garden, a pergola and a wall; sun-loving plants grow on the south side and shade-lovers on the north. The farther part of the garden has been restored to Jekyll's original design. From the lawn at the front of the house, grass paths lead through massed mature rhododendrons and azaleas to shady woods. In Gertrude Jekyll's day, 14 gardeners tended 15 acres; now 10 acres are worked by one and a half gardeners. Whinfold (see entry) is nearby.

PAINSHILL PARK ★★ 27
Portsmouth Road, Cobham, Surrey. Tel: (01932) 868113/864674

Painshill Park Trust ★ 1m W of Cobham on A245. Entrance on right, 200 yards E of A3/A245 roundabout ★ Limited parking ★ Teas and light refreshments ★ Toilet facilities inc. disabled ★ Partly suitable for wheelchairs (wheelchairs available) ★ Shop in Visitor Centre ★ Open 9th April to 15th Oct, Suns only, 11am – 6pm (last admission 5pm). Also all year by appointment for parties of 10 or more ★ Entrance: £3.50, concessions £3, children (5-16) £2.50. Children under 16 must be accompanied. School parties welcome

Painshill was developed by Charles Hamilton (1704–86), a great English landscape designer who acquired the lease in 1738 and got severely into debt for his ambitious plans. He should be better known and is described by the *Oxford Companion* as 'a brilliant and subtle designer (who) could create illusion and vary scene and mood. His work strikes a delicate balance between art and nature, between the artist and the plantsman'. His work was nearly lost to posterity but after 30 years of neglect and delay it was rescued at the eleventh hour when it was bought by Elmbridge Borough Council and an independent Trust was established in 1981. There are now 158 acres of which 14 are taken up by the lake. A great deal of work has already been done, and Charles Hamilton's garden is coming to life again. There are about 100 trees surviving at Painshill that were planted between 1738-1773, including the great cedar of Lebanon, the largest in England (120 x 32 feet) and the pencil cedar (*Juniperus virginiana*) approx 60 x 61½ feet – the tallest in England with a mountain ash growing from the trunk. Features include Gothic temple, water wheel, grotto island, abbey ruins, Turkish tent, replanted eighteenth-century style shrubberies and a vineyard.

PINEWOOD HOUSE ★   28
Heath House Road, Worplesdon Hill, Woking, Surrey.
Tel: (01483) 473241

Mr and Mrs Van Zwanenberg ★ 5m NW of Guildford. Turn off A322 opposite Brookwood Cemetery wall ★ Parking ★ ☆ Home-made teas ★ Toilet facilities ★ Specially planned for wheelchairs ★ House open with hand embroidery exhibits ★ Garden open April to Oct by appointment for parties of 2 to 25 persons ★ Entrance: £1.50 (house and garden)

In 1986, Mr and Mrs Van Zwanenberg built a new house in four acres of their original garden. They retained the water garden and rhododendrons massed against a backdrop of Scots pines, cedars and other fine trees. There is a young arboretum and a charming new walled garden with a fountain. An automated conservatory displays exotic plants.

POLESDEN LACEY ★   29
Great Bookham, Nr Dorking, Surrey. Tel: (01372) 452048/458203

The National Trust ★ 5m NW of Dorking, 2m S of Great Bookham off A246 Leatherhead – Guildford road ★ Parking 150 yards away ★ Refreshments: coffee, lunches, and teas in licensed restaurant in courtyard. Picnic site in grounds (not in formal areas) ★ Toilet facilities inc. disabled ★ Partly suitable for wheelchairs. Batricar available on pre-booked basis ★ Dogs on lead in estate grounds only ★ Shop ★ House open March, Sat and Sun, 1.30 – 4.30pm; 30th March to Oct, Wed – Sun, 1.30 – 5.30pm and Bank Holiday Mon and preceeding Sun, 11am – 5.30pm ★ Grounds open all year, 11am – 6pm (or dusk if earlier) ★ Entrance: £2.50 (house and grounds £5.50, parties £4.50 per person on weekdays only by prior arrangement with the Administrator)

This 30–acre garden has grown up over several centuries. Richard Brinsley Sheridan, the dramatist who owned the house for over 20 years, lengthened the Long Walk before he died here in 1816. The present house was built a few years later by Cubitt in the Greek classical manner for an owner who made extensive alterations and planted over 20,000 trees. The garden was further developed early this century and given to the Trust in 1944. The walled rose garden is in four square areas divided by paths and covered by wooden pergolas and the area is dominated by a water tower covered by an ancient Chinese wisteria. There are small gardens of peonies, bearded irises, beds of different kinds of lavender. A winter garden overshadowed by three iron trees. A long herbaceous border and a sunken garden. A fully detailed garden guide is available. The original parkland setting is to be restored over the next 10 years, allowing greater public access over the park and improved habitats for wildlife.

PYRFORD COURT   30
Pyrford Common Road, Pyrford, Woking, Surrey.
Tel: (01483) 765880

2m E of Woking. M25 Junction 10. Take A3 towards Guildford off to Ripley and then B367 Newark Lane. 1¾m on left at junction of Pyrford Common Road and Upshott Lane ★ Parking ★ Teas ★ Toilet facilities ★ Partly suitable for wheelchairs ★ Dogs on lead ★ Open by appointment and 13th, 14th May, 2 –

SURREY

6pm, 15th Oct, 12 noon – 4pm ★ Entrance: £2.50, children 80p

Transformed at the turn of the century by Lord and Lady Iveagh with advice from Gertrude Jekyll, this varied garden covers about 20 acres, both formal and woodland. The wild garden to the south is a blaze of colour in the autumn, especially the Japanese maples. The north lawn of around four acres is bordered by a high brick wall with a pillared loggia and features several pear-shaped Irish yews. Noticeable on the wall is a loquat, *Eriobotrya japonica*. The wisterias on the pergola walk are from Japanese raised seedlings imported about 85 years ago from Yokohama and are remarkable for their extremely long flower panicles. Further wisteria has been added to form part of the National collection. The ornamental grape, *Vitis coignetiae*, is a fine sight at the end of the pergola walk, brilliant when in autumn colours. By the stream is a rare flowering camellia (*C.* x *williamsii* 'Hiraethlyn') which flowers in October.

RAMSTER   31
Chiddingfold, Surrey. Tel: (01428) 644422

Mr and Mrs P. Gunn ★ 11½m S of Chiddingfold on A283 ★ Best season: spring ★ Parking ★ Refreshments: teas on Sat, Sun and Bank Holiday Mon. Lunches for pre-booked coach parties ★ Toilet facilities ★ Suitable for wheelchairs ★ Dogs on lead ★ Plants for sale ★ Embroidery for Gardeners exhibition, 6th to 19th May ★ Garden open 15th April to 30th July, daily, all 2 – 6pm and parties by appointment ★ Entrance: £2, children free

Owned by the same family for close to 70 years, these are 20 acres of peaceful woodland with views of lakes and hillsides filled with colour and interest. Planting includes Californian redwoods, cedars, firs, camellias, rhododendrons and azaleas plus the rarer *Styrax obassia*, *Tetracentron sinense*, and *Kalopanax pictus*. A camellia garden, magnolia bed and widespread bluebells and daffodils ensure flowers are on view throughout the spring. Especially notable is an avenue of *Acer palmatum* 'Dissectum'.

RISE TOP COTTAGE (formerly 2 The Cottage)   32
Off Maybourne Rise, Mayford, Woking, Surrey. Tel: (01483) 764958

Mr Trevor Bath ★ 3m S of Woking off A320. Along track at top of Maybourne Rise ★ Parking in Maybourne Rise ★ Teas ★ Plants for sale ★ Open 1st, 6th June, 10am – 5pm and by appointment mid-April to mid-July ★ Entrance: £1

Mr Bath began this delightful garden 25 years ago. There is a profusion of fascinating and unusual varieties of cottage plants: granny's bonnets (*Aquilegia vulgaris*), hardy geraniums (the owner is an expert), pulmonarias, comfreys and roses. Intersecting paths lead to an arbour; a small lawn, an unexpectedly formal water garden, a black mulberry tree and a gravel scree.

ROYAL HORTICULTURAL SOCIETY'S GARDEN ★★   33
Wisley, Woking, Surrey. Tel: (01483) 224234

Royal Horticultural Society ★ 7m from Guildford, 4m from Cobham, 1m from Ripley, W of London on A3 and M25 (junction 10) ★ Parking ★ Refreshments: licensed restaurant and self service cafeteria ★ Toilet facilities inc. disabled ★ Suitable for wheelchairs ★ Plants for sale ★ Shop ★ Garden open to non-members of the RHS, Feb to Oct, Mon – Sat only, 10am – 7pm or dusk if earlier, Nov to Jan, 10am – 4.30pm (Sun for RHS members only) ★ Entrance: by membership or £4.50, children (6–14) £1.75, under 6 free (1994 prices)

George Fox Wilson, a former treasurer of the R.H.S., established a famous woodland garden here *c.* 1880. After his death it was purchased by Sir Thomas Hanbury (owner of the famous La Mortola garden in Italy) and together with surrounding land it was presented to the R.H.S. and became the site of the fourth R.H.S. garden. In common with a number of gardens in the South East, Wisley was devastated by the storms of 1987 and 1990. This presented the opportunity for redevelopment and rejuvenation including a collection of Mediterranean plants on the southern side of Battleston Hill. Wisley fulfills its teaching role so splendidly that it warrants a two star classification. Impeccably planted and tended, the garden thrills the thousands of visitors it attracts each year who are understandably impressed by one of the finest alpine rock gardens in Europe, a fine range of plants in the glasshouse range and yards of quintessentially English, deep and richly-appealing herbaceous border. Bonuses available from a Wisley visit are that it is possible to browse among what is arguably the best selection of modern gardening books available anywhere in the world and to buy very well grown plants. A major redevelopment of Wisley as a teaching unit is planned including a national Centre for Horticultural Science to be open by the year 2000.

THE SAVILL GARDEN ★★   34
Wick Lane, Englefield Green, Surrey. Tel: (01753) 860222

Administered by the Crown Estate Commissioners ★ 5m from Windsor. From A30, turn into Wick Road and follow signs, or follow signs from Englefield Green ★ Parking ★ Refreshments: licensed self-service restaurant open Jan to 17th Dec (01784) 432326. Picnic area near car park ★ Toilet facilities inc. disabled ★ Suitable for wheelchairs ★ Plants for sale ★ Gift and book shop ★ Open daily: April to Sept, 10am – 6pm; Oct to March, 10am – 4pm. Closed 25th, 26th Dec ★ Entrance: £3.30, OAP £2.80, accompanied children under 16 free. Parties of 20 or more £2.80 per person. Guided tours are available – apply to Keeper of the Gardens

One of the finest woodland gardens anywhere. Covering some 35 acres it contains a fine range of rhododendrons, camellias, magnolias, hydrangeas and a great variety of other trees and shrubs producing a wealth of colour throughout the seasons, particularly in spring and summer – meconopsis and primulas in June especially. In the shadier areas a wonderful collection of hostas and ferns flourishes. Daffodils in impressive drifts dominate in the spring while lilies are the highlight of high summer. The tweedy autumn colours in the Savill Garden are almost as satisfying in their mellowness as its jauntier spring hues. A more formal area is devoted to modern roses, herbaceous borders, a range of alpines and a very interesting and attractive dry garden. Extensive new Temperate House opening spring 1995. Windsor Castle gardens are nearby.

SOUTH PARK FARM   35
South Godstone, Redhill, Surrey. (01342) 892141

Mrs P. Stewart-Smith ★ From the railway bridge over A22 at South Godstone travel 1m S. At Walker's Garden Centre turn right into Carlton road and follow signs for 1m ★ Parking in field ★ ☆Home-made teas ★ Toilet facilities ★ Suitable for wheelchairs ★ Open 17th to 19th June, 2 – 6pm ★ Entrance: £1.50, children free

A seventeenth-century barn enlivened with leaded windows is the centrepiece of the garden. This, with the farmhouse in the background, creates a dreamy setting. The walls support roses and honeysuckle, climbers and shrubs. Regale lilies thrive in a sheltered corner (an unbelievable 26 blooms were spotted on one stem during our inspection). There are peacocks and statuary on the lawns; a formal rose garden and a kitchen garden and views of the North Downs. The lake was enlarged when clay was dug to make bricks for the house and buildings. A walk around it passes shrub roses, a young handkerchief tree and a swamp cypress. Here is something which merits the term 'romantic garden'.

STREET HOUSE   36
Thursley, Godalming, Surrey. Tel: (01252) 703216

Mr and Mrs B.M. Francis ★ W of A3 between Milford and Hindhead, near road junction in village ★ Parking on village recreation ground. From A3, beyond the house ★ Teas ★ Toilet facilities ★ Dogs on lead ★ Plants for sale ★ Open several times April, June and Sept for charity (telephone for details). Private parties welcome by appointment ★ Entrance: £1.50, children 50p

Sir Edwin Lutyens spent his early years at this listed Regency house, and it was said that he first met Gertrude Jekyll here. There are three separate gardens around the house. A walled garden is full of interesting and unusual plants, trees and shrubs, including an immense acacia (*Robinia pseudoacacia*). The main lawn is surrounded by shrubs with a curving backdrop of fine limes, while the lower lawn is framed by dazzling rhododendrons and azaleas and has splendid views. There is an unusual astrological feature constructed with Bargate stone unearthed from the garden, and local ironstone.

SUTTON PLACE ★★   37
Guildford, Surrey. Tel: (01483) 504455

Sutton Place Foundation/ Mr Frederick Koch ★ 3m N of Guildford off A3 (directions will be given when appointment is made) ★ Best seasons: spring and summer ★ Open by appointment for pre-booked parties

Henry VIII gave Sutton Place to Sir Richard Weston in the early sixteenth century and it remained in the family until this century. Paul Getty lived here in the 1960s and 70s. In 1980 Stanley Seegar, the oil magnate, arrived and commissioned Sir Geoffrey Jellicoe to design a new garden. In 1986 Sutton Place was sold again and the gardens closed. Now the new owner, Frederick Koch (pronounced Coke), has formed the Sutton Place Foundation and there are plans to open the house as well as the garden. Sir Geoffrey created a series of gardens on a grand scale: some areas have been replanned. Mr Koch has made a rose garden in soft colours with a central arbour, the beds divided like a cake and edged with box. The walls are clothed in climbers and the borders punctuated by conical yews. A long rose arch separates it from a *potager* planted in blues. Beyond the wall a Jellicoe path with false perspective passes huge, decorative urns brought from Mentmore. Thoughtfully surrounded by yew hedges is Ben Nicholson's White Wall sculpture. A new Ellipse garden is approached by curving paths through a shrubbery planned to give scent throughout the year. In the centre is an elliptical pool bordered by pleached hornbeams. There is a new camellia garden and orchards of different varieties of apples, pears and plums, underplanted with bulbs. The 18–acre woodland garden goes down to the River Wey. Across the south front of the house is a vast lawn with mature trees. A dramatic Victorian fountain has been placed at the focal point of a yew bauble avenue leading from the mansion. Citrus trees grow in boxes in front of the house with herbaceous borders on either side, one in hot and one in cool colours. High arching pleached limes lead to Jellicoe's two–storey summerhouse, designed to balance a sixteenth–century one in the old walled garden. His Paradise Garden is a delight of tall rose arches, brick paths, little fountain pools and mixed planting. A moat with water lilies divides it from the house. The pool garden has a silver and old gold scheme and a Gertrude Jekyll shelter. The restoration and development of Jellicoe's garden have been successfully achieved and the best varieties of plants are grown. The high standard of work and maintenance is a credit to Head Gardener John Humphris and his 10 assistants.

VALE END 38
Albury, Surrey. Tel: (01483) 202594

Mr and Mrs J. Foulsham ★ 4¹/2m SE of Guildford. From Albury take A248 W for 1¹/2m ★ Parking ★ Refreshments ★ Toilet facilities ★ Dogs on lead ★ Plants for sale ★ Open 25th June, 23rd July, 10am – 5pm ★ Entrance: £1.50, children free

A one-acre walled garden on many levels in beautiful setting. Fine views from terrace across sloping lawns to mill pond and woodlands with a wide variety of herbaceous plants and roses, ornamental vegetable garden. This garden is entirely maintained by the owners and will interest plantsmen because on a light, well-watered soil, the owners have interspersed old favourites with less-known plants.

THE VALLEY GARDENS (Windsor Great Park) ★★ 39
Wick Road, Englefield Green, Surrey. Tel: (01753) 860222

Administered by the Crown Estate Commissioners ★ 5m from Windsor. From A30 turn into Wick Road and follow signs for Savill Garden (1m to W) and drive to car park adjoining Valley Gardens, avoiding a 2m round walk ★ Parking ★ Refreshments at Savill Garden ★ Plants for sale at Savill Garden ★ Open all year, 8am – 7pm or sunset when earlier. Possible closure if weather inclement ★ Entrance: £2.60 car and occupants (5p, 10p, 20p, 50p and £1 coins only) (1994 price)

One of Britain's most discriminating and experienced garden visitors, the late Arthur Hellyer, suggested that The Valley Gardens are among the best examples of the 'natural' gardening style in England. With hardly any artefacts or attempts to introduce architectural features they are merely a tract of undulating grassland (on the north side of Virginia Water) which is divided by several shallow valleys, that has been enriched by the introduction of a fine collection of trees and shrubs. It was started by the royal gardener Sir Eric Savill, when he ran out of room in the Savill Garden, to continue making 'natural' landscapes. One of the valleys is filled with deciduous azaleas. In another, 'The Punchbowl', evergreen azaleas rise in tiers below a canopy of maples. Notable too are collections of flowering cherries, a heather garden which amply demonstrates the ability to provide colour during all seasons, and one of the world's most extensive collections of hollies. Lovers of formal gardening might be forgiven for suggesting that the Valley Gardens have something of that rather too open, amorphous, scrupulously-kept feel to be found in America.

Virginia Water Lake, off the A30, adjacent to the junction with the A329, was a grand eighteenth-century ornamental addition to Windsor Great Park by the Duke of Cumberland, who became its ranger in 1746. It had dams, rockwork, a cascade and grotto. There was a fake 'Mandarin Yacht', a Chinese pavilion and a Gothic belvedere with a mighty single arch bridge spanning the water. Alas, almost all have disappeared but the woodland and the lovely one-and-a-half mile lake, full of fish and wildfowl survive, and there is still a colonnade of pillars and a 30ft waterfall.

VANN 40
Hambledon, Surrey. Tel: (01428) 683413

Mr and Mrs M.B. Caröe ★ 6m S of Godalming, E of A283 at Chiddingfold ★ Best season: spring ★ Parking as indicated ★ Refreshments: coffee, lunches and home-made teas in 'Barn' for parties by prior arrangement ★ Limited toilet facilities ★ Limited access for wheelchairs ★ Plants for sale if available ★ Open for three individual weeks between Easter and June, 2 – 6pm, and by appointment ★ Entrance: £2.50, children 50p. Parties by arrangement

The six different areas within this garden will provide some interest for most types of gardener. From the student of garden design viewing the water garden still containing plants selected and supplied by Gertrude Jekyll, to the admirer of the formal garden complete with clipped yews and regular brick paths, there is something for everyone. Of particular interest is the yew walk now re-planted with foliage plants – seemingly unattractive to deer – providing all year interest. Colourful annuals are introduced when the spring bulbs are over. Much publicised, it is remarkable that this garden is maintained by the family with only 14 hours' help weekly.

THE WALLED GARDEN 41
**Sunbury Park, Thames Street, Sunbury-on-Thames, Surrey.
Tel: (01784) 451499 (Community Services)**

Spelthorne Borough Council ★ In Sunbury-on-Thames via B375 Thames Street. Entrance through car park ★ Best seasons: spring and summer ★ Parking ★ Toilet facilities ★ Suitable for wheelchairs. Wheelchair available on request ★ Open daily except 25th Dec, 8am – dusk ★ Entrance: free

Although no house remains, this eighteenth-century walled garden has been developed since 1985 into a pleasant open space of about two acres designed to include garden styles from past centuries. Also four large areas of island beds display collections of plants from all parts of the world. The rose garden is composed entirely of species roses and varieties which were either introduced or widely planted during the reign of Queen Victoria. During the summer exhibitions of sculpture, paintings, etc, are on view and a band plays at published times.

THE WATER GARDENS, Kingston upon Thames
(see COOMBE WOOD)

WHINFOLD 42
Hascombe, Godalming, Surrey.

Mr and Mrs A Gash ★ 3¹/₂m SE of Godalming on B2130. Turn off on a bend near the top of Winkworth Hill ★ Parking in lane ★ Teas ★ Plants for sale ★ Open 2nd April, 14th May, 2 – 5pm ★ Entrance: £1, children free

Gertrude Jekyll designed this garden in 1897 and some specimen trees and shrubs still remain. A new pond has been made in the bluebell wood. There are two small, formal ponds further on. Around a long lawn, mature trees and rhododendrons frame distant views. Beyond, where the ground falls away steeply, are mature oaks and masses of bluebells. A splendid old handkerchief tree, *Davidia involucrata*, grows nearer the house. In April, there are magnolias, camellias and spring bulbs. Munstead Wood (see entry) is nearby.

WINKWORTH ARBORETUM 43
Hascombe Road, Nr Godalming, Surrey. Tel: (01483) 208477

The National Trust ★ 2m SE of Godalming, E of B2130 ★ Best season: spring/autumn ★ Parking inc. disabled. Coaches must book in advance ★ Refreshments: in tea room open March, weekends; April to 14 Nov, daily; 15 Nov to Christmas, weekends ★ Toilet facilities ★ Dogs on lead ★ Shop ★ Open all year, daily, dawn – dusk ★ Entrance: £2, children (5-15) £1

Winkworth is open 365 days of the year, so it's a great place to take the family for a walk on Christmas Day or any other! The 60 plant families and 150 genera grown here provide variety and interest throughout the year. In the spring there are the azaleas, rhododendrons, cherries and maples and in the autumn sorbus, liquidambars, acers and *Cotinus coggygria*. There is also a group of magnificent *Cotinus obovatus*, var. 'Chittam Woods' from the SE United States. Its hillside setting and two lakes give pleasing views from almost all of the site. Clearer labelling would be welcomed by the enthusiast and ignorant alike. Contains the National whitebeam collection.

WINTERSHALL MANOR 44
Bramley, Surrey. Tel: (01483) 892167

Mr Peter Hutley ★ 21¹/₂m S of Bramley on A281 from Guildford towards Horsham. Right turn to Selhurst Common, fork right and the Manor is on the left ★ Parking ★ Teas from 3.30pm ★ Toilet facilities ★ Suitable for wheelchairs ★ Open 5th Feb, 5th March, 7th May, 4th June, 2.30 – 5.30pm ★ Entrance: £2

This formal garden with roses and colourful herbaceous walk is steeped in history. The old mulberry tree planted by James II was badly damaged by the January 1990 gale but has fruited since. Garden railings were put up to celebrate the Battle of Waterloo. Walks through 100 acres of park and woodland with bluebells, rhododendrons and daffodils. Suitable areas for picnics are provided and there is a small chapel to St Francis for the contemplative. A path leads uphill past Stations of the Cross.

WISLEY
(see ROYAL HORTICULTURAL SOCIETY'S GARDEN)

SUSSEX (East)

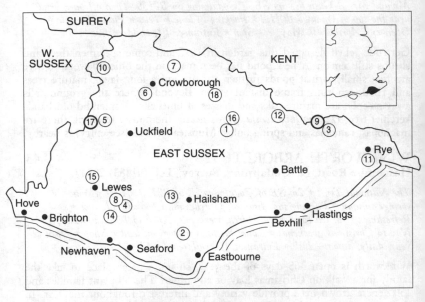

SURREY

W. SUSSEX

KENT

10

7

6

Crowborough

18

17 5

16

1

12

9 3

Uckfield

EAST SUSSEX

Rye

11

Battle

15

Lewes

13

Hailsham

8 4

Hove

Brighton

14

Bexhill

Hastings

2

Newhaven

Seaford

Eastbourne

Two-starred gardens are ringed in bold.

BATEMAN'S
Burwash, Etchingham, East Sussex. Tel: (01435) 882302

1

*The National Trust ★ ½m S of Burwash off A265 towards Lewes ★ Parking ★
Refreshments: light lunches, coffees, teas. Picnics in Quarry Garden and Copse ★
Toilet facilities, inc. disabled ★ Suitable for wheelchairs ★ Shop ★ House open and
mill which grinds flour on Sats in season ★ Garden open April to Oct, daily
except Thurs and Fri but open 14th April, 11am – 5pm (last admission 4.30pm)
★ Entrance: weekdays and Sats £3.50, children £1.80, Suns and Bank Holidays
£4, children £2. Pre-booked parties of 15 or more £3 per person (except Suns or
Bank Holidays) (1994 prices). All prices inc. house and mill*

Kipling may not be widely read these days, but his home from 1902-36 is
much visited. The house was built in 1634 and the rooms and study remain
as they were during the period when Kipling wrote many of his best-known
works. Much of the garden was his doing and contains formal lawns with
yew hedges, a rose garden and pond, a wild garden, and, on the right as you
descend from the car park, an exceptional herb garden.

BATES GREEN FARM
Arlington, Nr Polegate, East Sussex. Tel: (01323) 485152

2

*Mrs Carolyn McCutchan ★ 2½m SW of A22 at Hailsham, 2m S of Michelham
Priory (signposted) at Upper Dicker. Approach Arlington passing the Old Oak
Inn on right, continue for 350 yards, turn right along a small lane ★ Parking ★*

Refreshments ★ Toilet facilities ★ Partly suitable for wheelchairs ★ Plants sometimes for sale ★ Shop ★ Garden open March to Oct, Thurs, 10.30am - 6pm. Parties on other days by appointment ★ Entrance: £1.50

Successful and original groupings of plants here express the owner's flair for using colour and foliage to create atmosphere and effect. A splendid mature oak isolated after the '87 hurricane has been underplanted with foliage plants rejoicing in the dappled shade. Bark paths interweave between the planting and under the young trees. The warm and sheltered area of the former vegetable garden has colour-themed borders of sun-loving plants and foliage contrast. A serpentine path leads from the front of the old farmhouse to the pond where water-loving plants are skilfully grouped. Views from the pond are of the adjoining woodland where there are delightful walks in the bluebell season, which the owner's leaflet suggests would occupy up to one hour. Other specified walks extend from ½m upwards. Overall this might be described as a 'plantsman's artistic garden'.

BRICKWALL 3
Northiam, East Sussex. Tel: (01797) 223329

The Frewen Educational Trust ★ On B2088 Rye road ★ Best season: July ★ Parking ★ Suitable for wheelchairs ★ Dogs on lead ★ House open ★ Garden open 15th April to Sept, Sat and Bank Holiday Mons, 2 - 5pm ★ Entrance: £2, children under 10 free. Coach parties by arrangement

Brickwall is an interesting example of a Stuart garden, and care has been taken to use the plants chosen by Jane Frewen when she was making and planting it between 1680-1720, such as day lilies, bergamots, *Lychnis chalcedonica*, Cheddar pinks and columbines. There are large lavender beds, two old mulberries, groups of clipped yew, and a superb pleached beech walk. A striking modern addition is the Chess Garden with green and golden yew chessmen in iron frames, set in squares of white and black limestone chips. This garden is not far from Great Dixter (see entry) and a visit to both would make an excellent day out.

CHARLESTON FARMHOUSE ★ 4
Nr Firle, Lewes, East Sussex. Tel: (01323) 811265

The Charleston Trust ★ 6m E of Lewes on A27 ★ Best seasons: spring and midsummer ★ Parking 50p ★ Refreshments on Sat and Sun ★ Toilet facilities ★ Plants for sale ★ Shop ★ House open ★ Garden open April to 29th Oct, Wed - Sat (guided tours of house), Sun and Bank Holiday Mons (unguided), 2 - 6pm (last admission 5pm); also open 11am - 2pm from 19th July to 10th Sept ★ Entrance: £1.75, children 50p (farmhouse and garden £4.50, children £3)

In terms of pure gardening this does not deserve a grading, but it is of national interest because it was created by leaders of the Bloomsbury movement. The walled garden has been meticulously restored through painstaking research and the memories of people who visited when Vanessa Bell and Duncan Grant lived at the farmhouse and of those like Angelica Garnett and Quentin Bell who spent their childhood there. It is a delightful example of a garden created during the 1920s by an idiosyncratic group of highly creative people, and might be called an artist's garden. Useful notes and map available.

SUSSEX (East)

CLINTON LODGE ★ 5
Fletching, Nr Uckfield, East Sussex. Tel: (01825) 722952

Mr and Mrs Collum ★ 4m W of Uckfield from A272. Turn N at Piltdown from Fletching, 1½m in main village street surrounded by a yew hedge ★ Parking on street ★ Refreshments ★ Toilet facilities ★ Suitable for wheelchairs ★ Dogs on lead ★ Open 11th, 12th, 19th, 26th June, 2 - 6pm ★ Entrance: £2, children £1

This Caroline house was built for the first Lord Sheffield's daughter who married Henry Clinton. The garden of about six acres of clay soil is basically divided into areas by period. There is an Elizabethan herb garden with well-tended camomile paths and turf seats, and four knot gardens are being developed. A lawn and ha-ha at the rear of the house with views to distant woods create an eighteenth-century atmosphere, a white, yellow and blue Victorian herbaceous border with its 'hot' colours purposely absent, and a Pre-Raphaelite alley of white roses, clematis, purple vines and lilies; the twentieth century is represented in the area surrounding the swimming pool. There are also various walks of quince, pleached limes and a rose garden of old and English roses complete with fully-occupied dovecot. A *potager* along medieval lines is being developed with advice from Diana Baskervyle Glegg. Pillars of ceanothus and roses cover the walls in early summer, and less formal areas of orchard and wild flowers complete a garden of outstanding imagination and charm.

COBBLERS 6
Mount Pleasant, Tollwood Road, Jarvis Brook, Crowborough, East Sussex. Tel: (01892) 655969

Martin and Barbara Furniss ★ On A26 at Crowborough Cross take B2100 towards Crowborough and Jarvis Brook Station. At the second crossroads take Tollwood Road ★ Parking ★ Home-made teas ★ Toilet facilities ★ Partly suitable for wheelchairs ★ Unusual plants for sale ★ Open 14th, 29th May, 11th, 25th June, 9th, 23rd July, 6th, 20th, 28th Aug ★ Entrance: £3, children £1 (inc. tea)

Martin Furniss, an architect, created the garden from old meadows over 22 years ago. He is fascinated by the architectural forms of plants and this is reflected in inspired planting and the creation of vistas in all directions. The planting includes over 2000 varieties and species, ranging from rock and alpines on the terrace to the magnificent mixed borders and beds and, at the lowest part of the garden, a rhododendron walk. An outstanding feature is the water garden which is full of surprises and delight, and this, together with the 14 other mixed and herbaceous borders are visually bound together by ingenious brick paths and stone steps. During the four months that it is open, the garden will always be found to show colour and interest. It is both a plantsman's and an artist's garden.

CROWN HOUSE 7
Eridge Green, Nr Tunbridge Wells, East Sussex. Tel: (01892) 864389

Major and Mrs L. Cave ★ 3m SW of Tunbridge Wells. Take A26 Tunbridge Wells - Crowborough road. In Eridge take the Rotherfield turn S. House is first on the right ★ Parking ★ Home-made teas ★ Toilet facilities ★ Suitable for wheelchairs ★ Plants and home-made produce for sale ★ Open for NGS 8th, 9th

July, 2 - 6pm and by appointment May to Oct ★ Entrance: £1.50, OAP £1, children under 14 free

This gently sloping one and a half-acre garden contains several different areas of interest separated by old-established yew and beech hedges. At the front of the house are lily ponds surrounded by rare shrubs; on the east side the principal lawn is dominated by a raised, round bed which has as its centrepiece an umbrella of old-fashioned musk roses, surrounded by golden flame spiraea and nepetas. On the south side there are two more lily ponds, an alpine garden and a white garden, leading to a grass walk flanked on one side by a herbaceous border and on the other by a heather garden. The walk is terminated by a paved seating area enclosed by a trellis of roses and sweet peas surrounding an ornamental pond with fountain. On the south-west and west sides there is a formal rose garden, a herb garden and a rose walk leading to the aviary containing budgerigars, cockatiels and green parakeets. Panoramic views of the surrounding countryside.

FIRLE PLACE 8
Lewes, East Sussex.
Tel: (01273) 858335 (office and answer phone)

Viscount Gage ★ On A27 Lewes – Eastbourne road. Entrance 1m from house ★ Best season: summer ★ Parking ★ Refreshments: cold buffet, licensed 12.30 - 2pm, Sussex cream teas 3pm onwards (last orders 5pm) Wed, Thurs, Sun only. No picnics in grounds or park ★ Toilet facilities ★ Parkland suitable for wheelchairs ★ Dogs on leads ★ Selection of plants for sale ★ Shop ★ House open 2 - 5pm (unguided Connoisseurs Days first Wed of every month) ★ Garden open May to Sept, Wed, Thurs, Sun and Bank Holiday Mons, 12.30 - 5.30pm (last admission 5pm) ★ Entrance: £3.50, disabled persons £2.75, children (5-17) £2, under 5 free (house and garden). Parties of 25 or more by appointment £3 per person. Connoisseurs Day £4.50 per person. No charge for terrace

The accessible part of the garden is nowadays small although attractive. The house, with its honey-coloured Normandy stonework, lies at the foot of the South Downs and has long views over the parkland and a nearby lake. Immediately below the Georgian facade, a terrace (where tea can be taken on house open days) overlooks the formal area of Italianate terraces and balustrades, a fountain and a ha-ha. There are several seats from which to enjoy the surroundings.

GREAT DIXTER ★★ 9
Dixter Road, Northiam, East Sussex. Tel: (01797) 253107

The Lloyd family ★ ½m N of Northiam. Turn off A28 at Northiam post office ★ Parking ★ Toilet facilities ★ Plants for sale at nursery. Extensive choice of clematis ★ Shop ★ House open ★ Garden open April to 8th Oct, daily except Mon (but open Bank Holiday Mons), also probably 14th, 15th, 21st, 22nd Oct, all 2 - 5pm ★ Entrance: £2.50, children 25p (house and garden £3.50, children 50p. Concessionary rates for OAP and National Trust members on Fridays only when house and garden £3)

Probably too well-known to need describing, Great Dixter was bought by Nathaniel Lloyd in 1910. The fifteenth-century house was restored by Lutyens. The sunken garden was designed and constructed by Mr Nathaniel

Lloyd. His son Christopher has continued his family's fine gardening tradition, striving to maintain the garden with a dwindling labour force. Composed of a series of gardens, these include fine topiary, a magnificent long mixed border and a new tropical garden where vegetables and flowers mingle, and throughout the complex of gardens are pockets of wild flowers. The spring at Great Dixter is famous for the huge drifts of naturalised bulbs. Truly a plantsman's garden, but a joy for anyone who enjoys gardening in the finest tradition.

KIDBROOK PARK

10

Forest Row, East Sussex. Tel: (01342) 822275

Rudolph Steiner Trust ★ At Forest Row 1m W of A22. Entrance in Priory Road ★ Best season: summer ★ Parking ★ Toilet facilities (not disabled) ★ Suitable for wheelchairs ★ Dogs on lead ★ Probably open Aug, daily, 11am - 6pm ★ Entrance: £1, family £3 (1994 prices)

A sandstone house built in 1725, now used as Michael Hall School, and its park lie on the northern boundary of the Ashdown Forest. Work is in progress to restore the main elements of Repton's design, though this was hampered by the loss of 1500 trees during the 1987 gales. 'Swallow' spring, cascades, stepping stones, a pond and a twentieth-century weir add interest, together with wild and bog gardens. The parkland is obviously a shadow of its former glory. Maps show recommended walks through the 125 acres.

LAMB HOUSE

11

West Street, Rye, East Sussex.

The National Trust ★ In centre of Rye, in West Street, near the church ★ No parking near house ★ House open. Home of Henry James, American novelist, 1898-1916. Later, E.F. Benson, now a televised writer, lived there ★ Garden open April to Oct, Wed and Sat, 2 - 6pm (last admission 5.30pm) ★ Entrance: £2 (house and garden). No reductions for children or parties

Americans are frequent visitors to this house where Henry James wrote some of his best books and studied the English character, including its passion for gardening. Although not of considerable botanic interest, the high-walled garden has great charm and it is surprising to find it so big - one acre in the middle of overcrowded Rye. It is well-maintained by the Trust's tenants.

MERRIMENTS GARDEN

12

Hawkhurst Road, Hurst Green, East Sussex. Tel: (01580) 860666

Mr and Mrs Mark Buchele ★ On A229 (formerly A265) between Hawkhurst and Hurst Green ★ Best seasons: summer and autumn ★ Parking ★ Refreshments: coffee and biscuits ★ Toilet facilities ★ Suitable for wheelchairs ★ Plants for sale at adjoining nursery ★ Garden open April to Oct, daily, 10am - 5pm ★ Entrance: £1

This new (1991) four-acre garden has been planted by the owners of the adjoining nursery. It occupies a gently sloping, open site on the heavy Wealden clay of a former field. Physical disadvantages are being overcome with shelter planting and the heavy application of organic matter. The appearance of the garden in midsummer is a tribute to the perseverance and plant knowledge of its owners. The formal entrance leads to a main area surrounding water gardens and a pergola walk. Boldly curving beds are thematically planted according to colour or planting conditions such as damp ground. A natural area is being managed for meadow grassland. The many original associations of interesting and unusual plants make this a rewarding garden to visit now and a few more years should give greater character as the garden is developed further.

MICHELHAM PRIORY ★   13
Upper Dicker, Hailsham, East Sussex. Tel: (01323) 844224

Sussex Past ★ 10m N of Eastbourne off the A22 and A27. Signposted ★ Best season: spring/summer ★ Parking ★ Licensed refreshments, restaurant and picnic area for ticket holders ★ Toilet facilities inc. disabled ★ Suitable for wheelchairs ★ Dogs on lead in car park ★ Herbs and some herbaceous plants for sale ★ Shop ★ House and museum ★ Working watermill ★ Blacksmiths and Rope museum ★ Garden open 25th March to Oct, daily, 11am – 5.30pm and Suns in March and Nov, 11am – 4pm ★ Entrance: £3.50, OAP £2.90, children £1.90 (1994 prices)

A major feature is the Physic Garden, a reconstruction of a monastic physic garden, based on that at ninth-century St Gall, which was regarded as the ideal. The 11 beds contain medicinal plants for specific complaints. Many of them are the herbs of the hedgerows. A serpentine moatside border has been planted and there are plans to extend it. The monastery stewponds are also being planted up. and restocked. Mixed and herbaceous borders, and a small kitchen garden; research to re-create a replica medieval garden is underway. A few miles east of Hailsham is Herstmonceux Castle which has a garden worth visiting.

MONK'S HOUSE ★   14
Rodmell, Lewes, East Sussex.

The National Trust ★ 4m SE of Lewes off former A275 now C7. In Rodmell village follow signs to Church. Sign is 400 yards from the house ★ Parking further down narrow road ★ Toilet facilities ★ House open ★ Garden open April to Oct, Wed and Sat, 2 – 5.30pm (last admission 5pm) ★ Entrance: £2 (1994 price). No reduction for children or parties

The cottage home of Virginia and Leonard Woolf from 1919 until his death in 1969. Leonard Woolf had kept the village self-sufficient in vegetables, as well as showing them, and the original vegetable area is still thriving. There are three ponds, one in dewpond style. An orchard, underplanted with spring and autumn bulbs, contains a comprehensive collection of daffodils. The one and three quarter-acre garden is a mixture of chalk and clay, nurturing a wide variety of species. Flint stone walls and yew hedges frame the more formal herbaceous areas, leading to a typical Sussex flint church at the bottom of the garden. Among the interesting specimen trees are *Salix hastata* 'Wehrhahnii', Chinese lantern (20 feet tall), *Magnolia liliflora*, walnut, mulberry, and *Catalpa bignonioides* (Indian bean). Literary folk will want to compare and contrast this garden with the other Bloomsbury lot's house at Charleston Farmhouse (see entry).

OFFHAM HOUSE   15
Offham, Nr Lewes, East Sussex. Tel: (01273) 474824

Mr and Mrs H.N.A. Goodman ★ 2m N of Lewes on A275, ½m from Cooksbridge

SUSSEX (East)

Station ★ Best seasons: late spring, high summer ★ Limited parking on property, more on road ★ Refreshments ★ Toilet facilities ★ Suitable for wheelchairs ★ Dogs on lead ★ Plants for sale ★ Open 7th May, 4th June, 2 – 6pm ★ Entrance: £2, children 50p, under 12 free

This garden offers a wide variety of interest and perspectives. Lawns sweep from the extremely attractive house (with its well-blended, lush conservatory) to a colourful shrubbery, which contains shrub roses and a variety of trees, including an evergreen or holm oak, a tulip tree underplanted with bulbs, and a weeping mulberry; beyond is an arboretum with a weeping elm and collections of acers and sorbus. The colourful well-stocked herbaceous borders contain a variety of penstemons, euphorbias and salvias as well as an unusual sundial, contemporary with the house. Other features include a spring path with early purple orchids and fritillaries, a collection of lilacs, a cherry orchard (with several Japanese varieties), and an unusually long bed of peonies and aquilegias. A fine new addition is the herb garden, which is bursting with life: bergamots, alpine strawberries and marjorams, mixed with *Tricyrtis stolonifera*, *Phygelius aequalis* 'Yellow Trumpet', euphorbias and verbenas, are framed by box, lavenders and thymes. At the front of the house is a fountain and a splendid example of *Davidia* (pocket handkerchief tree). A particularly large and well-kept greenhouse is the backbone to this fine, well-tended garden.

PASHLEY MANOR ★   16
Ticehurst, East Sussex. Tel: (01580) 200692

Mr and Mrs James A. Sellick ★ On B2099 between Ticehurst and A21. Signposted ★ Parking ★ Refreshments inc. ploughman's lunch and home-made cakes served all day on the terrace in fine weather ★ Toilet facilities ★ Plants for sale ★ Open 15th April to 14th Oct, Tues – Thurs and Sat, 11am – 5pm. Also all Bank Holidays. Coach parties by appointment only ★ Entrance: £3, OAP £2.50

Pashley Manor is a Grade I listed Tudor timber-framed ironmaster's house of 1550 with a Queen Anne rear elevation dated 1720, standing in some eight acres of formal garden. Since 1981 Mr Sellick has undertaken with advice from Antony du Gard Pasley, a complete renovation of what was largely a Victorian garden. The planting is suble with emphasis on colour and form, pale colours blending with the carefully chosen foliage. The 1987 storm has opened up new vistas. From the terrace and over the magnificent fountain there is a view of the Mad Jack Fuller obelisk at Brightling Beacon several miles away. A series of enclosed gardens are surrounded by some beautiful eighteenth-century walls. Grass paths, some concealing the original Victorian gravel beneath, lead through camellia and rhododendron shrubberies. Natural springs feed a series of ponds falling away from the house and medieval moat. These springs together with the large fountain ensure that the sound of falling water is heard over the most of the garden. Access to a small island with recently erected temple is by a decorative iron bridge. Further projected developments include an extensive planting of tulips to complement the Tulip Festival held in April; an avenue of pleached trees underplanted with box so arranged to give a view through to the existing magnificent hydrangeas and planned garden of old-fashioned roses which will complement the Rose Festival to be held in June.

SHEFFIELD PARK GARDEN ★★   17
Nr Uckfield, East Sussex. Tel: (01825) 790231

The National Trust ★ 5m NW of Uckfield, midway between East Grinstead and Lewes E of A275 ★ Teas at Oak Hall (not National Trust). Picnics adjacent to the car park ★ Toilet facilities ★ Suitable for wheelchairs. Wheelchairs available ★ Shop ★ Garden open March, Sat and Sun, 11am - 4pm; April to 5th Nov, Tues - Sun and Bank Holiday Mons, 11am - 6pm (or dusk if earlier); 8th Nov to 16th Dec, Wed - Sat, 11am - 4pm (last admission one hour before closing) ★ Entrance: March, April, June to Sept and Nov: £3.50, children £1.80, pre-booked parties £2.50 per person. May and Oct: £4, children £2, pre-booked parties £3 per person (1994 prices)

One hundred and twenty-acre garden and arboretum with two lakes installed by 'Capability' Brown for the Earl of Sheffield in 1776. Repton also worked here in 1789 and was responsible for the string of lakes up to the mansion. Later still, the lakes were extended and cascades added. Between 1909 and 1934 a collection of trees and shrubs notable for their autumn colour was added, including many specimens of *Nyssa sylvatica*. These and other fine specimen trees, particularly North American varieties, provide good all-year-round interest. Features include good water lilies in the lakes, the Queen's Walk and, in autumn, two borders of the Chinese *Gentiana sino-ornata* of amazing colour. The Trust is continuing to open up new areas including a new stream area and the National collection of Ghent azaleas. Stewards on duty to answer questions.

WADHURST PARK   18
Wadhurst, East Sussex. Tel: (01892) 783693

Mrs M. Rausing ★ 6m SE of Tunbridge Wells on B2099. Turn right onto B2100 and after 1m turn left and then right at the T-junction. The entrance to Wadhurst Park is ahead after 1m ★ Parking in field ★ Teas ★ Toilet facilities ★ Partly suitable for wheelchairs ★ Plants for sale ★ Shop ★ Garden open one Sun in September for NGS, 2-5.30pm ★ Entrance: £1.50, children 50p

Wadhurst Park, as a Victorian mansion, was owned by Julius Drewe, founder of the Home and Colonial Stores before he commissioned Edwin Lutyens to build Castle Drogo on Dartmoor. Since then the Park has had a chequered history until the house was demolished in 1950. The present owners purchased the land in 1975 with a view to creating a deer park and planning a new house and garden. In a competition for the best country house built in the 1980s the New House at Wadhurst Park, designed by John Outram, was declared the winner. The garden, occupying a spectacular site overlooking the Sussex Weald, has been created under the guidance of Anthony du Gard Pasley and is still being developed. Around the house are formal gardens following the lines of the Victorian terraces. The Victorian conservatory has been restored by John Outram and now comprises a stove house, temperate house and cool house containing specimens of *Magnolia grandiflora*, camellia, *Trachelospermum jasminoides* and plumbago. Sheltered by the wall of the conservatory, the old kitchen garden has been renovated with espalier apple trees and mixed borders. Further away from the house, a long shrub border, azalea walk, wildflower meadow and woodland walk provide interest of all kinds and in all seasons.

SUSSEX (West)

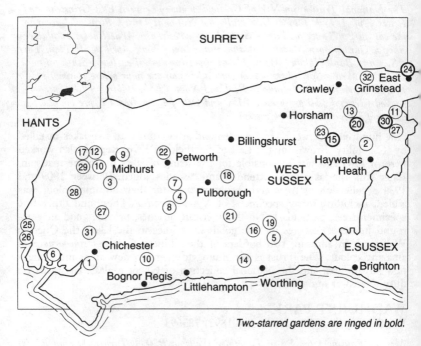

Two-starred gardens are ringed in bold.

APULDRAM ROSES   1
Apuldram Lane, Dell Quay, Chichester, West Sussex.
Tel: (01243) 785769

*Di Sawday ★ Turn off A259 (old A27) at signpost to Dell Quay, Apuldram ★
Best season: midsummer ★ Parking ★ Suitable for wheelchairs ★ Dogs on lead ★
Shop ★ Open daily except 24th Dec to 9th Jan 1996, Mon – Sat, 9am – 5pm,
Sun and Bank Holidays, 10.30am – 4.30pm ★ Entrance: charity collection box*

The garden has the brightest and latest HTs, floribundas, miniature and
patio roses, as well as climbers, several old roses, modern shrubs and standards. Every rose sold in the nursery is shown in a delightful enclosed
garden with grass paths. Visitors can also wander through the rose field, a
sheet of fragrance and colour in July.

BORDE HILL GARDEN ★   2
Haywards Heath, West Sussex.
Tel: (01444) 450326 or weekends (01444) 412151

*Borde Hill Gardens Ltd ★ 1½m N of Haywards Heath on Balcombe – Haywards
Heath road ★ Best season: March to May ★ Parking ★ Refreshments ★ Toilet
facilities ★ Suitable for wheelchairs ★ Dogs on lead ★ Plants for sale ★ Shop ★
Open 18th March to 1st Oct, daily, 10am – 6pm ★ Entrance: £3.50, OAP £3,*

children £1.50, family ticket £7.50, individual season ticket £12.50, family season ticket £25. Parkland only £1, children under 3 free

The garden of 40 acres was started by Col. Stephenson Clarke in 1893 and contains trees and shrubs, particularly rhododendrons, grown from seed collected by plant hunters like Douglas, Farrer, Forrest, Kingdon-Ward and Rock. Look out for *Umbellularia californica* whose leaves can cause sneezing, the Chusan palm *Trachycarpus fortunei* and *Rhododendron eximium*. An exceptional collection of ericaceous and other plants dear to the heart of the plantsperson. Being renovated after period of neglect, but still insufficient labels on rare plants. Enticing woods and attractive Brides Pool.

CASTERS BROOK 3
Cocking, Nr Midhurst, West Sussex. Tel: (01730) 813537

Mr and Mrs John Whitehorn ★ 3m S of Midhurst on A286 to Chichester. Turn sharp E at Cocking PO and the garden is 100 yards on right, next to the church ★ Parking ★ Teas ★ Open 18th, 25th June, 2 – 6pm and by appointment ★ Entrance: £1.50, children free

Extensive ponds with islands, trout, sculptures and a small bridge are memorable features of this interesting garden. The site slopes from the house down to the millpond and is on a series of levels, separated by beds and banks of lavender, musk and rugosa roses (both of which do well on chalk), santolina and *Alchemilla mollis*. There are dramatic plantings of iris, ferns and wild flowers round the ponds. Near the house are small secluded areas, including a fig court and a fruit and herb garden. Between the garden and the churchyard is a secret garden and a shady walk. A large mirror, a free-standing door frame placed near the water and dramatic pieces of sculpture – which may change from year to year – add surprise elements to the layout.

CHAMPS HILL 4
Coldwaltham, Pulborough, West Sussex. Tel: (01798) 831868

Mr and Mrs D. Bowerman ★ From A29 at Coldwaltham turn N towards Fittleworth. Champs Hill is 300 yards up on right ★ Parking ★ Refreshments: coffees and home-made teas (but not in March) ★ Open 5th 12th, 26th March, 2nd April, 6th, 7th, 13th, 14th, 20th, 21st May, 30th July, 5th, 6th, 13th, 19th, 20th Aug, all 1 – 6pm ★ Entrance: £1.50, children free

This fascinating heathland garden, with over 200 varieties of heather grown together with dwarf conifers and other interesting plants, is complemented by spectacular views of the Arun Valley and South Downs. The heathers are best viewed in March and Aug, but a walk in May through the 27 acres of natural woodland interplanted with a wealth of rhododendron and azalea species is a real bonus.

CHANTRY GREEN HOUSE 5
Church Street, Steyning, West Sussex.

Mr R.S. Forrow and Mrs J.B. McNeil ★ 5m N of Worthing, NW of Brighton off A283. Turn into Church Street from the high street opposite the White Horse Inn. House is 150 yards on left ★ Parking in Fletchers Croft car park opposite church ★ Teas ★ Open 17th, 18th June, 2 – 5pm ★ Entrance: £1.30, children 50p

Newly designed by Jack Grant White, this has some interesting features and many uncommon trees within its one acre. In a corner, an old wall fountain is the focus of a shady area planted with ferns and hostas. There is a water garden, a kitchen garden, an American garden and an arboretum with unusual trees including *Liriodendron tulipifera* 'Aureomarginatum', *Lagerstroemia indica*, the Crape myrtle and the Japanese loquat, *Eriobotrya japonica*. Many varieties of cistus are thriving in this sheltered and well-maintained town garden.

CHIDMERE HOUSE 6
Chidham, Chichester, West Sussex. Tel: (01243) 572287/573096

Mr T. Baxendale ★ E of Emsworth, W of Chichester, S off A259. Turn right at southern end of Chidham village ★ Best season: spring ★ Parking in road ★ Toilet facilities ★ Suitable for wheelchairs ★ Dogs on lead ★ Open certain days for charity in spring and summer and also by appointment, 2 – 7pm ★ Entrance: £1.20, children 40p

Chidmere gardens were laid out in 1930–36 by the present owner's father on the site of a farm and orchard. Modelled on Hidcote they incorporate impressive *allées* bordered by tall yew and hornbeam hedges together with a sizeable lake. The house (not open) is Tudor in origin and, together with the outbuildings, it has been blended into a setting which looks far older than the 1930s. Trees include *Gingko biloba*, *Prunus serrula* and *Davidia involucrata*. There is a good collection of flowering shrubs.

COATES MANOR 7
Fittleworth, Pulborough, West Sussex. Tel: (01798) 82356

Mrs G.H. Thorp ★ ¹/₂m S of Fittleworth off B2138 ★ Teas ★ Suitable for wheelchairs ★ Plants for sale ★ Open 11th, 12th, 13th June, 11am – 6pm and by appointment ★ Entrance: £1.50, children 20p

This one-acre garden has trees and shrubs which give long-term pleasure in the form of interesting foliage, berries and autumn colour. These include ferns such as *Polystichum setiferum divisilobum*, grasses such as *Stipa gigantea* like frozen waterfalls, *Phlomis italica* and *chrysophylla*, and thalictrum as well as a purple-leaved *Cotinus coggygria*, a golden *Catalpa bignonioides*, a white-trunked *Betula jacquemontii* x *papyrifera* and a *Liquidambar styraciflua* 'Worplesden' giving autumn colour. In addition to the two main gardens there is a small paved walled garden with honeysuckles, clematis, pinks and other scented flowers. The delightful old stone house is partly covered with variegated euonymus.

COOKE'S HOUSE ★ 8
West Burton, near Pulborough, West Sussex.

Miss J.B. Courtauld ★ Turn W off A29 at the foot of Bury Hill and continue for ³/₄m ★ Parking in field opposite ★ Partly suitable for wheelchairs ★ Open 22nd to 24th April, 6th to 8th May, 2 – 6pm and by appointment ★ Entrance: £1, children under 14 free (1994 prices)

Delightful garden surrounding Elizabethan house with views of wooded downs. It has the components of a great garden in miniature, each section perfectly articulated to vistas leading the eye beyond. Tiny paved rose garden and herb garden. Yew topiary of cubes, cones and birds about to take flight, overlooked by a stone heraldic lion. Steps up to path between borders of fiery tulips, later herbaceous plants. Shrubs underplanted with snakeshead fritillaries, Solomon's seal and bluebells. Meadow with cowslips. Judas tree, liriodendron, magnolias. Orchard. All immaculately cared for.

COWDRAY PARK GARDENS 9
Nr Midhurst, West Sussex. Tel: (01730) 812423 (Estate Office)

Lord Cowdray ★ 1m E of Midhurst S of A272 ★ Parking in field beside house ★ Open 14th May, 2 – 7pm ★ Entrance: £1

The rolling lawns of this opulent Edwardian pleasure garden, contained within a ha-ha and surrounding the amazingly eclectic house built round an ancient hunting lodge, evoke a more leisured age. Water garden, slightly overgrown, sunk garden and rock garden, now a gully packed with scented azaleas. The avenue of Wellingtonias, 90 years old, looking to the downs is the finest in the south of England. Terrace, Banksian rose, walks, views, rhododendrons.

DENMANS ★ 10
Denmans Lane, Fontwell, West Sussex. Tel: (01243) 542808

Mrs J.H. Robinson/ Mr J. Brookes ★ 5m E of Chichester. Turn S off A27, W of Fontwell racecourse ★ Parking ★ ☆Refreshments: dairy tea shop offering coffee, light lunches and teas from 10am – 5pm ★ Toilet facilities ★ Suitable for wheelchairs ★ Plants for sale ★ Shop ★ The Clock House is home to John Brookes' school of garden design running day courses on a variety of horticultural topics ★ Open daily except 24th, 25th Dec, 9am – 5pm or dusk if earlier ★ Entrance: £2.25, OAP £1.95, children over 5 £1.25, groups of 15 or more £1.75 per person if pre-booked

The owners originally ran this large site as a commercial enterprise until, in 1947, Mrs Robinson began planting in what was then the kitchen garden and stableyard of a grand house. Then in 1969 during a holiday on Delos, Greece, Mrs Robinson saw plants growing from rocks and stones, and returned inspired. She thereupon pioneered the concept of a gravel garden which needs no mowing. Plants grow informally from gravel in a vast greenhouse, in a walled garden, and along a dry winding river bed. Colour and interest rely on foliage contrast, purple cotinus beside golden philadelphus and robinia, variegated elaeagnus beside dark *Viburnum davidii*. *Verbascum bombyciferum* like woolly men from outer space, violas and alchemilla are allowed to self-seed. Good garden for out-of-season ideas – mounds of the architectural *Euphorbia wulfenii* 'Lambrook Gold' in April, tree poppies and species clematis like *C. jouiniana* 'Praecox' and *C. viticella* in late summer, bright willow shoots in winter. In 1980 the owner teamed up with the well-known garden designer John Brookes who has assisted in the evolution of Denmans as well as establishing his design school here.

DUCKYLS 11
Sharpthorne, Nr East Grinstead, West Sussex. Tel: (01342) 810352

Lady Taylor ★ 4m SW of East Grinstead, 6m E of Crawley. Take B2028 S at

SUSSEX (West)

Turners Hill and fork left after 1m to W Hoathly. Left at sign to Gravetye Manor garden on right ★ Parking ★ Toilet facilities ★ Partly suitable for wheelchairs ★ Dogs on lead ★ Plants for sale if available ★ Open for small parties by prior appointment ★ Entrance: £2, children £1

These 14 acres of terraced and hilly garden, with breathtaking views of woods and Weir Wood Reservoir, are established with rhododendrons and azaleas among carpets of bluebells, daffodils, fritillaries. Auriculas and double primroses near the house. Later come dogwoods and *Kalmia latifolia*, rambling roses and two small charming herbaceous borders beside the terrace. The rose garden, with beds of the white rugosa 'Blanc Double de Coubert', is being made into a parterre garden. Ponds and bog garden with gunnera and philadelphus. Only a portion of the garden is maintained to the same standard as that around the house, and dead trees from the 1987 storm remain, yet the place stays immensely attractive in its decayed grandeur.

HAMMERWOOD HOUSE GARDEN 12
Iping, Midhurst, West Sussex. Tel: (01730) 813635

The Hon Mrs Lakin ★ 3m W of Midhurst, 1m N of A272 ★ Parking ★ Refreshments ★ Toilet facilities ★ Suitable for wheelchairs ★ Dogs on lead ★ Open 7th, 14th May, 1.30 – 6pm ★ Entrance: £1.50, children free

This is a peaceful country garden, formerly part of a Regency vicarage, that has been planted with care and a fine eye for good plants. Although the rhododendrons and azaleas give it its most spectacular flowering season, there are some good camellias, magnolias, cornus and other specimen trees. Across a meadow from the main garden is the woodland walk by a stream. Bluebells and other wild flowers abound.

HIGH BEECHES GARDENS ★ 13
Handcross, West Sussex. Tel: (01444) 400589

High Beeches Gardens Conservation Trust ★ 1m E of A23 at Handcross, S of B2110 ★ Best seasons: spring and autumn ★ Parking ★ Refreshments on Suns in April, May and Oct and on event days ★ Toilet facilities inc. disabled ★ Open April to June, Sept and Oct, daily except Wed, 1 – 5pm. Event days 16th, 30th April, 28th May, 15th Oct ★ Entrance: £3, accompanied children under 14 free. Guided parties of 10 or more by appointment, £4 per person with lunches, etc. by arrangement any day or time

A garden bearing the mark of the Loder family, which is now being maintained by the Boscawen family as Col. Loder designed it in 1906. The early planting was influenced by John Millais, son of the Pre-Raphaelite artist; by Arthur Soames of Sheffield Park, Sussex; and by William Robinson whose philosophy of allowing plants to grow naturally has greatly influenced the development of the garden. A series of valleys or ghylls, the garden has a superb collection of rhododendrons and specimen trees. Willow gentians grow wild, and the front meadow, which has not been ploughed in living memory, is filled with native grasses and wild flowers. Wild flowers in the woodland garden which is outstanding for autumn colouring.

HIGHDOWN 14
Littlehampton Road, Goring-by-Sea, West Sussex. Tel: (01903) 8067

Worthing Borough Council ★ 3m W of Worthing, N of A259 ★ Best season: April ★ Parking ★ Refreshments at peak times ★ Toilet facilities inc. disabled ★ Open all year, Mon – Fri, 10am – 4.30pm, and first weekend in April to last weekend in Sept, weekends and Bank Holidays, 10am – 8pm ★ Entrance: free – donation box

Created by Sir Frederick Stern from a bare chalk pit in 1910, Highdown was donated to Worthing Corporation in 1968. Without a rhododendron or camellia in sight, Highdown makes a refreshing change for those used to gardening on acid soil. From such an unpromising site a garden has been created illustrating the scope and possibilities of a garden of chalk-loving plants. These include buddleia, mahonia, paulownia, althaea and paeonia, as well as rarities such as *Itea ilicifolia* and *Clerodendron trichotomum fargesii*.

LEONARDSLEE GARDENS ★★ 15
Lower Beeding, Nr Horsham, West Sussex. Tel: (01403) 891212

The Loder family ★ 3m SW of Handcross and M23 on the A279/A281 ★ Best season: mid-April to mid-June and autumn ★ Parking ★ Refreshments: café and licensed restaurant ★ Toilet facilities ★ Large selection of plants, esp. rhododendrons, for sale ★ Shop ★ Open April to Oct, daily, 10am – 6pm (May, 10am – 8pm) ★ Entrance: May: £4, April and June to Oct: £3, children £2

This garden was started by Sir Edmund Loder, who raised the famous Rhododendron Loderi hybrids, with their huge scented flowers, grown in gardens on acid soils throughout the world. This 240-acre valley with its six lakes, its collection of rhododendrons, azaleas, camellias, acers, magnolias, Snowdrop Tree, and other shrubs, and sweeps of bluebells combine to form a beautiful landscape in a peaceful setting. The immense scale and the mature trees give this garden, well known for its rhododendron collection, a special quality. In the late afternoon and early evening light the colours of the rhododendrons and azaleas glow and their heady scent fills the air. Rock garden with ferns and Kurume azaleas in perfect small scale. Excellent bonsai exhibition in walled Japanese garden. Alpine house with lewisias and other miniatures. Temperate greenhouse with banana, *Ceanothus thyrsiflorus repens* like a blue umbrella, and the white claws of *Clianthus puniceus* 'Albus'. New summer wildflower walk.

LITTLE THAKEHAM ★ 16
Merrywood Lane, Storrington, West Sussex. Tel: (01903) 744416

Mr and Mrs T. Ratcliffe ★ From London take A3 then A24 towards Worthing. 2m S of Ashington, at roundabout, return N up A24 for 200 yards. Turn left into Rock Road for 1m. At staggered crossroads turn right into Merrywood Lane. Little Thakenham is 300 yards on right. From Storrington, take B2139 to Thakenham. After 1m turn right into Merrywood Lane ★ Parking ★ ☆Teas ★ Toilet facilities ★ Partly suitable for wheelchairs ★ Open on one Sun in May, June and July

A superb Edwin Lutyens house (now a hotel) surrounded by an almost equally fine garden, now nearing the end of a three-year restoration period. The entrance court is very simple, squares of lawn, low pots overflowing with ivy, ferns and hostas against the walls. At the side of the building, a double

herbaceous border in soft colours owes a lot to Gertrude Jekyll. Peonies, thal-
ictrums, columbines, geraniums, dicentras and catmints combine to form an
archetypal English border. In front of the house, a paved parterre has a
large Arts and Crafts urn as a centrepiece. A long pergola walk, planted with
roses and almost blocked by two handsome acers at the beginning, leads to
the apple orchards which surround the garden. In spring you look over a sea
of blossom. Clematis, roses, romneyas and grey-leaved plants grow against the
house walls. There is a small water garden: a square pond with a fountain is
linked by a rill planted with ferns to another square, filled in and planted
with primulas, ferns and astilbes as a bog garden. There are also lawns,
specimen trees and banks of wild flowers.

MALT HOUSE 17
Chithurst, Rogate, West Sussex. Tel: (01730) 821433

*Mr and Mrs Graham Ferguson ★ From A272, 3½m W of Midhurst, turn N
signposted Chithurst. Or leave A3(M) at Liphook and follow old A3 W for 2m,
turn SE to Milland then follow signs to Chithurst for 1½m ★ Best season: early
summer ★ Parking ★ Refreshments ★ Toilet facilities ★ Plants for sale ★ Open 23rd,
30th April, 7th, 8th, 14th, 21st, 28th, 29th May, 2 – 6pm ★ Entrance: £1.50,
children 50p (1994 prices)*

Five-acre garden of flowering shrubs and trees, including fine prunus, rhododendrons and azaleas on steep slopes leading down to the Malt House and its
outbuildings. The pretty cottage is thickly hung with wisteria, one roof
intriguingly smothered with cotoneaster. Interesting underplanting includes
hostas, ferns, and the pink purslane *Claytonia sibirica*.

MILL HOUSE ★ 18
Nutbourne, Nr Pulborough, West Sussex. Tel: (01798) 813314

*Sir Francis and Lady Avery Jones ★ Nutbourne (Pulborough – not Chichester!)
turn right (going E) 80 yards after passing the Rising Sun pub. Last house in The
Street ★ Teas ★ Plants for sale ★ Open by appointment ★ Entrance: £1*

This garden surrounding a mill house is remarkably varied for its size.
Fascinating small herb garden (the owners define a herb as having been
historically of value to man and animals) with ancient dyes, medicines, scents,
wicks, insect repellents, detergents, etc. used since medieval times, all labelled.
Foamy border of perennials. The lawn slopes to a stream feeding pools edged
with gunnera, mimulus, astilbes, iris, hostas. Bridge and stepping stones to
shady wild flower banks on the far side. View to pond in countryside beyond.

NORTH SPRINGS 19
Fittleworth, West Sussex. Tel: (01798) 865731

*Mr and Mrs Michael Waring ★ Between Fittleworth and Wisborough Green.
Reached either from A272 outside Wisborough Green or A283 at Fittleworth.
Near Bedham turn off down lane ★ Parking ★ Open May to Sept by appointment
and 8th, 9th July, 2 – 6pm ★ Entrance: £2*

A hillside garden with good views, surrounded by 40 acres of woodland. Streams
cross the garden and there is a particularly well-planted pond surrounded by
gunnera, iris, *Lysichiton americanus* (skunk cabbage) and candelabra primulas.

There is a wide range of well-grown plants, with many different hebes and hostas, roses, ferns, geraniums and clematis as well as rhododendrons and azaleas.

NYMANS ★★ 20
Handcross, Nr Haywards Heath, West Sussex. Tel: (01444) 400321

The National Trust ★ At the southern end of Handcross village, off A23/M23 and A279. Signposted ★ Best seasons: spring and summer ★ Parking ★ Refreshments: in licensed restaurant ★ Toilet facilities, inc. disabled ★ Suitable for wheelchairs. Batricar available ★ Plants for sale ★ Shop ★ Garden open March to Oct, daily except Mon and Tues (but open 14th April and Bank Holiday Mons), 11am – 6pm (Sat and Sun 7pm) or sunset if earlier (last admission 1 hour before closing) ★ Entrance: £3.80, pre-booked parties £3 per person. Special joint party ticket which includes entry to Standen £5.50 available Wed – Fri

The story of this – one of the greatest of the great South Weald gardens – is fascinating. Bought over 100 years ago by Ludwig Messel, it was handed to the Trust in 1954 though a family link continues today. However the Great Storm of 1987 caused unimaginable destruction, and over 1000 trees and shrubs were replanted, the aim being to perfect the main structure and overall design, plus enriching the planting, much of which went back to Ludwig's time. There are over 30 acres here and the very minimum time required even for a brisk walk round the property is two hours. Whereas it is fashionable today to talk of 'rooms' Nymans is redolent with an equally imaginative quality – theatricality, many effects being introduced by two distinguished Messels, the late Countess of Rosse and her artist brother Oliver. Among the wonderful surprises are the Prospect at the end of the Lime Avenue, the Sunk Garden with its elegant stone loggia, and the Laurel Walk with its dramatically-placed statuary. Then mount the Wooden Erection to view the Croquet Lawn, Pergola, Lilac Border, Heather Garden and much else. Next, pass to the ruins of the mansion (caught fire 1947) and the house itself – probably open from 1996 – the Wall Garden and Rose Garden. If there is time, cross the main road to walk in the Wild Garden. The trees, well-labelled, are spectacular.

PARHAM HOUSE AND GARDENS ★ 21
Pulborough, West Sussex. Tel: (01903) 744888

4m SE of Pulborough on A283 ★ Parking ★ Refreshments in big kitchen 2.30 – 5.30pm. Picnic area ★ Toilet facilities ★ Suitable for wheelchairs (garden only) ★ Plants for sale ★ Shop ★ House open as garden but 2 – 6pm ★ Garden open 16th April to 1st Oct, Wed, Thurs, Sun and Bank Holidays, 1 – 6pm (last admission 5pm) ★ Entrance: £2.50, children £1 (house and garden £4.50, OAP £3.50, children £2). Pre-booked guided groups of 20 or more £4.50 per person. Pre-booked unguided groups £3.50 per person (1994 prices). There is a special House and Garden weekend

The gardens of this Elizabethan house are approached through the Fountain Court. A broad gravelled path leads down a slope through a wrought-iron gate guarded by a pair of Istrian stone lions to the walled garden of about four acres. This retains its original quadrant layout divided by broad walks and includes an orchard. In 1982 it was redesigned retaining its character and atmosphere; the borders were replanted to give interest for many months, with shrubs as well as herbaceous plants. A *potager* or vegetable garden and a rose garden have been introduced recently. A new project is a green border, planted along the outer west wall. In one corner is the enchanting miniature house, a delight for both children and adults. The pleasure grounds of about seven acres provide lawns and walks under stately trees to the lake, with views over the cricket ground to the South Downs. Veronica's brick and turf maze. This is a garden for all seasons, and in spring it is dominated by its splendid 'sacred' grove of Mount Fuji white flowering cherry, over 50 years old. Don't miss the annual Parham House Garden weekend in July featuring plant nurseries and flower arranging by the Parham House guides.

PETWORTH HOUSE ★ 22
Petworth, West Sussex. Tel: (01798) 342207

The National Trust ★ 6½m E of Midhurst on A272 in the centre of Petworth ★ Parking ½m N of Petworth on A283 ★ Refreshments: light lunches and teas in restaurant on days when house is open ★ Toilet facilities ★ Suitable for wheelchairs. Disabled arrangements with administration office ★ Dogs under control in deer park only ★ Shop ★ House open as Pleasure Ground, 1 – 5.30pm (last admission 5pm) ★ Pleasure Ground open 19th, 26th March; then April to Oct, daily except Mon and Fri (but open 14th April and Bank Holiday Mons), 12.30 – 6pm. Deer park open all year, daily (except 23rd to 25th June), 8am – sunset ★ Entrance: £4, children under 17 £2, under 5 free. Pre-booked parties of 15 or more £3.50 per person (house and grounds). Deer park free

The deer park grew from a small enclosure for fruit and vegetables in the sixteenth century to its present size of 705 acres over centuries, and is enclosed by an impressive five-mile-long stone wall. George London worked here as did 'Capability' Brown. The latter toiled from 1751-63 for the 2nd Lord Egremont modifying the contours of the ground, planting cedars and many other trees and constructing the serpentine lake in front of the house. It was one of Brown's earliest designs, planned while he was still at Stowe. Turner painted fine views of the park (as well as the interior of the house) and it is interesting to see these and have them in one's mind as one strolls around the park as he must have done many times while staying at Petworth. This is not a garden for the botanist, but it is a very splendid experience, all year round, for any lover of man's improvements over nature, and individual trees and shrubs, including Japanese maples and rhododendrons, deserve close study. It is interesting to contemplate that at the turn of the century Petworth had over two dozen gardeners (they were always counted in dozens).

SELEHURST 23
Lower Beeding, West Sussex.

Mr and Mrs M. Prideaux ★ 4½m S of Horsham on A281, directly opposite Leonardslee ★ Parking ★ Teas ★ Partly suitable for wheelchairs ★ Plants for sale ★ Open 14th May, 1 – 5pm, 25th June, 2 – 6pm ★ Entrance: £1.50

This well-established rhododendron and woodland garden now has a new chain of five ponds and a romantic bridge. There is much new tree and shrub planting and many new formal features. Near the house a rose and laburnum tunnel is underplanted with ferns, phormiums, artichokes, grasses and hostas in striking tapestry of foliage. There is newly-planted box parterre adjacent to the swimming pool garden. The pool is surrounded by standard roses under-pinned with day lilies and *Alchemilla mollis*. One striking border against a wall has rambler roses growing through tall iron frames, contrasting with silvery-leaved oleaster. There is a small conservatory and camomile lawn.

STANDEN ★★   24
East Grinstead, West Sussex. Tel: (01342) 323029

The National Trust ★ 2m N of East Grinstead signposted from A22 at Felbridge, and also B2110 ★ Best season: May/June ★ Parking ★ Refreshments ★ Toilet facilities ★ Partly suitable for wheelchairs ★ Dogs in lower car park and woodland walks only ★ Shop ★ House open 1.30 – 5.30pm ★ Garden open 18th, 19th, 25th, 26th March, 12.30 – 5.30pm; then April to Oct, Wed – Sun and Bank Holiday Mon, 2.30 – 6pm ★ Entrance: Wed, Thurs, Fri £2.50, children £1.25 (house and garden £4.80, children £2); Sat, Sun, 14th April and Bank Holiday Mons £3, children £1.50 (house and garden £4.80, children £2.40). Joint party ticket which includes entry to Nymans garden £5.50 available Wed – Fri.

The house and estate have close connections with William Morris, and the late Victorian garden reflects much of the romantic era of the latter part of the nineteenth century. It is made up of a succession of small, very English gardens. Perhaps the most outstanding is the little quarry, which has survived as a Victorian fernery. Good views from this hillside-garden across the Medway Valley. The house, designed by Philip Webb, will be of inter-est to architectural pundits.

STANSTED PARK   25
Rowlands Castle, Hampshire. Tel: (01705) 412265

The Earl and Countess of Bessborough ★ 1m N of Emsworth, just off the B2149 ★ Best season: early summer ★ Parking ★ Refreshments ★ Toilet facilities ★ Plants for sale ★ Shop ★ House open ★ Garden open 16th, 17th April; May to Sept, Sun, Mon (inc. Bank Holidays), Tues, 2 – 5.30pm (last admission 5pm) ★ Entrance: £2, children under 12 £1 (house and gardens £3.50, OAP £3, children under 12 £1.50. Parties of 20 or more £3, children £1 per person) (1994 prices)

A woodland walk with fine spring bulbs encloses walled gardens with good greenhouses with muscat vines and other organically-grown produce. There is an elegant Dutch-style rose garden, which is set off beautifully by the mellow red brick eighteenth–century house, and a fine arboretum which is quickly recovering from the gale damage of 1987. There is also a prettily-set cricket ground with cricket every Sunday, taking place in view of the tea room.

STANSTED PARK
VICTORIAN WALLED GARDENS   26
Rowlands Castle, Hampshire. Tel: (01705) 412833

1m N of Emsworth, just off B2149. Signposted ★ Parking ★ Refreshments: ice creams (teas and toilet facilities available at Stansted Park) ★ Suitable for wheelchairs ★ Plants for sale ★ Walled Garden open July to Sept, Sun – Tues, 2 – 5.30pm. Surreal Garden open Suns only, 2 – 5.30pm ★ Entrance: Walled Garden free. Surreal Garden £1.01 or a lobster, large shell, mirror, prism or other largish suitably surreal object

Victorian greenhouses have been renovated with a fine display of tender plants and the beds of the walled garden are planted with roses and herbaceous plants. Adjoining is a surreal 'Garden in Mind' created by Ivan Hicks for the television series *Dream Gardens*. Lilies grow in a room with telephone, bed, wardrobe and fireplace, a chair is perched in the air, a pair of legs is all that is left of someone who has dived into a dell of ferns. Underworlds and overworlds. Creepy fun.

STONEHURST 27
Ardingly, West Sussex. Tel: (01444) 892052 (Estate Manager)

Mr and Mrs D.R. Strauss ★ On B2028, 800 yards N of South of England Showground, Ardingly ★ Best season: spring and early summer ★ Parking ★ Refreshments ★ Toilet facilities ★ On charity days the nursery is open to the public for the sale of camellias, azaleas, rhododendrons and orchids only ★ Garden open 17th April, 14th, 29th May, 11am – 5pm. The Druid's Rocks may be seen by appointment ★ Entrance: £2.50, children £1 (1994 prices)

Thirty acres. Edwardian house set above valley, with contemporary brick balustrading, terrace, gazebos, observatory and summerhouses. Nearby are herbaceous border and lawns, with views of South Downs, valley and lakes. Slopes below are informally landscaped with steps, paths, grotto, rock garden and planted with shrubs, camellias, azaleas and specimen trees. Five lakes constructed before World War I fall into each other by a series of waterfalls. Black swans. Woodland walk to weird rock formations nearby, mentioned in the Domesday Book and Cobbett's Rural Rides. Woodland is a designated Site of Special Scientific Interest because of its lichens, liverworts and ferns.

TELEGRAPH HOUSE ★ 28
North Marden, Chichester, West Sussex. Tel: (01730 825) 206

Mr and Mrs D. Gault ★ Turn N on B2141 Chichester/South Harting road opposite North Marden ★ Parking ★ Teas on charity open days ★ Toilet facilities ★ Partly suitable for wheelchairs ★ Open by appointment May to Aug, 2 – 5pm and 17th, 18th June, 15th, 16th July, 2 – 6pm ★ Entrance: £1.50, children 75p

Built on the site of a semaphore station used to convey news from Portsmouth to the Admiralty, Telegraph House is approached up a magnificent one-mile drive of copper beeches, and sits in parkland (40-minute walk around a yew wood) with views to the Isle of Wight. Enclosed by immaculate yew and beech hedges, this intimate garden shows what can be done on thin chalky soil. There are many good plant combinations and fine use of foliage texture and colour: Bupleurum contrasts with golden marjoram and the crisp outlines of milk thistles. *Crocosmia* 'Lucifer' stands out against columnar golden yews, phlomis and artemisias. *Clematis* 'Lasurstern' rambles over the flowers of the common sage. *Hydrangea aspera*, abutilons, hybrid musk roses and cytisus all flourish.

TROTTON OLD RECTORY 29
Trotton, West Sussex.

Captain and Mrs John Pilley ★ 3m W of Midhurst on A272 ★ Best season: June ★ Parking in field ★ Open for NGS, 21st May, 25th June, 2 – 6pm ★ Entrance: £1.50, children 50p

The garden is not enormous but it contains many different areas, lavishly planted and with exciting plant combinations. There are two rose collections designed by Hazel le Rougetel. In the square rose garden directly outside the house pale pink English roses, underplanted with clumps of white pinks and punctuated with standard creamy white *R.* 'Hakuun' fill the air with their scent, captured in an enclosed space. A small circular rosarium with old roses in deep mauves and pinks as well as warmer yellows, combined with appropriate herbaceous plants. Mixed borders have flowers grouped in subtle yellows – the combination of cream phlomis and dark-stemmed *Ligularia przewalskii* is particularly good – and cooler colours. There are shady areas, with newly-planted shrubs including *Hydrangea* 'Tricolor', hostas and a new yew hedge which will enclose a Victorian obelisk, memorial to a much-loved horse and the graves of family pets. A large pond forms part of the boundary, planted with clumps of richly-coloured *Iris ensata* hybrids on the garden side and less exotic reeds and plants on the far side.

WAKEHURST PLACE GARDEN ★★ 30
Ardingly, Nr Haywards Heath, West Sussex.
Tel: (01444) 892701; enquiry line (0181) 332 5066

The National Trust/ The Royal Botanic Gardens, Kew ★ From London take A(M)23, A272, B2028 or A22, B2110 ★ Parking ★ Refreshments: self-service restaurant ★ Toilet facilities ★ Partly suitable for wheelchairs ★ Bookshop ★ Part of house open ★ Garden open all year daily, except 25th Dec and 1st Jan. Nov to Jan, 10am – 4pm; Feb and Oct, 10am – 5pm; March, 10am – 6pm; April to Sept, 10am – 7pm (last admission ½ hour before closing). Guided walks available 11.30am and 2.30pm most weekends ★ Entrance: £4, students and UB40 £2, children (5-16) £1.50, under 5 free, family ticket (2 adults and up to 4 children) £10. Season tickets available

Dating from Norman times, the estate was bought by Gerald W.E. Loder (Lord Wakehurst) in 1903. He spent 33 years developing the gardens, a work carried on by Sir Henry Price. The gardens have been managed by the Royal Botanic Gardens, Kew, since 1965. They have a fine collection of hardy plants arranged geographically and display four comprehensive NCCPG National collections – betula, hypericum, nothofagus and skimmia. Unique is the glade planted with species growing at 10,000 feet in the Himalayas. Wakehurst is a place for the botanist, plantsman and garden lover, offering features of year-round interest.

WEST DEAN GARDENS ★ 31
West Dean, Nr Chichester, West Sussex. Tel: (0124363) 303

Edward James Foundation ★ 5m N of Chichester on A286 ★ Best season: spring/ early summer ★ Parking ★ Toilet facilities ★ Suitable for wheelchairs ★ Open March to Oct, daily, 11am – 5pm (last admission 4.30pm) ★ Entrance: £3, OAP £2.50, children £1.50. Pre-booked parties of 20 or more £2.25 per person

This estate was acquired in 1891 by William James who planted fine trees in the 30 acres of informal nineteenth-century gardens which surround an impressive flint house by Wyatt. The range of plants was slightly limited by alkaline soil and severe frost pockets. There is a sunken garden, with a deep pond; 300-foot pergola built in 1911 by Harold Peto, which is swathed in roses and other climbers and leads to a charming gazebo. In addition to the romantic water garden and wild garden, there is a large working walled kitchen garden which contains an extensive range of recently-restored Victorian glasshouses and an amusing collection of antique lawnmowers and garden tools. There is also a two and a quarter-mile Circuit Walk which climbs through parkland to the 45-acre St Roche's Arboretum with its collection of trees and shrubs. The garden borders the Weald and Downland Museum of traditional rural life from 1400 to 1900. The house is now an Arts and Crafts college. The arboretum forms part of the gardens. If you are returning through Chichester, you may like to look in on the Bishop's Palace garden, near the Cathedral, Palace gatehouse and city walls.

YEW TREE COTTAGE ★   32
Turner's Hill Road, Crawley Down, West Sussex.
Tel: (01342) 714633

Mrs Hudson ★ 1m S of A264 on Down Lane opposite Grange Farm entrance on B2028, take right turn and the cottage is the second of semi-detached on left ★ Best season: spring/summer ★ Parking ★ Plants for sale ★ House open for small groups 50p extra ★ Garden open 24th, 25th June, 2 – 6pm and by appointment for small groups ★ Entrance: £1, children free

A plantsman's delight and an encouragement to all with small gardens, it is not surprising that this third of an acre plot has been a prizewinner. Developments continue and the vegetable garden is now a small Jekyll-style masterpiece. The front garden is divided between a scree with alpines and herbs and a shrubbery with a golden area including *Hypericum aurea*, physocarpus, forsythia and *Philadelphus aurea*. To the rear of the house a mature quince, underplanted with campanulas and rue, stands over a well, while the borders are bursting with colour and unusual plants. 'Ballerina' and 'Felicia' geraniums, *Mertensia asiatica*, pink phlomis, *Batisia australis*, toad lilies, and *Cheiranthus mutabilis* (*semperflorens*), sweet rocket and *Rhododendron impeditum* are but a few of the interesting plants in this exceptional garden.

TYNE & WEAR

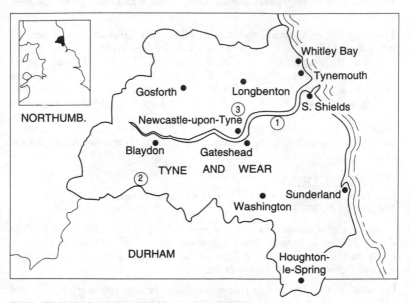

BEDE'S WORLD HERB GARDEN 1
Church Bank, Jarrow, Tyne and Wear. Tel: (0191) 4892106

Bede's World ★ 6m E of Gateshead off A185 ★ Best season: June/July ★ Parking ★ Refreshments: café ★ Toilet facilities ★ Suitable for wheelchairs ★ Dogs on lead ★ Plants occasionally for sale ★ House open all year ★ Garden open April to Oct, daily except Mon (but open Bank Holiday Mons), 10am – 5.30pm; Nov to Mar, 11am – 4.30pm, Suns, 2.30 – 5.30pm ★ Entrance: free (house and garden £2.50, concessions £1.25)

A small herb garden with a wide range in four sections: culinary, Anglo-Saxon medicinal, aromatic and medicinal. Also, narrow beds in second part of the garden based on the plans of the medicinal herb garden of St Gall (*c.* AD 816), and bricked area at top of garden with seating, planted around with rosemary, lavender and with two banks of herbs below it leading down to the St Gall area. Very interesting to the herbalist. A new 'Anglo-Saxon' farm has been developed on adjacent land, an 11-acre site with fields, crops and animals and Anglo-Saxon timber buildings. Some herbs and early vegetable strains will be grown there together with pond and stream plants and trees of species correct for the time of the Venerable Bede (AD 673-735).

GIBSIDE 2
Burnopfield, Newcastle-upon-Tyne, Tyne and Wear.
Tel: (01207) 542255

The National Trust ★ 6m SW of Gateshead, 20m NW of Durham from B6314, off A694 at Rowlands Gill ★ Light teas and picnic area in car park ★ Dogs on lead ★ Shop ★ Chapel open and service first Sun each month, 3pm. Concerts, guided walks and events throughout the year ★ Open April to Oct, daily except Mon (but open Bank Holiday Mons), 11am – 5pm ★ Entrance: £2.80, children £1.40

The chapel is an outstanding example of English Palladian architecture by James Paine. There is no 'real' garden but the fine avenue of Turkey oaks leading to the derelict Gibside Hall is memorable. The chapel is surrounded by woods managed by the Forestry Commission and has three Wellingtonia firs. There is a Victorian walled kitchen garden which is an open space waiting to be filled. Walks have been opened up with views to the ruined hall, orangery and other estate buildings in the park. In all, the Trust, assisted by English Heritage, has acquired 354 acres to secure the future of this great eighteenth-century landscape garden and protect the setting for the chapel.

JESMOND DENE 3
Jesmond, Newcastle-upon-Tyne, Tyne and Wear.
Tel: (0191) 2810973

Newcastle City Leisure Services Department ★ 1m E of city centre along Jesmond Road ★ Parking in Freeman Road ★ Refreshments: in café ★ Toilet facilities ★ Partly suitable for wheelchairs ★ Dogs on lead ★ Visitor Centre open at weekends ★ Garden open all year ★ Entrance: free

Presented to the city by Lord Armstrong, the famous engineer, in 1883 and only a mile from the city centre, this steep-sided thickly-wooded dene provides extensive walks in an entirely natural setting, complete with a waterfall, a ruined mill and some fine old buildings. There is a well-run pets' corner and from Freeman Road the upper park has a children's play area and pond. Quite exceptional condition for a city park.

1996 GUIDE

The 1996 *Guide* will be published before Christmas 1995. Reports on gardens for consideration are welcome at all times of the year but particularly by early summer (June) 1995 so that they can be inspected that year.

A report form is included in the *Guide* although experience shows that most people prefer to write a letter. Please address letters to the publishers, Vermilion, 20 Vauxhall Bridge Road, London SW1V 2SA. All letters are acknowledged by the editors.

All descriptions and other information are as accurate as possible at the time of going to press, but circumstances change and it is wise to telephone before making a long journey.

The *Guide* makes no charge for entries which are written by our own inspectors. The factual details are supplied by owners. It is totally independent and its only revenue is from sales of copies in bookshops.

WARWICKSHIRE

ALSCOT PARK

Alscot, Warwickshire.

1

*Mrs James West ★ 2¹/₂m S of Stratford-upon-Avon on A34 ★ Parking ★ Teas ★
Toilet facilities ★ Suitable for wheelchairs ★ Dogs ★ Plants for sale ★ Open 21st
May, 18th June, 8th July, 2 – 6pm ★ Entrance: £1, children free*

A typical eighteenth-century park with one of the earliest mock-Gothic houses
(not open), this has all the requisite main features – extensive lawns, fine trees,
orangery, deer park, river and lakes. There is a small garden round the house
but the main interest lies in the new garden developed by Mrs West near the
orangery, now the site of a pool area. Around it a large semi-formal garden
features old-fashioned roses, a mixed flower and vegetable garden and strong
lines of hedging, including several new imaginative curves. The herbaceous
borders here are the envy of dedicated gardeners all over the county.

ARBURY HALL ★ 2
Arbury, Nr Nuneaton, Warwickshire. Tel: (01203) 382804

Viscount and Viscountess Daventry ★ 10m from Coventry, 7m from Meriden at Astley off the B4102 Fillongley/ Nuneaton road ★ Best season: spring/ summer ★ Parking in adjoining field ★ Teas ★ Toilet facilities ★ Suitable for wheelchairs ★ Dogs on lead ★ Shop ★ House open as garden, Sun and Bank Holiday Mons ★ Garden open 16th April to 24th Sept, Sun and Mon, 2 – 6pm (last admission 5pm) ★ Entrance: park and gardens £2, children £1 (hall, park and gardens £3.50, children £2)

A delightful garden with a sense of peace. Bulbs at the start of the season followed by rhododendrons and azaleas, then roses in June and autumn colour from trees and shrubs. Formal rose garden and climbing roses. Lakes with wildfowl, parkland, the drive and bluebell woods. A canal system was installed years ago as a method of transport. Pollarded limes and the old walled garden are some of the features of this pleasant garden, along with the beautiful old trees. There is a museum in the old stables containing a collection of veteran cycles. Gift and craft shop in the Old Dairy.

CHARLECOTE PARK 3
Charlecote, Wellesbourne, Warwickshire. Tel: (01789) 470277

The National Trust ★ 1m W of Wellesbourne, 5m E of Stratford–upon–Avon ★ Parking ★ Refreshments: coffee, lunches, and teas in licensed restaurant (1865 Orangery). Picnics in deer park ★ Toilet facilities, inc. disabled behind Orangery ★ Mostly suitable for wheelchairs ★ Commercial plant nursery next to car park ★ Shop ★ House open as garden but closed 1 – 2pm (last admission 5pm) ★ Garden open April to Oct, Fri – Tues, 11am – 6pm. Closed 14th April. Parties by prior arrangement only ★ Entrance: house and garden £4, children £2, family ticket (2 adults and up to 4 children) £11. Party rates for parties of 15 or more and introductory talk available weekdays only by prior arrangement

More of picturesque and historic than garden interest. Home of Lucy family since the thirteenth century. Shakespeare reputedly poached the deer, which still populate the park alongside Jacob sheep. Park laid out by 'Capability' Brown who was directed not to destroy the avenues of elms, but they were later eliminated by Dutch elm disease. Orangery and wild garden. Of special interest is the Shakespeare border with plants which feature in the plays, ranging from herbs to quince and medlar, and old roses and carnations.

COOMBE ABBEY COUNTRY PARK 4
Nr Coventry, Warwickshire. Tel: (01203) 453720 Ranger Service

Just outside Coventry on A427 ★ Best season: June/ July ★ Parking ★ Refreshments: bar with snacks. Picnics allowed ★ Toilet facilities ★ Suitable for wheelchairs ★ Dogs on lead ★ Open daily, 9am – dusk ★ Entrance: free but pay and display parking charge all year. Seasonal price fluctuations

The great attraction is the wide range of activities to be enjoyed in the 150 acres. There is a courtyard with a pool, boating for children along with an adventure play area, a countryside centre, guided walks, a heron lake, pleasure cruises, a Victorian garden and a selection of beautiful old trees and shrubs. On the west front of the house is the terrace and parterre, and the grounds contain canals and woodland walks among oaks, chestnuts, conifers and copper beeches. A heather border, rhododendrons and herbaceous plants give further interest.

COUGHTON COURT 5
Alcester, Warwickshire. Tel: (01789) 762435

The National Trust/ Mrs C. Throckmorton ★ 2m N of Alcester on the A435 ★ Parking, inc. coaches ★ Refreshments: lunches and teas in restaurant ★ Toilet facilities ★ Suitable for wheelchairs ★ Dogs on lead in car park ★ Plants for sale ★ Shop ★ House open ★ Garden open 15th to 19th April, rest of April, Sats and Suns only; May to Sept, daily except Thurs and Fri; Oct, Sats and Suns only, all 11am – 5.30pm. Parties of 15 or more by arrangement ★ Entrance: £2.50, children £1.25 (house and garden £4.50, family ticket £12)

The garden of this mid-sixteenth-century house is developing and now has an orchard containing many varieties of apples, plums, cherries, quinces and damsons including old varieties. It also includes a rose circle. The main garden including the courtyard was designed by Christina Birch. The large lawn is bordered by cloistered lime walks. One can enjoy a peaceful stroll beside the River Arrow, where ferns, shrubs and willows have been planted, and see the lake with its various types of decorative waterfowl. A second lake was drained many years ago and is being made into a bog garden; the National Rivers Authority has restored the water meadow. A large walled garden is being developed to new designs also by Christina Birch and may be open later in 1995. There is a Gunpowder Plot exhibition in one of the stable buildings.

ELM CLOSE 6
Binton Road, Welford on Avon, Warwickshire. Tel: (01789) 750793

Mr and Mrs E.W. Dyer ★ 5m W of Stratford-upon-Avon on A439. Turn left after 4½ m to Welford ★ Parking pub car park nearby ★ Toilet facilities ★ Suitable for wheelchairs ★ Plants for sale ★ Open by appointment ★ Entrance: £1.50, children free

It is fascinating to see the wide range of plants in a relatively small garden. Clematis are trained over pergolas and climb through trees and shrubs, and there are dwarf conifers, a rock garden, hellebores, a pool, a fruit and vegetable garden, alpine troughs, raised beds and an excellent variety of bulbs; herbaceous plants and shrubs provide interest and colour throughout the year. All visitors are likely to be stimulated by new ideas.

FARNBOROUGH HALL 7
Farnborough, Warwickshire. Tel: (01295) 690202

The National Trust/ Mr and Mrs Holbech ★ 5m N of Banbury, ½m W off A423 or E off B4100 ★ Suitable for wheelchairs (grounds only – terrace walk is very steep) ★ Dogs on lead (grounds only) ★ House open ★ Grounds open April to Sept, Wed and Sat and 7th, 8th May; Terrace Walk only open Thurs and Fri, 2 – 6pm (last admission 5.30pm) ★ Entrance: garden and terrace walk £1.50, children 75p; terrace walk only (Thurs and Fri) £1, children 50p (house and grounds £2.70, children £1.35)

Grounds improved in the eighteenth century with aid of Sanderson Miller, the architect, landscape gardener and dilettante who lived at nearby Radway. The fine S-shaped terrace walk climbs gently along the ridge looking towards Edgehill. The owner, William Holbech, built the walk in order to greet his brother on the adjoining property. The *Oxford Companion* describes it as a majestic concept marking the movement towards the great landscaped parks at the end of the eighteenth century. Two temples along the walk and an obelisk at the end. The trees are beeches, sycamores and limes. Beyond the cedar tree is part of the site of the former orangery, now a rose garden and a yew walk with steps at the end leading into a field where there is a seat from which you see a fine view over the river and towards Edgehill and where the cascade fountain suppresses the otherwise invasive hum of the M40. This is a uniquely interesting site.

GREENLANDS   8
Wellesbourne, Warwickshire.

Mr Eric T. Bartlett ★ Leave Stratford-upon-Avon E on B4086. Garden is on the crossroads at Loxley/Charlecote by airfield ★ Parking in road ★ Teas ★ Toilet facilities ★ Suitable for wheelchairs ★ Dogs on lead ★ Plants for sale ★ Open 9th April, 14th May, 18th June, 23rd July, 11am – 5pm ★ Entrance: £1, children free

Although this one-acre garden has some uncultivated areas it has a sense of peace. There are several pools with a range of water plants and fish. Pergolas are planted with roses, clematis and fuchsias. A wide variety of perennials, grasses and variegated foliage. There are herbaceous borders, shaded areas with ferns and hellebores, and clematis and honeysuckle rambling through old trees. New areas being developed. This is a garden with many ideas for keen gardeners.

HICKECROFT   9
Mill Lane, Rowington, Warwickshire.

Mr Pitts ★ 6m NW of Warwick and 15m SE of Birmingham on B4439 between Hockley Heath and Hatton. Turn into Finwood Road (signposted Lowsonford) at Rowington crossroads and first left into Mill Lane ★ Parking in field opposite house ★ Tea and biscuits ★ Toilet facilities ★ Suitable for wheelchairs ★ Open 24th, 25th June, 2 – 5.30pm ★ Entrance: £1.50, children 50p (includes admission to another garden nearby)

This well-designed garden uses hedges to divide the different sections and there are surprises round most of the corners. The National collection of

---

Illustrations – The Best of Their Kind

If it is difficult to describe a garden in words, it is doubly difficult to give the essence of a garden in one single photograph. We have therefore chosen one outstanding garden to illustrate each of the main categories which appear in the *Guide* – from the stately landscape at one end of the scale to the pocket-handkerchief at the other. Each edition of the *Guide* will illustrate a new garden from each of the ten categories, the chosen gardens being, in the opinion of the editors, amongst the best in the land.

ROSE The British persist in putting rose gardens near the top of their planting priority, despite the difficulties of their cultivation. This two-acre walled garden at Wolseley Park, Staffordshire, is part of a new major leisure centre. Other modern rose developments are to be found at two castles, Warwick and Sudeley.

COTTAGE There is no really satisfactory definition of a cottage garden and the term is now applied to areas where there is no cottage in sight. That could not be said of Camp Cottage, Gloucestershire, a seventeeth-century half-timbered building surrounded by all the profusion of herbaceous plants, annuals, climbers, etc. It is a surprise to know that the owners only began to create this old-fashioned illusion in 1988.

TOWN *The main difference between a town and country garden is often a matter of size, but it can also be a matter of style. Here in Fulham Park Gardens, London, there is an air of theatricality which reflects the tastes of the owner, an actor turned landscape-gardener. It is a tiny garden, and plants are grown in vertical tiers so no space is wasted.*

HERB Medical, culinary or aromatic herbs were the plants of the earliest gardens and the current interest in gardening history means that herbs are enjoying a revival today, whether they are grown for visual or culinary reasons. Herbs would undoubtedly have been grown here at Hardwick Hall in the late-sixteenth century when Bess was boss.

GRAND FORMAL Though 'Capability' Brown is said to have destroyed numerous formalities by failing to see their capabilities, the British retained a taste for rectangles, circles and symmetry. There was a considerable resurgence of interest in the nineteenth century and though the Brits could never completely match the tradition of Le Nôtre and his French followers, they have done their best over the years as seen here at Blenheim.

digitalis is matched by a good range of euphorbias, grasses, geraniums and astrantias, and also hebes and potentillas. Colour contrasts, topiary, pools, trees planted at strategic points with roses growing up through them. Different materials are used for paths. There is an orchard with daffodils and a fruit and vegetable garden to enjoy. This garden should be open more regularly so that vistors could see it throughout the seasons.

ILMINGTON MANOR   10
Ilmington, Nr Shipston-on-Stour, Warwickshire. Tel: (01608) 682230

Mr D. Flower and Lady Flower ★ 4m NW of Shipston-on-Stour, 8m S of Stratford-upon-Avon ★ Parking in road ★ Teas ★ Toilet facilities ★ Suitable for wheelchairs ★ Plants for sale ★ Open by appointment and for NGS 9th April, 21st May, 25th June, 9th July, 2 – 6pm. Parties welcome ★ Entrance: £2, children free

Created from an orchard in 1919, this is now a mature garden with strong formal design which is full of surprises. There is also much to interest the plantsperson. To the right of the drive is a paved pond, with thyme of many varieties ornamenting the stones. Scented and aromatic climbers surround this area. Next, a walk up the pillar border presents an unusual combination of shrubs and herbaceous plants in colour groups. Then, up stone steps, is the formal rose garden and the long double border planted with old and modern shrub roses and herbaceous plants. The so-called Dutch garden is really an informal cottage garden with a profuse mixture of colour. There is much more – a trough garden, iris and foliage beds, a rock garden and, in the spring, plenty of daffodils and crocus. New plants and trees are still being added.

IVY LODGE   11
Radway, Warwickshire. Tel: (01295) 670371/670580

Mrs M.A. Willis ★ 7m NW of Banbury via A41 and B4086. 14m SE of Stratford-upon-Avon via A422 ★ Parking in village ★ Teas on open day ★ Suitable for wheelchairs ★ Open 23rd April, 25th June, 2 – 6pm for charity, and also by appointment ★ Entrance: £1, children free (1993 prices)

Radway nestles below Edgehill, and the garden of Ivy Lodge runs back across the former battlefield. Above on the skyline can be seen the mock castle, now a pub. In spring there is a profusion of bulbs and blossom; in summer a fine collection of roses. The village contains many cottages with interesting gardens and every other year (but not 1995) about a dozen are open to the public. Their attractions range from a good collection of garden gnomes to grander efforts such as pleached limes. In 1988-9 the village achieved the 'Best Kept Village' award but despite this it retains a marked villagey character.

JEPHSON GARDENS   12
**Royal Leamington Spa, Warwickshire.
Tel: (01926) 450000 (Amenities Officer – Warwick District Council)**

Warwick District Council ★ In centre of Leamington, main entrance off The Parade ★ Parking ★ Refreshments ★ Toilet facilities ★ Suitable for wheelchairs ★ Dogs on lead/ poop scoop ★ Open 8am (9am Sun and Bank Holidays) to ½ hour after dusk ★ Entrance: free

This spa town has always made a great effort in the floral decoration of its streets, and this activity can be enjoyed at its peak in the intensive bedding-out of the principal formal public garden. It is fine enough to be listed by English Heritage and, besides flowers, contains a remarkable collection of trees. Leamington has a string of parks and gardens running along the River Leam right across the town – an almost unique piece of town planning of a century ago. It is possible to walk their length – Mill Gardens, Jephson Gardens, Pump Room Gardens, York Promenade and Victoria Park. There are some fine listed examples of Victorian iron bridges, as well as earlier stone ones. On the outskirts of the nearby town, Kenilworth, is the ruined castle whose garden is worth a visit not so much for what it is, but in memory of what it has been.

LOXLEY HALL   13
Loxley, Nr Stratford-upon-Avon, Warwickshire. Tel: (01789) 840212

Col. A Gregory-Hood ★ 4m SE of Stratford-upon-Avon, N of A422 or W of A429 ★ Parking in field opposite ★ Teas ★ Toilet facilities ★ Suitable for wheelchairs ★ Open 28th May, 25th June, 2 – 7pm ★ Entrance: £1, children 20p

Divided by warm rose- and clematis-clad brick walls and well-clipped hedges into a series of smaller gardens which lead one from another past beds of iris, Loxley visitors pass through an arboretum to the secret garden bursting with old and new shrub roses. A magnificent ginkgo and an ancient mulberry seem quite at home beside pieces of modern sculpture, including a Philip King, as does the small Japanese garden. From the lawn there is a wide view over peaceful countryside. The adjacent church, built on a Saxon foundation, is open.

THE MILL GARDEN   14
Mill Street, Warwick, Warwickshire. Tel: (01789) 492877

A.B. Measures ★ Mill Street is off the A425 to the west just before reaching the Castle ★ Open 16th April to 15th Oct, Suns and Bank Holidays and at most other times. Parties by appointment ★ Collecting box for charities

This garden has a great sense of peace, nestling below the great towers of Warwick Castle (see entry) and beside the River Avon. The toll stocks in the garden recall the history of days gone by, and one can see the old bridge across which Shakespeare is said to have ridden to London. Good use of roses and clematis climbing through trees and large shrubs. Something of interest all year, including herbs, alpines and unusual plants. A garden of considerable variety and charm.

PACKWOOD HOUSE ★   15
Lapworth, Solihull, Warwickshire. Tel: (01564) 782024

The National Trust ★ 2m E of Hockley Heath on A3400, 11m SE of central Birmingham ★ Parking ★ Picnic site opposite main gates ★ Toilet facilities ★ Suitable for wheelchairs ★ Shop ★ House open ★ Garden open April to Sept, Wed – Sun and Bank Holiday Mons, 2 – 6pm (closed 14th April); Oct, Wed – Sun, 12.30 – 4.30pm (last admission ½ hour before closing). Parties of 15 or more by written arrangement ★ Entrance: £2 (house and garden £3.50, family £9.60)

Hidden away from a rather suburban part of Warwickshire this garden is notable for its intact layout with courtyards, terraces, brick gazebos and mount of the sixteenth and seventeenth centuries when the house was built. Even more remarkable is the almost surreal yew garden, unique in design. Tradition claims that it represents the Sermon on the Mount but in fact the 'Apostles' were planted in the 1850s as a four-square pattern round an orchard. Never mind, the result is now homogenous. There is a spiral 'mount' of yew and box, which is a delightful illusion. Note also the clever use made of brick. G. Baron Ash, who gave the property to the Trust, made a sunken garden in the 1930s and restored earlier design features. He also introduced colourful border planting, and now the gardens are worth seeing at all seasons of the year. In spring drifts of daffodils follow the snowdrops and bluebells carpet the copse while shrubs flower on red brick walls. The herbaceous border, the sunken garden, the terrace beds and climbing roses and honeysuckle are a riot of colour in summertime and autumn brings the changes in foliage. Baddesley Clinton is nearby and visited particularly by those who enjoy the restaurant. It is a medieval moated manor house with walled garden containing herbaceous borders and climbers. In the corners are collections of herbs and the greenhouses contain a vine and collection of pelargoniums. Pleasant walks round the lake.

RAGLEY HALL   16
Alcester, Warwickshire. Tel: (01789) 762090

Earl and Countess of Yarmouth ★ 1m from Alcester on A435 ★ Best season: spring ★ Parking ★ Refreshments: tearooms (small café open from 10am) ★ Toilet facilities inc. disabled ★ Partly suitable for wheelchairs ★ Shop ★ House open 11am – 5pm ★ Garden open 2nd April to 2nd Oct, 10am – 5.30pm ★ Entrance: £4, children £2.50, family (2 adults, 4 children) £12, (house, garden and park £5, OAP £4, children £3.50, family £16) (1994 prices)

Not a well-cultivated garden but the climbers on the pillar by the house, the rose garden and some lovely old trees are worthy of a visit. There is also a beautiful lake surrounded by lawns with picnic tables, an adventure area with very good facilities and woodland walks and country trails. The house is very popular with visitors.

RYTON ORGANIC GARDENS   17
(National Centre for Organic Gardening)
Ryton-on-Dunsmore, Coventry, Warwickshire. Tel: (01203) 303517

The Henry Doubleday Research Association ★ 5m SE of Coventry. Turn off A45 onto B4029 ★ Parking ★ Refreshments: restaurant serving organic food ★ Toilet facilities ★ Suitable for wheelchairs ★ Guide dogs only ★ Plants for sale ★ Shop ★ Open daily, except Christmas period, 9am – 5.30pm ★ Entrance: £2.50, concessions £1.75, children £1.25, under 4 free, parties £2 per person. Half-price admission from Nov to 13th April

Six acres including conservation area with pond, native woodland, wild flower meadow, wildlife garden, bee garden, soft fruit garden and trained fruit trees, rose garden, herbaceous and shrub borders, herbs, large vegetable plots including old varieties together with examples of compost-making, raised beds, mulching, green manure crops, use of deep beds and methods of attracting beneficial wildlife into the garden. Recently there has been more landscaping between the individual gardens. Also an alpine garden and a garden for blind and partially-sighted. A children's play area and picnic facilities make it somewhere for the family to visit and learn something for their own garden.

SHAKESPEARE GARDENS 18
Stratford-upon-Avon, Warwickshire. Tel: (01789) 204016

Shakespeare Birthplace Trust ★ Located in Stratford-upon-Avon and surrounding area ★ Parking in town car parks or open-top bus tour stops at each of the properties ★ Many tea shops in town ★ Toilet facilities in town ★ Shops in properties ★ Open March to Oct, weekdays, 9 or 9.30am – 5pm or 5.30pm, Sun, 10 or 10.30am – 5pm or 5.30pm; Nov to Feb, weekdays, 9.30 or 10am – 4pm, Sun, 10.30am or 1.30pm – 4pm. Closed all day 24th to 26th Dec and mornings of 1st Jan and 1st April ★ Entrance: to five Trust properties by individual charge or £7.50, children £3.50 inclusive

Some claim that little is known about Shakespeare and less still about his gardens. The Trustees have done their best to make them interesting adjuncts to the properties, mostly with tourists in mind. They include *The Birthplace Garden*, a small informal collection of over 100 trees, herbs, plants and flowers mentioned by the Bard. *Mary Arden's House*, the front a *mélange* of box, roses and flowers, the rear a stretch of lawn with, beyond, a wild garden. Country Museum with tools, etc. Light refreshments and picnic area. *Anne Hathaway's Cottage*; a re-creation of a typical English cottage garden at the end of the nineteenth century and the Tree Garden with examples of those mentioned in the Works. Garden Centre with plants and herbs for sale grown by the Trust's gardeners, and a small display of Victorian and Edwardian garden tools. *New Place/Nash's House*; the house Shakespeare bought for his retirement, but alas, demolished in the eighteenth century, and the foundations planted with a garden around which, it is suggested, his orchard and kitchen garden lay. Reconstructed Elizabethan knot garden with oak palisade and 'tunnell' or 'pleached bower' of that time. *Hall's Croft*; walled garden with little resemblance to its probable form in the period when it was owned by the Bard's son-in-law. *All the above are Trust properties and fee-charged*. Beyond the knot garden is a large free garden with separate access. Also free are *Bancroft Gardens* in front of the Theatre and the long stretch owned by the Royal Shakespeare Theatre, along the River Avon between the Swan Theatre and the church where Shakespeare is buried. Charlecote (see entry) is nearby.

SHERBOURNE PARK ★ 19
Sherbourne, Nr Warwick, Warwickshire. Tel: (01926) 624255/624506

Lady Smith-Ryland ★ ½m N of Barford, 3m S of Warwick on A429, close to junction 15 of the M40 ★ Parking ★ Lunches and teas for parties by prior arrangement ★ Open by appointment ★ Entrance: £2.50, OAP £2, children 12 and under free

A fine park surrounds the early Georgian house (1730), and adjacent Gilbert Scott church (1863), in which Lady Smith-Ryland has developed a series of imaginative smaller gardens characterised by inspired planting. In particular, the 'square' garden at an angle shows great originality. All the conventional features of the English garden – shrubs, herbaceous borders, roses, lilies and so on – are combined in most pleasing and sometimes surprising congruity. There is a temple and a small lake beyond the church. More of the grounds are being developed, and this will ultimately be one of the most distinguished in an area full of gardens of distinction.

TYSOE MANOR   20
Tysoe, Warwickshire. Tel: (0129680) 709

Mr and Mrs W.A.C. Wield ★ 5m NE of Shipston-on-Stour. Take the B4035 to Banbury. In Brailes turn left to Tysoe. The Manor is the first house on the left in Upper Tysoe ★ Parking ★ Teas in the village ★ Suitable for wheelchairs ★ Plants for sale when available ★ Open 10th Sept, 2 – 6pm and by special arrangement ★ Entrance: £1.50

There are many old trees including 125-year-old and 250-year-old walnut trees, and a cedar of Lebanon. The old orchard has apple trees hanging with mistletoe; honeysuckles climb through other trees. Masses of old shrub roses clothe the walls and the tops of some walls are covered with small plants. Wisteria and magnolia climb up the Manor and there is a *Cytisus battandieri* on the barn wall. The borders contain a wide range of hebes, abelias, alstroemerias, cryptomerias, mahonias and potentillas. New areas have been planted with rhododendrons, azaleas, berberis and other shrubs. There are iris, peonies, carnations and other plants providing all-year-round colour and interest.

UNIVERSITY OF WARWICK   21
Coventry, Warwickshire. Tel: (01203) 523713

Warwick University ★ Nearer to Coventry than Warwick, the most direct access is off the A46 signposted University of Warwick/Stoneleigh just S of Coventry ★ Parking difficult in term although there are short-term pay-and-display spaces ★ Refreshments: restaurant ★ Toilet facilities ★ Most parts of campus suitable for wheelchairs ★ Open all year. Term dates: 9th Jan to 18th March, 24th April to 1st July, 2nd Oct to 9th Dec ★ Entrance: free

The Oxbridge college gardens are much-publicised so it is interesting to see what a new university makes of its campus in botanical terms. The buildings here have been the subject of early controversy, but the landscaping of the surrounding area has done something to mellow their impact. The continuing work includes the creation of new landscaped sportsfields south of Gibbet Hill Road and the use of trees in landscaping larger areas, and in a smaller space, a wisteria-covered pergola in the Social Sciences quadrangle is interesting. Formal gardens are being created for some new residences. The university now has three lakes with a wetlands environment and nature reserve. Footpaths can be followed using the attractive leaflet 'Campus walks'.

UPTON HOUSE ★   22
Nr Banbury, Oxfordshire. Tel: (01295) 670266

The National Trust ★ 7m NW of Banbury on A422 ★ Parking. Coaches by arrangement with administrator ★ Light refreshments in tearoom ★ Toilet facilities, inc. disabled ★ Partly suitable for wheelchairs. Motorised buggy with driver available ★ Plants for sale by admission kiosk when available ★ House open ★ Garden open April to Oct, daily except Thurs and Fri, 2 – 6pm (last admission

*5.30pm). Parties of 15 or more and evening guided tours by arrangement ★
Entrance: £2.30 (house £4.60, family ticket £12.60). No reductions for parties*

The house itself, which dates from 1695, contains a fine collection of paint-ings including three super Stubbs. More interesting to the garden visitor is that it stands on limestone, 700 feet above sea level, on Edgehill, near the site of the famous battle. Below a great lawn, the garden descends in a series of long terraces, along one side of which is an impressive flight of stone steps, leading down to the large lake below. In the centre of the terraced area is a huge sloping vegetable garden, all well-labelled to indicate varieties. The grand scale of the plan is the main interest, but there are many unusual plants, particularly perennials and bog plants. This is a very fine example of terraced gardening and beautifully maintained by the Trust.

WARWICK CASTLE ★ 23
Warwick, Warwickshire. Tel: (01926) 495421

The Tussauds Group ★ In the centre of Warwick, which is off the A46 bypass and accessed from M40 junction 15 ★ Parking ★ Refreshments of all kinds in castle and town. Picnics in grounds ★ Toilet facilities ★ Shop ★ Castle open ★ Grounds open all year round except 25th Dec, March to Sept, 10am – 6pm, Oct to Feb, 10am – 5pm. Pre-booked garden tours for groups conducted by a consultant horticulturalist ★ Entrance: £7.75, OAP £5.50, student £5.95, children (4-16) £4.50 (1994 prices)

Warwick Castle stands on the banks of the River Avon, surrounded by 60 acres of beautiful grounds of which 30 acres were landscaped by 'Capability' Brown. Brown had previously been in employment as gardener to Lord Cobham at Stowe but after Lord Cobham's death in 1749 he decided to take on commissions of his own. His work at Warwick Castle for the Earl of Warwick (Francis Greville) is thought to have been his first independent commission for which he received much praise, encouragement and publicity. He removed the old formal garden outside the wall and shaped the grounds to frame a view using an array of magnificent trees, notably cedar of Lebanon. In 1753 Brown began to landscape the Castle courtyard. He removed steps, filled in parts of the yard and made a coachway surrounding the large level lawn. Then Brown worked on the creation of the Castle park which is on the other side of the eleventh-century Mound. In 1784 the next Earl constructed the conservatory at the top of Pageant Field which today houses a replica of the famous Warwick Vase. From here visitors can view the panorama before them – the Peacock Garden and the tree-lined lawn of Pageant Field which meanders down to the gently sloping banks of the River Avon. On the other side of the Castle entrance is the Victorian rose garden recreated in 1986 from Robert Marnock's designs of 1868.

One interesting way to see the castle walls is to go first to The Mill Garden (see entry), in Mill Street, Warwick, south of the town. Later from the castle grounds, the visitor can view this area from the riverside by crossing the bridge near the boat house. A newly re-opened garden in the town, still being restored but well worth a visit, is at Lord Leycester Hospital, a charitable foundation going back to Queen Elizabeth I's time. A walled area behind the Master's House, it has a Roman vase amongst its attractions, and can be seen at present on Saturdays, but will probably open more often as the year advances. The Hospital is open daily except Sundays, so it is best to telephone about garden opening times.

WOODPECKERS 24
**The Bank, Marlcliff, Nr Bidford-on-Avon, Warwickshire.
Tel: (01789) 773416**

Dr and Mrs A.J. Cox ★ 7m SW of Stratford-upon-Avon off B4085 between Bidford and Cleeve Prior ★ Best season: spring/summer ★ Parking in road and nearby car park ★ No refreshments but picnics allowed ★ Suitable for wheelchairs, if accompanied ★ Plants for sale ★ Open all year by appointment ★ Entrance: £1.50, children free

This two and a half-acre garden contains many good ideas and blends in with the surrounding countryside. Island beds and the terrace area with troughs provide all year round interest and colour and there are several borders of individual colours. There is a pool and bog garden, an ornamental vegetable garden with standard gooseberries and cordon apples grown on arches, a knot garden and a round greenhouse containing tender plants. A belvedere of framed English oak affords a fine view of the garden.

COUNTY GARDEN TRUSTS

The County Gardens Trust are independent charitable trusts which rely for their funding upon contributions, grants, sponsorship and membership income. Trust funds are dedicated to promote their objectives, which are to work with and alongside Parish, District and County Councils, The National Trust and garden or conservation societies to provide education, information, protection and creative projects for the improvement and conservation of the country's extensive garden heritage for the benefit of everyone. Examples can be found in many counties, for example in Hampshire, where the Trust has supported several new gardens and has been instrumental in reviving two hotel gardens listed in this year's *Guide*.

CUTTINGS

Readers may wish to be reminded that the taking of cuttings without the owners' permission can lead to embarrassment and, if it continues on a large scale, may cause owners to close their gardens to the public. This has to be seen in the context of an increasing number of thefts from gardens. At Nymans, the famous Sussex garden, thefts have reached such a level that the gardener will not now plant out any shrub until it is semi-mature and of such a size that its theft would be very difficult. Other owners have reported the theft of artefacts as well as plants.

DOGS, TOILETS & OTHER FACILITIES

If these are not mentioned in the text, then facilities are not available. For example if dogs are not mentioned, owners will probably not permit entry, even on a lead.

WILTSHIRE

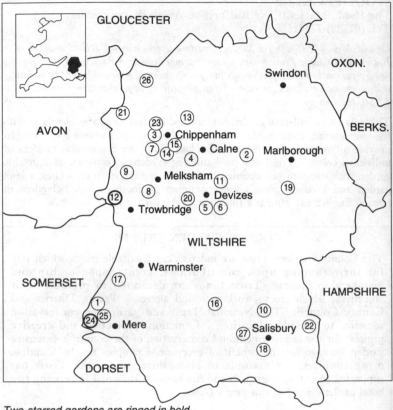

GLOUCESTER

Swindon

OXON.

㉖

㉑

AVON

㉓ ㉒
③
㉕ Chippenham
⑦ ⑭ Calne ②
④
⑨

Melksham
⑪
⑧
Trowbridge ⑳ ⑤ ⑥ Devizes
⑫

BERKS.

Marlborough

㉙

WILTSHIRE

Warminster

SOMERSET

⑰

HAMPSHIRE

①
㉕
㉔ Mere

⑯

⑩
Salisbury ㉒
㉗
⑱

DORSET

Two-starred gardens are ringed in bold.

ASHTREE COTTAGE ★   1
Kilmington Common, Warminster, Wiltshire. Tel: (01985) 844740

*Wendy and Len Lauderdale ★ 3m from Mere. Take B3092 N from Mere, turn
left beyond Stourton (signposted Kilmington) for 1m. The house is on the right,
200 yards beyond left turn to 'King Alfred's Tower' ★ Parking ★ Plants for sale ★
Open daily by appointment and several times for charity ★ Entrance: £2*

A densely-planted cottage garden built around a thatched cottage. A magnificent pergola covered with roses and clematis, and fringed with catmint,
dominates the front, and a series of lawns, each enclosed by shrubs and
herbaceous plants creates a riot of colour in summer. There are many
unusual plants, and some splendid and very varied phlox. The garden is kept
immaculately. Plants propagated from those within the garden are available
for sale in a small nursery adjacent and the stock seems very vigorous indeed.
Stourhead and Stourton (see entries) are nearby.

AVEBURY MANOR   2
Marlborough, Wiltshire. Tel (01672) 539251

The National Trust ★ 6m W of Marlborough, 1m N of A4 Bath road on A4361. The Manor is on the north side of the High Street, behind the church ★ Parking outer village ★ Refreshments adjacent ★ Toilet facilities in village ★ Suitable for wheelchairs ★ Shop adjacent ★ House open subject to restoration work (telephone (01672) 539388) ★ Archaeological Museum and Great Barn adjacent ★ Garden open April to Oct, daily, except Mon and Thurs (but open Bank Holiday Mons), 11am – 5.30pm (last admission 5pm) ★ Entrance: £2.20, children £1.40, pre-booked parties of 15 or more £2 per person, children £1.20

House and gardens purchased by The National Trust in 1991 after recent chequered history. Fine eighteenth-century walls in need of repair. Well-maintained rose garden in the shadow of the church tower. Splendid lavender walk on main entrance to the house, which on the south and west is framed by lawns and much topiary. Herbaceous borders neatly behind low box hedges. Originally the garden was enhanced with statuary, but this has recently been sold. There is much conservation work to be done, trees to be replaced and substantial replanting of the herbaceous beds. This will be undertaken by the Trust over the next few years, a project well worth watching. Visitors may care to know that clippings of the yew hedges are exported to Germany for processing into anti-cancer drugs.

BOLEHYDE MANOR   3
Allington, Chippenham, Wiltshire.

Earl and Countess Cairns ★ 1½m W of Chippenham on A420. Turn off to Allington then ½m on right ★ Parking ★ Toilet facilities ★ Suitable for wheelchairs ★ Plants for sale ★ Open 18th June, 2.30 – 6pm or by written appointment ★ Entrance: £1.50, children 50p

A sixteenth-century manor house with extensive gardens enclosed within high old stone walls and topiary to form a series of garden rooms. Interesting variety of climbers, roses and shrubs. A courtyard garden with many unusual half-hardy plants which are propagated from late summer cuttings and seeds. This, together with the greenhouse yard and the ornamental fruit and vegetable garden, has been developed over the past few years by the present owners and Melanie Chambers.

BOWOOD ★   4
Bowood House, Derry Hill, Calne, Wiltshire. Tel: (01249) 812102

The Earl and Countess of Shelburne ★ 4½m W of Calne, 5m SE of Chippenham, 8m S of M4. On A342 ★ Best seasons: spring and autumn ★ Parking ★ Licensed restaurant and garden tea-rooms ★ Toilet facilities ★ Suitable for wheelchairs ★ Garden centre specialising in unusual plants ★ Shop ★ House open. Also adventure playground for children 12 and under ★ Garden open April to 29th Oct, daily, 11am – 6pm or dusk if earlier ★ Entrance: £4.50, OAP £4, children £2.30 (1994 prices)

Bowood House and Pleasure Grounds cover over 100 acres and lie in the centre of 'Capability' Brown's enormous park. Other splendours include a tranquil lake, an arboretum and pinetum, Doric temple, cascade waterfall and hermit's cave. Thousands of flowering bulbs bloom in spring. The Robert Adam orangery (converted into a gallery) is particularly fine and in front of it are formal Bath-stone terraces with rose beds, standard roses and fastigiate yews. *Fremontodendron californicum* flourishes on the Italianate terrace. The rhododendron walks are situated in a separate 50-acre area, which is only open when the rhododendrons are flowering. Robert Adam's mausoleum ('a little gem' well worth a visit) is in this area.

BROADLEAS GARDEN 5
Broadleas, Devizes, Wiltshire. Tel: (01380) 722035

Lady Anne Cowdray/ Broadleas Garden Charitable Trust ★ 1m S of Devizes. Entrance through Devizes (signposted from Long Street) ★ Parking ★ Teas on Sun until end of Aug ★ Toilet facilities ★ Own-propagated plants for sale ★ Open April to Oct, Sun, Wed, Thurs, 2 – 6pm ★ Entrance: £2, children under 12 £1

This garden was bought just after World War II and started from nothing by Lady Anne Cowdray in a combe below Devizes. Mature and semi-mature magnolias grow on each side of a steep dell. As good as any Cornish garden, it is stuffed with fine things that one would think too tender for these parts. Large specimens of everything (much of it now 40 years old), *Paulownia fargesii, Parrotia persica*, all manner of magnolias, azaleas, hydrangeas, hostas, lilies and trilliums of rare and notable species, all very carefully labelled, but there has also been much new planting in recent years including many rhododendrons and camellias. It is a garden of tireless perfectionism, at its most stunning in spring when sheets of bulbs stretch out beneath the flowering trees. Rarely seen in such quantities for instance are the erythroniums or dogtooth violets. Many of the more unusual plants, both shrubs and perennials, are grown at Broadleas. There is also a woodland walk, a sunken rose garden and a silver border. This is serious plantsmanship and dendrology.

CHIFFCHAFFS
(see Dorset)

CLOCK HOUSE
(see Oxfordshire)

CONOCK MANOR 6
Devizes, Wiltshire.

Mr and Mrs Bonar Sykes ★ 5m SE of Devizes off A342 ★ Parking ★ Refreshments: tea and biscuits ★ Suitable for wheelchairs ★ Open 22nd May, 2 – 6pm ★ Entrance: £1.20, children under 18 free

Set between distant views of Marlborough Downs and Salisbury Plain, the Georgian house looks on to the lawns with specimen trees, ha-has and a recently-planted arboretum. From a Reptonesque thatched dairy near the house, a long brick wall and mixed shrub border lead to the stable block, in style early Gothic Revival, with a copper-domed cupola. Beyond, yew and beech hedges and brick walls frame the meticulously-kept kitchen garden and 1930s shrub walk. Box forms attractive bays and clipped balls. Pleached limes, a magnolia garden including malus, sorbus, prunus and many eucalyptus.

CORSHAM COURT 7
Corsham, Wiltshire. Tel: (01249) 712214

The Lord Methuen ★ 4m W of Chippenham on A4 ★ Best season: spring ★ Parking ★ Toilet facilities ★ Suitable for wheelchairs ★ Dogs on lead ★ House open ★ Garden open Jan to March, daily except Mon and Fri, 2 – 4.30pm; April to Sept, daily except Mon, 2 – 6pm; Oct to Nov, daily except Mon and Fri, 2 – 4.30pm. Open all Bank Holidays ★ Entrance: £3.50 with concessions. Garden season tickets available £10

Approaching from Chippenham, look out for a glimpse of this house on your left, once framed by an avenue of elms now replaced by some lime trees. Surrounded by a landscape of 'Capability' Brown's devising finished off by Humphry Repton (the lake and boat-house particularly), it is an example of this kind of gardening at its best. Rare and exotic trees look entirely at home: black walnuts, Californian redwoods, cedars, Wellingtonias, and the most astonishing layered Oriental plane tree, shading beeches, oaks, sycamores and Spanish chestnuts. There are 340 species of trees and 75,000 daffodils in the 20-acre arboretum. The bath-house designed by Brown is a treat and one can get through it into a world of entirely different mood. The Bradford porch leads out into a small enclosed flower garden with catalpa trees. Repton's roses trained over metal arches encircling a round pond are a rare surviving example of the elegance of early nineteenth-century flower gardens. Here the flower borders contain the unusual *Clerodendrum trichotomum* and enormous iron supports for roses and *Clematis* x *jackmanii*. There is a box-edged garden, hornbeam *allée*, urns, arbours and seats.

THE COURTS 8
Holt, Trowbridge, Wiltshire. Tel: (01225) 782340

The National Trust ★ 3m SW of Melksham, 3m N of Trowbridge, 2½m E of Bradford-on-Avon on B3107 ★ Best season: summer ★ Parking at the village hall ★ Suitable for wheelchairs ★ Open 2nd April to Oct, daily except Sat, 2 – 5pm. Out of season by appointment ★ Entrance: £2.80, children £1.40

Created by Sir George Hastings in 1900-1911, this has been an impressive garden and is still well worth visiting for both the plants and ideas. Extensive bog and water plants. The eighteenth-century house is set in formal areas of garden which give place to wild, bog and orchard gardens beyond. There are many lawns, much topiary, beguiling nooks and lots of good Edwardian features such as stone walls and paths, hedges, lily ponds and terraces. A garden in the Hidcote mould, it is being substantially restored under the care of the present head gardener. The large terrace has been rebuilt and has recently been replanted. Some superb specimen trees. A large part of the garden is given over to wild flowers, with close cut pathways winding through.

HAZELBURY MANOR 9
Nr Box, Corsham, Wiltshire. Tel: (01225) 810715

5m SW of Chippenham. From Box take A365 to Melksham, turn left onto B3109, take the next left, and then turn right immediately into private drive ★ Up for sale at the time of going to press and opening in 1995 doubtful

Very extensive formal gardens about a sprawling Elizabethan house, immaculately restored and rejuvenated. The massive rock garden at the front of the house is impressive although it couldn't be called in keeping with the house and makes as big a twentieth-century statement as the earlier Edwardian garden. This formal garden has a large lawn banked up on either side by high walks between clipped beeches. Every inch is extremely well looked after. In spring the alleys are all carpeted with brilliant polyanthus, cowslips and wall-flowers. Mammoth herbaceous borders blaze in summer. There is a beautiful laburnum arched walk, and other notable features are a lime walk and – nearer the house – a terraced alpine garden. Beyond the fortifications on the other side of the house is a new plantation of specimen trees, mostly conifers. There is a great deal to see and nothing is done by half measures. Very impressive.

HEALE GARDENS ★   10
Middle Woodford, Salisbury, Wiltshire. Tel: (01722) 73504

Mr Guy Rasch and Lady Anne Rasch ★ 4m N of Salisbury between A360 and A345 ★ Parking ★ Toilet facilities ★ Suitable for wheelchairs ★ Dogs on lead ★ Extensive range of plants for sale, many home-grown ★ Shop and Plant Centre open as gardens ★ House not open except to groups of 20 or more booked in advance ★ Gardens open all year, daily, 10am – 5pm ★ Entrance: £2.50

This is an idyllic garden with mature yew hedges. A tributary of the Avon meanders through it providing the perfect boundary and obvious site for the sealing-wax red Japanese bridge and the thatched tea-house which straddles the water. This was made with the help of four Japanese gardeners in 1910 and extends under the shade of *Magnolia* x *soulangiana* along the boggy banks planted with bog arums, *Rodgersia aesculifolia*, candelabra primulas and irises. There are two terraces immediately beside the house, one rampant with alchemilla, spurges and irises. The other has two stone lily ponds, designed by Harold Peto, and two small borders given height by nine-foot high wooden pyramids bearing roses, clematis and honeysuckles. The Long Border contains mostly hybrid musk roses backed by a simple but effective rustic trellis, and also many interesting herbaceous plants. The walled kitchen garden is possibly the most successful part of the garden – it achieves a very satisfying marriage between practicality and pleasure. It is not a regimented vegetable garden but the formal nature of rows of potatoes etc. are made into a feature and plots are divided by espaliered fruit trees forming an apple and pear tunnel, and by pergolas and hedges. The wonderful flint and brick wall provides protection for many plants including *Cytisus battandieri* and an ancient fig. This is a walled garden where one is encouraged to linger on the seats and in the shaded arbours and enjoy and admire the extraordinary tranquillity of the place. The plant centre is very comprehensive and the shop appeals to the discerning. Unique wrought-iron plant supports can be bought here. Look out for the ancient mulberry and the very old *Cercidiphyllum japonicum*, and *Magnolia grandiflora*.

HOME COVERT ★   11
Roundway, Devizes, Wiltshire. Tel: (01380) 723407

Mr and Mrs John Phillips ★ 1m N of Devizes. Signposted to Roundway off A361 on edge of built-up area NE of town. Turn left towards Rowde in village. House is ¼m beyond village, on left. Signposted ★ Parking ★ Teas on charity days

★ Partly suitable for wheelchairs ★ Open 26th April, 17th May, 21st June, 23rd July, 16th Aug, 2 – 6pm for charity and parties at all times by appointment ★ Entrance: £1.50, children free; £2 for appointment visits

Over the last 30 years this garden has been created by the present owners out of amenity woodlands of the now-demolished Roundway House. In front of the house there is a large lawn on a plateau edged with grasses, herbaceous plants and alpines producing much colour throughout the year. Beyond this, grass pathways meander through an informal collection of trees and rare shrubs. A steep path drops from the plateau to a water garden, lake, waterfall and bog garden, rich with colour from bog primulas and other moisture-loving plants. This area is shaded by fine specimen trees. Excellent collections of hostas and hydrangeas are scattered informally throughout and roses and clematis scramble over walks and through trees. Described as 'a botanical madhouse', this garden offers wonderful contrasts.

IFORD MANOR ★★   12
Bradford-on-Avon, Wiltshire. Tel: (01225) 863146

Mr and Mrs J.J.W. Hignett ★ 2m S of Bradford-on-Avon, 7m SE of Bath via A36. Signposted ★ Parking ★ Teas May to Aug, Suns and Bank Holiday Mons ★ Toilet facilities ★ Open April and Oct, Suns and 17th April, 2 – 5pm, May to Sept, Tues – Thurs, Sat, Sun and Bank Holiday Mons, 2 – 5pm. Other times and groups by appointment ★ Entrance: £2, OAP, students and children over 10 £1.50

It is always illuminating to see a famous architect and landscape gardener's own garden. Harold Peto found himself a near-ideal house in the steep valley through which the River Frome slides langorously towards Bath. The topography lent itself to the strong architectural framework favoured by Peto and the creation of areas of entirely differing moods. The overriding intention is Italianate with a preponderance of cypresses, juniper, box and yew, punctuated at every turn by sarcophagi, urns, terracotta, marble seats and statues, columns, fountains and loggias. In a different vein is a meadow of naturalised bulbs, most spectacularly martagon lilies. A path leads from here to the cloisters – an Italian-Romanesque building of Harold Peto's confection made with fragments collected from Italy. From here one can admire the whole, and the breathtaking valley and the walled kitchen garden on the other side.

KELLAWAYS   13
Chippenham, Wiltshire. Tel: (0124974) 203

Miss J.A. Hoskins ★ 3m NE of Chippenham on the East Tytherton road ★ Parking ★ Toilet facilities ★ Partly suitable for wheelchairs ★ Open by appointment ★ Entrance: £1.50, children 20p

June is a very rewarding time to visit because of the old roses which, cleverly underplanted, predominate throughout. Winter is another outstanding time, because of the profusion of winter-flowering shrubs. The Cotswold-stone seventeenth-century house has a stone terrace on the walled garden side bursting with thyme and wild strawberries. The clemency of the walls means that the owner can grow joyous things like sun roses, *Carpenteria californica* and other frailties. A serious cottage garden.

LACKHAM COUNTRY ATTRACTIONS 14
Lacock, Chippenham, Wiltshire. Tel: (01249) 443111

Lackham College ★ On A350 3m S of Chippenham, 4m N of Melksham. Signposted ★ Best season: June and July ★ Parking ★ Refreshments ★ Toilet facilities ★ Suitable for wheelchairs ★ Dogs (apart from guide dogs) in car park only ★ Plants for sale ★ Wiltshire Agricultural Museum on site ★ Open April to 29th Oct, daily, 11am – 5pm and by arrangement ★ Entrance: £3, concessions £2, children £1, season ticket £10, concession season ticket £6, family (2 adults, 4 children) £7, family season ticket £20. Parties of 10 or more (weekday rates) £1.85, concessions £1 per person. Evening parties by appointment

The garden is divided into distinct areas. Around the original house, now the focus of the College, is an Italian garden of balustrades and rose terraces, absolutely magnificent in late June. Many of the roses are very old hybrids, some French, some German, all clearly labelled. A long mixed herbaceous border links the house to the walled garden which contains collections of vegetables (including ornamental cabbages), fruit and flowers all neatly laid out and carefully labelled for instruction purposes. Fine greenhouses with a large citrus tree as well as a collection of unusual ornamental plants. The Agricultural Museum is excellent, and there is also a collection of rare-breed sheep and pigs, pleasant walks through the woodland and a well-placed bird hide perched above the Avon.

LACOCK ABBEY 15
Lacock, Chippenham, Wiltshire. Tel: (01249) 730227

The National Trust ★ 3m S of Chippenham off A350 ★ Best season: spring ★ Parking ★ Toilet facilities ★ Suitable for wheelchairs ★ NT shop in village ★ Abbey open as grounds except Tues, 1 – 5.30pm ★ Grounds and cloisters open April to Oct, daily except 14th April, 12 noon – 5.30pm (last admission 5pm) ★ Entrance: £2.10, children £1 (abbey, grounds and cloisters £4.20, children £2.20, parties £3.70 per person, children £1.90)

The thirteenth-century Abbey, set in meadows beside the River Avon, was turned into a private house by Sir William Sharington after the dissolution, and was later gothicised by Sanderson Miller in the eighteenth century. The informal gardens are best viewed in spring when floods of crocuses, daffodils, and later, fritillaries, replace the large drifts of snowdrops and aconites. Lady Elisabeth's Rose Garden, originally created for the mother of William Henry Fox Talbot, inventor of photography, has been recreated from the original photograph of 1840, which is probably the earliest known photograph of a garden. William Henry Fox Talbot was also an eminent botanist, and planted the gardens with many unusual trees which can still be seen today, including specimens of the American black walnut, the Judas tree and the swamp cypress.

LONG HALL 16
Stockton, Warminster, Wiltshire. Tel: (01985) 850424

Mr and Mrs N.H. Yeatman-Biggs ★ 7m SE of Warminster. S of A36 and W A303 Wylye interchange. Near Stockton church ★ Parking ★ Suitable for wheelchairs ★ Plants for sale in adjoining nursery open 2nd April to 1st Oct, Wed – Sun, 9.30am – 6pm (01985) 850914 ★ Garden open 6th May to 5th Aug, first Sat in the month; also 2nd April, 25th June, all 2 – 6pm. Parties by appointment ★ Entrance: £2, children free

A garden with plenty of atmosphere in a pretty village in the Wylye valley. A series of small hidden gardens, made intimate by clipped hedges and shrub planting, including a yellow garden, a blue garden and a fine red border. Old trees are to be found throughout including a magnificent medlar. A great spread of lawn sweeps away from the southern much older side of the house round which euphorbias and aquilegias grow in rich profusion. In spring there are drifts of aconites and daffodils, though there is plenty to see at all seasons of the year. The planting is rich and diverse and continually evolving as the garden is restored. Plenty of good stock in the plant sale here.

LONGLEAT 17
Warminster, Wiltshire. Tel: (01985) 844400

The Marquess of Bath ★ 3m W of Warminster, 4½m SE of Frome on A362 ★ Parking ★ Helicopter landing pad available by prior request ★ Refreshments: café, licensed restaurant, kiosks ★ Picnic area by lake ★ Toilet facilities ★ Suitable for wheelchairs ★ Dogs on lead ★ Shop ★ House open ★ Garden open daily except 25th Dec, Easter to Sept, 10am – 6pm, rest of the year, 10am – 4pm ★ Entrance: £2, OAP £1.50, children 50p, coaches free (garden only) (1994 prices)

This garden has been rearranged and tinkered with by most of the great names in English landscape history. There is nothing left to show today of the two earliest gardens here, the Elizabethan and that made by London and Wise in the 1680s which must have been one of the most elaborate ever made in England. Sadly it was barely half a century before 'Capability' Brown ironed out the formality and created a chain of lakes set amongst clumps of trees and hanging woods – best admired today from 'Heaven's Gate'. This was slightly altered by Repton in 1804 and added to in the 1870s when it became fashionable to collect exotic trees such as Wellingtonias and monkey puzzles and groves of rhododendrons and azaleas. In this century the fortunes of the garden came under the guiding hand of Russell Page. The park remains both beautiful and rewarding for all who delight in trees. The formal garden focused on the orangery to the south of the house was redeveloped in the nineteenth century. It was simplified and improved upon by Russell Page to great effect. The orangery itself is a dream of wisteria and lemon-scented verbenas. Near the house there is a small, trim rose garden, and a quarter of a mile to the south there is a pleasure walk in a developing arboretum, with many spring bulbs and wild flowers. To the immediate west of the house there is a small private garden, sometimes open to the public. Lord Bath says this was designed by Lawrence Fleming in 1965, around the two commas within the Yin and Yang symbols: bulbs and fruit trees in the first and a lily pond in the second. There is a large dovecote in one corner – inspired by the turrets on the roof at Longleat. Elsewhere, the safari park and other exhibitions are available to visitors.

MOMPESSON HOUSE 18
The Close, Salisbury, Wiltshire. Tel: (01722) 335659

The National Trust ★ In centre of Salisbury, N side of Chorister's Green in the Cathedral Close ★ Parking charged for in Close ★ Teas in Garden Room when house open ★ Toilet facilities ★ Suitable for wheelchairs in garden and ground floor of house ★ House open ★ Garden open April to Oct, daily except Thurs and Fri, 12 noon – 5.30pm (last admission 5pm) ★ Entrance: £3, children £1.50, parties £2.70 per person (house and garden)

If visiting Salisbury, the Cathedral and the Close are a must, and if you have been fortunate enough to find a parking space, take time also to visit this small walled garden, which is in the old English style. Its reposeful atmosphere is very refreshing. Summer is best, with the old-fashioned roses in bloom, but it is attractive throughout the open season.

OARE HOUSE ★   19
Oare, Nr Pewsey, Wiltshire. Tel: (01672) 62613

Mr H. Keswick ★ 2m N of Pewsey on A345 ★ Best season: spring/summer ★ Parking ★ ☆Teas on charity open days ★ Toilet facilities ★ Partly suitable for wheelchairs ★ Open 23rd April, 30th July, 2 – 6pm ★ Entrance: £1, children 20p

The 1740 house was extended by Clough Williams Ellis in the 1920s and the garden created from 1920 to 1960 first by Sir Geoffrey Fry and now by Mr Henry Keswick. The house is seen as the backdrop to a cathedral-like nave of limes, a worthy overture to many good things. The main garden is approached through a wisteria-covered pergola enlivened with a lily pond and tinkling fountain. Great yew hedges enclose a 'library' garden from which an elegant loggia (where splendid teas are served on open days) can be spied along a formal axis of pleached limes. Below is a long, corridor-like secret garden, known as 'the slip', where good brick walls have been used for interesting planting. The lawns to the west of the house are very much 'in the grand manner'. The eye rises over an immaculate lawn to the sweep of the Marlborough Downs seen at the end of a woodland ride. Substantial borders on either side of this lawn lead down to a swimming pool of equally grand proportions flanked by great herbaceous borders, one all gold achilleas and heleniums and the other filled with dahlias. The kitchen garden is equally grand. Fruit and vegetables are arranged around the edge in purposeful manner behind their lavender hedges, espalier fruit trees and shrub roses. The two axial paths are magnificent. One is dominated entirely by white roses, while in the other a mossy gravel path threads its way through a stunning tunnel of herbaceous plants with yellow and white violas spilling out beneath clumps of richly-coloured phlox and heleniums of many varieties. This is a garden worth every mile of a long detour.

THE OLD VICARAGE ★   20
Edington, Nr Westbury, Wiltshire.

J.N. d'Arcy ★ 4m from Westbury and West Lavington on the B3098. Signposted ★ Parking in church car park ★ Open once for charity in mid-June and by appointment ★ Entrance: £2, children free (includes The Monastery Garden and Bonshommes Cottage)

Every plant in this garden reflects the interests of the widely-travelled plantsman John d'Arcy. He made the garden on a shelf of greensand and about a third of the way up the steep escarpment on the northern side of Salisbury Plain. The views across Edington Priory and the Avon Vale towards the church tower of Steeple Ashton help to focus the vistas from the garden. Only about two acres but intensively cultivated, every area has trees, underplanted with shrubs, which are underscored in turn by herbaceous plants and bulbs. Together there is a succession of interest throughout the year. A sunken garden, pergola, gravel garden, hot walls, raised beds, peat beds and shaded areas all blend so that no feature dominates. Visitors will enjoy d'Arcy's successive manias for mahonias, phlomis, eryngiums and nepetas and an enduring enthusiasm for unusual trees and shrubs. He also holds the National collection of evening primroses. From his trip to the Caucasus comes the stunning *Echium rubrum*, from the Pamirs a collection of tulips and fritillaries and from China *Corydalis flexuosa*, a new introduction with electric-blue flowers.

POUND HILL HOUSE 21
West Kington, Wiltshire. Tel: (01249) 782781

Mr and Mrs Philip Stockitt ★ 2m NE of Marshfield ★ Parking at plant centre ★ Suitable for wheelchairs ★ Wide range of rare plants for sale ★ Open March to mid-Oct, Wed – Sun and Bank Holiday Mons, 2 – 6pm ★ Entrance: £1.50, OAP £1

An interesting update on the theme of the Cotswold garden, in two acres around a fifteenth-century stone house. Mrs Stockitt believes 'it's not contrived – gardening should be a refining process. And every year we have a new development.' The viewer takes in the effect from the yard through to an 'old-fashioned rose' garden (planted and labelled David Austin roses) leading to a Victorian vegetable garden with espaliered fruit trees, then through a clematis tunnel, culminating in a statue. Beyond there is an orchard, a Cotswold garden with topiary, yew-screened tennis court, herbaceous border and drystone walls showing off 'Ballerina' roses, topiary and two trelliswork obelisks. A water garden has recently been developed and in addition there are many shade-loving plants. This is surrounded by yew hedging to create another small garden. Another walk area has been created using *Betula utilis* var. *jacquemontii*, underplanted with *Pulmonaria officinalis* 'Sissinghurst White', spring bulbs and foxgloves. This leads on to a new rose walk with clipped sweet chestnuts and planted with old-fashioned roses. A terrace area has been developed with many interesting planters. Extensive retail area adjacent to the garden selling progenies from 2000 varieties of rarer plants from the nursery.

ROCHE COURT SCULPTURE GARDEN 22
East Winterslow, Nr Salisbury, Wiltshire.
Tel: (01980) 862244 and (0171) 235 5844

The Earl and Countess of Bessborough ★ 5m E of Salisbury off A30, S side, following the sign 'Roche Court, Winterslow' ★ Parking ★ Partly suitable for wheelchairs ★ Open May to Oct, Sat and Sun, 11am – 5pm; Nov to March by appointment only ★ Entrance: free

This is an exhibition of modern garden or 'public-place' sculpture by established sculptors such as Hepworth, Turnbull, Armitage and Flanagan, and younger artists from throughout the world. All works are for sale and information about them can be obtained from the New Art Centre, 168 Sloane

Street, London SW1X 9QF, (0171) 235 5844. The garden itself, with pleasant views of Wiltshire downland, is eminently suited to its rôle.

SHELDON MANOR   23
Chippenham, Wiltshire. Tel: (01249) 653120

Mrs Gibbs ★ 1½m W of Chippenham, S off A420, signposted ★ Best season: June ★ Parking ★ Refreshments: home-made buffet lunches and teas ★ Toilet facilities ★ Suitable for wheelchairs ★ House open from 2pm ★ Garden open 16th April to 1st Oct, Sun, Thurs and Bank Holidays, 12.30 – 6pm ★ Entrance: £1.75, OAP £1.50 (house and garden £3, OAP and students £2.75, children £1, under 11 free) (1994 prices)

The gardens of this ancient house are enclosed by barns and walls. The wonderful courts in front of the house have mostly been put to lawn but a whiff of formality remains in the form of yew hedges and lavender. It is best to visit in mid-June when the good collection of old-fashioned shrub roses, grown in grass, are blazing. The swimming pool is worth seeing as an example of the use of pleached trees and stone work to save it from looking as glaring as most do. Among the rare and interesting shrubs and plants look out for *Rosa gigantea* 'Cooperi', *Grevillea sulphurea*, *Carpenteria californica*, *Cytisus battandieri*, romneya, a white Judas tree and the Chilean fire bush.

STOURHEAD ★★   24
Stourton, Wiltshire. Tel: (01747) 840348

The National Trust ★ 3m NW of Mere at Stourton off the B3092 ★ Best season: May for rhododendrons – wonderful in winter when empty ★ Parking ★ Refreshments: in village hall restaurant or at Spread Eagle Inn at garden entrance ★ Toilet facilities ★ Suitable for wheelchairs. Wheelchairs and self-drive buggy available ★ Shop ★ House open April to Oct, daily except Thurs and Fri, 12 noon – 5.30pm or dusk if earlier (last admission 5pm) ★ Gardens open daily all year, 9am – 7pm (or dusk if earlier, except 19th to 22nd July when gardens close at 5pm) ★ Entrance: Mar to Oct: £4.20, children £2.20, family ticket £10, parties £3.60 per person; Nov to Feb: £3.20, children £1.50 (house and garden £7.50, children £3.50, family ticket £20, parties £7.20 per person)

Many people go to Stourhead to see the rhododendrons, which are astonishing. However they are not part of the original visionary design by Henry Hoare II in 1741-80, a paragon in its day and almost the greatest surviving garden of its kind. The sequence of arcadian images is revealed gradually if one follows a route anti-clockwise around the lake, having come from the house along the top and seen the lake from above. Each experience is doubly inspiring in that one enjoys the eye-catcher across the lake, almost unattainable and mirage-like, and later when one reaches one's goal – and always some other vision lures one on – the boat-house, the Temple of Flora, the bridge, Temple of Apollo, rock bridge, cascade (these two are tucked away and very surprising), the pantheon (now restored), thatched cottage and the grotto. The view from the Temple of Apollo (1765) was described by Horace Walpole as 'one of the most picturesque scenes in the world', by which he meant that it was as fine as a painting. To gain a better idea of how these buildings would have looked had the surrounding planting remained as it was originally, take a walk by Turner's Paddock Lake below the cascade. Between 1791 and 1838 Richard Colt Hoare planted many new species, particularly from America, tulip trees, swamp cypresses, Indian bean trees – the beginning of an arboretum. He also introduced *Rhododendron ponticum*. From 1894 the sixth Baronet replaced these with the latest kinds of hybrid rhododendron and azaleas, and a large number of copper beeches and conifers, such as the Japanese white pine, Sitka spruce and Californian nutmeg – all are record-sized specimens now. In early summer the scent of azaleas is delightful, but there have been complaints that the (non-historical) rhodos have now reached such proportions that they block off the (historical) view of the water from the walk. A new Reception building has been added which contains an informative exhibition.

STOURTON HOUSE FLOWER GARDEN ★   25
Stourton House, Stourton, Nr Warminster, Wiltshire.
Tel: (01747) 840417

Elizabeth Bullivant ★ 3m NW of Mere (on A303). Follow signposts to Stourhead, then immediately before Stourhead car park, look out for blue sign boards for Stourton House ★ Parking in Stourhead (NT) car park. Free ★ Refreshments: coffees, substantial home-made teas and sticky cakes ★ Toilet facilities, inc. disabled (in car park) ★ Suitable for wheelchairs ★ Unusual and rare plants for sale ★ Shop for dried flowers ★ Open April to Nov, Wed, Thurs, Sun and Bank Holiday Mons, 11am – 6pm or dusk if earlier. Also for groups of 12 or more on other days by arrangement ★ Entrance: £2, children 50p, groups £1.50 per person on open days, £2 per person on other days

This colourful five-acre garden contains treasures in friendly, small spaces: a wild garden, winter garden, secret garden, Apostles walk…seats abound. Rare plants and imaginative designs are everywhere; 250 different varieties of hydrangea, many species of magnolia, unusual daffodils and camellias; euphorbias, chocolate plants and a profusion of flowers for drying. A switch-back hedge of Leyland cypress encloses a herbaceous garden of island beds, lavishly planted, and a lily pond with many carnivorous plants and a great urn full of flowers. All-year-round interest.

THOMPSON'S HILL ★   26
Sherston, Nr Malmesbury, Wiltshire. Tel: (01666) 840766

Mr and Mrs J.C. Cooper ★ On B4040. At Sherston turn left opposite church down hill, then bear right up Thompson's Hill until you come to house No 1 ★ Best season: June ★ Parking in road ★ Plants for sale ★ Open by appointment and 18th June, 2 – 6.30pm ★ Entrance: £1.50, children 50p

Faultlessly-maintained half-acre garden created over the last 12 years on derelict ground. Terraced area behind house, planted in pots with many colours, enclosed by clipped yew hedges and three Gothic arches with climbing roses and clematis. Beyond, set in lawns, are island beds with mixed herbaceous planting. Old roses and grouped prunus add height and colour. New conservatory. An example of what can be achieved with taste and energy on an unpropitious site.

WILTON HOUSE ★ 27
Wilton, Salisbury, Wiltshire. Tel: (01722) 743115

The Earl of Pembroke ★ 2½m W of Salisbury on A30 ★ Parking ★ Refreshments: restaurant ★ Toilet facilities, inc. disabled ★ Suitable for wheelchairs ★ Plants for sale in garden centre (open all year) separate from main house and garden area ★ Shop ★ House open ★ Grounds open 11th April to 29th Oct, daily, 11am – 6pm, (last admission 5pm) ★ Entrance: £2.75, children £1.75 (house, grounds and exhibition areas £5.95, OAP £4.95, children (5-15) £3.95)

The first garden that one sees here is also the most recent, 'North Courtyard', designed by David Vickery in 1971. It incorporates formal pleached limes in rectangular layout, the geometry being further emphasised by a box parterre infilled with lavender and a central, torrential fountain which baffles the traffic noise outside. It has created a cool green space with immense style which manages to answer the architecture of the house. A wrought iron gate adjoining the courtyard leads to the East Front with wall-trained shrubs and extensive herbaceous borders. These borders will be replanted during the 1995/96 season as part of a five-year garden renovation programme. Looking to the south, the Palladian Bridge built in 1737 spanning the River Nadder is a fine focal point. Beside this stands a fine golden oak, *Quercus robur* 'Concordia', raised and grafted in 1843 at a nursery in Ghent. Going east along the broad gravel walk among many fine specimen trees set in eighteenth-century landscaped parkland, the visitor reaches the recently-established Walled Rose Garden containing a large collection of old-fashioned roses. This adjoins a fine pergola clothed with climbing plant species and newly-developed water garden containing roses, aquatic species and specimen fish. Beyond the water garden is the Whispering Seat with its unusual acoustic properties and a loggia facing the statue from the Arundel collection, all enclosed by a short avenue of *Quercus ilex* with the River Nadder a glistening vista in the distance. A newly opened riverside and woodland walk is being developed as a nature trail. For children there is fun and excitement in a large adventure playground. For historians, there is interest in searching out those parts of the garden which show the work of Isaac de Caus (*c*. 1632), the 8th Earl, the 9th 'Architect Earl', Sir William Chambers and James Wyatt (1801).

YORKSHIRE (North)

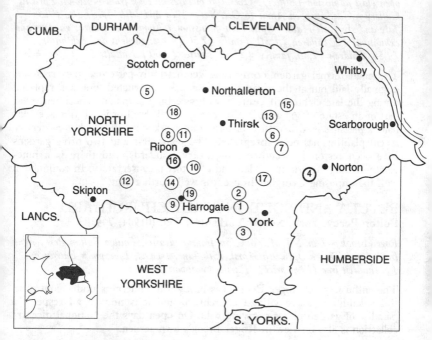

Two-starred gardens are ringed in bold.

ASKHAM BRYAN COLLEGE   1
York, North Yorkshire. Tel: (01904) 702121

Incorporated Charitable Trust ★ 4m W of York on A64 ★ Parking ★ Toilet facilities ★ Suitable for wheelchairs ★ Plants for sale ★ Open for College Open Day 3rd or 10th June, 12.30 – 5.30pm. Also parties by appointment ★ Entrance: £2.50 per car. Parties £2 per person for guided tour of grounds

This is one of the prime centres for the teaching of practical amenity horticulture. The grounds include numerous amenity features such as a limestone garden, woodland walk, bowling green, alpine house, lake, herbaceous and annual beds. The college will soon be host to the National spirea collection. The refurbished tropical house is the high point of the tour. Almost all the plants are clearly labelled and the grounds well worth a visit. There is a pitch and putt.

BENINGBROUGH HALL   2
Beningbrough, North Yorkshire. Tel: (01904) 470666

The National Trust ★ 8m NW of York off A19 York – Thirsk road at Shipton ★ Best seasons: spring and summer ★ Parking ★ Refreshments: restaurant. Picnics in walled garden ★ Toilet facilities ★ Suitable for wheelchairs. Self-drive scooter available ★ Annual regional NCCPG sale usually held here in Sept ★ House open (last admission 4.30pm). Over 100 pictures on loan from National Portrait Gallery ★ Gardens open April to Oct, Sat – Wed and 14th April; also Fri in July and Aug, all 11am – 5pm (last admission 4.30pm) ★ Entrance: gardens and exhibitions £3, children £1.50, family £7.50 (house, gardens and exhibitions £4.50, children £2.30, family £11.30, parties £3.60 per adult, £1.80 per child)

The main formal garden comprising geometrically-patterned parterres was originally laid out at the time the house was constructed, but was replaced during the late eighteenth century with sweeping lawns and specimen trees, part of an estate of 365 acres. Although generally well-ordered, this is essentially a pleasure garden with a historic framework amongst which considerable recent planting has been integrated. The wilderness and two privy gardens have been restored to eighteenth-century standards, and there is a nineteenth-century American garden and a Victorian conservatory. In conjunction with the imposing Georgian house it is well worth a visit.

BETULA AND BOLTON PERCY CHURCHYARD   3
Bolton Percy, York, North Yorkshire. Tel: (01904) 744383

Roger Brook ★ 7½m SW of York, 5m from Tadcaster. Follow Bolton Percy signs from A64 ★ Teas ★ Open 9th April, 25th June, 1st Oct, 1 – 5pm ★ Entrance: £1, children free (1994 price). Parties by appointment

The enthusiasm of Roger Brook has brought a wilderness under control in this splendid one-acre village churchyard and it is now in all respects a paradise of garden plants growing wild. On open days the National dicentra collection is also on view in Roger Brook's own garden.

CASTLE HOWARD ★★   4
York, North Yorkshire. Tel: (01653) 648444

Castle Howard Estates Ltd ★ 5m SW of Malton off A64 York – Scarborough road ★ Parking ★ Refreshments: cafeteria ★ Toilet facilities ★ Partly suitable for wheelchairs ★ Plants for sale in large plant centre ★ Shops ★ House open ★ Garden open 17th March to Oct, daily, 10am – 4.30pm. Special tours of woodland garden available for pre-booked groups ★ Entrance: £4, children £2, (house and garden £6, OAP £5, children (4 – 16) £3, parties £5 per person, children £2.50) (1994 prices)

Described as one of the finest examples of 'The Heroic Age of English Landscape Architecture', the grounds were first designed by Sir John Vanbrugh assisted by Nicholas Hawksmoor to complement the castle designed by Vanbrugh. This layout still generally exists, although in recent times features have been added, for example, the impressive fountains were designed by Nesfield. Although known principally as a very fine landscape, there is also much for the enthusiastic garden lover. There is one of the largest collections of old-fashioned and species roses in Europe. Ray Wood and the adjacent area accommodate very fine collections of magnolias, rhododendrons, sorbus and vaccinium, an adjunct to the newly extended arboretum which will soon be one of the largest and most important in the United Kingdom. Most of the plants are well labelled.

CONSTABLE BURTON HALL 5
Leyburn, North Yorkshire. Tel: (01677) 50428

Mr Charles Wyvill ★ 3m E of Leyburn on A684 ★ Best seasons: spring and early summer ★ Parking ★ Partly suitable for wheelchairs ★ Dogs on lead ★ Open April to mid-Sept, daily, 9am – 6pm ★ Entrance: £1, OAP and children 50p

In a walled and wooded parkland setting is the perfect Georgian Palladian mansion designed by John Carr of York in 1768. Built in beautiful honey-coloured sandstone it rises from the lawns shaded by fine mature cedars. A delightful terraced woodland garden of lilies, ferns, hardy shrubs, roses and wild flowers drops down to a lake enhanced by an eighteenth–century bridge (no access). Near to the entrance drive is a stream and rockery.

DUNCOMBE PARK 6
Helmsley, North Yorkshire.
Tel: (01439) 70213/71115 (during open hours)

Lord Feversham ★ 1m SW of Helmsley off A170 ★ Parking at Visitor Centre ★ Refreshments: at licensed tearoom. Picnic area ★ Toilet facilities ★ Shop ★ House open ★ Garden open April, Wed and Sun, and 14th to 19th April; May and June, Wed – Sun; July and Aug, daily; Sept, Wed – Sun; Oct, Wed and Sun; all 11am – 4.30pm (days and times may be changed for an event. Please telephone to check) ★ Entrance: £2.75 (house and grounds £4.50). Discounts for pre-booked groups visiting house and grounds

Home of the Duncombes for 300 years, the mansion has recently been restored to a family home by Lord Feversham. Its 35–acre garden, set in 300 acres of dramatic parkland, dates from *c.* 1715 and has been described as 'the supreme masterpiece of the art of the landscape gardener' by Sacheverell Sitwell. Tree-lined terraces, classical temples, statues, vast expanses of lawn and magnificent trees mostly dating from the original eighteenth–century planting. Tallest ash and lime trees according to the *Guinness Book of Records*. One of the earliest ha-has built. Views from terrace of the North York Moors. Yew walk. Orangery.

FOUNTAINS ABBEY
(see STUDLEY ROYAL)

GILLING CASTLE 7
Gilling East, North Yorkshire. Tel: (01439) 788206

The Right Reverend the Abbot of Ampleforth ★ 20m N of York on B1363 York – Helmsley road ★ Parking ★ Open July and August, daily, 10am – 4pm ★ Entrance: £1, children free

A lovely garden in outstanding scenery. The terraces have been constructed on the south-facing side of the garden, four of them tumbling down the slope from an expansive lawn at the top. Many old-fashioned flowers grow in the borders with a backdrop of majestic trees.

HACKFALL WOOD 8
Grewelthorpe, North Yorkshire.

Woodland Trust and Landmark Trust ★ 6m NW of Ripon, N of Grewelthorpe on the road to Masham, entrance on right ★ Limited parking ★ Dogs ★ Open all year ★ Entrance: free

The site is a spectacular 350-foot gorge cut out by the River Ure. Now battered by neglect, this romantic woodland garden, once painted by Turner and praised by Wordsworth, was laid out by William Aislabie between 1750 and 1765 as a counterpoint to the splendour of Studley Royal (see entry) created by his father. In the 112 acres of entirely overgrown semi-natural scenery, paths lead to a pool, grotto and a number of small arcadian ruins; the crumbling banqueting hall (which, once restored, may be for rent) commands magnificent views over the gorge. Restoration of the paths, sometimes soggy, is underway. Spring sees masses of flowering wild garlic and bluebells, tall ferns flourish in late summer amid beech, Turkey oak, elder and elm. English Heritage Grade I status.

HARLOW CARR BOTANICAL GARDENS ★   9
Crag Lane, Harrogate, North Yorkshire. Tel: (01423) 565418

Northern Horticultural Society ★ 1½m W of centre of Harrogate on B6162 Otley road ★ Parking ★ Refreshments: licensed restaurant and refreshment kiosk (10am – 5pm) ★ Toilet facilities, inc. disabled ★ Partly suitable for wheelchairs. Manual and electric wheelchairs available for loan ★ Guide dogs only ★ Plants for sale ★ Gift shop ★ Open all year, daily, 9.30am – 6pm or dusk if earlier ★ Entrance: £3.20, OAP £2.50, accompanied children free. Groups of 20 or more £2.50, children under 16 free

A 68-acre site established in 1949 by the Northern Horticultural Society as a centre for garden plant trials now also provides a wide range of horticultural courses for amateurs. It is said that if a plant prospers here it will grow anywhere in the north. Hosts the National collections of heather and rhubarb cultivars as well as those of hypericum, dryopteris and polypodium. Extensive streamside planting with one of the best collections of moisture-loving plants in the north of England. Large collections of rhododendrons, roses and alpines. Boasts a very fine alpine house and two extensive rock gardens.

NEWBY HALL AND GARDENS ★   10
Nr Ripon, North Yorkshire. Tel: (01423) 322583

R.E.J. Compton ★ 4m SE of Ripon on B6265, 3m W of A1 ★ Parking ★ Refreshments: licensed restaurant. Picnic area ★ Toilet facilities, inc. disabled ★ Suitable for wheelchairs (provided) ★ Dogs in area adjacent to picnic area only ★ Plants for sale ★ Shop ★ Open April to Sept, daily except Mon (but open Bank Holiday Mons), 11am – 5.30pm ★ Entrance: £3.30, OAP £2.60, children £2.20 (house and gardens £5.20, OAP £4, children £3) (1994 prices)

The family home of the owners who have set an exceptionally high standard of maintenance while retaining the atmosphere of an established and still lived-in country house. Newby Hall is late seventeenth-century with additions and interior by Robert Adam. There are 25 acres of formal gardens and some features remain from the eighteenth century, such as east to west walk marked by Venetian statuary, backed by yew and purple plum. The south face has long wide green slopes down to the River Ure, with herbaceous borders on either side backed by clipped hedges and flowering shrubs. Cross walks lead to smaller gardens full of interest. These include species roses, tropical, autumn, rock and a stepped water garden as well as a fine woodland area attributed to Ellen Willmott. National collection holder of genus *Cornus*. Children's adventure garden and miniature railway. Events are held in the summer, such as craft fairs, with special admission prices.

NORTON CONYERS   11
Ripon, North Yorkshire. Tel: (01765) 640601/640333

Sir James Graham, Bart ★ 3¹/₂m NW of Ripon, near Wath. 3m from A1 turn off at the Baldersby flyover, take the A61 to Ripon, turn right to Melmerby ★ Parking ★ Teas on charity open days. Buffet lunches, light refreshments and teas for booked parties by arrangement ★ Partly suitable for wheelchairs ★ Dogs on lead ★ Small garden centre specialising in unusual hardy plants and Pick Your Own fruit in June, July and Aug ★ House open as garden but also 16th, 17th April. £2.95, OAP £2, children (10–16) £2.50, rates for parties of 20 or more on application. Enquiries to Lady Graham ★ Garden open 7th, 8th May; 28th May to 10th Sept, Suns; also 24th – 29th July, daily, and 27th, 28th Aug; all 2 – 5pm ★ Entrance: free, though donations welcome

The lure of both the house and the garden lies very much with the past, especially the association of the house with Charlotte Brontë, who made it one of the models for Thornfield Hall in *Jane Eyre*. The eighteenth–century walled garden, with an orangery and herbaceous borders, covers two and a half acres. The plantings are modest but pleasant, being mostly of the cottage garden type, and give a historic feel.

PARCEVALL HALL GARDENS ★   12
Appletreewick, Skipton, North Yorkshire. Tel: (01756) 720311

Walsingham College (Yorkshire Properties) Ltd ★ 1m NE of Appletreewick off B6265 Pateley Bridge – Skipton road ★ Parking ★ Picnics in orchard ★ Dogs on lead ★ Plants for sale ★ Open April to Oct, daily, 10am – 6pm and for charity ★ Entrance: £2, children (3-12) 50p

A garden of great interest to the plantsperson, many of Sir William Milner's treasures having survived years of neglect. The garden is currently being restored and is well worth a visit, if merely to enjoy the spectacular views from the terrace. A fine range of rhododendrons, many originally collected in China, still grow happily here. Fishponds. Rock garden.

RIEVAULX TERRACE AND TEMPLES ★   13
Rievaulx, Helmsley, North Yorkshire. Tel: (014396) 340

The National Trust ★ 2¹/₂m NW of Helmsley on B1257 ★ Parking. Coach park 200 yards ★ Picnics ★ Toilet facilities ★ Suitable for wheelchairs on terrace. Electric self-propelled chair available, free of charge. Steps to temples ★ Dogs on lead ★ Shop and information centre ★ Two eighteenth–century temples and exhibition of landscape design in basement of Ionic temple ★ Open April to Oct, daily, 10.30am – 6pm or dusk if earlier (last admission 5pm). Ionic temple closed 1 – 2pm ★ Entrance: £2.50, children £1, parties £1.80 per person, children 80p

This is a unique example of the eighteenth–century passion for the romantic and the picturesque – that is, making landscape look like a picture. The work was done at the behest of Thomas Duncombe around 1754 and consists of a half-mile-long serpentine grass terrace high above Ryedale with fine views. At one end is a Palladian-style Ionic temple with furniture by William Kent and elaborate ceilings. At the other is a Tuscan temple with a raised platform from which are views to the Rye Valley. The concept is wonderfully achieved. Those who want to see flowers will have to concentrate their attention on the grass bank below the terrace which is managed for wildflower content – fine displays of cowslips, primroses, orchids, violets, bird's foot trefoils, ladies' bedstraws, etc. Also there is blossom throughout the season, such as cherry (bird and wild), blackthorn, rowan, whitebeam, elder and lilac.

RIPLEY CASTLE 14
Ripley, Harrogate, North Yorkshire. Tel: (01423) 770152

Sir Thomas Ingilby, Bart ★ 3½m N of Harrogate off A61 Harrogate – Ripon road ★ Best seasons: April/ May and July/ Aug ★ Parking ★ Refreshments: morning coffee and tea ★ Toilet facilities ★ Suitable for wheelchairs ★ Guide dogs only ★ Gift shop ★ Castle open at extra charge ★ Garden open March, Thurs – Sun, 11am – 4pm; April to Oct, daily, 11am – 5pm; Nov to Dec 23rd, 11am – 3.30pm ★ Entrance: £2.25, OAP £1.75, children £1. Parties of 25 or more £1.75 per person. Season ticket £15

A mid-eighteenth-century 'Capability' Brown landscape with formal gardens developed by Peter Aram for a family that has been here since the thirteenth century. A beautiful landscape, especially during spring at daffodil time. Magnificent specimen trees. The formal areas have seen better days, but the current owner is making considerable strides in their restoration. Lake with attractive Victorian iron bridge. Eighteenth-century orangery and summer-houses. Vegetable garden. Woodland walk to a temple with fine views. Extensive new plantings of a rich variety of spring-flowering bulbs have been made to complement the National collection of hyacinths here. The tropical plant collection formerly owned by Hull University at Cottingham Botanical Gardens is now at Ripley and is open to the public in the newly-restored listed greenhouses. There is also a lovely lakeside walk that takes the visitor through the deer park, giving fine views over the lake to the castle and grounds.

SLEIGHTHOLME DALE LODGE 15
Fadmoor, Nr Kirbymoorside, North Yorkshire. Tel: (01751) 431942

Dr and Mrs O. James ★ 3m N of Kirbymoorside. 1m from Fadmoor off A170 ★ Open by written appointment and 3rd June, 11.30am – 5pm, 15th, 16th July, 2 – 7pm ★ Entrance: £1.25, children 50p (1994 prices)

This garden occupies a unique position on the side of a wooded valley opening on to the moors. In the spring there is a blaze of blossom, wild daffodils and azaleas, and through the summer the walled garden, which runs steeply up the hill, is breathtaking in its colour and exuberance. As well as a mass of old-fashioned roses and delphiniums the owners have specialised in rare plants, notably meconopsis.

STUDLEY ROYAL AND FOUNTAINS ABBEY ★★ 16
Ripon, North Yorkshire. Tel: (01765) 608888

The National Trust ★ 2m SW of Ripon, 9m N of Harrogate. Follow Fountains Abbey sign off B6265 Ripon – Pateley Bridge road ★ Parking free at main visitor centre car park but £1.70 at Studley park ★ Refreshments: at Visitor Centre restaurant daily. Light lunches at Studley café. Picnic area ★ Toilet facilities ★ Suitable for wheelchairs. Self-drive powered 'runarounds' available by prior booking ★ Gift shop ★ Deer park open all year during daylight hours. Abbey and garden open all year, daily except 24th, 25th Dec and Fri in Nov to Jan, as follows: Jan to March and Oct to Dec, 10am – 5pm or dusk if earlier; April to Sept, 10am – 7pm. Free guided tours April to Oct, daily ★ Entrance: Deer park free. Gardens and Abbey £4, children £2, family rates available. Special rates for pre-booked coach parties. Tours and facilities available. Parking £2 at Studley Royal refundable if admission ticket purchased

The gardens were created by John Aislabie, who had been Chancellor of the Exchequer but whose finances were 'ruined' by the South Sea Bubble in 1720 and who retired here to his estate in 1722 and worked until his death in 1742 to make the finest water-garden in the country. The lakes, grotto springs, formal canal and water features plus buildings such as the Temple of Piety turn what is essentially a landscape with large trees and sweeping lawns into one of the most stunning of green gardens. The views from Colen Campbell's Banqueting House must also be savoured. Furthermore, there is the association with the largest and most complete Cistercian foundation in Europe, described by the *Oxford Companion* as probably the noblest monastic ruin in Christendom. This can be seen in the distance from the 'surprise view', through a door in a small building. Restoration of Anne Boleyn's seat, a timber gazebo with a fine view, is now complete. A further £3 million is being collected for the next phase of conservation which includes the repair of river banks, fords and bridges, restoration of Fountains Hall and Abbey Mill, and an on-going programme of woodland management and tree planting. Those who would like to see the dramatic 'surprise' view of the Abbey should take the turning for Studley Royal on B6265 and follow the road to arrive at the lake enterance. This also has the advantage of leading from the Hall via the Abbey to the lakeside Edwardian tearooms.

SUTTON PARK ★ 17
Sutton-in-the-Forest, York, North Yorkshire. Tel: (01347) 810249

Mrs N.M.D. Sheffield ★ 8m N of York on B1363 ★ Parking. Coaches by appointment ★ Refreshments: lunches, afternoon and high teas by appointment only ★ Toilet facilities ★ Suitable for wheelchairs (gardens only) ★ Plants sometimes for sale ★ Shop ★ Georgian house open April to Aug, Bank Holiday Suns and Mons only, 1.30 – 5.30pm (last admission 5pm). Parties of 25 or more by appointment 16th April to Oct, daily except Sat. Also ice-house ★ Gardens open 14th April to 1st Oct, daily, 11am – 5.30pm ★ Entrance: £1, children 50p (house and gardens £3.50, OAP £3, children £2, parties £4 per person) (1994 prices)

One of the most distinguished English garden designers of recent times, Percy Cane, came in 1962 to this Georgian house and its terraced site with views over parkland said to have been moulded by 'Capability' Brown. Cane started the elegant planting which has been most carefully expanded by the present owners. There are several fine features on the terraces – a tall beech hedge curved to take a marble seat, ironwork gazebos and everywhere soft stone. The woodland walk leads to a temple. A new water feature with exotic ducks has been created in the old walled-in garden.

THORP PERROW ARBORETUM ★   18
Bedale, North Yorkshire. Tel: (01677) 425323

Sir John Ropner, Bart ★ 2m S of Bedale, signposted off B6268 Masham road ★ Best seasons: spring and autumn ★ Parking ★ Refreshments: in tearoom. Picnic area ★ Suitable for wheelchairs. Electric wheelchair available ★ Dogs on lead ★ Plant Centre ★ Information Centre open ★ Arboretum open all year, dawn – dusk ★ Entrance: £2.75, OAP and children (5-16) £1.50

The arboretum was established many years ago and it is one of the finest collections of trees in the north of England, containing over 2000 species. In the 85 acres is a Victorian pinetum, sixteenth-century woodland and four National tree collections: ash, oak, walnut and lime. You can follow the tree trail, the nature trail or simply amble at your own leisure. Thousands of naturalised daffodils and bluebells in spring, glorious wild flowers in summer and stunning autumn colour. There are new plantings and continual improvements in the arboretum such as new interpretive signs.

VALLEY GARDENS ★   19
1 Valley Drive, Harrogate, North Yorkshire. Tel: (01423) 500600

Harrogate Borough Council ★ In centre of Harrogate, main entrance is near Pump Room Museum and Mercer Art Gallery ★ Best seasons: spring and summer ★ Parking ★ Refreshments: morning coffee, light lunches, teas ★ Toilet facilities ★ Suitable for wheelchairs ★ Dogs on lead ★ Open daily during daylight hours ★ Entrance: free

One of the best-known public gardens in the north of England, laid out earlier this century at the time Harrogate was fashionable as a spa. This is the site of the annual Harrogate Great Spring Flower Show, which sadly causes some damage in late April each year. While the stream garden and rock features have gone into decline in recent years, the standard of formal bedding remains very high. A very fine dahlia display is an annual feature.

NATIONAL COUNCIL FOR THE CONSERVATION OF PLANTS AND GARDENS

The NCCPG has just published the latest version of its *National Plant Collections Directory*. Anyone interested in particular families of plants who wants to see some of the rarer species and garden varieties will find this is an invaluable publication indicating where and when they can be seen. This edition, which offers information on about 550 collections comprising more than 50,000 plants, also contains articles by holders of the collections.

YORKSHIRE
(South & West)

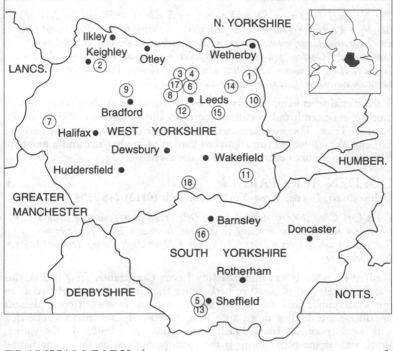

N. YORKSHIRE

Ilkley

Keighley
(2)

LANCS.

Otley

Wetherby

(3) (4)
(17) (6)
(8)
(1)

(14)

(9)

(7)

Halifax

Leeds

(12) (15)

(10)

Bradford

WEST YORKSHIRE

Dewsbury

Wakefield

HUMBER.

Huddersfield

(18)

GREATER
MANCHESTER

(11)

Barnsley

(16)

Doncaster

SOUTH YORKSHIRE

Rotherham

DERBYSHIRE

(5)
(13)

Sheffield

NOTTS.

BRAMHAM PARK ★   1
Wetherby, West Yorkshire. Tel: (01937) 844265

*Mr and Mrs G. Lane Fox ★ 5m S of Wetherby just off northbound A1 ★
Parking ★ Toilet facilities ★ Partly suitable for wheelchairs ★ House open at extra
charge ★ Park open 15th to 17th April, 8th, 27th to 29th May, 28th Aug and
18th June to 3rd Sept, Sun, Tues, Wed, Thurs, 1.15 – 5.30pm (last admission
5pm) ★ Entrance: £2, OAP £1.50, children £1 (house and gardens £3.50, OAP
£2.50, children £1.50). Reduced rates for parties of 20 or more*

Created by Robert Benson after the style of Le Nôtre nearly 350 years ago,
this is one of the few landscape gardens in the French style to survive in this
country. Although great storms removed many specimen beeches and
changed the layout of the avenues, the creator's concept has been maintained and his layout restored. Apart from their unique design, the gardens
also have a substantial rose garden which provides summer-long colour, and
an interesting herbaceous border. However, it is the splendid architectural
features and the trees which would have been familiar to the garden's creator,
in his day Chancellor of the Exchequer, that are outstanding; as visitors
wonder at the beauty of this garden they may well muse how many

Chancellors have left such a legacy to the nation. During restoration work in 1991 a massive eighteenth-century cascade was found. Apparently the family had tried to fill it in in the late eigtheenth century.

EAST RIDDLESDEN HALL 2
Bradford Road, Keighley, West Yorkshire. Tel: (01535) 607075

The National Trust ★ 1m SE of Keighley on S side of A650 and 3m NW of Bingley ★ Parking ★ Teas ★ Toilet facilities ★ Suitable for wheelchairs but prior notice required for refreshment room ★ Dogs on lead in grounds only ★ Shop ★ House open ★ Garden open April to Oct, Sat – Wed and 14th April; also Fri in July and Aug, 12 noon – 5pm (last admission 4.30pm). Pre-booking required for parties ★ Entrance: £3.25, accompanied children £1.50

A traditional seventeenth-century Yorkshire manor house. Neglected through much of nineteenth and twentieth centuries and restored in 1983-84 by the National Trust. The great barn is considered one of the finest in the north of England. A well-tended formal walled garden of modest size and a monastic fish pond in grounds running down to the river.

GOLDEN ACRE PARK ★ 3
Otley Road, Leeds, West Yorkshire. Tel: (0113) 246 3504

Leeds City Council ★ Off A660 Leeds – Otley road at approach to Bramhope ★ Parking ★ Refreshments: morning coffee, teas, lunches ★ Toilet facilities ★ Suitable for wheelchairs ★ Dogs ★ Gift shop ★ Open daily during daylight hours ★ Entrance: free

Until 1945, when it was purchased by Leeds Corporation for £18,500, this was a privately-owned pleasure park. Since then it has been developed as an important public park and minor botanic garden. It is sited on a pleasant undulating site leading down to a lake. Extensively-planted tree collection with most specimens labelled. Rhododendrons are a feature in the spring, along with alpine plants both in the rock garden and in the alpine house. Golden Acre Park is noted for its very fine collection of houseleeks or sempervivums as well as its heather collection. Demonstration plots are maintained where instruction is provided for home gardeners. The quality of plantings and vegetables for these improves annually. Now one of the demonstration gardens for Fleuroselect flowers.

HAREWOOD HOUSE ★ 4
Harewood, Leeds, West Yorkshire. Tel: (0113) 288 6331

The Earl and Countess of Harewood ★ 7m N of Leeds on A61 ★ Best seasons: April, early June and early Oct ★ Parking ★ Refreshments: light lunches, teas, etc., restaurant and bar, picnic area ★ Toilet facilities ★ Partly suitable for wheelchairs ★ Dogs on lead ★ Shop ★ Art gallery, bird garden and adventure playgrounds ★ House open as grounds, 11am – 5pm ★ Grounds open 25th March to Oct, daily, 10am – 7pm ★ Entrance: terrace gallery and grounds £3, OAP and children £1 (bird garden and grounds £4.50, OAP and children £2.50; house and grounds £5.75, OAP £5, children £3, family season ticket £25) (1994 prices)

Originally laid out in the 1770s by 'Capability' Brown the gardens and park still retain many of his characteristic features, most notably a majestic lake and a well-wooded horizon. Nineteenth-century rhododendrons enrich the edge of the lake and afford a fine sight reflected on its surface when flowering in early June. Other features in this woodland setting are a vaguely Japanese bog garden below the lake's cascade housing the National collection of hostas. Sir Charles Barry's terrace of the 1840s adds a formal contrast with its parterres and fountains, herbaceous borders and bedding. The terrace has just been restored and the intricate patterns of the parterre have been re-created to Barry's original designs after decades under grass. Large quantities of trees and shrubs in these excellently maintained grounds ensure a long season of interest.

HILLSBOROUGH WALLED GARDEN 5
Middlewood Road, Sheffield, South Yorkshire. Tel: (0114) 232 2474

Hillsborough Community Development Trust ★ Adjacent to Hillsborough Library ★ Parking for disabled only ★ Suitable for wheelchairs ★ Guide dogs only ★ Plants for sale ★ Garden open daily, summer, 9am – 8pm; winter 9am – 4pm ★ Entrance: free but donations welcome

The site embraces four different gardens: a wildlife area, a lawn with herbaceous borders, a woodland glade and a formal garden with raised beds for easy use by disabled gardeners. There are many features including a pergola, a pool, wallspout, arbour, herb garden, vegetable and nursery garden, greenhouse, and a garden for the visually handicapped. Planned as a project for children's nature studies, it now has strong links with arts bodies and provides employment training and community entertainments; it was awarded a Community Enterprise Scheme award in 1993. There is a Victorian heated garden wall, thought to be the most extensive in the Sheffield area. The garden was planned, created and is run by the community. As such it is not just an area to look at and enjoy, but everyone is encouraged to help with its upkeep. Tools are available on site and plants are always welcomed.

THE HOLLIES PARK ★ 6
Weetwood Lane, Leeds, West Yorkshire. Tel: (0113) 278 2030

Leeds City Council ★ Entrance off Weetwood Lane, off A660 Leeds – Otley road ★ Parking ★ Toilet facilities ★ Open daily during daylight hours ★ Entrance: free

The original layout is Victorian. The gardens were given to Leeds Corporation in 1921 by the Brown family in memory of a son killed during World War I. The fine informal, largely woodland garden features woody plants, especially rhododendrons, many rarely seen growing in this part of the North. Ferns flourish throughout the gardens and a varied collection of hydrangeas provide late summer colour. Many slightly tender subjects, such as eucryphia, embothrium and drimys, thrive in the pleasant microclimate. A number of National collections maintained by Leeds City Council is grown, including those of hemerocallis and deutzias, and probably the most comprehensive philadelphus collection in Europe.

LAND FARM 7
Colden, Nr Hebden Bridge, West Yorkshire. Tel: (01422) 842260

Mr and Mrs J. Williams ★ Off A646 between Sowerby Bridge and Todmorden. Call at the Visitors' Centre in Hebden Bridge for a map ★ Plants for sale ★ Open

*May to Aug, Sat, Sun and Bank Holiday Mons, 10am – 5pm. Parties welcome
★ Entrance: £2*

A four-acre garden created by the owners on a north-facing site 1000 feet up
in the Pennines. Designed as a low-maintenance garden, it nevertheless
contains a wide diversity of shrubs, herbaceous plants and alpines.

30 LATCHMERE ROAD   8
Leeds, West Yorkshire. Tel: (0113) 275 1261

*Mr and Mrs Joe Brown ★ NW of Leeds off A6120 (ring road to Bradford),
turn up Fillingfir Drive, right at pillar box, then left into Latchmere Road ★ No
parking in Latchmere Road ★ Plants for sale ★ Open by appointment to
horticultural societies, garden clubs and tourist groups and on 16th, 23rd July,
2.30 – 5.30pm ★ Entrance: £1, children 50p*

A garden of exceptional merit created from scratch over the last 30 years by
Mr and Mrs Brown, this is now one of the finest examples of garden design
in a small garden. Herbaceous plants, ferns, climbers and shrubs all
contribute to a series of mini-features which the visitor passes through in a
controlled circuit of the garden. These features include a clematis collection,
sink gardens, pools, patio and alpine garden.

LISTER PARK   9
Keighley Road, Bradford, West Yorkshire. Tel: (01274) 493313

*City of Bradford Metropolitan Council ★ 1½m N of Bradford centre (Forster
Square) on A650 Bradford – Keighley road ★ Best season: spring and summer ★
Parking in surrounding streets ★ Light refreshments: daily except Mon, 10am –
4pm ★ Toilet facilities ★ Suitable for wheelchairs ★ Dogs on lead ★ Cartwright
Hall, City Art Gallery and Museum open, April to Sept, Tues – Sun, 10am –
6pm, Oct to Mar, Tues – Sun, 10am – 5pm ★ Park open daily during daylight
hours ★ Entrance: free*

This used to be a well-tended park with an excellent garden and botanical
garden, including greenhouses with tropical plants. Recently there have been
signs of improvement although the botanical garden, which still exists,
appears untended, and the main reason for including the park in this guide is
that there is a formal floral display in front of Cartwright Hall and an interesting floral clock, a rare example of Victorian ingenuity, which is well worth
seeing by those living in or passing through the city, perhaps to visit the
National Museum of Photography, Film and TV.

LOTHERTON HALL   10
Aberford, West Yorkshire. Tel: (0113) 246 3510

*Leeds City Council ★ 3½m NE of Gosforth on B1217 ★ Best season: spring and
summer ★ Parking. Coaches by appointment ★ Refreshments and picnics ★ Toilet
facilities ★ Dogs except in bird garden ★ Shop ★ House open. Bird garden closed
Mon. Working shire horses ★ Garden open daily, 10.30am – dusk ★ Entrance: free*

A 10-acre garden which grows surprisingly tender shrubs and climbers rare
in this raw northern climate, protected by walls and tree shelters. The design
is thought to owe something to Ellen Willmott and is rather an Edwardian

period piece. Formal rose garden, an avenue of yews leading to a white summerhouse, walled garden, sunken garden with lily pond, a well-planted Japanese rockery glen of 1912 and a ha-ha now filled in and planted with primulas, astilbes and meconopsis. Sports lovers will be interested to see the tennis court, one of the earliest of brick construction, but some garden lovers have been disappointed at the lack of seasonal colour between spring and summer. Further restoration and improvement work is taking place and more period plants being introduced.

NOSTELL PRIORY 11
Nr Wakefield, West Yorkshire. Tel: (01924) 863892

The National Trust/Lord and Lady St Oswald ★ 6m SE of Wakefield on A638 ★ Best season: summer for rose garden ★ Parking ★ Light refreshments and teas. Picnic site ★ Toilet facilities inc. disabled ★ Suitable for wheelchairs. Batricar available ★ Dogs on lead ★ Gift shop ★ House open from 12 noon ★ Garden open April, May, June, Sept and Oct, Sat, 12 noon – 5pm and Sun and Bank Holiday Mons, 11am – 5pm; July to 10th Sept, daily except Fri, 12 noon – 5pm, Suns, 11am – 5pm ★ Entrance: £2.20, children £1.10, (house and garden £3.50, children £1.80, parties £3 per adult, children £1.50)

An eighteenth-century mansion set in open parkland with an attractive lake and a variety of well-established trees. A fine, well-tended and well-labelled rose garden is the main gardening feature with extensive lakeside gardens including magnolias (March to April), rhododendrons (May), summerhouse, Gothic archway and cock fighting pit. One of the most attractive Gothic buildings, with later additions by Robert Adams, once occupied by a couple who looked after the animals, is being restored. There is a children's playground and a picnic area. Special events and fairs are held during the season, some in marquees in front of the house, with a special admission charge.

ROUNDHAY PARK (Tropical World Canal Gardens) ★ 12
Roundhay Road, Leeds, West Yorkshire. Tel: (0113) 266 1850

Leeds City Council ★ Off A58 Roundhay Road from Leeds city centre ★ Parking ★ Refreshments: light snacks ★ Toilet facilities ★ Suitable for wheelchairs ★ Dogs ★ Open daily except 25th Dec, 10am dusk ★ Entrance: free

The intensively-cultivated canal gardens area was formerly the kitchen and ornamental gardens of the Nicholson family, who sold the site to the Leeds Corporation in 1871. The extensive parkland with its fine trees is an excellent setting for the pure horticultural extravaganza of the canal gardens with their formal bedding and generous collections of tropical plants in greenhouses. The collections are constantly being added to and are a Mecca for enthusiastic gardeners.

SHEFFIELD BOTANICAL GARDENS 13
Sheffield, South Yorkshire. Tel: (0114) 267 1115

Sheffield Council ★ ½m from A625, 1½m SW of Sheffield centre ★ Parking in surrounding streets ★ Toilet facilities inc. disabled ★ Suitable for wheelchairs ★ Dogs on lead ★ Plants for sale occasionally, by Friends of Botanical Gardens (FOBS) ★ Open daily during daylight hours ★ Entrance: free

An example of a botanical garden tended by a local authority, with support from and participation by local gardening societies and helpers. Flower displays are changed seasonally. All plants are well-labelled, including those in the special woodland area. The gardens, though close to Sheffield centre, are secluded with good seating and grass areas suitable for children and recreation. The gardens are improving and continually being brought back to their former glory.

SILVER BIRCHES   14
Ling Lane, Scarcroft, Leeds, West Yorkshire. Tel: (0113) 289 2335

Mr S.C. Thomson ★ 7m NE of Leeds in Ling Lane, Scarcroft off A58 Leeds – Wetherby road ★ Parking ★ Refreshment: tea ★ Partly suitable for wheelchairs ★ Plants for sale ★ Open by appointment from mid-April to Oct for parties and three times for charity probably in May and June ★ Entrance: £1, children 50p

A two and a half-acre garden with tastefully-added shrubs and conifers. Foliage plants are a significant component in the design. There are also good collections of roses, heathers and climbers as well as open water with a range of aquatic plants.

TEMPLE NEWSAM   15
Leeds, West Yorkshire. Tel: (0113) 264 5535

Leeds City Council ★ Signposted off junction of A63 and A6120 ring road E of Leeds ★ Best season: mid-May to early-Oct ★ Parking ★ Teas and snacks ★ Toilet facilities ★ Suitable for wheelchairs ★ Shop ★ House open daily except Mon, 10.30am – 6.15pm. Extra charge ★ Park open daily, 9am – dusk; National collections open Mon – Fri, 11am – 3pm, Sat and Sun, 11am – 2pm ★ Entrance: free

A pleasant oasis surrounded by urban Leeds. Set in the remnants of a 'Capability' Brown landscape of the 1760s (much reduced by a golf course and open-cast mining) is a wide diversity of gardens. Around the house an Italian paved garden and a Jacobean-style parterre surrounded by pleached lime walks are poorly maintained. A rhododendron and azalea walk leads to small ponds with a bog garden and arboretum, beyond which is a large walled rose garden and greenhouses containing collections of ivies, cacti and some rather dashing climbing pelargoniums. NCCPG collections of delphiniums, phlox and asters. Also within the large walled garden are traditional herbaceous borders considered to be amongst the best in England.

WENTWORTH CASTLE GARDENS ★   16
Stainborough, Barnsley, South Yorkshire. Tel: (01226) 772566

Barnsley Metropolitan Borough Council ★ Off M1 at Junction 37, 2m down minor road signposted Stainborough/Dodworth ★ Best season: spring ★ Parking ★ House and main buildings occupied by Northern College ★ Gardens open 28th, 29th May. Pre-booked conducted tours are available from April to July, Tues and Thurs, starting at 2pm at the car park ★ Entrance: £2, OAP £1, accompanied children under 16 free

One of the most exciting gardens in Yorkshire, laid out mainly under the direction of William Wentworth in 1740, it is currently undergoing a complete review of its activities. It contains one of the finest collections of rhododendrons in the North, which have been established during the past 15 years and form an invaluable educational resource. The owners at Wentworth are putting together an important development package which will preserve the fabric of the garden and yet enable its already valuable collections to be expanded. It has recently been designated the National collection for the Falconeri rhododendrons and there are many new plantings. The gardens have recently twinned with the Kumming Botanical Gardens in China and many rare species of Asiatic plants are being introduced. Interpretive signs and a guide book have been produced during the past year, greatly enhancing the enjoyment of a visit. There are extensive new plantings of magnolias, comprising one of the largest collections in northern England.

5 WHARFE CLOSE   17
Adel, Leeds, West Yorkshire. Tel: (0113) 261 1363

Mr and Mrs C.V. Lightman ★ E of A660 Leeds – Skipton road and N of the north Leeds ring road (A6120). Turn off ring road into Adel along Long Causeway/Sir George Martin's Drive to Derwent Drive ★ Best season: summer ★ Parking between bus terminus and shop ★ Teas ★ Plants for sale ★ Open some Suns during July and Aug, 2 – 5pm and by appointment ★ Entrance: £1

An interesting garden of about three-quarters of an acre which includes two ponds, a Japanese feature and woodland glade. There are large collections of both ivies and conifers and an amazing array of planted sinks and troughs, a passion of the gardener responsible for laying out the site.

YORKSHIRE SCULPTURE PARK   18
Bretton Hall, West Bretton, Wakefield, West Yorkshire.
Tel: (01924) 830302

Yorkshire Sculpture Park, Independent Charitable Trust ★ 6m SW of Wakefield at West Bretton. Leave M1 at junction 38 ★ Parking. Car parking charges £1 per day or part thereof. Coaches by prior arrangement ★ Refreshments in Bothy Café ★ Toilet facilities ★ Access Sculpture Trail suitable for wheelchairs ★ Dogs on lead ★ Shop and Information Centre ★ Open daily except 25th, 26th Dec and 1st Jan, summer, 10am – 6pm, winter, 10am – 4pm ★ Entrance: free but donation requested

A lecturer at the college initiated this great project for Britain's first permanent sculpture park in 1977, and the Yorkshire Arts Association was set up in the same year. The Palladian-style house and its 260 acres of formal gardens, woods, lakes and parkland provide a fine setting for temporary and permanent exhibitions. Work is not bought or given, but available on extended loan from artists, arts councils and, in a few cases, from the Tate Gallery. The layout makes it possible to view sculpture in 'garden' as well as the 'public' settings that demand a more monumental approach by the sculptor. Note the imaginative use of colour on wooden fencing which leads to the Access Sculpture Trail designed by Don Rankin with emphasis on access for disabled visitors. The sculptures here are being worked upon *in situ*, evolving with the gardens – an example of the subtle relationship between art and nature. Maintenance is patchy, and a difficult balance has to be kept between jolly areas for school parties and a certain amount of dignity round pieces by the likes of Moore.

IRELAND

Two-starred gardens are ringed in bold

ALTAMONT   1
Tullow, Co. Carlow, Republic of Ireland. Tel: (0503) 59128

*Mrs North ★ 5m from Tullow, about 1m off main Tullow – Bunclody road
(N80/81) ★ Parking ★ Home-made teas ★ Partly suitable for wheelchairs ★ Dogs
on lead ★ Plants for sale ★ Open 16th April to Oct, Suns and Bank Holidays, 2
– 6pm. Other times by appointment ★ Entrance: IR£2, children under 10 free*

The lily-filled lake surrounded by fine, mature trees forms a backdrop for a
gently sloping lawn. A central walkway formally planted with Irish yews and
roses leads from the house to the lake. There is a beautiful fern-leaved beech,
and other ancient beeches form the 'Nun's walk'. A long walk through the
demesne leads to the River Slaney with diversions to a bog garden, through
an Ice Age glen of ancient oaks undercarpeted with bluebells in spring. Mrs
North's passion for trees, old-fashioned roses and unusual plants is evident.
She is also starting residential gardening holidays.

ANNES GROVE ★   2
Castletownroche, Co. Cork, Republic of Ireland. Tel: (022) 26145

*Mr and Mrs F.P. Grove Annesley ★ 2m N of village of Castletownroche,
between Fermoy and Mallow ★ Parking ★ Picnic area ★ Toilet facilities, inc.
disabled ★ Partly suitable for wheelchairs ★ Dogs on lead ★ Open 17th March to
Sept, Mon – Sat, 10am – 5pm, Sun, 1 – 6pm ★ Entrance: IR£2.50, OAP and
students IR£1.50, children IR£1. Reductions for pre-booked groups*

This is an archetypal 'Robinsonian' alias wild garden, but such tags are not
helpful. Rhododendron species and cultivars arch over and spill towards the
pathways, carpeting them with fallen blossoms. Steep, sometimes slippery
paths descend at various places into the valley of the Awbeg river (which
inspired Edmund Spenser). The statuesque conifers planted in the valley
make a colourful tapestry behind the river garden, with *Primula florindae* and
P. japonica cultivars in profusion. The glory of Annes Grove is the collection
of rhododendron spp. wherein visitors may see hidden surprises – a superb
Juniperus recurva 'Castlewellan', a mature pocket handkerchief tree (*Davidia
involucrata*) and other exotic, flowering trees. Here is bird-song and the
crystal-clear Awbeg, water-buttercups and primroses – peaceful groves.

ANTRIM CASTLE GARDENS   3
**Randalstown Road, Antrim, Co. Antrim, Northern Ireland.
Tel: (01849) 428000; Fax (01849) 460360**

*Antrim Borough Council Arts and Heritage Service ★ Access from Randalstown
Road, Antrim (A6), 150 metres from Ballymena Road (A26) roundabout ★
Parking ★ Refreshments by arrangement for organised parties. No tea-room ★
Toilet facilities in Clotworthy House ★ Suitable for wheelchairs ★ Dogs ★
Interpretive display in Clotworthy House open 9.30am – 4.30pm ★ Grounds open
all year daily, 9.30am – dusk. Guided talks, tours and visits for parties at any
time by arrangement ★ Entrance: free*

A rare example of an estate where the main elements survive as laid out for a
late-seventeenth-century house (now demolished, although an Italianate tower
remains). The canals connected by a cascade are lined with clipped lime and
hornbeam hedges. Paths crisscross through the wooded Wilderness, the main

avenue of which leads to an airy clearing with a round pond reflecting sky and trees. A large parterre (three acres) has been planted up with varieties known in the late seventeenth century following a recent restoration project and is set off by a quincunx grove of standard hornbeam (new) and an immense yew hedge (old). All this could be viewed from the top of an Anglo–Norman motte. The motte retains its spiral path (difficult access) and it is worth a climb to the top to see the lower course of Sixmilewater river, the centre of the town of Antrim and the 37-acre ornamental site below, a fraction of a once vast desmesne stretching as far as the eye can see. The garden received a European Commission Architectural Heritage Award in 1993 and further programmes of conservation and restoration are planned.

ARD NA MONA ★★   4
Lough Eske, Donegal, Republic of Ireland. Tel: (073) 22650

Kieran and Amabel Clarke ★ On NW shore of Lough Eske, approached from Donegal, following signs for Harvey's Point ★ Best season: April and May ★ Parking ★ Open last week in Jan to last week in June by appointment ★ Entrance: IR£2

William Robinson would have been proud of this garden created by the Wallaces 1880-1932. Ard na Mona is 'Wild Gardening' at its most exuberant and refined. Imagine a Himalayan mountain slope cloaked with primeval rhododendron forest, 60 feet tall, with a carpet of fallen leaves underfoot embroidered in discarded flowers – you are close to imagining Ard na Mona. The rhododendrons are mainly over 100 years old, and they proclaim their age with proud clean trunks, coloured from cinnamon to purple, and canopies well beyond reach. Opened in 1992, this garden (once neglected, now again cared for) will welcome visitors (and bed and breakfast is offered in the house); rhododendron enthusiasts will need little more encouragement than the prospect of being in paradise.

THE ARGORY   5
Moy, Dungannon, Co. Tyrone, Northern Ireland.
Tel: (018687) 84753

The National Trust ★ 4m from Moy, 3m from M1 junction 14 (coaches must use junction 13 because of weight restrictions) ★ Parking 100 yards from house 50p ★ Refreshments: in tea room. Picnics welcome ★ Toilet facilities, inc. disabled ★ Suitable for wheelchairs ★ Dogs on lead ★ Shop ★ House open ★ Grounds and garden open 14th to 18th April, daily; rest of April, May, June and Sept, Sat, Sun and Bank Holiday Mons; July to Aug, daily except Thurs, all 2 – 6pm ★ Entrance: £2.20, children £1.10

The lawns of the pleasure ground slope down past yew arbours to two pavilions, one a pump house, the other a garden house. Beyond, the visitor can walk under pollarded limes along the banks of the Blackwater river. There are other woodland walks in this tranquil landscape. A splash of summer colour near the house attracts the eye to a very pretty enclosed early nineteenth–century sundial garden of box-edged rose beds.

BEECH PARK
(see THE SHACKLETON GARDEN)

BELVEDERE   6
Mullingar, Co. Westmeath, Republic of Ireland.
Tel: (044) 40861 and (044) 42820

*Westmeath County Council ★ 4m from Mullingar town, on Tullamore road ★
Parking ★ Toilet facilities ★ Gardens and walks suitable for wheelchairs ★ Dogs
on lead ★ Garden open May to Sept, 12 noon – 6pm ★ Entrance: IR£1, children
IR50p*

The Jealous Wall is one of those typically Gothic–Irish follies, built in 1760
to separate two squabbling brothers. It looks antique and is impressive.
Otherwise this garden does not abound in interest, but there are some fine
trees and a large walled garden, containing some bedding displays, and it is
pleasant to be on the terraces which drop in steps to the shores of Lough
Ennel, with views of its waters and islands.

BIRR CASTLE DESMESNE ★★   7
Birr, Co. Offaly, Republic of Ireland. Tel: (0509) 20056

*Earl of Rosse ★ In town of Birr, 82m W of Dublin ★ Parking outside castle gates
★ Coffee shop for lunch, tea, etc. at the entrance gates. Picnics in walled garden ★
Toilet facilities ★ Suitable for wheelchairs ★ Dogs on lead ★ Plants for sale ★
Shops ★ 1995 exhibition running May to Sept, daily, 2.30 – 5.30pm ★ Castle not
open ★ Desmesne open all year, daily ★ Entrance: Jan to Mar and Nov to Dec:
IR£2.60, children IR£1.30. April to Oct: IR£3.20, children IR£1.60, groups of
20 or more IR£2.60 per person, children IR£1.30*

The Victorian Gothic castle dominates vistas which strike through the park
and at whose centre is the slumbering 'Leviathan' (a giant telescope which
made Birr famous last century). Around, in profusion, are rare trees and
shrubs especially, many raised from seed received from central China in the
1930s. Over one of the rivers is a beautiful suspension bridge, and hidden
amongst laurels is a Victorian fernery with recently restored water-works.
Evergreen conifers, golden willows, carpets of daffodils, and world-record
box hedges, magnolias in the river garden, a newly replanted cherry avenue
and the original plant of *Paeonia* 'Anne Rosse' are mere selections of the
many attractions. It is invigorating to walk around the lake, glimpsing the
castle, examining the shrubs and trees (many of which are specially
labelled), and revelling in the peace and quiet of central Ireland – two
counties can be visited in one brief walk. It is fair to add that the beauties
of this garden, which owe so much to the late Anne, Countess of Rosse,
have given her international fame as a gardener. Birr has justly won several
national awards.

THE BOTANIC GARDEN PARK   8
Stranmillis Road, Belfast, Co Antrim, Northern Ireland.
Tel: (01232) 324902

*Belfast City Council Parks Department ★ Between Queen's University and the
Ulster Museum, Stranmillis ★ Parking outside ★ Refreshments: facilities in the
Ulster Museum ★ Toilet facilities ★ Suitable for wheelchairs ★ Dogs on lead ★
Open daily, 7.30am to dusk. Palm House and Tropical Ravine, summer,
weekdays, 10am – 5pm, weekends and public holidays, 2 – 5pm; winter,*

weekdays, 10am – 4pm, weekends and public holidays, 2 – 4pm. Guided tours and group visits at any time by arrangement ★ Entrance: free

Established in 1827, this became a public park in 1895. As well as two magnificent double herbaceous borders and a rose garden with 8,000 roses, there are two other reasons to visit this otherwise unexceptional park – the curvilinear iron and glass conservatory (1839 – 52), one of the finest Victorian glasshouses (Richard Turner built only the wings; the dome is by Young of Edinburgh). It was restored in the 1970s and contains a small collection of tropical plants with massed displays of 'pot mums' and the like in season (again well-grown and finely displayed, but not everyone's favourite). The Tropical Ravine House is the greater delight, and also recently restored. This is 'High Victoriana', with ferns, bananas, lush tropical vines and tree ferns, goldfish in the Amazon lily pond, and a waterfall worked with a chain-pull! Marvellous, evocative of bygone crinoline days.

BROOK HALL   9
65 Culmore Road, Londonderry, Northern Ireland.
Tel: (01504) 351297

Mr D. Gilliland ★ N of Londonderry about ¹⁄₂m from roundabout on west side of Foyle Bridge ★ Partly suitable for wheelchairs ★ Open by appointment ★ Entrance: by donation

This mature arboretum on the shores of Loch Foyle contains a good collection of trees and shrubs (including rhododendrons). Fortunately the planting was never cramped so fine specimens are seen to good advantage. *Azara microphylla* is a robust tree here, showing again that the north coast of Ireland has a remarkably temperate climate. The trees and shrubs are labelled and a catalogue has been prepared.

BUTTERSTREAM ★★   10
Trim, Co. Meath, Republic of Ireland.

Jim Reynolds ★ Best season: summer ★ Partly suitable for wheelchairs ★ Plants for sale ★ Open April to Sept, daily, 11am – 6pm ★ Entrance: IR£3

Like all the best gardens, this is a single-handed work of art. A series of compartments contains different arrangements of plants, ranging from a formal box-hedged garden of old roses and lilies, to an informal gold garden carpeted with ferns and hostas. In the main garden a selection of choice herbaceous perennials in an island bed encircled by wide borders processes through the summer from whites and blues to yellows and reds – phlox, kniphofia, lobelia, macleaya and allium are only a few of the genera represented. A formal pool, replete with water lilies and carp, is flagged in Liscannor stone and large terracotta pots of box topiary stand sentinel. A view across the rich pastures of adjoining farmland adds to the sense of a Tuscan villa garden. The large tennis lawn has a restrained gallery of clematis, deep purple hedges and a rustic summerhouse. New features include a Gothic pavilion, a small laburnum archway skirted by box and a maturing yew obelisk still caged in its wooden trellis. It is delightful to find a garden being developed with such enthusiasm and style.

CARNFUNNOCK COUNTRY PARK 11
Coast Road, Drains Bay, Larne, Co. Antrim, Northern Ireland.
Tel: (01574) 270541

Larne Borough Council ★ 4m N of Larne on the Antrim coast road ★ Best season:
spring/summer ★ Parking ★ Refreshments: in coffee shop ★ Toilet facilities ★
Suitable for wheelchairs ★ Dogs in country park, but guide dogs only in walled
garden ★ Shop ★ Country Park open all year at all times. Walled Garden open
Easter to Sept, 10am – 8pm; Oct to Easter 10am – 4pm. Maze (deciduous) open
June to Sept, Mon – Fri, 12 noon – 5pm, Sat and Sun, 1 – 6pm ★ Entrance:
country park and walled garden free, maze £1.20, children 60p

The main attraction is the Time Garden, a display of the history of time
with more than a dozen different sundials catching the sun in the shelter of
the old walled garden. This steep site was planted and landscaped, complete
with post-modernist pergolas and excess of hardworks, in 1990. Nearby,
9,000 hornbeams were used to make a maze in the shape of Northern Ireland
for the International Year of the Maze in 1991. Both features are in the
centre of parkland with walks among mature trees high up to an ice-house
and fine views of the sea. Activity centre with free child-play area.

CASTLE WARD 12
Strangford, Downpatrick, Co. Down, Northern Ireland.
Tel: (01396) 881204

The National Trust ★ 7m NE of Downpatrick, 1½m W of Strangford village on
A25, on S shore of Strangford Lough entrance by Ballyculter Lodge ★ Parking ★
Refreshments : light lunches and teas ★ Toilet facilities, inc. disabled ★ Suitable
for wheelchairs ★ Dogs on lead ★ Shop ★ House open different dates ★ Estate and
grounds open all year, dawn to dusk ★ Entrance: parking charge £3.50 (£1.75
when house and other facilities closed)

A beautifully-situated landscape park on a peninsula near the mouth of
Strangford Lough enhances the 1760s house with its classical west front and
a Gothic east front. Both house and decorative Lady Anne's Temple
command the heights. Below lie an impressive canal and yew walks, features
retained from the gardens of a previous early eighteenth-century house. The
sunken Windsor Garden has lost much of its intricate bedding but there are
colourful borders above leading to the rockery and a sentinel row of cordylines and Florence Court yews.

CASTLEWELLAN NATIONAL ARBORETUM ★★ 13
Castlewellan, Co. Down, Northern Ireland.

Forest Service, Dept of Agriculture (Northern Ireland) ★ In Castlewellan town,
25m S of Belfast, 4m W of Newcastle ★ Parking inc. disabled ★ Refreshments:
summer only ★ Toilet facilities ★ Partly suitable for wheelchairs ★ Dogs on lead ★
Open all year ★ Entrance: cars £2.50, minibuses £5, coaches £17.50

The walled garden, now called the Annesley Garden, contains an outstanding
collection of mature trees and shrubs, many planted before the turn of the
century by the Earl Annesley. Original specimens of some of Castlewellan's
cultivars thrive here, in fine condition. In the spring and summer there are
many rhododendrons in bloom, and scarlet Chilean fire-bushes (*Embothrium*

coccineum). In mid-summer, the snow-carpet is the fallen petals of the unequalled collection of eucryphia. The arboretum has a formal axis, with two fountain pools and steps. An herbaceous border runs along part of this. Beyond the walls is a new spring garden, planted with heathers, dwarf conifers and birch, and with flowering trees (malus, prunus, etc.) Signposted walks lead into the forest and round the magnificent lake. A caravan and camping ground within the forest park provides a wonderful base for exploring this part of Ireland and for visiting the other famous County Down gardens. Castlewellan is well known to everyone for the golden Leyland cypress that came from here – don't be dismayed – the arboretum contains many more wonderful plants, some unique, all in their prime. You will not see decrepit trees here – the maintenance and labelling is exceptionally good.

CREAGH GARDENS 14
Skibbereen, Co. Cork, Republic of Ireland. Tel: (028) 22121

Gwendoline Harold-Barry Trust ★ 4m from Skibbereen on road to Baltimore – on right through white-painted entrance gates ★ Parking. Small coaches only ★ Toilet facilities ★ Partly suitable for wheelchairs ★ Dogs on lead* Open all year, daily, 10am – 6pm ★ Entrance: IR£2, children IR£1

Definitely a garden for those who seek solitude and silence, far from traffic. Paths lead through woodland underplanted with rhododendron species and cultivars, and down to a sea estuary. A serpentine mill-pond is now fringed with gunnera, cordyline and hydrangea, the bold effect inspired by the paintings of 'Le Douanier' Rousseau. There are some fine tender species, including *Telopea truncata*, *Datura sanguinea*, several varieties of abutilon and a good collection of camellias. Take note also of the magnificent cryptogamic flora. In the walled garden there are angora rabbits and many old varieties of fowl. A valiant garden lovingly maintained wherein one feels the wilderness is being controlled, creating a truly wild, Irish pleasaunce.

CROM 15
**Newtownbutler, Co. Fermanagh, Northern Ireland.
Tel: (0136573) 8174**

The National Trust ★ 3m W of Newtownbutler on the Newtownbutler – Crom road ★ Parking ★ Picnics welcome ★ Toilet facilities, inc disabled ★ Partly suitable for wheelchairs ★ Dogs on lead ★ Visitor Centre with jetty to allow cruiser access. Boat hire available ★ Castle is not owned by the National Trust – please respect the areas marked private ★ Estate open April to Sept, Mon – Sat, 10am – 6pm, Sun, 12 noon – 6pm. Guided walks by arrangement ★ Entrance: £2.50 parking charge (1994 price)

Many lovely walks can be enjoyed at this heavily-wooded lough shore and island desmesne though no formal gardens remain. The Trust's aim is to keep up this estate as a nature conservation site. The notable features to visit are a pair of ancient and venerable yew trees. Cross the White Bridge to Inisherk Island and survey the naturally picturesque landscape enhanced by W.S. Gilpin in the 1830s for the present house. A wealth of interesting estate buildings are used as eye-catchers and surprises such as the Boat House, Tea House and the island folly, Crichton Tower. The local church and ruins of the seventeenth-century Old Castle are incorporated into the vistas.

DERREEN ★   16
Lauragh, Killarney, Co. Kerry, Republic of Ireland.

The Hon. David Bigham ★ 15m from Kenmare on road along S side of Kenmare Bay, towards the Healy Pass ★ Best season: April/May ★ Parking ★ Refreshments: in tea room in Gardener's Cottage near car park. Picnic area on lawn near car park ★ Toilet facilities ★ Open April to Oct, daily, 11am – 6pm ★ Entrance: IR£2 (1994 price)

The broad sweep of plush lawn and the bald outcroppings of rock by the house do not prepare visitors for the lushness of the walks which weave through native woodlands and palisades of jade-stemmed bamboo. The evocatively-named King's Oozy – a path that has a hankering to be a river – leads to a grove of tall, archaic tree-ferns (*Dicksonia antarctica*) with socks of filmy ferns. Wellies are the plantsman's only requirement to enjoy the rhododendrons that shelter among clipped entanglements of *Gaultheria shallon*. Probably one of the wettest places in Britain and Ireland, a fact you're reminded of by the lushness (and midges in season!)

DOWNHILL   17
Co. Londonderry, Northern Ireland.

The National Trust ★ 5m W of Coleraine on A2 coast road, 1m W of Castlerock ★ Parking at Bishop's Gate and at Lion Gate ★ Suitable for wheelchairs ★ Dogs on lead ★ Mussenden Temple open 14th to 18th April; rest of April, May, June and Sept, Sat, Sun and Bank Holiday Mons; July and Aug, daily, all 12 noon – 6pm ★ Grounds open all year ★ Entrance: free

For the architectural historian this is a must – the Mussenden Temple, sited on the clifftop with spectacular views along the coast of Northern Ireland, must be one of the most extraordinary libraries (that was its original purpose) in the world. The walk there is rough. The ruins of Downhill House, the Earl-Bishop's private house, are gaunt, and from the rear towards the Bishop's Gate Miss Jan Eccles has created a garden memorable for the miniature water meadow full of candelabra primroses (yellow and pink) with startling clumps of dark *Iris kaempferi*, embothriums, crinodendrons and many other unusual trees and shrubs. Old buttresses have now been cleared. Dressed stones from tumbledown buildings and armless statues are enveloped with happy plantings, bergenia and fuchsia, roses spilling from a rickety pergola. A gem of a garden to which the National Trust has been devoting more attention.

DRIMNAGH CASTLE   18
Longmile Road, Dublin 12. Tel: (1) 4502530

Christian Brother Community; leased to Drimnagh Castle Committee ★ 3m SW of city centre. Signposted ★ Parking in school grounds ★ House open, dependent on volunteer manning ★ Garden open April to Oct, Wed, Sat, Sun and Bank Holidays, 12 noon – 5pm; Nov to March, Sun and Bank Holidays, 2 – 5pm, and at other times by appointment ★ Entrance: castle and garden £1.50, OAP and students £1, children 50p

Drimnagh Castle, although well known to generations of small boys, lay in semi-ruins alongside a modern brick secondary school. A local voluntary committee aided by an Taisce and supported by the Christian Brother Community started restoring the castle some years ago. Five years ago the Irish Garden Plant Society was approached to design a new garden to replace the derelict one and Jim Reynolds of Butterstream (see entry) designed a seventeenth-century box garden with a hornbeam alley and perimeter beech hedge. This is a simple garden, intended to reflect the garden style of an old moated castle which has various elements dating from the fifteenth to eighteenth centuries. Not a plantsman's garden but a pleasant excursion with the castle being the main attraction.

DUNLOE CASTLE GARDENS   19
Hotel Dunloe Castle, Beaufort, Killarney, Co. Kerry, Republic of Ireland. Tel: (064) 44111

Killarney Hotels Ltd ★ 4m W of Killarney, off the Killorgan Road. Signposted ★ Parking ★ ☆ Refreshments ★ Toilet facilities in hotel ★ Suitable for wheelchairs ★ Dogs on lead ★ Open early May to Sept, but opening date varies – check with hotel ★ Entrance: free. Catalogue optional IR£1 (1994 price)

On a superb site facing the Gap of Dunloe lie the imposing buildings of the Hotel Dunloe Castle, opened in 1965, surrounded by acres of parkland and gardens with magnificent and unusual trees and shrubs. Visitors and hotel guests may wander freely and appreciate the well-kept lawns, colourful planting, walled garden and the ruined fort of Dunloe Castle. The more serious garden visitor will spot such tender specimens as *Eriobotrya deflexa*, *Glyptostrobus pensilis*, *Banksia marginata* and *Telopea oreades* with the aid of a catalogue compiled by Roy Lancaster which lists trees and shrubs of note and identifies their location on a plan. Early plantings of 1920 have been continually added to and the whole maintained impeccably. Take a two-hour stroll with the catalogue and then subject yourself to the culinary delights of a Grade A hotel restaurant.

EMO COURT   20
Emo, Co. Laois, Republic of Ireland. Tel: (0502) 26110

Mr Cholmeley-Harrison ★ 8m NE of Portlaoise on the R422 between the N7 and the R419 ★ Parking ★ Toilet facilities ★ Partly suitable for wheelchairs ★ House open mid-March to mid-Oct, Mon only, 2 – 6pm and by arrangement ★ Garden open daily 10.30am – 5.30pm ★ Entrance: IR£2, OAP and children IR£1 (house and gardens IR£4.50)

The garden is a splendid parkland setting for James Gandon's magnificent house, which dates, like many of the trees, from the end of the eighteenth century. There are fine specimen trees and arrays of Irish yews stand sentry on the lawns. Varied avenues and walks have been planned through the woodland, leading to vistas of the house and a large, but neglected, lake. Statues, cunningly sited among the glades, offer pleasing surprises. There are recent plantings of trees, shrubs and perennials, particularly azaleas and magnolias.

FERNHILL ★   21
Sandyford, Co. Dublin, Republic of Ireland. Tel: (1) 2956000

Mrs Sally Walker ★ On main Dublin – Enniskerry road, 8m from central Dublin

★ *Parking* ★ *Toilet facilities* ★ *Partly suitable for wheelchairs* ★ *Plants for sale* ★ *Open March to Nov, Tues – Sat, 11am – 5pm, Sun, 2 – 6pm, Bank Holiday Mons, 17th April, 5th June, 7th Aug, 30th Oct, 11am – 5pm* ★ *Entrance: IR£2.50, OAP IR£1.50, children IR£1*

The plantings of rhododendron species and cultivars provide spectacles of colour from early spring into mid-summer; many of the more tender rhododendrons flourish here. The garden is situated on the eastern slope of the Dublin Mountains and has a laurel lawn, some fine nineteenth-century plantings and an excellent flowering specimen of *Michelia doltsopa*. The walkways through the wooded areas wind steeply past many other shrubs, principally those that thrive on acid soil – pieris and camellias are also outstanding. There is a rock garden and a water garden near the house, and drifts of daffodils in the spring. In the summer there are the roses and a good collection of herbaceous plants, many as underplanting through the woodland.

FLORENCE COURT 22
Florencecourt, Enniskillen, Co. Fermanagh, Northern Ireland.
Tel: (01365) 348249; Fax (01365) 348873

The National Trust ★ *8m SW of Enniskillen, via A4 Sligo road and A32 Swanlinbar road, 4m from Marble Arch Caves* ★ *Parking* ★ *Refreshments: teas and lunches in the Granary Tea Room* ★ *Toilet facilities, inc. disabled* ★ *Suitable for wheelchairs. Batricar available* ★ *Dogs on lead* ★ *Shop* ★ *House open April, May and Sept, Sat, Sun and Bank Holidays; June to Aug, daily except Tues, all 1 – 6pm* ★ *Estate open all year, 10am – 7pm (Oct to March 4pm). Closed 25th Dec. Parties by arrangement* ★ *Entrance: Forest Park and Pleasure Gardens £1.50 per car (house £2.50, children £1.25, groups £1.80 per person (£3.50 after hours))*

The original, the mother of all Irish yews (*Taxus baccata* 'Fastigiata'), still grows in the original garden site – accessible by well-marked woodland paths and about a quarter of a mile from the splendid mansion at Florence Court. Well worth the walk, the gravel path allows glimpses of the mountains and the fine 'Brownian' park in front of the house. Some fine weeping beeches, Japanese maples and old rhododendrons grow in the pleasure grounds. There are ponds and a rose garden in the walled garden Strong shoes essential (especially in rainy season!) if you wish to pay respects to the venerable, 250-year-old tree. Ice-house, rose cottage, water-driven saw mill and recently-restored summerhouse, eel bridge and hydraulic ram. The nearby caves (open to public) are worth visiting too, making a rewarding day out, with some fine views.

FOTA ARBORETUM ★ 23
Fota Trust, Carrigtwohill, Co. Cork, Republic of Ireland.
Tel: (021) 812728

Fota Trust ★ *9m E of Cork city, on road to Cobh* ★ *Parking beside arboretum (also serving Fota Wildlife Park). IR£1 per car payable at automatic barrier* ★ *Refreshments at Wildlife Park* ★ *Toilet facilities in car park* ★ *Suitable for wheelchairs* ★ *Dogs on lead* ★ *Shop in Wildlife Park* ★ *Arboretum open April to Oct, daily, 10am – 6pm, Sun, 11am – 6pm* ★ *Entrance: free for arboretum*

Perhaps the wonders of Fota are best appreciated in summer when the obvious

distractions like camellias, embothriums, drimys, pieris and most of the rhododendrons have finished flowering. There is no lack of colour; the walls sparkle
with abutilons and cestrums, and the myrtles take on a pinkish hue. *Davidia
involucrata* may be bereft of handkerchiefs, but admire instead the elaborate
flowers of *Magnolia* x *wieseneri*, or the frothy white ones of *Eucalyptus dele-
gatensis*. Now is the time to appreciate the complicated growth of the Chilean
hazel, the immense canopy of the fern-leaved beech, a perfect *Pinus montezumae* and the marvellous bark of the stone pine. Note the wickedly spiny species
of *Colletia* and the elegance of *Restio subverticillatus*. Spend a few minutes in the
cool fernery. All this to the accompaniment of hoots and the chattering of
exotic birds and animals in the adjacent wildlife park and the antics of the red
squirrel. How disconcerting for the visitor to be left pondering on the future of
the house, closed indefinitely due to structural damage.

GLANLEAM HOUSE TROPICAL GARDENS 24
Valentia Island, Co. Kerry, Republic of Ireland. Tel: (066) 76176

*Mrs Meta Kreissig ★ On Valentia Island. Signposted from the bridge ★ Parking ★
Refreshments ★ Toilet facilities ★ Dogs on lead ★ Plants for sale ★ Open all year,
10am – 6pm ★ Entrance: IR£2.50, OAP and students IR£1.50, children IR£1*

Set on the northeast edge of Valentia Island, in a position rivalling Ilnacullin
(see entry), Glanleam's fame seems to date from the time of the nineteenth
Knight of Kerry who first planted exotics here, from whose extensive walled
garden produce was once exported. An organic vegetable garden is now
being developed. The present owner has replanted with care, using choice
tender species which bodes well for the future. The trail begins with a bog
garden, then falls away to the sea, fringing wooded slopes where areas have
been cleared for such architectural gems as *Butia capitata*, *Lithocarpus edulis*,
telanthophoras, fascicularias and puyas along with tree ferns, astelias and
correas. Higher up in the garden are myrtle groves wherein *Myrtus apiculata*
'Glanleam Gold' was spotted as a chance seedling around 1957, and here and
there can be seen the boles of what must have been enormous trees. Add to
this Soay sheep, bamboos and rushing streams banked with saxifrage, and
you have a garden to return to.

GLENVEAGH CASTLE ★★ 25
**Glenveagh National Park, Churchill, Letterkenny, Co. Donegal,
Republic of Ireland. Tel: (074) 37088/37090/37262**

*Office of Public Works ★ 15m NW of Letterkenny ★ Parking at Visitor Centre.
Access to garden and castle by official minicoaches only ★ Refreshments and meals
★ Toilet facilities ★ Castle open, IR£1 ★ Garden open 15th April to 30th Oct,
daily, 10am – 6.30pm (open to 7.30pm on Sun, June to Aug). Other times by
arrangement ★ Entrance: IR£1.50, OAP and groups per person IR£1, students
and children IR60p*

The centrepiece of the Glenveagh National Park is the garden around
Glenveagh Castle. The castle is set beside a mountain lough encircled with
high, peat-blanketed mountains, in the middle of windswept moorlands, a
most unpromising site. But, as in so many Irish gardens, surprises are count-
less. The lower lawn garden has fringing shrubberies and, beyond, steep
pathways wind through oak woods in which are planted scented, white-flow-

ered rhododendrons, and numerous other tender shrubs from southern lands. Terraced enclosures with terracotta pots of plants and sculpture are encountered unexpectedly. The *jardin potager* at the castle has rank on rank of ornamental vegetables and flowering herbs. This is a paradise for plantsmen and gardeners keen on seeing fine specimens of unusual aspect – *Pseudopanax ferox*, *Fascicularia bicolor*, and many more. Linger, and walk the mountain sides. Then take the last bus back to the remarkable heather-roofed Visitor Centre with its imaginative landscaping.

GLIN CASTLE GARDENS 26
Glin, Co. Limerick, Republic of Ireland. Tel: (068) 34173

Madam FitzGerald and the Knight of Glin ★ 30m W of Limerick on the N69 ★ Parking ★ Teashop with toilet facilities is situated a five-minute car ride away along the main road from Foynes ★ Suitable for wheelchairs ★ Castle open ★ Garden open May and June, daily, 10am – 12 noon, 2 – 4pm, otherwise by appointment (ring above number or (068) 36230) ★ Entrance: IR£3 (IR£2 per person for groups)

The formal garden could not be simpler with its lawns and two domed bays flanking a path to a sundial and an elegant *Parrotia persica*, beyond which is a meadow with daffodils and a woodland with fine old trees. Colourful in spring with magnolias and bluebells, in early summer rhododendrons are still providing a splash of colour in contrast to the cool tones of a large *Abutilon vitifolium* while the rather sombre grey walls of the castle are relieved by climbing plants. An outstanding feature is the walled garden on a steep slope, with its mathematically-neat rows of vegetables and herbs, figs, fruit, roses and clematis, a castellated henhouse, rustic temple with marble incumbent, and a lovely view across the Shannon over walls and undulating slate roofs of the old farmyard. If you like kitchen gardens, Glin's will please you. Glin is also noted for its landscape park which is 'defended' by three sets of Gothick castellated lodges built at the same time as the castle was battlemented in *c.* 1820-30. One set, on the main road, is the simple restaurant and shop, mentioned above.

GRAIGUECONNA ★ 27
Old Connaught, Bray, Co. Wicklow, Republic of Ireland.
Tel: (1) 2822273

Mr and Mrs John Brown ★ Drive from Dublin on the main Wicklow road. Turn off into Bray on a slip road. At the small garden centre or the first traffic lights turn right, follow road to Y-junction and the house is on this corner ★ Best season: May to July ★ Partly suitable for wheelchairs ★ Open for the Wicklow Festival and by appointment for groups of four or more ★ Entrance: IR£3

A three-acre garden, painstakingly cared for, surrounding a Georgian house. A fine collection of old shrub roses fills the walled garden with fragrance. The borders are filled with hellebores, primulas, lobelias, *Philadelphus mexicanus*, and other like shrubs. A small paved and gravel courtyard separates the main garden from the house and conservatory. Here tender plants soak up the southerly sun. A huge old plant of *Ceanothus* 'Emily Brown' vies with *Beschorneria yuccoides* for pride of place. Osteospermums and penstemons are used to great effect and everywhere there are clever colour combinations. The conservatory holds a small but fine collection of southern hemisphere plants – large datura, *Passiflora antioquiensis*, etc. The historic rock garden now contains ground cover, small shrubs, ferns and trees.

GUY L. WILSON DAFFODIL GARDEN ★   28
University of Ulster, Coleraine, Co. Londonderry, Northern Ireland. Tel: (01265) 44141

University of Ulster ★ On Cromore road, about 1m N of Coleraine town on road to Portstewart ★ Best season: spring ★ Parking ★ Dogs on lead ★ Open daily ★ Entrance: free

The daffodils in this garden represent one of the National collections (established under the patronage of the National Council for the Conservation of Plants and Gardens although it was commenced long before the NCCPG scheme). It is principally based on Irish-bred cultivars, particularly those of Guy Wilson; however, among the 1000-plus cultivars represented are daffodils from New Zealand and the USA, as well as Britain, and there are both old and modern cultivars. The daffodils are interplanted with shrubs in island beds. The setting is attractive, but the garden now shows signs of diminished care and attention due to cut-backs by the university. Vandalism clearly is a problem – flowers wantonly damaged and picked daffodils strewn on paths were seen on a recent visit. The labels have all been removed (to prevent theft) which makes a nonsense of the collection as an educational facility. The purpose of such a collection is to allow people to look and learn – we must sympathise with the problems faced by the university and hope that some imaginative scheme can be devised to allow visitors to discover the names of the host of daffodils.

HEYWOOD GARDEN ★   29
Ballinakill, Co. Laois, Republic of Ireland. Tel: (0502) 33563

Office of Public Works ★ Outside Ballinakill village. 3m from Abbeyleix (turn E in town following sign to Ballinakill) ★ Parking ★ Partly suitable for wheelchairs ★ Dogs on lead ★ Open May to Aug, 11am – 6pm by appointment ★ Entrance: IR£2, students and children IR£1

Edwin Lutyens' walled garden with pergola and lawns is acknowledged as his finest small-scale work in Ireland. It is a gem, now restored close to its original state as far as the walls and ornaments are concerned. The planting is being restored, in the style of Gertrude Jekyll with the advice of Graham Stuart Thomas. On the driveway leading towards the school buildings is an eighteenth-century folly. Heywood Garden has now been recognised as a heritage garden of historic and architectural importance and it is being maintained by the Office of Public Works.

ILNACULLIN
(commonly known as Garinish Island) ★★   30
**Glengarriff, Co. Cork, Republic of Ireland.
Tel: (027) 63040; Fax: (027) 63149**

National Parks and Monuments Service, Office of Public Works ★ On an island in Bantry Bay ★ Toilet facilities ★ Open March and Oct, daily, 10am – 4.30pm, Sun, 1 – 5pm, April to June and Sept, daily, 10am – 6.30pm, Sun, 1 – 7pm, July and

Aug, daily, 9.30am – 6.30pm, Sun, 11am – 7pm ★ Entrance: IR£2, OAP IR£1.50, students and children IR£1, family IR£5, groups of 20 or more IR£1.50 per person. Travel is by boat, charge for which was IR£5 return fare

The boat trip across the sheltered inlets of Bantry Bay, past sun-bathing seals, with views of the Caha Mountains, is doubly rewarding; landing at the slipway you gain entrance to one of Ireland's gardening jewels begun in the early 1900s. Most visitors cluster around the Casita – an Italianate garden – and reflecting pool, designed by Harold Peto, to enjoy (on clear days) spectacular scenery, and some quite indifferent annual bedding. But walk beyond, to the Temple of the Winds, through shrubberies filled with plants usually confined indoors – tree ferns, southern hemisphere conifers, rhododendron species and cultivars. A flight of stone steps leads to the Martello tower, and thence the path returns to the walled garden with its double-sided herbaceous border. Plant enthusiasts can spend many happy hours with such delights as *Lyonothamnus floribundus* var. *aspleniifolius* and myriad manuka (*Leptospermum scoparium*, the New Zealand tea tree); take a picnic and linger; if wet, bring boots or strong shoes and an umbrella. Wonderful. If lost for a thought, ponder on the fact that 'Capability' Brown never visited Ireland.

IRISH NATIONAL WAR MEMORIAL PARK 31
Dublin, Republic of Ireland.

Trustees of the Irish National War Memorial Committee and The Office of Public Works ★ In Islandbridge ★ Parking ★ Suitable for wheelchairs ★ Open all year, except 25th Dec, during daylight hours ★ Entrance: free

Sir Edwin Lutyens' Irish gardens (see also Heywood, Co. Laois) are not nearly as well-known as his English gardens. This memorial garden (1938, dedicated 1988), recently restored and planted anew, is typical of his reserved, calm style with sunken rose gardens, a simple altar stone, colonnades and formal plantings of trees. In the bookroom are volumes with the names of Irish men and women who died in World War I.

IVEAGH GARDENS 32
Clonmel Street, Dublin 2. Tel: (1) 6613111

Office of Public Works ★ Access via Clonmel Street or University College, Earlsfort Terrace ★ Metered parking nearby ★ Suitable for wheelchairs (Clonmel Street entrance only) ★ Dogs ★ Open all year, Mon – Sat, 8.30am – 7pm, Suns and Bank Holidays, 10am – 7pm (closes earlier Oct to March) ★ Entrance: free

This was one of the forgotten – and almost vanished – gardens of Dublin. Originally attached to Iveagh House, home of the Earls of Iveagh, it had been allowed to go into decay when Iveagh House became the Department of External Affairs (now Foreign Affairs), despite the fact that the University College had access to it through a small gateway in one of its walls for many years. The Office of Public Works has recently decided to open it to the public and begin restoration. Already it is becoming an interesting public garden appealing to the droves of workers who emerge for lunch from nearby offices. An old Victorian fountain is being renovated and the maze replanted. An old rose garden, long disappeared save for the pattern in the grass, will be replanted soon. Worth seeking out as an example of Georgian/early Victorian style.

JAPANESE GARDEN ★ 33
Irish National Stud, Tully, Kildare, Co. Kildare, Republic of Ireland. Tel: (045) 21617

Irish National Stud ★ 1m outside Kildare town, 25m SW of Dublin ★ Parking ★ Refreshments ★ Toilet facilities ★ Plants for sale ★ Shop ★ The Irish National Stud and Horse Museum open. Lego area for children ★ Garden open 17th March to Oct, daily, 9.30am – 6pm. Guided tours on request for groups of 20 or more ★ Entrance: IR£4, OAP and students IR£3, children IR£2 (Japanese Garden, Irish National Stud and Horse Museum)

Created between the years 1906-10. Devised by Colonel William Hall-Walker (later Lord Wavertree), a wealthy Scotsman of a famous brewery family, and laid out by the Japanese Eida and his son Minoru, the gardens, symbolising the 'Life of Man', are acclaimed as the finest Japanese gardens in Europe. This is not a plantsman's garden, for few of the plants are Japanese; to be sure there are some excellent old maples, but many of the trees and shrubs are clipped and shaped beyond reason. The overshadowing Scots pines are exquisite. A pathway meanders through artificial caves, into a watery stream, past the tranquil ponds and on to the weeping trees of the grave. Beautiful stone lanterns grace the garden which is in the style of a Japanese 'tea garden'. On a misty day with smoke from a distant fire billowing across, this visitor recalls it as mysterious, beautiful.

JOHN F. KENNEDY ARBORETUM ★ 34
New Ross, Co. Wexford, Republic of Ireland. Tel: (051) 88171

Office of Public Works ★ 8m S of New Ross ★ Parking ★ Refreshments: café mid–March to mid-Oct, Suns only; May to Sept, daily. Picnic area ★ Toilet facilities ★ Suitable for wheelchairs ★ Dogs on lead ★ Visitor Centre with Kennedy memorial and video ★ Arboretum open daily except 25th Dec and 14th April, May to Aug, 10am – 8pm, April and Sept, 10am – 6.30pm, Oct to March, 10am – 5pm ★ Entrance: IR£2, OAP IR£1.50, students and children IR£1, family IR£5. Heritage card available

A modern spacious arboretum laid out in botanical sequence with rides; from the summit of a nearby hill is a superb panorama of the arboretum and Co. Wexford. Best to begin at the viewpoint – turn left just beyond the main entrance and drive to summit car park to see the layout. At the arboretum be prepared for a long walk; fortunately those not keen on gardening tend to linger near the café so that the distant reaches are quiet and empty. Planting began in the 1960s and now 4500 different trees and shrubs are growing, ranging from conifers to flowering shrubs. Most species are represented by several specimens, and keen plantsmen can linger long examining the groups. Good labelling. A colourful planting of dwarf conifers is on the western side, a small lake on the east. While primarily a scientific collection, the arboretum is now achieving an established elegance.

KILLRUDDERY 35
Bray, Co. Wicklow, Republic of Ireland. Tel: (1) 2863405

Earl and Countess of Meath ★ 1m S of Bray on road to Greystones ★ Parking ★ Toilet facilities ★ Partly suitable for wheelchairs ★ House open with conducted tours at extra charge, and at other times for pre-arranged groups ★ Garden open May, June, Sept, daily, 1 – 5pm ★ Entrance: IR£1, OAP, students and children over 12 IR50p, under 12 free (house and gardens £IR2.50, OAP, students and children over 12 IR£1.50). All children must be accompanied

The joy of Killruddery, a seventeenth-century garden with nineteenth-century embellishments, is the formal hedges, known as 'The Angles', set beside the formal canals which lead to a ride into the distant hills. There is a collection of nineteenth-century French cast statuary, a sylvan theatre created in bay, and a fountain pool enclosed in a beech hedge. The excellent conservatory (nineteenth-century) alas, has a perspex dome (the cost of curved glass is horrendous!). The landscape features are unique, and Killruddery deserves to be better known, but it is not a garden for keen plantsmen without designer tastes.

KILMACURRAGH   36
Kilbride, Rathdrum, Co. Wicklow, Republic of Ireland.

Bill Dolan ★ From Dublin on the N11 road, turn right at The Old Tap pub. 1m further turn left at T-junction and watch for a gateway with curved granite wall and sequoiadendron trees ★ Parking in road ★ Partly suitable for wheelchairs but long walk from road ★ Open Feb – Nov, Mon – Fri, 10am – 4pm, Sat and Sun, 2 – 5.30pm ★ Entrance: IR£1.50

This garden is rated highly because of its atmosphere and magnificent ancient plants. It has no visitor facilities, but is open without hindrance to those who can find it. Behind the derelict eyesore of a house there is an incomparable avenue composed of alternating Irish yews and crimson rhododendrons – 'magical' is an overworked word, but the pattern of fallen blossoms on this pathway in May is magical. Beyond, paths wind through the arboretum, under rhododendrons taller and older than in most other gardens. The trees at Kilmacurragh include many unequalled specimens – rare conifers abound. If you can, visit it when crocus blossom is in the meadow, when the rhododendron flowers are tumbling down, at any time for elegant decrepitude. A secret pleasaunce; one hesitates to recommend it – for its secret then is lost.

KILWARLIN BATTLE GARDEN   37
Kilwarlin, Nr Hillsborough, Co. Down, Northern Ireland.

Moravian Church ★ Between Moira and Hillsborough – difficult to find but there are occasional signs to Moravian Chapel (OS ref J209588) ★ Open all year

One of Ireland's strangest 'gardens' comprising a series of grassy mounds that represents the site of the Battle of Thermopilae. Tucked away in the countryside near Moira, and reached by narrow country roads, the battle garden, created in the nineteenth century by the Rev. Zula (1834-44), is sited in the grounds of a small chapel. A place for those intrigued by the eccentricities of mankind.

KINOITH/BALLYMALOE COOKERY SCHOOL   38
Shanagarry, Cloyne, Co. Cork, Republic of Ireland.
Tel: (021) 646785/646727

Tim and Darina Allen ★ 23m E of Cork, between Cloyne and Ballycotton ★ Parking by the Cookery School ★ Refreshments by arrangement for groups only ★

Toilet facilities ★ Culinary herbs and herbaceous plants for sale ★ Open April to Sept, daily except Sun, 2.30 – 5pm and by arrangement for parties ★ Entrance: IR£3

The three formal gardens are an oasis of peace away from the intense activity of the Cookery School. The latest is planted with small fruit trees and a great variety of soft fruit. The largely organic vegetable garden appeals directly to the eye with its tapestry of edible flowers, red orach, ornamental cabbage and an asparagus bed confined by paths of old red brick. Note the newly-planted copper beech house, seakale in forcing pots and a novel use of rush matting. In the well-established herb garden, formal box hedging encloses mostly perennial culinary herbs, medicinal plants, runner beans and tall cardoons. A new pond garden has been completed with a folly reflected in the water and is now being planted. An old rose garden and new herbaceous borders are being developed out in the old orchard. These are working gardens, so expect some gaps, trimmed areas and new young plants.

LAKEMOUNT 39
**Barnavara Hill, Glanmire, Co. Cork, Republic of Ireland.
Tel: (021) 821052**

Brian Cross ★ 5m E of Cork, at the top of Barnavara Hill above Glanmire village ★ Restricted parking on road ★ Suitable for wheelchairs ★ Open April to Sept, daily, 11am – 5pm and by appointment ★ Entrance: IR£3

An immaculately-maintained two-acre hillside garden, with rhododendrons, azaleas and camellias in spring and plenty of summer interest, especially hydrangeas. There are paved areas on different levels, a pool and conservatory housing tender exotics, while to the rear of the house, a lawn slopes gently from a rock garden to beds with a mixed planting of trees, shrubs and herbaceous plants. This is an actively-evolving garden where new projects take shape and blend by means of skilful design and impeccable planting, which includes a wide range of unusual plants. The perfect antidote to too many wild Irish gardens.

LISMORE CASTLE GARDENS 40
Lismore, Co. Waterford, Republic of Ireland. Tel: (058) 54424

Duke and Duchess of Devonshire ★ Entrance in Lismore town ★ Parking ★ Toilet facilities inc. disabled in nearby Heritage Centre (old Courthouse) ★ Dogs on lead ★ Open 29th April to 10th Sept, daily, 1.45 – 4.45pm ★ Entrance: IR£2, children under 16 IR£1. Parties of 20 or more during normal working hours IR£1.80 per person, children IR80p (1994 prices)

The situation of the castle overlooking the River Blackwater is stunning. There are two gardens linked by the gatehouse entrance, the upper reached by a stairway in the gatehouse leads to terrace with vegetables and flowers, a reduced glasshouse by Joseph Paxton (an interesting ridge-furrow house) and a fine view from the main axis to the church spire. In the lower garden, a few steps down from the gatehouse are a few meritricious plants, but the principal feature, an ancient yew-walk carpeted softly with the dropped leaves, is wonderful. For that only can this be regarded as a garden of note – the rest is unremarkable. Yet Edmund Spenser is said to have written *The*

Fairie Queene here, and it is the Irish home of the Duke of Devonshire who has Chatsworth (see Derbyshire entry) to console him in England.

71 MERRION SQUARE   41
Dublin 2, Republic of Ireland. Tel: (1) 676281

Miss Sybil Connolly ★ On the W side of Merrion Square ★ Parking on roadway ★ Refreshments by arrangement ★ Toilet facilities ★ Eighteenth-century house and mews open ★ Garden open April to Oct, Mon – Fri, and Sat and Sun by appointment ★ Entrance: IR£3 (house, mews and garden IR£6; mews and garden IR£4)

This garden surprises the first-time visitor. It is 100 feet long and barely 30 feet wide. Not an easy shape to begin with but the owner has created a beautiful town garden which belies its position in the busy commercial hub of Dublin. A formal terrace framed with trellis, niches and containers of box and roses lead from the house down through a paved courtyard and into the garden. The old brick and blackstone walls are clothed with a fine specimen of wisteria, and roses, clematis, loniceras and actinidias add to the beauty of the old walls. Large specimens of *Cornus kousa*, *Pyrus salicifolia* 'Pendula', *Syringa vulgaris* 'Madame Lemoine' and *Viburnum plicatum* 'Mariesii' are stunning in season. *Paeonia* 'Joseph Rock' peeps from behind a small half-standard *Acer palmatum* var. *dissectum* 'Atropurpureum' and three semi-circular beds house old shrub roses and perennials. An old brick pathway winds past these beds and creates an impression of width and spaciousness, edged with well-kept lawn.

MOUNT CONGREVE ★★   42
**Kilmeaden, Co. Waterford, Republic of Ireland.
Tel: (051) 384115 (office)**

Mr Ambrose Congreve ★ Best season: spring ★ Open strictly by appointment ★ Entrance: IR£250 for visits organised by travel agents who specially ask for conducted tours but individuals are free to go around by themselves provided they have written or telephonic permission from the office

In emulation of Exbury, Ambrose Congreve has amassed an unequalled collection of rhododendron, camellia and magnolia species and cultivars, with many other trees as 'icing on the cake'. It is a staggering collection which cannot be adequately described in a single entry; 110 acres of shrubs, mass upon mass, since every cultivar is planted in groups. In addition to the flowering shrub collections, which include Mount Congreve hybrids, there are many other splendours, including a whole series of surprises, one of the most spectacular being a pagoda at the base of 80 ft cliffs. Highlights are memorable. In early March a forest of *Magnolia cambellii* offers pink to white goblets to the rooks. A languid walled garden, dominated by an ancient gingko, has a fine eighteenth-century vinery and range of glasshouses. In the borders, there is an extensive collection of herbaceous plants arranged in order of monthly flowering, May to July, a large arrangement for August plus a border for September and October – an unusual idea. There is far too much here to appreciate in one visit and it is satisfying to know the garden will eventually be left to the nation with a trust for maintenance for the first 25 years.

MOUNT STEWART HOUSE, GARDEN AND TEMPLE OF THE WINDS ★★ 43
Greyabbey, Newtownards, Co. Down, Northern Ireland.
Tel: (012477) 88387/88487; Fax: (012477) 88569

The National Trust ★ On Ards Peninsula, 5m from Newtownards on road (A20)
to Portaferry, 15m E of Belfast ★ Parking 300 yards ★ Refreshments: in tearoom
★ Toilet facilities ★ Partly suitable for wheelchairs. Batricar available ★ Shop ★
House open at different times ★ Garden open March, Suns only, 1 – 5pm; April
to Sept, daily, 10.30am – 6pm; Oct, Sat and Sun only, 10.30am – 6pm ★
Entrance: £2.70, children £1.35, parties £2 per person (house, garden and temple
£3.30, children £1.65, parties £2.60 per person). Different rates after-hours

Of all Ireland's gardens this is The One not to miss. Any adjective that
evokes beauty can be applied to it, and it's fun too. In the gardens in front of
the house is a collection of statuary, depicting British political and public
figures – dodos, monkeys and boars. The planting here is formal, with
rectangular beds of 'hot' and 'cool' colours. Beyond in the informal gardens
are mature trees and shrubs, a botanical collection with few equals, planted
with great panache and maintained with outstanding attention to detail.
Spires of giant lilies (*Cardiocrinum*), aspiring eucalyptus, banks of rhododendrons, ferns and blue poppies, rivers of candelabra primulas – and much
more. Walk along the lakeside path to the hill that affords a view over the
lake to the house. Rare tender shrubs such as *Metrosideros umbellata* flourish
here outside the walled family cemetery. Leading from it is the Jubilee
Avenue and its statue of a white stag. Mount Stewart is a whole day for
those keen on plants and it should be seen several times during the year truly
to savour its rich tapestry of plants and water, buildings and trees. The
Temple of the Winds, James 'Athenian' Stuart's banqueting hall of 1785, is
also memorable. Restoration of the topiary which once graced the Shamrock
garden has begun and more frames are being added year by year.

MOUNT USHER ★★ 44
Ashford, Co. Wicklow, Republic of Ireland. Tel: (0404) 40116/40205

Mrs Madelaine Jay ★ At Ashford, on main Dublin – Wexford road, 30m S of
Dublin ★ Parking ★ Refreshments: tea rooms, no picnics ★ Toilet facilities ★
Partly suitable for wheelchairs ★ Shopping courtyard ★ Open 17th March to Oct,
daily, 10.30am – 6pm ★ Entrance: IR£3, OAP, students and children IR£2.
Special group rates for groups of 20 or more

The Vartry river babbles through this exquisite garden over gentle weirs and
under bridges which allow visitors to meander through the collections. Mount
Usher is a plant-lovers' paradise. *Pinus montezumae* is always first port-of-call,
a shimmering tree, magnificent when the bluebells are in flower. The philosophy of Mount Usher eschews chemicals of all kinds, and the lawns are cut
in a cycle which allows the bulbs and wildflowers in them to seed naturally.
Throughout there are drifts of rhododendrons, fine trees and shrubs, including many that are difficult to cultivate outdoors in other parts of Britain and
Ireland. The grove of eucalyptus at the lower end of the valley is memorable;
a kiwi-fruit vine (*Actinidia chinensis*) cloaks the piers of a bridge, and beside
the tennis court is the gigantic original *Eucryphia* x *nymansensis* 'Mount
Usher'. In spring, bulbs, magnolias, and a procession of rhododendrons, in

summer eucryphias and leptospermums, in autumn russet and crimson leaves falling from maples – a garden for all seasons.

MUCKROSS HOUSE AND GARDENS ★ 45
Killarney National Park, Killarney, Co. Kerry, Republic of Ireland. Tel: (064) 31947/31440

National Parks and Wildlife Service; Office of Public Works ★ 4m from centre of Killarney, on road to Kenmare ★ Parking ★ Restaurant. Picnics ★ Toilet facilities ★ Suitable for wheelchairs ★ Dogs on lead ★ Craft shop ★ House open ★ Gardens open for pedestrians all year, with car access, 8am – 5pm (July and Aug, 8am – 7pm) ★ Entrance: free

The garden around Muckross House is almost incidental to the spectacle of the lakes and mountains of Killarney. It is principally renowned as a viewing area for the wild grandeur of the mountains. The lawns sweep to clumps of old rhododendrons and Scots pines, and there is a huge natural rock garden. Quiet corners abound along the lough-shore walks, and anyone interested in trees and shrubs is strongly recommended to head for the recently-developed arboretum area (it can be reached by car easily – follow the signpost – and it is a short walk from the house). There, good specimen trees surround a wooden pergola of imaginative design, and in the shaded woods beyond there are plantings of tender shrubs. This is a place for a whole day (or more) – the wild woods with their unique flora and ancient yews and the almost immortal strawberry trees (*Arbutus unedo*) are enticing and magical.

NATIONAL BOTANIC GARDENS, GLASNEVIN ★ 46
Glasnevin, Dublin 9, Republic of Ireland. Tel: (1) 8374388

Office of Public Works ★ 1m N of central Dublin situated between Finglas Road and Botanic Road close to Glasnevin Cemetery ★ Parking very limited in summer and at weekends ★ Refreshments: arrangements for groups only may be made in advance by writing to the Director ★ Toilet facilities ★ Suitable for wheelchairs except for main Palm House ★ Open daily except 25th Dec, summer, 9am – 6pm, winter, 9am – 4.30pm. Opening times for glasshouses are posted at entrance (closed 1 – 2pm and Sun am) ★ Entrance: free

A fine garden which still retains its Victorian exactitude with close-cut lawns and succulent carpet-bedding (in summer only!) The plant collection generally is fine, but in places the shrubs and trees are past their best. In the winter, the glasshouses are worth visiting; by spring there are daffodil-crowded lawns and flowering cherries; the summer highlight is the double, curving herbaceous border, and in autumn the fruit-laden trees and russet foliage can be magical. The Turner conservatory (1843 – 69), the finest in Ireland, is being restored. Glasnevin is undoubtedly worth visiting, especially by gardeners with a strong interest in shrubs and perennials; soil conditions preclude large-scale rhododendron planting. The newly-restored Alpine House contains, in season, collections of plants of considerable interest. Highlights are hard to enumerate, but a few outstanding plants may be mentioned: *Zelkova carpinifolia* (especially in winter a marvellous 'architectural' tree); the Chain Tent (*c.* 1836) with ancient wisteria; *Ochagavia carnea* (at Cactus House); cycads in Palm House; *Parrotia persica* (near entrance, wonderful in February and October); and of course 'The Last Rose of

Summer'! The Gardens hold the National collections of *Potentilla fruticosa* (shrubby cinquefoil) and *Garrya* (tassel bush).

PHOENIX PARK   47
Dublin, Republic of Ireland. Tel: (1) 8213021

Office of Public Works ★ On N side of the River Liffey. From city centre, follow signs to The West, or take No 10 bus to Phoenix Park ★ Parking ★ Toilet facilities ★ Dogs ★ Ashtown Castle Visitor Centre open with admission charge ★ Park open all year, daily, 7am – 11pm ★ Entrance: free

This is the largest enclosed park in any European city replete with a herd of fallow deer, some splendid monuments and great houses (not open to the public), including Aras an Uchtarain (the residence of the President of Ireland, and formerly the Vice-Regal Lodge). There is a new information centre, telling the history of the park, a short distance from the Phoenix monument which is now perched on the main avenue. Excellent information signs, well-designed and distinctive, provide information throughout. The planting is large scale – the avenues of horse chestnuts are spectacular in blossom, and in autumn, and gas lights twinkle at night the whole way along the ceremonious avenue. The People's Garden, near the main city entrance is the only part where there is intensive gardening, but Phoenix Park is a place to be 'lost' in among the hawthorns and the wild flowers, far away from (but within earshot of) Dublin city centre.

POWERSCOURT ★   48
Enniskerry, Co. Wicklow, Republic of Ireland. Tel: (1) 2867676

Slazenger family ★ 12m S of Dublin, just outside village of Enniskerry ★ Parking ★ Refreshments: licensed restaurant ★ Toilet facilities ★ Partly suitable for wheelchairs ★ Dogs on lead ★ Plants for sale ★ Shop ★ House a ruin after a fire in 1974. Occasional exhibitions and children's play area ★ Guided tours available ★ Open mid-March to Oct, daily, 9.30am – 5.30pm ★ Entrance: IR£2.80, OAP and students IR£2.30, children IR£1.70. Separate charge for waterfall

Powerscourt is a 'grand garden', a massive statement of the triumph of Art over the Natural Landscape. In its present form, with an amphitheatre of terraces and great central axis (mid-nineteenth century), the garden is largely the design of the inimitable Daniel Robertson. In some ways Powerscourt is beyond compare – the axis formed by the ceremonious stairway leading down to the Triton Pond and jet, and stretching beyond to the Great Sugarloaf Mountain, is justly famous – it can, however, be glimpsed in a few minutes (and that is what many tourists do). We recommend that you walk along the terrace towards the Pepperpot, through the mature conifers which Lord Powerscourt collected – a big-cone pine (*Pinus coulteri*), the tallest in Ireland and Britain, is here. A tree-trail, devised by Alan Mitchell, has recently been opened, and will amuse dedicated dendrophiles. Wander on, to the edge of the pond, and look up, along the stairway, past the monumental terraces to the facade of the burnt-out house. That's the view of Powerscourt that is breathtaking – a man-made amphitheatre guarded by winged horses. Statuary and the famous perspective gate; an avenue of monkey puzzles and a beech wood along the avenue; these add to Powerscourt's glory.

PRIMROSE HILL ★   49
Lucan, Co. Dublin, Republic of Ireland. Tel: (1) 6280373

Mrs Cicely and Mr Robin Hall ★ From Dublin follow the main road to the west. The village of Lucan is now by-passed so turn off at signs for Lucan, drive through the village and watch for steep, narrow laneway called Primrose Lane on left after Garda (police) station ★ Limited parking in village ★ Toilet facilities ★ Plants for sale ★ House open ★ Garden open February, daily, 1 – 5.30pm, other open days advertised in press and by poster, and at other times by appointment ★ Entrance: IR£2.50

This garden isn't much bigger than one acre yet it succeeds in housing a fine collection of snowdrops – the biggest and certainly the most named collection including some of their own 'Primrose Hill' seedlings which are glorious in flower. It is unusual for a garden to boast that February is its best month – but undoubtedly it is here, starting the visiting season, but to visit in late spring and summer when the borders are in full swathe with colour is an added joy. The herbaceous plants here are lovingly cared for and planted in humus-rich compost, in large clumps, giving a generous effect to the borders. Primulas are high on the priority list, so are lobelias (two named ones originated here), lilies, kniphofias and, of course, *P. auricula* 'Old Irish Blue', plus many others.

ROWALLANE ★★   50
Saintfield, Co. Down, Northern Ireland. Tel: (01238) 510131

The National Trust ★ ½m S of Saintfield on A7 Belfast – Downpatrick road ★ Parking ★ Refreshments: tea room with light refreshments, April and Sept, Sat and Sun; May to Aug, daily, 2 – 6pm ★ Toilet facilities ★ Partly suitable for wheelchairs ★ Dogs on lead ★ Shop ★ Open April to Oct, Mon – Fri, 10.30am – 6pm, Sat and Sun, 2 – 6pm; Nov to March 1996, Mon – Fri, 10.30am – 5pm. Closed 25th, 26th Dec and 2nd Jan ★ Entrance: April to Oct, £2.30, Nov to March, £1.20 (1994 prices). Parties outside normal hours extra charge by appointment only

While famous as a 52-acre rhododendron garden, and certainly excellent in this regard, Rowallane has much more to interest keen gardeners. In summer, the walled garden blossoms in lemon and blue while, around, hoheria cast white petals in the wind. In secluded places, a pocket handkerchief tree blows; there is a pale-yellow-leaved pieris, a restored Victorian bandstand (music-filled on some summer weekends) and orchid meadows. Rock garden with primulas, meconopsis, heathers, etc. and several areas of natural wild flowers. Any season will be interesting, and for the real enthusiast there are rhododendron species and cultivars in bloom from October to August. The original plant of *Viburnum plicatum* 'Rowallane' is in the walled garden as is the original *Chaenomeles* x *superba* 'Rowallane'; a feature is made of *Hypericum* 'Rowallane' at the entrance to the walled garden.

45 SANDFORD ROAD ★★   51
Ranelagh, Dublin 6, Republic of Ireland.

Helen Dillon ★ Best season: spring to late autumn ★ Parking in street ★ Toilet facilities ★ Limited access for wheelchairs ★ Plants for sale according to season ★ Open March, daily; April to June, Suns only; July and Aug, daily; Sept, Suns only, all 2 – 6pm. Groups at any time by arrangement ★ Entrance: IR£3, OAP IR£2

Within a walled rectangular garden, typical of Dublin's Georgian town houses, Helen Dillon has created one of the best designed and planted gardens in Ireland. As a central foil there is an immaculate lawn which enhances the colourful embroidery of the borders, which on exploration turn into a necklace of secret rooms with raised beds for rarities, such as lady's slipper orchids, or double-flowered *Trillium grandiflorum*. On the terrace, terracotta pots sprout more rare plants: *Trochocarpa thymifolia* and the blue sweet pea (*Lathyrus nervosus*). Clumps of *Dierama pulcherrimum* arch over the sphinxes, and a small alpine house and conservatory shelter the choicest – *Clematis florida* 'Sieboldii', *Lapageria rosea*, prize-winning ferns, alpines and bulbs. The mixed borders of shrubs and herbaceous perennials are changeful, each season revealing unusual plants and exciting colour combinations. A listing of the plants in Mrs Dillon's garden would not shame a large botanical garden. Each plant has its proper place, all is ordered with no forbidding sense of contrivance. The exuberance overwhelms the formality, and the garden is both a finely-designed pleasaunce and a plantsman's veritable nirvana.

SEAFORDE   52
Downpatrick, Co. Down, Northern Ireland.
Tel: (01396) 811225; Fax: (01396) 811370

Mr Patrick and Lady Anthea Forde ★ 22m from Belfast on the main Belfast – Newcastle road ★ Best seasons: April/ May and Sept ★ Parking ★ Refreshments in July and Aug, otherwise at weekends and on Bank Holidays ★ Toilet facilities ★ Suitable for wheelchairs ★ Plants for sale in nursery ★ Shop attached to butterfly house ★ Garden open 2nd Jan to 24th Dec, Mon – Sat, 10am – 5pm, Sun, 2 – 6pm (Nov to Feb, Mon – Fri only) ★ Entrance: £2, children £1.20

The fine landscaped park can be glimpsed en route to the vast walled garden, half of which is a commercial nursery with the attraction of a Butterfly House displaying a collection of tropical plants. The other half is an ornamental garden bedecked in late summer with blooms of eucryphia that make up the National collection. The hornbeam maze has a rose-clad arbour at the centre, the vantage point for which is a 1992 'Moghul Tower'. Beyond the walled garden is the 'Pheasantry', a verdant valley enclosed by mature trees, full of noteworthy plants collected over many years and still expanding.

THE SHACKLETON GARDEN ★★   53
Beech Park, Clonsilla, Co. Dublin, Republic of Ireland.
Tel: (1) 8212216

Jonathan and Daphne Shackleton ★ 1m from Clonsilla village on road to Lucan, 10m W of Dublin ★ Parking ★ Home-made teas ★ Toilet facilities ★ Suitable for wheelchairs ★ Plants for sale ★ Open March to mid-Oct, every Sun, and also Bank Holidays, 2 – 6pm. Groups and long-distance visitors by arrangement ★ Entrance: IR£2.50 (1994 price)

In an old walled garden of a Regency house, once bedded with vegetables in season, are raised beds and herbaceous borders brim-full of the choicest perennials and dwarf shrubs. The gems of this highly personal, indeed eclectic, collection begun about 1960 are celmisias (New Zealand mountain daisies), yet the raised beds contain many unusual and uncommon plants, all deliberately selected and superbly cultivated. The herbaceous borders which encircle the walled garden and line its intersecting pathways are planted with as great attention to excellence, and the collection of perennials is outstanding – meconopsis (esp. *M.* x *sheldonii*), phlox, papaver and iris cultivars are striking in season, and a listing of the entire assemblage would occupy a small book. The plants range from old-fashioned, cottage-garden types, some forgotten elsewhere, to the newest and best. There is an extensive range of old roses, fruit and vegetables, including an ornamental vegetable area. Throughout the summer, a series of gardening day courses makes use of the extensive plant collections. David Shackleton, who created this garden, garnering cultivars from Ireland and Britain, died in 1988; his idiosyncratic garden is a wonderfully vivid memorial.

SIR THOMAS AND LADY DIXON PARK 54
Upper Malone Road, Belfast, Northern Ireland.

Belfast Parks Department ★ S of Belfast city centre, on Upper Malone Road ★ Best seasons: spring and summer ★ Parking ★ Refreshments: in Stables Tea House ★ Toilet facilities ★ Suitable for wheelchairs ★ Dogs on lead ★ Park open all year; walled garden, 8am – sunset ★ Entrance: free

This 128-acre park, presented to the City of Belfast in 1959, is part of an estate established in the eighteenth century. The main feature today is the City of Belfast International Rose Garden where some 20,000 rose bushes can be seen in carefully-labelled beds that follow the contours of the park. One display has old varieties demonstrating the history of the rose. Elsewhere there are meadows by the River Lagan, a walled garden, continuing International Camellia Trials and a Japanese garden constructed in 1990. Attractions for all the family include a secluded children's playground and band performances in the summer.

ST ANNE'S ROSE GARDEN 55
Clontarf, Dublin, Republic of Ireland. Tel: (1) 331859

Dublin Corporation Parks Department ★ In NE Dublin. Take the coast road north and follow signs to Clontarf/Howth ★ Best season: June/July ★ Parking on road ★ Dogs on lead ★ Open all year, daily, until 1 hour before sunset ★ Entrance: free

A large well-looked-after rose garden spread over several acres of formal beds and tarmac paths. While it lacks the atmosphere and character of an old walled rose garden it does surprise the first-time visitor with its huge beds of single variety roses. Fragrance wafts across from old varieties like 'Fragrant Cloud' and 'Madame Isaac Pereire' but some of the varieties are now superceded by more fragrant ones. Its appeal owes much to these older hybrid teas and floribundas no longer commercially available, so it is worth spending an hour there before moving on to another garden.

STROKESTOWN PARK 56
Strokestown, Co. Roscommon, Republic of Ireland. Tel: (078) 33013

Westward Garage Ltd ★ 14m W of Longford on the N5 ★ Famine Museum in the four stable yards. Car park, refreshments and toilet facilities ★ Dogs on lead ★ Shop ★ House open ★ Park open June to mid-Sept, Tues – Sat and Bank

Holidays, 12 noon – 5pm. Parties by arrangement ★ Entrance: park free; house and garden IR£3, OAP IR£2, students, children and unemployed IR£1 (1994 prices)

The Neo-Palladian Strokestown Park House, entered from one of the broadest streets in Ireland, was purchased in 1979 by a local company who set in motion a restoration plan involving the refurbishment of the house, replanting of the remaining parkland and the creation of new gardens within the old walls. In the four-acre garden is what is said to be the largest herbaceous border (Rosemoor apart) in these islands, resplendent from the top – silver, blue and white – to the bottom – purple, red and yellow, is repeated for many of its 200 yards. Handsome gates from Rockingham near Boyle have been installed, the pool and the pergola have been completed, yew and beech hedge planted. The old summerhouse remains close by the area earmarked for a maze and croquet lawn. Future plans involve the Regency vinery and eighteenth-century banqueting folly in the adjoining two-acre garden. It is worth a trip from Cork just to see the herbaceous border.

TALBOT BOTANIC GARDEN ★ 57
Malahide Castle, Malahide, Co. Dublin, Republic of Ireland.
Tel: (1) 8462456

Dublin County Council ★ Malahide, 10m N of Dublin ★ Parking ★ Refreshments: lunches and teas in castle ★ Suitable for wheelchairs ★ Shop in castle ★ Castle open ★ Garden open May to Sept, daily, 2 – 5pm. Conducted tour of walled garden, Wed, 2pm ★ Entrance: IR£1, children free if accompanied (1994 prices)

Malahide Castle was the home of the Talbot family for many centuries; following the death of Lord Talbot de Malahide it was acquired by Dublin County Council. The garden consists of three parts – the outer demesne (now occupied by playing fields, well-kept lawns and shrubberies, pathways); the main shrubberies (open to the public as above) and the walled garden (open only by special arrangement and on Wednesdays for guided tours). The main shrubberies planted by Lord Talbot contain a varied mixture of trees and shrubs, some of which are outstanding and rare. However, the finest part of the collection is in the walled garden – here Lord Talbot planted such exotics as *Telopea truncata*, *Bomarea caldasii*, *Garrya* x *issaquahensis*, and numerous others. Olearia was a favourite genus and is well represented here. Australasian genera are also represented (e.g. pittosporum, grevillea, cyathodes, acacia); *Berberis valdiviana* and *Pseudopanax ferox* lurk in an out-of-the-way corner. By the castle is a large cedar of Lebanon with cyclamen below, and a spacious lawn.

TRINITY COLLEGE BOTANIC GARDEN 58
Palmerston Park, Dublin 6, Republic of Ireland. Tel: (1) 972070

School of Botany, Trinity College, Dublin ★ Adjacent to Palmerston Park, near Ranelagh, Dublin ★ Parking in street ★ Suitable for wheelchairs ★ Open Mon – Fri, 9am – 5pm. Appointment preferred ★ Entrance: free

This is essentially a research garden, but there is a small arboretum, order (family) beds and a collection of Irish native plants, as well as some glasshouses; a fragment of *Todea barbara* from a plant donated in 1892 grows in one glasshouse. Also a collection of *Saxifraga* sp., the rare Mauritius bluebell (*Nesocodon mauritianus*) and rare species recently collected from the Pitcairn group of islands. *Melianthus major* flowers well every year, and there are good specimens of *Betula utilis* cv. 'Trinity College' and *Sorbus hibernica*. For those in search of botanical curiosities.

TRINITY COLLEGE GARDEN
Dublin 2, Republic of Ireland. Tel: (1) 7021724 – Enquiries Office

Entrances in College Green, Nassau Street and Lincoln Place ★ No parking on site ★ Suitable for wheelchairs ★ Open daily, 8am – 10pm ★ Entrance: free

The gardens of this 40-acre urban campus contain an eclectic collection of trees in an impressive architectural setting. The most notable subjects are the pair of *Acer macrophyllum* in Library Square, which probably originate from the earliest introduction by David Douglas. One is the largest in Euope. The 600 specimens in the collection illustrate what may be grown in an urban setting. Good specimens of *Trachycarpus fortunei*, *Tilia mongolica*, *Betula ermanii*, *Ostrya carpinifolia* and *Sorbus sargentiana*. Also plantings originated by Lanning Roper and a range of more modern shrubs associated with new buildings. Guide to trees of Trinity College available in T.C.D. Library bookshop.

TULLYNALLY CASTLE   59
Castlepollard, Co. Westmeath, Republic of Ireland. Tel: (044) 61159

Thomas Pakenham ★ 1m NW of Castlepollard on road to Granard ★ Parking ★ Castle open mid-June to mid-Aug ★ Grounds open May to Sept, 2 – 6pm ★ Entrance: IR£2, children IR50p (1994 prices)

A Gothic entrance lodge gives onto an avenue of young oaks. The surrounding parkland has some outstanding mature trees. Terraces in front of the castle look south over a Romantic desmesne and lake landscaped in the late eighteenth century. Adjoining paths lead through the pleasure ground to a Victorian grotto (giving a view of Lough Derravaragh), flower garden and kitchen garden with an avenue of Irish yews. Another walk follows a stream garden down to the lower lake.

THE WAY THE FAIRIES WENT   60
Sneem, Co. Kerry, Republic of Ireland.

Sneem Development Co-operative ★ In village of Sneem, on 'Ring of Kerry' between Kenmare and Waterville ★ Parking nearby ★ Open permanently ★ Entrance: free

Close by the R.C. church on boggy land between the village and the river, Kerry-born artist James Scanlon has created an environmental sculpture garden featuring four stone-built 'pyramids', structures which echo other monuments of Kerry's ancient past. Visitors will find the use of stone, coloured glass and water intriguing, although some of the glass inserts have been tampered with, so that their reflections cannot be seen. There are trees and wild flowers around the sculptures, bluebells, flag irises and bullrushes. The sculptures, on a very human scale, were built by local men and seem especially apt in the landscape of Sneem with its two well-kept village greens.

SCOTLAND

Thurso
Wick
Ullapool
Dingwall
Inverness
SCOTLAND
Aberdeen
Fort William
Dundee
Perth
Oban
Stirling
Glasgow
Edinburgh
Galashiels
Dumfries
NORTHUMB.
Stranraer

Two-starred gardens are ringed in bold.

GURKHA BRIGADE ASSOCIATION IN SCOTLAND

LUNCHEON

OFFICERS MESS
ARMY HEADQUARTERS
CRAIGIEHALL

Saturday 17th June 1995
12 Noon for 1pm

ABBOTSFORD   1
Melrose, Roxburghshire, Borders. Tel: (01896) 2043

*Mrs P. Maxwell-Scott ★ 3m W of Melrose on A6091, turn SW on to B6360.
Just S of A72 ★ Parking ★ Teas and picnics ★ Toilet facilities ★ Suitable for
wheelchairs. Disabled enter by private entrance ★ Shop ★ House open ★ Garden
open 20th March to Oct, Mon - Sat, 10am - 5pm, Sun, 2 - 5pm ★ Entrance:
£2.60, children £1.30, parties £2 per person, children £1.10*

Sir Walter Scott's magnificent house, built between 1817 and 1821 to satisfy
his yearning to become a laird, has a garden that is rich in Scottish allusions.
A yew hedge to the south of the house has medallions from an old cross
inset, and a fountain in the same formal garden came from the same cross.
The River Tweed flows past the house and there are fine views across a
stretch of garden. Herbaceous beds lead to a Gothic-type fern house filled
with other plants beside ferns, such as orchids. However, the dedicated Scott
scholar will find most interest in the house, amongst historical relics collected
by the laird himself.

ACHAMORE GARDENS ★   2
Isle of Gigha, Argyll, Strathclyde. Tel: (015835) 267 or 268

*Mr and Mrs Derek Holt ★ Take A83 to Tayinloan then ferry to Gigha ★ Best
season: spring ★ Refreshments at hotel ★ Toilet facilities ★ Partly suitable for
wheelchairs ★ Dogs on lead ★ Open daily all year round ★ Entrance: £2, children
£1, collecting box*

An amazing idea to create such a superb garden on the Isle of Gigha. The
journey there is via most beautiful countryside finishing up with the ferry
trip, surrounded by squawking sea birds. In 1944 Sir James Horlick
purchased the whole island with the sole purpose to create a garden in which
to grow the rare and unusual. This was accomplished with the advice of
James Russell. A delightful woodland landscape was planted with a vast
collection of rarities from around the world. The garden is especially rich in
fine specimens of tender rhododendrons such as *R. lindleyii*, *R. fragrantissimum*, and *R. macabeanum* to name but a few. The overall effect of the garden
is tropical. There are many varieties of camellias, cordylines, primulas and
Asiatic exotica. A great number of genera are represented by very good specimens, thriving in Gigha's mildness. There is a very fine *Pinus montezumae* in
the walled garden; drifts of Asiatic primulas feature around the especially
pretty woodland pond. The rhododendrons are unsurpassed in variety,
quality and sheer visual magnitude. Gigha is a must, a Mecca for the keen
plantsman and avid gardener. Few gardens outside the national botanic
collections can claim such diversity and rarity.

ACHNACLOICH   3
Connel, by Oban, Argyll, Strathclyde. Tel: (0163171) 221

*Mrs T.E. Nelson ★ 3m E of Connel off A85 ★ Best season: April to June ★
Parking ★ Partly suitable for wheelchairs ★ Dogs on lead ★ Plants for sale ★ Open
2nd April to 29th Oct, daily, 10am - 6pm ★ Entrance: £1, OAP 50p, children free*

A castellated Scottish baronial house beautifully situated above the loch on a
rocky cliff. A curved drive sweeps past massed bulbs in spring, and later

there are azaleas and fine Japanese maples. Natural woodland with interlinked glades is beautiful in spring with bluebells, primroses and wood anemones. Other gaps are planted with primulas, magnolias, rare shrubs and rhododendrons. Good autumn colours. Fine views to Loch Etive and surrounding mountains. Garden walks recently extended.

ALLANGRANGE 4
Munlochy, Black Isle, Ross and Cromarty, Highlands.
Tel: (0146381) 249

Major and Mrs A. Cameron ★ Signposted from A9, 5m N of Inverness ★ Best season: May to July ★ Teas ★ Toilet facilities in house ★ Suitable for wheelchairs ★ Dogs on lead ★ Plants and prints for sale ★ Open probably 7th May, 11th June, 9th July for charity, 2 - 5.30pm and at other times by appointment ★ Entrance: £1.50, children 20p

A very attractive garden which spills down the hillside in a series of descending terraces merging naturally with the rolling agricultural landscape of the Black Isle. The formal part of the garden incorporates white and mauve gardens, many old and shrub roses, tree peonies and a small corner for plants of variegated foliage. In July climbing Himalayan roses, including *Rosa filipes* 'Kiftsgate', make a spectacular display. There is also a small pool garden, and to the rear of the house a woodland garden with unusual rhododendrons, primulas, meconopsis and *Cardiocrinum giganteum*. The hand of an accomplished flower painter, Elizabeth Cameron, shows itself everywhere.

ARBIGLAND 5
Kirkbean, Dumfries and Galloway. Tel: (0138788) 283

Captain and Mrs J.B. Blackett ★ From New Abbey, signposted on A710 Solway coast road ★ Best seasons: May to mid-June, Sept ★ Parking free ★ Teas, picnics on beach ★ Toilet facilities ★ Dogs on lead ★ Secluded private sandy beach which can be used by visitors ★ House open 20th to 29th May ★ Garden open May to Sept, Tues to Sun and 1st, 29th May, 28th Aug, 2 - 6pm ★ Entrance: £2, OAP £1.50, children 50p, under 5 free

The ancient 'broadwalk', lined with fine specimen trees, leads down towards the sea and the woodland garden. One area, called 'Japan', takes its name from the Japanese maples and azaleas which have been arranged around a small burn. Nearby is a large pool, especially attractive in the autumn when it reflects the colours of the trees that surround it; the border around the lawn is full of unusual and interesting plants. The formal sunken garden has been created in the foundations of the original house. The old walled garden, at present disused, dates from the original eighteenth-century house and nearby grows one of the finest *Pieris japonica* in Scotland, over 20 ft high.

ARBUTHNOTT HOUSE 6
Laurencekirk, Grampian.

The Viscount of Arbuthnott ★ 8m from Laurencekirk, 3m from Inverbervie on B967 between A90 and A94 ★ Parking ★ Tea and biscuits on charity open days ★ Toilet facilities ★ Plants for sale on charity open day ★ House open as garden ★ Garden open daily, 9am - 5pm ★ Entrance: £1.50, OAP and children £1

The enclosed garden dates from the late seventeenth century and with the policies is contained within the valley of the Bervie Water. The entrance drive is flanked by rhododendrons and the verges are full of primroses and celandines in spring. The drive crosses a fine bridge topped by imposing urns before reaching the house set high on a promontory with most of the garden sloping very steeply to the river. This garden is unusual in that it has always been treated as an extension of the house, rather than being laid out at some distance. The sloping part has four grassed terraces and this pattern is dissected by diagonal grassed walks radiating out in a manner reminiscent of the Union Jack. This fixed structure creates long garden 'rooms' and vistas as the garden is explored. The garden plan is very old but much of today's mature planting was done by a Lady Arbuthnott in the 1920s and this is continued by the present Lady Arbuthnott. Herbaceous borders, old roses together with shrub roses and ramblers, shrubs underplanted with hostas, primulas, meconopsis and lilies, lilacs and viburnums provide colour throughout the summer. A metal stag for target practice stands at the bottom of the slope by the lade (millstream).

ARDANAISEIG GARDEN AND HOTEL 7
Kilchrenan, Argyll, Strathclyde. Tel: (018663) 333

4m E from Kilchrenan on route B845 ★ Best seasons: April to July, and Oct ★ Parking ★ Refreshments at hotel, no children under 8 ★ Dogs on lead ★ Plants for sale ★ Hotel open, formerly Scottish baronial house ★ Garden open April to 30th Oct, 9am - 8pm ★ Entrance: by collection box at car park £1 (1994 price), children free

A picturesque 10-mile drive from Taynuilt down the peninsular makes a fitting introduction to this traditional Argyll garden. Attractive slate paths guide the visitor round 20 acres of well-planted woodland set behind an 1834 baronial house, now a very comfortable hotel, with lovely views across Loch Awe. The species and hybrid rhododendrons are particularly fine. Note the unusual curved walls of the walled garden.

ARDTORNISH 8
Lochaline, Morvern, Highlands. Tel: (01967421) 288 (Estate office)

Mrs John Raven ★ 30m from Corran. From Corran ferry, S of Fort William, cross to Morvern and take route left on A861 towards Lochaline, then left on A884. Gardens 2m before Lochaline on left ★ Best seasons: April to June and Oct ★ Parking ★ Dogs on lead ★ Plants for sale in kitchen garden ★ 12 units available as self-catering accommodation, 5 of them in the house ★ Open April to Oct, 10am - 4.30pm ★ Entrance: £1.50, children free. Collecting box

A plantsman's garden with a particularly fine and extensive collection of unusual shrubs, deciduous trees and rhododendrons set against a background of conifers, a loch and outstanding Highland scenery. The gardens have developed over the past 100 years or more following the first house on the site, established by a distiller from London in the 1850s. They are on a steeply sloping site and rainfall is heavy. Mrs Raven's late husband wrote a book, *The Botanist's Garden*, now republished, about their other garden, Docwra's Manor in Cambridgeshire (see entry), and he assisted his wife in following her parents' footsteps in trying to establish a plantsman's paradise

here. Apart from the area around the house, there is a pleasing air of informality about the gardens which include a boggy primula garden, Bob's Glen
with *Rhododendron thomsonii* and *prattii*, and a larger glen with still more
species and hybrid rhododendrons. There is a flourishing kitchen garden.

ARDUAINE GARDEN ★★   9
by Oban, Argyll, Strathclyde. Tel: (01852) 200366

*The National Trust for Scotland ★ On the A816, 20m S of Oban, 17m N of
Lochgilphead. Joint entrance with Loch Melfort Hotel ★ Parking ★ Refreshments
and toilet facilities at the hotel ★ Partly suitable for wheelchairs ★ Open all year,
daily, 9.30am - sunset ★ Entrance: £2, concessions and children £1 (1994 prices)*

Arduaine (pronounced Ardoony if you are asking the way) is a very special
place. Planted in the early 1900s by James Arthur Campbell possibly with
advice from his friend Osgood Mackenzie, creator of Inverewe Garden. Essex
nurserymen Edmund and Harry Wright restored the garden after they
acquired it in 1971. Given to the Trust by them in 1991, this is an outstanding 20-acre garden on a promontory bounded by Loch Melfort and the
Sound of Jura, climatically favoured by the North Atlantic Drift or Gulf
Stream. Nationally noted for rhododendron species azaleas, magnolias and
other rare trees and shrubs. The rhododendron species collection ranks high
in importance in Scotland.

BALLINDALLOCH CASTLE   10
Grantown-on-Spey, Banffshire, Highlands. Tel: (01807) 500206

*Mrs Oliver MacPherson Grant Russell ★ Halfway between Grantown-on-Spey
and Keith on A95. Signposted ★ Parking ★ Refreshments ★ Toilet facilities ★
Suitable for wheelchairs ★ Dog walking area ★ Shop ★ House open ★ Garden
open 14th April to Sept, daily, 10am - 5pm ★ Entrance: £1.50 (castle and
gardens £3.95)*

What a pleasure to find a garden of this scale and calibre set in the magnificent
Spey valley. The most attractive feature is undoubtedly the 1937 rock garden
which comes tumbling down the hillside onto the most impressive lawns in the
land. It takes three men two days to mow and edge it. The Russells have
completely renovated all borders over the last few years and are now landscaping the old walled garden into a rose and fountain garden opening in spring
1995. The daffodil season and the river/woodland walks are particularly lovely.
A small parterre at the side of the house shows how stunning humble nepeta
and *Alchemilla mollis* can be when all else is eaten by the deer.

THE BANK HOUSE   11
Glenfarg, Perth and Kinross, Tayside. Tel: (01577) 830275

*Mr and Mrs C.B. Lascelles ★ In Glenfarg village, 50 yards along Ladeside, by
Glenfarg Hotel ★ Best season: spring to late summer ★ Parking on road ★
Suitable for wheelchairs ★ Plants sometimes for sale ★ Open by appointment ★
Entrance: £2*

The principal garden is approached through a paved area with additional planting above low retaining walls. An apple and clematis tunnel leads the visitor
onwards to large curved beds set into lawns on a gently-sloping site. A horse-

shoe-shaped yew hedge underplanted with yellow archangel and star of Bethlehem is a fine spring feature. Bulbs and early-flowering herbaceous plants carry the display to summer. The owners have built up an eclectic collection of rare and unusual plants of much garden merit and these are grown to perfection using organic gardening techniques. The careful planting, with great regard to colour and form, makes for a very instructive visit. A smaller garden across the street, with a 'flowform cascade' water feature and a 'yin and yang' design circular bed, may be visited at any time. Ornamental trees have also been planted in a newly-acquired field, where a pond has been created.

BARGUILLEAN ANGUS GARDEN 12
Taynuilt, Argyll, Strathclyde.
Tel: (018662) 375/333; Fax: (018662) 652

Mr Sam S. MacDonald ★ 3m from Taynuilt. Minor road to Kilmore off A85 ★ Best season: April to June ★ Parking ★ Dogs on lead ★ Open March to Oct, daily, 8am - 9pm. Parties welcome by prior appointment in writing ★ Entrance: £1, children free

Nine-acre woodland garden with areas of established rhododendrons, azaleas and conifers and some rare trees and shrubs on a Highland hillside overlooking a lochan with views to Ben Cruachan. Much new planting with modern rhododendron hybrids, from the NW of the United States, among native birch and oak woodland makes for interesting comparisons with established rhododendron gardens of the west coast and is excellent for the evaluation of these cultivars for Scottish gardens. A very peaceful garden, achieving much in a difficult situation. Good nursery adjacent.

BEATRIX POTTER GARDEN 13
Birnam, Perthshire, Tayside.

Perthshire Tourist Board ★ 13m NW of Perth in the village of Birnam ★ Parking in road ★ Refreshments available locally ★ Toilet facilities in exhibition centre during open hours ★ Suitable for wheelchairs ★ Dogs on lead ★ Shop in exhibition centre ★ Exhibition in the Birnam Institute, 20 yards from the garden, open June to Sept, daily, 10am - 4pm (Sun 2 - 4pm) ★ Garden open all year ★ Entrance: free

There is always a certain rivalry between houses where a celebrity was born and others where he or she was conceived, lived or died. So it is with authors. Beatrix Potter, it seems, may have published her famous books from the Lake District, but the characters were invented when she stayed here near the family's Dalguise House, to which she came for 12 successive annual holidays and was a regular visitor to the Institute here. Her diaries have revealed that Peter Rabbit and his friends were modelled on local people and animals. This new garden commemorates the connection, with bronze sculptures of some of the best known characters amid rustic surroundings. Nursery interest rather than horticultural.

BEECHGROVE GARDEN ★ 14
Beechgrove Terrace, Aberdeen, Grampian. Tel: (01224) 625233

BBC Scotland ★ 1½m from city centre ★ Suitable for wheelchairs ★ Open daily except on filming days

This garden was begun in 1978 for use in conjunction with BBC Scotland's gardening programme of the same name. During 1990 the garden was cleared except for one area, now referred to as the 'established garden', and new gardens begun. These include two terrace gardens, a housing estate garden suitable for a family, a suburban garden for the more knowledgeable gardener and a 'clay corner' to demonstrate the possibilities for difficult soils. There is a conservatory and some small glasshouses. Examples of paving, fencing, vegetables, fruit, a children's play area, a small pool, troughs, etc, complete the garden. It is very interesting and instructive for the aspiring beginner but has less to offer the plantsman.

BELL'S CHERRYBANK GARDENS   15
Cherrybank, Perth, Tayside. Tel: (01738) 627330

United Distillers UK ★ On A9 into Perth city centre. Gardens located S of main road ★ Parking ★ Refreshments: light teas ★ Toilet facilities ★ Suitable for wheelchairs ★ Guide dogs only ★ Open May to Oct, daily, 9am – 5pm ★ Entrance: £1, OAP and children 50p (1994 prices)

This is a modern garden surrounding the commercial offices of United Distillers UK. It is in fact two gardens, the first laid out in the early 1970s, plus the Scottish National heather collection begun in 1983. Their aim is to have the world's largest collection of heathers. There are now over 830 varieties, all in superb condition. Other plant collections are well-maintained and beautifully designed. Interest is sustained throughout the total of 18 acres by water features, modern sculptures, pleasant vistas, a tiny putting green, tubular bells and an aviary. The children's play area includes a roundabout for wheelchair-bound children. There is a remarkable sundial designed by Ian Hamilton Finlay, the sculptor (see entry for Little Sparta).

BENT   16
Laurencekirk, Kincardineshire, Grampian.

Mr and Mrs James Mackie ★ 2¹/₂m from Laurencekirk on B9120 to Fettercairn ★ Parking ★ Refreshments on 2nd July ★ Toilet facilities ★ Suitable for wheelchairs ★ Plants for sale on 2nd July ★ Open for charity 21st May, 2nd July, 2 – 5pm. Parties welcome by appointment in writing ★ Entrance: £1.50, children 50p

A plantsman's garden in an open windy situation set into rich agricultural landscape. Old roses, hardy geraniums and grey-leaved plants are grouped in the shelter of the farmhouse walls. A collection of stone troughs is arranged on the paved terrace. A wide lawn leads to mixed borders of shrubs, hardy perennials, irises and lilies protected by sandstone walls. There is a small white garden edged with box. Fine old roses, including some rescued from derelict gardens in the surrounding area.

BIGGAR PARK ★   17
Biggar, Lanarkshire, Strathclyde. Tel: (01899) 20185

Capt. and Mrs David Barnes ★ S end of Biggar on A702, 30m SW of Edinburgh ★ Parking ★ Refreshments ★ Toilet facilities ★ Suitable for wheelchairs ★ Dogs on lead ★ Plants for sale ★ Open two afternoons for charity and by appointment ★ Entrance: £1.50 (1994 price)

A Japanese garden of tranquillity welcomes one to this well-planned 10-acre plantsman's garden. Sue Barnes' efficient labelling adds greatly to the enjoyment when walking through the woodland, the small arboretum and admiring the well-planted ornamental pond which have all been designed carefully to give year-round interest. This starts with a stunning display of daffodils which are followed by glades of meconopsis, rhododendrons and azaleas in early summer before the huge herbaceous borders burst into colour. The centrepiece, however, must be the outstanding walled garden reached through a fine rockery bank beside the eighteenth-century mansion house. The view through the wrought-iron gate stretches the length of a 50-yard double herbaceous border attractively backed by swags of thick ornamental rope hanging from rose 'pillars', whilst either side is divided into intensively planted sections divided by pleasing grass paths.

BLACKHILLS HOUSE   18
by Lhanbryde, Elgin, Moray, Grampian. Tel: (01343) 842223

Mr and Mrs John Christie ★ 4m E of Elgin off A96. Take B9103 southwards and then minor road ★ Best season: mid-April to early June ★ Parking ★ Teas on open days ★ Toilet facilities ★ Partly suitable for wheelchairs ★ Dogs on lead ★ Open one day in May and by appointment for charity ★ Entrance: £1.50, children 75p

The east coast of Scotland is not, with a few exceptions, noted for its rhododendron gardens but Blackhills in the Laich of Moray should be visited for its collection of species rhododendrons in early May and in late May for hybrids. Both sorts are spread under tree cover in a steep-sided valley with many fine specimen trees. These include a *Davidia*, a Japanese red cedar, Brewer's weeping spruce and a Chinquapin or golden chestnut (*Chrysolepsis chrysophylla*) - a rare chestnut relative from North America. The finest rhododendrons are those in the subsections Falconera, Grandia and Taliensa, but the genus is well represented as a whole. The wooded valley opens to reveal two lakes with plantings of maples and other Chinese plants. Mr Thomas North Christie who was responsible for the early planting in the 1920s corresponded at length and exchanged the latest introductions with his neighbour the Brodie of Brodie.

BLAIRQUHAN   19
Maybole, Ayrshire, Strathclyde. Tel: (016557) 239

James Hunter Blair ★ 7m SE of Maybole on B7045. Signposted ★ Parking ★ Refreshments ★ Toilet facilities ★ Suitable for wheelchairs ★ Dogs on lead ★ Shop ★ House open ★ Garden open 16th July to 13th Aug, daily except Mon, 1.30 - 6pm (last admission 4.15pm) ★ Entrance: £3, OAP and children £2 (house and garden)

Approached by a three-mile drive along the River Girvan giving good opportunities to admire the 1860 pinetum and the extensive wood and parkland. The three-acre walled garden has been redesigned with ornamental planting replacing the former vegetable beds and nursery trees. Visitors should allow time to see the house which was built in 1820 by William Burn for Sir David Hunter Blair, 3rd Baronet, and contains all the old furniture, arranged with great style by the present owner.

BOLFRACKS 20
Aberfeldy, Perthshire, Tayside. Tel: (01887) 820207

Mr J.D. Hutchison ★ 2m W of Aberfeldy on A827 towards Loch Tay ★ Parking ★ Limited plants for sale ★ Open April to Oct, daily, 10am - 6pm ★ Entrance: £1.50, children free. Honesty box at gate

There has been a garden on this site for 200 years, but the present garden was started by the owners' parents in the 1920s and reshaped by the owner over the last 20 years. Three acres of walled plantsman's garden, well laid out and planned to demonstrate the potential of an exposed hillside with a northerly aspect. Astounding views over the Tay Valley are matched by the garden's own interesting features. Gentians do well on this soil. Fine masses of bulbs in spring and good autumn colour. Peat walls and stream garden. The walled garden contains a collection of old and modern shrub roses.

BRANKLYN GARDEN 21
Dundee Road, Perth, Tayside. Tel: (01738) 625535

The National Trust for Scotland ★ ½m from Queen's Bridge on A85 ★ Best season: spring and early summer ★ Parking ½m from entrance. Coaches and disabled parking at gate ★ Toilet facilities ★ Some paths too narrow for wheelchairs ★ Plants for sale ★ NTS sales table ★ Open March to 23rd Oct, daily, 9.30am - sunset ★ Entrance: £2, OAP and children £1. Pre-booked parties of 20 or more £1.60 per person, OAP and children £1

John and Dorothy Renton created this garden nearly in sight and certainly within sound of the centre of Perth. Work commenced in 1922 and in 1955 Dorothy was awarded the Veitch Memorial Medal by the Royal Horticultural Society. Branklyn extends to nearly two acres with the main interest being in its Sino-Himalayan alpine and ericaceous plants and its magnificent scree/rock gardens. There is a splendid collection of dwarf rhododendrons. The National Trust for Scotland took over the garden in 1968, following the death of Dorothy Renton in 1966 and of her husband the following year. Essential work continues to maintain Branklyn's rightful reputation as an outstanding plantsman's garden with its main feature which has been described as 'a plantsman's paradise'. It is impossible to describe all the splendid things to be found here, from the fine trees to the comprehensive collection of dwarf and smaller rhododendrons, the meconopsis to the notholirions, and the garden will repay many visits.

BRECHIN CASTLE ★ 22
Brechin, Tayside. Tel: (013562) 4566 (Estate office)

The Earl and Countess of Dalhousie ★ 1m from Brechin, route A94 ★ Parking ★ Teas in garden ★ Open 28th May, 9th July for charity, 2 - 6pm ★ Entrance: £1, children 50p

There are two different pleasurable aspects to a visit to Brechin Castle. The early plantings of beech, especially coppers, oaks, cedars, maples, cercidiphyllum, *Cornus kousa*, assorted chamaecyparis and cherries make a stunning backdrop to more recent plantings. These consist of birches, notably *Betula utilis*, sorbus, rare maples from North America and Asia, and rhododendrons. Within the walled garden of some 13 acres, high curved walls allow climbing roses to develop fully and provide shelter for such delights as *Carpenteria californica*, *Rosa hugonis* and ceanothus. A long vista from the main gate is bounded by a fine castellated yew hedge on one side and at a central point there is another vista downwards to a circular lily pond. This view is flanked by mixed rhododendron, shrub and herbaceous planting. Other plants of note are *Rhododendron auriculatum*, summer-flowering and sweetly-scented, *Rhododendron* 'Elizabeth Lockhart' with bronze-purple foliage and a halesia.

BRODICK CASTLE ★★   23
Isle of Arran, Strathclyde. Tel: (01770) 302202

The National Trust for Scotland ★ On Isle of Arran, 2m from Brodick. Ferry from Ardrossan or Kintyre ★ Best seasons: late April/early May (woodland garden), May to Aug (formal garden) ★ Parking free ★ Restaurant dates as castle ★ Toilet facilities ★ Partly suitable for wheelchairs ★ Shop ★ Castle open April, Mon, Wed, Sat and 14th to 17th April; May to Sept, daily; Oct, Mon, Wed and Sat, all 1 - 5pm (last admission 4.30pm) ★ Gardens and country park open all year, 10am - 5pm ★ Entrance: £2, children £1 (castle and gardens £4, children £2, pre-booked parties of 20 or more £3.20 per person, schools £1.60 per child

High above the shores of the Firth of Clyde and guarding the approaches to Western Scotland is this castle of locally-quarried sandstone. Its garden was an overgrown jungle of rhododendrons until it was restored by the Duchess of Montrose after World War I. She was much helped after 1930 when her daughter married John Boscawen of Tresco Abbey (see entry): many trees and plants here came by boat then from Tresco in the Scillies. Others came from subscriptions to the second generation of great plant-hunters like Kingdon-Ward and, in particular, George Forrest, one of the greatest of all collectors. Plants from the Himalayas, Burma, China and South America, normally considered tender, flourish in the mild climate. A good display of primulas in bog garden. The walled formal garden to the east of the castle is over 250 years old and has recently been restored as a Victorian garden with herbaceous plants, annuals and roses. It is impossible to list all the treasures of the woodland garden, but perhaps the most surprising is the huge size of the specimens in the lower rhododendron walk where *R. sinograndee* are found with leaves up to two feet long. Memorable views.

BROUGHTON HOUSE   24
12 High Street, Kirkcudbright, Dumfries and Galloway. Tel: (01557) 30437

The National Trust for Scotland ★ In Kirkcudbright High Street ★ Parking ★ Toilet facilities ★ Open April to 23rd Oct, daily, 1 - 5.30pm (last admission 4.45pm). Pre-booked groups may be admitted outside opening hours ★ Entrance: £1.80, concessions 90p (1994 prices)

Created by a well-known artist who lived here from 1901-33, E.A. Hornel, the garden reflects his interest in oriental art. After his death the house became a museum and its surroundings were gradually restored. The garden opens with a sunken courtyard beyond which is a pleasant hybrid, something between 'fantasy Japan and fantasy old-world cottage'.

BUGHTRIG 25
Leitholm, Nr Coldstream, Berwickshire, Borders.
Tel: (01890) 840678

Major General and The Hon. Mrs Charles Ramsay ★ ½m E of Leitholm on
B6461 ★ Parking ★ Small picnic area ★ Open June to Sept, 11am - 5pm ★
Entrance: £1, OAP and children under 14 50p

This is a traditional six-acre Scottish garden, but hedged rather than walled
and much closer to the house than usual. It is an interesting combination of
herbaceous plants, shrubs, annuals, vegetables and fruit. It is surrounded by
fine specimen trees which provide remarkable shelter.

CALLY GARDENS NURSERY 26
Gatehouse of Fleet, Castle Douglas, Nr Kirkcudbright, Dumfries
and Galloway.

Mr Michael Wickenden ★ From Dumfries on the A75, take the Gatehouse
turning and turn left through the Cally Palace Hotel gateway. Gardens
signposted ★ Suitable for wheelchairs ★ Dogs ★ Open 15th April to 8th Oct, Sats
and Suns, 10am - 5.30pm ★ Entrance: free

A nursery in an old two and three-quarter-acre walled garden which has large
beds of herbaceous plants and many unusual varieties, well worth a visit by
plant collectors. Large range of perennial geraniums, kniphofias, crocosmias
and others - 3000 varieties in all. The Cally oak woods which surround the
nursery have nature trails.

CANDACRAIG 27
Strathdon, Grampian. Tel: (019756) 51226

Mrs E.M. Young ★ On A97 Huntly - Dinnet road then A944 (formerly B973)
Strathdon - Tomintoul road ★ Best season: June to Aug ★ Parking ★ Toilet
facilities ★ Suitable for wheelchairs ★ Plants for sale ★ Open May, June and
Sept, daily, 2 - 6pm; July and Aug, daily, 10am - 6pm and at other times by
appointment ★ Entrance: £1, children free

At an altitude of 1000 feet this old walled garden dates from 1820 and covers
a three-acre sheltered site in upper Donside. The garden is now being
systematically restored by its present owner and features herbaceous borders,
old roses, cottage garden flowers and a newly-formed spring garden with
pond and meadow. There is a Victorian summerhouse in Gothic style.

CARNELL ★ 28
Hurlford, Ayrshire, Strathclyde. Tel: (0156384) 236

Mr and Mrs J.R. Findlay and Mr Ian Findlay (The Garden House) ★ 4m from
Kilmarnock, 6m from Mauchline on A76, 1½m on Ayrshire side of A719 ★
Parking free ★ Tea and biscuits by arrangement ★ Dogs on lead ★ Plants for sale.
Also flowers, home-bakes and crafts ★ Sixteenth-century peel tower ★ Garden
open 30th July, 2 - 5pm. Private parties by appointment ★ Entrance: £2,
children under 12 free

Exquisite example of 100 yards of linear herbaceous borders facing a rectangular pool with informal planting as a contrast on the opposite bank. Also

interesting rock garden, lilies. Walled garden. Burmese and Japanese features including a Chinese gazebo and Burmese dragons, all mementos of Cdr. Findlay's travels. Climbing the slope behind the pavilion in the SE corner is the rock garden. Garden adjacent to house is now quite mature, the entrance to the desmesne being through an archway bedecked with a Kiftsgate rose. All plants and vegetables grown with organic compost produced *in situ*. The remarkable thing is that 80 years ago this was only an old limestone quarry which was re-designed as a garden.

CASTLE KENNEDY AND LOCHINCH GARDENS ★★   29
Stranraer, Wigtownshire, Dumfries and Galloway.
Tel: (01776) 702024

The Earl and Countess of Stair ★ 5m from Stranraer on A75 ★ Best season: April/ May ★ Parking ★ Teas ★ Toilet facilities ★ Partly suitable for wheelchairs ★ Dogs on lead ★ Plants for sale ★ Shop ★ Open April to Sept, daily, 10am - 5pm ★ Entrance: £2, OAP £1.50, children £1, parties of 30 or more £1.60 per person, OAP £1.20, children 80p

One of Scotland's most famous gardens set on a peninsular between two lochs and well worth a visit for its sheer 67-acre magnificence and spectacular spring colour. The gardens were originally laid out in 1730 around the ruins of his castle home by Field Marshal the 2nd Earl of Stair, who used his unoccupied Dragoons to effect a major remoulding of the landscape, combining large formal swathes of mown grassland with massive formal gardens, criss-crossed with avenues and *allées* of large specimen trees. The garden is internationally famous for its pinetum, currently being replanted, for its good variety of tender trees and for its species rhododendrons including many of Sir Joseph Hooker's original introductions from his Himalayan expeditions. The monkey puzzle avenue, now sadly a little tattered, was once the finest in the world and there is also one of noble firs and another of hollies under-planted with embothriums and eucryphias. An impressive 2–acre circular lily pond puts everyone else's in their proper place and a good walk from this brings you back to the ruined castle and its walled garden, well planted with theme borders.

CASTLE OF MEY ★★   30
Caithness, Highlands.

H.M. Queen Elizabeth the Queen Mother ★ 1¹/₂m from Mey ★ Parking ★ Teas ★ Toilet facilities ★ Suitable for wheelchairs ★ Dogs on lead ★ Open 19th, 27th, July, 2nd Sept for charity ★ Entrance: £1.50, OAP and children under 12, £1

The Castle originates from the late sixteenth century and was renovated by The Queen Mother in 1955. Gardening would not be possible in such an exposed position without the protection of the 'Great Wall of Mey'. Within the walled garden, The Queen Mother has collected her favourite flowers; many were gifts and have special meaning. The personal private feeling pervades the whole garden which is especially well-planted and maintained. The colour schemes are very good, blending the garden with the vast natural panorama within which it is situated.

SCOTLAND

CAWDOR CASTLE ★ 31
Cawdor, Nairn, Highlands. Tel: (01667) 404615

The Countess Cawdor ★ Between Inverness and Nairn on the B9090 off the A96 ★ Best season: summer ★ Parking ★ Refreshments in restaurant or snack bar. Picnic area ★ Toilet facilities ★ Partly suitable for wheelchairs ★ Shops ★ Castle open ★ Garden open May to 1st Oct, daily, 10am – 5.30pm ★ Entrance: £2.50 (castle and garden £4.50, OAP £3.50, children £2.50. Family ticket £12.50. Parties of 20 or more £4 per person)

Frequently referred to as one of the Highland's most romantic castles and steeped in history, Cawdor Castle is a fourteenth-century keep with seventeenth- and nineteenth-century additions. The surrounding parkland is handsome and well-kept, though not in the grand tradition of classic landscapes. To the side of the castle is the formal garden where recently-added wrought-iron arches frame extensive herbaceous borders, a peony border, a very old hedge of mixed varieties of *Rosa pimpinellifolia*, the Scots or Burnet rose, a rose tunnel, old apple trees with climbing roses, interesting shrubs and lilies. An abundance of lavender and pinks complete a rather Edwardian atmosphere. The castle wall shelters *Exochorda*, *Abutilon vitifolium*, *Carpenteria californica* and *Rosa banksiae*. Pillar-box red seats create an unusual note in this splendidly flowery garden but the owners like them. The walled garden below the castle is being developed with a holly maze, a thistle garden and a white garden. There are fine views everywhere of the castle, the park and the surrounding countryside which one can enjoy more actively by walking one of the five nature trails which vary in length from half to five miles.

CLUNY HOUSE ★ 32
by Aberfeldy, Perthshire, Tayside. Tel: (01887) 820795

Mr J. and Mrs W. Mattingley ★ 32m NW of Perth. N of Aberfeldy, over the Wade's Bridge, take the Weem – Strathtay Road. Cluny House is signposted about 3m along this road ★ Limited parking ★ Plants for sale and seed list available on request ★ Open March to Oct, 10am – 6pm ★ Entrance: £2, children free

Unlike most other gardens this is as truly wild as one can find - friendly weeds grow unchecked for fear of disturbing the NCCPG collection of Asiatic primulas. Sheltered slopes create a moist microclimate where all the plants flourish abundantly, including a Wellingtonia with the British near-record girth of 35½ft. Superb woodland garden where many of the plants were grown from seed propagated by Mrs Mattingley's father from seed acquired from the Ludlow/Sherriff expedition to Bhutan in 1948. Special treats are the carpets of bulbs, trilliums and meconopsis, a fine selection of Japanese acers, *Prunus serrula*, hundreds of different rhododendrons, *Cardiocrinum giganteum*, 6ft lysichitum and many fine specimen trees.

CORSOCK HOUSE 33
Corsock, Castle Douglas, Dumfries and Galloway.

Mr and Mrs M.L. Ingall ★ 10m N of Castle Douglas on A712. Also signposted from A75 onto B794 ★ Best season: May ★ Parking ★ Refreshments for May opening date ★ Toilet facilities ★ Dogs on lead ★ Open 28th May for charity and by arrangement ★ Entrance: £1, children 50p

A most attractive 20-acre woodland garden with exceptionally fine plantings both of trees (*Fagus sylvatica*, Wellingtonia, oak, Douglas fir, cercidiphyllum, acer) and of rhododendrons (*thomsonii*, *lacteum*, *loderi*, *prattii*, *sutchuenense*). The knowledgeable owner has contributed most imaginatively to the layout of the gardens over the last 20 years, creating glades, planting vistas of azaleas and personally building a temple and *trompe l'oeil* bridge which give the gardens a classical atmosphere. An impressive highlight is the large water garden, again cleverly laid out and with the water–edge plantings set off by a background of mature trees with good autumn colour.

CRARAE GARDEN ★★ 34
Minard, by Inveraray, Argyll, Strathclyde. Tel: (01546) 86614

Crarae Gardens Charitable Trust ★ 11m S of Inveraray on A83 ★ Best season: spring and autumn ★ Parking ★ Refreshments: teas and coffee ★ Toilet facilities ★ Lower slopes suitable for wheelchairs ★ Dogs on short lead ★ Shop ★ Open Easter to Oct, daily, 9am - 6pm, Nov to Easter, daily, during daylight hours ★ Entrance: £2.50, children £1.50, family (2 adults and 2 children) £7, wheelchair users free (1994 prices)

The gardens were originally started by the present owner's grandmother, Grace Lady Campbell, in the early part of this century. Inspired by her nephew, Reginald Farrer, a famous traveller and plant collector, she and subsequently her son, Sir George Campbell (1894-1967), spent many years creating this superb 'Himalayan ravine' set in a Highland glen. Using surplus seed from the great plant expeditions, numerous gifts from knowledgeable friends and the shared expertise of a network of famous horticulturalists, Sir George planted a variety of rare trees which were his first love, exotic shrubs and species rhododendrons which now form great canopies above the winding paths. These, together with many other plants from the temperate world, make a magnificent spectacle of colour and differing perspectives, the whole enlivened by splendid torrents and waterfalls. The autumn colouring of sorbus, acers, liriodendrons, prunus, cotoneasters and berberis is one of the great features of the garden.

CRATHES CASTLE GARDEN ★★ 35
Crathes Castle, Banchory, Grampian. Tel: (01330) 844525

The National Trust for Scotland ★ 3m E of Banchory and 15m W of Aberdeen on A93 ★ Parking 200 yards from gardens, signposted ★ Refreshments: licensed restaurant ★ Toilet facilities ★ Partly suitable for wheelchairs ★ No dogs in garden, but nature/dog trail in grounds ★ Plants for sale ★ Shop ★ Castle open April to Oct, daily, 11am - 5.30pm (last tour 4.45pm). Other times by appointment ★ Garden and grounds open daily, 9.30am - sunset ★ Entrance: £1.80, OAP and children 90p (castle, garden and grounds £4, OAP and children £2). Pre-booked parties of 20 or more £3.20 per person, children £1.60. Reductions for gardens only or castle only (1994 prices)

The first view of Crathes is breathtaking – a romantic castle set in flowing lawns. The building dating from 1596 looks much as it did in the mid-eighteenth century but there is no record of how the garden then looked, although yew topiary of 1702 survives. Sir James Burnett, who inherited the estate, was a keen collector, and his wife was an inspired herbaceous planter, and the garden today reflects their achievements. In all there are eight gardens, each with a different theme. Rare shrubs reflect Burnett's interest in the Far East where he served in the army. Splendid wide herbaceous borders with clever plant associations were Lady Burnett's creation, most famous of which is the white border. There are many specialist areas such as the trough garden; the large greenhouses contain a collection of Malmaison carnations. Extensive wild gardens and grounds with picnic areas, with 10 miles of marked trails. Often compared to Hidcote but with evident inspiration from Jekyll, Crathes has wonders for the plantsperson, the designer and the ordinary visitor.

CRUICKSHANK BOTANIC GARDEN   36
St Machar Drive, Old Aberdeen, Grampian. Tel: (01224) 272704

The Cruickshank Trust and University of Aberdeen ★ 1½m N from city centre in Old Aberdeen on A978. Public entry by gate in the Chanonry ★ Best season: May to Aug ★ Suitable for wheelchairs ★ Dogs on lead ★ Open all year, Mon - Fri, 9am - 4.30pm; also May to Sept, Sat and Sun, 2 - 5pm ★ Entrance: free. Children must be accompanied by an adult

Endowed by Miss Anne H. Cruickshank in 1898 to cater for teaching and research in botany at the University of Aberdeen and for the public good, the original six acres were designed by George Nicholson of Kew. That layout disappeared with World War I. The long wall, herbaceous border and sunken garden date from 1920 but much reverted to vegetable cultivation during World War II. In 1970, the garden was extended and a new rock garden made. A terrace garden was added by the long wall in 1980, a new rose garden in 1986 and the peat walls restored in 1988. The rock garden, with a series of connecting pools, has interesting alpines, bulbs and dwarf shrubs. A small woodland area is rich in meconopsis, primulas, rhododendrons and hellebores. Proximity to the North Sea does not permit good growth of large conifers, with the exception of dawn redwood and *Pinus radiata*. There are fine species lilacs, witch hazels and the long wall shelters more tender exotics. The total area of the present garden is 11 acres, of which four acres are planted as an arboretum - this is reached by a path from the summit of the rock gardens.

CULZEAN CASTLE COUNTRY PARK ★★   37
Maybole, Ayrshire, Strathclyde. Tel: (016556) 269

The National Trust for Scotland ★ 14m S of Ayr on A719 ★ Parking ★ Refreshments ★ Toilet facilities ★ Suitable for wheelchairs ★ Dogs under control ★ Plants for sale ★ Shop ★ Castle open ★ Country park and gardens open April to 30th Oct, 11am - 5pm ★ Entrance: £3, children £1.50, parties £2.50 per person, schools £1.25 per child; additional charge for castle (1994 prices)

Over 350,000 people a year visit Culzean, regarded by many as the flagship of The National Trust for Scotland. The castle was originally a medieval forti- fied house atop the Ayrshire cliffs, but was extensively restructured by Robert Adam from 1771 in what has become known as his 'Culzean' style. This is reflected in the many fine architectural features scattered throughout the grounds and in particular the handsome Home Farm Courtyard, now a visitor centre. The country-park landscape covers 563 acres with a network of woodland and cliff-top paths, and the gardens themselves cover a spacious 30 acres and include all the traditional elements of a grand garden at the turn of the century, the main elements being a fine fountained pleasure garden and a vast walled garden with herbaceous and vegetable plantings. Note the charming camellia house, currently under restoration.

DALMENY PARK 38
Mons Hill, South Queensferry, West Lothian. Tel: (0131) 331 4804

The Earl of Rosebery ★ 7m W of Edinburgh city centre off A90 ★ Parking ★ Mons Hill is open for charity one or possibly two Suns at end of Feb/beginning of March depending on the snowdrops. Admission charge

Mons Hill is a partly wooded hill of semi-natural hardwoods with several acres of wild snowdrops, and outstanding views towards the Pentland Hills, Edinburgh and the Firth of Forth, weather permitting. The snowdrops are over a quarter of a mile uphill from the car park and must be seen to be believed. However, Wellington boots are recommended. There is no possibility of taking wheelchairs or vehicles up the hill.

DALMENY HOUSE 39
South Queensferry, West Lothian. Tel: (0131) 331 4804

The grounds around Dalmeny House are open when the house is open May to Sept, Sun, 1 - 5.30pm, Mon and Tues, 12 noon - 5.30pm (last admission on all days 4.45pm). Parties by arrangement at other times ★ Teas ★ Suitable for wheelchairs ★ Entrance: grounds free. House (with collection) £3.20, children (10-16) £1.60, under 10 free. Parties of 20 or more £2.50 per person during normal opening hours (1994 prices)

Some one and a half miles from Mons Hill is the Garden Valley and other ornamental areas close to Dalmeny House. These feature rhododendrons, also azaleas and specimen trees.

DALNAHEISH 40
Carsaig Bay, Tayvallich, by Lochgilphead, Argyll, Strathclyde. Tel: (01546) 870286

Mrs Cynthia and Miss Jane Lambie ★ Telephone for directions ★ Best season: April to Sept ★ Limited parking ★ Plants occasionally for sale ★ Open April to Sept by appointment ★ Entrance: donation

This mother and daughter team have devoted many years making their one and three-quarter-acre seaside garden into a plantsman's pleasure. They stock it from seed, personally chosen and sent from all over the world with the result that they have a highly original selection of hardy plants, particularly variegated and scented ones. Cynthia has 15 varieties of fruit, and Jane specialises in aquilegias, astilbes and pittosporums. Winding up the natural stone paths and through a short woodland garden, visitors are lead to what must be one of the best-positioned picnic tables in Scotland, overlooking the Atlantic Sound of Jura and magnificent surrounding mountain scenery. Very rare cubic sundial dated 1738. Midge-repellent is sometimes necessary.

DAWYCK BOTANIC GARDEN   41
Stobo, Peebleshire, Borders. Tel: (01721) 760254

Royal Botanic Garden, Edinburgh ★ 8m SW of Peebles, 28m from Edinburgh on B712 ★ Parking ★ Refreshments ★ Partly suitable for wheelchairs ★ Guide dogs only ★ Plants for sale ★ Shop ★ Open 15th March to 22nd Oct, daily, 10am - 6pm and at other times by arrangement ★ Entrance: £2, concessions £1.50, children 50p, family £4.50. Discounts for parties of 11 or more. Season tickets covering Dawyck, Logan and Younger available - telephone Royal Botanic Garden (0131) 552 7171

This is a specialist garden of the Royal Botanic Garden, Edinburgh, the home of the famous Dawyck beech; the garden has a large variety of interesting mature trees and young plantings of trees and shrubs, including unusual rhododendrons. Landscaped burnside walks take the visitor through mature woodland clothing the steep slopes of the tributary of the River Tweed, a setting that abounds in wildlife.

DOCHFOUR ESTATE ★   42
Dochfour, Inverness, Highlands. Tel: (0146386) 218 (estate office)

Lady Burton ★ 6m W of Inverness on A82 ★ Best season: April to Oct ★ Parking ★ Suitable for wheelchairs ★ Plants and pick-your-own fruit for sale ★ Open all year except 25th Dec, Mon - Fri, 10am - 5pm; also April to Oct, Sat and Sun, 2 - 5pm ★ Entrance: £1.50, OAP and children 50p

The estate is bounded by the River Ness to the east, and overlooked by steeply-rising hills providing a dramatic backdrop to the extensive walled kitchen gardens. The formal landscaped gardens are contained within high yew hedges clipped at intervals to provide spectacular views of the loch below. Large areas of rhododendron, terraces of daffodils, vast grass parterres and magnificent trees.

DRUM CASTLE   43
**Drumoak, by Banchory, Kincardine and Deeside, Grampian.
Tel: (01330) 811204**

The National Trust for Scotland ★ Off A93, 3m W of Peterculter, 10m W of Aberdeen ★ Parking ★ Refreshments ★ Toilet facilities ★ Shop ★ House open 14th April to Sept, daily, 1.30 - 5.30pm (July and Aug opens 11am) ★ Garden open May to Oct, daily, 10am - 6pm ★ Entrance: garden and grounds £1.50, OAP and children 80p (castle, garden and grounds £3.50, OAP and children £1.80) (1994 prices)

Within the old walled garden of the castle, The National Trust for Scotland has established a 'garden of historic roses' which was officially opened in June 1991 as part of the Diamond Jubilee celebrations of the Trust. The four quadrants of the garden are designed and planted with roses and herbaceous or other plants appropriate to the seventeenth, eighteenth, nineteenth and twentieth centuries respectively. The central feature is a copy of the gazebo at Tyninghame, East Lothian (see entry), and a small garden house in one corner, now restored, acts as an interpretive centre. The grounds around the castle also contain interesting conifers, spacious lawns and woodland walks in the Old Wood of Drum.

DRUMMOND CASTLE ★★ 44
Muthill, Nr Crieff, Perthshire, Tayside. Tel: (01764) 681321

Grimsthorpe and Drummond Castle Trust Ltd ★ 2m S of Crieff on A822 ★ Best season: June and July ★ Parking ★ Toilet facilities ★ Partly suitable for wheelchairs ★ Open May to Oct, daily, 2 - 6pm (last admission 5pm) ★ Entrance: £3, OAP £2, children £1.50

The gardens to this fine castle were first laid out in 1630 by John Drummond, 2nd Earl of Perth. Next to the castle, across a courtyard, is the house and below both is the great parterre garden with, at its centre, the famous sundial made by the master mason to Charles I. When the garden was revived by Lewis Kennedy, who worked at Drummond from 1818 to 1860, he achieved what the *Oxford Companion* calls 'effectively the re-creation of an idea of the seventeenth-century Scottish garden'. The long St Andrew's cross design has Italian, French and Dutch influences. Beautiful white marble Italian statuary is set in arbours along the southern borders, giving an overall sense of tranquillity and order. The *Oxford Companion* believes that the old arrangement of filling the 'compartments' of the cross with shrubs and herbaceous plants was more effective than today's style, in which some may feel the structure is too prominent. The fruit and vegetable gardens and glasshouses should also be visited.

DUNDONNELL ★ 45
By Garve, Ross-shire, Highlands. Tel: (0185483) 206

Mr A.S. Roger and Mr N.M. Roger ★ 24m from Ullapool, 31m from Garve off A832 between Braemore Toll and Gruinard Bay ★ Parking ★ Teas ★ Toilet facilities ★ Partly suitable for wheelchairs ★ Plants for sale ★ Open 8th, 14th June, 6th, 12th July, 2 - 5.30pm ★ Entrance: £1.50, children 50p

Unlike many of the gardens of Scotland's west coast, Dundonnell does not rely on rhododendrons for its effect. It is a very individual garden of grassed walks, box-edged paths, enclosures made by borders of varying sizes all within a garden walled on three sides with the fourth side bounded by the river. Very old yew and holly trees are striking, and there are also many exotic trees and shrubs – Stewartia species, *Acer palmatum* 'Senkaki', *Quercus pontica*, species hydrangeas, *Decaisnea fargesii* and the bamboo *Chusquea couleou*. The laburnum tunnel is as unexpected as the extensive collection of bonsai, many of considerable size, grown in a slatted house. This is a very tranquil garden to be appreciated at a leisurely pace – even the heavy rainfall will not detract from its charm.

DUNROBIN GARDENS 46
Golspie, Sutherland, Highlands. Tel: (01408) 633177/633268

The Sutherland Trust ★ 1m N of Golspie on A9 ★ Parking ★ Refreshments: tea rooms ★ Toilet facilities ★ Shop ★ Castle open ★ Garden open 14th, 15th April, 10.30am - 4pm, 16th April, 1 - 4pm, 17th April, 10.30am - 4pm, May to 15th Oct, Mon - Sat, 10.30am - 5.30pm, Sun, 1 - 5.30pm (last admission 5pm and closes one hour earlier during May and Oct) ★ Entrance: £3.80, OAP £2.40, children £1.90, family £10, parties £3.50 per person, children £1.75

These Victorian formal gardens were designed in the grand French style to echo the architecture of Dunrobin Castle which rises high above them and looks out over the Moray Firth. They were laid out by the architect Charles Barry in 1850. Descending the stone terraces, one can see the round garden (evocative of the Scottish shield, the head gardener suggests), grove, parterre and herbaceous borders laid out beneath. The round ponds, some with fountains, are a particular feature, together with the wrought-iron Westminster gates. Roses have been replaced with hardy geraniums, antirrhinums, echiums and *Potentilla fruticosa* 'Abbotswood'. An eighteenth-century summerhouse which was converted into a museum in the nineteenth century is now also open to the public. In the policies (estate lands) there are many woodland walks.

EARLSHALL CASTLE 47
by St Andrews, Leuchars, Fife. Tel: (01334 839) 205

The Baron and Baroness of Earlshall ★ Follow signs from centre of Leuchars, A919 ★ Parking ★ Refreshments ★ Suitable for wheelchairs in garden ★ Guide dogs only ★ Plants for sale occasionally ★ Shop ★ Castle open as gardens ★ Gardens open by appointment for parties only ★ Entrance: £2.90, OAP £2.30, children £1, parties £2.30 per person (1994 prices) Note: at time of going to press this property was up for sale

A walled garden situated beside the sixteenth-century castle divided by yew hedges into a series of external 'rooms'. The most significant of these contains topiary 'chessmen' (although they are in fact planted in the form of four diagonal crosses, or Scottish saltires), and there is also a secret garden, orchard garden, herbaceous border and 'bowling green' with rose terrace, and attractively laid-out kitchen and herb gardens. Interesting garden architecture includes a gardener's cottage, dowry house, summerhouse and arbour, all bearing the stamp of Sir Robert Lorimer's eye for detail. Lorimer, famous for Kellie Castle (see entry), believed in the garden as a place of repose and solitude, formal near the house but becoming 'less trim as it gets further...and then naturally marries with the demesne that lies beyond'.

EDZELL CASTLE ★ 48
Edzell, Nr Brechin, Angus, Tayside. Tel: (01356) 648631

Historic Scotland ★ 4m N of Brechin. Take A94 and after 2m fork left on B966 ★ Parking ★ Picnic area ★ Toilet facilities ★ Suitable for wheelchairs ★ Dogs ★ Shop ★ Ruins and Visitor Centre (closed Thurs pm and Fri in winter) ★ Garden open April to Sept, Mon - Sat, 9.30am - 6pm, Sun, 2 - 6pm, Oct to March, Mon - Sat, 9.30am - 4pm, Sun, 2 - 4pm ★ Entrance: £2, OAP £1.25, children (6-16) 75p, under 6 free. 10 per cent reduction for parties of 11 or more

In 1604 Sir David Lindsay made a remarkable small walled garden at his fortress at Edzell; it remains today probably the oldest complete and unaltered garden in the country. By the time they came into the custody of H.M. Office of Works in 1932, the garden and castle had lain in ruins for over 150 years. Although the plantings are new, dating from the 1930s, they are elaborate examples in the manner of the period of the early seventeenth century. Meticulously-kept parterres of box, lawn, and bedding are contained within walls of unique and curious design. There are 43 panels of alternating chequered niches and sculptured symbolic figures. There are large recesses below for flowers. The whole is laid out to be viewed from a corner garden-house and the windows of the now-ruined castle. Edzell is quite a small and a charming example of an ordered Victorian Scottish Highland village. There are shops, a tea room and three hotels. A must for lovers of the historical and romantic.

FALKLAND PALACE GARDEN   49
Falkland, Fife. Tel: (01337) 857397

The National Trust for Scotland ★ 11m N of Kirkcaldy via A912. M9 junction 8 from Forth Road Bridge ★ Parking 100 yards from palace ★ Refreshments in village ★ Toilet facilities in town car park and next to NT shop ★ Suitable for wheelchairs ★ Shop ★ Palace open as garden (last tour of palace 4.30pm) ★ Garden open April to 23rd Oct, Mon – Sat, 11am – 5.30pm, Sun, 1.30 - 6pm ★ Entrance: £2, children £1 (palace and garden £4, children £2) (1994 prices)

This was originally the garden for the sixteenth-century palace which was the hunting lodge for the Stuart monarchs. Kings and queens from James II to Charles II enjoyed the Fife landscape and the grounds of the Renaissance palace. In the twentieth century the garden was a 'Dig for Victory' effort during World War II and was thereafter remodelled by the landscape designer Percy Cane. The palace itself lends a gracious and dignified atmosphere to this three-acre garden. The shrub island borders are now fully mature and provide a good illustration of how to break up large areas of lawn. In addition, visitors can see the royal tennis court (i.e. real tennis) where occasional competitions of this old game are still staged. Features include an outdoor chequers game near the herb garden. Orchard. Interesting village houses nearby.

FINLAYSTONE   50
Langbank, Renfrewshire, Strathclyde. Tel: (0147554) 285

Mr George Gordon Macmillan of Macmillan ★ 8m W of Glasgow Airport, on A8 W of Langbank ★ Best season: spring and autumn ★ Parking ★ Refreshments: at 'Celtic Tree' in walled garden ★ Toilet facilities ★ Suitable for wheelchairs ★ Dogs on lead (off lead in woodland) ★ Shop and visitor centre open 12 noon – 4.30pm ★ House open, April to Aug, Sun, 2.30 – 4.30pm ★ Garden open all year, daily, 10.30am – 5pm ★ Entrance: £1.50, OAP and children £1

Designed in 1900 and enhanced and tended over the last 50 years by the late Lady Macmillan, much respected doyenne of Scottish gardens, and her family, this spacious garden is imaginatively laid out over 10 acres with a further 70 acres of mature woodland walks. Large, elegant lawns framed by long herbaceous borders, interesting shrubberies and mature copper beech look down over the River Clyde. John Knox's tree, a Celtic paving 'maze' laid out by Lady Macmillan's daughter-in-law Jane, a paved fragrant garden with the handicapped in mind and a new bog garden are all added attractions. The walled garden is planted in the shape of a Celtic ring cross.

GLAMIS CASTLE   51
Glamis, by Forfar, Angus, Tayside.
Tel: (01307) 840242/840243 (Estates Office)

Earl of Strathmore and Kinghorne ★ 5m W of Forfar on A94 ★ Parking, inc. coaches ★ Refreshments: in Castle Restaurant 10.30am to 5.30pm ★ Picnic area ★ Toilet facilities ★ Suitable for wheelchairs ★ Shops ★ Castle open, guided tours ★ Garden open April to 30th Oct, daily, 10.30am - 5.30pm ★ Entrance: £2.20, OAP, students and children (5-16) £1.10, disabled persons free (castle and grounds: £4.50, OAP and students £3.50, children (5-16) £2.40, family ticket £13). Reductions for groups

At the end of a long, tree-lined avenue and against the backdrop of mountain and moorland, the turrets and spires of Glamis Castle beckon the visitor to explore its secrets and to enjoy the tranquillity of its grounds. Although much older, the park was landscaped in the 1790s by a garden designer working under the influence of 'Capability' Brown, and the avenue was replanted about 1820. Near the Castle, on the lawn, there is an intriguing baroque sundial, 21 feet tall and with a face for every week of the year. On the east side of the Castle is a two-acre Italian garden consisting of high yew hedges, herbaceous borders, fountains and seventeenth-century-style gazebos, and the creation of this quiet haven is commemorated by an engraved stone. Glamis was the childhood home of Queen Elizabeth, the Queen Mother, and in celebration of her 80th birthday, a new pair of wrought iron gates was erected here. A nature trail winds through the magnificent Douglas firs in the policies.

GLASGOW BOTANIC GARDENS 52
Great Western Road, Glasgow, Strathclyde. Tel: (0141) 3342422

Glasgow City Council ★ Near the centre of Glasgow, corner of Great Western Road and Queen Margaret Drive ★ Parking outside ★ Toilet facilities ★ Suitable for wheelchairs ★ Dogs on lead ★ Gardens open daily, 7am - dusk. Kibble Palace Glasshouse open 10am - 4.45pm (4.15pm in winter). Main Range open 1 - 4.45pm (from 12 noon on Sun and to 4.15pm in winter) ★ Entrance: free

A pleasant afternoon's walk with well-maintained herbaceous, shrub and annual borders. Large shrubs have been added to obstruct children who caused so much damage when planting was more open. Re-landscaping here should be completed soon. The 'Systematic Garden' has plants grouped together in family beds, representing the more important genera and families of plants hardy in Scotland. The use of this garden for study is emphasised, while at the same time it is labour-intensive, so there are problems of maintenance and there have been many losses. That said, the chief attraction, and well worth visiting, is the old Kibble Palace glasshouse of 1873 where naked marble statues keep warm in a temperate zone climate. In the series of interconnecting neighbouring glasshouses are displays of orchids, begonias, cacti and tropical plants - all meticulously maintained. It has to be said that some visitors find this disappointing for a botanic garden, though the Council proposes to give attention to the interpretation/educational aspect as resources become available and considerable improvements are planned in the months and years ahead.

GLENARN ★ 53
Rhu, Dunbartonshire, Strathclyde. Tel: (01436) 820493

Michael and Sue Thornley ★ On A814 between Helensburgh and Garelochhead. Go up Pier Road to Glenarn Road ★ Parking ★ Refreshments on special open days only ★ Toilet facilities ★ Dogs on lead ★ A few plants for sale ★ Open 21st March to 21st June, dawn - dusk ★ Entrance: £1

Established in the 1930s in a Victorian garden by the Gibson family and fed by the famous plant expeditions of that decade, this is a very special woodland garden. Well-kept paths meander round a 10–acre sheltered bowl, sometimes tunnelling under superb giant species rhododendrons (including a falconeri grown from Hooker's original seed in 1849), sometimes allowing a glorious vista across the garden to the Clyde estuary, and sometimes stopping the visitor short to gaze with unstinted admiration at 40-foot magnolias, pieris, olearias, eucryphias and hoherias. Michael and Sue Thornley, both professional architects, acquired Glenarn some years ago and with almost no help are successfully replanting and restoring where necessary, whilst still retaining the special atmosphere created by such magnificent growth. An especially pleasing finale is provided by winding down through a nook-and-cranny rock garden - not suitable however for those who find walking very difficult.

GLENBERVIE   54
by Drumlithie, Stonehaven, Kincardineshire, Grampian.
Tel: (01569) 740226

Mr and Mrs C.S. MacPhie ★ 8m from Laurencekirk, 6m from Stonehaven off A940 Laurencekirk - Stonehaven road. On a minor road 3m W of Drumlithie village ★ Parking ★ Partly suitable for wheelchairs ★ Open one day for charity ★ Entrance: £1.50, children 80p

Two very different gardens may be enjoyed at Glenbervie - a traditional Scottish walled garden on a slope and a woodland garden by a stream. Occupying one wall of an enclosed garden is a fine example of a Victorian conservatory with a great diversity of pot plants and climbers on the walls creating a spectacular display. Elsewhere in the walled area is a typical mix of herbaceous plants, fruit, vegetables and summer bedding. There are many shrub and old roses, and on walls and pillars many climbing and rambler roses. In spring there are good displays of bulbs. The woodland garden with its drifts of primulas, ferns and interesting shrubs is beautiful in early summer. There are fine trees near the house.

GLENDOICK GARDENS   55
Glendoick, by Perth, Tayside.
Tel: Nursery (01738) 860205; Garden centre (01738) 860260

Mr and Mrs Peter Cox and Kenneth Cox ★ 8m from Perth, 14m from Dundee on A85 ★ Parking in grounds ★ Toilet facilities ★ Partly suitable for wheelchairs ★ Garden centre open all year at the main road ★ Open 7th, 14th, 21st, 28th May, 2 - 5pm. Parties must pre-book ★ Entrance: £1.50, children under 5 free

One of the world's most comprehensive collections of rhododendrons is contained within the grounds of this fine Georgian mansion which has an association with Bonnie Prince Charlie, who is reputed to have visited the Laird of Glendoick one dark night in 1745. The plant collection was started by the late Euan H.M. Cox and the present owners planted an arboretum in 1993 in memory of the 100th anniversary of his birth. The woodland garden which has also been extended is full of wild naturalised plants as well as introductions. Border and conservatory near the house. Through the walled garden is the old Japanese garden, much decayed but with fine trees.

GLENWHAN GARDEN ★ 56
**Dunragit, by Stranraer, Wigtownshire, Dumfries and Galloway.
Tel: (015814) 00222**

Mr and Mrs Knott ★ 7m E of Stranraer, 1m off A75 at Dunragit. Signposted ★ Parking ★ Refreshments: in licensed restaurant ★ Toilet facilities ★ Partly suitable for wheelchairs ★ Guide dogs only ★ Plants for sale ★ Shop ★ Garden open April to Sept, daily, 10am - 5pm ★ Entrance: £1.80, OAP £1.50, children under 12 50p, toddlers free. Party rates available

This very exciting 12-acre garden has commanding views over Luce Bay and the Mull of Galloway, and is set in an area of natural beauty, with rocky outcrops and Whinnie Knowes. Difficult to believe that it was only started in 1979 and was developed by the owners and one man. Because of the Gulf Stream and consequent mild climate exotic plants thrive amongst the huge collections of trees, shrubs and plants. Seats and walkways abound in this maze of hilly plantings mostly overlooking the central lochans and bog gardens. Collections, whether of genera or reminders of friends or particular themes of interest, are to be seen everywhere. The garden continues to expand and progress at a steady rate, and the creator of this private garden, Tessa Knott, has worked hard, illustrating and inspiring proof that the making of a large garden can be possible. She has had no formal horticultural training and began as a complete amateur in the plant world.

GOWRANES ★ 57
Kinnaird by Inchture, Perthshire, Tayside. Tel: (01828) 86752

Professor and Mrs Park ★ 11m from Perth and Dundee, 3m from Inchture. Follow signs for Kinnaird turn off A90 Perth - Dundee road ★ Best seasons: spring and early summer ★ Parking ★ Toilet facilities ★ Open by appointment ★ Entrance: £2, children free

A garden full of surprises, lovingly carved out of a difficult sloping rocky site with magnificent views over the Carse of Gowrie. The house is partly surrounded by stone-flagged terraces overflowing with plants. Lower-level lawns are planted with specimen trees such as *Abies koreana* and *Prunus serrula*. From here maze-like paths lead you up and down through cool, intensive plantings of shade-loving plants, rhododendrons, camellias, azaleas, ferns, meconopsis and many others. At the bottom of the slope there is a rushing burn that has been formed into a series of pools and waterfalls. This marks the western boundary. Great masses of primulas have seeded themselves here amongst the gunneras, hostas and *Lysichiton americanus*. The site was originally a pig farm and, much to the horror of the present owners, many 'bodies' were found during the garden construction but, as they say, they probably contributed to the healthy and lush-looking plants.

GREENBANK GARDEN ★ 58
Nr Clarkston, Glasgow, Strathclyde. Tel: (0141639) 3281

The National Trust for Scotland ★ From Clarkston Toll take Mearns Road for 1m. Signposted ★ Parking ★ Refreshments ★ Toilet facilities ★ Suitable for wheelchairs ★ Dogs on lead, but not in walled garden ★ Plants for sale ★ Shop ★ Garden open all year, daily except 1st, 2nd Jan and 25th, 26th Dec, 9.30am - sunset ★ Entrance: £2, children £1 (1994 prices)

Large old walled garden of eighteenth-century house divided into many sections, imaginatively offering practical demonstrations to illustrate the design and planting of small gardens. The colour combinations are especially good. All the plants are in very good condition and admirably labelled. An old hard tennis court in the corner has been converted into a spacious and pleasant area with ideas for disabled and infirm gardeners, with raised beds and a waist-high running-water pond. Wheelchair access to the glasshouse and potting shed allows disabled people to attend classes and work here. Woodland walks are filled with spring bulbs and shrubs and there are usually Highland cattle in the paddock. Advice Centre programme available.

HILL OF TARVIT MANSION-HOUSE 59
Cupar, Fife. Tel: (01334) 653127

The National Trust for Scotland ★ 2½m S of Cupar off A916 ★ Parking ★ Picnic area ★ Toilet facilities ★ Partly suitable for wheelchairs ★ Plants for sale, especially one weekend in early Oct ★ Shop in house ★ House open 1st, 2nd, 8th, 9th, 14th to 17th, 22nd, 23rd, 29th, 30th April; May to 23rd Oct, daily, 1.30 - 5.30pm (last admission 4.45pm) ★ Garden open daily, 9.30am - sunset ★ Entrance: £1, children 50p (honesty box) (house and garden £3, children £1.50, parties of 20 or more £2.40 per person) (1994 prices)

The garden surrounds the charming Edwardian mansion, designed in 1906 for a jute magnate by Sir Robert Lorimer who also laid out the grounds to the south of the mansion-house. There is a lovely rose garden. Good-size borders are filled with an attractive variety of perennials, annuals and heaths, and the grounds as a whole contain many unusual ornamental trees and shrubs now reaching maturity. The views over Fife are particularly fine. The garden is maintained by The National Trust for Scotland which regularly upgrades the plantings to include newer and unusual specimens. A good garden for amateurs and keen plantspersons. A massive plant sale is held each October - there is no entry charge and the public queue at the gate well before the 10.30am opening.

THE HIRSEL 60
Coldstream, Berwickshire, Borders. Tel: (01890) 882834

Lord Home of the Hirsel, KT ★ 50m from Edinburgh, 60m from Newcastle, W of Coldstream on A697 ★ Parking ★ Refreshments: café in main season. Picnic areas ★ Toilet facilities ★ Suitable for wheelchairs ★ Dogs on lead ★ Craft workshops ★ Grounds open daily during daylight hours ★ Entrance: parking charge £2 per car

Hirsel House is not open but at all seasons of the year the grounds have much of interest and enjoyment for the visitor who values the peace and ever-changing beauty of the countryside. There is something for the ornithologist, botanist, forester, zoologist, historian and archaeologist. In spring, snowdrops and aconites and then acres of daffodils herald the coming summer. The birds, resident and migrant, of which 169 have been definitely identified within the estate boundaries, start busying themselves around their nesting sites. From mid/late-May to mid-June the rhododendron wood, Dundock, is justly famous for its kaleidoscopic colouring and breathtaking scents. Rose beds, herbaceous and shrub borders follow through the summer. In October and November, the leaves turning on trees and shrubs provide attractive autumn colouring, and hundreds of duck, geese and gulls make the lake their nightly home. In winter the same trees are stark but magnificent in their skeletal forms against storm clouds and sunsets.

HOUSE OF PITMUIES ★★ 61
Guthrie, by Forfar, Tayside. Tel: (01241) 828245

Mrs Farquhar Ogilvie ★ 1½m from Friockheim, route A932 ★ Best season: May to July ★ Parking ★ Refreshments: off A932 ½m W at Trumpeton Forge Tea-room open daily, except Tues, 12 noon - 5pm ★ Partly suitable for wheelchairs ★ Dogs on lead ★ Home-grown plants and soft fruit for sale in season ★ House open for parties and teas by appointment ★ Garden open daily, April to Oct, 10am - 5pm and at other times by appointment ★ Entrance: £2 by collection box

In the grounds of an attractive eighteenth-century house and courtyard, these beautiful walled gardens lead down towards a small river with an informal riverside walk and two unusual buildings, a turreted dovecot and a Gothic wash-house. There are rhododendron glades with other unusual trees and shrubs, but pride of place must go to the spectacular semi-formal gardens behind the house. Exquisite old-fashioned roses and a series of long borders containing a dramatic palette of massed delphiniums and other herbaceous perennials in July constitute one of the most memorable displays of its type to be found in Scotland.

HOUSE OF TONGUE ★ 62
Tongue, by Lairg, Sutherland, Highlands. Tel: (0184755) 209

Countess of Sutherland ★ 1m N of Tongue off A838 ★ Parking ★ Open by appointment and 29th July for charity ★ Entrance: £1, children 50p

Sheltered from wind and salt by tall trees, this walled garden is a haven in an otherwise exposed environment. Adjoining the seventeenth-century house, it is laid out after the traditional Scottish acre with gravel and grass walks between herbaceous beds and hedged vegetable plots and orchard. A stepped beech-hedged walk leads up to a high terrace which commands a fine view over the Kyle of Tongue. The centrepiece of the garden is Lord Reay's sundial (1714), a sculpted obelisk of unusual design.

INNES HOUSE GARDEN 63
Elgin, Moray, Grampian. Tel: (01343) 842228

Mr and Mrs Mark Tennant ★ Off A96 on B9103 in direction of Lossiemouth, 5m E of Elgin ★ Parking ★ Suitable for wheelchairs ★ Dogs on lead ★ Open to parties for house and garden by prior appointment only

An extensive ornamental garden divided into compartments, the whole framed by a wide variety of mature and interesting trees. The gardens were partially replanned and reorientated by the present owner's great grand-mother in 1912 when yew hedges were planted, providing a central walk leading to a lily pond. A charming rose garden has been created on the site of the original chapel with the chapel font and cross in the centre. The large trees are a major feature of the property - 47 varieties are represented, many estimated to be over 200 years old, including rare oaks, Californian 'Madrona' and Chinese beech. A complete tree list is available.

INVERESK LODGE AND VILLAGE GARDENS 64
Nr Musselburgh, East Lothian, Lothian. Tel: (0131) 2265922

Various owners inc. The National Trust for Scotland (Lodge) ★ 6m E of Edinburgh, S of Musselburgh via A6124 ★ Best season: summer ★ Parking ★ Garden open all year, Mon – Fri, 10am - 4.30pm, Sat and Sun, 2 - 5pm (but closed Sats Oct to March). Privately-owned gardens in the village open one day for charity with teas ★ Entrance: £1, honesty box (1994 price)

This large seventeenth-century house in the village of Inveresk, now owned by The National Trust for Scotland, is situated on a steeply sloping site. The high stone retaining-walls are well-planted with a wide range of climbers. There are numerous flowerbeds; a particularly good border is devoted to shrub roses. A peat bed permits a greater diversity of planting. The garden has been completely remade since it came under the ownership of the Trust. No attempt has been made to re-create a period style. The garden is 'modern' in most respects, semi-formal, well-planted, very well-maintained and offers a wide selection of plants flowering from spring through autumn. The village itself is a unique, unspoilt example of eighteenth-century villa development with houses dating from the late seventeenth and early eighteenth centuries. All have well laid-out gardens enclosed by high walls and containing a wide range of shrubs and trees as well as some unusual plants.

INVEREWE GARDEN ★★ 65
Poolewe, Ross and Cromarty, Highlands. Tel: (0144586) 200

The National Trust for Scotland ★ 6m NE of Gairloch on A832 ★ Parking ★ Refreshments ★ Toilet facilities ★ Partly suitable for wheelchairs ★ Plants for sale ★ Shop and Visitor Centre ★ Garden open all year, daily, 9.30am - sunset ★ Entrance: £3, concessions £1.50, parties £2.40 per person, concessions £1.20 (1994 prices)

This garden is spectacular. Created from 1865 on the shores of the sea loch, Loch Ewe, it covers the entire Am Ploc Ard peninsular. Planned as a wild garden around one dwarf willow on peat and sandstone, it has been developed as a series of walks through herbaceous and rock gardens, a wet valley, a rhododendron walk and a curved vegetable garden and orchard. This is a plantsman's garden (labelling is discreet) containing many tender species from Australia, New Zealand, China and the Americas, sheltered by mature beech and pine trees. New Zealand plants include the National collections of the genera *Olearia* and *Ourisia*. The garden is well-tended and way-marked. Note: midge-repellent is advised and on sale at main desk.

JOHNSTON GARDENS 66
Viewfield Gardens, Aberdeen, Grampian. Tel: (01224) 276276

Aberdeen City Council ★ In Aberdeen, ¼m S of Queens Road (A944 to Alford), ¼m W of junction with ring road ★ Best seasons: spring and summer ★ Parking ★ Toilet facilities ★ Partly suitable for wheelchairs ★ Open daily, 8am - one hour before dusk ★ Entrance: free

When Johnston House was demolished and the grounds sold for redevelopment, it was impossible to utilise the deepest area of the ravine. This was converted into a water and rock garden by the City of Aberdeen Parks and Recreation Department. The result is a very congenial oasis of trees, shrubs and mature

...ndrons surrounding a small lake complete with an island, rustic bridges
an... ...sident waterfowl. The rock and scree gardens have some interesting
plants, and primulas and astilbes edge the outlet from the lake in summer.

JURA HOUSE 67
Ardfin, Isle of Jura, Strathclyde. Tel: (0149682) 315

*Riley–Smith family ★ On Jura, 5m SE of the ferry terminal off A846. Vehicle
ferries from Kennacraig by Tarbert to Port Askaig, Islay, and from Islay to
Feolin, Jura ★ Best season: summer ★ Parking ★ Toilet facilities ★ Dogs on leads
★ Plants for sale ★ Open all year, 9am – 5pm ★ Entrance: £2 (inc. booklet),
children under 16 free. Collecting box*

A circular walk around the Jura House estate illustrates the rich natural
history and geology of the island. Starting from the car park, the visitor walks
through native woodland and follows the fuchsia–clad banks of the burn to
where it plunges into a ravine, filled with ferns and lichens, over the raised
beach to the sea. Spectacular views of the Islay coast accompany the steep
path down to the shore. Dykes and rock formations are home to wild scree
plants and scrubby trees, and here is an example of *Machair* – dune grassland. After the climb back up the cliff, signs guide the visitor to the garden
of Jura House. This organic walled garden is a sheltered haven with many
unusual plants, including a collection of Australasian origin. Linger awhile
before continuing on the woodland path back to the Lodge.

KAILZIE GARDENS ★ 68
Peebles, Peebleshire, Borders. Tel: (01721) 20007

*Lady Angela Buchan-Hepburn ★ 2¹/₂m from Peebles on B7062 ★ Parking ★ Tea
room and restaurant ★ Toilet facilities ★ Suitable for wheelchairs ★ Dogs on lead
★ Shop ★ Open April to 30th Oct, 11am – 5.30pm ★ Entrance: £1.80 – £2
(depending on season), children 50p*

'A Pleasure Garden' is the description in one of the advertisements for
Kailzie (pronounced Kailie) and very apt it is too. The gardens of 17 acres
are situated in a particularly attractive area of the beautiful Tweed Valley and
are surrounded by breathtaking views. The Old Mansion Home was pulled
down in 1962 and the vast walled garden, which still houses the magnificent
greenhouse, was transformed by Angela Buchan-Hepburn from vegetables to
a garden of meandering lawns and island beds. Full of interesting shrubs and
plants for drying, there are many surprises including a herb garden, choice
flower area, secret gardens, loving seats invitingly placed under garlanded
arbours and several pieces of statuary which have been thoughtfully sited. A
magnificent fountain at the end of the herbaceous borders leads on to woods
and huge stately trees, and from here you may stroll down the Major's walk
which is lined with laburnum and underplanted with rhododendrons, azaleas,
blue poppies and primulas. From here you can go to the small duck pond. A
fishing pond for trout is being opened.

KELLIE CASTLE 69
Pittenweem, Fife. Tel: (01333) 720271

The National Trust for Scotland ★ 3m NNW of Pittenweem on B9171 towards

Arncroach ★ Best season: summer ★ Parking 100 yards, closer parking for disabled ★ Limited refreshments in castle ★ Toilet facilities, not for disabled ★ Partly suitable for wheelchairs ★ Shop ★ Castle open 14th to 17th April; May to Oct, daily, all 1.30 – 5.30pm ★ Garden and grounds open all year, daily, 9.30am – sunset ★ Entrance: £1, children 50p (castle and garden £3, OAP and children £1.50) (1994 prices)

The garden appears to be sixteenth-century in plan, embellished by Professor James Lorimer and his family in late Victorian times. Entered by a door in a high wall, the garden is small (one acre) and inspires dreams within every gardener's reach. Simple borders, such as one of catmint, capture the imagination as hundreds of bees and butterflies work the flowers. Areas of lawn are edged with box hedges, borders, arches and trellises. In one corner, behind a trellis, is a small romantic garden within a garden. A large, green-painted commemorative seat designed by Hew Lorimer provides outstanding focal interest at the end of one of the main walks. The head gardener is establishing a collection of old and unusual vegetable varieties and employing only organic gardening methods, putting heart back into the soil through liberal use of compost. Roses on trellis and on arches abound.

KILBRYDE CASTLE 70
Dunblane, Perthshire, Central. Tel: (01786) 823104

Sir Colin Campbell ★ Off A820 Dunblane – Doune road ★ Best season: April to July ★ Parking ★ Partly suitable for wheelchairs ★ Open 12th March, 9th, 30th April, 21st May, 11th June, 9th July, 13th Aug, 10th Sept, 8th Oct, 2 – 5pm for charity and also by appointment ★ Entrance: £2, OAP and children £1.50

A good example of a partly-mature 20-acre garden created over the last 15 years by the enthusiastic owner and his highly knowledgeable helper, who are constantly introducing new features and plant content. Imaginatively-placed borders filled with constant colour on wide lawns sloping down to a woodland water garden. A good collection of bulbs in March to April followed by rhododendrons, azaleas and shrub roses. Plantings of clematis.

KILDRUMMY CASTLE GARDENS ★ 71
Nr Alford, Aberdeen, Grampian. Tel: (019755) 71203/71277

Kildrummy Castle Garden Trust ★ 2m from Mossat, 10m from Alford, 17m from Huntly. Take A944 from Alford, following signs to Kildrummy, left on A97. From Huntly turn right on to A97 ★ Parking: car park free inside hotel main entrance. Coaches park in hotel delivery entrance ★ Picnics at car park only ★ Toilet facilities, inc. disabled ★ Suitable for wheelchairs ★ Dogs on lead ★ Plants for sale ★ Visitor centre and video room ★ Woodland walks, children's play area ★ Open April to Oct, daily, 10am – 5pm ★ Entrance: £1.70, children (5-16) 50p

The gardens are set in a deep ravine between the ruins of a thirteenth-century castle and a Tudor-style house, now the hotel. The rock garden, by Backhouse of York (1904), occupies the site of the quarry which provided the stone for the castle. The narrowest part of the ravine is traversed by a copy of the fourteenth-century Auld Brig O'Balgownie, Old Aberdeen bridge built by Col. Ogston in 1900. This provides a focus for the water garden commissioned from a firm of Japanese landscape gardeners at the same period.

Backhouse continued the planting. In April the reflections in the still water of the larger pools increase the impact of the luxurious *Lysichiton americanus*, and later come primulas, a notable *Schizophragma hydrangeoides*; there are fine maples, rhododendron species and hybrids, oaks and conifers. Although a severe frost pocket the garden can grow embothriums, dieramas and other choice plants. A garden for all seasons, but especially beautiful in autumn, with the colchicums and brilliant acers, all sheltered by specimen trees.

KINROSS HOUSE 72
Kinross, Tayside.

Sir David Montgomery ★ N of Dunfermline, E of M90, in the centre of Kinross ★ Toilet facilities ★ Suitable for wheelchairs ★ Plants for sale ★ Open May to Sept, daily, 10am – 7pm ★ Entrance: £2, children 50p

There are four acres of formal walled garden round the mansion designed in the 1680s, restored early this century, all beautifully maintained. The walls, surmounted by fine statuary, have decorative gates. This is a formal garden of herbaceous borders, some with colour themes, and rose borders round the fountain. Yew hedges in interesting shapes, with well-placed seating for those in a contemplative mood or wishing to view Loch Leven Castle on the nearby island. It was here that Mary Queen of Scots was imprisoned in1567 and though it has no garden, it would be churlish not to walk to the pier to make the short boat trip to its sombre walls.

KITTOCH MILL 73
Carmunnock, Strathclyde. Tel: (0141) 6444712

Pat and Howard Jordan ★ On the B759 Busby – Carmunnock road. Signposted ★ Best season: June ★ Limited parking ★ Plants for sale ★ Open by appointment and 11th, 25th June, 2 – 5pm ★ Entrance: £1

A charming small garden created by the owners and set above the mill-stream waterfall adjacent to a Site of Special Scientific Interest. This is surely a place of pilgrimage for all hosta lovers as Pat and Howard have the NCCPG collection of this popular plant. Over 250 different varieties, all professionally labelled, grow in luxurious clumps without a slugbite in sight.

LANGWELL 74
Berriedale, Caithness, Highlands. Tel: (015935) 278

Lady Anne Bentinck ★ 2m from Berriedale on the A9 Helmsdale – Wick road ★ Parking ★ Teas ★ Partly suitable for wheelchairs ★ Open 6th, 13th Aug, 2 – 5.30pm ★ Entrance: £1.50 (1994 price)

The bare landscape of Caithness does not support too many gardens of interest, but here in the shelter of the Langwell Water is one of the happy exceptions. Reached by a two-mile drive through mature woodland this old walled garden provides the shelter necessary to grow a good range of plants. A map of 1877 already shows a formal plan but the present-day cruciform layout, centred on a sundial, dates from 1916 when it was made by John Murray. Murray's hedges of thuya have had to be removed recently but new hedges have been planted. The main area is kept in the old tradition of a mixture of flower borders, fruit and vegetables and there is a small rockery area. At the bottom end is a formal pool surrounded by yew hedging and hidden to one side a small pool filled with water soldiers, *Stratiotes aloides*.

LAWHEAD CROFT 75
Tarbrax, West Calder, West Lothian, Lothian.

Sue and Hector Riddell ★ 12m from Balerno, 6m from Carnwath on A70 towards Tarbrax ★ Best season: summer ★ Parking ★ Refreshments on open days ★ Toilet facilities ★ Mostly suitable for wheelchairs ★ Open for parties by appointment and twice yearly for SGS (telephone for details). Closed 2nd to 4th June ★ Entrance: £1.50

Nearly 1000ft up in the midst of the bleak Lanarkshire moors, Sue and Hector Riddell have planted shelter belts and laboriously carved out a luxuriant garden. Grass walks lead from one interesting border to another, all full of unusual plants. Colour associations and leaf contrasts are carefully thought out. There is an enchanting series of garden rooms all with a different theme. A garden of great ideas including an excellent bonsai collection. Recently most of the vegetable garden has been swept away and replanted in a great sweep of curved, tiered and circular beds of spectacular and original design.

LECKMELM SHRUBBERY AND ARBORETUM 76
Little Leckmelm House, Lochbroom, Ullapool, Ross-shire, Highlands.

Mr and Mrs Peter Troughton ★ 4m S of Ullapool on A835 ★ Best season: May/June ★ Parking in walled garden ★ Open April to Sept, daily, 10am - 6pm ★ Entrance: £1, OAP and children 50p

Planted in about 1870, this was derelict for 50 years until reclamation started in 1984. A 10-acre woodland garden with many fine examples of species rhododendron. There are many different mature pine and cypress trees, bamboos, shrubs and a magnificent weeping beech. A simple quiet woodland garden, well worth a visit.

LEITH HALL ★ 77
Kennethmont, by Huntly, Aberdeen, Grampian. Tel: (014643) 216

The National Trust for Scotland ★ 1m W of Kennethmont on B9002 and 34m NW of Aberdeen ★ Parking ★ Refreshments: in tea room. Picnic area ★ Toilet facilities, inc. disabled ★ Suitable for wheelchairs ★ Dogs (not in walled garden) ★ Stalls on charity open days ★ Hall open inc. exhibition: May to Sept, 2 - 6pm; Oct, weekends, 2 - 5pm (last tour ¾ hour before closing) ★ Garden and grounds open all year, daily, 9.30am - sunset ★ Entrance: £1 by honesty box (hall and gardens £3.50, OAP £1.80, children £1.80, pre-booked parties £2.80 per person) (1994 prices)

The gardens of Leith Hall have been expanded and upgraded. But it is the old garden, remote from the house, that offers the greatest pleasure to the garden enthusiast. This comprises large borders and a big, well-stocked rock garden. The design is simple, romantic and allows a tremendous display of flowers during the whole of summer and early autumn. Especially fine is the magenta *Geranium psilostemon* and a border of solid catmint running from top to bottom of the garden. There are no courtyards and no dominating architecture, just massive plantings of perennials and the odd rarity amongst the rocks. Woodland walks, views and excellent opportunities for birdwatching around the lake.

THE LINN 78
Cove, Dunbartonshire, Strathclyde. Tel: (0143684) 2242

Dr J. Taggart ★ 6m S of Garelochhead, 2m from Cove off B833 on Rosneath Peninsular ★ Limited parking ★ Entirely unsuitable for wheelchairs ★ Dogs on lead ★ Plants for sale in nursery open daily except Thurs ★ Garden open March to Oct, daily, dawn – dusk ★ Entrance: £1 contribution by donation box on cherry tree

A woodland garden of three acres with extensive water – several ponds with a stream running through. Pines, conifers and eucalyptus (30-40 species of the latter). Markers 1-50 signpost a walk which takes visitors to all parts of the garden using a keyed leaflet. The garden has been developed in its present form by the owner since 1971.

LITTLE SPARTA ★★ 79
Dunsyre, Nr Lanark, Lanarkshire, Strathclyde.

Dr Ian Hamilton Finlay ★ Turn off A721 at Newbigging for Dunsyre. 1m W of Dunsyre is an unmarked very rough farm track up to Little Sparta, marked at the foot by a sign saying 'Stonypath, Little Sparta'. Alternatively take A702 from Edinburgh, turning off at Dolphinton, where the road is signposted to Dunsyre ★ Best season: June ★ Parking ★ Guide dogs only ★ Open by appointment in writing (SAE please) from mid-June to Sept ★ Entrance: free

Sir Roy Strong recently described this as the most original contemporary garden in the country. On arrival at the gate to the property a beautifully-carved wooden sign 'Stonypath' greets you, giving a hint of the fine craft that combines with the art of this admired scultptor. Hamilton Finlay believes that a garden should appeal to all the senses and particularly should provoke thought, both serious and trivial, and he has therefore revived the art of emblematic gardening which died out in Britain in the seventeenth century. He achieved an international reputation in the process. It is impossible to describe Little Sparta briefly, except to say that he has transformed a sizeable hill farmstead (starting in 1966 with the idea of establishing a testing-ground for his sculptures) into a garden full of images, allusions and symbols. Not all are easily understood or interpreted, which doesn't matter as this is a garden not a crossword puzzle.

LOCHALSH WOODLAND GARDEN
(Balmacara Estate) ★ 80
Lochalsh House, Balmacara, Kyle, Ross-shire, Highlands.
Tel: (0159986) 325

The National Trust for Scotland ★ 3m E of Kyle of Lochalsh off A87 ★ Best season: spring ★ Parking (½m walk to garden) on a limited basis. Arrangements can be made for the less active to park closer. Please telephone ahead of visit ★ Open all year, daily, 9am – sunset ★ Entrance: £1, children 50p (1994 prices)

The garden is approached down the wooded road through the village of Glaick on the lochside. From there, across the water, rise the magnificent mountains of Skye and Knoydart. Woodland planting on this steep-sided, 11-acre site began in 1887 around Lochalsh House, and the canopy of beeches, larches, oaks and pines is now outstanding. Ornamental plantings began in the late 1950s with large-leaved rhododendrons, followed, during the 1980s to the present day, with shrubs from China, Japan, the Himalayas and Australasia. Paths created through the woods give a choice of walks, both in terms of gradient and length. Beside these and in glades, logs have been used to build curved, raised beds for the new plantings, which include many hydrangeas, fuchsias, bamboos and ferns.

LOGAN BOTANIC GARDEN ★★ 81
Port Logan, by Stranraer, Dumfries and Galloway.
Tel: (01776) 860231

Royal Botanic Garden, Edinburgh/ Estate of Sir Ninian Buchan-Hepburn, Bt ★ 14m S of Stranraer, off the B7065. Signposted ★ Best seasons: spring and summer ★ Parking ★ Refreshments: in licensed salad bar ★ Toilet facilities, inc. disabled ★ Suitable for wheelchairs ★ Plants for sale ★ Shop and Visitor Centre ★ Garden open 15th March to Oct, daily, 10am - 6pm and at other times by arrangement ★ Entrance: £2, concessions £1.50, children 50p, family ticket £4.50. Discount for bus parties. Season tickets covering Dawyck, Logan and Younger available. Note: Logan House adjoining has been sold and may not, as formerly, be open one day a year for charity

Situated midway down the narrow peninsular of the Mull of Galloway, this enjoys a relatively mild winter climate, thanks to the Gulf Stream. The garden was gifted as an annexe to the Royal Botanic Garden, Edinburgh, in 1969. There is a fascinating collection of plants including Australian tree ferns *Dicksonia antarctica*, New Zealand cabbage palms *Cordyline australis*, Chusan palms *Trachycarpus fortunei* from China and many of the more tender rhododendrons in the walled garden. Also here are camellias, magnolias and spring bulbs. As the season progresses, rhododendrons, primulas, meconopsis and other acid-loving plants come into bloom on the peat walls. Other plants of particular interest during the late spring include the Chatham Island forget-me-not *Myosotidium hortensia*, the Chilean flame tree *Embothrium coccineum*, *Crinodendron hookerianum* also from Chile and many sweetly-scented, but tender, rhododendrons. During the summer the beds in the walled garden are a botanical blaze of colour thanks to the many half-hardy perennial plants which are bedded out each year. These include different diascias, osteospermums, salvias, felicias and argyranthemums. Also during the summer months, unusual flower spikes, which can reach 18 feet, are produced on the *Echium pininana*, a native of the Canary Isles. The New Zealand Christmas tree *Metrosideros umbellata* and the red and yellow Australian bottle brushes also flower at this time. The woodland garden has interesting and exotic plants including many different eucalyptus species, New Zealand daisy bushes, olearia species, New Zealand tea trees, *Leptospermum* species, South American *Berberis* species and many other rarities from the Southern Hemisphere including a number of the more tender conifer species. Probably the most fascinating plant in the woodland garden is the giant native of Brazil *Gunnera manicata*, whose leaves can reach up to 10 feet across and 10 feet high.

MALLENY GARDEN 82
Balerno, Midlothian, Lothian. Tel: (0131449) 2283

*The National Trust for Scotland ★ In Balerno village, off A70 Edinburgh -
Lanark road ★ Best seasons: summer and autumn ★ Parking ★ Suitable for
wheelchairs ★ Gardens open all year, 10am - dusk ★ Entrance: £1, OAP 50p
(honesty box) (1994 prices)*

Aptly described as The National Trust for Scotland's secret garden, Malleny
seems an old and valued friend soon after meeting and reflects the thoughtful
planning by the head gardener and his talented wife. An impressive Deodar
cedar reigns over this three-acre walled garden assisted by a square of early
seventeenth-century clipped yews and by yew hedges. As well as containing
the NCCPG collection of nineteenth-century shrub roses and a permanent
display from the Scottish Bonsai Association, Malleny's 12ft wide herbaceous borders are superb, as is the large glasshouse containing a continual
display of flowering plants. Don't forget to admire the attractive herb and
ornamental vegetable garden, laid out in traditional manner.

MANDERSTON ★ 83
Duns, Borders. Tel: (01361) 883450

*The Lord Palmer ★ 2m E of Duns on A6105 ★ Best season: early Aug, woodland
garden May and June ★ Parking ★ Refreshments: tea room in grounds ★ Toilet
facilities ★ Partly suitable for wheelchairs ★ Dogs on lead ★ Plants for sale ★ Shop
★ House open ★ Gardens open mid-May to Sept, Sun and Thurs, 29th May and
28th Aug or parties by appointment ★ Entrance: £5 (house and garden). Reduced
rate for coach parties (1994 prices)*

One of the last great classic houses to be built in Britain, Manderston was
modelled on Robert Adams' Kedleston Hall in Derbyshire (see entry). It was
described in 1905 as a 'charming mansion inexhaustible in its attractions' and
this might equally well apply to the gardens which remain an impressive
example of gardening on the grand scale. Four magnificently formal terraces
planted in Edwardian style overlook a narrow serpentine lake and a
Chinoiserie bridging dam tempts one over to the woodland garden on the far
side, thus elegantly effecting the transition from formal to informal. No
expense was spared creating the gardens and this air of opulence and good
quality is much evident in the formal walled gardens to the north of the
house. They are a lasting tribute to the very best of the Edwardian era when
100 gardeners were employed to do what two now do to the same immaculately high standard. Gilded gates open on to a panorama of colourful planting on different levels, with fountains, statuary and a charming rose pergola
all complementing each other. Even the greenhouses were given lavish treatment with the walls created from lumps of limestone to resemble an exotic
planted grotto. Fifty-six acres in total of formal and informal beauty.

MEGGINCH CASTLE 84
Errol, by Perth, Tayside.

*Lady Strange ★ 8m E of Perth off A85 Perth - Dundee road ★ Best season: Aug
★ Suitable for wheelchairs ★ Dogs on lead ★ Open every Wed, 2 - 5pm, and in
Aug daily, 2 - 5pm ★ Entrance: £2, children £1*

Originally a fifteenth-century tower house, Megginch, meaning Beautiful Island, was considerably restructured by Robert Adam in 1790 and also by successive generations and this gives the gardens and the Gothic courtyard of 1806 a timeless atmosphere. A fountain parterre to the west of the house is of particular interest for its yew and variegated holly topiary, including an unusual topiary yew crown planted to commemorate Queen Victoria's Jubilee. A few yards away is a thousand-year-old yew, at 72 feet the highest in Scotland. Try and visit Megginch during August when a stunning 120-yard double border – the length of the eighteenth-century walled garden – is a glorious blaze of annual plantings. So many dahlias can rarely have been displayed. An adjacent walled garden of the same period contains an interesting astrological garden with relevant plants pertaining to each sign.

MELLERSTAIN ★★   85
Gordon, Etterick, Borders. Tel: (0157381) 292

The Earl of Haddington ★ Halfway betwen Galashiels and Coldstream. Turn S in Gordon on A6089 and turn W after 2m or turn off B6397 2m N of Smailholm ★ Parking ★ Teas ★ Toilet facilities ★ Suitable for wheelchairs ★ Charity gift shop and craft gallery ★ House open. Extra charge ★ Garden open May to Sept, daily except Sat, 12.30 - 5pm ★ Entrance: £1.50, children free (1994 prices)

A bastion of formal garden layout with dignified terraces overlooking an 'arranged' landscape. The house of Mellerstain is a unique example of the work of the Adam family; both William and son, Robert, worked on the building. The garden is formal, comprised of very dignified terraces, balustraded and 'lightly' planted with climbers and simple topiary because even when labour was plentiful there were a mere six gardeners employed, though they had to supply flowers and vegetables for the London establishment as well as here. The great glory of the garden is the landscape complete with lake and woodlands in the style of Brown and Repton, but designed early this century by Sir Reginald Blomfield. The view of the Cheviot Hills from the terraces is one of the finest to be found in this lovely area of the Scottish Borders. Mellerstain is a must for lovers of the formal landscape.

MERTOUN   86
St Boswells, Roxburghshire, Borders. Tel: (01835) 23236

The Duke of Sutherland ★ 2m NE of St Boswells on B6404 ★ Parking ★ Toilet facilities ★ Suitable for wheelchairs ★ Open April to Sept, Sat, Sun and Bank Holiday Mons, 2 - 6pm ★ Entrance: £1, children 50p

Overlooking the Tweed and with Mertoun House in the background, this is a lovely garden to wander round and admire the mature specimen trees, azaleas, daffodils and a most attractive ornamental pond flanked by a good herbaceous border. The focal point is the immaculate three-acre walled garden which is everything a proper kitchen garden should be. Walking up from a 1567 dovecot, thought to be the oldest in the county, through a healthy orchard the visitor reaches the traditional box hedges, raised beds and glasshouses of the main area. Neat rows of vegetables, herbs and bright flowers for the house vie for attention with the pruning of the figs and peaches in the well-stocked glasshouses.

MONTEVIOT 87
Nr Jedburgh, Borders. Tel: (01835) 830380 (mornings)

Turn off A68 on B6400 to Nisbet. Entrance second turning on right ★ Parking ★ Refreshments at Harestanes Countryside Visitor Centre, ½m; on-site refreshments for parties by pre-booking ★ Toilet facilities ★ Partly suitable for wheelchairs ★ Dogs on lead ★ Plants for sale ★ Open April to Aug, Mon – Thurs, 2 – 5pm; also one day early in the year ('Daffodil' day) and 16th July, 2 – 5pm for charity. Parties book with the Administrator ★ Entrance: £2, OAP and children (10–14) £1, under 10 free

The river garden which runs down to the River Teviot has been extensively replanted with herbaceous perennials and shrubs to a more informal design. Beside it, the semi-enclosed terraced rose gardens overlooking the river have a large collection of hybrid teas, floribundas and shrubs. The pinetum is full of unusual trees reaching great heights, and nearby a water garden has recently been created, planted with hybrid rhododendrons and azaleas. A circular route around the gardens is laid out. Fine views.

THE MURRELL 88
Aberdour, Fife.

John E. Milne ★ Off A921/B9157 Inverkeithing – Kirkcaldy road opposite Croftgarry Farm ★ Best seasons: spring and summer ★ Parking ★ Toilet facilities ★ Plants for sale ★ Open April to Sept, Mon – Fri, 10am – 5pm. Also on certain days for charity and at other times by appointment in writing ★ Entrance: £1.50, concessions £1

The garden, laid out in 1910, is adjacent to a house in the Arts and Crafts style by a well-known local architect Frank Deas, who had worked with Lutyens. The garden has been much extended and replanted by the present owner over the last nine years. It is now much more mature and because of its climatic situation many of the tender plants are shown to best advantage. Walls and terraces with buttresses shelter tender plants not commonly seen in local gardens – cistus, pittosporums, tricuspidarias, carpenterias, phormiums, and *Paeonia suffruticosa*. The walled garden is being developed with mixed borders of perennials, shrubs and roses. Bog plants thrive alongside a stream at the bottom of the garden beyond a formal rose and iris garden.

NETHERBYRES 89
Eyemouth, Berwickshire, Borders. Tel: (018907) 50337

Colonel S.J. Furness ★ ¼m from Eyemouth on A1107 ★ Parking by house ★ Suitable for wheelchairs ★ Open twice yearly in April and July for charity and April to Sept for small parties by appointment ★ Entrance: £2, children £1

Although the Victorian conservatory and vineries were demolished quite recently to make way for a modern house and conservatory, the garden is worth seeing for the unique elliptical walls which date from before 1750. The present layout dates from the 1860s, and is one of the few Scots walled gardens with a traditional mix of fruit, flowers and vegetables still in private hands. A central gazebo feature has recently been added.

PITMEDDEN GARDEN ★   90
Pitmedden, Ellon, Aberdeenshire, Grampian. Tel: (01651) 842352

*The National Trust for Scotland ★ 1m W of Pitmedden village on A920 and 1m
N of Udny. 14m N of Aberdeen ★ Parking ★ Refreshments: tea room. Picnic
area ★ Toilet facilities inc. disabled ★ Suitable for wheelchairs and wheelchairs
supplied ★ Museum of Farming Life ★ Gardens, museum, etc, open May to Sept,
daily, 10am - 5.30pm (last admission 5pm) ★ Entrance: £3, concessions and
children £1.50 (1994 prices)*

Like Edzell Castle, the Great Garden at Pitmedden exhibits the taste of
seventeenth-century garden-makers and their love of patterns made to be
viewed from above. The rectangular garden is enclosed by high terraces on
three sides and by a wall on the fourth. Very ornamental patterns are cut in
box on a grand scale, infilled with 40,000 annuals. The overall impact is striking when viewed from the period stone gazebo at the north of the garden or
when walking along the terraces. Simple topiary and box hedging are abundant. There is a rather curious contemporary fountain made from fragments
preserved at Pitmedden from the Cross Fountain at Linlithgow. Fine borders
of herbaceous plants line the south- and west-facing walls of the parterre
garden. When the Trust acquired Pitmedden in 1952 all that survived was
the masonry. Since nothing remained of the original design, contemporary
seventeenth-century plans for the garden at the Palace of Holyroodhouse in
Edinburgh were used in re-creating what is seen today.

PLANTINGS   91
108 Main Street, Thornhill, Stirling, Central. Tel: (01786) 850683

*Mr and Mrs Robin Price ★ 10m W of Stirling on A873. In Thornhill main street
opposite church ★ Parking in street ★ Plants for sale in nursery open Fri and Sat ★
Garden open each Sat from May – July ★ Entrance: £1 by collection box*

Beautifully-designed small island bed garden made by the owners in the last six
years. Not only is it immaculate, it is also packed with choice herbaceous plants
and old-fashioned roses which is not surprising as Robin Price's extremely good
nursery garden centre, which is adjacent to the garden, specialises in these
plants. Well worth a visit to see how to create an instant garden.

POLLOK HOUSE   92
Glasgow, Strathclyde. Tel: (0141) 6320274

*City of Glasgow Council ★ 3½m from city centre, well signposted. A736 in
Pollokshaws ★ Parking ★ Teas (reservations (0141) 6497547 ★ Toilet facilities ★
Suitable for wheelchairs ★ House open and gallery ★ Garden open all year except
25th Dec and 1st Jan, Mon - Sat, 10am - 5pm, Sun, 11am - 5pm ★ Entrance: free*

A visit to Pollok House offers a full day's entertainment. The house itself
features a lovely formal terrace of box parterres, beautifully planted and maintained by Glasgow Parks. There are borders near the water and a nineteenth-
century woodland garden on the ridge nearby. Stone gazebos with ogee roofs.
The grounds are famous for their bluebells in spring. Pollok House holds the
famous Stirling Maxwell collection of European paintings. In the grounds is
the famous Burrell Collection, one of the world's finest galleries of the deco-

rative and fine arts. The building was designed to encompass the woodland and the parkland around is beautifully planted and maintained.

PRIORWOOD GARDEN 93
Melrose, Ettrick and Lauderdale, Borders. Tel: (0189682) 2493

The National Trust for Scotland ★ On A6091 in Melrose ★ Parking ★ Shop ★ Open April to 24th Dec, Mon - Sat, 10am - 5.30pm. Also May to Oct, Sun, 2 - 5.30pm ★ Entrance: £1 (honesty box) (1994 price)

Purchased by The National Trust for Scotland in 1974, this was originally the walled garden belonging to Priorbank House, now Melrose Youth Hostel. The garden has been developed for the production of dried flowers and by drying them in sand - as the ancient Egyptians did - the range of plants has been greatly increased to include some 700 varieties of annual and herbaceous plants. Another aspect of the garden is the orchard which has been designed to show the development of the apple tree in Britain. The eighteenth-century garden walls are complemented with ornamental ironwork thought to be the work of Lutyens.

ROYAL BOTANIC GARDEN ★★ 94
Edinburgh, Lothian. Tel: (0131) 5527171

Department of Agriculture and Fisheries for Scotland ★ 1½m N of city centre at Inverleith ★ Parking ★ Terrace café ★ Toilet facilities ★ Suitable for wheelchairs ★ Plants for sale ★ Shop ★ Exhibition hall and Inverleith House gallery open ★ Garden open daily except 25th Dec and 1st Jan: Mar to April, 10am - 6pm; May to Aug, 10am - 8pm; Sept to Oct, 10am - 6pm and Nov to Feb, 10am - 4pm. Garden tours operate April to Sept, daily except Sat, 11am and 2pm from the West Gate ★ Entrance: free, voluntary contributions invited for the Glasshouse Experience

Set on a hillside with magnificent panoramic views of the city, the Royal Botanic Garden, Edinburgh, is one of the finest botanic gardens in the world; arguably the finest garden, physically, of its type in Britain. The 75 acres of gardens are filled with hundreds of thousands of plants, trees and shrubs from all over the world with a particular emphasis on Himalayan and Chinese species. The rhododendron collection is vast, the rock garden is among the finest in the world, and the heather collection is renowned. The glasshouses hold enormous collections of tropical, sub-tropical and xerophytic plants and were among the earliest to be internally landscaped. The home demonstration gardens are very well done. The perennial border is one of the largest in the UK, approaching 600 feet. The many paths meander through numerous areas of specific interest, all beautifully planted and maintained to the very highest degree. The overall standard of horticulture is superb. The specimen trees are amongst the finest in Britain - the birch collection is unequalled. This is a garden that takes years to know well. Improvements continue to be made, including a new herb garden by the West Gate at Inverleith, with a snack bar within fragrance distance, initially open weekends only.

STEVENSON HOUSE 95
Nr Haddington, East Lothian. Tel: (0162082) 3376

Mrs Dunlop/ Brown Dunlop Country Houses Trust ★ Parking ★ Self-service teas ★ Toilet facilities ★ Suitable for wheelchairs ★ House open July to mid–Aug, Thurs, Sat and Sun, 2 – 5pm. Conducted tour at 3pm (by arrangement on other days) ★ Garden open May to Oct, daily, 2 – 5pm ★ Entrance: 50p, children under 12 free (house and garden £3) (1994 prices). Children must be accompanied

The main lawn is surrounded by exuberant flowerbeds with interesting and unusual planting, a rockery and many fine trees. One is quite unprepared for the size and diversity of planting in the old walled kitchen garden reached through a small door. Extending nearly two acres, the kitchen garden was designed in the eighteenth-century to feed a household of 20 or 30. Today, while three-quarters of the garden has been grassed over, shrubs and trees have been planted to prevent any impression of emptiness; an economical area is kept under cultivation providing vegetables for the family and the old herbaceous border has been revived. The overall impression is of an ornamental pleasure garden carefully restored to provide attractive views from the house and a quiet retreat for the owners.

STOBO CASTLE WATER GARDENS 96
Peebles, Borders. Tel: (01721) 760245

Hugh and Charles Seymour ★ 6m SW of Peebles on the B712, 12m E of Biggar ★ Parking ★ Refreshments ★ Toilet facilities ★ Dogs on lead ★ Plants for sale ★ Open by appointment and for SGS in mid–June ★ Entrance: £1.50

The enduring appeal of water is exemplified here where the planting, although most attractive, takes second place to the visual impact of clear water flowing down a series of cascades and waterfalls. Japanese bridges and stepping stones invite frequent crossing from side to side and peaceful rills stray from the main torrent to create one huge water garden. In fine landscape garden tradition, man has contrived to manipulate nature – in this case a large earth dam across a steep valley – into something of classical delight. The dam was faced with stone to create a magnificent waterfall and the resulting flow is impressive even in dry summers. The lovely mature trees, such as *Cercidiphyllum japonicum, Kalopanax pictus* var. *maximowiczii* and many Japanese maple varieties obviously date from this period, which ended with the outbreak of World War I.

TEVIOT WATER GARDEN 97
Kirkbank, Eckford, Kelso, Borders. Tel: (01835) 850253

Mr and Mrs Denis Wilson ★ Between Kelso and Jedburgh on A698 ★ Refreshments in restaurant ★ Plants for sale ★ Open April to Sept, Mon – Sat, 10am – 4.30pm, Sun, 11am – 4pm ★ Entrance: free

A remarkable garden has been achieved here only about five years after beginning work on a stony riverside field. The ground falls steeply down to the Teviot river and has been cleverly terraced with ponds linked by falling water. The wide range of planting combines carefully-selected bog and water plants with bamboos, shrub roses and unusual herbaceous. Back in the house is a successful smokery and a good restaurant, and there is a small nursery specialising in the needs of the water garden plus unusual herbaceous offerings.

THREAVE GARDEN ★   98
Stewartry, Castle Douglas, Dumfries and Galloway.
Tel: (01556) 502575

The National Trust for Scotland ★ 1m W of Castle Douglas off A75 ★ Parking ★ Refreshments: restaurant April to Oct, daily, 10am – 5pm ★ Toilet facilities ★ Suitable for wheelchairs ★ Shop ★ Visitor centre. Exhibition April to Oct, daily, 9.30am – 5.30pm ★ Garden open all year, daily, 9.30am – sunset ★ Entrance: £3, children £1.50, party rates: £2.40, OAP and children £1.20 (1994 prices)

The Threave estate, which extends to 1500 acres, includes the famous 65-acre garden which has been used as a School of Horticulture since 1960 and caters for young gardeners. Numerous perennials, annuals, trees and shrubs are used in imaginative ways and are maintained by the resident horticultural students. For the visitor the main interest is the working walled garden with its range of glasshouses, vegetables, orchard and well-trained fruit. This can be contrasted with the less formal woodland and rock gardens, heath garden and arboretum. The garden is famous for its collection of daffodils which are complemented in spring by rhododendrons and flowering trees and shrubs.

TILLYPRONIE   99
Tarland, Grampian. Tel: (013398) 81238

The Hon. Philip Astor ★ 4¹/₂m from Tarland via A97 Dinnet – Huntly road ★ Parking ★ Teas ★ Toilet facilities ★ Partly suitable for wheelchairs ★ Dogs on leads ★ Open 27th Aug for charity, 2 – 5pm ★ Entrance: £1, children 40p

Set on the south-facing slope of a hill at over 1000 feet above sea level this is a cold garden, but shelter belts dating from the mid-1800s ensure that a wide range of plants can be grown. More shelter planting was added in the period 1925-51. The overall layout was completed in the 1920s and was the work of George Dillistone of Tunbridge Wells. The terraces below the house date from the same period and support narrow herbaceous borders. The house walls provide shelter for less hardy climbers and trained *Buddleia davidii* cultivars make a good display in August. Curved stone steps lead between extensive heather gardens onto lawns which sweep down to the ponds which have colourful plantings of astilbes, filipendulas, lysichitons, primulas and ferns. There are fine specimens of *Picea breweriana* and many other conifers and an area devoted to dwarf varieties. Spectacular views over rich farmland and nearby hills end with the Grampians on the horizon. The small pinetum set in pine and birch forest was planted by the late Lord Astor.

TOROSAY CASTLE AND GARDENS   100
Craignure, Isle of Mull, Argyll, Strathclyde.
Tel: (01680) 812421; Fax: (01680) 812470

Mr Christopher James ★ 1¹/₂m from Craignure. Steamer 6 times daily 14th April to 15th Oct (2 to 4 times daily Oct to April) from Oban to Craignure. Motor boat during high season. Miniature steam railway from Craignure ferry. Or Lochaline to Fishnish ferry, then 7m S on A849 ★ Best season: May ★ Teas ★ Toilet facilities ★ Partly suitable for wheelchairs ★ Dogs on lead ★ Shop ★ Castle open, mid-April to mid-Oct, 10.30am – 5.30pm. Admission extra ★ Garden open all year, daily, 9am – 7pm (or dusk in winter) ★ Entrance: £1.50, OAP, students, children £1

House in baronial castle style by Bryce (1858). Main garden formal Italian based on a series of descending terraces with unusual statue walk. This features one of the richest collections of Italian rococo statuary in Britain and alone justifies the crossing from Oban to Mull. Vaguely reminiscent of Powis Castle (see entry in Wales), this is a dramatic contrast with the rugged island scenery. The peripheral gardens are also a contrast - an informal water garden and Japanese garden looking out over Duart Bay; also a small rock garden. Rhododendrons and azaleas are a feature but less important than in other west coast gardens. Collection of Australian and New Zealand trees and shrubs.

TYNINGHAME HOUSE ★ 101
Tyninghame, Nr East Linton, Lothian.

Tyninghame Gardens Ltd ★ 25m E of Edinburgh between Haddington and Dunbar. N of A1, 2m E of A198 ★ Parking ★ Teas ★ Suitable for wheelchairs ★ Open for charity 28th May, 9th July, 2 - 6pm ★ Entrance: £2

Tyninghame is renowned for the gardens created by the Dowager Lady Haddington from 1947 onwards, which have been described as of 'ravishing beauty'. They consist of a formal rose garden, terraces, a secret garden, an Italian garden and an area of woodland. When her husband died in 1986, her son reluctantly sold the house, but those who worried about the garden's future need not to have feared, as the conversion and addition of two houses was handled by Kit Martin with great sensitivity. Tyninghame is close to the sea, with fine views in all directions, and those who are able to visit it on the open days will have a rare opportunity of seeing how the unique character of the garden has been maintained, perhaps enhanced, by the architectural changes around it, and by the dedicated work of Mrs Clifford and others who are restoring the garden towards the glories of the Haddington days.

WEST DRUMMUIE GARDEN 102
West Drummuie, Golspie, Sutherland, Highlands.
Tel: (01408) 633493

Mrs Elizabeth Woollcombe ★ 1m S of Golspie. At the white milestone on right, turn up the hill to garden sign ★ Limited parking ★ Comfort and other amenities in Golspie ★ Suitable for wheelchairs ★ Plants for sale ★ Open late March to early Oct, Weds only, 10am - 12.30pm, 2 - 5.30pm or by appointment ★ Entrance: free

For those who venture so far north, this is one of the Highland's horticultural treasures. Anywhere with a sign on the doorstep saying 'In the garden' must be special, and sure enough, visitors will find Elizabeth Woollcombe with her dogs and bantams (which eat the slugs) working almost single-handed in this remarkable small garden. For 18 years she has propagated all her favourite treasures. Notices sternly advise the visitor not to touch the numerous propagating pots and only when considered ready for sale are they put in rustic table containers all around the garden - usually near the parent plant. Although she specialises in meconopsis (inc. monocarpic types), there is always a good selection of primulas, gentians, geraniums, herbaceous and bog plants, tropaeolums and shrubs. Elizabeth even makes baskets from her phormium leaves.

YOUNGER BOTANIC GARDEN ★★   103
Benmore, Dunoon, Argyll, Strathclyde. Tel: (01369) 6261

Royal Botanic Garden Edinburgh ★ At Dunoon 1m from junction of A885 and A815 ★ Best season: May to June ★ Teas at main entrance ★ Toilet facilities ★ Suitable for wheelchairs ★ Open daily, 15th March to Oct, 10am - 6pm and at other times by arrangement ★ Entrance: £1.50, concessions £1, children 50p. 10% discounts for groups of 11 or more. Season tickets covering Dawyck, Logan (see entries) and Younger available

Benmore's 100 acres of woodland gardens have been under development since 1820. The gardens are approached along Britain's finest Wellingtonia (*Sequoiadendron giganteum*) avenue. The tallest is more than 150 feet. Numerous other fine specimen conifers are to be found throughout the gardens. There are exceptionally fine monkey puzzles (*Araucaria araucana*) that retain their lower branches. But Benmore is most famous for its extensive rhododendron and magnolia collections on the hillside beside the River Eachaig in one of Britain's most breathtaking natural settings; the Highlands at their best. Myriad paths take the visitor along the mountainside through vast plantations of rare shrubs and trees. Marvellous vistas open from time to time. The only obviously man-made feature is a great rectangular lawn enclosed on three sides by walls but open to the mountains on the fourth. This garden is bisected by borders filled with a collection of dwarf conifers. A handsome pavilion overlooks it all. There are other informal beds filled with Australian and New Zealand shrubs and herbaceous plants. Benmore is well worth a visit both for its natural beauty and its vast specimen plant collections. Be prepared for a full day's outing, a great deal of walking, and rain.

THE NATIONAL TRUST FOR SCOTLAND

In Scotland, gardens are in the care of the National Trust for Scotland, 5 Charlotte Square, Edinburgh, EH2 4DU (tel: (0131) 226 5922), from whom information may be obtained.

OPENING DATES AND TIMES

Times of access given are the best available at the moment of going to press, but some may have been changed subsequently. In the entries, the times given are inclusive – that is, an entry such as May to Sept means that the garden is open from 1st May to 30th Sept inclusive and 2 – 5pm also means that entry will be effective during that period. Please note that many owners will open their gardens to visitors by appointment. They will often arrange to give a personally-conducted tour on these occasions.

WHEELCHAIR USERS

Please note that entries which describe a garden as 'suitable for wheelchairs' refer to the garden only. If there is a house open, it may or may not be suitable for wheelchairs.

WALES

Two-starred gardens are ringed in bold.

ASHFORD HOUSE 1
Talybont, Brecon, Powys. Tel: (01874) 87271

Mr and Mrs Anderson ★ 1m E of Talybont on B4558 ★ Teas ★ Toilet facilities ★ Partly suitable for wheelchairs ★ Dogs on lead ★ Plants for sale ★ Open April to Oct, Tues, 2 – 6pm and by appointment ★ Entrance: £1.50, children free

Ashford House garden is about one acre with a further three acres of woodland and wild garden. The walled garden has a good selection of shrubs and herbaceous plants and long raised beds containing an interesting collection of alpines which are the owners' prime interest. The wild garden is being interplanted with rhododendrons and other shrubs and contains a healthy wild pool with frogs and dragonflies. Mrs Anderson propagates plants for sale from material in the garden.

BLAENGWRFACH ISAF 2
Bancyffordd, Dyfed. Tel: (01559) 362604

Mrs Gail Farmer ★ 2m W of Llandyssul on Newcastle Emlyn road. First left by Halfmoon pub, 1½m until farm track on right ★ Best season: spring ★ Parking very limited ★ Teas 1m away in village ★ Plants for sale ★ Shop, adjacent craft workshops ★ Garden open April to June by appointment, 10am – 5pm; also in Oct for autumn colour ★ Entrance: 75p (1994 price)

Created over the last 15 years from a green field site, this is essentially a cottage garden, but recent plantings of trees and shrubs to attract wildlife and plants suitable for pressed flowers give great diversity. Autumn colour.

BODNANT GARDEN ★★ 3
Tal-y-Cafn, Colwyn Bay, Gwynedd. Tel: (01492) 650460

The National Trust ★ 7m S of Llandudno, just off A470 ★ Best season: April to Oct ★ Official car park 50 yards from garden nursery ★ Lunches, teas and light refreshments in Pavilion Restaurant ★ Toilet facilities ★ Partly suitable for wheelchairs ★ Plants for sale in adjacent nursery ★ Garden open mid–March to Oct, daily, 10am – 5pm (last admission 4.30pm) ★ Entrance: £3.90

Bodnant is one of the finest gardens in the country, not only for the magnificent collections of rhododendrons, camellias and magnolias but also for its beautiful setting above the River Conway and the extensive views of the Snowdon range. The gardens, which cover 80 acres, have many interesting features, the most well known being the laburnum arch which is an overwhelming mass of bloom in late May and early June. Others include the lily terrace, curved and stepped pergola, canal terrace, Pin Mill and dell garden. These, together with the outstanding autumn colours, make Bodnant a garden for all seasons. The whole effect was created by four generations of the Aberconway family (who bought Bodnant in 1874) and aided by three generations of the Puddle family as head gardeners. Work has begun to restore the Rose Terrace's patterned brickwork. In the Dell is the tallest redwood in the country, the 148ft *Sequoia sempervirens*.

BODRHYDDAN 4
Rhuddlan, Clwyd. Tel: (01745) 590414

*Lord Langford ★ Take A5151 Rhuddlan – Dyserth road and turn left.
Signposted ★ Parking ★ Teas. Picnic area ★ Suitable for wheelchairs (garden and
ground floor of house) ★ House open ★ Garden open June to Sept, Tues and
Thurs, 2 – 5.30pm ★ Entrance: £2, children under 16 £1 (house and garden)*

The main feature of the garden is a box-edged parterre designed by William
Nesfield. Other points of interest are clipped yew informal walks, three pools
(one with rainbow trout), new plantings and ancient specimens of oak. There
is also a 1612 pavilion by Inigo Jones which houses St Mary's Well, revered
since pagan times and said to have been used for clandestine marriages.

BODYSGALLEN HALL ★   5
Llandudno, Gwynedd. Tel: (01492) 584466

*Historic House Hotels ★ Take A55 (North Wales Expressway) from Chester and
at the intersection turn onto A470 towards Llandudno. Hotel and garden are 1m
on right ★ Parking ★ ☆ Refreshments ★ Open all year, daily ★ Entrance: free to
all guests and visitors using the facilities of the hotel*

The owners have restored both house and gardens of this seventeenth-
century country house to a high standard. The naturally-occurring limestone
outcrops provide an interesting array of rockeries and terraces. One of the
major features is a knot garden sympathetically planted with herbs, another is
a formal walled rose garden. A number of well-established and interesting
trees and shrubs can be seen, including medlar and mulberry. A woodland
walk adds a further dimension.

BRYN DERWEN   6
Wrexham Road, Mold, Clwyd. Tel: (01352) 756662

*Roger and Janet Williams ★ ½m from Mold Cross on old Mold – Wrexham road
(B5444), opposite Alun School and Sports Centre ★ Plants for sale when
available ★ Open by appointment only ★ Entrance: £1, children 25p*

A small town garden planted with a wide variety of interesting plants including alliums, cistus, euphorbias, ferns, hostas and grasses to give colour all year
round. The planting is intensive and imaginative.

BRYN MEIFOD   7
Graig, Glan Conwy, Colwyn Bay, Clwyd. Tel: (01492) 580875

*Dr and Mrs K. Lever ★ Just off A470, 1½m S of Glan Conwy. Follow signs for
Aberconwy Nursery ★ Parking ★ Toilet facilities ★ Plants for sale in adjacent
nursery open all year, Tues – Sun, 9am – 5pm ★ Garden open by appointment
during nursery working hours ★ Entrance: by collecting box*

The garden, situated next to the Lever's nursery renowned for the quality of
plants sold, is being extended and modified. In effect a new garden is being
created within the framework of an existing established one, a process of
interest in itself. The planting is imaginative and includes some unusual
plants in skilfully designed settings which display them to best effect. There
is a lack of artificiality in what is currently a lovely garden with the promise
of even more to come, for example a scree area being planted with alpines
and turf beds for choice ericaceous plants.

BRYNMELYN 8
Cymerau Isaf, Ffestiniog, Gwynedd. Tel: (0176676) 2684

Mr and Mrs A.S. Taylor ★ 2m SW of Ffestiniog on A496 ★ Parking in lay-by opposite junction to Manod (½m to garden along path at lower gate bearing right after garage) ★ Open May to July, 10am – 1pm, 2 – 5pm. Telephone first before 10am or after 9pm ★ Entrance: collecting box

An interesting garden, not only for its range of plant material, but also for its wild mountainside setting. Divided into smaller gardens each with its own theme and character, it lends itself well to the overall informal style with nature reserve and woodland.

BRYN-Y-BONT 9
Nantmor, Nr Beddgelert, Gwynedd. Tel: (0176686) 448

Miss J. Entwisle ★ 2½m S of Beddgelert, turn left over the Aberglaslyn Bridge onto A4085. After 500 yards turn left up hill marked Nantmor. Bryn-y-Bont is second house on right ★ Parking ★ Plants for sale ★ Open by appointment and also for small pre-booked parties ★ Entrance: £1, children free

This is a well-designed garden taking full advantage of the view over the Glaslyn Vale. Mixed borders and rhododendron beds give way to a woodland area where a variety of trees is being introduced.

CAE HIR ★ 10
Cribyn, Lampeter, Dyfed. Tel: (01570) 470839

Mr W. Akkermans ★ From Lampeter take A482 towards Aberaeron. After 5m at Temple Bar take B4337 signed Llanybydder. Cae Hir is 2m further on left ★ Best season: summer ★ Parking ★ Refreshments ★ Plants for sale ★ Shop ★ Open daily, 1 – 6pm ★ Entrance: £1.50, OAP £1.25, children 50p

Beautiful and peaceful six-acre garden on an exposed west-facing slope, entirely created and maintained by the owner from four overgrown fields of rough grazing, starting in 1985. Many unusual features found unexpectedly around each corner including red, yellow and blue sub-gardens, bonsai 'room', stonework ponds. Lovely views and plenty of seating. Water garden, bog garden and white garden are new.

CARROG ★ 11
**Llanddeiniol, Llanrhystud, Nr Aberystwyth, Dyfed.
Tel: (01974) 202369**

Mrs Williams ★ 6m S of Aberystwyth on private road off A487 ★ Best seasons: spring and summer ★ Parking ★ Toilet facilities ★ Suitable for wheelchairs ★ Dogs on lead ★ Open by appointment ★ Entrance: £1, children 30p

From the flowers of varied spring bulbs to the autumn colours of rare maples and birches, this garden is alive with interest for the plant lover. Grass paths wend amongst collections of sorbus, eucalyptus and sweetly scented old-fashioned roses, with rhododendrons flowering well into summer. The walled garden is home for many treasures, such as fremontodendron, rare lilac species and *Abutilon megapotamicum*. Orchids in conservatory.

CEFN BERE 12
Cae Deintur, Dolgellau, Gwynedd. Tel: (01341) 422768

Mr and Mrs Maldwyn Thomas ★ N of Bala – Barmouth road (not bypass) near Dolgellau. From the town, turn at top of the main bridge, turn right within 100 yards, then second right behind school, continue up hill to left hand bend. Cefn Bere is fourth house on right ★ Parking at roadside ★ Refreshments in Dolgellau ★ Toilet facilities ★ Open spring and summer months by appointment only ★ Entrance: collecting box

This relatively small garden has a very diverse plant collection amassed over the last 35 years. Planted informally but within a formal framework, it is a delight to amateur and professional gardeners alike. The alpine house, bulb and peat frames are well worth seeing; so too are the old-fashioned roses.

CEFN ONN PARK ★ 13
Cardiff, South Glamorgan.

Cardiff City Council ★ From Cardiff centre take A469 under M4. Turn first right then left opposite Lisvane Station. From elsewhere, at M4 junction 32, turn S of A470. Take first left to T-junction, turn right, turn left at church, turn left at T pass under M4, first right then left opposite Lisvane Station ★ Best seasons: spring and early summer ★ Parking ★ Toilet facilities ★ Suitable for wheelchairs ★ Dogs on lead ★ Open all year during daylight hours ★ Entrance: free

Cefn Onn Park is something out of the ordinary for a city. It retains a little of the formality common in such areas, with straight gravelled paths running through the centre, but from there on the similarity ends. No large areas of bedding plants, rather, large areas of informally-planted azaleas and rhodo-dendrons. Layer upon layer of colour and perfume reaching up into the upper storey of trees, which can only be appreciated by standing on the bank opposite in order to see them at all. The camellias and magnolias here have also become trees, rather than bushes, and the visitor may have to guard against a cricked neck trying to see everything. Small streams and pools could be quite attractive, but were suffering from the usual park problem caused by those few visitors who find it impossible to take their rubbish home. It may also be a little dull once the rhododendrons are over.

CENTRE FOR ALTERNATIVE TECHNOLOGY 14
Machynlleth, Powys. Tel: (01654) 702400

C.A.T. ★ 2½m N of Machynlleth on A487 ★ Parking inc. coaches at base of site, but for elderly and disabled at top of steep drive. Also access by water balance cliff railway from 8th April to 29th Oct ★ Self-service vegetarian restaurant ★ Toilet facilities ★ Partly suitable for wheelchairs ★ Guide dogs only ★ Plants for sale ★ Shop ★ Open daily, 10am – 5pm, but telephone for winter openings ★ Entrance: £4.50, OAP, claimants and students £3.50, children £2.50, family ticket (2 adults and up to 4 children) £12.50 (1994 prices). Discounts for those arriving by public transport or bicycle

High in a former slate quarry, and at the heart of the environmentally-friendly community here, is the most exciting garden. Compactly laid out, using natural and recycled materials to form harmoniously-shaped raised beds, ponds and walks, the garden is vibrant (in June) with colour and insect life drawn to the organically-grown flowers and companion-planted vegetables. There are suggestions, too, for urban gardeners and displays of land reclamation, wildlife gardening, composting, weed and pest control. Wind turbines in different sizes and designs could be considered unusual (but highly functional) garden sculptures.

CHIRK CASTLE ★   15
Chirk, Clwyd. Tel: (01691) 777701

The National Trust ★ ½m W of Chirk village off A5, up private drive of 1½m ★ Best season: spring ★ Parking 200 yards from garden ★ Refreshments: light lunches and teas, picnic area in car park ★ Toilet facilities ★ Partly suitable for wheelchairs ★ Shop ★ Castle open as gardens 12 noon – 5pm (last admission 4.30pm) ★ Gardens open 2nd April to 29th Sept, daily except Mon and Sat (but open Bank Holiday Mons and Mon in July and Aug); 1st to 29th Oct, Sat and Sun only, 11am – 6pm (last admission 4.30pm) ★ Entrance: £2, children £1(castle and garden £4, children £2, family (2 adults and 2 children) £10, parties £3.20 per person)

A six-acre garden of trees and flowering shrubs including rhododendrons and azaleas. Interesting formal gardens with some excellent nineteenth-century topiary in yew. Also a rockery garden. Herbaceous borders, ha-ha and folly. The castle dates from 1300 but is set in an eighteenth-century landscaped park.

CLYNE GARDENS ★★   16
Black Pill, Swansea, West Glamorgan. Tel: (01792) 401737

Swansea City Council ★ From Swansea take Mumbles road, turn right at Woodman Roast Inn ★ Best season: spring ★ Parking ★ Refreshments in garden during May, otherwise at Woodman Roast Inn ★ Toilet facilities ★ Suitable for wheelchairs ★ Dogs on lead ★ Open all year, 8am – dusk. For garden tours contact (01792) 302420 ★ Entrance: free

Fifty acres of well-kept garden to interest everyone from the beginner to the more knowledgeable. Near the entrance gates is a planting of young magnolias and a varied selection of rhododendrons and azaleas. This area leads on to a magnificent group of large-leaved rhododendrons, at their best in April. Clyne Gardens holds the National collection of rhododendron section Falconeri, but even these tree-like rhododendrons are looked down upon by *Magnolia campbellii*. Clearly defined paths lead the visitor through other areas where the National collections of rhododendron section Triflorum, pieris and enkianthus flourish in this woodland garden; the perfume from *Rhododendron fragrantissimum* is heady and unforgettable. The bog garden is a prehistoric forest of *Gunnera manicata* linked by a colourful ribbon of primulas to the lake and waterfall spanned by a Japanese bridge. Many more rare and interesting trees and shrubs are there for the discerning visitor to discover.

COLBY WOODLAND GARDEN   17
Colby Lodge, Amroth, Narberth, Dyfed. Tel: (01834) 811885

The National Trust ★ Adjoining Amroth beside Carmarthen Bay ★ Best season: April and May ★ Parking 50 yards from garden. Disabled may park closer.

Coaches by prior arrangement ★ Refreshments: in tearoom. Picnic area ★ Toilet facilities ★ Partly suitable for wheelchairs ★ Dogs on lead ★ Shop ★ Gallery open ★ Garden open April to 30th Oct, daily, 10am – 5pm (last admission 4pm) ★ Entrance: £2.60, children £1.10, parties of 15 or more £2.10 per person, children 90p

This early nineteenth-century estate garden round a Nash-style house is now mainly woodland with some formal gardens. The walled garden is planted informally for ornamental effect. The woodland garden is planted extensively with rhododendrons and contains some interesting tree species. Indeed, the garden has one of the Trust's largest collections of rhododendrons and work started in 1994 on a three-year programme to improve the garden's layout and planting.

CWM-PIBAU 18
New Moat, Clarbeston Road, Haverfordwest, Dyfed.
Tel: (01437) 532 454

Mrs Drew ★ From Haverfordwest take A40 through Robeston Wathen. Turn left on B4313. Follow signs to New Moat. 3m from Clarbeston Road on outskirts of New Moat, there is a concealed drive on left. Continue up ½m drive, keeping left ★ Parking ★ Toilet facilities ★ Dogs on lead ★ Open by appointment for charity ★ Entrance: £1

Created by Mrs Drew since 1978 and therefore still very young. It has as a background some mature woodland, and the driveway to the house is very long and rather uneven. Parking is at the start of the drive and visitors should be aware that it is quite a long, uphill walk back (although on charity days it is possible to get a lift down and back to the car). A good many rhododendrons have been planted along the side of the drive which leads to lawns and herbaceous plantings near the house. Paths are then signposted to take the visitor down through shrub plantings and along a stream planted with moisture-lovers. This area is still very young, but leads on to five more acres of woodland with embothriums and rhododendrons.

THE DINGLE ★ 19
Crundale, Haverfordwest, Dyfed. Tel: (01437) 764370

Mrs A.J. Jones ★ 3m NW of Haverfordwest ★ Best season: spring to autumn ★ Parking ★ Teas ★ Toilet facilities ★ Suitable for wheelchairs ★ Plants for sale in small nursery adjoining ★ Shop ★ Open daily except Tues, March to Oct, 10am – 6pm ★ Entrance: £1, children 50p, season ticket £4

This is a secluded plantsman's garden where foliage and plant structure play an important part in the layout and design. A collection of many rare and unusual plants, including over 150 different old-fashioned and species roses. Formal beds, scree beds, herbaceous borders, water garden and woodland walks all blend within an informal framework.

THE DINGLE ★ 20
Welshpool, Powys. Tel: (01938) 555145

Mr and Mrs Roy Joseph ★ 3m N of Welshpool. Take A490 to Llanfyllin for 1m and then turn left at sign for Dingle Nursery or Frochas. After 1¾m fork left ★

Best seasons: early June and, for autumn colour, mid-Oct ★ Parking ★ Toilet facilities ★ Partly suitable for wheelchairs ★ Nursery adjacent ★ Garden open daily except Tues, 9am – 5pm ★ Entrance: £1 for charity, children free

Four acres of very steep south-facing garden, planted with many evergreens for year-round interest. Beds have been created with colour schemes in mind and plants have been carefully chosen to harmonise. A large pool at the bottom, with a woodland garden beyond, gives another dimension to the garden and a breathing space before climbing back to the house.

DOLWEN ★ 21
Cefn Coch, Llanrhaedr-ym-Mochnant, Powys. Tel: (01691) 780411

Mrs Frances Denby ★ On B4580 Oswestry – Llanrhaedr road. Turn sharp right in village at Three Tuns Inn ★ Parking ★ Refreshments ★ Toilet facilities ★ Plants for sale ★ Shop ★ Open May to Sept, Fri and last Sun in months May to Aug, 2 – 4.30pm ★ Entrance: £1

A woodland and water garden situated high in the hills with very good views. The owner has used the land to good advantage. The whole area is very rocky, and large boulders have been used imaginatively to create pools and support bridges across a stream. There is an interesting collection of waterside plants.

DONADEA LODGE 22
Babell, Clwyd. (01352) 720204

Mr and Mrs Patrick Beaumont ★ Turn off A541 Mold – Denbigh at Afonwen, signposted Babell and at the T-junction, turn left; or take A55 to St Asaph, B5122 to Caerwys and third turn on the left ★ Parking ★ Suitable for wheelchairs ★ Plants for sale ★ Open 14th May to July by appointment, and 16th July, 2 – 6pm ★ Entrance: £1.50, children 30p

On a very long site this garden demonstrates what creative design can achieve. On one side an avenue of mature lime trees is a fine feature in its own right. The other side is a mixed border of bays and small islands, each with its own restrained and carefully thought-out colour scheme often achieved with unusual plants in unexpected but entirely effective combinations. A particular feature is the use of roses and clematis.

DYFFRYN BOTANIC GARDEN 23
St Nicholas, Cardiff, South Glamorgan. Tel: (01222) 593328

South and Mid Glamorgan Council ★ 4m W of Cardiff on A4232 turn S on A4050 and then W to Dyffryn ★ Parking ★ Refreshments and picnics ★ Toilet facilities ★ Suitable for wheelchairs ★ Dogs on lead ★ Plants for sale ★ Shop ★ House now a conference centre run by Mid Glamorgan and South Glamorgan County Councils. Open air theatre in garden. Butterfly house. Extra charge ★ Garden open all year, daily, 9am – dusk ★ Entrance: £1.50, OAP and children £1 (1994 prices)

Dyffryn is one of Wales' largest landscaped gardens and has been described as one of its best-kept secrets (though the word 'best-kept' is now a bad pun). An Edwardian garden, created out of a Victorian original between 1906 and 1914, it was designed by Thomas Mawson, a leading landscape architect rather over-shadowed by his contemporary Edwin Lutyens. Mawson's services were commissioned by the owner Reginald Cory, a distinguished horticulturalist whose special interest was Eastern plants such as those introduced to Britain by E.H. Wilson. To the south of the fine house is a large open lawn with orna-mental lily pond and, to the west, a series of 'rooms' each enclosed by yew hedges. These are the Roman garden (closed), the paved court, the 'swimming pool' garden and the round garden. Beyond these is the west garden with large beds and borders and fine trees and shrubs. There is a Japanese garden, lily pool garden and a vine walk. The arboretum, labelled as a wildlife reserve, contains some of the finest *Acer griseum* (paper bark maple) in the country. A fine cacti collection is contained inside the range of traditional display glasshouses within the walled garden but these very much have gone downhill. Recent visitors have complained of extensive dereliction and poor maintenance.

ERDDIG ★ 24
Wrexham, Clwyd. Tel: (01978) 313333

The National Trust ★ 2m S of Wrexham off A525 ★ Best season: spring ★ Parking 200 yards from garden ★ Refreshments: licensed restaurant for light lunches and teas. Picnic area in car park ★ Toilet facilities inc. disabled ★ Suitable for wheelchairs (wheelchairs provided but house difficult) ★ Dogs on lead in grounds ★ Plants for sale ★ Joiner's shop manufacturing quality garden furniture ★ House open (last admission 4pm) ★ Garden open 14th April to 30th Oct, daily except Thurs and Fri (but open 14th April), 11am – 6pm ★ Entrance: £3.20, children £1.60, pre-booked parties £2.50 per person, family (2 adults and 2 children) £8 (house and garden £5, children £2.50, pre-booked parties £4 per person. Mid-week (except July to Aug) £4.50)

Erddig's gardens, a rare example of early eighteenth-century formal design, were almost lost along with the house. They have been carefully restored. The large walled garden contains varieties of fruit trees known to have been grown there during that period and there is a canal garden and fish pool. South of the canal walk is a Victorian flower garden. Later Victorian addi-tions include the parterre and yew walk. National ivy collection here; also a narcissus collection. Parties may have conducted tours with the head gardener by prior arrangement. Apple Day is celebrated at Erddig in October.

FARCHYNYS COTTAGE 25
Bontddu, Gwynedd. Tel: (0134149) 245

Mrs G. Townshend ★ On A496 Dolgellau – Barmouth road, after Bontddu on right. Signposted ★ Best season: spring ★ Parking ★ Teas ★ Plants for sale when available ★ Open April to Oct, daily except Sat and Wed, 2.30pm – 6pm ★ Entrance: £1

This woodland garden overlooking the Mawddach estuary is set in natural oak and conifer woodland which adds to its attraction. There is much new planting, but azaleas, rhododendrons and magnolias are well established and would repay a spring visit when a system of pools, some now established, should be in operation.

FOXBRUSH 26
Aber Pwll, Port Dinorwic, Gwynedd. Tel: (01248) 670463

Mr and Mrs B.S. Osborne ★ 3m from Bangor on old Caernarvon road, avoiding new bypass, enter village and the house is on the left after high estate wall, opposite layby. Signposted Felinheli ★ Parking in layby opposite for cars and coaches ★ Refreshments ★ Toilet facilities ★ Suitable for wheelchairs ★ Plants for sale ★ Craft shop ★ Garden open 16th, 17th April, 11am – 5pm and by appointment ★ Entrance: £1

The present owners have created this garden since they bought the site of an old mill in 1968. It is a very difficult area to garden as it is subject to extensive flooding by the stream running through its entire length. The garden is part-walled with extensive planting of this feature, and the current three acres of varied planting are also being extended each year. Many wheelbarrows are planted as small landscapes, just the right height for wheelchairs.

GLANSEVERN 27
Berriew, Welshpool, Powys. Tel: (01686) 640200/640812

Mr and Mrs R.N. Thomas ★ From Welshpool take A483 S. After 5m the entrance is on left by bridge over River Rhiew ★ Parking ★ Toilet facilities ★ Partly suitable for wheelchairs ★ Plants for sale on Mon evenings and by appointment ★ Open by appointment all year, 2 – 6pm ★ Entrance: £2, children 10p

Large mature garden. A three-acre lake with islands where swans, ducks and other waterfowl breed. The streams, which form a water garden and feed the lake, are planted along the banks with moisture-loving plants and shrubs. A large area of lawn contains mature trees, herbaceous borders. Fountain with surround and walk planted with wisteria. Restored rockery and grotto.

HAFOD GARREGOG 28
Nantmor, Caernarfon, Gwynedd. Tel: (0176686) 282

Hugh and Angela Mason ★ 5m N of Penrhyndeudraeth ★ Parking ★ Partly suitable for wheelchairs ★ Dogs on lead ★ Open 14th May, 25th June, 11am – 5pm and April to Sept by appointment ★ Entrance: £1, children free

Created by the owners since 1971 in a woodland setting with fine mountain views above the River Hafod this is now one of the more interesting little gardens of North Wales. There is much foliage colour at all seasons from rhodendrons, azaleas, flowers and trees. There is a vegetable garden and water garden.

HEN YSGOLDY 29
Llanfrothen, Penrhyndeudraeth, Gwynedd. Tel: (01766) 771231

Mr and Mrs Michael Jenkins ★ From Llanfrothen via B4410 to Rhyd, after ½m turn left. Garden is first on right opposite drive to Fronheulog ★ Limited parking ★ Open April to Sept by appointment ★ Entrance: by charity box

A site with two streams, several different levels within the two acres, a natural sloping rock face turned into a heather garden and a naturally-formed rockery. Rich alluvial soil and an extremely mild and sheltered position afford maximum and varied growing conditions. The result is a garden of continually unfolding aspects of established trees and shrubs, including magnolias, rhododendrons, azaleas and embothriums which have been supplemented by a rich and varied collection of herbaceous plants; hostas, crocosmias, ligularias and ferns.

MAENAN HALL 30
Nr Llanrwst, Gwynedd. Tel: (01492) 640441

The Hon. Christopher McLaren ★ 2m N of Llanrwst on E side of A470, ¼m S of Maenan Abbey Hotel ★ Parking ★ Teas ★ Suitable for wheelchairs ★ Plants for sale ★ Open 21st May, 20th Aug, 10.30am – 5pm (last admission 4.30pm) ★ Entrance: £1.50, children 50p

Created in 1956 by the late Christabel Lady Aberconway, formal gardens surround the Elizabethan and Queen Anne house. Beyond are less formal gardens in mature woodland. The present owners have extended the planting of ornamental trees and shrubs in both formal and informal settings. Azaleas, rhododendrons and camellias, the latter situated in a dell at the base of a cliff, will make a spring visit rewarding, whilst a large number of eucryphias will be spectacular in late summer. There are many distinctive aspects of the garden including a fine collection of roses.

NEWCASTLE HOUSE ★★ 31
8 West Road, Bridgend, Mid-Glamorgan. Tel: (01656) 766880

Mr Fraser-Jenkins ★ From Bridgend town centre go 400 yards up Park Street, turn right to St Leonards Road and right into West Road ★ Parking ★ Toilet facilities ★ Property on market, but may be open one day in May and in June for charity, 2 – 5pm, also by appointment at other times 2- 5pm ★ Entrance: £2

This brings new meaning to the term 'plantsman's garden' for here is indeed a creation by an unusually knowledgeable plantsman. It is a relatively small town garden, made up of several smaller, interconnected gardens totally surrounded by walls. The lush planting within means each area is self-contained and yet leads on to the next, giving the visitor a feeling of being many miles from civilisation rather than a short distance from a busy town centre. Unusual trees abound here, and the sympathetic walls are hosts to a variety of shrubs and climbers, some well-known like roses and clematis, others rarely heard of and even more rarely seen. Rhododendrons, camellias, pieris and other lime-haters defy the rules and flourish in a garden overlying limestone. The fern lovers can see the NCCPG collection of *Dryopteris*; go in June and you will see a huge specimen of *Buddleia colvillei* dripping with its unusual flowers. Cold greenhouses shelter plants too tender for even this favoured garden.

PANT-YR-HOLIAD ★ 32
Rhydlewis, Llandysul, Dyfed. Tel: (01239) 851493

Mr and Mrs G. Taylor ★ From Cardigan take coast road to Brynhoffnant. Take B4334 towards Rhydlewis for 1m, turn left and garden second left ★ Parking ★ Teas and biscuits ★ Toilet facilities ★ Partly suitable for wheelchairs ★ Plants for sale ★ Open mid-April to Sept, once a month, Suns, 2 – 5pm (telephone for dates). Parties by appointment ★ Entrance: £1.50, children £1 (1994 prices)

This five-acre woodland garden, created by the owners since 1971, was started in an area of natural woodland backing on to the farmhouse. Over the years since then, hundreds of rhododendrons (species and hybrids) have been planted along the banks. Acers, eucalyptus, eucryphias and many other rare and unusual trees are now reaching maturity, and the paths wander in and around to give something to please the eye wherever the visitor may care to look. A stream runs through the middle of the garden, creating a boggy area which is home for iris and primulas as well as the numerous species of ferns which abound here and also giving a congenial home to a *Rhododendron macabeanum*. A fairly recent addition to the garden is a summer walk along which slate-edged beds are filled with herbaceous plants, including a collection of penstemons. A small pergola has a seat, surrounded by roses, from which the lovely view over the valley may be enjoyed, and the remainder of the walk is beneath more arches of climbing roses. Nearer the house is a walled garden, alpine beds, and a series of pools for ornamental waterfowl.

PENCARREG ★   33
Glyn Garth, Nr Menai Bridge, Gwynedd. Tel: (01248) 713545

Miss G. Jones ★ 1½m NE of A545 Menai Bridge towards Beaumaris, Glan Y Menai drive is a turning on the right, Pencarreg is 100 yards down on right ★ Parking in layby on main road, limited parking on the courtyard for small cars and disabled ★ Suitable for wheelchairs ★ Open all year by appointment only ★ Entrance: by charity box

This beautiful garden, with a wealth of species planted for all-year interest, has colour which has been achieved by the use of common and unusual shrubs. A small stream creates another delightful and sympathetically-exploited feature. The garden terminates at the cliff edge and this, too, has been skilfully planted. The views are remarkable.

PENLAN-UCHAF FARM GARDENS   34
**Cwm Gwaun, Gwaun Valley, Nr Fishguard, Dyfed.
Tel: (01348) 881388**

Mr and Mrs Vaughan ★ 7m from Fishguard take B4313 to Maenclochog signed Cwm Gwaun (Pontfaen). 4½m from Newport take A487 to Cwm Gwaun. Situated next to Sychpant Forest car park ★ Parking. Up to 35-seater coaches permitted ★ Refreshments ★ Toilet facilities ★ Partly suitable for wheelchairs ★ Dogs on lead ★ Open 25th March to Nov, daily, 9am – dusk ★ Entrance: £1.50, children 75p, disabled persons and children under 3 free

A medium-sized garden on a hillside near the top of the Gwaun Valley. The drive is very steep, but the view from the tea room is worth the effort. A young garden but the owners have realised that its position will make many trees and shrubs an impossibility so they have chosen alpines and summer bedding. Some 25,000 spring bulbs, and fuchsias, geraniums and annuals give plenty of colour later. A raised herb garden, suitable for wheelchair visitors and the blind, is being developed.

PENRHYN CASTLE ★   35
Bangor, Gwynedd. Tel: (01248) 353084; Fax: (01248) 371281

The National Trust ★ 1m E of Bangor on A5122 ★ Best seasons: spring and summer ★ Parking ★ Refreshments: hot meals and teas. Picnics in grounds ★

Toilet facilities inc. mother and baby facilities and disabled ★ Suitable for wheelchairs, golf buggy available for garden and park if pre-booked ★ Dogs on lead in grounds only ★ Shop ★ Castle open as for gardens, 12 noon – 5pm, July to Aug opens 11am (last audio tour 4pm, last admission 4.30pm) ★ Garden open 29th March to 29th Oct, daily except Tues, 11am – 6pm ★ Entrance: £2, children £1 (castle and garden £4.40, children £2.20, parties £3.50 per person)

Large garden covering 48 acres with some fine specimen trees, shrubs and a Victorian walled garden in terraces with pools, lawns and a wild garden. Although the site of the house dates from the eighteenth century, the gardens are very much early Victorian, dating from the building of the present castle by Thomas Hopper. A giant tree fern, which will dwarf any children which visit the garden, has been sent from Tasmania to take its place in a specialist collection that also includes another giant, gunnera, and the Australian bottle brush plant. They can be found in the spectacular bog garden beyond the walled garden.

PICTON CASTLE ★   36
The Rhos, Haverfordwest, Dyfed. Tel: (01437) 751379

Picton Castle Trust ★ 4m E of Haverfordwest on A40. Signposted ★ Best season: spring ★ Parking ★ Refreshments ★ Toilet facilities ★ Suitable for wheelchairs ★ Dogs on lead ★ Plants for sale ★ Shop ★ Castle open mid-July to mid-Sept, also Easter Sun and Bank Holidays. Conducted tours Sun and Thurs ★ Garden open April to Sept, daily except Mon (but open Bank Holiday Mons), 10.30am – 5pm ★ Entrance: £2, OAP and children £1 (castle and grounds £3, OAP and children £1.50) (1994 prices)

Picton Castle gardens have a history going back many hundreds of years, but it is only since 1954 that the gardens in their present form have come into being. Fortunate in having wind shelter planted many years ago, the garden flourishes and has an air of maturity although it is described by its former owners as being young. Some of the shrubs are also quite ancient; a rhododendron 'Old Port' on the edge of the lawn is believed to be several hundred years old. There are not many labels on the rhododendrons as a great number are hybrids bred by the present head gardener and un-named. The walled garden is being reclaimed vigorously to provide variety and more colour in high summer.

PLANTASIA   37
Swansea, West Glamorgan.

Swansea City Council ★ Clearly signposted from city centre ★ Parking ★ Refreshments nearby ★ Toilet facilities ★ Suitable for wheelchairs ★ Plants for sale ★ Shop ★ Open all year, daily except Mon, 10am – 5.30pm ★ Entrance: £1 (1994 price)

Plantasia is a hothouse of some 2000 square yards divided into three zones – arid, tropical and humid. It contains over 5000 plants on permanent display from cacti to orchids. The former orchid house is now a butterfly house. Included in the main section of the building are varieties of plants from tropical and subtropical areas of the world interesting for their flowers or foliage. This is also an aviary for exotic birds and home to collections of reptiles and invertebrates.

PLAS BRONDANW GARDENS 38
Llanfrothen, Gwynedd. Tel: (01766) 770484/770814

5m NE of Porthmadog between Llanfrothen and Croesor ★ Parking ★
Refreshments for groups by prior arrangement and in summer only ★ Partly
suitable for wheelchairs ★ Open all year, daily, 9am – 5pm ★ Entrance: £1.50,
children 25p

This garden, in the grounds of the house given to Sir Clough Williams-Ellis
by his father, is quite separate from the village of Portmeirion (see entry), and
was created by the architect over a period of 70 years. His main objective was
to provide a series of dramatic and romantic prospects inspired by the great
gardens of Italy. It includes architectural features, such as the orangery; visitors should walk up the avenue that leads past a dramatic chasm to the
folly, from which there is a fine view of Snowdon. Indeed mountains are
visible from the end of every vista. Williams-Ellis made a prodigious investment in hedging and topiary and the present-day head gardener has calcu-
lated that the former, if laid out, would cover four acres. It is mostly yew.
Hydrangeas and ferns flourish in the damp climate. The present custodian,
the architect's grand-daughter, is trying to enhance the strong formal structure by flower planting.

PLAS NEWYDD 39
Llanfairpwll, Anglesey, Gwynedd. Tel: (01248) 714795

The National Trust/ The Marquess of Anglesey ★ 1m SW of Llanfairpwll ★ Best
season: spring ★ Parking ¼m from house and garden ★ Refreshments: light lunches
and teas ★ Toilet facilities inc. disabled ★ Suitable for wheelchairs ★ Plants for
sale in adjacent nursery (not NT) ★ Shop ★ House open inc. military museum ★
Garden open 31st March to 29th Sept, daily except Sat, 12 noon – 5pm (last
admission 4.30pm); 1st to 29th Oct, Fri and Sun only, 12 noon – 5pm. In May
to Aug gardens open at 11am ★ Entrance: £1.90 (house and gardens £3.80,
children £1.90, family £9.50, parties £3 per person)

An eighteenth-century house by James Wyatt, also an attraction because it
contains Rex Whistler's largest wall painting. Humphry Repton's suggestion
of 'plantations...to soften a bleak country and shelter the ground from violent
winds' has resulted in an informal open-plan garden, with shrub plantings in
the lawns and parkland, which slopes down to the Menai Straits and frames
the view of the Snowdonia peaks. There is a formal Italian-style rose garden
to the front of the house. A new arbour has replaced a conservatory on the
top terrace with a tufa mound from which water falls over cascades down to
a pool on the bottom terrace. The pool has a new Italianate fountain to add
to the overall Mediterranean effect of this formal area within the parkland.
The influence of the Gulf Stream enables the successful cultivation of many
frost-tender shrubs and a special rhododendron garden is open in the spring
when the gardens are at their best, although they are expertly tended
throughout the year. Major restoration of the Italianate Terrace Garden
continues. New features include a deep grotto with watery tufa rockery, a
pond and fountain.

PLAS PENHELIG ★ 40
Aberdovey, Gwynedd. Tel: (0165472) 676

Mr and Mrs A.C. Richardson ★ At Aberdovey, between the two railway bridges ★ Best season: spring ★ Parking ★ Teas ★ Toilet facilities ★ Plants for sale ★ Open April to Oct, Wed – Sun, 2.30 – 5.30pm ★ Entrance: £1, children 50p (1994 prices)

A traditional Edwardian estate garden of seven acres reclaimed over the past 10 years. An informal garden with lawns, terraces, pools, fountains, orchard, rock garden and herbaceous borders. Spring bulbs, azaleas, rhododendrons, magnolias, euphorbias, roses and some mature tree heathers of immense size. The jewel is the half-acre walled garden, including 900 square feet of glass with vines and peaches.

PLAS-YN-RHIW 41
Pwllheli, Gwynedd. Tel: (01758) 88219

The National Trust ★ 12m from Pwllheli on S coast road to Aberdaron ★ Best season: spring ★ Parking 80 yards from house and garden. No coaches ★ Toilet facilities, inc. disabled ★ Shop ★ House open but to limited numbers ★ Garden open 2nd April to 29th Sept, daily except Sat, 12 noon – 5pm; Oct, Suns only, 12 noon – 4pm (last admission ½hr before closing) ★ Entrance: £2.30, children £1.15

Essentially a cottage garden around a partly medieval manor house, on west shore of Hell's Mouth Bay. Flowering trees and shrubs, rhododendrons, camellias and magnolias, divided by formal box hedges and grass paths extending to three quarters of an acre. The Trust has recently extended Plas-yn-Rhiw to include 150 acres of woodland, purchased from the Forestry Commission. Snowdrop wood on high ground above garden.

PORTMEIRION ★ 42
Penrhyndeudraeth, Gwynedd. Tel: (01766) 770 228 (Hotel reception)

2m SE of Portmadoc near A487 ★ Parking at top of village ★ Self-service restaurant open 10am – 5pm. Ice Cream Parlour ★ Toilet facilities ★ Shops ★ Village open to hotel non-residents daily, 9.30am – 5.30pm ★ Entrance: £3, OAP £2.40, children £1.30, under 5 free. Reduced prices Nov to March

Architect Sir Clough Williams-Ellis' wild essay into the picturesque is a triumph of eclecticism with Gothic, Renaissance and Victorian-styled buildings arranged as an Italianate village around a harbour and set in 70 acres of subtropical woodlands crisscrossed by paths. This 'light opera' is played out against the backdrop of the Cambrian mountains and the vast empty sweep of estuary sands. The gentle humour of the architecture extends to the plantings in both horizontal and vertical planes – in formal gardens and in the wild luxuriance which clings to rocky crags. One visitor was overheard to remark that 'only the plastic geckos were missing' to give that full Italian feeling. Portmeirion provides one of Britain's most stimulating objects for an excursion, and during the period of the June festival in nearby Criccieth there are nine other good gardens open in the district. Write (with SAE) to Criccieth Festival Office, PO Box 3, 52 High Street, Criccieth, Gwynedd LL52 0BW for details.

POST HOUSE GARDENS ★   43
Cwmbach, Whitland, Dyfed. Tel: (01994) 484213

Mrs Jo Kenaghan ★ From Carmarthen W on A40, take B4298 through Meidrim. Leave by centre lane signposted Llanboidy, turn right at crossroads signposted Blaenwaun then right at next crossroads to Cwmbach ★ Best seasons: spring and early summer ★ Parking in official car park ★ Tea and coffee on request ★ Toilet facilities ★ Partly suitable for wheelchairs ★ Plants for sale ★ Open all year during daylight hours ★ Entrance: £1.50, OAP £1, children 50p

Some five acres of woodland valley garden, begun in 1978, wind along the bank of the River Sien. Paths lead through shrubberies to a large pool with golden orfe and grass carp, then by a bridge across the river and back by stepping stones to a bog garden (also reached by path). Steps lead up to paths at higher levels which meander between shrubberies housing many species and hybrid rhododendrons and on through a rose garden planted with old roses. Above the pond a summerhouse provides seating from which to see *Rosa filipes* 'Kiftsgate' and 'Himalayan Musk Rose', now rampant through and over adjacent trees; several other seats give views of different areas. Near the entrance to the garden a glasshouse (built over an old mill) and a conservatory extend the range of well-known and unusual plants, which together with the wild flowers and wooded background make up this interesting garden.

POWIS CASTLE ★★   44
Welshpool, Powys. Tel: (01938) 554338

The National Trust ★ ¾m from Welshpool on A483, well signposted ★ Parking ★ Refreshments: Teas and light lunches ★ Toilet facilities ★ Partly suitable for wheelchairs (but not castle) ★ Plants for sale ★ Shop ★ Castle open ★ Garden open April to June, and Sept to Oct, daily except Mon and Tues. In July and Aug, daily except Mon but open Bank Holiday Mons, 11am – 6pm. 'Meet the gardener' tours by special arrangement ★ Entrance: £3.60, children (5-17) £1.80, under 5 free (garden and museum); £5.80, children (5-17) £2.90, under 5 free (castle, garden and museum) (1994 prices)

This is a garden originally laid out in 1720 based on even earlier designs. The original formal design of the courtyard round the statue of Fame has been reinstated. Most notable features are broad hanging terraces interestingly planted with huge clipped yews. On the second terrace, brick alcoves opposite fine lead urns and figures above the orangery below. Some fruit trees remain on the terraces, where in the nineteenth century advantage was taken of the microclimate to grow fruit and vegetables until a kitchen garden was established. The latter is now a flower garden. Unusual and tender plants and climbers prosper in the shelter of walls and hedges. This garden is not for the faint-hearted because it is very steep, but it's well worth the effort to relish the views which are as fine as any, anywhere. A good collection of old roses. Excellent guide book available with lists of plants.

RAGLAN CASTLE   45
Raglan, Gwent. Tel: (01291) 690228

Cadw: Welsh Historic Monuments ★ Close to and signposted from A40 at Raglan ★ Parking ★ Toilet facilities ★ Open all year: April to Oct, daily, 9.30am – 6.30pm;

Nov to March, Mon – Sat, 9.30am – 4pm, Sun, 2 – 4pm (last admission ½hr before closing) ★ Entrance: £2, OAP and students £1.50 (1994 prices)

Belonging mainly to the fifteenth century, Raglan Castle was as much a product of social grandeur as it was a military stronghold. Extensively damaged by Cromwell's demolition engineers, the fine apartments at the castle still hint at its splendour. Vestigial extensive water gardens can be seen below the terraces on two sides. The guidebook's plan of the gardens coupled with the early landforms which can still be detected, such as rather grand terraces, will prove attractive to those interested in garden history.

SAUNDERSFOOT BAY LEISURE PARK   46
Broadfield, Saundersfoot, Dyfed. Tel: (01834) 812284

Mr Ian Shuttleworth ★ On B4316 ½m from centre of Saundersfoot ★ Parking ★ Toilet facilities ★ Suitable for wheelchairs ★ Dogs on lead ★ Plants for sale ★ Open 28th March to 2nd Oct, daily, 10am – 5pm ★ Entrance: free

An unusual garden as it has been designed around a 20-acre holiday caravan park. Different and interesting shrubs have been used as hedges round the caravans; there are large herbaceous borders and unusual trees and shrubs surround the whole park. The central area of lawns is framed by mixed herbaceous and shrub borders, and leading past a colourful planting of conifers to a laburnum walk is a large water feature. The park also holds the National collection of *Potentilla fruticosa*.

SINGLETON BOTANIC GARDENS ★   47
Singleton Park, Swansea, West Glamorgan. Tel: (01792) 302420

Swansea City Council ★ Access from Gower Road, Swansea ★ Parking on road ★ Refreshments during Aug ★ Toilet facilities ★ Suitable for wheelchairs ★ Open all year, daily, summer, 9am – 6pm, winter, 9am – 4.30pm ★ Entrance: free

A four and a half-acre garden with herbaceous borders, rockeries, rose beds and an interesting collection of trees and shrubs. Hedges with a variety of different shrubs. Newly-erected temperate and tropical glasshouses contain an extensive collection of rare and unusual plants, including orchids, bromeliads and epiphytes.

TREDEGAR HOUSE   48
Newport, Gwent.

Newport Borough Council ★ Signed from M4 junction 28 and A48 ★ Parking ★ Open April to Sept, Wed – Sun, 11.30am – 4pm ★ Entrance: £1 (house and garden £3.50, concessions £2.70)

One of the finest Restoration houses in the country. The house, as restored, is remarkable, with pictures from Dulwich and furniture from the V&A. The reason for it being in this *Guide* is that researchers in the Orangery Garden discovered physical evidence of a coloured garden, a unique piece of archaeology. The result is the first coloured gravel garden to be re-created in this country and well worth seeing.

TREM-AR-FOR 49
125 Cwm Road, Dyserth, Clwyd. Tel: (01745) 570349

Mr and Mrs L. Whittaker ★ Take A5151 Dyserth – Rhuddlan road. Turn left at crossroads signed Cwm, fork left and at traffic de-restriction sign house on left ★ Best season: spring ★ Parking ★ Plants for sale when available ★ Open by appointment only ★ Entrance: £1 by collecting box

This small three-quarter-acre garden offers dramatic views of Snowdon and Anglesey and is of great interest to the enthusiastic gardener. Its steep lime-stone terraces are filled with many rare and interesting plants with special emphasis on alpines.

TRETOWER COURT 50
Tretower, Crickhowell, Powys. Tel: (01874) 730279

Cadw: Welsh Historic Monuments ★ 3m NW of Crickhowell. Access signposted from Tretower village off A479 ★ Parking ★ Toilet facilities ★ Open all year: April to Oct, daily, 9.30am – 6.30pm; Nov to March, Mon – Sat, 9.30am – 4pm, Sun, 2 – 4pm ★ Entrance: £1.50, OAP and students 90p (1994 prices)

This late medieval home is set in the beautiful Usk valley. An earlier castle is located across an open meadow to the rear. Stretching south from the Court is a charming re-creation of a mid-fifteenth-century pleasure garden. Planted as recently as 1991, it is maturing well and its design is faithful to the late medieval period.

VAYNOR PARK 51
Berriew, Welshpool, Powys. Tel: (01686) 640406

Mr and Mrs W. Corbett-Winder ★ 1m from Berriew off B4385 Welshpool – Newtown Road ★ Parking ★ Refreshments and toilet facilities in Berriew ★ Open May, daily, 10am – 6pm and June to Oct by appointment ★ Entrance: £1 donation for charity

Mature parkland garden with fine old trees. Woodland with rhododendrons, azaleas, old rambling roses, herbaceous borders, a rose garden, formal herb garden and fine views of surrounding countryside.

WINLLAN 52
Talsarn, Lampeter, Dyfed. Tel: (01570) 470612

Mr and Mrs Ian Callan ★ 8m NNW of Lampeter on B4342 ★ Best season: May/June ★ Parking ★ Partly suitable for wheelchairs ★ Dogs on lead ★ Open May and June, daily, 2 – 6pm, and July and Aug by appointment only. Coaches by appointment ★ Entrance: £1, children 50p, under 12 free

This six-acre garden has been created by the owners mainly as a haven for the wildlife which is disappearing so rapidly countrywide. After 18 years the garden is home to over 200 species of wild flowers, including five species of wild orchid, and more appear all the time; these in turn attract the butterflies which thrive on the rich flora of the meadow. A small area was planted up as a woodland with some 35 species of mainly native trees in 1982 and again this has its attendant wild flowers and birds. Beyond the wood is a hay meadow, and along the length of the garden is the river creating another habitat. Although there is a small area of conventional garden the emphasis is on native wild plants and a small pond is a very lively habitat for frogs, toads and dragonflies.

YNYSHIR HALL 53
Eglwysfach, Machynlleth, Powys. Tel: (01654) 781209

Mr and Mrs R. Reen ★ On A487 Aberystwyth — Machynlleth road in village of Eglwysfach ★ Best season: May/June ★ Parking ★ ☆Refreshments ★ Toilet facilities ★ Dogs on lead ★ Open all year ★ Entrance: £1

Although the house was once owned by Queen Victoria, the 12 acres of gardens were not really developed and extensively planted until in the hands of William Mappin who owned the Hall from 1930-70. During this time many unusual trees were planted and the grounds were landscaped. Water played an important part in the garden, and the present owners have discovered pools and a water course which are being cleared and replanted. The trees are now nearing maturity and are very fine specimens which create a noble background for a variety of rhododendrons, azaleas, camellias and other shrubs. Early visitors can see massed plantings of daffodils and fritillaries, moving on to magnolias and other later-flowering shrubs, finishing the season with autumn colour from the maples. There is a famous 'Ironstone tree' dating from the period when Queen Victoria visited the Hall. The 500 acres of woodland round the house were given to the RSPB by Mappin. The Hall itself is now a hotel.

WELSH HISTORIC GARDENS TRUST

Formed in 1989 the Trust has since formed ten branches to make a network throughout Wales. The membership has topped 600 and apart from national projects involving the Trust office, the branches undertake projects locally. Its national aims are to initiate and assist in the conservation of gardens, parks and designed landscapes that are of historic, cultural and aesthetic importance in the Welsh heritage, and to raise public awareness of the decline in particular cases. In order to compile a gazetteer, members are being encouraged to help within the branch.

WHEELCHAIR USERS

Please note that entries which describe a garden as 'suitable for wheelchairs' refer to the garden only. If there is a house open, it may or may not be suitable for wheelchairs.

CHANNEL ISLANDS

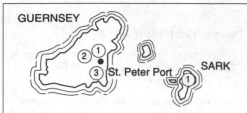

GUERNSEY

2 1
3 St. Peter Port

SARK
1

CHANNEL ISLANDS

JERSEY

4 5 2
3 6
St. Helier

Gorey

GUERNSEY

CANDIE GARDENS   1
Candie Road, St Peter Port, Guernsey. Tel: (01481) 46263

*States of Guernsey ★ In St Peter Port, off Candie Road ★ Parking nearby ★
Refreshments ★ Toilet facilities ★ Dogs on lead ★ Guernsey Museum and Art
Gallery open (wheelchair access) ★ Garden open all year, 8am to sunset (5pm in
winter) ★ Entrance: free*

Situated on a slope overlooking the harbour at St Peter Port, there are
wonderful views over the islands of Herm and Sark from these gardens.
Created over 100 years ago, they contain statues of Queen Victoria and
Victor Hugo. The Lower Gardens used to be the walled fruit and vegetable
garden of Candie House (now the Priaulx Library) but have since been laid
out as a public garden with palms and a maidenhair tree. Walls give shelter
to *Fremontodendron californicum*, mallows and a lemon tree. In fact a surprising variety of plants normally grown indoors flourish here, notably camellias,
daturas and hibiscus. The first greenhouse on Guernsey is said to have been
constructed in the gardens in 1792 by Peter Mourant and two of these
greenhouses can still be seen, with thick timbers and narrow panes. The
Guernsey Museum and Art Gallery built around an original Victorian bandstand and the Priaulx reference and genealogical library are here. Current
plans, following advice from garden expert Peter Thoday of BBC2's *Victorian
Kitchen Garden*, are for a two–year restoration of the gardens to their original
1898 state.

LES ROUVETS TROPICAL GARDENS   2
Rue de L'Arquet, St Saviours, Guernsey. Tel: (01481) 63566

*Michael Smith ★ 5m W of St Peter Port ★ Best season: July to Sept ★ Parking
★ Refreshments Easter to Sept ★ Toilet facilities ★ Suitable for wheelchairs ★
Shop open Easter to Sept ★ Plants for sale ★ Open all year, daily, 10am – 5pm
★ Entrance: £1.20, OAP 80p, children 60p, disabled persons free (1994 prices)*

A collection of tropical plants built up under two owners over 20 years, set in
four greenhouses, each with its own climatic theme, including the Madeira
house, cactus house and citrus house. Bananas, avocados, pineapples, coffee,
palms, hibiscus, bougainvilleas and cotton are just some of the exotic plants
and trees that can be seen in this unusual collection.

SAUSMAREZ MANOR EXOTIC WOODLAND
GARDEN   3
St Martin, Guernsey. Tel: (01481) 35571

*Mr Peter de Sausmarez ★ 1½m S of St Peter Port, off Fort Road ★ Parking ★
Refreshments ★ Toilet facilities ★ Partly suitable for wheelchairs ★ Dogs on lead ★
Rare plant sale on 31st May ★ Manor open mid-week in summer ★ Dolls House
collection ★ Garden open daily, 10.30am – 5.30pm or dusk if earlier. Guided
tours for groups by appointment ★ Entrance: £1.50, children 50p, disabled persons
and babies free (1994 prices)*

Set around two small lakes in an ancient wood is a garden which has been
crammed with the unusual and rare to give an exotic feel. It is strewn with
plants from many parts of the world, particularly the sub-tropics and the
Mediterranean, which survive in Guernsey's southern mellow maritime
climate. Collections of yuccas, ferns, camellias (nearly 300), bamboos, hebes,
bananas, echiums, lilies, palm trees, fuchsias, as well as hydrangeas, hostas,
azaleas, pittosporums, clematis, rhododendrons, cyclamens, impatiens, giant
grasses etc., all jostle with indigenous wild flowers. No pesticides are used so
wildlife flourishes and appears in season.

JERSEY

DOMAINE DES VAUX   1
St Lawrence, Jersey.

*Mr and Mrs Marcus Binney ★ 2m N of St Helier ★ Parking ★ Open one Sun, 2
– 5pm for charity (check with Jersey Tourist Board (01534) 24779). Private
parties by prior arrangement in writing to the owners ★ Entrance: £2*

Marcus Binney, architectural correspondent of *The Times*, has a passion for
the preservation of architecture and landscape and these tastes are very much
reflected in his and his wife's delightful garden. It is in two completely
contrasting parts. The top is a formal Italianate garden, set around and above
a sunken rectangular lawn, and the borders are a riot of unusual and familiar
perennials and shrubs. The lower garden is a semi-wild and quite steep valley
with a string of ponds connected by a stream. Of particular note are the
camellias in both gardens and an interesting collection of conifers in a small
arboretum. The formal garden is perfect and was created by the previous

generation, Sir George and Lady Binney, and designed by Walter Ison who created the strong architectural form. Lady Binney planted with an eye for colour in foliage as much as in flowers, as is evidenced by the grey and silver borders facing the yellow, gold and bronze ones. The Binneys have planted a small formal herb garden on a triangular theme and are creating a *jardinière*.

ERIC YOUNG ORCHID FOUNDATION 2
Victoria Village, Trinity, Jersey. Tel: (01534) 861963

The Eric Young Charitable Trust , 1 1/2m N of St Helier , Parking , Toilet facilities , Suitable for wheelchairs , Open all year, Thurs – Sat, 10am – 4pm , Entrance: £2, OAP £1.50, students and children £1

This exquisite private orchid collection was built up by the late Eric Young, who came to Jersey after World War II. In 1958 he merged his own collection with that of a Sanders nursery which was closing down and continued to acquire new plants which have been described as 'the finest private collection of orchids in Europe, possibly the world'. The purpose-built centre, which has won many awards, consists of five growing houses and a landscaped display area where visitors may view these exotic flowers in close detail. From November to April there are cymbidiums, paphiopedilums, odontoglossums and calanthes, while from May to June cattleyas, miltonias and odontoglossums and from June to October, phalaenopsis, miltonias and odontoglossums. The beauty of these flowers is inversely proportional to the difficulties of their names. Meanwhile, those wishing to see native orchids in season may find a walk in Les Blanches Banques, the sand dunes behind St Ouen's Bay, rewarding.

HOWARD DAVIS PARK 3
St Saviour, Jersey.

In St Helier, between St Clement's Road and Don Road ★ Car park in Cleveland Road nearby ★ Refreshments ★ Toilet facilities, inc. disabled ★ Suitable for wheelchairs ★ Open all year, daily: Oct to March, 8.30am – 4.30pm; April to May, 8am – 8pm; June to Sept, 8am – 10pm ★ Entrance: free (nominal charge for bandstand seats)

Given by T.B. Davies, a great benefactor of the island, in memory of his son who was killed in World War I, this is the most famous of Jersey's public gardens. Colourful sub-tropical trees and plants flourish here and the bandstand is the venue for an excellent variety of live entertainment from May to September. Other public parks in St Helier are Parade Gardens, off Parade Place, and Victoria Park, off St Aubins Road/Cheapside. Both contain interesting statues.

JERSEY LAVENDER 4
Rue du Pont Marquet, St Brelade, Jersey. Tel: (01534) 42933

David and Elizabeth Christie ★ 3m W of St Helier near Pont Marquet Country Park ★ Best season: June/July ★ Parking ★ Light refreshments and teas ★ Toilet facilities ★ Suitable for wheelchairs ★ Dogs ★ Shop for lavender products ★ Plants for sale ★ Open 22nd May to 23rd Sept, Mon – Sat, 10am – 5pm ★ Entrance: £1.75, children free (1994 prices)

This lavender farm was started in 1983 and now covers eight acres. Visitors are invited to walk around the main fields, planted with four varieties of lavender, to enjoy their different colours and scents. Harvesting is done by hand, starting in late June, and the distillation and perfume bottling processes may also be seen. There is an extensive garden of herbs including the NCCPG collection of lavenders.

JERSEY ZOOLOGICAL PARK 5
Les Augres Manor, Trinity, Jersey. Tel: (01534) 864666

Jersey Wildlife Preservation Trust ★ 2½m NW of St Helier ★ Parking ★ Refreshments ★ Toilet facilities ★ Suitable for wheelchairs ★ Open daily except 25th Dec, 10am – 6pm (or dusk in winter) ★ Entrance: £4.60, OAP £3.10, children £2.60. Party rates available (1994 prices)

While most visitors will undoubtedly, and rightly, go to Jersey Zoo to see the animals described by its founder Gerald Durrell in *Menagerie Manor*, and in support of the breeding and conservation programmes for endangered wildlife which are run so successfully here, the parkland and water gardens are in themselves a good reason to visit. Surrounding the sixteenth-century manor and extending to 25 acres, they contain trees, shrubs and rare and exotic flowers from around the world because the Trust has aimed to grow plants native to the animals' habitats.

SAMARÈS MANOR 6
St Clement, Jersey. Tel: (01534) 70551

Mrs Obbard ★ 1m E of St Helier ★ Best seasons: late spring and mid-summer ★ Parking ★ Refreshments: restaurant specialising in vegetarian cuisine ★ Toilet facilities ★ Suitable for wheelchairs ★ Dogs on lead ★ Shops ★ Plant centre ★ Manor (guided tours daily except Sun, am. £1.50 extra) and Craft Centre open ★ Garden open April to Oct, daily, 10am – 5pm ★ Entrance: £2.90, OAP £2.40, children £1.50, under 5 free (1994 prices)

The name Samarès is derived from the French for salt marsh and, nearby in marshy land, sea salt was once extracted. It is not known who built the existing manor house, which has passed through many owners, but the grounds have developed gradually. They were famed for their trees by 1680. The present garden was the work of Sir James Knott who bought the property in 1924, and had it developed employing 40 gardeners at a cost of £100,000. Really two quite different gardens: a herb garden, claimed to be one of the largest and comprehensive in Britain, specialising in culinary and medicinal herbs in a partially-walled garden leading to a lakeside area, and a Japanese garden. Of particular note are the camellias, the *Taxodium distichum* in the lake and the rocks imported from Cumberland. This is not just a garden but a whole way of life based on herbs and farm animals with daily talks and demonstrations.

SARK

LA SEIGNEURIE 1
Sark. Tel: (01481) 832345 (Sark Tourism)

Seigneur Mr J.M. Beaumont ★ ¹/₂m NW of Creux Harbour, Sark ★ Best season: summer ★ Parking for bicycles ★ Toilet facilities ★ Open 3rd April to 27th Oct, Mon – Fri, 10am – 5pm. Also Sats during July and Aug for charity ★ Entrance: 70p, children 30p

The grounds and walled garden of La Seigneurie, the residence of the Seigneurs of Sark, are beautifully maintained. Visit in spring and early summer for the camellias, azaleas and rhododendrons and later for roses, old-fashioned annuals and in autumn for the glowing colours of dahlias and fuchsias. The walled garden contains clematis, geraniums, lapagerias, abutilons, osteospermums and many sub-tropical and tender plants. The ornamental rose garden with box hedge surrounds has three beds devoted to the rose 'Dame of Sark' named after the late Dame Sibyl Hathaway, the Seigneur's grandmother, who was responsible for much of the planning and planting in the garden. There is a *potager,* wild pond area, a restored Victorian greenhouse with vines and bougainvilleas, a hedge maze for children, and a small outdoor museum with antique canons. The Gothic *columbier* (the dovecot being the prerogative of the lord of the manor) may still be seen behind the house.

GARDENS IN FRANCE

In addition to the books by Barozzi and Abb mentioned opposite, the Marie de Paris has produced a useful leaflet with an introduction by Jacques Chirac on the gardens of Paris. There are six tours *'par thème'*, a calendar of dates from March to November and a suggested programme for 4th – 23rd June. The leaflet can be obtained from 3 avenue de la Porte d'Auteuil, Paris 16 e arr., tel: 40.71.76.47.

EUROPE

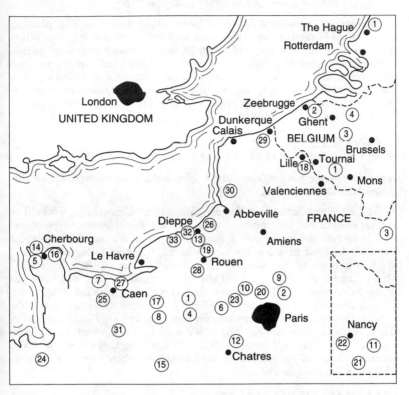

This does not pretend to be an exhaustive guide to the best gardens open to the public in France and Belgium. We have selected about 30 which have been seen recently by inspectors and are considered worthy of a visit by those driving in northern Europe for a day or two. Those staying longer may of course see fine gardens further afield, particularly in the Loire. Giverny, the Monet garden, is rather too far for a quick drive and admission is being curtailed because it is often over-crowded, particularly at weekends. For Paris visitors a paperback book *Guide des 400 jardins publics de Paris* by Jacques Barozzi is useful. Those travelling further afield will wish to use Barbara Abb's *French Gardens: A Guide*, available from bookshops here. All opening times should be checked beforehand, although those given here have been supplied by the owners.

FRANCE

ARBORETUM D'HARCOURT   1
27800 Harcourt, Normandie. Tel: 32.46.29.70; Fax: 32.46.53.38

*Association des Amis du Domaine d'Harcourt ★ 6km SE of Brionne via D137 ★
Open 15th March to 14th June, daily except Tues, 2 – 6pm; 15th June to 14th*

Sept, daily, 10am – 7pm; 15th Sept to 15th Nov, daily except Tues, 2 – 6pm. Guided tours for parties by appointment ★ Entrance: 25F, children 10F, under 6 free, parties 20F per person, children 10F, guide's fee 250F

A nine-hectare arboretum set in a forest of 94 hectares. The planting began in 1852 and among the oaks and beeches are many conifers discovered on the west coast of North America around that time: swamp cypresses and giant sequoias, thuyas from California and Oregon and two *Pseudotsuga menziesii* that were among the first introduced to France, now over 40m high. Look out, too, for the 32m high *Liquidambar styraciflua* and newer plantings of tulip trees and walnuts from the east coast of America. (Not yet inspected)

CHANTILLY 2
60500 Chantilly. Tel: 44.57.03.62/44.57.08.00

Institute de France ★ 40km N of Paris ★ Open daily, 10am – 6pm ★ Entrance to garden 17F, children 10F

Andre Le Nôtre believed that this design was one of his greatest works. The original château had been built on its watery site for defensive purposes and he transformed the moats into a magnificent water feature. The equestrian statue on the great terrace is the focal point for the long T-shaped canal and the formal pools of the parterre. The Grand Château (which houses the Musée Condé) was rebuilt *c.* 1880 after the original building was destroyed in the Revolution and is set to one side, completely surrounded by water. Like all Le Nôtre's work, it is very splendid. On a more intimate scale is the *hameau*. Earlier than Marie Antoinette's plaything at Versailles, it consists of tiny brown and white cottages, one with a working water wheel, set around a small lawn. The pretty 'Maison de Sylvie' is worth seeking out in the woods on the same side of the grounds as the Capitanerie where there is a Salon de Thé and a Brasserie for the needy.

CHÂTEAU DE BAZEILLES 3
08140 Bazeilles. Tel: 24.27.09.68

M. Guilhas ★ 3km S of Sedan via N43 ★ Open all year except Mon, 10am – 12noon, 2 – 6pm ★ Entrance: free

A formal garden in the course of restoration. The seven-hectare park is entered by magnificent wrought iron gates and a gravelled forecourt. At the back of the château are four rectangular pools. Set among the box-edged groups of trees are some fine buildings. A striking orangery (now a restaurant) with a curved and tiled roof, and at the far end of the shady garden beyond the pools are two very fine classical pavilions and an old dovecot. The château is pure Louis XV style. The stable block is a hotel and the estate is well-signed.

CHÂTEAU DE BEAUMESNIL 4
27410 Beaumesnil. Tel: 32.44.40.09

Fondation Furstenburg-Beaumesnil ★ 40km W of Evreux and 13km SE of Bernay on D140 ★ Open May to Sept, daily except Tues. Groups by telephone appointment

La Quintinie, the horticulturalist who worked with Le Nôtre at Versailles, was the designer of the gardens, unchanged since their creation in 1640. The formal garden of the moated château is divided into sections; one is in the shape of a half-moon with a curved parterre. There is an unusual labyrinth, a circular mound based around the foundations of the medieval keep. It is very well kept and there are walks around the lake and park.

CHÂTEAU DE BEAUREPAIRE 5
50690 Martinvast. Tel: 33.52.02.23

SCI du Domaine de Beaurepaire ★ 7km from Cherbourg ★ Open Jan to 2nd April 2 – 6pm; 8th April to 1st Nov, daily, 2 – 7pm ★ Entrance: to 2nd April 20F, teenagers and groups 15F per person ; from 8th April 30F, teenagers and groups 20F per person

The park was created in the English style in 1820. There are extensive lakes, streams and waterfalls. Pyramids, cascades and a model farm *c*. 1850. Rhododendrons, palm trees and tulip trees grow well in this wooded park as do some fine conifers and other rare species.

CHÂTEAU DE BIZY 6
27200 Vernon.

M and Mme Patrice Vergé ★ In Vernon, on the Seine, SE of Rouen ★ Open April to 1st Nov, daily except Mon, 9am – 12noon and 2 – 6pm; 2nd Nov to March, Sat and Sun, 2 – 5pm and parties by appointment on weekdays only ★ Entrance: 32F, children 16F, parties 24F per person

The garden at Bizy can only be visited before or after the guided tour of the château, a nineteenth-century building with pillared facade. Original eighteenth-century stables and part of the eighteenth-century château remain as does a remarkable water feature designed by a nephew of Le Nôtre. The elaborate cascades, fountains and statuary are particularly fine. Unfortunately there is no water and so the whole composition is lifeless and disappointing although important work is being done with Les Monuments Historiques to put the water back. From the terrace there is an attractive view over the park with its baroque statues and a shady lime walk leads to a circle of yews around a statue of Venus.

CHÂTEAU DE BRÉCY 7
14480 Saint-Gabriel, Brécy.

M and Mme Didier Wirth ★ 10km E of Bayeux off D12 or 24km W of Caen by motorway ★ Open 16th April to Oct, Tues, Thurs and Sun, 2.30 - 6.30pm. At other times by appointment ★ Entrance: 15F

This compact seventeenth-century garden is the ideal antidote for the garden visitor convinced that French formal gardens must be grand and boring. Part of its charm is the contrast between the surrounding pastoral landscape and the architectural sophistication of the formal garden created in the Italian style *c*. 1630. It is quite small and rises away from the house in five terraces, each different and all designed to give the illusion of a long perspective from the château to a pair of wrought iron gates on the skyline. The first terrace has an elaborate design of clipped box; the others are simpler with central pools or cones of clipped evergreen. The stonework is beautiful with rows of stone urns decorated with fruit, two-headed lions, pavilions, pilasters and statues encrusted with lichen. All is well kept. Major structural work will take place in the garden in the next two years.

CHÂTEAU DE CANON   8
14270 Mezidon. Tel: 31.20.05.07/31.20.02.72

M and Mme de Mézerac ★ 20km E of Caen, via the RN13 and 6km S on the D152 ★ Open Easter to 30th June, Sat, Sun and holidays, 2 - 6pm; July to Sept, daily, 2 - 7pm. Also at other times by prior arrangement ★ Entrance: 25F

Unchanged since its creation in the mid-eighteenth century, the garden is particularly interesting for its combination of French and English picturesque styles and for its Anglo-Chinese garden. This mixture of styles plus the devotion and care of the owners make it a delight. The back façade of the château is reflected in a large rectangular pool. At the far end a semi-circle of busts in Carrara marble gaze across the water towards the house. In the picturesque wooded grounds there are some striking follies, a Chinese pavilion in brilliant red lacquer, a white marble temple, a pigeon loft with a classical facade and a ruined château. The prettiest area is a series of linked walled enclosures, designed originally to provide micro-climates where fruit could be grown but now exuberantly planted with flowers and at its best in July and August.

CHÂTEAU DE COMPIÈGNE   9
62000 Compiègne. Tel: 44.40.03.38

70km NE of Paris by A1 exit 9. On the edge of the town ★ Open April to Oct, daily, 7am - sunset; Nov to March, 8am - sunset ★ Entrance: free

The Petit Parc at Compiègne has been undergoing important restoration in recent years. The garden was started during the reign of Louis XV but the magnificent vista which stretches to the horizon was ordered by Napoleon I. The prospect from the balustraded terrace is particularly imposing. Below the terrace is a 1400-metre-long trellised covered walk or *berceau* planted with climbers. This was also built for Napoleon who wanted his new empress, Marie Louise, to be able to walk from the palace to the woods under its light shade.

CHÂTEAU DE CORBEIL-CERF   10
60110 Corbeil-Cerf. Tel: 44.52.02.43

Mme de Lubersac ★ 20km S of Beauvais ★ Open on written request for parties from Easter to All Saints Day ★ Entrance: 20F (château and garden 40F)

Surrounding the small château of Corbeil-Cerf are a series of rides cut through the forest. In the front, garlands of ivy link lime trees together. To the north is a fine vista defined by clipped hedges and green arches containing statues and urns. Four other gardens were designed by René Pechère in 1960: a rose garden, a knot garden, an 'English garden' and a green garden where box bushes form four tables and a bay. (Not yet inspected)

CHÂTEAU DE GERBEVILER 11
54830 Gerbeviller. Tel: 83.42.70.15/83.42.71.57

Princesse d'Arenberg ★ 10km S of Luneville, 38km from Nancy ★ Open 15th May to 15th Oct, Sat and Sun, 2 - 5pm and on other days for parties by appointment ★ Entrance: 15F, children free, parties 12F per person

The original château at Gerbeviller was burnt down in World War I and the present single-storied building was erected in 1920. To one side there is a kitchen garden and behind, a long meadow slopes towards a pretty seventeenth-century pavilion of rosy pink brick. On one side of the meadow, shaded by the surrounding trees, is an elaborate grotto, lined with shells, tufa and red and white stone chippings. This is in need of restoration but is still worth seeing.

CHÂTEAU DE MAINTENON 12
28130 Maintenon. Tel: 37.23.00.09

Fondation du Château de Maintenon ★ 18km N of Chartres, 25km W of Rambouillet ★ Open April to Oct, daily, 2 - 6pm; Nov to March, Sat and Sun, 2 - 5pm ★ Entrance: 30F, children 22F, under 6 free, groups 24F per person, pre-booked guided tours (in French) 38F per person, students 17F per person

In front of the château is a small classical parterre of grass, crushed brick, and box hedges designed by Le Nôtre for Madame de Maintenon. The château and garden are surrounded by the rivers Eure and Voise and there is a view to the uncompleted aqueduct which was planned to carry the waters of the Eure all the way to Versailles for Louis XIV's fountains. Racine also worked here on two of his plays.

CHÂTEAU DE MIROMESNIL 13
76550 Offranville.

Mme de Vogué ★ 8km S of Dieppe ★ Open May to 15th Oct, daily except Tues, 2 - 6pm ★ Entrance: moderate charge

Guy de Maupassant was born in this seventeenth-century château set in magnificent beech woods. The *potager* (kitchen garden) is still maintained in the traditional way with perfect rows of vegetables surrounded by mixed borders of roses, delphiniums, peonies and campanulas. Broad grass paths divide the beds and the soft pink brick walls support clematis and gnarled fruit trees.

CHÂTEAU DE NACQUEVILLE 14
50460 Urville-Nacqueville, Nr Cherbourg, Manche. Tel: 33.03.27.89/33.03.56.03

M and Mme Azan ★ 6km W of Cherbourg ★ Open Easter to Sept, daily except Tues and Fri unless holidays. Guided visits hourly from 2 - 5pm

It is difficult to believe that this English-style park created in 1830 and the château were damaged in the last war. All is now restored and the peaceful green valley is sheltered by wooded escarpments. A small stream thickly bordered with arum lilies falls into a long lake surrounded by rhododendrons, azaleas and gunneras. There is a walk from the gatehouse where cars are parked to the château and the guided tour (55 minutes) could allow more time to enjoy the garden fully.

CHÂTEAU DE SASSY   15
St Christophe de Jajolet, 61570 Mortrée. Tel: 33.35.32.66

M and Mme d'Andriffet-Pasquier ★ 9km S of Argentan on road to Sées via R158 ★ Open all year ★ Entrance: 25F, parties 15F per person

A garden for lovers of French formal style. The château of soft pink brick looks over descending terraces to a parterre with symmetrical scrolls and flourishes of clipped box against a surface of crushed brick. A small pavilion of brick and stone, equally perfect in its symmetry, abruptly terminates the central perspective. Clipped hedges, moats and trained lime trees separate the garden from the surrounding woods and fields. The whole effect is very satisfying. Unfortunately the steps leading down to the formal garden are unsafe and it can only be viewed from above. As with many formal gardens, however, this is not a particular deprivation.

CHÂTEAU DE VAUVILLE   16
50440 Beaumont-Hague, E Cherbourg. Tel: 33.52.71.41

M and Mme Pellerin ★ 17km E of Cherbourg ★ Open Easter to Oct, Sun and Tues only, 2 - 6pm, Sat in June and July. Guided tours (¾ hour). Special visits by prior arrangement ★ Entrance: 30F, children 15F

The layout of this four-hectare garden is very informal with broad grass paths and grassy pockets around which are planted exotic and succulent plants more often seen around the Mediterranean than the English Channel. Agaves, aloes and clumps of echiums are planted throughout and they remain outside all year. The garden was started in 1947 and suffered from cold and wind in the mid-80s. Recent warmer years have encouraged a flourishing rebirth. Yuccas, agapanthus and tritonias are all burgeoning, accompanied by bamboos, brooms and Corsican cistus.

CHÂTEAU DE VENDEUVRE   17
14170 Saint-Pierre-sur-Dives.

M and Mme de Vendeuvre ★ 27km SE of Caen on N13 and the D40, 4km SW of St Pierre ★ Light refreshments in the Salon de Thé ★ Toilet facilities ★ Museum of Miniature Furniture ★ Garden open 15th March to May and 15th Sept to Oct, weekends and holidays, and June to 15th Sept, daily, 2 - 7pm. By appointment for groups

There is an impressive view of the château from the road through splendid wrought-iron gates. Above the approach there are some interesting plantings of trees and shrubs and this is carried on at the back of the château. The classical lake reflects the building and the resident swans. New hedges and trees will eventually add interest to this aspect of the garden. In direct contrast to this tranquil area is a new water garden inspired by Chatsworth. This is in the early stages of construction but already it provides fun and excitement. A natural stream links the musical Japanese bridge (which should trigger water jets when people tread on it), the tree fountain, the classical pavilion and other constructions, including an extremely beautiful stone pyramid. The planting is limited as yet but sympathetically chosen and placed.

CHÂTEAU DE VERT BOIS   18
59910 Bondues, Nr Lille. Tel 20.46.23.16

M. Albert Prouvost ★ Leave Lille on N17 to Ostend. After village take right fork on to N352. Signs to château. ★ Open: Suns and Hols except between 7th July and 20th Aug, 2.30 - 6pm ★ Guided tours including entry price

The eighteenth-century château is surrounded by a circular moat planted with several magnificent weeping willows. On the far side of the château is a paved formal garden. In front are two tiny buildings, one a pavilion, the other a chapel. A small bridge over the moat leads to a double herbaceous border enclosed by yew hedges and originally designed by Russell Page. The atmosphere is one of great tranquillity.

CLERES   19
76690 Cleres. Tel: 35.33.23.08

Musée National d'Histoire Naturelle ★ 41km S of Dieppe and 22km N of Rouen ★ Open March – Nov daily, 9am – 6pm, but closed 12noon – 1.30pm in spring and autumn. ★ Entrance: 25F, children 15F (groups of 25-plus at reduced rate)

The walls of the château are thickly covered with climbers, roses, *Akebia lobata* and wisteria as well as *Actinidia chinensis*, the Chinese gooseberry or Kiwi fruit and the other well-known actinidia, *A. kolomikta* with leaves of white, pink and green. In front are beds filled with a multitude of low-growing colourful plants such as aubrieta and alyssum. Cleres is owned by the French Natural History Museum and peacocks, cranes, waterfowl, antelope and wallabies are free to wander round the garden. A wild flower meadow slopes down to a lake and streams planted with bot sedges and *Gunnera manicata*. A hilly grassed area with a group of handsome copper beeches leads to animal enclosures where antelopes and emus are kept. Aviaries. This is a good place to visit for a family with young children.

ERMENONVILLE/
PARC JEAN JACQUES ROUSSEAU   20
60950 Ermenonville

45km N of Paris, via A1, exit Saint-Witz, then D922. Entrance to the garden is in the village (not through the camping site) ★ Open daily except Tues, 2 - 6.30pm ★ Entrance: 12F, groups of 20 or more 6F per person

The Parc Jean Jacques Rousseau is in the same tradition as the gardens of Stowe or Painshill: a natural landscape of grass, trees and water embellished with statues or small follies that are intended to create a particular mood. This garden, now far smaller than its original 900h, regettably impinged upon by a campsite and severed from its château by a now busy road, was designed by the Marquis de Girardin in the years following 1766. The Marquis was the last patron of Jean Jacques Rousseau and much influenced by his ideas of the superiority of nature and natural man. From the lake you can descend into the grotto of the Naiads under a small cascade or sit on the 'Banc de la Reine' named after Marie

Antoinette who was reputed to have cut off some of her hair in homage to
Rousseau at this spot. After gazing at the Ile de Peupliers and the tomb of
Rousseau (the great man himself was later reburied in Paris) you can
wander across the Arcadian meadow and afterwards ascend to look at the
prehistoric dolmen and visit the Temple of Philosophy. Roofless and with
fallen columns, this is unfinished because Philosophy itself is always
incomplete. Full notes of the various features are available in English.

HAROUE 21
54740 Haroue. Tel: 83.52.40.14; Fax: 83.52.44.19

*Princesse Minnie de Beauvau-Craon ★ 30km S of Nancy. Take the motorway
towards Epinal and exit Haroue ★ Open April to 11th Nov, daily, 2 - 6pm and
every morning by appointment for parties of 20 or more. Parties can telephone the
owner in London on (0171) 373 6498 or fax (0171) 373 5954 ★ Entrance: 35F*

The formal garden at the back of the château was designed in traditional
French style by Emilio Terry in 1957. Eighteenth-century statues in white
marble alternate with clipped shrubs to form a striking central area confined
by a narrow canal and contrasting with the fields beyond. There is a wooded
area, with eight paths radiating between the trees from a central pool, which
was designed in 1942 and behind the stable block is a flower garden designed
originally by Russell Page in 1952, replanted in 1987 by Cindie Simon. This
has been replanted recently in the scheme of pink, white and grey. Beds of
rose 'Margaret Merrill' together with flowering shrubs and herbaceous plants
are surrounded by clipped box and trained hornbeam. A circular dovecot in
softly-coloured brick makes an attractive background.

JARDIN BOTANIQUE DU MONTET 22
**100 rue du Jardin Botanique, 54600 Villers-les Nancy.
Tel: 83.41.47.47; Fax: 83.27.86.59**

*Jardin Botanique du Montet ★ SW of the city centre ★ Open April to Sept,
daily, 2.00 - 5.00pm (Sun and Bank Holidays 6pm); Oct to March, Wed to
Sun and Bank Holidays, 2 - 5pm. Closed 25th Dec, 1st Jan ★ Entrance: 15F,
children (7-16) 8F, under 7 free*

The Jardin Botanique du Montet is the largest and newest botanic garden
in France and it is still being developed. The garden covers 24 hectares
and there are five principal collections. An historical collection displays
plants grown in groups according to their date of introduction. The
ornamental collection is founded on plants bred by local horticulturalists
such as F.F. Crousse and Victor Lemoine. There is a collection of alpine
plants arranged in geographical areas. The systematic collection is where
the plants are arranged in their orders, from the most primitive forms at
the top of the site to the most highly-developed plants at the bottom. The
final intriguing group is the homoeopathic collection. There are 10
greenhouses, five open to the public, including a tropical pool house and
one containing useful plants, like coffee and bananas.

JARDIN D'AMBLEVILLE 23
95710 Bray-et-Lû. Tel: 34.67.71.34

Madame Stephanie de Laubadère ★ 12km from Giverny and Vernon ★ Open 15th April to 15th Oct, Sat and Sun, and 1st May, 1st July, 1st Aug, 10.30 - 6.30pm. Groups by appointment

The Italian gardens were created by the present owner's grandmother between the two world wars and one of the terraces is inspired by the garden of the Villa Gamberaia at Fiesole. An arcaded yew hedge curves around a semi-circular pool and paths are marked by citrus trees in Italian pots. A second terrace is studded with topiary, an essay in Renaissance symbolism realised in stone, water and evergreens and contrasting with the surrounding rural landscape.

JARDIN DE LA BALLUE   24
35720 Bazouges-la-Pérouse. Tel 45.48.78.90

41km N of Rennes, SW of Pontorson ★ Parking ★ Open: March to 15th April and 5th Aug to 15th Sept, daily, 10am - 12noon and 2.30 - 6pm and by appointment for groups. The garden has a new owner so check by phone before visiting

A series of theatrical gardens in the baroque or mannerist style of the sixteenth and seventeenth centuries. An orchard in containers (*verger*), another garden with weeping trees, another with giants, another with exotica, and a *jardin à la française* with many diagonals. Altogether 12 'surprises' for the visitor.

JARDIN DE PLANBESSIN   25
14490 Castillon, Basse Normandie. Tel: 31.92.56.03

M and Mme Sainte-Beuve ★ SW from Bayeux towards St Lô, turn through Castillon to Planbessin ★ Parking ★ Plants for sale ★ Open Mon - Fri, 2 - 5pm and Sat by appointment ★ Entrance: 20F

The garden provides a delightful setting for the plants available in the nursery. The owners regularly visit English gardens whose influence is reflected in the layout of the separate 'rooms'. Plantbessin has only been in existence for seven years but good use has been made of existing trees and the whole site already has a timeless and settled feel to it. The water garden is cool and fresh, thanks to good use of light green foliage and white flowers, the herbaceous borders very colourful, moving through pinks and blues to yellows and oranges, the whole held together by more clever use of foliage. Also Japanese and herb gardens. In all a plantsman's delight, with a system of numbers attached which can be looked up in the nursery catalogue for plant identification and cultural information.

JARDIN DES PEPINIÈRES FRÉDÉRIC COTELLE   26
76370 Derchigny. Tel: 35.83.61.38

M and Mme F. Cotelle ★ 2km E of Dieppe on D925 ★ Open every day except Suns and Bank Holidays, 10am - 12noon and 2 - 6pm. Closed Christmas - New Year ★ Entrance: 25F

A garden created by a nurseryman and his painter wife round their nursery of unusual plants. The nursery specialises in herbaceous plants, heathers, shrubs and old roses and these are used in a fresh and subtle way in the borders of the garden. Plants are grouped with attention paid to their foliage, colour and texture beside long grass walks. Look out for area devoted to ground-cover plants that enjoy full sun and another to plants that need moisture.

JARDIN DES PLANTES CAEN 27
Rue Desmoneux, 14000 Caen.

NW of Caen city centre ★ Open daily, 8 - 8pm or sunset. Glasshouses 14.00 - 17.00. Guided tours some Sat afternoons ★ Entrance: free

This pleasant public garden with a clearly-labelled botanic section was founded in 1736 and the park area added in 1805 so it has a well-established appearance and numbers of fine mature trees. Austrian black pines, sugar maples and the ironwood *Ostrya virginiana* are underplanted with uncommon shrubs like *Diervilla sessilifolia* and *Aronia prunifolia*. The plant order beds in the botanic garden include wild flowers of Normandy, collections of tulips and utilitarian and medicinal plants. A rock garden and a circular pond planted with water and marginal plants add to the enjoyment. *Vallée des jardins*, another garden owned by the municipality, is opposite.

JARDIN DES PLANTES DE ROUEN 28
114 ter avenue des Martyrs de la Résistance, 76100 Rouen. Tel: 35.72.36.36

SW of city centre ★ Open daily: winter 8am - 5.30pm; summer 8am - 8pm. Guided visits daily except weekends and 17th April, 1st, 8th May, 5th June, 14th July, 15th Aug, 1st Nov, 25th Dec ★ Entrance: free

A public park with interesting plants, including a specimen of the unusual twisted beech, the Faux de Verzy. The Jardin des Plantes opened here in the 1830s and the attractive greenhouses contain collections of succulent and useful plants. There are also tropical and temperate glasshouses with collections of orchids and bromeliads and the water lily, *Victoria amazonica*. Order beds have collections of wild flowers native to Normandy, sedums and sempervivums and water plants. There is also a large rock bank. All very well maintained.

JARDIN DES SCULPTURES DE DUNKERQUE 29
59386 Dunkerque.

The gardens surround the Musée d'Art Contemporain, off Avenue des Bains ★ Open daily, 10am - 7pm

Created in 1979 on an unpropitious site whipped by winds from the North Sea, the garden includes eighteenth-century sculptures. Curved paths of interlocking bricks wind round outcrops of rock creating enclaves for statues or seats. Rusting iron is used as a fencing material and bold plantings of salt-resistant plants like elaeagnus, sea buckthorn and marram grass create a striking and unusual landscape.

JARDIN DE VALLOIRES 30
80120 Argoules. Tel: 22.23.53.55

North of Abbeville on N1 or halfway to Montreux on D175 ★ Refreshments ★
Plants for sale ★ Shop ★ Open Easter to Oct, daily, 10am - 7pm (8pm in June to
Aug); Oct to Easter by prior arrangement ★ Entrance: 31F

Wide lawns, flowers in subdued colours, a rosery and a cloister re-created
with yew columns and parterre, all backed by the splendid Abbaye
buildings, evoke the peace and calm formerly enjoyed by the Cistercian
monks. Begun only in 1989, but incorporating some mature plants, the
garden's aim is to display extensive collections of trees and shrubs and to
preserve continuity of plants. The lawns are bordered on one side by blue
flowers, edging a marsh and bog garden, and on the other by a steep bank
of white flowers backed by yellow, leading up to island beds with many
different themes: golden foliage; autumnal tints; decorative fruits; nectar-
rich plants; plants with unusual growth or foliage.

PARC ET JARDINS DU CHÂTEAU D'HARCOURT   31
14220 Thury-Harcourt. Tel: 31.79.65.41

Duc and Duchesse d'Harcourt ★ 26km S of Caen ★ Open April and Oct, Sun
and public holidays, 2.30 - 6.30pm; May to Sept, daily, 2.30 - 6.30pm and by
appointment in writing for parties of 15 or more ★ Entrance: 20F (23F July to
Oct), children 7F, under 12 free, parties 15F per person

The dramatic ruins of the Château de Thury-Harcourt, destroyed during the
last war, announce the entrance to the park and gardens. The path leads to a
meadow hedged with spring-flowering trees and shrubs. A walk along the
poplar-lined river bank is reached through a tunnel of hornbeam. A spring
and a summer garden dazzle the visitor by their variety, brilliance and the
profusion of the flowerbeds and the perfection of their layout. The gardens
are at their best in high summer, and extend in total to 70 hectares.

PARC FLORAL DES MOUTIERS   32
76119 Varengeville-sur-Mer.

Mallet family ★ 5km W of Dieppe ★ Open mid–March to mid–Nov, 10 - 12noon,
2 - 6pm. Guided tours by written appointment. Once inside visitors can stay
longer than opening time ★ Entrance: 30F/40F depending on season, children (6-
12) 10F, groups 25F/30F per person (1994 prices)

The influence of Gertrude Jekyll can be seen in this garden designed by
Edwin Lutyens at the beginning of the century. Near the house are formal
features: a long, rose-covered brick pergola leading to a Chinese pavilion,
typical Lutyens stone and tile seats, flower borders, a white garden and,
made in recent years, a rose garden with climbing roses trained in the
French way. The mixed borders are punctuated with rugosa roses, tree
peonies and buddleias. In the rectangular box-edged beds of the white
garden, 'White Triumphator' tulips are followed by thickly-underplanted
'Iceberg' roses. There is a magnolia collection, many in the magnolia
orchard, others in the woodland garden. This is the largest part of the Parc
Floral. Rhododendrons, azaleas and viburnums grow beneath fine specimens
of ilex, pine, oak and blue cedar. The ground is a carpet of wild flowers.
This is a garden to please any visitors whatever their special interest.

LE VASTERIVAL   33
76119 Varengeville-sur-mer. Tel: 35.85.12.05

Princess Sturdza ★ 1km W of Varengeville-sur-mer on the D75 ★ Open all year round by appointment only for parties of 15-50 people. Visit lasts 2 - 2½ hours ★ Entrance: parties of 15-29 110F per person, parties of 30 or more 120F per person

A garden created since 1957 by an outstanding plantswoman. It can only be seen by joining a group that the Princess Sturdza or one of her assistants takes in charge. The garden, informal in layout and immaculately cultivated, contains 11,000 species. Each plant is placed in the best possible position for its own growth and next to other plants that, by contrast of form, texture and colour, enhance its appearance. Exciting rarities like *Ginkgo biloba* 'Horizontalis' and *Pterostyrax corymbosa* grow alongside more usual but beautifully combined plants. *Cornus controversa* 'Variegata' is contrasted with an underplanting of ferns. *Clematis* 'Niobe' grows through a willow-leaved pear. The planting is in four tiers: trees, shrubs, ground cover including herbaceous, and bulbs. This ensures interest at all seasons of the year, particularly winter with many hellebores, heaths and daphnes.

BELGIUM

BRUSSELS
Brussels itself has a number of gardens open at all times, including Abbey de la Cambre, Bois de la Cambre, the Jean Massart Experimental Garden and the park in the City Centre. Ten kilometres north of Brussels is the National Botanic Garden, open daily 9am to sunset. Once a year, usually in April/May, the King of Belgium opens the conservatories in the Royal Palace at Laeken on the Northern outskirts of the city. For this brief period they are open daily, except Mondays and Fridays, but there are some evening openings from 9 - 11pm. Described as three acres of spectacular nineteenth-century ornamental architecture, they are well worth a visit as they house the world's oldest and most important collection of camellias.

Those motoring in the Dunkirk - Lille area (or willing to make a detour from Calais-St Omer) should consider a visit to Château de Beloeil, just across the border. If driving from Ostend to Brussels (or prepared to make a detour from Dunkirk) there are three gardens which might be visited en route although in each case prior appointment must be made. In addition there is the *Kasteel van Loppem*, a few kilometres from Ostend, just South of Bruges, open daily sunrise to sunset, where the main feature is a large maze. These gardens are listed 2, 3,and 4 below.

CHÂTEAU DE BELOEIL   1
Owner: Prince de Ligne ★ About two-thirds of the way between Tournai and Mons just N of the E42 motorway ★ Open daily, April to Oct, 10 - 6pm ★ Entrance: 180BF (château and park 280BF)

Exceptional gardens with a great lake of six hectares with gardens on each side consisting of separate 'rooms' each with individual themes.

Spectacular high hedges, some as high as seven metres, long lines of pleached limes and other features, such as a foliage 'building'.

15 GRAAF VAN HOORNESTRAAT 2
B-9850 Nevele.

Owner: Dr A. De Clercq ★ 3km from motorway E40, exit 12 ★ Open by appointment only

A one and a half-hectare (4 acre) plantsman's garden, specialising in rhododendrons and azaleas, with their best season in early May.

KASTEEL VAN LEEUWERGEM 3
B-9620 Zottegem. Tel: 32.9.360 0873; Fax: 32.9.361 0138

Owner: Baron Baudouin delle Faille d'Huysse ★ 2km NE of Zottegem, 18km W of Aalst via E40 ★ Open for groups by appointment ★ Entrance: 120BF per person (château and gardens)

Famous for its eighteenth-century *théâtre de verdure*, an outdoor building in vegetation rare in Europe (see also Château de Beloeil). The house has a splendid simplicity which is mirrored in the classicism of the garden design.

PARK VAN BEERVELDE 4
Beervelde-Dorp 75, B-9080 Lochristi. Tel: 32.9.355 5540

Comte Renaud de Kerchove de Denterghem ★ 20km E of Ghent via E17 ★ Open for flower shows 12th to 14th May and 6th to 8th Oct and also open for parties by arrangement ★ Entrance: 200BF for flower shows, parties 100BF per person

An eight-hectare park in the English landscape style, mainly famous for its azaleas in May.

NETHERLANDS

Easy for anyone going from Harwich to the Hook or flying to Rotterdam.

LEIDEN BOTANIC GARDEN 1
Rapenburg 3, PO Box 9516, 2300 RA Leiden.
Tel: 31.71.277.249/31.71.275.144

Open daily, April to Sept, Mon - Sat, 9am - 5pm, Sun 10am - 5pm; Oct to March closed Sat ★ Entrance: f3.50, OAP and children f1.50, parties of 15 or more f2.50

In 1594 Clusius (Charles de l'Ecluse) became director of the Leiden Botanic Garden, and his garden there has been reconstructed in the same area as the original, based on a 1594 manuscript. About one-third of the plants in his sixty beds were medicinal - the rest were of botanical interest (his garden not open at weekends). The general garden includes the Von Siebold Memorial Garden, rosarium and tropical greenhouses.

Specialist Gardens

ARBORETA

Many of the gardens in the *Guide* are extensively treed, and this list concentrates on mature arboreta, in which the trees are labelled.

Avon *Vine House*
Bedfordshire *Luton Hoo, The Swiss Garden*
Cheshire *Cholmondeley Castle Gardens, Jodrell Bank Arboretum, Tatton Park*
Cornwall *Pencarrow*
Cumbria and the Isle of Man *Holker Hall, Muncaster Castle*
Derbyshire *Chatsworth House, Derby Arboretum*
Devon *Bicton College of Agriculture, Bicton Park*
Dorset *Deans Court, Forde Abbey, Melbury House, Minterne*
Durham *Bowes Museum Garden*
Essex *Cracknells, Saling Hall*
Gloucestershire *Batsford Arboretum, Westonbirt Arboretum*
Hampshire and the Isle of Wight *Macpennys Nursery and Woodland Gardens, Nunwell House, The Sir Harold Hillier Gardens and Arboretum*
Hereford and Worcester *Eastnor Castle, Hergest Croft Garden*
Hertfordshire *The Beale Arboretum*
Kent *Bedgebury National Pinetum, Belmont, Emmetts Garden, Ladham House, Riverhill House Gardens*
Lincolnshire *Grimsthorpe Castle, Riseholme Hall*
London (Greater) *Cannizaro Park, Isabella Plantation, Royal Botanic Gardens, Kew*
Manchester (Greater) *Haigh Hall Gardens*
Merseyside *Ness Gardens*
Midlands, West *University of Birmingham Botanic Garden*
Norfolk *Holkham Hall*

Oxfordshire *University Arboretum*
Shropshire *Hodnet Hall*
Suffolk *The Rookery*
Surrey *Coverwood Lakes and Garden, Royal Horticultural Society's Garden, Winkworth Arboretum*
Sussex, East *Sheffield Park Garden*
Sussex, West *High Beeches Gardens, Leonardslee Gardens, Nymans, Wakehurst Place, West Dean Gardens*
Warwickshire *Arbury Hall*
Wiltshire *Bowood, Broadleas Garden, Corsham Court*
Yorkshire, North *Castle Howard, Thorp Perrow Arboretum*
Yorkshire, South & West *Wentworth Castle Gardens, Temple Newsam*
Ireland *Brook Hall, Castlewellan National Arboretum, Fota Arboretum, John F. Kennedy Arboretum*
Scotland *Castle Kennedy and Lochinch Gardens, Cruickshank Botanic Garden, Leckmelm Shrubbery and Arboretum, Monteviot*
Wales *Dyffryn Botanic Garden*

HERB GARDENS

Many gardeners now grow herbs for the kitchen, and this listing is mainly devoted to those who make an ornamental feature of the necessity.

Avon *Goldney Hall*
Bedfordshire *Toddington Manor*
Cambridgeshire *Emmanuel College*
Cheshire *Cheshire Herbs, Little Moreton Hall, Norton Priory Museum and Gardens*
Cornwall *Mary Newman's Cottage*
Cumbria and the Isle of Man *Acorn Bank Garden, Levens Hall*
Derbyshire *Hardwick Hall, The Herb Garden*
Dorset *Cranborne Manor Gardens,*

Edmondsham House, Sandford Orcas
Manor
Essex *Fanners Green, Tye Farm*
Gloucestershire *Alderley Grange,
Barnsley House, Painswick Rococo
Garden, Sudeley Castle*
Hampshire and the Isle of Wight
*Gilbert White's House and Garden,
Hollington Herb Garden*
Hereford and Worcester *Staunton
Park*
Hertfordshire *Hatfield House,
Knebworth House*
Kent *Iden Croft Herbs, Leeds Castle,
Long Barn, Marle Place, Scotney
Castle, Sissinghurst Garden,
Stoneacre*
Lancashire *Leighton Hall, Sellet Hall
Gardens*
Lincolnshire *Doddington Hall, Gunby
Hall*
London (Greater) *Chelsea Physic
Garden, Hall Place, Museum of
Garden History, 7 St Georges Road*
Norfolk *Besthorpe Hall, Congham
Hall Hotel, Norfolk Lavender Ltd*
Northamptonshire *Hill Farm Herbs,
Holdenby House Gardens, Sulgrave
Manor*
Northumberland *Herterton House,
Hexham Herbs*
Nottinghamshire *Rufford Country
Park*
Oxfordshire *Blenheim Palace*
Somerset *Combe Sydenham Country
Park, Gaulden Manor, R.T. Herbs
and Garden*
Suffolk *Helmingham Hall*
Surrey *Royal Horticultural Society's
Garden*
Sussex, East *Bateman's, Clinton
Lodge, Crown House, Michelham
Priory, Offham House*
Sussex, West *Mill House, Parham
House and Gardens*
Tyne and Wear *Bede's World Herb
Garden*
Wiltshire *Broadleas Garden*
Yorkshire, North *Harlow Carr
Botanical Gardens*
Scotland *Earlshall Castle, Falkland

Palace Garden, Kailzie Garden,
Malleny House Gardens, Monteviot*
Wales *Bodysgallen Hall, Pant-yr-
Holiad, Penlan-Uchaf Farm
Gardens*
Channel Islands *Sausmarez Manor
Exotic Woodland Garden, Guernsey*

HERBACEOUS BORDERS

Buckinghamshire *Cliveden*
Cambridgeshire *Anglesey Abbey*
Cheshire *Tatton Park*
Cornwall *Lanhydrock*
Cumbria *Sizergh Castle*
Devon *Arlington Court, Castle Drogo,
Coleton Fishacre Garden, Killerton,
Knightshayes*
Gloucestershire *Hidcote Manor
Garden*
Kent *Sissinghurst Garden*
Lincolnshire *Gunby Hall*
Manchester (Greater) *Dunham
Massey*
Norfolk *Blickling Hall, Felbrigg Hall,
Oxburgh Hall*
Northumberland *Wallington*
Somerset *Barrington Court Garden,
Lytes Cary Manor, Montacute
House, Tintinhull House Garden*
Staffordshire *Shugborough*
Suffolk *Melford Hall*
Sussex, West *Nymans*
Warwickshire *Packwood House*
Wiltshire *The Courts*
Yorkshire, North *Beningbrough
Hall*
Wales *Bodnant Garden, Powis Castle*

JAPANESE AND CHINESE
GARDENS

Cheshire *Tatton Park*
Dorset *Compton Acres*
Kent *Mount Ephraim*
London (Greater) *Capel Manor,
Holland Park*
Nottinghamshire *Newstead Abbey*
Surrey *Coombe Wood*

SPECIALIST GARDENS

Wiltshire *Heale Gardens, Wilton House*
Yorkshire, West *Harewood House*
Ireland *Japanese Garden*
Scotland *Arbigland, Manderston, Torosay Castle and Gardens*

ORGANIC GARDENS

Bedfordshire *The Lodge*
Devon *Fardel Manor*
Dorset *Dean's Court, Edmondsham House*
Gloucestershire *Snowshill Manor*
Humberside *The Cottages*
Lancashire *Pendle Heritage Centre*
Somerset *Greencombe*
Warwickshire *Ryton Organic Gardens*
Ireland *Kinoith/Ballymaloe Cookery School*
Scotland *The Bank House, Carnell, Kellie Castle*
Wales *Centre for Alternative Technology*

ROCK GARDENS

Bedfordshire *Luton Hoo*
Cheshire *Arley Hall and Gardens, Cholmondeley Castle Gardens, Tatton Park*
Cornwall *Pencarrow*
Derbyshire *Chatsworth*
Dorset *Forde Abbey*
Hampshire *Exbury Gardens*
Hereford and Worcester *Spetchley Park*
Kent *Mount Ephraim*
Leicestershire *Whatton House*
Norfolk *Sandringham House*
Northamptonshire *Lamport Hall Garden*
Northumberland *Bide-a-Wee Cottage, Chillingham Castle*
Warwickshire *Warwick Castle*
Yorkshire, North *Newby Hall and Gardens*
Scotland *Manderston, Torosay Castle and Gardens*

ROSE GARDENS

Most of the entries are for rose gardens, though some may be included because they have a number of unusual varieties although not a rose garden as such. It is hoped that owners of listed gardens have labelled their rose varieties. Many beautiful roses will of course be found in other gardens not listed.

Bedfordshire *Luton Hoo*
Berkshire *Folly Farm*
Buckinghamshire *Chicheley Hall, Cliveden, The Manor House Bledlow*
Cambridgeshire *Duxford Mill, Elton Hall, St John's College Cambridge*
Cheshire *Bridgemere Garden World, Cholmondeley Castle Gardens, Tatton Park, Tirley Garth*
Cumbria and the Isle of Man *Dalemain, Graythwaite Hall, Holker Hall*
Derbyshire *Haddon Hall, Kedleston Hall, 210 Nottingham Road*
Devon *Doctyn Mill, Rosemoor Garden*
Dorset *Cranborne Manor*
Durham *Raby Castle Gardens, University of Durham Botanic Garden, Westholme Hall*
Essex *Panfield Hall, Saling Hall, RHS Garden Hyde Hall*
Gloucestershire *Abbotswood, Barnsley House, Hunts Court, Kiftsgate Court, Misarden Park Gardens, Painswick Rococo Garden, Stancombe Park, Sudeley Castle*
Hampshire and the Isle of Wight *Broadhatch House, Exbury Gardens, Fairfield House, Gilbert White's House and Garden, Jenkyn Place, Mottisfont Abbey, Northcourt, Stratfield Saye, Ventnor Botanic Garden*
Hereford and Worcester *Eastnor Castle, Hergest Croft, How Caple Court, Spetchley Park*
Hertfordshire *Benington Lordship, Gardens of the Rose, R. Harkness & Co, Hatfield House*

Kent *Chartwell, Emmetts Garden, Godinton Park, Goodnestone Park, Hever Castle, Leeds Castle, Mount Ephraim, Penshurst Place, Scotney Castle, Sissinghurst Garden, Smith's Hall, Squerryes Court, Walnut Tree Farm Gardens*

Leicestershire *Arthingworth Manor, Ashwell House, Belvoir Castle*

Lincolnshire *Ayscoughfee Hall and Gardens, Burghley House, Doddington Hall, Grimsthorpe Castle, Hall Farm and Nursery, Manor House*

London (Greater) *Avery Hill Park, Cannizaro Park, Capel Manor, Fenton House, Gunnersbury Park, Hall Place, Hampton Court Palace, Priory Gardens, Queen Mary's Rose Garden, Royal Botanic Gardens, Syon Park*

Manchester (Greater) *Heaton Hall*

Merseyside *Ness Gardens, Speke Hall*

Midlands, West *Birmingham Botanical Gardens, University of Birmingham Botanic Garden*

Norfolk *Norfolk Lavender Ltd, Mannington Hall*

Northamptonshire *Boughton House, Holdenby House, Kelmarsh Hall, Rockingham Castle, Sulgrave Manor*

Northumberland *Belsay Hall, Chillingham Castle, Hexham Herbs*

Nottinghamshire *Holme Pierrepont Hall*

Oxfordshire *Blenheim Palace, Greys Court, Oxford Botanic Garden, Rousham, Stonor Park, Wroxton Abbey*

Shropshire *Benthall Hall, David Austin Roses, Hodnet Hall, The Paddocks, Weston Park*

Somerset *The Bishops Palace, Bittescombe Mano, Combe Sydenham Country Park, Gaulden Manor, Wootton House*

Staffordshire *Eccleshall Castle Gardens, Shugborough, Trentham Gardens, Wolseley Garden Park*

Suffolk *Euston Hall, Helmingham Hall, Somerleyton Hall*

Surrey *Albury Park Mansion, Bradstone Brook, Loseley Park, Polesden Lacey, Royal Horticultural Society's Garden, The Walled Garden*

Sussex, East *Crown House, Great Dixter, Duckyls*

Sussex, West *Apuldram Roses, Hammerwood House Garden, Nymans, Parham House, Stansted Park*

Warwickshire *Arbury Hall, Farnborough Hall, Ilmington Manor, Ragley Hall, Ryton Organic Gardens, Warwick Castle*

Wiltshire *Avebury Manor, Bowood, Broadleas, Corsham Court, Heale Garden, Iford Manor, Lackham Country Attractions, Longleat, Pound Hill House, Wilton House*

Yorkshire, North *Castle Howard, Newby Hall and Gardens, Norton Conyers*

Yorkshire, South & West *Bramham Park, Harewood House, Lotherton Hall, Nostell Priory, Temple Newsam*

Ireland *Sir Thomas and Lady Dixon Park*

Scotland *Arbigland, Blairquhan, Cawdor Castle, Drum Castle, Dunrobin Gardens, Earlshall Castle, Hill of Tarvit, The Hirsel, Malleny Gardens, Manderston, Mellerstain, Monteviot, Tyninghame House*

Wales *Bodysgallen Hall, The Dingle Haverfordwest, Vaynor Park*

SPECIALIST GARDENS

WATER AND BOG GARDENS

Most of these entries are for water gardens or features; bog gardens are also included.

Avon *Goldney Hall*
Berkshire *Scotlands*
Buckinghamshire *Gracefield, Manor House (Lyde Garden), Stowe Landscape Garden*
Cambridgeshire *Duxford Mill*
Cheshire *Cholmondeley Castle Gardens, Dorfold Hall, Stapeley Water Gardens*
Cornwall *Chyverton, Pencarrow, Trebah*
Derbyshire *Chatsworth*
Devon *Coleton Fishacre Garden, Doctyn Mill, Gidleigh Park, Marwood Hill*
Dorset *Charlton Cottage, Compton Acres, Forde Abbey, Mapperton, The Old Mill, Shute House, Stour House*
Essex *The Beth Chatto Gardens, Feeringbury Manor, Glen Chantry, The Magnolias, Saling Hall, Volpaia*
Gloucestershire *Abbotswood, Frampton Court, Hodges Barn, Lydney Park Gardens, Ryelands House, Sezincote, Westbury Court Garden*
Hampshire and the Isle of Wight *Barton Manor, Exbury Gardens, Greatham Mill, Longstock Park Gardens, Spinners*
Hereford and Worcester *Burford House Gardens, Hergest Croft Garden, How Caple Court, Lakeside, Whitfield*
Hertfordshire *Hill House, Hopleys*
Humberside *Burnby Hall Gardens, Burton Constable Hall*
Kent *Godinton Park, Ladham House, Mount Ephraim*
Leicestershire *Prebendal House*
London (Greater) *Golders Hill Park, Hampton Court Palace, Kensington Gardens, Walpole Park*
Manchester (Greater) *Fletcher Moss Botanical Gardens and Parsonage Gardens*
Norfolk *Goodnestone Water Gardens, Hoveton Hall Gardens, How Hill Farm, Lake House, Mannington Hall*
Northumberland *Chillingham Castle*
Nottinghamshire *Newstead Abbey*
Oxfordshire *Buscot Park*
Shropshire *Brownhill House, Dudmaston, Hodnet Hall, The Paddocks, Preen Manor*
Somerset *Ambleside Aviaries and Gardens, Bittescombe Manor, Gaulden Manor*
Staffordshire *Heath House, Wolseley Garden Park*
Suffolk *Haughley Park*
Surrey *Coombe Wood, Coverwood Lakes and Gardens, High Meadow, Pinewood House, Vann, The Valley Gardens*
Sussex, East *Kidbrook Park, Sheffield Park Garden*
Sussex, West *Mill House, West Dean Gardens*
Wiltshire *Bowood House, Heale Gardens, Stourhead, Wilton House*
Yorkshire, North *Newby Hall and Gardens, Studley Royal and Fountains Abbey*
Yorkshire, South & West *Harewood House, Roundhay Park*
Ireland *Creagh Gardens, Fernhill, Japanese Garden*
Scotland *Ardtornish, Corsock House, Crarae Glen Garden, Kilbryde Castle, Kildrummy Castle Gardens, Manderston, Monteviot, Stobo Castle Water Gardens, Teviot Water Gardens, Torosay Castle and Gardens*
Wales *Bodrhyddan, Cae Hir, The Dingle Haverfordwest, The Dingle Welshpool, Dolwen, Foxbrush, Glansevern, Hafod Garregog*

WILD GARDENS AND WILDERNESSES

The term wild garden/wilderness includes a range of types of garden, including wildlife gardens, which have been specifically designed to avoid the formal, cultivated garden. In general, the wild garden forms only a part of the total area.

Cambridgeshire *Docwra's Manor, St John's College Cambridge*

Cheshire *Dorfold Hall*

Cornwall *Heligan, Trebah*

Cumbria and the Isle of Man *Dalemain, Hutton-in-the-Forest, Levens Hall, Muncaster Castle*

Derbyshire *Chatsworth*

Devon *Arlington Court, Greenway House*

Dorset *Athelhampton, Charlton Cottage, Dean's Court, Edmondsham House, Kesworth, Mapperton, Parnham House*

Essex *Olivers*

Gloucestershire *Painswick Rococo Garden, Stancombe Park*

Hampshire and the Isle of Wight *The Manor House*

Hereford and Worcester *How Caple Court*

Hertfordshire *Hatfield House, Knebworth House*

Humberside *The Cottages*

Kent *Godinton Park, Hole Park, Marle Place, Penshurst Place, Riverhill House Gardens, Smith's Hall*

Lancashire *Sellet Hall Gardens*

Leicestershire *Belvoir Castle*

Lincolnshire *Doddington Hall, Fulbeck Hall, Grimsthorpe Castle*

London (Greater) *Camley Street Natural Park, Hampton Court Palace, Isabella Plantation, Syon Park, Trinity Hospice, Waterhouse Plantation*

Manchester (Greater) *Lyme Park*

Midlands, West *Castle Bromwich Hall Gardens*

Norfolk *Elsing Hall, Fairhaven Garden Trust, How Hill Farm, Mannington Hall, The Old Rectory Holt*

Northamptonshire *Canons Ashby House, Cottesbrooke Hall, Delapre Abbey, Rockingham Castle Gardens*

Northumberland *Belsay Hall, Chillingham Castle, Hexham Herbs*

Nottinghamshire *St Helen's Croft*

Oxfordshire *Christ Church Meadow Oxford, Mill House, Wilcote House*

Shropshire *Millichope Park*

Somerset *Combe Sydenham Country Park, Hadspen Garden and Nursery*

Staffordshire *Eccleshall Castle Gardens*

Suffolk *Helmingham Hall, Shrubland Hall*

Surrey *Hatchlands, Pyrford Court, The Royal Horticultural Society's Garden, The Savill Garden*

Sussex, East *Michelham Priory*

Sussex, West *Duckyls, Hammerwood House Garden, High Beeches Gardens, Nymans, Stonehurst, West Dean Gardens*

Warwickshire *Charlecote Park, Ryton Organic Gardens, Warwick Castle*

Wiltshire *Corsham Court, The Courts, Stourton House Flower Garden*

Yorkshire, North *Betula and Bolton Percy Churchyard, Constable Burton Hall, Hackfall Wood, Norton Conyers*

Yorkshire, South & West *Bramham Park*

Ireland *Annes Grove, Downhill*

Scotland *Ardtornish, Candacraig, Cawdor Castle, Crarae Glen Garden, Manderston, Mellerstain*

Wales *Penrhyn Castle, Post House Gardens, Winllan*

Channel Islands *Sausmarez Manor Exotic Woodland Garden, Guernsey, Domaine Des Vaux, Jersey*

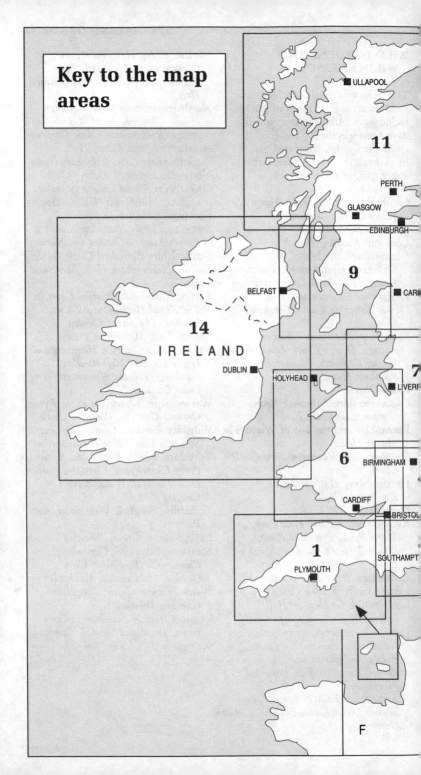

Key to the map areas

ULLAPOOL

11

PERTH

GLASGOW

EDINBURGH

9

BELFAST

CAR

14
IRELAND

DUBLIN

HOLYHEAD

7

LIVERP

6

BIRMINGHAM

CARDIFF

BRISTOL

1

SOUTHAMPT

PLYMOUTH

F

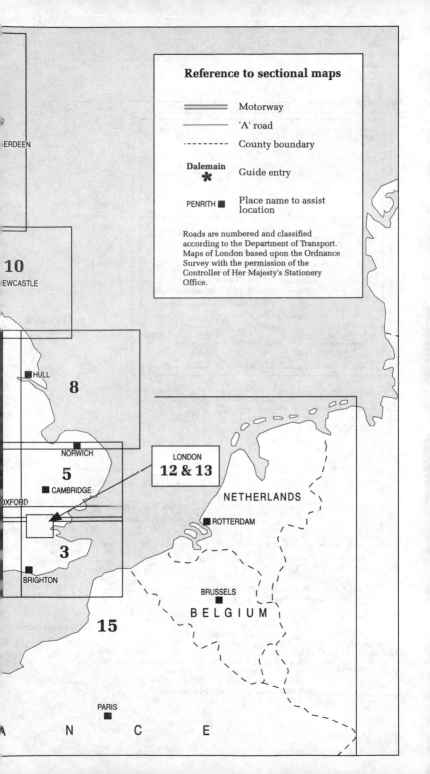

Reference to sectional maps

▬▬▬	Motorway
▬▬▬	'A' road
- - - - -	County boundary
Dalemain ✱	Guide entry
PENRITH ■	Place name to assist location

Roads are numbered and classified according to the Department of Transport. Maps of London based upon the Ordnance Survey with the permission of the Controller of Her Majesty's Stationery Office.

ERDEEN

10
EWCASTLE

■ HULL

8

■ NORWICH

5

■ CAMBRIDGE

OXFORD

LONDON
12 & 13

NETHERLANDS

■ ROTTERDAM

3

■ BRIGHTON

BRUSSELS ■

B E L G I U M

15

PARIS ■

A   N   C   E

1

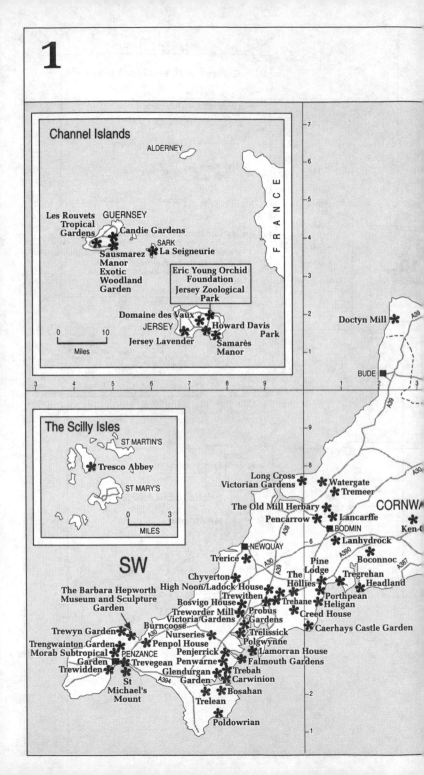

Channel Islands

ALDERNEY

FRANCE

Les Rouvets Tropical Gardens
GUERNSEY
Candie Gardens
SARK
Sausmarez Manor Exotic Woodland Garden
La Seigneurie

Eric Young Orchid Foundation
Jersey Zoological Park

Domaine des Vaux
JERSEY
Howard Davis Park
Jersey Lavender
Samarès Manor

0   10
Miles

Doctyn Mill

BUDE

The Scilly Isles

ST MARTIN'S
Tresco Abbey
ST MARY'S

0   3
MILES

Long Cross Victorian Gardens
Watergate
Tremeer

The Old Mill Herbary
Pencarrow
Lancarffe
BODMIN
Ken-C

CORNWA

Lanhydrock

NEWQUAY

Boconnoc

Trerice

Pine Lodge
Tregrehan
Headland

SW

Chyverton
High Noon/Ladock House
The Hollies
Trewithen
Trehane
Porthpean
Heligan

The Barbara Hepworth Museum and Sculpture Garden

Bosvigo House
Treworder Mill Victoria Gardens
Probus Gardens
Creed House

Trewyn Garden
Burncoose Nurseries
Penpol House
Trelissick
Polgwynne
Caerhays Castle Garden

Trengwainton Garden
Morab Subtropical
PENZANCE
Trevegean
Penjerrick
Penwarne
Lamorran House

Trewidden
St Michael's Mount
Glendurgan Garden
Carwinion
Falmouth Gardens
Trebah

Trelean
Bosahan

Poldowrian

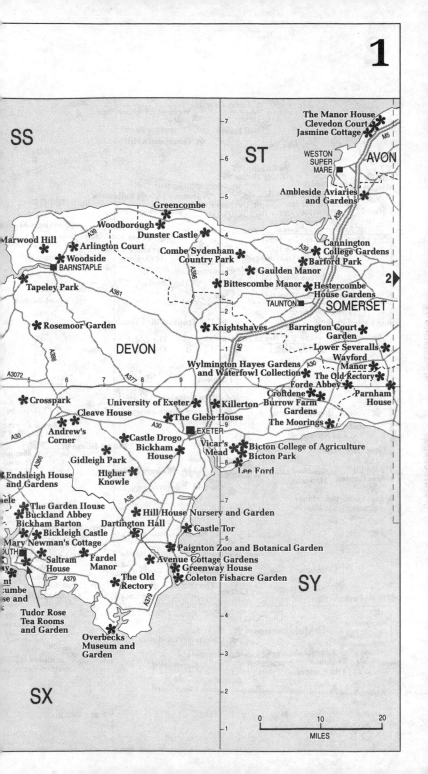

1

SS

ST

The Manor House
Clevedon Court
Jasmine Cottage

WESTON
SUPER
MARE

AVON

M5

Ambleside Aviaries
and Gardens

Greencombe

Woodborough

Marwood Hill

Dunster Castle

Arlington Court

Woodside
BARNSTAPLE

Combe Sydenham
Country Park

Cannington
College Gardens

Barford Park

Gaulden Manor

Tapeley Park

Bittescombe Manor

Hestercombe
House Gardens

TAUNTON

SOMERSET

2

Rosemoor Garden

DEVON

Knightshayes

Barrington Court
Garden

Lower Severalls

Wayford
Manor

Wylmington Hayes Gardens
and Waterfowl Collection

The Old Rectory

Forde Abbey

Parnham
House

Crosspark

University of Exeter

Killerton

Croftdene
Burrow Farm
Gardens

Cleave House

The Glebe House

Andrew's
Corner

EXETER

The Moorings

Castle Drogo
Bickham
House

Vicar's
Mead

Bicton College of Agriculture

Gidleigh Park

Bicton Park

Endsleigh House
and Gardens

Higher
Knowle

Lee Ford

The Garden House
Buckland Abbey

Hill House Nursery and Garden

Bickham Barton

Dartington Hall

Castle Tor

Bickleigh Castle

Mary Newman's Cottage

Paignton Zoo and Botanical Garden

Saltram
House

Fardel
Manor

Avenue Cottage Gardens

Greenway House

The Old
Rectory

Coleton Fishacre Garden

SY

Tudor Rose
Tea Rooms
and Garden

Overbecks
Museum and
Garden

SX

| 0 | 10 | 20 |

MILES

2

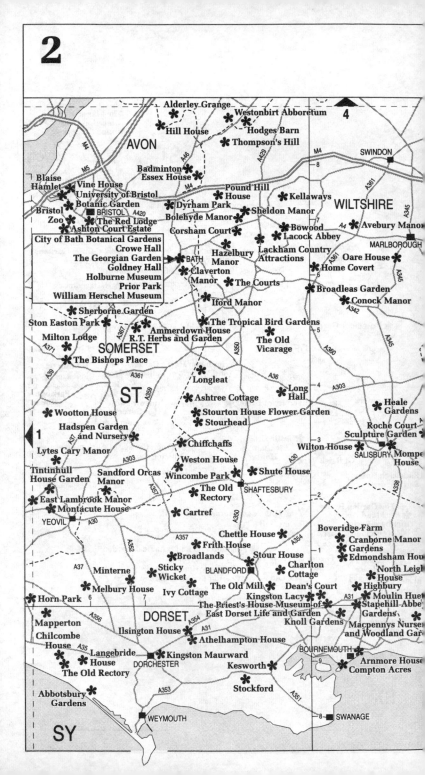

Alderley Grange

Westonbirt Abboretum

Hill House

Hodges Barn

Thompson's Hill

AVON

SWINDON

Badminton
Essex House

Pound Hill
House

Kellaways

WILTSHIRE

Blaise
Hamlet

Vine House
University of Bristol
Botanic Garden

Bristol
Zoo

The Red Lodge
Ashton Court Estate

Dyrham Park

Bolehyde Manor

Corsham Court

Sheldon Manor

Bowood
Lacock Abbey

Avebury Manor

MARLBOROUGH

City of Bath Botanical Gardens
Crowe Hall
The Georgian Garden
Goldney Hall
Holburne Museum
Prior Park
William Herschel Museum

BATH

Hazelbury
Manor

Claverton
Manor

The Courts

Lackham Country
Attractions

Oare House
Home Covert

Iford Manor

Broadleas Garden

Conock Manor

Sherborne Garden

The Tropical Bird Gardens

Ston Easton Park

Ammerdown House
R.T. Herbs and Garden

The Old
Vicarage

Milton Lodge

SOMERSET

The Bishops Place

Longleat

Long
Hall

ST

Ashtree Cottage

Wootton House

Stourton House Flower Garden

Heale
Gardens

Hadspen Garden
and Nursery

Stourhead

Roche Court
Sculpture Garden

Lytes Cary Manor

Chiffchaffs

Weston House

Wilton House

SALISBURY Mompe
House

Tintinhull
House Garden

Sandford Orcas
Manor

Wincombe Park

Shute House

The Old
Rectory

SHAFTESBURY

East Lambrook Manor
Montacute House

YEOVIL

Cartref

Boveridge Farm

Chettle House

Cranborne Manor
Gardens

Frith House

Stour House

Edmondsham Hou

Broadlands

Charlton
Cottage

North Leigh
House

Minterne

Sticky
Wicket

BLANDFORD

Highbury

Melbury House

Ivy Cottage

The Old Mill

Dean's Court

Moulin Hue

Horn Park

Kingston Lacy

Stapehill Abbe
Gardens

DORSET

The Priest's House Museum of
East Dorset Life and Garden

Knoll Gardens

Macpennys Nurser
and Woodland Gar

Mapperton

Ilsington House

Chilcombe
House

Langebride
House

Athelhampton House

BOURNEMOUTH

Kingston Maurward

The Old Rectory

DORCHESTER

Kesworth

Arnmore House
Compton Acres

Abbotsbury
Gardens

Stockford

WEYMOUTH

SWANAGE

SY

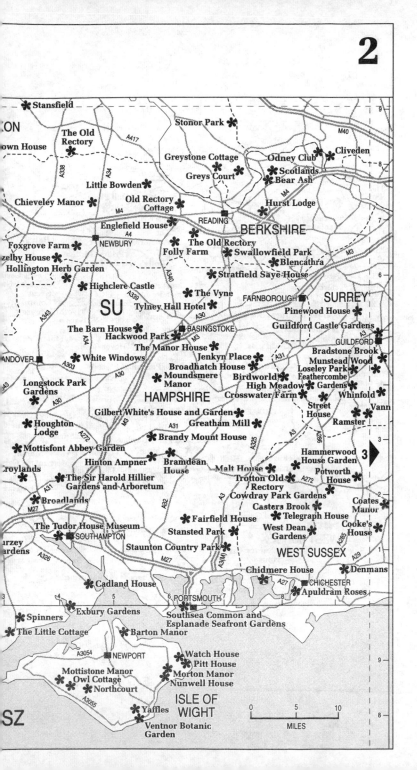

2

Stansfield

KON
The Old
Rectory
own House

Stonor Park

A417

Greystone Cottage

Odney Club · Cliveden

A338
A34

Greys Court

Scotlands
Bear Ash

Chieveley Manor

Little Bowden

Old Rectory
Cottage

M4

Englefield House

READING

Hurst Lodge

BERKSHIRE

Foxgrove Farm
zelby House
Hollington Herb Garden

A4
NEWBURY

The Old Rectory
Folly Farm

Swallowfield Park
Blencathra

A340

Stratfield Saye House

Highclere Castle

The Vyne

SU

A339

Tylney Hall Hotel

FARNBOROUGH

SURREY

A30

Pinewood House

The Barn House
Hackwood Park

BASINGSTOKE

Guildford Castle Gardens

A34

GUILDFORD

M3

The Manor House

Bradstone Brook

ANDOVER

A303

White Windows

Jenkyn Place

A31

Munstead Wood
Loseley Park

A30

Broadhatch House
Moundsmere
Manor

Birdworld

Feathercombe

High Meadow Gardens
Crosswater Farm

Longstock Park
Gardens

A30

HAMPSHIRE

Whinfold

A272

Street
House

Vann

Gilbert White's House and Garden

Ramster

Houghton
Lodge

A31

Greatham Mill

A325

A3

A286

Mottisfont Abbey Garden

Brandy Mount House

roylands

Hinton Ampner

Bramdean
House

Hammerwood
House Garden

3

A31

The Sir Harold Hillier
Gardens and Arboretum

Malt House

Potworth
House

Trotton Old
Rectory

A272

Broadlands

M27

A32

Cowdray Park Gardens

A3

Coates
Manor

Fairfield House

Casters Brook

Telegraph House

Cooke's
House

The Tudor House Museum

Stansted Park

West Dean
Gardens

A285

urzey
ardens

SOUTHAMPTON

Staunton Country Park

WEST SUSSEX

A29

A326

M27

A3(M)

1

Chidmere House

Denmans

Cadland House

A27

PORTSMOUTH

CHICHESTER

6

7

8

Apuldram Roses

Spinners

Exbury Gardens

Southsea Common and
Esplanade Seafront Gardens

The Little Cottage

Barton Manor

A3054

NEWPORT

Watch House
Pitt House

9

Mottistone Manor
Owl Cottage

Morton Manor
Nunwell House

Northcourt

ISLE OF
WIGHT

A3055

Yaffles

0

5

10

SZ

Ventnor Botanic
Garden

MILES

8

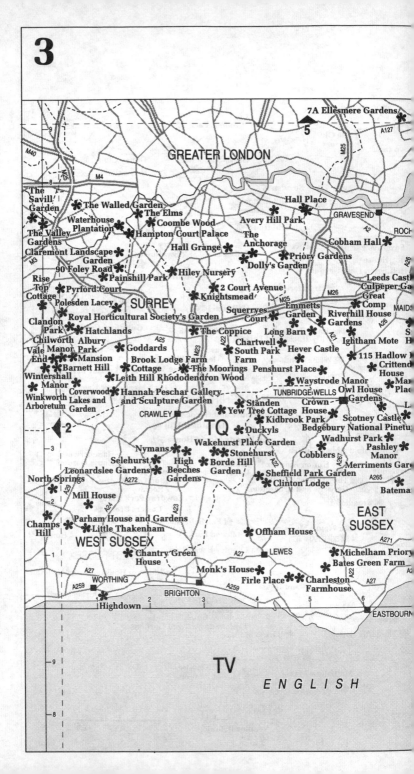

3

5 7A Ellesmere Gardens

GREATER LONDON

GRAVESEND

ROCH

The Savill Garden

The Walled Garden
The Elms
Coombe Wood
Avery Hill Park
Waterhouse Plantation
Hampton Court Palace
The Valley Gardens
The Anchorage
Cobham Hall
Claremont Landscape Garden
Hall Grange
90 Foley Road
Priory Gardens
Painshill Park
Dolly's Garden
Hiley Nursery

Leeds Castle
Culpeper Ga
Great Comp
Riverhill House Gardens
MAIDS

Rise Top Cottage
Pyrford Court
2 Court Avenue
Knightsmead
SURREY
Polesden Lacey
Royal Horticultural Society's Garden
Squerryes Court
Emmetts Garden
Clandon Park
Hatchlands
The Coppice
Long Barn
Ightham Mote
S H
Chilworth
Albury
Vale Manor Park End
Goddards
Chartwell
Hever Castle
115 Hadlow
Mansion
Brook Lodge Farm Cottage
South Park Farm
Crittend House
Barnett Hill
Penshurst Place
Leith Hill Rhododendron Wood
Wintershall Manor
Coverwood Lakes and Garden
Hannah Peschar Gallery and Sculpture Garden
Waystrode Manor
Mar Plac
Winkworth Arboretum
TUNBRIDGE WELLS
Owl House Gardens
L
CRAWLEY
Standen
Crown House
Scotney Castle
Yew Tree Cottage
Kidbrook Park
Bedgebury National Pinetu
TQ
Duckyls
Nymans
Wakehurst Place Garden
Wadhurst Park
Pashley Manor
Selehurst
High Beeches Gardens
Stonehurst
Cobblers
Leonardslee Gardens
Borde Hill Garden
Merriments Gar
North Springs
Sheffield Park Garden
Batema
Mill House
Clinton Lodge

EAST SUSSEX

Champs Hill
Parham House and Gardens
Little Thakenham
Offham House
WEST SUSSEX
Michelham Priory
Chantry Green House
LEWES
Bates Green Farm
Monk's House
Firle Place
Charleston Farmhouse
WORTHING
BRIGHTON
EASTBOURN
Highdown

TV
ENGLISH

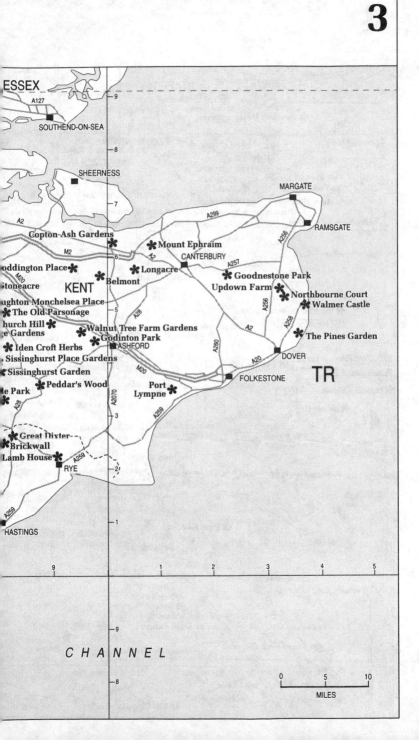

ESSEX

A127

SOUTHEND-ON-SEA

SHEERNESS

MARGATE

RAMSGATE

A2

A299

A256

Copton-Ash Gardens

M2

Mount Ephraim

CANTERBURY

oddington Place

A2

Longacre

A257

Goodnestone Park

toneacre

KENT

Belmont

Updown Farm

Northbourne Court

ughton Monchelsea Place

A28

A256

A258

Walmer Castle

The Old Parsonage

M20

A5

hurch Hill

Walnut Tree Farm Gardens

A2

The Pines Garden

e Gardens

Godinton Park

Iden Croft Herbs

ASHFORD

DOVER

Sissinghurst Place Gardens

A260

A20

TR

Sissinghurst Garden

FOLKESTONE

le Park

A28

Peddar's Wood

A2070

Port

Lympne

A259

Great Dixter

Brickwall

A259

Lamb House

RYE

A259

HASTINGS

C H A N N E L

0   5   10

MILES

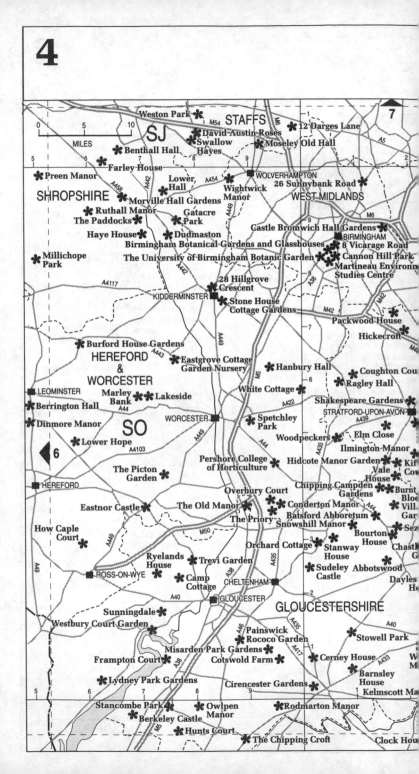

4

7

Weston Park ✱
M54
STAFFS
✱ 12 Darges Lane
M6
A5

SJ
✱ David Austin Roses
✱ Swallow
Hayes
✱ Moseley Old Hall

✱ Benthall Hall
✱ Farley House

✱ Preen Manor
A458
A442
Lower,
Hall ✱
A454
✱ Wightwick
Manor
WOLVERHAMPTON ■
26 Sunnybank Road ✱
WEST MIDLANDS
M6

SHROPSHIRE
✱ Morville Hall Gardens
✱ Ruthall Manor
The Paddocks ✱
✱ Gatacre
Park
A449

✱ Haye House
✱ Dudmaston
Castle Bromwich Hall Gardens ✱
BIRMINGHAM ■
✱ 8 Vicarage Road
Cannon Hill Park
Martineau Environm
Studies Centre

Birmingham Botanical Gardens and Glasshouses ✱
The University of Birmingham Botanic Garden ✱

✱ Millichope
Park
A4117
A442

28 Hillgrove
Crescent ✱
KIDDERMINSTER ■
✱ Stone House
Cottage Gardens
M42
A38

✱ Packwood House
✱ Hickecroft

✱ Burford House Gardens
A443
HEREFORD
&
WORCESTER
✱ Eastgrove Cottage
Garden Nursery
✱ Hanbury Hall
M5
A449
✱ Coughton Cou
✱ Ragley Hall
6

■ LEOMINSTER
Marley ✱✱ Lakeside
Bank
A44
White Cottage ✱
✱ Berrington Hall
WORCESTER ■
A22
Shakespeare Gardens ✱
STRATFORD-UPON-AVON
A439

✱ Dinmore Manor
SO
A449
A44
✱ Spetchley
Park
Woodpeckers ✱
✱ Elm Close
✱ Ilmington Manor

◄ 6
✱ Lower Hope
A4103
✱ Hidcote Manor Garden ✱ Kif
Vale Cow
House

■ HEREFORD
✱ The Picton
Garden
Pershore College
of Horticulture ✱
Chipping Campden ✱✱
Gardens ✱ Burnt
Bloo
Vill.

✱ Eastnor Castle
✱ The Old Manor
Overbury Court ✱
✱✱ Conderton Manor
The Priory ✱ ✱ Batsford Abboretum
Snowshill Manor ✱
A44 Gar
✱ Sez

✱ How Caple
Court
M50
Orchard Cottage ✱
3
Stanway ✱
House
✱ Bourton
House
Chast

A449
A435
Trevi Garden ✱
Ryelands
House ✱
✱ Sudeley Abbotswood
Castle
Dayles
H

■ ROSS-ON-WYE
✱ Camp
Cottage
CHELTENHAM ■
A40
A46
A435
2

A49
GLOUCESTER ■
GLOUCESTERSHIRE

✱ Sunningdale
✱ Westbury Court Garden
A38
Painswick ✱
Rococo Garden ✱
✱ Stowell Park
A40
A433

✱ Frampton Court
Misarden Park Gardens ✱
Cotswold Farm ✱
A417
✱ Cerney House
W
M

✱ Lydney Park Gardens
Cirencester Gardens ✱
✱ Barnsley
House
✱ Kelmscott Ma

✱ Stancombe Park
✱ Owlpen
Manor
✱ Rodmarton Manor
✱ Berkeley Castle
M5
✱ Hunts Court
✱ The Chipping Croft
Clock Hou

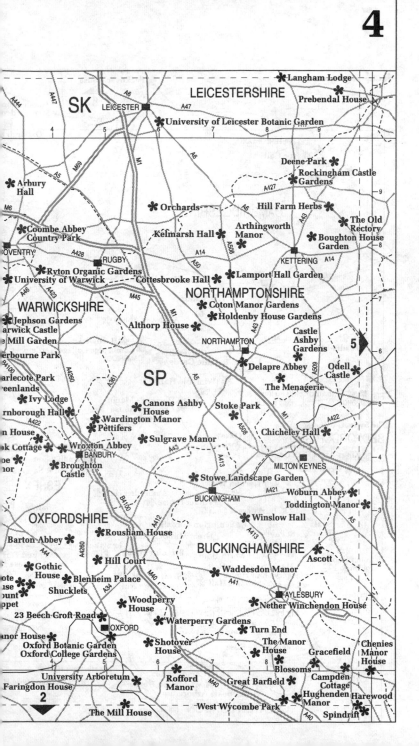

4

LEICESTERSHIRE

SK

LEICESTER

* Langham Lodge
Prebendal House

* University of Leicester Botanic Garden

Deene Park *
Rockingham Castle
Gardens

* Arbury
Hall

* Orchards

Hill Farm Herbs *

The Old
Rectory

* Boughton House
Garden

* Coombe Abbey
Country Park

COVENTRY

Kelmarsh Hall *

Arthingworth
Manor

KETTERING

* Ryton Organic Gardens
* University of Warwick
Cottesbrooke Hall *

* Lamport Hall Garden

RUGBY

NORTHAMPTONSHIRE

WARWICKSHIRE

* Coton Manor Gardens
* Holdenby House Gardens

* Jephson Gardens
Warwick Castle
e Mill Garden

Althorp House *

Castle
Ashby
Gardens

5

erbourne Park

NORTHAMPTON

arlecote Park
reenlands

SP

Odell
Castle *

* Delapre Abbey

* Ivy Lodge

The Menagerie

rnborough Hall

* Canons Ashby
House

Stoke Park
*

n House

* Wardington Manor
* Pettifers

Chicheley Hall *

k Cottage *

* Wroxton Abbey

* Sulgrave Manor

oe *
nor

* Broughton
Castle

BANBURY

MILTON KEYNES

* Stowe Landscape Garden

Woburn Abbey *

BUCKINGHAM

Toddington Manor *

OXFORDSHIRE

* Winslow Hall

* Rousham House

BUCKINGHAMSHIRE

* Barton Abbey

Ascott

* Hill Court

* Waddesdon Manor

* Gothic
House *
Shucklets

* Blenheim Palace

AYLESBURY

* Woodperry
House

* Nether Winchendon House

ote
use
unt
ppet

23 Beech Croft Road *

* Waterperry Gardens

* Turn End

nor House *
Oxford Botanic Garden
Oxford College Gardens

* Shotover
House

The Manor
House *

Gracefield

Chenies
Manor
House

OXFORD

University Arboretum *

Rofford
Manor

Blossoms

* Great Barfield *

Campden
Cottage *

Faringdon House

2

* West Wycombe Park

Hughenden
Manor *

Harewood

The Mill House *

Spindrift

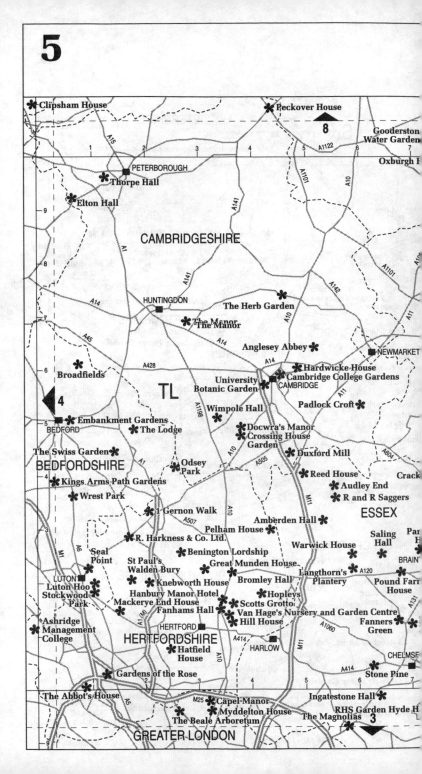

5

Clipsham House
Peckover House
8
Gooderstone Water Garden
Oxburgh Hall

A15

1 · A15 2 · 3 · 4 · 5 · A1122 6 · 7

PETERBOROUGH
Thorpe Hall
A1101
A10

A141
A142

Elton Hall
A1
9

A1101

CAMBRIDGESHIRE
8

A141
A142

A45
HUNTINGDON
The Herb Garden
7
A14
The Manor
A10
A45

A1
Anglesey Abbey
NEWMARKET

6
Broadfields
A428
A14
Hardwicke House
Cambridge College Gardens

TL
University Botanic Garden
CAMBRIDGE
A11

A1198
Wimpole Hall
Padlock Croft

Embankment Gardens
5
BEDFORD
The Lodge
Docwra's Manor
Crossing House Garden
A10
A505
A604

Duxford Mill

4

The Swiss Garden
BEDFORDSHIRE
A1
Odsey Park
Reed House
Crack
4
Kings Arms Path Gardens
Audley End
R and R Saggers

Wrest Park
A10
1 Gernon Walk
ESSEX

A507
Amberden Hall
3
Pelham House
Saling Hall
Par H
R. Harkness & Co. Ltd.
Warwick House
A6
Seal Point
Benington Lordship
BRAIN
St Paul's Walden Bury
Great Munden House
Langthorn's Plantery
A120
LUTON
Knebworth House
Bromley Hall
Pound Farm House
2
Luton Hoo
Stockwood Park
Hanbury Manor Hotel
Hopleys
A1(M)
Mackerye End House
Scotts Grotto
A131
Ashridge Management College
Fanhams Hall
Van Hage's Nursery and Garden Centre
Fanners Green
Hill House
HERTFORD
A1060
CHELMSF
Hatfield House
HERTFORDSHIRE
A414
HARLOW
M11

Gardens of the Rose
A10
Stone Pine

The Abbot's House
A5
Capel Manor
Ingatestone Hall
M25
Myddelton House
RHS Garden Hyde H
The Beale Arboretum
The Magnolias
3
GREATER LONDON

2 · 3 · 4 · 5 · 6

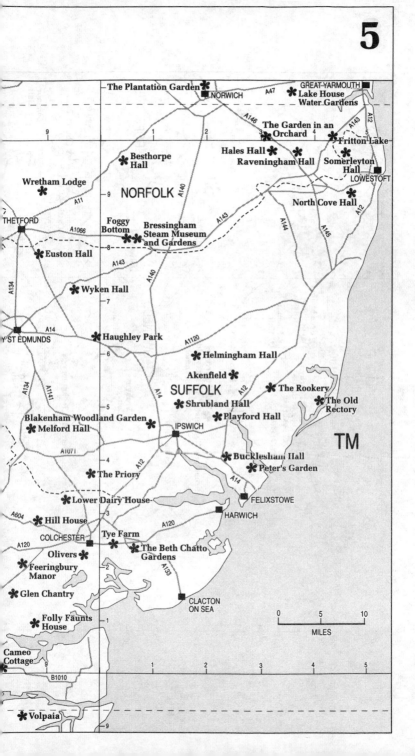

5

The Plantation Garden ✽
✽ NORWICH
GREAT-YARMOUTH ■
✽ Lake House
Water Gardens

A47

A146

The Garden in an ✽
Orchard

Fritton Lake

Hales Hall ✽ ✽
Raveningham Hall

Somerleyton
Hall ✽
LOWESTOFT ■

✽ Besthorpe
Hall

Wretham Lodge
✽

NORFOLK

A140

North Cove Hall ✽

THETFORD ■

A11

A1066

Foggy
Bottom

A143

Bressingham Steam Museum
and Gardens ✽✽

A140

A143

A144

A146

✽ Euston Hall

A134

✽ Wyken Hall

A143

—7

A134

✽ Haughley Park

A1120

—6

Y'ST EDMUNDS ■

A14

✽ Helmingham Hall

A134

A1141

A14

Akenfield ✽

SUFFOLK

✽ The Rookery

Blakenham Woodland Garden ✽
✽ Melford Hall

Shrubland Hall ✽

A12

✽ The Old
Rectory

A1071

—4

A12

✽ Playford Hall

IPSWICH ■

TM

—5

✽ The Priory

A14

✽ Bucklesham Hall
✽ Peter's Garden

A604

✽ Lower Dairy House

—3

A14

FELIXSTOWE ■

✽ Hill House

COLCHESTER ■

Tye Farm
✽

A120

HARWICH ■

A120

✽ Olivers
✽
Feeringbury
Manor

✽ The Beth Chatto
Gardens

A133

—2

✽ Glen Chantry

CLACTON
ON SEA ■

✽ Folly Faunts
House

—1

0   5   10

MILES

Cameo
Cottage ✽

B1010

—9

1   2   3   4   5

✽ Volpaia

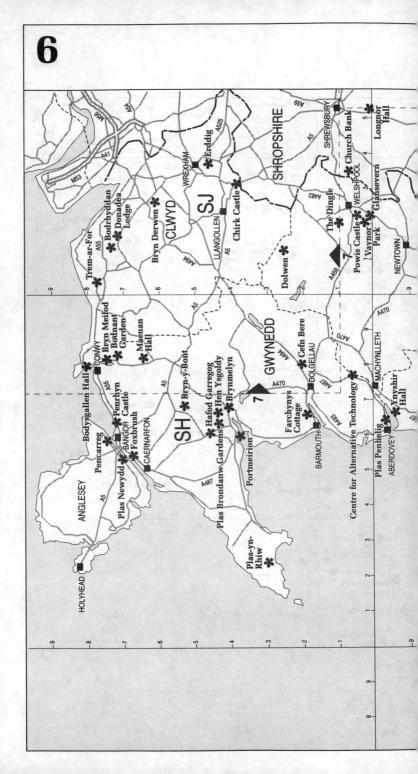

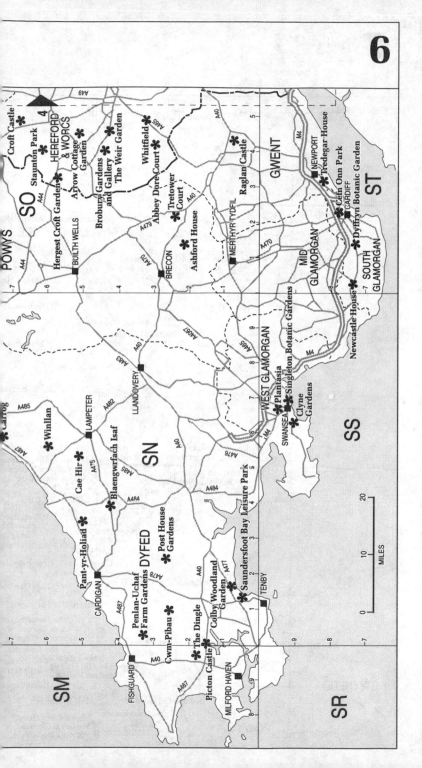

6

POWYS
SO

Croft Castle ✱
Staunton Park ✱
HEREFORD
& WORCS
Arrow Cottage ✱
Garden
Brobury Gardens ✱   The Weir Garden ✱
and Gallery   Whitfield ✱
Hergest Croft Garden ✱   Abbey Dore Court ✱
BUILTH WELLS   Tretower ✱
Court
A40
Ashford House ✱   Raglan Castle ✱
BRECON   MERTHYR TYDFIL
                           GWENT
                           NEWPORT
                           Tredegar House ✱
                           Cefn Onn Park ✱
                           CARDIFF
                           Dyffryn Botanic Garden ✱
MID
GLAMORGAN
                           SOUTH
                           GLAMORGAN
Newcastle House ✱   ST

Carrog ✱
Winllan ✱
LAMPETER
Cae Hir ✱
Blaengwrfach Isaf ✱
SN
Pant-yr-Holiad ✱
DYFED
Post House ✱
Gardens
WEST GLAMORGAN
Plantasia ✱
Singleton Botanic Gardens ✱
SWANSEA
Clyne ✱
Gardens
SS

Penlan-Uchaf ✱
Farm Gardens
Cwm-Pibau ✱
The Dingle ✱
CARDIGAN
Colby Woodland ✱
Garden
Saundersfoot Bay Leisure Park
TENBY
Picton Castle ✱
FISHGUARD
MILFORD HAVEN
SM
SR

MILES
0   10   20

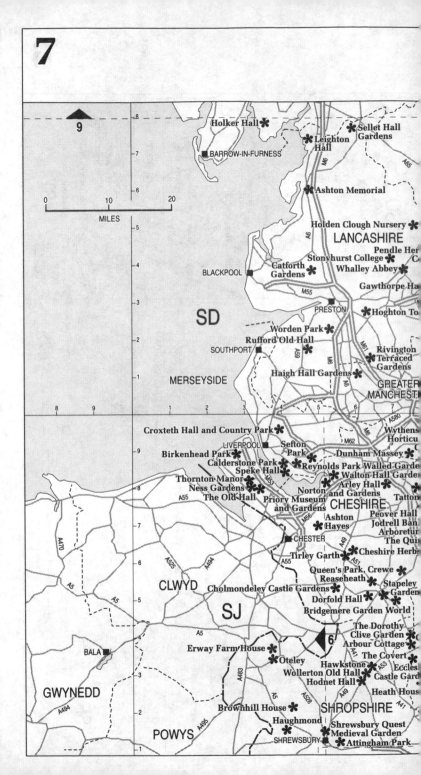

7

9

Holker Hall ✳

✳ Sellet Hall
Gardens

✳ Leighton
Hall

■ BARROW-IN-FURNESS

✳ Ashton Memorial

Holden Clough Nursery ✳

LANCASHIRE

Pendle Her
C
Stonyhurst College ✳

Catforth
Gardens ✳

Whalley Abbey ✳

Gawthorpe Ha

■ BLACKPOOL

SD

PRESTON ■

✳ Hoghton To

Worden Park ✳

Rufford Old Hall ■

✳ Rivington
Terraced
Gardens

■ SOUTHPORT

Haigh Hall Gardens ✳

MERSEYSIDE

**GREATER
MANCHEST**

0   10   20

MILES

Croxteth Hall and Country Park ✳

Wythens
Horticu

Birkenhead Park ✳

LIVERPOOL ■

Sefton
Park ✳

Dunham Massey ✳

Calderstone Park ✳
Speke Hall ✳

Reynolds Park Walled Garde

Thornton Manor ✳

Walton Hall Garde

Ness Gardens ✳

Arley Hall ✳

The Old Hall ✳

Priory Museum
and Gardens ✳

Norton
and Gardens ✳

CHESHIRE

Tatton

■ CHESTER

Ashton
Hayes ✳

Peover Hall
Jodrell Ban
Arboretur
The Qui

Tirley Garth ✳

✳ Cheshire Herb

Queen's Park, Crewe ✳

CLWYD

Cholmondeley Castle Gardens ✳

Reaseheath ✳

✳ Stapeley
Garden

Dorfold Hall ✳

SJ

Bridgemere Garden World ✳

BALA ■

The Dorothy
Clive Garden ✳

Erway Farm House ✳

Arbour Cottage ✳

6

✳ The Covert

Oteley ✳

Hawkstone ✳

✳ Eccles

GWYNEDD

Wollerton Old Hall ✳

Castle Gard

Hodnet Hall ✳

Heath Hous

Brownhill House ✳

SHROPSHIRE

Haughmond ✳

Shrewsbury Quest
Medieval Garden ✳

POWYS

SHREWSBURY ■

Attingham Park ✳

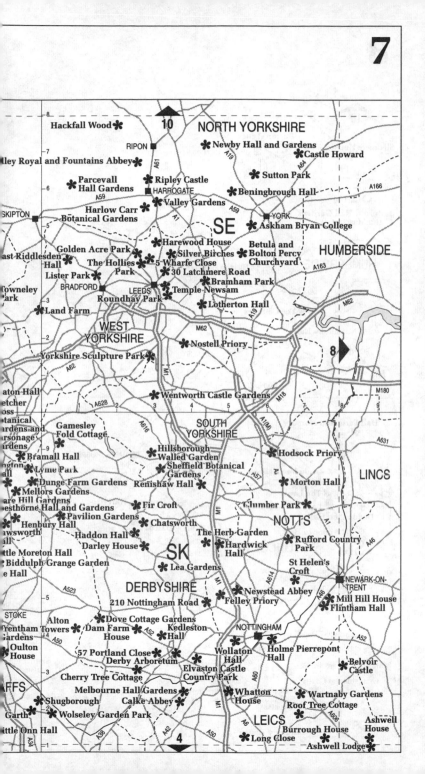

Hackfall Wood ✽

10

NORTH YORKSHIRE

RIPON ■

✽ Newby Hall and Gardens   ✽ Castle Howard

A19   A64

ley Royal and Fountains Abbey ✽   A61

✽ Sutton Park

✽ Parcevall Hall Gardens ✽   ✽ Ripley Castle   ✽ Beningbrough Hall   A166

HARROGATE ■   A59

Harlow Carr ✽   ✽ Valley Gardens   A59

SKIPTON   Botanical Gardens

A1

SE

ast Riddlesden Hall ✽   Golden Acre Park ✽   ✽ York

✽ Askham Bryan College

HUMBERSIDE

Harewood House ✽

✽ Silver Birches   Betula and Bolton Percy Churchyard

The Hollies ✽ Park   ✽ 5 Wharfe Close

Lister Park ✽   ✽ 30 Latchmere Road   A163

owneley ark   BRADFORD ■   ✽ Bramham Park

LEEDS ■   ✽ Temple Newsam

Roundhay Park ✽   M62

✽ Land Farm   ✽ Lotherton Hall

WEST YORKSHIRE   M62   A19   M62   M180

Yorkshire Sculpture Park ✽   ✽ Nostell Priory   **8** ▶

M1

A62   ✽ Wentworth Castle Gardens   M18   M180

aton Hall   A628   2   3   4   5   A1(M)   A631

etcher oss

tanical ardens and rsonage rdens   Gamesley Fold Cottage   **SOUTH YORKSHIRE**   A57

✽ Bramall Hall   Hillsborough Walled Garden ✽   ✽ Hodsock Priory   **LINCS**

ngton all   ✽ Lyme Park   Sheffield Botanical Gardens ✽

✽ Dunge Farm Gardens   Renishaw Hall ✽   ✽ Morton Hall

✽ Mellors Gardens   A57

are Hill Gardens   ✽ Fir Croft   ✽ Clumber Park

esthorne Hall and Gardens ✽   Pavilion Gardens ✽   **NOTTS**

✽ Henbury Hall   ✽ Chatsworth   A1

awsworth   Haddon Hall ✽   The Herb Garden ✽   ✽ Rufford Country Park   A46

ill   Darley House ✽   ✽ Hardwick Hall

ttle Moreton Hall   **SK**   St Helen's Croft

Biddulph Grange Garden   ✽ Lea Gardens   NEWARK-ON-TRENT ■

e Hall   A523   **DERBYSHIRE**   M1   ✽ Newstead Abbey   A46   ✽ Mill Hill House

STOKE   -5   210 Nottingham Road ✽   ✽ Felley Priory   ✽ Flintham Hall

Alton Towers ✽   ✽ Dove Cottage Gardens   Kedleston Hall ✽   A614

rentham ardens   Dam Farm House ✽   A52   NOTTINGHAM ■   A52

Oulton House   Wollaton Hall ✽   Holme Pierrepont Hall

57 Portland Close ✽   ✽ Derby Arboretum   ✽ Belvoir Castle

Cherry Tree Cottage ✽   Elvaston Castle Country Park   A60

FFS   Melbourne Hall Gardens ✽   Calke Abbey ✽   ✽ Whatton House   ✽ Wartnaby Gardens

Garth ✽   ✽ Shugborough   Roof Tree Cottage ✽   Ashwell House

ittle Onn Hall   ✽ Wolseley Garden Park   A42   **LEICS**   A46

A34   A38   A50   A6   Burrough House ✽   Ashwell Lodge ✽

4 ▼   ✽ Long Close

8

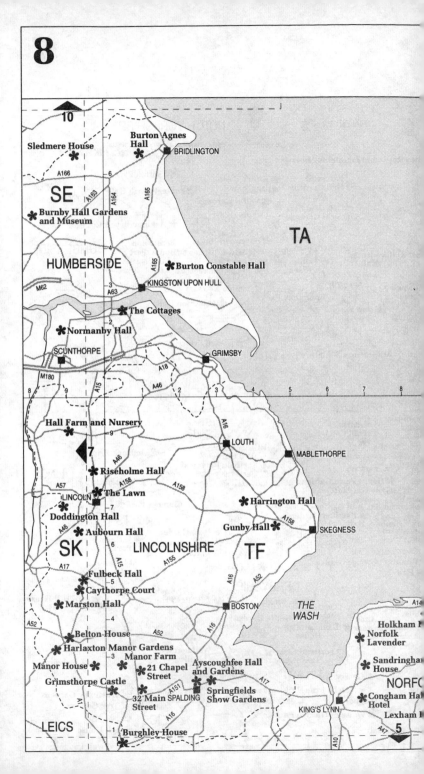

10

Sledmere House

7

Burton Agnes Hall

■ BRIDLINGTON

A166

6

A183 A164 A165

SE

Burnby Hall Gardens and Museum

TA

4

HUMBERSIDE

A165 **Burton Constable Hall**

M62 A63 3 ■ KINGSTON UPON HULL

The Cottages

2

Normanby Hall

SCUNTHORPE ■ GRIMSBY

A18

M180 A15 A46

8 9 1 2 3 4 5 6 7 8

Hall Farm and Nursery

9

A16

7

A46 **Riseholme Hall** ■ LOUTH ■ MABLETHORPE

A57 A158 A158

LINCOLN ■ **The Lawn**

7 **Harrington Hall**

Doddington Hall

A46 **Aubourn Hall** **Gunby Hall** A158 ■ SKEGNESS

6

SK LINCOLNSHIRE TF

A155 A16

A15 A52

A17

Fulbeck Hall

5 **Caythorpe Court**

Marston Hall

4 A16

A52 ■ BOSTON *THE WASH*

A14

Belton House A52

Harlaxton Manor Gardens **Manor Farm** **Holkham**

3 **Norfolk Lavender**

Manor House A16

Sandringham House

21 Chapel Street **Ayscoughfee Hall and Gardens**

Grimsthorpe Castle

A151 A17 NORFO

32 Main Street SPALDING **Springfields Show Gardens** **Congham Hall Hotel**

A16 ■ KING'S LYNN

LEICS **Lexham**

1 **Burghley House** A10 A47 5

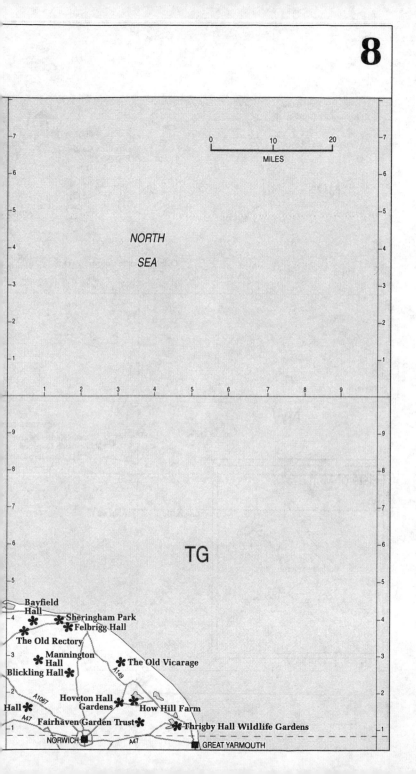

8

0 10 20
MILES

7
6
5
4
3
2
1

NORTH

SEA

1 2 3 4 5 6 7 8 9

9
8
7
6
5
4
3
2
1

TG

Bayfield
Hall
✹ Sheringham Park
✹Felbrigg Hall
✹
The Old Rectory

✹ Mannington
Hall   ✹ The Old Vicarage
Blickling Hall✹   A149

Hall ✹   A1067
Hoveton Hall ✹✹
Gardens   How Hill Farm

A47
Fairhaven Garden Trust ✹   ✹Thrigby Hall Wildlife Gardens

NORWICH ■   GREAT YARMOUTH ■
A47

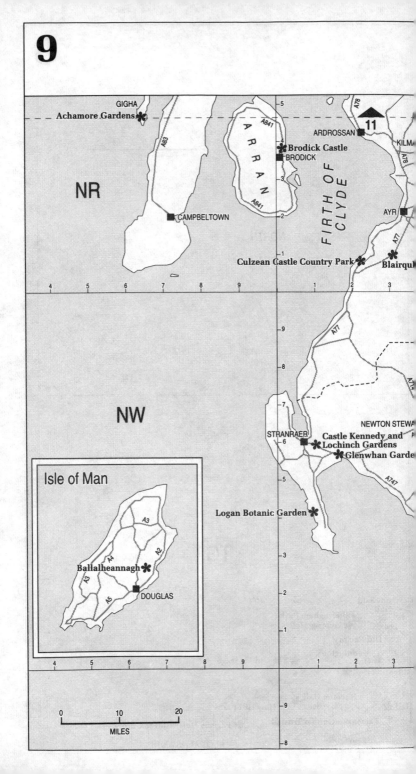

9

GIGHA
Achamore Gardens ✽

NR

A841

A841

CAMPBELTOWN

A83

ARDROSSAN

KILM

A78

A78

A R R A N

Brodick Castle ✽
BRODICK

F I R T H O F

C L Y D E

AYR

11

A77

Culzean Castle Country Park ✽

Blairqu

A77

NW

A77

A71

NEWTON STEWA

STRANRAER
**Castle Kennedy and
Lochinch Gardens** ✽
Glenwhan Garde ✽

A747

Logan Botanic Garden ✽

Isle of Man

A3

A2

A4

Ballalheannagh ✽

A3

A5

DOUGLAS

0   10   20
MILES

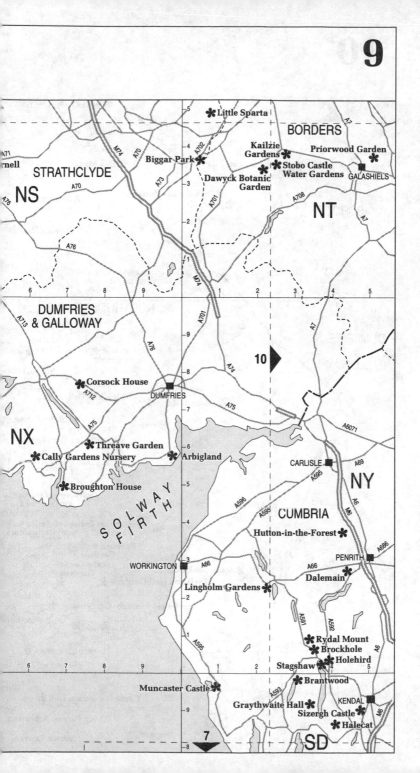

* Little Sparta

BORDERS

Kailzie
Gardens *   * Priorwood Garden

STRATHCLYDE   Biggar Park *

NS   * Stobo Castle
          Water Gardens
          Dawyck Botanic   GALASHIELS
          Garden

NT

DUMFRIES
& GALLOWAY

10 ▶

* Corsock House

DUMFRIES

NX

* Threave Garden
* Cally Gardens Nursery   * Arbigland

CARLISLE

NY

* Broughton House

SOLWAY
FIRTH

CUMBRIA

Hutton-in-the-Forest *

PENRITH

WORKINGTON   A66

Dalemain *

Lingholm Gardens *

* Rydal Mount
* Brockhole
* Holehird
Stagshaw *

Muncaster Castle *   * Brantwood   KENDAL

Graythwaite Hall *
Sizergh Castle *
* Halecat

7 ▼   SD

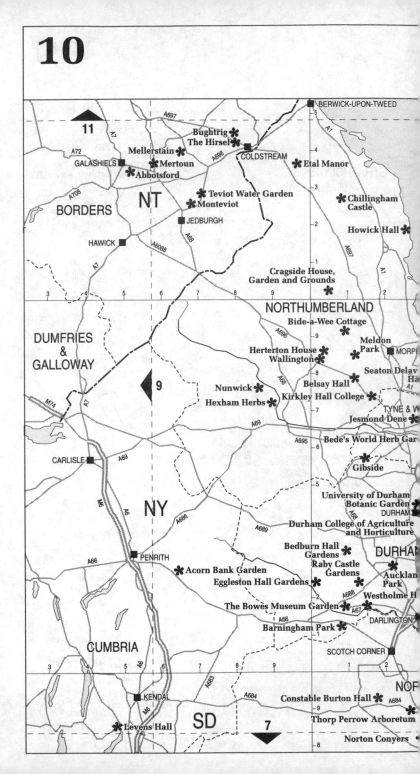

11

BERWICK-UPON-TWEED

A697

A72

A7

Bughtrig
The Hirsel ❋

Mellerstain ❋

GALASHIELS

Mertoun ❋
Abbotsford ❋

A698

COLDSTREAM

❋ Etal Manor

A1

A708

BORDERS

NT

Teviot Water Garden ❋
Monteviot ❋

❋ Chillingham
Castle

JEDBURGH

A68

Howick Hall ❋

HAWICK

A6088

❋ Cragside House,
Garden and Grounds

A697

A1

NORTHUMBERLAND

DUMFRIES
&
GALLOWAY

9

Bide-a-Wee Cottage
❋

A696

Meldon
Park ❋

MORPE

Herterton House ❋
Wallington ❋

Seaton Delav
Ha

M74

A7

Nunwick ❋

A68

Belsay Hall ❋

A1

Hexham Herbs ❋

Kirkley Hall College ❋

TYNE & W

A69

Jesmond Dene ❋

CARLISLE

A69

A695

Bede's World Herb Gar ❋

Gibside ❋

M6

A6

NY

A696

A689

University of Durham
Botanic Garden ❋

DURHAM

Durham College of Agriculture
and Horticulture

A66

PENRITH

Bedburn Hall
Gardens ❋

DURHA

❋ Acorn Bank Garden

Eggleston Hall Gardens ❋

Raby Castle
Gardens ❋

Aucklan
Park ❋

The Bowes Museum Garden ❋

A688

Westholme H ❋

A67

DARLINGTON

Barningham Park ❋

A66

CUMBRIA

SCOTCH CORNER

A683

KENDAL

M6

A684

NOF

Constable Burton Hall ❋

A684

SD

7

Thorp Perrow Arboretum

Levens Hall ❋

Norton Conyers

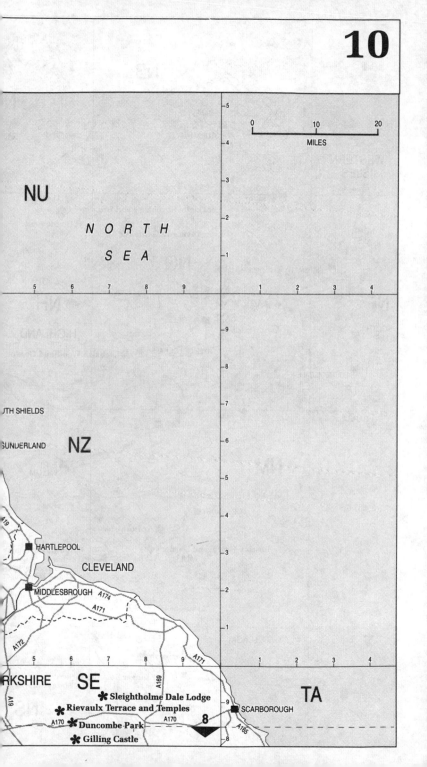

10

0   10   20
MILES

NU

NORTH

SEA

5   6   7   8   9   1   2   3   4

9

8

7

UTH SHIELDS

SUNDERLAND   NZ

6

5

4

A19

■ HARTLEPOOL   3

CLEVELAND

■ MIDDLESBROUGH   A174   2

A171

A172   1

5   6   7   8   9   A171

RKSHIRE   **SE**   A169   **TA**

✳ **Sleightholme Dale Lodge**

✳ **Rievaulx Terrace and Temples**   9   ■ SCARBOROUGH

A19   A170   ✳ **Duncombe Park**   A170   **8**   A165

✳ **Gilling Castle**   8

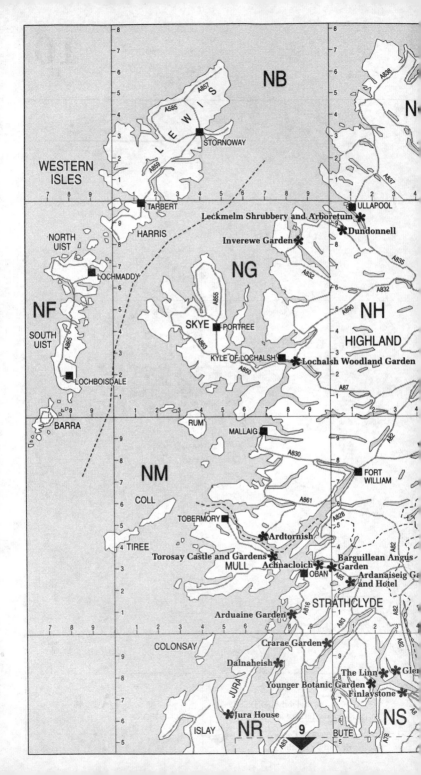

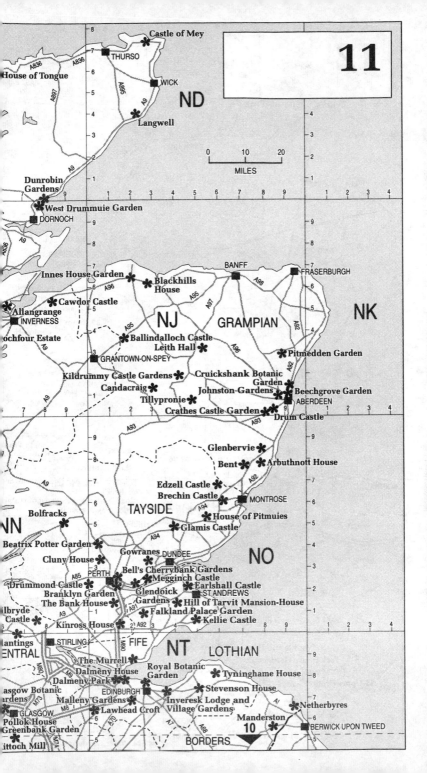

11

Castle of Mey

THURSO

WICK

House of Tongue

ND

Langwell

0   10   20
MILES

Dunrobin Gardens

West Drummuie Garden

DORNOCH

Innes House Garden

BANFF

FRASERBURGH

Blackhills House

Cawdor Castle

Allangrange

INVERNESS

NJ

GRAMPIAN

NK

ochfour Estate

Ballindalloch Castle

Leith Hall

GRANTOWN-ON-SPEY

Pitmedden Garden

Kildrummy Castle Gardens

Cruickshank Botanic Garden

Candacraig

Johnston Gardens

Beechgrove Garden

Tillypronie

Crathes Castle Garden

ABERDEEN

Drum Castle

Glenbervie

Bent

Arbuthnott House

Edzell Castle

Brechin Castle

MONTROSE

Bolfracks

TAYSIDE

House of Pitmuies

Glamis Castle

Beatrix Potter Garden

Gowranes

DUNDEE

NO

Cluny House

Bell's Cherrybank Gardens

PERTH

Megginch Castle

Earlshall Castle

Drummond Castle

Branklyn Garden

Glendoick Gardens

ST ANDREWS

The Bank House

Hill of Tarvit Mansion-House

lbryde Castle

Falkland Palace Garden

Kellie Castle

Kinross House

antings

STIRLING

FIFE

NT

LOTHIAN

ENTRAL

The Murrell

Dalmeny House

Royal Botanic Garden

Tyninghame House

Dalmeny Park

asgow Botanic ardens

Malleny Gardens

EDINBURGH

Stevenson House

Netherbyres

GLASGOW

Lawhead Croft

Inveresk Lodge and Village Gardens

Pollok House

Greenbank Garden

Manderston

10

BERWICK UPON TWEED

ittoch Mill

BORDERS

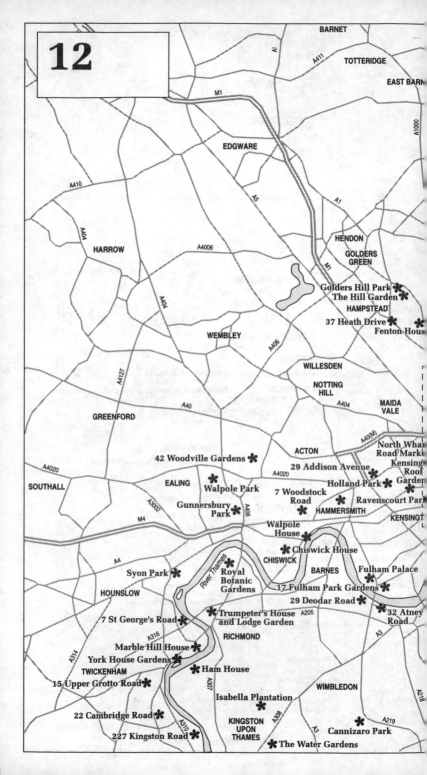

12

BARNET

TOTTERIDGE

EAST BARN

EDGWARE

HENDON

GOLDERS
GREEN

HARROW

Golders Hill Park ✳
The Hill Garden ✳

HAMPSTEAD

WEMBLEY

37 Heath Drive ✳ ✳
Fenton Hous

WILLESDEN

NOTTING
HILL

MAIDA
VALE

GREENFORD

ACTON

North Whar
Road Mark
Kensing
Roof
Garden

42 Woodville Gardens ✳

29 Addison Avenue ✳

SOUTHALL

EALING

Walpole Park ✳

7 Woodstock
Road ✳

Holland Park ✳ ✳

Ravenscourt Par

Gunnersbury ✳
Park

HAMMERSMITH

KENSINGT

Walpole ✳
House

KENSING

Syon Park ✳

Royal
Botanic
Gardens ✳

Chiswick House ✳

CHISWICK

BARNES

Fulham Palace ✳

HOUNSLOW

17 Fulham Park Gardens ✳ ✳

29 Deodar Road ✳

32 Atney
Road ✳

7 St George's Road ✳ ✳

Trumpeter's House ✳
and Lodge Garden

RICHMOND

Marble Hill House ✳

York House Gardens ✳

TWICKENHAM

Ham House ✳

15 Upper Grotto Road ✳

WIMBLEDON

Isabella Plantation ✳

22 Cambridge Road ✳

KINGSTON
UPON
THAMES

Cannizaro Park ✳

227 Kingston Road ✳

✳ The Water Gardens

GURKHA BRIGADE ASSOCIATION
IN SCOTLAND

LUNCHEON

OFFICERS MESS
ARMY HEADQUARTERS
CRAIGIEHALL

Saturday 17th June 1995
12 Noon for 1pm

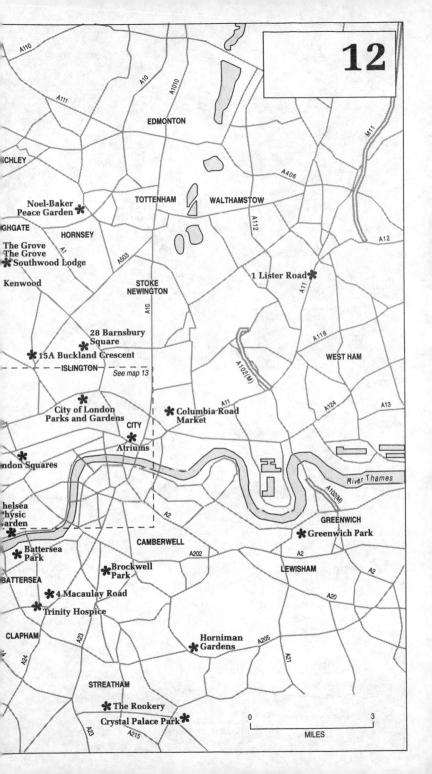

12

A110

A10

A1010

EDMONTON

A111

M11

A406

A12

TOTTENHAM

WALTHAMSTOW

ICHLEY

GHATE

A112

Noel-Baker
Peace Garden ✳

HORNSEY

The Grove
The Grove
✳ Southwood Lodge

A1

A503

A10

1 Lister Road ✳

A11

Kenwood

STOKE
NEWINGTON

A10

28 Barnsbury
Square ✳

A118

WEST HAM

✳ 15A Buckland Crescent

A1021(M)

— ISLINGTON — *See map 13*

A124

A13

City of London ✳
Parks and Gardens

CITY

✳ Columbia Road
Market

A11

ndon Squares ✳

Atriums ✳

River Thames

A1021(M)

A2

helsea
hysic
arden

GREENWICH

✳ Greenwich Park

CAMBERWELL

A2

✳ Battersea
Park

✳ Brockwell
Park

A202

LEWISHAM

A2

BATTERSEA

✳ 4 Macaulay Road

A20

✳ Trinity Hospice

CLAPHAM

A23

Horniman ✳
Gardens

A205

A21

A24

STREATHAM

✳ The Rookery

Crystal Palace Park ✳

A23

A215

0   3

MILES

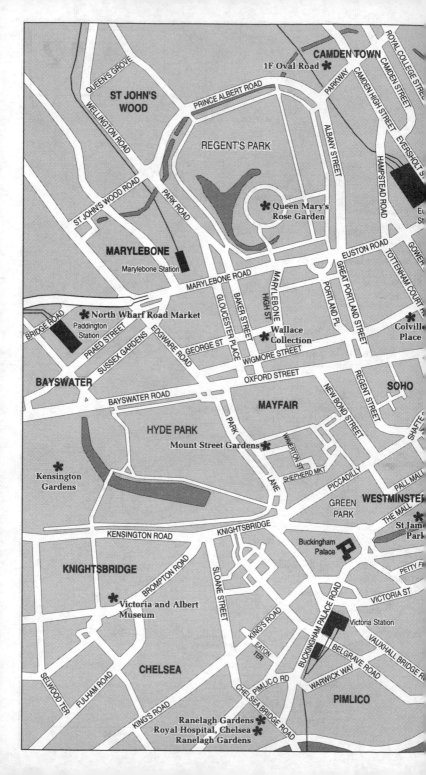

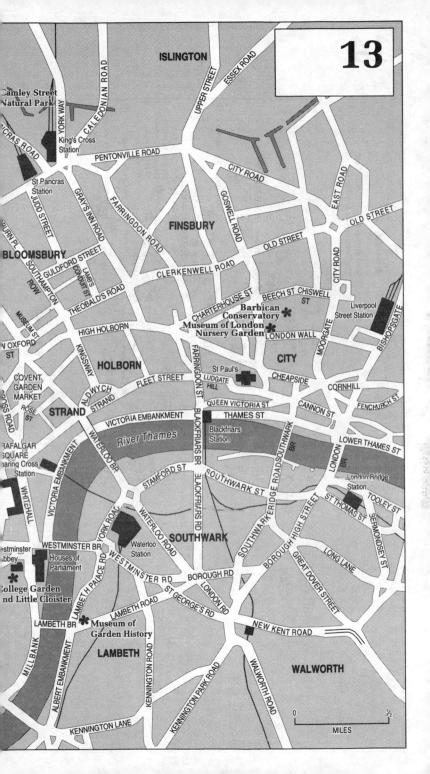

14

ATLANTIC

OCEAN

Belfast

Sir Thomas & Lady Dixon Park

The Botanic Garden Park

Carnfunnock Country Park

Guy L. Wilson Daffodil Garden

Antrim Castle Gardens

Belfast — see box above

Mount Stewart House, Garden & Temple of the Winds

Castle Ward

Rowallane

Castlewellan National Arboretum

Seaforde

Kilwarlin Battle Garden

Downhill

Brook Hall

NORTHERN IRELAND

The Argory

Florence Court

Crom

NEWRY

LONDONDERRY

Glenveagh Castle

Ard na Mona

SLIGO

Strokestown Park

Tullynally Castle

A36

M2

M1

A1

A37

A2

A6

A5

N15

A32

A29

A28

N4

N5

N17

N17

N2

N3

N4

N1

N2

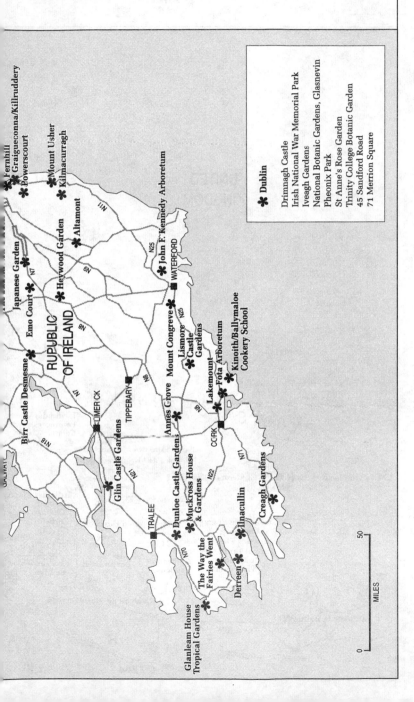

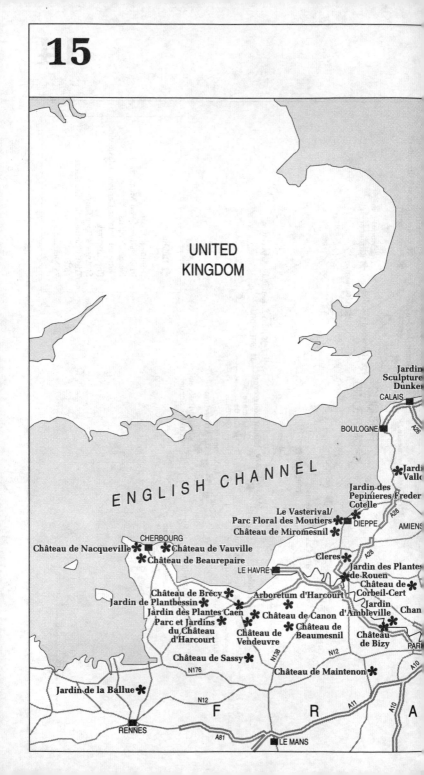

UNITED
KINGDOM

ENGLISH CHANNEL

Jardin
Sculpture
Dunker

CALAIS

BOULOGNE

Jardi
Vallo

Jardin des
Pepinieres Freder
Cotelle

Le Vasterival/
Parc Floral des Moutiers
Château de Miromesnil

DIEPPE

AMIENS

A28

CHERBOURG

Château de Nacqueville
Château de Vauville
Château de Beaurepaire

LE HAVRE

Cleres

Jardin des Plantes
de Rouen
Château de
Corbeil-Cert

Jardin
d'Ambleville

Chan

Château de Brécy
Jardin de Plantbessin
Jardin des Plantes Caen
Parc et Jardins
du Château
d'Harcourt

Arborétum d'Harcourt

Château de Canon

Château de
Vendeuvre

Château de
Beaumesnil

Château
de Bizy

PARI

Château de Sassy

Château de Maintenon

N138

N12

A10

Jardin de la Ballue

N176

N12

A11

F   R   A

RENNES

A81

A10

LE MANS

NORTH
SEA

AMSTERDAM ■
NETHERLANDS

Leiden Botanic Garden ✳

THE HAGUE ■

■ ROTTERDAM

OSTENDE ■

Graaf van ✳
rnestraat
Kasteel van ✳
Leeuwergem

Château de Vert Bois ✳

✳ Château de
Beloeil

✳ Park van Beervelde
GHENT ■ **B E L G I U M**
■ Brussels ✳

■ ANTWERP

✳ Château de
Bazeilles

Château de ✳
Compiègne

rmenonville/
arc Jean
acques Rousseau

■ REIMS

A4

■ METZ

■ NANCY

Jardin Botanique du Montet ✳

✳ Château de
Gerbeviller

✳ Haroue

0   KILOMETRES   100
0   MILES   50

N   C   E

INDEX

Gardens which are illustrated in the inserts of photographs are denoted by *col. ill.* following the garden entry page reference.

INDEX

INDEX

Report Form

The next edition of the *Guide* will be improved if readers will write to tell us (i) if gardens are not included which you think should be (ii) if you visit a garden in the *Guide* and want to confirm its merits or propose an upgrading (iii) if you visit a garden and believe its merits are overestimated by our inspector. The report form below can be used for this purpose, or you may send your comments on a sheet of paper. Handwriting is not always distinct, so if possible please print difficult words or Latin names for plants. Also please print your name clearly. All those who write will help to improve the standards of garden visiting by making good gardens open to the public known to a wider circle. The great thing is to enjoy your garden visiting, just as our inspectors have done. Happy visiting in 1995.

Send your comments to:
The Good Gardens Guide, Vermilion, Random House,
20 Vauxhall Bridge Road, London SW1V 2SA

GOOD GARDENS GUIDE REPORT FORM

To the Editors of the Good Gardens Guide:

From my own experience the following garden should/should not be included in the *Guide*

GARDEN NAME

Address:

Postcode

Telephone:

Name of Owner(s):

DESCRIPTION

1. Location:

2. Opening times:

3. Best season:

4. Entrance charge:

5. Plants for sale:

6. House open/times:

Continued overleaf...

GOOD GARDENS GUIDE REPORT FORM Continued

7. Type of garden:

8. Features/condition:

9. Brief details of its main characteristics:

Sent in by ....